Fodor's Road Guide USA

New Jersey
New York

First Edition

Fodor's Travel Publications
New York Toronto London Sydney Auckland
www.fodors.com

Fodor's Road Guide USA: New Jersey, New York

Fodor's Travel Publications
President: Bonnie Ammer
Publisher: Kris Kliemann
Executive Managing Editor: Denise DeGennaro
Editorial Director: Karen Cure
Director of Marketing Development: Jeanne Kramer
Associate Managing Editor: Linda Schmidt
Senior Editor: Constance Jones
Director of Production and Manufacturing: Chuck Bloodgood
Creative Director: Fabrizio La Rocca

Contributors
Editor: Julie Stonberg
Additional Editing: David Cashion, Kathy Green, Amy Hegarty, Anthony Laudato, and Candy Moulton
Writing: Mitchell Davis (New York), Janue Gottlieb (New York), Frank F. Herron (New York), Jane Miller (New York), Lisa Ramirez (New York), Nancy Roberts (New York), Jill Sue Schensul (New Jersey), Jan Sheridan (New York), Tom Steele (New York), June Sullivan (New York), Mitchell Uscher (New York), and Michael Virtanen (New York), with Marla Cukor, Rich Eastman, Amanda Erickson, Katherine Kane, Ellen McCurtin, Sidharth Murdeshwar, and Frances Schamberg
Research: Niladri Basu, Jennifer Cohen, Jonah Eagan, Doug Hirlinger, Kristina Klurman, Alia Levine, Tenisha Light, and Alexei Taylor
Black-and-White Maps: Rebecca Baer, Robert Blake, David Lindroth, Todd Pasini
Production/Manufacturing: Robert B. Shields
Cover: Frank Whitney/The Image Bank (background photo), Bart Nagle (photo, illustration)
Interior Photos: Pete Morelewicz (New Jersey), Artville (New York)

First Edition
ISBN 0-679-00502-1
ISSN 1528-154X

Special Sales
Fodor's Travel Publications are available at special discounts for bulk purchases for sales promotions or premiums. Special editions, including personalized covers, excerpts of existing guides, and corporate imprints, can be created in large quantities for special needs. For more information, contact your local bookseller or write to Special Markets, Fodor's Travel Publications, 280 Park Avenue, New York, NY 10017. Inquiries from Canada should be directed to your local Canadian bookseller or sent to Random House of Canada, Ltd., Marketing Department, 2775 Matheson Boulevard East, Mississauga, Ontario L4W 4P7. Inquiries from the United Kingdom should be sent to Fodor's Travel Publications, 20 Vauxhall Bridge Road, London SW1V 2SA, England.

PRINTED IN THE UNITED STATES OF AMERICA
10 9 8 7 6 5 4 3 2 1

CONTENTS

Great Road Trips

Of all the things that went wrong with Clark Griswold's vacation, one stands out: The theme park he had driven across the country to visit was closed when he got there. Clark, the suburban bumbler played by Chevy Chase in 1983's hilarious *National Lampoon's Vacation,* is fictional, of course. But his story is poignantly true. Although most Americans get only two precious weeks of vacation a year, many set off on their journeys with surprisingly little guidance. Many travelers find out about their destination from friends and family or wait to get travel information until they arrive in their hotel, where racks of brochures dispense the "facts," along with free city magazines. But it's hard to distinguish the truth from hype in these sources. And it makes no sense to spend priceless vacation time in a hotel room reading about a place when you could be out seeing it up close and personal.

Congratulate yourself on picking up this guide. Studying it—before you leave home—is the best possible first step toward making sure your vacation fulfills your every dream.

Inside you'll find all the tools you need to plan a perfect road trip. In the hundreds of towns we describe, you'll find thousands of places to explore. So you'll always know what's around the next bend. And with the practical information we provide, you can easily call to confirm the details that matter and study up on what you'll want to see and do, before you leave home.

By all means, when you plan your trip, allow yourself time to make a few detours. Because as wonderful as it is to visit sights you've read about, it's the serendipitous experiences that often prove the most memorable: the hole-in-the-wall diner that serves a transcendent tomato soup, the historical society gallery stuffed with dusty local curiosities of days gone by. As you whiz down the highway, use the book to find out more about the towns announced by roadside signs. Consider turning off at the next exit. And always remember: In this great country of ours, there's an adventure around every corner.

HOW TO USE THIS BOOK

Alphabetical organization should make it a snap to navigate through this book. Still, in putting it together, we've made certain decisions and used certain terms you need to know about.

LOCATIONS AND CATEGORIZATIONS

Color map coordinates are given for every town in the guide.

Attractions, restaurants, and lodging places are listed under the nearest town covered in the guide.

Parks and forests are sometimes listed under the main access point.

Exact street addresses are provided whenever possible; when they were not available or applicable, directions and/or cross-streets are indicated.

CITIES

For state capitals and larger cities, attractions are alphabetized by category. Shopping sections focus on good shopping areas where you'll find a concentration of interesting shops. We include malls only if they're unusual in some way and individual stores only when they're community institutions. Restaurants and hotels are grouped by price category then arranged alphabetically.

RESTAURANTS

All are air-conditioned unless otherwise noted, and all permit smoking unless they're identified as "no-smoking."

Dress: Assume that no jackets or ties are required for men unless otherwise noted.

Family-style service: Restaurants characterized this way serve food communally, out of serving dishes as you might at home.

Meals and hours: Assume that restaurants are open for lunch and dinner unless otherwise noted. We always specify days closed and meals not available.

Prices: The price ranges listed are for dinner entrées (or lunch entrées if no dinner is served).

Reservations: They are always a good idea. We don't mention them unless they're essential or are not accepted.

Fodor's Choice: Stars denote restaurants that are Fodor's Choices—our editors' picks of the state's very best in a given price category.

LODGINGS

All are air-conditioned unless otherwise noted, and all permit smoking unless they're identified as "no-smoking."

AP: This designation means that a hostelry operates on the American Plan (AP)—-that is, rates include all meals. AP may be an option or it may be the only meal plan available; be sure to find out.

Baths: You'll find private bathrooms with bathtubs unless noted otherwise.

Business services: If we tell you they're there, you can expect a variety on the premises.

Exercising: We note if there's "exercise equipment" even when there's no designated area; if you want a dedicated facility, look for "gym."

Facilities: We list what's available but don't note charges to use them. When pricing accommodations, always ask what's included.

Hot tub: This term denotes hot tubs, Jacuzzis, and whirlpools.

MAP: Rates at these properties include two meals.

No smoking: Properties with this designation prohibit smoking.

Opening and closing: Assume that hostelries are open year-round unless otherwise noted.

Pets: We note whether or not they're welcome and whether there's a charge.

Pools: Assume they're outdoors with fresh water; indoor pools are noted.

Prices: The price ranges listed are for a high-season double room for two, excluding tax and service charge.

Telephone and TV: Assume that you'll find them unless otherwise noted.

Fodor's Choice: Stars denote hostelries that are Fodor's Choices—our editors' picks of the state's very best in a given price category.

NATIONAL PARKS

National parks protect and preserve the treasures of America's heritage, and they're always worth visiting whenever you're in the area. Many are worth a long detour. If you will travel to many national parks, consider purchasing the National Parks Pass ($50), which gets you and your companions free admission to all parks for one year. (Camping and parking are extra.) A percentage of the proceeds from sales of the pass helps to fund important projects in the parks. Both the Golden Age Passport ($10), for those 62 and older, and the Golden Access Passport (free), for travelers with disabilities, entitle holders to free entry to all national parks, plus 50% off fees for the use of many park facilities and services. You must show proof of age and of U.S. citizenship or permanent residency (such as a U.S. passport, driver's license, or birth certificate) and, if requesting Golden Access, proof of your disability. You must get your Golden Access or Golden Age passport in person; the former is available at all federal recreation areas, the latter at federal recreation areas that charge fees. You may purchase the National Parks Pass by mail or through the Internet. For information, contact the National Park Service (Department of the Interior, 1849 C St. NW, Washington, DC 20240-0001, 202/208—4747, *www.nps.gov*). To buy the National Parks Pass, write to 27540 Ave. Mentry, Valencia, CA 91355, call 888/GO—PARKS, or visit www.national-parks.org.

IMPORTANT TIP

Although all prices, opening times, and other details in this book are based on information supplied to us at press time, changes occur all the time in the travel world, and Fodor's cannot accept responsibility for facts that become outdated or for inadvertent errors or omissions. So always confirm information when it matters, especially if you're making a detour to visit a specific place.

Let Us Hear from You

Keeping a travel guide fresh and up-to-date is a big job, and we welcome any and all comments. We'd love to have your thoughts on places we've listed, and we're interested in hearing about your own special finds, even the ones in your own back yard. Our guides are thoroughly updated for each new edition, and we're always adding new information, so your feedback is vital. Contact us via e-mail in care of roadnotes@fodors.com (specifying the name of the book on the subject line) or via snail mail in care of Road Guides at Fodor's, 280 Park Avenue, New York, NY 10017. We look forward to hearing from you. And in the meantime, have a wonderful road trip.

THE EDITORS

Important Numbers and On-Line Info

LODGINGS

Adam's Mark	800/444—2326	www.adamsmark.com
Baymont Inns	800/428—3438	www.baymontinns.com
Best Western	800/528—1234	www.bestwestern.com
	TDD 800/528—2222	
Budget Host	800/283—4678	www.budgethost.com
Clarion	800/252—7466	www.clarioninn.com
Comfort	800/228—5150	www.comfortinn.com
Courtyard by Marriott	800/321—2211	www.courtyard.com
Days Inn	800/325—2525	www.daysinn.com
Doubletree	800/222—8733	www.doubletreehotels.com
Drury Inns	800/325—8300	www.druryinn.com
Econo Lodge	800/555—2666	www.hotelchoice.com
Embassy Suites	800/362—2779	www.embassysuites.com
Exel Inns of America	800/356—8013	www.exelinns.com
Fairfield Inn by Marriott	800/228—2800	www.fairfieldinn.com
Fairmont Hotels	800/527—4727	www.fairmont.com
Forte	800/225—5843	www.forte-hotels.com
Four Seasons	800/332—3442	www.fourseasons.com
Friendship Inns	800/453—4511	www.hotelchoice.com
Hampton Inn	800/426—7866	www.hampton-inn.com
Hilton	800/445—8667	www.hilton.com
	TDD 800/368—1133	
Holiday Inn	800/465—4329	www.holiday-inn.com
	TDD 800/238—5544	
Howard Johnson	800/446—4656	www.hojo.com
	TDD 800/654—8442	
Hyatt & Resorts	800/233—1234	www.hyatt.com
Inns of America	800/826—0778	www.innsofamerica.com
Inter-Continental	800/327—0200	www.interconti.com
La Quinta	800/531—5900	www.laquinta.com
	TDD 800/426—3101	
Loews	800/235—6397	www.loewshotels.com
Marriott	800/228—9290	www.marriott.com
Master Hosts Inns	800/251—1962	www.reservahost.com
Le Meridien	800/225—5843	www.lemeridien.com
Motel 6	800/466—8356	www.motel6.com
Omni	800/843—6664	www.omnihotels.com
Quality Inn	800/228—5151	www.qualityinn.com
Radisson	800/333—3333	www.radisson.com
Ramada	800/228—2828	www.ramada.com
	TDD 800/533—6634	
Red Carpet/Scottish Inns	800/251—1962	www.reservahost.com
Red Lion	800/547—8010	www.redlion.com
Red Roof Inn	800/843—7663	www.redroof.com
Renaissance	800/468—3571	www.renaissancehotels.com
Residence Inn by Marriott	800/331—3131	www.residenceinn.com
Ritz-Carlton	800/241—3333	www.ritzcarlton.com
Rodeway	800/228—2000	www.rodeway.com

Sheraton	800/325—3535	www.sheraton.com
Shilo Inn	800/222—2244	www.shiloinns.com
Signature Inns	800/822—5252	www.signature-inns.com
Sleep Inn	800/221—2222	www.sleepinn.com
Super 8	800/848—8888	www.super8.com
Susse Chalet	800/258—1980	www.sussechalet.com
Travelodge/Viscount	800/255—3050	www.travelodge.com
Vagabond	800/522—1555	www.vagabondinns.com
Westin Hotels & Resorts	800/937—8461	www.westin.com
Wyndham Hotels & Resorts	800/996—3426	www.wyndham.com

AIRLINES

Air Canada	888/247—2262	www.aircanada.ca
Alaska	800/426—0333	www.alaska-air.com
American	800/433—7300	www.aa.com
America West	800/235—9292	www.americawest.com
British Airways	800/247—9297	www.british-airways.com
Canadian	800/426—7000	www.cdnair.ca
Continental Airlines	800/525—0280	www.continental.com
Delta	800/221—1212	www.delta.com
Midway Airlines	800/446—4392	www.midwayair.com
Northwest	800/225—2525	www.nwa.com
SkyWest	800/453—9417	www.delta.com
Southwest	800/435—9792	www.southwest.com
TWA	800/221—2000	www.twa.com
United	800/241—6522	www.ual.com
USAir	800/428—4322	www.usair.com

BUSES AND TRAINS

Amtrak	800/872—7245	www.amtrak.com
Greyhound	800/231—2222	www.greyhound.com
Trailways	800/343—9999	www.trailways.com

CAR RENTALS

Advantage	800/777—5500	www.arac.com
Alamo	800/327—9633	www.goalamo.com
Allstate	800/634—6186	www.bnm.com/as.htm
Avis	800/331—1212	www.avis.com
Budget	800/527—0700	www.budget.com
Dollar	800/800—4000	www.dollar.com
Enterprise	800/325—8007	www.pickenterprise.com
Hertz	800/654—3131	www.hertz.com
National	800/328—4567	www.nationalcar.com
Payless	800/237—2804	www.paylesscarrental.com
Rent-A-Wreck	800/535—1391	www.rent-a-wreck.com
Thrifty	800/367—2277	www.thrifty.com

Note: Area codes are changing all over the United States as this book goes to press. For the latest updates, check www.areacode-info.com.

Fodor's Road Guide USA

New Jersey
New York

New Jersey

New Jersey's nickname, "the Garden State," may seem strange to those whose knowl-edge of the state consists of New Jersey jokes or views of the steely urban landscape surrounding Newark International Airport. But New Jersey is, in fact, full of gardens. It is home to the third-largest state park system in the country, and throughout its communities you will see plenty of green space and unique natural habitats.

Tourism is one of New Jersey's largest industries, mainly because of Atlantic City's position as a major gambling center. Atlantic City draws more visitors a year—37 million—than Las Vegas. For many years the Jersey Shore was receiving most of the state's visitors, but today New Jersey's forests, inland lakes, low mountain areas, histor-ical sites, and cultural institutions are being more actively promoted and woven into package tours linking sites in numerous regions of the state.

Although New Jersey is the fifth-smallest state in the country, it ranks ninth in popu-lation. Much more than just a bedroom community for New York, New Jersey is a major industrial center and an important nexus of transportation on the East Coast. In recent years, especially, it's been luring major corporations to its side of the Hudson and has become a leader in the pharmaceutical field.

Only 50 mi of New Jersey (along the northern border with New York State) is not bordered by water—the Atlantic Ocean is to the east, the Delaware River is to the west, and the Delaware Bay is to the south. New Jersey is home to several mountain chains, including the Appalachians in the northeast and the Kittatinny Mountains along the northwest corner of the state (from the New York border to the Delaware Water Gap). The latter range includes High Point State Park, which is home to the state's highest elevation of 1,803 ft. Along the Hudson River run the Palisades, the cliffs after which the "cliff-hanger" of early movies was named. The Palisades afford heart-stopping views of the Manhattan skyline.

CAPITAL: TRENTON	POPULATION: 8,115,011	AREA: 7,419 SQUARE MI
BORDERS: NY, PA, DE, ATLANTIC OCEAN	TIME ZONE: EASTERN	POSTAL ABBREVIATION: NJ
WEB SITE:	WWW.STATE.NJ.US/TRAVEL/		

The northern part of New Jersey has not only the mountains, but much of New Jersey's forests and farmlands as well. From about the middle of the state, running southward, are the Pinelands, a sandy-soiled area that contains unique flora and fauna and was designated a national Biosphere Reserve in the 1970s.

History

The first occupants of New Jersey were the Lenni Lenape Indians, who lived in what is now New Jersey, Delaware, eastern Pennsylvania, and southeastern New York.

Henry Hudson was the first European to arrive in the area, sailing into Newark Bay in 1609. The Dutch came to colonize and bought land from the Lenni Lenape, who began moving farther inland. Under the auspices of the Dutch West India Company, patroon-ships—manorial estates—were offered to colonists to encourage settlement and small colonies sprung up on the present sites of Hoboken, Jersey City, and Glouces-ter.

Because of its strategic location, New Jersey saw a lot of action during the American Revolution. General George Washington led many famous battles here (including ones in Trenton, Princeton, and Monmouth), and his troops spent two hellish winters in Morristown. The sites of the battles, and many of the places Washington actually slept, have been preserved as state and national historic sites.

While the first major economic activities in the state were agricultural, by the late 18th century agriculture had been supplemented by mining and the processing of iron, much of it used to manufacture ammunition for the Revolution. The sandy soil of the south helped that region to become a major glass manufacturer, and lumber and leather also became major industries throughout the state.

Andrew Hamilton created America's first planned industrial city in Paterson, building a textile industry by tapping into the water power of the city's dramatic Great Falls. Potteries, shoe factories, and brickworks were built. Roads were improved, the Morris Canal and the Delaware and Raritan canals were chartered, and the Camden and Amboy Railroad completed a line from New York to Philadelphia. The first locomotives were turned out in Paterson; the first lightbulb and the first phonograph came from Thomas Edison's ateliers in Menlo Park; and the first condensed soup was made at the Campbell's plant in Camden.

And so New Jersey grew, with major urban centers as well as tracts of farmland. New Jersey became for example, and still is, a major grower of cranberries. It has also become the leading producer of chemicals and pharmaceuticals in the country. New Jersey's growth and development did not come without difficulties, however. The six-day race riots in Newark in July 1967, drew attention to the urgent need for social and political reform in many of the state's urban centers and numerous toxic waste sites. Plenty of Superfund dollars have been spent here, fueling the state to literally clean up its act. Today, New Jersey boasts some of the cleanest ocean water and beaches in the country.

Bruce Springsteen, Frank Sinatra, Governor Christine Todd Whitman, and William

NJ Timeline

1524	1618	1638	1655
Sailing for France, Verrazano (possibly) explores New Jersey's shores.	Dutch found Village of Bergen (Jersey City)	Swedish settlers establish forts in South Jersey and along the Delaware River, founding New Sweden.	Under Peter Stuyvesant, the Dutch force Swedes to give up forts in South Jersey. New Netherlands is established.

INTRODUCTION
HISTORY
REGIONS
WHEN TO VISIT
STATE'S GREATS
RULES OF THE ROAD
DRIVING TOURS

Carlos Williams have all added some panache to the state. The Meadowlands Sports Complex, which hosted the World Cup in 1994, reintroduced New Jersey to the world, pointing out that it was much more than an alternative airport to fly into on your way to New York City.

Regions

1. THE SKYLANDS REGION

The northeast quarter of the state is known as the Skylands, made up of Morris, Sussex, Warren, Hunterdon, and Somerset counties. Parts of two national parks are within its borders: the Delaware Water Gap National Recreation Area to the west, and the Great Swamp National Wildlife Refuge to the east. In between are state forests, the state's best skiing in and around Vernon, and the Kittatinny and Appalachian mountains.

More than 8 million visitors a year come to hike in the Morristown National Historic Park, explore the many sites from the American Revolution, visit the antiques-filled towns of Frenchtown and Lambertville along the Delaware River, and shop the discount outlets in Flemington and the upscale stores in Short Hills. The Morris Museum is one of the best in the state, and the Franklin Mineral Museum and Sterling Hill mines have some of the most unique geological specimens in the world. The U.S. Golf Association's museum and the Biking Hall of Fame are both in the Skylands, and the minor-league baseball team, New Jersey Cardinals, are establishing a large and loyal following at their stadium, Skylands Park.

Towns listed: Augusta, Basking Ridge, Belvidere, Bernardsville, Chatham, Chester, Clinton, Flemington, Franklin, Frenchtown, Gladstone, Griggstown, Hackettstown, Hope, Lambertville, Madison, Milford, Morristown, Parsippany, Short Hills, Somerset, Somerville, Stanhope, Stockton, Summit, Vernon, Walpack Center

2. THE GATEWAY REGION

This northeast region of the state is called the gateway because the George Washington Bridge and the Lincoln and Holland tunnels connect it to New York. The nickname is also apropos because this region claims the historic gateway to America—Ellis Island—as well as Liberty State Park in Jersey City. Though predominantly urban and industrial, the region is visited by more than 12 million people annually. The region encompasses the counties of Passaic, Bergen, Essex, Hudson, Union, and Middlesex.

Hoboken, to the south, has become a junior Greenwich Village, with a thriving arts and music scene, beautiful old brownstones, eclectic eateries, a notable history (it's the birthplace of both Frank

1661	1664	1665	1675	1702
First recorded school at Bergen (Jersey City).	Dutch surrender New Netherlands to England; proprietorship is granted to Lord Berkeley and Sir George Carteret (Hudson River to Delaware River).	Concessions and agreement establish government for the colony of New Jersey.	John Fenwick establishes a Quaker colony at Salem in West Jersey.	East and West Jersey proprietorships end and become a united colony again under New York governors.

Sinatra and baseball), and desperately few parking places. Newark, home to Newark International Airport and the extensive Newark Museum, has seen revitalization of late, including the addition of the New Jersey Performing Arts Center, a state-of-the-art facility that opened to much acclaim in October 1997. The area also boasts the Paper Mill Playhouse in Millburn, and the John Harms Center for the Arts in Englewood. East Rutherford is home to the Meadowlands Sports Complex, which includes: Giants and Jets football at Giants Stadium; the 10,000-seat Continental Airlines Arena (home of the state's hockey and basketball teams, as well as concerts); plus the Meadowlands Racetrack for both harness and thoroughbred racing. Some of the great minds of the 20th century have called this region home, including Thomas Alva Edison (West Orange), and William Carlos Williams (Paterson and Rutherford). If shopping is your thing, Secaucus is the grandmother of all outlet shopping.

Towns listed: Bergenfield, Caldwell, Clifton, East Rutherford, Edison, Elizabeth, Englewood, Fort Lee, Hackensack, Hoboken, Ho-Ho-Kus, Jersey City, Lyndhurst, Mahwah, Metuchen, Millburn, Montclair, Montvale, Mountainside, Newark, New Brunswick, Paramus, Paterson, Plainfield, Ramsey, Ridgewood, Ringwood, River Edge, Rutherford, Saddle Brook, Secaucus, Teaneck, Union, Wayne, West Orange, Woodbridge

3. THE SHORE REGION

The "shore" is the northern shore region—Monmouth and Ocean counties—and home to nearly three dozen beaches, among them the Sandy Hook Gateway National Recreation Area, where you can mix history with your nature walks and sunning. Many of the state's 23 lighthouses are here, including the Sandy Hook Lighthouse and the historic Twin Lights of Navesink across the bay. The shore towns range from all-out amusement piers and party hot spots in Seaside Heights, to the ecologically protected Island Beach State Park, to the colorful Victorian enclave of Ocean Grove, which was originally a Methodist camp meeting ground. In the warmer months, locals and visitors enjoy the beaches, rides, and attractions at Six Flags Great Adventure Theme Park and Safari in Jackson, and performances at the PNC Bank Arts Center in Holmdel.

Towns listed: Asbury Park, Belmar, Eatonton, Freehold, Jackson, Lakewood, Long Beach Island, Matawan, Ocean Grove, Point Pleasant, Point Pleasant Beach, Red Bank, Rumson, Sandy Hook, Seaside Heights, Seaside Park, Spring Lake, Tinton Falls, Toms River, Waretown

4. THE DELAWARE RIVER REGION

Although this region includes Camden, Trenton, and Princeton, much of the rest of it has been overlooked by tourists, which is one more reason to visit. Here you'll find the otherworldly Pine Barrens, a 1.1-million-acre preserve that is home to tree frogs, meat-eating lady slipper plants, and many other natural wonders not found anywhere else in the world. For a different sort of edification, go to Princeton, at the northern end of

1738	1746	1766	1777	1787
New Jersey becomes a separate royal colony from New York and receives its own governor, Lewis Morris.	Princeton University is founded as the College of New Jersey and opens in Elizabeth the next year.	Rutgers, the State University of New Jersey, is founded as Queens College.	New Jersey State Seal issued.	New Jersey becomes a state.

the region, with its world-renowned university, museums, McCarter Theater, fine restaurants and hotels, and history—including the Princeton Battlefield and homes once lived in by everyone from Albert Einstein to Thomas Mann. More history can be found in such charming Delaware River towns as Bordentown, Burlington, and Salem.

Towns listed: Batsto, Bordentown, Burlington, Camden, Cherry Hill, Gibbstown, Haddonfield, Hightstown, Medford, Mount Holly, Mount Laurel, Princeton, Salem, Trenton

5. THE GREATER ATLANTIC CITY REGION

Atlantic City is such a big tourist draw—37 million people visit annually—that it needed its own tourism region. Since Resorts Casino Hotel, the region's first casino, opened in May 1978, Atlantic City has become a gambling mecca, with 13 casino-hotels and more in the planning stages. Although most visitors have traditionally been day-trippers from around the area, Atlantic City developers are now broadening their scope of influence, with a world-class convention-center complex, better boardwalk attractions, and a citywide revitalization project.

Even without stepping foot in a casino, you could spend a week in this region with never a dull moment—whether you're shopping in the historic town of Smithville, getting a dose of wildlife at the Edwin B. Forsythe National Wildlife Refuge in Brigantine, or golfing at one of the area's dozen or so courses. This region is also home to the Marine Mammal Stranding Center and Sea Life Museum, which rescues and returns stranded marine life to their natural environments; the Ocean Life Center that opened in Gardner's Basin in 1999; and the Wetlands Institute near Stone Harbor. Renault Vineyards, in Little Egg Harbor, is the oldest in the country. And of course, a chance to march through the belly of Lucy the Elephant in Margate is alone worth an hour of your time.

Towns listed: Atlantic City, Mays Landing, Somers Point, Stone Harbor

6. THE SOUTHERN SHORE REGION

Anchoring the southern shore region is the classic Victorian town of Cape May, itself a National Historic Landmark featuring 600 restored Victorian homes. The year-round resort has a full schedule of events, from Dickensian Christmas, to an enormous Victorian Week celebration in October, to bird-, whale-, and dolphin-watching tours. North of Cape May is Wildwood, with its four amusement piers and wonderful, wide, 3-mi beach. The area also has several historic villages, such as Cold Spring, which provides glimpses of 18th-century farm life. Wheaton Village in Millville is home to both the Down Jersey Folklife Center and the Museum of American Glass, which has a collection of more than 7,000 objects from handblown paperweights to Tiffany lamps.

The oft-overlooked East Point Lighthouse, built in the 1800s, is a highlight of this part of the Coastal Heritage Trail. The Town of Bridgeton is New Jersey's largest historic district with 2,200 Colonial, Federal, and Victorian buildings. Ocean City, known as "America's Greatest Family Resort," offers a 2½-mi boardwalk of rides, food, and fun; the Ocean

1789	1790	1804	1805	1831
New Jersey became the first state to ratify the Bill of Rights.	Trenton selected as state capital.	Alexander Hamilton/Aaron Burr duel at Weehawken on July 11. Hamilton is killed.	Robert Fulton builds the first ship dry dock in Jersey City. It is the first in the country.	The Morris Canal is opened.

City Music Pier; more than 200 holes of miniature golf; unique shops; and parades and festivals throughout the year. A bit farther south, the shores of Sea Isle City, Avalon, and Stone Harbor offer wide, pristine beaches and wetlands for bird-watching.

Towns listed: Bridgeton, Cape May, Cape May Court House, Millville, Ocean City, Sea Isle City, Stone Harbor, the Wildwoods

When to Visit

New Jersey is 166 mi long; while this may not seem very large, that distance, plus the differences in elevation between sea level at Cape May in the south and the Kittatinny Mountains in the north, create marked variations in weather patterns in the state.

Temperature differences between the northern and southern parts are greatest in winter and smallest in summer. The average number of freeze-free days in the northern highlands is 163, 179 in the central and southern interior, and 217 along the coast. Precipitation ranges from 51 inches in the north-central parts of the state to 40 inches in the south. Snow may fall from mid-October to the end of April in the highlands, and from mid-November to mid-April in southern counties. Fall months are usually driest. In the oceanfront zone in the southeast, coastal storms—sometimes called nor'easters—that bring strong winds and heavy rains are most frequent between October and April. Rarely does a winter go by that there isn't at least one significant coastal storm. Sometimes there are more than five.

The record high temperature for the state was 110°F, on July 10th, 1936; the low was minus 34°F, in River Vale, in 1904. The shore can be cooler in summer, of course, than inland, and the northern part of the state, which has more foliage, is beautiful in the fall. The Pine Barrens, which can be too hot and unshady in summer for hiking, is another place best visited in autumn, and in September the cranberry harvest begins. While snowmaking is good at the major ski areas in Vernon, call ahead to make sure it's been cold enough to actually make it. It can be more moderate near the shore region, but generally there is not a huge difference in temperatures throughout the state. The shore does, however, feel the complete wrath of the nor'easters that rip through every once in a while, destroying boardwalks and beaches.

The shore is a great place to cool off in summer, but it can be crowded and the traffic coming and going, especially on weekends, can be daunting. If you prefer to have more of the beach to yourself, the water's still warm well after Labor Day. In winter, the shore exudes a bleak, windy, yet alluring beauty; many bed-and-breakfasts, particularly in Cape May and Spring Lake, stay open year-round or close for only one month.

CLIMATE CHART
Average high/low temperatures (°F) and monthly precipitation in inches

	JAN.	FEB.	MAR.	APR.	MAY	JUNE
ATLANTIC CITY	39.5/26.8	41.5/28.8	48.8/36.0	57.3/44.1	65.7/53.6	74.4/62.3
	3.27	3.02	3.36	3.25	2.96	2.56

1838
F. B. Morse and Alfred Vail demonstrated telegraph in Morristown.

1840
Cranberries are first cultivated in the state.

1846
Baseball played between the Knickerbockers and the New Yorks at Elysian Fields, Hoboken on June 19; New Yorks win 23 to 1.

1855
The first normal school in New Jersey is founded at Trenton.

1869
First intercollegiate football game in the country is played on November 6 in New Brunswick between Rutgers and Princeton.

INTRODUCTION
HISTORY
REGIONS
WHEN TO VISIT
STATE'S GREATS
RULES OF THE ROAD
DRIVING TOURS

	JULY	AUG.	SEPT.	OCT.	NOV.	DEC.
	80.1/68.3	79.8/68.0	73.8/61.8	64.3/51.0	54.8/41.7	45.5/32.5
	3.31	3.84	2.65	2.40	3.19	3.29
	JAN.	FEB.	MAR.	APR.	MAY	JUNE
NEWARK	37.7/23.4	40.5/25.4	50.8/33.4	61.9/42.7	72.4/53.2	82.3/62.8
	3.39	3.04	3.87	3.84	4.13	3.22
	JULY	AUG.	SEPT.	OCT.	NOV.	DEC.
	87.0/68.6	85.4/67.4	77.6/59.9	66.7/48.2	55.4/39.2	42.9/29.1
	4.50	3.91	3.66	3.05	3.91	3.45

FESTIVALS AND SEASONAL EVENTS
WINTER

Dec. **George Washington's Crossing of the Delaware.** This famed event is reenacted on Christmas Day at the original site of the march in 1776, on the state border at Titusville in what is now Washington Crossing State Park. The event actually starts in the Pennsylvania part of the park. | 609/737–0623.

Dec., Jan. **Christmas in Cape May.** During this annual event, Cape May's Victorian homes go all-out with traditional holiday decorations. There are special tours, crackling fires, and live performances of Charles Dickens's *A Christmas Carol.* You'd be hard pressed to find a more postcard-pretty winter scene. | 609/884–5404 or 800/275–4278.

Feb., Mar. **New Jersey Flower and Patio Show.** Now in its third decade, this event features 82,000 square ft of landscaped gardens and floral designs. Changing exhibits and lectures take place throughout the show, which is held at the Garden State Convention and Exhibit Center in Somerset. | 732/469–4000.

SPRING

Mar. **Atlantique City Spring Festival.** Held in Atlantic City's Convention Center, this is the world's largest indoor antiques and collectibles show, with dealers from around the country and overseas. There is also a fall version held the third week in October. | 800/526–2724.

May **Wildwood International Kite Festival.** One of the world's largest sport kite competition, drawing competitors from around the world. Competitions include stunt flying and indoor flying and are held in Wildwood where Rio Grande St. meets the ocean. | 215/736–3715.

1870	1877	1879	1893	1917
The first boardwalk in Atlantic City is completed by Alex Boardman; Monmouth Park is opened.	Thomas A. Edison invents the phonograph at Menlo Park.	Edison invents the incandescent lamp; first commercially produced electric lightbulb is manufactured in 1890.	Edison's film studio, the Black Maria, opens in West Orange.	Fort Dix is established.

SUMMER

June **Heritage Days at Mill Hill Park.** Held in Trenton, this event attracts 100,000 visitors annually. The two-day festival celebrates New Jersey's cultural diversity, with food, exhibits, crafts, children's activities, and continuous music of all sorts. | 609/695–7107.

Riverfest. This Red Bank food and jazz festival showcases local restaurants and features scenic cruises on the Navesink, crafts, and other festivities. | 732/741–0055.

July **QuickChek New Jersey Festival of Ballooning.** This event at Solberg Airport in Readington is one of the largest summertime balloon fest on the East Coast, with more than 100 balloons, an old-time air show, daily concerts, fireworks, and arts and crafts. You'll find the airport 10 mi west of Somerville. | 973/882–5464 or 800/HOT–AIR9.

Aug. **Sussex Air Show.** Called "The Biggest Little Air Show in the World," this event, at Sussex Airport, has a lineup of the best plane performers around. There's amazing aerobatics, gliders, and comic acts, as well as war plane flyovers and exhibits. Model planes also get exhibit space and their own flight time. Food, crafts, music, in a pastoral—if sometimes dusty—location. | 973/875–0783 or 973/875–7337.

AUTUMN

Sept. **Miss America Week and Pageant.** Held at the Atlantic City Convention Center, this event is more than just pretty faces on the big televised night: it's a whirlwind of activities and competitions, including the Miss America Parade. | 609/344–5278.

Wings 'n' Water Festival. Sponsored by the Wetlands Institute in Stone Harbor, this festival features a weekend of events and activities designed both to entertain and to educate. Check out the exhibits and activities at the institute, as well as hikes and tours throughout the area. | 609/368–1211.

Oct. **Victorian Week.** This event is such a big deal that it stretches for more than a week. Held in the lovely Victorian resort town of Cape May, which is on the National Register of Historic Places, the event includes guided historic house tours, workshops, fashion shows, antiques shows, entertainment, and all things gingerbread. | 609/884–5404.

1921	1928	1932	1937	1951
First Miss America Pageant is held in Atlantic City.	Newark Airport is opened.	Lindbergh baby is kidnapped at Hopewell.	German airship *Hindenburg* explodes over Lakehurst.	The first 53 mi of the New Jersey Turnpike is opened.

State's Greats

INTRODUCTION
HISTORY
REGIONS
WHEN TO VISIT
STATE'S GREATS
RULES OF THE ROAD
DRIVING TOURS

While vacationers come to New Jersey for gambling and the state's 127 mi of shoreline, New Jersey is much more than just another pretty beach or changing slot machine. The state boasts some of the most unique and plentiful wildlife and flora in the country. Cape May, at the tip of the state, is home to many species of butterflies and an opportune stop-off for birds along the busy Atlantic Flyway migration. The waters are so full of fish that many marine mammals that used to just pass through on their migrations now call them home. The **Great Swamp National Wildlife Refuge** offers a protected wetlands environment, and the Pinelands are so unique that they merit Biosphere Reserve status. Among the state's noteworthy hiking trails are the Appalachian Trail in the northeast, and the Long Path along the Palisades, which goes all the way north to the Adirondacks. History is evident all over this state, too, since General George Washington used the region as a strategic stronghold against the British. The area is also full of firsts, from baseball, to the electric lightbulb, to the first planned industrial city (Paterson). And of course there's shopping, from the outlet malls of Secaucus to the upscale shops of Short Hills, as well as antiques caches in small towns like Chester and Bridgeton.

Beaches, Forests, and Parks

New Jersey has 127 mi of shoreline, and you can find just about any type of beach you want here. For boardwalk fun with the kids, try Wildwood, Ocean City, Point Pleasant Beach, or Seaside Heights. For a quieter ambience, try Spring Lake, which has no development at all along its boardwalk. If you're a fan of lighthouses, the **Twin Lights** of the Navesink, in the Highlands, has a nice museum and great vantage points. **Barnegat Lighthouse,** at the northern tip of Long Beach Island, is the most photographed at the shore. And from the top of the **Cape May Lighthouse,** you'll get sweeping views of the festive boardwalk in the Wildwoods and maybe, if you're lucky, you'll spot the spray of a passing whale or jumping dolphin.

New Jersey also has an extensive park system. For great views, visit **High Point State Park** in Sussex County. The Delaware Water Gap National Recreation Area, spanning Pennsylvania and New Jersey, offers access to the Appalachian trail as well as other good hiking spots, not to mention some fine canoeing. You can also canoe in the Pine Barrens, along its tea-color water. The ride isn't heart-stopping—no white water here—but it's a peaceful way to pass a day in nature. Beware, though: the rivers can be very nearly jammed with boat traffic in summer, so it's best to go in autumn. For some history mixed in with your hiking, try the Long Pond Ironworks State Park in Ringwood, where you can see vestiges of the old ironworks and the community that grew up around them. Ditto for **Allaire State Park,** in Lakewood,which has a much better developed living history program.

1955	1967	1969	1978	1995
The Garden State Parkway is opened.	Cold War summit between LBJ and Kosygin is held at Glassboro. Newark racial riots kill 26 people and injure 1,500.	New Jerseyan Edwin "Buzz" Aldrin of Glen Ridge lands on the moon with Neil Armstrong.	Opening of legalized gambling in Atlantic City.	Christine Todd Whitman becomes the state's first female governor.

Culture, History, and the Arts

You don't need to cross the river to get world-class entertainment. New Jersey offers numerous performing arts venues drawing top performers and troupes to the area. In Englewood there is the **John Harms Center for the Arts.** The **Count Basie Theater** keeps Red Bank and environs along the shore hopping, and the **New Jersey Performing Arts Center** has quickly established itself as a major draw for entertainment in the Newark area, pulling in audiences from all parts of the state and drawing new business to the area as well. In Millburn, the **Paper Mill Playhouse** has won national acclaim for its top-notch theater productions and in Holmdel, the **PNC Bank Center** has great acoustics and is a comfortable outdoor venue for shows and festivals. Another outdoor stage that rocks in summer is the the **Blockbuster–Sony Music Entertainment Centre** on the Camden waterfront—an easy ferry ride over from Philadelphia.

Historic sites are many and varied, from the corner in Hoboken marking the Elysian Fields, where the first game of baseball was played, to the **Morristown National Historic Park,** where Washington and his men held forth in the terrible winters of 1779–80. In Edison, you can visit the site where Thomas Alva Edison invented the lightbulb, as well as the oldest Quaker burial ground in the United States.

Some of the state's top-notch museums include: the **New Jersey State Museum** in Trenton, which houses a planetarium; the **Morris Museum** with varying exhibits and a natural history area; the **Wheaton Glass Museum,** home to one of the largest collections of American glass in the country; the **Newark Museum,** which also has a planetarium; and the beautiful **Ballantine House,** in Newark.

Sports

The state is filled with hiking and biking trails, including many in the Rails to Trails program, which turned old railroad right-of-ways into recreational paths. Fishing enthusiasts can enjoy both lake and ocean fishing, and there are hundreds of places to charter a boat for the day. Canoeing, kayaking, and boating can be enjoyed from the tea-color streams in the Pine Barrens to the mighty Hudson and Delaware rivers.

Although the mountains here don't soar as high as those of its New England neighbors, New Jersey offers a variety of skiing options. The largest of the state's resorts is **Mountain Creek,** formerly Vernon Valley/Great Gorge, which has the most extensive trails system but often the most extensive lift lines, too. A smaller alternative nearby is **Hidden Valley,** with fewer trails but only a limited number of skiers allowed on the hills every day, keeping lift lines to a minimum. Less advanced skiers should try **Campgaw** in Bergen County. Many areas also cater to snowboarders. Note that skiing in the state can sometimes be icy, because of all the melting and refreezing the slopes may see in a day.

Golf courses abound in New Jersey, including many terrific public courses. The **Marriott Seaview Resort** in Absecon is among the finest in the state. The greater Atlantic City Golf Association can hook you up with tee times, lodging options, and package deals that include both.

Other Points of Interest

Casinos, casinos, casinos. We probably don't have to remind you that New Jersey has them—at least in Atlantic City. Although most visitors to the casinos are still day-trippers, city officials and the state Division of Tourism are working together to make it more attractive as a vacation destination so visitors will be inclined to stay longer.

STATE PARKS

A $35 State Park Pass provides free entrance for one calendar year to state parks and forests that charge parking or daily walk-in fees. Camping fees are separate, and not

INTRODUCTION
HISTORY
REGIONS
WHEN TO VISIT
STATE'S GREATS
RULES OF THE ROAD
DRIVING TOURS

covered by the pass. For more information, contact the **N.J. Division of Parks and Forestry, State Park Service** | Box 404, Trenton, NJ | 609/984–0370 or 800/843–6420.

Rules of the Road

License requirements: To drive in New Jersey you must be at least 17 years old and have a valid driver's license. Residents of Canada and most other countries may drive as long as they have valid licenses from their home countries.

Right turn on red: Everywhere in the state you may make a right turn at a red light after a full stop unless otherwise posted.

Seat belt and helmet laws: All drivers and front-seat passengers must wear seat belts. Children under age 10 must wear a seat belt at all times, whether they are in the back or the front. Children under age four must be in a federally approved child safety seat. Motorcyclists must wear helmets and are required to keep their headlights and tail-lights on at all times.

Speed limits: New Jersey is testing a 65-mph speed limit on some major highways. In areas of heavier traffic, though, 55 is still the speed limit, and, of course, on local roads the limit is usually 30 mph. Speed limits often change from town to town, so be sure to check the speed limit signs carefully.

Other: Headlights must be on whenever windshield wipers are on.

For more information: Contact the State Department of Transportation at | 609/292–6500, 888/486–3339 in NJ.

The South Jersey Shore Driving Tour
FROM ATLANTIC CITY TO CAPE MAY

Distance: Approximately 50 mi, depending on detours. Time: 2 days
Breaks: Stay overnight in Cape May or the Wildwoods; many bed-and-breakfasts have a two-night minimum on weekends, so if you're only staying one night or B&Bs aren't your style, check out the many 1950s-style motels in North Wildwood.

This tour, from Atlantic City to the southernmost tip of the state, will take you to some of the best of the Jersey Shore, including sterling examples of its boardwalks, natural habitats, and collections of historic architecture. While you can spend time on a beach sunbathing, for sure, there are also some great attractions and diversions inland, including horseback riding, touring the Intracoastal Waterway, and hiking. This is prime real estate in summer, and traffic can be nightmarish on Friday going south and Sunday coming north. Try visiting in spring or fall, when the crowds have thinned and the birds are stopping in along the Atlantic Flyway.

❶ In **Atlantic City**, you can choose from any of 13 casinos. But if you're not into gambling, it's still fun to check out the boardwalk and look at some of the over-the-top archi-tecture (most notably the **Trump Taj Mahal Casino Resort**) and over-the-top people (from street characters to kids with multiple body piercings). At the **Garden Pier,** visit the Atlantic City Historical Museum, small but with a wonderful array of memorabilia from the times of Mr. Peanut and full-body bathing suits. North of Atlantic City is the pristine **Edwin B. Forsythe National Wildlife Refuge,** which has an 8-mi driving loop as well as two short hiking trails and watchtowers. To get there, take the Garden State Parkway North, exit at Atlantic City Service Plaza, Milepost 41, and follow signs for Jim

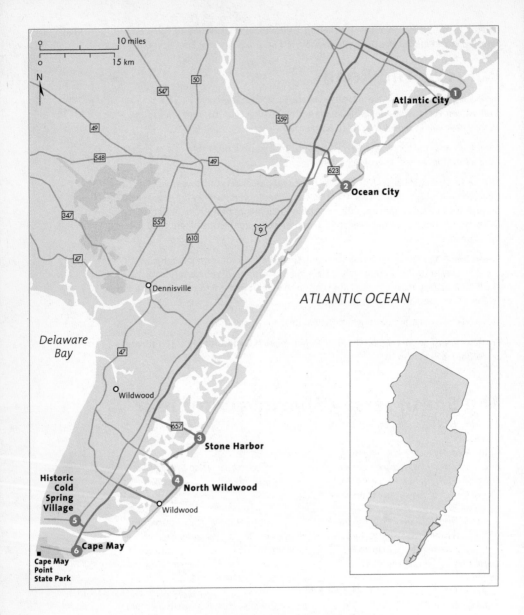

Leeds Rd. Turn right onto Leeds and left at Great Creek Rd., then continue 3 mi to Route 9. Go south on Route 9 and take a left onto Lily Lake Road.

❷ In **Ocean City** you can play on the boardwalk of "America's Greatest Family Resort," as the town calls itself. Ocean City has 2 mi of beach and boardwalk, and no doubt in summer you'll find yourself either watching or participating in one of the wacky contests or festivals the town is known for.

❸ Return to the Garden State Parkway via Route 623 and proceed south to Exit 10 (Route 657/Stone Harbor Boulevard), which will take you into **Stone Harbor.** Visit the **Wetlands Institute** which has easy, flat hikes as well as exhibits of marine life in the wetlands

INTRODUCTION
HISTORY
REGIONS
WHEN TO VISIT
STATE'S GREATS
RULES OF THE ROAD
DRIVING TOURS

environment. The second weekend in September the institute sponsors a huge **Wings 'n' Water Festival** in Stone Harbor and several of the surrounding towns.

❹ In **North Wildwood** you'll begin to see the kitschy 1950s architecture of the diners and motels that line block after block near the beach. You can take an official tour, called the **Doo-Wop Trolley Tours,** on Tuesday or Thursday, or drive by and enjoy it on your own anytime; the buildings are particularly photogenic at sunrise and sunset. Next you can head for Morey's Piers and check out the biggest Ferris wheel on the East Coast, along with a slew of other rides at not only Morey's but four other piers. The boardwalk really rocks most nights in season, which has grown to include part of October, when the crowds are not as thick. Buy some curly fries or some Kohr's custard (after you go on the rides) then pick up a paddle-wheeler cruise of the Intracoastal Waterway aboard the *Delta Lady*.

❺ Proceed west on Wildwood Boulevard (Route 47) to Garden State Parkway south. Continue on the Parkway to Route 109/U.S. 9 west to Cold Spring, where you will find the **Historic Cold Spring Village**, a collection of vintage houses from around the state. Often on weekends there are crafts fairs and entertainment suitable for kids.

❻ From Cold Spring Village take U.S. 9 east to Route 633 south into **Cape May**, where you'll find an awesome collection of restored Victorian houses in a city that restored itself to National Historic Landmark starting in the 1970s. There are lots of cute shops along the Washington Mall, if you're into Victoriana. The Mid-Atlantic Center for the Arts (MAC) offers all sorts of architectural tours, most of which include the **Emlen Physick Estate**, a huge gray mansion that has been carefully restored and is home to MAC. Favorites include walking tours, trolley tours, candlelight tours, and if you are there in October take the Haunted Haunts of Cape May tour. MAC also spearheads numerous festivals, including the extremely popular **Victorian Week** in October, and a Dickens-theme week during Christmas season. Cape May's strategic position along the Atlantic Flyway means great bird-watching, from a hawk-sighting watchpoint on the boardwalk at the **Cape May Point State Park** to sightings of songbirds and even monarch butterflies. At the other end of the parking lot from the birders is the Cape May Point Lighthouse, open to the public after a $2 million restoration. You can climb the 199 steps to the top, where you'll be rewarded with great views of the ocean and the shoreline back to Wildwood, and if you keep your eyes peeled you may even see some dolphins splashing about in the ocean. If not, you can take a whale-and-dolphin-watch cruise aboard any of several sightseeing boats in the Cape May marina near the bridge on Route 9 coming into town.

To return to your starting point, take the Garden State Parkway north to the Atlantic City Expressway, and then drive east to Atlantic City.

Morris County Driving Tour
FROM MORRISTOWN TO SHORT HILLS

Distance: Approximately 60 mi   Time: 2 days
Breaks: Treat yourself to a night at the Hilton at Short Hills, the state's top-rated hotel, along with dinner in the gourmet Dining Room and maybe a couple of treatments in the hotel's full-service spa.

You're not going to have to cover a lot of ground on this two-day tour. The Morristown area is just jammed with history; you could spend the whole weekend in Morristown

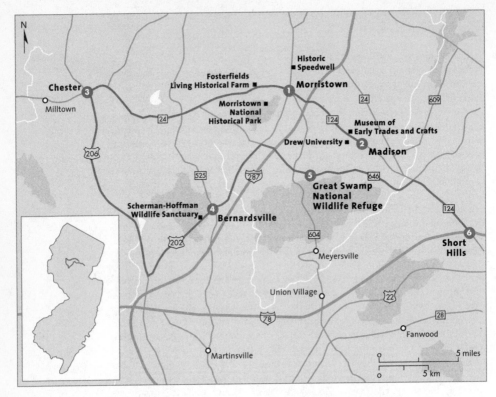

N

Chester
Milltown
24
206
525

Fosterfields
Living Historical Farm ■

Morristown ■
National
Historical Park

Historic
■ Speedwell

Morristown 1

24
124

Drew University ■
287

Museum of
■ Early Trades and Crafts

Madison 2

609

5
646

Great Swamp
National
Wildlife Refuge

124

Scherman-Hoffman
Wildlife Sanctuary■ 4 Bernardsville

202

604

Meyersville

Short
Hills 6

Union Village

22

78
28

Martinsville

Fanwood

5 miles

5 km

itself. But in Morris County you'll find some beautiful backcountry roads (Route 24 is particularly inspiring) and big houses, and a few charming little towns in which to have a fine meal or do some shopping. The area is lovely during foliage season; stay away from the Great Swamp National Wildlife Refuge in summer—it really is swampy and the black flies and skeeters will chase you away fast.

❶ Begin your tour in **Morristown**. A good orientation point is the Town Green, which has been the heart of the town for 250 years. During the 1700s, the Green was used as a pasture for animals and as a training ground for the local militia. In 1755, a log cabin was constructed on the western corner of the Green to serve as the town's courthouse and jail. A pillory and a scaffold were also located on the Green, and numerous executions took place here until 1833. The looming Civil War monument, *Soldier at Rest,* was erected in 1871. Cross the street to the **Presbyterian Church of Morristown**, formed in 1733. During the American Revolution (George Washington reportedly worshipped and took communion here), the church became a hospital for soldiers. The present church, the third one constructed on the site, dates from 1893–94; the burial ground dates to 1731 and holds town founders and soldiers from the American Revolution. From the town green you can head off to visit several historic homes that are linked for the annual **Holly Walk Tour** in December. Among them are **Acorn Hall**, home of the Morris County Historical Society, and **Macculloch Hall**, a Federal-style brick mansion completed in 1819 for George Perrot Macculloch, "Father of the Morris Canal." Macculloch's vision for a canal that would connect Pennsylvania's coal mines to Morris County's iron foundries was realized by 1831. Today the mansion and gardens are open to the public and house a collection of 18th- and 19th-century English and American fine and decorative arts. The mansion holds a major collection of the works of political cartoonist

Thomas Nast. The wonderful **Morris Museum** features interesting temporary exhibits in the Geraldine R. Dodge Gallery, plus a good science-based collection including rocks and minerals, dinosaur bones and fossils, and some small live animals.

Morristown includes classic **Historic Speedwell,** a National Historic Landmark Site and the former home of Judge Stephen Vail. It's best known as the spot where Alfred Vail and Samuel P. Morse perfected the electromagnetic telegraph in 1838 and where the engine for the first trans-Atlantic steamship, the SS *Savannah,* was produced in 1818. The 7-acre site includes the Vail mansion and the Telegraph Factory; the ironworks itself is gone. The **Morristown National Historical Park** preserves sites that were occupied by General George Washington during the Revolution, in 1777, and again from 1779–80, including Washington's Headquarters and **Jockey Hollow. Fosterfields Living Historical Farm** is a 200-acre site on which chores are still performed the old way. You can tour the Willows mansion, the home on the estate, or just picnic or run around on the wide expanses of lawn in the park. It's a great spot to stop with the kids.

② From Morristown head east on Route 124 to **Madison** where the **Museum of Early Trades and Crafts** houses a collection of 18th- and 19th-century tools and hands-on displays for children, and has demonstrations most weekends that kids especially will enjoy. **Drew University** is home to the **New Jersey Shakespeare Festival,** a professional troupe dedicated to presenting the works of the Bard and his contemporaries; the troupe recently moved into a $7.5 million facility, renovated in 1998: the F. M. Kirby Shakespeare Theatre.

③ From Madison head west on Route 124 back through Morristown to Routes 510/24 to **Chester,** where you can find great antiquing. In the 1860s, this small, sweet place was another boomtown when iron ore was discovered. Chester's "Brick House" tavern remains today, now as the Publick House serving meals and offering accommodations. Chester has caught on big time with the baby-boomer crowd.

④ From Chester head south on U.S. 206 to U.S. 202 east to **Bernardsville**. The local Audubon Society offers hikes in the 250-acre **Scherman-Hoffman Wildlife Sanctuary**; the nighttime owl prowl is especially fun.

⑤ From Bernardsville take U.S. 202 northeast to Route 646 east to the **Great Swamp National Wildlife Refuge,** which lies between Chatham and Basking Ridge. The 6,700-acre swamp was once a glacial lake. The Lord Stirling Environmental Education Center adjacent to the refuge is a good starting point; from the center you can take a board-walk trail to bird observation blinds.

⑥ From Great Swamp National Wildlife Refuge, take Route 646 east to Route 124 east to **Short Hills. The Mall at Short Hills** is an oasis of shopping in New Jersey, where the famous malls of Paramus are closed due to Blue Laws on Sunday. The Mall at Short Hills is home to upscale shops, including Tiffany, Neiman Marcus, and Nordstrom. Head north on Route 24 to return to Morristown.

ASBURY PARK

MAP 9, H6

(Nearby towns also listed: Belmar, Ocean Grove, Spring Lake, Tinton Falls)

In the late 1800s Asbury Park was a hot resort town, but over the years, it was plagued by fires and storms. A building boom in the early 1920s added some notable structures by the architects Warren and Wetmore, designers of New York's Grand Central

Terminal. You'll find more than a mile of beaches and struggling boardwalk ventures, but it's best not to go roaming the side streets and areas farther into Asbury on your own. The town is mostly known for music—Bruce Springsteen named an album after it. A local artists' community is helping to bring some life to the old town, though, and the Berkeley Carteret remains a wonderful and comfortable place to stay overnight.

Information: Asbury Park Chamber of Commerce | 100 Lake Ave., Asbury Park, 07712 | 732/775–7676 | chamber@mail.com | www.asbury.net/chamber.

Attractions
Stone Pony. This club is synonymous with Bruce Springsteen and the E Street Band, who used to play there, as did Southside Johnny and the Asbury Jukes. The club, which closed in 1998, reopened under new management in May 2000 with an impressive summer lineup of musical talent. | 913 Ocean Ave. | 732/502–0600.

ON THE CALENDAR
JUNE: *12th Annual Asbury Park Jazz Festival.* Bring your family and a beach blanket to Sunset Park for this weekend festival with performances by national and local jazz-gospel artists. | 732/775–2100.
JUNE–AUG.: *Thursday Concert Series.* Hear big-band jazz, Dixieland, and swing every Thursday evening beginning at 7, in the Arthur Pryor Band Shell. | 732/775–2100.
AUG.: *Paradise Street Festival.* This annual celebration of African and African-American culture, held in Sunset Park on the first weekend of August, features traditional music, food, and dance. Vendors offer clothing and jewelry, arts and crafts, and food and drink. | 732/988–0711.
DEC.: *Christmas Tree Lighting.* Join Santa and his associates in Sunset Park as they celebrate the Christmas season with this December 1 tradition. | 732/775–2100.

Dining
La Nonna Piancone's Cafe. Italian. This casual Italian eatery in Bradley Beach, a neighboring town, has an open kitchen and brick archways, and is known for filet mignon. Try the mozzarella tower or zuppa di pesce (fish soup). You can dine outside at sidewalk tables. | 800 Main St., Bradley Beach | 732/775–0906 | No lunch Sun. | $9–$22 | AE, D, DC, MC, V.

Lodging
Berkeley-Carteret. This hotel, an elegant resort destination in the 1920s, '30s and '40s, is a reminder of Asbury Park in its heyday. It received a $20 million renovation in 1985 and its enviable location, right on the water, provides spectacular views from many rooms. Other views however, are not as appealing, such as the ones of stretches of abandoned buildings south of the hotel. The hotel has an interesting past, including having at one time been owned by the Mararishi Mahesh Yogi, who wanted to turn it into a transcendental meditation center (Asbury Park prevented this). The current owner has plans to restore it to its former grandeur, and help rejuvenate Asbury Park in the process. Restaurant, bar, complimentary Continental breakfast. Cable TV. Pool. Tennis court. Health club. Laundry service. Some pets allowed. | 1401 Ocean Ave. | 732/776–6700 or 800/776–6011 | fax 732/776–9546 | 246 rooms, 4 suites | $129–$159 rooms, $179–$219 suites | AE, D, DC, MC, V.

ATLANTIC CITY

MAP 9, F10

(Nearby town also listed: Ocean City, Somers Point)

Atlantic City has long held the moniker of "America's Favorite Playground," and—like Las Vegas—is in the midst of reinventing itself yet again. In the late 1800s Atlantic City was a fashionable seaside resort, where the innovation of the boardwalk was born:

in 1870, it was a series of boards laid across the beach to the hotels and to the train, to keep visitors from tracking in the sand. The boards were taken up each winter, until finally a permanent structure was built in 1880, and a more permanent one put in place after a storm in 1889.

Also born in Atlantic City was saltwater taffy, "amusement piers" with their oft-bizarre attractions including the Diving Horse, Dr. Couney's Premature Infant Exhibit, and marathon dance contests. In 1940, the Convention Center became home to the Miss America Pageant, a legacy that the city dearly holds onto today (the Sheraton Convention Center has a bar featuring the footwear of various Miss America contestants).

After experiencing a lull in the middle of the 20th century, Atlantic City began to make a comeback with gambling in the 1980s, but there was little more than casinos in the town, and most visitors were day-trippers. Today the city is going for a much broader client base. You'll see high profile spots like Planet Hollywood, the Hard Rock Cafe, and a Ripley's Believe It or Not museum on the boardwalk, as well as rides, shopping, and a convention center and hotel complex nearby. There are currently 13 major casinos, and Steve Wynn, who left town many years ago to establish his empire in Vegas, is planning a new Mirage resort for the city in the near future. Service has also increased at the Atlantic City Airport just outside town.

Stop by the $4 million Visitor Welcome Center, about a mile east of the toll plaza on the Atlantic City Expressway. You'll find information about not only the attractions along the boardwalk but also on Historic Gardner's Basin, the Historic Village of Smithville, Edwin B. Forsythe National Wildlife Refuge, and other things to do within a short drive of the one-armed bandits.

Information: **Atlantic City Convention and Visitors Authority** | 2314 Pacific Ave., Atlantic City, 08401 | 800/BOARDWK or 888/AC–VISIT | www.atlanticcitynj.com.

TRANSPORTATION INFORMATION

Airports: Atlantic City International Airport | 101 Atlantic City Airport, off the Atlantic City Expwy, Exit 9, in Egg Harbor Township | 609/645–7895.
Spirit Airlines, Inc. (800/772–7117) offers flights between Atlantic City and Cleveland, Tampa, Ft. Lauderdale, Orlando, Ft. Myers, and Myrtle Beach. **US Airways Express** (800/428–4322) offers flights between Atlantic City and Philadelphia and Baltimore.
Bus Lines: Atlantic City is the most popular bus destination in the world. **New Jersey Transit** (800/582–5946), **Greyhound** (800/231–2222), **Grayline of New York** (800/669–0051), and **Academy Bus Lines** (800/992–0451 | www.academybus.com) provide scheduled service to Atlantic City from the NY/NJ Port Authority terminal in New York City. The Atlantic City Municipal Terminal is at Michigan and Atlantic Avenues.
Other: Trains to Atlantic City are offered through **New Jersey Transit.** Its Philadelphia–Atlantic City Rail Line runs 13 trains per day between Philadelphia (30th Street Station) and the Atlantic City Rail Terminal, with local stops. Free shuttle service is available between the Atlantic City Rail Terminal and all casinos. Call 800/AC–TRAIN in New Jersey, or 215/569–3752 in Pennsylvania for information. | www.njtransit.state.nj.us.

Attractions

ART AND ARCHITECTURE
Lucy, the Margate Elephant. Built in 1881 as a publicity stunt by a real estate developer from Philadelphia, this six-story National Historic Landmark remains a strange and fun attraction just outside Atlantic City. You can take a tour through the inside of the elephant. | 9200 Atlantic Ave., Margate | 609/823–6473 | $4 | Apr.–mid-June, weekends 10–4; mid-June–Labor Day, Mon.–Thurs. 10–8, Fri.–Sat. 10–5.

BEACHES, PARKS, AND NATURAL SIGHTS

Absecon Lighthouse. This 1857 lighthouse was designed by George Meade, stands 171 ft tall, and is the oldest man-made tourist attraction on the Jersey shore. The lighthouse is just north of downtown Atlantic City. | Pacific and Rhode Island Aves. | 609/927–5218 or 609/449–1360 | $4 | Mar., weekends 11–4 Memorial Day–Labor Day, Thurs.–Mon. 11–4 (daily in July and Aug.).

Edwin B. Forsythe National Wildlife Refuge, Brigantine Division. Nearly 40,000 acres of coastal habitats—including 3,000 acres of woodlands—are protected in this refuge. You'll see plenty of winged visitors, among them peregrine falcons and bald eagles. Human visitors can take an 8-mi Wildlife Drive or walk the two short foot trails. To get there, head west on Route 30, then right on Route 9. After about 5 mi, make a right on Great Creek Rd. | Great Creek Rd. and Rte. 9, Oceanville | 609/652–1665 | $4 per vehicle | Daily dawn–dusk.

CULTURE, EDUCATION, AND HISTORY

Historic Gardner's Basin. Once a home to pirates, privateers, and whalers, this site is now a restored maritime village with a waterfront park complete with historic vessels, an aquarium, museum, and two restaurants. | 800 North New Hampshire Ave. | 609/348–2880 | $7 | Daily 10–5.

Ocean Life Center. This facility is a hands-on learning center for kids and adults alike. Highlights include a 750-gallon touch tank and gorgeous views from the observation deck and widow's walk. | 609/348–2880 | $7; special rates for children and senior citizens | Daily 10–5; closed Thanksgiving, Christmas, New Year's Day.

MUSEUMS

Marine Mammal Stranding Center and Museum. This unique research and rescue center is on call to rescue stranded dolphins, seals, sea turtles, and whales that travel up this way and into New York Harbor. The museum has exhibits on marine life. | 3625 Atlantic-Brigantine Blvd. | 609/266–0538 | www.mmsc.org | $1 suggested donation | Memorial Day–Labor Day, daily 11–5; Labor Day–Memorial Day, weekends noon–4.

Noyes Museum. You'll find contemporary American and folk art, crafts, and a superb bird decoy collection in this compact but wonderful museum. | Lily Lake Rd. | 609/652–8848 | $3; special rates for children | Wed.–Sun. 11–4.

Ripley's Believe It or Not! Museum. Housed in a bizarre building that looks as if it's about to be destroyed by a wrecking ball, this eclectic museum has, among its equally bizarre treasures, a lock of George Washington's hair and a collection of actual shrunken heads. | 1441 Boardwalk | 609/347–2001 | $9; special rates for children | Memorial Day–Labor Day, daily 10–10. Labor Day–Memorial Day, 10–6.

SHOPPING

The Shops on Ocean One. This upscale shopping complex, on a pier off the boardwalk across from Caesars, has restaurants and a food court. | 1 Atlantic Ocean | 609/347–8082 or 609/347–8086 | Free | Jan.–May, daily 10–7; June–Aug., daily 10–9; Sept.–Dec., daily 10–8.

SPORTS AND RECREATION

Golf. The Greater Atlantic City Golf Association, a coalition of area golf courses and hotels, offers local stay-and-play packages. The Marriott Seaview Resort in Absecon is among the finest in the state. | Greater Atlantic City Golf Association: 1742 Mays Landing | 800/GOLF–222 | www.gacga.com/ | Year-round.

Storybook Land. Just west of Atlantic City, the 20-acre Storybook Land has 50 larger-than-life buildings and displays illustrating the tales of famous childhood stories. There's also rides and a picnic area. | 6415 Black Horse Pike, Egg Harbor Township | 609/641–7847 or 609/646–0103 | fax 609/646–4533 | www.storybookland.com/homens3.htm | $12.25 | Daily 10–5.

SIGHTSEEING TOURS/TOUR COMPANIES

Atlantic City Jitney. Jitneys have been an Atlantic City tradition since 1915, although the former white bread-truck vehicles have recently been replaced with sleek powder-blue ones. The jitney routes cover all of Atlantic City, including landmarks such as the Absecon Lighthouse, Northeast Inlet, Historic Gardner's Basin, City Hall, and the Convention Center. | 201 Pacific Ave. | 609/344–8642 | fax 609/345–5069 | www.virtualac.com/jitney | $2 | Weekdays 8:30–4.

OTHER POINTS OF INTEREST

Convention Center. This $268-million facility opened in May 1997 as the Northeast's largest convention center. | 1 Ocean Way | 609/449–2000 | fax 609/449–2090 | Free | Weekdays 9–5.

Convention Hall. Although it's currently closed for renovations, this classic old-fashioned grand edifice is worth checking out from the outside, especially if you're a Miss America fan. The famous pageant has been held here for more than 60 years. | 2301 Boardwalk, between Mississippi and Florida Aves. | 609/449–2000 or 888/222–3683.

Garden Pier. An oasis of culture in Atlantic City, the Garden Pier is home to the wonderful Atlantic City Historical Museum, as well as the Atlantic City Art Center. | Boardwalk and New Jersey Ave. | 609/347–5844 | Free | Daily; museum 10–4.

Historic Town of Smithville and the Village Greene at Smithville. Originally built in 1787, Smithville today is an enclave of shops and stores specializing in early-American antiques. Special events are held throughout the year. To get there, head north along Route 9. | 615 Moss Hill Rd., Smithville | 609/652–4040 | Free | Daily.

Renault Winery. Established in 1864, Renault is the oldest vineyard in the country. Along with tours, tastings, and a museum, it also has an elegant restaurant and a wine café. To get here, head west on Route 30 for approximately 16 mi, then head right on North Bremen Avenue. | 72 N. Bremen Ave. Egg Harbor City | 609/965–2111 | www.renaultwinery.com | $2 | Mon.– Sun. noon–4.

ON THE CALENDAR

MAR., OCT.: *Atlantique City Spring and Fall Festivals.* These huge antique shows are held at the Convention Center on the last weekend in March and the third weekend in October. | 800/526–2724.

MAY: *Thoroughbred racing.* Catch the excitement of live horse racing daily at the Atlantic City Race Track. | 609/641–2190.

MAY–AUG.: *Smithville Fife and Drum Corps Concert and Parade.* These musical events are held the last weekend of May, June, July, and August in the historic town of Smithville, just north of Atlantic City. | 609/652–0440 or 609/652–7777.

JUNE: *Annual NJ Seafood Festival.* Held the second weekend in June in Historic Gardner's Basin, this delicious festival features food sampling, live music, rides, games, and exhibits. | 609/347–4386.

JUNE: *Beach Fest.* Claiming to be the largest free festival in the East, Beach Fest, held along the boardwalk between the Taj Mahal and the Hilton, incorporates concerts, sporting events, a food court, dance parties, and more into one weekend—usually the third in June. | 609/484–9020.

JUNE: *Spring Fling, Chevy Thing.* Antique Chevrolets are on display in Historic Smithville, along with food and entertainment. This event is generally held on a Saturday or Sunday in mid-June. | 609/748–6160.

MID-JUNE: *ShopRite LPGA Classic.* This is the only LPGA event played in New Jersey, and it takes place at the Marriott's Seaview Resort in Absecon, 15 mi west of Atlantic City. Call for dates. | 609/383–8330 | www.shopritelpga.com.

AUG: *Wedding of the Sea.* This local Catholic tradition, commemorating the Old Testament story of the appearance of the Virgin Mary to the Fishermen of Venice and always celebrated on August 15, regularly draws 10,000 faithful to the Atlantic City boardwalk.

The bishop of the Diocese of Camden leads his choir down to the water, where he tosses a wreath into the ocean, symbolizing the marriage of the city and the sea. | 609/344–8536.

SEPT.: *Festival Latino Americano.* Celebrate Hispanic culture in Historic Gardner's Basin with entertainment, dancing, food, and crafts. This festival is usually held on the second weekend in September. | 609/645–4520.

SEPT., OCT: *Miss American Week and Pageant.* Conceived in 1921 as a "Bathing Beauty" contest intended to extend the summer tourist season by one more week, this small local pageant has grown into a national tradition. The event is held in the Boardwalk Convention Center at Mississippi Avenue and the Boardwalk. Call for dates. | 609/344–5278.

Dining

INEXPENSIVE

★ **Angelo's Fairmount Tavern.** Italian. Locals flock to this unassuming restaurant, known for its Italian standards as well as steaks and seafood since 1935. | 2300 Fairmount Ave. | 609/344–2439 | No lunch weekends | $9–$26 | AE, D, MC, V.

Harley Dawn Diner. American. Settle in for homemade meatloaf, mashed potatoes, and fresh seafood at this old-fashioned diner, 30 mi west of Atlantic City. Pies are baked daily. There's a kids' menu and senior specials. Breakfast is also available. | 1402 Black Horse Pike, Folsom | 609/567–6084 | $6–$15 | AE, D, DC, MC, V.

Irish Pub and Inn. Irish. Enjoy live Irish music nightly at this informal pub, where favorite dishes include corned-beef sandwiches, turkey dinners, and beef stew. The $1.95 lunch special is one of the city's great bargains. The bar is open 24 hours, and you can order dinner until 7:30 AM. In midtown, right off the boardwalk. | 164 St. James Pl. | 609/344–9063 | $5–$7 | No credit cards.

Mama Mott's. Italian. This cozy center-city restaurant has a Little Italy feel, with candles, chandeliers, and plenty of red and gold. It's known for shrimp, lobster, and flounder Orleans. Try the zuppa di pesce. There's live piano music on Saturday nights. | 151 S. New York Ave. | 609/345–8218 or 800/293–0805 | No lunch | $8–$39 | AE, DC, MC, V.

White House Sub Shop. Delicatessen. More than 17 million hefty sandwiches have been made at the White House since 1946. Midtown location. | 2301 Arctic Ave. | 609/345–1564 or 609/345–8599 | $5–$10 | No credit cards.

MODERATE

Angeloni's. Italian. Wine bottles line the walls of this Ducktown restaurant, whose extensive wine list is famous. Enjoy typical Italian beef, veal, and seafood served family-style. The *braciole*—rolled veal stuffed with sausage, cheese and italian seasonings—is very popular. | 2400 Arctic Ave. | 609/344–7875 | fax 609/344–9141 | $11–$30 | AE, D, DC, MC, V.

Captain Young's Seafood Emporium. Seafood. Nautical motif (including huge stuffed fish on the walls), a spectacular ocean view, and fresh seafood are the draws here. Try lobster, flounder, swordfish or shrimp scampi. Rumor has it the original Captain Young liked to fish out of his bedroom window upstairs. | 1 Atlantic Ocean | 609/344–2001 | $10–$27 | AE, D, DC, MC, V.

Dock's Oyster House. Seafood. Owned and operated by the Dougherty family since 1897, the city's oldest restaurant serves seafood in a setting of wood and stained glass engraved with nautical scenes. Try the pan-seared ahi tuna and fresh soft-shell crab. Piano bar. Kids' menu. | 2405 Atlantic Ave. | 609/345–0092 | Closed Dec., Jan. No lunch Mon. | $15–$42 | AE, DC, MC, V.

Grabel's. Continental. This restaurant is known for standards such as veal chops, steak, jumbo shrimp, and crab cakes. There's a kids' menu, a piano bar from Thursday through Sunday, and a large dance floor to hit between courses. | 3901 Atlantic Ave. | 609/344–9263 | No lunch | $15–$22 | AE, DC, MC, V.

Knife and Fork Inn. Seafood. Step into a turn-of-the-20th-century European eating club when you enter this restaurant, in a 1912 landmark inn. It's well known for Lobster Thermadore and Lobster Newberg, but the bouillabaisse and crab cakes are also popular. Non-seafood eaters can enjoy filet mignon. Enjoy live music on weekends in July and August. No smoking. | 29 S. Albany Ave. | 609/344–1133 | fax 609/344–4890 | www.knifeand-forkinn.com | $20–$42 | AE, D, DC, MC, V.

Los Amigos. Mexican. This cozy bar and restaurant, minutes from the boardwalk casinos, serves burritos, Mexican pizza, and other south-of-the-border fare. There's fresh tuna and salmon daily and a wide variety of tequilas. Open-air dining on the patio. Kids' menu. | 1926 Atlantic Ave. | 609/344–2293 | Closed Sun. No lunch weekends | $10–$21 | AE, MC, V.

Old Waterway Inn. Contemporary. This cozy waterfront spot, 2 mi from the Venice Park section of the boardwalk, has lots of dark cherrywood and a fire burning all year. Stick with their famous charbroiled steak, or try the pan-seared red snapper with green coconut curry sauce. An enclosed outdoor dining area overlooks the water. Kids' menu. | 1700 W. Riverside Dr. | 609/347–1793 | Closed Jan. No lunch | $16–$25 | AE, DC, MC, V.

Ram's Head Inn. American. This pastoral retreat, 8 mi from Atlantic City, is one of New Jersey's top restaurants. It's filled with the works of local artists and soft piano music plays as you enjoy drinks by the fireplace. In season, you can dine outdoors in a flower-filled courtyard with a fountain. Try creamy chicken potpie with dumplings in a copper kettle, glazed crisp roasted duckling with rice, and Maryland Crabmeat Imperial in a pastry crust. Live music. Kids' menu. | 9 W. White Horse Pike, Absecon | 609/652–1700 | Jacket required | Closed Mon. No lunch weekends | $18–$30 | AE, D, DC, MC, V.

Renault Winery. Continental. A guitarist sets the mood at this elegant 1864 winery, known for six-course seafood, poultry, and beef meals served, of course, with appropriate wines. For lunch, check out the winery's Garden Café, which offers lighter fare. Live music. Sunday brunch. To get there, head west on Route 30, approximately 30 mi. | 72 N. Bremen Ave., Egg Harbor City | 609/965–2111 | Reservations essential | $30–$35 | AE, D, DC, MC, V.

Scannicchio's. Italian. This intimate, candlelit, classic Italian restaurant is often cited on "Best of" lists. There are eight fish specials daily, and an extensive pasta menu. Popular dishes include stuffed veal, calamari, and filet mignon stuffed with crab, shrimp, and scallops. Don't skip the homemade cannoli. | 119 S. California Ave. | 609/348–6378 | Reservations essential weekends | No lunch | $11–$25 | AE, MC, V.

Tun Tavern Brewery and Restaurant. American. All-natural lagers are made in the brewery, which can be toured. The restaurant is known for salads, sizzling strip steaks, and barbecued strawberry salmon. Kids' menu. | 2000 Kirkman Blvd. | 609/347–7800 | $13–$19 | AE, DC, MC, V.

EXPENSIVE

Brighton Steakhouse. Continental. Lots of dark wood and leather create an upscale, subdued atmosphere at this classic steak house, in the Sands Hotel. The Chateaubriand for two is very popular, as are the lobster and shrimp dishes. There are six different desserts each month, and 21 wines by the glass. | Indiana Ave. and Brighton Park | 609/441–4300 | Call for hrs, which change monthly | $21–$60 | AE, D, DC, MC, V.

Chef Vola's. Italian. This small, romantic, and very exclusive Italian restaurant is known for steak, veal, and homemade pasta. Patrons are mostly regulars. | 111 S. Albion Pl. | 609/345–2022 | Reservations essential | Closed Mon. No lunch | $13–$35 | No credit cards.

★ **La Palais.** French. Look up from your rack of lamb with rosemary and pine nuts, or your individual dessert soufflé, and you'll see yourself in one of the many ornate mirrors scattered throughout the dining room of this restaurant, which you'll find in the Resorts

ATLANTIC CITY

INTRO
ATTRACTIONS
DINING
LODGING

Casino Hotel. Live piano music nightly. Sunday brunch. | North Carolina Ave. and Boardwalk | 609/344–6000 or 800/438–7424 | Closed Mon., Tues. | $32–$60 | AE, D, DC, MC, V.

Lodging

INEXPENSIVE

Atlantic City-Boardwalk Days Inn. This oceanfront motel has sweeping water views and beach access. It's adjacent to the Tropicana Casino and an easy walk to several others. There is also an outdoor pool with a great view of the ocean. Restaurant, bar, room service. In-room data ports, cable TV. Pool. Free parking. | Boardwalk and Morris Ave. | 609/344–6101 or 800/544–8313 | fax 609/348–5335 | www.atlanticcitydaysinn.com | 105 rooms | $40–$175 | AE, D, MC, V.

Atlantic City Hilton. Located right on the boardwalk, this Hilton has a casino and a theater that features major musical performers. The rooms are bright and airy, and some have ocean views. 7 restaurants, bar (with entertainment). Cable TV. Pool. Barbershop, beauty salon, hot tub. Gym. Business services. Parking fee. | Boston Ave. and Pacific Ave. | 609/347–7111 or 800/257–8677 | fax 609/340–4858 | www.hilton.com | 850 rooms | $99–$225 | AE, D, DC, MC, V.

Atlantic City's Howard Johnson Hotel. This oceanfront hotel is steps from the boardwalk, next to Tropicana Casino, and two blocks from the Atlantic City Hilton Casino. Restaurant, bar. Cable TV. Pool. Hot tub, sauna. Exercise room. Laundry service. Business services. No pets. Free parking. | Chelsea Ave. and Boardwalk | 800/695–4685 or 800/406–1411 | fax 609/344–0878 | www.hojo.com | 121 rooms | $53–$179 | AE, D, MC, V.

Clarion Bayside Resort. This two-story hotel is on the bay, just 2 mi from the casinos. Rooms overlook either the pool, the Bay, or the Atlantic City skyline. The golf shop offers packages to nine area courses, along with free shuttle service. Restaurant, bar. Some microwaves, some refrigerators, cable TV. Pool, wading pool. Massage, sauna. Tennis. Exercise equipment. Gym. Laundry facilities. Business services, airport shuttle. Free parking. | 8029 Black Horse Pike, West Atlantic City | 609/641–3546 | fax 609/641–9740 | 110 rooms | $60–$160 | AE, D, DC, MC, V.

Comfort Inn-Boardwalk. This hotel is 100 yards from the beach and the casinos and 1 mi from the Convention Center. Smaller than many of the area hotels, it prides itself on offering personal attention to its guests. Complimentary Continental breakfast. In-room data ports, some microwaves, some refrigerators. Cable TV. Laundry facilities. No pets. Free parking. | 154 S. Kentucky Ave. | 609/348–4000 | fax 609/348–0072 | www.comfortinn.com | 80 rooms | $80–$107 | AE, D, DC, MC, V.

Comfort Inn–North. About 3 mi northeast of the Atlantic City boardwalk, this seven-story hotel remains convenient to the casinos, but is less expensive than others that are directly on the beach. Some rooms have views of the Atlantic City skyline. To get there, head west on Route 30. Complimentary Continental breakfast. Cable TV. Exercise equipment. Business services. Free parking. | 539 E. Absecon Blvd., Absecon | 609/641–7272 | fax 609/641–1239 | www.comfortinn.com | 205 rooms | $75–$150 | AE, D, DC, MC, V.

Econo Lodge Boardwalk. This chain hotel is half a block from the boardwalk in the heart of the casino district, and the interior was updated in 1999. Complimentary Continental breakfast. Cable TV. Pool. Free parking. | 117 S. Kentucky Ave. | 609/344–9093 or 800/323–6410 | fax 609/340–8065 | www.econolodge.com | 51 rooms | $89–$116 | AE, D, MC, V.

Fairfield Inn by Marriott. This comfortable chain hotel is about 5 mi from the beach and casinos, and offers free weekend shuttle service to the Tropicana Casino. Some rooms have city skyline views. You can rent video games to use in your room. From Atlantic City, head west on Route 30. Complimentary Continental breakfast. Some refrigerators, cable TV. Pool. Business services. No pets. Free parking. | 405 E. Absecon Blvd., Absecon | 609/646–5000 | fax 609/383–8744 | www.fairfieldinn.com | 200 rooms | $69–$159 | AE, D, DC, MC, V.

Flagship Resort. This modern, salmon-color, 32-story, all-suites hotel is across from the board-walk (facing Brigantine and the Absecon Inlet) and away from the casino action. Every suite has a private terrace with a view. Restaurant. Microwaves, refrigerators, cable TV. Pool. Health club. Free parking. | 60 N. Main Ave. | 609/343–7447 or 800/647–7890 | 300 suites | $90–$145 | AE, D, MC, V.

Hampton Inn. On Route 30 in Absecon, the Hampton Inn is 4 mi from the Atlantic City International Airport and less than 10 mi from many area attractions, including the board-walk and casinos. Guest rooms are done in subdued colors and furnished with antique reproductions. There are five sizes of rooms to choose from. Complimentary Continental breakfast. In-room data ports, cable TV. Pool. Hot tub. Laundry facilities. Business services, airport shuttle. Free parking. | 240 E. White Horse Pike, Absecon | 609/652–2500 | fax 609/652–2212 | www.hamptoninn.com | 129 rooms | $89–$129 | AE, D, DC, MC, V.

Hampton Inn–West. Also called the Hampton Inn–Bayside, this six-story hotel overlooks the beach and offers beach access and rentals. It's 3 mi from Atlantic City's boardwalk and casinos, and 6 mi from the Atlantic City International Airport. To find it, head west on Route 40. Complimentary Continental breakfast. Some refrigerators, cable TV. Business services, airport shuttle. Free parking. | 7079 Black Horse Pike, West Atlantic City | 609/484–1900 | fax 609/383–0731 | www.hampton-inn.com | 143 rooms | $66–$159 | AE, D, DC, MC, V.

Holiday Inn–Boardwalk. This modern Holiday Inn in Atlantic City's central business district overlooks the boardwalk and the beach. Casinos are a few feet away. The lobby has a marble floor and a lounge area. Many rooms have ocean views. Restaurant, bar. In-room data ports, cable TV. Pool. Business services. Free parking. | Chelsea Ave. and Boardwalk | 609/348–2200 | fax 609/348–0168 | www.holiday-inn.com/hotels/acybw | 216 rooms, 4 suites | $79–$189, $289 suites | AE, D, DC, MC, V.

Super 8–Absecon. This motel is on U.S. 30 in Absecon and offers proximity to area attractions at lower prices than many of the establishments on the Atlantic City Boardwalk. Two of the rooms have hot tubs. Cable TV. Business services. Free parking. | 229 E. U.S. 30, Absecon | 609/652–2477 | fax 609/748–0666 | www.super8.com | 58 rooms | $50–$175 | AE, D, DC, MC, V.

Tropicana Casino. Welcome to oceanfront gambling heaven, where slots, table games, poker, and even "Asian Games" such as Pai Gow (a form of dominoes) are available around the clock. 5 restaurants, 2 bars. In-room data ports, cable TV. 2 pools. Barbershop, beauty salon, hot tub. Tennis court. Shops. Business services, parking (fee). | Brighton Ave. and Boardwalk | 609/340–4000 or 800/257–6227 | fax 609/343–5211 | www.tropicana.net | 1,624 rooms | $78–$300 | AE, D, MC, V.

MODERATE

★ **Bally's Park Place.** Choose between the art-deco style of the main building or the modern brass and marble luxury of the tower at this beachfront property. 9 restaurants, bar. Some refrigerators, cable TV. 2 pools. Barbershop, beauty salon, hot tub, massage. Gym. Business services. Parking (fee). | Boardwalk at Park Place | 609/340–2000 or 800/225–5977 | fax 609/340–4713 | www.parkplace.com | 1,268 rooms | $125–$245 | AE, D, DC, MC, V.

Caesars Atlantic City Hotel/Casino. The numbers at Caesars are impressive: 120,231 square ft, 1,138 rooms, 24 casinos, 3,595 slot machines, a theater seating 1,100 that offers "world-class entertainment," and on and on. It's also right on the beach, and many of the luxurious rooms and suites have breathtaking views of the ocean. 11 restaurants, 3 bars. Cable TV. Pool. Barbershop, beauty salon, hot tub, massage. Tennis. Exercise equipment. Shops. Business services, airport shuttle. Parking (fee). | 2100 Pacific Ave. | 609/348–4411 or 800/443–0104 | fax 609/347–8089 | www.caesars.com | 1,138 rooms | $150–$225 | AE, D, DC, MC, V.

Claridge Casino/Hotel. Built in 1930, the Claridge is one of the older hotels in the area. It has a handsome redbrick facade and several rooms with ocean views. There is a casino (with three floors of gambling) and theater on the premises. 5 restaurants, bar, room service. Refrigerators, cable TV. Pool. Beauty salon, hot tub, massage, sauna. Exercise equipment, gym, health club. Business services. Free parking. | Indiana Ave. and Boardwalk | 609/340–3400 or 800/257–8585 | fax 609/340–3875 | 504 rooms | $130–$180 | AE, D, DC, MC, V.

Harrah's Atlantic City Casino Hotel. Located on the bayside, this 16-story, three-tower property overlooks a marina and features live entertainment, including top Broadway productions and top celebrity vocalists. With seven restaurants, a health club, a casino, and modern, luxurious rooms, many guests feel no need to leave the hotel during their stay. 7 restaurants, bar. Cable TV. Pool. Health club. Parking (fee). | 777 Harrah's Blvd. | 609/441–5000 or 800/242–7724 | fax 609/348–6057 | 1,174 rooms | $125–$269 | AE, D, DC, MC, V.

Sands Hotel Casino. The Sands is expanding and renovating. The lobby and restaurant were updated in 2000 and room renovations are ongoing. The Copa Lounge is already a classic venue for singers, bandleaders, and other acts, and the hotel has purchased an additional building to add more gambling and entertainment. Restaurant, bar (with entertainment). Cable TV. Beauty salon. Spa. Exercise equipment. Business services, parking (fee). | Indiana Ave. and Boardwalk | 609/441–4000 or 800/257–8580 | fax 609/441–4180 | 523 rooms | $155–$275 | AE, D, DC, MC, V.

Trump Plaza Hotel and Casino. Visible from anywhere in town, this imposing white Trump building is the first hotel off the expressway. It's close to trains and buses, and right on the boardwalk. Ultramodern guest rooms have lots of mirrors, and suites have hot tubs. One side of the hotel overlooks the ocean; the other overlooks the city. 12 restaurants, 3 bars (with entertainment). In-room data ports, some refrigerators, cable TV. Pool. Beauty salon, hot tub, massage. Tennis. Exercise equipment, gym. Shops, video games. Business services. Parking (fee). | Mississippi Ave. and Boardwalk | 609/441–6000 or 800/677–7378 | fax 609/441–2603 | 904 rooms | $185–$325 | AE, D, DC, MC, V.

Trump Taj Mahal Casino Resort. This huge, white, well-lit modern building has rooms overlooking the ocean or the city, and suites with master bedrooms, living rooms, dining areas, and hot tubs. And, of course, there's the casino. 6 restaurants, 3 bars (with entertainment). Some refrigerators, cable TV. Pool. Barbershop, beauty salon, hot tub, massage. Gym. Bicycles. Shops, video games. Business services. Parking (fee). | 1000 Boardwalk | 609/449–1000 or 800/825–8786 | fax 609/449–6818 | www.trumptaj.com | 1,250 rooms, 246 suites | $175–$375 | AE, D, DC, MC, V.

Trump's Marina Casino Hotel. With helicopter service and the state's largest marina at its disposal, this hotel on an inlet (about six blocks from the boardwalk) caters to a sophisticated clientele. Decorated with a fanciful medieval theme, it hosts major sporting and entertainment events. 7 restaurants, 2 bars (1 with entertainment). In-room data ports, cable TV, in-room VCRs. Pool, wading pool. Barbershop, beauty salon, hot tub, massage. 2 tennis courts. Basketball, gym. Shops, video games. Business services. Parking (fee). | Heron Ave/Brigantine Blvd. | 609/441–2000 or 800/777–8477 | fax 609/441–8541 | 728 rooms | $125–$200 | AE, D, DC, MC, V.

EXPENSIVE

Marriott's Seaview Resort. Built in 1915, this grand Gatsby-style mansion just north of Atlantic City has lovely spacious rooms and suites with modern amenities and views of the surrounding woodlands. Some rooms have wet bars. Restaurant, bar, room service. In-room data ports, some refrigerators, cable TV. 2 pools. Hot tub, spa. 36-hole golf course, two 18-hole golf courses, putting green, 8 tennis courts. Exercise equipment. Laundry facilities. Business services. Parking (fee). | 401 S. New York Rd., Absecon | 609/748–1990 | fax 609/652–6917 | www.marriott.com | 297 rooms | $214–$244 | AE, D, DC, MC, V.

AUGUSTA

(Nearby town also listed: Franklin)

In the heart of New Jersey's rural Sussex County, Augusta is best known for being the home of the Sussex County Fairgrounds, at which numerous events take place throughout the year. In 1994, the addition of Skylands Park made it also the home of the New Jersey Cardinals, a minor-league baseball team.

Information: Sussex County Chamber of Commerce | 120 Hampton House Rd., Newton, 07860 | 973/579–1811 | fax 973/579–3031 | www.sussexcountychamber.org.

Attractions

Peters Valley Craft Education Center. From May to October, students come from all over to take classes in crafts ranging from blacksmithing to photography, taught by master craftspeople. The enclave also has a nice crafts store and a gallery. The annual juried crafts show takes place the last weekend in September. | 19 Kuhn Rd. | 973/948–5200 | fax 973/948–0011 | www.pvcrafts.org | Free | Office weekdays 9–5; gallery hours change seasonally.

Stokes State Forest. Highlights of Stokes' 15,735 acres include the very popular Tillman Ravine, a cool retreat in summer, and the view from Sunrise Mountain. The park, 8 mi north of Augusta, also rents cabins and has camping facilities. | 1 Coursen Rd., Branchville | 973/948–3820 | Free | Daily dawn–dusk.

Sussex County Fairgrouds. This 125-acre facility plays host to The New Jersey State Fair, the Sussex County Farm and Horse Show, craft festivals, and other events throughout the year. | Plains Rd. | 973/948–5500 | fax 973/948–0147 | www.sussex-county-fair.org/ | Variable | 9–4 Tue.–Fri., office hrs.

Swartswood State Park. This relatively small, 1,600-acre park, 9 mi west of Augusta, has hiking trails, water sports, and picnic facilities, as well as a winter ice-skating rink and cross-country ski trails. | 1091 E. Short Dr. and Rte. 619, Swartswood | 973/383–5230 | Parking: $5 weekdays, $7 weekends and Memorial Day–Labor Day | Daily 8–6.

ON THE CALENDAR

MAR.: *Spring Fest Flower and Garden Show.* This annual event showcases the work of area landscaping/gardening professionals, and includes lectures, demonstrations, and horticultural items for sale. At the Sussex County Fairgrounds. | 973/948–2090.

MAY: *Garden State Horse Show.* Held at the Sussex County Fairgrounds the first weekend in May, this event is New Jersey's largest hunter/jumper horse show. | 508/698–6810.

JUNE–SEPT.: *NJ Cardinals Baseball.* Cheer on this minor-league baseball team and participate in different family activities throughout the summer at Skylands Park. | 973/579–7500 | www.njcards.com.

AUG.: *Sussex County Farm and Horse Show.* Agricultural exhibits, concerts, crafts, food, and more make up the largest county fair in the state, held at the Sussex County Fairgrounds on the first Friday in August. | 973/948–5500 | www.newjerseystatefair.org.

SEPT.: *NJ State Square and Round Dance Camporee.* This festival offers dances, workshops, crafts, and games. It's held the first weekend after Labor Day at the Sussex County Fairgrounds. | 908/722–8157.

Dining

Calamity Café. American. This classic country diner, less then 2 mi from Augusta, is the perfect place to stop for a burger and a milk shake. Naturally they do breakfast too, so if you're up early, grab a stool at the counter and a cup of coffee, and soak in the retro atmosphere. Dinner is only served on Friday nights. | 11 Main St., Branchville | 973/948–2007 | $4–$10 | No credit cards.

Lodging

Wooden Duck. This cozy inn is set on 17 acres of rolling hills and woodlands in a quiet area contiguous to Kittatinny State Park (about 6 mi south of Augusta). The area is great for walking and hiking, and there is an outdoor pool and patio for sunbathing. Inside, there's a fireplace and a collection of videos, games, and books. Complimentary breakfast. Cable TV, in-room VCRs. No pets. No smoking. | 140 Goodale Rd., Newton | 973/300–0395 | fax 973/300–0395 | www.woodenduckinn.com. | 7 rooms | $100–$120 | AE, D, MC, V.

BASKING RIDGE

MAP 9, F4

(Nearby towns also listed: Bernardsville, Morristown)

If you like pastoral mixed in with civilization, then Basking Ridge should appeal to you. Within its boundaries, you'll find large, beautiful houses, as well as huge tracts of open space, including the 400-acre Lord Stirling Park, with its active environmental center, and the western edge of the Great Swamp National Wildlife Refuge. A fun way to head off into nature is on horseback, at the Lord Stirling Riding Stables.

Information: Somerset County Chamber of Commerce | 360 Grove St., Bridgewater, 08807 | 908/725–1552 | fax 908/722–7823 | www.somersetcountychamber.org.

Attractions

Great Swamp National Wildlife Refuge. This 7,600-acre tract of wetlands is in the midst of lovely, laid-back countryside, with 9½ mi of hiking trails, boardwalks, and wildlife-watching blinds. It is swampy, so watch out for deerflies and mosquitoes in summer! | 152 Pleasant Plains Rd. | 973/425–1222 | Free | Daily dawn–dusk.

Lord Stirling Park and Environmental Education Center. This park claims 450-acres of the Great Swamp Basin as its own. You can hike the 10 mi of trails and learn about the enviroment and ecology of the refuge through one of the educational center's programs. | 190 Lord Stirling Rd. | 908/766–2489 | Free | Daily 9–5.

Lord Stirling Stables. You can arrange to travel the 10 mi of trails or the outdoor jumping course at Lord Stirling Park on your very own steed. Riders must qualified to ride or take a lesson and be at least 12 years of age. | 256 S. Maple Ave. | 908/766–5955 | Daily 9–5.

ON THE CALENDAR

MAY: *Annual Carving and Wildlife Art Show and Sale.* More than 50 artists participate in this festival of environmental and animal-themed art, now in its 20th year. The artwork, from wood carvings to ceramics, is available for sale. The festival takes place the weekend after Mother's Day, in Lord Stirling Park. | 908/766–2489 | www.park.co.somerset.nj.us.

MAY: *Charter Day.* Enjoy sidewalk sales, craft demonstrations, music, and food at this mid-May festival. | 908/204–3049.

SEPT.: *Tour of Basking Ridge.* Spend Labor Day pedaling in either a 5-, 20-, or 40-mi bicycle race around the town. | 908/204–3049.

OCT.: *Lord Stirling 1770s Festival.* This period fair re-creates life in Basking Ridge during colonial times with arts and crafts, music, costumes, children's games, and food. The fair is held in Lord Stirling Park, on Lord Stirling Rd., 5 mi south of Basking Ridge. | 908/766–2489 | www.park.co.somerset.nj.us.

DEC.: *Festival of Trees.* View extra-special Christmas trees at this annual exhibition showcasing trees decorated with different cultural and personal themes. At Lord Stirling Park. | 908/766–2489.

Dining

Grain House. American. Cozy and welcoming, this restaurant has fireplaces and antiques, and three private dining rooms. In warm weather, you can eat on the umbrella-shaded patio. The food is classic American: pork chops, steaks, and mashed potatoes with gravy. | 225 Rte. 202, | 973/579–7500 | $19–$25 | AE, DC, MC, V.

Lodging

Olde Mill Inn at Basking Ridge. In the rolling landscape of the Somerset Hills on 10 acres with English gardens, gazebos, a courtyard, and more, the inn is a popular place for weddings and other events. Guest rooms are luxuriously furnished and the staff is attentive and friendly. Golf is nearby. Restaurant, bar, room service (evenings), complimentary Continental breakfast. Cable TV. Exercise room. Library. Baby-sitting. Laundry service. Business services. | 225 Rte. 202 | 908/221–1100 | fax 908/221–1560 | www.oldemillinn.com | 85 rooms | $180–$350) | AE, D, DC, MC, V.

BATSTO

(Nearby towns also listed: Mays Landing, Medford)

Batsto is in the heart of the Pine Barrens region, within Wharton State Forest. The town is on the map as a former center of iron mining, and the historic village that grew up

THE JERSEY DEVIL

The "Jersey Devil" is the state's own Bigfoot. Its haunt is the Pine Barrens, where it was allegedly born, and where, strangely, many of the region's more unusual flora and fauna can be found. There are, of course, several theories regarding the creature's origins, but the most popular purports that the Devil was the 13th child of Mother Leeds, who was fed up with having children and asked the Devil to take the child away after it was born. At birth, the child suddenly changed into the ugliest of creatures and flew away up the chimney. He remains to this day, wandering the region and venturing out at night to scare people and animals with his piercing screams and grotesque appearance. Portrayed with horns, a forked tail, and a body that is part man and part animal, the Jersey Devil has been blamed for everything from tearing the roof off a car to killing and dismembering animals. Skeptics take note: as recently as 1987, a German shepherd was torn to shreds 25 ft from the chain which had been tied to him. Around the body were strange tracks that no one could identify.

While those who believe in or have heard or seen the Jersey Devil often fear him, many are rather fond of this mythical creature. In fact, the state's hockey team is named after the old fellow. And proponents of the area's ecology also think the Jersey Devil may in fact be protecting the area, and won't hurt anyone who loves New Jersey's very special ecosystem.

© Artville

around the mining operation is a reminder of a once-very-different time. History, not iron, is the draw today, with visitors coming to view the ironmaster's mansion as well as demonstrations of crafts that were once performed here as part of daily life.

Information: **Historic Batsto Village** | Rte. 542, Wharton State Forest, Batsto, 08037 | 609/561–3262.

Attractions

Batsto State Historic Site. This is the site of a former bog iron and glassware industrial center, which operated between 1766 and 1867. The ironworks was an important supplier to the Continental army during the Revolutionary War. Tours of the old mansion, crafts demonstrations by resident artisans, and special summer outdoor events are offered. | Wharton State Forest: Rte. 542 | 609/561–3262 | Free; mansion tours $2 | Daily 9–4.

Tomasello Winery. This full-production winery, established in 1933, offers tours and wine tastings. It's about 5 mi west of Batsto. | 225 White Horse Pike, Hammonton | 609/561–5700 or 800/MMM–WINE | Admission varies, depending on event | Call for reservations and event schedule.

Wharton State Forest. This 110,017-acre forest, in the heart of the Pine Barrens, is the largest single tract of land in the state park system. You'll find rivers and streams for canoeing, a major section of the Batona Trail for hiking, and historic Batsto Village. | Rte. 542 | 609/561–0024 | Free; parking $3 on weekends | Memorial Day–Labor Day, daily 9–4. The **Atsion Recreation Area,** on Route 206, offers swimming and camping facilities. You'll find a large lake and a concession stand with drinks and hot snacks. The lake is about 5 mi from Medford. | 609/268–0444 | Free | Daily 9–4.

ON THE CALENDAR

OCT.: *Batsto Country Living Fair.* You'll find a huge open-air antiques market, homemade food and craft items, depictions of local Native American life during Revolutionary times, and more, on the third Sunday of October in Batsto village. | 609/561–0024.

Dining

Sweetwater Casino. American. You can watch the boats head in and out of the marina from this casino-restaurant on the banks of the Mullica River, and if you're lucky you might spot an osprey swoop down for a fish. Steak, stuffed lobster, and chicken dishes make up the classic American menu. About 5 mi west of Batsto, in Hammonton | 2780 7th Ave. (Rte. 643), Hammonton | 609/965–3285 | $10–$20 | AE, MC, V.

Lodging

Ramada Inn. You'll find this comfortable, family-friendly Ramada about 5 mi west of Batsto, near Wharton State Park's fishing, canoeing, hiking, and horseback riding. The Tomasello Winery is 2 mi away. Restaurant, bar, complimentary Continental breakfast. In-room data ports, some refrigerators, cable TV. Pool. Business services. No pets. | 308 White Horse Pike, Hammonton | 609/561–5700 or 888/298–2054 | fax 609/561–2392 | www.ramadainn.com | 100 rooms | $45–$110 | AE, D, DC, MC, V.

BELMAR

MAP 9, G6

(Nearby towns also listed: Asbury Park, Ocean Grove, Spring Lake)

Belmar is quintessential Jersey Shore: kids having fun, a laid-back atmosphere, a great mile-long beach, and a busy boardwalk with plenty of places to sit and have an ice-cream cone. There are beach playgrounds and a nature trail along the oceanfront, and down along Route 35 is the Belmar Marina, where more than two dozen party and charter fishing boats are available to rent.

Information: Belmar Tourism Development Commission | 601 Main St., Belmar, 08723 | 732/681–3700 | www.belmar.com.

Attractions

Belmar-Playland Rooftop Golf. Play miniature golf, practice your baseball swing, try skee-ball, or tackle numerous video games at this all-encompassing amusement center. There are rides and even an Italian restaurant on the premises. | 1400 Ocean Ave. | 732/681–5115 | $5 | May–Oct., daily 10 AM–midnight, weather permitting.

ON THE CALENDAR

MAR.: *St. Patrick's Day Parade.* Bands, bagpipers, floats, and marching units make up this parade, one of the state's largest. It starts at Main Street in South Belmar. | 732/280–2648.

MAY: *Fly Away Classic Kite Flying Festival.* You can try out different kites at this festival, held on the beach at 4th Ave., as well as watch skilled kite competitions and demonstrations. | 732/280–8084.

JUNE: *AVP Professional Volleyball.* Watch games on the beach all weekend, and meet some of the pros. | 732/681–0005.

JUNE: *New Jersey Seafood Festival.* Seafood is one of the state's favorite (and most delicious) natural resources, and this is one of the state's biggest celebrations of seafood. There's tastings, entertainment, kid's activities, a crafts fair, exhibits, and more. The festival is held the second weekend in June on Silver Lake at the ocean, between 5th and 6th Aves. | 732/681–3700.

JULY: *The Free United Firemen's Carnival.* This long-standing carnival features five nights of rides, games, and food. It's usually the second week of the month, at the Belmar Marina and Route 35. | 732/681–3332.

JULY: *Sand Castle Contest.* Prizes are offered in various age categories at this annual event, which draws thousands of entrants. The contest is generally held at 18th Ave. and the beach. Call for the date. | 732/681–0005.

AUG.: *Belmar 5-Mile Run.* More than 2,000 typically run in this race along the ocean, which takes place the weekend before Labor Day. | 732/681–2900.

SEPT.: *Belmar Kite Festival and the New Jersey Stunt Kite Championships.* This fall festival on the beach features single and team precision kite flying and kite-flying lessons. | 732/280–8084.

OCT.: *Fall Harvest Festival.* Scarecrow-making, pumpkin-decorating, and a chile cook-off are just some of the seasonal activities at the Fall Harvest Festival, held on the Sunday of Columbus Day weekend on Main St. between 8th and 10th Sts. There's also music, antiques, and crafts. | 732/681–2900.

Dining

Armadillo Crossing. Southwestern. You can eat outside here at sidewalk tables in the front or back, and there's a garden with a raw bar. Inside, the dining room is relaxed and fun, and full of Americana in the form of old tools, toys, and photos. Be daring and try the alligator sausage, or play it safe with the Cajun grilled tuna. Enjoy live music ranging from jazz to flamenco on Wednesday and Friday evenings. | 1605 Main St., South Belmar | 732/280–1880 | Reservations not accepted | Closed Sun., Mon. mid-Sept.–mid-May. No lunch | $12–$18 | AE, MC, V.

Klein's Fish Market & Waterside Cafe. Seafood. Eat in or take out at this bustling, no-frills, family-run eatery known for the freshest seafood in town. | 708 River Rd. | 732/681–1177 | No lunch | No credit cards.

Matisse Restaurant. Contemporary. Portobello Wellington with goat cheese and rack of lamb with watercress and burgundy jus are characteristic of the menu at this chic bistro.

BYOB. | 1400 Ocean Ave. | 732/681–7680 | www.matissecatering.com | Closed Mon., Tue. No breakfast. No lunch | $15.95–$23.95 | AE, MC, V.

Lodging

Belmar Motor Lodge. The two-story brick Belmar is directly across the street from the Belmar Marine Basin. Rooms are sunny, but nothing fancy. Cable TV. Pool. Laundry facilities. | 732/681–6600 or 800/848–8382 | fax 732/681–6604 | 55 rooms | $90–$120 | AE, DC, MC, V.

Inn at the Shore This charming 1880 Victorian home, owned by Rosemary and Tom Volker since 1994, is decorated with an eclectic mix of antiques, wicker, floral fabrics, quilts, teddy bears, and angels. Relax on the wraparound porch or in the cozy library. A sumptuous breakfast includes pancakes, homemade pastries, and gourmet coffee. There is a Murder Mystery weekend package in November which includes two nights lodging, two gourmet breakfasts, dinner for two, a welcoming wine and cheese event, and of course, a murder mystery. Clues are planted around the inn and around town. Bicycles are available for you to use. Complimentary breakfast. Cable TV, some in-room VCRs. Free parking. | 301 4th Ave. | 732/681–3762 | fax 732/280–1914 | www.theinnattheshore.com | 12 rooms | $85–$135 | AE, MC, V.

Morning Dove Inn. You'll feel light as a feather in the airy pastel-hue rooms of this lakefront inn, which also happens to be a block from the ocean. Each room is named after a different bird. Check out the Swan Suite or the Blue Heron Room. TV in common area. Massage. No pets. No smoking. | 204 5th Ave. | 732/556–0777 | www.morningdoveinn.com | 6 rooms, 2 suites | $100–$175 | MC, V.

Seaflower Bed & Breakfast. Built in the late 1890s, this Dutch Colonial home is but two blocks away from the beach and the boardwalk. Complimentary breakfast. TV in common area. No pets. | 732/681–6006 | 5 rooms | $90–$165 | MC, V.

BELVIDERE

MAP 9, D3

(Nearby town also listed: Hackettstown, Hope)

The Pequest River flows through the center of Belvidere, emptying into the Delaware River. The Pequest first attracted Native Americans to the area, and European settlers followed in the 18th century. For many years Belvidere served as the shipping point of iron ore from the Oxford Furnace to Philadelphia and Trenton. Today it is a quiet, upscale community with tree-lined streets and rural countryside. The "downtown" area includes the County Court House complex and a small retail center. Matarazzo Farms and Four Sisters Winery is a big draw to the area, offering not only pick-your-own fruits and vegetables but special events such as powwows and wine fests.

Information: **Belvidere Chamber of Commerce** | 334 Water St., Belvidere, 07823 | 908/859–5161 | www.phillipsburgnj.com.

Attractions

Four Sisters Winery at Matarazzo Farms. This winery hosts grape-crushing parties, hayrides, and a farmers' market, in addition to the usual tastings and tours. | 10 Doe Hollow La., Rte. 519 | 908/475–3671 | www.tomasellowinery.com | Free | Daily 9–6.

ON THE CALENDAR

JUNE: *Return to Beaver Creek Powwow.* This festival, which takes place the second weekend of June at Matarazzo Farms, is one of the top Native American festivals on the East Coast. It features dancers, crafts, entertainment, seminars, music, and food. | 908/475–3872.

JUNE–OCT.: *Walking Tours of Historic Hope.* Saturday, beginning at 10 AM at the Inn at Millrace Pond. | 908/459–9177.

AUG.: *Jersey Fresh Food and Wine Festival.* Taste local wines and other New Jersey products, listen to live music, and stomp on a few grapes at Matarazzo Farms on the third weekend of August. | 908/475–3872.

Dining

Thisilldous Eatery. American. This homey, casual spot, complete with lunch counter and swivel stools, serves breakfast and lunch at bargain prices. For breakfast, order an omelet filled with anything you want. Burgers, soups and salads make up the lunch menu. Try the french fries—they're made from scratch. | 320 Front St. | 908/475–2274 | No lunch Sun. | $4–$6 | AE, MC, V.

Lodging

Thisilldous Inn. This tiny inn, in a row house on the main street of town, is a block from a park and half a mile from the Delaware River. Simple, comfortable rooms are decorated in pastels and florals. Complimentary breakfast. Cable TV. | 320 Front St. | 908/475–2274 | fax 908/475–1946 | www.thisilldous.com | 2 rooms | $65 | AE, MC, V.

BERGENFIELD

(Nearby towns also listed: Englewood, Hackensack)

Just a few miles from Manhattan, Bergenfield was originally a farming town, but today, with a population of 24,827, qualifies as an unofficial suburb of New York City. Bergenfield has its own downtown area though, and you can easily spend an entire day shopping and dining along the town's main strip, the heavily traveled Washington Avenue.

Information: **Bergenfield Chamber of Commerce** | 35 South Washington Ave., Bergenfield, 07621 | 201/387–8300 | unavailable | www.bergenfield.com.

Attractions

Bergenfield Museum. If you're looking for artifacts and information on the history of Bergenfield and North Jersey, it's probably somewhere in this quaint museum, which opened in 1976, and has been popular ever since. While there is no large permanent display, there are two or three special exhibits; quilts and war memorabilia have been the focus in the past. The museum was set to move to a new location at press time. | 84 Hickory Ave. | 201/384–8656 | www.bergenfield.com | Free | Mon., Thurs., Sat. 1–4 PM.

Cooper's Pond Park. In addition to its signature pond, this park also has an old cemetery and church. Popular year-round, the park hosts concerts in the summer and ice-skating in the winter. | West Church St.; on Easy Church and Prospect Ave. | Free | Year-round. Weekdays dawn to dusk.

Memorial Field. This much-used park has baseball fields, tennis and basketball courts that are free and open to the public. There's also a shady pavilion, lots of open grounds and greenery, and a lovely picnic area. | New Bridge Rd.; Between the railroad tracks and Prospect Ave. | Free | Year-round. Weekdays dawn to dusk.

ON THE CALENDAR

JUNE: *Annual Sidewalk Sale.* During this townwide celebration, Bergenfield's Washington Ave. is closed to traffic and the road becomes a pedestrian mall for the day with food, entertainment, and kiddie rides. There's even a petting zoo with pony rides. | 201/384–8555.

OCT.: *Halloween Parade.* Kids (and some adults, too) dress up and parade across town during this annual event. After awards for best costumes have been handed out, participants trick or treat along the main strip. | 201/387–8300.

DEC.: *Christmas Tree Lighting.* Everyone in town—including Santa—comes out to celebrate Bergenfield's annual entry into shopping season. | 201/387–8300.

Dining

Cellar Bar & Grill. Continental. On a Friday or Saturday night, this casual, family oriented restaurant is often the hottest spot in town. Locals order the chef's signature Black Forrest steak by the truckload. (The ingredients of the special marinade are a closely guarded secret.) In terms of decor, the restaurant derives its charm from the many antiques scattered throughout the place. | 47 Legion Drive, Bergenfield | 201/385–5781 | Closed Mon. and Sun. in July and Aug. | $12–$21 | AE, DC, MC, V.

Chez Dominque. French. This tiny, romantic spot is among the region's top French restaurants. It's hard not to be entranced by Chez Dominque's exposed wooden beams and simple country French feel. Chef Dominque Payraudeau takes great pride in the signature dishes: Black Angus steak in peppery brandy sauce, rack of lamb, and confit of duck. The homemade smoked salmon and seafood gazpacho are also delicious. | 4 Bedford Ave. | 201/384–7637 | Reservations essential | Closed Sun. and Mon. No lunch Tues., Sat. | $21–$32 | MC, V.

Tommy Fox's Publick House. Irish. You can order just about anything here from hamburgers and fish and chips, to innovative entrees like potato crusted salmon—a dish of the kitchen's own creation. The atmosphere is Irish pub: fun and lively. It gets busy, too, so be prepared to hang out at the famous mahogany bar until a table opens up. | 32 South Washington Ave. | 201/384–0900 | $8–$22 | AE, D, DC, MC, V.

BERNARDSVILLE

MAP 9, E4

(Nearby towns also listed: Basking Ridge, Chester, Morristown)

Bernardsville became a town in 1924, when it split from Bernards Township. In the horse country of the Somerset Hills, Bernardsville is a suburban-rural mix, which makes property very desirable. If you arrive by train, take time to admire the historic Bernardsville Train Station. The Morristown National Park and the Scherman-Hoffman Wildlife Sanctuary afford many outdoor recreational activities, such as hiking and biking.

Information: **Somerset County Chamber of Commerce** | 360 Grove St., Bridgewater, 08807 | 908/725–1552 | fax 908/722–7823 | www.somersetcountychamber.org.

Attractions

Scherman-Hoffman Wildlife Sanctuary. This 265-acre sanctuary, run by the New Jersey Audubon Society, offers guided hikes and moonlight walks. | 11 Hardscrabble Rd. | 908/766–5787 | Free | Grounds daily dawn–dusk; nature center Tues.–Sat. 9 AM–5, Sun. noon–5.

ON THE CALENDAR

FRIDAY AND SATURDAY YEAR-ROUND: *Guided tours at Scherman-Hoffman Wildlife Sanctuary.* Audubon Society experts lead guided nature walks Friday and Saturday mornings throughout the year. | 908/766–5787 | Free | Fri. and Sat. 8 AM–9 AM.

APR.–NOV.: *Heritage Trail Association Bus Tour.* Tour historic sites throughout Somerset County. Walking tours are also available. | 732/356–8856.

Dining

Bernards Inn. Contemporary. Enjoy sophisticated French-influenced American food, such as sautéed lobster with fava beans and chanterelles, warm smoked salmon and spinach salad, and apple galette for dessert. The turn-of-the-20th-century inn has a jazz lounge and two dining rooms, as well as a front patio for outdoor dining. | 27 Mine Brook Rd. | 908/766–0002 or 888/766–0002 | Reservations essential Fri., Sat. | Jacket required | Closed Sun. | $37–$57 | AE, DC, MC, V.

Le Petit Chateau. French. This welcoming and elegant country restaurant is known for its excellent classic French cooking. Try the foie gras, the braised short ribs, and the Grand Marnier souffle. The dining room has lovely white-and-rose wallpaper, fresh flowers, candlelight, and harp music. The wine cellar holds nearly 1,000 labels. | 121 Claremont Ave. | 908/766–4544 | Closed Mon. No lunch weekends | $16–$28 | AE, DC, MC, V.

Lodging

Bernards Inn. This elegant mission-style inn, built in 1907, is small enough to feel intimate, yet large enough to cater to your every need. Antiques-filled rooms have thick robes, bottled water, and biscotti and fruit. Luxurious bathrooms are stocked with Caswell and Massey soap. It's across the street from the turn-of-the-20th-century train station. Restaurant, bar, complimentary Continental breakfast, room service. In-room data ports, cable TV, some in-room VCRs. Business services. | 27 Mine Brook Rd. | 908/766–0002 or 888/766–0002 | fax 908/766–4604 | www.bernardsinn.com | 20 rooms | $170–$225 | AE, DC, MC, V.

Somerset Hills. Nestled in the Watchung Mountains near the crossroads of historical Liberty Corner, 8 mi south of Bernardsville, this Colonial-style building has suites as well as regular rooms, and all rooms on the second floor have balconies overlooking a wildlife preserve. Restaurant, bar. In-room data ports, some kitchenettes, some microwaves, some in-room hot tubs, cable TV. Pool. Exercise equipment. Business services. Pets allowed. | 200 Liberty Corner Rd., Warren | 908/647–6700 or 800/688–0700 | fax 908/647–8053 | shhotel@aol.com | www.shh.com | 108 rooms, 3 suites | $135–$150; $150–$375 suites | AE, DC, MC, V.

BORDENTOWN

MAP 9, E6

(Nearby towns also listed: Burlington, Princeton, Trenton)

In the 18th century, Bordentown, on the Delaware River, became a center of trade for the region, as well as a Quaker outpost. The area was a hotbed of Revolutionary activity—Thomas Paine fomented rebellion here and his spirit is remembered with a statue and a plaque on one of the town's side streets. Figures ranging from Joseph Bonaparte, brother of Napoleon and ex-king of Spain, to Clara Barton, founder of the American Red Cross, have historical ties to the community. The Old City Hall has a notable Queen Anne-style clock tower with a Seth Thomas clock that has been ticking since 1884. Ocean Spray has a major processing plant here, hence the cranberry festivities in autumn.

Information: **Greater Bordentown Chamber of Commerce** | Box 65, Bordentown, 08505 | 609/298–7774.

Attractions

Clara Barton Schoolhouse. Clara Barton began the state's first free public school in this one-room schoolhouse in 1852. Barton later founded the American Red Cross. | 142 Crosswicks St. | 609/298–3334 | Free | By appointment only.

Self-guided walking tour. Stroll through the town's historic district past an old schoolhouse and the Old City Hall. | 609/298–7774 | Free | Daily.

ON THE CALENDAR

MAY: *Annual Street Fair.* Food, drinks, gifts, souvenirs, games, and entertainment line Farnsworth Ave. on the third weekend of the month. | 609/298–7774.

OCT.: *Annual Cranberry Festival.* This event has fine arts and crafts, antiques, a vintage vehicle show, a Miss Cranberry Fest Pageant, a cranberry cook-a-thon, and music and entertainment. It takes place the first weekend of the month on Farnsworth Ave. | 609/298–7774.

OCT.: *Ghost Walk.* If you're in town around Halloween, check out this spooky evening tour of ghostly and (supposedly) haunted local sites. | 609/298–3334.

Dining

Farnsworth House. Contemporary. Enjoy no-nonsense fresh seafood in Bordentown's historic district. Specials include Chilean sea bass, grilled swordfish, and other catches of the day. | 135 Farnsworth Ave. | 609/291–9232 | $14–22 | AE, MC, V.

Lodging

Best Western Bordentown Inn. This hotel is in a prime fishing area, just east of the Delaware River and the New Jersey/Bucks County, Pennsylvania border. Trenton is 10 mi to the north and Fort Dix and Maguire A.F.B. are 10 mi west. There's a nice blue-tiled, indoor pool area with an attached hot tub. Restaurant. Refrigerators, cable TV. Pool. Sauna. Exercise room. No pets. | 1068 Rte. 206 | 609/298–8000 or 800/780–7234 | fax 609/291–9757 | www.bestwestern.com | 101 rooms | $98–$132 | AE, D, DC, MC, V.

Days Inn. This two-story chain is 15 minutes from Great Adventure theme park. It prides itself on being family friendly and efficient. Restaurant, bar (with entertainment). Some refrigerators, cable TV. Pool. Laundry facilities. Business services. Pets allowed. | 1073 U.S. 206 | 609/298–6100 | fax 609/298–7509 | www.daysinn.com | 131 rooms | $45–$95 | AE, D, DC, MC, V.

BRIDGETON

MAP 9, D10

(Nearby town also listed: Millville, Salem)

Settled in 1686, Bridgeton has New Jersey's largest historical district, with 2,200 Colonial, Victorian, and Federal buildings. You can get maps for self-guided tours of the district at the town's tourist information center. In the middle of town is the 1,100-acre Bridgeton City Park, which includes the Nail House Museum; the New Sweden Farmstead Museum, a 17th-century farmstead with restored log cabins; and the Cohanzick Zoo.

Information: **Bridgeton Historical District** | 50 E. Broad St., Bridgeton, 08302 | 856/451–4802 or 800/319–3379 | www.historicbridgeton.com.
Bridgeton Area Chamber of Commerce | 53 S. Laurel Rd., Bridgeton, 08302 | 856/455–1312 | fax 856/453–9795.

Attractions

City Park. With hiking, boating, a zoo, a farm museum, and more, this 1,100-acre green oasis is a major presence in the town. | Mayor Aitken Dr. | 856/451–9208 | Free | Daily.
Cohanzick Zoo. Established in 1934, this zoo was the first of its kind in New Jersey. There are over 200 species of birds and mammals from around the world including rare specimens such as white tigers, bald eagles, and ring-tailed lemurs. | Bridgeton City Park | 856/455–3230 | Free with $1 parking donation | Daily 9–5.
In 1988, the King and Queen of Sweden came to Bridgeton to formally dedicate the **New Sweden Farmstead Museum,** a painstaking re-creation of a 17th-century farmstead in the tradition of those built by early Swedish settlers. The log structures include a main residence, bath/smokehouse, stable, barn, storehouse, and blacksmith shop. Many contain original Swedish/Finnish artifacts. | 856/455–9785 | $3; special rates for children, students, senior citizens, and families | May–Labor Day, Wed.–Sun. Call for hrs.

Nail House Museum. This 1815 building houses exhibits of early iron tools and regional history. | Bridgeton City Park, 1 Mayor Aitken Dr. | 609/455–4100 | Free | Apr.–Dec., Tues.–Fri. 10–3:30; weekends 11–4.

George J. Woodruff Museum of Indian Artifacts. This museum at the Bridgeton Free Public Library displays artifacts from the early Lenni Lenape tribe that lived in the area. | 150 E. Commerce St. | 856/451–2620 | Free | Weekdays 2–4, Sat. 10–noon.

Old Broad St. Church. Considered one of the finest architectural specimens in the state, this brick Presbyterian meetinghouse was built in 1792. | Broad St. | 856/455–0809 | Free | Daily.

Parvin State Park. This 1,135-acre park, on the edge of the Pine Barrens, contains as much in the way of interesting history as it does wildlife. The park was home to the Civilian Conservation Corps from 1933 to 1941; a summer camp for the children of displaced Japanese-Americans in 1943; a prisoner-of-war camp for German soldiers in 1944; and temporary housing for Eastern Europeans who fled their homes in 1952. Still evident in the park are remains from the earliest Native American settlers. The park offers hiking, biking (the trails are wheelchair-accessible), camping, swimming and boating in Parvin Lake, and an interpretive visitor center. Head north on Route 553, approximately 10 mi. | 701 Almond Rd., Pittsgrove | 856/358–8616 | $1 for the beach, $10 for camping | Daily.

ON THE CALENDAR

MAY: *Kids' Fest.* This one-day event, held at the Cohanzick Zoo on the first Saturday of the month, has magic shows, face painting, refreshments, and other kid-friendly activities. | 856/455–3230, ext. 242.

JUNE: *Annual Strawberry Festival.* Head to Dutch Neck Village (about 2 mi west of Bridgeton) on the first Saturday in June, for crafts, strawberry shortcake, entertainment, kiddie rides and activities, and more. | 856/451–2188 | www.dutchnechvillage.com.

AUG.: *Annual Peach Festival.* Essentially a flea market and food sale to benefit area nonprofits, this event has live music and kiddie rides, and plenty of peaches and peach ice cream for sale. You'll find it just west of Bridgeton, in Dutch Neck Village, on the first Saturday in August. | 856/451–2188.

OCT.: *Annual Fall Festival.* This one-day craft show, just west of Bridgeton in Dutch Neck Village, has a diverse array of handicrafts and lots of apple-centered treats. | 856/451–2188.

NOV.: *Sunday at the Village.* Take advantage of specials, giveaways, and other promotions at this holiday open house at the shops in Dutch Neck Village, just west of Bridgeton. This event takes place on the third Sunday in November. | 856/451–2188.

DEC.: *Annual Walk of Lights.* Christmas comes alive in Dutch Neck Village. Walkways are lined with luminaria, and there are carolers in the streets. There's also a bonfire, a live nativity scene, and special appearances by Santa and Mrs. Claus. Just west of Bridgeton, on the first Friday and Saturday of the month. | 856/451–2188.

DEC.: *Christmas Open House Tour.* Historic district homes are decorated for the season and open for tours. | 856/451–9208.

Dining

Country Rose Restaurant. American. This Dutch Neck Village restaurant is known for its homemade breads, soups, and desserts. Dinner specials usually include fresh seafood. Breakfast is served daily and there is a kids' menu. No smoking. | 97 Trench Rd. | 856/455–9294 | No dinner Mon.–Wed. | $9–$16 | AE, D, DC, MC, V.

Lodging

Days Inn Bridgeton. This family and budget-friendly chain hotel is in Bridgeton's historic district, minutes from the Cohanzick Zoo. Complimentary Continental breakfast. Cable TV. | 500 Broad St. E | 609/455–1500 or 800/544–8313 | fax 609/451–1556 | www.daysinn.com | 32 rooms | $45–$55 | AE, DC, MC.

BURLINGTON

(Nearby towns also listed: Bordentown, Mount Holly)

First settled in 1624, and permanently settled by the Quakers in 1677, Burlington City offers more than three centuries of history, with dozens of historic sites and structures, including the 300-year-old Burlington Quaker Meetinghouse, which is still used for meetings. Modern-day Burlington features neighborhoods of historic homes and a mile-long scenic promenade along the Delaware River, where special events take place.

Information: Burlington Chamber of Commerce | 900 Briggs Rd., Suite 110, Mt. Laurel, 08054 | 856/439–2520. **Burlington County Historical Society** | 457 High St., Burlington, 08016 | 609/386–4773 | bchistoryctr@juno.com.

Attractions

Burlington County Historical Society. The society maintains a historic complex including the Bard-How House, the James Fenimore Cooper House, and the Captain James Lawrence House, complete with period furnishings and decorative arts, as well as the Aline Wolcott Museum Galleries, presenting regional exhibits. It also maintains the Delia Biddle-Pugh research library and archives, which includes the James Fenimore Cooper collection—the author was born here and returned as an adult. | 457 High St. | 609/386–4773 | fax 609/386–4828 | bchistoryctr@juno.com | $5 | Mon.–Thurs. 1–4, Sun. 2–4.

Burlington Quaker Meeting House. The original hexagonal structure was built on this site in 1683. After it was used as a barracks during the Revolutionary War, a larger ediface was built in the mid-1780s to serve as a place for the community's Quakers to gather. In 1995, major refurbishments turned the house into a banquet and function hall while preserving much of the original meeting room. | 340 High St. | 609/386–4828 | Free | Tours by appointment.

Old St. Mary's Church. Built in 1703, this is the oldest Episcopal church in New Jersey. A newer St. Mary's was built across the churchyard between 1846 and 1854 by Richard Upjohn, who was also the architect for Trinity Church in Manhattan. The church cemetery is home to past prominent local politicians. | 145 W. Broad St. | 609/386–0902 | Free | Daily 9–3.

Rankokus Indian Reservation. This 350-acre site, 5 mi south of Burlington, is home to the Powhatan Renape Nation. There is a museum, a gallery of contemporary art, and a re-creation of an ancestral woodland village that even includes buffalo. There are also festivals twice a year, including a juried Indian art festival in autumn. | Rancocas Rd., between the Garden State Pkwy. and Spur 541, Rancocas | 609/261–4747 | www.powhatan.org | Museum open by appointment.

ON THE CALENDAR

APR.: *The Meerwald Historic Oyster Schooner Sunset Sail.* New Jersey's Official Tall Ship sails from Burlington's Riverfront Promenade. | 856/785–2060.

JUNE: *Historic Yorkshire Community Yard Sale.* Residents buy tables and sell their wares to benefit the Historic Yorkshire Alliance on the first Saturday of June. Goods range from valuable antiques to attic trinkets. | 609/386–8657.

AUG.: *Festival of Lights and Fireworks.* Enjoy this annual concert, decorated boat parade, and fireworks display along the Riverfront Promenade. | 609/386–0200.

SEPT.: *Annual Wood Street Fair and High Street Art Show.* This show, held on the first Saturday after Labor Day, provides an opportunity for area artisans to display and sell their wares. | 609/386–0200.

OCT.: *Biketoberfest.* A motorcycle show headlines this festival, held downtown and on the promenade. Food and street entertainment accompany the show. | 609/387–7265.

Dining

Café Gallery. Continental. Dine formally upstairs at this two-story spot, or eat downstairs in the more casual gallery/café. Sunday brunch is popular, as are the hamburgers and salads. There's a vegetarian special on the menu every day. | 219 High St. | 609/386–6150 | $14–$22 | AE, DC, MC, V.

Thommy G's. Italian. This building was a bank in its previous life, and its 24-ft-high ceilings and towering arched windows remain intact. The cooking is Italian with Louisiana accents and the private dining rooms (once the bank's vaults) are a special draw. | 354 High St. | 609/239–8133. | $12–$20 | AE, V.

Lodging

Best Western Burlington Inn. You'll enjoy waking up to complimentary coffee and donuts in your room at this Best Western, 5 mi southeast of Burlington. Rooms are large, and there's a fireplace in the lobby. Restaurant, complimentary Continental breakfast. Some refrigerators, some in-room data ports, cable TV. Exercise room. Business services. Some pets allowed. | 2020 Rte. 541, Mt. Holly | 609/261–3800 or 800/780–7234 | fax 609/267–0958 | www.bestwestern.com. | 64 rooms | $97–$111 | AE, D, DC, MC, V.

CALDWELL

MAP 4, B6

(Nearby towns also listed: Montclair, Wayne)

Caldwell is in Western Essex County and is named in honor of Reverend James Caldwell, who was chaplain of the Third New Jersey Brigade from 1776 to 1781. His church was used as a hospital by the Continental Army until it was burned by a Loyalist in 1780. The Revolutionary War was fought in the center of town on Bloomfield Avenue. The town is also the birth place of Grover Cleveland (born March 18, 1837), the only United States President to serve two nonconsecutive terms.

Information: **West Essex Chamber of Commerce** | 3 Fairfield Ave., West Caldwell, 07006 | 973/226–5500 | fax 973/403–9335 | www.wecc.org. **Borough of Caldwell** | 1 Provost Sq., Caldwell, 07006 | 973/226–6100 | fax 973/403–1355 | www.caldwellnj.com.

Attractions

Grover Cleveland Birthplace State Historic Site. Besides being the only American president to have ever won the office in nonconsecutive elections, Grover Cleveland was also the only president born in New Jersey. His birthplace is now a national park and museum. | 207 Bloomfield Ave. | 201/226–1810 | Free | Wed.–Fri. 9–noon and 1–6, Sat. 9–noon and 1–5, Sun. 1–6.

ON THE CALENDAR

JULY/AUG.: *Concerts at the West Caldwell Gazebo.* Spread a blanket on the green and enjoy music of all genres, from jazz and classical to country and western. There's also children's programs. | 973/226–3621.

NOV.: *Annual Craft Show.* For more than 25 years, this craft show at the Caldwell College Student Center has featured stained glass, wood, textiles, ceramics, antiques, jewelry, and refreshments. | 973/226–2885.

Dining

Mezzanotte Café & Grill. Italian. "Mezzanotte" means "midnight" in Italian, and this Tuscan café and grill is indeed open until the witching hour. Known for huge bowls of great pasta, this spot is a favorite haunt of the New Jersey Devils. | 115 Bloomfield Ave. | 973/403–8500 | fax 973/403–0419 | Closed Mon. | $14–$25 | AE, DC, MC, V.

Lodging

Radisson Fairfield. The Radisson is about 3½ mi northwest of downtown Caldwell, in neighboring Fairfield. Restaurant. Cable TV. Pool. Sauna. Exercise room. Business services. | 690 U.S. 46, Fairfield | 973/227–9200 or 800/333–3333 | fax 973/227–4308 | www.radisson.com | 204 rooms | $100–$250 | AE, D, DC, MC, V.

CAMDEN

MAP 9, D7

(Nearby towns also listed: Cherry Hill, Haddonfield, Mount Laurel)

Camden was originally settled in 1681, and although the city today has a lot going for it, it also has its share of problems. With the development of the Camden waterfront, including an extensive aquarium and the Walt Whitman House, there are certainly reasons to visit, but not yet to stay overnight. (For that, try Cherry Hill or Philadelphia or surrounding communities.) Still, Camden is on the rise, and worth the trip on its own, although many visitors combine it, via ferry, with a day on the Philly waterfront.

Information: **Delaware River Tourism Council** | C/o NJ State Aquarium at Camden, 1 Riverside Dr., Camden, 08103 | 856/365–3300 ext. 230 | www.njaquarium.org. **Camden County Office of Constituent Services** | Court House, 520 Market St., 15th floor, Camden, 08102 | 856/225–5431.

Attractions

Blockbuster–Sony Music Entertainment Centre. Built in 1995, this is a unique, year-round facility. In summer, it's a 25,000-person-capacity open amphitheater. During colder weather, the E-Centre, as it's called, converts to a fully enclosed, climate-controlled theater which can accommodate anywhere from 1,600 to 7,000 people. The center offers concerts, theatrical productions, and family entertainment. It is next to the New Jersey State Aquarium, on 14 acres along the Delaware River. | 1 Harbor Blvd. | 856/365–1300 | www.ecentre.com.

Camden County Historical Society–Pomona Hall. Pomona Hall has been restored to its 1788 appearance, complete with period furnishings and open-hearth cooking demonstrations. This beautiful South Jersey plantation house is considered the finest example of Georgian-style architecture in the state. Bottles and other products of southern New Jersey's most important early industry, glassmaking, are on display, as well as Victrolas and advertising art from the Victor Talking Machine Company. | Park Blvd. and Euclid Ave. | 856/964–3333 | $2; children under 12 free | Tues., Thurs. 12:30–4:30; Sun. 1–5; closed Aug.

New Jersey State Aquarium. Eighty exhibits hold more than 4,000 fish and aquatic animals representing some 500 species. The Aquarium's main exhibit, Ocean Base Atlantic, takes visitors on an immersive, interactive journey, beginning on the beach of a Caribbean Outpost and ending in a Deep Atlantic Sea Lab looking into the Aquarium's breathtaking 760,000 gallon Open Ocean Tank. | 1 Riverside Dr. | 856/365–3300 | www.njaquarium.org | $12; special rates for children, students, and senior citizens | Mid-Apr.–mid-Sept., daily 9:30–5:30; mid-Sept.–mid-Apr., weekdays 9:30–4:30, weekends 10–5.

Tomb of Walt Whitman. Camden resident Walt Whitman died in this city on March 26, 1892. His tomb is not far from that of haiku poet Nick Virgilio. | Harleigh Cemetery: 1640 Haddon Ave. | 856/963–0122 | Free | Daily.

Walt Whitman House State Historic Site. The unassuming home of the great poet is in the middle of a run of Greek revival row houses, virtually across from the city prison. The house offers a good idea (and tours help paint the picture) of the quirky manner in which the poet lived. | 330 Mickle Blvd. | 856/964–5383 | Free | Wed.–Sat. 10–noon and 1–4, Sun. 1–4.

APR.: *Black Maria Film and Video Festival*. This showcase for independent, award-winning films and videos is held on the Rutgers Camden campus. You'll see all kinds of films, from documentaries and animation to feature-length movies. | 856/225–6676.

OCT.: *Sea Monster Masquerade*. Spooky fish-related activities at the New Jersey State Aquarium include a "haunted" dive show and Halloween-themed games. | 800/616–5297.

NOV.: *Fish Tale Festival*. Storytellers, authors, and entertainment add to the exhibits at the New Jersey State Aquarium. | 800/616–5297.

Dining

Hank's Bar & Grille. Casual. This lively restaurant and bar is popular with locals who want to get a burger and beer, shoot pool, and listen to the jukebox. It's a no-frills place with friendly service and inexpensive food. | 2nd & Market St. | 856/541–6651 | $4–$6 | No credit cards.

CAPE MAY

MAP 9, E12

(Nearby towns also listed: Stone Harbor, the Wildwoods)

Cape May, the nation's oldest seashore resort, was a bustling town in the 19th century, but then it slowly faded from favor. In the 1970s, many of the dilapidated, yet beautiful old Victorians ("painted ladies" as they were called) were bought for next to nothing, renovated, and opened as bed-and-breakfasts. Now an official National Historic Landmark City, Cape May boasts more than 600 of these restored structures. Well-orchestrated tours and other events are scheduled throughout the year by the Chamber of Commerce and the Mid-Atlantic Center for the Arts. And Cape May is definitely not just for summer, so you may also have a hard time getting a room during Victorian Week or the Christmas season if you don't plan well ahead.

Information: **Chamber of Commerce of Greater Cape May** | Box 556, Cape May, 08204 | 609/884–5508 | fax 609/884–2054 | www.capemaycountychamber.com. **Cape May County Chamber of Commerce** | 13 Crest Haven Rd., Cape May Court House, 08210 | 609/465–7181 | fax 609/465–5017 | inquiry@cmccofc.com | www.capemaycounty-chamber.com. **Mid-Atlantic Center for the Arts** | 1048 Washington St., Cape May, 08204 | 609/884–5404 | www.capemaymac.org/.

PACKING IDEAS FOR HOT WEATHER

- ❑ Antifungal foot powder
- ❑ Bandanna
- ❑ Cooler
- ❑ Cotton clothing
- ❑ Day pack
- ❑ Film
- ❑ Hiking boots
- ❑ Insect repellent
- ❑ Rain jacket
- ❑ Sport sandals
- ❑ Sun hat
- ❑ Sunblock
- ❑ Synthetic ice
- ❑ Umbrella
- ❑ Water bottle

*Excerpted from *Fodor's: How to Pack: Experts Share Their Secrets*
© 1997, by Fodor's Travel Publications

Attractions

Cape May–Lewes (DE) Ferry. A 70-minute trip aboard one of five modern ferries in the fleet shuttles foot passengers and cars between the two resort areas. Sometimes dolphins swim along for company. Food is available on board. To catch the ferry from Cape May, go to the Terminal Building at Lincoln Drive. To catch the ferry from Lewes, Delaware, board at 43 Henlapen Drive. | 800/643–3779, 609/886–1725, or 302/645–6313 | www.capemay-lewesferry.com | $6.50–$20; special rates for children | Daily 8:30–4:30.

Cape May Lighthouse. This 1859 lighthouse is in Cape May Point State Park. It is one of the oldest operating lighthouses in the United States, and is being completely restored by the Mid-Atlantic Center for the Arts. The 157½-ft structure includes a small museum and offers wonderful views of the shoreline. | Cape May Point State Park, Lighthouse Ave. | 609/884–5404 | www.capemaymac.org | $4 to climb stairs | Apr.–Nov., daily 10–4; Dec.–Feb., weekends 11-4.

Emlen Physick Estate. This Stick-style mansion built in 1879 is attributed to architect Frank Furness. The house features many of the original furnishings as well as textiles and objets d'art. It's home to the Mid-Atlantic Center for the Arts, which was formed in an effort to save the structure, one of the town's crowning glories. It offers a look at Victorian architecture, decorative arts, customs, and the lives of one particular Cape May family, the Physicks. The Physick Estate is also home to the restored Carriage House Gallery which hosts changing exhibits. | 1048 Washington St. | 609/884–5404 | $5–$15 | Daily for tours; call for schedule.

Historic Cold Spring Village. Over 20 antique structures, built between 1702 and 1897, were brought in from sites throughout Cape May County and laid out to represent a small 19th-century South Jersey farming village. Village craftspeople in period costumes demonstrate age-old crafts using traditional tools, methods, and materials. | 720 Rte. 9 | 609/898–2300 | www.hcsv.org | $5; special rates for children and senior citizens | Late June–Sept., daily 10–4:30.

The Nature Center of Cape May. Explore 18 acres of beach, meadow, and marsh habitat at this N.J. Audubon Center. Tours, exhibits, and educational activities are also available. | 1600 Delaware Ave. | 609/898–8848 | Free | Tues.–Sat. 10–3.

Tours. There are almost as many ways to see Cape May as there are things to do here. The Mid-Atlantic Center for the Arts, for example, offers a wide variety of tours almost every day of the year. **The Mid-Atlantic Center for the Arts' boat tours** include sightseeing cruises around Cape May, tours of Delaware Bay (July and August), and, on D-Day, a morning cruise to see historic sites on both sides of the Delaware Bay. | Departs from Miss Chris Fishing Center, at the marina at the entrance to Cape May | 609/884–5404 | $14; special rates for children | Late Apr.–mid-Oct. daily tours at 10 AM).

Other boat tours include the M/V *Whale Watcher,* which is a 75-ft catamaran specifically designed for nonobtrusive, up-close wildlife viewing. The Cape May Whale Watch and Research Center offers cruises with an on-board naturalist who identifies species of whales, dolphins, and other marine mammals. | 3rd Ave. | 609/884–5404 | $50; special rates for children and senior citizens | Call for schedule.

Two different **"Tall Ship Adventures"**—one on the Intracoastal Waterway and the other on the high seas—are boat tours aboard the schooner *Schooner Yankee.* You can fancy yourself a pirate or a magnate aboard this 80-ft-long, 64-ft-high ship. Help with the navigation and sailing, or relax and enjoy the ride | 609/884–1919 | www.schooneryankee.com | $29.50 | May–Sept., daily).

The interiors of five restored Victorian buildings are featured during the **Cape May INNteriors Tour and Tea.** An elegant afternoon tea buffet completes the two-hour tour. | Washington St. Mall at Ocean St. | 609/884–5404 or 609/884–1309, ext. 12 | $15 | Reservations essential | May–Sept., Mon. 12–2; Oct.–Apr., dates vary.

Combination tours include a guided trolley tour of Cape May's historic district paired with a tour of the Physick Estate. | Washington St. Mall at Ocean St. | 609/884–5404 | $11; special rates for children and senior citizens | Call for schedule).

The **Harbor Safari** tour begins at the Cape May Nature Center. A marine biologist guides visitors through Cape May's beach and marsh habitats, teaching them about plants and animals in South Jersey. The 90-minute tour includes the visit to the Nature Center, the upland beach areas and, depending on the tides, the beach habitat or the butterfly meadow | 1600 Delaware Ave. | 609/884–5404 | $5 | Hrs vary.

Cute red trolleys ply the town's streets, and you can take a 30-minute **trolley tour** of the east, west, or beachfront area of town. Combination trolley/Physick Estate tours are also offered, along with Garden Trolley Tours, Romantic Moonlight rides, and Stairways to the Stars, a trolley ride combined with a trip to the top of the Cape May Point Lighthouse to stargaze. | Ticket booth is at Washington St. Mall at Ocean St. | 609/884–5404 | $5.50 | Call for schedule).

Washington Street Mall. Positioned in the heart of the historic district, this outdoor mall has a variety of specialty shops and restaurants. | 609/884–5011 | fax 609/898–9868 | info@mallcapemay.com | www.mallcapemay.com | Free | Call for hrs.

ON THE CALENDAR

APR.: *Cape May Annual Tulip Festival.* Tiptoe through the tulips, or view them from a trolley. Enjoy music and arts and crafts. | 609/884–5508.

APR.: *Cape May's Spring Festival.* This 10-day celebration of the season has special events and tours, including Garden Trolley Tours, historic house tours, lectures, and more. | 609/884–5404.

MAY: *Cape May Bird Observatory Spring Weekend.* Guided walks, boat trips, speakers, and birding are part of this three-day nature festival. | 609/884–2736.

MAY: *Crafts and Antiques on Memorial Day.* The high quality and large variety of merchandise at this annual show at the Cape May Convention Hall make it popular with collectors. | 609/884–5404.

MAY: *World Series of Birding.* Count as many bird species as you can in this environmental contest at the Cape May Bird Observatory. | 609/884–2736.

JUNE: *Cape May Music Festival.* The restaurants, cafés, and public spots of Cape May are alive with music during this monthlong festival of symphonies, songs, folk, pops, and jazz. | 609/884–5404.

OCT.: *Ceili Dance Weekend.* Irish dance workshops and lessons are held at Convention Hall. | 609/884–9565.

OCT.: *Victorian Week.* A must for Victoriana fans, this huge event runs for 10 days and features tours, lectures, vintage fashion shows, vaudeville, crafts, and antiques. | 609/884–5404.

OCT., NOV.: *Cape May Autumn Weekend/The Bird Show.* Commune with nature at such events as hawk, owl, and bat demonstrations, as well as lectures and field trips. The demonstrations take place at Convention Hall. | 609/884–2736.

NOV.–JAN.: *Christmas in Cape May.* Candlelight House Tours, evening Holly Trolley Rides, readings of Dickens's *A Christmas Carol*, wine-and-cheese tastings, a Christmas feast, a brass-band concert, and more make Cape May worth visiting in this season. | 800/275–4278 | www.capemaymac.org.

Dining

Alexander's Inn. French. The elegant, romantic, Victorian dining room dates from 1883 and has a solarium. Waiters wear tuxedos, and you can sample three types of caviar. Try interesting dishes such as domestic rabbit with a Portuguese chocolate sauce and cream of crab and wild mushroom soup. Don't skip dessert—Alexander's makes its own desserts and ice cream. There's an elegant five-course Sunday brunch. BYOB. No smoking. | 653 Washington St. | 609/884–2555 | Closed Mon., Tues. No lunch Wed.–Sun. | $25–$40 | AE, D, DC, MC, V.

Axelsson's Blue Claw Restaurant. Continental. This modern waterfront restaurant is designed to look like a captain's stateroom, with a marble fireplace, European draperies, and dark wood walls. It's known for seafood, beef, veal, and seasonal game preparations.

Try the fresh oysters, the blue claw crab cakes, or the Fisherman's Kettle (an assortment of seafood served in a copper pot). | 991 Ocean Dr. | 609/884–5878 | No lunch | $24–$43 | D, DC, MC, V.

Ebbitt Room. Eclectic. Enjoy cocktails on one of the three porches of this elegant restaurant close to the beach. Inside the candlelit dining room you'll find antique chairs, silk window treatments, and a fire burning all year. Dishes include filet mignon with a truffle red wine sauce, pan-roasted Chilean sea bass, barbecued salmon with sweet mango chutney, and grilled tuna on black risotto. There's piano music and valet parking in season. | 25 Jackson St. | 609/884–5700 | No lunch | $23–$30 | AE, D, DC, MC, V.

410 Bank Street. Cajun/Creole. Housed in this 1850s summer cottage is one of southern New Jersey's top restaurants. Most people dine outside, either on the partially covered patio or on the front porch. It's known for mesquite-grilled fish and steaks and home-smoked meats. Try smoked prime rib, barbecued jumbo shrimp, blackened striped bass, and fresh Maine lobster tails. BYOB. | 410 Bank St. | 609/884–2127 | Closed Nov.–Apr. No lunch | $24–$34 | AE, D, DC, MC, V.

Frescos. Italian. This small, modern cottage is known for seafood and homemade pasta with a Mediterranean flair. Try the shrimp with feta cheese, tomato and basil over fresh fettuccine, the braised veal shank, or the boneless duck. Outdoor dining on an enclosed porch. Kids' menu. BYOB. No smoking. | 412 Bank St. | 609/884–0366 | Closed Nov.–Apr. No lunch | $17–$29 | AE, D, DC, MC, V.

Lobster House. Seafood. You can order shellfish from both inside and out at this large, popular spot on the wharf. Inside there's a cocktail lounge and lots of nautical touches. Outside, you can sit on the dock and watch the ships come in. There's a raw bar and a kids' menu. | Fisherman's Wharf, on Shillenger Landing Rd. | 609/884–8296 | No lunch Sun. | $19–$25 | AE, D, MC, V.

Mad Batter. Contemporary. Housed in a lovely old building, this restaurant is known for fresh seafood and desserts. Try classic crab *mappatello*—a pastry puff filled with fresh crabmeat, spinach, and ricotta cheese, baked and served with a roasted red pepper-white wine cream sauce—the Jackson Street crab cakes, or the orange almond French toast. The dining room has purple walls, a green ceiling, Victorian lamps, and art that changes monthly. Dine outside on the front porch or the garden terrace. Kid's menu. Sunday brunch. BYOB. | 19 Jackson St. | 609/884–5970 | Breakfast also available; closed Jan. | $14–$26 | AE, D, DC, MC, V.

Merion Inn. American. This turn-of-the-20th-century dining room has been serving since 1885, and its beautiful mahogany bar is the oldest in Cape May. Try the Crab Imperial, stuffed lobster tail, steaks, or the daily seafood special. Dine outside on an enclosed porch. Pianist. Kids' menu. | 106 Decatur St. | 609/884–8363 | Closed Jan.–Mar. | $15–$30 | AE, D, DC, MC, V.

Peaches at Sunset. Contemporary. Tropically inspired dining rooms have local artwork, and a screened porch overlooks gardens. Try the sea bass with a jade sauce, avocado crab cake, grilled breast of duck with Mexican orange chipotle glaze, or the rack of lamb. Kids' menu. BYOB. No smoking. | 1 Sunset Blvd. | 609/898–0100 | Closed Mon.–Thurs. from Oct.–May. No lunch | $18–$28 | AE, D, DC, MC, V.

Union Park Dining Room. Continental. Chef owned and operated, this upscale gourmet restaurant specializes in seafood, but also has a great rack of lamb. Try the veal medallions with Maine lobster. BYOB. | 727 Beach Ave. | 609/884–8811 | Closed Jan., weeknights in Feb. No lunch | $23–$28 | AE, MC, V.

Washington Inn. Contemporary. This 1840s Victorian Plantation home has five dining areas: the Fireplace room; the front porch (which is enclosed); the patio dining room, enclosed with a small running waterfall; the Garden room, with a plant-filled atrium; and the wine cellar room with over 10,000 bottles on display. Dishes include pan-seared halibut, grilled veal loin with pesto mashed potatoes, and soft-shell crab. Kids' menu. | 801

Washington St. | 609/884–5697 | Reservations essential Sat. | No lunch | $19–$30 | AE, D, DC, MC, V.

Water's Edge. Continental. Aptly named, this restaurant overlooks the water. Indoors, peach walls and modern art makes for a clean, California-style look. Enjoy the view outdoors on a candlelit patio. Try double-cut port chops with a jerk barbecue sauce, cashew-crusted grouper with a sautéed banana rum sauce, or filet mignon with a horseradish béarnaise sauce. Kids' menu. | Pittsburgh Ave. and Beach Dr. | 609/884–1717 | fax 609/884–1885 | No lunch May–mid-Oct. | $22–$48 | AE, D, DC, MC, V.

Lodging

The Abbey. In the heart of the historic district, this Gothic Revival–style B&B is decorated with Victorian antiques, and the main house looks like an abbey (although it never actually was one). Complimentary breakfast. Refrigerators. No room phones. Library. No kids under 12. No smoking. | 34 Gurney St. | 609/884–4506 | fax 609/884–2379 | www.abbeybedandbreakfast.com | 14 rooms | $80–$235 | Closed Jan.–early Mar. | D, MC, V.

Angel of the Sea. Originally in the center of town, this 1850 Victorian was relocated to the beach in 1891. (Because of its size the house had to be cut in half to make the move). In 1963 the building was moved once again, from the beach to its present location across the street. Complimentary breakfast. Cable TV, no room phones. Beach. Business services. No kids under 8. No smoking. | 5 Trenton Ave. | 609/884–3369 or 800/848–3369 | fax 609/884–3331 | www.angelofthesea.com | 27 rooms | $155–$285 | AE, D, MC, V.

Atlas Inn. Although the name might suggest otherwise, this "Inn" is really a full-service beach resort, complete with just about everything you could possibly want on vacation, especially if you're traveling with kids. There's a pool with a sundeck and kid's area; there are barbecue grills you can use; and there's even a baseball-theme restaurant on the premises, loaded with Babe Ruth memorabilia. Modern and airy guest rooms all have private balconies, many with ocean views. Restaurant, bar, complimentary breakfast. Microwaves, refrigerators, cable TV. Pool. Sauna. Exercise room. Laundry facilities. | 1035 Beach Dr. | 609/884–7000 or 888/285–2746 | fax 609/884–0301 | www.atlasinn.com | 90 rooms | $140–$187 | AE, D, MC, V.

Captain Mey's Bed & Breakfast. Tea is served every afternoon at this antiques-filled Victorian Inn, built in 1890 and named for the Dutch discoverer of Cape May. The inn counts a wraparound veranda, a walled courtyard, and a tulip garden among its charms, and it's walking distance from the beach (two blocks) and the Washington Mall (half a block). Complimentary breakfast. | 202 Ocean St. | 609/884–7793 or 800/981–3702 | www.bbianj.com/captainmeys | 5 rooms | $85–$225 | AE, MC, V.

Carroll Villa. This family-owned and -operated B&B is housed in an 1882 Italian Villa–style mansion with antiques-furnished rooms. Restaurant, complimentary breakfast. TV in common area. Business services. | 19 Jackson St. | 609/884–9619 | fax 609/884–0264 | mbatter@cyberenet.com | www.carrolvilla.com | 22 rooms | $105–$175 | AE, D, MC, V.

Chalfonte. Loyal guests return yearly to stay in this 1876 Victorian Inn, with its rocking chairs, sweeping veranda, original furnishings, and southern-style courtesy. Restaurant, bar. | 301 Howard St. | 609/884–8409 | fax 609/884–4588 | www.chalfonte.com | 78 rooms, 2 cottages | $70–$100 | MC, V.

Hotel Macomber. Bring your old furs to "The World's Smallest Teddy Bear Factory," in this turn-of-the-20th-century hotel, and have them transformed into charming little bears. This was the last historic landmark building built in Cape May, and the lobby includes a comfortable sitting room and solarium with a view of the water across Beach Avenue. Relax in a rocking chair on one of the oceanfront verandas or rent a bike and pedal to town. Guest rooms are cheerfully decorated in keeping with the Victorian theme. Restaurant. Cable TV. | 727 Beach Dr. | 609/884–3020 | fax 609/884–9036 | www.covesoft.com/capemay/macomber | 23 rooms | $45–$95 off-season, $150–$255 in-season | Closed Jan.–mid-Feb. Open weekends only from mid-Oct.–Dec. and mid-Feb.–Apr. | MC, V.

★ **Mainstay Inn.** Located two blocks from the historic district, this B&B consists of two restored Victorian buildings. Although the rooms are furnished with period antiques, the luxury suites have a more contemporary look, with hot tubs, kitchens, and fireplaces. All guests get beach passes. Complimentary breakfast. No smoking. | 635 Columbia Ave. | 609/884–8690 | www.mainstayinn.com | 9 rooms, 7 suites | $170–$225, $225–$350 suites | No credit cards.

Marquis De Lafayette. There are two buildings that make up this property: a six-story building with regular hotel rooms and a three-story building with suites. The six-story structure houses the Pelican Club restaurant on the top floor. All rooms have ocean views. Restaurant, bar (with entertainment), complimentary breakfast. Some kitchenettes, cable TV. Pool. Sauna. Laundry facilities. Business services. Some pets allowed (fee). | 501 Beach Dr. | 609/884–3500 or 800/257–0432 | fax 609/884–3871 | 67 rooms, 6 suites | $129–$249; $219–$389 suites | AE, D, DC, MC, V.

Montreal Inn. This oceanfront hotel is within walking distance of Cape May's historic district and the Washington Mall. Although the structure is your basic concrete building, guests have been returning for 20–30 years, and you must book rooms at least one year in advance. Restaurant, bar, room service. In-room data ports, some kitchenettes, microwaves, refrigerators, cable TV. Pool, wading pool. Hot tub. Miniature golf, putting green. Exercise equipment. Video games. Laundry facilities. Business services, airport shuttle. | 1028 Beach Dr. | 609/884–7011 or 800/525–7011 | fax 609/884–4559 | montrealinn@aol.com | www.cape-mayfun.com | 70 rooms | $98–$180 | Closed late Oct.–mid-Mar. | AE, D, MC, V.

Mt. Vernon. Located directly across from the ocean and five blocks from the historic district, this hotel has a modern sundeck and airy rooms with wall-to-wall carpeting. Restaurant. Some kitchenettes, some microwaves, refrigerators, cable TV. Pool, wading pool. | 1st Ave. and Beach Dr. | 609/884–4665 | www.capenet.com/capemay/mtvernon | 25 rooms | $66–$158 | Closed Nov.–early Apr. | No credit cards.

Queen Victoria. This Victorian B&B is actually made up of two 1880 buildings: Prince Albert Hall and the Queen Victoria. The ocean is a block away. There is a guest pantry area, and suites have in-room hot tubs. Complimentary breakfast. Cable TV. Bicycles. | 102 Ocean St. | 609/884–8702 | fax 609/884–1666. | www.queenvictoria.com | 17 rooms, 6 suites | $190–$220, $265–$280 suites | MC, V.

Queen's Hotel. Owned by the same people who own the Queen Victoria, this 1876 building is also only a block from the ocean, but it's smaller and very private. Some microwaves, refrigerators, some in-room hot tubs, cable TV. Business services. No smoking. | 601 Columbia Ave. | 609/884–1613 | fax 609/884–1666 | www.queenshotel.com | 8 rooms, 3 suites | $175–$220, $245–$255 suites | MC, V.

Southern Mansion at the George Allen Estate. Built in 1863, this mansion was one of the few buildings left standing after a huge fire destroyed Cape May in the late 19th century. After falling into a state of disrepair, it was purchased in 1994 and completely renovated. The feel is still Victorian though, and antiques fill the lobby and rooms. Restaurant, picnic area, complimentary Continental breakfast, room service. In-room data ports, cable TV. Pool. Massage. Business services. No kids under 12. No smoking. | 720 Washington St. | 609/884–7171 or 800/381–3888 | fax 609/898–0492 | www.capenet.com/capemay/allen | 25 rooms | $185–$300 | AE, D, MC, V.

Virginia Hotel. This hotel has a sleeker, more contemporary look than many others in town, but you can still find some Victorian touches, such as fringed lamp shades and potted palms. Rooms all have down comforters and some have private porches overlooking historic Jackson Street. Guests receive beach passes, chairs, and towels. Restaurant, bar, complimentary Continental breakfast, room service. In-room data ports, some in-room hot tubs, cable TV, in-room VCRs. Business services. | 25 Jackson St. | 609/884–5700 or 800/732–4236 | fax 609/884–1236 | www.virginiahotel.com | 24 rooms | $130–$345 | AE, D, DC, MC, V.

Wooden Rabbit. This pretty inn distinguishes itself from the crowd by virtue of the fact that is *not* Victorian. A Federal house built in 1838, the inn is named for the many rabbits–from illustrations to stuffed toys–that grace its rooms. Fireplaces warm up the common rooms and afternoon tea is served on the glassed-in sunporch. Complimentary breakfast. No pets. No smoking. | 609 Hughes St. | 609/884–7293 | fax 609/898–0842. | 2 rooms, 2 suites | $160–$190 | D, MC, V.

CAPE MAY COURT HOUSE

MAP 9, E11

(Nearby towns also listed: Sea Isle City, Stone Harbor)

North of Cape May is Cape May Court House, which considers itself part of Cape May for marketing purposes. This municipality doesn't get quite the attention of Cape May, but it's definitely worth a stop, especially since it's not much of a detour on the way to Cape May. The main attractions are the marvelous Leaming's Run Gardens (actually in Swainton 4 mi away) and the Cape May County Park and Zoo, a good place to go with kids.

Information: Cape May County Tourism Dept. | 4 Moore Rd., Cape May Court House, 08210 | 609/463–6415 | www.thejerseycape.net. **Cape May County Chamber of Commerce** | Box 74, Cape May Court House, 08210 | 609/465–7181 | fax 609/465–5017 | www.capmaycounty.com.

CAPE MAY
COURT HOUSE

INTRO
ATTRACTIONS
DINING
LODGING

Attractions

Cape May County Historical Museum. The holdings of the Cape May County Historical and Genealogical Society are displayed in the John Holmes House, a prerevolutionary structure itself on the State and National Registers of Historical Places. The collection includes furnishings, costumes, textiles, tools, and decorative and practical objects used in the county from the 17th century to the mid-20th century. There is a barn as well as a library with a collection of old Cape May County family bibles and works by local authors. | 504 Rte. 9 N | 609/465–3535 | fax 609/465–4274 | $2.50 | Apr.–Dec., Tues.–Sat. 9–3; Jan.–Mar., Sat. 9–3.

Cape May County Park. This shady oasis, with picnic facilities, walking trails, a concession stand, and strollers for rent, is a good place to take the family if you're burned out on the beach. | U.S. 9 at Crest Haven Rd. | 609/465–5271 | Free | Daily.
The small but well-kept **Cape May County Zoo,** in the county park, includes nice walkways through animal habitats, and an aviary known as the "World of Birds" attraction. | 609/465–5271 | Free | Daily 10–4:45.

Leaming's Run Gardens. This is the largest annual garden in the United States—actually a series of 22 separate theme gardens along a walking path. As you walk through, remember that everything you see has been started from seeds. In August, the gardens become an attraction for migrating butterflies. Also on the property you'll find a little museum of life in the 1700s (when the Leaming family settling here), a small farm with goats, sheep, and chicken, and a gift shop with dried flowers and garden-related items. It's about 5 mi north of Cape May Court House. | 1845 Rte. 9 N, Swainton | 609/465–5871 | www.njsouth.com/leamingsrun.htm | $7 | Mid-May–mid-Oct., daily 9:30–5.

Triple R Ranch. Take an hour-long horseback ride through wooded trails. Led five times daily, the rides are geared toward beginners and use western saddles. | 210 Stagecoach Rd. | 609/465–4673 | $25 | Daily rides at 9:30, 11, 1, 2:30, 4.

ON THE CALENDAR

JULY: *Avalon Recreation Five Mile Run.* Compete in a 5-mi race, or join a 1-mi "fun run" in Avalon. | 609/967–3066.

Dining

Back Yard Restaurant. American. Dine outside surrounded by flowers under a grape arbor, or in the air-conditioned glass-walled interior of this romantic restaurant, 3 mi southeast of Cape May Court House. Try the curried shrimp or the roast duck, and leave room for the key lime tart. | 222 81st St.,Stone Harbor | 609/368–2627. | $22–$26 | AE, V.

Lodging

Doctor's Inn at King's Grant. This small inn, housed in an 1854 Victorian building, features antique furnishings, stained glass, and a garden with a gazebo. Restaurant, complimentary breakfast. Some refrigerators, some in-room hot tubs, cable TV, in-room VCRs. Sauna. Exercise equipment. No smoking. | 2 N. Main St. | 609/463–9330 | fax 609/463–9194 | 6 rooms | $140–$175 | AE, D, MC, V.

Hy–Land Motor Inn. This two-story highway motor inn caters to families and is 3 mi from Stone Harbor beach. Cable TV. Pool. Business services. | 38 E. Mechanic St. | 609/465–7305 | fax 609/465–8776 | 34 rooms | $55–$130 | AE, MC, V.

Peter Shields Inn. You'll find ocean views and eclectic Victorian charm in this 1907 Georgian Revival mansion. Some guest rooms have claw-foot bathtubs, others have working fireplaces. All are furnished with antiques. Bicycles are available. Some in-room fireplaces, cable TV. No room phones. Exercise equipment. Free parking. | 1301 Beach Ave. | 609/884–9090 | fax 609/884–9098 | www.petershieldsinn.com | 9 rooms | $175–$350 | AE, D, DC, MC, V.

CHATHAM

MAP 9, F4

(Nearby towns also listed: Madison, Millburn, Morristown, Short Hills, Summit, Union)

Originally known as Day's Bridge in 1730, this village on the Passaic River was renamed in 1773 in honor of William Pitt, the Earl of Chatham, an ardent supporter of America's civil liberties. The transition from agriculture and mills to a 2.4-square-mi commuter town was accelerated in 1837 with the advent of the Morristown & Essex Railroad. In 1871, an Irish settlement was introduced through the New York Homestead Asssociation's parcelling of 148 lots for immigrant laborers fleeing the Potato Famine. Today Chatham's tree-lined streets are home to about 8,000 residents. Visitors come for the outdoor recreational facilities of the Passaic River and the Great Swamp National Wildlife Refuge.

Information: **Chatham Chamber of Commerce** | 27 Bowers La., Chatham, 07928 | 973/635-2444 | fax 973/635-8420. .

Attractions

Great Swamp Outdoor Education Center. This nature center, adjacent to the Great Swamp National Wildlife Refuge, has 2 mi of trails for hiking and walking. The center also holds a variety of public programs. | 247 Southern Blvd. | 973/635–6629 | Free | Sept.–June, daily 9:30–4:30.

ON THE CALENDAR

APR.: *Earth Day Celebration.* Join an environmental theme party which includes educational exhibitions, lectures and seminars, as well as crafts and games for the kids. This event is held every year on Earth Day at the Great Swamp Outdoor Education Center. | 973/635–6629.

Dining

Restaurant Serenade. French. Dine in simple candlelit elegance at this romantic spot with lots of windows. Popular dishes include fried Maine oysters with seaweed salad, seared yellowfin tuna, and creamless asparagus soup. For dessert try the warm chocolate tart. | 6 Roosevelt Ave. | 973/701–0303 | Reservations essential Sat. | Closed Sun. No lunch Sat. | $21–$32 | AE, D, DC, MC, V.

Scalini Fedeli. Italian. This elegant spot in a 250-year-old home is one of the best Italian restaurants in the state. The dining room has vaulted ceilings and is candle lit. It's known for veal, lamb, and seafood dishes, as well as rich desserts. Try roasted Chilean sea bass with sun-dried tomato sauce, braised lamb shanks with risotto, and roasted rack of lamb. BYOB. | 63 Main St. | 973/701–9200 | Reservations essential | Jacket required | Closed Sun. No lunch Sat. | $52 prix fixe | AE, MC, V.

Lodging

Parrot Mill Inn. Built as a mill house in 1790, this building was actually moved from its original location on the Fishawack River to its present incarnation on Main Street. Guest rooms in the English country-style house are decorated with antiques, paintings, and seasonal fresh flowers. The inn is named for the Parrot family, who lived in the mill house for generations. Complimentary Continental breakfast. In-room data ports, cable TV. No pets. No smoking. | 47 Main St. | 973/635–7722 | fax 973/701–0620 | www.parrotmillinn.com | 10 rooms | $115–$135 | AE, D, MC, V.

CHERRY HILL

MAP 9, D8

(Nearby towns also listed: Camden, Haddonfield, Medford, Mount Laurel)

This once-agricultural area is now an oasis of upscale civilization, and a strategic place to stay the night if you're exploring Camden or some of New Jersey's Western Bulge, or even Philadelphia. You'll find loads of options for accommodations, and also the Cherry Hill Mall, which was the first enclosed mall in the Northeast. Another shopping feature of note is the Garden State Park Flea Market.

Information: **Greater Cherry Hill Chamber of Commerce** | 1060 Kings Hwy. N, Suite 200, Cherry Hill, 08034 | 856/667–1600 | fax 856/667–1464 | chamber@cherryhillnj.com | www.cherryhillnj.com.

Attractions

Barclay Farmstead. A 32-acre Quaker farm from 1684, this property includes a three-story brick farmhouse dating from 1816, plus an operating forge barn, blacksmith, and shop. | 209 Barclay La. | 856/795–6225 | fax 856/795–9722 | $2, $1 children and senior citizens | Tues.–Fri. 9–4; tours available by appointment.

Cherry Hill Mall. The Cherry Hill Mall was the first enclosed mall in the Northeast. Over 175 stores are here, including department stores such as Strawbridge & Clothier, Macy's, and JC Penney. Food court selections include anything from deli sandwiches to sushi. | Rte. 38 and Haddonfield Rd. | 856/662–7440 | Free | Sun.–Thurs. 10–9, Fri. and Sat. 10–10.

Garden State Discovery Museum. This children's museum (geared toward ages 1–10) features lots of hands-on exhibits. Kids can climb inside a bubble, bandage a wounded teddy bear, and even try rock climbing. | 16 N. Springdale Rd. (Rte. 295, Exit 34A) | 856/424–1233 | fax 856/424–6516 | www.discoverymuseum.com | $7; special rates for senior citizens | Tues.–Sun. 9:30–5:30.

Garden State Park Flea Market. This outdoor market at the Garden State Racetrack draws more than 400 vendors. | Rte. 70 and Cornell Ave. | 856/665–8558 | Free | Mid-Mar.–Dec., Wed. and Sun. 8–3.

ON THE CALENDAR
MAY: *May Day Celebration.* Kick off a monthlong celebration with the Family Renaissance Fair at the Garden State Discovery Museum. | 856/424–1233.
AUG.: *New Jersey State Fair.* Held at the Garden State Park, this fair celebrates the state's accomplishments and products. It includes rides, headline entertainment, and exhibits. | 856/667–1600.
NOV.: *Annual South Jersey Fall Food and Wine Festival.* Join local vintners and merchants at the Cherry Hill Hilton for wine tasting and food-related fun. | 800/524–0043.

Dining
La Campagne. French. Also a cooking school, this restaurant is in a 160-year-old farmhouse. The dining rooms have fireplaces, fresh flowers, and French music. Try the rack of lamb or the duck breast. Dine outdoors on a covered garden terrace. Kids' menu. Sunday brunch. | 312 Kresson Rd. | 856/429–7647 | Closed Mon.; closed Sun. July–Aug. | $24–$30 | AE, MC, V.

Los Amigos. Southwestern. If you're in the mood for a fiesta, hit this casual, lively spot about 5 mi south of Cherry Hill. Tequila shrimp is the most popular dish, and the shrimp and cheese enchilada is a close second. Kids' menu. | 461 Rte. 73 N, West Berlin | 856/767–5216 | Closed Mon. No lunch | $12–$30 | AE, MC, V.

Old Hickory Smokehouse. Barbecue. You'll find down-home, old-fashioned barbecue, smoked over real hickory, cherry, and apple logs, about 20 minutes south of Cherry Hill. Try the barbecue brisket, the huge baby-back ribs, or the chicken in homemade barbecue sauce. Closes at 8 on weekdays, 9 on weekends. Kids' menu. BYOB. | 234 Rte. 73, Berlin | 856/753–1323 | Closed Mon. | $19–$27 | AE, D, MC, V.

Red, Hot and Blue. Barbecue. Part of a chain, this spot has blues memorabilia and jazz-playin' pigs on the walls. Known for pork, "wet" or "dry" pork ribs, catfish, and salads. Live blues Friday and Saturday. Kids' menu; kids eat free on Thursday and Sunday. All-you-can-eat ribs on Tuesday and Wednesday. | Rte. 70 and Sayer Ave. | 856/665–7427 | $9–$17 | AE, DC, MC, V.

Siri's Thai French Cuisine. Thai. In the Track Town Shopping Center, this family-run restaurant is a refreshing contrast in appearances. Dark wood accents and a palette of golds and blues are punctuated by fresh flowers and clean white tablecloths. Signature dishes include chicken with basil and chiles, and bouillabaisse with lemongrass. | 2117-19 Rte. 70 W | 856/663–6781 | No lunch Sun. | $13–$29 | AE, MC, V.

Lodging
Days Inn–Brooklawn. With its triangular roof, the three-story building looks more like a house than your typical roadside hotel. Yet this Days Inn, 10 mi north of Cherry Hill and 10 minutes from Philadelphia, takes pride in its chain's attributes, namely quality at budget prices. All rooms have balconies. Complimentary Continental breakfast. In-room data ports, cable TV. Pool. Exercise equipment. Laundry facilities. Business services. | 801 U.S. 130, Brooklawn | 856/456–6688 or 800/544–8313 | fax 856/456–1413 | 115 rooms | $65–$75 | AE, D, DC, MC, V.

Econo Lodge. Reasonably priced and proud of its "Mr. Clean Housekeeping Certification", this hotel is a mile from the Cherry Hill Mall and 3 mi from the New Jersey State Aquarium. Restaurant, bar. Cable TV. Business services. | 515 Rte. 38 | 609/665–3630 or 800/55-ECONO | fax 856/662–7861 | www.econolodge.com | 73 rooms | $38–$45 | AE, D, DC, MC, V.

Four Points by Sheraton. This Sheraton is 45 minutes from Atlantic City and less than 20 minutes from the Philadelphia International Airport. It's got a large work area and other accommodations for the business traveler, and a nice pool. The Garden State Racetrack is also nearby. Restaurant, bar. In-room data ports, cable TV. Pool. Business services, airport shuttle. | 1450 Rte. 70 E | 856/428–2300 | fax 856/354–7662 | 213 rooms | $79–$155 | AE, D, DC, MC, V.

Hampton Inn. This four-story hotel is 15 mi from the Philadelphia International Airport and 9 mi from the city itself. Atlantic City and Six Flags Great Adventure are 40 mi and 25 mi away respectively. It's in a semi-residential area, about 5 mi south of Cherry Hill. Complimentary Continental breakfast. In-room data ports, cable TV. Pool. Business services. Pets allowed. | 121 Laurel Oak Rd. Voorhees | 856/346–4500 | fax 856/346–2402 | 122 rooms | $99 | AE, D, DC, MC, V.

Holiday Inn. Take advantage of the hotel's facilities, and from May through September, consider picking a horse at the Garden State Race Track across the highway. This six-story hotel is in a commercial area. Restaurant, bar, room service. In-room data ports, cable TV. 2 pools, wading pool. Exercise equipment. Laundry facilities. Business services. Pets allowed. | Rte. 70 and Sayer Ave. | 856/663–5300 | fax 856/662–2913 | www.basshotels.com/holiday-inn | 186 rooms | $119 | AE, D, DC, MC, V.

Hilton. This lovely suburban hotel is 10 minutes from Philadelphia's historic and business districts and 10 minutes from the Pennsylvania Convention Center. There's an Olympic-size outdoor pool. Restaurant, bar. In-room data ports, some refrigerators, cable TV. Pool, wading pool. Exercise equipment. Business services. | 2349 W. Marlton Pike | 856/665–6666 | fax 856/662–3676 | www.hilton.com | 408 rooms | $99–$149 | AE, D, DC, MC, V.

Residence Inn by Marriott. This hotel was designed for extended business travel, but it is equally suited for tourists. Rooms are spacious and comfortable, with contemporary furnishings in subdued colors. Some rooms have fireplaces. You can get dinner delivered from local restaurants. Complimentary Continental breakfast. In-room data ports, kitchenettes, cable TV. Laundry facilities, laundry service. Business services. Pets allowed (fee.). | 1821 Old Cuthbert Rd. | 609/429–6111 or 800/331–3131 | fax 856/429–0345 | www.marriott.com | 96 suites | $118–$179 | AE, D, DC, MC, V.

Rodeway Inn. Located 2½ mi northeast of Cherry Hill, this motel features spacious, well-lit rooms, some with whirlpool baths. It's 1½ mi from the Cherry Hill Mall, 4 mi from the Garden State Racetrack and 8 mi from Philadelphia. Complimentary Continental breakfast. Cable TV. Business services. No pets. | 2840 Rte. 73 N, Maple Shade | 856/235–3200 | fax 856/235–6191 | www.econolodge.com | 50 rooms | $45–$55 | AE, D, DC, MC, V.

Sleep Inn. Near the Cherry Hill Mall (3 mi) and the Moorestown Mall (5 mi), this chain motel is also just a 15-minute drive from Philadelphia. Complimentary Continental breakfast. In-room data ports, cable TV. Exercise room. Video games. Business services. | 208 Rte. 130 N, Cinnaminson | 856/829–0717 or 800/SLEEP–INN | fax 856/829–2321 | www.choicehotels.com | 52 rooms | $71 | AE, D, DC, MC, V.

CHESTER

MAP 9, E4

(Nearby towns also listed: Bernardsville, Gibbstown, Hackettstown, Morristown, Stanhope)

You'll find a wonderful oasis of antiques here, 30 minutes away from the bustle of Morristown in Morris County. The town has a definite British flavor: try Sally Lunn's for a lovely afternoon tea, and the Publick House for dinner and perhaps to stay overnight. Unfortunately, it's so cute and there were so many untapped antiques stores just waiting with great stuff to sell, Chester is now yuppie city on the weekends. Still very much worth a visit, however.

Information: **Historic Chester Business Association** | Box 320, Chester, 07930 | 908/879–4814 | www.chesternj.com.

Attractions

Cooper Mill County Park. The working gristmill here is listed on the State and National Registers of Historic Places. You can take a tour in summer. | Rte. 513 | 908/879–5463 | www.parks.morris.nj.us/cooper/index.html | $2 | Grounds: daily 10–5. Mill: July–Aug., Fri.–Tues. 10–5; May–June and Sept.–Oct., weekends 10–5.

Flanders Valley Golf Course. You'll love the views from the Red/Gold course. To get here, take Route 206 north and make a right on Flanders Bartley Road. | 81 Pleasant Hill Rd. | 973/584–5382 | Apr.–Nov.

Hacklebarney State Park. The Black River runs through this 892-acre sanctuary, about 3 mi southwest of Chester. It's one of the less-frequented state parks, and you'll find excellent hiking. In the 19th century this was an iron-ore mining area, and some remnants can be seen. Three rare or endangered species of plants are found here: American ginseng, leatherwood, and Virginia pennywort. | 119 Hacklebarney Rd., Long Valley | 908/879–5677 | Free; parking $5 weekdays, $7 weekends and Memorial Day–Labor Day | Daily.

ON THE CALENDAR

FEB.: *Cabin Fever Days.* Area shops make the best of their slow season with promotions and general good cheer. | 908/879–4814.

OCT.: *Civil War Encampment.* The 33rd New Jersey Infantry Regiment demonstrates camp life at the Cooper Gristmill, 1 mi west of Chester. | 908/879–5463.

NOV., DEC.: *Late Nights in Chester.* To accommodate seasonal shoppers, many stores stay open Thursday and Friday until 9 PM. | 908/879–4814.

Dining

Lamplighter Pub & Restaurant. Continental. This family-run restaurant serves basic Italian and American food in three dining areas. The Pub features sandwiches and appetizers. The more formal Lamplighter Room and the cozy Fireside Room serve lunch and dinner. | 190 Rte. 24 | 908/879–4080 | fax 908/879–8311 | $8–$18 | AE, DC, D, MC, V.

Sally Lunn's English. You must stop in at this Victorian-style tea shop while you're in town either for full lunch service or dessert and, of course, for tea. For lunch, choose between one of Sally Lunn's famous pot pies (chicken, lamb, or oyster are special favorites) or a delectable turnover—a pastry filled with meat, turnips, potatoes, and leeks. Delicious casseroles,

KODAK'S TIPS FOR USING LIGHTING

Daylight
· Use the changing color of daylight to establish mood
· Use light direction to enhance subjects' properties
· Match light quality to specific subjects

Dramatic Lighting
· Anticipate dramatic lighting events
· Explore before and after storms

Sunrise, Sunset, and Afterglow
· Include a simple foreground
· Exclude the sun when setting your exposure
· After sunset, wait for the afterglow to color the sky

From *Kodak Guide to Shooting Great Travel Pictures* © 2000 by Fodor's Travel Publications

soups, and salads are also very popular. The dessert menu is ever-changing and inexhaustible. Try the traditional trifle: pound cake topped with tropical fruits then soaked in a cranberry-raspberry jello, and topped again with raspberry sauce, homemade custard and whipped cream. For the chocolate addict, there are seven different kinds of chocolate cake. | 15 Perry St. | 908/879–7731 | Closed Mon. No dinner | $7.50–$10 | AE, MC, V.

Lodging

Ledgewood-Days Inn/Lake Hopatcong. There's boating, fishing, camping, and swimming within 5 mi of this modern chain hotel, which is 7 mi north of Chester near state parks galore. Restaurant. Pool. Laundry service. | 1691 U.S. 46, Ledgewood | 973/347–5700 or 800/544–8313 | fax 973/347–6356 | www.daysinn.com | 98 rooms | $69–$95 | AE, MC, V.

Publick House. This inn, which dates back to 1810, served as the keystone of the town when it was a stagecoach stop between New York and Philadelphia. The craft, candy, and country stores of central Chester are footsteps away. Rooms are adorned with antiques. Restaurant, bar, complimentary breakfast. No room phones, TV in common room. | 111 Main St. | 908/879–6878 | fax 908/879–6553 | 10 rooms | $60–$90 | AE, CB, D, MC, V.

CLIFTON

MAP 4, C6

(Nearby towns also listed: East Rutherford, Paterson, Rutherford)

Clifton is an 11.3-square-mi city on the Passaic River with a population count of about 76,000. Prior to the 17th-century, Clifton was a major Lenape Indian gathering place. The city's known roots date back to 1693 when the area was called the Acquakanock Patent which was later partitioned into four divisions—the Wesel Division evolved into present day Clifton, incorporated in 1917. Today the city is a shopping oasis and a bustling upscale suburban community. Some of the more photogenic old warehouses have been turned into outlet malls.

Information: **North Jersey Regional Chamber of Commerce** | 1033 Rte. 46, Box 110, Clifton, 07011 | 973/470–9300 | fax 973/470–9245 | www.njrcc.org.

Attractions

Hamilton House Museum. This red sandstone house (named for its last owner Henry Hamilton, who died in 1972) was built in 1817 by Anna and John Vreeland on a site 500 ft south of its present location. Hamilton stipulated in his will that if the property was sold the house must either be moved or torn down. When the land was sold after Hamilton's death, the city put iron rollers under the house and moved it to its present location. Each room in the house is furnished to represent a different period of the 19th century, as well as reflect the lives of the different families who lived there. | 971 Valley Rd. | 973/744–5707 | Donation suggested | First Sun. of every month 2–5; call for appointment.

ON THE CALENDAR
NOV., DEC.: *Annual Holiday Candlelight Tour.* The Hamilton House Museum is decorated for the season and illuminated by candlelight. Docents tell stories of past holidays. There's also singing and refreshments. | 973/744–5707.

Dining

Chengdu 46. Chinese. Casually elegant Asian decor, done in dark woods and grays, makes this restaurant refreshingly cheery and unstuffy. Try the Peking duck, Empress chicken, and Dragon-Phoenix Match (lobster and shrimp with chicken). | 1105 Rte. 46 E | 973/777–8855 | Closed Mon. | $15–$38 | AE, DC, MC, V.

Lodging

Howard Johnson. This four-story chain hotel's location on Route 3 allows for convenient access to the New Jersey Turnpike and the Garden State Parkway. There's an IHOP on the premises, with a "grab and go" breakfast. Restaurant, bar, complimentary Continental breakfast. In-room data ports, cable TV. Pool. Business services. Some pets allowed. | 680 Rte. 3 W | 973/471–3800 | fax 973/471–2125 | www.hojo.com | 116 rooms | $89–$139 | AE, D, DC, MC, V.

Ramada Inn Clifton. You'll find this Ramada in a suburban area, 2 mi from the the Meadowlands Sports Complex and 7 mi from the Lincoln Tunnel. Restaurant, bar (with entertainment), room service. Some refrigerators, cable TV. Pool. Exercise equipment. Business services. | 265 Rte. 3 E | 973/778–6500 or 888/298–2054 | fax 973/778–8724 | www.ramada.com | 225 rooms | $94–$149 | AE, DC, MC, V.

CLINTON

MAP 9, D4

(Nearby towns also listed: Flemington, Frenchtown, Milford, Somerville)

Clinton, which likes to call itself "the quintessential small town," is an old mill town nestled into Hunterdon County's pastoral hills. Lovely Victorian homes, cherry tree–lined streets, and a river meandering through it make Clinton a picture-perfect hamlet. The town's icon—indeed, a recognizable edifice throughout the state—is the landmark Red Mill, home of the Hunterdon Historical Society. The Red Mill is across the 200-ft-wide waterfall of the Raritan River from the Stone Mill, which houses the Hunterdon Museum of Art. The historic center of town was recently entered into the State and Federal Registers of Historic Places.

Information: Hunterdon County Chamber of Commerce | 2200 Rte. 31, Suite 15, Lebanon, 08833 | 908/735–5955 | fax 908/730–6580 | hunterdon@sprintmail.com | www.hunterdon-chamber.org.

Attractions

Hunterdon Museum of Art Across the old iron bridge from the Red Mill, this art museum is in an historic stone structure dating from 1836, when it operated as a gristmill. | 7 Lower Center St. | 908/735–8415 | Free | Apr.–Oct., Tues.–Sun. 11–5.

Red Mill/Hunterdon Historical Museum. The town's signature structure, the Red Mill (which dates to 1810), is on the grounds of this museum. Exhibits of the town's 190-year history are on display over the four floors of the mill. Much of the rest of the 9-acre site is the Mulligan Quarry, which was operated in 1848 by three Irish immigrant brothers and remained in Mulligan hands until the early 1960s. | 56 Main St. | 908/735–4101 | $5; special rates for children and senior citizens | Apr.–Oct., Tues.–Sat. 10–4, Sun. noon–5.

Round Valley State Park. The focal point of this 3,639-acre park is the Round Valley Reservoir, the deepest lake in New Jersey. This is one of the few state parks that allows wilderness camping. Other activities include boating, canoeing, swimming, and picnicking. In winter, there's cross-country skiing and sledding. Clinton is 4 mi away. | 1220 Lebanon-Stanton Rd., Lebanon | 908/236–6355 | Free; Memorial Day–Labor Day, parking $5 weekdays, $7 weekends | Daily.

Spruce Run Recreation Area. The Spruce Run reservoir covers 1,290 acres, with 15 mi of shoreline for recreation. The third-largest reservoir in the state, it's popular with hikers, picnickers, boaters, and fishermen. The park also includes basketball courts and space for 70 tents and trailers. Winter sports include ice fishing, cross-country skiing, and ice-boating. | 1 Van Syckels Rd. | 908/638–8572 | Memorial Day–Labor Day, parking $5 weekdays, $7 weekends; Labor Day–Memorial Day, free parking | Weekdays 8–8, weekends 6–8.

JAN.–FEB.: *HMA Annual Members' Exhibition.* The Hunterdon Museum of Art kicks off its winter season with this group show, in which the museum's members are invited to display and sell to the public artwork they've made. | 908/735–8415.

MAY: *Irish River Festival.* Celebrate Irish culture at the Hunterdon Historical Museum with music, dancing, food, and drinks. Takes place the third Sunday in May. | 908/735–4101.

AUG.: *Annual Motorcycle Show.* Local motorcycle enthusiasts work with the museum to put on this outdoor pageant, which features food, music, and motorcycles, and which usually takes place on the third Sunday in August. | 908/735–4101.

OCT.: *Harvest Jubilee.* This autumn harvest celebration, on the last weekend of the month, features family and children's activities, craft demonstrations, children's theater, guided tours, and food. | 908/735–4101.

OCT.: *Infamous Annual Milford Bed Race and Fall Festival.* This is a hilarious competition of people-powered beds. Past entries have included a rolling bar, the Titanic, and a beer-bottle bed. It's on Bridge Street in Milford, 14 mi outside Clinton. There's also food, crafts, and entertainment. | 908/995–0188.

Dining

Clinton House. Continental. Classic dishes such as blue-ribbon steak au poivre, broiled lamb chops, and wiener schnitzel have inspired a loyal following at this elegant 18th-century inn and restaurant. They also have great seafood. Try the pepper-crusted tuna or lobster tails. | 2 W. Main St. | 908/730–9300 | fax 908/735–5490 | $14–$30 | AE, D, DC, MC, V.

Lodging

Holiday Inn Select. Relax in your comfortable room or stroll down to the antiques-furnished lobby with high ceilings and windows overlooking a pond. Restaurant, bar (with entertainment), room service. In-room data ports, cable TV. Pool. Exercise equipment. Business services. | 111 Rte. 173 | 908/735–5111 | fax 908/730–9768 | www.holiday-inn.com | 142 rooms | $130 | AE, D, DC, MC, V.

Riverside Victorian. This 1852 Mansard-style inn, listed on the Historic Registry, is decorated with antiques, family heirlooms, and Victorian reproductions. Guest rooms have thick comforters and soft robes. Breakfast includes gourmet coffee and homemade pastries. The inn is within walking distance of historic sites. Complimentary breakfast. In-room data ports, cable TV, in-room VCRs. Business services. No pets. No smoking. | 66 Leigh St. | 908/238–0400 | www.riversidevictorian.com | 6 rooms | $85–$115 | AE, D, MC, V.

Stewart Inn. You'll find this Inn about 3 mi west of Clinton, in a 1770 stone house in the country. Guest rooms have antiques and four-poster beds, and two of the rooms have fireplaces. Make friends with the farm animals on the grounds. Complimentary breakfast. Pool. Business services. No kids under 12. No smoking. | 708 S. Main St. Stewartsville | 908/479–6060 | fax 908/479–4211 | 7 rooms | $95–$125 | AE, D, MC, V.

EAST RUTHERFORD

MAP 4, D6

(Nearby towns also listed: Clifton, Hackensack, Lyndhurst, Rutherford, Secaucus)

East Rutherford (pop. 8,107) is in the heart of the the Meadowlands, named for the the rolling meadows that expanded over the land before massive industrialization urbanized the area. The town is home to the Meadowlands Sports Complex, which is enough to keep it hopping year-round. You'll also find the Meadowlands Race Track, and the Continental Arena here. Sports fans come from all around to watch football, hockey, and basketball games, and to watch ice shows and concerts.

Attractions

Meadowlands Marketplace/Flea Market. The state's premier outdoor market has nearly 1,000 vendors. | Giants Stadium, Parking Lot 17, off Rte. 3 W | 201/935–5474 | fax 201/935–5495 | www.fleamkt.com | Thurs. and Sat. 9–5.

Professional sports. Professional sports galore can be found in New Jersey's Meadowlands Sports Complex, which includes the Continental Airlines Arena, Giants Stadium, and the Meadowlands Racetrack. The complex also hosts major concerts and fairs. The **NBA's New Jersey Nets** play in the 20,000-seat Continental Airlines Arena (50 Rte. 120, off Rte. 3 W | 201/935–8888 | $25–$80), as do the **NHL's New Jersey Devils** (201/935–6050 | $20–$74). Both the **NFL's New York Giants and New York Jets** play at the 77,716-seat Giants Stadium (Rte. 3 W | 201/935–3900 | $40–$55).

ON THE CALENDAR

JUNE: *FIFA Women's World Cup Soccer.* See the 1999 World Champion USA Women's Soccer Team play at Giants Stadium. | 212/338–9074.

JUNE, JULY: *Meadowlands Fair.* Enjoy rides, food, games, stage shows, and attractions at Giants Stadium. From the last week of June through the first week of July. | 201/933–0199.

OCT: *Chiller Theatre Expo.* This weekend-long event is devoted to horror, drawing fans from across the country. There's an expo with vendors, a ghoulish model kit contest, and a costume ball with live music. The expo, held the last weekend in October at the Sheraton Hotel, is perfect for Halloween. | 201/896–0500.

Dining

Park & Orchard. Contemporary. Housed in a former machine shop, this perennially packed restaurant serves no red meat, nor does it use any refined sugar, bleached flour, or artificial preservatives. The results are delicious grilled poultry and fish, complemented with wines from the restaurant's estimable list of 2,000-plus vintages. Save room for the coconut custard pie. Although reservations aren't accepted, you can call ahead to put your name on the waiting list. | 240 Hackensack St. | 201/939–9292 | $13–$25 | AE, DC, MC, V.

Romanissimo. Italian. Serving both modern and traditional Italian food, Romanissimo's glass-enclosed space overlooks a garden, and a banquet room has brass chandeliers and a stone fireplace. Try the stuffed pork chop Milanese, or the rack of lamb. | 1 Hoboken Rd., East Rutherford | 201/939–1128 | www.romanissimo.com | No lunch weekdays | $17–$23 | AE, D, DC, MC, V.

Sonoma Grill. Contemporary. This roomy restaurant (it seats 110) features sleek, modern interiors, an impressive wine list, and lots of steak, pork, and game. Live jazz Friday. Kids' menu. | 64 Hoboken Rd. | 201/507–8989 | Closed Sun. | $28–$48 | AE, DC, MC, V.

Lodging

Fairfield Inn Meadowlands. Geared toward business travelers, this hotel is 5 mi from the Lincoln Tunnel and 2 mi from Teterboro airport. The Meadowlands Sports Complex is less than a half mile away, and the Secaucus outlets are 2 mi away. Complimentary Continental breakfast. Cable TV. Exercise room. Laundry service. | 850 Rte. 120 S | 201/507–5222 or 800/228–2800 | www.marriott.com | 141 rooms | $109–$129 | AE, D, DC, MC, V.

Sheraton Meadowlands Hotel and Conference Center. This 21-story hotel has the largest ballroom in northern New Jersey and features two "club" floors dedicated to serving business travelers and guests who want a little extra luxury. (Naturally these rooms cost a little more.) Guest rooms feature complimentary Starbuck's coffee and coffeemakers. In-room data ports. | 2 Meadowlands Plaza | 201/896–0500 or 888/625–5144 | fax 201/896–9696 | www.sheraton.com. | 425 rooms | $179–$219 | AE, D, DC, MC, V.

EATONTOWN

(Nearby towns also listed: Freehold, Lakewood, Red Bank, Tinton Falls)

Although Eatontown traces its origins to 1670, when Thomas Eaton built a gristmill in the area, the town was not officially recognized until 1873. Today, Eatontown is home to one of New Jersey's largest malls (Monmouth Mall) as well as lots of open space: two major parks, an arboretum, and a wildlife sanctuary.

Information: Monmouth County of Economic Development and Tourism | 31 E. Main St., Freehold, 07728 | 800/523–2587 | www.visitmonmouth.com.

Attractions

80 Acre Park. Nature trails, two baseball fields, a basketball court, and a playground are at this, the newest of the town's parks. | Industrial Way E. and Wall St. | 800/861–5515 | Free | Daily dawn–dusk.

Bliss Arboretum. You can walk through trails, smell the pine trees, and catch a glimpse of passing wildlife at this botanical reserve. | Wycoff Rd. | 800/861–5515 | Free | Daily dawn–dusk.

Monmouth Mall. Here you'll find 150 stores, a 15-screen Sony Theater, and a food court. | Rte. 35 and Rte. 36 | 732/542–0333 | Free | Mon.–Sat. 10–9:30, Sun. 11–6.

Wampum Lake Park. Four memorials commerating American war veterans, nature trails, and five picnic tables surround this 10-acre lake. | Rte. 35 and West St. | 800/861–5515 | Free | Daily dawn–dusk.

ON THE CALENDAR

JULY: *Independence Day Parade and Picnic.* Fourth of July festivities are held in Wolcott Park. | 732/389–7600.
DEC.: *Tree lighting.* Carolers, Santa Claus, and general holiday cheer make up this joint Christmas/Chanukkah celebration, in front of Borough Hall. | 47 Broad St. | 732/389–7600.

Dining

Grist Mill. American. Fifteen lunch and dinner specials are served here daily. It's a relaxed, friendly place to get a cheeseburger, Kansas City sirloin, or their signature Sautéed Chicken Vinnie. There is outside dining on the patio and a kids' menu is available. | 1213 Sycamore Ave. | 732/542–3131 | $10–$16 | AE, DC, MC, V.

Tokyo's Japanese Cuisine. Japanese. Excellent sushi and sashimi draw crowds to this small luncheonette-style eatery. The menu also has all the traditional Japanese noodle dishes. BYOB. | 26 Rte. 35 | 732/389–1673 | No lunch weekends | $8–$16 | AE, D, MC, V.

Lodging

Crystal Motor Lodge. This budget-friendly motel is conveniently on U.S. 35, near malls and multiplexes. Restaurant. In-room data ports, microwaves, refrigerators, cable TV. Pool. Laundry facilities. Business services. | 170 Main St. | 732/542–4900 | fax 732/542–1718 | 77 rooms | $70–$85 | AE, D, DC, MC, V.

Ocean Place Conference Resort & Spa. This shore resort, which used to be a Hilton, provides a full-service business or vacation environment in a beautiful oceanside location. All rooms have ocean views. 2 restaurants, bar (with entertainment). In-room data ports, cable TV. 2 pools. Barbershop, beauty salon, hot tub, massage. Tennis. Gym. Shops. Children's programs (ages 3–12). Business services. | 1 Ocean Blvd., Long Branch (10 mi east of Eatontown) | 732/571–4000 | fax 732/571–3314 | 254 rooms | $295–$325 | AE, D, DC, MC, V.

Sheraton–Eatontown Hotel and Conference Center. This Sheraton is convenient to area attractions, including the Garden State Arts Center, which is 10 mi away. Restaurant, bar. In-room data ports, refrigerators, cable TV. 2 pools. Hot tub. Exercise equipment. Business services. | 6 Industrial Way E | 732/542–6500 | fax 732/542–6607 | 208 rooms | $154 | AE, D, DC, MC, V.

EDISON

MAP 9, F5

(Nearby towns also listed: Metuchen, New Brunswick, Somerset, Woodbridge)

George Washington rode through Edison on the way to his inauguration in New York in 1789. Another historic figure stayed—Thomas Alva Edison, for whom the town has been named. Edison, aka "The Wizard of Menlo Park" (a neighborhood of Edison), established his "invention factory" here because it was the highest point along the Pennsylvania Railroad between New York and Philadelphia. Today the town's industrial prowess continues with Raritan Center, the largest industrial park east of the Mississippi, home to 45,000 workers during the day.

Information: **Edison Chamber of Commerce** | 100 Menlo Park Dr., Suite 209, Edison, 08837 | 732/494–0300 | fax 732/494–4141 | www.edisonchamber.com.

Attractions

Edison Memorial Tower. A National Historic Landmark, this marvelous Art Deco tower was erected in 1937 as a tribute to Thomas Edison, who invented the lightbulb, the phonograph, and about 400 other things here. It includes an exhibit of Edison memorabilia. The tower is in dire need of repairs; a campaign is under way to raise funds for that purpose. | Christie St. | 732/549–3299 | Free | Wed.–Sun. 10–4.

Garden for the Blind. The plants are identified in Braille in this lovely L-shape public garden, and the walkways are wide enough to accommodate a wheelchair. At the crux of the "L" there is a section called the "Circle of Senses" in which strongly fragrant plants such as lavender and spearmint are planted, along with plants like Lamb's Ear, which is particularly soft to the touch. It's in Iselin, about 2 mi east of Edison. | Iselin Library 1081 Green St., Iselin | 732/283–1796 | Free | Daily dawn–dusk.

ON THE CALENDAR

MAY: *Book and Arts Fair.* Literature fans will enjoy the sales, signings, exhibits, and entertainment at this event. | 732/248–7298.

JUNE–SEPT.: *Plays in the Park.* This long-running summer theater series is held outdoors in Roosevelt Park. | 732/548–2884.

Dining

Bennigan's. American. Fast, friendly service and reliable food in a pub atmosphere make this a popular place to relax and unwind. | 65 Rte. 1 | 732/549–2859. | $6–$15 | AE, V.

Charlie Brown's Steakhouse. American. One of New Jersey's largest steak-house chains, Charlie Brown's offers casual dining, a full salad bar, and your basic prime rib, steaks and seafood choices. You can eat outdoors on a patio with plants and umbrellas. Kids' menu. | 222 Plainfield Ave. | 732/494–6135 | $11–$31 | AE, MC, V.

Lodging

Clarion Hotel. Catering mostly to business travelers, this Clarion is busiest during the week. A little posher than the chain average, it won the "Best Clarion of the Year" in 1998, and three consecutive Clarion Gold Awards (1997, '98, and '99.) Restaurant, bar, complimentary breakfast, room service. In-room data ports, refrigerators, cable TV. Exercise equipment. Business services. | 2055 Lincoln Hwy. | 732/287–3500 | fax 732/287–8190 | 169 rooms | $99–$149 | AE, D, DC, MC, V.

Red Roof Inn Edison. This family-friendly motel is convenient to Rutgers University, JFK Medical Center, and the Menlo Park and Woodbridge malls. Spacious rooms have desks and easy chairs. Cable TV. Business services. | 860 New Durham Rd. | 732/248–9300 | fax 732/248–9326 | 133 rooms | $66 | AE, DC, MC, V.

ELIZABETH

(Nearby town also listed: Newark)

Close to the New Jersey Turnpike, Elizabeth is the quintessential industrial New Jersey town, the kind that the unenlightened may think is representative of the state. In truth, it does make a rather large impact, especially since it's one of the first things many visitors see if they come into Newark International Airport and head south. But the city has a long and colorful history of its own. Settled in 1664, Elizabeth was the first capital of the state and the first home of Princeton University. Its port was and still is an important commercial center. Today Elizabeth has a number of informal historic districts, such as The Port, Peterstown, Keighry Head, Elmora, and the North End, and residents sometimes refer to where they live by these names.

Information: Greater Elizabeth Chamber of Commerce | c/o First Bank Americano, 339 N. Broad St., 07208-3704 | 908/355–7600 | fax 908/355–0911 | gecc@juno.com | www.elizabethchamber.com, or www.elizabethnj.org/.

Attractions

Belcher-Ogden Mansion. Tour this restored Georgian mansion which dates back to the colonial era. | 1046 E. Jersey St. | 908/351–2500 | Free | Open by appointment.

Boxwood Hall State Historic Site. This was the home of Elias Boudinot, president of the Continental Congress, and then Jonathan Dayton, one of the signers of the U.S. Constitution. It's a staid Georgian structure noted for its wide halls, spacious rooms, Dutch tiles, and fireplaces with finely carved mantels and paneling. | 1073 E. Jersey St. | 973/648–4540 | Free | Weekdays 9–noon and 1–5.

First Presbyterian Church and Graveyard. This colonial church and cemetery also contains a small museum. This is the third structure on the site, which saw its first church in 1665. The present building was completed in 1789, with the parish house added in 1864. | 42 Broad St. and Caldwell Pl. | 908/353–1518 | Free | Daily by appointment.

Warinanco Park. A popular skating center for hockey and ice-skating, this park also has outdoor tennis and boating in season. | St. Georges Ave. at Linden Ave. | 908/298–7849 | $5 | Daily.

ON THE CALENDAR
OCT.: *A Journey Through Union County's History.* Travel through four centuries in one weekend with this tour of 20 house museums around the county. | 908/558–2550.

Dining
Manolo's. Spanish. Cream-color walls trimmed with dark wood, and white-on-white table settings give this restaurant a European bistro feel. Favorite dishes include the Spanish chorizo and the breast of chicken stuffed with crab and shrimp. | 91 Elizabeth Ave. | 908/353–7674 | No lunch | $12–$23 | AE, MC, V.

ELIZABETH

INTRO
ATTRACTIONS
DINING
LODGING

Lodging

Hilton–Newark Airport. Located directly across from the airport, this modern, 12-story Hilton is close to all major highways and 10 minutes away from the Jersey Garden mall, built in 1998. Restaurant, bar, room service. In-room data ports, cable TV. Pool. Hot tub. Exercise equipment. Business services, airport shuttle. | 1170 Spring St. | 908/351–3900 | fax 908/351–9556 | www.hilton.com/hilton | 375 rooms | $89–$229 | AE, D, DC, MC, V.

Hampton Inn Newark Airport. This chain hotel is ½ mi from Newark International Airport and offers free popcorn and fresh cookies in the lobby on weeknight evenings. Restaurant, complimentary Continental breakfast, room service. Cable TV. Hot tub, sauna. Exercise room. Laundry service. Airport shuttle. No pets. | 1128-38 Spring St. | 908/355–0500 or 800/426–7866 | fax 908/355–4343 | www.hamptoninn.com | 152 rooms | $89–$100 | AE, D, DC, MC, V.

ENGLEWOOD

MAP 4, E5

(Nearby towns also listed: Bergenfield, Hackensack, Teaneck)

Englewood is a classic Bergen County enclave, with a Starbucks, nice boutiques, a couple of good restaurants, and, up on the hill in Englewood Cliffs, some very beautiful and expensive homes. Brooke Shields grew up here; Eddie Murphy lives here, too. You can score some unique clothing on Dean Street and lose yourself in nature at Flat Rock Brook Park, all in the course of a day.

Information: Bergen County Division of Cultural and Historic Affairs | 21 Main St., Room 203 W, Hackensack, 07601 | 201/646–2780.

Attractions

Flat Rock Brook Park. This 150-acre park is one of the last remnants of the Palisades Forest. The preserve is managed by the Flat Rock Brook Nature Association, which holds special events and demonstrations throughout the year. There are 3½ mi of hiking trails that wind through or around wetlands, ponds, cascading streams, and woodlands. An 800-ft boardwalk loop trail, with rest areas and interpretive signs, accommodates those unable to walk the woodland trails. No pets are allowed. | 443 Van Nostrand Ave. | 201/567–1265 | www.flatrockbrook.org | Free | Daily dawn–dusk.

John Harms Center for the Arts. Built in 1926 as a silent movie house and vaudeville performance venue called The Plaza, the theater is now named after a local resident who led restoration efforts. With 1,400 seats, it is northern New Jersey's largest theater, and hosts celebrity appearances, plays, dance and musical performances, and children's shows throughout the year. The local production of *The Nutcracker* is a holiday staple. | 30 N. Van Brunt St. | 201/567–3600 | www.johnharms.org | Box office Mon.–Sat. 11–6.

ON THE CALENDAR

DEC.: *The Nutcracker.* This classic holiday story is performed annually by the New Jersey Ballet at the John Harms Center for the Arts. | 201/567–3600.

Dining

Baumgart's. Pan-Asian. An eclectic 1950s-style chrome and black-and-white interior belies the menu's Eastern flair. Known for dim sum and cold sesame noodles. Kids' menu. Sunday brunch. BYOB. | 45 E. Palisade Ave. | 201/569–6267 | $13–$23 | AE.

Jamie's. Contemporary. Jamie Milkman, the chef-owner, is known for her innovative American cuisine. Elegant and romantic, this restaurant enjoys a loyal local following. For lunch, order the grilled salmon burger with red onion marmalade. For dinner, try the roast duck with raspberry peppercorn sauce. | 54 Sylvan Ave.,Englewood Cliffs | 201/568–4244 | $18–$28 | AE, V.

Lodging
Radisson Hotel Englewood. This full-service hotel is convenient to New York City, abundant shopping, and major highways. The rooms are spacious and suites are available. It's geared toward business travelers and tourists who want easy access to the city for less money than it would cost to stay there. In-room hot tubs. Pool. Health club. Business services, airport shuttle. Some pets allowed. | 401 Van Brunt St. | 201/871–2020 or 800/333–3333 | fax 201/871–7116 | www.radisson.com | 194 rooms | $119–$220 | AE, MC, D, DC, V.

FLEMINGTON

MAP 9, E5

(Nearby towns also listed: Clinton, Somerville, Stockton)

In 1785, Flemington was chosen as the County Seat of Hunterdon and, despite a huge fire in 1826 that destroyed the old courthouse and an attempt by the City of Lambertville to have the Seat moved, Flemington held tight and remains the County Seat today. The courthouse, which still stands on Main Street, was the site of the infamous Lindbergh kidnapping trial. Today, 65% of Flemington is listed in the National Register of Historic Places. Along with history, Flemington is known for its well-established outlet shopping, particularly at the 65-store enclave of Liberty Village.

Information: Hunterdon County Chamber of Commerce | 2200 Rte. 31, Suite 15, Lebanon, 08833 | 908/735–5955 | www.hunterdon-chamber.org.

Attractions
Black River and Western Railroad. With a claim to fame as the only standard-gauge steam train in the state, this short-line railroad operates shopping and sightseeing tours between Flemington and neighboring towns. Special events include tours on rare passenger trains in April, staged train robberies in May and September, and Black River's freight train operations in July. | Center Shopping Area, Stango Rd. | 908/782–9600 | www.brwrr.com | $8; special rates for children | July, Aug., Thurs.–Sun.; Apr.–June and Sept.–Dec., Sat., Sun., and holidays. Tours are at 11:30, 1, 2:30, plus 4 on weekends.

Case Cemetery. The most notable grave here is that of the peaceful Chief Tuccamirgan, dating from 1750. The families of the chief and John Philip Case were close friends, and the chief had requested permission to be buried in the cemetery of the Case family. A monument at his grave today replaces the pile of stones that slowly disappeared over the years. | 56 Bonnell St. | www.flemington.net/points/grave.html | Free | Daily.

Fleming Castle. It might not warrant castle status today, but when the house was built in 1756 it was considerably larger than the surrounding huts and Indian dwellings. Owned by Samuel Fleming, the town's namesake, the house today is under the auspices of the Daughters of the American Revolution. | 5 Bonnell St. | 908/735–5955 | Free | Open during Flemington Victorian Days; call for info.

Liberty Village Outlet. You can save from 25%–65% at the 60 designer outlet stores at this shopping complex. Polo, Donna Karan, and Timberland, to name a few, have branches here. | Church St. | 908/782–8550 | Free | Call for hrs.

Northlandz. Here you'll find the world's largest miniature railway, which took 25 years to design and build. Other highlights include a 2,000-pipe organ, the amazing "Le Peep" dollhouse with 94 rooms and an indoor swimming pool, a doll museum, a railway ride, and an art gallery. | 495 Rte. 202 S | 908/782–4022 | $14; special rates for children and senior citizens | Weekdays 10:30–5, weekends 10–6.

Volendam Windmill Museum. In a section of Hunterdon County with a Dutch past, this 60-ft-tall windmill is a living museum with a working model of the wind-powered mills of Volendam, Holland, that used to grind grain into flour. | Adamic Hill Rd. | 908/995–4365 | $3. | June–Sept., weekends noon–4:30.

ON THE CALENDAR

MAY: *Lindbergh and Hauptmann: The Trial of the Century.* Witness live reenactments of the famous Lindbergh kidnapping trial in its original courtroom. | 908/782–2610.

AUG., SEPT.: *Flemington Fair.* Head to the Flemington Fairgrounds until Labor Day for rides, games, car races, 4-H displays, animals, music, vendors, food, and a demolition derby. | 908/782–2413.

SEPT., OCT.: *Challenge of Champions.* This season-ending NASCAR extravaganza features three categories of auto racing, plus merchandise, souvenirs, and more. | 908/782–2413.

Dining

California Grill. American. Casual and family friendly, this restaurant has fresh, sophisticated cooking. There is an open kitchen and a spacious, simple dining room with Native American design accents. Kids will like the aquarium at the restaurant's entrance. The salads are especially good; they're big and include such surprises as poached pears. Try the sesame tuna or one of the many pizzas. | Rte. 31-202 Circle | 908/806–7141 | Reservations not accepted | Closed Mon. No lunch Sun. | $7–$19 | AE, MC, V.

Harvest Moon Inn. American. Known for its vegetable garden and extensive wine list, this restaurant, about 5 mi sound of Flemington, is housed in an historic Federal-style building with fireplaces, beamed ceilings, and a large oak bar. Try the grilled vegetable Napoleon with roasted peppers and goat cheese, and sautéed Long Island duck breast. Pianist Friday and Saturday evenings. Kids' menu. | 1039 Old York Rd., Ringoes | 908/806–6020 | Closed Mon. No lunch Sat. | $18–$34 | AE, D, DC, MC, V.

Union Hotel. American. During the infamous Lindbergh kidnapping trial, this hotel, across from the courthouse, housed participants from both sides. The dining room retains the history of the place, with a 1935 mural, a tin ceiling, and other details. The menu is basic steak and seafood. Entertainment Thursday–Saturday evenings. Kids' menu. | 76 Main St. | 908/788–7474 | $18–$25 | AE, MC, V.

Lodging

Main Street Manor Bed & Breakfast. Rooms are appointed with early 20th-century antiques and feather beds at this three-story Victorian home built in 1901. Antique shops, restaurants, and the courthouse where the Lindbergh baby trial was held in 1933 are within walking distance. Complimentary breakfast. No room phones, TV in common room. | 194 Main St. | www.mainstreetmanor.com | 908/ 782–4928 | 5 rooms | $100–$160. | AE, MC, V.

Ramada Inn. This two-story chain hotel is next to an outlet mall and convenient to historic districts. There's a movie theater and several restaurants around the corner. Restaurant, bar, complimentary Continental breakfast. Some kitchenettes, cable TV. Pool. Laundry facilities. | 250 U.S. 202 and Rte. 31 | 908/782–7472 | fax 908/782–1975 | 103 rooms | $97–$102 | AE, D, DC, MC, V.

FORT LEE

MAP 4, E6

(Nearby towns also listed: Hackensack, Teaneck)

Once known as the "Hollywood on the Hudson," Fort Lee was at the center of northeast moviemaking when the industry began to take off, and numerous classics such as the *Perils of Pauline* (those "cliff-hangers" hung off the cliffs of the Palisades) were filmed here. Today, Fort Lee's location at the foot of the George Washington Bridge makes it the first stop in New Jersey coming off the bridge from New York and a classic bedroom community. It is the most populated town per square mile in Bergen County, and has one of the highest volumes of vehicular traffic in the nation. The city does have single-family homes, but what you'll notice are its high-rises, taking advantage of those spectacular Manhattan views and the prime real estate prices. Many fine restaurants, boutiques, and ethnic delis line the main drags of town. You'll notice the influence of the growing Asian population, now about a quarter of the residents, in bilingual signs and excellent restaurants.

Information: Greater Fort Lee Chamber of Commerce | 210 Whitman Ave., Fort Lee, 07024 | 201/944–7575 | fax 201/944–5168 | ftleechamb@aol.com | www.fortlee.com.

Attractions

Fort Lee Historic Park. Stroll through history while enjoying fabulous views of Manhattan at this site along the Palisades cliffs. Named for Revolutionary War General Charles Lee, this was a strategic stronghold during the war, and you can still see gun batteries and firing stations. The museum on the grounds has artifacts from the war, and, in summer, park rangers give informative talks. Concerts are also held in the park. | Hudson Terr. | 201/461–1776 | Free, $4 to park in season | Wed.–Sun. 10–5.

George Washington Bridge. This two-level suspension bridge, opened on October 25, 1931, spans the Hudson River between Manhattan and Fort Lee. There are walkways on both the north and south sides so visitors can walk or cycle across. The bridge can also be viewed from Ft. Lee Historical Park, on a bluff just south of the bridge. On a clear day, the bridge offers great views of the city and at night it is lit up with lights that outline the cables. | Rte. 95 | Free.

ON THE CALENDAR

MAY: *Madonna Carnival.* This celebration of the *original* Madonna has kiddie rides and food for all. You'll find this event at the Madonna Rectory, 340 Main St. | 201/944–2727.

Dining

Laziz. Middle Eastern. Kebobs, stews, vegetarian dishes, and other staples of the Middle Eastern diet are complemented by innovations like the Navanj Polow lamb or chicken. Meals are served in a dining room with high celings, exotic artwork, and a large mirror on the right side which encompasses the entire wall. | 89 Main St. | 201/461–9339 | fax 201/461–8499 | Closed Mon. No breakfast | $9–$16 | AE, MC, V.

Sally Ling's. Chinese/Japanese. Specializing in Yu-Hsiang cooking, the chicken, beef, and seafood dishes made in this spicy style are especially popular. Chow meins, General Tso's Chicken, and other Chinese staples are joined by gourmet selections like the Beijing Duck, Grand Marnier Prawns, and fried whole fish. | 1636 Palisades Ave. | 201/346–1282 | fax 201/346–1431 | No breakfast | $9–$28 | AE, MC, V.

Lodging

Best Western Fort Lee. With New York City less than 2 mi away across the Hudson River, this hotel is an economical alternative for visitors who don't want to pay Manhattan prices. Another nearby draw is the Palisades Interstate Park, less than a mile away. Complimentary Continental breakfast. In-room data ports, refrigerators, cable TV, in-room VCRs. Exercise room. Laundry facilities. Business services. No pets. | 2300 Rte. 4 W | 201/461–7000 or 888/HOTEL–NJ | fax 201/461–3338 | www.bestwestern.com | 60 rooms | $116–$139 | AE, DC, MC, V.

Hilton-Fort Lee. At the gateway to New York City, this 15-story Hilton offers luxurious amenities for business travelers and tourists. It's five minutes from the George Washington

Bridge, and 15 minutes from midtown Manhattan. 2 restaurants, bar, room service. In-room data ports, cable TV. Pool. Hot tub. Exercise equipment. Business services. | 2117 Rte. 4 E | 201/461–9000 | fax 201/585–9807 | 236 rooms | $139–$219 | AE, D, DC, MC, V.

Holiday Inn. Located right off the George Washington Bridge, this is the closest Holiday Inn to New York City. Giants Stadium is a few minutes away, and there's a shopping mall and movie theater nearby. Restaurant, bar, room service. Cable TV. Pool. Business services. | 2339 Rte. 4 E | 201/944–5000 | fax 201/944–0623 | 175 rooms | $109–$149 | AE, D, DC, MC, V.

FRANKLIN

MAP 9, F2

(Nearby towns also listed: Augusta, Vernon, Walpack Center)

Franklin and nearby Sterling Hill are home to more mineral species than any other location on earth, and many that can't be found anywhere else. Another of the area's geological claims to fame is its wealth of fluorescent minerals—more than 80 varieties—which glow spectacular colors under ultraviolet light. Franklin's Mine Hill became a metal bonanza, producing a half billion dollars worth of zinc, iron, and manganese over a period of 106 years. It stopped producing in 1986, due to depressed oil prices. In 1997, the Franklin Heritage Museum opened on Main Street, featuring old photographs and memorabilia from the area.

Information: **Skylands Tourism Council of New Jersey** | 2 Locust St., Columbia, 07832 | 908/496–8598 | www.njskylands.com.

Attractions

Franklin Heritage Museum. The Franklin Historical Society opened this museum in 1997 in the former "Time Office" of the New Jersey Zinc Company to house its memorabilia, collections, and artifacts. Much of the homespun collection deals with the zinc mining past as well as the history of Franklin and the area. | 95 Main St. | 973/209–1232 | Free | Weekends, hrs. vary.

Franklin Mineral Museum. The emphasis here is on the minerals found in the area, which is home to one of the most productive zinc mining operations in the world. Along with local specimens are rocks, polished and rough, from around the world. A replica of the mining operation shows the process from start to finish. The Jensen wing has fossils, Native American relics, more rocks, and minerals. Outside, visitors can sift through the Buckwheat Dump, a mine waste pile dating from the 1870s. | 32 Evans St. | 973/827–3481 | www.franklin-mineralmuseum.com | $4, additional $5 to visit Buckwheat Dump, $8 combination tickets available | Apr.–Nov., Mon.–Sat. 10–4, Sun. 11–4:30; weekends only in Mar.

Sterling Hill Mining Museum. This once-prolific zinc mine, 3 mi south of Franklin, has been turned into a terrific museum, complete with a ⅕-mi underground mining tour, a museum of old mining equipment, and a collection of minerals, including a room full of the fluorescent minerals for which the area is famous. Out back is a rock pile for kids and adult rock hounds to dig through. | 30 Plant St., Ogdensburg | 973/209–7212 | $9 | Mar.–Nov., daily 10–5, with tours of the mines at 1 and 3.

ON THE CALENDAR

APR.: *Annual New Jersey Earth Science Association Gem and Mineral Show and Outdoor Swap.* Enjoy fluorescent and mineral displays, jewelry and mineral sales, miniworkshops, and a Children's Corner at this all-day affair at the Robert E. Littell Community Center, formerly the Franklin Armory. | 973/209–7212.

DEC.: *Open House.* For a holiday celebration including tours and refreshments, head to the Franklin School on North Broad Street. | 973/827–9775.

Dining

Shelby's. Contemporary. Although out of the way—it's 10 mi north of Franklin—and a bit on the expensive side, this charming restaurant, in a beautiful old bank building, is worth the trip. Try the potato-wrapped red snapper and the streusel-topped apple pie. | 4 Main St.,Hamburg | 973/209–0300 | $15–$27 | AE, MC, V.

Lodging

Hotel & Spa at Crystal Springs. Accommodations at this golf and spa resort, 10 mi north of Franklin, range from one-bedroom condominiums to town houses. Many condominiums have slope-side access to Mountain Creek Ski Area and link-side access to the Spa Golf Club. All have private decks with sweeping views of the rolling countryside. Kitchens, cable TV. | Rte. 94,Vernon | 973/827–2222 | fax 973/827–8115 | www.greatgorgegolf.com | 90 rooms | $94–$170 | AE, D, DC, MC, V.

FREEHOLD

(Nearby towns also listed: Eatontown, Lakewood)

Founded in 1715, Freehold is not quite on the Jersey Shore, but it does provide a first glimpse of Monmouth County's pastoral scenery, with its horse farms and county parks. To the west, in Manalapan, is the Monmouth Battlefield State Park. Bruce Springsteen was born in the borough of Freehold, though not in the town of Freehold, which didn't have a hospital at the time.

Information: Freehold Township | 1 Municipal Plaza, Freehold, 07728 | 732/294–2000 | fax 732/462–7910 | info@twp.freehold.nj.us | twp.freehold.nj.us. **Western Monmouth Chamber of Commerce** | 36 W. Main St., Freehold, 07728 | 732/462–3030 | fax 732/462–2123 | admin@wmchamber.com | www.wmchamber.com.

Attractions

Covenhoven House. This home, built in 1752, belonged to Elizabeth and William Covenhoven. It was occupied by British General Clinton before the Battle of Monmouth in June of 1778. Today, school groups visit for the popular hearth cooking program and several special annual events. | 150 W. Main St. | 732/462–1466 | $2 | May–Sept., Tues., Thurs., Sat. 10–4, Sun. 1–4.

Monmouth Battlefield State Park. The 1,800-acre park was the site of the longest infantry battle of the American Revolution. The visitor center has information on the battle, including artifacts and maps. A landscape restoration project is recreating fences, lanes, and woodlots as they would have been during the Revolutionary War period. You'll find picnic facilities and food concessions, hiking, and nature and bridle trails. The annual weekend-long reenactment of the June 28, 1778 battle is a popular event in the area. | 347 Freehold Rd. | 732/462–9616 | www.state.nj.us/dep/forestry/parknj/parks/monbat.htm | Free | Daily. In Monmouth Battlefield State Park and run by the New Jersey Audubon Society, **Owl Haven,** once a home for injured owls, is now a museum and nature center with over 60 New Jersey bird specimens, a butterfly garden, and a "magic" herb garden. Field trips, children's education programs, and evening birding workshops are offered, and "Mystery Van Trips" take visitors where the birding is best for the season. | 250 Rte. 522 | 732/780–7007 | www.njaudubon.org | Free | Tues.–Sat. 10–5, Sun. 1–5, or by appointment.

Monmouth County Historical Museum and Library. Changing exhibits on the county's history are displayed in the library. The Monmouth County Historical Association maintains four historic houses: the Covenhoven House, Holmes-Hendrickson House, Allen House, and Marlpit Hall. | 70 Court St. | 732/462–1466 | www.monmouth.com/~mcha | $2 | May–Oct., Tues., Thurs., Sat. 10–4, Sun. 1–4.

Turkey Swamp Park. This 849-acre Monmouth County park includes a 17-acre lake for boating, fishing, and ice-skating. You'll also find miles of trails, an archery range, playgrounds, a campground, and picnic facilities. It offers electric and water hookups. | 66 Nomoco Rd. | 732/462–7286 | Free | Daily.

ON THE CALENDAR

MAY: *Craftfest.* Craft-lovers will enjoy this annual juried show at Monmouth County Fairgrounds. | 732/946–3229.

JUNE: *Annual Freehold Area AAUW Used Book Sale.* Thousands of books are for sale at this fund-raising event, which benefits the Freehold Area American Association of University Women. | 732/780–9037.

JUNE: *Battle of Monmouth.* The longest infantry battle of the American Revolution is reenacted at Monmouth Battlefield State Park during the last weekend of the month. | 732/462–9616.

JULY: *Monmouth County Fair.* This slice of classic Americana has cotton candy, farm animals, fresh produce, rides, and games. At the East Freehold Park Showgrounds. | 732/842–4000.

OCT.: *Turkey Swamp Park Day.* A scarecrow contest, pumpkin painting, an archery demonstration, and other activities will put you in a seasonal frame of mind. | 732/842–4000 ext. 237.

DEC.: *Annual Holiday House Tour.* Buy tickets at 36 West Main Street, and take a self-guided tour of houses, churches, and other noteworthy Freehold sites. | 732/462–3584.

Dining

Ferrari's Ristorante. Italian. Join the locals for good standard Italian food. Ferrari's is in a busy strip mall on Route 9 and is often crowded, but good service and huge servings make it worthwhile. | 3475 Rte. 9 N | 732/294–7400 | No lunch weekends | $8–$25 | AE, DC, MC, V.

Golden Bell. Italian. If you're hankering for a late-night snack, this decades-old diner is open 24 hours on weekends, and stays open until 1 AM during the week. The menu is mostly Italian, with some stir-fry and burgers thrown in. Kids' menu. | 3320 U.S. 9 | 732/462–7259 | Breakfast also available | $8–$22 | AE, D, DC, MC, V.

Lodging

Colts Neck Inn. This reasonably priced family-run inn is right on the highway about 10 mi east of Freehold, just 15 minutes from the Jersey shore. There's a restaurant next door, and a mall and racetrack about 10 minutes' drive away. Two suites are available with microwaves. Bar, complimentary Continental breakfast. Refrigerators, cable TV. Business services. | 6 Rte. 537, Colts Neck | 732/409–1200 or 800/332–5578 | fax 732/431–6640 | 49 rooms | $99–$175 | AE, DC, MC, V.

Freehold Gardens. Although there are no actual gardens here, there are flowers planted along the grounds, and plants fill the lobby. Walk to harness racing at Freehold Racetrack or drive to the mall and Six Flags Great Adventure Theme Park (15 mi). Suites have refrigerators and microwaves. Restaurant, complimentary Continental breakfast, room service. Cable TV. Pool. Business services. | 50 Gibson Pl. | 732/780–3870 | fax 732/780–8725 | 114 rooms | $115–$145 | AE, DC, MC, V.

Hepburn House Bed & Breakfast Inn. Charming antiques-filled rooms and suites with bay windows overlook the Battle of Monmouth Monument Park in this 1886 Queen Anne Victorian. It's also an easy walk to downtown shops and restaurants. As a guest, you can have complimentary sherry. Cable TV. Free parking. No pets. No kids under 12. No smoking. | 15 Monument St. | 732/462–7696 | fax 732/780–1195 | horenkamp@aol.com | www.hepburn-house.com | 3 rooms, 2 suites | $85–$135 | AE, MC, V.

FRENCHTOWN

(Nearby towns also listed: Clinton, Lambertville, Milford)

Located along the Delaware River, this former mill and market town has reinvented itself for the 21st century as a quaint shopping district. Its eclectic shops and businesses are housed in restored Victorian homes and other 19th century structures that have long and colorful histories. Art, antiques, and gift stores abound. Best of all—you can cover most of Frenchtown's shopping district on foot.

Information: Frenchtown Business & Professional Association | Box 425, Frenchtown, 08825 | 800/989–3388 | fax no | webmaster@frenchtown.com | www.frenchtown.com.

Attractions

The Delaware and Raritan Canal Toe Path Park. A favorite spot of bikers throughout the region, this bikeway runs about 35 mi from Boundbrook to Trenton alongside the Delaware River. Finding an entrance can be tricky; your best bet is to get on at Route 29 South, or at the towpath at Bridge Street. | | 609/397–2949 | Free | Daily/all year.

ON THE CALENDAR

AUG./FEB.: *Decoys & Wildlife Gallery*. People travel from all over the world to visit this upscale and unusual art gallery, which specializes in handpainted decoys and wildlife-themed artwork. The semi-annual open houses are free and open to the public, and showcase artists throughout the country. During a show, it's not unusual to see crowds lined up outside the gallery to meet the artists and see their handiwork. Prices are steep—$50,000 to $100,000 for some top-shelf items. | 908/ 996–6501.

JULY: *Bastille Day*. The streets come alive as Frenchtown goes European. During the day, participants take part in a crosstown race for charity. Merchants and street vendors sell their wares in the streets and local restaurants set up shop on the sidewalk. Fireworks top off the night. | 800/989–3388.

Dining

Cornerstone Cafe. American. Locals flock to this low-key spot for the nightly specials and friendly waitstaff. Sunday night's offering, a huge "Tom Turkey dinner," is legendary. The decor is low key, and portions are huge. Open for breakfast, lunch, and dinner. | 3312 12th Street | 908/996–2885 | cornerstonecafe@frenchtown.com | www. frenchtown.com/cornerstone | $10–$18 | No credit cards.

Frenchtown Cafe. American. On weekends, people wait in line for hours outside this nostalgic former ice cream parlor-turned eatery to get a seat. Black and white photographs of old Frenchtown dot the walls, and creative breakfast specialties like "The Mess" (ham and potatoes and onions with eggs all mixed up together) and cooked-on-premises turkey and road beef fill the menu. | 44 Bridge Street | 908/996–0663 | $3–$7 | MC, V.

The Frenchtown Inn. French. Constructed originally in 1838, this inn was refurbished in 1985 and although it no longer serves as a hotel, it is consistently rated one of the state's best restaurants. Its eclectic menu and extensive wine line are trademarks, and house specialties include beef Wellington and a selection of homemade pâtés. There are two dining rooms—one refined and upscale (with no smoking allowed) and the other a more casual bistro. | 7 Bridge Street | 908/996–3300 | fax 908/996–7113 | ttomko@frenchtowninn.com | www.frenchtowninn.com | Reservations essential | Closed Mon. | $23–$28 | AE, D, MC, V.

Lodging

The Guest House At Frenchtown. If you're looking for an unusual and private experience, you'll find it at this two-bedroom Colonial fieldstone home dating from the 1780s on a 70-acre estate. Available for rent by the night or week, it's a cozy bed and breakfast sort of place, with a fairly well stocked fridge. But unlike the typical B&B, you have the whole place to yourself, since the caretakers live elsewhere. For an additional fee, you can order meals cooked by a chef, or take a private hot air balloon ride straight from the backyard. Complimentary breakfast. In-room data ports, full kitchen, microwave, cable TV, VCR. Massage. Hiking. No pets allowed. No smoking. | 85 Ridge Road | 908/996–7474 | fax no | brownhomestd@earthlink.net | www.frenchtownguesthouse.com | 1 unit | $165–$185 | AE, MC, V.

The Widow McCrea House. This restored 1878 Victorian home bills itself as the perfect romantic weekend getaway. You get a bottle of wine upon checking in, and a fancy breakfast is served by candlelight on weekends. You can borrow a bike for an afternoon ride, and then return for free tea and cordials by the fireplace. Horseback riding, hot air ballooning, and river sports are nearby, along with plenty of shopping and antiquing. Complimentary breakfast. In-room data ports, refrigerators, cable tv, VCR. Bicycles. Business services. No pets. No smoking. | 53 Kingwood Avenue | 908/996–4999 | fax 908/806–4496 | bpatalano@sprintmail.com | www.widowmccrea.com | 4 rooms and a cottage | $115–$145 per night | AE, MC, V.

Blackwell's National Hotel. Built in 1851, this is one the oldest hotels in the country. Capitalizing on its long history, the owners have outfitted all the rooms with antique double beds and other period treasures. Downstairs, there's a cozy pub with a fireplace, the Rath Skeller. The upstairs restaurant and a bar, the Gibson, are open late. 2 restaurants. Cable TV, Pets allowed. | 31 Race St. | 908/996– 4871 | www.frenchtown.com | 5 rooms | $50–$125 | AE, D, DC, MC, V.

GIBBSTOWN

MAP 9, C8

(Nearby town also listed: Chester)

Also known as the Township of Greenwich, Gibbstown is about 20 mi south of Philadelphia, and Interstate 295 makes it easy to zip up to Philly as well as down to Wilmington, Delaware. Gibbstown got its name from Ethan Gibbs, a local blacksmith who donated land for the construction of a municipal building. The town now has a population of about 5,102 and a land area of 9.3 square mi.

Information: **Gloucester County Office of Business and Economic Development** | 115 Budd Blvd., Woodbury, 08096 | 856/384–6930 or 856/423–1038.

Attractions

Greenwich Lake Park. Part of the Gloucester County Department of Parks and Recreation, Greenwich Lake Park is great for fishing, swimming, and boating. Fishing is permitted year-round, and the New Jersey Department of Fish and Game stocks the 40-acre lake with trout. For swimmers, there is lifeguard supervision from June until Labor Day. The boat launch is open weekends from the start of trout season to Memorial Day; after that, it is open daily until Labor Day. | Tomlin Station Rd. | 856/468–0100 | Free | Apr.–Nov., daily dawn–dusk.

Hunter-Lawrence-Jessup House. Judge John Sparks built this house in 1765; the Reverend Andrew Hunter, a chaplain in the Revolutionary Army, owned it in 1792; and six years later it became the home of John Lawrence. Lawrence's younger brother, James, lived in the house until 1813, when he was fatally wounded on the deck of his ship. His dying words, "Don't give up the ship," have since become the watchword of the U.S. Navy. In 1924 the Gloucester County Historical Society purchased the building and has maintained it as an 18-room museum ever since. | 58 N. Broad St. | 856/845–7881 | fax 856/845–0131 | www.rootsweb.com/~njglouce/gchs | $2 | Mon., Wed., and Fri. 1–4, last weekend of every month 2–5.

Nothnagle Home. This one-room cabin, built in the mid-1600s, is the oldest standing wooden structure in North America. Built completely without nails, its ingenious architecture and rustic furnishings are shown by appointment. The cabin is attached to the (much newer) private home of Harry and Doris Rink, who conduct the tour. | 406 Swedesboro Rd. | 856/423–0916 | www.fieldtrip.com/nj/94230916.htm | Free | By appointment.

Dining
Panda House. Chinese. This is the place to go for shrimp fried rice and steamed dumplings. They serve an inexpensive daily lunch special and takeout is available. | 401 Harmony Rd. | 856/423–6525 | $6–$17 | AE, V.

Lodging
Ramada Inn. Travelers in search of affordable accommodations need look no further then this comfortable chain with soundproofed rooms, blackout window drapes, and a 24-hour coffee shop. It was remodeled in 1998. Philadelphia is just 15 minutes away by car. Restaurant, bar (with entertainment). Cable TV. Pool. Laundry facilities. Business services. | 299 Swedesboro Ave. | 856/423–6600 | fax 856/423–0757 | 124 rooms | $59–$69 | AE, D, DC, MC, V.

Holiday Inn Select. Located 20 minutes from Philadelphia 15 mi south of Gibbstown, this Holiday Inn received a Quality Excellence Award in 1998. Restaurant, bar (with entertainment), room service. In-room data ports, cable TV. Pool. Hot tub. Exercise equipment. Video games. Laundry facilities. Business services. | 1 Pureland Dr. (Exit 10 at I–295), Swedesboro | 856/467–3322 | fax 856/467–3031 | 149 rooms | $84–$109 | AE, D, DC, MC, V.

GLADSTONE

MAP 9, E4

(Nearby towns also listed: Griggstown, Somerville)

Gladstone is one of the twin communities incorporated in 1912. The northern end of the borough adopted the name Gladstone in 1890 to designate the terminating point of the Delaware & Lackawana Railroad—it was named for Britain's Prime Minister. The southern end is Peapack, a name derived from the Lenni–Lanape and believed to mean a "place where water is located." The early rural economy supported many blacksmiths. In the 1800s, the major enterprise was limestone mining and processing. Today the quaint and charming 5.8-square-mi community of 2,500 is the home of the United States Equestrian Stables, Hamilton Farms. Jackie Kennedy Onassis had a house in this upscale pastoral community, which is generally known as Peapack-Gladstone because of the two closely linked small towns.

Information: **Somerset County Chamber of Commerce** | Box 833, Somerville, 08876-0833 | 908/725–1552 | fax 908/722–7823 | dsieberg@somersetcountychamber.org | www.somersetcountychamber.org.

Attractions
Leonard Buck Garden. Wooded trails lined with wildflowers link the different sections of this beautiful rock garden, said to be one of the finest in the country, and rare, exotic plants are tucked among the rocks. Although it is man-made, the garden was designed to be ecologically correct, appearing as though it formed naturally. You can arrange guided tours for up to 15 people for a $30 group fee. The garden is actually in Far Hills, which borders Gladstone to the east. | 11 Layton Rd., Far Hills | 908/234–2677 | $1 per person | Mon.–Sat. 10–4, Sun. 12–4.

ON THE CALENDAR
JUNE: *U.S. Equestrian Team Festival of Champions.* This event showcases Olympic dressage, show jumping, endurance, and combined driving at Hamilton Farm, Pottersville Road in Gladstone. | 908/234–1251.
SEPT.: *Gladstone Driving Event.* Catch the nation's premier equestrian driving competition the third weekend in September, at Hamilton Farm. | 908/234–0151.

Dining

Rudolfo Ristorante. Italian. Clubby and elegant with dark wood walls and fresh flowers, this spot boasts an extensive and sophisticated wine list. Try the seafood salad with Japanese octopus; the duck confit marinated with juniper, thyme, rosemary, and savory; the seafood ravioli; and the homemade anise and amaretto biscotti. | 12 Lackawanna Ave. | 908/781–1888 | No lunch weekends | $14–$26 | AE, MC, V.

GRIGGSTOWN

MAP 9, E5

(Nearby towns also listed: Gladstone, Somerville)

Rural and picturesque Griggstown is on the Delaware River and the Raritan Canal in Franklin Township. It was the home of the legendary Revolutionary War spy John Honeyman. Honeyman was a butcher, who delivered meat to the British and returned with information about their position. As he passed back and forth through the lines he noted the strength and deployment of the King's troops, information that paved the way for Washington's victory at Trenton. In 1873 the bridge-tender station housed a wireless telegraph used to notify the tender of approaching ships, and many believe this was the first commercial use of the telegraph in America. The Griggstown Historic District has numerous 19th-century buildings.

Information: Somerset County Chamber of Commerce | Box 833, Somerville, 08876-0833 | 908/725–1552 | fax 908/722–7823 | dsieberg@somersetcountychamber.org | www.somersetcountychamber.org.

Attractions

Mule Tenders Barracks Museum. This museum, in the Delaware and Raritan Canal State Park (which passes through several towns), features photos, artifacts, and models. The wooden canal bridge, the museum, the bridge tender's house and station, and the site of the Griggstown Mill are along the canal. Canoes can be rented at a private rental concession. The Griggstown Lock is less than a mile south on the towpath. | 4 Griggstown Causeway | 732/873–3050 | Free | Hrs vary.

Dining

Aranka's Hungarian American Restaurant. Hungarian. The food at Aranka's, less than 4 mi east of Griggstown, is flavorful and substantial. Baked pork with gravy, goulash, and stuffed cabbage are all house specialties, and the sugar-dusted dessert crepes with fruit fillings are not to be missed. Aranka's grows all its own vegetables and herbs. | 3185 Rte. 27, Franklin Park | 732/297–8060 | Closed Mon. No lunch Sat. | $9–$18 | AE, V.

Lodging

Hillsborough-Days Inn. You'll find this chain hotel just north of Griggstown, in a quiet neighborhood convenient to area businesses via Route 206. There is a cocktail hour for guests on Monday and Wednesday evenings. Restaurant, complimentary Continental breakfast. Cable TV. Pool. Beauty salon. Tennis. Health club, fishing. | 118 Rte. 206 S, Hillsborough | 908/685–9000 or 800/544–8313 | fax 908/685–0601 | www.daysinn.com | 102 rooms | $62–$99 | AE, DC, D, V.

HACKENSACK

(Nearby towns also listed: Bergenfield, East Rutherford, Englewood, Fort Lee, Paramus, Paterson, River Edge, Rutherford, Saddle Brook, Teaneck)

Founded in 1647, the County Seat of Bergen County has a pretty courthouse and a funky, varied main street where you can get anything from Thai to Mexican food (and don't miss the famously teeny White Manna chrome diner on River Street). Upscale Riverside Square Mall, on Route 4, and the main Fairleigh Dickinson University campus are both at the north end of town. To the south is the top-notch Hackensack Medical Center.

Information: Hackensack Chamber of Commerce | 302 Union St., Hackensack, 07601 | 201/489–3700.

Attractions

Aviation Hall of Fame Museum. Aircraft, artifacts, photographs, and documents pertaining to New Jersey's part in aeronautical history are displayed here, including exhibits on Buzz Aldrin, Charles Lindbergh, and Wally Schirra. Visitors can walk around a Martin 202 airliner, watch planes taking off from the old control tower, or visit the Educational Center at Teterboro Airport. Teterboro is 2 mi away from Hackensack. | 400 Fred Wehran Dr., Teterboro | 201/288–6344 | $5 | Tues.–Sun. 10–4.

The Church on the Green. This was one of the first churches, in Bergen County, built in 1686, and its little cemetery contains the graves of the Bogerts, a prominent family during the early settling of the area. | 42 Court St. | 201/342–7050 | Free | Daily.

The Ice House. This is the largest ice-skating facility in the state. | 111 Midtown Bridge Approach | 201/487–8444 | www.icehousenj.com | $8; special rates for children and seniors | Call for hrs.

Steuben House State Historic Site. The beautifully cared-for stone Steuben House (the curator lives in part of it) is a Revolutionary landmark. Its architecture and historic furnishings recall the Bergen Dutch, an agricultural community whose language and culture blended contributions from Dutch, Angolan African, German, English, French, Scotch, and Scandinavian settlers. Folk-music concerts are held in summer, and the Christmastime Dutch-style tours are always a sellout. | 1209 Main St. | 201/487–1739 | Free | Wed.–Sat. 10–5, Sun. 2–5.

USS*Ling* Submarine. The *Ling* is a Balaoclass World War II–era submarine, permanently berthed at the New Jersey Naval Museum on the Hackensack River. The dedicated volunteer staff of the Submarine Memorial Association will answer questions and take you on a tour of the sub, or you can just browse the old photos or view the small collection of military equipment. | 75 River St. | 201/342–3268 | Free; $4 for submarine tour | Weekends 10–4.

ON THE CALENDAR
JULY: *Fireworks.* Celebrate Independence Day at Foschini Park with the locals. | 201/489–3700.

Dining

Miyoshi. Japanese. Sit at a table or at the sushi bar at this small, unpretentious restaurant with friendly service and quality food at low prices. Located on a side street, it's known for fresh sushi and sashimi, as well as tempuras, udons, and a delicious ginger-based salad dressing. Kids' menu. | 21 Mercer St. | 201/489–0007 or 201/489–0008 | No lunch Sat., Sun. | $8–$23 | AE.

Stony Hill Inn. Continental. In a lovely stone 1818 hillside house, this is a popular special-occasion spot, known for crab cakes, veal, chicken, pasta, and seafood. Inside you'll find several antiques-filled dining rooms, each with its own personality. Don't skip the homemade pastries. Live music Friday and Saturday. | 231 Polifly Rd. | 201/342–4085 | No lunch weekends | $16–$30 | AE, DC, MC, V.

White Manna Diner. American/Casual. Don't blink when you pass Manna—you might miss it. The ultimate in greasy spoon experiences, this red and white hamburger joint on the banks of the Passaic River has been a local favorite since the 1930s. The place is tiny, and you can practically touch both walls when inside. There are no booths or tables—twenty stools surround a tiny grill, where you watch as your burger is prepared. Not to be confused with the White Mana in Jersey City that once graced the World's Fair, Manna's history is less illustrious. But it has an undeniable charm and a die-hard following. Breakfast also served. | 358 River St. | 201/342–0914 | No dinner Sat. Closed Sun. | $1–$5 | No credit cards.

Lodging

Best Western Oritani. This brick hotel is a 45-minute bus ride to Manhattan, and very close to shopping at the upscale Riverside Square Mall. Restaurant, bar, complimentary Continental breakfast. Cable TV. Pool. Exercise equipment. Business services. | 414 Hackensack Ave. | 201/488–8900 | fax 201/488–5456 | www.bestwestern.com/best.html | 99 rooms | $95–$115 | AE, D, DC, MC, V.

Hilton at Hasbrouck Heights. The New York skyline is visible from the back rooms of this 12-story Hilton, which is convenient to bus lines and Giants Stadium. Hackensack is 2 mi away. Restaurant, bar. In-room data ports, cable TV. Pool. Exercise equipment. Business services. | 650 Terrace Ave., Hasbrouck Heights | 201/288–6100 | fax 201/288–4717 | www.hilton.com | 355 rooms | $119–$229 | AE, D, DC, MC, V.

Holiday Inn Hasbrouck Heights. Located just 1 mi from Teterboro airport (2 mi from Hackensack) this hotel is geared toward business travelers. There is a main building and a special executive tower which features work areas in each room. Rooms in both buildings are done in beige, dark greens, and burgundy. Restaurant, room service. In-room data ports, cable TV. Pool. Exercise room. Laundry facilities. | 283 Rte. 17 S | 201/288–9600 or 800/465–4329 | fax 201/288–4527 | www.basshotels.com/holiday-inn | 247 rooms | $144–$175 | AE, D, MC, V.

HACKETTSTOWN

MAP 9, E3

(Nearby towns also listed: Belvidere, Chester, Hope, Stanhope)

Settled in the mid-1700s, Hackettstown today is in very quiet Warren County. The happening little town is undergoing a revitalizaton of its downtown area. In addition to being the home of M&M's (Mars candy), it is the center of an enthusiastic local music scene.

Information: **Hackettstown Area Chamber of Commerce** | 600 High St., Hackettstown, 07840 | 908/852–1253 | fax 908/852–5622 | chamber@hackettstown.com | www.hackettstown.com/chamber/.

Attractions

Allamuchy Mountain State Park, Stephens Section. The 727-acre Stephens section, about 10% of the whole park, features remains of one of the Morris Canal's 28 locks and a section of the old canal's towpath. Campsites are available April–October. | 800 Willow Grove St. | 908/852–3790 | www.state.nj.us./dep/forestry/parknj/parks/stephen.htm | Free; $10 to camp | Daily.

Rockport Pheasant Farm. The pheasants raised here are used to stock public lands. Visitors will also see peacocks, deer, and turkeys. | 700 Rockport Rd. | 908/852–3461 | Free | Daily 7–dusk.

APR., MAY: *Hackettstown Spring Festival.* Town merchants and restaurants participate in the largest local event of the year, which includes a carnival, entertainment, and more. | 908/852–1253.

Dining
Mattar's. Italian. Locals and critics love the warm lobster salad and Cornish game hen at this spot, just north of Hackettstown or Route 517. Original artwork hangs in the pink and mauve dining room, which overlooks a fountain and garden. | Rte. 517 and Ridge Rd., Allamuchy | 908/852–2300 | fax 908/852–1941 | No lunch weekends | $20–$25 | AE, DC, MC, V.

Lodging
Inn at Millrace Pond. Built in 1769, this three-building colonial inn is set on 23 acres. Romantic common areas include a timbered beam dining room and a cozy lounge with a fireplace. Rooms have colonial-style furniture, some with their own fireplaces. Restaurant, complimentary Continental breakfast. No TV in some rooms. Tennis. Library. Business service, airport shuttle. | 313 Johnsonburg Rd., Hope | 908/459–4884 or 800/746–6467 | www.innatmillracepond.com | 17 rooms | $110–$160 | AE, D, DC, MC, V.

Inn at Panther Valley. This large country inn, 3 mi north of Hackettstown, has a lovely courtyard with a gazebo. Rooms in the back overlook a pond and a golf course. Restaurant, bar. Cable TV. | Rte. 17 (Exit 19 off Rte. 80), Allamuchy | 908/852–6000 | fax 908/850–1503 | 100 rooms | $90–$150 | AE, D, MC, V.

HADDONFIELD

MAP 9, D8

(Nearby towns also listed: Camden, Cherry Hill)

Just down the road from Cherry Hill along Kings Highway, Haddonfield, now one of the most affluent communities in this area, started out as a stopover along the main road between Burlington and Salem. The town was also a stop on the Underground Railroad. The Historic District, comprising over 400 structures and including most of the central business district, is listed on both the State and National Registers of Historic Places. William Parker Foulke, a member of the Academy of Natural Sciences of Philadelphia, excavated the fossils of *Hadrosaurus foulkii*—a duck-billed dinosaur—from a marl pit here in 1858; it was America's first dinosaur skeleton. A marker at the end of Maple Avenue places the site of the discovery.

Information: **Visitors Center** | 114 Kings Hwy. E, Haddonfield, 08033 | 856/216–SALE | www.haddonfieldnewjersey.org. **Borough Hall** | 242 Kings Hwy. E, Haddonfield, 08033-0969 | 856/429–4700 | fax 856/795–1445 | www.boro.haddonfield.nj.us/.

Attractions
Indian King Tavern. The state of New Jersey was officially founded here in 1777, when the Assembly passed legislation creating an independent state and adopted its great seal. The tavern itself, built in 1750 and named for the local Lenni Lenape Indians, is a classic example of 18th-century colonial tavern architecture. | 233 Kings Hwy. E | 609/429–6792 | Free | Sat. 10–noon and 1–4, Sun. 1–4, Wed.–Fri. 9–noon 1–4.

MAY: *May Fest.* Costumed guides lead tours of the quaint, downtown, historic shopping district, highlighted by streetside flower vendors. | 856/216–7253.
JULY: *Summer Rotary Concert Series.* Head downtown on Friday nights for this summer concert series. | 856/216–7253.

JULY: *Haddonfield Crafts and Fine Arts Festival.* More than 200 artisans and crafts-people from around the country attend this outdoor festival, held in the center of town. | 856/216–7253.

DEC.: *First Night Haddonfield.* The whole town participates in this New Year's Eve party. | 856/216–7253.

Dining

Villa Rosa Restaurant & Pizzeria. Italian. Popular with the locals, this family-oriented restaurant has good food, generous portions, and a huge menu. Try the meatball parmi-giana, a house specialty, or one of their vegetarian dishes like eggplant rollatini. | 1 Kings Hwy. E | 609/428–9239 or 609/428–9240. | $4–$10 | No credit cards.

Lodging

Econo Lodge. This motel, less than 3 mi from Haddonfield, is convenient to Philadelphia (5 mi from the city and 8 mi from the airport), and 4 mi from the Cherry Hill Mall. There is also a movie theater, a bowling alley, and a health club nearby. Complimentary Continental break-fast. Cable TV. No pets. | 301 S. Blackhorse Pike, Bellmawr | 856/931–2800 or 800/55–ECONO | fax 856/931–6633 | www.econolodge.com | 46 rooms | $58–$69 | AE, D, DC, MC, V.

Haddonfield Inn. This renovated Queen Anne Victorian with a wraparound porch is near more than 200 shops and restaurants. A full complimentary gourmet breakfast is served in the dining room or on the porch. There are fireplaces in the common areas and in every room. Complimentary breakfast. Cable TV. Some in-room hot tubs. Business services. No smoking. | 44 West End Ave. | 856/428–2195 or 800/269–0014 | www.haddonfieldinn.com | 8 rooms, 1 suite | $155–$215 | AE, D, DC, MC, V.

HIGHTSTOWN

MAP 4, F6

(Nearby town also listed: Trenton)

If you're on your way to Princeton, Hightstown is a good place to stop for a place to sleep, or to satisfy any other driving-related need. The town has a population of a few thousand, and they've built a strong community with good services, from auto parts to restaurants.

Information: Hightstown-East Windsor Chamber of Commerce | Box 87, Hightstown, 08520 | 609/448–4412 | fax 609/448–1672.

Attractions

Richard L. Swig Arts Center. This art center, on the 280-acre Peddie School campus, houses the Mariboe art gallery as well as various musical, theater, and dance performance venues. | S. Main and E. Ward Sts. | 609/490–7550 | fax 609/426–9019 | www.peddie.org | Free | Week-days 8–3.

ON THE CALENDAR

OCT., DEC., APR.: *Jazz Fridays.* The Peddie School hosts this three-part series of jazz performances. | 609/490–7550.

Dining

Coach and Four. Continental. Moderate prices and generous servings make this a local favorite, especially among the older crowd. The dining room, done in red and gold, has chandeliers, candles, and fresh flowers. There is dancing and live entertainment on weekends. Signa-ture dishes include pistachio-crusted salmon, potato-wrapped sea bass, and pasta put-tanesca. | 351 Franklin St. (Rte. 33) | 609/443–9600 | Closed Mon. No lunch Sat. | $13–$20 | AE, MC, V.

Lodging

East Windsor-Hightstown Days Inn. This three-floor chain hotel just south of Hightstown is halfway between New York and Philadelphia. It's 8 mi from Six Flags Great Adventure Theme Park and 2 mi from Assunpink Creek Wildlife Management Area. Restaurant, bar, complimentary Continental breakfast, room service. Cable TV. Pool. Video games. Laundry facilities, laundry services. | 460 Rte. 33 E, East Windsor | 609/448–3200 or 800/544–8313 | fax 609/448–8447 | www.daysinn.com | 100 rooms | $59–$139 | AE, D, DC, MC, V.

Ramada Inn. This four-story building with spacious rooms is just south of Hightstown, near a shopping mall. It's about 15 minutes by car to Princeton. Bar. Cable TV. Pool. Sauna. Exercise equipment. Laundry facilities. Business services. Pets allowed. | 399 Monmouth St., East Windsor | 609/448–7000 | fax 609/443–6227 | www.ramada.com | 200 rooms | $72–$129 | AE, D, DC, MC, V.

Town House. This reasonably priced hotel, near New York City train service, caters to business travelers. Restaurant, bar (with entertainment), complimentary Continental breakfast. In-room data ports, refrigerators, some in-room hot tubs, cable TV. Pool, wading pool. Pets allowed. | 351 Franklin St. | 609/448–2400 or 800/922–0622 | fax 609/443–0395 | 104 rooms, 20 suites | $69–$99, $69–$119 suites | AE, D, DC, MC, V.

HOBOKEN

MAP 4, D7

(Nearby towns also listed: Jersey City, Newark)

HOBOKEN

INTRO
ATTRACTIONS
DINING
LODGING

The home of baseball, Frank Sinatra, and *On the Waterfront*, Hoboken, founded in 1640, is today something of an extension of Manhattan, with its easy access to and from the New York City borough via the PATH train. The town's brownstone-lined Washington Street is a center of activity, including a still-healthy music scene led by the long-standing Maxwell's. Some of the unique neighborhood quality has been eroded by the installment of chain establishments such as McDonald's and KFC. If you're bringing a car, prepare for angst, especially on weekends when the situation can be as bad as Manhattan's Greenwich Village.

Information: Hoboken Chamber of Commerce | 1 Newark St., Suite 1A, Hoboken, 07030 | 201/222–1100 | fax 201/222–9120 | www.hobokenchamber.com.

Attractions

Stevens Institute of Technology. Stevens is on a scenic, 55-acre, parklike campus, near the Hudson River. Situated on a promontory known as Castle Point (because the Stevens family actually built their "castle" there), it commands fabulous views of Manhattan. A leading technical institute, the college has a student population of about 3,400. | Castle Point on Hudson St. | 201/216–5105 | www.stevens-tech.edu | Free | Daily.
Formerly the Stevens Center, the **Wesley J. Howe Center** is the nerve center of the college. It includes a bowling alley, restaurants, a gift shop, and conference rooms. | Free | Daily, 24 hrs.
The **Samuel C. Williams Library**'s special Leonardo da Vinci Collection contains one of the finest collections of da Vinci prints, manuscripts in facsimile, and books in the Western Hemisphere. The library also houses historical documents relating to Hoboken and the archives of the Institute, including history and art treasures of the Stevens Family and the Castle, displayed in a grand gallery. | At Castle Point across from Howe Center | 201/216–5105 | fax 201/216–8319 | www.lib.stevens-tech.edu/. | Free | By appointment only.
The **Davidson Laboratory**'s Hydrodynamic and Ocean Engineering research center has an international reputation in marine craft development and testing, as well as advanced research in coastal engineering, marine environmental engineering, and underwater acoustics. | 711 Hudson St. | 201/216–5300 | www.dl.stevens-tech.edu | Free | Daily.

ON THE CALENDAR

MAY: *Hoboken Arts and Music Festival.* More than 250 artists, crafters, and photographers gather for music and food—the festival is held on Washington St., between Newark St. and 7th St. on the first Sunday in May. Usually a name headliner like Joan Jett or Patti Smith finishes up the festivities on the big outdoor music stage. | 201/420–2207.

JULY: *St. Ann's Italian Festival.* This huge annual event brings downtown to life with great food, music, rides, games, and people-watching. | 201/659–1116.

OCT.: *Fall Foliage Iron Horse Express Train.* Leave from Hoboken Terminal for an all-day excursion on a giant steam locomotive. | 888/324–0614.

Dining

Arthur's Tavern. American. This casual tavern, with its colorful stained-glass panels, has five dining rooms (on two floors) serving 24- and 48-ounce Delmonico rib-eye steaks and burgers. There's also some seafood on the menu. | 237 Washington St. | 201/656–5009 | No lunch Sun. | $8–$15 | AE, D, DC, MC, V.

Baja. Mexican. Loud Mexican and Spanish music, bright lights, cactuses, and 100 different kinds of tequila set a high energy scene for fajitas, quesadillas, and other south-of-the-border fare. Go for the Baja special—it's a local favorite. | 104 14th St. | 201/653–0610 | No lunch Mon.–Thurs. | $16–$31 | AE, D, DC, MC, V.

Bangkok City. Thai. Simple, pretty interiors with pale polished wood floors and Thai art on the walls serve as the backdrop for an extensive, classic Thai menu. The $6.95 lunch special is a great value. For dinner try the steamed seafood with ginger and bean thread noodles. The iced Thai coffee is a cool treat. | 335 Washington St. | 201/792–6613 | fax 201/792–0444 | $9–$14 | AE, MC, V.

Café Michelina. Italian. Enjoy classic Italian cooking in an old-fashioned family-friendly 16-table dining room. Try lobster ravioli, or any of the veal and chicken dishes. | 423 Bloomfield St. | 201/659–3663 | No lunch | $8–$15 | MC, V.

Clam Broth House. Seafood. This big, often noisy restaurant has been a Hoboken institution since 1899, as demonstrated by the photos of famous patrons that line the walls. It's known for lobster, seafood platters, bouillabaisse, and steaks. | 34 Newark St. | 201/659–4860 | $10–$22 | AE, D, DC, MC, V.

Grimaldi's. Italian. You can dine inside or out on the sidewalk in front of this small pizzeria that serves up the usual pies, toppings, and antipasto choices. | 133 Clinton St. | 201/792–0800 | www.grimaldis.com/hoboken | Closed Mon. No lunch Tues.–Thurs. | $9–$17 | AE, MC, V.

Margheritas's. Italian. Enjoy pasta, chicken, and seafood in a casual café-style atmosphere on "the strip." There are specials everyday, and you can dine outside in front for prime people-watching. BYOB. | 740 Washington St. | 201/222–2400 | Closed Mon. No lunch Sun. | $16–$30. | MC, V.

Oddfellows Restaurant. Cajun. This slice of Cajun country in Jersey serves authentic jambalaya, seafood gumbo, blackened catfish, and more, amid pictures of Mardis Gras and other New Orleans artifacts. You can eat outside in an enclosed courtyard. Sunday brunch. | 80 River St. | 201/656–9009 | No dinner Sun. | $11–$18 | AE, MC, V.

Lodging

Sheraton Suites at Lincoln Harbor. This Sheraton is 2 mi from Hoboken and just across the river from New York City. It has terrific views of the city skyline, and there's a courtesy shuttle to New York, making it ideal for Manhattan-bound tourists. There's an Italian restaurant on the premises. Restaurant, complimentary breakfast. Cable TV. Pool. Health club. Business services. | 500 Harbor Blvd. Weehawken, | 201/617–5600 or 800/325–3535 | fax 201/617–5627 | www.sheraton.com | 347 suites | $179–$319 | AE, MC, V.

HO-HO-KUS

(Nearby town also listed: Paramus)

Founded in 1790, Ho-Ho-Kus is a quiet, upscale community that likes its tranquility. Events at its central jewel, the Hermitage, are done with taste and refinement.

Information: **Ho-Ho-Kus Chamber of Commerce** | Box 115, Ho-Ho-Kus, 07423 | 201/444–6664 | fax 201/444–6292 | www.hohokuschamber.com.

Attractions
The Hermitage. This stone 1847 Gothic Revival house features docent-led tours and pro-grams—from Victorian lecture series to parlor theater productions—year-round. Nestled among century-old trees on 5 wooded acres of land, this national landmark museum has been an impressive fixture in Bergen County for more than 200 years. It's had its share of noteworthy visitors, too: George Washington, Alexander Hamilton, and James Monroe are counted among its former guests, and Aaron Burr was married to widowed owner Theo-dosia Prevost here in 1782. | 335 N. Franklin Tpk. | 201/445–8311 | $4 | Wed.–Sun. 1–4.

ON THE CALENDAR
DEC.: *Holidays at the Hermitage.* Magic lantern shows were the precursors to movies when it came to mass entertainment up on a screen, and this special magic lantern show will transport you back to the pre-movie 1890s. Participate in sing-alongs, musical instrument playing, and other activities. | 201/445–8311.
DEC.: *Dickens' "A Christmas Carol."* Take in a parlor performance of the holiday classic at the Hermitage. | 201/445–8311.

Dining
Ho-Ho-Kus Inn. Continental. This romantic 1790 sandstone building was a private home for many years. It has a fireplace, five dining rooms, and a patio, and is the preferred place for private functions in the area. There is a good wine list, and favorite dishes include roasted Chilean sea bass and the black pasta. | 1 E. Franklin Tpk. | 201/445–4115 | fax 201/445–9604 | Closed Sun. No lunch Sat. | $18–$25 | AE, DC, MC, V.

HOLMDEL

(Nearby towns also listed: Freehold, Red Bank, Toms River)

After years of being part of Middletown and then Raritan when the latter split from the former, Holmdel officially became its own town in 1857, and was named after the Holmes family, who owned most of the land in the area. (Residents originally sought to name their home Baptist Town, but the name was rejected when it was discovered that a town by that name already existed in New Jersey.) Located right off the turn-pike, Holmdel today is best known for the PNC Bank Arts Center and abundant park-land.

Information: **Shore Region Tourism Council** | Box 1162, Toms River, 08754 | 732/BIG–WAVE. **County of Monmouth Department of Economic Development/Tourism** | 31 E. Main St., Freehold, 07728 | 800/523–2587 | www.visitmonmouth.com. **Western Monmouth Chamber of Commerce** | 31 W. Main St., Freehold, 07728 | 732/462–3030 | admin@wmcham-ber.com. | www.wmchamber.com/.

Attractions

Holmdel Park/Longstreet Farm. This 342-acre county park has hiking trails, fishing, an activity center, small food concessions, and gardens. In winter there's ice-skating, sledding, and cross-country skiing. The park is also home to Longstreet Farm, a living history museum which has demonstrations of everyday farm chores in the 1890s. | Longstreet Rd. | 732/842–4000 | Free (charge for groups) | Park daily dawn–dusk; farmhouse Mar.–Dec., weekends noon–3:30.

Holmes-Hendrickson House. Located next door to Longstreet Farm, this charming Dutch-style 1754 home has been meticulously restored and is full of wonderful mid-18th-century furnishings. Be sure to seek out one of the helpful, knowledgeable docents. | 62 Longstreet Rd. | 732/462–1466 | $2 | May–Oct., Tues., Thurs.–Sun. 10–4.

NJ Vietnam Veterans War Memorial. This huge open-air memorial bears the names of the 1,555 New Jerseyans who died in the conflict. Beside it is the Vietnam Era Educational Center, with information about this tumultuous period in American history. Take Exit 116 off the Garden State Parkway and follow signs. | 800/648–VETS | fax 732/335–1107 | www.njvvmf.org/ | Daily; educational center Tues.–Sat. 10–4 or by appointment.

PNC Bank Arts Center. A great place for a summer concert, with seating in the band shell or on the lawn under the stars, the center attracts top names in pop, rock, and country music. It also hosts a series of ethnic festivals in summer and fall. You can snack at your car in the parking lot before a show, or have a picnic at Telegraph Hill Park next door. The Center hosts a Christmas-lights show in the parking lot in December and January. | Garden State Pkwy., Exit 116 | 732/335–0400 | www.artscenter.com.

ON THE CALENDAR

JUNE, SEPT.: *Cultural Festivals.* The PNC Arts Center holds all-day Italian, Irish, Polish, Slovak, African, and German festivals on weekends during June and September with ethnic entertainment, food, and crafts. | Garden State Pky. (Exit 116) | 732/442–9200.

Dining

Jerry & Harvey's Noshery. Delicatessen. This family-friendly Jewish deli in neighboring Marlboro serves up reliably good sandwiches and soups. Takeout and delivery are also available. | 96 Rte. 9 (Rte. 520), Marlboro | 732/972–1122 | $4–$12 | AE, V.

Lodging

Wellesley Inn. This chain hotel is just 3 mi from the beach, Keansburg Amusement Park, and Keyport's Antique District. It's right across the Garden State Parkway from Holmdel, in the town of Hazlet. Complimentary Continental breakfast. Refrigerators, cable TV. Business services. Some pets allowed (fee). | 3215 Rte. 35, Hazlet | 732/888–2800 | fax 732/888–2902 | 89 rooms | $159 | AE, D, DC, MC, V.

HOPE

MAP 9, E3

(Nearby towns also listed: Belvidere, Hackettstown)

Although its Colonial-era architecture and stone-covered buildings give it the look and feel of a small New England town, Hope was actually built by the Moravians, who originally settled here in 1769. Nestled not far from the Delaware Water Gap in the Skylands Region, Hope has plenty of local attractions nearby, including shopping outlets, museums and recreational activities.

Information: **Hope Chamber of Commerce** | 1301 Hope Bridgeville Road, Blairstown, 07825 | 908/459–5700 | www.hopenj.org.

Attractions

Land of Make Believe. Geared towards kids 13 and under, this 40-year-old amusement park features the largest wading pool in the country, water rides, a Spin-o-saurus Rex ride that spins riders inside a dinosaur, and the Windjammer, which simulates hang gliding. Old favorites like Tilt-a-Whirl and the Thriller roller coaster round out a manageable day of fun. The park, on Jenny Jump Mountain, won a Governor's Tourism Award. | 354 Great Meadows Rd. | 908/459–5100 | www.lomb.com | $15.50 | Memorial Day–mid-June, weekends 10–6; mid-June–Labor Day, daily 10–6.

Hemknoll Farm. Flower lovers will bask in Hemknoll Farms' amazing selection of hybrid daylilies. The farm is just a few miles from Hope and is considered the largest displayer of daylilies on the East Coast. It has over 1,000 registered hybrids, which are in full bloom in July and remain a lovely sight through August. | 316 Great Meadows Road; Take Interstate 80 off at Exit 12, they are about 10 mi down the road | 908/459–5778 | fax 908/459–5058 | hemknoll@worldnet.att.new | Shown by appointment.

ON THE CALENDAR

DEC.: *Christmas Craft Market.* One of the region's most celebrated craft shows, this huge Christmas-themed event is held in various historic buildings around town. | 908/459–5127.

Dining

The Village Cafe. American. This historic residence, once home to the town mill keeper, is the area's coziest eatery. The chairs and tables don't match, and the decor is garage sale antique chic. However, the food is good and servers are friendly. They're known for Brandied Chicken—boneless chicken breast in a brandy cream sauce with snow peas and mushrooms, served over pasta—and Seafood Marinara—sautéed shrimp and scallops in a marinara sauce over pasta. Breakfast is served on weekends. | 3 Millbrook Road | 908/459–4860 | fax 908/459–4873 | $11–$19.

The Inn At Mill Race Pond Restaurant. American. This simple, unpretentious inn is a good choice for a casual dinner at the end of a long day of sightseeing and exploring. The rack of lamb is excellent, and the menu is diverse. Locals come for the venison medallions or the chicken breast stuffed with sun-dried tomatoes, spinach, wild mushrooms, and roasted garlic. There is a tavern within the restaurant, which features a scaled-down version of the regular menu and a nicely stocked bar. Sunday brunch. | 113 Johnsonburg Road, Hope | 908/459–4884 | fax 908/459–5276 | millrace@epix.net | www.innatmillracepond.com | Reservations required on weekends | $19–$29 | AE, D, DC, MC, V.

Lodging

The Inn At Mill Race Pond. This unusual inn is actually a converted 18th century grist mill. It has 17 rooms and a number of nice amenities, such as a video and book library for guests to use free of charge. The rooms have queen-size beds, and are decorated in early-American shaker style, with period antiques lending to their charm. 1 Restaurant SEE ABOVE Complimentary breakfast. In-room data ports. Pond. Tennis. Library. Pets allowed. No smoking. | 113 Johnsonburg Road, Hope | 908/459–4884 or 800/746–6467 | millrace@epix.net | www.innatmillracepond.com | 17 rooms | $120–$170 | AE, D, DC, MC, V.

Bethel Farms Bed & Breakfast. You'll find this beautifully restored 1700's stone farm house on four acres in the center of Hope. In winter, there's a bottomless crock of hot cider in the kitchen, and you'll be greeted with a basket of fresh fruit and homemade cookies all year. Only one of the three rooms has a private bathroom, but the common bathroom has a fun, oversized, claw-footed tub. You'll be invited to tour Bethel's private 61-acre farm just up the road. Complimentary breakfast. In-room data ports, cable TV in some rooms, VCRs. Laundry facilities. No pets allowed. No smoking. | 419 Route 519, Hope | 908/459–4895 | 3 rooms | $95–$135 | MC, V.

JACKSON

MAP 9, F7

(Nearby towns also listed: Lakewood, Toms River)

Often called the "Gateway to the Jersey Shore," Jackson is, at 100 square mi, the largest municipality in Ocean County and the third largest in the state. It's been rated as one of the top five places in New Jersey to live, and many new residents have migrated here in recent years from more congested areas. The town is more lively since the Great Adventure Outlet Mall, a 90-store shopping mecca, and a state-of-the-art Municipal Justice and Recreational Complex were added.

Attractions

Cream Ridge Winery. Tours and tastings are available at this family-owned and -operated winery, known for its cherry, plum, and cranberry wines. It's about 4 mi west of Jackson. | 145 Rte. 539, Cream Ridge | 609/259–9797 | fax 609/259–1865 | www.creamridgewinery.com | Daily 11–5.

★ **Six Flags Great Adventure Theme Park/Six Flags Wild Safari Animal Park.** This is the largest theme park in the country, with a contiguous 350-acre wild animal park that is home to 1,200 (mostly) free-roaming animals. You drive your own car through, so be warned that the monkeys can get rambunctious. | 732/928–1821 | www.sixflags.com/greatadventure/ | $45 theme park, $15 safari only, $46 combination ticket | Themepark: Memorial Day–Labor Day, daily 10–10; Wild Safari: Memorial Day–Labor Day, daily 9–4.

ON THE CALENDAR

OCT.: *Fall Forestry and 4H Festival.* Hike, take a hayride, tour the greenhouse, and bring acorns for fall planting. On the 1st Saturday of the month at the Forest Resource Education Center. | 732/928–0029.

Dining

Pasta House. Italian. The name says it all. This country, kid-friendly restaurant serves up great pastas. Try the gnocchi or the penne with vodka sauce. | 250 N. Hope Chapel Rd. | 732/363–4111 | $10–$16 | AE, V.

JERSEY CITY

MAP 9, H4

(Nearby towns also listed: Hoboken, Newark)

Founded in 1629 and adjacent to Hoboken, Jersey City has some similar brownstone architecture but until recently never garnered the attention or panache of its neighbor. This relative anonymity may have saved the place and the rents—until now. People are beginning to venture forth to buy up less expensive apartments with lots of style; the amenities are sure to follow. The waterfront has always been a center of tourist activity, with Liberty State Park, and, more recently, the Liberty Science Center. Here, too, you can catch the ferry to Ellis Island and the Statue of Liberty (which both New Yorkers and New Jerseyans claim as their own).

Information: **Hudson County Chamber of Commerce** | 574 Summit Ave., Jersey City, 07306 | 201/436–4333.

Attractions

Jersey City Museum. This museum focuses on 19th-, 20th-, and 21st-century paintings and prints, with the emphasis on contemporary work. | 472 Jersey Ave. | 201/547–4514 | fax 201/547–5655 | Free | Tues.–Sat. 10:30–5 (until 8 on Wed.).

Liberty State Park. This bustling waterfront park offers a spectacular view of the Statue of Liberty and the Manhattan skyline. From here you can catch the ferry to the Statue of Liberty and Ellis Island Immigration Museum. There's also an interesting waterfront path, part of the N.J. Coastal Heritage Trail. Take Exit 14B off the New Jersey Turnpike. | Morris Pesin Dr. | 201/915–3400 | www.libertystatepark.com | Free; parking $5 weekdays, $7 weekends and Memorial Day–Labor Day | Daily.

A public/private partnership raised $68 million to build the **Liberty Science Center,** which opened in January 1993. Since then, more than 3 million visitors have made it one of the area's most popular attractions. Three themed floors—Environment, Health, and Invention—feature interactive exhibits designed to be both educational and fun. Play virtual reality basketball, visit with a giant insect, or lose yourself in a towering IMAX movie presentation. There are also traveling exhibits from around the world, and overnight programs for kids. | 251 Phillip St. | 201/200–1000 | www.lsc.org | $10–$15 | Daily 9:30–5:30.

ON THE CALENDAR

JUNE: *Pathmark Multicultural Arts Festival.* One of the largest multicultural arts festivals in the country, this event lasts for 16 days and is held in three states. Events are at different venues throughout town. | 914/762–8878.

JULY: *Fireworks on the Fourth.* The Manhattan skyline is the backdrop for this annual free fireworks display at Liberty State Park. | 201/915–4301.

SEPT.: *New Jersey Harbor Heritage Day.* Celebrate down at the harbor with food, music, boats, clam bakes, sailing races, a children's area, and more. | 201/915–3412.

OCT.: *Downtown Artists Studio Tour.* Local artists open their studios for a weekend-long exhibit. | 201/547–5522.

Dining

Laico's. Italian. There are actually two Laico's in Jersey City. The first opened in about 1975 and is one of the city's dining landmarks. Fittingly, the home of this newer Laico's, Summit House, is itself a historic landmark dating back to 1690. Choose from an extensive and classic Italian menu complemented by a good wine list. | 510 Summit Ave. | 201/963–0657 | Closed Sun. | $11–$20 | AE, D, DC, MC, V.

White Mana Diner. American/Casual. One of the stars of the "Diner State," White Mana is a relic of the 1939 New York World's Fair and a historic landmark. Round and white-tiled, it was designed to be the nation's first fast food joint. The burgers are billed by locals as the best in the area. | 470 Tonnele Ave. | 201/963–1441 | Open 24 hrs | $2–$5 | No credit cards.

Lodging

Doubletree Club Suites Jersey City. Located a half mile from the Holland Tunnel and the New Jersey Turnpike, this hotel is also 9 mi from Newark Airport. Most suites have sweeping views of the Manhattan skyline. Geared toward business travel, the hotel offers complimentary shuttle service to the local companies. In-room data ports, cable TV. Exercise room. Video games. Laundry service. | 455 Washington Blvd. | 201/499–2400 or 800/222–8733 | fax 201/499–2406 | www.hilton.com/doubletree | 199 suites | $191–$259 | AE, DC, MC, V.

LAKEWOOD

MAP 9, G7

(Nearby towns also listed: Eatontown, Freehold, Jackson)

Founded in 1800, Lakewood has a number of large historic homes, including that of George Jay Gould, which is now part of a Catholic university. Lakewood is also a good jumping-off point for hikes through the pine trees that originally drew people to the region. There are a variety of bicycle trails and camping facilities in the area, as well as popular fishing spots.

Information: Lakewood Chamber of Commerce | 395 Rte. 70, Lakewood, 08701 | 732/363–0012 | fax 732/367–4453.

Attractions

Allaire State Park. This 3,000-acre park, 6 mi from Lakewood, has camping, picnicking, canoeing, hiking, biking, horseback riding, cross-country skiing, a playground, and more. | Allaire Rd off Rte. 54 N, Farmingdale | 732/938–2371 | Free; weekend parking $3 Memorial Day–Labor Day | Daily.

Located within Allaire State Park Park, **Historic Allaire Village** centers around the restored Howell Furnace, which produced pig iron in the early 1800s. An entire town grew up around the operation, and several buildings, including a church, general store, bakery, blacksmith shop, tin shop, and row houses, remain. Nineteenth-century crafts and trades demonstrations are offered, and the gift shop is a nice place to shop for hand-dipped candles, homemade preserves, and other old-fashioned gifts. Candlelight tours, crafts markets, and other events are held throughout the year. | Rte. 524, Farmingdale | 732/938–2253 | www.allairevillage.org | free | May–Labor Day, Wed.–Sun. 10–4; Feb.–Dec., Fri. 10–2, some weekends 10–4.

Also in the park, the **Pine Creek Railroad** toots along a ¾-mi loop, spouting steam and delighting children. The narrow-gauge trains are operated by the New Jersey Museum of Transportation. The trains depart every half hour. | 732/938–5524 | $2 | Aug., daily 12–4; Oct., weekends 12–4.

Georgian Court College. The 150-acre Gould Estate, complete with Georgian and Renaissance architecture and elaborate gardens, was built by George Jay Gould in 1898. In 1924 the Sisters of Mercy converted it into a four-year institution of higher learning. It's a national historic landmark, and you're invited to visit the arboretum, a project of the Biology Department. | 900 Lakewood Ave. | 732/364–2200 | www.georgian.edu | Free | Daily.

Ocean County Park. You'll find hiking trails and exotic trees imported from around the world on this 323-acre park, which was once a Rockefeller estate. | 659 Ocean Ave. | 732/506–9090 | Free | Sept.–Aug., daily.

ON THE CALENDAR

FEB.: *Annual Irish Afternoon.* Music, bagpipes, food, beer, and singing make up this Irish festival at the Georgian Court College. | 732/364–2200, ext. 236.

JUNE: *South Jersey Canoe and Kayak Classic.* You'll find more than 100 boats, model boats, free paddling, clinics, antiques, and food at this wet-and-wild event in Ocean County Park on the first weekend of June. | 609/971–3085.

Dining

The Quiet Man. Continental. Named for the 1952 movie starring John Wayne (the owner, then a waiter, met him in Ireland when he was on location and became a fan), this pub is cozy, fun, and serves top-notch comfort food like homemade chicken potpie and fish-and-chips. There's also more contemporary dishes on the menu, such as balsamic grilled tuna steak and spinach salad. Live music (guitar and piano) adds to the scene. This spot is actually in Dover, the next town south of Lakewood on Route 623. | Rte. 46 and Hudson Ave., Dover | 973/366–6333 | $10–$19 | AE, MC, V.

Lodging

Best Western Leisure Inn. This two-story hotel is 15 minutes by car from the beach, 20 minutes from two malls, and 30 minutes from Six Flags Great Adventure Theme Park. Locals describe it as a "friendly place." Restaurant, bar. In-room data ports, cable TV. Pool. Laundry facilities. Business services. Pets allowed. | 1600 Rte. 70 | 732/367–0900 | fax 732/370–4928 | 105 rooms | $95–$135 | AE, D, DC, MC, V.

Rodeway Inn. This chain motel is halfway between Six Flags Great Adventure Theme Park (11 mi) and the shore (10 mi). Cable TV. Business services. No pets. | 450 Madison Ave. | 732/363–8530 or 800/228–2000 | fax 732/363–1647 | www.hotelchoice.com | 30 rooms | $90 | AE, MC, V.

LAMBERTVILLE

(Nearby towns also listed: Frenchtown, Stockton, Trenton)

Rightfully known as the "Jewel of Jersey's West Coast," this lovely town was at one time a key stop on the Old York Road, taking business travelers and tourists from New York to Philadelphia. It was also a bustling commercial center, thanks to the water power provided by the Delaware River. In the last decade or so the town has capitalized on its inventory of beautiful old Federal and Victorian buildings, and has turned some of the old factory buildings along the river into warrens for antiques. Antiquing, in fact, seems to be the main industry in Lambertville these days, along with eating. Some lovely B&Bs, as well, make Lambertville a viable and less-crowded alternative to New Hope, across the bridge in Pennsylvania.

Information: Lambertville Area Chamber of Commerce | 239 N. Union St., Lambertville, 08530 | 609/397–0055 | fax 609/397–1530 | www.lambertville.org.

Attractions

Marshall House. Currently the home of the Lambertville Historical Society, this house was once the home of James Wilson Marshall, the man who first discovered gold in California. | 62 Bridge St. | 609/397–0770 | www.lambertvillehistoricalsociety.org | Free | Apr.–Oct. weekends 1–4.

ON THE CALENDAR

APR.: *Shad Festival.* The annual event celebrates the return of the shad to the Delaware River, with arts and crafts, entertainment, a nighttime Shad Fest Boogie party, and, oddly, lots of shad sandwiches. Events take place at different locations throughout town. | 609/397–0055.

JUNE: *Hidden Gardens of Lambertville.* The oldest continually running women's club in New Jersey hosts its annual garden tour. | 609/397–0051.

OCT.: *Lambertville Historical Society Autumn House Tour.* Tour the town's Federal, Victorian, and contemporary homes. | 609/397–0770.

Dining

Anton's at the Swan. American. Grilled lamb, served with couscous and mango chutney, is a signature dish at Anton's, a romantic candlelit spot whose dark-wood interior, with antiques and oil paintings and a wood-burning stove, suggests turn-of-the-century Paris. You can start with a bacon, leek and Gruyère tart as an appetizer, or with an arugula salad topped with peppered pears and blue cheese. | 43 S. Main St. | 609/397–1960 | Closed Mon., no lunch | $18–$32 | AE, D, DC, MC, V.

Church Street Bistro. French. This cozy French bistro is at its best in summer when you can eat outside in their charming courtyard. The interiors have pretty wainscotting and pots and pans hang from the ceiling. The menu is small and sophisticated (as is the wine list), with classics such as their signature cassoulet. Save room for the pear poached in red wine sauce with vanilla ice cream and chocolate sauce. | 11½ Church St. | 609/397–3653 | Closed Tues. No lunch Mon. | $12–$21 | AE, MC, V.

David's Yellow Brick Toad. French. Experience Provence with entrées like *bouillabaise* (fish and shellfish stew in a white-wine-and-herb base) and rack of lamb with a thyme crust. There's lighter fare available as well, including a wasabi tuna burger with tomato and sesame relish and French dip on a garlic baguette. In warm weather you can dine outdoors in the patio overlooking the country garden. | 19 North Union St. | 609/397–2596 | No lunch weekdays. Sun. brunch. Closed Mon. | $19–$25 | No credit cards.

Lambertville Station. American. Dine in one of three Victorian-style dining areas furnished with dark wood and brass in a lovely setting on the banks of the Delaware River. Try the special alligator chile, the seafood Pescatore, and the smoked duck pasta. Live jazz on weekends. Kids' menu. Sunday brunch. | 11 Bridge St. | 609/397–8300 | Sun. brunch | $15–$22 | AE, DC, MC, V.

Lodging

Chimney Hill Bed and Breakfast. Set on 8 acres, this romantic 1820 stone manor home offers a quiet country escape. Rooms have canopied beds and fireplaces, and a spacious living room and sunroom invite guests to relax. Complimentary breakfast. Some kitchenettes, no room phones. Business services. No kids under 12. | 207 Goat Hill Rd. | 609/397–1516 | fax 609/397–9353 | www.virtualcities.com/ons/nj/t/njt9701.htm | 12 rooms | $89–$225 | AE, MC, V.

Inn at Lambertville Station. Rooms are named after famous cities (i.e. Paris, New Orleans, Venice, San Francisco) and have views of the Delaware River and plenty of antiques. Suites have fireplaces. There's a lovely deck off the lobby. Restaurant, bar, complimentary Continental breakfast. Some refrigerators, cable TV. Laundry facilities. Business services. | 11 Bridge St. | 609/397–4400 or 800/524–1091 (except NJ) | fax 609/397–9744 | 45 rooms, 8 suites | $95–$135 rooms; $135–$235 suites | AE, DC, MC, V.

York Street House. Industrialist George Massey built this elegant manor house for his wife in honor of their 25th wedding anniversary in 1909. Rooms are furnished with period antiques. In the first-floor common rooms there's a baby grand piano, an original Waterford crystal chandelier, and a fireplace. | 42 York St. | 609/397–3007 or 888/398–3199 | fax 609/397–9677 | 6 rooms | $85–$185 | AE, V.

LONG BEACH ISLAND

MAP 9, G9

(Nearby town also listed: Waretown)

In many ways Long Beach Island is the New Jerseyite's Jersey Shore. Less well known than its fellow beaches to the south and north, this 18-mi-long, mile-wide barrier island is home to about 20 communities, and offers everything from modest motels to megabucks neighborhoods and plenty in between.

The northern end of Long Beach Island is crowned by the historic Barnegat Lighthouse, affectionately known as "Old Barney." Open to visitors, this landmark is in a small gem of a state park. At the island's south end is a wildlife refuge and the bustling Beach Haven, a center for shopping, recreation, and nightlife.

In between are miles of hamlets such as Beach Haven Terrace, Surf City, North Beach, and the more posh and picturesque Harvey Cedars and Loveladies—all sharing Long Beach Boulevard, which runs down the middle of the island and is lined with movie theaters, seafood markets, restaurants, shops, miniature golf, and ice cream stands.

(Long Beach Boulevard is also known in places as Ocean Avenue, Bay Avenue, or just The Boulevard.)

In the late 1700s, the island attracted whalers, fishermen, and hunters. Later, Quaker farmers began ferrying across the bay in summer, but the history of Long Beach as a summer resort didn't begin until the 1880s, when the railroad first came to the island. In 1914 a bridge for vehicular traffic was completed and by that time, hotels and summer homes were already cropping up, particularly in Beach Haven. Today, the popular mode of transportation on the island is bicycles. A word to motorists: the speed limit everywhere is 30 mph.

Long Beach Island has more than a dozen towns that fall under the umbrella of Long Beach Township (including Loveladies, Brant Beach, and Holgate) as well as the independent towns of Barnegat Light, Harvey Cedars, Surf City, Ship Bottom, and Beach Haven. Each has its own beach rules and sets its own prices on beach tags, which are required from mid-June through Labor Day.

Barnegat Light (not to be confused with Barnegat, which sits on the mainland across Barnegat Bay), at the northern end, is the quietest and least commercial part of the island. Fisherman dock their boats here after long days at sea, and Barnegat Light State Park, at the very tip of the island, is home to "Old Barney," a lighthouse which although no longer used, remains to this day a symbol of the entire island.

Dubbed "The Queen City," **Beach Haven** lies toward the south end, and is ground zero for the island's activity. In August especially, swarms of people are drawn to the beaches, restaurants, ice-cream shops, and other amusements, such as Fantasy Island, the Thundering Surf water slide, and lots of shopping. The Surflight Theatre presents professional-quality shows, and the Long Beach Island Historical Museum features exhibits and gives walking tours of the town's Victorian architecture. Some restaurants and hotels are open year-round, and it may be more peaceful to visit in winter and hole up on the beach at the Engleside Inn.

The township of **Harvey Cedars,** the smallest on the island, was established in 1894 but was inhabited long before that by hardy shore whalers and a few tavern owners. The name is thought to be a corruption of "Harvest Cedars," referring to both the makeshift living quarters inhabited by colonial farm laborers and the cedar trees that are plentiful in the area. Today this town is mostly residential, and you can rent some homes by the week or the month.

Named when a young woman was rescued from the hull of an overturned ship stranded off shore, **Ship Bottom** is the first town you'll hit coming onto the island. As a result, the beach tends to be crowded with day-trippers, but the atmosphere is still basically low-key. Besides location, the mile-long beach is also distinguished by the presence of a snack bar—something you won't find on the other island beaches.

Surf City, the town north of Ship Bottom near the center of the island, was originally settled in the 1800s by whaling families. Today the area is family oriented and, of course, there's plenty of surfing. The area between North First and North Third streets is a designated surfing section.

The Township of Long Beach includes the villages of Beach Haven Crest, Beach Haven Gardens, Beach Haven Inlet, Beach Haven Park, Beach Haven Terrace, Brant Beach, Brighton Beach, Haven Beach, High Bar, Harbour, Holgate, Loveladies, North Beach, North Beach Haven, Peahala Park, South Beach Haven, Spray Beach, and The Dunes. The 12 mi of divided beach—spanning two-thirds of the Long Beach Island coastline and including 52 beaches in all—account for 10% of the Jersey shoreline's 122 mi of sandy beach. The southern section tends to be more commercialized, and the exclusive Loveladies is in the quieter, more secluded northern end. Often ignored because of its distance from the action, Holgate's beach near the wildlife refuge is worth checking out. Boxed in by by dunes, with most of Holgate's residential neighborhood out of view, it feels cozy and remote, and has a peaceful, family atmosphere.

Information: Long Beach Island Chamber of Commerce | 265 W 9th St., Ship Bottom, 08008 | 609/494–7211 | fax 609/494–5807 | www.discoversouthernocean.org.

Attractions

Barnegat Lighthouse State Park. One of the last remnants of maritime forest in New Jersey can be found in this 32-acre park. Dominated by black cherry, eastern red cedar, and American holly, the forest is an important resting and feeding area for migratory birds; a short self-guided trail leads you through. There are picnic and fishing areas. | Broadway and the Bay | 609/494–2016 | www.state.nj.us/dep/forestry/parks/barnlig.htm | Free, parking fee | Daily.

The second-tallest lighthouse in the U.S., **Barnegat Lighthouse** stands at the northernmost end of the island in Barnegat Lighthouse State Park. The lighthouse was deemed inadequate by mariners when it first went into commission in 1834. The tower that stands today was built in its place in 1856, four times as tall as its predecessor. The light was extinguished in 1944. Tours are available. | Broadway at the bend | 609/494–2016 | Oct.–Apr. weekends 9–3:30; May–Sept. daily 9–4:30.

Beach Haven Guided Walking Tours. Tour 25 houses and six B&Bs in Beach Haven's downtown Victorian district. | Beach and Engleside Aves. | 609/492–0700 | $5 | June–Sept., Tues. and Fri. 10:30 AM.

Fantasy Island Amusement Park. This Victorian-style family spot has rides, games, food, and an ice-cream parlor. | 320 W. 7th St., Beach Haven | 609/492–4000 | www.fantasyislandpark.com | Pay per ride | Daily noon–"when the crowd dies out."

Hartland Miniature Golf & Arcade. Bring the kids and play 18 holes. If that isn't enough, you can head over to the arcade for video games and then recharge your batteries with an ice cream or hot dog at their snack bar. | 28th St. and Blvd., Ship Bottom | 609/494–7776 | $4 | Apr.–Nov., daily 10:30 AM–11:30 PM; Nov.–Apr., weekends 10 AM–9 PM.

Harvey Cedars Marina/Wildlife Refuge. Experience an unparalleled method of approaching wildlife as you take a guided kayak tour around the salt marshes of the Edwin B. Forsythe National Wildlife Refuge. Tours are prefaced with a brief lecture and paddling lesson. | 6318 Long Beach Blvd., Harvey Cedars | 609/494–0111 | $45 for 2 hrs.

Long Beach Island Foundation for the Arts & Sciences. This popular and well-respected arts center, in Loveladies, holds summer classes for adults and children in ceramics, painting, sculpture, and printmaking. | 120 Long Beach Blvd. | 609/494–1241 | fax 609/494–0662.

Long Beach Island Historical Museum. Housed in the charming Holy Innocents' Episcopal Church, dating from 1882, this museum displays exhibits from turn-of-the-20th-century island life. Walking tours are offered through Victorian Beach Haven Tuesday and Friday mornings; educational programs are given throughout the summer for adults and children. | Engleside and Beach Aves., Beach Haven | 609/492–0700 | www.nealcomm.com/nonprof/lbimusm.html | $2 suggested donation | June 26–Sept. 8, daily 2–4 and 7–9.

ON THE CALENDAR

MAR: *Annual Long Beach Island Quilt Show.* Quilts old and new are displayed and sold. Proceeds benefit the Southern Ocean County Hospital. | 609/494–4232.

MAY–OCT.: *Surflight Theatre season.* Take in mostly musical fare at this summer stock/repertory theater. There's also a Christmas show. | 609/492–9477.

JUNE: *Day at the Bay Festival.* This two-day event in Ship Bottom has crafts, food, a bike/trike race, and musical entertainment. | 609/494–0558.

JUNE–SEPT.: *Stories-by-the-Sea.* The Alliance for a Living Ocean office offers storytelling on Monday afternoons, from 2 to 3 PM, in North Beach Haven. | 609/492–0222.

JULY: *Fireworks.* There's an annual Fourth of July display on the Bay. | 609/492–2800.

JULY, AUG.: *Eco-Tour of a Barrier Island.* Tours, offered once a week, leave from Chamber of Commerce lot in Ship Bottom. | 609/492–0222.

When it Comes to Getting Cash at an ATM,

Same Thing.

Whether you're in Yosemite or Yemen, using your Visa® card or ATM card with the PLUS symbol is the easiest and most convenient way to get cash. Even if your bank is in Minneapolis and you're in Miami, Visa/PLUS ATMs make getting cash so easy, you'll feel right at home. After all, Visa/PLUS ATMs are open 24 hours a day, 7 days a week, rain or shine. And if you need help finding one of Visa's 627,000 ATMs in 127 countries worldwide, visit **visa.com/pd/atm**. We'll make finding an ATM as easy as finding the Eiffel Tower, the Pyramids or even the Grand Canyon.

It's Everywhere You Want To Be®

Mother Nature does some of her prettiest work in New Jersey.

You see it reflected in the eyes of a child as she watches a stunning sunset say good-bye to another perfect day. You see it in the smiling faces of families who can't wait to come back to our sparkling sandy beaches...year after year. In fact, everywhere you turn it seems that Mother Nature has worked a little bit harder to make summertime in New Jersey unforgettable.

But Mother Nature isn't the only thing that's unforgettable about New Jersey. In Atlantic City, you'll be dazzled by the long list of entertainment, world-class dining, and, of course, casinos. To slow it down a bit, why

not go whale watching or soak up the historic charm of Victorian Cape May.

And we know the whole family will be thrilled by the rides and attractions of Six Flags Great Adventure & Wild Safari.

From sand castles to sunsets, lighthouses to Long Beach Island, New Jersey and you...are perfect together. For a FREE Travel Guide to plan your next vacation, call 1-800-VISIT-NJ, ext. 1425, or visit our Web site at www.visitnj.org.

New Jersey & You
Perfect Together®

TRAVEL & TOURISM
NEW JERSEY COMMERCE & ECONOMIC GROWTH COMMISSION

AUG.: *Annual Arts and Crafts Festival.* This two-day festival in Loveladies features traditional arts and crafts for sale. Refreshments are available. | 609/494–1241.

AUG.: *Annual Long Beach Island Lifeguard Tournament.* This annual event, now entering its fourth decade, gives the island's heroic and highly skilled beach patrol a chance to demonstrate their ocean skills in 16 competitive events over two days. In Loveladies. | 609/361–1000.

SEPT: *LBI Chowderfest Weekend.* Chow down at this annual seafood fest featuring music, a chowder cook-off, local restaurant competitions, and more. | 800/292–6372.

DEC.: *Christmas Parade.* Catch the Christmas spirit in Ship Bottom with floats, antique cars, fire engines, bands, and more. | 609/597–3211.

Dining

Barnegat Light Deli. Delicatessen. Located at the Barnegat Light Marina, this deli has fishing box lunches as well as daily breakfast and lunch specials. They also carry groceries, sundries, and fresh produce. Next door is a full-service bait-and-tackle shop. | 1501 Bayview Ave. | 609/494–6611 | No dinner | $5–$12 | AE, V.

Beach House Restaurant. Seafood. This informal restaurant with weathered shingles, white shutters, and a covered porch serves great seafood. Try the house favorite—a generously sized serving of fried flounder, scallops, and shrimp accompanied by one of their famous broiled jumbo lump crab cakes. Kids' menu. | 13015 Long Beach Blvd., Beach Haven Terrace | 609/492–1997 | Breakfast also available weekends; no lunch | $9–$16 | AE, MC, V.

Charles' Seafood & Angus Steakhouse. Seafood. There are five casually elegant dining rooms at this serious surf 'n' turf, the most popular being the romantic back porch overlooking a fountain. Try the Florida rock shrimp farfalle, the New Orleans catfish gumbo, or their signature 16-ounce filet mignon. | 87th St. and Boulevard St., Beach Haven Crest | 609/492–8340 | $9–$19 | AE, MC, V.

Green Gables. Continental. In an elegant 100-year-old inn, this restaurant offers a prix fixe three- or five-course meal. They also serve high tea, complete with tea sandwiches, pastries, and a pot of your favorite brew. In warm weather, the choice seats are on the front porch. | 212 Centre St. | 609/492–3553 | Thurs.–Sun. | greengableslbi@aol.com | Reservations essential | $75 for 5 courses, $45 for 3 courses | AE, D, DC, MC, V.

Panzone's Pizza. American/Casual. Located on the main thoroughfare, this family-run pizzeria is one of three Panzone's on Long Beach Island. Among the long list of reasonably priced menu items are specialty pizzas, Sicilian style pizza, steak sandwiches, chicken steaks, and other hot sandwiches and hoagies. Takeout is available. | 22nd St. and Long Beach Blvd., Beach Haven | 609/494–1114 | Breakfast also available | $4–$15 | AE, MC, V.

Wheel House. Seafood. Lobster and crab are the specialties here; you can't go wrong with lobster bisque, lobster rolls, King Crab legs, or soft-shell crabs. This is a good place to bring the family after a day at the beach. Kids' menu. Takeout is available. | 21st St. and Long Beach Blvd., Ship Bottom | 609/494–1717 | $6–$16 | AE, D, DC, MC, V.

Lodging

Amber St. Inn. Romance abounds in this antiques-filled 1885 Victorian house, less than a block from the beach. Relax in the garden or on the patio. Complimentary breakfast. No TV in rooms, TV in common room. No kids under 12. No smoking. | 118 Amber St., Beach Haven | 609/492–1611 | www.bbianj.com/amber/ | 6 rooms | $150–$200 | Closed late Oct.–Feb. | No credit cards.

Coral Seas Oceanfront Motel. Oceanfront rooms with balconies, spacious double suites, and poolside accommodations are all available at this comfortable motel on the beach. All rooms have two double beds. The motel prides itself on being a quiet, peaceful place to stay. Refrigerators, cable TV. Pool. No pets. | 21 Coral St., Beach Haven | 609/492–1141 | fax 609/492–1411 | www.lbi.net/coral/index.htm | 50 rooms | $169–$189 | AE, MC, V.

Ebb Tide Motel. You'll find this cheerfully pink, family-friendly motel about 150 ft from the beach. Beach passes and blankets are provided, and there's a fully equipped kitchen you can use. If you don't feel like cooking, restaurants are an easy walk. Cable TV. No pets. | 115 E. 7th St., Ship Bottom | 609/494–1785 or 888/514–4482 | fax 609/494–2169 | 16 rooms | $45–$159 | AE, MC, V.

Engleside Inn. Pastel-color rooms have ocean views and private balconies at this beachfront inn, close to shops and restaurants. Some rooms have whirlpools and/or a heart-shape tub. Restaurant, bar. Some kitchenettes, refrigerators, cable TV, in-room VCRs (and movies). Pool. Business services. Some pets allowed. | 30 Engleside Ave., Beach Haven | 609/492–1251 or 800/762–2214 | fax 609/492–9175 | www.engleside.com | 72 rooms | $170–$328 | AE, D, DC, MC, V.

Hurley's at Holgate Motel. This cozy two-story motel is set just 75 ft from the water. Rooms are simple and cheerfully furnished. There are outdoor barbecues and tables, bike racks, and complimentary coffee and juice in the mornings. All rooms have their own deck with outside tables and chairs. Refrigerators, cable TV. No pets. | 4804 South Long Beach Blvd., Beach Haven Inlet | 609/492–2266 | fax 609/492–9227 | 5 rooms | $75–$150 | AE, D, MC, V.

North Shore Inn. This quiet inn opened in 1998 after extensive remodeling. It's one block from the beach (beach badges are provided for guests) and a short walk to the Barnegat Lighthouse State Park and Bird Sanctuary. Guest rooms are more beach motel than "inn." Cable TV. | 806 Central Ave., Barnegat Light | 609/494–5001 | fax 609/494–7172 | information@northshoreinn.com | www.northshoreinn.com | 14 rooms, 14 efficiencies | $45–$135 | AE, MC, V.

Sand Castle. Rooms at this B&B are light and airy and elegantly furnished in an updated Victorian style. Each room has its own private entrance, and either a pool or an ocean view. There's a music room with a grand piano, an enclosed sunroom, a rooftop deck, and a barbecue area. Beach tags, towel, chairs, and bicycles are available to guests at no charge. Afternoon tea is served daily. Complimentary breakfast. Cable TV, VCR. Pool. Hot tub. Exercise equipment. No kids under 12. No smoking. | 710 Bayview Ave., Barnegat Light | 609/494–6555 | fax 609/494–8655 | www.sandcastlelbi.com | 5 rooms, 2 suites | $125–$350 | AE, MC, V.

Sea Horse Inn. This two-story motel is right on the main drag of Brant Beach, next to Hagler's Marina. The nicest view is from the apartment suite which overlooks the marina and bay. Refrigerators, cable TV. Pool. | 3rd Ave. and Long Beach Blvd., Brant Beach | 609/494–5392 | info@seahorselbi.com | www.seahorselbi.com | 25 rooms | $85–$150 | AE, MC, V.

Spray Beach Motor Inn. This family-oriented inn has poolside and ocean-view rooms, and is close to shops and food in Beach Haven. Restaurant, bar. Some kitchenettes, refrigerators, cable TV. Pool. Business services. | 24th Ave. and Oceanfront | 609/492–1501 | fax 609/492–0504 | 88 rooms | $170–$235 | Closed Jan. | AE, MC, V.

Surf City Hotel. This hotel is just a block from the beach (beach tags are available to guests) and is quite a social hub due to the attached restaurant, bar, and lounge with live entertainment and clam bar. If you're looking for a lively place to stay on the island this is it. Restaurant, bar. Some refrigerators, cable TV. No pets. | 8th St. and Long Beach Blvd. | 609/494–7281 or 800/353–3342 | fax 609/494–5271 | 25 rooms | $70–$160 | AE, MC, V.

LYNDHURST

MAP 4, D6

(Nearby towns also listed: East Rutherford, Rutherford, Secaucus)

Founded in 1917, Lyndhurst is a tiny town in the center of the Meadowlands area. There are a few historic buildings and casual restaurants, but the town is otherwise very quiet and without visitor attractions. DeKorte Park (which you can see from Route 17 on the way into Manhattan) provides the town with a bit of natural beauty.

Information: **Meadowlands Regional Chamber of Commerce** | 201 Rte. 17 N, Rutherford, 07070 | 201/939–0707 | www.lyndhurstonline.com.

Attractions

DeKorte Park. This is a truly environment-friendly park: part of it is built on the former site of the town dump, or rather landfill, where plants have been reestablished to lure back wildlife squeezed out by development. Likewise, the benches, trash cans, and wheelchair-accessible boardwalk are made of recycled plastic boards. The mile-long marsh trail presents you with a canyon of towering reeds one moment, then a placid vista of gadwalls (wild ducks) and the Jersey Turnpike and the New York City skyline the next. Visitors may walk the entire barrier-free trail system, which is open daily, weather permitting. Trail guides are available at the Environment Center reception desk, and free guided natural history walks are offered every second and fourth Sunday. | 2 DeKorte Park Plaza | 201/460–8300 | www.hmdc.state.nj.us | Free | Weekdays 9–5, weekends 10–3.

Hackensack Meadowlands Environment Center. The Trash Museum teaches kids about the effects of all those disposable goods, and the benefitsof recycling. If you visit before you hit the trail, you may be more aware of the presence of trash in the park, from beer cans to plastic bags. The center also has a small exhibit on wetlands environments, and a great overlook of the marsh. Various temporary exhibits of wildlife art and photography are hung throughout the year. | DeKorte Plaza | 201/460–8300 | www.hmdc.state.nj.us | $2 | Mon.–Sat. 9–5.

Little Red Schoolhouse. A one-room, Queen Anne–style schoolhouse, more than a century old, has been restored to its original appearance by the Lyndhurst Historical Society. It was in use until 1980. | Riverside and Fern Aves. | 609/465–9393 | Free | 2nd and 4th Sun. of month 2–4.

ON THE CALENDAR

APR., JULY, AUG., SEPT.: *J & C's Giant Flea Market, Craft & Collectible Show.* This flea market, held one Sunday each month at the Town Hall Park, has over 75 vendors selling a variety of unique merchandise. | 201/997–9535.

Dining

Medieval Times Dinner & Tournament. Continental. This medieval-theme restaurant serves a prix fixe four-course feast, which includes a jousting tournament and show performed by costumed actors. | 149 Polito Ave. | 201/933–3352 or 800/828–2945 | fax 201/438–2062 | $40; special rates for children | AE, MC, V.

Lodging

Novotel. Outlet shopping at the Meadowlands is close to this hotel, as is Giants Stadium and the Meadowlands racetrack. Or, catch a bus that stops at the corner of the hotel and take a 15-minute ride to New York City. Restaurant, bar (with entertainment). In-room data ports, refrigerators, cable TV. Pool. Hot tub, massage. Exercise equipment. Laundry facilities. Business services. Some pets allowed. | 1 Polito Ave. | 201/896–6666 or 800/668–6735 | meadmail@aol.com | 219 rooms | $109–$119 | AE, D, DC, MC, V.

Quality Inn Meadowlands. This chain hotel features spacious modern rooms and proximity to Giants Stadium and the Meadowlands racetrack. Restaurant, bar, room service. In-room data ports, cable TV. Pool. Video games. Laundry facilities. Business services, airport shuttle. | 10 Polito Ave. | 201/933–9800 or 800/468–3588 | fax 201/933–0658 | www.qual-ityinn.com | 150 rooms | $109–$129 | AE, D, DC, MC, V.

MADISON

MAP 9, F4

(Nearby towns also listed: Chatham, Morristown)

This pretty, upscale town in Morris County, just outside of Morristown, was founded in the late 1600s. Benefiting from three higher-education institutions—Drew University, Fairleigh Dickinson University, and the College of Saint Elizabeth—the town enjoys a variety of cultural programs. Drew University is home to the F.M. Kirby Shakespeare Theatre, where the resident company, the New Jersey Shakespeare Festival, offers classic productions.

Information: **Madison Chamber of Commerce** | Box 152, Madison, 07940 | 973/377–7830 | www.rosenet.org.

Attractions

Drew University. Started as a Methodist seminary in 1867, this small university (about 2,300 students) in Madison is known for its excellent liberal arts education. Former New Jersey Governor Thomas Kean is the university's 10th president. The school's 186 wooded acres include ancient hardwoods, namely the Hardin Oak, estimated to be 400 years old. The newly renovated F. M. Kirby Shakespeare Theatre is home to the New Jersey Shakespeare Festival, a highly acclaimed professional theater company in residence. | 36 Madison Ave. | 201/408–3000 or 973/408–3000 | www.drew.edu | Free | Daily.

F.M. Kirby Shakespeare Theater. Since 1972, this professional troupe has made its own at this Drew University theater. Hamlet, Othello, A Midsummer Nights Dream, and other classics are performed throughout the season at 308-seat facility. | 36 Madison Ave. | 973/408–5600 | www.njshakespeare.org | Free | June.–Dec.; (Box office) Mon. 10–6, Tue.–Sat. 10–7, Sun. noon–6.

Fairleigh Dickinson University–Florham-Madison Campus. One of three Fairleigh campuses (the others are in Hackensack-Teaneck and Wroxton, England), this 166-acre facility is dedicated to liberal arts, science, and business administration. The campus encompasses Florham, a former country estate of early 20th-century socialites Florence Vanderbilt and Hamilton Twombly, and the grounds were designed by Frederick Law Olmsted. The principal buildings, designed in Georgian style in the 1890s, have been adapted for educational use. The 100-room mansion, with its marble staircases and fireplaces, is a replica of a wing in King Henry VIII's Hampton Court and a campus centerpiece. In addition to classrooms and offices, the mansion holds the chestnut-paneled former billiard room and the Lenfell Hall drawing room. Enrollment is about 3,700. | 285 Madison Ave. | 973/443–8500 | www.fdu.edu/visitorcenter/fmwelcome.html | Free | Daily.

Florence and Robert Zuck Arboretum. The Zuck Arboretum was created in 1980 to honor Drew University faculty members Robert and Florence Zuck. Its ponds are home to turtles, goldfish, catfish, and muskrats. Migrating Canada geese, ducks, and great blue herons stop at the arboretum to rest. | 36 Madison Ave. | 973/408–3000, ext. 3358 | Free | Daily.

Museum of Early Trades and Crafts. The museum's changing exhibits provide a look at the life and work of those who settled this region. Part of the James Library Building on Main Street, it's listed on the State and Federal Register of Historic Sites. | Main St. and Green Village Rd. | 973/377–2982 | fax 973/377–7358 | www.rosenet.org/metc | $3.50 | Tues.–Sat. 10–4, Sun. noon–5.

ON THE CALENDAR

JUNE–DEC.: *New Jersey Shakespeare Festival.* The state's only professional theater company dedicated to Shakespeare also offers intensive acting/theater training programs. | 36 Madison Ave. | 973/408–3278.

Dining

3 Central Avenue. Italian. Chef-owner Michael DiIonno transformed this storefront into a charming trattoria with black-and-white interiors and live music (usually classical guitar) during the week. His innovative twists on Italian and other cuisine have been well received—try the pork loin medallions with Caribbean pineapple grille sauce. | 3 Central Ave. | 973/514–1333 | No lunch weekends | $12–$20 | AE, MC, V.

Garlic Rose. Contemporary. This casual bistro is dedicated to the mighty garlic clove. The walls of the restaurant were hand painted by local artists, and ceramic garlic cloves hang from the ceiling. Try the Garlic Rose pork chop, the San Francisco Cioppini, or the Calamari Del Mediterranean. | 41 Main St. | 973/822–1178 | No lunch Sun. | $12–$23 | AE, MC, V.

Lodging

Madison Hotel. This white, four-story, green-shuttered Victorian inn has a beautiful glass conservatory that's especially pretty when lit with candles. In Convent Station, the hotel is convenient to Interstate 287 and is just 2.8 mi northwest of downtown Madison. Room service. Cable TV. Pool. Sauna. Exercise room. | 143 Readington Rd.,Convent Station | 973/285–1800 or 800/526–0729 | fax 973/540–8566 | 191 rooms | $129–$229 | AE, D, DC, MC, V.

MAHWAH

(Nearby town also listed: Ramsey)

At nearly 27 square mi, Mahwah is the largest township in Bergen County. You'll find quiet suburban homes, along with the bustling Sheraton Crossroads Complex. Earlier this century it was home to one of the largest Ford Motor plants in the country. Today it is the national headquarters for Sony Electronics. The looming Sheraton Crossroads hotel is an obvious place for a stopover on the way to or from New York State, just down Route 17.

Information: Greater Mahwah Chamber of Commerce | Box 506, Mahwah, 07430 | 201/529–5566 | fax 201/529–8122 | info@mahwah.com | www.mahwah.com.

Attractions

Campgaw Mountain. This 1,374-acre wooded county park with hiking and horseback riding trails offers campsites, some with shelters, by permit only. In winter you can ski on three relatively uncrowded beginner to intermediate trails. | 200 Campgaw Rd. | 201/327–3500, 201/327–7800 ski information | Free | Daily.

Campgaw Mountain Ski Center. Ski day and night, and stay overnight. | 200 Campgaw Rd. | 201/327–7800 | Dec.–Mar.

Darlington County Park. You'll find three lakes among the 178 acres in this park—one for fishing—as well as wooded picnic areas, white-sand beaches, a playground, tennis and handball courts, and a wildlife observation area. | 600 Darlington Ave. | 201/646–2680 or 201/327–3500 | Free. | Apr.–Nov., daily.

Ramapo Valley Reservation. Busy with hikers, particularly in the fall, the reservation includes 15 mi of trails, plus Scarlet Oak Pond and McMillan Reservoir. Picnics and camping are permitted. | 584 Ramapo Valley Rd. | 201/327–3500 or 201/825–1388 | Free | Apr.–Nov., daily.

ON THE CALENDAR

JULY: *The A and P Tennis Classic.* This event features the biggest names in women's tennis, three major concerts, games, contests, beer and wine tasting, and hot-air balloons. | 201/825–9100.

Dining

Nobody's Inn. American. This family-owned and -operated restaurant has live music on weekends, two fireplaces, and outdoor seating on a patio. Menu staples include burgers, sandwiches, Yankee pot roast, and pork chops. | 150 Franklin Tpk. | 201/529–2357 | $10–$17. | AE, MC, V.

Lodging

Courtyard Mahwah. This hotel, convenient to many area companies, is geared toward business travel. It's also 2 mi from Darlington Golf Course and 1 mi from Campgaw Ski Area. Restaurant, bar. In-room data ports, cable TV. Pool. Hot tub. Exercise room. Laundry service, laundry facilities. Business services. No pets. | 140 Rte. 17 S | 201/529–5200 or 800/321–2211 | fax 201/529–1991 | www.marriotthotels.com | 146 rooms, 12 suites | $143–$174 | AE, MC, V.

Ramada Inn Mahwah. A free shuttle takes business travelers to nearby companies from this modern hotel. Deluxe rooms are available. Restaurant, bar, room service. In-room data ports, cable TV. Pool. Exercise equipment. Laundry facilities. Business services. | 180 Rte. 17 S | 201/529–5880 | fax 201/529–4767 | 128 rooms | $109–$119. | AE, D, DC, MC, V.

Sheraton Crossroads. A glass building with corporate offices and guest rooms make up this modern business-oriented hotel. Rooms are spacious, and some have mountain views. Others overlook the landscaped grounds, which include gardens, a fountain, and a fishpond. The Illusions nightclub plays disco favorites every night but Sunday. 2 restaurants, bar (with entertainment). Refrigerators, cable TV. Pool. Tennis. Exercise equipment. Shops. Business services. Some pets allowed. | Crossroads Corporate Center, Rte. 17 N | 201/529–1660 | fax 201/529–4709 | 228 rooms | $179–$215 | AE, D, DC, MC, V.

MATAWAN

MAP 9, G5

(Nearby town also listed: Freehold)

The borough of Matawan, at the head of the Matawan Creek, has a rich history as a shipping center. Today, Matawan is a suburban commuter community; Matawan's train station—one of the busiest in the state—is the northernmost stop within Monmouth County on New Jersey Transit's North Jersey Coast Line.

Information: Matawan Borough | 150 Main St., Box 424, Matawan, 07747 | 732/290–2001 | fax 732/290–7585 | www.matawan.com. **Downtown Matawan Alliance** | Box 432, Matawan, 07747 | 732/566–9570.

Attractions

Cheesequake State Park. Covering a transitional zone between two different ecosystems, the park offers a sampling of much of the state's ecology, concentrated in a relatively small 1,284 acres. Several marked trails lead you through open fields, saltwater and freshwater marshes, a white cedar swamp, Pine Barrens, and a northeastern hardwood forest. You'll also find an excellent interpretive center, bike trails, picnic areas, and facilities for camping. | 300 Borden Rd. | 732/566–2161 | Free; $10 per night to camp; parking $5 weekdays, $7 weekends and Memorial Day–Labor Day | Daily.

Keyport Antique District. Stroll through these streets near the bay, about 1 mi northeast of Matawan, and browse at the numerous unique antiques shops and boutiques. | West and East Front, Main and Broad Sts., Exit 117 of Garden State Pkwy. Keyport | Free.

ON THE CALENDAR

JUNE–NOV.: *Matawan Flea Market.* Check out the goods on the first Tuesday of every month, but get there early. The market opens at 6:30 AM and hard-core flea market hunters are out before dawn! | 732/566–5657 or 732/583–7363.

Dining

Buttonwood Manor. Continental. Try the "Tableside for Two," which includes chateaubriand and rack of lamb, at this popular lakeside special-occasion spot. Aside from the picture-perfect setting, it's known for steak, veal, and fresh seafood. Live music Friday and Saturday. Kids' menu. | 845 Rte. 34 | 732/566–6220 | $14–$27 | AE, DC, MC, V.

Peter's Fishery. Seafood. You'll eat off plastic plates and it's BYOB, but locals swear by the food at Peter's. Takeout is also available. | 930 Rte. 34 (Rte. 79) | 732/583–5666 | $6–$11 | AE, D, DC, MC, V.

Lodging

The Hazlet. Located just east of Matawan across the Garden State Parkway, this hotel is 3 mi from the beach, 2 mi from Keansburg Amusement Park, and 1 mi from the Keyport Antique District. Restaurant, bar (with entertainment). Cable TV. Pool. Business services. | 2870 Rte. 35, Hazlet | 732/264–2400 | fax 732/739–9735 | 120 rooms | $92 | AE, D, DC, MC, V.

Wellesley Inn. There are movie theaters, a water park, several amusement parks, and shopping near this well-situated three-story chain hotel, just east of Matawan. Complimentary Continental breakfast. Refrigerators, cable TV. Business services. Some pets allowed (fee). | 3215 Rte. 35, Hazlet | 732/888–2800 | fax 732/888–2902 | 89 rooms | $159 | AE, D, DC, MC, V.

MAYS LANDING

MAP 9, E10

(Nearby towns also listed: Batsto, Somers Point)

Mays Landing, in the southern reaches of the Pinelands, offers access to the Great Egg Harbor National Scenic and Recreational River. It is the county seat of Atlantic County, and is home to both the 1,900-acre Lake Lenape Park and Estell Manor, a 1,742-acre park featuring historic buildings, trails, and a nature center. You'll also find a community college, winery, and a 150-store mall here.

Information: **Greater Mainland Chamber of Commerce** | 6712 Washington Ave., Suite 201, Egg Harbor Township, 08234 | 609/646–2214.

Attractions

Estell Manor Park. This popular 1,700-acre park has a fitness trail and facilities for camping, boating, volleyball, softball, orienteering, and hiking. In addition to its interpretive natural exhibits, the Warren E. Fox Nature Center in the park offers historic tours and lectures, workshops, summer nature programs, and school group tours. It even has its own library stocked with literature related to local history and ecology. Also within the park are two historic sites, the Estellville Glassworks and the Bethlehem Loading Company munitions factory. Bikes and other equipment are available to borrow, for free, at the nature center. | 109 Rte. 50 | 609/645–5960 or 609/625–1897. | www.aclink.org/parks/estell.htm | Free | Daily.

Lake Lenape Park. This park and recreation center was opened on Memorial Day, 1907 by the Leiling Family. You'll find a fishing pier, boats, canoes, a carousel, nature trails, and even a small lighthouse. | 109 Rte. 50 | 609/645–5960 or 609/625–1897 | Free | Daily dawn–dusk.

Dining

Inn at Sugar Hill. Contemporary. Set on a knoll of the same name on the northeastern banks of the Great Egg Harbor, this restaurant and inn was once the private mansion of William Moore, an entrepreneur and state senator, who built it in 1846. Although it has received praise for its sophisticated cooking, it remains somewhat of a secret. Try the island marinated grilled chicken or the Sugar Hill crab cakes. | 5704 Mays Landing Rd. | 609/625–2226 | fax 609/625–3838 | No lunch weekends or Mon. | $13–$23 | AE, MC, V.

Lodging

Abbott House. This elegant Victorian mansion with gingerbread moldings was built by prominent lawyer Joseph Abbott and his wife Adeline. Relax on the bluff overlooking the Great Egg Harbor River, swim in the pool, or enjoy complimentary afternoon tea in the belvedere, with views of Mays Landing. Rooms with hand-painted walls and bay windows are furnished with antiques, wicker, and quilts. Complimentary breakfast. Pool. No smoking. | 6056 Main St. | 609/625–4400 | www.bbianj.com/abbott | 3 rooms, 1 suite | $85–$95 | AE, D.

MEDFORD

MAP 9, E8

(Nearby towns also listed: Batsto, Cherry Hill, Mount Laurel)

Nestled in the Pine Barrens, Medford is a hub of business and culture for the Southern Burlington County region. The well-preserved Medford Village area has an historic Main Street, with shops and restaurants. The Medford Historic Society and the Historic Medford Village Business Association are both vigilant in maintaining the history of the town.

Information: **Burlington Chamber of Commerce** | 900 Briggs St., Suite 110, Mt. Laurel, 08054 | 856/439–2520 | www.bccoc.com.

Attractions

Woodford Cedar Run Wildlife Refuge. The Elizabeth Woodford Pine Barrens Education Center and Children's Museum has hands-on exhibits for kids, along with small animals to see and touch. Visitors are encouraged to walk the 1-mi trail around Cedar Run Lake to see the animals in the rehabilitation compound. | 6 Sawmill Rd. | 856/983–0326 | www.cedar-run.org | Free | Wed.–Fri. 1–4, weekends 10–4.

ON THE CALENDAR

MAY: *Medford Jazz Festival.* Jazz music by regional artists fills Historic Medford Village for an entire weekend. | 609/654–2512.
MAY: *Memorial Day Parade.* Enjoy an old-fashioned parade down Main Street with high-school marching bands, scout troops, and more. | 609/654–2512.
JUNE: *Air Victory Museum Open House and Spring Dance.* Take a free tour of the museum and check out the historic airplanes and other exhibits. | 609/267–4488.
JUNE: *Festival of Art and Music.* This festival, held on Main St., features four stages of entertainment and more than 70 regional artists and crafters. | 609/654–0488.
JUNE: *Quilt Show and Sale.* Local quilters display their wares on Church Road at Kirby's Mill. | 609/654–2512.
DEC.: *Medford Eve.* Midnight fireworks top off this night of family entertainment in Historic Medford Village. | 609/654–2512.
DEC.: *Medford's Village Dickens Festival.* Main Street takes on the spirit of *A Christmas Carol,* and Santa presides over a Dickens character costume contest. On the first weekend of the month. | 609/654–2512.

Dining

Beau Rivage. French. Surrounded by woods overlooking Lake Pine, Beau Rivage is a classic French country restaurant. Dine on the charming and rustic first floor, or upstairs in the elegant Louis XVI room. Signature dishes include fillet of Dover sole and lobster bisque flambé with crabmeat, complemented by an extensive wine list. | 128 Taunton Blvd. | 856/983–1999 | fax 856/988–1136 | Jacket and tie | Closed Mon. No lunch weekends | $16–$26 | AE, MC, V.

Braddock's Tavern. Continental. Choose formal dining or the more casual pub in this historic building with its carefully preserved colonial atmosphere. Braddock's is known for prime rib and sautéed veal. Kids' menu. Sunday brunch. The restaurant is 15 minutes from Mount Laurel. | 39 S. Main St. | 609/654–1604 | fax 609/654–8180 | $20–$36 | AE, D, DC, MC, V.

Lodging
Main Stay Bed & Breakfast. Centrally located on Main Street in downtown Medford, this charming Victorian inn has hardwood floors, stained-glass windows, and chestnut staircases. Complimentary Continental breakfast. No pets. No smoking. | 45 S. Main St. | 609/654–7528 | 8 rooms | $55–$95 | AE, MC, V.

METUCHEN

(Nearby towns also listed: Edison, Plainfield, Woodbridge)

Named after an Indian chief called Matouchin who lived between 1630 and 1700, the town is believed to have been founded and developed during those years as well. Today, this Middlesex County town is basically a residential commuter community, about 25 mi (and a 45-minute train ride) from New York City.

Information: **Metuchen Area Chamber of Commerce** | 323 Main St., Metuchen, 08840 | 732/548–2964 | fax 732/548–4094 | mmc@metuchenchamber.org | www.metuchenchamber.org.

Attractions
St. Francis of Assisi Cathedral. This lovely cathedral, named for the patron saint of animals, hosts concert series of choral and orchestra music. | 32 Elm Ave. | 732/548–0100 | Free | Daily.

ON THE CALENDAR
JUNE: *Metuchen Street Festival.* Craftspeople, artisans, and vendors of all types offer artwork, clothing, jewelry, and plenty to eat. There are also activities for the kids. | 732/548–2964.
SEPT.: *Town-wide garage sale.* As many as 400 households participate in this enormous garage sale. The Chamber of Commerce provides a map to all locations, or you can just wander through the town. | 732/548–2964.
OCT.: *Country Fair.* You'll find hundreds of booths, kiddie rides, and other activities at this annual fair, held on Main Street. | 732/548–2964.

Dining
Metuchen Inn. Contemporary. White linen and tiny table lamps are set against blue and green walls in this charming Victorian Inn. Try the barbecued Peking duck breast with snow-pea salad or the seared diver scallops with vanilla corn cake. There is live music Tuesday, Friday, and Saturday, and in winter the fireplaces make for a cozy, intimate meal. | 424 Middlesex Ave. | 732/494–6444 | No lunch Sat., Sun. | $18–$25 | AE, MC, V.

MILFORD

(Nearby towns also listed: Clinton, Frenchtown)

The Lenni Lenape Indians peacefully sold this land to European traders in the early 1700s. Residents of the town made their living trapping animals for their pelts in the richly forested area until the discovery of iron. Milford remained an iron working town until after WWII, when people began to discover the springs, lakes, and other recreational opportunities around town. Today, the town is a sportsman paradise with plenty of lakes, hiking trails, and camping facilities.

Information: **The Milford Guild** | CARE/OF PO BOX L, Milford, 08848 | 908/995–4854.

Attractions

The Baker. A trip to Milford isn't complete without a visit to The Baker, the best known bakery in the area. People travel from all over just to pick catch a whiff of the pastries for sale here. The bagels are so-so, but it's worth the trip to sample one of the dozens of flavors of unique, organic breads. | 60 Bridge Street | 908/995–4040 | fax 908/995–9669 | askus @the-baker.com | www.the-baker.com | Year-round.

Toys and Fun. This high-end toy store prides itself on selling only "family-centered" toys — no electronic or video games. For the "big" kids, you can also pick up kayaks and inflatable boats—perfect for using in the nearby Delaware River, which is less than a $1/4$ mi away. | 71 Bridge Street | 908/995–9770 | fax 908/996–3745 | Year-round.

The Volendam Wind Mill and Museum. Located about $3^{1}/_{2}$ mi northwest of Milford, this amazing windmill is about as close to Holland as you can get in New Jersey. An exact replica of a Danish wind-driven grain mill, it is over 60 ft high, and has 86 ft long sail arms. Visitors can usually tour the interior of the mill, but at press time it was closed for renovations. | 231 Adamic Hill Road., Holland Township. | 908/995–4365 | $2.50.

ON THE CALENDAR

OCT.: *Halloween Parade.* This annual parade and awards ceremony is a longtime town tradition. The kids dress up in costume and trick-or-treat afterwards. There's free cider and doughnuts. | 908/995–4854.

DEC.: *Christmas in Milford.* The start of the Holiday season is marked by Santa's arrival in Milford, along with food, holiday music, and special ice sculptures created for the occasion. | 908/995–4854.

Dining

Cookies Milford Cafe. American. Cookies is one of the area's best kept secrets. The food has a French flair, but the portions are American-style large and practically no one goes home without a "doggie-bag". Entrée's like salmon and meatloaf are popular, and the prices can't be beat. Breakfast is served on Sunday. | 56 Bridge Street | 908/995–2000 | $8–$14 | AE, MC, V.

Milford Oyster House. Seafood. Located in an 1829 Colonial home, the Oyster house is famous not only for its food, but also for the fresh selection of fish and produce sold at the adjoining marketplace. Friday is crabcake day, but come early. They often sell out before dinner. | 17 Bridge Street | 908/995–9411 | fax 908/995–2245 | publican@shipinn.com | www.milfordoysterhouse.com | $19–$24 | No credit cards.

The Ship Inn Restaurant & Brewery. British. Described as the "best of merry old England" this popular eatery is best-known as New Jersey's first brew pub, and it was a speak-easy during Prohibition. The fare is English, Scottish, and Irish, as in fish-and-chips and bangers and mash. There's live music every Friday and Saturday night, and a great selection of home-brewed beer. | 61 Bridge Street | 908/995–0188 | $7–$19 | AE, MC, V.

Lodging

Chestnut Hill on The Delaware. Rooms at this warm and fuzzy inn have names such as "The Rose Garden Room," the "Peaches and Cream Room" and "The Teddy Bear Room" (which is filled with 140 stuffed bears). Guests stay in one of two Victorian homes. The main house has an old-fashioned formal drawing room with a piano and a pump organ. The view of the Delaware is majestic from all over the property, and there's plenty of skiing and hiking nearby. Complimentary breakfast. In-room data ports, kitchenettes, refrigerators, microwaves, hot tubs, cable TV, VCRs. Massage. Tennis, hiking. Bicycles. Library. Laundry service. Business services. | 63 Church Street, Milford, | 908/995–9761 | fax 908/995–0608 | chhillinn@aol.com | www.chestnuthillnj.com | 8 total, 6 main house, 2 cottages | $100–$$200 | No credit cards. Personal checks only.

MILLBURN

(Nearby towns also listed: Chatham, Newark, Short Hills, Summit, Union)

Founded in the 1720s, this township is comprised of two areas: the town center and adjoining residential sections is Millburn proper, while the residential area to the north and west is known as Short Hills *(see below)*. Millburn is home of the well-regarded Paper Mill Playhouse theater.

Information: **Millburn-Short Hills Chamber of Commerce** | 343 Millburn Ave., Suite 303, Millburn, 07041 | 973/379–1198 | fax 973/376–5678 | mshcc@millburn.com | www.millburn.com/chamber. **Township of Millburn** | 375 Millburn Ave., Millburn, 07041 | 973/564–7073 | fax 973/564–7468 | www.twp.millburn.nj.us.

Attractions

Paper Mill Playhouse. One of the most acclaimed nonprofit professional theaters in the country, this state theater was a forerunner of the regional theater movement in America. Everyone from the Gish sisters to E. G. Marshall has played here, and some of the theater's musicals, dramas, and comedies have been featured on PBS's *Great Performances.* The F. M. Kirby Carriage House Restaurant, run by the owners of New York's Palio, is affiliated with the theater. | Brookside Dr. | 973/379–3636 or 973/376–4343 | www.papermill.org | Wed.–Sun.

ON THE CALENDAR
SEPT.: *Art Fair.* This annual outdoor show and sale of fine art and crafts takes place downtown. | 973/379–1198.
DEC.: *"The Nutcracker."* If you're in town this time of year, don't miss this annual performance by the New Jersey Ballet, with the Paper Mill Orchestra, at the Paper Mill Playhouse. | 973/376–4343.

Dining
Café Main. American. This attractive café is convenient for an evening at the Paper Mill Playhouse. Try one of the wine-tasting dinners. Entertainment Thursday–Saturday. | 40 Main St. | 973/376–4444 | $19–$33 | AE, D, DC, MC, V.

Ling Ling. Chinese. Tasty and healthy food is the goal here. The chef uses only cholesterol-free canola oil and the freshest seasonal ingredients. There is an open kitchen and the dining area is white and cheerful. Try the salt-and-pepper shrimp. Takeout is also available. | 59 Main St. | 973/912–8838 | fax 973/912–9136 | $11–$21 | AE, D, MC, V.

Lodging
Holiday Inn Springfield. This four-story hotel is 4 mi from Millburn, 4 mi from Kean College and 5 mi from the Paper Mill Playhouse, an Equity Company with elaborately staged plays and musicals. Restaurant, bar. In-room data ports, cable TV. Pool. Exercise room. Laundry service. Business services. Pets (cats and dogs) allowed. | 304 Rte. 22 W, Springfield | 973/376–9400 or 800/465–4329 | fax 973/376–9534 | www.basshotels.com/holiday-inn | 195 rooms | $110–$112 | AE, MC, V.

MILLVILLE

MAP 9, D10

(Nearby towns also listed: Bridgeton, Mays Landing)

The town gets its nickname, the "Holly City," from the trees cultivated at the former Holly Farm in East Millville. There are other parks, lakes, streams, and wildlife areas here, as well as the surprising, compact Millville Army Airfield Museum, which gives a glimpse of the area's World War II history.

Information: **Millville Chamber of Commerce** | 415 N. High St., Millville, 08332 | 856/825–2600 | fax 856/825–5333. | chamber@xes.com | www.millvillechamber.com.

Attractions

Army Airfield Museum. Set in the original base headquarters' building from when the airstrip was army operated, exhibits here display WW II aviation artifacts of local and national interest. Programs and tours focus on educating you about Millville's role in domestic defense. | Building 1, Millville Municipal Airport | 609/327–2347 | $1 donation suggested | Weekdays 10–2, weekends 10–4.

Museum of American Glass. This museum contains the largest collection (6,500 objects) of American glass in the country, with pieces ranging from early functional items and decorative objects to contemporary sculpture. | 1501 Glasstown Rd. | 609/825–6800 or 800/998–4552 | fax 609/825–2410 | www.wheatonvillage.org | $7 adults ($6 off-season) | Jan.–Mar., Wed.–Sun. 10–5; Apr.–Dec., daily 10–5.

ON THE CALENDAR

MAY: *Wheels and Wings Freedom Weekend.* The Army Air Field Museum hosts this antique auto show and historic aircraft fly-in. | 856/327–2347.
JUNE: *Bottle Show.* Bottle dealers converge from all over the Mid-Atlantic to display and sell their treasures at Wheaton Village. | 800/998–4552.
JULY: *Cumberland County Agricultural Fair.* Enjoy games, agricultural exhibits, food, rides, and family entertainment at the Cumberland County Fairgrounds. | 856/453–2125.
AUG.: *Annual Car Show.* Antique and unusual cars parade down High Street in downtown Millville. | 856/825–2600.
NOV.–JAN.: *The Holidays at Wheaton Village.* Special exhibits, hands-on activities, and holiday entertainment spice up the season. | 800/998–4552.

Dining

Best Food in Town. Chinese. This family-run restaurant serves plenty of sesame noodles and chicken fried rice. The menu is extensive and the service is fast. Takeout is popular. | 1712 E. Main St. | 856/327–8885 | $6–$15 | No credit cards.

Lodging

Country Inn by Carlson. Local touches, such as handblown glass made in nearby Wheaton Village, distinguish this homey country-style inn. Many of the rooms overlook a lake. Restaurant, bar, complimentary Continental breakfast. Some refrigerators, cable TV. Pool. Business services. No pets. | 1125 Village Dr. | 856/825–3100 or 800/456–4000 | fax 856/825–1317 | 96 rooms, 4 suites | $85, $135 suites | AE, D, DC, MC, V.

MONTCLAIR

(Nearby towns also listed: Caldwell, West Orange)

Montclair and Upper Montclair have attracted upscale types to its beautiful tree-lined streets and big homes. Founded in 1666, present-day Montclair seems to have more than its share of writers and artists, and downtown Montclair has some unique boutiques, (good shopping for clothes you won't find anywhere else), secondhand stores, and restaurants. It even has two movie theaters, including one that plays art films—a rarity in these parts. Also adding to the spirited demographics is Montclair State University.

Information: **Montclair Chamber of Commerce** | 26 Park St., Suite 2025, Montclair, 07042 | 973/744–7660 | fax 973/744–2578 | office@montclairchamber.org | www.montclairchamber.org OR www.montclair.org.

Attractions

Israel Crane House. The Montclair Historical Society owns and operates this Federal-style 1796 mansion, home to seven generations of one family. The restored house is furnished with beautiful examples from the Decorative Arts movement, and its grounds include a country store, a craft building, and a kitchen garden. The Clark House, a restored Victorian housing the Historical Society offices and the Terhune Library, shares the site. | 110 Orange Rd. | 973/744–1796 | $3 | Sept.–June, Sun. 2–5 or by appointment.

Montclair Art Museum. Seven galleries, housed in a neoclassic Greek revival building, hold more than 15,000 works of high-quality American and Native American art in a variety of media. The American collection covers the 18th to the 21st centuries; the Native American collection consists of both traditional and contemporary ethnographic and fine art objects. The museum, opened in 1913, has the works and personal papers of Morgan Russell, an originator of Synchromism, the first American modernist art movement. The property also includes the Van Vleck Arboretum, a collection of native and rare trees. | 3 S. Mountain Ave. | 973/746–5555 | fax 973/746–0920 or 973/746–9118 | www.montclair-art.com | $5 | Tues., Wed., Fri., Sat. 11–5; Thurs., Sun. 1–5.

Summerfun Theater, Inc./Weiss Art Center. Recent Broadway shows are performed once a week here at the only professional summer-stock theater in the state. | Lloyd Rd. and Bloomfield Ave. | 973/256–0576.

ON THE CALENDAR

APR., MAY: *Montclair Roadside Attractions/ Annual One-Act Festival of New Jersey Playwrights.* Winning plays are presented in three series at the 12 Miles West Theatre Company. | 973/746–7181.

MAY: *Herb/Plant Sale.* This annual four-day event, sponsored by the Montclair Historical Society, is held on the lawns of the 1796 Israel Crain House. Merchandise from the Country Store is also available. | 973/744–1796.

MAY: *May Pole.* Young revelers braid streamers around a maypole to commemorate May Day at this annual spring event. Events take place at different venues throughout town. | 973/744–1796.

MAY, JUNE: *Presby Memorial Iris Gardens Bloom Season.* This world-famous floral display, held in Upper Montclair, boasts, among its delights, more than 4,000 varieties of iris. | 973/783–5974 | community.nj.com/cc/presbyiris.

JUNE: *Montclair Theatre Cafe.* The 12 Miles West Theatre Company presents this series of offbeat short plays and scenes in an intimate café setting. | 973/746–7181.

JUNE: *Montclair African American Heritage Parade and Festival.* This annual celebration of African American culture features music, food, and dance. Vendors sell clothing and jewelry, arts and crafts, and food and drink. | 973/509–0350.

JULY: *Fourth of July Parade and Fireworks.* Celebrate Independence Day Montclair-style with a parade and fireworks. | 973/509–4915.

SEPT.: *Montclair Blues and Jazz Festival.* Big and not-so-big names in music lend their talents to this annual event, which begins in the auditorium of the local high school, then proceeds through the town's many music clubs. | 973/509–4910.

OCT.: *Annual Craft As Art Festival.* Enjoy juried crafts displays along with exotic and natural foods at the Montclair Art Museum. | 973/746–5555.

OCT.: *Apple Harvest Festival.* Eat lots of apple-related snacks, and tour the Historic Israel Crane House. | 973/744–1796.

OCT.: *Booktoberfest.* This literary festival, with book sales, storytelling, music, games, and rides, benefits the Montclair Public Library. | 973/744–0500.

DEC.: *First Night Montclair.* Montclair's New Year's Eve Celebration of the Arts features more than 100 performers of music, dance, comedy, and magic. There are clowns and all-day arts workshops for the kids, where they can make their own musical instruments for the festive parade which caps the event. | 973/744–3427 | www.firstnight-montclair.org.

Dining

Blue Sky American Bistro & Café. Contemporary. This restaurant is chic, comfortable, and fun. The loftlike space, with exposed brick, sky-blue halogen lighting, and silver stars on the floor, is as modern and sophisticated as the food. Try the endive, pear, and arugula salad and the pan-roasted duck, or go for the grilled ostrich medallions and mashed potatoes with Guinness-stout sauce. Desserts are made fresh daily. | 400 Bloomfield Ave. | 973/746–2553 | fax 973/746–7430 | No lunch Mon., Sat., no dinner Sun. | $16–$28 | AE, MC, V.

Palazzo. Mediterranean. A variety of original soups and salads start off your meal at as you dine at one of the small tables encircling the piano in the center of the dining room. Highlights of the dinner menu are veal medallions, risotto, and the Pollo alla Giardiniera. | 11 S. Fullerton Ave. | 973/746–6778 | Closed Mon. No lunch weekends | $14–$18 | AE, DC, D, MC, V.

Taro Restaurant. Pan-Asian. Huge bamboo shoots and other trappings of the Far East welcome you to the dining room of this two-story establishment. The eclectic dinner selections range from sliced beef with noodles to Chilean sea bass and Peking duck. | 32 Church St. | 973/509–2266 | fax 973/509–0154 | No lunch Sun. | $7–$24 | AE, MC, V.

Lodging

Marlboro Inn. This Tudor mansion, built in 1840 and run as a hotel since 1890, combines European charm with a touch of old Hollywood glamour. Bette Davis, Joan Crawford, Helen Hayes, and even the Crown Prince of Lichtenstein have stayed here. Some refrigerators, in-room data ports, cable TV. | 334 Grove St. | 973/783–5300 or 800/446–6020 | fax 973/783–8709 | www.marlboroinn.com | 29 rooms | $105–$190 | AE, DC, MC, V.

MONTVALE

MAP 4, D4

(Nearby towns also listed: Paramus, Ridgewood)

Located at Exit 172 off the Garden State Parkway, Montvale, founded in 1894, is the first town you'll hit driving south on the parkway from New York State. Stop off at the extensive Tourist Information Center, right on the parkway, for brochures and information about all of New Jersey. Montvale itself is a large business center.

Information: **Borough of Montvale** | One Memorial Dr., Montvale, 07645 | 201/391–5700 | fax 201/391–9317 | www.montvale.nj.us.

Dining

Marcy's Ristorante. Italian. House specialties at this cozy, family-oriented restaurant, less than 2 mi from downtown Montvale, include fried calamari, three-cheese pizza, and eggplant rollatini. There's an excellent wine list. Kids' menu. | 117 Kinderkamack Rd., Park Ridge | 201/391–2424 | $10–$14 | AE, D, DC, MC, V.

Valentino's. American. This top-notch restaurant offers excellent service in a dark, comfortable atmosphere. The menu includes veal, chicken, pasta, and fresh seafood. Less than 2 mi from Montvale. | 103 Spring Valley Rd., Park Ridge | 201/391–2230. | Jacket required | Closed Sun. No lunch Sat. | $14–$27 | AE, DC, MC, V.

Lodging

Holiday Inn. Business travelers often stay at this hotel for the 40-minute commute to New York City. Rooms are basic and modern. Restaurant, bar (with entertainment), room service. In-room data ports, cable TV. Pool. Exercise equipment. Business services. | 100 Chestnut Ridge Rd. | 201/391–7700 | fax 201/391–6648 | 190 rooms | $94–$145 | AE, D, DC, MC, V.

Marriott–Park Ridge. Renovated in 2000, this four-story Marriott less than 2 mi from Montvale has an atrium lobby and modern rooms. Its extensive grounds include a small lake. Restaurant. In-room data ports, cable TV. Pool. Hot tub. Exercise equipment. Business services. Some pets allowed. | 300 Brae Blvd., Park Ridge | 201/307–0800 | fax 201/307–0859 | www.marriott.com | 289 rooms | $99–$209 | AE, D, DC, MC, V.

Woodcliffe Lake Hilton. Set on 21 acres with rolling hills and fruit orchards, this sprawling hotel has lots of luxuries, including major sports facilities and a state-of-the-art amphitheater that seats 250. The hotel is 1 mi from Montvale. Restaurant, bar, room service. In-room data ports, cable TV. Pool. Putting green, tennis court. Basketball, racquetball. Playground. Laundry services. Business services. | 200 Tice Blvd., Woodcliffe Lake, | 201/391–3600 or 800/445–8667 | fax 201/391–4286 | www.hilton.com | 336 rooms | $206 | AE, D, DC, MC, V.

MORRISTOWN

MAP 9, F4

(Nearby towns also listed: Basking Ridge, Bernardsville, Chatham, Chester, Madison, Parsippany)

Morristown is the seat of Morris County, and is loaded with restaurants, shops, clubs, theaters, and antiques, not to mention an historic Village Green. The town played a prominent role in the Revolutionary War, and, during the Gilded Age, it housed more millionaires than any other city in the United States. Morristown's National Historic District includes a strolling garden and Macculloch Hall, a museum known for its collection of Thomas Nast's political cartoons. Across the street sits Nast's own home, Villa Fontana, where he created the modern image of Santa Claus.

Information: **Morris County Chamber of Commerce** | 10 Park Ave., Morristown, 07960 | 973/539–3882 | fax 973/539–3960 | www.morrischamber.org.

Attractions

Acorn Hall. This 1853 home is now occupied by the Morris County Historical Society. Along with beautiful mid-Victorian furnishings, the galleries offer exhibits on state and local history. Lovely gardens also recall the era. | 68 Morris Ave. | 973/267–3465 | $5; special rates for children, students, and senior citizens | Mar.–Dec., Mon., Thurs. 10–4, Sun. 1–4.

Fosterfields Living Historical Farm. Turn-of-the-20th-century farming techniques are demonstrated at this 200-acre farm, and the Willows mansion is open for tours. | 73 Kahdena Rd. | 973/326–7645 | www.morrisig.com/vgreen/foster.htm | $4 | Apr.–Oct., Wed.–Sat. 10–5, Sun. noon–5.

Historic Speedwell. This site is part of the estate of Stephen Vail, whose father, Alfred, worked with Samuel B. Morse to develop the telegraph in his factory here, and gave the first demonstration of it in 1838. Exhibits explain the history of the Speedwell Iron Works, the development of the telegraph, early farm equipment, and the SS *Savannah*, a steam-driven paddle wheeler that, despite the doubts of the general public, managed to cross and recross the Atlantic. | 333 Speedwell Ave. | 973/540-0211 | www.speedwell.org/ | $5; special rates for children | May–Oct., Thurs. noon–5, Sun. noon–5.

Macculloch Hall Historical Museum. This beautiful columned mansion in the Morristown Historic District is both a Macculloch and Miller family museum, and a home for the W. Parsons Todd Collection of 18th- and 19th-century American and English fine and decorative arts. It's perhaps best known, however, for the Thomas Nast Collection of some 2,000 19th-century political cartoons. The artist, who lived on Macculloch Avenue for 30 years, created the donkey and elephant icons of the Democratic and Republican parties, as well as the jolly depiction of the modern-day Santa Claus. The museum also has an historic garden. | 45 Macculloch Ave. | 973/538-2404 | fax 973/538-9428 | www.machall.org/ | $3 | Wed., Thurs., Sun. 1–4.

Morris Museum. One of the state's best, this museum features interesting, varied temporary exhibits in the Geraldine R. Dodge Gallery, as well as a good science-based permanent collection that includes rocks and minerals, dinosaur bones and fossils, and some small live animals. | 6 Normandy Heights Rd. | 973/538-0454 | www.morrismuseum.org | $5; special rates for children, students, and senior citizens. Free Thurs. 1–8 | Tues., Wed., Fri., Sat., 10–5; Thurs. 10–8; Sun. 1–5.

USEFUL EXTRAS YOU MAY WANT TO PACK

- ❏ Adapters, converter
- ❏ Alarm clock
- ❏ Batteries
- ❏ Binoculars
- ❏ Blankets, pillows, sleeping bags
- ❏ Books and magazines
- ❏ Bottled water, soda
- ❏ Calculator
- ❏ Camera, lenses, film
- ❏ Can/bottle opener
- ❏ Cassette tapes, CDs, and players
- ❏ Cell phone
- ❏ Change purse with $10 in quarters, dimes, and nickels for tollbooths and parking meters
- ❏ Citronella candle
- ❏ Compass
- ❏ Earplugs
- ❏ Flashlight
- ❏ Folding chairs

- ❏ Guidebooks
- ❏ Luggage tags and locks
- ❏ Maps
- ❏ Matches
- ❏ Money belt
- ❏ Pens, pencils
- ❏ Plastic trash bags
- ❏ Portable TV
- ❏ Radio
- ❏ Self-seal plastic bags
- ❏ Snack foods
- ❏ Spare set of keys, not carried by driver
- ❏ Travel iron
- ❏ Travel journal
- ❏ Video recorder, blank tapes
- ❏ Water bottle
- ❏ Water-purification tablets

Morristown National Historical Park. General George Washington and his Continental Army camped here through the winter of 1779–80, and there are many historical buildings and sites throughout the park. | Morristown National Historical Park/Washington Place | 973/539–2085 | www.nps.gov/morr/index.htm | $4, free for children under 17 | Daily.

Built between 1772 and 1774 for businessman Jacob Ford Jr., the Georgian-style **Ford Mansion** was used by General Washington as his military headquarters in the winter of 1779–80. | Tours daily 10–4, on the hr.

In May 1777, soldiers dug trenches and raised embankments at **Fort Nonsense** to fortify the crest, which was a strategic overlook for the area. The site later became known as Fort Nonsense because some claimed it had only been built to keep the troops occupied. | Daily dawn–dusk.

At the **Historical Museum,** a 25-minute film of 18th-century soldier life teaches you that if the ammunition didn't kill you, the diseases probably would have. A self-guided tour of the museum focuses on the history and artifacts of the area. | Daily 9–5.

Jockey Hollow is the site of the encampment of the 13,000 Continental Army soldiers in the winter of 1779–80, the worst winter in 100 years. When the soldiers first arrived at Jockey Hollow, they had to sleep out in the snow until supplies arrived for them to build huts. Replicas of these huts, open to visitors, stand in the fields of Jockey Hollow today. | Daily dawn–dusk.

The **Wick House** was on the Wick Farm, which belonged to one of the most prosperous families in the area during the late 1700s. The home is roomy and well constructed, and reminiscent of the family's New England origins. The home later became winter headquarters for General Arthur St. Clair. Its 1,400 acres, and adjacent acreage on other farms, were the campgrounds for Washington's soldiers. | Daily 10–4:30.

Presbyterian Church of Morristown. The original church here was built in 1738. The present building, the third one on the site, dates from 1893–94. The burial ground dates to 1731 and holds town founders and soldiers from the American Revolution. | 57 Park Pl | 973/538–1776 | fax 973/538–7879 | www.pcmorristown.org | Free | Open by appointment. Office, weekdays 9–5.

Schuyler-Hamilton House. Famous for housing President Washington's surgeon, this historical landmark home and museum was built in 1760. | 5 Olyphant Pl. | 973/267–4039 | www.morrisig.com/vgreen/schuyler.htm | $5 | Tues., Sun. 2–5 and by appointment.

"Soldier at Rest." This looming Civil War monument that anchors the Morristown Green was erected in 1871. | Morristown Green, in the center of town | Free | Daily.

ON THE CALENDAR

APR.: *New Jersey Daffodil Society's Annual Show.* This popular judged daffodil show, held at the Haggerty Educational Center, includes educational exhibits. | 973/326–7600.

MAY: *Spring on the Farm–1899.* Butter making, feed grinding, children's games, and baby animals abound at the Fosterfields Living Historical Farm. | 973/326–7645.

JUNE: *Garden State Iris Society Late Blooming Iris Show.* Learn about the culture and care of Irises, and enjoy the beautiful displays. | 973/326–7600.

SEPT.: *Annual Frelinghuysen Arboretum Harvest Show and Plant Sale.* This event includes a judged flower show, a plant sale, and family entertainment. | 973/326–7600.

OCT.: *Annual New Jersey State Chrysanthemum Show and Sale.* Learn everything you ever wanted to know about chrysanthemums at this show held usually at the Haggerty Education Center. | 973/326–7600.

OCT.: *Corn Husking By Hand.* For two weekends, visitors can help pick and harvest the corn crop at the Fosterfields Living Historical Farm. | 973/326–7645.

OCT.: *Gesneriad Society Annual Show and Plant Sale.* Plants in the African violet family and gloxinia family are for sale at this popular show held usually at the Haggerty Education Center. | 973/326–7600.

DEC.: *First Night Morris County.* A town-wide New Year's eve celebration features dozens of musical acts, clowns and magicians, children's activities, and art exhibits. |

973/538–2555.

DEC.: *Gingerbread Wonderworld.* Gingerbread creations by artists of all ages are on display at the Haggerty Education Center. | 973/326–7600.

DEC.: *Holly Walk Tour.* Historic homes and museums are decorated for holiday tours. | 973/539–2085.

Dining

El Salvaoreno. Mexican/Spanish. An ornate mural of an ancient Aztec village encompasses the entire wall on the right side of this eatery. Pupusas, the national snack of El Salvador, Tex-Mex choices, paella, pollo con arroz, and seafood are on the varied menu. | 104 Speedwell Ave. | 973/889–1777 | Closed Mon. | $7–$13 | AE, D, MC, V.

Grand Café. French. The former chef of Manhattan's *Maxim's* presides over this formal, elegant, clubby French restaurant, known for rack of lamb, veal, and quail. | 42 Washington St. | 973/540–9444 | Jacket required | Closed Sun. No lunch Sat. | $24–$32 | AE, D, DC, MC, V.

Nagano. Japanese. Wooden chairs seat you at matching tables or the sushi bar at this elegant yet simple little restaurant. Sushi, maki, and sashimi can be ordered a la carte or in a combination style. Beef and chicken hibachi dishes are also served. | 23 Washington St. | 973/540–9120 | fax 973/540–9187 | No breakfast. No lunch Sun. | $10–$22 | AE, D, MC, V.

Rod's Steak and Seafood Grill. Continental. Call ahead for private dining in renovated railway cars at this prime beef and seafood house. Note the interesting brass chandelier in the bar. Entertainment Wednesday–Saturday. Kids' menu. Sunday brunch. | 1 Convent Rd., Convent Station | 973/539–6666 | Breakfast also available weekdays; no lunch Sat. | $20–$33 | AE, DC, MC, V.

Lodging

Best Western Morristown Inn. The Morristown Museum, with a variety of fine arts exhibits, is within walking distance of this three-story brick Best Western. Restaurant. In-room data ports, some kitchenettes, cable TV. Exercise equipment. Laundry facilities. Airport shuttle. | 270 South St. | 973/540–1700 | fax 973/267–0241 | www.bestwestern.com/best.html | 60 rooms | $98–$135 | AE, D, DC, MC, V.

Headquarters Plaza. Renovated in 1999, this 16-story corporate-style hotel is in historic Morristown, and close to the Meadowlands. Restaurant, bar. In-room data ports, cable TV. Pool. Gym. Children's programs (ages 5–12). Business services, airport shuttle. | 3 Headquarters Plaza | 973/898–9100 or 800/225–1942 (except NJ), 800/225–1941 (in NJ) | fax 973/292–0112 | www.travelweb.com/thisco/lri | 256 rooms | $199–$249 | AE, DC, MC, V.

Westin Morristown. This luxurious Georgian-style hotel underwent a $5 million renovation in 1998, and now the comfortable spacious rooms even have ergonomic chairs and desks. There is dancing in the lounge, and the hotel is 2 mi from the Papermill Playhouse. 2 restaurants, 2 bars (with entertainment), room service. In-room data ports, cable TV. Pool. Basketball, health club, volleyball. Laundry facilities, laundry service. Business services. No pets. | 2 Whippany Rd. | 973/539–7300 or 888/625–5144 | fax 973/984–1036 | www.westin.com | 200 rooms | $199 | AE, D, DC, MC, V.

MOUNT HOLLY

MAP 9, E7

(Nearby town also listed: Burlington)

Established by Quakers, this historic and beautiful town has a one-room schoolhouse, 18th-century homes, and a prison dating from 1810. It is the county seat of Burlington County, and has one of the oldest continuously occupied court houses in the country.

KODAK'S TIPS FOR TAKING GREAT PICTURES

Get Closer
- Fill the frame tightly for maximum impact
- Move closer physically or use a long lens
- Continually check the viewfinder for wasted space

Choosing a Format
- Add variety by mixing horizontal and vertical shots
- Choose the format that gives the subject greatest drama

The Rule of Thirds
- Mentally divide the frame into vertical and horizontal thirds
- Place important subjects at thirds' intersections
- Use thirds' divisions to place the horizon

Lines
- Take time to notice lines
- Let lines lead the eye to a main subject
- Use the shape of lines to establish mood

Taking Pictures Through Frames
- Use foreground frames to draw attention to a subject
- Look for frames that complement the subject
- Expose for the subject, and let the frame go dark

Patterns
- Find patterns in repeated shapes, colors, and lines
- Try close-ups or overviews
- Isolate patterns for maximum impact (use a telephoto lens)

Textures that Touch the Eyes
- Exploit the tangible qualities of subjects
- Use oblique lighting to heighten surface textures
- Compare a variety of textures within a shot

Dramatic Angles
- Try dramatic angles to make ordinary subjects exciting
- Use high angles to help organize chaos and uncover patterns, and low angles to exaggerate height

Silhouettes
- Silhouette bold shapes against bright backgrounds
- Meter and expose for the background illumination
- Don't let conflicting shapes converge

Abstract Composition
- Don't restrict yourself to realistic renderings
- Look for ideas in reflections, shapes, and colors
- Keep designs simple

Establishing Size
- Include objects of known size
- Use people for scale, where possible
- Experiment with false or misleading scale

Color
- Accentuate mood through color
- Highlight subjects or create designs through color contrasts
- Study the effects of weather and lighting

From *Kodak Guide to Shooting Great Travel Pictures* © 2000 by Fodor's Travel Publications

Information: Delaware River Tourism Council | c/o N.J. State Aquarium at Camden, 1 Riverside Dr., Camden, 08103 | 856/365–3300 ext. 230. **Burlington Chamber of Commerce** | 900 Briggs St., Suite 110, Mt. Laurel, 08054 | 856/439–2520 | www.bccoc.com.

Attractions

Burlington County Historic Prison. Built in 1810, this prison was designed by Robert Mills, the architect of the Washington Monument. It was the first fireproof building, and until it closed in 1965, it was the oldest prison in continuous operation. | 609/265–5858 | free for now, but they may start charging admission | May–Sept., 4th weekend of every month, 10–4; tours can also be scheduled upon request.

ON THE CALENDAR

MAY: *Mount Holly Spring Fest and Heritage Day Festival.* Enjoy a juried arts and crafts show, guided tours, music, and a parade in downtown Mount Holly. | 609/267–0170.

MAY: *Hot Rod Car and Cruise Night.* More than 1,000 American classic cars and hot rods line the streets of Historic Mount Holly. | 609/267–0170.

JULY: *Christmas in July.* Mill Race Village is decked out for Christmas offering special sales and promotions. | 609/267–8600, ext. 20.

SEPT.: *Autumn Festival.* Downtown Mount Holly. | 609/267–0170.

SEPT.: *Dog Day Afternoon.* Mill Race Village celebrates man's best friend with shelter exhibits, adoption information, obedience trials, seeing-eye dog demonstrations, and dog accessories. | 609/267–9505.

OCT.: *Today's Pleasures Tomorrow's Treasures.* Head to Peachfield Plantation, about 5 mi northwest of Mount Holly, for a needlework exhibit. | 609/893–5636.

Dining

Robin's Nest. French. This restaurant, which also does catering, is a four-time winner of the Chatsworth Cranberry Festival's dessert category. The charming space is filled with hundreds of whimsical objects collected by owner JoAnn Winzinger, many of which are antiques. Try the Sonoma butterfly shrimp or the rosemary chicken. | 609/261–6149 | No dinner Mon., Tues. | $12–$22 | AE, V.

Lodging

Best Western Burlington Inn. Located off the New Jersey Turnpike, this motel is between Mt. Holly and Burlington. It is 20 minutes by car from Six Flags Great Adventure Theme Park. There are meeting facilities and a comfortable lobby with a fireplace where coffee and donuts are served in the mornings. Restaurant. Cable TV. Exercise room. Some pets allowed. | 2020 Rte. 541 | 609/261–3800 or 800/780–7234 | fax 609/267–958 | www.best-western.com | 61 rooms | $97–$111 | AE, D, DC, MC, V.

MOUNT LAUREL

MAP 9, E7

(Nearby towns also listed: Camden, Cherry Hill, Medford)

Mount Laurel is really a suburb of the Philadelphia suburb of Cherry Hill, and, like Cherry Hill, it's convenient to Philly and to Camden. You'll find some of the largest hotels in the area here, and Mount Laurel is also home to the National Ballet of New Jersey.

Information: Delaware River Tourism Council | c/o N.J. State Aquarium at Camden, 1 Riverside Dr., Camden, 08103 | 856/365–3300, ext. 230.

Attractions

Peachfield Plantation. The lands of historic Peachfield Plantation were laid out and named by Deputy Governor John Skene in 1686, and were sold by his widow Helena to pioneer Henry Burr in 1695. Burr and his sons built the stone house on the site between 1725 and 1732. Today it is maintained as one of the principal historic sites in the County of Burlington. You'll find it about 6 mi northeast of Mount Laurel. | 180 Burrs Rd., Westhampton | 609/267–6996 | Varies according to group size | May–June and Sept.–Oct.; by appointment only.

Rancocas State Park. Known as birding heaven, this park has hiking trails for exploring 1,200 acres of Pine Barrens ecosystem. The Rancocas Nature Center, at the eastern end of the park, has educational exhibits and a well-stocked bookstore and gift shop for binoculars, maps, and other trail needs. | 794 Rancocas Rd. | 609/261–2495 | Free; parking $5 weekdays, $7 weekends and Memorial Day–Labor Day | Daily.

ON THE CALENDAR

NOV.: *The Nutcracker.* Four performances of this classic Christmas ballet, danced by members of the New Jersey State Ballet and students from its school, are held at the Mount Laurel Middle School. | 5113 Church St. | 609/235–5342.

Dining

Charley's Other Brother. Continental. A rather bland outside belies the warm interior, with its Tiffany-style lamps and fresh seafood and steak. The front Grill Bar has an exhibition-style kitchen and a more casual atmosphere. There are extensive beer, wine, and cigar selections. Kids' menu. | 1383 Monmouth Rd. | 609/261–1555 | fax 609/261–7577 | www.charleysotherbrother.com | No lunch Sun. | $20–$45 | AE, D, DC, MC, V.

The Pacific Grille. Contemporary. Influences from Art Deco to Asian can be felt in the food and the feel of this eclectic restaurant in a suburban shopping center. Friendly service and popular dishes like the jambalaya and the Pacific Island fresh fruit fritters have earned it a loyal following. | 1200 S. Church St. | 856/778–0909 | Closed Mon. | $14–$18 | AE, MC, V.

Lodging

Days Inn. Forty minutes from Six Flags Great Adventure theme park and Atlantic City, this hotel, less than 7 mi south of Cherry Hill, is also convenient to Fort Dix and McGuire Air Force Base. Restaurant, bar. In-room data ports, refrigerators, cable TV. Pool. Laundry facilities. Business services. | 550 Fellowship Rd. | 856/235–7400 | fax 856/778–9729 | www.daysinn.com | 148 rooms | $75 | AE, D, DC, MC, V.

Howard Johnson. This HoJos is right off the turnpike, near several fast-food restaurants. Restaurant, bar. Cable TV. Pool. Sauna. Playground. Business services. Pets allowed. | Rte. 541 | 609/267–6550 | fax 609/267–2575 | 90 rooms | $75–$85 | AE, D, DC, MC, V.

Isaac Hilliard House. This small 18th-century Victorian house has period furnishings and a lovely side garden. There are only four rooms: the Rose Room, the Cranberry Room, the Raspberry Room, and the Isaac Hilliard Suite. The latter is the most deluxe, with a canopied four-poster bed, a remote-control gas fireplace, a VCR and tapes, and a sweetheart bathtub. The inn is 8 mi outside of Mount Laurel. Complimentary breakfast. Cable TV. Pool. No smoking. | 31 Hanover St., Pemberton | 609/894–0756. | 4 rooms (3 with shower only) | $75–$155 | AE, MC, V.

McIntosh Inn. Part of a privately owned chain of hotels, the McIntosh has country decor and is 15 minutes from the Pennsylvania border, about 6 mi northeast of Cherry Hill. Cable TV. Business services. | 1132 Rte. 73 S | 856/234–7194 or 800/444–2775 | fax 856/231–8516 | 93 rooms | $56–$69 | AE, DC, MC, V.

Radisson Mount Laurel. This 10-story luxury hotel, in the heart of downtown Mount Laurel, was renovated in 1998. Philadelphia is 10 minutes away, the Moorestown Mall is 1 mi away, and the Cherry Hill Mall is 4 mi away. Take advantage of a free shuttle that will take you anywhere within a 5-mi radius of the hotel. Restaurant, bar. In-room data ports, cable TV. Pool. 2 tennis courts. Basketball, health club. Laundry service. Business services. No pets. | 915 Rte. 73 | 856/234–7300 or 800/333–3333 | fax 856/802–3911 | www.radisson.com | 283 rooms | $99–$169 | AE, D, DC, MC, V.

Ramada Plaza. This five-story chain hotel is centrally located between Atlantic City and Philadelphia, and convenient to area attractions. It's 15 mi from the New Jersey State Aquarium. It's about 6 mi northeast of Cherry Hill. Restaurant, bar, complimentary Continental breakfast. Cable TV. Pool. Exercise equipment. Business services. | 555 Fellowship Rd. | 856/273–1900 | fax 856/273–8562 | www.ramada.com | 100 rooms | $74–$99 | AE, D, DC, MC, V.

MOUNTAINSIDE

MAP 4, B7

(Nearby towns also listed: Plainfield, Union)

This quiet Union County town gets its name because it's on the side of the Watchung Mountains, and affords overviews of Manhattan, 24 mi away. Once mostly farmland, a great deal of the town is still preserved as parkland and Watchung Reservation land. Although the town straddles busy Route 22, strict zoning has kept its stretch of the highway free of fast-food chains and car dealerships.

Information: **Mountainside Borough** | 1385 Rte. 22, Mountainside, 07092 | 908/232–2400 | fax 908/232–6831 | www.mountainsidenj.com.

Attractions

Watchung Reservation. This 2,000-acre woodlands in Union County has riding stables, a nature center, and a ghost town. | 452 New Providence Rd. | 908/527–4900 | www.union-countynj.org | Free | Daily.

The **Trailside Nature and Science Center** includes a museum and exhibits on the environment, as well as a planetarium. For kids, there's the Discovery and Fluorescent Mineral Rooms, and a summer camp. You can explore more than 13 mi of marked hiking trails. | 452 New Providence Rd. | 908/789–3670 | Free | Daily 1–5.

ON THE CALENDAR

APR.: *Wildlife Sunday.* The Trailside Nature and Science Center presents live animal exhibits, discussions, and children's activities. | 908/789–3670.

SEPT.: *Harvest Festival.* On the last Sunday of the month, the Trailside Nature and Science Center hosts exhibits, entertainment, and demonstrations of colonial life in America. | 908/789–3670.

NOV.: *The Great Pumpkin Sail.* Bring your own jack-o-lantern to be set sail on a lake the evening after Halloween. | 908/527–4900.

DEC.: *Holiday Tree Lighting Ceremony and Charity Drive.* Santa Claus makes an appearance at this annual event, which also features a Sheriff's K-9 Unit demonstration, children's fingerprinting, and more. Participants bring food and/or toys to donate to charity. | 908/527–4900.

Dining

Spanish Tavern. Spanish. Diners familiar with the original Spanish Tavern in Newark will recognize the burgundy-and-pink table settings, the lively crowds, and menu items such as the hearty homemade soups, Spanish escargot, and paella Valencia—a rice and seafood dish with shrimp, chicken, fish and sausage. | 1239 Rte. 22 E | 908/232–2171 | $15–$20 | AE, D, DC, MC, V.

NEWARK

(Nearby towns also listed: Elizabeth, Jersey City, Lyndhurst, Millburn, Union, West Orange)

The nation's third-oldest city (and New Jersey's largest) was founded by Puritans and incorporated as a township in 1666. Despite a decline in industry in recent decades, which has helped to make it one of the poorest cities in America, Newark remains a major industrial center. Downtown you'll find the University of Medicine and Dentistry of New Jersey, a Rutgers University campus, Seton Hall Law School, New Jersey Institute of Technology, and several major hospitals. The New Jersey Performing Arts Center, built in 1997, has helped revitalize the downtown area, spurring the opening of cafés and restaurants. Bringing a further boost to downtown is Riverfront Stadium, the 6,000-seat home of the Minor League Newark Bears, which opened in April 1999. Other landmarks include the Newark Museum, Newark Symphony Hall, Sacred Heart Cathedral, Newark Public Library, and nearly 800 acres of parkland. The Ironbound District is a famous Portuguese enclave whose restaurants draw visitors from around the area.

Information: Newark Regional Business Partnership | One Newark Center, 22nd floor, Newark, 07102 | 973/522–0099 | fax 973/824–6587. **City of Newark** | 920 Broad St., Newark, 07102 | 973/733–6400 | fax 973/733–5352 | www.ci.newark.nj.us or www.gonewark.com.

Attractions

Branch Brook Park. At 486 acres, this is the largest park in Essex County. With more than 2,200 ornamental cherry trees of four different species, it holds claim to the largest cherry blossom display in the world come April. In addition to the usual complement of fishing, tennis, hiking, baseball, and soccer fields, the multiculturally aware park also has bocce alleys, a cricket crease, and a Gaelic football field. | 973/482–7649 | Free | Daily.

Minor Basilica of the Sacred Heart. Organ recitals and tours are offered at this French Gothic cathedral, famous for its stained glass. | 89 Ridge St. | 973/484–4600 | Free | Daily.

New Jersey Historical Society. This museum has interactive exhibits, a research library, and children's activities. | 52 Park Pl. | 973/596–8500 | Free | Tues.–Sat. 10–5.

New Jersey Performing Arts Center. The $180-million performing arts complex, opened in 1997, includes two theaters, two restaurants, parking facilities, and an open plaza area. The largest arts center built in the Northeast in the last 30 years, NJPAC is home to the New Jersey Symphony Orchestra, and draws top entertainment from around the world. | 1 Center St. | 973/648–8989 or 888/466–5722 | fax 973/642–5229 | www.njpac.org | Performances year-round.

Newark Museum. The 80 galleries that make up the state's largest museum complex display 18th- to 21st-century American painting, sculpture, and decorative arts; Native American, African, Pacific, and Asian Art; a world-renowned Tibetan collection; antiquities from Greece, Rome, and Egypt; and numismatics. The Dreyfuss Planetarium is on the first floor, and the grounds' garden contains a 1784 schoolhouse, the Newark Fire Museum with antique fire trucks, and contemporary American sculptures. The Museum's renovation was designed by architect Michael Graves. Secure parking is available for a fee. | 49 Washington St. | 973/596–6550 | www.newarkmuseum.org | Free | Wed.–Sun. noon–5 (until 8:30 Thurs.).

ON THE CALENDAR

MAR.: *Annual Newark Teen Arts Festival.* Public-school students exhibit their work at the Newark Museum. | 973/596–6550.

APR.: *Essex County Cherry Blossom Festival.* This showcase of Japanese cherry tree blossoms in Branch Brook Park is the largest of its kind in the United States. There's also a 10K run. | 973/268–3500.

JUNE: *Pathmark Multicultural Arts Festival.* One of the largest multicultural arts festivals in the country, this event lasts for 16 days and travels through three states. Events are scattered throughout the city. | 914/762–8878.

NOV.–JAN.: *Christmas in the Ballantine House.* Celebrate the holidays at this restored Victorian house, part of the Newark Museum. | 973/596–6550.

Dining

Don Pepe. Portuguese. The equation at Don Pepe's is simple: one family-style dinner equals several days' worth of leftovers. You won't believe the size of the lobsters. | 844 McCarter Hwy. (Raymond Blvd.) | 973/623–4662 | $25–$37 | AE, D, DC, MC, V.

Fornos of Spain. Spanish. This elegant restaurant has three dining areas: the garden room with cool green hand-painted murals; the white-walled dining room with polished wood trim and chandeliers; and the more casual bar room. Classic Spanish and Portuguese seafood dishes, along with veal, chicken, and pork, make up the menu. Takeout is available. | 47 Ferry St. | 973/589–4767 | fax 973/589–1482 | $10–$16 | AE, MC, V.

Maize. Contemporary. Maize opened in 2000 and has caught the attention of foodies with its sophisticated southern-influenced fare. Try cornmeal-coated catfish with tomato-and-black-bean salsa or ginger-citrus-flavored duck. The dining room, done in gold and white, is quite elegant, as is the wine list. Save room for a slice of Kentucky Bourbon pecan pie. | 50 Park Pl. | In the Robert Treat Hotel | 973/639–1200 | No lunch Sun. | $15–$25 | AE, D, DC, MC, V.

Rothschild's. American. The appearance is a bit dated—vinyl lounge chairs and brass chandeliers—but the food is up-to-date and the prices are good. Burgers, grilled chicken sandwiches, and gourmet pizzas are menu staples. | 160 Frontage St. | In the Holiday Inn North | 973/344–4700 | fax 973/466–9311 | $6–$10 | AE, D, DC, MC, V.

Seabra's Marisqueira. Portuguese. This family-friendly restaurant in the Ironbound section of Newark serves up lots of classic Portuguese seafood dishes in a cheerful blue-and-white dining room that conjures up images of the ocean. Try the *mariscada* (lobster, clams, mussels, shrimp, and scallops served in a tomato-cognac sauce) or the traditional paella *a marinheira*. | 87 Madison St. | 973/465–1250 | fax 973/491–6330 | No lunch | $12–$17 | AE, D, DC, MC, V.

Spain Restaurant. Spanish. You'll feel like you're in Spain at this cheerful restaurant with exposed beams and muraled walls. Classic Spanish seafood entrées like camarones rellenos (shrimp stuffed with scallops and crabmeat) and veal dishes make up the menu. Leave your car at the hotel and indulge in a pitcher of homemade sangria. Takeout is available. | 419 Market St. | 973/344–0994 | fax 973/344–2669 | $10–$16 | AE, MC, V.

Lodging

Courtyard by Marriott. Newark Airport is only 1 mi away from this three-story hotel geared toward business travel. Suites have refrigerators. Restaurant, bar, room service. In-room data ports, microwaves, cable TV. Pool. Hot tub. Exercise equipment. Laundry facilities. Business services, airport shuttle. | 600 U.S. 1/9 | 973/643–8500 | fax 973/648–0662 | 146 rooms | $165–$205 | AE, D, DC, MC, V.

Days Inn–Newark Airport. This standard, modest, eight-story chain hotel features suites with well-lit work areas and other corporate services. Restaurant, bar. Cable TV. Exercise equipment. Laundry facilities. Business services, airport shuttle. | 450 U.S. 1 S | 973/242–0900 | fax 973/242–8480 | www.daysinn.com | 191 rooms | $104–$175 | AE, D, DC, MC, V.

Hilton Gateway. This modern hotel is connected to the PATH train, which takes visitors to Manhattan in a matter of minutes. Suites have a wet bar and provide bathrobes, and there's a nice outdoor pool. Restaurant, bar, room service. Cable TV. Pool. Exercise equipment. Shops. Business services, airport shuttle. | Gateway Center, Raymond Blvd. | 973/622–5000 | fax 973/824–2188 | www.hilton.com | 253 rooms | $169–$249 | AE, D, DC, MC, V.

Holiday Inn International Airport–North. All the rooms of this extremely busy hotel were renovated in 1999. Restaurant, bar (with entertainment), room service. In-room data ports, cable TV. Exercise equipment. Business services, airport shuttle. | 160 Frontage Rd. | 973/589–1000 | fax 973/589–2799 | www.holiday-inn.com | 234 rooms | $199–$249 | AE, D, DC, MC, V.

Howard Johnson. This three-story hotel is affordable and convenient, with useful amenities. It was renovated in 1999. Restaurant. In-room data ports, cable TV. Laundry facilities. Business services, airport shuttle. | 50 Port St. | 973/344–1500 | fax 973/344–3311 | 170 rooms | $79–$99 | AE, D, DC, MC, V.

Marriott–Airport. Roll out of bed and catch your flight from this 10-story Marriott which was renovated in 2000. The huge lobby has two restaurants. Restaurant, bar, room service. Cable TV. 2 pools. Hot tub. Exercise equipment. Business services, airport shuttle. | Newark International Airport | 973/623–0006 | fax 973/623–7618 | 590 rooms | $89–$229 | AE, D, DC, MC, V.

Ramada Inn Newark International Airport. This hotel is directly across from Newark International Airport. It has a nicely landscaped courtyard and outdoor patio. Restaurant, room service. Cable TV. Pool. Exercise room. Laundry service. Airport shuttle. | 550 Rte. 1 | 973/824–4000 or 888/298–2054 | fax 973/824–2034 | www.ramada.com | 347 rooms | $109–$119 | AE, D, DC, MC.

Robert Treat Hotel. Across the street from the New Jersey Performing Arts Center and the New Jersey Historical Society, this hotel is home to the upscale restaurant Maize (*see above*). Spacious and staidly elegant rooms are furnished with antique reproductions. Restaurant, bar. In-room data ports, cable TV. Exercise room. Laundry service. | 50 Park Pl. | 973/622–1000 | fax 973/622–6410 | www.roberttreathotel.com | 170 rooms, 3 suites | $125 | AE, D, DC, MC, V.

Sheraton–Newark Airport. This modern hotel is 20 minutes from New York City and five minutes from downtown Newark. The atrium lobby has several bars and restaurants, and there is a fitness center nearby which you can use. 2 restaurants, 2 bars (with entertainment). In-room data ports, cable TV. Pool. Hot tub. Exercise equipment. Video games. Business services, airport shuttle. | 128 Frontage Rd. | 973/690–5500 | fax 973/465–7195 | www.sheraton.com | 502 rooms | $99–$189 | AE, D, DC, MC, V.

Four Points Sheraton Barcelo Newark. This hotel is 1 mi from Newark Airport and offers guests a free ride there every 20 minutes. The Statue of Liberty and Liberty Science Center are both about 5 mi away and the Meadowlands Sports Complex is 9 mi. Restaurant, bar, room service. In-room data ports, cable TV. Pool. Health club. Laundry service. Airport shuttle. | 901 Spring St. | 908/527–1600 or 800/325–3535 | fax 908/527–1327 | www.sheraton.com | 260 rooms | $139 | AE, D, DC, MC, V.

NEW BRUNSWICK

MAP 9, F5

(Nearby towns also listed: Edison, Somerset, Somerville, Woodbridge)

Founded in 1681, the centrally located seat of Middlesex County is both a manufacturing center, thanks to the Raritan River and the rail lines, and a thriving cultural center. Its State Theatre, once a vaudeville and silent-movie palace, is a busy center for the performing arts. New Brunswick is also home to Rutgers, the State University of New Jersey, and Johnson and Johnson, whose office building was designed by architect I. M. Pei.

Information: **Middlesex County Cultural and Heritage Commission** | 703 Jersey Ave., North Brunswick, 08901 | 732/745–4489 | www.newbrunswick.com.

Attractions

Buccleuch Mansion. This mansion, in the 78-acre Buccleuch Park, houses a collection of 18th-century antiques. | Easton Ave.; Across from St. Peter's Hospital | 732/745–5094 | Free | June–Oct., Sun. 2–4.

Crossroads Theatre. Take in a performance by one of the country's premier African-American theater companies. | 7 Livingston Ave. | 732/249–5560 | fax 732/249–1861 | www.crossroadstheatre.com | Sept.–May, Wed.–Sun.

George Street Playhouse. The George Street Playhouse is dedicated to developing new plays and musicals, often those headed for Broadway. | 9 Livingston Ave. | 732/246–7717 or 732/846–2895 | www.georgestplayhouse.org | Sept.–May.

Hungarian Heritage Center. This center for Hungarian Americans features folk art and exhibits by Hungarian artists. | 300 Somerset St. | 732/846–5777 | $5 donations suggested | Tues.–Sat. 11–4, Sun. 1–4.

Rutgers–The State University of New Jersey. Founded in 1766 as Queens College, the country's eighth-oldest institution of higher learning was renamed in 1825 to honor Colonel Henry Rutgers, a Revolutionary War hero. Today Rutgers is a leading public university with a diverse student body of almost 50,000, offering over 100 undergraduate majors and graduate programs. The New Brunswick campus is the largest of Rutgers' three regional campuses. | 65 Davidson Rd. | 732/932–7881 or 732/932–1766 | www.rutgers.edu | Free | Daily.
The **Geology Museum's** collection emphasizes the natural history and geology of New Jersey, and includes fossils from dinosaurs and fish to flowers. It also has Egyptian and Native American artifacts, with the latter primarily belonging to the indigenous Lenni Lenape. | 85 Somerset St. | 732/932–7243 | Free | Mon. 1–4, Tues.–Fri. 9–noon.
The **Jane Voorhees Zimmerli Art Museum,** on the campus of Rutgers University, has a wide and adventurous collection, including Nonconformist Art from the Soviet Union, French graphic art, stained glass, and the collection of the National Association of Women Artists. | 65 Davidson Rd. | 732/932–7237 | www-rci.rutgers.edu/~zamuseum/visitorinfo/visinfo.html | $3 | Sept.–July, Tues.–Fri. 10–4:30, weekends noon–5; closed Memorial Day, July 4, Labor Day, Thanksgiving, Dec. 24–Jan. 2.
Seasonal events and educational workshops are presented at the **Rutgers University Display Gardens,** a 50-acre garden and arboretum. | Ryder's La. (U.S. 1) | 732/932–8451 | Free | Daily dawn–dusk.

State Theatre. This restored vaudeville theater from the 1920s has concerts, musicals, dance performances, children's shows, and more. | 15 Livingston Ave. | 732/246–7469 | www.statetheatrenj.org | Tues.–Sun.

ON THE CALENDAR

JAN.–JUNE: *The Meadows Foundation Candlelight Concert Series.* Enjoy music in historic colonial settings. | 732/828–1812 or 732/249–6770.
MAR.: *Annual Genesis Festival.* New plays by commissioned writers are read on stage at the State Theatre, and there are post-performance discussions with the playwrights. | 732/249–5560.
APR.: *New Jersey Film Festival.* International, independent, documentary, and experimental films and videos are premiered at Rutgers University and the historic State Theater. | 732/932–8482.
APR.: *New Jersey Folk Festival.* Enjoy a day of crafts, children's games, musical entertainment, and food at the oldest folk festival in New Jersey. The festival is held at Douglass College. | 732/932–9174.

MAY: *Annual Spring Fest.* This festival brings crafters, vendors, children's activities, demonstrations, and entertainment to the Middlesex County Fair Grounds. | 732/238–6669.

MAY: *Spring Flower Fair.* Get ready for summer with this flower show and sale at Rutgers Gardens. | 732/932–8451.

JUNE: *Hungarian Festival.* This long-standing festival, held on the first Saturday of the month, has food, exhibits, music, folk dancing, fencing demonstrations, and games. | 732/846–5777 or 732/249–4756.

JUNE: *New Brunswick Food and Music Festival.* Taste food from more than 30 area restaurants, listen to live music, and participate in other activities for the whole family. | 732/545–4849.

JUNE–JULY: *New Jersey International Film Festival.* Held at Rutgers University and the historic State Theater, this festival premieres independent and foreign films. | 732/932–8482.

JULY: *Independence Day.* New Brunswick celebrates July 4th with a 45-minute pyrotechnic display by Garden State Fireworks in Boyd Park, and a performance of John Philip Sousa by the New Brunswick Symphony Orchestra. | 732/745–5125.

JULY: *Raritan River Festival.* Free activities over the July 4th weekend include music, fireworks, children's rides, family games, canoe rides, a cardboard canoe contest, and more. | 732/745–5125.

JULY: *Rutgers Gardens Open House.* Tour the gardens of Rutgers University at this annual open house, which also features lectures and children's activities. | 65 Davidson Rd. | 732/932–8451.

AUG.: *Hispanic Riverfront Festival.* The Puerto Rican Action Board sponsors this weekend event along the Raritan River in Boyd Park. | 732/828–4510.

SEPT.: *New Jersey Book Fair.* Featuring more than 75 booksellers and libraries, this fair also has author appearances, book signings, lectures, live music, an international food court, and children's activities. | 732/545–0026.

Dining

Frog and the Peach. Contemporary. This eclectic eatery serves up "world-influenced" food in a downtown historic building, built in 1876. Dishes include pan-seared tuna, organic chicken with fettuccine, sautéed sea scallops on sesame noodles, and sushi arrangements served with pickled vegetables and wasabi oil. Dine outside on a plant-filled patio. | 29 Dennis St. | 732/846–3216 | www.frogandpeach.com | Reservations essential | No lunch Sat., Sun. | $20–$36 | AE, D, DC, MC, V.

La Fontana. Italian. They'll make you whatever you want to eat here, as long as it's Italian. The menu includes lots of ornate seafood, pasta, and other favorite dishes. Try the hickory-smoked chicken over wild field greens or the seafood risotto. The restaurant offers theater/dining packages with nearby George Street Playhouse. Kids' menu. | 120 Albany St. | 732/249–7500 | Jacket required | Closed Sun. No lunch Sat. | $28–$44 | AE, DC, MC, V.

Makeda. Ethiopian. African prints decorate this ethnic eatery, which includes an exotic gift boutique. It's known for lamb, chicken, seafood, and beef, as well as vegetarian options. There's live music Thursday–Sunday. | 338 George St. | 732/545–5115 | www.makedas.com | Closed Mon. | $18–$38 | AE, D, DC, MC, V.

Marita's Cantina. Mexican. This casual Rutgers-area restaurant has a southwestern feel, and is open until 1 AM. It's known for fajitas and margaritas, and you can eat outside on a patio. Live music Thursday and Saturday. Kids' menu. | 1 Penn Plaza | 732/247–3840 | No lunch Sun. | $9–$17 | AE, DC, MC, V.

Old Man Rafferty's. American. Rutgers students can be found most nights around Rafferty's lively bar, or eating hamburgers in the comfortable booths. Kids' menu. | 106 Albany St. | 732/846–6153 | $12–$18 | AE, D, MC, V.

Rusty Nail. American. This casual spot has been serving New Brunswick for more than half a century. Steaks and seafood are the specialty. There's a salad bar and a kids' menu. | 1609 Rte. 130 | 732/821–4141 | $11–$16 | AE, MC, V.

Szechwan Gourmet. Chinese. Swords, masks, and colorful umbrellas adorn the walls, and General Tso's chicken is the most popular dish. | 3 Livingston Ave. | 732/846–7878 | $5–$14 | AE, D, DC, MC, V.

Tumulty's Pub. American. Dark wooden rafters and brass lamps give Tumulty's an old-world charm. Steaks, burgers, and the heart of lettuce salad (a head lopped in half) are very popular. Live music in the bar Thursday–Sunday. Kids' menu. | 361 George St. | 732/545–6205 | $12–$22 | AE, D, DC, MC, V.

Lodging

Embassy Suites. This hotel, about 4 mi east of New Brunswick, was renovated in 1996 and has modern luxurious suites. It's about a 10-minute drive from the town's many shops and restaurants. Restaurant, bar, complimentary breakfast. In-room data ports, microwaves, refrigerators, cable TV. Pool. Hot tub. Exercise equipment. Video games. Laundry facilities. Business services. | 121 Centennial Ave. Piscataway | 732/980–0500 | fax 732/980–9473 | www.embassy-suites.com | 224 suites | $210 | AE, D, DC, MC, V.

Hilton and Towers. This renovated atrium hotel sits within the Tower Center Business Complex, right off the New Jersey Turnpike. Light, luxury, and waterfalls abound, and the rooms are modern. Suites have Jacuzzis and wet bars. Restaurant, bar, room service. In-room data ports, refrigerators, cable TV. Pool. Hot tub. Exercise equipment. Business services, airport shuttle. | 3 Tower Center Blvd. East Brunswick | 732/828–2000 | fax 732/828–6958 | bhtsales@injersey.com | www.hilton.com | 405 rooms | $99–$249 | AE, D, DC, MC, V.

Hyatt Regency. Located just 2½ blocks from trains and close to New Brunswick's commercial area, this extravagant Hyatt has a lovely staircase in the lobby and a huge ballroom on the ground floor. Restaurant, bar (with entertainment). In-room data ports, cable TV. Pool. Hot tub. Tennis. Exercise equipment. Business services. | 2 Albany St. | 732/873–1234 | fax 732/873–6666 | www.hyatt.com | 286 rooms | $155–$224 | AE, D, DC, MC, V.

Ramada Inn. This hotel was opened in 1998 and is in the Route 1 business corridor. Geared toward business travel, it has major conference and banquet facilities. It's also convenient to Rutgers and Kean College. Restaurant, bar, complimentary Continental breakfast. In-room data ports, cable TV. Pool. Hot tub. No pets. | 999 Rte. 1 | 732/246–3737 | fax 732/448–9670 | www.ramada.com | 131 rooms | $75–$125 | AE, D, DC, MC, V.

Ramada Inn. This relatively inexpensive hotel provides many of the amenities found in neighboring, more pricey options. Restaurant, bar (with entertainment), room service. Cable TV. Pool. Exercise equipment. Business services. | 195 Rte. 18, East Brunswick | 732/828–6900 | fax 732/937–4838 | 137 rooms | $79–$149 | AE, D, DC, MC, V.

University Inn & Conference Center. This university-owned and -operated hotel and conference center is set amid 21 peaceful acres on the Rutgers campus. Each room has a view of the surrounding woods. Complimentary breakfast. In-room data ports, refrigerators, cable TV. Business services. No smoking. | 178 Ryder's La. | 732/932–9144 | fax 732/932–6952 | univinn@rci.rutgers.edu | www.univinn.rutgers.edu | 36 rooms | $84–$115 | AE, MC, V.

Wellesley Inn. This three-story hotel is 10 minutes from Rutgers. There's a landscaped approach to the hotel, with a fountain. Complimentary Continental breakfast. In-room data ports, cable TV. Pets allowed. | 831 Rte. 1 | 732/287–0171 or 800/444–8888 | fax 732/287–8364 | www.wellesleyinnandsuites.com | 100 rooms | $70 | AE, D, DC, MC, V.

OCEAN CITY

(Nearby towns also listed: Atlantic City, Somers Point)

With year-round entertainment, 8 mi of beach, and 3 mi of boardwalk with amuse-ments and shops, Ocean City is one of the shore's major family resorts. You'll also find fine restaurants, a vibrant downtown shopping area, golf and fishing facilities, and many places to stay, including historic inns and B&Bs. In summer, the Greater Ocean City Chamber of Commerce, in conjunction with the Bed and Breakfast Guild of Ocean City, offers inn-to-inn tours on Thursday afternoons.

Information: **Ocean City Tourism** | Ocean City, 08226 | 800/BEACH–NJ | www.oceanci-tyvacation.com. **Ocean City Chamber of Commerce** | Rte. 52, 9th St. Causeway, Box 157, Ocean City, 08226 | 609/399–2629 | fax 609/398–3932 | www.oceancityvacation.com.

Attractions

Ocean City Historical Museum. Here you'll find exhibits of local artifacts and old postcards. The Sindia Room highlights Ocean City's most famous shipwreck. | 1735 Simpson Ave. | 609/399–1801 | Free | Weekdays 10–4, Sat. 1–4, and by appointment.

ON THE CALENDAR

APR: *Ocean City Doodah Parade.* Classic comedians such as the Marx Brothers, Lucille Ball, and Laurel and Hardy are honored at this annual parade, which features clown troupes and other comic fare. It's followed by a comedy show and banquet at the Music Pier. | 609/525–9300.

MAY: *Clown Festival.* Clown around with professionals at this four-day event on the Boardwalk. | 609/525–9300.

MAY: *Martin Mollusk Day.* The famous hermit crab, Martin Z. Mollusk, attempts to see his shadow; if he does, summer has arrived in Ocean City a week early. | 609/525–9300.

MAY: *Spring Block Party.* Enjoy more than 400 crafters, entertainment, food, merchant sidewalk sales, and children's fun and games. On Asbury Avenue, from 5th to 14th Streets. | 609/525–9300.

JUNE: *Ocean City Flower Show.* More than 500 horticulture exhibitors take part in this annual event, which also has a special garden and railroad-train exhibit. The show is held at the Music Pier on the boardwalk on Moorlyn Terrace. | 609/525–9300.

JUNE, JULY: *July Jubilee.* Treasure hunts, special contests, and other fun events take place the week leading up to July 4. | 609/525–9300.

JULY: *A Night in Venice.* Conjure up the canals with a water parade of decorated boats and 300 waterfront homes on Great Egg Harbor Bays. | 609/525–9300.

JULY: *Ocean City Lifeguard's Association Biathlon.* Compete in or watch this annual 1-mi swim and 4-mi run, held on the beach, usually at 35th Street. | 609/767–1337.

JULY: *Sand Sculpting Contest.* Everyone is welcome to compete in this good-natured public contest. Kids, teens, adult and family categories. | 609/525–9300.

AUG.: *Baby Parade.* Locals and visitors participate in this 90-year tradition. Parents promenade their youngsters in carts, carriages, and costumes. | 609/525–9300.

AUG.: *Twins Contest.* Categories include most-similar-looking and least-similar-look-ing. There's even a prize for most-similar-looking nontwins. | 609/525–9300.

AUG.: *Weird Contest Week.* If you have a talent for saltwater-taffy sculpting, french-fry sculpting, or wet-shirt throwing, this is the week to hit town. Don't miss the Miss Mis-cellaneous contest. | 609/525–9300.

SEPT.: *Super 50s Weekend.* More than 600 street rods are on display, along with enter-tainment, dances, food, games, and contests. | 609/525–9300.

DEC.: *Ocean City Air Festival.* Ocean City Airport hosts a display of antique airplanes. | 609/525–9300.

Dining

Chef Paolo's That's Amore Italian Restaurant. Italian. Everything from soup to pasta is made from scratch at this 10-table eatery whose chef/owner used to own a restaurant in Florence. The ravioli is a must-try. Choose from fillings such as lobster, crab, shrimp, and, in the fall, sweet potato and pumpkin. | 506 9th St. | 609/399–5800 | Closed mid-Oct.–Apr. | $10–$23 | AE, MC, V.

Cousin's. Italian. Since the Carnuccio family opened this homey family-style restaurant in 1980, they have taken on catering duties and even published their own cookbook. Seafood, chicken, and steak are staples. Try the chicken saltimbucca or the jumbo fried shrimp. Early bird specials, children's menu, and family-size take-out menu available. | 104 Asbury Ave. | 609/399–9462 or 800/286–1963 | $15–$22 | AE, MC, V.

Deauville Inn. American. If you're looking for the perfect sunset dining experience, try this waterfront restaurant housed in a former hotel built in 1880, 7 minutes from Ocean City. The main fare is seafood, and there are daily specials. Eat outdoors overlooking the water, and enjoy live music on summer weekends. Kids' menu. Early bird dinners. | 201 Willard Rd. Strathmere | 609/263–2080 | www.deauvilleinn.com | Closed 2 days a wk Nov.–Mar. (check web site for days) | $14–$38 | AE, MC, V.

Lodging

Beach Club Hotel. This boardwalk hotel has a spacious sundeck and a beachfront pool. Cozy poolside and oceanfront rooms are available. Restaurant, room service. Cable TV. Pool, wading pool. Laundry facilities. Business services. | 1280 Boardwalk | 609/399–8555 | fax 609/398–4379 | www.beachclubhotel.com | 82 rooms | $210–$275 | Closed mid-Oct.–Apr. | AE, MC, V.

Castle by the Sea. Located a block from the beach and the boardwalk, this inn serves a gourmet three-course breakfast and a free afternoon tea with homemade sweets. (And if that's not enough, you'll get bedside chocolates with turn-down service.) Rooms are romantic and cozy with Victorian touches. Complimentary breakfast. Cable TV. | 701 Ocean Ave. | 609/398–3555 or 800/622–4894 | 8 rooms, 1 cottage | $99–$219 | AE, D, MC, V.

Days Inn. This four-story chain hotel is less than 50 ft from the ocean, and some rooms have ocean views. Suites have kitchenettes. Cable TV. Pool. Laundry facilities. Business services. | 7th and Boardwalk (Box 415) | 609/398–2200 | fax 609/391–2050 | www.daysinn.com | 80 rooms | $185–$220 | Closed mid-Oct.–mid-Apr. | AE, D, DC, MC, V.

Impala Island Inn. Rooms surround the pool at this inn, and some are more modern than others. Some also have ocean views. It's a block from the boardwalk, with rides at Playland and treats at the Peanut Shop. Restaurant, room service. Refrigerators, cable TV. 2 pools, wading pool. Business services. | 1001 Ocean Ave. | 609/399–7500 | fax 609/398–4379 | www.beachclubhotel.com | 109 rooms in 2 buildings | $140–$174. | AE, MC, V.

Koo Koo's Nest Bed & Breakfast. Enjoy complimentary afternoon tea on a wraparound porch overlooking Tabernacle Park. This inn provides guests with beach tags and will arrange on-site massage appointments. Rooms are simple and cheerful, each with its own distinct look. Complimentary breakfast. Cable TV. Hot tub. No pets. No smoking. | 615 Wesley Ave. | 609/814–9032 | reservations@kookoosnest.com | www.kookoosnest.com | 7 rooms | $40–$135 | AE, MC, V.

Northwood Inn Bed & Breakfast. This family-friendly inn has a rooftop hot tub, a billiard room, a library with videos, and free afternoon snacks. Bicycles and beach passes are provided and massage appointments can also be set up. The rooms are named for flowers and decorated (fittingly) in pastels and floral prints. Complimentary breakfast. Cable TV, in-room VCRs. | 401 Wesley Ave. | 609/399–6071 | info@northwoodinn.com | www.northwoodinn.com | 5 rooms, 2 suites | $80–$220 | AE, MC, V.

Pavilion. This beach hotel is convenient to concerts at the music pier and slippery amusements at the water park. It has a country-club atmosphere, and some rooms face the ocean.

Restaurant, room service. Refrigerators, cable TV. Pool, wading pool. Laundry facilities. Business services. | 801 Atlantic Ave. | 609/399–2600 | 80 rooms | $135–$145 | AE, D, MC, V.

Port–O–Call. The motto at this hotel? "The only thing we overlook is the ocean." Renovated in 1999, it features modern rooms, many of which have private balconies. Restaurant, room service. In-room data ports, refrigerators, cable TV. Pool. Barbershop, beauty salon, sauna. Exercise equipment. Laundry facilities. Business services, airport shuttle. | 1510 Boardwalk | 609/399–8812 or 800/334–4546 | fax 609/399–0387 | www.portocallhotel.com | 99 rooms | $225–$240 | AE, D, DC, MC, V.

Serendipity. This homey inn, built in 1912 (and renovated in 1999), is decorated in pastels with wicker furniture and ceiling fans. A garden veranda shaded with vines makes for a lovely picnic area, and you can eat breakfast inside or out. It's less than a block from the ocean. Picnic area, complimentary breakfast. Cable TV, no room phones. No kids under 10. No smoking. | 712 9th St. | 609/399–1554 or 800/842–8544 | fax 609/399–1527 | www.serendipitynj.com | 6 rooms (2 with shared bath) | $85–$159 | AE, D, MC, V.

Wild Dunes Inn. Rent your own cozy one-bedroom suite in the heart of the beach district. Microwaves, refrigerators, cable TV. Pool, wading pool. Laundry facilities. | 801 10th St. | 609/399–2910 | fax 609/398–4379 | www.ocbeachclub.com | 28 suites | $230–$242 | AE, MC, V.

OCEAN GROVE

MAP 9, H6

(Nearby towns also listed: Asbury Park, Belmar)

This town was established in 1869, when a group of spiritual leaders assembled as the Ocean Grove Camp Meeting Association. Since then, Ocean Grove has been a meeting place for Methodists who live in small tent-bungalows all summer long. On the tree-lined streets you'll find the largest assemblage of authentic Victorian architecture in the nation, listed in the National Register of Historic Places. Its Main Street has experienced a slight yuppie revival in recent years, with a few nice places to eat and shop.

Information: **Ocean Grove Chamber of Commerce** | 45 Pilgrim Pathway, Ocean Grove, 07756 | 732/774–1391 or 800/388–GROVE | www.oceangrovenj.com. **Ocean Grove Camp Meeting Association** | 54 Pitman Ave., Ocean Grove, 07756 | 732/775–0035 or 800/773–0097 | www.oceangrove.org.

Attractions

Great Auditorium. A soaring, spacious structure, dating from 1894, the Great Auditorium is the largest enclosed auditorium in New Jersey. It was built to hold up to 10,000 worshipers, and expanded in 1907 to accommodate the Hope-Jones pipe organ, which still delivers concerts on Wednesday evenings and Saturday afternoons. Evangelists like Billy Graham and Norman Vincent Peale hold special gatherings here. With its surprisingly fine acoustics it is also the home of a thriving summer Saturday-night concert series. | 54 Pitman Ave. | 732/775–0035 | Call for hrs/schedule.

ON THE CALENDAR

MAY–SEPT.: *Saturday Night Shows.* Popular entertainers, from The Lettermen to the Duke Ellington Orchestra, perform in the Great Auditorium. | 732/775–0035 or 800/773–0097.

JUNE: *Giant Spring Flea Market.* Three hundred vendors assemble on the Ocean Pathway for great finds and plenty of food and drink the first weekend in June. | 732/774–1391.

JULY: *Annual Open House Tour.* The Historical Society leads this tour of houses with historic, cultural, and architectural significance. | 732/774–1869.

DEC.: *Celebrate the Season.* Welcome Christmas with tree lighting, caroling, and cookie contests in Auditorium Park. | 732/774–1391.

DEC.: *Victorian Holiday Festival.* Houses and inns are open for touring, and there are special concerts around town. | 732/774–1391.

Dining

Moonstruck. Mediterranean. Enjoy fresh broiled seafood and big, crisp salads in a romantic, candlelit dining room about 3 mi west of Asbury Park. Local artists' work is displayed on the walls. In summer, you can eat outside at sidewalk tables. BYOB. | 57 Main Ave. | 732/988–0123 | Reservations not accepted | Closed Mon. and Jan.–mid-Feb. No lunch | $17–$41 | MC, V.

Secret Garden Restaurant. Contemporary. This enchanting restaurant, with its gauzy white curtains and pink tablecloths, is a popular place for Sunday brunch. For dinner, try the grilled duck breast with figs and plum sauce, the flame-broiled sea scallops, or the trout with roasted pumpkin-seed butter. It's in the Manchester Inn. | 25 Ocean Pathway | 732/775–0616 | Closed Labor Day–Memorial Day | $11–$18 | AE, MC, V.

Lodging

The Cordova. Built in 1885, the Cordova is listed on the National Registry of Historic Places, and some guests should probably be listed as well—they've been returning for more than 30 years. Accommodations range from small rooms with no bathrooms to cottages. Located a block from the beach and boardwalk. No TV in some rooms, TV in common area. Tennis, bicycles. Library. | 26 Webb Ave. | 732/774–3084 | fax 732/207–4720 | 20 rooms, 2 cottages | $46–$159 | No credit cards.

PARAMUS

MAP 4, D5

(Nearby towns also listed: Hackensack, Ho-Ho-Kus, Montvale, Paterson, Saddle Brook, Teaneck)

Settled in 1660, the self-titled "Shopping Crossroads of the Northeast" is famous for its three huge malls and two smaller ones, which have a major impact on the flow of traffic on Routes 17 and 4. These roads are also a Who's Who of fast-food chains and diners. The sometimes-contested Blue Laws keep the town quieter on Sunday.

Information: The Greater Paramus Chamber of Commerce | 58 E. Midland Ave., Paramus, 07652 | 201/261–3344 | fax 201/261–3346 | staff@paramuschamber.com | www.paramuschamber.com.

Attractions

Bergen County Van Saun Park. The 140-acre park's most popular features are its small zoo, including an area for farm animals, and its miniature railroad. There are tennis and picnic facilities, but reserve in advance on summer holidays. | 216 Forest Ave. | 201/262–2627 or 201/262–3771 | $2 | Daily.

Bergen Museum of Art and Science. Featuring changing exhibits, this museum focuses on prominent New Jersey artists. The "Youth Gallery" opened in 1998, and showcases the work of young artists. Another highlight is the museum's two mastodon skeletons, which were found in New Jersey. The Nature Room has live fish, frogs, turtles, snakes, and plants. | 327 E. Ridgewood Ave. | 201/265–1248 | $3 | Daily 10–5.

New Jersey Children's Museum. This interactive play and learning center was designed for children under age 8. | 599 Industrial Ave. | 201/262–5151 | www.njcm.com | $8 | Daily 9–5.

Sportsworld Indoor Amusement Park. This 60,000-square-ft space has more than 150 games, rides, and attractions. | 200 Rte. 17 N | 201/262–1717 | fax 201/299–5961 | $10 | Daily 10 AM–midnight (weekends until 2 AM).

Dining
Orange Lantern. American/Casual. Originally converted from a gas station in the 1930s, this restaurant, now in its third generation of ownership by the Faatz family, features burgers, sandwiches, and pizzas at hard-to-beat prices. If you're a sports fan (any sport will do), you'll feel right at home; the Orange Lantern throws parties for the Super Bowl, the World Series, and the Stanley Cup Finals. | 15 Firehouse La. | 201/652–4443 | fax 201/652–9222 | $4–$7 | AE, V.

Lodging
Howard Johnson Lodge. Convenient to the Garden State Parkway, this is the place to stay if you're looking to shop in Paramus's nine malls. The Garden State and Paramus Park malls are within 1½ mi. Cable TV. Pool. Laundry service. | 393 Rte. 17 | 201/265–4200 or 800/406–1411 | fax 201/265–0247 | 81 rooms | $95–$130 | AE, D, DC, V.

Radisson. The Paramus Park Mall is directly behind this modern two-story hotel, and Sportsworld (with rides and games) is 10 minutes away by car. The hotel was renovated in 2000, and the rooms have contemporary, streamlined furnishings in neutral colors. Restaurant, bar, room service. In-room data ports, refrigerators, cable TV. Laundry facilities. Business services. Some pets allowed. | 601 From Rd. | 201/262–6900 | fax 201/262–4955 | www.radisson.com | 119 rooms | $89–$169 | AE, D, DC, MC, V.

PARSIPPANY

MAP 9, F3

(Nearby town also listed: Morristown)

Parsippany–Troy Hills, as the municipality is officially known, covers 25 square mi and is close to Interstate 80, Interstates 287 and 280, U.S. 46, U.S. 202, and Routes 10 and 53. Parsippany's proximity to these arteries encourages business growth, and allows it to serve as a major hub for meetings and conventions. As a result, you have your choice of major hotels, but with all that business traffic, you'd better book in advance.

Information: **Parsippany Area Chamber of Commerce** | Parsippany Pl., 959 Rte. 46 E, Suite 101, Parsippany, 07054 | 973/402–6400 | fax 973/334–2242 | president@pacc-nj.org | www.pacc-nj.org or www.Parsippany.net.

Attractions
Craftsmen Farms/Gustav Stickley Museum. This museum, right next to Parsippany in Morris Plains, is the former home of Gustav Stickley, leader of the arts-and-crafts movement. In addition to permanent displays, it has special exhibitions and weekend programs for the public. | Manor La., off Rte. 10 W, Morris Plains | 973/540–1165 | fax 973/540–1167 | $5 | Wed.–Fri. noon–3, Sat. 10–4, Sun. 11–4.

ON THE CALENDAR
MAY: *Memorial Day Parade.* This holiday parade is followed by a festival. | 973/263–7255.
JULY: *Fireworks.* The July 4th tradition is held at Parsippany Hills high school. | 973/263–4350.

Dining
Harold's New York Deli. Delicatessen. Family-style meals with huge sandwiches, matzoh balls, and great desserts make this New York–style deli a favorite of local noshers. Takeout is available. | 707 Rte. 46 E | 973/335–3339 | Breakfast also available | $6–$15 | AE, V.

Il Capriccio. Italian. Enjoy top-rated northern Italian cuisine in a classic Venetian-style atmosphere. Il Capriccio is known for fish, chicken, and veal. Try one of the wine-tasting dinners, the *Costolette d'Agnello al Barbaresco* (sautéed rack of lamb), Midnight Cake, or the imported zuccotto with raspberry sauce. Pianist weeknights. Parsippany is 2 mi away. | 633 Rte. 10 E Whippany | 973/884–9175 | Reservations essential | Closed Sun. | $17–$28 | AE, D, MC, V.

Marakesh. Middle Eastern. This restaurant, adorned like a Moroccan palace with tiles, carvings, and paintings, serves nightly family-style, seven-course dinners. Belly dancers perform on the weekends. Use silverware if you want, but the traditional way is to eat with your hands! | 321 Rte. 46 E | 973/808–0062 | fax 973/808–2851 | Closed Mon. No lunch | $22 prix fixe | MC, V.

Reservoir Tavern. Italian. This family-style restaurant is well liked by locals who grew up eating its pizza. Reliably good Italian food and huge amounts of it are served up at reasonable prices. | 90 Parsippany Blvd. | 973/334–5708 | $6–$14 | AE, V.

Tartufo. Italian. The dining room is pretty and modern with metal Art Deco wall sconces, sheer curtains, and white linen tablecloths. The spicy *Spezzatino di Pollo Arrabiato*—chicken in a spicy tomato sauce—is a specialty, and the tuxedoed waiters are experts in choosing a wine to go with your meal. An organic menu is also available. | 810 Rte. 46 | 973/334–5421 | Closed Sun. No lunch Sat. | $9–$20 | MC, V.

Lodging

Days Inn. Located at the junction of Interstates 80 and 287, this chain hotel is close to area businesses as well as shopping. It was renovated in 1999 and has antique-style furnishings. Cable TV. Laundry service. Pets allowed (fee). | 3159 Rte. 46 E | 973/335–0200 or 800/544–8313 | fax 973/263–3094 | 119 rooms | $69–$149 | AE, D, DC, MC, V.

Embassy Suites. This five-floor chain hotel is in Parsippany's downtown business district and is geared toward the executive traveler on a long-term assignment. It's less than a mile from several Fortune 500 and other companies, as well as chain restaurants such as Chili's and Bennigan's. Enjoy the sundeck between meetings. Restaurant, bar. In-room data ports, cable TV. Pool. Exercise room. Video games. Baby-sitting, playground. Laundry facilities, laundry service. No pets. | 909 Parsippany Blvd. | 973/334–1440 or 800/362–2779 | fax 973/402–1188 | www.embassysuites.com | 274 suites | $189–$229 | AE, D, DC, MC, V.

Hampton Inn. This four-story hotel has rooms that are comfortable, though not luxurious. Complimentary Continental breakfast. Some kitchenettes, cable TV. Hot tub. Exercise equipment. Business services. | 3535 U.S. 46 E | 973/263–0095 | fax 973/263–6133 | www.hampton-inn.com | 109 rooms | $124–$159 | AE, D, DC, MC, V.

Hilton. This huge Hilton has a well-tended front area with a fountain, a massive Grand Ballroom, and a full business center. Restaurant, bar (with entertainment), room service. In-room data ports, refrigerators (in suites), cable TV. Pool. Hot tub. Tennis. Exercise equipment. Playground. Business services, airport shuttle. Some pets allowed. | 1 Hilton Ct. | 973/267–7373 | fax 973/984–6853 | www.hilton.com | 508 rooms, 5 suites | $89–$119 rooms; $109–$395 suites | AE, D, DC, MC, V.

Holiday Inn. You'll find this Holiday Inn across from Wendy's restaurant. It has a nice outdoor pool with lawn chairs, and some rooms have a poolside view. Modern rooms were renovated in 1997. Restaurant. Cable TV. Pool. Exercise equipment. Laundry facilities. | 707 U.S. 46 | 973/263–2000 | fax 973/299–9029 | www.holiday.com | 153 rooms | $69–$119 | AE, D, DC, MC, V.

Howard Johnson Express Inn. The express HoJo doesn't have a restaurant on the premises, but it's an excellent inexpensive option. Complimentary Continental breakfast. Refrigerators, cable TV. Laundry facilities. Business services. | 625 U.S. 46 | 973/882–8600 | fax 973/882–3493 | www.hojo.com | 117 rooms | $69–$79 | AE, D, DC, MC, V.

Ramada Inn. This two-story hotel was built in 1970 and renovated in 1996. In Parsippany's business district, it is close to all major highways, and adjacent to a 22,000-square-ft. health club. There's also a poolside grill. In-room data ports, cable TV. Pool. Laundry service. Pets allowed. | 949 Rte. 46 E | 973/263–0404 or 888/298–2054 | fax 973/263–4057 | www.ramada.com | 72 rooms | $80–$105 | AE, D, DC, V.

PATERSON

(Nearby towns also listed: Clifton, Hackensack, Paramus, River Edge, Wayne)

Although today Paterson is often written off as a rather blighted area, it has an impressive history. Founded in 1792 by Alexander Hamilton, it was America's first planned industrial city, famous for inventions in cotton processing and locomotive production. The city was also known for its silky textiles, and Lambert Castle—the former home of silk baron Catholina Lambert—is a local must-see. The city covers 8 square mi and has more than 140,000 residents, making it the largest in Passaic County and the third largest in the state. The 75-ft-high Great Falls are still a major draw, and the surrounding 89 acres is a National Historic District.

Information: Greater Paterson Chamber of Commerce | 100 Hamilton Plaza, Paterson, 07505 | 973/881–7300 | www.greaterpatersoncc.org.

Attractions

American Labor Museum/Botto House National Landmark. Explore period rooms, exhibits, and the garden at this former Italian immigrant's home where silk workers rallied in 1913. Located just next door to Paterson, in neighboring Haldeon. | 83 Norwood St., Haldeon | 973/935–7953 | fax 973/935–7291 | Wed.–Sat. 1–4, and by appointment.

Garret Mountain Reservation. This urban park has some wonderful views of Paterson's hodgepodge of spires, smokestacks, and big-city sprawl. | Rifle Camp Rd., West Paterson | 973/881–4832 | Free | Daily.

Great Falls Historic District. Paterson's Great Falls, at about 75 ft, is the second-largest waterfall by volume east of the Mississippi. The falls' waterpower spurred on the development of Paterson as the first planned industrial city. The hulking old warehouses you see today are reminders of that heyday. | 65 McBride Ave. Extension | 973/279–9587 | Free | Daily. Exhibits at the **Paterson Museum** explain the town's role as the nation's first planned industrial city. The museum itself is in the Thomas Rogers Building, where locomotives were once built (an example of one is in front of the building). You'll see historic photos, textiles and textile-making equipment, hulls from the first submarines (invented by a Paterson schoolteacher), and changing art exhibits. Occasional poetry readings and other art events are scheduled. | Thomas Rogers Building, 2 Market St. | 973/881–3874 | www.fieldtrip.com/nj/18813874.htm | $2 | Tues.–Fri. 10–4, weekends 12:30–4:30.

Lambert Castle. An actual castle perched on a hillside overlooking the city, this was the home of silk industrialist Catholina Lambert. Today it's the home of the Passaic County Historical Society, restored to offer an interpretation of Victorian life. Some events still take place here, although most of the castle is closed for extensive renovation. The Historical Society also maintains its genealogical service and library here. | 3 Valley Rd. | 973/881–2761 | www.dclink.com/castles/lambert.htm | $5 | Weekdays 10–9, weekends 10–5.

Rifle Camp Park. This 160-acre park includes an observatory with a 14-inch telescope, and hosts many public night viewings. The Nature Center has a variety of guided nature walks, children's activities, and photography and astronomy clubs. | Rifle Camp Rd. | 973/523–0024 | Free | Daily.

APR.–MAY, NOV.–DEC.: *Holiday House Boutique at Lambert Castle Museum.* As many as 200 craftspeople and artisans contribute works to this twice-yearly fund-raising event. | 973/881–2761.
JUNE: *Pathmark Multicultural Arts Festival.* One of the largest multicultural arts festivals in the country, this event lasts for 16 days and travels through three states. | 914/762–8878.
SEPT.–OCT.: *House Tour.* Tour area homes, including spectacular mansions and architectural curiosities. | 973/345–2700.

Dining
Meson Galicia. Spanish. This restaurant is in Paterson's Little Italy, next to Lou Costello Park. Classic Spanish dishes like mariscada (lobster, clams, mussels, shrimp, and scallops served in a tomato-cognac sauce) and paella Valencia are menu staples along with a good selection of Italian dishes, reflecting the neighborhood. The warm interiors are done in dark wood and exposed brick with red accents in the place settings. | 58-60 Ellison St. | 973/684-4250 | fax 973/684–5425 | $9–$23 | AE, V.

Lodging
Holiday Inn Totowa. There is a movie theater, plenty of restaurants, and shopping within 2 mi of this hotel, which is 3 mi south of downtown Paterson. Restaurant, complimentary Continental breakfast, room service. In-room data ports, cable TV. Pool. Exercise equipment. Business services. | 1 Rte. 46 W, Totowa | 973/785–9000 | fax 973/785–3031 | 155 rooms | $99–$139 | AE, D, DC, MC, V.

PLAINFIELD

MAP 9, F4

(Nearby towns also listed: Metuchen, Mountainside)

Founded in 1685, Plainfield boasts six historic districts, with Victorian, colonial, and Federal architecture. The city has a very active cultural calendar, and serves as an urban center for numerous surrounding communities, including North Plainfield, Dunellen, Green Brook, Watchung, Scotch Plains, Fanwood, and Warren.

Information: Central Jersey Chamber of Commerce | 120 W. 7th St., Suite 217, Plainfield, 07060-1798 | 908/754–7250. **City of Plainfield** | 515 Watchung Ave., Plainfield, 07060-1798 | 908/753–3000 | fax 908/753–3500 | comments@plainfield.com | www.plainfield.com.

Attractions
Cedarbrook Park & Shakespeare Garden. Stroll among roses and sundry bushes, stone monuments, and beneath grape vines in this meticulously landscaped garden. | Mathewson Dr., Plainfield | 908/527–4900 | Free | Daily.

Drake House Museum. Built in 1746 by Isaac Drake, this house was taken over by George Washington as his headquarters during the Battle of Short Hills, fought June 25–27, 1777. John S. Harberger of New York City, founder of Manhattan Bank, bought it in 1864, adding more rooms in the au courant Victorian style. You can see both influences in the house today. In the Harberger Library is the museum's most prized possession, Julian Scott's huge painting, *The Death of General Sedgewick*, which was restored in 1998. The house has changing exhibits on local history and art. | 602 W. Front St. | 908/755–5831 | www.members.tripod.com/~drakehouse/index.html | $3 | Sun. 2–4.

JUNE, JULY: *Festival of the Arts.* Local artists and craftspeople offer their work for sale at the Library Park. There are refreshments and kids activities. | 908/753–3222.
JULY, AUG.: *Annual Central Jersey July 4th Celebration.* A tradition for more than 75 years, the day includes an elaborate parade, drawing more than 80,000 people. | 908/753–3000.

Dining
Giovanna's. Italian. The bright dining room at this reliably good trattoria has lovely wall sconces and an airy false skylight. Pillars separate this room from a second, cozier room with a fireplace. The grilled swordfish and salmon Portofino are popular dishes, and are complemented by a decent wine list. | 1462 South Ave. | 908/753–6900 | $15–$20 | AE, V.

Lodging
Holiday Inn. This three-story hotel in the business district of South Plainfield is 40 minutes by car from New York City and 15 minutes from shopping and movies at the Menlo Park Mall. Restaurant, room service. In-room data ports, refrigerators, cable TV. Pool. Hot tub. Exercise equipment. Laundry facilities. Business services. Some pets allowed. | 4701 Stelton Rd., South Plainfield | 908/753–5500 | fax 908/753–5500, ext. 620 | 17 rooms | $69–$114 | AE, D, DC, MC, V.

Pillars Bed & Breakfast. This private and elegant Victorian mansion with stained-glass windows and fireplaces is surrounded by gardens. Large, luxurious suites have antique furnishings, canopy beds, and Stickley furniture. Other amenities include terry-cloth robes, turn-down service, and complimentary evening sherry. Complimentary breakfast. In-room data ports, cable TV, in-room VCRs. Some pets allowed. No kids 2yrs.–12yrs. No smoking. | 922 Central Ave. | 908/753–0922 or 888/–PILLARS | pillars2@juno.com | www.pillars2.com | 7 suites | $99–$165 | AE, MC, V.

POINT PLEASANT

MAP 9, H7

(Nearby towns also listed: Lakewood, Point Pleasant Beach)

This small coastal town of 3.5 square mi is along the Manasquan River and the Barnegat Bay, less than a mile from the Atlantic Ocean. It was once home to the Leni-Lenape Indians. In the early 1700s, Europeans settled in the area and survived for hundreds of years as fishermen, farmers, and boat builders. In the center of Point Pleasant, there is a small business area made up of privately owned businesses that pride themselves on offering quality products and services that are often hard to come by in more urban areas. Citizens claim they never have to make the trek to bigger cities, because everthing they need is right here. Point Pleasant's population is about 18,000.

Information: Point Pleasant Chamber of Commerce | Box 797, Point Pleasant, 08742 | 732/295–8850. | www.community.nj.com/cc/PointPleasant.

Attractions
Point Pleasant Historic Society Museum. This museum houses local memorabilia. | 416 New Jersey Ave. | 732/892–3091 | $1 | Tours by appointment.

JULY: *New Jersey Offshore Powerboat Races.* This 10-mi national powerpoint competition starts in front of Jenkinson's Pavilion. | 732/727–4765.

Dining

Clark's Bar & Grill. American. This marina-side restaurant serving burgers, grilled chicken, and seafood has great views of the Manasquan River. In good weather you can eat outside at the sidewalk café. Entertainment and dancing make for a lively singles scene on weekends. Brunch is served Sunday. | 847 Arnold Ave. | 732/899–1111 | $10–$18 | AE, V.

Lodging

Steeple View Bed & Breakfast Cottage. You don't have to worry about the other guests here, because there won't be any. Built in 1885, this unique inn has only a single guest cottage. The main building, which houses the dining room and a parlor, has a white picket fence, a porch with wicker furniture, and a peaceful parklike backyard. In the cottage there's a sitting room, a romantic bedroom with ivy-stenciled walls, a private bath, a wet bar, a refrigerator and microwave, and lots of books and games. Complimentary breakfast. Cable TV. Pool. No pets. No kids under 12. No smoking. | 1107 Front St. | 732/899–8999 | fax 732/899–4845 | steepleview@pointpleasantbeach.com | www.pointpleasantbeach.com | 1 cottage | $175 | MC, V.

POINT PLEASANT BEACH

MAP 9, H7

(Nearby towns also listed: Lakewood, Point Pleasant, Spring Lake)

The quintessential shore town of Point Pleasant Beach is between the Manasquan Inlet and the Metedeconk River. You'll find lots of good seafood and Italian cuisine in down-home surroundings, as well as an oasis of antiques, the largest trove being the Point Pleasant Antiques Emporium, a three-floor building with more than 125 vendors. Jenkinson's Boardwalk, with its aquarium, miniature golf course, and busy calendar of events, is a major player in the area, and is open year-round.

Information: Point Pleasant Beach Chamber of Commerce | 517A Arnold Ave., Point Pleasant Beach, 08742 | 732/899–2424 | www.pointpleasantbeachnj.com.

Attractions

Jenkinson's Boardwalk. This boardwalk has games, an amusement park, and arcade, shops, restaurants, miniature golf, a nightclub, and an aquarium. | 500 Boardwalk | 732/295–4334 | fax 732/295–2181 | www.jenkinsons.com | Free | Apr.–Oct., daily 9 AM–2 AM amusement park and arcade; Oct.–Mar., weekdays 11 AM–5 PM, weekends 10 AM–5 PM, amusement park closed.

Point Pleasant Antique Emporium. You'll find more than 125 individual dealers here, spread out over three floors. | Bay and Trenton Aves. | 732/892–2222 | Free | Daily 11–5.

ON THE CALENDAR

APR.: *Earth Day Celebration.* Celebrate the earth at Jenkinson's Aquarium with seminars on local and global environmental issues; face painting and kiddie crafts. | 732/899–1212.

MAY: *Miller Lite Pro/Am Beach Volleyball.* Professionals and amateurs compete in this televised tournament. Vendors offer food, merchandise, and souvenirs. | 732/506–9449.

MAY–SEPT. *Fireworks/Laser Light Show.* Head to the beach on Thursdays for fireworks and Tuesdays for an open-air laser light show. | 732/295–4334.

MAY–OCT.: *Cruise Nights.* Antique and collectible cars, hot rods, and trucks cruise the streets for show downtown on the first Friday of each month. | 732/899–2424.

JUNE: *Antiques festival.* Dealers of various types of antiques set up their wares along Arnold Avenue. | 732/899–2424.

JULY: *Boatfest.* Racing boats are on display. | 732/899–2424.

JULY: *Offshore Powerboat Parade, Boat Fest, Offshore Grand Prix.* Powerboats are on display, along with food, arts and crafts, and entertainment. High-power speedboats race in the ocean, visible from the beach. | 732/899–2424.

SEPT.: *Festival of the Sea.* This seafood festival includes arts and crafts, 1- and 5-mi runs, and fireworks. | 732/899–2424.

OCT.: *Octoberfest.* Celebrate the season on the first weekend of October with food, drink, and music. | 732/899–2424.

Dining

Broadway. American. A truly nautical spot, you'll find fisherman here at all hours. Awesome and affordable is how locals describe the food. Crab cakes, burgers, cod fish, pot roast platters, and grilled salmon are just some examples. | 106 Randall Ave., at corner of Broadway and Ocean Ave. | 732/295–1500 | Breakfast also available | $5–$11 | AE, MC, V.

Europa South. Portuguese. This cavernous restaurant with live Latin music on weekends is a popular place to salsa, cha-cha, and rhumba as well as eat. Order a pitcher of sangria at the bar while you're waiting for a table. When you finally do sit down, try the shrimp marinated in garlic and olive oil or the Portuguese-style filet mignon with ham and olives. | 521 Arnold Ave. | 732/295–1500 | Closed Mon. | $15–$24 | AE, DC, MC, V.

Frankie's Bar&Grill. American. A local favorite, this restaurant has a homey feel, with brick interior, dark woods, two fireplaces, and tons of knick-knacks. There's an extensive appetizer menu; dinners include a grilled chicken sandwich with bacon and Meunster cheese, filet mignon with fresh mozzarella and eggplant, plus lots of pasta, steak, and seafood. | 414 Richmond Ave. | 732/892–6000 | $7–$20 | AE, D, MC, V.

Spike's. Seafood. With makeshift wooden tables and a working fish market inside, this restaurant looks casual but tastes divine. Fresh seafood is the only choice here, but choices can be hard, with everything from Spike's lobster roll (lobster on a hot dog roll) to shrimp Parmesan. | 415 Broadway | 732/295–9400 | $12–$23 | AE, D, MC, V.

Lodging

Amethyst's Beach Motel. This family-friendly motel overlooks Jenkinson's Boardwalk. Breakfast is served on the poolside patio and guests have access to a picnic area where they can barbecue and play volleyball. Microwaves are available at no extra charge, and efficiencies are available for longer stays. Complimentary Continental breakfast. Refrigerators. Pool. | 202 Arnold Ave. | 732/899–3600 | fax 732/899–7754 | 42 rooms | $129–$169 | AE, D, MC, V.

White Sands Ocean Front Resort. Four buildings of this resort are right on the ocean, and one is across the street. Extremely popular in summer, White Sands is family-run and family-oriented. The hotels have beach themes and rooms with ocean views. Restaurant, complimentary breakfast (in season). In-room data ports, some kitchenettes, some in-room hot tubs, cable TV. 2 outdoor pools, 1 indoor pool, hot tub, sauna, wading pool. Outdoor hot tub, massage, sauna, spa. Health club, exercise equipment. Business services. No pets. | 1205 Ocean Ave. | 732/899–3370 | www.thewhitesands.com | 130 rooms, 2 suites | $210–$260 | AE, D, DC, MC, V.

PRINCETON

MAP 9, E6

(Nearby towns also listed: Bordentown, Trenton)

Settled in the late 17th century as "Prince Town" in honor of Prince William of Orange and Nassau, Princeton is today a sophisticated university town. Many great minds taught or were educated here, including Edward Albee, F. Scott Fitzgerald, and Albert Einstein. You'll find some good (preppie) shopping stores, and an array of dining options.

Information: Chamber of Commerce of the Princeton Area | Princeton Forrestal Village, 216 Rockingham Row, Princeton, 08540 | 609/520–1776 | fax 609/520–9107 | ccpa@ix.netcom.com | www.princetonol.com/biz/ccpa/index.html.

Attractions

Bainbridge House. This 1766 Georgian brick house contains a museum with changing exhibitions, a library, and photo archives. Two temporary exhibitions are presented on the main floor each year, from the permanent collections of furniture, paintings, clothing, household objects, and other items illustrative of 18th- and 19th-century life. It is the headquarters of the Historical Society of Princeton, which also conducts a walking tour of Princeton on Sunday. | 158 Nassau St. | 609/921–6748 | Free | Mar.–Dec., Tues.–Sun. noon–4; Jan., Feb., weekends noon–4.

Drumthwacket. Drumthwacket comes from the Scottish words *drum,* meaning hill, and thwacket, meaning woods, although now you might notice more lawn than woods. Built in 1835, today Drumthwacket serves as the Governor's Mansion. Forty-minute tours are offered of this stately Greek Revival home. | 354 Stockton St. (U.S. 206) | 609/683–0057 | www.princetonol.com/groups/drumthwacket | Free | Wed. noon–2; closed Jan., Aug.

Historic Morven. Originally built in 1758 by Richard Stockton, one of the signers of the Declaration of Independence, this building was home to N.J. governors from 1954 to 1980. The historic gardens were restored in 1997; there are also horticultural exhibits. | 55 Stockton St. | 609/683–4495 | fax 609/683–1415 | Free | Weds.–Fri. 11–2, or by appointment.

Kuser Farm Mansion and Park. This 22-room mansion was the home of the Kuser family, who helped found the 20th Century Fox Film Company. Tour 17 rooms, including a theater with an 18-ft CinemaScope screen. | 390 Newkirk Ave. | 609/890–3684 | fax 609/890–3630 | Free | May–Nov., Thurs.–Sun. 11–3, last tour at 2:00; Feb.–Apr., grounds dawn–dusk; Feb.–Apr. weekends 11–3.

Lake Carnegie. Andrew Carnegie financed this 3½-mi-long lake, completed in 1906, so the Princeton crew team would not have to row on the Delaware and Raritan Canal, then dangerously crowded with steamships. Watch students practice and race here today. It is also one of the Olympic training centers for the U.S. crew team. | 609/258–3000 | www.princeton.edu | Free.

Princeton Battle Monument. This limestone monument, dedicated in 1922, was designed by the prominent Beaux Arts sculptor Frederick MacMonnies and architect Thomas Hastings. On the sides of the monument are the seals of the United States and the original 13 states, including New Jersey. Commemorating the Battle of Princeton, which took place on January 3, 1777, the sculpture depicts Washington leading his troops into battle, as well as the death of General Hugh Mercer. The actual Battlefield Park is on Mercer Street, 1¼ mi west of the center of town. | 609/520–1776 | Free | Daily.

Princeton Cemetery. Aaron Burr and Grover Cleveland are among the notable people buried here. Gravestones date back to the 1700s. | 29 Greenview Ave. | 609/520–1776 | Free | Daily.

Princeton University. Founded as the College of New Jersey in 1746 in Elizabeth, this top university opened in its present location in 1756 and adopted its current name in 1896. Located on a scenic 500-acre campus, Princeton is home to over 6,000 undergraduate and graduate students. | 609/258–3603 | www.princeton.edu | Free | Daily.
One of New Jersey's largest cultural centers, **McCarter Theatre** was built in 1929 and hosts professional music, drama, and other performances. | 91 University Pl. | 609/258–2787.
The 20-piece outdoor **Putnam Collection of Sculpture** is a memorial to an alumnus who was killed in World War II. The collection features the work of major 20th-century sculptors and can be found throughout the university campus. The *Oval with Points* sculpture is a campus landmark and valued at over $1 million. | Free | Daily.

The **Woodrow Wilson School of Public and International Affairs** was named to honor Princeton's famous alumnus whose distinguished career included serving as President of Princeton University, Governor of New Jersey, and President of the United States. The school seeks to educate public-affairs leaders, and to produce research that will improve public policy. | Robertson Hall | 609/258–4817 | Free | Daily.

Terhune Orchards This 225-acre family farm has apple-cider making and a bakery. There is an Apple Day farm festival in September. | 330 Cold Soil Rd. | 609/924–2310 | fax 609/924–8569 | Free | Weekdays 9–5, weekends 9–6.

ON THE CALENDAR
MAY: *Kite Day.* Kite Day is actually a weekend, and it includes a farm festival, kite flying, food, live music, wagon rides, and entertainment. | 609/924–2310.
MAY: *Memorial Day Parade.* This annual tradition begins north of Franklin Corner Road and continues up Princeton Pike, ending at Lawrence Veterans' Park. | 609/844–7067.
DEC.: *"A Christmas Carol."* Don't miss this holiday fixture at the McCarter Theatre. | 609/258–6500.

Dining

Alchemist and Barrister. Continental. Choose from four different seating options: two colonial-style dining rooms, a traditional pub, or an enclosed patio. And the menu is just as eclectic. For the health conscious there's pan-roasted chicken breast with fat-free mashed potatoes; vegans will love the vegetarian burrito with Spanish rice; and meat lovers shouldn't miss the tasty grilled rib eye of pork with sage-roasted yams and caramelized onions. | 28 Witherspoon | 609/924–5555 | www.alchemistandbarrister.com | $18–$30 | AE, MC, V.

The Annex. Continental. Students, professors, and locals have been mingling at this popular spot for 50 years. The large menu includes lots of veal, fried shellfish, and other seafood dishes. Kids' menu. | 128½ Nassau St. | 609/921–7555 | www.annexrestaurant.com | Closed Sun. | $6–$27 | AE, MC, V.

The Ferry House. Eclectic. You can truly taste America's "melting pot" at this upscale eatery serving American food with an international flair. Diverse dishes include roast baby rack of New Zealand lamb with a mustard-basil crust, black bean tortilla, and coriander au jus, sautéed salmon over herb mashed potatoes with steamed French green beans and saffron vanilla butter. Presentation is key and the food looks as good as it tastes. The restaurant is quaint and cozy, with dark walls and local artwork. | 32 Witherspoon St. Princeton, | 609/924–2488 | www.theferryhouse.com | No lunch weekends | $23–$32 | AE, DC, MC, V.

Good Time Charley's. American. Dine fireside in cozy booths with caricatures decorating the walls, or in the grill room with its five TVs. Try the lobster ravioli, crispy shrimp and walnuts, or the Danish baby-back ribs. There's live music on Friday and Saturday nights, and once a month there's murder mystery performance with dinner included. Good Time Charley's is about 10 mi north of Princeton | 40 Main St., Kingston | 609/924–7400 | www.gtcharleys.com | No lunch Sat. | $13–$21 | AE, D, DC, MC, V.

Harriet's. French. This casual bistro has a relaxed, friendly atmosphere. Popular dishes include coq au vin and escargot. BYOB. | 18 Witherspoon St. | 609/683–4771 | fax 609/683–0207 | Reservations essential Fri., Sat. | Closed Sun. No lunch Sat. | $18–$32 | AE, D, DC, MC, V.

Lahiere's. Continental. Princeton students dine with visiting parents at this long-standing, well-heeled establishment, known for beef and fresh seafood. | 5-11 Witherspoon St. | 609/921–2798 | www.lahieres.com | Closed Sun. | $18–$31 | AE, DC, MC, V.

Rusty Scupper. Seafood. Dine outdoors, fireside, or in the popular loft, with its large tables, numerous TVs, and pool tables. Try the crawfish étouffée with dirty rice, handmade crab ravioli in tomato fennel cream sauce, or seafood cioppino. Salad bar. Kids' menu. | 378 Alexander Rd. | 609/921–3276 | www.rustyscupperrestaurant.com | $18–$45 | AE, D, MC, V.

Lodging

Best Western Palmer Inn. This chain hotel is half a mile from the Princeton University campus. Many of the rooms overlook a landscaped courtyard and some have private balconies. Charlie Brown's Steakhouse is in the hotel. Restaurant, bar, complimentary Continental breakfast. In-room data ports, some kitchenettes, cable TV, in-room VCRs. Pool. Sauna. Exercise room. Laundry service. Business services. | 3499 Rte. 1 S | 609/452–2500 or 800/688–0500 | fax 609/452–1371 | www.bestwestern.com | 105 rooms | $89–$99 | AE, DC, MC, V.

The Forrestal. This hotel is on 25 wooded acres but is contemporary in design and furnishings. There are walking trails on the grounds and there's a picnic area with tables. You'll have access to a day spa for massages, facials, and body wraps as well. Restaurant, bar. In-room data ports, minibars, cable TV. Pool. Hot tub. Tennis. Exercise equipment. Business services, airport shuttle. | 100 College Rd. E | 609/452–7800 or 800/222–1131 | fax 609/452–7883 | www.forrestal.com | 285 rooms, 15 suites | $149–$675 | AE, D, DC, MC, V.

Holiday Inn. This six-story chain hotel is 10 minutes from Princeton University and 30 minutes from Great Adventure amusement park. Restaurant, bar. Refrigerators, cable TV. Pool. Exercise equipment. Business services. | 4355 U.S. 1 | 609/452–2400 | fax 609/452–2494 | 242 rooms | $159–$179 | AE, D, DC, MC, V.

Hyatt Regency. A mile from downtown Princeton and close to businesses such as Johnson and Johnson and Bristol Myers Squibb, this modern Hyatt has a huge open lobby surrounded by upper-floor rooms. There are plants everywhere and interesting blue lighting in the evening. Restaurant, bar (with entertainment). In-room data ports, cable TV. Pool. Hot tub. Tennis. Exercise equipment. Business services, airport shuttle. | 102 Carnegie Center | 609/987–1234 | fax 609/987–2584 | 348 rooms | $129–$234 | AE, D, DC, MC, V.

Marriott. This six-story chain hotel is next to a shopping center. It was renovated in 2000. Restaurant, bar (with entertainment). In-room data ports, refrigerators, cable TV. Pool. Hot tub. Gym. Laundry facilities. Business services. | 201 Village Blvd. | 609/452–7900 or 800/242–8689 | fax 609/452–1123 | 294 rooms | $184–$204 | AE, D, DC, MC, V.

Nassau Inn. Part country inn, part fancy hotel, this place has been around since 1756, but you certainly can't tell from the modern rooms. It's in the heart of downtown Princeton, and the staff delivers chocolate cookies to your room. For a splurge, book the Christopher Reeve Suite (three rooms) for $860 per night. Restaurant, bar (with entertainment). In-room data ports, cable TV. Exercise equipment. Business services. | 10 Palmer Sq. | 609/921–7500 or 800/627–7286 (except NJ) | fax 609/921–9385 | lorginjam@aol.com | www.nassauinn.com | 216 rooms | $335–$860 | AE, DC, MC, V.

Novotel. You'll find this chain hotel in a corporate park overlooking woods, with a bright, remodeled lobby and café. Rooms were renovated in 2000. Restaurant, bar, room service. In-room data ports, cable TV. Pool, hot tub. Exercise equipment. Laundry facilities. Business services. Some pets allowed. | 100 Independence Way | 609/520–1200 | fax 609/520–0594 | 180 rooms | $69–$169. | AE, D, DC, MC, V.

Peacock Inn. Each room in this 1775 building, just three blocks from the Princeton University campus, is unique. All rooms have fireplaces and are done in period antiques. Complimentary breakfast. Cable TV. Business services. Pets allowed (fee). | 20 Bayard La. | 609/924–1707 | fax 609/924–0788 | http://peacockinn.tripod.com | 17 rooms (7 with shared bath) | $145–$165 | AE, MC, V.

Red Maple Farm. This small 1740 colonial inn, 4 mi from Princeton University, is set on 2 acres of flowers, fruit trees, and berry bushes. You can borrow bikes to tour local roads. Cable TV, in-room VCRs. Library. Business services. | 211 Raymond Rd. | 732/329–3821 | 4 rooms | $65–$85 | AE, DC, MC, V.

Residence Inn by Marriott. Rent either a studio or bi-level suite, with a kitchen and a living area. Some have fireplaces and two bathrooms. Picnic area, complimentary Continental breakfast. Kitchenettes, microwaves, cable TV. Pool. Hot tub. Laundry facilities. Business services. Some pets allowed (fee). | 4225 U.S. 1 | 732/329–9600 | fax 732/329–8422 | residenceinn.com/ttnpr | 208 suites | $79–$194 | AE, D, DC, MC, V.

Summerfield Suites Hotel Princeton. This hotel is two minutes from Princeton's Forrestal Center and Corporate Center, and 10 minutes from the university campus. Several restaurants are also close by. One-, two-, and three-bedroom suites are available. Complimentary breakfast. In-room data ports, kitchenettes, cable TV. Pool. Spa. Exercise room. Laundry facilities. | 4375 U.S. Rte. 1 S | 609/951–0009 or 877/999–3223 | fax 609/951–0696 | www.summerfieldsuites.com | 124 suites | $139–$239 | AE, D, DC, MC, V.

RAMSEY

MAP 9, G2

(Nearby towns also listed: Mahwah, Ringwood)

Nestled against the Ramapo Mountains, Ramsey is the last major shopping and dining oasis you'll hit off Route 17 before heading toward the New York border or Harriman and Bear Mountain state parks. Though it may not seem like it from the highway, Ramsey is also a beautiful residential community, a key location for residents working in major corporate headquarters and industries in northern New Jersey.

Information: **Skylands Tourism Council of NJ** | 3117 Rte. 10 E, Denville, 07834 | 908/496–8598 or 800/4–SKYLAN | www.njskylands.com.

RAMSEY

INTRO
ATTRACTIONS
DINING
LODGING

Attractions

James A. McFaul Wildlife Center. Programs at this center, about 10 mi north of Ramsey, seek to educate the public about natural surroundings. | Crescent Ave., Wycleff | 201/891–5571 | www.fieldtrip.com/nj/18915571.htm | Free | Tues. and weekends 8–4:45.

Old Stone House Museum. This 1740 pre-Revolutionary Dutch house was a tavern during the Revolutionary War. Today it's a hands-on museum with displays of 18th-century artifacts. Tours can be arranged. | 538 Island Rd. | 201/327–2208 or 201/327–6467 | Donation | Call for schedule.

Dining

Madison's Deli and Gourmet Catering. Delicatessen. Madison's is a casual, comfortable place to grab lunch and a cup of coffee. You'll find lasagna, roasted chicken, and burgers on the menu along with sandwiches. Kids' menu. | 10 E. Main St. | 201/327–0640 | fax 201/327–0667 | Breakfast also available | $6–$14 | AE, V.

Lodging

Best Western: The Inn at Ramsey. This hotel is near several Fortune 500 companies and adjacent to a shopping center and a multiplex cinema. Golf is available nearby. Restaurant, bar, complimentary Continental breakfast, room service. In-room data ports, some kitchenettes, cable TV, in-room VCRs. Hot tub, sauna. Laundry service. Business services. Pets allowed (fee). | 1315 Rte. 17 S | 201/327–6700 or 800/780–7234 | fax 201/327–6709 | www.bestwestern.com | 80 rooms | $89–$154 | AE, D, DC, MC, V.

Wellesley Inn. This three-story quiet, family-oriented hotel was renovated in 1997. Complimentary Continental breakfast. Refrigerators, cable TV. Business services. Some pets allowed (fee). | 946 Rte. 17 N | 201/934–9250 or 800/444–8888 | fax 201/934–9719 | 89 rooms | $74–$124 | AE, D, DC, MC, V.

RED BANK

(Nearby towns also listed: Eatontown, Holmdel, Rumson, Sandy Hook, Tinton Falls)

Red Bank and its surrounding area was purchased from Native Americans in 1665. Well situated on the Navesink River at the relative start of the Jersey Shore, today Red Bank is a cultural, energetic town with lots to do, from theater-going to canoeing. But by far the favorite activity is perusing the antiques shops that line the streets.

Information: Eastern Monmouth Area Chamber of Commerce | 170 Broad St., Red Bank, 07701 | 732/741–0055 | fax 732/741–6778 | emacc@monmouth.com | www.emacc.org.

Attractions

Allen House. Built prior to 1700, this house has been influenced by Dutch and English building styles. It has been restored to look like the 18th-century tavern it once was—the Blue Ball tavern—but the museum does not actually sell food or drinks. | 400 Sycamore Ave., on the intersection of Hwy. 35 and Sycamore Ave. | 732/462–1466 or 732/747–6260 | $2; special rates for children and senior citizens | May–Sept., Tues., Thurs., Sun. 1–4; Sat. 10–4.

Count Basie Theater. This 1,406-seat theater hosts major artists as well as community theater groups. Performances range from opera and dance to rock concerts. | 99 Monmouth St. | 732/224–8778 | fax 732/842–9323 | www.theatre-link.com/cbt | Box office, weekdays 12–6.

Monmouth Museum. One of the top five museums in New Jersey, this modern building on the campus of Brookdale Community College, about 10 mi west of Red Bank, has changing exhibitions. The Becker Children's wing features special educational interactive exhibits on natural history, ecology, and art. | Newman Springs Rd., Lincroft | 732/747–2266 | www.monmouthmuseum.org | $4 | Tues.–Sun. 10–4:30.

Red Bank Antiques Center. Three buildings in this complex sell various antiques from 150 dealers. | 226 W. Front St. | 732/842–4336 | Free | Mon.–Sat. 11–5, Sun. 12–5.

ON THE CALENDAR

JUNE: *Riverfest.* This jazz and food festival in Marine Park features local and national performers, crafts, and more. | 732/741–0055.
OCT.: *Two-River Folk Festival.* Marine Park's environmental festival has music and food. | 888/447–8696.

Dining

Molly Pitcher Inn. Continental. The elegant chicken potpie is a tradition in this formal dining room overlooking the river. The Inn is also known for seafood and pasta. Pianist Friday–Sunday. Kids' menu. Sunday brunch. | 88 Riverside Ave. | 732/747–2500 | Jacket required | Breakfast also available | $20–$30 | AE, DC, MC, V.

Murphy Style Grill. Steak. This is one of two Murphy's (the other is in Old Bridge). The dining areas are green and white with paintings and prints on the walls. The 24-ounce steak is its signature, and it also has grilled chicken, seafood, and an assortment of sandwiches and salads. In good weather, you can eat outside at sidewalk tables. | 26 Broad St. | 732/530–6659 | $10–$16 | AE, DC, MC, V.

No Joe's Café. American/Casual. After a day of antiquing, you can come to this casual eatery for a cup of gourmet coffee. A variety of soups complement the turkey and chicken salad sandwiches served on panini bread during lunchtime. Sunday brunch. | 51 Broad St. | 732/530–4040 | Breakfast also available. No dinner Sun. | $4–$7 | No credit cards.

Shadowbrook. French. Stroll the breathtaking formal gardens at this 1907 Georgian mansion with blazing chandeliers and fireplaces. Try the shellfish fra diavolo or veal française.

| 732/747–0200 or 800/634–0078 | www.shadowbrook.com | Jacket required | No lunch | $22–$33 | D, DC, MC, V.

Lodging

Courtyard by Marriott. This Marriott is 20 minutes from the beach and close to quaint shops and restaurants. It was built in the late 1980s and renovated in 1998. Restaurant, bar. In-room data ports, some refrigerators, cable TV. Pool, hot tub. Exercise equipment. Laundry facilities. Business services. | 245 Half Mile Rd. | 732/530–5552 | fax 732/530–5756 | www.marriott.com | 146 rooms | $69–$169 | AE, D, DC, MC, V.

Molly Pitcher Inn. Originally built in 1928 and deemed a national landmark, this inn overlooking the Navesink River underwent a total renovation in 1993. Rooms, some of which have balconies overlooking the pool and marina, are elegantly furnished with reproduction antiques. Restaurant, bar. Cable TV. Pool. Health club. Baby-sitting. Laundry service. | 88 Riverside Ave. | 732/747–2500, 800/221–1372 out of state | fax 732/747–2713 | mollypitcher@msn.com | 107 rooms | $110–$170 | AE, D, DC, MC, V.

RIDGEWOOD

MAP 4, C5

(Nearby towns also listed: Ho-ho-kus, Montvale)

Originally called Godwinville, this town's name was changed to Ridgewood in 1866. Ridgewood Avenue is home to unusual boutiques, and you can stop at about every third store for a fancy coffee or something to eat. A great school system makes this a desirable place for families to settle down.

Information: **Ridgewood Chamber of Commerce** | 199 Dayton St., Ridgewood, 07450 | 201/445–2600 | chamber@webridgewood.com | www.webridgewood.com.

Attractions

Schoolhouse Museum. Once a one-room schoolhouse, the main feature is still the main schoolroom, which has the original teacher's platform, blackboard, school desks, potbelly stove, kerosene ceiling lamps, and an 1850s map of the United States. The museum also offers a homespun glimpse of life in Bergen County, displaying household pieces from the 18th through the 21st centuries. | 650 E. Glen Ave. | 201/652–4584 or 201/447–3242 | www.fieldtrip.com/nj/16524584.htm | Free | May–late Oct., Sun. 10–4.

ON THE CALENDAR

JULY: *Fireworks and Parade.* July 4th is hugely popular in this town, which overloads with traffic and revelers for the annual festivities. | 201/445–2600.
SEPT.: *Annual Ridgewood Country Street Fair.* Join locals for arts, crafts, food, music, and children's activities. | 908/996–3036.
DEC.: *First Night Ridgewood.* The town's New Year's Eve celebration features music, dance and comedy performances, storytelling, clowning, magic, and more, at sites all around town. | 201/447–1739.

Dining

Café Winberie. Contemporary. This Art Deco bistro is warm and elegant with lots of polished wood, tiled floors, and potted palms. The fire-roasted rosemary chicken and southwestern vegetarian chile are standout dishes. Cozy up with a cappuccino and the chocolate fondue or the apple tart for dessert. | 30 Oak St. | 201/444–3700 | fax 201/444–9414 | $7–$15 | AE, D, DC, MC, V.

Village Green Café. Contemporary. A black and white checkered floor and various works of art on the walls highlight this small dining room. Braised New Zealand Lamb Shank, roasted free range chicken, and seafood selections with original sauces and presentations are some dinner menu selections. | 36 Prospect St. | 201/445–2914 | fax 201/251–9510 | Closed Sun. No breakfast | $9–$29 | MC, V.

RINGWOOD

MAP 9, G2

(Nearby town also listed: Ramsey)

Formerly an iron ore mining center, Ringwood today remains a hub of activity in the Ramapo Mountain area, a still-pastoral part of the state. Many Bergen County residents migrate to this Passaic County oasis for more space and lower taxes (not to mention a few bears). You'll find good restaurants, strip malls, big houses, and lots of parkland. Ringwood is home not only to the state park and botanical gardens, but to the very active Weis Ecology Center, a less-crowded summer alternative with good picnic facilities and hiking.

Information: **Ringwood Chamber of Commerce** | Box 62, Ringwood, 07456 | 973/835–7998 | fax 973/728–7971 | www.ringwoodchamber.com.

Attractions

Ringwood State Park. The 5,237-acre park includes hiking trails, streams, picnic areas, as well as Ringwood Manor, the state's botanical gardens, Shepherd Lake, and Norvin Green Forest. | 1304 Sloatsburg Rd. | 973/962–7031 | www.state.nj.us/dep/forestry/divhome.htm | Free; parking $5 weekdays, $7 weekends and Memorial Day–Labor Day | Daily.

Long Pond Ironworks State Park. You can hunt, fish, or bird-watch in this park, located within a formerly prosperous ironworking community. There's also boating and cross-country skiing. | Ringwood State Park, 1304 Sloatsburg Rd. | 973/962–7031 | Free; parking $5 weekdays, $7 weekends and Memorial Day–Labor Day | Daily.

Dedicated in 1984, the **NJ Botanical Gardens at Skylands** are the state's official gardens, and were originally laid out by Frederick Law Olmsted, of Central Park fame. Although operating on a limited budget, the 96 acres of gardens—from formal to wild and boggy—are a wonderful place to spend an afternoon. Skylands Manor, the gorgeous stone mansion on the property, is only open on special dates, and it's unfurnished. Ranger-led hikes and botanical walks, along with occasional plant sales, are held on weekends. | Morris Rd. | 973/962–7031 or 973/962–7527 | Free | Daily 8–4:30.

Ringwood Manor. The former home of both ironmaster Robert Erskine and ironmaster Abram S. Hewitt (of the Cooper Hewitt Museum in Manhattan), the manor house is restored, furnished with many of Hewitt's classy and unusual finds, and open for tours. It is also used for art exhibits and special events. Erskine is buried at the little cemetery on the property, and some say his ghost still walks the place. | Morris Rd. | 973/962–7031 or 973/962–7527 | Free | Daily 8–8.

Weis Ecology Center. This privately owned, 160-acre nonprofit preserve and environmental education center has hiking, picnic facilities, educational walks, and special programs. | 150 Snake Den Rd. | 973/835–2160 | Free | Wed.–Sun. 8:30–4:30.

ON THE CALENDAR

JUNE–JULY: *Annual Photography Competition.* All photographers are invited to participate in this annual event. Juried works hang in the Barn Gallery at Ringwood Manor State Park. | Sloatsburg Rd. | 201/251–8598.

DEC.: *Skylands Manor Holiday Open House.* The beautiful stone manor in the botanical gardens is open to the public. | 973/962–9534.

Dining

Skyline Diner. Continental. This is a classic road-trip stop. The food is good and so are the prices. Grab a booth for a quick lunch and a bottomless cup of coffee. | 16 Greenwood Lake Tpk., | 973/831–5777 | $5–$10 | AE, V.

RIVER EDGE

(Nearby towns also listed: Hackensack, Paterson)

River Edge, like many Bergen County towns, is a small bedroom community just a few miles from the Big Apple. However, the town sets itself apart from the rest with its unique collection of historical sites, fine restaurants and an active cultural center. There aren't any lodgings here, but there are dozens of hotels in nearby Paramus.

Information: River Edge Chamber of Commerce | 705 Kinderkimack Road | 201/576–9400 | fax 201/894–4474.

Attractions

The Steuben House. Named for a Prussian-born hero of the American Revolution, this restored sandstone mansion dates back to 1713. Opened as a museum in 1939, it showcases collections of the Bergen County Historical Society such as "Betsy Coxe," a beeswax girl touted as the oldest doll in America. The home is furnished with a rare collection of authentic Bergen Dutch decorations. | 1209 Main St. | 201/343–9492 or 201/487–1739 | www.carrol.com/bchs | Free | Wed.–Sat. 10–5 PM, Sund. 2–5 PM.

Campbell-Christie House. This historic Colonial was moved from New Milford to River Edge in 1977, and renovated shortly afterwards. The tavern has been restored to its former glory, and features a kitchen with a working open hearth. | 1209 Main St. | 210/343–9492 | www.carrol.com/bchs | Free | Second Sun. of each month.

River Edge Cultural Center. As the home base of Bergen County's active artists community, the cultural center sponsors varying exhibits during the year. The center also hosts free shows year-round, which vary from art shows to performances of theater, music, dance and film. | 201 Continental Ave. | 201/634–0158 | recultural@juno.com | Free. Events Free as well | Mon., Wed. and Sat. 2–4 p.m.

Van Saun Park. This 140-acre park is a popular outing spot for parents with young kids. There's a duck pond, pony rides, a newly installed carousel and a miniature train that circles the Bergen County Zoological Park, which is also housed here. For adults, there is a 12-court tennis center and a four acre pond that's perfect for fishing and ice skating. | Forest and Continental Avenue (half the park is in Paramus, the other half is in River Edge) | 201/646–2680 or 201/262–3771 (zoo) | fax 201/986–1788 | Free to the park. $1–$2 for Zoo during the summer on Friday, Saturday, Sunday and holidays. Nominal charge for train and merry go round | Daily. Dawn to dust. Zoo opened daily from 10–4:30 PM.

ON THE CALENDAR

JULY: *Fourth of July Celebration.* Locals describe this huge parade and fair as River Edge's annual "homecoming" party. The early morning parade marches through town, and then heads over to Veteran's Memorial Park, where there are activities for kids and a town-wide bake sale. After the last brownie has been devoured, the night's topped off with a huge fireworks display. | 201/576–9400.

DEC.: *Jersey Dutch Christmas Concerts.* Take an evening tour through River Edge's historic collection of homes while being serenaded by musicians playing 18th century holiday music. | 201/343–9492.

Dining

Fuki Sushi. Japanese. The decor here is low-key and traditional Japanese, but the sushi is anything but. The two full-time sushi chefs will make you anything you want, and it's all delicious and fresh. The house specialty (named after the town's main street) Kinderkamack Roll consists of a spicy salmon inside with yellow tail on top. | 828 Kinderkamack Rd. | 201/225–0160 | Sat. and Sun. closed for lunch | $20–$25 | AE, MC, V.

Dinallo's. Italian. English pub meets Italian café at this popular dinner spot. Local families come for the family-style Sunday night dinner: a mix of all-you-can-eat pasta with meats such as bracciole, sausage, meatballs pork ribs, and spare ribs mixed in. | 259 Johnson Ave. | 201/342–1233 | fax 201/342–7214 | Required on the weekends | $13–$25 | AE, D, MC, V.

Sanduccis Restaurant. Italian. Family photos of the owners' Italian relatives back "in the old country" line the walls of this casual eatery. Checkered table clothes adorn the tables, and they've recently built a mosaic-tiled bread and biscotti bar that serves expresso and cappuccino in the main dining area. Their bread and biscotti cookies are all homemade, baked on premises and available for purchase. Try the gourmet pizzas. | 570 Kinderkamack Rd. | 201/599–0600 | www.sanduccis.com | $8–$16 | AE, D, MC, V.

Lodging

Ramada Inn. Easily accessible from the Garden State Pkwy., Rte. 80, and Rte. 17, this Ramada, 2 ½ mi outside of River Edge, is also only about 15 mi from midtown Manhattan. Restaurant. Cable TV. Pool. Exercise equipment. Laundry facilities. Business services. No pets. | 375 W. Passaic St., Rochelle Park | 201/845–3400 | fax 201/845–0412 | 173 rooms | 60 rooms | $169–$179 | AE, D, DC, MC, V.

RUMSON

MAP 9, H5

(Nearby towns also listed: Red Bank, Long Branch)

One of the most upscale and exclusive communities in Jersey's shore area, Rumson was recently dubbed by Money Magazine as the third best place to live in the United States. The city is mostly a bedroom community where mansions dot the tree-lined streets. Residents of the area include Connie Chung and Bruce Springsteen, to name a few.

Information: **Borough Hall** | 80 East River Rd., Rumson, 07760 | 732/842–3300 | www.rumsonboro.com.

Attractions

Rumson Road or River Road. If you love looking at stately mansions and million dollar estates, you'll enjoy driving through Rumson's main thoroughfares, Rumson Road or River Road. The houses are extraordinary and most of them are visible from the road. **Information:** Borough Hall | 80 East River Rd., Rumson, | 732/842–3300 | www.rumsonboro.com.

ON THE CALENDAR

MAY: *Rumson Run.* Everyone in town comes out to run or cheer in this annual 5k race for charity. | 732/842–3300.

DEC.: *House Tour.* Get a sneak peak inside five privately owned mansions and estates in the Rumson area. Tickets aren't cheap—it's for charity—but if you enjoy looking at how the "other half" lives, you won't be disappointed. | 732/224–6970.

Dining

Fromagerie. French. With its elegant French sconces, tapestry-upholstered chairs, and crystal candelabras, this restaurant feels like a mini-Versailles. Fromagerie, which means "cheese shop" in French, is known across the Tri-state area as one of the premiere French restaurants on the East Coast. The food is delicious, and the service is seamless. The specialty is a Dijon mustard-crusted Colorado rack of lamb. For an appetizer, try the foie gras with roasted Black Mission figs. | 26 Ridge Rd. | 732/842–8088 | www.fromagerierestaurant.com | Reservations essential | Jacket required | No lunch Sun. | $24–$37 | AE, D, MC, V.

Raven & the Peach. Continental. The owner's a Casablanca fan and it shows in this art deco eatery, painted in light blue with palm trees and ceiling fans everywhere. It attracts a young, hip crowd and there's entertainment on weekends. The menu is innovative; a signature house dish is wasabi crusted sea bass. Located in Fair Haven, it's less than a mile from Rumson. | 740 River Rd., Fair Haven | 732/747–5494 | fax 732/747–3633 | Closed for lunch on weekdays | $26–$31 | AE, MC, V.

What's Your Beef. Steak. Diners place their orders at a glass "meat counter," at this 32-year-old steak house, by picking out the size and cut of beef they'd like, and telling the chef how long to cook it. Antiques and World War II posters decorate the walls, and there is also some fish, chicken and pasta on the menu. | 21 West River Rd. | 732/842–6205 | Closed for lunch | $11–$27 | AE.

RUTHERFORD

MAP 4, D6

(Nearby towns also listed: Clifton, East Rutherford, Hackensack, Lyndhurst, Secaucus)

A pleasant and notably affordable Bergen County town just off Route 17, Rutherford has a varied downtown area with specialty shops along Park Avenue. Rutherford is home to the Meadowlands Museum and the Meadowlands William Carlos Williams Center for the Arts, whose schedule includes movies, children's theater productions, concerts, and ballet. Rutherford is also a stone's throw from the Meadowlands Sports Complex in East Rutherford. Note that Rutherford is a "dry" town and many restaurants here are of the bring-your-own variety.

Information: **Rutherford Chamber of Commerce** | Box 216, Rutherford, 07070 | 201/933–5230 | www.rutherfordi.com/. **Meadowlands Regional Chamber of Commerce** | Meadows Office Complex, 201 Rte. 17 N, Rutherford, 07070 | 201/939–0707 | fax 201/939–0522 | www.meadowlands.org.

Attractions

Meadowlands Center for the Arts. Movies, concerts, exhibitions, demonstrations, and all manner of performances take place at this venue throughout the year. There is also a gallery with rotating displays and a Japanese restaurant on the premises. | One Williams Pl, Rutherford | 201/939–6969 | Variable.

Meadowlands Museum. Set in a Dutch-American house, exhibits chronicle local history and arts at this museum. Antique toys, pre-electric kitchenware, and colonial homecrafts are also on display. | 91 Crane Ave. | 201/935–1175 | Donations suggested | Mon., Wed., Fri. 1–4, Sun. 2–4.

ON THE CALENDAR
APR.: *Rutherford House Tour.* Tour local homes of cultural and architectural significance. | 201/939–7483.

Dining

Cafe Matisse. Contemporary. A motley collection of colorful artwork and floral patterns contrast the simple blue and white chairs and tablecloths at this small bistro. Peppered tuna loin with toasted sesame crusted scallops and noisettes of lamb on a zucchini pancake are typical of the ever changing menu. You can order a la carte or prix fixe. | 167 Park Ave. | 201/935–2995 | www.cafematisse.com | Closed Mon. and Tue. No breakfast. No lunch | $57, 3–course prix–fixe; $35 per entree | AE.

Lodging

Rutherford-Meadowlands Extended Stay America. This business efficiency hotel is 1 mi off Exit 16-W on the NJ Turnpike and 22 mi north of Newark International Airport. In-room data ports, kitchenettes, refrigerators, cable TV, Exercise room. Laundry facilities. Business services. No pets. | 2300 Rte. 4 W | 201/635–0266 or 800/EXT–STAY | fax 201/635–0267 | www.extstay.com | 60 rooms | $114 | AE, DC, MC, V.

SADDLE BROOK

MAP 4, D5

(Nearby towns also listed: Clifton, Hackensack, Paramus, Paterson, Teaneck)

This Bergen County town covers an area of 2.69 mi and has a population of about 13,296. The town is composed of a comfortable mix of residences, with relatively affordable prices, and businesses that make Saddlebrook a convenient stopping-off point along Interstate 80.

Information: **Gateway Regional Tourism Council** | Box 602, Little Ferry, 07643 | 201/436–6009.

Dining

GoodFellas. Italian. This family-owned Italian restaurant, about 2 mi from the center of Saddle Brook, serves exceptional food in a romantic dining room with hand-painted walls, cherry wainscoting, and lace window panels. Try the Farfalle del Pacifico, a bow-tie pasta dish in a light garlic sauce with rock shrimp, asparagus, chopped tomato, and basil. Saddle Brook is 10 minutes away. | 661 Midland Ave.,Garfield | 973/478–4000 | fax 973/478–0506 | $12–$24 | AE, MC, V.

Villa Nicastro. Italian. Roasted chicken, stuffed shrimp, and veal piccata are some of the specialties of this family-owned and family-friendly spot. Kids' menu. The restaurant is 15 minutes from Saddle Brook. | 15 Terhune Ave.,Lodi | 973/777–6800 | fax 973/777–7701 | Closed Sun. | $9–$16. | AE, V.

Lodging

Holiday Inn. Rooms here all have executive work areas. The hotel is 2 mi from the Garden State Plaza Mall and 5 mi from Teterboro Airport. Restaurant, bar. In-room data ports, cable TV. Pool. Exercise equipment. Business services. | 50 Kenney Pl. | 201/843–0600 | fax 201/843–2822 | www.holiday-inn.com | 146 rooms | $109–$169 | AE, D, DC, MC, V.

Marriott. This hotel is in a commercial area on an intersection of two major highways, about 25 mi from Newark International Airport and 10 mi from the George Washington Bridge. Built in 1965, it was renovated in 1999. Restaurant, bar. Cable TV. 2 pools. Hot tub. Exercise equipment. Business services. | I-80 and Garden State Pkwy. | 201/843–9500 | fax 201/843–7760 | 245 rooms | $89–$199 | AE, D, DC, MC, V.

Ramada Hotel. Built in 1974 and renovated in 2000, this five-story hotel is in a suburban area about five minutes from the Garden State Plaza Mall. It's also convenient to Paramus shopping. It's in Rochelle Park, about ½ mi from Saddle Brook. Restaurant, bar (with entertainment), room service. Cable TV. Pool. Exercise equipment. Laundry facilities. Business services. | 375 W. Passaic St.,Rochelle Park | 201/845–3400 | fax 201/845–0412 | 173 rooms | $99–$169 | AE, D, DC, MC, V.

Saddle Brook Howard Johnson-Plaza Hotel. Renovated in 1995, this Howard Johnson is 12 mi from New York City and 7 mi from the Meadowlands Sports Complex. Restaurant, bar, room service. Cable TV. Pool. Beauty salon, hot tub. Exercise room. Laundry service. No pets. | 129 Pehle Ave. | 201/845–7800 or 800/406–1411 | fax 201/845–7061 | 141 rooms | $69–$109 | AE, D, DC, MC, V.

SALEM

(Nearby town also listed: Bridgeton)

Salem was founded in the late 1600s, and limited modern-day intrusions have helped preserve the beauty of the town's colonial and Victorian period houses. Salem's port also still remains a gateway to the Northeast and beyond. The Salem County Historical Society operates a museum and four interconnected 18th-century historic buildings, with period furniture, fine and decorative arts, antique vehicles, and rare New Jersey glassware.

Information: Salem County Chamber of Commerce | 91A S. Virginia Ave., Carneys Point, 08069 | 856/299–6699 | fax 856/299–0299 | www.salemnjchamber.com. **Salem County Dept. of Economic Development** | 978 Market St., Salem, 08079 | 856/935–7510, ext. 8532. | fax 856/935–8596.

Attractions

Fort Mott State Park. This peaceful, 104-acre park on the Delaware River (about 5 mi north of Salem) contains the remainder of an elaborate 19th-century river defense system. You can walk along the 750-ft concrete parapet and imagine the cannon and gun emplacements. A small visitor center offers information and exhibits on the history of the fort and other sites in the area that are linked by the New Jersey Coastal Heritage Trail. Just outside the park is the odd, black Finn's Point Lighthouse, made of wrought iron and dating from 1876. | 454 Ft. Mott Rd., Pennsville | 856/935–3218 | Free | Daily.

Salem County Historical Society Museum and Library. An 18th-century house showcases Salem county history. | 79–83 Market St. | 856/935–5004 | www.salemcounty.com/schs/index.html | $3 | Tues.–Fri. and 2nd Sat. of each month noon–4, Sun. noon–3:30.

Salem Oak. This 425-year-old white oak tree, also known as the Centennial Oak, is 61 ft tall and 21½ ft in circumference. Salem lore has it that John Fenwick treatied with Native Americans beneath its branches upon his arrival here in 1675. The oak is so important to the community that each branch and acorn that falls from it is gathered and preserved. | First Presbyterian Church's cemetery, Grant St. | Free.

ON THE CALENDAR

MAY: *Salem County House and Garden Tour.* Tour homes, gardens, and historic sites in Mannington, Pilesgrove, and Woodstown, illustrating three centuries of architecture in Salem County. | 856/935–5004.

Dining

Welcome Chinese Restaurant. Chinese. Stop here for great spring rolls and chicken lo mein. Fast, friendly service and reliably good food keeps locals coming back. Takeout is available. | 163 W. Broadway | 856/935–1137 | $7–$16 | AE, V.

Lodging

Brown's Historic Home Bed & Breakfast. This 1738 house has King of Prussia marble fireplaces and a lovely backyard with a waterfall and lily pond. Complimentary breakfast. Cable

TV. Pets allowed. | 41-43 Market St. | 609/935–8595 | fax 609/935–8595 | 3 rooms | $55–$100 | AE, D, MC, V.

SANDY HOOK

(Nearby town also listed: Red Bank)

Across the Shrewsbury River, north of Highlands, is a 6-mi spit of land that boasts a strategic location at the mouth of New York Harbor, as well as beautiful beaches and holly forests. In addition, its location along the Atlantic Flyway has allowed for 300 species of birds to be identified here. You can learn about both Sandy Hook's military and navigational importance at the Gateway National Recreation Area, which has a lighthouse and a fort. Most inns and eateries are actually in Highlands, right next door.

Information: Gateway Regional Tourism Council | Box 602, Little Ferry, 07643 | 201/641–7632.

Attractions

Fort Hancock. This fort was established in 1895 as a defense for New York Harbor. The museum, in the former post guardhouse, has a bookstore and exhibits. History House is a restored 1898 lieutenant's residence on "Officers Row" overlooking Sandy Hook Bay; its exhibits offer a glimpse into the daily life of personnel at Fort Hancock. Visitors can also see Battery Potter, the oldest gun battery at the site. | Gateway National Recreation Area, Sandy Hook Unit | 732/872–5970 | Free | Weekends 1–5.

Fort Hancock Post Theater. This former movie theater for the fort community now offers theatrical productions. Proceeds go toward the theater's restoration. | Hartshorne Rd., Building 67 Z | 732/291–7733 | Weekends 1–5.

Sandy Hook Lighthouse. This is America's oldest lighthouse, and ownership was transferred from the Coast Guard to the National Park Service in 1996. | Gateway National Recreation Area: Fort Hancock | 732/872–5970 | www.njlhs.burlco.org/sandyhk.htm | Free | Call for tour hrs.

Twin Lights State Historic Site. These "twin" brownstone light towers, built in 1862 to mark the western entrance to New York Harbor, are 64 ft high and 320 ft apart, connected by an 18-room brownstone keeper's and crew dwelling. The north tower was taken out of service in 1898, but was kept ready as an emergency light. The north tower is open to the public, and on display is the original Fresnel lens. Twin Lights was the first to use these lenses in America, and also the first to use electricity. The extensive lighthouse museum also has information on the U.S. Lifesaving Service. | Lighthouse Rd., Highlands | 732/872–1814 | www.njlhs.burlco.org/twinlights.htm | Free | Memorial Day–Labor Day, daily 10–5; Labor Day–Memorial Day, Wed.–Sun. 10–5.

ON THE CALENDAR

APR., OCT: *Clean Ocean Action's Annual Spring Beach Sweeps.* A brunch, themed entertainment, and a fashion show in Sandy Hook National Park support protection of the ocean. There's one in April and one in October. | 732/872–0111.

JUNE: *Highlands Chamber of Commerce Clam Festival.* This festival, which includes clams, other seafood, music, a carnival, fireworks, tall ships, and lighthouse tours, is across the river (less than 1 mi away) in Highlands. | 732/872–1224.

JUNE–AUG.: *Sandy Hook Beach Concert Series.* Listen to a different band every week at this Wednesday-evening beach concert series, sponsored by the Sandy Hook Foundation and National Park Service. Music ranges from reggae to Irish to rock and others. Concerts are free, and start at 6 PM. | 732/872–5970.

Dining

Bahrs Landing. Seafood. This casual waterfront spot, about 2 mi south of Sandy Hook, is known for fresh seafood. The decor is nothing special, but try the seared salmon topped with shrimp over sautéed spinach, or the fisherman's platter. Kids' menu. | 2 Bay Ave., Highlands | 732/872–1245 | Reservations not accepted | $22–$42 | AE, D, DC, MC, V.

Careless Navigator. Seafood. This lively spot has great seafood, live music and dancing, water views, and outdoor patio dining. They also have a kids' menu, a popular Sunday brunch, and a late-night menu. Try the whole lobster or the stuffed flounder, and wash it down with their 20-ounce Bloody Mary. | 1 S. Bay Ave., Highlands | 732/872–1616 | $10–$16 | AE, D, DC, MC, V.

Doris and Ed's. Seafood. This top-rated shore restaurant, about 2 mi north of Sandy Hook, is in a 100-year-old hotel which looks out over the bay. Try the poached Atlantic salmon in a Champagne mussel stew, the grilled tuna with ginger scallion, or the red scamper with rock shrimp. Kids' menu. | 348 Shore Dr., Highlands | 732/872–1565 | www.doris-and-eds.com | Closed Mon., Tues. and Jan.–Feb. No lunch | $21–$33 | AE, DC, MC, V.

Lodging

Water Witch House. This small, charming, redbrick inn, named after the James Fenimore Cooper novel, was built in 1910 as a summer cottage. It sits in the Highland Hills overlooking the town and the Sandy Hook and Raritan bays. Guest rooms are furnished with antiques and have water views. It borders Sandy Hook. Complimentary breakfast. Refrigerators. No smoking. | 254 Navesink Ave., Highlands | 732/708–1900 | www.water-witch-house.com | 3 rooms, 1 suite | $129–$259 | No credit cards.

SEA ISLE CITY

MAP 9, E11

(Nearby towns also listed: Cape May Court House, Stone Harbor)

This small, private island is entirely surrounded by water and is connected to the mainland by bridge. Primarily a summer beach community, it offers abundant water

KODAK'S TIPS FOR PHOTOGRAPHING WEATHER

Rainbows
- Find rainbows by facing away from the sun after a storm
- Use your auto-exposure mode
- With an SLR, use a polarizing filter to deepen colors

Fog and Mist
- Use bold shapes as focal points
- Add extra exposure manually or use exposure compensation
- Choose long lenses to heighten fog and mist effects

In the Rain
- Look for abstract designs in puddles and wet pavement
- Control rain-streaking with shutter speed
- Protect cameras with plastic bags or waterproof housings

Lightning
- Photograph from a safe location
- In daylight, expose for existing light
- At night, leave the shutter open during several flashes

From Kodak Guide to Shooting Great Travel Pictures © 2000 by Fodor's Travel Publications

sports, fishing, recreation, free concerts and a family oriented nightlife, with most events taking place on the boardwalk. As far as accommodations go, they have mostly private rental units – so make sure you have a reservation somewhere before you make the trip down. Sea Isle City is also known for campgrounds, which are close to the beach. If you go in the off-season, things are cheaper, but fewer attractions are open.

Information: **Sea Isle City Tourism Development Commission** | Box 622, 08243 | 609/263–TOUR 8687, 609/263–6110 | www.seaislecity.org.

Attractions

The Beach. Sea Isle City has 7 mi of as unspoiled-as-you-can-get-in-New Jersey beaches, and an asphalt boardwalk that is easy to walk, rollerblade, bike or push a baby stroller across. There's a small amusement park geared for kids here called "Fun City," and a variety of food and gift shops. | Kennedy Blvd. and the Promenade | 609/263–TOUR | fax 609/263–6110 | www.seaislecity.org | $4 | Open year-round.

Play By The Bay. Built by locals, this huge Habitrail of a playground is guaranteed to please kids of all ages. For parents who hate losing sight of their kids "in the tubes," they've built an elevated observation center, which also offers a great view of the ocean and the bay. | 60th and Central Ave., in Dealy Field | 609/263–TOUR | fax 609/263–6110 | www.seaislecity.org | Free | Year-round.

ON THE CALENDAR

FEB.: *Polar Bear Plunge.* Volunteers (many of them senior citizens) don bathing suits and agree to take a brief plunge in the Ocean – which hoovers just about the freezing point at this time of year– to help raise money for charity. | 609/263–TOUR.

JUNE: *Skimmer Weekend.* This three-day "welcome back summer" celebration has Dixieland music, a dance party on the promenade, pony rides and other special events for kids. | 609/263–TOUR.

JUNE/JULY/AUG.: *Free Concerts Under The Stars.* These popular free concerts are held on the boardwalk, Monday and Wednesday evenings in mid-June–Aug. from 7:30-9 p.m. Artists vary between country, big bands, and contemporary rock bands. In addition, every Thursday evening, the town sponsors a dance party for the entire family on the promenade. | 609/263–TOUR.

JULY: *Sara the Turtle Festival.* Over 5,000 people (and growing yearly) show up at this unique festival, created to promote awareness about endangered turtles. There are free puppet shows, coloring books and a live turtle exhibit with snappers from around the world. There's a diaper derby race for kids who crawl, and "turtle" races for toddlers and young kids. | 609/263–TOUR.

SEPT.: *Fall Family Festival.* This weekend event is considered the largest seaside festival on the Jersey coast. There's live music, dancing and over 350 vendors hawking their goods at the weekend-long flea market and crafts fair. There's also an Antique Auto Show, free guided trolley tours, and a sand sculpting contest. The festivities are topped off by a fireworks display over the water. | 609/263–TOUR.

Dining

Busch's Seafood Restaurant. Seafood. Operating since 1882, this is probably the most popular eatery on Sea Isle City. On Tuesdays and Sundays, try the famous "she" crab soup. They don't take reservations for small parties, but with three dining rooms and two full service bars, the wait's never too long. There's live music in the lounge on weekends. | 8700 Lands Avenue | 609/263–2626 | bushesseafood@technology21.com | www.bushesseafood.com | Closed Mon. | $16–$25 | AE, MC, V.

Carmen's Seafood Restaurant. The food here is incredibly fresh, and the house specialty, the Ala' Carmen Deluxe, contains just about every kind of shellfish there is. The service is friendly, and the casual, open air surroundings are comfortable and relaxing. | 343 43rd

Place | 609/263–4300 | Apr–Oct. Summer from 8 AM to 10 PM Fall 5 PM -10 PM | $15–$25 | No credit cards, ATM inside.

Deauville. Continental. Located right on the water, Deauville features outside dock-side dining, as well as indoor seating. It's just a short mile or two drive from Sea Isle City and there's entertainment on summer weekends. The food is adequate, but the atmosphere is truly relaxing. Locals come for the she-crab soup—made with jumbo crab meat in a cream sauce—or the flounder, also stuffed with crabmeat. You can get their crab cakes broiled or fried. | 201 Willard Rd., Strathmere | 609/263–2080 | fax 609/391–1327 | deauville3@aol.com | www.deauville.com | Oct.–Mar. closed Tues. and Wed. | $12–$35 | AE, MC, V.

Lodging
The Colonnade Inn. Every room here is unique, and filled with antiques and charming, hand-picked Victorian items. The staff serves afternoon tea and lemonade in summer. Complimentary breakfast. In-room data ports, in-room safes, kitchenettes, microwaves, refrigerators, hot tubs, cable TV, VCRs. Massage. Beach. Business services. | 4600 Landis Ave. | 609/263–0460 | ecavella@collonadeinn.com | www.colonnadeinn.com | 24 (mix of rooms, suites and apartments) | $88–$250 | MC, V.

La Costa Motel. One block from the ocean, this touristy spot is bustling in the summer, so get reservations early. There are no ocean views from the rooms. Atlantic City casinos are about 18 mi north. There's a nice lounge area, and a pool bar, as well as a restaurant on the premises. Restaurant, bar. Kitchenettes, microwaves, refrigerators, cable TV. Pool. No pets. No smoking. | 4000 Landis Ave. | 609/263–1111 | 33 rooms | $135–$150 | DC, MC, V | Closed weekdays from Oct.–Mar.

Sea Isle Inn. A short walk from the beach, most of the accomodations in this friendly motel are suites or efficiencies. The hotel doesn't have many amenities, but it's roomy and conveniently near attractions, nightlife and dining. Prices drop drastically in the off-season. Cable TV. Outdoor pool. Tennis. Beach, dock. Playground. No pets. | 6400 Landis Ave. | 609/263–4371 | seaisleinn@aol.com | www.eisolutions.com/seaisleinn | 53 rooms | $96–$174 | DC, MC, V.

SEASIDE HEIGHTS

MAP 9, H7

(Nearby towns also listed: Point Pleasant, Seaside Park, Toms River)

One of the shore's major amusement boardwalks is here, with tons of food concessions and rides ranging from tame carousels to the harrowing Sling Shot. Coolers of 32-quart capacity and less are permitted but are subject to inspection, as alcohol is not permitted on the beach.

Information: Borough of Seaside Heights | Box 38, 901 Boulevard, Seaside Heights, 08751 | 732/793–9100 or 800/SEA–SHOR | www.seaside-heights.nj.org | seasideheights@injersey.com.

Attractions
Seaside Heights Beach and Boardwalk. This 1½-mi stretch of beach boasts New Jersey's only beach sky ride, along with lots of arcades and amusement rides, an antique carousel, miniature golf, and food. | 800/SEASHOR | Apr.–Oct. daily 10 AM–11 PM.

ON THE CALENDAR
MAR.: *Annual St. Patrick's' Day Parade.* Join in this celebration of all things Irish. | 800/SEA–SHOR.
AUG.: *Crab Races and Seafood Festival.* Come down and buy a crab, then race it. | 732/349–0220.

SEPT.: *Annual Clownfest.* Armies of clowns converge on the town for some serious clowning around at this three-day festival. | 732/349–0220.

Dining

Heights Diner. Casual. This classic diner is off the Seaside Heights Boardwalk—great for people-watching as you enjoy a burger and fries. Superthick milk shakes dare you to drink them with a straw. | 14 Ocean Terr. | 732/830–3900 | $5–$13 | AE, V.

Lodging

Boardwalk Sea Gull Motel. Formerly the Sunset motel, this small family-friendly board-walk-side establishment is convenient to all the Seaside Heights arcades and casinos, as well as the state's only beach sky ride. Restaurant. Some microwaves, refrigerators, cable TV. No pets. | 1119 Ocean Terr. | 732/793–1735 | 11 rooms | $90–$144 | Closed mid-Sept.–Memorial Day | No credit cards.

SEASIDE PARK

MAP 9, H7

(Nearby towns also listed: Seaside Heights, Toms River)

The quieter southern neighbor of Seaside Heights, Seaside Park has the Funtown Pier and boardwalk in the north section. The pier has both kiddie rides and grown-up attractions, including mini–Formula 1 racers. You'll find nearly 2 mi of beach area protected by dunes, ideal for a relaxing and peaceful day. Seaside Park is home to the beautiful Island Beach State Park.

Information: Shore Region Tourism Council | Box 1162, Toms River, 08754 | 732/244–9283.

Attractions

★ **Island Beach State Park.** This picturesque, 10-mi strip of sand dunes from Seaside Park to Barnegat Inlet is home to a local population of red foxes. The Forked River Coast Guard Station Interpretive Center has an herbarium with more than 100 pressed specimens of barrier beach plant life. The former Life Saving Station 14 is one of a series that was manned by "surfmen" credited with saving many shipwreck victims. Five self-guided nature trails, blazed in 1998, feature exhibits highlighting the flora and the fauna of the park. Arrive early in the morning in summer. | 732/793–0506 | Free; parking $6 weekdays, $7 weekends and holidays Memorial Day–Labor Day, $4 daily rest of the year | Daily.

Seaside Park Boardwalk. This stretch of boardwalk has an amusement pier (Funtown Pier), gazebos, games, and food. | Porter Ave. and Boardwalk | 732/914–0100 | Free.

ON THE CALENDAR

SEPT.: *Island Beach State Park Beach–Plum Festival.* This festival has a juried craft show, live entertainment, children's activities, exhibits, canoe tours, and nature hikes. | 732/793–5525.

Dining

Bum Roger's Tavern & Restaurant. Seafood. Head to this casual beachy watering hole in Island Beach State Park for lobsters, burgers, and beer. Try the Baltimore-style hot and spicy crabs. | 23rd and Central Ave., S. Seaside Park, | 732/830–2770 | $11–$21 | AE, V.

Lodging

Belvedere Motel. This two-story park-in-front-of-your-room motel is one block from the beach and half a mile from Island Beach State Park. It is clean, nicely furnished, and has no phones in the rooms, leaving plenty of time for Seaside Park's popular summer pastime—fishing. Ask at the front desk for a good place to buy bait, and wait for the striped bass to bite. Some kitchenettes, refrigerators, cable TV, no room phones. | 1209 S.W. Central Ave. | 732/793–7373 | fax 732/793–1533 | 23 rooms | $75–$105 | MC, V.

Island Beach Motor Lodge. Located on a private beach, this 1970 building has standard motel rooms, efficiency suites, and penthouses. Some of the rooms are oceanfront. Some kitchenettes, refrigerators, cable TV. Pool, wading pool. Laundry facilities. | 24th St. and Central Ave. | 732/793–5400 | 76 rooms | $97–$205 | D, MC, V.

Windjammer. You'll find basic amenities here, about a mile from the hustle and bustle of the beach. You can rent a standard hotel room or a 2½-room "apartment." Restaurant, bar. Some kitchenettes, cable TV. Pool. Laundry facilities. | 1st Ave. and Central Ave. | 732/830–2555 | 63 rooms | $95–$130 | AE, MC, V.

SECAUCUS

MAP 4, D6

(Nearby towns also listed: East Rutherford, Lyndhurst, Rutherford)

Plenty of copy-cat mall outlets have sprung up around the country, but Secaucus is home to the original, now boasting more than 140 stores lining the streets of Meadowlands Pkwy. (exit off Rte. 3). It's not much in the way of charm, but it's rich with sales and great finds, made even sweeter by New Jersey's lack of sales tax on clothing. Foreigners arrange entire trips around a visit to the outlets, which sell everything from Searle coats to Samsonite products. Secaucus is also home to high-rise apartments, corporate headquarters, big hotels, and movie theaters.

Information: Town of Secaucus | Municipal Government Center, 1203 Paterson Plank Rd., Secaucus, 07094 | 201/330–2066. **Gateway Regional Tourism Council** | Box 602, Little Ferry, 07643 | 201/436–6009. **Hudson County Chamber of Commerce** | 253 Washington St., Jersey City, 07302-3809 | 201/435–7400 | www.hudsonchamber.org.

Attractions

Harmon Cove Outlet Center. One of the enclosed malls in the Meadowlands outlet complex, residents from surrounding states come to the 60 outlets to purchase clothing with no sales tax assessment. | 20 Enterprise Dr. | 201/348–4780 | Free | Mon.–Wed. 10–6, Thurs. 10–8, Fri. and Sat. 10–7, Sun. 11–6.

Meadowlands Exposition Center. Numerous trade, consumer and corporate shows, as well as other special events, take place here throughout the year. | Harmon Meadow, 355 Plaza Dr. | 201/330–7773 | fax 201/330–1172.

ON THE CALENDAR
JUNE/AUG.: *The East Lynne Company theater productions.* Dedicated to the "performance and preservation of American theater," this company produces works of 19th- and early-20th-century playwrights. | 281 Lincoln Ave. | 201/863–6436.

Dining
Bareli's. Italian. This old-fashioned Italian restaurant is fancy and on the expensive side, but generally lives up to its reputation for excellence. Try the shrimp sautéed with brandy and cream, or the veal scaloppine Navona— veal with a light lemon sauce. There's piano music on Friday and Saturday, and the dining room has a fireplace. | 219 Rte. 3 E (Mill Creek Dr.) | 201/865–2766 | Jacket and tie | Closed Sun. | $15–$28 | AE, MC, V.

SECAUCUS

INTRO
ATTRACTIONS
DINING
LODGING

Herbert's. American. Herbert's has over 30 varieties of beer to go with its burgers, sandwiches, and pizza, but people really come here to play pool on one of the 24 Gold Crown III billiard tables. | 600 Plaza Dr. | 201/330–7665 | $6–$10 | AE, V.

Lantana. Italian. This elegant and pricey restaurant, with its stained-glass windows and sleek interior, is known for unique pastas and seafood dishes. Dover sole is a house specialty. | 1148 Paterson Plank Rd. (Rte. 3) | 201/867–1065 | Reservations essential | $14–$25 | AE, MC, V.

Lodging

Courtyard Secaucus Meadowlands. This seven-story hotel is 1.4 mi from the Meadowlands Sports Complex, 1½ mi from the Secaucus outlets, and 3 mi from New York City. Two public golf courses (Paramus and Overpeck) are also nearby. Restaurant, room service. In-room data ports, cable TV. Exercise room. Laundry service. Business services. No pets. | 455 Harmon Meadow Blvd. | 201/617–8888 or 800/321–2211 | fax 201/319–0035 | 165 rooms | $109–$185 | AE, MC, V.

Crowne Plaza–Meadowlands. This full-service hotel was built in 1975, and underwent a 15 million-dollar renovation in 1999. The lobby has large plants and couches. Restaurant, bar. In-room data ports, cable TV. Pool. Hot tub. Exercise equipment. Business services. | 2 Harmon Plaza | 201/348–6900 | fax 201/864–0963 | www.crowneplaza.com | 305 rooms | $139–$189 | AE, D, DC, MC, V.

Embassy Suites. This nine-story hotel geared toward business travel is close to two movie theaters, restaurants, Giants Stadium, and nonoutlet shopping at Harmon Meadow Plaza. Restaurant, bar, complimentary breakfast. In-room data ports, microwaves, refrigerators, cable TV. Pool, hot tub. Exercise equipment. Laundry facilities. Business services, airport shuttle. | 455 Plaza Dr. | 201/864–7300 | fax 201/864–5391 | www.promus.com | 261 suites | $169–$229 suites | AE, D, DC, MC, V.

Hampton Inn Secaucus Meadowlands. Located within a corporate and shopping complex in the northeastern section of Secaucus, this hotel is convenient to the New Jersey Turnpike and the Lincoln Tunnel. Complimentary Continental breakfast, room service. In-room data ports, cable TV. Exercise room. Laundry service. No pets. | 250 Harmon Meadow Blvd. | 201/867–4400 or 800/426–7866 | fax 201/865–7932 | 151 rooms | $125–$140 | AE, D, DC, V.

Holiday Inn. This hotel, in a downtown/business area, is close to the Meadowlands and about 5 mi from the New York City theater district. Restaurant, bar, room service. In-room data ports, refrigerators, cable TV. Exercise equipment. Laundry facilities. | 300 Plaza Dr. | 201/348–2000 | fax 201/348–6035 | www.basshotels.com/holiday-inn | 160 rooms | $139–$169 | AE, D, DC, MC, V.

Radisson Suite. Accommodations are two-room suites here, and the music you hear on the way could be coming from the Radisson's banquet facility, frequently the site of wedding parties and other catered events. Renovations are scheduled for 2001. Restaurant, bar. In-room data ports, minibars, refrigerators, cable TV. Pool. Exercise equipment. Laundry facilities. Business services. Some pets allowed. | 350 Rte. 3 W | 201/863–8700 | fax 201/863–6209 | www.radisson.com | 151 suites | $149–$259 | AE, D, DC, MC, V.

SHORT HILLS

MAP 4, B7

(Nearby towns also listed: Chatham, Millburn, Summit, Union)

A tony Union County enclave, Short Hills lies to the northwest of Millburn, with which it is municipally linked. Short Hills does have its own post office and railroad station, but it might be most widely known for the upscale Mall at Short Hills and the Short Hills Hilton, where even locals head for a weekend away.

Information: Millburn-Short Hills Chamber of Commerce | 343 Millburn Ave., Suite 303, Box 651, Millburn, 07041 | 973/379–1198 | fax 973/376–5678 | mshcc@millburn.com | www.millburn.com/chamber.

Attractions

Cora Hartshorn Arboretum and Bird Sanctuary. These 16 acres of undeveloped woodlands are home to hundreds of varieties of birds, wildflowers, and trees. The arboretum sponsors field trips, classes, lectures, and workshops in nature study and crafts. | 324 Forest Dr. S | 973/376–3587 | www.hartshornarboretum.com | Free | Mon., Fri. 9–3; Tues., Thurs. 9–4:30; Sat. 9:30–11:30.

The Mall at Short Hills. This New Jersey shopping oasis has upscale shops like Tiffany, Neiman Marcus, and Nordstrom. | 1200 Morris Tpk. | 973/376–7350 | Free | Daily, hrs vary seasonally.

ON THE CALENDAR

MAY: *Short Hills Spring Jewelry and Silver Sale.* Jewelry, watches, silver, and china are for sale to benefit the New Eyes for the Needy, Inc., an organization that assists visually impaired Americans. | 973/376–4903.

Dining

The Dining Room. Continental. Dine in an elegant English drawing room of the Hilton at Short Hills, the state's top hotel. This upscale eaterie is known for seasonal seafood, game, and veal. A vegetarian menu is available. Sunday brunch. | 41 John F. Kennedy Pkwy. | 973/379–0100 | Jacket required | Closed Sun. year-round and Sun.–Mon. June–mid-Sept. No lunch | $52–$72 | AE, D, DC, MC, V.

Stage House Inn. French. Known for Provence-inspired cuisine like charlotte of Maine crab and pan-roasted cod with crispy potatoes, peas, and black truffle sauce, this romantic 1737 inn has three cozy fireplaces and an outdoor patio. Short Hills is 15 minutes away. | 366 Park Ave., Scotch Plains | 908/322–4224 | www.stagehouseinn.com | Jacket required | No lunch Sun. | $30–$35 | AE, D, MC, V.

Lodging

Best Western Westfield Inn. Cook your own dinner, try the restaurant downstairs, or drive 25 mi to New York City for innumerable dining and entertainment possibilities. This two-story inn is in a suburban/residential area, 25 mi from Short Hills. Restaurant, complimentary Continental breakfast. Some kitchenettes, cable TV. Laundry facilities. Business services. | 435 North Ave. W, Westfield | 908/654–5600 | fax 908/654–6483 | 40 rooms | $130–$150 | AE, D, DC, MC, V.

★ **Hilton at Short Hills.** Less than an hour's drive from mid-Manhattan, this elegant suburban hotel offers many facilities of a fine resort. The hotel is across from the Mall at Short Hills, which is home to many of the nation's top stores. Restaurant (*see* The Dining Room, *above*), bar (with entertainment), room service. In-room data ports, some refrigerators, cable TV. 2 pools. Beauty salon, hot tub, massage. Gym. Business services. | 41 John F. Kennedy Pkwy. | 973/379–0100 | fax 973/379–6870 | www.spaatshorthills.com | 304 rooms, 37 suites | $145–$369 | AE, D, DC, MC, V.

Grand Summit Hotel. Built in 1929 and opened just a few months before the stock market crash, this hotel became home to many wealthy town residents who lost their own homes and estates. Today the Tudor-style building has vaulted beamed ceilings, rare chestnut paneling, a flagstone fireplace, and spacious, elegantly furnished rooms. It's 2.4 mi southwest of downtown Short Hills. Restaurant, room service. Pool. Exercise room. Laundry service. Business services, airport shuttle. | 570 Springfield Ave. | 908/273–3000 or 800/346–0773 | fax 908/273–4228 | www.grandsummit.com | 150 rooms | $149–$249 | AE, MC, V.

SOMERS POINT

MAP 9, F10

(Nearby towns also listed: Atlantic City, Mays Landing, Ocean City)

You'll find Somers Point just across the Ninth Street causeway from Ocean City, on the "mainland." A popular resort in the 1800s, the town today has several good seafood restaurants, as well as fine marinas and good bay fishing. Somers Point is also home to the South Jersey Regional Theater, whose season runs from October to June. The Atlantic County Historical Society has a museum of local history here.

Information: Greater Atlantic City Chamber of Commerce | 1125 Atlantic Ave., Atlantic City, 08401 | 609/345–5600 | www.atlanticcitynj.com. **Somers Point City Hall** | 1 W. New Jersey Ave., Somers Point, 08244 | 609/927–9088. ·

Attractions

Somers Mansion. Somers Mansion, built around 1725, is the oldest house in Atlantic City. It contains 18th- and 19th-century artifacts and period furniture. | 1000 Shore Rd. | 609/927–2212 | fax 609/927–1827 | Free | Wed.–Sat. 10–noon and 1–4, Sun. 1–4.

South Jersey Regional Theater. This troupe puts on major productions of dramas, musicals, and comedies throughout the year at the Gateway Playhouse. | Bay Ave. | 609/653–0553 | $10–$15 | May–Sept.; call for reservations.

Atlantic County Historical Museum. Victorian clothing, early county photos, maritime artifacts and weapons, as well as an original Edison phonograph are on display. The facility also serves as a genealogical and historical research library. | 907 Shore Rd. | 609/927–5218 | Free; $5 research fee | Wed.–Sat. 10–3:30.

ON THE CALENDAR

APR.: *Annual Jazz Festival.* Enjoy jazz at different locations within walking distance of each other, in the New Road area. | 609/927–5253.
APR.: *Somers Point Bayfest.* This annual celebration in Historic Bayfront features crafts, music, entertainment, and food. | 609/927–5653.

Dining

Crab Trap. Seafood. Known for excellent seafood, this 40-seat restaurant overlooks Great Egg Harbor Bay. Specialties include broiled clams casino, rosemary pork loin chops, crab cakes, deviled clams, and sesame-crusted tuna steak. Live music Wednesday, Friday, and Saturday. Kids' menu. | 2 Broadway | 609/927–7377 | www.thecrabtrap.com | $19–$38 | AE, D, DC, MC, V.

Hatteras Coastal Cuisine. Contemporary. An eclectic mix of dishes plus delicious homemade breads and desserts have contributed to a buzz about this place. The dining room is cool and fresh with blue tablecloths, crystal, and fresh flowers. Try the Virginia country ham, the shrimp and oyster jambalaya, or the lemongrass-seasoned fresh fish with Japanese vegetables. Enjoy ocean views all year, and eat outdoors in summer on the porch or in the covered courtyard. | 801 Bay Ave. | 609/926–3326 | fax 609/653–4595 | No lunch weekends | $7–$16 | AE, D, DC, MC, V.

Mac's. American. Enjoy casual family dining at this medieval-theme restaurant, decorated with a King Arthur mural and suits of armor. Dishes include pasta, mussels, veal, and a Seafood Shore Platter. Kids' menu. | 908 Shore Rd. | 609/927–4360 | No lunch | $15–$32 | AE, D, MC, V.

Lodging

Pier 4 on the Bay. This modern four-story hotel on the bay, about 2 mi from Ocean City, was renovated in 1999. Half the rooms have water views. Complimentary Continental breakfast. Microwaves, refrigerators, cable TV. Pool. Laundry facilities. Business services. | 6 Broadway, Somers Point | 609/927–9141 or 888/927–9141 | fax 609/653–2752 | 72 rooms, 8 suites | $49–$79 rooms; $99–$119 suites | AE, D, DC, MC, V.

Residence Inn Atlantic City-Somers Point. This 120-suite hotel is near beaches, a health club, and four golf courses. Complimentary breakfast. In-room data ports, kitchenettes, cable TV. Pool. Laundry facilities, laundry service. Business services. Pets allowed (fee). | 900 Mays Landing Rd. | 609/927–6400 or 800/331–3131 | fax 609/926–0145 | www.residenceinn.com | 120 suites | $89–$99 | AE, D, DC, MC, V.

SOMERSET

MAP 9, F5

(Nearby towns also listed: Edison, New Brunswick)

Somerset is a section of Franklin Township. The Garden State Convention and Exhibit Center is the town's main claim to fame, due to its central location, facilities, and services. There are a fair number of historic homes here, as well, that are maintained, periodically restored, and open to the public.

Information: **Franklin Township Chamber of Commerce** | 1717 Amwell Rd., Somerset, 08873 | 732/873–1717 | www.franklinchamber.org.

Attractions

Garden State Convention and Exhibit Center. Trade shows, banquets, meetings, and festivals are held throughout the year at this 62,000 square ft facility. | 50 Atrium Dr. | 732/469–4000 | fax 732/563–4500 | sales@gsec.com | www.gsec.com | Free | Daily.

The Meadows Foundation. The foundation oversees six historic properties: the Wickle House, Hageman Farm, Blackwells Mills, Van Liew-Suydam House, Wyckoff-Garretson House, and Franklin Inn. Restoration of the Wickle House included the addition of an outdoor stage, formal gardens, a canal bridge, wetland boardwalk, program center, nature trail, and youth camping site. The Wickle House is the site of many community events, including the Meadows Foundation's Candlelight Concert Series. The foundation also conducts open houses and special community events throughout the year. | 1289 Easton Ave. | 732/828–7418 | www.themeadowsfoundation.pair.com/ | Houses: special events only; Meadows Park: daily.

ON THE CALENDAR

JAN.–JUNE: *The Meadows Foundation Candlelight Concert Series.* Enjoy music in a historic colonial setting. | 732/828–1812 or 732/249–6770.

FEB., MAR.: *New Jersey Flower and Patio Show.* Wander among the exhibits, or attend some of the many seminars. There's also plenty for sale. At the Garden State Exhibit Center. | 732/469–4000.

MAY: *Sugarloaf Spring Crafts Festival.* This juried show at the Garden State Exhibit Center attracts more than 250 craftspeople. | 800/210–9900.

MAY, JUNE: *New Jersey Renaissance Festival and Kingdom.* Jousting, juggling, jesters, crafts, food, and general medieval fun make this event worthwhile. The festival is generally held on Davidson Avenue. | 732/271–1119.

JULY: *Garden State Cat Show.* The Garden State Convention Center is crawling with felines from around the country for this prestigious cat show. | 732/469–4000.

AUG.: *Antiques Weekend in Somerset.* Antiques of all kinds are for sale at this annual event at the Garden State Convention Center. | 732/469–4000.

OCT.: *Sugarloaf Fall Crafts Festival.* More than 300 artists attend this juried event at the Garden State Exhibit Center. | 800/210–9900.

DEC.: *Antique and Collectible Toy, Train, and Doll Show.* You'll see exhibitors from around the world, buying, selling, and trading at the Garden State Exhibit Center. | 718/979-4797.

DEC.: *Holiday House Tours.* Take a driving tour of area homes. | 732/249-6770.

DEC.: *Sinterklass Festival.* The Dutch Santa arrives at the Van Wickle House, on Easton Avenue, riding his white horse amid music, dancing, crafts, and historic house tours. | 732/249-6770.

Dining

Pooja Exotic Indian Cuisine. Indian. Feast on tandoori, seafood, chicken, lamb, vegetarian dishes, and biryanis, all served with chutney. The ingredients are fresh (no packaged curries or canned vegetables) and careful attention is paid to the customer's specifications for spiciness. | 1075 Easton Ave. | 908/220-0051 | No lunch Sun. | $7-$15 | AE, V.

Lodging

Doubletree Somerset Executive Meeting Center. This six-story hotel on 16 landscaped acres is adjacent to the Garden State Convention and Exhibit Center and near many Fortune 500 companies. Quailbrook golf course is 1 mi away. Restaurant, bar, room service. In-room data ports, cable TV. 2 pools. 2 tennis courts. Exercise room. Laundry service. Business services. No pets. | 200 Atrium Dr. | 732/469-2600 or 800/222-8733 | fax 732/469-4617 | 360 rooms | $129-$184 | AE, D, DC, MC, V.

Holiday Inn-Somerset. You'll find this six-story modern, corporate hotel near Somerset's malls and restaurants. It was renovated in 2000. Restaurant, bar, room service. In-room data ports, cable TV. Pool. Exercise equipment. Business services, airport shuttle. | 195 Davidson Ave. | 732/356-1700 | fax 732/356-0939 | www.holiday-inn.com | 284 rooms | $79-$139 | AE, D, DC, MC, V.

Madison Suites. You'll stay in a two-level suite here, with a kitchenette, bathroom, and sitting area on one level and the sleeping area upstairs. The property was renovated in 1998, and there's a shopping plaza nearby. Complimentary Continental breakfast. In-room data ports, microwaves, refrigerators, cable TV. Business services. | 11 Cedar Grove La. | 732/563-1000 | fax 732/563-0352 | www.utell.com/static/welcome_19129.html | 83 suites | $124-$160 | AE, D, DC, MC, V.

Marriott-Somerset. With its towers and well-maintained grounds, this Marriott is a handsome option among the business district's many hotels. It was renovated in 1997. Restaurant, bar In-room data ports, refrigerators, cable TV. Pool. Hot tub. Tennis. Gym. Business services. | 110 Davidson Ave. | 732/560-0500 | fax 732/560-3669 | www.marriott.com | 440 rooms | $79-$199 | AE, D, DC, MC, V.

SOMERVILLE

MAP 9, E5

(Nearby towns also listed: Clinton, Flemington, Gladstone, Griggstown, New Brunswick)

Somerville is in the middle of the state, at the south end of the Watchung Mountain range. If you're going to be passing through, visit the beautiful Duke Gardens, but remember to call at least a week in advance to make reservations, especially in summer.

Information: **Somerset County Chamber of Commerce** | 360 Grove St., Bridgewater, 08807 | 908/725-1552 | fax 908/722-7823 | www.somersetcountychamber.org.

Attractions

Duke Gardens. The fabulous gardens in Victorian greenhouses on Doris Duke's 6,000-acre estate reflect the traditions of various countries. | Off Rte. 206 S, | 908/722–3700 | $5 | Oct.–May, weekdays 9–4, tours by appointment.

Golf House–USGA Museum and Library. You'll find the world's largest collection of golfing memorabilia, books, and art here. Yes, the club Alan Shepard swung on the moon is included. The Golf House Theater shows vintage footage throughout the day. The museum displays 10,000 golf balls; twice that many are tested every year at the state-of-the-art Research and Test Center on the site. It's about 15 mi north of Somerville. | 1 Liberty Corner Rd., Far Hills | 908/234–2300 | www.usga.org/golfhouse | Free | Daily.

U.S. Bicycling Hall of Fame. Founded in 1986, this museum is a primary source of bicycling history and artifacts. Its location here is appropriate, since the town is home to America's oldest continuously run bicycle race, the Tour of Somerville. | 135 W. Main St. | 908/722–3620 | Weekdays 1–3; call for appointment.

Wallace House State Historic Site. George Washington stayed in this former home of a wealthy merchant in the winter of 1778–79. | 38 Washington Pl. | 908/725–1015 | Free | Wed.–Sun. 10–noon and 1–4.

The **Old Dutch Parsonage State Historic Site** is the former home of Jacob Hardenbergh, who founded what is now Rutgers University. | 65 Washington Pl. | 908/725–1015 | Free | Wed.–Sun. 10–noon and 1–4.

ON THE CALENDAR

JAN.: *Winter Candlelight Tours.* Intimate candlelight tours of the historic Wallace House and Old Dutch Parsonage help visitors envision life in a simpler age. | 908/725–1015.

MAR.: *Cruzin' Friday Nights.* Watch vintage cars glide through town accompanied by music. | 908/526–3499.

MAR.: *St. Patrick's Day Parade.* Celebrate this Irish holiday with the locals along Main Street. | 908/725–4190.

MAY: *Kugler-Anderson Memorial Tour of Somerville.* Locals call this the "Kentucky Derby of Cycling." It's the nation's oldest continuous bicycle race. | 908/725–7223.

JUNE: *7th Raritan Street Fair.* Running along Somerset Street in Raritan (which borders Somerville to the west), this festival features crafts, food, music, and family activities. | 908/996–3036.

JUNE: *Tin Man Triathlon.* Run a 10K in Bridgewater, cycle 23 mi from Round Valley Recreation Area (in Hunterdon County) back to Bridgewater, then complete the 1.2-mi swim back at Round Valley. Or just watch. | 908/725–2300.

JUNE–AUG: *Concerts on the Green.* Band concerts are held on the lawn of the Somerville Borough Hall. | 908/541–1600.

DEC.: *Holiday Diversion at the Wallace House.* Christmas in the 18th-century is brought to life with dance, interpreters, and food. | 908/725–1015.

Dining

La Scala. Italian. Try the rigatoni stuffed with spinach and ricotta cheese, or the homemade lobster ravioli at this cozy, romantic, northern Italian restaurant. | 117 N. Gaston Ave. | 908/218–9300 | fax 908/218–0055 | $10–$16 | AE, DC, MC, V.

Ryland Inn. French. Housed in an 1800 stagecoach on a 55-acre setting, this top-rated restaurant has five antiques-filled dining rooms and a library. The food is modern regional French, with daily specials depending on available ingredients. Try the lobster tart, the crispy black sea bass, or any of the tasting menus. The inn is about 8 mi west of Somerville. | U.S. 22 W, Whitehouse | 908/534–4011 | Jacket required | Closed 1st wk Jan. No lunch weekends | $30–$42 ($75 prix fixe) | AE, D, DC, MC, V.

Lodging

Days Inn–Hillsborough. This modern Days Inn, built in 1991, is convenient to restaurants, a movie theater, and the Bridgewater Commons Mall. It's about 3 mi south of Somerville. Complimentary Continental breakfast. In-room data ports, cable TV. Pool. | 118 U.S. 206, Hillsborough | 908/685–9000 | fax 908/685–0601 | 100 rooms | $89–$99 | AE, D, DC, MC, V.

Holiday Inn. Located 3 mi east of Somerville across from the Garden State Exhibit Center (and 15 minutes from Rutgers and several Fortune 500 companies), this Holiday Inn is geared toward the business traveler. The rooms have modular desks and rolling office chairs to make working more comfortable, and the hotel provides free access to a nearby health club. Restaurant, bar. In-room data ports, cable TV. Pool. Laundry service. Business services. Some pets allowed. | 197 Davidson Ave., South Bound Brook | 732/356–1700 or 800/465–4329 | fax 732/356–2355 | www.basshotels.com/holiday-inn | 284 rooms | $139–$159 | AE, MC, V.

SPRING LAKE

MAP 9, H6

(Nearby towns also listed: Asbury Park, Belmar, Point Pleasant Beach)

At one time called the Irish Riviera, Spring Lake has remained a quietly beautiful seaside town, with 2 mi of noncommercial boardwalk. The pristine beaches and sand dunes belie street after street of huge turn-of-the-20th-century houses behind them. About two dozen of them have been turned into B&Bs, and a cute shopping district offers 60 boutiques and small restaurants. There is, in fact, a lake called Spring, as well as two other lakes in the town.

Information: Greater Spring Lake Chamber of Commerce | Box 694, Spring Lake, 07762 | 732/449–0577 | www.springlake.org.

Attractions

Spring Lake Theatre Co. The summer season of this community theater includes classic Broadway musicals like "My Fair Lady" and "Anything Goes." | Third and Madison Ave. S | 732/449–4530.

St. Catharine's Church. Designed in the neo-classical style, the interior of this large cathedral is stunning—a huge portrait of the apostles, done in the Italian Renasiannce tradition, adorns the ceiling. | 215 Essex Ave. | 732/449–4530 | Free | Mon.–Thurs. 9–7:30, Fri. 9–4 (Rectory).

ON THE CALENDAR

JULY: *Spring Lake Mile Ocean Swim.* Jump in for this 1-mi open water endurance swim, or cheer on others. | 732/449–0800.

NOV.: *NJBBIA Annual Open House.* Tour more than 60 B&Bs all over the state. Proceeds benefit the Coalition for Battered Women. | 732/449–3535.

DEC.: *Spring Lake Christmas Hospitality Tour.* Victorian inns and hotels are decorated for the season. | 732/449–0577.

Dining

Beach House. American. The Beach House overlooks the ocean, and is a relaxed summer place to have lunch or dinner. The menu includes sandwiches, seafood, pasta, steaks, and daily specials. | 16 Mercer Ave. | 908/449–8800 | Closed mid-Oct.–May | $7–$13 | AE, MC, V.

The Breakers on the Ocean. Italian. Drop-dead-gorgeous ocean views have made this classically romantic restaurant a popular place for weddings. It's in the grand 100-year-old Breakers hotel, and you can sit poolside or on the veranda for breakfast and lunch. For dinner, try the veal rollatini, the New York strip steak, or the roasted red snapper with shiitake mushrooms and herbs. Treat yourself to the decadent Chocolate Thunder and New York Cheesecake any time. | 1507 Ocean Ave. | 732/449–7700 | fax 732/449–0161 | $10–$23 | AE, MC, V.

Eggiman's Tavern. American. This friendly, unpretentious spot is a great place to drop by for a steak or lobster and a beer. Popular with locals, it's open year-round until 1 AM. | 2031 Rte. 1 | 732/449–2626 | $8–$15 | AE, DC, MC, V.

Family Tree. Continental. If you're looking for a restaurant that appeals to parents *and* kids, try the Family Tree, about 3 mi south of Spring Lake. It's small (only 20 tables), casual, and lively, and has a very energetic staff. There are more than 10 specials every night, and the menu is full of fish, steak, veal, and pork chops. Pianist Friday and Saturday. Kids' menu. | 2420 Rte. 35, Manasquan | 732/528–5950 | $12–$19 | AE, D, DC, MC, V.

Old Mill Inn. American. Formal dining takes place downstairs, while a more casual atmosphere is available upstairs. Both levels have a wall of windows looking out over panoramic lakeside views. There's seafood, roast duck, veal, lamb chops, and pasta dishes, as well as prime aged steaks and filet mignon. You can eat outside on a small deck in front of a pond. Entertainment Friday and Saturday. Kids' menu. Sunday brunch. | Old Mill Rd., Spring Lake Heights | 732/449–1800 | www.oldmillinn.com | $24–$38 | AE, MC, V.

The Porch. American. This cozy bar and grill serves up reliably good burgers, BBQ ribs, and pasta dishes and runs daily specials such as "kids eat free Monday" and "2 for 1 burger Tuesday." There's a late-night menu, and live music on weekends. Takeout is available. | 810 Rte. 71 | 732/449–5880 | $10–$16 | AE, V.

The Sandpiper. Continental. For a romantic dinner, try this 15-room Victorian inn close to the beach. The menu includes grilled Atlantic salmon, veal and shrimp Milanese, and stuffed filet mignon. Kids' menu. Sunday brunch. BYOB. | 7 Atlantic Ave. | 732/449–4700 or 800/U–B HAPPY | $20–$30 | DC, MC, V.

Sister's Cafe. Contemporary. This clubby, modern, storefront restaurant has two dining areas and a service bar, and is known for excellent innovative food. Try the rock shrimp with scallion dumplings or the New York strip streak with green peppercorn sauce—but save room for the crème brûlé for dessert. | 1321 3rd Ave. | 732/449–1909 | Closed Mon. No dinner Sun. | $10–$18 | MC, V.

Whispers. Contemporary. This elegant 50-seat restaurant, in the Hewitt Wellington Hotel, serves beautifully presented dishes at tables set with fresh flowers, candles, and fine china. Try the breaded halibut in a saffron beurre blanc and sample the bourbon-flavored crème brûlé. | 200 Monmouth Ave. | 732/974–9755 | No lunch | $15–$26 | AE, V.

Lodging

Ashling Cottage. This 1877 gothic house, originally built as a summer cottage, is a block from both the beach and Spring Lake. Rooms have antiques and reproductions and floral patterns prevail throughout. Breakfast is served in the solarium which has views of both the ocean and the lake. Guests are provided with beach passes and blankets. For rainy days there is a collection of books and games to pass the time. Smoking is allowed on the front porch only. Complimentary breakfast. No air-conditioning in some rooms, cable TV, in-room VCRs. No pets. | 106 Sussex Ave. | 732/449–3553 or 888/274–5464 | fax 732/974–0831 | www.ashlingcottage.com | 10 rooms | $75–$170 | Closed mid-Nov.–Apr. | No credit cards.

Bay Head Gables. The architect Stanford White designed this Georgian-style, cedar-shake "cottage," which was built in 1914. It's 4 mi from Spring Lake. Complimentary breakfast. TV in common area. No smoking. | 200 Main St., Bay Head | 732/892–9844 | fax 732/295–2196 | www.bayheadgables.com | 11 rooms | $150–$215 | Closed Jan. | AE, D, MC, V.

Breakers. This all-white restored Victorian oceanfront hotel has a private beach. Some rooms have oceanfront views, and there's one deluxe room with a fireplace and a whirlpool. You can rent two rooms next to each other and join them. Restaurant. Refrigerators, cable TV.

SPRING LAKE

INTRO
ATTRACTIONS
DINING
LODGING

Pool. Hot tub. Business services. | 1507 Ocean Ave. | 732/449–7700 | fax 732/449–0161 | www.breakershotel.com | 67 rooms | $175–$350 | AE, DC, MC, V.

Chateau. This lovely 1888 Victorian lakefront inn is close to the quaint Spring Lake 3rd Avenue shopping area. The lobby has a fireplace, and rooms have marble bathrooms and Casablanca ceiling fans. Luxury suites have fireplaces and wet bars. There's a three-day minimum stay in July and August. Microwaves, cable TV, in-room VCRs (and movies). Pool. Bicycles. Business services. | 500 Warren Ave. | 732/974–2000 | fax 732/974–0007 | www.chateauinn.com | 38 rooms | $175–$275 | AE, D, DC, MC, V.

Comfort Inn. This highway hotel is not far from the action in both Belmar and Point Pleasant Beach. Suites have refrigerators and microwaves. Complimentary Continental breakfast. Pool. In-room data ports, cable TV. Exercise equipment. Business services. | 1909 Rte. 35 | 732/449–6146 | fax 732/449–6556 | www.comfortinn.com | 70 rooms | $96–$175 | AE, D, DC, MC, V.

Doolan's. The friendly Doolan family owns and runs this motel, seven blocks from the ocean. The lobby and banquet rooms are frequently used for weddings, and the restaurant and bar are popular local hangouts. The hotel was built in the 1930s with a wing added 20 years later. Restaurant, bar (with entertainment). Complimentary Continental breakfast. Cable TV. Pool. | 700 Rte. 71 | 732/449–3666 | fax 732/449–2601 | www.doolans.com | 60 rooms | $75–$180 | AE, D, DC, MC, V.

Hewitt Wellington. This carefully renovated old property is on Spring Lake and two blocks from the ocean. The lobby and common rooms retain early 1900s' architecture and details. Rooms have modern furnishings, marble baths, and carpeting. Restaurant, complimentary Continental breakfast. In-room data ports, refrigerators, cable TV. Pool. Business services. No kids under 12. | 200 Monmouth Ave. | 732/974–1212 | fax 732/974–2338 | www.hewittwellington.com | 29 rooms | $175–$270 | AE, D, DC, MC, V.

Hollycroft Inn. Located on a bluff above Como Lake (at the northern edge of Spring Lake), this inn is a popular base for bird-watching and fishing. Rooms in the rustic Adirondack-style lodge have brass-and-iron beds and crafts collected by the owners, and all but one have lake views. The beach is four blocks away and bicycles, beach passes, towels, and chairs are available to guests. Complimentary breakfast. No pets. No smoking. | 506 Northern Blvd. | 732/681–2254 or 800/679–2254 | fax 732/280–8145 | 7 rooms, 1 suite | $125–$275. | AE.

La Maison. Owned by a Francophile, this French country-style inn serves wine and cheese every afternoon. Sleep in under your duvet, or greet the morning with an elegant full breakfast including fresh-squeezed orange juice and cappuccino. Beach tags, towels, and chairs are available to guests. Rooms have outbound-only phones. Complimentary breakfast. Cable TV. Some pets allowed. No smoking. | 404 Jersey Ave. | 732/449–0969 or 800/276–2088 | fax 732/449–4860 | 5 rooms, 2 suites, 1 cottage | $145–$250 | AE, D, DC, MC, V.

Normandy Inn. This Victorian-style inn has fireplaces, porches, a private garden, and loads of antiques. Complimentary breakfast. Cable TV. Bicycles. Business services. | 21 Tuttle Ave. | 732/449–7172 | fax 732/449–1070 | www.normandyinn.com | 19 rooms | $143–$295 | AE, D, DC, MC, V.

Sandpiper. Right across the street from the beach, this pretty, upscale inn features rooms with ocean views and 12-ft ceilings. Free afternoon snacks are served. Restaurant, complimentary Continental breakfast. Refrigerators, cable TV. Pool. No kids under 16. Business services. | 7 Atlantic Ave. | 732/449–6060 or 800/824–2779 | fax 732/449–8409 | www.sandpiperinn.com | 15 rooms (8 with shower only) | $175–$250 | AE, D, MC, V.

Sea Crest by the Sea. Anglophiles will feel right at home in this Queen Anne–style inn, where you can enjoy afternoon tea following a game of croquet. Each of the antiques-furnished guest rooms has a theme, such as the Teddy Roosevelt suite, which has both Roosevelt memorabilia and a collection of teddy bears. Guests are provided with beach tags, towels, chairs, and bicycles. Complimentary breakfast. Some refrigerators, cable TV, in-room VCRs.

No pets. No smoking. | 19 Tuttle Ave. | 732/449–9031 or 800/803–9031 | fax 732/974–0403 | 10 rooms, 2 suites | $159–$259 | AE, MC, V.

Travelodge. This chain hotel is walking distance (½ mi) from Spring Lake. It was built in 1975 and renovated in 1993. Complimentary Continental breakfast. Cable TV. Pool. Business services. | 1916 Rte. 35, Wall | 732/974–8400 | fax 732/974–8401 | 52 rooms (2 with shower only) | $79–$124 | AE, D, DC, MC, V.

Victoria House Bed & Breakfast. This gingerbread Queen Anne–style inn, with original stained glass and gothic shingles, was built in 1882. The guest rooms are furnished with antiques, and breakfast is served on the veranda overlooking the English country garden. On rainy days, curl up with a book in front of the parlor fireplace. Complimentary breakfast. No TV in some rooms. No pets. No kids under 14. No smoking. | 214 Monmouth Ave. | 732/974–1882 or 888/249–6562 | fax 732/974-2132 | www.victoriahouse.net | 8 rooms | $115–$325 | AE, D, MC, V.

White Lilac Inn. This large white house, built in 1880, has two wraparound porches. Four of the guest rooms have fireplaces. Complimentary breakfast. No room phones, no TV in some rooms. No kids under 14. | 414 Central Ave. | 732/449–0211 | www.whitelilac.com | 9 rooms | $119–$219 | Closed Jan., open New Year's Eve | AE, D, MC, V.

STANHOPE

MAP 9, E3

(Nearby towns also listed: Chester, Hackettstown)

The completion of the Morris Canal in 1831 transformed Stanhope into a major outlet for goods shipped into upper Sussex County. Remains of the canal can be seen today, and the canal itself is on the National Register of Historic Places, yet many interrelated sites and structures in Stanhope have been overlooked. Modern-day attractions include Waterloo Village and the Wild West theme park. For a change of pace, try the Stanhope House, a hotbed of regional blues activity, and the Whistling Swan, one of the top-rated inns in the state.

Information: **Stanhope Progressive Chamber of Commerce** | Box 642, Stanhope, 07874 | 973/691–2499 | fax 973/691–4995 | www.stanhopechamber.com.

Attractions

Hopatcong State Park. The focal point of the park is man-made Lake Hopatcong, 9 mi long and a draw for visitors since its construction in the 1860s. In the area's heyday more than 40 hotels drew the upper crust hoping to escape the urban heat. The park, at the southwest end of the lake, is a popular spot for fishing, boating, and swimming in summer, as well as ice-boating and fishing in winter. The historical museum has exhibits on local American Indian history, the Morris Canal (for which the lake was made), as well as great photos of the old Bertrand Island Amusement Park. The park is actually in Landing, less than a mile from Stanhope. | Southwestern shore of Lake Hopatcong | 973/398–7010 or 973/398–2616 | www.hopatcong.org/museum/ | Free; parking $5 weekdays, $7 weekends and Memorial Day–Labor Day | Park: daily; museum: Mar.–May and Sept.–Nov., Sun. 1–4.

Stanhope House. Built in 1790, this structure has been a private residence, a tavern, a hotel, and even a brothel. However, since the early 70s, the house has become legendary as a venue for the blues. World-famous musicians have played here and still do. Concerts, fairs, and ethnic festivals take place here in spring, summer, and fall. | 45 Main St. | 973/347–0458 | fax 973/426–9506 | www.stanhope-house.com | Variable | Call for hrs.

Waterloo Village Restoration. Among the more than two dozen buildings in this re-creation of the historic village, first settled in 1758, are a blacksmith shop, a sawmill, and a reconstructed Lenni Lenape Indian village. Concerts, fairs, and ethnic festivals happen in spring, summer, and fall. | 525 Waterloo Rd. | 973/347–0900 | www.waterloovillage.org | $9; special rates for children and senior citizens | Apr.–Nov., Wed.–Sun., call for hrs (which differ every month).

Wild West City. You can take a stagecoach ride and get held-up, see a Pony Express race, witness a gun fight, or pan for gold at this Old West recreational theme park. You'll find the park off Route 206 N, 2 mi northwest of Stanhope. | Lackawanna Dr., Netcong | 201/347–8900 | www.wildwestcity.com | $7.50, $1.50 per ride | May 1–Jun. 19 weekends 10:30–6, Jun. 19–Labor Day daily 10:30–6, Labor Day–Columbus Day weekends 10:30–6.

ON THE CALENDAR
APR.–NOV.: *Waterloo Village.* The village hosts concerts, demonstrations, and lectures throughout the season. | 973/347–0900.
MAY: *Waterloo Antiques Fair.* Waterloo Village hosts New Jersey's largest outdoor antiques show. | 973/347–0900.
MAY: *Waterloo Art and Fine Craft Show.* Browse the works of talented artists and craftspeople and enjoy food from local restaurants. In Waterloo village. | 973/347–0900.
JUNE: *Annual Garden State Craft Brewers' Festival.* Sample beers from New Jersey's brewpubs and microbrews at Waterloo Village. There's music and pub food too. | 973/347–0900.
JUNE: *Michael Arnone's 10th Annual Crawfish Fest.* More than 12,000 pounds of boiled crawfish are on hand for the biggest Crawfish Boil in the Northeast, at the Waterloo Concert Field. | 212/539–8830 or 973/347–0900.
JUNE: *Wine Festival.* Sample and buy wines from New Jersey wineries in Waterloo Village. | 973/347–0900.
SEPT.: *Dodge Poetry Festival.* Attend workshops, readings, and performances at the largest poetry festival in North America, held in Waterloo Village. | 973/347–0900.
SEPT.: *Garden State Wine Grower's Fall Wine and Cheese Classic.* Enjoy great food, music, and New Jersey wine tastings and competitions at Waterloo Village. | 908/475–3671.
SEPT.: *Scandinavian Fest.* Celebrate the cultures of Norway, Iceland, Denmark, Finland, Sweden and Estonia, with entertainment, imported gifts, demonstrations, and dancing, in Waterloo Village. | 732/542–8150.

Dining
Barone's. Italian. Originally a farm, this property just north of Stanhope was converted into a tavern in 1807, and then restored by the Barone family, who turned it into an elegant restaurant with a more casual "tavern" downstairs. Signature dishes at Barone's include chicken balsamico and filet mignon piedmontese. The wine list contains over 10,000 bottles in stock, including special private reserve wines. Downstairs, the Lockwood Tavern serves pizza, beer, and burgers. | 77 Rte. 206 Byram | 973/347–1812 | fax 973/347–1693 | $10–$17 | AE, DC, MC, V.

Black Forest Inn. German. This restaurant has a decidedly Germanic flair, with hunting paintings on the wall and stained glass. It's known for veal, seafood, and *Maultaschen* (the German version of pierogi or ravioli). | 249 U.S. 206 N | 973/347–3344 | www.blackforestinn.com | Closed Tues. | $21–$39 | AE, DC, MC, V.

Lodging
Days Inn. This link in the Days Inn chain, about 15 mi south of Stanhope, offers amenities for both business travelers and tourists. Take advantage of the recreational facilities or shop at two malls less than 2 mi away. Restaurant, bar (with entertainment). Cable TV. Pool. Laundry facilities. Business services. | 1691 Rte. 46, Ledgewood | 973/347–5100 | fax 973/347–6356 | www.daysinn.com | 100 rooms | $87 | AE, D, MC, V.

Whistling Swan Inn. The rooms in this 1905 Victorian have period antiques such as brass canopy beds and claw-foot tubs. The inn is near wineries, antiquing, and Waterloo Village.

It's also walking distance from Lake Musconetcong, where you can rent a boat for a leisurely row. Complimentary breakfast. Cable TV. | 110 Main St. | 973/347–6369 | fax 973/347–3391 | www.bbianj.com/whistlingswan | 10 rooms | $99–$150 | AE, D, DC, MC, V.

Wooden Duck. The Wooden Duck takes its name from a collection of handcrafted wooden ducks on display in the lobby, but in fact you'll see plenty of real wildlife in the fields and woodlands of this 17-acre picturesque property. Five of the guest rooms are in the Estate House, and two are in the Horseless Carriage House. There are two deluxe rooms, with fireplaces, private balconies, and tubs for two. It's 8 mi north of Stanhope. Complimentary breakfast. In-room data ports, cable TV, in-room VCRs (and movies). Pool. Business services. No kids under 8. No smoking. | 140 Goodale Rd., Newton | 973/300–0395 | www.woodenduckinn.com | 7 rooms | $110–$175 | AE, D, MC, V.

STOCKTON

MAP 9, D5

(Nearby towns also listed: Lambertville, Flemington)

There are only about 600 residents in Stockton, and the town measures less than 1 square mi, but it's worth the trip if you enjoy scenic country roads, intimate B&B's and fine dining. Since it's right near the Delaware River, you can also spend the day canoeing, tubing, or just lazing alongside the shore. Artsy meccas like New Hope, PA and Lambertville are a few miles away.

Information: Hunterdon County Chamber of Commerce | 2200 Route 31, Suite 15, Lebanon, 08833 | 908/735–5955 | fax 908/730–6580 | hunterdon@sprintmail.com | www.hunterdon-chamber.org. .

STOCKTON

INTRO
ATTRACTIONS
DINING
LODGING

Attractions

The Green Sergeant Bridge. Take a step back in time as you walk or drive over what's considered last existing covered bridge in New Jersey. Located at the end of Lower Creek Road, this scenic wooden passageway is just a few miles from Stockton. | Sergeantsville; Off Lowercreek Rd. | 908/735–5955 | fax 908/730–6580 | hunterdon@sprintmail.com | www.hunterdon-chamber.org | Free.

The Tow Path. A former mule pathways, this 60 mi long gravel trail is one of the busiest bike paths in the country. Shaded by trees and calm country winds, the most heavily-traveled part of the path is the southern section, which goes from Lambertville to Frenchtown. | 84 Park Ave., Flemington; you can get on or off in numerous places along its 60 mi stretch | 908/788–5553 | fax 908/788–8583 | www.hart-tma.com | Year-round.

The Academy Books and Bindery. This is one of only a handful of "book binders" remaining in America. They don't sell books here, but will bind together limited editions if commissioned. They have a nice outdoor sculpture garden on the front lawn, full of large works donated by local artists. | 829 Rosemont-Ringoes Road, Stockton | 609/397–4035 | Free | Call for hours.

Dining

The Café at Rosemont. Contemporary. Built as a general store in 1896, this homey restaurant 3 mi from Stockton is half Vermont inn and half hip bistro. The food is fresh and the menu changes seasonally. In summer most of the produce and fish is local. For brunch, they make a homemade black bean chili, and at dinner try the lemongrass coconut shrimp pasta. While waiting for a table, you can tour their organic gardens. | 88 Kingwood-Stockton Rd., at Rte. 519 and 604, Rosemont | 609/397–4097 | Closed Mon. | $13–$22 | MC, V.

Meils. American. Housed in a former gas station, this unusual upscale restaurant is famous for it's "comfort food," such as meatloaf, chicken pot pie, and potato pancakes. The decor is eclectic; walls are covered with a mix of local artwork and cooking-themed antiques. BYOB. | Rte. 29; Corner of Bridge and Main St. | 609/397–8033 | No reservations | $12–$22 | No credit cards.

Lodging

The Woolverton Inn. Surrounded by a 400-acre nature preserve, this quiet B&B is a sanctuary from the outside world. Featherbeds, hot tubs and fireplaces give it an upscale feel—although the prices are competitive with most B&B's in the area. There are fresh flowers and robes in your room, and you can order your breakfast in bed. In season, the roses and the herb garden make the air incredibly aromatic. They are also famous for homemade turkey breakfast sausage, made with apple and sage grown on the grounds. Complimentary breakfast. Some in-room data ports, some refrigerators, hot tubs, some VCRs, no TV or phones in some rooms. Massage. Water sports. Bicycles. No pets. No smoking. | 6 Woolverton Road, Stockton | 609/397–0802 or 888/264–6648 | sheep@woolvertoninn.com | www.woolvertoninn.com | 9 rooms now, 13 after 1/2001 | $115–$285 | AE, MC, V.

The Stockton Inn. The drawings of Bambi illustrator Kurt Wiese are painted on the dining room walls of this lovely inn, and the grounds have water falls and a trout pond. The individually decorated spacious rooms are spread through four buildings, and some have fireplaces, balconies and canopy beds. The on-site restaurant, The Stockton Inn, is one of the best in the region. And, although they don't have room service per se, if you've got a late-night craving for the famous crab cakes the chef will whip you up a batch (as long as he's still awake) and send them to your door. Restaurant with bar, picnic area, complimentary breakfast. Cable TV. No pets. | One Main St., Rte. 29, Stockton | 609/397–1250 | fax 609/397–8948 | www.stocktoninn.com | 11 rooms | $60–$165 | AE, D, DC, MC, V.

STONE HARBOR

MAP 9, E11

(Nearby towns also listed: Cape May, Cape May Court House, Sea Isle City, the Wildwoods)

With Wildwood and Cape May nearby, Stone Harbor doesn't get quite the crush of tourists that its fine beaches and shopping district might otherwise warrant. Instead, it remains a rather quaint seashore community. The proximity of beach and town allows visitors to stroll from sand and water to ice-cream parlors and gift shops. It's also home to two wildlife sites: the Stone Harbor Bird Sanctuary and the Wetlands Institute.

Information: Stone Harbor Chamber of Commerce | 212 96th St., Stone Harbor, 08247 | 609/368–6101 | www.stoneharborcoc.com. **Southern Shore Region Tourism Council** | c/o Greater Ocean City Chamber of Commerce, Box 157, Ocean City, 08226 | 609/399–1412 | www.oceancityvacation.com.

Attractions

Stone Harbor Bird Sanctuary. This sanctuary provides an open-air view of hundreds of species of shore birds. | 3rd Ave. and 114th St. | 609/368–5102 | Free | Mon.–Fri. 9 AM–8 PM; Sat.–Sun. 10 AM–8 PM.

Wetlands Institute. The facility offers exhibits and hiking trails geared towards appreciation of the Jersey Shore's highly prized wetlands ecology. Every September is the terrific Wings 'n' Water Festival weekend. | 1075 Stone Harbor Blvd. | 609/368–1211 | $5 | Mid-Oct.–mid-May, Tues.–Sat. 9:30–4:30; mid-May–mid-Oct., Mon.–Sat. 9:30–4:30, Sun. 10–4.

VACATION COUNTDOWN Your checklist for a perfect journey

Way Ahead

- ❑ Devise a trip budget.
- ❑ Write down the five things you want most from this trip. Keep this list handy before and during your trip.
- ❑ Book lodging and transportation.
- ❑ Arrange for pet care.
- ❑ Photocopy any important documentation (passport, driver's license, vehicle registration, and so on) you'll carry with you on your trip. Store the copies in a safe place at home.
- ❑ Review health and home-owners insurance policies to find out what they cover when you're away from home.

A Month Before

- ❑ Make restaurant reservations and buy theater and concert tickets. Visit fodors.com for links to local events and news.
- ❑ Familiarize yourself with the local language or lingo.
- ❑ Schedule a tune-up for your car.

Two Weeks Before

- ❑ Create your itinerary.
- ❑ Enjoy a book or movie set in your destination to get you in the mood.
- ❑ Prepare a packing list.
- ❑ Shop for missing essentials.
- ❑ Repair, launder, or dry-clean the clothes you will take with you.
- ❑ Replenish your supply of prescription drugs and contact lenses if necessary.

A Week Before

- ❑ Stop newspaper and mail deliveries.
- ❑ Pay bills.
- ❑ Stock up on film and batteries.
- ❑ Label your luggage.
- ❑ Finalize your packing list—always take less than you think you need.
- ❑ Pack a toiletries kit filled with travel-size essentials.
- ❑ Check tire treads.
- ❑ Write down your insurance agent's number and any other emergency numbers and take them with you.
- ❑ Get lots of sleep. You want to be well-rested and healthy for your impending trip.

A Day Before

- ❑ Collect passport, driver's license, insurance card, vehicle registration, and other documents.
- ❑ Check travel documents.
- ❑ Give a copy of your itinerary to a family member or friend.
- ❑ Check your car's fluids, lights, tire inflation, and wiper blades.
- ❑ Get packing!

During Your Trip

- ❑ Keep a journal/scrapbook as a personal souvenir.
- ❑ Spend time with locals.
- ❑ Take time to explore. Don't plan too much. Let yourself get lost and use your Fodor's guide to get back on track.

MAY: *Sail Into Summer Family Festival.* Stone Harbor welcomes the season with a boat show, a seafood festival, exhibits, music, a family treasure hunt, bay cruises, and food booths. | 609/368–6101.

MAY: *Memorial Day Parade and Ceremony.* Stone Harbor marks the beginning of summer with a parade and beach opening ceremony. | 609/368–6101.

SEPT.: *Wings 'n Water Festival.* The Wetlands Institute comes to life with artists who paint and carve birds and fish, model boats, crafts, food, and wildlife. | 609/368–1211.

Dining

Back Yard Restaurant. Contemporary. Dine outside under a grape arbor surrounded by flowers, or inside in air-conditioned glass-walled comfort. Either way you're in for a romantic treat. Try the curried shrimp or the roast duck, and save room for the key lime tart. | 222 81st St. | 609/368–2627 | Closed Sun. No lunch | $22–$26 | AE, V.

The Mirage. Continental. The three dining rooms in this restaurant have touches of ancient Egypt. Try the shrimp martini, the honey-marinated port medallions, and the corn-bread pudding. Pianist Friday–Sunday. Kids' menu. It's about 4 mi from Stone Harbor. | 7888 Dune Dr., Avalon | 609/368–1919 | www.desertsand.com/miragemenu.htm | Breakfast also available, closed Nov.–Mar. | $15–$36 | MC, V.

Lodging

Colonial Lodge. This two-story redbrick motel is a block from the beach and three blocks from tennis courts, a basketball court, restaurants, and shops. There is a deck for sunbathing. Beach tags are provided, but you have to rent chairs and umbrellas. The hotel will set up a golf game for you at nearby Avalon Golf Club. Some microwaves, some refrigerators, cable TV. No smoking. | 181 93rd St., at Second Ave. | 609/368–2202 | 20 rooms | $55–$169 | AE, V.

SUMMIT

MAP 4, B7

(Nearby towns also listed: Chatham, Millburn, Short Hills, Union)

Picturesque Summit offers oak-lined streets and Victorian architecture. The downtown shopping district is made up of boutiques and unique shops, and the Short Hills Mall is just down the road. The Grand Summit Hotel is an historic and well-run place to stay overnight or to drop in for the extensive Sunday brunch buffet.

Information: **Suburban Chambers of Commerce** | 71 Summit Ave., Summit, 07902-0824 | 908/522–1700 | fax 908/522–9252 | info@suburbanchambers.org | www.suburbanchambers.org.

Attractions

New Jersey Center for Visual Arts. The center has six contemporary art exhibitions a year, as well as classes and a sculpture garden and park. | 68 Elm St. | 908/273–9121 | fax 908/273–1456 | $5 | Weekdays 9–5, weekends 12–4, park and garden open 24 hours.

DEC.: *Holiday House Tour.* A half dozen private homes, decorated for the season, are open for self-guided tours in Summit and Short Hills. Each year different homes are featured; residents volunteer to showcase their yuletide decorating prowess. | 908/273–8787.

Dining

La Focaccia. Italian. Close tables, lace curtains, and a tiled fireplace make this 75-seat storefront restaurant feel cozy and intimate. Tuscan cuisine is at the heart of the menu, and dishes like the roasted game hen and the grilled Portobello mushrooms are particularly good. Warm baskets of focaccia bread are brought to the table when you sit down. Try the Tiramisu for dessert. | 523 Morris Ave. | 908/277–4006 | Closed Sun. No lunch Sat. | $10–$18 | AE, V.

Lodging

Grand Summit Hotel. Opened just a few months before Black Tuesday, at the beginning of the 1929 Stock Market Crash, this elegant Tudor hotel became home to many wealthy town residents who lost their own homes and estates. The building has vaulted beamed ceilings, rare chestnut paneling, and a flagstone fireplace. Rooms are luxuriously spacious and elegantly furnished. Cable TV. Some in-room hot tubs. | 908/273–3000 | 570 Springfield Ave. | 150 rooms, 12 suites | $169 rooms, $299 suites | www.hartshornarboretum.com.

TEANECK

MAP 4, D5

(Nearby towns also listed: Englewood, Fort Lee, Hackensack, Paramus, Saddle Brook)

Teaneck is a neat residential town, only 15 minutes from Manhattan, and close to Routes 4 and 17, Interstate 80, and U.S. 46. It is the most populous town in Bergen County, with nearly 48,000 residents, including a large and active Jewish community, so some businesses are closed for the Sabbath. Bustling Cedar Lane is a great place to stroll, get some ice cream, see a $4 first-run movie, or shop for Judaica. Fairleigh Dickinson University has some of its campus here, and the public library has art exhibits, films, and musical performances throughout the year.

Information: **Teaneck Chamber of Commerce** | 206 The Plaza, Teaneck, 07666 | 201/837–0020 | www.teaneck.org.

Attractions

Fairleigh Dickinson University–Teaneck-Hackensack Campus. Fifty-five buildings on 88 acres accommodate 6,500 students concentrating in business, hard sciences, and health-care programs. The hub of sports activity is the Rothman Center, with myriad facilities and seating for 5,000. The center often hosts computer shows, markets, job fairs, and other area events. | 1000 River Rd. | 201/692–2000 | www.fdu.edu | Free | Daily.
The mission of **American Stage Company,** in residence at FDU, is to promote American theater through performing classics and premiering new works by contemporary authors. The company offers classes in the performing arts, staged readings, and workshops, as well as main-stage performances. | 201/692–7720, 201/692–7744 box office.

ON THE CALENDAR

MAY: *Cedar Lane Alive!* Teaneck's family celebration of the arts has live music on two stages, kiddie rides, crafts, games, a pie-eating contest, and food. | 201/907–0493.

Dining

Hiro. Japanese. Hiro has three locations in Teaneck (this was the first to open) and is known for its freshly prepared sushi and sashimi as well as classic tempura, teriyaki, and soba noodle dishes. The staff make a point of directing patrons who want a nonsmoking environment to the tatami dining room at the 254 DeGraw location. | 299 Queen Anne Rd. | 201/692–1002 | fax 201/692–1004 | No lunch Sun. | $7–$18 | AE, V.

Lodging

Marriott Glenpointe Hotel. This 15-story glass hotel caters mostly to business travelers, although it's in a suburban area. It was renovated in 2000, and 64 rooms are set aside strictly for corporate travel. The Port Imperial ferry to New York City is 6 mi away. Restaurant, bar. In-room data ports, refrigerators, cable TV. Pool. Hot tub. Gym. Business services. | 100

Frank W. Burr Blvd. | 201/836–0600 | fax 201/836–0638 | www.marriott.com | 341 rooms | $99–$226 | AE, D, DC, MC, V.

Clinton Inn Hotel. This three-story hotel prides itself on having the charm of a country inn but the convenience of a full-service hotel. It's set off from the highway on a quiet street. Restaurant, bar, room service. Cable TV. Exercise room. Laundry service. | 145 Dean St., Tenafly | 201/871–3200 or 800/275–4411 | fax 201/871–3435 | 120 rooms | $120 | AE, MC, V.

TINTON FALLS

MAP 9, G6

(Nearby towns also listed: Asbury Park, Eatontown, Red Bank)

Just off the New Jersey Turnpike in Monmouth County, Tinton Falls, founded in 1675, has numerous hotels for an overnight in the area. There's hiking and biking trails, as well as swimming in the area's many ponds.

Information: **Monmouth County Dept. of Public Information/Tourism** | 6 W. Main St., Freehold, 07728 | 800/523–2587 | www.visitmonmouth.com.

ON THE CALENDAR

APR.: *Monmouth Festival of the Arts.* See the work of more than 225 artists and create your own art in hands-on workshops. Classes and exhibitions take place at many area shops. | 732/747–8278.

Dining

Piccola Italia. Italian. Marble columns, crystal, and Art Deco chairs set an elegant tone for this reasonably priced restaurant with consistently good food in Ocean, which borders Tinton Falls to the east. Try the baby spinach salad, the angel-hair pomadoro with shrimp, or the homemade porcini gnocchi. | 837 W. Park Ave., Ocean, | 732/493–3090 | No lunch Sat.–Mon. | $7–$20 | AE, MC, V.

Lodging

Courtyard Tinton Falls. This hotel is geared toward business travelers, but is also convenient to the beach (3 mi), Fort Monmouth (1 mi), Monmouth University (5 mi), Monmouth Racetrack and Monmouth Malls (both 2 mi). Restaurant, bar. In-room data ports, cable TV, in-room VCRs. Pool. Exercise room. Laundry service. Business services. No pets. | 600 Hope Rd. | 732/389–2100 or 800/321–2211 | fax 732/389–1727 | www.courtyard.com | 121 rooms | $135 | AE, D, DC, MC, V.

Holiday Inn Tinton Falls. Built in 1976, this four-story brick building was renovated in 1999. The hotel is right off Garden State Parkway, in a quiet suburban area. Restaurant, bar, room service. In-room data ports, refrigerators, cable TV. Pool. Exercise equipment. Laundry facilities. Business services. | 700 Hope Rd. | 732/544–9300 | fax 732/544–0570 | 171 rooms | $79–$129 | AE, D, DC, MC, V.

Red Roof Inn. This three-story chain hotel is 2 mi from downtown and convenient to area dining and attractions. It's about 35 mi from Newark International Airport. All rooms on the top two floors have balconies. The hotel was renovated in 1998. In-room data ports, cable TV. Some pets allowed. | 11 Centre Plaza | 732/389–4646 | www.redroof.com | fax 732/389–4509 | 119 rooms | $69–$99 | AE, D, DC, MC, V.

Residence Inn by Marriott. This chain hotel is 5 mi from the shore and approximately one hour by car from New York City. Great Adventure is about 40 mi away. Picnic area, complimentary Continental breakfast. In-room data ports, kitchenettes, microwaves, cable TV. Pool. Laundry facilities. Business services. Pets allowed. | 90 Park Rd. | 732/389–8100 | fax 732/389–1573 | 96 suites | $119–$139 | AE, D, DC, MC, V.

Sunrise Suites Tinton Falls. This three-story hotel is 1 mi from Eatontown Industrial Park, 6 mi from the shore, and close to several area restaurants. There is a complimentary cocktail hour evenings Monday-Thursday. Kitchenettes, cable TV. Pool. Spa. Exercise room. Laundry facilities, laundry service. Business services. Pets allowed. | 3 Centre Plaza | 732/389–4800 or 877/999–3223 | fax 732/389–0137 | www.summerfieldsuites.com | 96 suites | $149 | AE, D, DC, MC, V.

TOMS RIVER

MAP 9, G7

(Nearby towns also listed: Holmdel, Lakewood, Seaside Heights, Seaside Park, Waretown)

Located just slightly west of the Jersey Shore, Toms River is a bastion of suburbia that is becoming more and more popular as a retirement community. Delightful Cattus Island County Park, with biking and hiking trails, is worth a detour.

Information: Toms River-Ocean County Chamber of Commerce | 1200 Hooper Ave., Toms River, 08753 | 732/349–0220. | fax 732/349–1252 | www.tomsrivercoc.com.

Attractions

Cooper Environmental Center at Cattus Island County Park. It's a good idea to stop here for an orientation to the 500-acre Cattus Island County Park. The center also has occasional concerts and environmental lectures. | 1170 Cattus Island Blvd. | 732/270–6960 | www.fieldtrip.com/nj/8270696o.htm | Free | Daily 10–4.

Ocean County Historical Museum. This museum, housed in a Victorian home, has historical exhibits and a genealogy library. | 26 Hadley Ave. | 732/341–1880 | www.islandhts.com | $2 adults, children free | Tues. and Thurs. 1–3, Sat. 10–4.

ON THE CALENDAR
JUNE: *NJ Chili Cook-off.* Hot stuff in Huddy Park—this is one of the most popular events in Toms River. Test your taste buds or partake in some country dancing. | 732/349–0220.
JULY: *Annual Wooden Boat Festival.* World-class boats gather in Huddy Park. There are family activities and refreshments all day. | 732/349–9209.
SEPT.: *Olde Time Antiques and Collectibles Faire.* More than 100 dealers bring thousands of items to this one-day event, usually held at the Toms River Historical Society. | 732/341–1880.
SEPT: *Pet Parade/Festival.* Pets and their people promenade to the waterfront. Prizes are awarded for the best pet trick, costume, and other categories. | 732/349–0220.
OCT.: *Big "C" Day.* Celebrate Cattus Island County Park's anniversary, with seining, nature walks, van tours, exhibits, and kids' activities. | 732/270–6960.
OCT.: *Halloween Parade.* Get spooked at one of the largest Halloween parades in the state, held October 31 on Main St. | 732/349–0220.

Dining
International House of Pancakes. Fast food. If you're craving chocolate-chip pancakes at 3 AM on a Tuesday you can have them here. Open 24/7, IHOP serves all the buttermilk, banana nut, and (fill in the blank) pancakes you can eat. They also have burgers, sandwiches, bacon and eggs, and other items. | 178 Rte. 37 E | 732/349–4555 | $6–$11 | AE, D, DC, MC, V.

Jeffrey's. Contemporary. Owner Jeffrey Schneekloth has created a romantic dining space right on Toms River's Main Street in two cozy rooms, brightened with lace curtains and fresh flowers. Menu highlights include oyster stew with leeks, cream, and sambuca; halibut on mustard smashed potatoes; and homemade sorbets—try the sour cherry. | 73 Main St. | 732/914–9544 | Closed Mon. | $18–$26 | AE, D, DC, MC, V.

Natural Foods General Store Cafe. Vegetarian. Part of a natural-foods store, this café has homemade fat-free soup, sandwiches, fresh salad, and daily entrée specials such as home-made pizza, tofu, baked vegetarian ziti, or shepherd's pie. Try the famous "Colossalm," a sandwich made with tahini, nutritional yeast, grated carrots, cucumbers, tomatoes, let-tuce, and "nayonaise" on pita bread. | 675 Batchelor St. | 732/240–0024 or 732/240–9320 | fax 732/240–0641 | $5–$9 | AE, V.

Old Time Tavern. American. This cheerful, rustic restaurant, with wooden booths and a 200-year-old fireplace, is known mainly for steak. Kids' menu. | N. Main St. | 732/349–8778 | $12–$27 | AE, DC, MC, V.

Lodging

Budget Inn. The main bus terminal in Toms River is a block away from this standard three-story brick chain hotel. Restaurant, bar, room service. Cable TV. Laundry facilities. Business services. | 2 W. Water St. | 732/341–6700 or 800/244–3631 | fax 732/244–4415 | 50 rooms | $69–$79 | AE, D, DC, MC, V.

Econo Lodge Lakehurst. This motel is 2 mi west of Toms River, and halfway between Six Flags Great Adventure Theme Park and the shore. Discounted tickets to Six Flags are avail-able for guests, and several fast-food restaurants are nearby. The motel also maintains a baby-sitting list and guests can rent VCRs and movies. Complimentary Continental break-fast. In-room data ports, some refrigerators, cable TV. No pets. | 2016 Rte. 37 W, Lakehurst | 908/657–7100 or 800/55–ECONO | fax 732/657–1672 | www.econolodge.com | 45 rooms | $80–$90 | AE, MC, V.

Holiday Inn. This Holiday inn is 2 mi from fishing and boating on Toms River. The modern rooms are "nothing fancy" but it's a decent place to spend the night, especially if you're traveling with your pet. Restaurant, bar (with entertainment), room service. Refrigerators, cable TV. Pool. Hot tub, sauna. Laundry facilities. Business services. Pets allowed. | 290 Rte. 37 E | 732/244–4000 | www.basshotels.com/holiday-inn | 123 rooms | $95–$115 | AE, D, DC, MC, V.

Howard Johnson. This two-story Hojo is down the street from the Ocean County Mall, the Seacourt Pavillion, and the Toys R Us plaza. Restaurant, bar. In-room data ports, cable TV. Pool. Business services. Some pets allowed (fee). | 955 Hooper Ave. | 732/244–1000 | fax 908/505–3194 | 96 rooms | $90–$110 | AE, D, DC, MC, V.

Pier One Motel & Restaurant. This motel is just over the bridge from Seaside Heights and the shore, but if you don't feel like venturing out it has its own private beach. Six Flags Great Adventure Theme Park is 13 mi west on Route 37, and on weekends there is live music in the motel lounge. Restaurant, bar. Cable TV. Beach. Pets allowed in winter only. | 3430 Rte. 37 E | 732/270–0914 | fax 732/270–9412 | 22 rooms | $65–$165 | AE, V.

Quality Inn. This two-story hotel is 8 mi from Island State Park. It was built in 1990, and already renovated once, in 1999. The bar has live entertainment on weekends. Restaurant, bar, complimentary Continental breakfast. In-room data ports, cable TV. Pool. Playground. Business services. | 815 Rte. 37 W | 732/341–2400 | fax 732/341–6469 | 100 rooms | $100–$145 | AE, D, DC, MC, V.

Ramada Inn. This three-story hotel is actually two buildings, one of which has suites. It's about 10 minutes from Seaside Heights on the Jersey shore. Restaurant, bar, complimen-tary Continental breakfast, room service. In-room data ports, cable TV. Pool. Hot tub. Ten-nis. Exercise equipment. Laundry facilities. Business services. | 2373 Rte. 9 | 732/905–2626 | fax 732/905–8735 | 153 rooms | $122–$165 | AE, D, DC, MC, V.

TRENTON

(Nearby towns also listed: Bordentown, Hightstown, Lambertville, Princeton)

Founded in 1679, New Jersey's capital city is a center of government, commerce, and history. George Washington crossed the Delaware to get to the Battle of Trenton, and you'll find many historic sites throughout the town. The Trenton Downtown Association oversees the Special Improvement District, coordinates the Heritage Days Festival (as well as an outdoor farmers market), and furthers the development of an arts-and-culture district that includes living and working space for artists.

Information: Trenton Convention and Visitors Bureau | Lafayette and Barrack Sts., Trenton, 08608 | 609/777–1771 recorded information, 609/777–1770 staff | fax 609/292–3771 | trentoncvb@voicenet.com | www.trentonnj.com. **Mercer County Chamber of Commerce** | 214 W. State St., Trenton, 08608 | 609/393–4143 | fax 609/393–1032 | www.mercerchamber.org.

NEIGHBORHOODS

Mill Hill is a neighborhood of gaslit streets and 19th-century row houses. Now designated a National Historic District, this downtown area dates back to 1679, when Quaker settlers built the first gristmill on the banks of the Assunpink Creek. It was also the site of the Second Battle of Trenton, a turning point in the Revolutionary War. The area, which was on its way to demolition in the mid-1960s, got a shot in the arm when Trenton's then-Mayor Arthur Holland and his wife Betty moved into Mill Hill in 1964, to demonstrate their commitment to rebuilding the neighborhood. Many houses are still being restored, but the sense of pride is more than obvious. The Old Mill Hill Society (Box 1263, Trenton, NJ, 08607-1263) has been conducting a house tour of the neighborhood every December for the last 30 years. Among the landmarks to visit in this neighborhood are Mill Hill Park, a nice expanse of greenery that was once the site of the Battle of Trenton, as well as the site of the city's first mill, and the Douglass House at Front and Montgomery streets.

The **State House Historic District** is a compact row of wonderful old houses along State Street, between Willow and Calhoun, the State House buildings. The homes, well-preserved examples of 19th-century architecture, once belonged to many of the prominent families in Trenton, including the inventive Roeblings, whose legacy in the town remains the John A. Roebling Sons factory. John A. Roebling, who invented wire rope and was the driving force behind the Brooklyn Bridge (he died during its construction), set up factories in Trenton in the mid-1800s. Today many of the historic district buildings are owned by professional organizations and businesses who can afford the top rents they command.

Another area worth a visit (especially if you're hungry) is **Chambersburg,** better known as the "Little Italy" of Trenton. Just minutes from the State House, the neighborhood is usually defined as being bordered by Hamilton Avenue and Lalor Street, between Chambers and Broad streets. You'll find numerous excellent Italian restaurants in this well-kept working class enclave, as well as the Mercer County Arena, home of the Trenton Titans ice hockey team.

TRANSPORTATION INFORMATION

Airports: The **Trenton/Mercer Airport** (609/882–1600) has little regularly scheduled service; limited to East Wind Airlines. **Philadelphia International Airport** (215/937–6800) is the largest major airport close to Trenton.
Amtrak: Schedules and fares can be obtained by calling 800/USA–RAIL.

Other: In addition to Amtrak, Trenton is a major stop on the **New Jersey Transit's** Northeast Corridor Line (800/772–2222 or 800/626–RID) as well as on the **SEPTA (Southeastern Pennsylvania Transportation Authority)** (215/580–7800).

Attractions

ART AND ARCHITECTURE

New Jersey State House. Built in 1792, it's the second-oldest state capitol building in continuous use in the country. | 125 W. State St. | 609/633–2709 | Free | Tours weekdays May–Sept., Sun.–Fri. 10–3, Sat. noon–3; Oct.–Apr., Tues., Wed., Fri., Sat. 9–5.

William Trent House. This house was built by New Jersey's fifth chief justice in 1719. Today it offers a look at life during that time. | 15 Market St. | 609/989–3027 | $2 | Daily 12:30–4.

BEACHES, PARKS, AND NATURAL SITES

Cadwalader Park. Edward C. Hill, the designer of New York City's Central Park, built this 100-acre park in 1887. The park is also home to the Trenton City Museum. | West State St. | 609/989–3632 | Free | Daily dawn–dusk.

Washington Crossing State Park. The visitor center, near the site of the landing of Washington and his troops, describes the crossing as well as the conditions during the Revolutionary War at this 991-acre historic site and recreation area. A collection of Revolutionary War artifacts contains nearly 900 military items from both American and British armies. | 355 Washington Crossing-Pennington Rd. | 609/737–0623 or 609/737–9304 | www.nj.com/outdoors/parks/washington.html | Free; parking $5 weekdays, $7 weekends and Memorial Day–Labor Day | Wed.–Sun. dawn–dusk.

Ferry House State Historic Site. The Johnson Ferry House is believed to be where Washington and his officers discussed military strategy while the army continued crossing the Delaware. Here visitors will find period rooms interpreting the 18th-century life of the ferry keeper and his family. | 355 Washington Crossing-Pennington Rd. | 609/737–2515 | Free; parking $3 Memorial Day–Labor Day | Wed.–Sat. 10–4, Sun. 1–4.

CULTURE, EDUCATION, AND HISTORY

The College of New Jersey. Formerly Trenton State, the college was established in 1855 by the state legislature as The Normal School, New Jersey's first, and the nation's ninth, teacher training school. The campus has 38 buildings on its 265 acres, and more than 5,000 full-time undergraduate students. | 609/771–1855 | 2000 Pennington Rd. | Free | Daily.

The **College Art Gallery** is on the first floor of Holman Hall. It exhibits six shows annually, including a faculty show and student art show. | 609/771–2198 | Free | Feb.–May and Sept.–Dec., Sun.–Fri. noon–3.

Sovereign Bank Arena. Opened in October 1999, Trenton's newest performance venue is a $53 million building, which presents sports and family entertainment. The Arena is home to two expansion franchises as of 2000: the Trenton Titans of the East Coast Hockey League, and the Trenton Shooting Stars of the International Basketball League. | 550 S. Broad St. | 609/656–3200 | www.sovereignbank-arena.com.

MUSEUMS

New Jersey State Museum. This 1895 museum displays artworks and objects of interest in the areas of natural history, archaeology/ethnology, cultural history, and fine art. Hands-on workshops, talks, performances, children's theater, group tours, and sky shows in the adjoining 150-seat planetarium are also offered. | 205 W. State St. | 609/292–6464 | fax 609/599–4098 | www.state.nj.us/state/museum/musidx.html | Free | Tues.–Sat. 10–4, Sun. noon–4.

All space on the first level of the four-story **Main Building** is devoted to changing exhibitions. Other galleries allocated for short-term exhibitions are devoted to showcasing New Jersey Arts, as well as the New Jersey State Museum's permanent collections. Second-floor and lower-level exhibitions feature the natural history of New Jersey, and selections from the New Jersey State Museum's collection of fine arts, cultural history, archaeology, and ethnology.

The 416-seat **Auditorium** is used for lectures, concerts, and other special events.| 609/292–6464.

The 150-seat, state-of-the-art **Planetarium** features sky shows and demonstrations. | 609/292–6303 | $1.

The Old Barracks Museum. Barracks dating from 1758, when they housed British troops drawn into the French and Indian War, have been turned into a museum. (The barracks also saw service during the American Revolution.) The museum has four furnished hospital rooms and an officers house with period furnishings. There's also an interactive "History Lab," where visitors can explore the working environments of the historian, historic architect, archaeologist, and curator, using the barracks' own restoration as a case study. | Barrack St. | 609/396–1776 | www.barracks.org/main/main.html. | $6 | Daily 10–4.

ON THE CALENDAR

JAN.: *Super Science Weekend.* This event is the New Jersey State Museum's annual extravaganza of exhibits, workshops, hands-on experiments, and other programs. | 609/292–6464.

FEB.: *African-American History Program.* This annual program, held at the Old Barracks Museum, commemorates the role of African-Americans in the Revolution. | 609/396–1776.

JUNE: *Heritage Days at Mill Hill Park.* Attracting more than 100,000 visitors annually, this two-day festival celebrates New Jersey's cultural diversity with food, exhibits, crafts, children's activities, and music. | 609/695–7107.

DEC.: *Battle of Trenton Celebration.* Citywide events commemorate Washington's victories over the Hessians and the British. | 609/396–1776.

DEC.: *George Washington's Crossing of the Delaware.* A reenactment of this famed 1776 event is held on Christmas Day at the original site, in what is now Washington Crossing State Park. It's on the state border at Titusville. | 609/737–0623.

Dining

MODERATE

Marsilio's. Italian. A venerable Trenton favorite, Marsilio's is especially busy at lunch, when one plate of the popular chicken cacciatore is served after another. | 541 Roebling Ave. | 609/695–1916 | Closed Sun. | $19–$44 | AE, MC, V.

Sal De Forte's. Italian. This restaurant, in the predominately Italian neighborhood of Chambersburg, has remained an institution in the community since 1960. Homemade breads and soups lead to an array of pasta, chicken, and seafood dishes for dinner. | 449 S. Broad St. | 609/396–6856 | No breakfast. No lunch weekends | $13.95–$24.95 | AE, DC, MC, V.

EXPENSIVE

Anthony Merlino's Waterfront. Continental. Relax in the dark-paneled dining rooms or lounge by the fireplaces. This place is known for veal, beef, and seafood. | 1140 River Rd. | 609/882–0303 | No lunch Sat. | $15–$30 | AE, D, DC, MC, V.

Diamond's. Italian. This restaurant is known for its classic seafood, steak, and veal dishes. The veal Saltimbocca—veal with prosciutto, provolone, and spinach is very popular. | 132 Kent St. | 609/393–1000 | No lunch Sat., Sun. | $12–$35 | AE, D, DC, MC, V.

Urban World Cafe. Contemporary. Join a hip young crowd at this Trenton hot spot for poetry readings, live music, and standout dishes at reasonable prices. Try the pan-seared ahi tuna or the Tijuana tortilla with chicken and black bean sauce. | 449 S. Broad St. | 609/989–7777 | No lunch Sat., no dinner Sun. | $13–$16 | AE, MC, V.

Lodging

Howard Johnson's Lawrenceville., This two-story motel was built in 1962 and renovated in 1996. It is near Princeton University (8 mi), Rider College (2 mi), Trenton College (4 mi), and Mercer County Park (3 mi). It's in Lawrenceville, less than 4 mi from downtown Trenton. Restaurant, bar, complimentary Continental breakfast. Cable TV. Pool. Business services. Some pets allowed. | 2995 Rte. 1,Lawrenceville | 609/896–1100 or 800/406–1411 | fax 609/895–1325 | www.hojo.com | 104 rooms | $70–$125 | AE, DC, D, MC, V.

UNION

(Nearby towns also listed: Chatham, Elizabeth, Millburn, Newark, Short Hills, Summit)

Of all the cities named Union, this town claims its fame by being the first. Union was known as Connecticut Farms, until it separated from Elizabeth in 1808. At that time the area's nutrient-rich soil was producing bountiful crops of all kinds and it sustained the farming community for many years after. Today, many of the town's residents are employed with Shearing Plow, a pharmaceutical company, or the local hospital. A large retirement community resides here as well. There's a small but active nightlife scene downtown with a few sports bars and theaters. Union is also home to Keane University.

Information: **Union Township Chamber of Commerce** | 355 Chestnut St., Union, 07083 | 908/688–2777 | fax 908/688–0338. | www.unionchamber.com.

Attractions

The Model Railroad Club Inc. This 50-year-old club built and runs one of the largest model railroad layouts in the world. Its annual show runs the three weekends after Thanksgiving. | 295 Jefferson Ave. | 908/964–9724 | www.tmrci.com/ | $2 | Sat. 1–4.

ON THE CALENDAR
MAY: *Union Center Street Fair.* Downtown comes alive with arts, crafts, food, music, and children's activities. | 908/996–3036.

Dining

Ristorante da Benito. Italian. Da Benito's dining room is modern and understated with dark wood accents, sheer window panels, and a wall mural. Dishes such as the fennel-stuffed lemon-glazed chicken and the pan-roasted salmon over homemade fusilli are two examples of the chef's talent. | 222 Galloping Hill Rd. | 908/964–5850 | Closed Sun. No lunch Sat. | $16–$26 | AE, DC, MC, V.

Lodging

Holiday Inn. This hotel, less than 4 mi from downtown Union, is 8 mi from Newark International Airport, 5 mi from Bowcraft Amusement Park, and 1 mi from a multiplex theater. You can work out at the nearby Bally's health club. Restaurant, bar. In-room data ports, cable TV. Pool. Exercise room. Laundry service. Business services. Some pets allowed. | 304 Rte. 22 W,Springfield | 973/376–9400 or 800/465–4329 | fax 973/376–9534 | www.basshotels.com/holiday-inn | 190 rooms | $112 | AE, D, DC, MC, V.

VERNON

(Nearby towns also listed: Franklin, Walpack Center)

Vernon is sleepy Sussex County's hub of activity and has a population count of about 23,000. Founded in 1792, today it is home to the state's most challenging ski slopes, as well as more than 10 top-notch golf courses. The Appalachian Trail goes through the town, drawing hikers to the area. The rugged terrain keeps most of Vernon, except for a growing downtown, from being developed. Most residences are nestled in small valley hamlets. Among the 68 square mi of Vernon, 48% of it is protected as sacred wetlands or is part of a National Park, such as High Point.

Information: **Sussex County Chamber of Commerce** | 120 Hampton House Rd., Newton, 07860 | 973/579–1811 | www.sussexcountychamber.org.

Attractions

Hidden Valley Resort. Hidden Valley is a small, manageable ski area with shorter lift lines due to a limited number of tickets sold each day. It's good for families. | Breakneck Rd. | 973/764–4200 | hidval@warwick.net | www.hiddenvalleynj.com | Mid-Dec.–Mar.

High Point State Park. This 14,000-acre park, one of the most popular in the state, include's New Jersey's highest point (hence the name). The 220-ft High Point Monument offers sweeping views of the Pocono Mountains toward the west, the Catskill Mountains to the north, and the Wallkill River valley in the southeast. Among the hiking trails is the Appalachian Trail. The park has facilities for cross-country skiing, boating on Sawmill and Steenykill lakes, picnicking, swimming, and camping April–October. It's in Sussex, about 30 mi north of Vernon. | 1480 Rte. 23, Sussex | 973/875–4800 | Free; parking $7 | Daily.

Mountain Creek. Formerly Vernon Valley/Great Gorge Ski Resort, the property was taken over in 1998 by developers who pumped $25 million into improving what was already the biggest ski resort in the state. | Rte. 94 | 973/827–2000 | www.mountaincreek.com | Apr.–Oct., daily.
Mountain Creek's summer water and amusement park, formerly known as Action Park, **Mountain Creek Water Park** is the largest water park in the region with 26 rides, slides and pools. Don't miss the H2 "Oh No," a 99-ft speed slide, the Colorado River Ride (with more than 12,000 ft of light water rapids), or the 18-ft leap from the canyon cliff. There are also concerts and special festivals outdoors. | Rte. 94 | 973/827–2000 | $25 | June–Oct. daily 10–7.

ON THE CALENDAR

AUG.: *Sussex Air Show.* One of the East Coast's largest, this air show at Sussex Airport has world-class performers, old-time barnstorming, and vintage planes. | 973/875–7337 or 973/875–0783.

Lodging

Alpine Haus Bed & Breakfast Inn. This 1880s Federal-style inn is adjacent to Mountain Creek Ski Resort and Water Park, close to the Appalachian Trail, and minutes from Hidden Valley Ski area and the Great Gorge Golf Reserve. The antiques-furnished guest rooms are named after mountain wildflowers, and the suites have fireplaces. In summer, breakfast is served outside on a covered porch with sweeping views of Vernon Valley. Complimentary breakfast. | 217 Rte. 94 | 973/209–7080 | fax 970/209–7090 | alpinehs@warwick.net | www.alpinehausbb.com | 8 rooms, 2 suites | $110–$180 | AE, V.

Legends Resort and Country Club. Rooms have a scenic view of mountains and a golf course. The resort is just outside Vernon. Restaurant, bar (with entertainment). Some kitchenettes, cable TV. 2 pools, wading pool. Hot tub, sauna. Driving range, 27-hole golf course, putting green, tennis. Hiking. Downhill skiing, sleigh rides. Children's programs, playground. | Rte. 517 North, McAfee | 973/827–6000 or 800/835–2555 | fax 201/827–3767 | 350 rooms | $99–$139 | AE, D, DC, MC, V.

WALPACK CENTER

MAP 9, E2

(Nearby towns also listed: Franklin, Vernon)

This small town is actually within a 70,000-acre park: the Delaware Water Gap National Recreation Area. Nature lovers can easily spend an entire weekend exploring the 40 mi of the Delaware River preserved in the park, which is famous for its spectacular views of the Appalachian Mountains. It's one of the few places in the Garden State where you can see free-flowing waterfalls, streams, and tranquil forest areas—all in a single afternoon. And for those in the mood to explore the days of yore, visit the many "ghost town" villages within the park. A word of caution, make sure you pack plenty of provisions before you go. There are scant few place to buy food, water, or other necessities in the immediate vicinity.

Information: **Kittatinny Point Visitor Center** | 3 Hwy. 80, Columbia, 07832; I–80 to the Delaware Water Gap, at the Millbrook Exit, the last exit in NJ | 908/496–4458 | fax 570/588–2780 | Email dewa_interpretation@nps.gov | www.nps.gov/dewa | Mon.–Sun. 9–5.

Attractions

National Recreation Area. Outdoor enthusiasts will feel as though they've died and gone to hiker's heaven. There are more than 60 mi of trails here, and you can also camp, fish, hunt, swim, rock climb, bicycle, canoe or picnic. In season, designated sections are open for ice-fishing, ice-skating, cross-country skiing, and snowmobiling. | 570/588–2451 (PA information) or 908/496–4458 (NJ information) | Certain areas for parking are free, elsewhere, a $5-$7 charge applies. Other recreational fees vary | Year-round. Dawn to dusk.

Peters Valley. One of only a handful of nationally recognized "craft education centers," this working artist's village offers the chance to take a self-guided walking tour through eight different art studios houses in historic buildings dating back to the late 1700's. The craft gallery is open all year, and on weekends, you can stroll through the studios and watch artists at work. Peters Valley is within the Delaware Water Gap National Recreation Area. | 19 Kuhn Rd., Layton; Located on Rte. 615 and Kuhn Rd. | 973/948–5200 | pv@warwick.net | www.pvcrafts.org | Free | Mid-May to mid-Sept., Sat. and Sun. 2–5 PM.

Historic Villages of Walpack Center, Millbrook Village, and Van Campen Inn. Meander through time as you explore the remnants of several architecturally significant 19th century villages and homes, all within the Delaware Water Gap National Recreation Area. Although some of the homes have sparse furnishings, the knowledgeable staffers make the homes come alive. Tour the Van Campen Inn, a former lodge that in its heyday was visited by luminaries of the American Revolution. Self-guided tours are allowed. There is a terrific view along Old Mine Road as you approach the villages. | Old Mine Rd. | 908/496–4458 | Free | Mostly weekends in the summer, call for availability of guided tours.

ON THE CALENDAR

OCT.: *Millbrook Days.* Demonstrations, tours, programs, and activities celebrate rural farm life of the 1800's. Enjoy a hayride and a free apple-butter cooking workshop. | 908/496–4458.

SEPT.: *Peters Valley Craft fair.* This two-day juried craft fair features 200 exhibitors from around the country, free music and food vendors galore. | 973/948–5202.

OCT.: *Van Campen Days.* Local volunteers dress in costumes and conduct live re-enactments of the French and Indian War periods. Staffers also perform demonstrations of colonial-era crafts like lacemaking and caning. | 908/496–4458.

OCT.: *Octivities.* Decorate pumpkins and make Halloween-themed crafts. Great for kids. | 908/496–4458.

Dining

The Walpack Inn. Steak. If you've ever fantasized about eating in a greenhouse, don't miss this spot, snuggled in the heart of the Delaware Water Gap National Recreation Area's magnificent park. The greenhouse room – a glass enclosed dining area overflowing with flowering plants and ferns - is amazing, and you'll see deer grazing just a few feet away outside on the lawn. Hunting enthusiasts might be more inclined to choose the wildlife room, with the expected animal trophies mounted on the walls. The salad bar is plentiful and the Swedish Bread is a house specialty. | Route 615 (no address), Walpack Center | 973/948–9849 or 973/948–6505 | fax 973/948–9849 | walpakinn.com | Open Fri.–Sat. dinner only 5-10 PM Sun. 12–8 PM | $12–$34 | MC, V.

The Deli Depot. Delicatessen. Located in a 1916 building, the Deli Depot is the place to grab a quick sandwich and some groceries to go. There's a small outside eating area, but no wait staff. You'll have to cross (NJ) state lines to get here, it's in PA about 20 mi from the Kittatinny Visitor Center in NJ. | (no mailing address) Corner of Bushkill Falls Road and Route 209, Bushkill, PA | 570/588–0444 | Year-round | $3–$6 | MC, V.

The Delaware View House. If you need some bait, a bag of chips and a drink, this general store is the only place on the map. There isn't much else, but if you're thirsty and your thermos is empty, you'll be glad you stumbled on in. | Intersection of Old Mine Rd. and Blue Mountain Lake Rd., Delaware Water Gap National Recreation Area Park (near Flatbrookville, located in the park); About 13 mi north of Interstate 80 | Open weekends in the summer | $3–$6.

Lodging

Columbia Day's Inn. Perfect for a budget-minded traveler who'll be out exploring most of the day, this motel offers a scenic view of the Delaware Water gap, clean rooms, and lots of nearby attractions. If you've exhausted the park's offerings, you can drive a few miles to "civilization," where the nearby Pocono and Shawnee resort areas have golfing, skiing and other activities. The restaurant is open 24 hours, and three local fast food spots are within walking distance. Restaurant. Business services. Some pets allowed. | Post Office Box 305, Columbia, NJ; Exit 4 off Route 80. About 15–20 mi from Walpack | 908/496–8221 or 800/DAYS–INN | fax 908/496–4809 | www.daysinn.com | 35 rooms | $58–$62 | AE, D, DC, MC, V.

Worthington State Forest Campgrounds. This bustling campground is one of the most popular camping spots in the area. Be warned however, it's rather primitive. While you'll find shower facilities and flush toilets, there are no water or electric hookups. Pets aren't allowed, and reservations are required. | 908/841–9575 | www.webari.com /njparks | 69 family tent sites | $10–$15 | MC, V.

The Walpack Inn Cabin. For those who long to camp out but don't really want to give up the comforts of home, this "luxury," cabin is just the thing. It sleeps up to seven and has three bedrooms, and yes, there's indoor plumbing, although no TV or phone. The kitchen is modern and fully equipped, and it's also only a short walk to the acclaimed Walpack Inn. Rent it by the night or by the week – but make sure you reserve far in advance, it books up quickly. | $100–200 per night.

WARETOWN

MAP 9, G8

(Nearby towns also listed: Long Beach Island, Toms River)

This town of 5,700, whose population increases dramatically in the summer, sits along Bonagat Bay. The little town survived as a fishing village in the 1800s and many people still enjoy fishing as a pastime in this coastal spot. Commuting to Atlantic City, New York, or Newark is very common here. Bluegrass, country, and folk music have been enjoyed by this community for years—every week there is live entertainment at the Albert Music Hall. As the home of the Pinelands Cultural Society, Waretown also hosts the concert, "Sounds of the Jersey Pines," at Albert Hall every Saturday night.

Information: **NJ Pinelands Commission** | 15 Springfield Rd., New Lisbon, 08064 | 609/894–7300 | fax 609/894–7330 | info@njpines.state.nj.us | www.state.nj.us/pinelands.

Attractions

Albert Music Hall. A group of old-time musicians from the Pine Barrens used to gather every Saturday night, beginning about 25 years ago, at the home of Joe and George Albert, and play until the sun came out. In 1997, an actual Albert Music Hall building (complete with porch) was constructed for this Pine Barrens institution, where on a given Saturday you might be entertained by anyone from a master spoon-player to an amateur crooner at "Sounds of the Jersey Pines." Bring your instrument and you'll get a chance to join in. | 125 Wells Mills Rd. (Rte. 532) | 609/971–1593 | www.alberthall.org/main.html | $4 | Sat. 7:30–11:30.

Wells Mills County Park. Hike, bike, and bird-watch in more than 800 acres of Pinelands. The Nature Center runs educational programs on weekends. | 905 Wells Mills Rd. | 609/971–3085 | Free | Daily.

ON THE CALENDAR

SEPT.: *Ocean County Bluegrass Festival.* Enjoy live bluegrass music with food and crafts, at the Albert Music Hall. | 609/971–1593.

OCT.: *Chatsworth Cranberry Festival.* Celebrate the harvest of the berry in South Jersey with tons of food and baked goods made from cranberries, along with contests, bog tours, entertainment, and displays. Events take place at different shops and restaurants around town. | 609/859–9701.

OCT.: *Halloween Show.* This festival of live bluegrass, country, and folk music is made seasonal with a costume contest and Halloween refreshments. At Albert Hall. | 609/971–1593.

DEC.: *Holiday Show.* Bring the kids to meet Santa at Albert Music Hall and sing old-time Christmas tunes. | 609/971–1593.

Dining

Burrito House. Mexican. For good, authentic, and inexpensive Mexican food, this little no-frills storefront restaurant does the trick. The huge burritos are made with fresh ingredients. Takeout is available. | 304 Rte. 9 (Seneca Rd.) | 609/698–9800 | $5–$10 | MC, V.

Lodging

Sea Pine Motor Inn. This highway motel is 10 mi from Long Beach Island and close to a park and a national wildlife refuge. Restaurant, bar. Cable TV. Pool. No pets. | 529 Rte. 9 | 609/693–6600 | fax 609/971–3222 | 38 rooms | $45–$100 | AE, D, MC, V.

WAYNE

(Nearby town also listed: Paterson)

The first European got a glimpse of Wayne, or Pompton Valley, around 1694. Before that the land had been inhabited by the Lenni-Lenape Indian Tribe. Their legacy can be read in the names of the natural sites and the streets of the area. In 1695 Wayne was purchased from the East Jersey Company by the English in New York and it remained a simple farming community throughout the 18th and 19th centuries. Once the railroad was built in the early 20th century, vacationers from New York City began to explore this natural haven. Now many of Wayne's 50,000 citizens commute to Manhattan, happy to have a spacious home with a yard to come home to.

Information: Tri-County Chamber of Commerce | 2055 Hamburg Tpk., Wayne, 07470 | 973/831–7788 | fax 973/831–9112 | business@tricounty.org | www.tricounty.org.

Attractions
Dey Mansion. George Washington used this home as a headquarters in 1780. Tours are offered, along with lectures, concerts, and craft shows. | 199 Totowa Rd. | 973/696–1776 | $1 | Tues.–Wed., Fri.–Sun. 1–4.

Schuyler-Colfax House. Wayne's oldest home, built in 1696 by pioneer settler Arent Schuyler, was a private home for eight generations of his family. In 1966, it was named an historical site by the state, and became a Wayne Township Museum. | 2321 Hamburg Tpk. | $1 | Weekends 1–4.

Terhune Memorial Park–Sunnybank. The grounds of the former home of Albert Payson Terhune, author of *Lad* and other dog stories, have been made into a park. Look for the marked graves of favorite dogs. The house itself was torn down many years ago. | Terhune Dr. | Free | Daily.

ON THE CALENDAR
SEPT.: *Tri-County Chamber of Commerce's 5th Annual Antique/Classic Car Show.*
View old cars and trucks in the State Farm Insurance parking lot. There's also car memorabilia, food, and Golden Oldies music. | 973/831–7788.

Dining
Brunello's Ristorante. Italian. Brunello's has excellent northern Italian food served in a pretty dining room with murals and marble accents. Recommended dishes include the Florida rock shrimp appetizer, the tequila-cured salmon entrée, and the 32-ounce Porterhouse steak. There is live piano music Thursday–Saturday evenings. | 120 Terhune Dr. | 973/616–0999 | fax 973/616–0504 | www.brunelloristorante.com | No lunch Sat. | $13–$24 | AE, V.

Lodging
Best Western Executive Inn. At this four-story "business traveler's home away from home" one can stay in to enjoy nightly entertainment at the Images lounge or take the free shuttle to area restaurants and businesses including the Willowbrook Mall. It's about 5 mi from Wayne. Restaurant, bar (with entertainment), complimentary breakfast, room service. In-room data ports, refrigerators, some in-room hot-tubs, cable TV. Pool. Hot tub. Exercise equipment. Laundry facilities. Business services. | 216 U.S. 46 E, Fairfield | 973/575–7700 | fax 973/575–4653 | 170 rooms | $61–$88 | AE, DC, MC, V.

Holiday Inn. Guests have privileges at a nearby fitness center and at the Golden Bear driving range and miniature golf course. Restaurant, bar (with entertainment), room service. In-room data ports, cable TV. Pool. Business services. | 334 U.S. 46 E | 973/256–7000 | fax 973/890–5406 | 140 rooms | $79–$119 | AE, D, DC, MC, V.

Holiday Inn Totowa. You'll find a movie theater and plenty of restaurants and shopping within 2 mi of this modern five-story chain hotel in Totowa, about 3 mi from Wayne. Rooms have roll-out workstations. Restaurant, complimentary Continental breakfast, room service. In-room data ports, cable TV. Pool. Exercise equipment. Business services. | 1 U.S. 46 W, Totowa | 973/785–9000 | fax 973/785–3031 | 155 rooms | $104–$139 | AE, D, DC, MC, V.

Howard Johnson. Although there's no restaurant in this two-story HoJo's, there are several within walking distance, including the Greenhouse Cafe. The hotel is scheduled for a complete overhaul in 2001. Complimentary breakfast. Some in-room data ports, some refrigerators, cable TV. Pool. Laundry facilities. Business services, airport shuttle. Some pets allowed. | 1850 Rte. 23 | 973/696–8050 | fax 973/696–0682 | www.hojo.com | 149 rooms | $75–$105 | AE, D, DC, MC, V.

Meadowlands Plaza Hotel. This hotel is 1 mi from the Willowbrook Mall, 1½ mi from the Essex County Airport, 5 mi from the Meadowlands Sports Plaza, and 25 minutes by car from New York City. There are conference facilities and a jogging track. Restaurant, complimentary Continental breakfast. In-room data ports, cable TV. Laundry services. Business services. | 286 Rte. 46, Fairfield | 973/227–4333 | fax 973/227–5399 | 70 rooms | $70–$75 | AE, D, DC, MC, V.

Radisson Fairfield. If Gotham beckons, it's about 35 minutes from this full-service five-story hotel to New York City. Built in the 1970s, the hotel was renovated in 2000. It's in Fairfield, about five minutes west of Wayne. Restaurant, bar (with entertainment), room service. In-room hot tubs, cable TV. Pool. Exercise equipment. Business services. | 690 U.S. 46 E, Fairfield | 973/227–9200 | fax 973/227–4308 | 204 rooms | $189–$209 | AE, D, DC, MC, V.

Ramada Inn Fairfield. Located off Interstate 80 and Route 46, this chain hotel, 3.6 mi southwest of downtown Wayne, has an an indoor pool with a retractable roof and a pretty courtyard. The restaurant on the premises, the Sports Bar & Grille, broadcasts national sporting events from two satellite dishes. There's happy hour every weeknight. Restaurant, bar, room service. In-room data ports, cable TV. Pool. Exercise room. Laundry service. | 38 Two Bridges Rd., Fairfield | 973/575–1742 or 888/298–2054 | fax 973/575–9567 | www.ramadainn.com | 176 rooms | $69–$119 | AE, D, DC, MC, V.

WEST ORANGE

MAP 4, C6

(Nearby towns also listed: Montclair, Newark)

West Orange (pop. 40,802) was settled in the 1600s by Puritans from Milford, Connecticut, who were opposed to the religious leniency there. The green valleys and ridges that drew the early settlers are still there and you'll find large, lush parks and golf courses in the area. Take time to explore the hiking trails and bridle paths at the Eagle Rock and South Mountain reservations. Thomas Edison resided here from 1886 until he died in 1931. Today, West Orange is a suburban community 5 mi from Newark and 20 mi from New York City.

Information: **West Orange Chamber of Commerce** | Box 83, West Orange, 07052 | 973/731–0360 | fax 973/676–8725 | www.westorange.com.

Attractions

Eagle Rock Reservation. A 400-acre wooded oasis in the midst of Central Jersey's urban sprawl, this park is situated on the crest of the Watchung's First Mountain. During the 19th century, it was a weekend retreat for Manhattanites, but today it remains largely undeveloped and has hiking and bridle trails. Lookout Point offers a great view of the Manhattan skyline (which is why many people find the Highlawn Pavilion restaurant, a historic structure dating from 1910 and within the reservation, so romantic). | Prospect Ave. and Eagle Rock Ave. | 973/268–3500 or 973/731–3000 | Free | Daily.

★ **Edison National Historic Site.** Thomas Edison's former research laboratory and his home are preserved at this site. The laboratory and its surrounding factories employed thousands of workers, and gave birth to many of Edison's inventions. Park rangers give tours through the chemistry laboratory, machine shop, the library, and through a replica of the Black Maria, the first motion picture studio. Glenmont, built in 1880, is a Victorian mansion on a 15-acres in Llewellyn Park, the country's first private residential community. | Main St. and Lakeside Ave. | 973/736–0550 | Free | Tours available Weds.–Fri. 12:30–4, weekends 10–4.

South Mountain Reservation. This is the largest tract of parkland in Essex County, covering nearly 2,100 acres in the central section of the county, extending through the municipalities of West Orange, Maplewood, and Millburn. Enjoy 10 picnic areas, 20 mi of hiking and walking trails, 27 mi of carriage roads for jogging, horseback riding, and cross-country skiing, and more. | 560 Northfield Ave. | 973/268–3500 or 973/731–5801 | Free | June–Sept., daily; Oct.–May, weekends.

South Mountain Arena includes two indoor ice-skating rinks, and the New Jersey Devils hockey team's training facilities are here. The arena is also used for special events. | 560 Northfield Ave. | 973/731–3828 | Price varies with event | Daily 10–9.

The 16-acre **Turtle Back Zoo** includes domestic and wild animals, and a train ride. At press time, the zoo was building an otter house. | 560 Northfield Ave. | 973/731–5800 or 973/731–5801 | $5 | Apr.–Nov., daily; Nov.–Apr., weekends.

ON THE CALENDAR

MAY: *Essex County Fair.* This typical county fair, held in the South Mountain Arena, includes educational and agricultural exhibits, 4-H displays, rides, games, food, and family activities. | 973/268–3551.

NOV.–JAN.: *Christmas at Glenmont.* An exhibit at the Edison National Historic Site shows how Thomas Edison and family would have celebrated the holidays. | 973/736–0550.

Dining

Highlawn Pavilion. Continental. During World War I, Thomas Edison worked in the upstairs rooms here on various top-secret Navy projects. Today, this 1909 building is furnished with beautiful antiques, such as 400-year-old Venetian lanterns and 15th-century chairs in the courtyard lobby. Try the grilled salmon-smoked polenta cake, the seared diver scallops, or the white-corn and fava-bean risotto. Pianist Thursday–Saturday. | Eagle Rock Reservation | 973/731–3463 | www.highlawn.com/index.html | Jacket required | No lunch Sat., Sun. | $19–$32 | AE, D, DC, MC, V.

The Manor. Continental. In a manor house, this grandly decorated and bustling special-occasion place offers a view of formal gardens, which include a waterfall. The menu has seafood, chicken, veal, and a wide selection of desserts. Pianist Tuesday–Sunday, live band Friday–Saturday. | 111 Prospect Ave. | 973/731–2360 | www.themanorrestaurant.com | Jacket required | Closed Mon. No lunch Sat. | $25–$33 | AE, D, DC, MC, V.

Pals Cabin. American. This Essex County institution started as a 10-ft-by-12-ft hot dog stand in 1932. Today it's known for steaks, seafood, fresh-ground burgers, and cream of mushroom soup. Sunday brunch. | 265 Prospect Ave. | 973/731–4000 | www.palscabin.com | Breakfast also available | $14–$25 | AE, D, MC, V.

Lodging

Turtle Brook Inn. Walk to restaurants and the 16-acre Turtle Brook Zoo from this modern inn. Complimentary Continental breakfast. In-room data ports, cable TV. | 555 Northfield Ave. | 973/731–5300 or 800/731–3002 | fax 973/731–0263 | www.turtlebrookinn.com | 45 standard rooms, 9 deluxe rooms, 2 suites | $85–$95 | AE, D, DC, MC, V.

WILDWOOD
(See The Wildwoods)

WILDWOOD CREST
(See The Wildwoods)

THE WILDWOODS

MAP 9, E12

(Nearby towns also listed: Cape May, Stone Harbor)

"The Wildwoods," as they're called, are made up of three areas: Wildwood, Wildwood Crest, and North Wildwood, each with a slightly different flavor. Wildwood is where three of the famous amusement piers are, and is home to the national marbles and stunt kite-flying tournaments. Wildwood and Wildwood Crest are also popular for their great collection of 1950s architecture, including some classic old motels. Sunset Lake, in Wildwood Crest, offers fishing, boating, and beautiful sunsets. Wildwood is a long-time summer vacation spot, with 5 mi of wide (sometimes too wide for kids or the less energetic) white beaches plus 3 mi of boardwalk with amusement rides, games, shops, and restaurants. Special events, historic sites (including a lighthouse), and proximity to Cape May make it an especially busy and varied New Jersey shore town.

Information: **Wildwood Chamber of Commerce** | 1 Rte. 47 S, Wildwood, 08260 | 609/729–1934 or 800/WW–BY–SEA | fax 609/522–5420 | www.wildwoods.org.

Attractions

The Boardwalk. The boardwalk, which celebrated its centennial in 1999, encompasses more than 2 mi of "boards" with five amusement piers, the bulk of them owned by the Morey family. Morey's Pier itself boasts the tallest Ferris wheel in America. There are water parks, bumper cars, and five major roller coasters, along with some bungeelike thrill rides. You'll find all sorts of visitors here, from heavy-metal types to grandparents. | On the ocean | 800/786–4546 boardwalk information, 888/MOREYS–1 Morey's Piers | www.wildwoods.org or www.moreyspiers.com | Free | Daily.

Doo-Wop Trolley Tours. Tours of so-called "doo-wop" 1950s-era architecture, preserved in the town's rich stock of old-fashioned motels, are offered on this 45-minute tour. Tour goers will learn about the shapes, images, and symbols associated with the designs, about "fractured geography," and about the space-age infatuation of the day. | Information booth at Washington St. Mall, on Washington St. and Ocean St. | 609/884–5404 | $10 | June–Sept., Tues. and Thurs., call for hrs.

Hereford Inlet Lighthouse. Built in 1874, the small, high Victorian lighthouse has a charming, quiet place on the beach in North Wildwood, and is open for visits. | 1st and Central Aves. | 609/522–4520 | www.woodbridgenj.com/bararts.html | $3 | Weekdays 9–7.

Ocean Discovery Center. This marine environment educational center offers individualized boat and beach tours. | 6006 Park Blvd., Wildwood | 609/523–8989 or 800/942–5373 | Varies with tours | Tours by appointment May–Nov.

Sunset Lake & Turtle Gut Park and Memorial. This area marks the site of an American Revolution battle fought in Cape May County. | New Jersey and Miami Aves, Wildwood Crest | 609/522–7788 | Free.

Wyland's Whaling Wall. This huge wall mural (220 ft by 30 ft) depicting life-size whales and dolphins was painted by acclaimed marine artist Wyland. It's on the Boardwalk Mall at Garfield Ave. | Wildwood | Free.

ON THE CALENDAR

APR.: *Easter Festivities.* Celebrate the holiday with vendors, a craft show, an Easter fashions show, and more, at the Wildwoods Convention Center. | 609/729–9000.

MAY: *Annual East Coast Boardwalk Nationals Car Show.* More than 1,500 classic cars are on display, along with plenty of engine noise. There are also awards, concerts, crafts, and vendors. | 609/523–8051.

MAY: *Annual Wildwoods International Kite Festival.* America's largest kite festival includes world-renowned kite builders and competitors, sport kite competitions, kite buggy racing, indoor competitions, illuminated night kite flying, and kite making. At the Wildwoods Convention Center. | 215/736–3715.

MAY: *Pirates Weekend with Captain Kidd.* Hunt for treasure on the beach, win prizes, and enjoy the parade. In North Wildwood Beach. | 800/882–7787.

MAY: *Wildwood's Boardwalk Bash Clown Convention.* Celebrate the art of clowning with lectures, vendors, workshops, competitions, and a parade. At the Wildwoods Convention Center. | 609/909–9411.

JUNE: *Annual Polka Spree by the Sea.* Top polka bands provide nonstop music for listening and dancing, at the Wildwoods Convention Center. | 908/359–5520.

JUNE: *Seafood Festival.* Events at this North Wildwood weekend-long festival include a 5-mi run, crafts, seafood, and an antique car show. Festival events take place all over town, call for locations. | 800/882–7787.

JUNE: *National Marbles Tournament.* Champions from around the country vie for national honors and scholarships at Ringer Stadium. | 301/724–1279.

JUNE–SEPT.: *Events on the Boardwalk* Mondays through Labor Day Weekend, the Cape Atlantic Irish Piper Brigade marches on the Wildwoods Boardwalk from 16th to Cresse Avenues. Thursday night is Family Fun Night on the boardwalk with parades, clowns, string band performance, and more. Fridays bring fireworks on the beach at Pine Avenue. | 609/523–1602.

YOUR CAR'S FIRST-AID KIT

- ❏ Bungee cords or rope to tie down trunk if necessary
- ❏ Club soda to remove stains from upholstery
- ❏ Cooler with bottled water
- ❏ Extra coolant
- ❏ Extra windshield-washer fluid
- ❏ Flares and/or reflectors
- ❏ Flashlight and extra batteries
- ❏ Hand wipes to clean hands after roadside repair
- ❏ Hose tape

- ❏ Jack and fully inflated spare
- ❏ Jumper cables
- ❏ Lug wrench
- ❏ Owner's manual
- ❏ Plastic poncho—in case you need to do roadside repairs in the rain
- ❏ Quart of oil and quart of transmission fluid
- ❏ Spare fan belts
- ❏ Spare fuses
- ❏ Tire-pressure gauge

*Excerpted from *Fodor's: How to Pack: Experts Share Their Secrets*
© 1997, by Fodor's Travel Publications

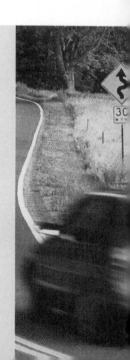

JULY: *Annual Doo Wop Music Festival.* Celebrate the 1950s with music, vendors, crafts, food, and memorabilia at the Wildwoods Convention Center. | 609/729–9000.

JULY: *N.J. State Barbecue Championship.* Bring your appetite to North Wildwood for some of the best barbecue around. The contest takes place on 2nd and New Jersey Avenues. | 856/881–8062.

JULY–SEPT.: *Summer Concert Series.* Enjoy 21 free concerts in North Wildwood, every Thursday and Saturday evening, featuring top artists from the 1950s through today. The venue changes each year, so call ahead. | 800/882–7787.

SEPT.: *Thunder on the Beach.* Watch monster trucks do their thing, along with plenty of food, entertainment, and truck rides. On the Boardwalk, at Young Avenue. | 609/523–8051.

Dining

Captain's Table. Seafood. Dine overlooking the water in what feels like the inside of a ship. Lobster tail is the most popular dish, but the menu has plenty of other seafood choices too. Kids' menu. | 8800 Atlantic Ave. | 609/522–2939 | Breakfast also available; closed mid-Oct.–Mother's Day. No lunch | $15–$44 | AE, D, DC, MC, V.

Garfield Giardino. Italian. Traditional dishes like Veal Saltimbocca are served, along with a variety of pasta sauces. The decor is modern, and the restaurant feature entertainment in July and August. Kids' menu. | 3800 Pacific Ave., Wildwood | 609/729–0120 | No lunch July, Aug. Nov.–mid-Mar. | $21–$43 | AE, D, DC, MC, V.

Groff's. American. You'll find old-fashioned comfort food at its best at this restaurant, which first opened in 1932 and is still owned and run by the original family. Think pork chops with apple sauce, fried chicken, and lemon meringue and coconut cream pies. One of the original waitresses, a former Miss Wildwood now in her 80s, still works here in summer. | 423 E. Magnolia, Wildwood | 609/522–5474 | Closed late Sept.–mid-May. No lunch | $9–$26 | AE, D, DC, MC, V.

Luigi's. Italian/American. A friendly atmosphere, where you can get favorites done right, like spaghetti with meat sauce, or fettucine Alfredo, served at tables that comfortably accommodate families. Kids' menu. | 4119 Pacific Ave. | 609/522–8571 | Closed mid-Oct.–Easter. No lunch | $16–$45 | AE, D, DC, MC, V.

Papa Joe's Bayside Pizza Pasta House. Pizza. This neighborhood pizza joint is loved by locals who come for white pizza, seafood pasta dishes, hoagies, and milk shakes. Takeout is available and delivery is free. | 6710 New Jersey Ave., Wildwood Crest | 609/729–3236 | $4–$10 | AE, V.

Snuffy's. American. This corner luncheonette (and town landmark, according to locals) was opened in 1940 by Snuffy and Flo Smith and is still run by the Smiths and their kids. There is a different $3.95 soup-sandwich-and small beverage lunch special every day. | 101 E. Aster Rd., Wildwood Crest | 609/522–1825 | Breakfast also available; no dinner Sept.–June | $3–$10 | No credit cards.

Triangle Restaurant. Italian. This tiny restaurant, named for its triangle-shape building on a triangle shape-lot, serves big portions of fresh, classic Italian food—from seafood and ravioli to veal parmigiana. Large parties may find themselves too close for comfort. | New Jersey and Walnut Aves, North Wildwood | 609/522–4947 | $9–$15 | AE, V.

Lodging

Aqua Beach Resort. The paint on the walls of your room is supposed to match the color of the ocean. For the real thing, enjoy the view from the hotel's sundeck or from your own private balcony (if you're in a suite.) There are also eight separate cottages on the property. Restaurant. Some kitchenettes, microwaves, cable TV. Pool, wading pool. Hot tub. Video games. Children's programs. Laundry facilities. Business services. | 5501 Ocean Ave., Wildwood Crest | 609/522–6507 or 800/247–4776 | fax 609/522–8535 | info@aquabeach.com | www.aquabeach.com | 123 rooms | $70–$265 | Closed mid-Oct.–mid-Apr. | D, MC, V.

Aquarius. Rooms here have bedrooms, living rooms, two televisions, and ocean views. Microwaves, refrigerators, cable TV. Pool, wading pool. Laundry facilities. | 4712 Ocean Ave., Wildwood | 609/729–0054 or 800/982–1831 | 28 rooms | $110–$165 | Closed mid-Oct.–mid-Apr. | AE, D, MC, V.

Cara Mara Motel. This motel, just yards from the beach, has a playground, barbecue grills, sundecks, shuffleboard, and local trolley service to the casinos. Many rooms have ocean and pool views. Efficiencies and suites are also available. Refrigerators, cable TV. Pool. Laundry facilities. | 6701 Atlantic Ave., Wildwood Crest | 609/522–6951 | fax 609/729–7669 | www.caramara.com | 45 rooms | $31–$201 | Closed mid- Oct.–mid Apr. | AE, V.

Candlelight Inn. You'll find such treasures as an 1855 sofa and an 1890 Eastlake piano in this restored 1905 home, just three blocks from the ocean. Antiques-filled guest rooms are decorated in Victorian style, and free afternoon snacks are served daily. Complimentary breakfast. No air-conditioning in some rooms, no room phones. Hot tub. Business services. No kids allowed. No smoking. | 2310 Central Ave., North Wildwood | 609/522–6200 or 800/992–2632 | fax 609/522–6125 | info@candlelight-inn.com | www.candlelight-inn.com | 10 rooms | $125–$200 | AE, D, MC, V.

Cape Cod Inn. The trolley stops right outside this family-friendly three-story hotel, which is eight blocks from the beach and boardwalk. Miniature golf is nearby. Picnic area. Some kitchenettes, microwaves, refrigerators, cable TV. Pool, wading pool. Playground. Laundry facilities. Business services. | 6109 Atlantic Ave., Wildwood Crest | 609/522–1177 | fax 609/729–2353 | 50 rooms | $135–$170 | Closed mid-Oct.–mid-Apr. | AE, D, MC, V.

Carideon. You'll find murals of Mediterranean settings and cozy furniture in every room. Refrigerators, cable TV. Pool, wading pool. Video games. Laundry facilities. | 2200 Atlantic Ave., North Wildwood | 609/729–7900 | 34 rooms | $58–$110 | Closed Oct.–Apr. | AE, D, DC, MC, V.

El Coronado Motor Inn. All the rooms here have ocean views and private balconies at this somewhat more upscale hotel. Guests can join in organized pool volleyball games. Restaurant. In-room data ports, some kitchenettes, microwaves, refrigerators, cable TV. Pool, wading pool. Hot tub, sauna. Video games. Children's programs (ages 3–11). Laundry facilities. Business services. | 8501 Atlantic Ave., Wildwood Crest | 609/729–1000 or 800/227–5302 | fax 609/729–6557 | www.elcoronado.com | 113 rooms | $94–$247 | Closed mid-Oct.–Apr. | AE, D, MC, V.

Flamingo Terrace Motel. With its comically cheerful pink-and-turquoise facade, its white balconies, and even the occasional palm tree, the Flamingo Terrace is like a little slice of Miami in Wildwood. The motel is within walking distance to the beach, boardwalk, churches, restaurants, and movies. Rooms are basic and comfortable, and many have views of the pool. Refrigerators, cable TV. Pool. Laundry facilities. No pets. | 229 E. Pine Ave., Wildwood | 609/522–5113 | www.beachcomber.com/Wildwood/flamingo.html | 28 rooms | $50–$200 | MC, V.

Ivanhoe. The Ivanhoe Panoramic Hotel, five minutes from Cape May and 30 minutes from Atlantic City, rents family suites (bungalows) as well as standard rooms. You can't get much closer to the beach—you don't even have to cross the street—but the room decor is early 1980s. Microwaves, refrigerators, cable TV. Pool, wading pool. Laundry facilities. Business services. | 430 E. 21st Ave., North Wildwood | 609/522–5874 | www.ivanhoemotel.com | 40 rooms, 3 suites | $80–$110, $300 suites | AE, D, DC, MC, V.

Le Voyageur. This three-story hotel is a block from the beach and the boardwalk. Many of the rooms look out at the pool. It's not upscale, but perfectly fine. Picnic area. Some kitchenettes, refrigerators, cable TV. Pool, wading pool. Video games. Laundry facilities. | 232 E. Andrews Ave., Wildwood | 609/522–6407 or 800/348–0846 | fax 609/523–1834 | www.levoyageurmotel.com | 33 rooms | $80–$115 | Closed Nov.–mid-Apr. | AE, MC, V.

Park Lane. All rooms at this three-story hotel have views of the pool or of Wildwood Crest beach. There's a sundeck that looks out over the ocean. Rooms are basically modern standard. Picnic area. Some kitchenettes, refrigerators, cable TV. Pool, wading pool. Laundry facilities. | 5900 Ocean Ave., Wildwood Crest | www.parklanemotel.net | 609/522–5900 | 36 rooms | $114–$175 | Closed late Sept.–Apr. | MC, V.

Pope Cottage Bed & Breakfast. This white Victorian inn, built as a summer home by Louis Pope in 1907, is an easy three-block walk to the ocean. It's also walking distance from Sunset Lake, the boardwalk, a bicycle rental shop, a bakery, and several restaurants. Charming rooms are furnished with a mix of antiques and reproductions. Some rooms share baths. Complimentary breakfast. No smoking. | 5711 Pacific Ave., Wildwood Crest | 609/ 523–9272 | fax 609/523–2208 | www.bbonline.com/nj/popecottage/index.html | 5 rooms | $110–$140 | MC, V.

Rio Motel. This waterfront motel has an ocean observation deck, shuffleboard, and miniature golf. It's two blocks from a municipal beachfront playground and tennis court, and guests have golf privileges at both the public or Greater Wildwood Club courses. Rooms are cheerful and sunny with private balconies. Restaurant. Cable TV. Pool. Golf privileges, miniature golf. Baby-sitting. Laundry facilities. | Rio Grande Ave. and the Ocean, Wildwood | 609/522–1461 or 800/900–8876 | riomotel@bellatlantic.net | www.beachcomber.com/Wildwood/rio.html | 115 rooms | $42–$156 | MC, V.

WOODBRIDGE

MAP 9, G5

(Nearby towns also listed: Edison, Metuchen, New Brunswick)

Woodbridge Township, which contains the community of Woodbridge along with Avanel, Colonia, Fords, Hopelawn, Iselin, Keashey, Menlo Park, Terrance, Port Reading, and Sewaren, is the oldest township in the state. Not to be confused with Wood-Ridge, Woodbridge is the brawny center of operations for Middlesex County, with plentiful shopping at the Woodbridge Center, plus some good restaurants and an active arts center. Its central location makes it a strategic stop for food and lodging.

Information: Woodbridge Metro Chamber of Commerce | 52 Main St., Woodbridge, 07095 | 732/636–4040 | fax 732/636–3492 | www.woodbridgenj.com.

Attractions

Barron Arts Center. Listed on the National Register of Historic Places, this 1877 Richardsonian Revival–style building, with stained glass and a clock tower, is home to an active arts scene for central New Jersey. A once-a-month Poet's Wednesday is a forum for local talent; concerts and art exhibits are scheduled throughout the year. | 582 Rahway Ave. | 732/634–0413 | www.twp.woodbridge.nj.us | Free | Weekdays 11–4.

Woodbridge Center. Dozens of shops, five restaurants, and five department stores are at this major area mall. | 250 Woodbridge Center Dr. | 732/636–4600 | www.woodbridgecenter.com | Free | Mon.–Sat. 10–9:30, Sun. 11–6.

ON THE CALENDAR

JUNE–AUG.: *Mayor's Summer Concert Series.* Popular artists such as the Duprees, the Party Dolls and the Tommy Dorsey Band have performed in this nine-week outdoor series also known as Woodbridge MusicWorks. The concerts are free, and held on Monday evenings behind the Woodbrige High School. | 732/602–6045.

Dining

J. J. Bitting Brewing Company. American. Housed in a 100-year old building that was once the J. J. Bitting Coal and Feed Depot, the J. J. Bitting Brewing Company was the first brewery to operate in Woodbridge Township after prohibition was repealed. The menu has burgers, pizza, ribs, and sandwiches, but the real attraction is the homemade beers and ales. Outdoor seating available on a deck overlooking Main Street. | 33 Main St. | 732/634–2929 | fax 732/634–4402 | $5–$15 | AE, D, MC, V.

Lodging

Hilton. The tasteful decorative touches at this 11-story Hilton include mahogany paneling and a fountain and Italian marble in the lobby. Rooms were renovated in 1999. Restaurant, bar (with entertainment). In-room data ports, some refrigerators, cable TV, in-room VCRs. Pool. Hot tub. Gym. Business services. | 120 Wood Ave. S, Iselin | 732/494–6200 | fax 732/603–7777 | www.hilton.com | 200 rooms | $107–$177 | AE, D, DC, MC, V.

Sheraton at Woodbridge Place. This Sheraton, set on extensive grounds, underwent a $7½ million renovation in 1999. Restaurant, bar. In-room data ports, cable TV. 2 pools. Hot tub. Exercise equipment. Video games. Business services. | 515 U.S. 1 S, Iselin | 732/634–3600 | fax 732/634–0258 | www.sheraton.com | 295 rooms, 14 suites | $109–$160, $400–$600 suites | AE, D, DC, MC, V.

Woodbridge Days Inn. This two-story motel was built in 1963 and renovated in 1991. It is 3 mi from the Woodbridge Mall and Expo Hall. It's in Iselin, 2 mi west of downtown Woodbridge. Complimentary Continental breakfast, room service. Cable TV. Laundry service. Pets allowed. | Rte. 1 S, Iselin | 732/634–4200 or 800/544–8313 | fax 732/634–7840 | 76 rooms | $75–$130 | AE, DC, MC, V.

New York

If the words "New York" bring to mind images of skyscrapers, Broadway, subways, and round-the-clock activity (not to mention other less pleasant pictures), what you're really thinking about is New York City, the frenzied tail that wags the statewide dog. With its bright lights and dark corners, this thriving and frantic metropolis reigns as a national and world capital in everything from fashion and food to culture and business, and often seems to eclipse the rest of the state, whose name it shares.

Many say they want to avoid or ignore the city, but 25 million people visit it every year. And many of those and others find, by accident or by reading guides such as this, that there's also plenty more to New York than that fabulous town at the mouth of the Hudson River, which, believe it or not, occupies far less than 1% of the state.

As a whole, New York State embodies some of the best that nature, and humans, have to offer. In addition to Gotham in the south, there's another spectacular tourist attraction to the west —Niagara Falls. These top two sites can give you a thunderous introduction to a state that defies labels, but somehow can't escape them. Venture away from the well known, and you are likely to make some wonderful discoveries.

Nature lovers will find spectacles ranging from the warm beaches of Long Island and the high peaks of the Adirondacks to the sparkling waters of the Finger Lakes and the mysterious hills and valleys of the Catskills.

Sports-lovers can see the best, and sometimes the worst, of professional athletics at all levels. Arenas, museums, and tracks throughout the state honor and cater to the best in horse racing, baseball, boxing, fly-fishing, auto racing, sailing, winter sports, soccer, and other pastimes.

Arts and literature lovers can enjoy the museums and shows of Manhattan, the haunts of Washington Irving in the Hudson River valley, and the cultural offerings of the Chautauqua Institution, just to name a few.

CAPITAL: ALBANY	POPULATION: 18,169,100	AREA: 49,576 SQUARE MI
BORDERS: CANADA, CT, MS, NJ, PA, VT	TIME ZONE: EASTERN	POSTAL ABBREVIATION: NY
WEB SITE:WWW.ILOVENY.STATE.NY.US		

Thrill seekers can ride one of the tallest roller coasters in the East at Darien Lake, climb into a raft and tumble through the rapids of North Country rivers, and explore caverns and cliffs in the Catskills.

New York's state motto is "Excelsior," meaning "ever upward," and things certainly do seem to go up in New York. Cynics point to the taxes, poverty, and a general sense of misery based on observations of city sidewalks and rural shacks. They also might argue that "upward" hardly describes the state of manufacturing and farming in New York, since both industries have lost thousands of jobs. But when it comes to health services, the arts, banking, finance, entertainment, and publishing, things are moving up. Agriculturally, the state holds its own, as a leading supplier of apples, cherries, grapes, maple syrup, onions, sweet corn, and dairy products.

Internal contradictions abound. The state has city ponds and churning waterfalls, urban sprawl and virgin wilderness, fabulous wealth and numbing poverty, crystal-clear lakes and murky rivers, rednecks and blue bloods, engineering triumphs and bureaucratic boondoggles. The Empire State boasts both the nation's largest city and the biggest wilderness area east of the Mississippi (both of which could borrow the Adirondacks' "forever wild" designation). And that's just the way it should be.

The state's tensions are widely documented. The Upstate-Downstate rift is the most well known, and it's nearly as old as the hills that give upstate New York so much of its character. In the early 19th century, New York City politicians scorned a plan to build what was to become the Erie Canal. Little did they know that the project would catapult the city from an also-ran position on the East Coast to the great center of commerce that it became in the 1800s.

Political and racial tensions sometimes eclipse the geographical ones, but conflict seems to be part of the state's history, for better or worse. After all, about 30% of all the battles of the Revolutionary War were fought in New York, which was considered then, as now, a key strategic part of the emerging nation. If you have sharp eyes and open ears, you will pick up on the geographical, political, economic, and cultural diversity that makes New York such an engaging place to live in and to visit.

Some of the many famous people with ties to New York include Susan B. Anthony (women's rights leader); Clara Barton (Red Cross founder); Samuel Clemens, a.k.a. Mark Twain (author); Glenn Curtiss (the father of naval aviation); Frederick Douglass (abolitionist); Millard Fillmore (U.S. president); Lou Gehrig (athlete); Julia Ward Howe (author); Washington Irving (author); Logan (Cayuga Nation orator); John Wesley Powell (geologist); John D. Rockefeller (businessman); Franklin D. Roosevelt (U.S. president); Theodore Roosevelt (U.S. president); Shanandoah (Native American leader); Elizabeth Cady Stanton (women's rights leader); Joseph Smith (the founder of the Mormon religion); Martin Van Buren (U.S. president); Walt Whitman (poet); and Frank W. Woolworth (businessman).

History

About 32 years after Christopher Columbus reached land in the Western Hemisphere, Giovanni da Verrazano slipped into what was to become New York Harbor. He, and the

NY Timeline

ca. 1300	1524	1570	1609
Iroquois Indians find a spectacular waterfall and name it "Niagara," which means "thunder of the waters."	Giovanni da Verrazano is the first European to step on New York soil.	Mohawk, Oneida, Onondaga, Cayuga, and Seneca nations form the Iroquois League (which the Tuscarora Nation later joins in 1722).	Henry Hudson sails up the river that will bear his name and claims the area for the Dutch.

INTRODUCTION
HISTORY
REGIONS
WHEN TO VISIT
STATE'S GREATS
RULES OF THE ROAD
DRIVING TOURS

droves of Europeans and others who followed, were relative latecomers. People had roamed the woodlands, shorelines, and glens for thousands of years. At the time of European explorations, the Algonquins lived in much of the Hudson Valley, on Manhattan, and on Long Island, while the Iroquois ruled the west.

Thanks to Henry Hudson's travels and claims in the early 1600s, the Dutch occupied the area and called it New Netherlands. In 1626, just over 100 years after Verrazano spotted New York, Peter Minuit, the first Dutch governor of the colony, bought Manhattan Island from the Algonquins for $24 worth of tools and trinkets. Only 40 years later, the British acquired the land and changed the name to New York. The Dutch influence lingers in some place names in the Hudson Valley, such as Kinderhook ("children's corner") or any place whose name ends in "-kill" ("stream").

The colony played a key role in the American Revolution and nearly one-third of the battles were fought on New York soil. The area's importance, however, really rose with the development of the Erie Canal in the mid-1800s and New York City's phenomenal growth as a center of commerce. That, in turn, led to its natural place as a port-of-choice for millions of immigrants from Europe and other parts of the world who poured into this country at the end of the 19th century and beginning of the 20th century.

New York City, and many areas in the state, continue to draw immigrants (legal and illegal) from other nations. Despite economic problems, such as New York City's financial crisis of the 1970s, the city and state continue to play key roles in the nation's life—financially, socially, politically, and artistically.

Regions

Note: Area codes in southeastern New York State are changing. The code 845 must now be used to reach many numbers in the former 914 area. Parts of Columbia, Delaware, Dutchess, Greene, Orange, Putnam, Rockland, Sullivan, and Ulster counties are affected.

1. ADIRONDACKS

The park for which this region is named covers 6.1 million acres, an area larger than the state of New Jersey, making it the biggest U.S. park outside Alaska. The area linked to the park stretches from Lake Champlain and Lake George to the Mohawk River on the south and the St. Lawrence River valley on the north and west. This region is dotted with small villages and hamlets, most with populations less than 1,000. The park has 46 rugged mountains that are more than 4,000 ft tall, mountains considered by some to be the oldest in the world. The incredible 2,300 lakes and 30,000 mi of streams, along with 2,000 mi of trails, offer plenty of opportunities for hiking, canoeing, fishing, and other outdoor activities.

Towns listed: Adirondack Park, Ausable Chasm, Blue Mountain Lake, Bolton Landing, Boonville, Crown Point, Diamond Point, Glens Falls, Gloversville, Hague, Keene Valley,

1624	1626	1664	1777	1779
Fort Orange (which is eventually renamed Albany) is established as the first permanent European settlement in New York.	Governor Peter Minuit buys Manhattan Island from Native Americans for 60 guilders (about $24).	New Amsterdam (Holland) becomes New York (Great Britain).	American colonists defeat the British in the Battle of Saratoga.	The military campaign by American generals Clinton and Sullivan in central and western portions of the state disperses Iroquois.

Lake George Village, Lake Luzerne, Lake Placid, Long Lake, Malone, North Creek, Old Forge, Paul Smiths, Plattsburgh, Queensbury, Rouses Point, Saranac Lake, Schroon Lake, Speculator, Ticonderoga, Tupper Lake, Warrensburg, Wilmington.

2. CAPITAL/SARATOGA

The Hudson and Mohawk rivers meet here, forming a natural hub for commerce and activity. Mohicans originally inhabited the area, and the Dutch set up a trading post in 1614. By 1686, Albany was the leading fur-trading settlement in the colonies, which were by now under British control. The Battle of Saratoga in 1777 turned the tide of the military campaigns during the Revolution and prevented the British from controlling the key Hudson River valley. Saratoga Springs became one of the nation's premier resorts, and gave us some of our more treasured food items, including the club sandwich, pie à la mode, and the potato chip. Saratoga Springs remains a cultural and recreational draw with horse racing and summer music festivals. The region hugs the borders with Vermont and Massachusetts to the east, touches the shores of picturesque and busy Lake George to the north, follows the lower Mohawk River valley to the west, and reaches down the Hudson River to Selkirk.

Towns listed: Albany, Amsterdam, Colonie, Johnstown, Saratoga Springs, Schenectady, Troy.

3. CATSKILLS

The Algonquins called this area "Onteora," or "land in the sky." Later, writer Washington Irving referred to the Catskills as "these fairy mountains" and this is perhaps the most visited, written-about, and painted mountain range in the country. Rising between the Hudson River to the east and the upper Delaware and Susquehanna rivers to the south and west, the Catskills provided an early outlet for those who had the time and money to leave the hustle and bustle of New York City for some peace and quiet. The first resort, the Catskill Mountain House, was built in the 1820s near Haines Falls. World-class trout streams flow through the region, which spawned the sport of fly-fishing. This is also a popular area for hiking, with a range of trails, especially in the Shawangunk Mountains (called the Gunks) on the southern fringe of the region.

Towns listed: Cairo, Delhi, Hunter, Kingston, Liberty, Monticello, Mt. Tremper, Port Jervis, Roscoe, Roxbury, Shandaken, Stamford, Windham, Woodstock.

4. CHAUTAUQUA-ALLEGANY

This area covers the southwestern part of the state, bordering Pennsylvania to the south, Lake Erie to the west, and the Buffalo and Finger Lakes regions to the north and east, respectively. This region in the foothills of the Allegheny Mountains includes the Chautauqua Institution (one of the nation's most respected educational and cultural institutions), the state's largest ski resort, an active and industrious Amish community, the beautiful Allegany State Park, and the expansive Allegany Indian Reservation,

1784	**1788**	**1802**	**1807**	**1825**
While touring the state, George Washington refers to New York as "the seat of the empire," a statement that spawned the nickname, the Empire State.	New York becomes the nation's 11th state.	U.S. Military Academy is built in West Point.	The first successful steamship run (Robert Fulton's *Clermont*) ends in Albany.	The Erie Canal opens.

which includes the city of Salamanca. This is also big-time hunting country with large numbers of white-tailed deer and wild turkey.

Towns listed: Arcade, Bemus Point, Chautauqua, Dunkirk, Fredonia, Jamestown, Olean, Salamanca, Wellsville, Westfield.

INTRODUCTION
HISTORY
REGIONS
WHEN TO VISIT
STATE'S GREATS
RULES OF THE ROAD
DRIVING TOURS

5. FINGER LAKES

Whether clawed out by retreating glacier sheets as geologists argue, or pressed into the earth by the hand of the Great Spirit as the Iroquois legends say, these north–south valleys and lakes provide memorable sights and unique agricultural opportunities. This region, which stretches from the Pennsylvania border in the south to Lake Ontario in the north, is home to waterfalls and glens. The Finger Lakes' geography makes this a good place for vineyards; the lakes are so deep they don't freeze in winter, which means a cooler spring and warmer fall. Grapes like that. So do wine makers, because visitors flock to the region to sample the results. History, education, auto racing, and all water sports bubble to the surface throughout the area.

Towns listed: Auburn, Avon, Bath, Canandaigua, Corning, Cortland, Elmira, Endicott, Geneseo, Geneva, Hammondsport, Hornell, Ithaca, Naples, Palmyra, Penn Yan, Rochester, Seneca Falls, Skaneateles, Victor, Waterloo, Watkins Glen.

6. HUDSON RIVER VALLEY

Navigator Henry Hudson hoped he'd found a route through North America to Asia when he sailed up what would become his namesake waterway. Eventually Hudson noticed what the Algonquins had long known: the Hudson River is really an estuary, with tides felt as far north as Albany. The Algonquins called the river "Muhheahkantuck," or "the river that flows both ways." The beauty of the 315-mi-long river captured the imagination of many of America's early landscape painters, who were collectively known as the Hudson River School. The river's beauty also prompted many to build spectacular mansions overlooking the Hudson, some of which are now open to the public. The towns and villages along the Hudson River have long been a favorite destination for antiques hunters and history buffs. By the early 1970s, the 75-million-year-old river had become quite polluted. More recently, a cleanup effort has begun to improve its condition.

Towns listed: Catskill, Ellenville, Fishkill, Garrison, Goshen, Hudson, Hyde Park, Middletown, Monroe, Newburgh, New Paltz, Poughkeepsie, Pound Ridge, Rhinebeck, Saugerties, Walden, Warwick.

7. LEATHERSTOCKING

The curious name of this region is a reminder of the area's pioneer past; it comes from the leather leggings the frontiersmen wore to protect their ankles and shins. Nestled between the Adirondacks to the north and the Catskills to the south, the region

1826	1827	1848	1872	1891
Joseph Smith meets Angel Moroni in Palmyra, thus founding Mormonism.	Slavery is abolished in New York.	The first conference on women's rights is held in Seneca Falls.	Chautauqua Institution begins as a vacation school for Sunday-school teachers.	Carnegie Hall opens in New York City.

extends west from the Capitol region to Syracuse, a key city on the Eric Canal. It was the Canal that brought prosperity and settlers to this fertile heartland of the state in the early and mid-1800s, and many of the cities and towns floated, then foundered a bit, with its fortunes. Today, the main attractions in this region are the halls of fame for baseball, boxing, and soccer. High-stakes bingo, opera, and hidden caverns are also draws.

Towns listed: Bainbridge, Binghamton, Canajoharie, Canastota, Cazenovia, Cobleskill, Cooperstown, Deposit, Greene, Hamilton, Herkimer, Ilion, Liverpool, Norwich, Oneida, Oneonta, Owego, Richfield Springs, Rome, Syracuse, Utica.

8. LONG ISLAND

This island stretches about 120 mi to the east of New York City, along the southern coast of Connecticut, and splits into two forks at its far eastern end. The spectacular sandy stretches of Long Beach, Jones Beach, and Fire Island hug the southern flank of the island. While Long Island is known for its suburban sprawl, it also has rural farms and vineyards, charming seaside villages, and spectacular mansions of the omnipresent rich and famous. The waters have yielded plenty of world-record catches for hardworking and lucky fishermen.

Towns listed: Amagansett, Amityville, Babylon, Bay Shore/Brightwaters, Bridgehampton/Water Mill, Cold Spring Harbor, East Hampton, Eastport/Moriches, Fire Island National Seashore, Freeport, Garden City, Glen Cove, Great Neck, Greenport, Hampton Bays, Huntington, Jamesport/Aqueboque/Laurel, Jericho, Long Beach, Mastic/Mastic Beach, Mattituck, Montauk, Northport, Orient Point, Oyster Bay, Patchogue, Plainview/Old Bethpage, Port Jefferson, Port Washington, Quogue/East Quogue, Riverhead, Rockville Center, Roslyn, Sag Harbor, Sayville, Shelter Island, Smithtown, Southampton, Southold, Stony Brook, Syosset, Westbury/Old Westbury, Westhampton Beach.

9. NEW YORK CITY

New York City teams with life, and all the good and bad that go with it. The Big Apple is the state's most popular tourist destination, and most of the world-class attractions are in Manhattan, an island only 12 mi long and 3 mi wide. But the city actually includes five boroughs (Manhattan, the Bronx, Brooklyn, Queens, and Staten Island) covering 301 square mi. Thanks to some solid bedrock and plenty of landfill, the city houses about 7.3 million people (2.3 million of them in Brooklyn alone). The Bronx is part of the mainland, while Manhattan and Staten Island are their own islands, and Brooklyn and Queens swarm over the far western end of Long Island.

Town listed: New York City

10. NIAGARA-FRONTIER

Anchored by the tenacious city of Buffalo and the inescapable Niagara Falls, this region is wedged between Lake Erie to the west and Lake Ontario to the north, and

1892	1898	1898	1900	1901
Adirondack Park is established.	The Bronx, Brooklyn, Manhattan, Queens, and Staten Island become the five boroughs of New York City.	Statue of Frederick Douglass goes up in Rochester. It's the first statue in the nation to honor an African American.	First subway tunnel built in New York City.	President William McKinley is shot dead in Buffalo.

INTRODUCTION
HISTORY
REGIONS
WHEN TO VISIT
STATE'S GREATS
RULES OF THE ROAD
DRIVING TOURS

shares the Niagara River with Canada. Buffalo has rebounded partly from an economic battering in the 1970s and now boasts a lively waterfront area and theater district to go with its collection of wonderful architectural landmarks. Between the lakes lie acres of rolling farmland, part of the Great Lakes Plain, which stretches north from the Appalachian Plateau.

Towns listed: Albion, Amherst, Batavia, Buffalo, Clarence, East Aurora, Grand Island, Hamburg, Lockport, Medina, Niagara Falls, Williamsville.

11. THOUSAND ISLANDS

The 50-mi section of the St. Lawrence River that begins at Lake Ontario's eastern end teems with fish, islands, and ships. The region was long held in awe by Native Americans, who referred to it as "the Garden of the Great Spirit." The powerful St. Lawrence River served as a vital staging area during the War of 1812, as well as a route for rum-runners and other smugglers. Today this area, shared by both Canada and the United States, has a wide variety of recreational activities to choose from, including sailing, scuba diving, fishing, and hiking.

Towns listed: Alexandria Bay, Canton, Clayton, Fulton, Massena, Ogdensburg, Oswego, Potsdam, Sackets Harbor, Watertown.

12. LOWER HUDSON VALLEY

Steeped in natural beauty, this region is also known for its quaint towns, antiques shops, and National Historic sites. One of the most important battles of the American Revolution, led by General George Washington, was held in what is today the town of White Plains. Many people who work in New York City choose to live in this part of the state because it is just a quick commute from Manhattan. Some of the towns in the lower Hudson Valley are inland, while others lie along the scenic Hudson River and Long Island Sound.

Towns listed: Brewster, Canaan, Carmel/Lake Carmel, Croton-on-Hudson, Elmsford, Hartsdale, Hawthorne, Hillsdale, Mahopac, Mamaroneck, Millbrook, Mt. Kisco, New Rochelle, North Salem, Nyack, Peekskill, Piermont, Rye, Scarsdale, Spring Valley, Stony Point, Suffern, Tarrytown, White Plains, Yonkers.

When to Visit

The high-water tourist season is, not surprisingly, in summer. New York's waterways attract people with boats, swimsuits, fishing poles, and sun-tan lotion, while the mountains of the Catskills, Adirondacks, and Allegheny foothills offer invigorating hikes and cool refuges. There's still plenty to do in New York throughout the year, however; after all, the water tumbles over Niagara all year long and theater lights shine in Manhattan every day.

The spring ushers in the major-league baseball season, and fans flock through the fall to games played by the New York Yankees in the Bronx, and the New York Mets in

1930	1939	1964	1947	1952
The nation's first supermarket (King Kullen) opens on Long Island.	National Baseball Hall of Fame opens in Cooperstown.	Buffalo wings invented at the city's Anchor Bar and Restaurant.	Levittown, Long Island, is created as the nation's first instant suburb. It contains 17,400 houses.	Construction of the United Nations headquarters in New York City is finished.

Queens. Beginning in late September, the Adirondacks shimmer with spectacular fall foliage and, soon after, other areas of the state (such as the Catskills and Finger Lakes) follow suit with spectacular autumn vistas of their own. Vineyards celebrate harvests and new issues in fall, which is a great time to visit the wineries along the Hudson River and Lake Erie, among the Finger Lakes, and on Long Island. During winter, the Tug Hill plateau east of Lake Ontario is the place to go. The area receives more than 200 inches of snow every season, courtesy of the lake and the wind patterns above it.

Winter is also a popular time to visit New York City. The Big Apple's seasonal delights include ice-skating in Rockefeller Center and Central Park, the annual Christmas tree lighting ceremony at Rockefeller Center, festive and imaginative holiday window dressings at major department stores, and Radio City Music Hall's annual Radio City Christmas Spectacular, which has been attracting both tourists and locals since 1933.

The weather varies wildly throughout the state. The hottest day on record was July 22, 1926, when the thermometer hit 108°F in Troy. The coldest reading was -52°F in Old Forge on Feb. 18, 1879. Overall, annual average temperatures range from a low of 40°F in the Adirondacks to about 55°F in New York City. Away from coastal areas, there's plenty of snow in New York, with a statewide seasonal average of 40 inches. More than half the state receives over 70 inches of snow per year.

In summer, temperatures range from 70 to 85°F in the higher elevations of the Adirondacks and Catskills. The summer air can be much more humid in the lower Hudson River valley and the New York City area. You may find that spring and fall are the best times to visit New York City.

CLIMATE CHART
Average High/Low Temperatures (°F) and Monthly Precipitation (in inches)

	JAN.	FEB.	MAR.	APR.	MAY	JUNE
ALBANY	30/17	30/11	33/14	44/25	58/35	70/45
	3.49	2.36	2.27	2.93	2.99	3.41
	JULY	AUG.	SEPT.	OCT.	NOV.	DEC.
	79/55	84/60	81/58	73/49	62/39	47/34
	3.62	3.18	3.47	2.95	2.83	3.83
	JAN.	FEB.	MAR.	APR.	MAY	JUNE
BUFFALO	37/26	32/17	42/26	54/36	66/47	75/57
		2.7	2.31	2.68	2.87	3.14
	JULY	AUG.	SEPT.	OCT.	NOV.	DEC.
	80/62	78/60	71/53	72.9/60.0	59/43	52.1/35.8
	3.55	3.08	4.17	3.48	3.09	4.23

1962
New York City's largest ticker-tape parade is held for astronaut John Glenn.

1969
Woodstock Music Festival is held near Bethel.

1969
New York City's first automatic bank teller appears.

1980
Winter Olympics are held in Lake Placid.

2000
The New York Yankees win their 26th World Series.

INTRODUCTION
HISTORY
REGIONS
WHEN TO VISIT
STATE'S GREATS
RULES OF THE ROAD
DRIVING TOURS

ISLIP	JAN.	FEB.	MAR.	APR.	MAY	JUNE
	31/14	35.9/21.3	37.8/21.7	45.9/30.8	57.1/39.5	67.2/49.4
		3.69	3.48	4.1	4.23	3.94
	JULY	AUG.	SEPT.	OCT.	NOV.	DEC.
	75.4/58.7	80.8/65.7	80.8/65.1	64/51	63.4/45.7	42/31
	3.82	3.46	4.04	3.89	3.55	4.47

NEW YORK CITY	JAN.	FEB.	MAR.	APR.	MAY	JUNE
	39/27	48/35	59/44	70/54	79/63	84/69
	3.42	3.27	4.08	4.2	4.42	3.67
	JULY	AUG.	SEPT.	OCT.	NOV.	DEC.
	82/68	75/61	60/41	51/37	35/21	34/18
	4.35	4.01	3.79	3.56	3.72	3.25

SYRACUSE	JAN.	FEB.	MAR.	APR.	MAY	JUNE
	33/15	43/25	56/36	68/46	77/54	82/59
	2.34	2.15	2.77	3.33	3.28	3.79
	JULY	AUG.	SEPT.	OCT.	NOV.	DEC.
	79/58	72/51	48/33	35/18	35/23	41.9/26.5
	3.81	3.51	3.24	2.93	3.67	4.05

FESTIVALS AND SEASONAL EVENTS

WINTER

Dec. **Christmas season, New York City.** One of the tallest and most lavish Christmas trees in the country is on display in Rockefeller Center, just above the skating rink. Early each December, thousands of people gather to watch the ceremonial tree lighting, which is telecast live. The city's shop windows, especially along Fifth Avenue in midtown, are magnificently decorated, and many display animated puppets acting out Christmas stories. The season culminates in the famous ball drop on New Year's Eve in Times Square, which is televised all over the world. Then, in Central Park, a Midnight Run, hosted by the New York Road Runners Club, begins at the perennially festive Tavern on the Green. | 212/632–3975 tree lighting information, 212/768–1560 Times Square ball drop.

Dickens Christmas, Skaneateles. The village turns back the clock to the 1800s to celebrate the holidays. | 315/685–2268.

SPRING

Mar. **St. Patrick's Day Parade, New York City.** Irish societies and others turn out for this huge parade that has been an annual event since 1762. | 212/484–1222.

Apr.–May **Lake Ontario Bird Festival, Mexico.** Watch songbirds and raptors return to the North along the Atlantic flyway. | 315/349–8322.

May **Lilac Festival, Rochester.** The 1,200 lilac bushes in Highland Park, among other attractions, draw up to 500,000 people during this 10-day event. | 716/546–3070.

Lucy-Desi Hometown Celebration, Jamestown. Celebrates the lives and careers of Lucille Ball and Desi Arnaz | 716/484–7070.

Tulip Festival, Albany. Thousands of tulips bloom in Washington Park during this celebration of the area's Dutch heritage. | 518/434–2032.

SUMMER

June
Belmont Stakes, Elmont. This is the final race of the Triple Crown. | 516/488–6000.

The General's Lady, Newburgh. The birthday of Martha Washington is celebrated with music, food, and craft demonstrations at Washington's Headquarters. | 518/562–1195.

June–Sept.
Chautauqua Institution Season, Chautauqua. Every summer, this institution offers lectures, art exhibitions, and outdoor symphonies, as well as theater, dance, and opera performances. | 800/836–ARTS.

July
Baseball Hall of Fame Weekend, Cooperstown. The annual induction ceremony of new members takes place at the National Baseball Hall of Fame. Down the street, you can catch a Hall of Fame baseball game in Doubleday Field. | 888/425–5633 or 607/547–7200.

Finger Lakes Wine Festival, Watkins Glen. Tastings, seminars, demonstrations, and music about the history, production, and appreciation of wine are held at the International Raceway. | 607/535–2481.

French Festival, Cape Vincent. This 30-year-old festival celebrates the French heritage of the village. | 315/654–2481.

Hill Cumorah Pageant, Palmyra. Using a cast of 600, this outdoor theatrical production tells the story of the Mormon Church. Seating for 9,000 is provided for the seven performances. | 315/597–2757.

July–Aug.
Shakespeare in the Park, New York City. Held in the magical open-air Delacorte Theater in Central Park, these plays often feature high-profile actors. The productions are usually Shakespeare plays, although recent summers have included Wilder's *The Skin of Our Teeth* and the musical *On the Town*. | 212/539–8500 or 212/539–8750 (seasonal phone at the Delacorte).

July–Sept.
Thoroughbred racing at Saratoga Race Course, Saratoga Springs. The big races are the Whitney Handicap, the Breeders Cup, and the Travers. | 718/641–4700.

Aug.
International Celtic Festival, Hunter. Bagpipes and drummers mix with Highland games and entertainment. | Hunter Mountain Ski Bowl, Southside, Rte. 23A | 518/263–4223.

Mostly Mozart Festival, New York City. Free outdoor afternoon concerts and casual indoor evening concerts held at Lincoln Center showcase special soloists, with the orchestra under the baton of Gerard Schwarz. | 212/875–5103.

NASCAR Racing, Watkins Glen International Race Track. Join thousands of fans to watch top drivers compete in the state's only NASCAR race, the Winston Cup. | 607/535–2481.

New York State Fair, Syracuse. The largest agricultural fair in the state brings rides, demonstrations, and world-class musical entertainment to the Empire Expo Center. | 800/234–4797.

Hampton Classic Horse Show, Bridgehampton. This equestrian competition draws plenty of celebrities. | 516/537–3177.

INTRODUCTION
HISTORY
REGIONS
WHEN TO VISIT
STATE'S GREATS
RULES OF THE ROAD
DRIVING TOURS

AUTUMN

Sept.
Feast of San Gennaro, New York City. The city's oldest and most crowded festival covers 12 blocks in Little Italy. On Mulberry Street from Canal to Houston streets. | 212/764–6330 or 800/225–5697.

Great Grape Festival, Naples. Enjoy entertainment, displays, demonstrations, and wonderful pies. | 716/374–5184 or 716/374–2240.

Hudson Valley Garlic Festival, Saugerties. More than 45,000 people come to what some fondly call a "stink fest." It includes music and food and takes place the last weekend of the month. | 914/246–6982.

Sept.–Oct.
New York Film Festival, New York City. Since 1963, the city's most prestigious film event has drawn movie lovers and filmmakers alike to preview features and shorts from all over the world. Often the stars and filmmakers participate in panel discussions following their screenings. Advance tickets are usually essential; some screenings are sold out a month in advance. | 212/875–5610.

Nov.
Macy's Thanksgiving Day Parade, New York City. Santa Claus and other celebrities and performers make appearances at this traditional parade, which marks the official beginning of the Christmas season. Gigantic balloons (if it's not too windy) float down Central Park West from 77th Street to Broadway and Herald Square, where Macy's flagship store stands. | 212/494–4495.

Nov.–Jan.
Radio City Christmas Spectacular, New York City. Since 1933 these performances have featured the Rockettes, along with singers, dancers, special effects, and a live orchestra. Even Santa Claus shows up. | 212/247–4777 or 212/307–7171.

State's Greats

New York truly seems to have it all: miles of beaches, an expansive state park system, breathtaking mountains, apple orchards, professional sports, world-class museums and educational institutions, important historical sites, Great Lakes, one of the seven natural wonders of the world, an inimitable metropolis, and much, much more. Whatever your reason (or reasons) for visiting the Empire State, you are not likely to be disappointed.

Beaches, Forests, and Parks

Jones Beach State Park covers 2,413 acres on Long Island's south shore, and is a great place to swim. (Bathers can choose from the oceanfront, the bay, or the pools.) However, since it's only 25 mi from midtown Manhattan, it's also crowded. The 2-mi boardwalk and Jones Beach Theater, which presents a diverse lineup of entertainment, are worth checking out.

If you're more interested in finding an unforgettable place to take a walk, you will want to visit **Letchworth State Park,** near Geneseo, which is called the Grand Canyon of the East. As the foliage turns in autumn, the scenes become even more beautiful and memorable. The park's 66 mi of trails vary in difficulty, but there's something for everybody here. (Even the roadway offers wonderful sights.) In the wintertime, this fabulous year-round destination has cross-country skiing and snowmobiling.

Of the many Finger Lakes area parks that include waterfalls and glens, **Watkins Glen State Park** is the grandest of them all, providing a dramatic look at just how much power water has to shape land over time.

Yes, **Niagara Falls** is a tourist-trap of the highest order, but it's still worth the trip. For a change, try the falls in March and witness what happens when mist freezes on the rocks and trees. It's the most powerful waterfall in the state, but it's not the tallest. That honor goes to the falls in Trumansburg's **Taughannock Falls State Park,** which are 30 ft taller than Niagara Falls.

Culture, History, and the Arts

Manhattan's **Museum Mile** along Fifth Avenue is home to world-class museums, including The **Metropolitan Museum of Art,** the western hemisphere's largest art museum, and the **Frick Collection,** the city's premier small art museum. The latter collection is housed in a stunning Beaux Arts–style mansion, which belonged to businessman Henry Clay Frick. Famed architect Frank Lloyd Wright's six-story spiral design for the **Solomon R. Guggenheim Museum** is striking, and the museum houses some of the finest examples of modern art. Upstate, Buffalo's **Albright-Knox Art Gallery** has modern and contemporary art displayed in a Greek Revival–style building. The comprehensive collection covers all major artists from the United States and Europe over the past five decades, and the Gallery was the first museum in the United States to buy works of Picasso and Matisse. If you're looking for a more subdued cultural experience, Ogdensburg's **Frederic Remington Art Museum** is a quiet, out-of-the-way museum that presents spectacular work painted, drawn, and sculpted by one of the great artists of the Old West, who also happens to be a native New Yorker.

The **Corning Glass Center,** in Corning, could be the third-most-popular destination in the state (behind New York City and Niagara Falls). The artwork and craftsmanship of the glass objects on display are spectacular and the collection goes back to 1400 BC. Children will find the displays and demonstrations particularly memorable.

One of the most significant cultural institutions in the nation, the **Chautauqua Institution** on Chautauqua Lake draws people from around the country with musical performances, theater productions, classes, and lectures.

If you are interested in American history, visit the **Saratoga National Historic Park,** located 8 mi south of Schuylerville. This is the site of the 1777 Battle of Saratoga, which turned the tide of the American Revolution. The 9½-mi scenic drive through the park will help you understand the battle and its significance. Another good history site is the 55-building **Genesee Country Village** in Mumford, which hosts demonstrations about life in the 1800s, many of which are geared towards children. If you are curious about military history, the place to go is the **U.S. Military Academy** at West Point, on the west bank of the Hudson River.

The splendid **Vanderbilt Mansion National Historic Site** in Hyde Park exemplifies the Gilded Age and conveys the wealth and privilege of one of the state's most prominent families.

Sports

New York's parks, mountains, rivers, beaches, and hallowed arenas offer plenty of outlets for the sports enthusiast—participants and spectators alike.

You can go white-water rafting on the Hudson and Black rivers, and the Catskills and Adirondacks are popular places for hiking. Long Island's location on the Atlantic Ocean means you can go deep-sea fishing, which can yield memorable catches and equally memorable sights. Trophy fishing on the Salmon River and throughout the Great Lakes and St. Lawrence River attracts anglers from around the world.

The **National Baseball Hall of Fame** in Cooperstown is a wonderful mecca for baseball fans, while the **Catskill Fly Fishing Center,** between Livingston Manor and Roscoe, showcases the history of fly-fishing, which was developed where the Willowemoc and Beaverkill rivers meet, just west of Roscoe. If you are after coho and chinook salmon trophies, visit the **Salmon River,** near Pulaski, where the state record chinook (47 pounds, 13 ounces) was caught. The **Saratoga Race Course** in Saratoga Springs is the nation's oldest thoroughbred track. The big race is the Travers Stakes, held on the fifth Saturday of the season. If you like rock climbing, the **Shawangunks,** or Gunks, just west of New Paltz are mountains to visit.

INTRODUCTION
HISTORY
REGIONS
WHEN TO VISIT
STATE'S GREATS
RULES OF THE ROAD
DRIVING TOURS

Rules of the Road

License requirements: Licensed 16-year-olds may drive, with restrictions. Those 18 and older have no restrictions. In New York City, you must be 18 or older to drive, even with a valid out-of-state license.

Right turn on red: Permitted in most areas, unless otherwise posted. Not allowed in New York City.

Seat belt and helmet laws: Seat belts are required for driver, front-seat passengers, and back-seat passengers between the ages of 4 and 10. Children younger than 4 must be in child restraints. Motorcyclists are required to wear helmets.

Speed limits: 65 mph on rural interstates; 55 mph on nonrural interstates. Watch signs on all roads.

For more information: Contact the State Police Headquarters at 518/457–6811 or 800/842–2233

Finger Lakes and Thousand Islands Driving Tour

FROM ITHACA TO ALEXANDRIA BAY

Distance: 290 mi   Time: 4 days
Breaks: You might want to stop overnight in Corning, Geneva, or Sackets Harbor.

This drive takes you through the Finger Lakes Region, up to the southern shore of Lake Ontario, and along part of the state's Seaway Trail, which hugs what some consider to be the nation's "fourth seacoast": the Great Lakes and St. Lawrence River.

❶ Begin in **Ithaca,** a city of gorges that sits on the southern end of Cayuga Lake, the longest of the Finger Lakes. Here, you can enjoy an early morning stroll at Ithaca Falls, which is downtown, **Buttermilk Falls State Park,** which is just south of the city on Route 13, or at some of the gorges that cut through the **Cornell University** campus on a hillside

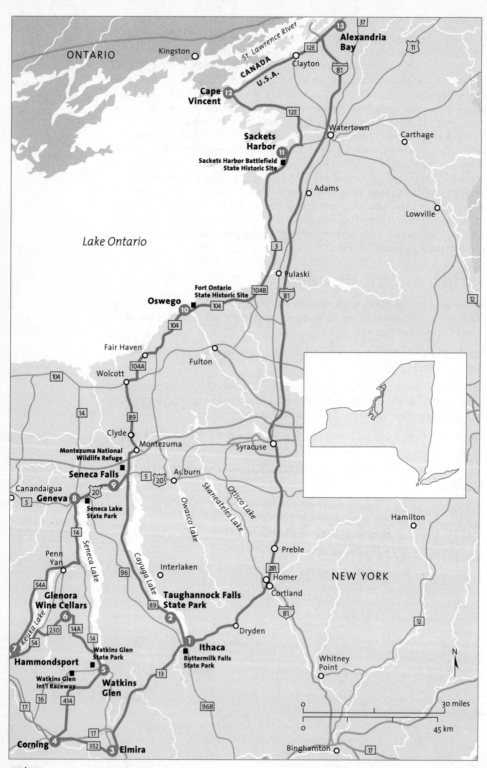

ONTARIO

Kingston

St. Lawrence River

CANADA

U.S.A.

Alexandria Bay **13**

37

12E

Clayton

81

11

Cape Vincent **12**

Watertown

12E

Carthage

Sackets Harbor **11**

Sackets Harbor Battlefield State Historic Site

Adams

Lowville

Lake Ontario

3

Pulaski

Fort Ontario State Historic Site

104B

81

12

Oswego **10**

104

104

Fair Haven

Fulton

104A

Wolcott

104

14

89

Clyde

Montezuma

Syracuse

Montezuma National Wildlife Refuge

Seneca Falls **9**

5 20

Auburn

Otisco Lake

Canandaigua

20

Geneva **8**

Seneca Lake State Park

5

Hamilton

14

Owasco Lake

Skaneateles Lake

Penn Yan

Seneca Lake

Preble

96

Interlaken

NEW YORK

Glenora Wine Cellars **6**

54A

Cayuga Lake

281

Homer

Cortland

230

14A

89

Taughannock Falls State Park **2**

Dryden

81

12

54

14

7

Watkins Glen State Park

1 **Ithaca**

Buttermilk Falls State Park

Hammondsport

16

230

5 **Watkins Glen**

Whitney Point

Watkins Glen Int'l Raceway

13

17

414

96B

Corning **4**

17

352

3 **Elmira**

Binghamton

17

30 miles

45 km

N

INTRODUCTION
HISTORY
REGIONS
WHEN TO VISIT
STATE'S GREATS
RULES OF THE ROAD
DRIVING TOURS

east of the city. One of the best views of the lake and city is from the **Herbert F. Johnson Museum of Art** (on Central Ave., on the northwest side of the campus), which was designed by I. M. Pei. Depending on how much time you have, you'll also want to see Cornell Plantations and Sapsucker Woods.

❷ From Ithaca, take a quick drive north on Route 89, which climbs out of the city and follows the west bank of Cayuga Lake. Stop at **Taughannock Falls State Park** (8 mi north of Ithaca on Rte. 89). A short walk brings you to the highest waterfall in the state. At 215 ft, it eclipses Niagara by approximately 30 ft.

❸ Retrace your route back through Ithaca and head south on Route 13 toward **Elmira.** There you will find **Mark Twain's Study** (on the campus of Elmira College, off Park Pl.), an unusual octagon-shaped building where he wrote *The Adventures of Huckleberry Finn* and other books. Twain is buried in the city's **Woodlawn Cemetery** (1200 Walnut St.). Next door to that graveyard, you'll find the **Woodlawn National Cemetery** (1825 Davis St.) in which about 3,300 Confederate prisoners and Union soldiers are buried. If you need a lift after that, head to the **National Soaring Museum** at Harris Hill Park, where gliding began in this country. You can take a ride yourself or simply enjoy the world's largest exhibit of sail planes and historic gliders.

❹ Head west on Route 352 to **Corning** where the **Corning Glass Center** beckons. The center is one of New York State's major tourist attractions. A new Glass Innovation Center complements the already established exhibits of glass objects. Also worth seeing are the **Rockwell Museum** and the city's historic **Market Street district** (between Denison Pkwy. and Tioga Ave.), which has plenty of restaurants.

❺ **Watkins Glen** is to the northeast, on Route 414. If you're a race fan, you'll want to peek at the layout of the famous **Watkins Glen International Raceway.** But without question the main attraction of the area is the glen itself, in **Watkins Glen State Park** (Franklin St.), which stretches west from the city's main street and includes nearly 20 waterfalls and a deep walk-through canyon. You can also leave from here for a cruise on one of the Finger Lakes, with **Captain Bill's Seneca Lake Cruises** (1st and Franklin Sts.).

❻ A pretty drive north on Route 14 takes you along the west shore of Seneca Lake. You can pick from any of a number of wineries on this road or throughout the region. One popular choice is the **Glenora Wine Cellars** (5435 Rte. 14, Dundee), which is about 8 mi north of Watkins Glen. An inn and restaurant offer spectacular views of Seneca Lake.

❼ Backtrack a bit, or cut over to Route 14 A which takes you north to Dundee. Head west on Route 230, which covers the highlands west of Seneca Lake and brings you on a swooping curve toward the most unusual looking of the Finger Lakes: Keuka (which Native Americans called "broken lake"). At Route 54, head south toward the delightful village of **Hammondsport,** at the southern end of the lake. You can easily spend a day here with the **Glenn H. Curtiss Museum** (dedicated to the father of naval aviation), the **Great Western Winery Visitor Center,** and the peaceful village square. The *Keuka Maid* offers another chance for a lake cruise if you haven't taken one already.

Again, wineries beckon. Try **Heron Hill Winery** (9249 Rte. 76) or **Bully Hill Vineyards** (8843 Greyton H. Taylor Memorial Dr.) which has its own museum dedicated to charting the growth of the wine industry in the area and to Walter S. Taylor and the corporate takeover battles he waged. Head north from the village along Route 54A. At one time this was considered one of the prettiest drives in the world. Some trees have cut into the sight lines from the road, which hugs the shore and offers wonderful views of the lake and Bluff Point, which splits the lake's northern arms. You'll pass through **Penn Yan** and rejoin Route 54 as it swings east, back to the west shore of Seneca Lake.

⑧ Go north on Route 14 and head for **Geneva**, where you can spoil yourself with a meal at **Belhurst Castle** (Rte. 14 S) or **Geneva on the Lake**, or have a picnic at the expansive **Seneca Lake State Park** (1 mi east of Geneva on U.S. 20/Rte. 5) just to the east of the city. You may choose to visit the **Rose Hill Mansion** (3 mi east of Geneva, on the northeast shore of Seneca Lake on Rte. 96A, just south of U.S. 20—Use N.Y. Thruway exit 41 or 42), a wonderfully restored 1839 mansion that's one of the finest examples of Greek Revival architecture in America.

⑨ Follow Route 20 east to **Seneca Falls** for a look at some of the key places in the history of the women's rights movement: The **Elizabeth Cady Stanton House**, **Wesleyan Chapel Declaration Park**, and **National Women's Hall of Fame**. You can stretch your legs at the **Montezuma National Wildlife Refuge** (5 mi east of Seneca Falls on U.S. 20/Rte. 5), which is perched on the north end of Cayuga Lake. The refuge is a major stopover for migrating birds and features a walking tour that takes you close to the waterfowl. With some luck, you'll spot a bald eagle.

⑩ Head north on Route 89 and meet the Seaway Trail at Wolcott. Follow the signs (along Route 104A) to Fair Haven, on the shore of Lake Ontario. The trail takes you through **Oswego** right by the **Ft. Ontario State Historic Site** where you can catch daily military drills echoing the 1800s from mid-spring through early autumn. From Oswego, the Seaway Trail follows Routes 104, 104B, and 3, which takes you north along the beautiful eastern end of Lake Ontario. At the Pulaski River, depending upon the season and your inclination, you might want to watch the fisher folk. This area lures anglers from all over the world. (The county sells more than 65,000 fishing licenses a year, one of the most in the state.) The eastern shore of Lake Ontario features some fragile barrier beaches, dunes, and lagoons.

⑪ At **Sackets Harbor**, you can stroll the battlefield where two engagements of the War of 1812 took place. The village's historic district is worth strolling through. In summer the harbor is likely to be bustling with cruising activity.

⑫ The Seaway Trail leaves Route 3, eventually links with Route 12 E, and takes you to Cape Vincent, where Lake Ontario meets the St. Lawrence River. The **Tibbetts Point Lighthouse** marks the spot. Farther along Route 12 east is **Clayton**, which retains a genuine river city feel and features the must-see **Antique Boat Museum**. The local **Thousand Islands Inn** is the birthplace of Thousand Island dressing.

⑬ The much more commercialized and busier **Alexandria Bay** lies in the center of the 50-mi-long Thousand Islands area. Here you'll find historic **Boldt Castle** (on Heart Island) and plenty of opportunities to get out on the water and begin counting the islands.

The simplest way to get back to Ithaca is to head south on Interstate 81 to exit 13 in Preble. Go south on Route 281 until it hits Route 13, which takes you to Ithaca.

Seaway Trail along Lake Erie Driving Tour

FROM THE NEW YORK/PENNSYLVANIA BORDER TO HISTORIC OLD FT. NIAGARA

INTRODUCTION
HISTORY
REGIONS
WHEN TO VISIT
STATE'S GREATS
RULES OF THE ROAD
DRIVING TOURS

Distance: Approximately 110 mi, excluding detours   Time: 1–3 days

Breaks: If you like lakeside camping, make reservations at one of three state parks along the route (Lake Erie, Evangola, and Four Mile Creek). If you prefer indoor sleeping, there are many motels and hotels in Buffalo, or in the city of Niagara Falls.

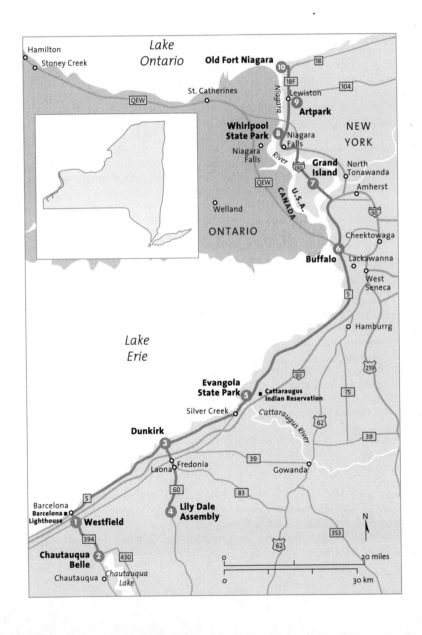

This scenic driving tour along the well-marked Seaway Trail takes you through three of western New York's most interesting counties—Chautauqua, Erie, and Niagara. The tour starts near the New York/Pennsylvania border and ends at Old Ft. Niagara in the northwestern part of Niagara County. The best time of year to take this tour is between May and November; in summer you'll be refreshed by cool breezes off the lake, and in fall you'll enjoy the grape harvest in Chautauqua County's wine country. The winter, however, can be pleasant too, as Lake Erie has a moderating influence on the amount of snowfall the area receives. Along the way, you'll enjoy beautiful countryside, breathtaking lake views, many beaches and boat launches, lighthouses, quaint villages, an historic fort, and the natural wonder of Niagara Falls.

❶ This tour begins near the New York/Pennsylvania border, heading north on Route 5. At Barcelona Harbor, look for a National Landmark lighthouse, which was the first lighthouse to be fueled by natural gas.

Continue heading away from Lake Erie by driving southeast on Route 394, past Interstate 90, until you come to the historic town of **Westfield**, which is home to Welch's grape juice. Near Westfield's town square you'll find antiques and craft shops, as well as the Federal-style McClurg Mansion, which was built in 1820. Guided tours are offered from May through November for a modest fee.

❷ Traveling farther inland along Route 394 you will come to Mayville, located on Chautauqua Lake. Here you will find the *Chautauqua Belle*, an old steamboat that once carried passengers the length of the lake; today the boat offers 1½-hour narrated cruises. From Mayville, take Route 394 back towards Barcelona and proceed north on Route 5. A few miles north of Barcelona is Blue Water Beach, a place to camp, fish, or picnic while looking across the seemingly endless lake towards Canada.

❸ Driving 15 mi north on Route 5 to **Dunkirk**, you can visit the **Dunkirk Historical Lighthouse and Veterans Park Museum**. The lighthouse was built in 1875, and is filled with memorabilia from various branches of the military.

❹ From Route 5, take Route 60 south to the **Lily Dale Assembly** on Cassadaga Lake. This is the largest spiritualist center in the world. Throughout the summer people flock here for lectures, workshops, and services on such subjects as spiritual healing and clairvoyance.

Backtracking to Route 5, drive north just past the town of Silver Creek. Make a left on Allegheny Road and continue north to the hamlet of Sunset Bay. This seasonal town contains a warren of summer cottages, a sandy beach, and a few good restaurants, which take advantage of the fantastic sunsets over Lake Erie.

Return to Route 5 and you'll soon enter the northern end of the Cattaraugus Indian Reservation. Native American homes are visible when driving south on Route 438 along Cattaraugus Creek.

❺ Leaving the reservation, head north on Route 5. Travel west on Lotus Point Road, then north on Lakeshore Road. Here you may choose to rest or stay overnight at **Evangola State Park**, which has a long beach and spacious lawns of freshly mown grass along either side of its tree-lined drive. Lake Erie Beach and Wendt Beach Park (adjacent to Sturgeon Point Marina) are also along Lakeshore Road. The summer homes in the area range from rental cottages to mansions.

6 At the town of Pinehurst, Lakeshore Road joins Route 5. As you stay on Route 5, you will start to see industrial **Buffalo**, including old steel factories on either side of the highway.

Route 5 is nicknamed the Skyway because it rises above the magnificent grain elevators lining Buffalo Creek on the way to downtown Buffalo. (Note: You don't want to be on the Skyway in a driving rain or during a high wind warning.) To the west of the roadway are expansive views of Lake Erie and Buffalo's inner harbor, while to the east you have a bird's-eye view of downtown Buffalo, which includes City Hall, the Old County Building, and the Old Post Office. High above **Buffalo and Erie County Naval and Military Park** Route 5 joins Interstate 190 from the east. Stay on Interstate 190 north as you approach the Peace Bridge, which crosses over into Canada.

7 Now you are leaving Lake Erie as it spills into the Niagara River. You'll soon have another opportunity to witness breathtaking views as you take Interstate 190 over the arching bridge to **Grand Island**. Taking the first exit after the bridge, you will join the Robert Moses Parkway (which hugs the river known for its ever-mounting rapids), and enter the city of Niagara Falls.

8 After experiencing the falls, continue north on Robert Moses Parkway for about 3 mi to **Whirlpool State Park**, located near Niagara University. You'll want to stop and look into Niagara Gorge, where you can see a perpetual whirlpool created at the place where the Niagara River changes its course 90 degrees.

9 Your next stop on the Robert Moses Parkway might be the historic village of Lewistown, which was settled in 1796. Taking Route 18F due west from the Parkway you'll find **Artpark**, at the foot of S. 4th Street. This 200-acre state park on a bluff overlooking Niagara Gorge is the only New York state park dedicated to the performing arts.

10 Continue north on Route 18F for your last stop on this driving adventure—the New York State Historic Site of **Old Ft. Niagara**, right at the mouth of the Niagara River where it empties into Lake Ontario. The earliest part of the fort was built as a French castle in 1726 and the fort later played a critical role in the French and Indian War (1754–63). Self-guided tours are available throughout the year, and living-history demonstrations and reenactments are held from the spring through the fall.

To return to your starting point, take Route 18F to Interstate 90 to Route 5.

ADIRONDACK PARK

INTRO
ATTRACTIONS
DINING
LODGING

ADIRONDACK PARK

MAP 3, J3

Adirondack Park is unlike any other in the country. Covering one-third of the total land in New York State (just over 6 million acres), the park includes both public and private land. There are forests, mountains, and valleys; farmlands, towns, and villages; lakes, ponds, and rivers. The state constitution designates that about one-third of the park remain "forever wild" and you'll see old-growth forests as well as wildflower-filled meadows here. The opportunities for recreation and sports are many: you can climb, hike, ride, cross-country ski, water-ski, and scuba dive. There are 2,000 mi of foot trails, and hundreds of miles of canoe routes. Many campgrounds are open through the fall foliage and hunting seasons. Visitors centers in Paul Smiths and Newcomb serve as designated education and orientation centers for all of Adirondack Park. Both centers offer walks, slide presentations, and various educational programs.

Information: Adirondack Park Agency | Rte. 73, Ray Brook, 12977 | 518/891–4050.

ALBANY

(Nearby towns also listed: Amsterdam, Cobleskill, Colonie, Saratoga Springs, Schenectady, Troy)

Settled in 1624, Albany is the second-oldest permanent European settlement within the country's 13 original colonies. Initially, under the control of the Dutch, the city was called Fort Orange, but after the British took over in 1664, it was renamed for the Duke of York and Albany. Following the American Revolution, Albany experienced rapid growth and development. In 1797, it was chosen to be the Empire State's capital. Located on the Hudson River, it served as a transportation hub in the 19th century. Today, it has a population of approximately 100,000. Government is important in this city, but you will also find a variety of cultural and historical attractions.

Information: **Albany County Convention and Visitors Bureau** | 25 Quackenbush Sq., 12207 | 518/434–1217.

TRANSPORTATION INFORMATION
Airport: Albany International Airport | 737 Albany Shaker Rd. | 518/242–2200.
Bus Lines: Greyhound | 34 Hamilton St. | 518/434–8980.
Driving Around Town: Driving around Town: I–90 cuts laterally through Albany, approximately 2 mi north of downtown. I–87 comes from the south and skirts the western side of the city, while I–787 branches off from I–87 and runs parallel to the Hudson River on the city's eastern side. Access to downtown is provided by a spur off I–787. Because rush-hour traffic can frustrate travel on the highways, plan on getting into the downtown area by 9:30 or 10 AM, when most people are already at work.

Visitor parking in the downtown area is found in three parking areas: beneath the Empire State Plaza, on levels P-1 and P-3; in the Pepsi Arena parking garage; and in the Cathedral and Madison Avenue Parking lot, just south of the New York State Museum. The rate for an entire day in one of the plaza areas is $8; there is no charge if you park after 2 PM. For the Cathedral and Madison Avenue lots, the price is $7 for an entire day. Metered parking is also available in this area, but can be difficult to find on weekdays. The speed limit for downtown streets is 30 mph.

Neighborhoods

Downtown Albany. The downtown area, although dominated by the marble expanses of Governor Nelson A. Rockefeller Empire State Plaza, includes many other fine architectural sights. The State Capitol is an obvious example, but others are easily found, like the Romanesque City Hall, built in the 1880s. In addition to the many public buildings, there are also historic residences, restaurants, and shops. Bordering this area to the west is Washington Park, a large public park with its own lake and the site of many annual festivals and events.

Mansion Hill. South of the Empire State Plaza is a historic district known as Mansion Hill. As the city grew more prosperous in the late 1800s, many wealthy residents built homes in this area, convenient to the downtown markets and port. Although the historic structures suffered neglect for many years, today, through federal grants, they have been renovated. Victorian style is characteristic of many of the homes; many, especially those that cluster around the Cathedral of the Immaculate Conception, are in the Gothic Revival style. Adding prestige to the neighborhood is the fact that the Governor resides on Eagle Street.

WALKING TOUR

A tour of Albany should begin at the Governor Nelson A. Rockefeller Empire State Plaza, the sprawling complex at the city's center. At the northeastern corner of the plaza stands the New York State Capitol, one of the finest examples of American 19th-century public architecture. It's well worth a visit inside to view the Million Dollar Staircase and the Legislative and Executive Chambers. Walking out of the capitol onto the plaza, you'll have a dramatic view of the complex; to your left stands the Egg, a modernist structure that houses two theaters. To your right are the four Agency buildings and in front of you, beyond the reflecting pools, is the New York State Museum. As you walk toward the museum, you'll pass several examples of modernist and contemporary sculpture, complementing the plaza's dramatic layout.

After a visit to the many treasures within the museum, exit to another dramatic view of the plaza, this time with the capitol in the distance. Turn right and stroll to the Corning Tower, where you can take an elevator to the 42nd floor for a panoramic view of the city. Stroll past the tower to the plaza's southeastern side. Here you'll have a view of the Pepsi Arena, home to the Albany Firebirds, River Rats, and Attack. Continue in a northeasterly direction until you pass the capitol. Turn left at Washington Avenue and walk northwest one block to the Albany Institute of History and Art. From here, backtrack on Washington Avenue; the City Hall will be in front of you at the end of the street. At City Hall, turn left on Eagle Street, then right on Columbia Street. Stroll down Columbia to Pearl and turn left to find the Capitol Repertory Theater. Follow Pearl to Clinton Avenue and the Palace Theatre. Follow Clinton east to reach the Visitor's Center and Henry Hudson Planetarium.

Attractions

ART AND ARCHITECTURE

Historic Cherry Hill. Philip Van Rensselaer, one of the region's original Dutch settlers, built this home in 1787. | 523½ S. Pearl St. | 518/434–4791 | $3.50 | Feb.–Dec., tours Tues.–Sat. 10–3, Sun. at 1, 2, 3.

New York State Capitol. This National Historic Landmark, built from 1867 to 1899 in eclectic styles, has elaborate carvings and murals. | Washington Ave. and State St., Concourse at Empire State Plaza, Room 106 | 518/474–2418 | Free | Tours daily at 10, noon, 2, 3.

Schuyler Mansion State Historic Site. This is the Georgian mansion of Philip Schuyler, a Revolutionary War general of the Albany militia. | 32 Catherine St. | 518/434–0834 | fax 518/434–3821 | www.nysparks.com | $3 | Mid-Apr.–Oct., Wed.–Sat. 10–5, Sun. 1–5; Nov.–mid-Apr., by appointment only.

BEACHES, PARKS, AND NATURAL SIGHTS

Five Rivers Environmental Center. Hiking and ski trails can be found here, about 10 mi from downtown, along with outdoor education programs and an exhibit center with animals. You can picnic on the grounds. | 56 Game Farm Rd., Delmar | 518/475–0291 | fax 518/439–8044 | Free | Grounds open daily dawn–dusk; visitors center Mon.–Sat. 9–4:30, Sun. 1–4:30.

CULTURE, EDUCATION, AND HISTORY

Capital Repertory Theatre. Enjoy eclectic professional theater, familiar and new, in a small and intimate setting. | 111 N. Pearl St. | 518/445–4531.

Palace Theatre. Home to the Albany Symphony Orchestra, the Berkshire Ballet, and the Capital Ballet, this former movie palace is the place to go for musical and dance performances, as well as family entertainment. | 19 Clinton Ave. | 518/462–4531 | Call for schedule.

State University of New York at Albany. Established in 1844, the university boasts NCAA Division I sports teams and a public art gallery. Approximately 16,000 students are enrolled here. | Uptown campus at 1400 Washington Ave.; downtown campus at 135 Western Ave. | 518/442–3300 | fax 518/797–5270 | www.albany.edu | Free | Daily.

USS *Slater*. This historic naval ship was the last of 565 destroyer ships used by military personnel through World War II and the Cold War. | Quay and Broadway on the Hudson River | $5 | Apr.–early Nov., Thurs.–Sun. 1–4 | 518/431–1943 or 518/434–0405.

MUSEUMS

Albany Institute of History and Art. Hudson River School paintings, as well as collections of silver, furniture, and contemporary art, illuminate four centuries of regional history at one of the oldest museums in the United States. While renovations are in progress, to be completed in Spring 2001, the museum is maintaining a branch downtown at 63 State Street, featuring exhibitions, programs, and a small shop. | 125 Washington Ave. | 518/463–4478 | fax 518/462–1522 | www.albanyinstitute.org | Call for information | Weekdays 10–5.

Bronck Museum. This is the oldest surviving home in the Hudson Valley, located about 20 mi outside of Albany. Eight generations of the Peter Bronck family lived here, from 1663 to 1939. Today, it houses collections of the Greene County Historical Society. Take Interstate 87 to exit 21B. | Pieter Bronck Rd., on U.S. 9 W, Coxsackie | 518/731–6490 or 518/731–8862 | $4 | Memorial Day–mid-Oct., Tues.–Sat. 10–4, Sun. 1–5.

New York State Museum. A showcase for New York State history, geography, and art, this museum has a recreated Iroquois Longhouse, as well as a hands-on learning center for children. | Empire State Plaza, Cultural Education Center | 518/474–5877 | fax 518/486–3696 | www.nysm.nysed.gov | Free | Daily 9:30–5.

SPORTS AND RECREATION

Pepsi Arena. The area hosts both professional and college sports games, along with concerts and conventions. | 51 S. Pearl St. | 518/487–2000 | Call for schedule.

SIGHTSEEING TOURS

Dutch Apple Cruises Inc. Two- and three-hour Hudson River cruise options include brunch, dinner, and moonlight excursions. Book 48 hours in advance. | 137 Broadway at Quay | 518/463–0220 | fax 518/463–0235 | $10–$29 | Mid-Apr.–Oct., weekdays 8–5.

OTHER POINTS OF INTEREST

Albany Visitor's Center and Henry Hudson Planetarium. Pick up visitor information, or pay a visit to the domed theater, 53 ft wide by 30 ft high, to view the night sky. The center also has a restaurant. | 25 Quackenbush Sq.; Clinton Ave. at Broadway | $4.50 | Weekdays 9–5, weekends 10–4; planetarium show open only on Sat. | 518/434–0405.

Governor Nelson A. Rockefeller Empire State Plaza. This 96-acre complex includes the capitol building, the New York State Museum, the state library, a performing arts center, the Vietnam memorial, and much more. | Between Madison and Washington Aves. | 518/474–2418 | fax 518/473–2956 | Free | Weekdays 9–5; tours daily 10, noon, 2, 3.

ON THE CALENDAR

MAY: *Tulip Festival*. Thousands of tulips are at their peak during this 3-day festival celebrating Albany's Dutch heritage in Washington Park on Madison Avenue. Traditions include scrubbing the streets and crowning a Tulip Queen. | 518/434–2032.

MID-AUG.: *Altamont Fair*. This weeklong, three-county fair (Albany, Schenectady, and Greene) brings a circus, horse shows, and livestock, as well as a midway and entertainment to the fairgrounds in Altamont, Route 146. | 518/861–6671.

SEPT.: *Capital District Scottish Games*. Pipe bands, Highland dance, and traditional contests are the highlights of this Celtic arts festival at the Altamont Fairgrounds, Route 146. | 518/438–4297.

DEC.: *First Night Albany*. More than 40 downtown locations usher in the New Year with music, food, theater, and children's entertainment. At midnight, fireworks are set off over the Hudson River. Stroll, or ride free buses. Badges are sold at various sites, including City Hall, Eagle Street. | 518/434–2032.

Dining

INEXPENSIVE

Beff's. American. Known for its burgers, wings, and specialty pizzas, this homey Irish pub/sports bar on the west side of town serves family-style food. | 15 Watervliet Ave. | 518/482–2333 | $6–$8 | AE, DC, MC, V.

Bleecker Cafe. Continental. This reasonably priced, international bistro in the heart of the historic Center Square neighborhood serves steaks, Greek entrées, seafood, and salads. Saturday and Sunday brunch. | 32 Dove St. | 518/463–9382 | fax 518/462–1182 | $10–$12 | AE, D, MC, V.

Jillian's. American. This high-energy, casual, theme restaurant serves pizza, burgers, and sandwiches inside a downtown entertainment complex. You can play interactive video games, shoot pool at one of their 12 tables, or take a turn on the dance floor. If you want to eat outside, you can choose from four different levels of outside decks. Kids' menu. | 59 N. Pearl St. | 518/432–1997 | fax 518/432–9772 | $6–$13 | AE, MC, V.

MODERATE

Big House Brewing Co. American. Original and special seasonal brews are served in this five-story converted downtown warehouse with authentic brick walls, high ceilings, and curbside dining. Known for its baby-back ribs, nachos, and burgers, the restaurant also serves a buffet. College kids hang out here on weekend nights, but during the week professionals make up the crowd. Three theaters and the Pepsi Arena are nearby. Take advantage of the outside patio or the dance club upstairs. Live blues Tuesday, and Thursday through Saturday. Kids' menu. | 90 N. Pearl St. | 518/445–2739 | fax 518/463–4594 | No lunch Sun. | $10–$18 | AE, D, DC, MC, V.

C. H. Evans Brewing Co. at the Albany Pump Station. American. This 1837 converted brick warehouse, listed on the National Register of Historic Places, houses a microbrewery and restaurant serving eclectic American fare with Caribbean and Indian influences. Located downtown, this restaurant is known for burgers, meat loaf, and jambalaya. Family-style service. Kids' menu. | 19 Quackenbush Sq. | 518/447–9000 | fax 518/465–1410 | $12–$22 | AE, D, DC, MC, V.

Gingerman Wine Bar and Restaurant. American. Named for J. P. Donleavy's novel, *The Ginger Man,* this wine bar and restaurant has Irish photos on the walls and a sprawling bar. College students and professionals come here for the pastas, sandwiches, salads, steaks, and seafood, as well as the extensive wine list and, of course, the Guinness. Located midtown. Patio seating is available. | 234 Western Ave. | 518/427–5963 | fax 518/427–1917 | Closed Sun. No lunch Sat. | $12–$18 | AE, D, MC, V.

Hudson Harbor Steak and Seafood Restaurant. Seafood. Once a ticket office for day-liner boats, this downtown restaurant near the waterfront has stone floors and a fireplace. Try the coquilles St. Jacques or the seafood delight. Tables with umbrellas provide just enough shade on the outside patio. | 351 Broadway | 518/426–5000 | fax 518/427–0630 | Closed Sun. No lunch Sat. | $12–$18 | AE, D, DC, MC, V.

Elda's. Italian. Crisp linen tablecloths, carved-wood chairs, and high ceilings with chandeliers create the setting for northern Italian food that draws both young people and business professionals. Located in Center Square on the corner of State Street, the restaurant is a block from the state capitol, the Capital Repertory Theatre, and Washington Park. You can also eat outside on the patio. | 205 Lark St. | 518/449–3532 | fax 518/426–0951 | $18–$22 | AE, D, DC, MC, V.

Lombardo's. Italian. Young professionals, legislators, couples, and tourists flock here to eat northern and southern Italian fare in a dining room where casual clothes mix easily with jackets and ties. Lombardo's is known for veal, pasta, and seafood. The Pepsi Arena is just one block away and down the street is the Governor's Mansion and the State Library. | 119-121 Madison Ave., at S. Pearl St. | 518/462–9180 | Closed Sun. No lunch Sat. | $12–$18 | D, DC, MC, V.

McGeary's. American. This Irish pub down the street from the Capital Repertory Theater has live music Wednesday through Saturday. Although known for chicken wings, the kitchen also serves a full menu, including club sandwiches, pasta, Caesar salad, and clam chowder. You can eat outside at one of the tables with green umbrellas. | 4 Clinton Sq. | 518/463–1455 | fax 518/456–1456 | Closed Sun., except in football season | $11–$15 | AE, D, MC, V.

Red's. Seafood. Besides its huge portions (which are available in half sizes), this restaurant is known for fresh seafood, shellfish, pasta, and hand-cut steak. There is a lobster tank on site. Try the gulf shrimp. Kids' menu. Sunday brunch. In West Coxsackie, 2 mi south of exit 21B off Interstate 87. | 12005 Route 9 W, West Coxsackie | 518/731–8151 | fax 518/731–8199 | Closed Mon. | $12–$18 | AE, D, DC, MC, V.

Quintessence. Continental. The cuisine changes nightly at this funky Art Deco diner. Monday is Italian night, Tuesday is seafood, Wednesday is German, Thursday is International, Friday is Asian, and Sunday is Mexican. Known for chicken teriyaki. Sunday brunch. | 11 New Scotland Ave. | 518/434–8186 | fax 518/434–2700 | Breakfast also available | $9–$15 | AE, D, DC, MC, V.

EXPENSIVE

Albany Mansion Hill Inn and Restaurant. Continental. Located in the Mansion District, Albany's second-oldest neighborhood, this restaurant serves seasonal, vegetarian, and pasta dishes. You can eat outside in the landscaped courtyard which has a fishpond. | 115 Philip St., at Park Ave. | 518/465–2038 | fax 518/434–2313 | www.mansionhill.com | Closed Sun. No lunch | $20–$30 | AE, D, DC, MC, V.

Bongiorno's. Italian. This cozy restaurant serving northern and southern Italian cuisine appeals to both college students and professionals. Candles and fresh flowers are on each of the 10 tables. Try the zuppa di pesce, tortellini primavera, or veal picante. Near Washington Park, the State Museum, and the Lark Street boutiques. | 23 Dove St. | 518/462–9176 | fax 518/465–0846 | Closed Sun. No lunch Sat. | $18–$23 | AE, DC, MC, V.

Bumpers Cafe. American. The chairs are made of actual car parts in this unique 1950s automotive-theme restaurant located in North Albany. The menu features standard American fare with an Asian, Mideast twist. Burgers and sandwiches are popular. Try the chicken pistachio, or pork tenderloin with ginger coconut milk. Live music on Friday; jazz music at Sunday brunch. | 64 Colvin Ave. | 518/489–9418 | fax 518/437–3410 | Breakfast also available Mon.–Sat.; no dinner Sun. | $15–$20 | AE, D, DC, MC, V.

Café Capriccio. Italian. A favorite of the Albany political establishment, this downtown eatery serves northern Italian and Mediterranean food in small booths with beautiful lighting. Try the eggplant with four cheeses or the calamari pasta. Near the Pepsi Arena. | 49 Grand St. | 518/465–0439 | No lunch | $14–$22 | AE, D, MC, V.

Jack's Oyster House. Continental. If you want great seafood, this downtown Albany landmark with tiled floors, white tablecloths, dark wood, and polite service is a winner. Oysters and clams are on the menu, along with steak and prime rib. Signature dishes include calves' liver with bacon and the jack seafood grill. The pasta, chicken fingers, and hamburgers are favorites. The restaurant is down the hill from the state capitol building and next door to the Pepsi Arena. Kids' menu. | 42 State St. | 518/465–8854 | fax 518/434–2134 | $18–$22 | AE, D, DC, MC, V.

Justin's. American. One of Albany's busiest hot spots, this restaurant in Central Square draws an eclectic crowd of students, families, and the political elite. The American cuisine is spiced with Latin American, Asian, and southern influences. Try the *ropa vieja,* ultra-tender braised Cuban brisket. Sunday brunch. | 301 Lark St. | 518/436–7008 | fax 518/432–4122 | $18–$23 | AE, D, MC, V.

La Serre. Continental. Poached salmon, rack of lamb, beef steak, and veal dishes attract a traditional old Albany crowd to this cozy spot. A raw bar serves cold seafood. Open-air dining is available at umbrellaed tables. Kids' menu. | 14 Green St. | 518/463–6056 | fax 518/463–3830 | Closed Sun. No lunch | $19–$30 | AE, DC, MC, V.

L'Ecole Encore. Continental. This casual restaurant in a former home on the border of Albany and Gilderland is known for steaks, chops, pasta, and seafood. Try the artichokes, chicken broccoli strudel, or angel-hair shrimp fra diavolo. Dine outside from June to September on an umbrella-shaded patio. Jazz on Thursday. Sunday brunch. | 337 Fuller Rd. | 518/437–1234 | $17–$22 | AE, D, DC, MC, V.

Nicole's Bistro at the Quackenbush House. American. Once the home of Pieter Quackenbush, one of Albany's original Dutch settlers, the 17th-century building that houses this French-American bistro has been standing longer than any building in Albany. Try the rack of lamb with rosemary dijon crust, or the roast lamb or pheasant served with garlic mashed potatoes. The grounds include the re-creation of a colonial herb garden and outside dining is available. Right next door is the Albany Visitor's Cultural Center and just across the street is the Palace Theatre, which was built in the 1930s. | 25 Quackenbush Sq. | 518/465–1111 | fax 518/465–3911 | Closed Sun. No lunch Sat. | $25–$30 | AE, D, DC, MC, V.

★ **Ogden's.** Contemporary. You'll find this turn-of-the-20th-century building on a quiet side street, just off the main downtown thoroughfare. Inside, the rooms are paneled with oak. Try the sea bass, lobster pasta, or one of the veal dishes. Extensive wine list. Private dining available. | 42 Howard St. | 518/463–6605 | fax 518/463–6568 | Closed Sun. No lunch Sat. | $15–$20 | AE, MC, V.

Yono's. Indonesian. This upscale restaurant in the Armory Center draws a mostly business crowd with its curry and coconut-milk dishes and quiet, intimate Colonial setting. Try the rack of lamb and rijstaffel, and the chocolate rendezvous, which has several small, delectable dessert options tastefully arranged on one communal tray. There's a balcony. | 64 Colvin Ave. | 518/436–7747 | fax 518/437–3410 | Jackets required | Closed Sun.–Tues. | $18–$30 | AE, D, DC, MC, V.

Lodging

INEXPENSIVE

Fairfield Inn. Across the street from the SUNY Albany campus, and 5 mi from downtown Albany, this no-frills chain offers simple rooms. Complimentary Continental breakfast. Pool. Hot tub. Free parking. | 1383 Washington Ave. | 518/435–1800 | fax 518/435–1800 | 91 rooms, 8 suites | $90–$100 | AE, D, DC, MC, V.

Pine Haven Bed and Breakfast. This late-1800s Victorian mansion retains its original character with an array of antiques. In summer you can relax in a wicker rocking chair on the front porch, and in winter you can drink cocoa and warm yourself by the lobby fireplace. Complimentary Continental breakfast. Free parking. | 531 Western Ave. | 518/482–1574 | 5 rooms (3 with shared bath) | $49–$79 | AE, D, MC, V.

Susse Chalet Inn. Located 10 minutes by car from Albany, and ½ mi from Interstate 87, this inn makes it easy for you to avoid Albany traffic and hop right on the highway. It's also within walking distance of restaurants, a mall, and a gym where you'll have health-club privileges. Complimentary Continental breakfast. Laundry facilities. Free parking. | 1383 Washington Ave. | 518/459–5670 | fax 518/459–0069 | www.sussechalet.com | 97 rooms | $70 | AE, D, MC, V.

MODERATE

Best Western Airport Inn. This hotel off Interstate 87 and near the Albany International Airport has a lawn and roses. Restaurant, bar, room service. In-room data ports, some refrigerators, cable TV. Pool. Business services, airport shuttle. Free parking. | 200 Wolf Rd. | 518/458–1000 | fax 518/458–2807 | bwaai@crisny.org | 153 rooms | $89 | AE, D, DC, MC, V.

Comfort Inn and Suites. Each standard room at this chain hotel has two phone lines. Three suites have in-room hot tubs. Complimentary Continental breakfast. In-room data ports, some microwaves, some refrigerators, some in-room hot tubs, cable TV. Pool. Gym. Business services. Free parking. | 1606 Central Ave. | 518/869–5327 or800/233–9444 | fax 518/456–8971 | www.comfortinn.com | 52 rooms, 56 suites | $89, $109 suites | AE, D, DC, MC, V.

Howard Johnson Hotel. Some rooms at this chain hotel have desks, tables, and pull-out sofas. The hotel is 20 minutes from the Albany International Airport. Restaurant, complimentary Continental breakfast. In-room data ports, cable TV. Pool. Tennis. Gym. Business services. Some pets allowed. Free parking. | 416 Southern Blvd. | 518/462–6555 | fax 518/462–2547 | 135 rooms | $82 | AE, D, DC, MC, V.

Ramada Limited. Basic lodging near the Albany International Airport is available in this chain motel. Complimentary Continental breakfast. Microwaves, refrigerators, some in-room hot tubs, cable TV. Exercise equipment. Business services. Pets allowed (deposit). | 1630 Central Ave. | 518/456–0222 | fax 518/452–1376 | ramada-albany@travelbase.com | 105 rooms | $74–$94 | AE, D, DC, MC, V.

EXPENSIVE

Albany Courtyard by Marriott. Catering mostly to business travelers, this hotel features, among other business-related services, large work desks in every room. It's right off Interstate 87 and close to the Albany International Airport. In-room data ports, cable TV. Pool. Gym. Laundry facilities. Business services, airport shuttle, free parking. No pets. | 168 Wolf Rd. | 518/482–8800 | fax 518/482–0001 | www.courtyard.com | 78 rooms | $104–$129 | AE, D, DC, MC, V.

Hampton Inn. King-size beds are available in some rooms at this chain hotel, which is close to Interstate 87 and the Albany International Airport. Complimentary Continental breakfast. In-room data ports, cable TV. Pool. Laundry facilities. Business services, airport shuttle. Free parking. | 10 Ulenski Dr. | 518/438–2822 | fax 518/438–2931 | www.hampton-inn.com | 154 rooms | $99–$116 | AE, D, DC, MC, V.

Ramada Inn of Albany. This hotel is 3 mi from downtown Albany and the state capitol building and 6 mi from Albany International Airport. Restaurant, bar, complimentary breakfast, room service. In-room data ports, cable TV. Pool. Beauty salon. Exercise equipment. Business services, airport shuttle. Pets allowed. Free parking. | 1228 Western Ave. | 518/489–2981 | fax 518/489–8967 | ramadaonwestern@msn.com | www.sovereignhotels.com | 195 rooms | $98 | AE, D, DC, MC, V.

VERY EXPENSIVE

Crowne Plaza. This hotel is downtown, less than a mile from the State Museum, and within a few blocks of a half-dozen restaurants and nightspots. The state capitol complex is two blocks away. Restaurant, room service. In-room data ports, some refrigerators, cable TV. Pool. Hot tub. Gym. Business services, airport shuttle, parking (fee). | State and Lodge Sts. | 518/462–6611 | fax 518/462–2901 | 371 rooms, 15 suites | $140 rooms, $134–$179 suites | AE, D, DC, MC, V.

Desmond Hotel and Conference Center. This Colonial-style hotel, less than a mile from the Albany International Airport, has courtyards and both a casual and formal restaurant. Some rooms have balconies. The game room has two pool tables and video games. 2 restaurants, room service. In-room data ports, some microwaves, some refrigerators, cable TV. 2 pools. Hot tub. Exercise equipment. Video games. Business services, airport shuttle, free parking. | 660 Albany-Shaker Rd. | 518/869–8100 or 800/448–3500 | fax 518/869–7659 | www.desmondhotels.com | 333 rooms | $139–$149 | AE, D, DC, MC, V.

Holiday Inn–Turf. This eight-story hotel has a central courtyard area, and is near Interstate 87 and Albany International Airport. 2 restaurants, room service. In-room data ports, refrigerators, some in-room hot tubs, cable TV. 2 pools. Barbershop, beauty salon, hot tub, sauna. Tennis courts. Gym. Business services, airport shuttle, free parking. | 205 Wolf Rd. | 518/458–7250 | fax 518/458–7377 | info@holidayinnturf.com | www.holidayinnturf.com | 309 rooms | $130 | AE, D, DC, MC, V.

Mansion Hill Inn and Restaurant. This inn in the heart of downtown Albany was built in 1861 and has a central courtyard. Guest rooms are large and uncluttered, with antique reproduction pieces and tasteful watercolor prints. Restaurant, complimentary breakfast, room service. Cable TV. Pets allowed. Free parking. | 115 Philip St. | 518/465–2038 | fax 518/434–2313 | www.mansionhill.com | 8 rooms | $155–$175 | AE, D, DC, MC, V.

Marriott. You'll find rooms with pull-out couches, king-size beds, or two double beds at this chain hotel near Interstate 87 and the Albany International Airport. Outside there's a patio and pool with a view. Two shopping malls are within 5 mi. Suites have meeting rooms. 2 restaurants, bar, complimentary Continental breakfast. In-room data ports, cable TV. 2 pools. Hot tub. Exercise equipment. Laundry facilities. Business services, airport shuttle. Pets allowed. Free parking. | 189 Wolf Rd. | 518/458–8444 | fax 518/458–7365 | 359 rooms, 3 suites | $139–$184, suites $514–$678 | AE, D, DC, MC, V.

★ **Morgan State House.** You'll be in the center of Albany in this late 19th-century town house, but you'll still have a view of either Washington Park or the house's own well-tended flower garden. This inn prides itself on the luxuries it provides, from down comforters to gourmet breakfast. Complimentary breakfast. | 393 State St. | 888/427–6063 or 518/427–6063 | fax 518/463–1316 | info@statehouse.com | www.statehouse.com | 13 rooms, 1 suite | $135–$200 rooms, $250 suite | AE, D, DC, MC, V.

ALBION

MAP 3, D5

(Nearby towns also listed: Batavia, Lockport, Medina, Rochester)

The village of Albion was established at the crossing of the Erie Canal and Oak Orchard Road, which served as a conduit for people and goods en route from Batavia. Once the canal was surveyed, people bought land in 40-acre parcels. By the time the village was three years old, it had a population of 500 and was selected as the county seat of Orleans County. The residents called their village Albion after the name often used in poetic allusions to England and the White Cliffs of Dover. George Pullman, who made his fortune designing sleeping cars for the railroad, grew up here. In his will, he left money to build Pullman Memorial Church in memory of his parents.

Information: Greater Albion Chamber of Commerce | 101 N. Main St., 14411 | 716/589–7727.

Attractions
Watts Farms Country Markets. On weekends, you can take a 30-min train trip through the apple orchard. A country gift shop and market sells fresh fruits and 25 flavors of fudge. | 3121 Rte. 98 | 716/589–8000 or 800/274–5897 | fax 716/589–8001 | www.wattfarms.com | kwatt@eznet.net | Free | May–Dec., Mon.–Sat. 9–8, Sun. 10–9.

ON THE CALENDAR
JUNE: *Albion Strawberry Festival.* The strawberry desserts are delectable and the free family entertainment includes 5K and 8K footraces. There are also arts and crafts, antique and classic cars, and a chicken barbecue. | 716/589–7727.

AUG.: *The Great Orleans Unique Flying Machine Expo and Hot Air Balloon Family Fest.* Watch the hot-air balloons, or take a balloon or helicopter ride at the Pine Hill Airport. Meanwhile, on the ground, there's a pancake breakfast and craft show, and antique cars and military equipment are on display. | 716/589–4363.

SEPT.: *AKC All-Breed Dog Obedience Show.* Canines are judged for obedience at Bullard Park, off Route 31. | 716/638–5041.

Dining

Navarra's Restaurant. Italian. In downtown Albion you'll find this Sicilian family restaurant where everything is homemade, from the lasagna to the veggie burgers to Grandma's delicious desserts. If you're feeling somewhat adventurous, try the calamari or tripe. Full bar and salad bar. | 20 N. Main St. | 716/589–9860 | Closed Sun. | $5–$10 | D, MC, V.

Tillman's Historic Village Inn. Continental. The Village Inn first opened in 1824 to serve stagecoach travelers along the Ridge Road in Orleans County. It is now owned and operated by the Tillman family, who provide a cordial atmosphere and generous meals. It's known for prime rib, steaks, chops, ribs, and chicken. Kids' menu. | 14369 Ridge Rd. | 716/589–9151 | $15–$30 | AE, D, DC, MC, V.

Lodging

Fairhaven Inn. Once a home, this tiny cobblestone inn in the center of the Cobble Stone Museum Complex dates to 1837. Next door is a creek. Antique-style furnished rooms have modem-ready phones and coffeemakers. Cable TV. | 14369 Ridge Rd. | 716/589–9151 | 4 rooms | $55 | AE, D, DC, MC, V.

Friendship Manor Bed and Breakfast. This 1880 house sits on an acre of land with lovely rose gardens and an herb garden. The rooms are done in country Victorian, and have some antique furniture. No alcohol allowed on premises. Picnic area, complimentary breakfast. Pool. Tennis. Bicycles. No smoking. | 349 S. Main St. | 716/589–2983 | fax 716/589–1162 | baker@iinc.com | 4 rooms | $65 | AE, D, MC, V.

Tillman's Historic Village Inn. Located 3 mi north of Albion, this rural inn sits amid flourishing gardens and within view of Proctor Brook. All rooms have two double beds, eclectic antiques, and large desks. | 14369 Ridge Rd. | 716/589–9151 | www.tillmansvillageinn.com | 4 rooms | $55 | AE, D, DC, MC, V.

ALEXANDRIA BAY

MAP 3, H3

(Nearby towns also listed: Clayton, Watertown)

The vacation center and heart of the Thousand Islands area, Alexandria Bay sits on the edge of the St. Lawrence River. In the late 1800s, the village was a popular resort and steamboat stop, attracting wealthy visitors who built homes on the islands. Today, Alexandria Bay caters to tourists who want a quick look at the islands. Restaurants and motels abound. The centerpiece attraction is Boldt Castle, on Heart Island, right across from the village.

Information: Alexandria Bay Chamber of Commerce | Box 365, 11 Market St., 13607 | 800/541–2110 or 888/HEART–TI | www.thousandislands.com/alexbay.

Attractions

Aqua Zoo. More than 30 exhibits show creatures from lakes, oceans and rivers around the world. On Route 12, 3½ mi off Route 81. | 43681 Rte. 12 | 315/482–5771 | www.abay.com/aquazoo/ | $4.75 | May–Sept., daily 10–7; Apr. and Oct., weekends 11–7.

Boat trips. Narrated cruises run throughout the islands. Some companies run dinner-time cruises. **Uncle Sam Boat Tours.** July and August is the peak time for the 2½-hour tours that go through the Canadian side of the islands, but the fall foliage is also memorable. Sightseeing cruises last 2¼ hours, and there is an unlimited stopover at Boldt Castle. Boats have heated, enclosed lower decks. Lunch cruises leave at 12:30 PM. Dinner cruises run at 7 PM Tuesday, and Thursday through Sunday. Reservations are required. | 47 James St. | 315/482–2611 or 800/ALEX BAY | fax 315/482–2611 | www.usboattours.com | $9–$27, depending on cruise | May–Oct., daily 10–7; tours leave at 10, 11:30, 12:30, 2, 3, 4:30.

Empire Boat Lines. Empire offers a shuttle to Boldt Castle every 30 minutes, as well as narrated 90-minute cruises to the castle. Dinner cruises are also available. | 5 Fuller St. | 315/482–TOUR or 888/449–ALEX | www.boattours.com | $5 for ferry; other cruise prices vary | Memorial Day–Labor Day, daily; tours leave at 10, noon, 2, 4.

Rockport Boat Line. This Canadian cruise line conducts 1-hr tours to bring passengers within sight of Boldt Castle and Millionaire's Row. | 23 Front St.; 401 Hwy./Extension Thousand Islands Pkwy.; head east across the bridge to Rockport, Ontario | 613/659–3402 or 800/563–8687 | info@rockportcruises.com | www.rockportcruises.com | $11 | Mid-Apr.–Jun., tours leave at 10, noon, and 2. July–Oct., tours leave every hour on the hour from 9–5.

Boldt Castle. George C. Boldt, proprietor of the Waldorf-Astoria Hotel in New York, began building this Rhineland-style castle on Heart Island for his wife, Louise, in 1900. Four years later, when she died suddenly, he ordered work stopped on the 120-room castle. The building remained deserted for 73 years, abused by vandals and weather. Since 1977, millions of dollars have been poured into restoration work. It's worth a trip to the island to see the castle and its fleet of wooden boats. The yacht house has an additional admission fee. | Box 428 | 315/482–2501 or 800/8–ISLAND | www.boldtcastle.com | $4.25; $2.50 for yacht house | May–June and Sept.–Oct., daily 10–6:30; July–Aug., daily 10–7:30.

Keewaydin State Park. This 180-acre park about a mile outside of town has 41 campsites, hot showers, and flush toilets. | 45165 Rte. 12 | 315/482–3331 | www.nysparks.state.ny.us/parks/ | Free; parking $6 May–Sept. | Daily.

Kring Point State Park. This 51-acre park, about 5 mi outside town, has 100 camping sites, hot showers, picnic areas, boating, fishing, swimming, and cross-country skiing. | 25950 Kring Point Rd., Redwood | 315/482–2444 | www.nysparks.state.ny.us/parks/ | $5; parking $6 May–Sept. | May–Oct., daily.

COUNTING ISLANDS

French explorer Jacques Cartier supposedly gave the region its name in the 1600s when he saw the islands before him and exclaimed "Les mille îles." Cartier's little rhyme offered his best explorer's-eye view of the situation. His estimate, "the thousand islands," was effective in its staying power and simplicity. Cartier was, of course, off by, well, nearly a "mille."

So how many islands are there? Good question. The first task is to define an island. How about: it must remain above water all year and support at least two trees. With that in mind, a tourism brochure hedges at "nearly 1,900." Other cautious pronouncements read "more than 1,700," "more than 1,800," or "1,800 or so." Sources bristling with confidence give 1,874 and 1,834. About half of the islands appear to be in Canada. Perhaps that influenced the number a forward-thinking Cartier was counting?

© Artville

Minna Anthony Common Nature Center. There are eight trails and an interpretive center at this 600-acre wildlife sanctuary in Wellesley Island State Park. A Braille Trail gives access to blind or partially sighted people. | 44927 Cross Island Rd., Fineview | 315/482–2479 | $6 per car | July–Aug., Mon.–Sat. 8:30–8:30, Sun. 8:30–4:30; Sept.–June, daily 8:30–4:30.

Thousand Islands Skydeck. The Skydeck rises 400 ft above the river on the Canadian side. One of the three decks is enclosed, and binoculars are available. An on-site restaurant is tucked between the spans of the Thousand Islands International Bridge. Off Interstate 81, about ½ mi from Canadian customs. | Hill Island, Lansdowne, Ontario, Canada | 613/659–2335 | fax 613/659–2285 | U.S.$6.95 | Apr.–Oct., daily 8:30 AM–dusk.

ON THE CALENDAR

AUG.: *Bill Johnson's Pirate Days.* Pirates invade the village for two weekends, and the mayor hands over the keys to the city to the marauders. Midweek festivities include music and other entertainment throughout downtown Alexandria Bay. | 800/561–1595.
AUG.: *Festival of the Islands.* Eastern Ontario's largest family festival has waterfront concerts, a parade, sidewalk sales, and plenty of entertainment. At Town Park, in Ganonoque, off Route 401. | 315/482–9531.

Dining

Admirals' Inn. American. Family-style food is served in this Victorian inn, whose signature dish is fried haddock. Don't skip the homemade desserts. Open-air dining on the patio. Kids' menu. | 33 James St. | 315/482–2781 | Closed Oct.–Mar. | $15–$18 | AE, D, DC, MC, V.

Captain's Landing. American. This family-oriented restaurant actually floats on the water, and features views of Boldt Castle and the Sea Way Canal. The foundation was once used as a dredge on the New York State Canal system. The oak-trimmed dining room has antique buffet tables. Try the prime rib (also served Cajun style), seafood pasta, porterhouse steak, chicken Carolina, or shrimp scampi. The restaurant is part of Captain Thompson's Resort. Kids' menu. Open-air dining on the deck. All-you-can-eat breakfast buffet July–August. | 49 James St. | 315/482–7777 and 800/ALEXBAY | Closed mid-Oct.–May | $10–$22 | AE, D, MC, V.

Cavallario's Steak and Seafood House. Continental. More than 20 appetizers are on the menu at this semi-dressy Alexandria Bay institution, including tender, savory ribs, hot-pepper poppers, and steamed mussels. The exterior of Cavallario's is designed to look like a medieval castle, with turrets and banners. Inside, two suits of armor flank the entrance to the dining area, which is lit with chandeliers and set with white linen tablecloths. Live entertainment on Fridays and Saturdays. Kids' menu. | 24 Church St. | 315/482–9867 | www.thousandislands.com/cavallarios | Reservations essential Sat. and holidays | Closed early Nov.–mid-Apr. No lunch | $16–$22 | AE, DC, MC, V.

Chez Paris Restaurant. Eclectic. Run by the same family since 1945, this lunch spot specializes in fresh-pressed hamburgers, followed by homemade peach and blueberry cobbler. Kids' menu. | 24 Church St. | 315/482–9825 | Breakfast also available; no dinner | $6–$8 | No credit cards.

C.P. Roman's Bayside Barbeque. American. Seafood and barbecue are the focus at this nautical-theme restaurant. Three decks directly above the water are available for open-air dining. | 4 Church St. | 315/482–4583 | $9–$14 | AE, D, MC, V.

Dockside Pub. American. This sports bar and restaurant is close to the shore and always seems to have something going on, despite billing itself as the village's "best-kept secret." The Dockside is best known for clams, shrimp, and burgers. | 17 Market St. | 315/482–9849 | $5–$10 | MC, V.

Golden Apple Inn and Restaurant. Continental. This restaurant is worth the drive across the border. It's known for delicious prime rib, Canadian lamb, veal, chicken, and pasta. Salad bar. Sunday brunch. | 45 King St. W, Ganonoque, Ontario, Canada | 613/382–3300 or 888/739–6150 | Closed Jan.–Mar. | $15–$30 | AE, MC, V.

Homestead Spot Restaurant. American. Built by settlers in the late 1700s, this limestone building is one of the oldest in the area. The tradition of history is carried on inside as well: antique chairs and desks serve as decorations, and the same family has run the restaurant since 1948. The menu has mostly seafood and steak. Try the surf-and-turf platters for a taste of both. Kids' menu. | 15 Church St. | 315/482–2740 | Breakfast also available; closed Oct.–May | $13–$23 | AE, D, DC, MC, V.

Jacques Cartier Dining Room. French. A pianist sets a romantic mood at this elegant restaurant with views of Boldt Castle and the St. Lawrence River. Salads, broiled sea bass, veal, New York–cut prime rib, and lobster are on the menu, along with flaming desserts. Part of the Riveredge Resort Hotel, the restaurant is 5 mi from downtown. Kids' menu. Sunday brunch. | 17 Holland St. | 315/482–9917 | www.riveredge.com/jacques.htm | $19–$30 | AE, D, DC, MC, DC.

Lodging

Bach's Alexandria Bay Inn. You'll be surrounded by the water of the St. Lawrence River, as well as Alexandria Bay, at this restored, antiques-filled Victorian mansion. Though within walking distance of all the local restaurants and boat tours, it's removed enough for one to feel truly peaceful sipping lemonade on the wraparound porch. Complimentary breakfast. No kids. | 2 Church St. | 315/482–9697 | 9 rooms | $80–$160 | AE, D, MC, V.

Boardwalk Resort of Alexandria. A central location, dock access, and a view across the bay to Boldt Castleall characterize this lodging, which also has efficiency rooms with full kitchenettes. Guest rooms have excellent views of the St. Lawrence River, and the tourist-friendly shopping and dining hotspots in downtown Alexandria Bay are a short stroll along the water from the resort. Some kitchenettes, some in-room hot tubs. Pool, lake. Beach, dock, boating, fishing. | 41 Walton St. | 315/482–9371 | www.boardwalkresorts.com | 37 rooms, 3 suites | $89–$119, suites $139–$200 | AE, D, DC, MC, V.

Bonnie Castle Resort. This luxury resort on the St. Lawrence River has 68 rooms with hot tubs, a dining room overlooking the river, a poolside café, and a nightclub that can hold 750 people. Some rooms have balconies. Restaurant, bar, room service. Refrigerators, some in-room hot tubs, cable TV. 2 pools. Hot tub, sauna. Driving range, miniature golf, tennis. Dock. Business services, airport shuttle. | Holland St. | 315/482–4511 or 800/955–4511 | fax 315/482–9600 | bcastle@gisco.net | www.bonniecastle.com | 128 rooms, 68 hot tub rooms, 2 presidential suites | $124–$175, suites $175–$240 | AE, D, DC, MC, V.

Capt. Thomson's Resort. This is a two-level motel on the waterfront, directly across from Boldt Castle. Some rooms have a view of the St. Lawrence River. The rooms have cherry-wood furnishings. The outdoor pool is heated. Restaurant (see Captain's Landing). Some kitchenettes, cable TV. Pool, wading pool. Water sports, boating, fishing. Airport shuttle. | 45 James St. | 315/482–9961 or 800/253–9229 | fax 315/482–2611 | www.captthomsons.com | 69 rooms | $70–$185 | Closed Nov.–Apr. | AE, D, DC, MC, V.

Channelsyde Motel. Each room faces the river at this quiet motel halfway between the Thousand Islands International Bridge and the village of Alexandria Bay. There is also a sandy beach. Some refrigerators, cable TV. Beach, dock, boating, fishing. | 21061 Point Vivian Rd. | 315/482–2281 | channelsyde@1000islands.com. | www.1000islands.com/channel | 12 rooms | $65–$90 | Closed Nov.–Apr. | MC, V.

Edgewood Resort. Built in 1886, this is the oldest continuously operated resort in northern New York. The 75-acre grounds are on the riverfront, and boat tours are available. Most of the rooms have balconies. All are furnished lodge style with king- or queen-size log beds. Restaurant, bar. Some in-room hot tubs, cable TV. Pool. Playground. Business services. | Edgewood Park Rd. at the 1000 Islands International Bridge | 315/482–9922 or 888/334–3966 | fax 315/482–5210 | edgewood@1000islands.com | www.edgewoodresort.com | 160 rooms | $94–$279 | Closed Nov.–Mar. | AE, DC, MC, V.

Fisherman's Wharf Motel. All rooms are within 25 ft of the waterfront, with most over-looking the harbor and St. Lawrence Seaway. Some queen-size water beds are available. You can fish off the dock. Refrigerators, cable TV. Beach, dock, fishing. | 16 Sisson St. | 315/482–2230 | fwharf@1000islands.com | www.thousandislands.com/wharf | 24 rooms | $80–$90 | Closed mid-Oct.–mid-Apr. | D, MC, V.

Hart House Bed and Breakfast. In 1899, this "cottage" was shipped across the frozen St. Lawrence River to Wellesley Island, where it took its place as part of the exclusive Thousand Islands Club. Since that time, the cottage has been restored as a B&B, and today the house overlooks the third hole of the Thousand Islands Golf Course. Some suites have four-poster beds, hot tubs, and fireplace. Afternoon tea is served in the Summer Great Room, and the five-course breakfast is enjoyed via candlelight. There's also a wedding chapel on the property. Restaurant, complimentary breakfast. In-room hot-tubs, No pets. No smoking. | 21979 Club Rd., Wellesley Island | 315/482–5683 or 888/481–5683 | fax 315/482–5683 | info@harthouseinn.com | www.harthouseinn.com | 5 rooms, 2 suites | $95–$215, suites $215–$245 | D, MC, V.

Hill's Motor Court. Both rooms and cabins are available at this hotel on the river, about a block from downtown. Some accommodations have kitchens, and others have roomside docking for your boat. 2 docks, fishing. No pets. | 24 Bethune St. | 315/482–2741 | www.thousandislands.com/hills | 12 rooms, 7 furnished cabins | $65–$95 | Closed mid-Oct.–Apr. | D, MC, V.

Ledges Resort. This small, family-oriented motel offers a quiet atmosphere away from the hustle and bustle of the village. Six acres provide plenty of room for outdoor activity on the grounds, and there is a large riverside deck. King-size beds are available. Picnic area. Cable TV. Pool. Dock, fishing. Airport shuttle. | 718 Anthony St. | 315/482–9334 | ledges@thousandislands.com | www.1000islands.com/ledges | 28 rooms | $98–$155 | Closed Nov.–Apr. | AE, D, MC, V.

Northstar Resort Motel. This motel is only two blocks from downtown on an inlet. Some rooms have decks. Restaurant, bar. Some refrigerators, cable TV. Pool. Docks, boating. Playground. Pets allowed. | 116 Church St. | 315/482–9332 | fax 315/482–5825 | northstar@gisco.net | 66 rooms | $89–119 | AE, D, MC, V.

Otter Creek Inn. Located two blocks from downtown, this two-story stone-and-cedar building overlooks the upper bay of the St. Lawrence River. Non-smoking rooms are available. You can make arrangements through the Inn to go fishing with a professional guide, as well. Picnic area. Some refrigerators, cable TV. Dock, fishing. | 2 Crossmon St. | 315/482–5248 | 32 rooms | $65–$89 | Closed Nov.–Mar. | D, DC, MC, V.

Pine Tree Point Resort. This eight-building complex is on its own private peninsula east of the village. All rooms in the two-story Cliffs building have views of the seaway and Boldt Castle. The Voyageur Dining Room has live jazz in the evening and serves Sunday brunch. Restaurant, bar (with entertainment), picnic area, room service. Cable TV. Pool. Hot tub. Docks, fishing. Playground. Business services. | 70 Anthony St. | 315/482–9911 or 888/746–3229 | fax 315/482–6420 | 96 rooms | $79–$189 | Closed Nov.–Apr. | AE, D, DC, MC, V.

Pinehurst Motel and Cottages. Set on 23 acres about 3 mi from downtown, this lovely spot maintains a private dock that gives guests access to the St. Lawrance River. A go-cart track, minigolf course, aquarium, and sandwich shop are all across the street. Rooms are simple, with views of the Thousand Islands Bridge and some phenomenal sunsets over the water. Many guests return every year. Pool. | 20683 Pinehurst Rd. | 315/482–9452 | www.thousandislands.com/pinehurst | 30 rooms, 21 cottages | $58–$68 rooms, $325 cottages (7-day minimum stay in summer) | MC, V.

Riveredge Resort Hotel. This four-story hotel on the St. Lawrence River has views of Boldt Castle and over 2,000 ft of dock space with power, water, and cable TV hookups. Guest rooms here are rather unique; many have private hot tubs, and some are bi-level loft rooms with sitting areas downstairs and sleeping quarters upstairs. Most rooms have water views. 2

restaurants *(see* Jacques Cartier), bar, room service. Some in-room data ports, minibars, some in-room hot tubs, cable TV. 2 pools. Hot tub, massage. Exercise equipment. Docks. Laundry facilities. Business services, free parking. | 17 Holland St. | 315/482–9917 or 800/365–6987 | fax 315/482–5010 | enjoyus@riveredge.com | www.riveredge.com | 88 rooms, 27 hot tub suites, 14 loft rooms | $268–$348, suites $348–$368, loft rooms $328 | AE, D, DC, MC, V.

Rock Ledge Motel. One-story buildings located right on the river within walking distance of Keewaydin State Park. In addition to rooms and cottages, efficiency cabins with kitchens are available. Complimentary Continental breakfast. Cable TV. Room phones. Playground. | Rte. 12 | 315/482–2191 or 800/977–9101 | www.1000islands.com/rockledge | 14 motel rooms, 5 cabins, 5 cottages | $57–$75 rooms, $85 cabins, $48–$60 cottages | Closed Nov.–Mar. | MC, V.

Ship Motel. Surrounded by shops and restaurants about four blocks from the town park, the Ship Motel is truly in the center of things in Alexandria Bay. Rooms are tastefully furnished in blue. Although there is no restriction, this motel does not encourage guests to bring children. Cable TV. Free parking. | 12 Market St. | 315/482–4503 | www.thousandislands.com/theship/ | 40 rooms | $65–$85 | AE, D, MC, V.

Sir Robert Peel Motor Lodge. Located about 2 mi from downtown, this family-friendly hotel has a pool, a large playground, and a patio. Most rooms have two double beds and sliding glass doors to the patio. Pool. Playground. | 44810 State Rte. 12 | 315/482–2691 or 315/482–5246 | 24 rooms | $35–$60 | MC, V.

AMAGANSETT

MAP 3, F2

(Nearby towns also listed: East Hampton, Montauk)

Amagansett, a popular tourist area just east of East Hampton, became known in the 1960s as the "jewel in the crown of the Hamptons." Amagansett is an Indian word meaning "place of good water" and from its earliest beginnings, the town's tranquil setting was perfectly suited to fishing and offshore whaling. The area was originally settled by two brothers, Abraham and Jacob Schellinger, whose father, a New Amsterdam merchant, had moved to rural East Hampton after the English took over New York City from the Dutch. Downtown Main Street has retained many of its original buildings as private residences, shops, and bed-and-breakfasts. Along with excellent dining, it is home to many small shops and outlets.

Information: East Hampton Chamber of Commerce | 79A Main St., East Hampton, 11937 | 631/324–0362 | info@easthamptonchamber.com.

Attractions

Atlantic Ave. Beach. Swimming and looking for seashells are popular pastimes at this public beach. It's convenient to the center of town, and there are food concessions right on the sand, making it possible to stay all day. There's a life guard on duty from Memorial Day to Labor Day—after that, you're on your own. | End of Atlantic Ave. in downtown Amagansett | 631/324–2417 | $10 | Daily 10–5 between Memorial Day and Labor Day.

Miss Amelia's Cottage Museum. Built in 1725 and full of beautifully-preserved Colonial furniture—including a few exceptionally rare pieces—this museum and adjacent carriage house has artifacts and exhibits illustrating Amagansett life from the colonial period through the 20th century. | 129 Main St. | 631/267–3020 | $2 | Fri.–Sun. 10–4.

Town Marine Museum. Fishing vessels are on display on the grounds of this museum. Other permanent and changing exhibits focus on whaling, fishing, and the coastal ecology. There's even a kids' jungle gym built from an old fishing trawler. On the ocean. | 300 Bluff Rd. | 516/267–6544 or 516/324–6850 | $4 | July–Aug., 10–5 daily; June and Sept., 10–5 weekends.

ON THE CALENDAR

AUG.: *Annual East Hampton Sand Castle Contest.* Participants often produce spectacular sand sculptures in this annual contest. There are five different age categories for children, and trophies and prizes are awarded. A T-shirt artist is on hand and celebrities occasionally drop in. | 631/324–6250.

Dining

Gordon's. Continental. High ceilings and a chandelier give this restaurant charm. Try any of the fresh seafood, veal, or duck dishes. No smoking. | 231 MainSt. | 631/267–3010 | Reservations essential weekends | Closed Mon. and Feb. No lunch in summer | $20–$30 | AE, D, DC, MC, V.

Lobster Roll. Seafood. This local landmark is the proverbial shanty by the sea. Its booths are filled with people coming and going from the beach, which is just a few hundred yards away. It's known for lobster rolls, burgers, and grilled shrimp, and you can eat outside at picnic tables. Family-style service. Kids' menu. Beer and wine only. No air-conditioning. No smoking. | 1980 Montauk Hwy. | 631/267–3740 | Closed Nov.–Apr. and weekdays Apr. and Oct. | $8–$17 | MC, V.

Mount Fuji. Japanese. A full sushi and Japanese menu provides plenty of choices. Try the amber roll, which is made of crabmeat and avocado topped with spicy tuna, then very lightly breaded and quickly fried tempura-style and garnished with scallions. You can sit at-table, Western-style, or on tatami mats on the floor. Quench your thirst with a Japanese beer or sake from the full bar. | 631/267–7600 | $8–$20.

Lodging

Mill Garth. This two-story antiques-filled bed-and-breakfast is a mile from the beach and within walking distance of Amagansett restaurants and shops. Suites in the main house have living rooms and kitchenettes, and additional lodging is available in charming separate cottages. There's a lovely terrace, and guests receive complimentary beach passes. Picnic area, complimentary Continental breakfast. Some room phones, no TV in some rooms. | 23 Windmill La. | 631/267–3757 | 2 rooms, 4 suites, 5 cottages | $200 rooms, $485 suites, $325 cottages | MC, V.

Ocean Vista. The beach is steps away from this quiet seaside inn. Rooms have either one or two queen-size beds. Two restaurants are within walking distance. Pool. Tennis. | 2136 Montauk Hwy. | 631/267–3448 | fax 631/267–7730 | www.oceanvistaresort.com | 46 rooms, 2 suites | $160–$215 | AE, MC, V.

Sea Crest on the Ocean. Situated on the beach, this deluxe resort has some fantastic ocean views, as well as access to private sand beaches and barbecue pits for sunset grilling amongst the dunes. One- and two-bedroom guest accommodations have fully-equipped kitchenettes, and many have direct beach access. Picnic area. Some kitchenettes. Pool. 2 tennis courts. Beach. Laundry facilities. Business services. | Navajo La., Montauk Hwy. | 631/267–3159 | fax 631/267–6840 | duneresort@aol.com | 74 rooms | $75–$535 | D, MC, V.

AMHERST

MAP 3, C6

(Nearby towns also listed: Buffalo, Clarence, East Aurora, Grand Island, Hamburg, Lockport, Niagara Falls, Williamsville)

The Township of Amherst covers 53 square mi, bordering Tonawanda Creek to the north and Buffalo to the south. The town was named after Amherst, Massachusetts, and Sir Jeffery Amherst, who led the British forces in America during the final phase of the French and Indian War (1754–63). At that time, western New York was claimed by the state of Massachusetts, and it became part of New York State only after the American Revolution. Here you will find the Amherst Museum, a group of restored buildings that illustrate regional history. Amherst is also home to the North Campus of the State University of New York at Buffalo. The town's population is 121,717.

Information: **Amherst Chamber of Commerce** | 325 Essjay, Suite 200, Williamsville, 14221 | 716–632–6905.

Attractions

Amherst Museum. A small town of historic buildings, including a one-room schoolhouse, a church, and homes, has been moved to this site and restored to reflect western New York life during the 1800s. Exhibits showcase local history and agriculture, period artifacts, and costumes. (*For special events, see* On the calendar *listings.*) Off Interstate 90 via exit 49; north on Transit Road to Tonawanda Creek Road; left on Tonawanda Creek Road. | 3755 Tonawanda Creek Rd. | 716/689–1440 | fax 716/689–1409 | $4 | Apr.–Oct., Tues.–Fri. 9:30–4:30, weekends 12:30–4:30; Nov.–Mar., Tues.–Fri. 9:30–4:30.

ON THE CALENDAR

AUG.: *Annual Scottish Festival and Highland Games.* Celebrate Scotland's heritage with athletic competitions, pipers, dancers, children's games, traditional food, and more. At the Amherst Museum. | 716/689–1440.
AUG.: *Blacksmith Hammer-In.* Blacksmiths display their crafts and demonstrate their skills at the Amherst Museum. | 716/680–1440.
SEPT.: *Harvest Festival and Craft Show.* The area's agricultural heritage is honored with this old-fashioned day of family fun and celebration. Enjoy crafts, bluegrass entertainment, a pumpkin patch, and a farmers market. At Amherst Museum and other locations. | 716/689–1440.
DEC.: *Victorian Christmas Tours.* The Amherst Museum dresses itself up for a 19th-century Christmas. | 716/689–1440.

Dining

Alice's Restaurant. American. If you crave breakfast food after 11 AM, you'll appreciate this classic American eatery where it's served all day. The chicken fingers are also popular, and don't skip the homemade strawberry pie. | 3122 Sheridan Dr. | 716/834–4182 | $6–$9 | No credit cards.

Cafe in the Square. American. This European-style eatery is built around an interior courtyard, and jazz or classical music sets a casual tone. The food, however, is gourmet, with the menu changing as frequently as crops in local gardens. Typical entrées include lemon roasted pine-nut chicken breast, or salmon wrapped in rice paper. | 4476 Main St. | 716/839–5330 | $13–$19 | AE, D, DC, MC, V.

Fanny's Restaurant. Continental. A romantic night out in Amherst should include this candlelit bi-level restaurant. An extensive (mostly California) wine list will complement your meal of traditional seafood, lamb, steak, or pasta. There's live jazz on Friday night. | 3500 Sheridan Dr. | 716/834–0400 | No lunch weekends | $16–$40 | AE, DC, MC, V.

The Juicery. Eclectic. Healthy fast food is not a contradiction here, where vegetarian delights such as the Super Veggie outweigh meat options. Everything's served in a pita. Dine in or take out. | 3131 Sheridan Dr. | 716/446–0256 | Breakfast also available; no dinner weekends | $2–$5 | No credit cards.

Siena. Italian. This restaurant, only 2 mi from the SUNY campus, draws an upscale crowd with authentic Italian cuisine from the Tuscany region. Try any of the fresh pasta, fresh fish, or authentic veal dishes. | 4516 Main St. | 716/839–3108 | Reservations not accepted | No lunch weekends | $9–$25 | AE, MC, V.

Lodging

Hampton Inn. This modern four-story building, 8 mi from Buffalo Niagara International Airport, is close to area dining. Complimentary Continental breakfast. In-room data ports, cable TV. Pool. Exercise equipment. Business services, airport shuttle. | 10 Flint Rd. | 716/689–4414 | fax 716/689–4382 | www.hampton-inn.com | 196 rooms | $80–$100 | AE, D, DC, MC, V.

Holiday Inn Buffalo Amherst. This two-story chain hotel is located between Buffalo and Niagara Falls, near SUNY Buffalo. It's also less than a mile from shopping areas. Restaurant. In-room data ports, cable TV. Pool. Hot tub. Exercise equipment. Laundry facilities. Business services. | 1881 Niagara Falls Blvd. | 716/691–8181 | fax 716/691–4965 | 199 rooms | $90 | AE, D, DC, MC.

Lord Amherst. This two-story hotel near the Buffalo Niagara International Airport has large spacious rooms done in colonial style, and bathrooms with double sinks. It's 2 mi from local restaurants and 20 mi from Niagara Falls. Restaurant, bar, complimentary breakfast. In-room data ports, cable TV. Pool. Exercise equipment. Laundry facilities. Business services. Some pets allowed. | 5000 Main St. | 716/839–2200, 800/544–2200 reservations | fax 716/839–1538 | 100 rooms | $72–$89 | AE, D, DC, MC, V.

Marriott. This 10-story hotel in the heart of Amherst's business district has a lobby with a marble finish and a restaurant that serves Tuscan food. Restaurant, bar. In-room data ports, microwaves, cable TV. Pool. Hot tub. Gym. Video games. Business services, airport shuttle. Some pets allowed. | 1340 Millersport Hwy. | 716/689–6900 | fax 716/689–0483 | www.marriotthotels.com/bufny/default.asp | 356 rooms | $80–$175 | AE, D, DC, MC, V.

Motel 6. There are few surprises at this standard-issue motel, which borders the campus of the University of Buffalo. Pets allowed. | 4400 Maple Rd. | 716/834–2231 | fax 716/834–0872 | 94 rooms | $54–$60 | AE, D, DC, MC, V.

Red Roof Inn. This hotel is 20 minutes from downtown Amherst by car and just a mile from the University of Buffalo. Rooms have video games. Cable TV. Business services. Some pets allowed. | 42 Flint Rd. | 716/689–7474 | 108 rooms | $60–$80 | AE, D, DC, MC, V.

Super 8. This chain hotel has a faux exposed-timber exterior and a breakfast nook adjacent to the main lobby. The University of Buffalo campus is directly across the street, and both the airport and Amtrak station are 10 mi away. Complimentary Continental breakfast. Cable TV. | 1 Flint Rd. | 716/688–0811 or 800/800–0811 | fax 716/688–2365 | www.super8.com | 103 rooms | $55–$78 | AE, D, DC, MC, V.

University Manor. Located in the center of Amherst, near shopping and restaurants, the University Manor nonetheless remains a quiet place to stay, nestled in a tree-shaded, mostly residential area. Some in-room data ports. Cable TV. Some in-room hot tubs. | 3612 Main St. | 716/837–7400 | 20 rooms, 2 suites | $50–$70, $129 suites | AE, D, DC, MC, V.

AMITYVILLE

MAP 3, D3

(Nearby town also listed: Babylon)

Since revolutionary times when George Washington was a visitor here, Long Island has been a summer playground, and in the early 1900s Amityville was no exception. It's reported that during the town's swinging heyday, Al Capone owned property here, and celebrities such as Annie Oakley and Will Rogers enjoyed its shores.

There are really two Amityvilles: downtown Amityville village, which rings the harbor; and the large residential area that sweeps north, east, and west behind it. The village harbor area boasts restaurants and shopping areas, including some malls, and is best known for antiques, craftspeople, and restored Victorian homes.

Information: **Chamber of Commerce** | Box 885, 11701 | 631/598–0695 | www.amityville.com.

Attractions

Lauder Museum. An 1880s Victorian parlor is one of the highlights of this museum, which focuses on local history. | 170 Broadway | 631/598–1486. | Donations accepted | Tues., Fri., Sun. 2–4.

Tackapausha Museum and Preserve. This natural-history museum, on 80 tranquil acres that include 5 mi of nature trails and picnic areas, is about 2 mi southwest of Amityville proper in the nearby village of Seaford. | Washington Ave., Seaford | 516/571–7443 | Preserve free; museum $2 | Tues.–Sat. 10–4, Sun. 1–4.

ON THE CALENDAR

JUNE: *Annual Strawberry Festival.* Strawberries take center stage along with hand-made arts and crafts and music at the Old Grace Church in Massapequa, just 2 mi west of Amityville. | 516/799–2023.

Dining

Amato's. Italian. Amato's offers two-story dining with cozy booths and tables. Cool brick walls add to an intimate old-world atmosphere. For dinner, try the chicken parmigiana, a tender breast of chicken lightly breaded and baked with tangy marinara sauce and melted mozzarella cheese. Live music on Wednesdays. Sunday brunch. | 330 Merrick Rd. | 516/598–2229 | Closed Mon. | $18–$30 | AE, D, DC, MC, V.

Big Daddy's. Cajun/Creole. This lively spot, known for catfish, shrimp, crawfish, and pasta, captures the festive spirit and taste of New Orleans. Try the cub scout brownie sundae, a heated rich chocolate brownie topped with a heaping scoop of vanilla ice cream and caramel sauce. Kids' menu. In Massapequa, 2 mi west of Amityville. | 1A Park La., Massapequa | 516/799–8877 | Closed Sun. No lunch | $20–$30 | AE.

AMSTERDAM

MAP 3, K6

(Nearby towns also listed: Albany, Canajoharie, Johnstown, Saratoga Springs, Schenectady, Troy)

This former industrial hub is located on the New York State Barge Canal, about 30 mi west of Albany. Amsterdam was settled in 1785, and became home to the Dutch, Germans, and British. Amsterdam has a population of 20,000, and the noise and bustle of shipping traffic has been largely replaced by a quieter, though no less enthusiastic, flow of tourists. Visitors come here to partake of Amsterdam's surrounding natural beauty, to steep themselves in the Colonial history of the area, or to pay homage to the Oneida and Mohawk Native American influences in the region.

Information: **Amsterdam Chamber of Commerce** | Box 309, 366 W. Main St., 12010 | 518/842–8200 | www.montgomerycountyny.com.

Attractions

Kanatsiohareke Mohawk Traditional Community. This is the site of the last Mohawk Indian village in the county, which existed from 1700 to 1767. Tribal families re-acquired it in a 1993 auction. The grounds include natural springs, a bed-and-breakfast, and a crafts store. | 4934 Rte. 5, Fonda; between Fonda and Palatine Bridge | 518/673–5092 (bed–and–breakfast) | fax 518/673–5575 | Free | Daily.

National Shrine of the North American Martyrs. Three Catholic priests killed by Mohawk Indians in the 1640s are remembered at this shrine, located about 6 mi west of Amsterdam. The priests had traveled from France and settled here to convert the Indians. This is also the birthplace of Blessed Native American Kateri Tekakwitha. The immense coliseum church has 72 doors and offers mass daily. | 144 Shrine Rd., Auriesville | 518/853–3033 | fax 518/853–3051 | www.klink.net/~jesuit | Free | Early May–late Oct., daily 10–4.

Noteworthy Indian Museum. A re-created Iroquois longhouse is on exhibit here, along with 4,000 pieces from a 60,000-piece collection of Mohawk Valley Native American artifacts, owned by the founder of the museum, Thomas Constantino, who was a paper manufacturer. On the corner of Prospect and Church Streets, ½ mi from downtown. | 100 Church St. | 518/843–4761 | Donations accepted | July–Aug., Tues.–Sat. 10–6; Sept.–June, by appointment.

Schoharie Crossing State Historic Site. Five miles west of Amsterdam is the only site with remains of all three stages of the Erie Canal, including an old aqueduct. The earliest parts date to 1817. The site has a small-boat launch, hiking, cross-country skiing, and a bike path. | 129 Schoharie St., Fort Hunter | 518/829–7516 | fax 518/829–7491 | www.montgomerycountyny.com | Free | Visitors center May–Oct., Wed.–Sat. 10–5, Sun. 1–5; outdoor areas open year-round.

Walter Elwood Museum. This old schoolhouse in downtown Amsterdam houses exhibits devoted to carpet making and other industries that once thrived in the Mohawk Valley. Native American artifacts are also on display. | 300 Guy Park Ave. | 518/843–5151 | www.montgomerycounty.com | Free | July–Aug., Mon.–Thurs. 8:30–3:30, Fri. 8:30–1; Sept.–June, weekdays 8:30–4.

ON THE CALENDAR
JUNE: *Canal Days.* This mid-summer event celebrates the building of the Erie Canal and the prosperity it brought to Amsterdam and Montgomery County with live music, lots of food, guided walking tours of the canal and local historical sites, and much more. | 518/842–8200.

Dining

Adirondack Pizza. Italian. Though hot wings, pasta, and pizza are the fare, this isn't your average pizza joint. Names of dishes are inspired by the surrounding Adirondack Mountains. (The Snowy Mountain pizza, for example, is smothered in veggies before being covered in mozzarella). Rustic murals evoke surrounding rivers and forests, and a carved moose in the center welcomes you. | 4803 State Hwy. 30 | 518/842–9744 | $4–$8 | AE, MC, V.

Happi Daze Charcoal Pit. American. Homemade food, 1950s music, and 1950s prices make you want to treat your friends. You can watch through the circular glass window at the center of this diner as the chefs cook your meal. Soft-serve ice cream with chunks of fresh cheesecake swirled in is a unique treat. | 254 Forest Ave. | 518/843–8265 | Closed Sept.–Apr. | $1–$6 | No credit cards.

Raindancer Steak Parlour. American. This casual restaurant 3 mi north of Amsterdam serves prime rib, lobster, and Alaska king crab legs. Salad bar. Kids' menu. Early bird dinners. | 4582 Rte. 30 | 518/842–2606 | fax 518/842–2943 | Reservations essential holidays | $15–$20 | AE, D, DC, MC, V.

Lodging

Best Western Amsterdam. This five-story chain hotel is about 8 mi from the Shrine of the North American Martyrs and 10 mi from Great Sacandage Lake and the surrounding parkland. Park and museum. Restaurant, bar. In-room data ports, cable TV. Pool. Shops. Business services. Some pets allowed. | 10 Market St. | 518/843–5760 | fax 518/842–0940 | 125 rooms | $70 | AE, D, DC, MC, V.

Blue Moon Motel. This small motel is 9 mi north of Amsterdam, in the foothills of the Adirondacks. Room themes range from nautical to oriental, and all have queen-size beds. Cable TV. Free parking. | 3778 State Hwy. 30 | 518/883–9990 | www.maxpages.com/bluemoon34 | 16 rooms, 2 suites | $59, suites $70 | AE, MC, V.

Kanatsiohareke Mohawk Traditional Community. Stay in cozy rooms at this family-oriented bed-and-breakfast on the grounds of the region's only active Mohawk Indian community just west of Amsterdam. Walking trails are on-site. Complimentary breakfast. No rooms phones, no TV. | 4934 Rte. 5, Fonda | 518/673–5092 | fax 518/673–5575 | 4 rooms | $65 | No credit cards.

Super 8 Motel. This chain offers basic lodging near Interstate 90. Complimentary Continental breakfast. In-room data ports, cable TV. Business services. | Rte. 30 S | 518/843–5888 | fax 518/843–5888 | 67 rooms | $74 | AE, D, DC, MC, V.

ARCADE

(Nearby towns also listed: East Aurora, Hamburg)

Much of New York history has been influenced by the railroad, and small towns like Arcade were once part of rail networks that shipped agricultural goods. Arcade still has its old-fashioned depot which dates to 1880 and from there you can board the Arcade and Attica Railroad, an old-fashioned train powered by steam engine, for a trip through the rolling countryside. Arcade is home to just a little over 2,000 people today.

Information: **Arcade Chamber of Commerce** | 278 Main St., 14009 | 716/492–2114.

Attractions

Arcade and Attica Railroad. All aboard an authentic 1915 steam train, featuring regular 90-minute round-trip excursions through the beautiful rural countryside of Wyoming County, stopping at the Curriers Station Stop for a visit to a small railroad museum. Don't expect a smooth ride: this is old-time 90-minute chug, chug. You can also take a peek at the private car Grover Cleveland, mayor of Buffalo in 1881, used to travel the country during his presidency. The car is complete with a bed, bar, and writing desk. Call for special trips featuring Civil War reenactments, Murder Mystery and Dinner Theatre evenings, Haunted House runs during the Halloween season, and Santa rides at Christmas time. | 278 Main St. (Rte. 39) | 716/496–9877 | $8.50 | Office open Memorial Day–Oct., 10–5. Call for rail schedule.

Beaver Meadow Audubon Nature Center. You can explore 324 acres here, with 8½ mi of trails through open meadows and forests, stopping to snack at your choice of three picnic areas. Kettle and Beaver ponds add some diversity and extra wildlife. | 1610 Welch Rd. | 716/457–3228 | $2 | Trails always open; visitors center Tues.–Sat. 10–5, Sun. 1–5.

ON THE CALENDAR
FEB.: *Arcade Winter Festival.* Softball in the snow and a snowshoe contest are among the winter fun activities sponsored by the village. There is also a parade, a hockey tournament, a tug-of-war, kids games, crafts, and a chile tasting. | Downtown Arcade | 716/492–2114.

Dining

Moore's Sugar Shack and Pancake House. Café. Feast on "all-you-can-eat" pancakes amid country antiques at this restaurant about 3 mi from Arcade. You can also get ham, bacon, eggs, and other breakfast staples. Tours of the adjacent syrup-making facility are given in-season, and you can buy the same delicious maple syrup used in the restaurant at the Sugar Shack shop. | Galen Hill Rd., Freedom | 716/492–3067 | Closed Dec.–Feb. Closed Mon. Mar.–Apr. No dinner | $4–$7 | No credit cards.

Yorkshire Inn. American. This country restaurant is known for prime rib and fish fry. The dining room is green and gold, and features quilts and crafts for sale. | Rte. 16, Yorkshire | 716/492–1331 | Breakfast also available | $15–$25 | MC, V.

Lodging

Arcade Hotel. Located in the heart of Arcade and a mile from Routes 16 and 98, this hotel makes a good a stopping point if you're on your way to Niagara Falls. All-size beds are available in the sparingly decorated rooms. Cable TV. Free parking. | 574 W. Main St. | 716/492–3600 | fax 716/496–0062 | 15 rooms | $40 | AE, D, MC, V.

Arcade Village Motel. This is a quiet, comfortable, one-story motel in the country. Local phone calls are free and the motel offers 10% discount cards for the restaurant. Restaurant. Microwaves, refrigerators, cable TV. | 574 W. Main St. | 716/492–3600 or 888/254–1268 | 15 rooms | $40 | AE, D, DC, MC, V.

Inn at Houghton Creek. There's cross-country skiing within 1/2 mi and several restaurants within 2–10 mi driving distance. Houghton is 13 mi south of Letchworth Park. Cable TV. Business services. No smoking. | 9722 Genesee St., Houghton | 716/567–8400 | fax 716/567–4842 | 17 rooms | $59 | AE, DC, MC, V.

AUBURN

MAP 3, G6

(Nearby towns also listed: Cazenovia, Geneva, Liverpool, Seneca Falls, Skaneateles, Syracuse, Waterloo)

Auburn sits at the northern end of Owasco Lake, one of the Finger Lakes, in a farming area. Founded in 1793, it has some remarkable historic buildings, including the homes of Harriet Tubman (a leader of the Underground Railroad), and William Henry Seward (secretary of state under President Lincoln). The Auburn Correctional Facility, New York's oldest prison, was a model for modern American prisons, with its tiers of tiny cells.

Information: **Cayuga County Tourism** | 131 Genesee St., 13021 | 315/255–1685 or 800/499–9615 | cctourism@cayuganet.org | www.cayuganet.org/tourism.

Attractions

Cayuga Museum/Case Research Lab. Cayuga County history is the focus at this museum, which features exhibits on Native Americans, the Erie Canal, the Civil War, the women's rights movement, and the city's industrial history. The Case Research Lab, in a building behind the museum, is where Theodore W. Case and E. I. Sponable successfully developed sound film. | 203 Genesee St. | 315/253–8051 | Free | Tues.–Sun. noon to 5; closed Jan.

Schweinfurth Memorial Art Center. Regional and national works are on display here and the center hosts an annual quilt show and "Made in New York" juried show. | 205 Genesee St. | 315/255–1553 | $3 suggested donation | Feb.–Dec., Tues.–Sat. 10–5, Sun. 1–5.

Emerson Park. This 133-acre park, 3 mi from town, includes a recreation area with two bathing beaches, three boat-launch sites, and a large playground. Canoes and paddleboats are available to rent. Lifeguards are on duty July–August. | Rte. 38A | 315/253–5611 | Free; parking $2 | May–Sept., daily dawn–dusk.

The **Merry-Go-Round Playhouse** is upstate New York's largest professional summer theater. | Emerson Park | 315/255–1305 administration, 800/457–8897 box office | $19–$26; special rates for students and senior citizens | Performances Mon.–Sat. 8 PM and some matinees 2 PM; closed Sun.

The **Iroquois Center** offers hands-on exhibits, including a scale-model longhouse and items from the Owasco and Cayuga cultures. Across the street from Emerson Park. | Rte. 38A | 315/253–8051 | Donations accepted | Memorial Day–Labor Day, Wed.–Sun. 11–4.

The **Ward W. O'Hara Agricultural Museum** includes a blacksmith shop, and an 1890-era general store, kitchen, and veterinarian's office. Children are encouraged to try out some of the tools. | Emerson Park | 315/253–8051 | $2 suggested donation | Memorial Day–Labor Day, Wed.–Sun. 1–5.

Finger Lakes Drive-In. One of the country's few remaining outdoor movie venues is 3 mi west of Auburn. | Rtes. 5 and 20 | 315/252–3969 | $5 | May–Labor Day nightly.

Fort Hill Cemetery. For centuries, Native Americans used this site as burial grounds, but with the advent of European colonization, the land was appropriated by Christians as their own. Among those buried here are William Seward, Harriet Tubman, and Miles Kehoe (who fought with General Custer at Little Big Horn). The site includes a monument to Mingo Indian orator Chief Logan. | 19 Fort St. | 315/253–8132 | Free | Mon.–Sun. dawn–dusk.

Harriet Tubman Home. Harriet Tubman, an escaped slave, risked her life to make 19 trips into the South to bring 300 other slaves to freedom. She's known as the "Moses of her people." Her bed and her Bible are among the items displayed. | 180 South St. | 315/252–2081 | Free | Feb.–Oct., Tues.–Fri. 10–3, Sat. by appointment.

Hoopes Park Flower Gardens. This small lake has ducks, rose gardens, and a rock gazebo. Band concerts are held Monday and Wednesday evenings in July and August. | E. Genesee St. and S. Herman | 315/252–9300 | Free | Daily 7 AM–9 PM.

Seward House. Housed in a distinguished Federal-style home built in 1816–17, this museum honors William H. Seward, a governor of New York, U.S. senator, and secretary of state under Presidents Lincoln and Andrew Johnson. Seward is best remembered for arranging the purchase of Alaska from Russia in 1867. Nearly everything in the house is original, including some grocery bills. | 33 South St. | 315/252–1283 | $3.25 | Feb.–June, Tues.–Sat. 1–3; July–mid-Oct., Tues.–Sat. 10–4, Sun. 1–4; mid-Oct.–Dec., Tues.–Sat. 1–4.

Sterling Renaissance Festival. For seven weekends during summer, this festival celebrates the high and low life of England in the time of Elizabeth I. And like England, it's open rain or shine. From Auburn, take Route 38 north to Route 104A. | 15431 Farden Rd., Sterling | 315/947–5783 or 800/879–4446 | fax 315/947–6905 | www.sterlingfestival.com | $14.99 | Weekends 10–7.

Willard Memorial Chapel and Welch Memorial Building. The beautiful stained-glass windows and chandeliers in this chapel were designed by Tiffany Glass and Decorating Company. | 17 Nelson St. | 315/252–0339 | Donations accepted ($2 suggested) | Tues.–Fri. 10–4, or by appointment.

ON THE CALENDAR

JUNE: *Old Ways and Dairy Day.* Ward O'Hara Agricultural Museum celebrates old-fashioned dairy-farm operations during this festival. | 315/252–5009 and 800/499–9615.
JULY: *Cayuga County Fair.* If you like music and big trucks, you won't want to miss this fair, held at the Cayuga County Fairgrounds in Weedsport, about 5 mi from Auburn on Route 34 N. | 315/834–6606 or 800/499–9615.

Dining

Balloons. Italian. Serving since 1939, this restaurant across from the Auburn Correctional Facility is a fixture in the city. The friendly service and care-worn interior more than make up for the restaurant's somewhat imposing neighbor. For dinner, try the lasagna—a multi-layered mix of tastes and textures, sided with buttery garlic bread. | 65 Washington St. | 315/252–9761 | Closed Mon. No lunch | $18–$24 | D, MC, V.

Lasca's. Italian. Go hungry to this this casual, very popular family-friendly spot—the portions are huge! You could very easily split an order of pasta primavera or a dish of tender gnocchi in light cream sauce. Kids' menu. | 252 Grant Ave. | 315/253–4885 | Closed Mon. and 1st 2 weeks Feb. | $12–$20 | D, MC, V.

Springside Inn. Continental. This red clapboard Victorian, right across from Owasco Lake, looks like a gingerbread house. Try the prime rib. Jazz on Wednesdays; piano music on Saturdays. Kids' menu. Sunday brunch. | 6141 W. Lake Rd. (Rte. 38 S) | 315/252–7247 | www.springsideinn.com | Closed Mon. and Tues. Jan.–Feb. | $8–$20 | AE, MC, V.

Lodging

Budget Inn. This downtown inn is within walking distance of restaurants and shops. Rooms have either one queen or two double beds. Cable TV. Free parking. | 61 State St. | 315/253–3296 | 20 rooms | $45–$50 | AE, D, MC, V.

Days Inn. Renovated in 1996, this two-story hotel is less than ½ mi from both the William Seward House and the Auburn Family Restaurant. Days Inn gives out 10% discount coupons to nearby restaurants. It's next door to the YMCA. Complimentary Continental breakfast. In-room data ports, cable TV. Tennis. Gym. Laundry facilities. Business services. Pets allowed. | 37 William St. | 315/252–7567 | fax 315/252–7567 | 51 rooms | $39–$59 | AE, D, MC, V.

Holiday Inn. This five-story convention center has spacious rooms ranging from standard two-bed rooms to two-room hot-tub suites. Restaurant, bar. Some in-room hot tubs, cable TV. Pool. Exercise equipment. Laundry facilities. Business services. | 75 North St. | 315/253–4531 | fax 315/252–5843 | hiauburn@earthlink.net | 163 rooms, 2 suites | $109–$129 rooms, $200–$300 suites | AE, D, DC, MC, V.

Springside Inn. Once a private school, this memorable red clapboard Victorian is across the road from Owasco Lake. Rooms are sunny, and the house has several big porches. Restaurant (*see* Springside Inn), complimentary Continental breakfast. No room phones. | 6141 W. Lake Rd. (Rte. 38 S) | 315/252–7247 | www.springsideinn.com | 8 rooms (5 with bath) | $47–$65 | MC, V.

Super 8. This two-story chain motel is just 5 min by car from restaurants, shopping, and the local supermarket. Complimentary Continental breakfast. In-room data ports, cable TV. Business services. | 9 McMaster St. | 315/253–8886 | fax 315/253–8329 | 48 rooms | $45–$59 | AE, D, DC, MC, V.

Whispering Winds Motel. This scenic spot is a good choice if you're touring the Finger Lakes. It's 10½ mi from Auburn and ½ mi from Lake Skaneateles. All rooms have views of the well-tended rose garden. Complimentary Continental breakfast. Some refrigerators. Pool. | 4223 Genesee Rd. | 315/685–6056 | 12 rooms | $58–$68 | AE, D, MC, V.

AUSABLE CHASM

MAP 3, L2

(Nearby towns also listed: Plattsburgh, Rouses Point)

Over millions of years, the Ausable River carved deep into the sandstone here in the Champlain valley, leaving cliffs, waterfalls, and rapids. The chasm made by the river in this small northern Adirondack town was opened to the public in 1870, and is the oldest tourist attraction in the country.

Information: **Ausable Chasm Co** | U.S. 9, Box 390, 12911 | 518/834–7454.

Attractions

Ausable Chasm. This 500-million-year-old mass of sculpted stone formations became the country's first tourist attraction in 1870. A deck allows you to view formations such as Elephant Head and Table Rock. Other activities include rafting and boat rides. A refreshment center, gift shop, and miniature golf are on-site. | U.S. 9 | 518/834–7454 or 800/537–1211 | $17–$19 | Mid-May–mid-Oct., daily 9:30–4.

Lodging

Ausable Chasm Motel. Located about 10 mi south of Plattsburgh, this one-story motel is on the grounds of the chasm, close to rafting and fishing. Cable TV. | 1137 Mace Chasm Rd. | 518/834–9990 | fax 518–834–1104 | 8 rooms | $34 | Closed Oct.–May | AE, DC, MC, V.

AVON

(Nearby towns also listed: Canandaigua, Geneseo, Geneva, Rochester, Victor)

Avon provides a western gateway to the Finger Lakes region. The village is a farming and canning center, with lots of horse breeding nearby. Mineral springs once attracted many to health resorts here, and the water still bubbles in Avon Driving Park.

Information: Livingston County Chamber of Commerce | 4235 Lakeville Rd., Building 2, Suite A, Geneseo, 14454 | 716/243–2222 or 800/538–7365 | livchamber@aol.com | www.livchamber.com.

Attractions

Five Arch Bridge. Built in 1856 by the Genesee Valley Railroad, this limestone bridge was used until 1941 and has been preserved ever since. A peaceful spot to visit, it is in the center of a small park named after the bridge. | Rte. 39, west of the village | 716/226–2425 | Free.

Genesee Country Village and Museum. Guides in period dress show how things were done in the 19th century at this group of meticulously restored buildings including a blacksmith's shop, a Greek Revival mansion, a land office, and a bookshop. A self-guided tour takes three–four hours. About 10 mi from Avon off Route 36. | 1410 Flint Hill Rd., Mumford | 716/538–6822 | www.gcv.org | $11 | Mid-May–Oct., Tues.–Fri. 10–4, weekends 10–5; open Mon. that fall on a holiday 10–5.

ON THE CALENDAR
AUG.: *Avon Corn Festival.* This event has crafts, live music, a small midway section, and plenty of food from fritters to fresh corn on the cob. Organized by the Avon Rotary Club, it takes place in the town traffic circle on the second weekend of the month. | 716/226–9623.

Dining

Avon Inn. Continental. Located in a delightful 19th-century country inn close to Rochester and Letchworth State Park, this restaurant offers seasonal fireside dining. A porch with umbrellaed tables at the rear of the building lets you eat near the garden. Known for chicken and steak. Kids' menu. You can also stay at the inn. | 55 E. Main St. | 716/226–8181 | Closed Mon., Tues. | $15–$25 | AE, D, MC, V.

Fratelli's Restaurant. Italian. Bring your appetite to this family-oriented eatery that serves huge portions, including a 20-ounce strip steak. Kids' menu. | 2995 Lakeville Rd. | 716/346–6160 | Closed Mon. No lunch Sun. | $6–$18. | D, MC, V.

Tom Wahl's. American. The Wahlburger, a ground-steak burger with a special sauce, is the signature dish at this large restaurant with room for 180 inside and 280 outside. Root beer is served in frosted mugs. | Rtes. 5 and 20 | 716/226–2420 | $5–$10 | D, MC, V.

Lodging

Avon Inn. This country inn built in the early 1800s has antiques and a fireplace. Restaurant (*see* Avon Inn), complimentary Continental breakfast, room service. Cable TV, room phones. Business services. | 55 E. Main St. | 716/226–8181 | fax 716/226–8185 | 14 rooms | $75 | AE, D, MC, V.

Genesee Country Inn. This three-story stone-and-stucco building overlooks 9 acres of mill ponds, waterfalls, gardens, and woodlands. The grounds include a trout pond and gazebo. Both the Genesee County Fairgrounds and Nature Center are within walking distance. There is a deck and grill by the pond. Serves a gourmet breakfast. About 10 mi from Avon. Restaurant, complimentary breakfast. Room phones. No pets. No smoking. | 948 George St., Mumford | 716/538–2500 or 800/NYSTAYS | www.geneseecountryinn.com | 9 rooms | $85–$150 | AE, D, MC, V.

White Oak Bed and Breakfast. This turn-of-the-20th-century mansion sits on a wide street with grand trees lining the sidewalks. Although the area is not entirely rural, you will see horses grazing on an adjacent lot, and there is a garden on the property. Inside there's lots of wood—mahogany, cherry, and walnut—and antiques. Complimentary breakfast. | 277 Genesee St. | 716/226–6735 | www.whiteoakbandb.com | 3 rooms | $85–$115 | MC, V.

BABYLON

MAP 4, J7

(Nearby town also listed: Amityville)

Babylon is one of the oldest towns in the nation. Its earliest inhabitants, the Massapequa, Secatogue, and Matinecock Indians, began deeding property to settlers in 1653. Once a farming community, it evolved into a summer resort, and then, after World War II, grew into a bedroom community for people working in New York City. Along with fathering the first all-black professional baseball team in America, Babylon was home to Guglielmo Marconi, who created the forerunner of commercial radio, and millionaire August Belmont, whose large estate became Belmont State Park.

Deerpark Avenue in downtown Babylon village is a thriving retail district, and lovely Argyle Park has a lake and flowing fountains. Babylon's residential areas are tranquil, especially near the water, where one can still find caution signs announcing turtle nesting areas. The ocean offers views of Fire Island Inlet and the marshes of Great South Bay.

Information: **Babylon Village Chamber of Commerce** | 64 Bayview Ave., 11702 | 631/661–2229.

Attractions
Argyle Park. Bubbling fountains make this attractive park a nice place to relax. | Babylon Village, on Montauk Hwy. | 631/669–1500 | Free | Daily.

ON THE CALENDAR
OCT.: *Town of Babylon Arts and Crafts Fair.* Enjoy arts and crafts, food vendors, and music at the Town Hall Park in Lindenhurst, only 3 mi from Babylon. | 631/893–2100.

Dining
All Ocean Restaurant. Eclectic. An extensive menu of French, Cajun, and California-style food draws a crowd of loyal regulars to this family-owned restaurant. A full wine and beer list, piano music, and pictures of fish and the sea make for a relaxing evening. | 69 Deer Park Ave. | 631/669–2333 | Closed Mon. No lunch weekends | $10–$23 | AE, D, DC, MC, V.

BAINBRIDGE

MAP 3, H7

(Nearby towns also listed: Binghamton, Delhi, Greene, Norwich, Oneonta)

Bainbridge, a village in the southern tier of the Adirondacks, lies about 30 mi northeast of Binghamton, along the Susquehanna River and Interstate 88. Every year, around Memorial Day, the village hosts one of the largest canoe races in the country, which draws competitors from all over the world.

Information: **Bainbridge Chamber of Commerce** | Box 2, 13733 | 607/967–8700.

ON THE CALENDAR
MAY: *General Clinton Canoe Regatta.* On Memorial Day weekend, 2,800 people gather from all over the world to compete in these canoe races, including the world championship Flatwater Endurance race. | 607/967–8700 | www.canoeregatta.org.
JUNE OR JULY: *Bainbridge Dog Show.* More than 5,000 dogs of all breeds woof it up at the Clinton Park Campground during this weekend show in late June or early July. Enter your pooch by calling the Chamber of Commerce to register. | 607/967–8700.

Dining

Bob's Diner. American. This authentic 1950s diner, directly off Highway 88, has been serving three meals a day since before the 1950s. Try the French toast or a daily special. | 26 Main St. | 607/967–3111 | Breakfast also available | $5–$8 | No credit cards.

Olde Jericho Tavern. American. Located in an 18th-century building. Buffet lunch and dinner. Kids' menu. | 4 N. Main St. | 607/967–5893 | Closed Mon. | $12–$18 | D, MC, V.

River Club. Continental. This restaurant is in an old rail station on the Susquehanna River, just south of Bainbridge. The seafood buffet and prime rib are popular. You can dine outside on the deck. Kids' menu. Sunday brunch. | 1 Maple St., Afton | 607/639–3060 | Closed Mon.–Wed. No lunch Thurs.–Sat. | $12–$16 | AE, MC, V.

Unadilla House. American. The restaurant in this old, homey hotel serves steaks, prime rib, seafood, and chicken. It's 9 mi from Bainbridge, in the middle of town near Main Street. | 63 Main St., Unadilla | 607/369–7227 | Closed Sun. | $10–$25 | AE, D, MC, V.

Lodging

Algonkin Motel. This country motel sits alongside the Susquehanna River amid hills wooded with pines and maples. Beds are queen or double. Cable TV. Business services. Free parking. | 2626 State Hwy. 7 | 607/967–5911 | 25 rooms | $40–$65 | AE, D, MC, V.

Super 8. Located north of Bainbridge on Interstate 88, this two-story chain motel in the village of Sidney is within walking distance to the post office, grocery store, and fast-food restaurants. Cable TV. Business services. | 4 Mang Dr., Sidney | 607/563–8880 | fax 607/563–8889 | 39 rooms | $59–$77 ($71–$93 Fri., Sat.) | AE, D, DC, MC, V.

BATAVIA

MAP 3, D6

(Nearby towns also listed: Albion, Buffalo, Clarence, Geneseo, Rochester)

Batavia is the county seat of the largely agricultural Genesee County. The town's unusual name comes from the Dutch, who purchased 3.3 million acres of land in western New York and then sold them from the Holland Land Office here in Batavia. The office's 1815 Greek Revival building on Main Street is now preserved as a museum. Stop at the museum for an inexpensive walking guide to the town and the cemetery. Although many of Main Street's original buildings were removed in the 1960s to create a more "modern" look, some striking examples of Romanesque, Italianate, and Victorian buildings still remain.

Information: **Genesee County Chamber of Commerce** | 210 E. Main St., 14020 | 716/343–7440.

BATAVIA

INTRO
ATTRACTIONS
DINING
LODGING

Attractions

Batavia Downs Race Track. This pioneering track, off I–90, introduced night harness racing in 1940. | 8315 Park Rd.; off I–90 | 716/343–3750 | Call for information | Mon.–Sun. 11:30 AM–11 PM.

Holland Land Office Museum. Now a National Historic Landmark, this office was once used by the Holland Land company to sell over 3 million acres of western New York State in the early 1800s. The museum displays artifacts from the Land Office days, and exhibits focus on 19th-century life in Genesee County. | 131 W. Main St. | 716/343–4727 | Donations accepted | Tues.–Sat. 10–4.

Iroquois National Wildlife Refuge. The more than 10,000 acres of wildlife habitat here attract migratory waterfowl and other birds, as well as resident wildlife. There are overlooks and nature trails for biking, photography, and cross-country skiing. The refuge is 24 mi north of Batavia. | 1101 Casey Rd., off Rte. 63, Alabama | 716/948–5445 | Free | Daily dawn–dusk.

Le Roy House. The family of Jacob Le Roy lived here in 1823, and the building was donated to the Le Roy Historical Society in 1942. The kitchen has a brick oven that is still used for open-hearth cooking and all seven rooms are decorated in period furnishings. The home also has two exhibits rooms, and a very large collection of Morganville pottery. The house is east of Batavia. | 23 E. Main St., Le Roy | 716/768–7433 | Free | Tues.–Fri. 10–4, Sun. 2–4.

Jell-O Gallery. Behind the Le Roy house is where Jell-O was invented in Le Roy, and this gallery documents Jell-O history. Original artwork used in early Jell-O advertisements is on display. | 23 E. Main St., Leroy | $3 | Mon.–Sat. 10–4, Sun. 1–4.

Six Flags Darien Lake Theme Park and Camping Resort. Five roller coasters are among the more than 100 rides at this "superpark." There's also shows, a water park, a concert amphitheater, and a hotel and campground. | 9993 Allegany Rd., off Rte. 77, Darien Center | 716/599–4641 | fax 716/599–4053 | www.sixflags.com | $29.99 | Mid-May–Oct., daily 10:30–10.

ON THE CALENDAR

JUNE: *Balloons Over Batavia.* Over 30 hot-air balloons take to the skies during this festival. Balloon and parachute rides are available and there is entertainment, and arts and crafts. At the Genesee Country fairgrounds, Route 5. Take exit 48, off I–90. | 716/343–1490.

JUNE–AUG.: *Concerts in the Park Series.* Bring a blanket or lawn chair to Centennial Park and listen to Broadway tunes, swing, pop, and classical music played by the Batavia Concert Band. | 716/343–5991.

JUNE–OCT.: *Genesee County Farmer's Market.* You can buy fresh fruit, vegetables, plants, baked goods, cheese, pepperoni, and flowers on Route 63, at the Kmart parking lot in Batavia, off Lewiston Rd. | Tues.–Fri. 8–5 | 716/343–9491.

JULY: *Annual Art Picnic in the Park.* Celebrate the 4th of July with fireworks, horse-drawn wagon rides, folk arts performances, and a huge arts-and-crafts show and sale. At Centennial Park. | 716/343–9313.

JULY: *Genesee County Agricultural Fair.* Rides, concessions, grandstand shows, 4-H events, entertainment, and agricultural exhibits come to the Genesee County Fairgrounds, off Route 5. | 716/344–2424.

Dining

Pontillo's Pizza and Pasta. Italian. This well-known family restaurant has an open kitchen and a health-conscious menu, which incorporates lower-fat and all-natural ingredients into entrée recipes. Buffet lunch buffet. | 500 E. Main St. | 716/343–3303 | $5–$10 | AE, D, DC, MC, V.

Red Osier Landmark, Inc. Continental. The bountiful prime-rib dinners range from the 1½-lb Queen size to the 4½-lb Call Cut at this old-fashioned inn 8 mi from Batavia. Steak and seafood are also served. Early bird dinners. | Rte. 5, Stafford | 716/343–6972 or 888/343–6972 | www.redosier.com | Closed Mon. No lunch | $10–$40 | AE, MC, V.

Sunny's. Italian. This family restaurant in the center of Batavia has a circular mirror in the dining room and neon lighting. Kids' menu. Early bird dinner. | Genesee Country Mall | 716/343–4578 | Closed Sun. | $10–$30 | AE, D, DC, MC, V.

Lodging

Batavia Motel. Located 3 mi from Highway 90, in downtown Batavia, this hotel has been run by the same family since 1965. You can fish in the backyard, in a small creek that runs through the property. Beds are either queen or full size. | 3768 W. Main St. | 716/343–5531 | fax 716/345–4254 | $35–$89 | 22 | AE, D, DC, MC, V.

Best Western. This chain hotel is 2 mi from the Genesee County Airport and 30 mi from the Buffalo International Airport. Restaurant, bar. In-room data ports, cable TV. Pool. Business services. Some pets allowed. | 8204 Park Rd. | 716/343–1000 | fax 716/343–8608 | 75 rooms | $80–$110 | AE, D, DC, MC, V.

Days Inn. This two-story hotel is a 45-min drive from Niagara Falls and Darien Lake. Complimentary Continental breakfast. Cable TV. Pool. Business services. Pets allowed. | 200 Oak St. | 716/343–1440 | fax 716/343–5322 | 120 rooms | $58 | AE, D, MC, V.

Holiday Inn. This link in the chain is a five-story building near Darien Lake and Batavia Downs thoroughbred racetrack. Restaurant, bar. In-room data ports, some refrigerators, cable TV. 2 pools. Exercise equipment. Business services. Some pets allowed. | 8250 Park Rd. | 716/344–2100 or 800/877–6145 | fax 716/344–0238 | 196 rooms | $84 | AE, D, DC, MC, V.

Microtel Inns and Suites. Located on the edge of a suburban area 1 mi from downtown, this lodging option has rooms and suites. There are a few restaurants within walking distance. Complimentary Continental breakfast. Pool. Hot tub. Exercise equipment. | 8210 Park Rd. | 716/344–8882 | fax 716/344–7187 | www.microtelinnandsuites.com | 52 rooms, 23 suites | $102–$105 | AE, D, DC, MC, V.

Park Oak. A renovated facility offering affordable rooms. Complimentary Continental breakfast. Cable TV. Business services. No smoking. | 301 Oak St. | 716/343–7921 | fax 716/343–6701 | 23 rooms | $38 | AE, D, MC, V.

BATH

MAP 3, D3

(Nearby towns also listed: Corning, Hammondsport, Hornell)

The first planned community in western New York, Bath was founded in 1793 and sits in the middle of a rich farming area. The Conhocton River, which skirts the village, is a local attraction for people who like to fish for trout. The Veterans' Administration Medical Center continues a long tradition in Bath of caring for soldiers and sailors, many of whom are buried in the village's national cemetery.

Information: Greater Bath Area Chamber of Commerce | 10 Pulteney Sq. W, 14810 | 607/776–7122.

Attractions

Elm Cottage Museum. This 1828 house has original domestic items from the mid-1800s in rooms set up as if they were still being lived in. Pictures, clothes, even physician's equipment are on display. | Cameron Park, MaGee House | 607/776–9930 Chamber of Commerce | Free | Weekdays 10–3.

ON THE CALENDAR

JUNE: *Steuben County Dairy Festival.* The downtown fairgrounds host dairy-related demonstrations and musical entertainment. | 607/776–7122.

AUG.: *Steuben County Fair.* Catch the amusements, rides, exhibits, and country-and-western music at this fair, which has been held for over 180 years. At the fairgrounds downtown. | 607/776–4801.

Dining

Judy's Restaurant. American. Judy's has been serving a full American menu (and three meals a day) since 1978. Try the Friday fish fries, the steak, or any of the daily specials. Kids' menu. | 14 W. Steuben St. | 607/776–7578 | $4–$9 | No credit cards.

Loafin' Tree. American. This casual family-style restaurant within the village limits has an adjoining gift shop that sells collectibles. Kids' menu. | 143 Geneva St. | 607/776–7734 | $7–$15 | AE, D, MC, V.

Tally-Ho Restaurant. American. This spot, known for steaks, chicken, chops, and seafood, is about 5 mi from Bath. | W. Main St., Kanona | 607/776–7759 | $7–$15 | AE, D, MC, V.

Lodging

Budget Inn. Located 2 mi from Route 17, this inn is in Bath's business area and within walking distance of many restaurants and shops. Rooms have either two double beds or a king. Complimentary Continental breakfast. Cable TV. Free Parking. | 330½ W. Morris St. | 607/760–7536 | 20 rooms | $40 | AE, D, MC, V.

Caboose Motel. Sleep in an old railroad car at this motel, 12 mi from Bath. The "caboose" rooms are furnished with bunk beds and train seats. Caboose rooms are not available October–April. Restaurant, picnic area. In-room data ports, cable TV. Pool. Playground. Business services. Some pets allowed. | 8620 Rte. 415, Avoca | 607/566–2216 | fax 607/566–3817 | 18 rooms, 5 caboose rooms | $45–$50 rooms, $75 caboose rooms | Closed Dec.–Mar. | MC, V.

Days Inn. This five-story downtown hotel is within walking distance of several restaurants. No-smoking rooms are available. Restaurant, bar. Cable TV. Pool. Laundry service. Business services. Pets allowed. | 330 W. Morris St. | 607/776–7644 | fax 607/776–7650 | 104 rooms | $75 | AE, D, DC, MC, V.

Holland American Country Inn. This simple, independently run motel is primarily the haunt of business travelers. Guest rooms have desks big enough to spread your work out on, and the immediate area has a number of dining establishments to choose from. Cable TV. | Rte. 415 | 607/776–605 | eander@shell10.vivanet.com | 16 rooms | $44 | AE, D, MC, V.

Super 8. This chain hotel is downtown. Guest rooms are spaced along two floors with interior corridors, and all are equipped with modern, modular furniture. Cable TV. Business services. Pets allowed. | 333 W. Morris St. | 607/776–2187 | fax 607/776–3206 | 50 rooms | $59–$62 | AE, D, MC, V.

BAY SHORE/BRIGHTWATERS

MAP 3, D3

(Nearby towns also listed: Babylon, Mastic/Mastic Beach, Sayville)

Originally purchased from the local Secatogue Indians, Greater Bay Shore was established by an English Royal Patent in 1701. Located about 40 mi east of New York City, Bay Shore is close to Robert Moses Beach and Jones Beach. Fire Island is just a short ferry ride away across Great South Bay. Houses ring the active waterfront, which attracts locals and visitors to its public launching ramps, abundant dock space, and excellent restaurants. The Bay Shore Marina is one of the largest publicly owned marinas on the East Coast and renowned boat shows and fishing tournaments are held here. Bay Shore is also home to the headquarters of the national baked goods company, Entenmanns.

Information: Chamber of Commerce of Greater Bay Shore and the Business Improvement District | 102 E. Main St., Box 5110, Bay Shore, 11706 | 631/665–7003.

Attractions

Bayard Cutting Arboretum. Trees and gardens are the attraction at this site on the Connetquot River 8 mi east of Bay Shore. A mansion overlooks the great lawn that sweeps down to the water, and paths lead you past a variety of trees, including pine and swamp cypress. Wildflowers, daffodils, and rhododendrons bloom in season. The mansion has a snack bar. | Montauk Hwy., East Islip | 631/581–1002 | $5 per car | Tues.–Sun. 10–dusk.

Gibson-Mack-Holt House. This museum was once a typical tradesmen's house of the 1850s, and is still authentically furnished. Permanent collections include more than 100 antique photographs of the surrounding areas, a Victorian herb garden, a two-seater outhouse, and a chicken coop. A research library consisting of postcards, maps, old newspapers, and books on the Bay Shore/Brightwaters area is in the basement. Alternating exhibits display memorabilia and artifacts ranging from world wars to sports and crafts. | 22 Maple La. | 631/665–7003 | Free | Tues. and Sat. 2–4; closed Jan.–Feb.

Sagtikos Manor. The original section of this private estate was built between 1692 and 1697. During the Revolutionary War, the manor served as a military headquarters. Sagtikos is an Indian word meaning "snake that kisses." The manor now houses a substantial collection of antiques and historical exhibits depicting the structure's early days. | Montauk Hwy., between Gardiner Dr. and Manor La., West Bay Shore | 631/665–0093 or 631/321–8829 | www.sagtikosmanor.com | $3 | July–Aug., Wed.–Thurs. and Sun. 1–4; June, Sun. 1–4.

ON THE CALENDAR

JULY–AUG.: *Summertime in the Park Concerts.* The Dr. George S. King Park on west Main street comes alive with Brown Bag Lunch concerts on Tuesdays; Magic Carpet Story Hour on Wednesday mornings; and evening concerts on Thursdays and Fridays. | 631/665–7003.

AUG.: *Long Island Feis and Piping Competition.* Celebrate Irish culture with step-dancing competitions, piping, singing, and soda-bread baking. | 631/736–1230.

OCT.: *Entenmanns' Great South Bay Run.* Open to anyone, this 10K race begins on Main Street and ends at Great South Bay. A half marathon is also run. Prizes are awarded. | 631/665–7003.

OCT.: *Town of Islip Apple Festival.* This event includes pie eating, apple-cider making, autumnal contests, and crafts. At the Islip Grange, corner of Broadway and Montauk Highway in Islip, 6 mi east of Bay Shore. | 631/224–5430.

Dining

Molly Malone's. Irish. Corned beef and cabbage with boiled potatoes are served at this cozy restaurant that is also known for fresh seafood. The old Irish theme is carried out in the Tiffany-style lamps throughout the bar and dining areas. Try the Whistle Stop cheesecake and Mississippi mud pie. Open-air dining on the deck. Live Irish music and singers Tuesdays through Sundays. Reggae music on the deck Fridays at 6 and Sundays 2–9. Kids' menu. Sunday brunch in winter. Dock space. | 124 Maple Ave. | 631/969–2232 | $19–$25 | AE, MC, V.

Porky and Glenn's Fish House. Seafood. Steamers, mussels, and fresh fish are the mainstays at this casual, nautical-theme restaurant with an open-air view of the water. Steak and chicken are also available and you can eat outside on the deck under a tent canopy. Family-style service. Kids' menu. Live music Wednesday and Friday–Sunday. Sunday brunch buffet. | 28 Cottage Ave. | 631/666–2899. | $12–$25 | AE, D, DC, MC, V.

Lodging

Hampton Inn. This chain hotel east of Bay Shore has cribs and connecting rooms available. Complimentary Continental breakfast. Cable TV. Gym. Business services, airport shut-

BAY SHORE/
BRIGHTWATERS

INTRO
ATTRACTIONS
DINING
LODGING

. tle. No pets. | 1600 Veterans Memorial Hwy. (Rte. 454), Islandia | 631/234–0400 | fax 631/
234–0415 | www.hamptoninn.com | 121 rooms | $149–$169 | AE, D, DC, MC, V.

BEMUS POINT

MAP 3, B7

(Nearby towns also listed: Chautauqua, Jamestown)

The largest community on the north shore of Chautauqua Lake, Bemus Point was first
settled by the William Bemus family in 1806. In March of that year, the family loaded
themselves and all their possessions on sleds. The sleds were then hand-pushed down
the length of the lake from their temporary home in Westfield to what is now Bemus
Point. During summer months, the area's population swells with vacationers coming
from all over New York and Canada to enjoy the lake and the Chautauqua Institution,
located on the opposite shore.

Information: **Mayville Area Chamber of Commerce** | Box 22, Mayville, 14757 | 716/753–
3113.

Attractions

Long Point on Lake Chautauqua State Park. This busy, 320-acre day use state park on the
shores of Lake Chautauqua has a swimming beach and bathhouse, and the most modern boat launching facility on the lake. There is also a marina and playground and you
can go fishing, biking, hiking, snowmobiling, and cross-country skiing. No camping. | 4459
Rte. 430 | 716/386–2722 | $5 per vehicle | Daily.

Stow Ferry. The ferry leaves from the village of Bemus Point and goes across Chautauqua
Lake to Stow. You can take your bike, car, or just yourself. | 15 Water St. | 716/753–2403 | Cruise
prices vary—call for specific rates | Daily cruises at 11, 1:15, 3.

ON THE CALENDAR

JULY, AUG.: *Art in the Park.* Local artists exhibit and sell their art at Bemus Point Town
Park. | 716/569–5624.

Dining

Bemus Point Inn. Continental. This informal restaurant serves breakfast all day and is known
for its huge cinnamon rolls. Sandwiches, finger foods, salads, and desserts are also popu-
lar. Open-air dining on the patio. | Main St. | 716/386–2221 | Breakfast also available; no din-
ner | $6–$12 | AE, D, MC, V.

Italian Fisherman. Contemporary. Eat indoors or outside on the multilevel deck that has
a built-in barbecue. The restaurant is known for seafood specialties and Italian dishes. Open-
air dining. Raw bar. Live music and theme nights. Kids' menu. | 61 Lakeside Dr. | 716/386–
7000 | Closed late Sept.–Apr. | $12–$19 | AE, MC, V.

Ye Hare 'N' Hounds Inn. Continental. This 1915 English country inn has fireplaces and lots
of windows overlooking Chautauqua Lake. Try the fresh seafood or the seafood Julienne,
a combination of baked seafood and rack of lamb. Open-air dining on the porch. | 64 Lake-
side Dr. | 716/386–2181 | No lunch | $12–$19 | AE, D, MC, V.

Lodging

Bemus Point Lakeside Cottages. Cabins sit across the street from Chautauqua Lake, about
50 ft from water. A variety of restaurants and shops are within walking distance, and Interstates 430 and 96 are just ¼ mi away. Dock area. No room phones, no in-room TVs. Laun-
dry facilities. | 50 Lakeside Dr. | 716/386–2535 | red@madbbs.com | 20 cottages; 10 1-bedroom,
10 2-bedroom | $90–$100 | MC, V.

Hotel Lenhart. Built in 1890, this four-story Victorian hotel in downtown Bemus Point still has some original furniture. The spacious veranda faces Chautauqua Lake and the beach is just across the street. The Village Casino is nearby. Restaurant, bar. Tennis. Dock. Business services, airport shuttle. | 22 Lakeside Dr. | 716/386–2715 | fax 716/386–5404 | lenhart36@aol.com | 50 rooms (34 with bath) | $115–$135 | Closed Labor Day–Memorial Day | MAP | No credit cards.

BINGHAMTON

MAP 3, H8

(Nearby towns also listed: Bainbridge, Deposit, Endicott, Greene, Owego)

Binghamton lies at the intersection of Interstates 81 and 88, 10 mi north of the Pennsylvania border. The Chenango and Susquehanna rivers meet here. Founded in 1787, today Binghamton is the home of a state university, a symphony orchestra, minor-league hockey and baseball, a zoo, and science museums.

Information: Broome County Chamber of Commerce | Box 995, 13902-0995 | 607/772–8860.

Attractions

Binghamton Municipal Stadium. The Binghamton Mets baseball team makes this their home from April through September. | Henry St. | 607/723–6387 | $6 grandstand seating, $7 box seating | www.bmets.com | Hrs vary with games.

Binghamton University, State University of New York. Established in 1946 as Triple Cities College in Endicott, New York, Binghamton University was incorporated into the State University of New York system in 1950 and moved here in 1961. The sprawling 606-acre campus on the banks of the Susquehanna River has a 117-acre nature preserve. Approximately 12,000 students are enrolled. Located on Vestal Parkway E off Rte. 434. | 607/777–2000 or 607/777–3535 | www.binghamton.edu | Free | Daily.

The **Anderson Center for Performing Arts** is a 1,200-seat concert hall with a retractable rear wall, which allows lawn seating. The hall is at the end of parking lot C. | 607/777–ARTS or 888/bingfest | www.anderson.binghamton.edu | Hrs vary with shows.

Binghamton Visitor Center. Get information on the city, and watch a 12-minute film that narrates the history of Binghamton. Other exhibits explore the local industrial history. The center shares an address with Roberson Museum and Science Center. | 30 Front St. | 607/772–0660 | Tues.–Sat. 10–5, Sun. 12–5.

Broome Center for the Performing Arts. This restored vaudeville house is home to the Binghamton Philharmonic, Pop Series, Tri-Cities Opera, and Broadway Theatre League. A small exhibit of photographs and memorabilia in honor of Twilight Zone creator and Binghamton native Rod Serling are on permanent display. | The Forum, 236 Washington St. | 607/778–2480 | Call for schedule.

Broome County Veterans Memorial Arena and Convention Center. The Binghamton Icemen, a minor-league hockey team, play at this multipurpose facility which is used for concerts, trade shows, and conventions. | 1 Stuart Pl. | 607/778–6626 | Call for schedule.

Chenango Valley State Park. In addition to 216 campsites and 24 cabins, this park has a golf course, trails, boat docks, and a special sand-bottomed swimming area in a diked-off corner of the lake. Stop at the interpretive center for maps and information, and say hello to the center's resident turtle. About 15 mi northeast of Binghamton off Route 369. | 153 State Park Rd., Chenango Forks | 607/648–5251, 800/456–2267 reservations | $6 per vehicle | Apr.–Oct., daily.

Discovery Center of the Southern Tier. This children's museum has hands-on exhibits. | 60 Morgan Rd. | 607/773–8661 | www.tier.net/discovery | $3.50 | Tues.–Thurs. and Sat. 10–4, Sun. noon–5; open 1st Fri. of the month 10–8.

Roberson Museum and Science Center. Science exhibits and a planetarium are housed in this restored 1907 building. Other displays showcase regional art, history, and folk life. | 30 Front St. | 607/772–0660 | $6 | Tues.–Sat. 10–5, Sun. 12–5; planetarium shows weekends at 2.

Ross Park Zoo. Snow leopards, African lions, and red wolves are among the more than 200 animals who call this zoo home. Founded in 1875, it is the fifth-oldest zoo in the country. | 60 Morgan Rd. | 607/724–5454 | www.tier.net/rossparkzoo | $4 | Mar.–Nov., daily 10–5; closed Dec.–Feb.

ON THE CALENDAR

JULY: *Carousel Festival.* Six hand-carved 1920s carousels are on display at various sites in Binghamton, Johnson City, and Endicott. | 607/772–0660 or 607/754–7832.
JULY–AUG.: *Binghamton Summer Music Festival.* Enjoy musical events at venues in and around Binghamton, including the Anderson Center at Binghamton University. | 888/BINGFEST or 607/777–4777.
AUG.: *Balloon Rally and Spiedie Fest.* Head to the Tri-Cities Airport for hot-air balloons, crafts, antique cars, music, and, of course, the local food specialty: the "spiedie" sandwich, which comes with your choice of marinated chicken, veal, or pork. | 607/761–2475.

Dining

Argo. American. This downtown family restaurant has a large menu and breakfast specials. It's known for fresh seafood, chicken, steak, and Italian dishes. Beer and wine only. | 117 Court St. | 607/724–4692 | Breakfast also available | $10–$15 | AE, D, MC, V.

Giovanni's Restaurant. Italian. The emphasis here is gourmet food without a too-formal atmosphere. Try the sampler platter: eggplant Parmesan, lasagna, and stuffed shells. Kids' menu. Across the street from Interstate 81. | 1290 Upper Front St. #2 | 607/722–5417 | $6–$16 | AE, D, DC, MC, V.

Number Five. Continental. The 1897 building that houses this restaurant is a National Historic Landmark. For dinner, the juicy, grilled-to-order prime rib can't be beat—it's sided with rosemary red potatoes and fresh steamed vegetables. Entertainment on Friday and Saturday. | 33 S. Washington | 607/723–0555 | No lunch | $25–$35 | AE, D, DC, MC, V.

The Spot. American. This Greek diner just three minutes from downtown is open all night and serves fresh seafood, lamp chops, chicken, and hamburgers. Desserts are homemade. Kids' menu. Open 24 hours. | 1062 Front St. | 607/723–8149 | $12–$18 | AE, D, DC, MC, V.

Lodging

Best Western Regency Hotel. This 10-story hotel downtown is near the Chenango River and surrounded by popular chain restaurants and smaller, family-owned spots. Guest rooms are replete with modern, polished-wood furniture and neutral-colored carpet. Restaurant, bar, room service. In-room data ports, some in-room hot tubs, cable TV. Pool. Sauna. Exercise equipment. Business services. | 225 Water St. | 607/722–7575 | fax 607/724–7263 | www.admin@bingregency.com | www.bingregency.com | 203 rooms | $79 | AE, D, DC, MC, V.

Comfort Inn. This hotel on a commercial strip in Nimmonsburg, a suburb north of Binghamton, is surrounded by restaurants. Complimentary Continental breakfast. In-room data ports, some microwaves, cable TV. Laundry facilities. Business services. Pets allowed. | 1156 Front St., Nimmonsburg | 607/722–5353 | fax 607/722–1823 | www.macomfy@aol.com | www.comfortinn.com | 67 rooms | $80 | AE, D, DC, MC, V.

Days Inn. Restaurants are nearby this four-story chain hotel on a commercial strip north of Binghamton, in Chenango Bridge. Picnic area, complimentary Continental breakfast. In-room data ports, cable TV. Pool. Business services. | 1000 Front St., Chenango Bridge | 607/724-3297 | fax 607/771-0206 | 104 rooms, 1 suite | $95 rooms, $200 suite | AE, D, DC, MC, V.

Del Motel. This motel, ½ mi from Highway 81 on the outskirts of town, has views of the surrounding mountains. Local art is displayed some of the rooms. Complimentary Continental breakfast. | 609 Court St. | 607/775-2144 | 25 rooms | $35 | AE, D, MC, V.

Foothills Motel. Set in the Catskill foothills, but only a mile from the intersection of Hwys. 17 and 81, this is a good choice if you'll be passing through for a night. Adjoining rooms are available. Cable TV. Laundry facilities. Free parking. | 591 Court St. | 607/775-1515 | 20 rooms | $38 | MC, V.

Grand Royale. This six-story inn is close to Binghamton University. Complimentary Continental breakfast. In-room data ports, cable TV. Business services. Some pets allowed (fee). | 80 State St. | 607/722-0000, 888/242-0323 reservations | fax 607/722-7912 | 55 rooms, 6 suites | $88 rooms, $158 suites | AE, D, DC, MC, V.

Holiday Inn–Arena. This high-rise hotel in Binghamton's business district overlooks the Chenango River and is across from the Broome County Arena. Restaurant, bar, room service. In-room data ports, some refrigerators, cable TV. Pool. Shops. Laundry facilities. Business services. Pets allowed (fee). | 2-8 Hawley St. | 607/722-1212 | fax 607/722-6063 | www.holiday-inn.com | 229 rooms, 11 suites | $90 rooms, $129 suites | AE, D, DC, MC, V.

Howard Johnson's. You'll find this Hojo on the northern end of Binghamton, just off the college campus, and within 2 mi of many restaurants. Complimentary Continental breakfast. Cable TV. Business services. Some pets allowed. | 690 Old Front St. | 607/724-1341 | fax 607/773-8287 | 107 rooms | $54 | AE, D, DC, MC, V.

Parkway. This roadside motel is near the Ross Park Zoo, southwest of Binghamton. Restaurant, bar. Some kitchenettes, microwaves, cable TV. Pool. | 900 Vestal Pkwy. E, Vestal | 607/785-3311, 607/754-4961 reservations | fax 607/785-8117 | 58 rooms | $55 | AE, D, DC, MC, V.

Ramada Inn. This Ramada puts you downtown within walking distance of a department store and restaurants. Room have either a queen-, double-, or king-size bed. Complimentary Continental breakfast. Pool. Sauna. | 65 Front St. | 607/724-2412 | fax 607/722-4000 | www.ramada-ny.com | 135 rooms | $72-$89 | AE, D, DC, MC, V.

Red Roof Inn. The Red Roof Inn is a two-story chain hotel 2 mi from Binghamton University and near restaurants and shopping. In-room data ports, cable TV. Business services. | 590 Fairview St., Johnson City | 607/729-8940 | fax 607/729-8949 | 107 rooms | $60 | AE, D, DC, MC, V.

Super 8 Motel. This chain hotel is between Route 17 and Interstate 81. Restaurant. Pool. | Rte. 11, Upper Court St. | 607/775-3443 or 800/800-8000 | fax 607/775-2368 | 104 rooms | $56 | AE, D, DC, MC, V.

BLUE MOUNTAIN LAKE

MAP 3, J4

(Nearby towns also listed: Long Lake, North Creek, Old Forge)

Perched on the edge of Blue Mountain Lake is this tiny village, home to only a few hundred people. The area is a mecca for outdoor lovers, who come here to the geographic heart of the Adirondack Park for the boating, swimming, fishing (largemouth bass, lake trout, brook trout, and whitefish), and the excellent hiking trails. Two major attractions, the Adirondack Museum and the Adirondack Lakes Center for the Arts, have made the village a cultural center. There are also boat-launching ramps, a canoe-

BLUE MOUNTAIN
LAKE

INTRO
ATTRACTIONS
DINING
LODGING

launching site, and a public beach, along with plenty of restaurants, lodging, outfitters, and shops in town.

Information: **Indian Lake Chamber of Commerce** | PO Box 724, Indian Lake, NY 12842 | www.indian-lake.com/ | 518/648–5112 or 800/328–5253.

Attractions

Adirondack Lakes Center for the Arts. This multi-arts center presents a wide variety of programs, from classical concerts to coffeehouse entertainment, films, plays, exhibits, and workshops. Galleries display regional and national artwork. | Box 205, Rte. 28 | 518/352–7715 | alca@telenet.net | Sept.–June, weekdays 10–4; July–Aug., weekdays 10–4, Sat. 10–4, Sun. noon–4.

Adirondack Museum. Over 100,000 Adirondack artifacts are in the collection of this acclaimed museum that explores the history and culture of the Adirondack region. Twenty-three indoor and outdoor exhibit areas examine nearly every feature of Adirondack life, including environmental and health-care issues, resort life, and wood crafts. A library, snack bar, and shop are on site. | Box 99, Rte. 30 | 518/352–7311 | www.adkmuseum.org | $10 | Mid-June–mid-Oct., daily 9:30–5:30.

Blue Mountain. This 3,759-ft crag towers over the waters of Blue Mountain Lake. If you hike the well-maintained 2-mi trail to the mountain's peak, you'll be rewarded with a spectacular view of 165 mountains and 16 lakes. The trailhead is 1.3 mi from town on Route 30. | 518/352–7600 | Free | Daily.

© Artville

ADIRONDACK STYLE

Ah, the Adirondacks, where you freeze in below-zero temperatures and mile-high piles of snow in winter, and swat flies and mosquitoes the rest of the year. The Adirondacks is not a place for the untrained or the faint of heart. And yet, during the late 1800s, people of these dispositions began to flock here to enjoy the cooler temperatures of summer, the unspoiled hunting and fishing, and the almost opulent scenery.

Wealthy families arrived from New York City and Boston, bringing servants, fancy clothing, their best china for tea, and the expectations and tastes of the well-bred and well-to-do city folk that they were. What they discovered was a land indeed rich in resources and beauty, but a remote and harsh land, too. One tale claims that the region's indigenous people were known as the "Ratirondack," or the "people who eat bark"—an indication of both their abilities and the difficulty of life in the Adirondack region.

To satisfy the newcomers' desire for large, comfortable summer homes, and to overcome the expense of importing materials, local builders relied on their innate sense of "make do" and used what they found in the area—lots of wood and stone—to construct fantastic homes in what came to be known as the "Adirondack style." Some of these "great camps" exist today, and are popular tourist attractions. Visitors who can afford to will happily take home a sample of Adirondack Twig Furniture as a memento of a vacation in the "howling wild" of the North.

Great Camp Sagamore. Sagamore Lodge and the 26 adjoining buildings that make up Great Camp Sagamore were built in the late 1800s by William West Durant, a prominent Adirondack figure. Designed in a Swiss chalet-style, the lodge was built with native spruce, cedar, and granite and its rustic style set a precedent among wealthy vacationers' retreats. Bought and expanded by the Vanderbilt family in the early 1900s, Sagamore is now owned and run by a nonprofit organization that sponsors meetings, seminars, and classes, and rents rooms by the night or week. Classes and activities include canoeing, rustic furniture making, mosaic twig decoration, mountain music and dance, and more. Daily tours take you to a blacksmith shop, furniture shop, ice house, and livestock buildings, as well as the main lodge. The camp is about 30 mi southwest of Blue Mountain Lake. | Box 146, Rte. 28, Raquette Lake | 315/354–5311 | Tours $9 | Tours mid-June–Labor Day, daily 10 and 1:30; Labor Day–Columbus Day, weekends 10 and 1:30.

Raquette Lake Navigation. Cruise the waters of beautiful Raquette Lake aboard the *W.W. Durant*, a 60-ft double-deck ship. Two-hour lunch trips, Sunday champagne cruises, dinner cruises, foliage cruises, and moonlight cruises are among the options. The dining room is enclosed and heated and there is a full bar. South on Route 28. | Box 100 | 315/354–5532 | fax 315/354–5852 | rivnav@telenet.net | www.raquettelakenavigation.com | $5–$40 | Memorial Day–early Nov., daily.

ON THE CALENDAR

JUNE: *No-Octane Regatta*. At this event sponsored by the Adirondack Museum, you'll only see boats that run without a motor—sailboats, sloops, rowboats, canoes, and guide boats. Some of these craft are found only in the Adirondacks. There is a grand parade of wooden boats on Blue Mountain Lake, a toy boat regatta, workshops, and food. | 518/648–5112 or 800/328–LAKE.

Dining

Blue Mountain General Store. If you're planning a picnic, stock up here on your choice of soda, beer, snacks, sandwiches from a full deli, and basic grocery items. There are picnic tables in back. | Corner of Rtes. 28 and 30 | 518/352–7318 | AE, D, MC, V.

Potter's Restaurant. American. The only real restaurant in Blue Mountain Lake, this gorgeous Swiss chalet–style dining room overlooks Blue Mountain Lake. Prime rib, fresh seafood, and a salad bar are available every day. Homemade fruit pies or strawberry shortcake are a great finale. | Junction of Hwys. 28 and 30 | 518/352–7664 | Closed Tues. | $9–$23 | MC, V.

Lodging

Blue Mountain Lake Inn. This 1860 three-story Victorian bed-and-breakfast is across from a public beach. The rooms have a rustic country feel. Complimentary breakfast. | Rte. 28 | 518/352–7600 | 6 rooms, 1 cabin. Shared bath | $70–$110 | Closed Columbus Day–Memorial Day | AE, MC, V.

Burke's Cottages. All cottages on this 3-acre site east of Blue Mountain Lake have lake views. Each has a full kitchen and bath, but you must bring your own linens and towels. A minimum two-night stay is required. Picnic area. Kitchenettes. Cable TV. Beach, dock. No pets allowed. | Lake Shore Dr., Indian Lake | 518/648–5258 | fax 518–648–5258 | 6 cottages | $95–$135 per night (up to 6 people) | No credit cards.

Chief Sabael Cottages. Some of these large, fully equipped cottages have fireplaces, and all have kitchens. There are also four efficiency units. The cottages are available from Memorial Day to Columbus Day only, and in July and August you have to stay for at least a week. Some kitchenettes. Picnic area. Tennis. Beach, docks. | Lake Shore Rd., Sabael | 518/648–5200 | 6 cottages, 4 apartments | $410–$850 cottages (weekly), $55 apartments | No credit cards.

1870 Bed and Breakfast. This attractive farmhouse on 40 acres has a fireplace, a big front porch, and flower, fruit, and vegetable gardens. East on Route 30 about 10 mi outside Blue Mountain Lake. Complimentary breakfast. TV in common area. | 36 W. Main St., Indian Lake | 518/648–5377 | bandb@telenet.net | 5 rooms (2 with shared bath) | $62 | No credit cards.

Great Camp Sagamore. Although bunkhouses can occasionally be rented by the night when available, most are offered as part of weekend or full-week instructional programs that are run here. The rooms sleep 72 in summer and 60 during the off-season. Restaurant. No room phones, no TV. Tennis. Hiking. Beach, boating. | Box 146, Rte. 28, Raquette Lake | 315/354–5311 | fax 315–354–5851 | sagamore@telenet.net | www.sagamore.org | 30 rooms | $199 | Closed Nov.–Apr. | AP | MC, V.

Hedges. Early-morning views from this property are of the mist-covered lake and surrounding Adirondack Mountains. Wildlife thrives here, and so will you if you're willing to disconnect yourself from some trappings of the modern world. No room phones, no TV. 2 tennis courts. Beach. | Hedges Rd. | 518/352–7352 | 18 rooms, 13 cabins | $155–$175 rooms, $180 cabins | Closed Oct. 15–June 15 | No credit cards.

Hemlock Hall. Both the lake and the woods are visible from the wraparound porch at this 1890s mountain lodge. The rooms are done in rustic Victorian style. Canoes, Sunfish sailboats, paddleboats, and kayaks are available for use. Restaurant. No air-conditioning, no room phones. Hiking. Beach, boating. Library. Playground. | Hemlock Hall Rd. | 518/352–7706 | 12 rooms in 2 buildings (3 with shared bath), 13 cottages | $92–135 rooms, $135–$145 cottages | Closed mid-Oct.–mid-May | MAP July–Aug. | No credit cards.

Lone Birch Motel. This homey country motel is just 500 ft from Indian Lake. The condos and cottage have kitchens. There are entrances to snowmobiling and cross-country skiing trails from the property. 10 mi east of Blue Mountain. Cable TV. | Rte. 28, Indian Lake | 518/648–5225 | lmoore@telenet.net | www.tvenet.com/indianlake | 4 rooms, 3 condo style units, 1 cottage | rooms $50, condos $70–$80, cottage $110 | AE, MC, V.

Mountain Motel. This motel is ¼ mi from Blue Mountain Lake and 1 mi from the Adirondack Museum. The 2 mini-suites have fully-equipped kitchenettes. Microwaves, kitchenettes, refrigerators, cable TV. Pets allowed. | Rtes. 28 and 30 | 518/352–7781 | 4 rooms, 2 suites | $45–$65 | MC, V.

Potter's Resort and Restaurant. This family-run resort dates to the 1800s, and some visitors seem to have been coming almost that long. The resort is on Blue Mountain Lake, surrounded by the Adirondacks—so quiet you can hear a pin drop in your wood cabin. The restaurant serves three meals a day—the only food within walking distance. Beach, fishing. | Junction of Rtes. 28 and 30 | 518/352–7664 | 10 rooms, 6 cottages | $80–$95 per night, $495–$1,130 per wk | Closed Labor Day–Memorial Day | MC, V.

Steam Boat Landing. Located right on Blue Mountain Lake, this lovely spot has cabins with hardwood floors and lake views. Like most accommodations in this vacation area, the same crowd comes back year after year. The general store is nearby. Some kitchenettes, no room phones. | 123 U.S. Hwy. 140 | 518/352–7323 | 7 rooms, 6 cottages | $52 rooms, $98 cabins | Closed end Oct.–Apr. | No credit cards.

BOLTON LANDING

MAP 3, L4

(Nearby towns also listed: Diamond Point, Glens Falls, Hague, Lake George Village, Lake Luzerne, North Creek, Queensbury, Schroon Lake, Ticonderoga, Warrensburg)

Bolton Landing, a community of some 2,000 year-round residents, hugs the western shore of Lake George about 10 mi north of Lake George Village. While most Adirondack communities can boast scenic settings, Bolton Landing's surroundings place it high among equals. Long settled by Native Americans, in the 1800s Bolton Landing became a place where the well-heeled went to spend the summer and the area was known as "Millionaire's Row." Small coves and islands dot the shore of Lake George here and one large island is the home of Sagamore Resort, a famous Adirondack Hotel. Although it is quieter and less "touristy" than Lake George Village, you can still expect a good deal of summer traffic.

Information: Chamber of Commerce | Box 368, 12814 | 518/644–3831.

Attractions
Veterans Memorial Park. The small public beach has a playground, a gazebo, and an arts-and-crafts building. You can play volleyball here. | Lake Shore Dr. | 518/644–3831 | Free; $4.25 per vehicle July–Aug. | Daily.

Dining
Cate's Italian Garden. Eclectic. Excellent gourmet pizza, seafood specialties like sea bass, pasta, a full wine list, and homemade desserts make it hard to decide what to order. With flowers and candles at each table and a cherry-wood interior, this is a place not to miss. | 7054 Main St. | 518/644–2041 | $9–$15 | AE, D, MC, V.

Char Steer. American. Drive a mile south of Bolton Landing and you'll find this wood-and-brick restaurant surrounded by mountains and filled with photographs of local land-scapes. It serves prime rib, seafood, and pasta, and there's a full wine list. | 4587 Lake Shore Dr. | 518/644–9818 | Closed Oct.–May | $9–$15 | AE, MC, V.

Tavern on the Pond. American. Eat inside in a candlelit dining room with a fire, or on the outdoor porch overlooking Dula Pond. Try the fish-and-chips special or the Dula Pond chicken sandwich with Swiss cheese. And don't forget: it's a tavern, complete with 15 types of tequila, scotch, and vodka. | 4905 Lake Shore Dr. | 518/644–5520 | $6–$17 | AE, MC, V.

Trillium. Continental. This highly acclaimed, elegant restaurant at the Sagamore Resort is known for char-grilled jerk duck breast, roasted sliced pork tenderloin, and pan-seared striped bass. Homemade baked goods and ice cream are also on the menu. | 110 Sagamore Rd. | 518/743–6110 | Reservations essential | Jacket required | No lunch | $30–$60 | AE, D, DC, MC, V.

Villa Napoli Restaurant. Italian. A mile from Bolton Landing, this restaurant in a former estate specializes in Tuscan dining, going beyond just serving Italian food (although it does import the desserts from Italy). Pavarotti or Vivaldi plays in the background, while you sit in the quaint dining area, either inside with candlelight or out on the porch where a creek runs by. Osso buco is a specialty. | 4610 Lake Shore Dr. | 518/644–9750 | $11–$22 | AE, MC, V.

Lodging
Bluebird Cottages. These lakefront cottages on a private beach have full kitchens. Row-boats are available. Cable TV. Lake. Boating. | 4632 Lake Shore Dr. | 518/644–2136 | 17 cottages | $100–$170 | Closed Columbus Day–May 15 | No credit cards.

Bonnie View Resort. This rustic lakefront resort has rooms and cottages. Three restaurants are nearby. A golf course is 1½ mi away, and horseback riding is 3 mi away. Picnic area. Some kitchenettes, cable TV. Pool. Tennis. Beach, boating. Playground. | 4685 Lake Shore Dr. | 518/644–5591 | 22 rooms, 28 cottages | $79–$109 rooms, $505–$1192 cottages (7–day minimum stay) | Closed mid-Oct.–mid-May | D, MC, V.

Carey's Lakeside Cottages. Some of the units at this one-story building on the water have fireplaces. Restaurant. Cable TV. | Lakeside Drive | 518/644–3091 | 35 rooms | $72–$88 | Closed Nov.–Mar. | No credit cards.

Horicon Heights. Here you'll find rustic, 50-year-old cabins on 10 wooded acres bordering Lake George. Kitchenettes. Beach, dock. | 5592 Lake Shore Dr. | 518/644–9440 | fax 518–644–9440 | 6 cabins | $300–$525 per week | Closed mid-Oct.–mid-May | No credit cards.

House of Scotts. This inn with a beautiful view of Lake George is next to a public beach. Rooms have mission oak–style furniture. Restaurant. Cable TV. Pool. | 4943 Lake Shore Dr. | 518/644–9955 | 6 rooms | $60 | Closed Nov.–mid-Apr. | AE, D, MC, V.

Melody Manor. This two-story building on 9 acres overlooks 300 ft of lakefront. Restaurant, bar, picnic area. Cable TV. Pool. Tennis. Beach, boating. | 4610 Lake Shore Dr. | 518/644–9750 | 40 rooms | $112–$135 | Closed late Oct.–Apr. | AE, DC, MC, V.

Sagamore Resort. Expect to be pampered at this epitome of the grand old hotel. Horse-drawn carriages tour the grounds, and some of the rooms have fireplaces. Restaurant *(see Trillium)*, bar, room service. In-room data ports, some microwaves, cable TV. Pool. Beauty salon, hot tub, spa. 18-hole golf course, putting green, tennis. Gym, racquetball Beach, dock, boating, bicycles. Ice-skating, cross-country skiing. Shops. Children's programs (ages 3–12), playground. Business services, airport shuttle. | 110 Sagamore Rd. | 518/644–9400 or 800/358–3585 | fax 518/644–2604 | www.thesagamore.com | 100 rooms in hotel, 240 suites in lodge | $240–380 rooms, $340 suites | AE, D, DC, MC, V.

Seminole Lodge. Fully equipped cottages on the water. Cable TV. Beach, dock, boating. | 186-1 Palisades Rd., Brant Lake | 518/494–3029 | fax 518/434–5439 | 10 cottages | $55–$90 | Closed Columbus Day–Memorial Day | No credit cards.

Victorian Village. This hotel on the lake south of Bolton Landing has a beach front view. Restaurants are within walking distance. No air-conditioning in some rooms, cable TV. Tennis. Beach, boating. | 4818 Lake Shore Dr. | 518/644–9401 | 30 rooms | $71–$79 | Closed mid-Oct.–mid-May | MC, V.

BOONVILLE

MAP 3, I5

(Nearby town also listed: Old Forge)

A small town on the border of the Adirondack region, Boonville is one of the gateway towns to the Adirondack Park. The town was named after Garret Boon, an agent of the Holland Land Company, which owned land in the area at the turn of the 18th century. Railroading put the town on the map in the mid-1800s, and you can still see remnants of a more affluent past in the grand old homes along Schuyler Street.

Information: **Boonville Area Chamber of Commerce** | 122 Main St., Box 163, 13309 | 315/942–5112.

Attractions

Constable Hall. The restored 1800s Georgian mansion of William Constable is now a National Historic Landmark. Nine miles northeast of Boonville, the 14 rooms contain Constable's original furnishings as well as period artifacts. There are also formal gardens. | John St., Constableville | 315/397–2323 | $3 | June–mid.-Oct., Tues.–Sat. 10–4, Sun. 1–4.

Dodge-Pratt-Northam Art and Community Center. This community arts center is housed in a large Victorian building in the middle of town. | 106 Schuyler St. | 315/942–5133 | Free | Mar–late Dec., Tues.–Sat.10–4.

Erwin Park. This 20-acre park has a sand-bottom pool, a picnic area, a playground, and tennis and basketball courts. | Rte. 12 | 315/943–2061 | $2 per vehicle and $1 per person | July–Aug., daily.

Pixley Falls State Park. A 50-ft waterfall is one of the highlights of this state park near Boonville just outside the border of the Adirondack region. You can camp streamside at one of the 22 campsites, hike, fish, hunt, and cross-country ski. Picnic facilities, pavilions, and nature trails are also available. South of Boonville on Route 46. | Rte. 46 | 315/942–4713 or 315/337–

4670 | $6 per vehicle; $5 per vehicle when beach is closed; free before 8 AM or after 6 PM and Nov.–Mar. | Daily.

Snow Ridge Ski Area. Snow Ridge has 22 trails, 7 lifts, a restaurant, ski school, and baby-sitting. Head north out of Boonville on Route 12D to Route 26. | 4501 West Rd., Turin | 315/348–8456 or 800/962–8419 | Dec.–Apr., depending on ski season.

ON THE CALENDAR

AUG.: *New York State Woodsmen's Field Days.* Watch lumberjacks from as far away as Canada, Australia, and New Zealand compete in the premiere lumberjack contest in the United States. At the Boonville Oneida County Fairgrounds, Route 294. | 315/942–4593.

Dining

Buffalo Head. American. This rustic restaurant about 7 mi southeast of Boonville serves large portions of beef, seafood, poultry, pasta, and salads. Kids' menu. Southeast of Boonville. | N. Lake Rd., Forestport | 315/392–6607 | Breakfast also available | $9–$16 | AE, D, DC, MC, V.

Hulbert House. German. On summer Fridays there is an all-you-can-eat special at this casual family restaurant. Known for sauerbraten with homemade noodles, prime rib, salmon, and halibut. Salad bar. Buffet. Kids' menu. All-you-can-eat special: May–mid.-September, Friday 5–9. | 106 Main St. | 315/942–4318 | $10–$20 | AE, DC, MC, V.

Whelley's Four Seasons Restaurant. American. This casual eatery with a jukebox and fireplace is 2½ mi from downtown Boonville, overlooking the Black River. It serves a Friday fish fry that's known around town, along with steak and seafood and a full bar. | 3446 Moose River Rd. | 315/942–9036 | $8–$15 | No credit cards.

Lodging

Boonville Hotel. Built in 1860, this downtown hotel, with its 1940s cocktail lounge complete with copper ceilings and the original while leather booths, is one of Boonville's longstanding landmarks. The bar is a popular tourist site, and the rooms are often rented out by groups of snowmobilers. The accommodations, which all overlook Water Street, are not exactly luxurious—they're comparatively small and all share a bathroom at the end of the hall. Pets allowed. | 103 Water St. | 315/942–2124 | fax 315/942–2124 | 8 rooms, shared bath | $40 | AE, D, MC, V.

Headwaters Motor Lodge. This two-story building just north of Boonville is near historic Constable Hall and the Old Canal Locks through which barges used to pass. Rooms have Colonial-style furniture. It's 6 mi from downhill and cross-country skiing. Complimentary Continental breakfast. In-room data ports, some kitchenettes, refrigerators, cable TV. Some pets allowed. | Headwaters Motor Lodge, Rte. 12 | 315/942–4493 | fax 315/942–4626 | 37 rooms | $50–$55 | AE, D, MC, V.

Sugarbush Bed and Breakfast. This bed-and-breakfast at the foothills of the Adirondacks was built in the early 1800s by John Sherman, grandson of Roger Sherman, a signer of the Declaration of Independence. At one time a private boys' school, Sugarbush now has a spacious veranda, lovely gardens and orchards, and individually decorated rooms. Complimentary breakfast. No TV in many rooms. | 8451 Old Poland Rd., Barneveld | 315/896–6860 or 800/582–5845 | www.adirondacktravel.com/sbush.html | 5 rooms, 2 suites | $55–$145 | AE, MC, V.

BREWSTER

MAP 3, C1

(Nearby towns also listed: Carmel/Lake Carmel, Mahopac, North Salem, Pound Ridge)

Country roads wind through hillside scenery in this village. Founded in 1730, Brewster developed along with the iron mining and dairy industries in the 19th century. In

1864, the Borden Milk Factory was constructed here, and more than 200 dairy farmers supplied the region with 20,000 gallons of milk each day.

Main Street is still the heart of the village and maintains much of its original character. The town, which now has a population of 2,000, boasts an active railroad station, antiques shops, and many turn-of-the-20th-century buildings.

Information: **Brewster Chamber of Commerce** | 31 Main St., 10509 | 845/279–2477 | www.brewsterchamber.com.

Attractions
Southeast Museum. An educational and cultural institution established in 1963, the Southeast Museum provides exhibition programs, lectures, conferences, children's activities, tours, and cultural events. It's in the 1896 Old Town Hall, one of Putnam County's largest landmark buildings. Local history exhibits examine the Harlem Line Railroad, the Borden Milk Condensery, and the Croton Reservoir System. | 67 Main St. | 845/279–7500 | fax 845/279–1992 | www.southeastmuseum.org | $3 suggested donation | Apr.–Dec., Tues., Wed., Sat. 10–4, Fri. 12–5.

Thunder Ridge Ski Area. Of the 32 trails on the 100 acres of this ski area, 40% are for beginners. The remainder are divided evenly between intermediate and advanced trails. You can also go night skiing. North of Brewster on Route 22. | Rte. 22, Patterson | 845/878–4100 | fax 845/878–2279 | www.thunderridgeski.com | $25 | Dec.–Mar., daily.

Dining
The Arch. French. A massive fireplace, vibrant yellow walls, and fresh flowers create an elegant backdrop for the seasonal specialties served here. Outside, colorful gardens surround the stone cottage that houses the restaurant. Specials include mangrove snapper and grilled antelope steak. Kids' menu. Sunday brunch. Open-air dining on patio. | Rte. 22 | 845/279–5011 | www.archrestaurant.com | Jacket required | Closed Mon., Tues. | $25–$50 | AE, D, DC, MC, V.

BRIDGEHAMPTON/WATER MILL
MAP 3, E2

(Nearby towns also listed: Amagansett, East Hampton, Sag Harbor, Southampton)

The beautiful beaches are just part of the attraction at these two quiet, graceful Hampton communities. Elegant Bridgehampton has attractive antiques shops, art galleries, and restaurants in which you can sip wine made from grapes grown in local vineyards. This is also polo country, and Bridgehampton is home to the prestigious annual Hampton Classic Horse Show.

Water Mill is the nation's only community with a functional, working water mill and windmill. Water Mill's beautiful farms and wineries also draw visitors.

Information: **East Hampton Chamber of Commerce** | 79A Main St., East Hampton 11937 | 631/324–0362.

Attractions
Duck Walk Vineyards. A Normandy-style château sits on 56 beautiful acres of vineyards. You can taste the wine and take a tour. | 231 Montauk Hwy., Water Mill | 631/726–7555 | Free | Daily 11–6.

Poxabogue County Park. These attractive 26 acres include a ½-mi nature walk. | Poxabogue La. | 631/854–4949 | Free | Daily dawn–dusk.

Sagg Main Beach. Southampton town beach offers 1,500 ft of ocean beach. Lifeguards are on duty; facilities include showers, rest rooms, a food stand, picnic tables, and volleyball.

Beachgoers must get a parking permit. | 314 Surf Side Dr., Bridgehampton | 631/283–6011 | Call for permit and parking fees | Lifeguards: May 31–June 25, weekends 10–6; June 26–Sept. 6, daily 10–6.

Water Mill Museum. Originally built in 1644, the oldest operating water mill on Long Island is still fully operational today. You can work the lathe and learn the arts of quilting and weaving. Uncle Fred's workshop, also on site, has handmade toys. Just 3 mi south of East Hampton, 500 ft off Route 27. | 41 Old Mill Rd., Water Mill | 631/726–4625 | $3 suggested donation | June–Sept., Thurs.–Mon. 11–5, Sun. 1–5.

ON THE CALENDAR

AUG.: *Hampton Classic Horse Show.* North America's largest outdoor hunter/jumper horse show draws 40,000 spectators. | 240 Snake Hollow Rd., Bridgehampton | 631/537–3177.

AUG: *Members Art Show.* An evening reception launches this four-day art show in which local artists and craftspeople display their work at the Water Mill Museum. | 631/726–4625.

Dining

Bobby Van's. American. The French doors and the large fans continually spinning overhead give this restaurant a distinctly *Casablanca* feeling. It's known as much for people-watching near its open doors as for its food. Popular dishes include: classic prime aged beef, fresh fish, chicken, and pasta. Raw bar. Pianist in winter. Sunday brunch. No smoking. | 2393 Main St., Bridgehampton | 631/537–0590 | Reservations essential Fri., Sat. | $35–$50 | AE, D, DC, MC, V.

95 School Street. American. The emphasis is on fresh local seafood at this restaurant with two candlelit dining rooms and white walls hung with mirrors. Try diver scallops with potato gratin, or crab cakes with avocado, mango, and tomato. | 95 School St., Bridgehampton | 516/537–5555 | Reservations essential | No lunch | $19–$26 | AE, DC, MC, V.

Old Stone Pub. Steak. This simple, charming restaurant in a 200-year-old farmhouse is known for its oversize portions of broiled steak and lamb chops. East of Bridgehampton. | 3516 Montauk Hwy., Sagaponack | 631/537–3300 | Closed Tues. No lunch | $35–$45 | AE.

Lodging

Inn at Box Farm. Originally a colonial farmhouse dating back to the late 1600s, this shingled house has been expanded over the years and derives its form and style from early English and Dutch traditional houses. Rooms are furnished with antiques and the beds are covered with thick comforters. Beaches are within ½ mi of the inn. Complimentary breakfast. No smoking. | 78 Mecox Rd., Water Mill | 631/726–9507 | fax 631/726–5074 | inn@box-farm.com | www.boxfarm.com | 12 rooms | $150–$250 | AE, D, DC, MC, V.

BUFFALO

(Nearby towns also listed: Amherst, Batavia, Clarence, East Aurora, Grand Island, Hamburg, Niagara Falls, Williamsville)

Snow, the Buffalo Bills, and the gateway to Niagara Falls are just some of the things that come to mind when most people think of Buffalo. While it is true that the city is hit by at least one to four memorable snowstorms a year, Buffalo doesn't actually receive a great deal of snow compared to many other cities in New York. Buffalo is indeed a great sports town with tough professional teams, but it is also the home of Buffalo Wings, Beef on Weck (thin-sliced, juicy roast beef and fresh horseradish on a pretzel-salt and caraway-seed encrusted hard roll) and Sponge Candy (a sweet confection with an airy, toffee-like center inside a chocolate shell). Spectacular nearby Niagara Falls is Buffalo's greatest attraction, yet the city also boasts world-class architecture, a foremost cancer-research institute, and one of the four research universities of the State University of New York.

The city's growth began in the early 1800s when ships from the Great Lakes transported millions of bushels of grain from Midwest farms to Buffalo. In 1825, the completion of the Erie Canal connected Buffalo to Albany, and Lake Erie to the Hudson River, allowing the grain to be distributed along the East Coast, and Buffalo became known as the "Queen City on the Lake." Railroad tracks laid along the route of the Erie Canal continued the great migration of products. Laborers were needed to handle the boats, grain, and, later, the steel mills. The thousands of immigrants who came to fill those jobs brought rich ethnic diversity to Buffalo.

Buffalo's success as a commercial crossroads resulted in a booming economy at the turn of the 20th century, and Delaware Avenue, known as Millionaire Row, was lined with majestic mansions. It was in one of these mansions that Theodore Roosevelt was inaugurated President after President William McKinley was assassinated in 1901.

Buffalo hosts great jazz and theater productions, as well as art exhibitions. Over 10 resident theater companies put on a broad range of plays in the downtown Theater District on Main Street not far from the waterfront. In summer months, Shakespeare plays are performed outside for free in Delaware Park, across the street from the internationally known Albright-Knox Art Gallery, which has an outstanding collection of 20th-century American Art.

Information: **Greater Buffalo Convention and Visitors Bureau** | 617 Main St., Suite 400 | 716/852–0511.

TRANSPORTATION INFORMATION

Airports: Buffalo Niagara International Airport. Nonstop service is available to 24 cities. More than 3 million passengers arrive and depart annually. | Genesee St. off Rte. 33 | 716/630–6000 | www.buffaloairport.com.

Amtrak. Provides national rail service. | 75 Exchange St. | 716/856–2075.

Bus Lines: Greyhound provides national bus service. | 181 Ellicott St. | 716/855–7531, 800/231–2222 reservations.

Driving Around Town: Buffalo is reached most easily from the south and east by the New York State Thruway, I–90, a toll road. I–190 provides access from the north. The beltway around the city is composed of these highways plus I–290. Congestion on the highways is light even during rush hours; the worst of it is on I–90 going west between exits 53 and 55 during the morning (7–8:30) and east in the early evening (4:30–5:30). In general the speed limit for residential streets is 30 mph. A good mix of one-way and two-way streets makes travel convenient. Downtown parking can be found on the street, in metered lots, open-air lots, and parking garages. Rates for meters are $1 per hour with a 2-hr maximum. Fines for expired meters begin at $20. Daily rates for lots and garages vary from $4.25 to $5, while 1/2-hr rates begin at $1.50. At the northern end of town, near the State College, parking can be found on the street, in residential neighborhoods, or on the campus itself.

NEIGHBORHOODS

Downtown. Architectural treasures fill Buffalo's downtown. During the late 1800s and early 1900s, the city enjoyed an economic boom that resulted in the construction of many ornate structures, including some of the world's first skyscrapers. Buildings range in style from the Art Deco City Hall to the Beaux-Arts Theatre Place. In addition to handsome facades, many buildings have exquisite interiors and are open to the public during business hours on weekdays. Posters inside often give a brief history of the building and its construction.

Theatre District. This small area at the north end of Main Street between Chippewa and Tupper Streets includes Shea's Performing Arts Center and Tralfamadore Café.
Elmwood Avenue. An area along Elmwood Avenue is famous for its record shops, boutiques, used book stores, hip bars, and eateries, all aimed at the twenty-somethings who fill Buffalo's six institutions of higher learning. The youthful feel extends along Elmwood from Allentown, at North Street, to the State College, in the 1300 block of Elmwood. Structures here are mostly two-story red-brick buildings, though there are some Victorian homes too, especially closer to Allentown.

WALKING TOUR

Begin your tour at one of the country's finest examples of Art Deco architecture, the City Hall in the large plaza of Niagara Square. The Guaranty Building stands three blocks southeast of the plaza on the corner of Church and Pearl Streets. Three blocks due east of the plaza and City Hall is Lafayette Square, on which stands the Public Library. Along Main Street, you'll see fine examples of late 19th-century architecture, many in the Renaissance style. On Main at Huron Street is the Hyatt Regency Hotel, and two blocks farther on is the Theatre District with Shea's Performing Arts Center and the Tralfamadore Café.

From the downtown area you can take the Light Rapid Rail System north to the Allen Street stop or drive 1 mi north to Allen Street. At the station, you'll be in the center of Allentown, surrounded by many Victorian homes, boutiques, and restaurants. Just north of Allen Street, on Delaware Avenue, is the Wilcox Mansion: Theodore Roosevelt Inaugural National Historic Site.

DRIVING TOUR

From Delaware Avenue, drive ¼ mi east to Elmwood Avenue and follow it north for 2 mi to the Albright-Knox Art Gallery. Along the way you'll pass many of the city's best shops and restaurants. Once at the gallery, you can park your car and walk across the street to the campus of Buffalo State College where you'll find the Burchfield-Penney Art Center and the Buffalo Center for the Arts. Walk across the Scajaquada Creek, still along Elmwood, to reach the Buffalo and Erie County Historical Society. Then you can drive east on Nottingham Road, skirting the northern border of Delaware Park, until you reach the Buffalo Zoological Gardens. From the zoo, backtrack along Nottingham Road to Delaware, then drive south on Delaware for approximately a mile to Delavan Avenue and the entrance to Forest Lawn Cemetery.

From the cemetery, drive east on Delavan Avenue until you reach Route 198. Take this highway south until you come to Martin Luther King Jr. Park. The Buffalo Museum of Science is at the northwest corner of the park.

Attractions

ART AND ARCHITECTURE

City Hall. This outstanding building in the heart of downtown is one of the country's Art Deco architectural masterpieces. Go up to the observation deck for a spectacular view of both the city and the Lake Erie waterfront. | Niagara Sq. | 716/851–5891 | fax 716/851–4791 | Free | Weekdays 8–5.

Frank Lloyd Wright residences. Several examples of the work of renowned architect Frank Lloyd Wright can be found in Buffalo. The Darwin Martin House is in Wright's early Prairie style. | Darwin Martin House: 125 Jewitt Pkwy.; Barton House: 118 Summit Ave.; Tillinghast | 716/856–3858 | $10 | Tours Sat. 10, Sun. 1; summer, also Wed. 1 PM.

Guaranty Building. America's earliest skyscraper was designed by Louis Sullivan and built in 1895–96. Also known as the Prudential Building. | 28 Church St. | 716/852–0511.

BEACHES, PARKS, AND NATURAL SIGHTS

Buffalo and Erie County Botanical Gardens. Even in the middle of winter, you can enjoy the sights and scents of the tropics under the domes of this Victorian glass conservatory. The 12 greenhouses shelter exotics, cacti, fruit trees, palms, and orchids. Guided tours by reservation. | 2655 S. Park Ave. | 716/827–1587 | fax 716/828–0091 | www.buffalogardens.com | Donations accepted | Weekdays 9–4 (Wed. 9–6), weekends 9–5.

Tifft Nature Preserve. Five miles of nature trails, boardwalks, and a cattail marsh make this wildlife refuge near the Lake Erie shore an ideal place for hiking, bird-watching, and picnics. Part of the Buffalo Museum of Science. | 1200 Fuhrmann Blvd. | 716/825–6397 | fax 716/824–6718 | www.sciencebuff.org | webmaster@sciencebuff.org | $2 suggested donation | Daily dawn–dusk; visitors center Tues.–Sun. 9–5.

CULTURE, EDUCATION, AND HISTORY

Allentown. The streets in this historic district are lined with buildings in a mix of architectural styles dating from the mid-1800s through the turn of the 20th century. Allentown's rough boundaries are Main Street to the east, Edward Street to the south, North Street to the north, and Cottage and Pennsylvania streets to the west. Local sightseeing companies offer architectural tours. | 234 Allen St. (Historic District Office) | 716/881–1024 | Free | Historic district office Tues.–Fri. 9–5, Sat. 9:30–1:30.

Buffalo and Erie County Historical Society. This is one of the oldest regional historical societies in the country, and the largest in western New York. Tens of thousands of old books, artifacts, photographs, and manuscripts document the region's history. The building was originally designed for the Pan-American Exhibition in 1901 and is now a historical landmark. | 25 Nottingham Ct., at Elmwood Ave. | 716/873–9644 | fax 716/873–8754 | bech@buffnet.net | www.intotem.buffnet.net/bechs | $4 | Tues.–Sat. 10–5, Sun. 12–5.

Buffalo and Erie County Naval and Military Park. A guided missile cruiser, destroyer, and a World II submarine are on display at this 6-acre waterfront site, the largest naval park of its kind in the nation. | 1 Naval Park Cove | 716/847–1773 | fax 716/847–6405 | www.buffalonavalpark.org | npark@ci.buffalo.ny.us | $6 | Apr.–Oct., daily 10–5; Nov., weekends 10–4.

Buffalo and Erie County Public Library. This modern library downtown houses more than 3 million books on 58 mi of shelving. The Mark Twain Room features a rare book collection and other memorabilia. | 1 Lafayette Sq. | 716/858–8900 | fax 716/858–6211 | www.buffalolib.org | $1 | Labor Day–Memorial Day, Mon.–Wed., Fri., Sat. 8:30–6, Thurs. 8:30–8, Sun. 1–5; call for hrs rest of year.

WHAT TO PACK IN THE TOY TOTE FOR KIDS

- ❏ Audiotapes
- ❏ Books
- ❏ Clipboard
- ❏ Coloring/activity books
- ❏ Doll with outfits
- ❏ Hand-held games
- ❏ Magnet games
- ❏ Notepad
- ❏ One-piece toys
- ❏ Pencils, colored pencils
- ❏ Portable stereo with earphones
- ❏ Sliding puzzles
- ❏ Travel toys

*Excerpted from *Fodor's: How to Pack: Experts Share Their Secrets*
© 1997, by Fodor's Travel Publications

Buffalo State College. This arts-and-sciences school has a 115-acre urban campus in the historic Elmwood district. | 1300 Elmwood Ave. | 716/878–6100 | fax 716/878–3039 | www.buffalostate.edu | Free | Daily.

Forest Lawn Cemetery. Countless trails wind through this beautiful, 270-acre, parklike cemetery within the heart of Buffalo. President Millard Fillmore is among the notable people buried here. Trolley rides and walking tours are available in summer months. | 1411 Delaware Ave. | 716/885–1600, 716/583–8687 reservations | fax 716/881–6482 | Free | Tours June–Sept.

Klienhans Music Hall. The Buffalo Philharmonic Orchestra plays a variety of classical and pop concerts throughout the year at this hall renowned for its excellent acoustics. Civic, religious, and cultural activities also take place here. | Symphony Circle | 716/883–3560 | fax 716/883–7430 | Call for hrs.

Shea's Performing Arts Center. This center built in the style of a European Opera House presents opera, dance, concerts, children's shows, and touring plays. The building is included in the National Register of Historic Places. | 646 Main St. | 716/847–1410 | fax 716/847–1644 | sheas@sheas.org | www.shea.org | Call for schedule.

State University of New York at Buffalo. Millard Fillmore was the first chancellor of this public university founded in 1846. Today, the university is home to some 20,800 graduate and undergraduate students. The university's main campus complex is located in suburban Amherst, while the south campus is located within the city of Buffalo. | 3435 Main St. | 716/645–2000 | fax 716/645–6498 | www.buffalo.edu | Free | Daily.

Buffalo Center for the Arts. Performances and visual arts programs and exhibits take place here on the North campus of the State University of New York at Buffalo. | 103 Center for the Arts | 716/645–2787 | fax 716/645–6929 | www.wings.buffalo.edu/arts/ | cfa@cfabuffalo.edu | Box office hrs Tues.–Fri. 12–5.

Studio Arena Theatre. Western New York's premier resident theater puts on seven mainstage and two second-stage productions annually. The smaller second-stage theater is just across the street. | 710 Main St. | 716/856–5650 or 800/77–STAGE | fax 716/856–3415 | www.studioarena.org | $15–$37.50 | Sept.–May; call for schedule.

Tralfamadore Café. This performance space features light dramas and first-class jazz, blues, r&b, and rock acts. The box office opens 2 hrs prior to shows. | 622 Main St. | 716/851–8725 | fax 716/851–8728 | tralf@buffnet.net | Call for hrs.

Wilcox Mansion: Theodore Roosevelt Inaugural National Historical Site. After President William McKinley was assassinated at the Pan-American Exposition in 1901, Theodore Roosevelt was inaugurated as the nation's 26th president in the library of this mansion. You can take guided tours, and view exhibits and gardens. Architectural walking tours are also available. | 641 Delaware Ave. | 716/884–0095 | fax 716/884–0330 | www.nps.gov/thri | $3 | Weekdays 9–5, weekends 12–5.

MUSEUMS

African-American Cultural Center. Houses the African world studies archives, the Paul Robeson Theater, and Tas'hama Children's peer Performance Dance Group. | 350 Masten Ave. | 716/884–2013 | fax 716/885–2590 | Admission varies per event | Mon.–Sat. 10–6.

The **Paul Robeson Theater** was founded in 1968 and named for the multigifted singer/actor/scholar/athlete/activist. It has a Mother's Day dinner theater. | 350 Masten Ave. | 716/884–2013 | fax 716/885–2590 | $14.50 | Jan.–May and Sept.–Dec., Fri., Sat. 8 PM, Sun. 6 PM.

Albright-Knox Art Gallery. Twentieth-century art is wonderfully well represented here. The gallery's collections are especially rich in postwar American and European art, including Pollock, Johns, and Warhol. Works by Picasso, van Gogh, Monet, Matisse, and Renoir are here as well. On Sunday afternoons, there are free jazz performances on the massive steps leading up to the Greek Revival museum. | 1285 Elmwood Ave. | 716/882–8700 | fax 716/882–1958 | www.albrightknox.org | bmccall@albrightknox.org | $4 | Tues.–Sat. 11–5, Sun. 12–5.

BUFFALO

INTRO
ATTRACTIONS
DINING
LODGING

Buffalo Museum of Science. Exhibits cover everything from anthropology to zoology. One special exhibit uses the stories of three mummies to explore what daily life was like in ancient Egypt for ordinary citizens. Special family and children's events and activities. | 1020 Humboldt Pkwy., off Rte. 33 | 716/896–5200 | fax 716/897–6723 | www.sciencebuff.org | webmaster@sciencebuff.org | $6 | June–Aug., Tues.–Sun. 10–5; Sept.–May, Tues.–Thurs., Fri. 10–10, weekends 10–5; observatory open Fri. evenings.

Burchfield-Penney Art Center. This premier showcase for western New York artists spotlights the works of watercolorist Charles Burchfield, and handcrafted objects from the Roycroft Arts and Crafts community. | Buffalo State College, 1300 Elmwood Ave. | 716/878–6011 | fax 716/878–6003 | www.burchfield-penney.org | burchfield@buffalostate.edu | Free | Tues.–Sat. 10–5, Sun. 1–5.

Pedaling History Bicycle Museum. More than 300 rare and unique bicycles are on display here, at one of the largest bicycle museums in the world. South of Buffalo in Orchard Park. | 3943 N. Buffalo Rd., Orchard Park | 716/662–3853 | fax 716/662–4514. | bicyclemus@aol.com | www.pedalinghistory.com | $4.50 | Mon.–Sat. 11–5, Sun. 1:30–5.

QRS Music Rolls, Inc. The world's oldest and largest manufacturer of player piano rolls features historic instrument displays. | 1026 Niagara St. | 716/885–4600 or 800/247–6557 | fax 716/885–7510 | $2 | Tours weekdays at 10 and 2.

Steel Plant Museum. Photos, exhibits, and memorabilia pay tribute to western New York's steel workers, and what was once the largest steel plant in the world, Bethlehem Steel. It's housed in a beautiful Carnegie Library in Lackawanna, south of Buffalo. | 560 Ridge Rd., Lackawanna | 716/823–0630 | Mon. and Wed. 1–9; Tues., Thurs.–Sat. 10–5; closed Sat. July–Labor Day.

SHOPPING

Broadway Market. This traditional European indoor marketplace features more than 40 vendors of ethnic delicacies, such as kielbasa, perogi, and bratwurst. | 999 Broadway, off Rte. 62 | 716/893–0705 | fax 716/893–2216 | manager@broadwaymarket.com | www.broadwaymarket.com | Free | Weekdays 8–5, Sat. 7–5.

SPORTS AND RECREATION

Marine Midland Arena. This state-of-the-art sports-and-entertainment complex downtown near the waterfront hosts hockey, basketball, and football games, as well as top concert and family shows. | 1 Seymour Knox III Plaza | 716/855–4100 | fax 716/855–4110 | www.sabres.com | Call for hrs.

Professional sports. Buffalo is home to major sports teams, such as the NFL's **Buffalo Bills** (Ralph Wilson Stadium, 1 Bills Dr., Orchard Park Stadium | 716/648–1800 or 800/BBTICKS | info@buffalobills.com | www.buffalobills.com | Call for schedule) and the NHL's **Buffalo Sabres** (HSBC Arena, 1 Seymour Knox III Plaza | 716/649–1280 | fax 716/649–0030 | www.sabres.com | Call for schedule).

SIGHTSEEING TOURS/TOUR COMPANIES

Gray Line bus tours. Gray Line offers a variety of sightseeing tours in the Buffalo and Niagara Falls areas. Try the Rainbow Tour to Ontario, or the Niagara Falls Adventure Tour, both about 12 mi due north of downtown Buffalo. | 3466 Niagara Falls Blvd. N, Tonawanda | 716/283–1378 | fax 716/692–4398 | www.grayline-niagarafalls.com | Daily.

Miss Buffalo Clipper Cruises and Niagara Clipper Cruises. Take an excursion on the water along the international border with Canada, or pass through the historic Black Rock Lock and Canal. Other cruises view Buffalo's original lighthouse and old Fort Erie. Reservations are needed for many cruises. | Miss Buffalo: 79 Marine Dr. (departure is next to Buffalo Naval and Military Park); Niagara Clipper: 650 River Rd., North Tonawanda | 716/856–6696 | fax 716/856–8901 | www.missbuffalo.com | May–Oct.; call for specific tour times.

OTHER POINTS OF INTEREST

Buffalo Zoological Gardens. Endangered Siberian tigers, Asian elephants, and pancake tortoises are among the over 1,000 wild and exotic animals found in this natural setting in Delaware Park. The grounds also include a children's zoo and petting area, as well as the interactive **World of Wildlife Discovery Center.** | 300 Parkside Ave. | 716/837–3900 | fax 716/837–0738 | www.buffalozoo.org | $7; parking $3 per car, $6 per bus | May–Sept., weekdays 10–5, weekends 10–5:30; Oct.–Apr., daily 10–4.

ON THE CALENDAR

APR.: *Spring Flower Show.* The Buffalo and Erie County Botanical Gardens put on fragrant displays of hyacinths, daffodils, and lilies. | 716/827–1587.

APR.–SEPT.: *NHRA Drag Racing, Stock Car Racing.* Amateurs and professionals take part in these National Hot Rod Association drag and stock-car races at the Lancaster Motor Sports Park, in Lancaster, 10 mi east of Buffalo off Route 33. | 716/759–6818.

MAY: *Greek Hellenic Festival.* Kick off warm weather with authentic Greek food, music, dancing, displays, bazaars, and costumes. | At the Hellenic Greek Church, Delaware Ave. at West Utica | 716/882–9485.

JUNE: *The Allentown Arts Festival.* This nationally acclaimed fine arts–and–crafts show brings nearly 500 exhibits, music, food, colorful spectacles, and outstanding people-watching to the Allentown district. | 716/881–4269.

JUNE: *Juneteenth Festival.* This two-day, family-oriented festival commemorates the end of slavery with food, music, entertainment, and a parade at Martin Luther King Park, Best Street and Fillmore Avenue. | 716/857–2121.

JUNE–AUG.: *Plaza Event Series.* These free lunchtime summer performances bring jazz, big bands, dance, top 40, gospel, and community theater to the M and T Plaza on Main Street. Don't forget your bag lunch. | 716/842–5405.

JUNE–AUG.: *Shakespeare in the Park.* Bring a picnic basket and a blanket and enjoy the magic of these free evening performances of full-length plays. Performances take place behind the Rose Gardens in Delaware Park. | 716/856–4533.

JUNE–AUG.: *Thursday at the Square Concert Series.* Free musical shows during summer months with a diverse lineup of entertainment, and complimentary food and drink. | Lafayette Sq., downtown | 716/856–3150.

JULY: *Canal Fest of the Tonawandas.* Nautical displays and a midway with rides and games are set up along the Eric Canal for eight days. | Erie Canal Banks | 716/692–3292.

JULY: *A Taste of Buffalo.* Western New York's biggest outdoor festival takes on Main Street with more than 150 culinary specialties from outstanding eating establishments offered at nominal prices. | 716/831–9376.

DEC.: *First Night Buffalo.* Artists perform at this New Year's Eve celebration held at the Buffalo and Erie Country Historical Society. Midnight is marked with a blaze of fireworks. This event is alcohol and drug free. | 716/635–4959 | www.firstnight.buffnet.net.

Dining

INEXPENSIVE

Anchor Bar and Restaurant. American. This restaurant claims to have been the originator of Buffalo wings. A buffalo's head hangs on the wall along with antiques from old ships. Jazz Friday and Saturday. | 1047 Main St. | 716/886–8920 | $5–$16 | AE, D, DC, MC, V.

Blackthorn. American. Photographs of Ireland adorn the walls of this friendly family restaurant with a mahogany-and-oak dining room. The extensive menu includes seafood and steak. Buffet lunch. | 2134 Seneca St. | 716/825–9327 | $9–$15 | AE, DC, MC, V.

Ilio Dipaolo's. Italian. This casual family restaurant in a southern suburb of Buffalo is known for steak, seafood, and Italian specialties. Kids' menu. Early bird dinners. No smoking. | 3785 Park Ave., Blasdell | 716/825–3675 | No lunch weekends | $8–$18 | AE, D, MC, V.

Old Man River. American. There are no tables at this small, old-timey spot; just a few booths and a long Formica sandwich counter. You can eat in or take your burger or sandwich to go. The restaurant also has a clam-and-lobster bar in summer. Kids' menu. | 375 Niagara St., Tonawanda | 716/693–5558 | Closed Nov.–Feb. | $7–$12 | No credit cards.

Prima Pizza Pasta. Italian. You have your choice of two floors at this restaurant known for pizza, chicken fingers, chicken wings, and pasta. | 396 Pearl St. | 716/852–5555 | $7–$15 | D, MC, V.

MODERATE

Al-E-Oops. Barbecue. If you're craving barbecue, this is your place. Just outside Buffalo proper in the eastern suburb of Lancaster. Try the ribs or the chicken. Kids' menu. | 5389 Genesee St., Lancaster | 716/681–0200 | Closed Mon. | $10–$18 | MC, V | Tues.–Thurs. 11:30–10, Fri. 11:30–midnight, Sat. 3–midnight, Sun. 3–9.

Coda. French. The limited but delicious menu at this small restaurant with lace tablecloths changes weekly. It has health-conscious, low-fat menu items and prix-fixe meals. No smoking. | 350 Pennsylvania Ave. | 716/886–6647 | Reservations essential | Closed July–Aug. No lunch | $12–$18 | No credit cards.

Coles. American. This award-winning restaurant has been around since the 1940s. Try the swordfish sandwich. | 1104 Elmwood Ave. | 716/886–1449 | $15–$25 | AE, D, DC, MC, V.

Park Lane Tavern and Oyster Bar. American. This restaurant in the heart of town is housed in a mansion-style building. Dark hardwood floors and low lighting create the backdrop for steak, seafood, and pasta. | 33 Gates Cir. | 716/881–2603 | No lunch Fri., Sat. | $16–$26 | AE, MC, V.

Rue Franklin West. French. French doors open onto a beautiful landscaped courtyard. The changing menu offers modern French dishes such as fresh seafood, venison, wild striped bass, and rack of lamb. In summer, dine on the courtyard surrounded by the garden. | 341 Franklin St. | 716/852–4416 | Closed Sun., Mon. No lunch | $18–$23 | AE, DC, MC, V.

Salvatore's Italian Gardens. Italian. Candles, white tablecloths, and cherry-wood furniture are a romantic complement to the steak, prime rib, lobster, and seafood served here. The restaurant is near Genesee Street, close to Buffalo International Airport. Entertainment Friday and Saturday. Kids' menu. | 6461 Transit Rd. | 716/683–7990 | No lunch | $13–$43 | AE, D, MC, V.

EXPENSIVE

Fiddle Heads. American. The casual, experimental cuisine changes seasonally at this restaurant where you have a choice of two different dining areas. One has an arty, downtown-Manhattan watering-hole feel, while the other has dim lighting and a more low-key, sedate demeanor. Try pesto chicken on homemade focaccia, grilled Portobello and Italian deli sandwiches, or the pizza of the day. | 62 Allen St. | 716/883–4166 | Closed Sun., Mon. | $25–$30 | D, MC, V.

Lord Chumley's. Continental. Serves a variety of dishes, including mussels Rockefeller, Gulf shrimp cocktail, roasted duck, pepper steak, stuffed mushrooms, and jambalaya. The main dining area has acres of polished hardwood, soft gold lighting, and linen tablecloths. Lord Chumley's is a favorite spot for couples out on the town for a romantic evening. Entertainment. No smoking. | 481 Delaware St., between Virginia St. and Allen St. | 716/886–2220 | No lunch | $21–$52 | AE, D, DC, MC, V.

Lodging

INEXPENSIVE

Broadway Motel. This is a basic, one-level motel in the eastern suburb of Cheektowaga, about 7 mi outside downtown Buffalo near the airport. Cable TV. | 3895 Broadway, Cheektowaga | 716/683–2222 | 22 rooms | $34 | D, MC, V.

MODERATE

Comfort Suites. This chain hotel offers standard suites near the Buffalo airport. Complimentary Continental breakfast. In-room data ports, microwaves, refrigerators, cable TV. Pool. Hot tub. Tennis. Exercise equipment. Laundry facilities. Business services, airport shuttle, free parking. | 901 Dick Rd. | 716/633–6000 or 800/228–5150 | fax 716/633–6858 | www.comfortinn.com | 100 suites | $51–$125 | AE, D, DC, MC, V.

Days Inn. This Days Inn is directly across from the airport and within a 5-min drive of two large shopping malls. Restaurant, complimentary Continental breakfast, room service. In-room data ports, cable TV. Pool. Business services, airport shuttle. Free parking. | 4345 Genesee St. | 716/631–0800 or 800/DAYS–INN | fax 716/631–7589 | www.daysinn.com | 130 rooms | $59–$99 | AE, D, DC, MC, V.

Lenox. This 19th-century hotel stands in the Allentown district around the corner from the Theodore Roosevelt Inauguration Site. Though the building has been renovated a number of times since it was built, it retains its turn-of-the-century charm with high ceilings, hardwood floors, and spacious rooms. No air-conditioning in some rooms, in-room data ports, some kitchenettes, cable TV. Laundry facilities. Business services. Parking (fee). | 140 North St. | 716/884–1700 or 800/82–LENOX | fax 716/885–8636 | 156 rooms | $51–$125 | AE, D, DC, MC, V.

Microtel Inn And Suites. A two-story hotel. Complimentary Continental breakfast. Cable TV. Some pets allowed. | 1 Hospitality Centre Way, Tonawanda | 716/693–8100 or 800/227–6346 | fax 716/693–8750 | 100 rooms | $50–$75 | AE, D, DC, MC, V.

EXPENSIVE

Beau Fleuve. Each of the five rooms at this bed-and-breakfast in the historic Linwood district is furnished to celebrate one of the various nationalities of the people who settled Buffalo. You can sleep in the French, the Polish, or the Irish room, among others, and in the morning, walk down an oak staircase past stained-glass windows to the dining room where a candlelit gourmet breakfast is waiting. Complimentary breakfast. No smoking. Free parking. | 242 Linwood Ave. | 716/882–6116 | beauflve@buffnet.net | www.beaufleuve.com | 5 rooms | $95 | D, MC, V.

Best Western Inn Downtown. This five-story chain is close to the theater district and shopping. Cable TV. Health club. Business services, free parking. | 510 Delaware Ave. | 716/886–8333 or 800/528–1234 | fax 716/884–3070 | 61 rooms | $101 | AE, D, DC, MC, V.

Holiday Inn–Downtown. You'll find this Holiday Inn in historic Allentown across from the Wilcox Mansion, where Theodore Roosevelt was inaugurated. It's also near the downtown business district. Restaurant, bar, room service. In-room data ports, cable TV. Pool, wading pool. Laundry facilities. Business services, airport shuttle, free parking. Some pets allowed. | 620 Delaware Ave. | 716/886–2121 or 800/465–4329 | fax 716/886–7942 | www.basshotels.com/holiday-inn | 168 rooms | $76–$125 | AE, D, DC, MC, V.

VERY EXPENSIVE

Adam's Mark Hotel. Stay here for spacious rooms and suites convenient to downtown activities. The lounge has live music and a pianist. Restaurant, bar. Some in-room hot tubs, cable TV. Pool. Health club. Shops. Free parking. | 120 Church St. | 716/845–5100 or 800/844–ADAM | fax 716/845–5377 | 486 rooms, 7 suites | $159 rooms, $235 suites | AE, D, DC, MC, V.

Homewood Suites Hotel. The apartment-style suites at this hotel have fully equipped kitchens, work desks, and sofa beds in the living room. Complimentary Continental breakfast. Some in-room hot tubs. Pool. Gym. Airport shuttle. Parking (fee). | 760 Dick Rd. | 716/685–0700 or 800/CALL–HOME | 77 suites | $109–$189 | AE, D, DC, MC, V.

Hyatt Regency Buffalo. This 1923 building in the theater district has a glass atrium addition. The beds have feather pillows and the desks are paired with ergonomic chairs. 3 restaurants, bar, room service. In-room data ports, in-room hot tubs (in suites). Beauty salon. Business services. Free parking. | 2 Fountain Plaza | 716/856–1234 | fax 716/852–6157 | www.hyatt.com | 395 rooms | $119 | AE, D, DC, MC, V.

Mansion on Delaware Ave. A beautiful old Buffalo mansion, renovated in 2000. Restaurant, bar. Complimentary Continental breakfast. Some kitchenettes, microwaves, some refrigerators, cable TV. | 414 Delaware | 716/855–1970 or 800/448–8355 | fax 716–689–4382 | 28 rooms | $145–$320 | AE, D, DC, MC, V.

Pillars Hotel. This downtown hotel offers larger-than-typical standard rooms, suites, and extended-stay rooms. Connected to the Roswell Park Cancer Institute and Buffalo General Hospital, it is also close to the Children's Hospital. The 27-inch color TVs are connected to Sony PlayStations. No-smoking rooms are available. Restaurant. Kitchenettes, cable TV. Health club. Library. Business services. | 125 High St. | 716/845–0112 or 877/633–4667 | fax 716/845–0125 | www.medinns.com | 100 rooms | $109–$149 | AE, D, DC, MC, V.

Radisson. Directly across from the airport is this chain hotel with an elegant lobby. Major malls are just 10 min away by car. Restaurant, bar (with entertainment). In-room data ports, cable TV. Pool. Hot tub. Exercise equipment. Business services, airport shuttle. Parking (fee). | 4243 Genesee St., Cheektowaga | 716/634–2300 | fax 716/632–2387 | www.radisson.com | 274 rooms, 54 suites | $119–$127 rooms, $139 suites | AE, D, DC, MC, V.

Radisson Suites. Suites at this downtown hotel have king-size beds, full-size pull-out sofas, and separate living areas. Restaurant, bar, complimentary Continental breakfast. In-room data ports, some microwaves, refrigerators, cable TV. Exercise equipment. Business services. Free parking. | 601 Main St. | 716/854–5500 or 800/333–3333 | fax 716/854–4836 | www.radisson.com | 146 suites | $129 | AE, D, DC, MC, V.

CAIRO

MAP 3, K7

(Nearby towns also listed: Catskill, Hudson, Hunter, Roxbury, Shandaken, Windham)

Tucked at the Catskill's northern peak, Cairo is a small community of old homes and shops. It is just a short ride from East Durham. Both towns are renowned for their celebration of Irish heritage.

Information: **Green County Chamber of Commerce** | 159 Jefferson Heights Blvd., Catskill, 12414 | 518/943–4222.

Attractions

Zoom Flume Waterpark at the Country Place Resort. The Catskills' largest water park has water slides, activity pools, and river rides. About 2 mi north of East Durham off Route 145. | East Durham | 518/239–4559 or 800/888–3586 | www.zoomflume.com | $16.95 | June–Sept., weekdays 10–6, weekends 10–7.

ON THE CALENDAR

MAY: *East Durham Irish Festival.* During the biggest celebration of the year in this Irish enclave, The M. J. McQuill Irish Cultural and Sports Center comes alive with bands, bagpipers, and dancers. On Route 145 E in East Durham. | 800/434–FEST | www.eastburham.org.

Lodging

Greenville Arms 1889 Inn. Rooms at this Victorian bed-and-breakfast have been individually furnished with antiques and quilts, and some have fireplaces. Tea is served in the afternoon. Downhill skiing is 18 mi away. Northeast of East Durham, at Route 32. Complimentary breakfast. No room phones, TV in common area. Pool. Hot tub. Business services.

No kids under 12. | South St., Greenville | 518/966–5219 | fax 518/966–8754 | stay@greenvillearms.com | 15 rooms | $115–$215 | Closed Nov.–Apr. | MC, V.

Pickwick Lodge. This country getaway has miles of marked hiking trails. Dining room, bar. No room phones, no TV in rooms. Pool. Putting green, tennis. Hiking. | Winterclove Rd., Round Top | 518/622–3364 | 50 rooms (25 with shared bath) | $120–$130 | AP | MC, V.

Winter Clove Inn. This early 19th-century Colonial house has an expansive front porch, acres of hardwood inside, and a vast collection of antique and antique reproduction furniture. Restaurant. No air-conditioning in some rooms, no room phones, TV in common area. 2 pools. playground. | Winter Clove Rd. off Rte. 32 | 518/622–3267 | 50 rooms | $80–$90 (2–night minimum stay) | AP | MC, V.

CANAAN

(Nearby towns also listed: Catskill, Hillsdale, Hudson)

Bordered by the beautiful Berkshire Mountains, this small (population 2,000) Columbia County town has great charm and serene beauty. It was settled by New Englanders from Massachusetts in 1778. The rustic region is known for its pristine lake—Queenchy Lake—as well as for its delightful inns. It is also close to many Berkshire attractions and ski resorts.

Information: Canaan Town Clerk | Rte. 5 S, 12029 | 518/781–3144.

Lodging

Inn at Silver Maple Farm. Once a barn, this inn on 10 acres has exposed beams and pine floors. Several of the individually furnished rooms have antique trunks and custom-made cupboards. Complimentary breakfast. Refrigerators, cable TV, some room phones. Outdoor hot tub. No kids under 12. No smoking. | Rte. 295, west of Canaan | 518/781–3600 | fax 518/781–3883 | info@silvermaplefarm.com | www.silvermaplefarm.com | 9 rooms, 2 suites | $95–$175 rooms, $225–$275 suites | AE, D, MC, V.

Mill House. Exposed beams, wood-paneled walls, and a large stucco fireplace give this 1940s inn a European flair. Its 3 acres of grounds have lovely mountain views. Some of the individually decorated rooms have fireplaces. Free afternoon tea is served daily. Complimentary Continental breakfast. No TV in some rooms. Pool. No smoking. | Rte. 43, Stephentown | 518/733–5606 | fax 518/733–6025 | fxt2@taconic.net | www.themillhouseinn.com | 12 rooms, 5 suites | $105 rooms, $115–$160 suites | Closed Sept., Nov., and mid-Mar.–mid-May | AE, V.

CANAJOHARIE

(Nearby towns also listed: Amsterdam, Cobleskill, Herkimer, Ilion, Johnstown, Richfield Springs)

Canajoharie is on Route 5S on the southern side of the Mohawk River. Founded in 1730, Canajoharie is today home to a large, operating Beech-Nut food-processing plant. The wealth of its industrial past is evident in the Canajoharie Library and Art Gallery, which has a collection of fine art donated by the late Beech-Nut factory owner, Bartlett Arkell.

Information: Montgomery County Chamber of Commerce | Box 144, St. Johnsville, 13452 | 518/842–8200.

Attractions

Canajoharie Library and Art Gallery. Winslow Homer, John Singer Sargent, and George Bellows are some of the painters whose work is displayed here. | 2 Erie Blvd. | 518/673–2314 | Free | Mon.–Wed., Fri. 10–4:45, Thurs. 10–8:30, Sat. 10–1:30.

Fort Klock. This 1750 limestone house and trading post, about 2 mi east of St. Johnsville, was a stronghold built to protect settlers from the Indians during the French and Indian War. There are early-American tools, a gathering room, and living history tours. | Rte. 5, St. Johnsville | 518/568–7779 | $1 | Late May–early Oct., Tues.–Sun. 9–5.

Fort Plain Museum. You can see Revolutionary War artifacts and Indian collections at this museum housed in a Greek Revival home on the west side of Fort Plain. The home was built in 1848 on what had been the site of a Revolutionary War fortification in the late 1700s. Northwest of Canajoharie | 389 Canal St., Ft. Plain | 518/993–2527 | Free | May–Sept., Wed.–Sun. noon–5; rest of the year by appointment.

Dining

Village Restaurant. Eclectic. This downtown diner across the street from Interstate 90 is favored by locals craving a Spanish omelet or baked ziti. Everything is made from scratch, and seasonal decorations keep things interesting. Half orders made for kids. Breakfast available. | 59 Church St. | 518/673–2596 | No dinner Fri.–Wed. | $4–$5 | No credit cards.

Lodging

Rodeway Inn. Queen- and king-size beds are available at this hotel, which is within a few blocks of restaurants and convenience stores. Some kitchenettes, cable TV. Business services. | E. Grand St., Rte. 5, Palatine Bridge | 518/673–3233 | fax 518/673–5011 | 30 rooms | $85 | AE, D, DC, MC, V.

CANANDAIGUA

MAP 3, E6

(Nearby towns also listed: Avon, Geneseo, Geneva, Palmyra, Penn Yan, Rochester, Seneca Falls, Victor, Waterloo)

This resort community sits at the north end of Canandaigua Lake, the westernmost of the major Finger Lakes. The first white settlers arrived in 1789, and it was here that the 1794 Pickering Treaty, which gave whites the right to settle in the Great Lakes basin, was signed. One of the few islands in the Finger Lakes, Squaw Island, lies at the north end of the lake. Legend has it that many Iroquois women and children escaped slaughter by hiding there during the 1779 Clinton-Sullivan campaign to drive the Iroquois out of central New York because of their allegiance to the British.

Long a favorite vacation destination for residents of nearby Rochester, Canandaigua also boasts attractions like the Sonnenberg Gardens. It is the smallest city in the state of New York with a population of 20,000.

Information: **Canandaigua Chamber of Commerce** | 113 S. Main St., 14424 | 716/394–4400.

Attractions

Bristol Mt. Ski and Snowboard Resort. With a 1,200-ft vertical drop, this is the highest ski area between the Adirondacks and the Rockies. The area has 22 slopes and trails. The longest run is 2 mi; 100% snowmaking. | 5662 Rte. 64 | 716/374–6000 | $12–$38 | Nov.–Mar.

Canandaigua Lady. You can take a leisurely cruise on the Finger Lakes in a reproduction of a 19th century double-decker paddlewheeler. The operating company offers narrated tours and brunch, lunch, and dinner cruises. Call for reservations. | 169 Lakeshore Dr. | 716/394–5365 | Excursions $12, meal cruises $20–$40 | May–Oct., Tues.–Sun.; call for hrs.

Capt. Gray's Boat Tours. Tours range from 1-hr cruises to excursions across the Finger Lakes that take 3 hrs or longer. | 770 S. Main St. | 716/394–5270 | info@captgrays.com | www.captgrays.com | Call for prices | July–Labor Day, daily 1- and 2-hr tours; Aug.–mid-Oct., alternate Sun., 3-hr and longer tours.

Finger Lakes Performing Arts Center. The outdoor amphitheater offers weekend summer concerts by the Rochester Philharmonic Orchestra, as well as national rock, jazz, and pop music concerts. | Rte. 364 and Lincoln Hill Rd. | 716/394–7190 | Call for schedule.

Finger Lakes Race Track. Since it opened in 1962, this track has hosted some of the world's top jockeys and thoroughbreds. Eight miles north of Canandaigua, just east of the intersection of Routes 96 and 332. | 5857 Rte. 96 | 716/924–3232 | www.fingerlakesracetrack.com. | $2 | Call for schedule.

Granger Homestead. This Federal-era house was completed in 1816 by Gideon Granger, postmaster general for Presidents Jefferson and Madison. The carriage house has 44 horse-drawn vehicles, including an undertaker's hearse. | 295 N. Main St. | 716/394–1472 | $4 | May, Sept.–Oct., Tues.–Fri. 1–5; June–Aug., Tues.–Sun. 1–5.

Onanda Park. This 80-acre park about 10 mi south of town has a wide, sandy swimming beach, ballparks, hiking trails, and on-shore fishing. The park's name comes from the Iroquois word for "tall fir." | West Lake Rd. | 716/394–0315 | $3 for town residents, $8 for non-residents on weekend holidays | Daily dawn–dusk.

Ontario County Historical Society. The original Native American Six Nations' copy of the Pickering Treaty with the signatures of Iroquois leaders Red Jacket, Cornplanter, Little Beard, and others is housed in this brick building along with other local artifacts. You can also pick up a walking tour map of the village here. | 55 N. Main St. | 716/394–4975 | $2 | Tues.–Sat. 10–4:30, Wed. 10–9.

Sonnenberg Gardens. The grounds at this sprawling estate form a magnificent example of late-Victorian gardening and design. Four thousand rosebushes fill the rose garden and there are eight other gardens, including Italian, Japanese, and rock gardens. Another garden contains only blue and white flowers. There are two gift shops and a restaurant, the Green House Cafe Restaurant, open Tuesday–Sunday 10–4. Wine tasting starts June 22. | 151 Charlotte St. | 716/394–4922 | $8.50 | Mid-May–mid-Oct., daily 9:30–5:30.

ON THE CALENDAR

JULY: *Ontario County Fair*. 4H activities, stock-car racing, and a demolition derby come to the Ontario County Fairgrounds on County Road 10. | 716/394–4987.
AUG.: *Pageant of Steam*. Old tractors are on display and you can watch demonstrations of grain threshing and wood cutting. On Gehan Road, 3 mi east of Canandaigua, off Routes 5 and 20. | 716/394–8102.
AUG.: *Phelps Sauerkraut Festival*. Rides for children, a classic auto show, parade, music, food, and fireworks. | 315/462–3376.
AUG.: *Waterfront Art Festival*. Hundreds of arts-and-crafts exhibitions, with entertainment. | Kershaw Park | 716/454–2620.

Dining

Bristol Harbour. Contemporary. Sample the fresh salmon, lobster bisque, or spinach-and-artichoke dip while looking out over Canandaigua Lake at this restaurant/resort. | 5410 Seneca Point Rd. | 716/396–2200 or 800/288–8248 | fax 716/394–9254 | $10–$15 | AE, MC, V.

Canandaigua Inn on the Lake. Contemporary. You'll have good views of Canandaigua Lake, Squaw Island, and the nearby city pier at this restaurant. Try the filet mignon, pan-roasted salmon, or rigatoni tossed with prosciutto and sautéed calf's liver. Open-air dining. | 770 S. Main St. | 716/394–7800 or 800/228–2801 | $15–$25 | AE, D, MC, V.

Captain Yogi's. Seafood. Located about 4 mi south of town on a main road, this New England fish shanty still feels off the beaten path. It's known for seafood, steaks, burgers, and chicken. Salad bar. | 4520 E. Lake Rd. | 716/394–1166 | Closed Mon., Tues. | $8–$15 | AE, D, DC, MC, V.

Holloway House. American. In the early 19th century, this building, about 9 mi west of Canandaigua, was an inn and stagecoach stop. It is now known for seafood, roast duck, turkey, steak, and lamb. Kids' menu. Early bird dinners. | 29 State St., East Bloomfield | 716/657–7120 | Closed Mon. and mid-Dec.–Mar. | $13–$25 | AE, MC, V.

Kellogg's Pan-Tree Inn. American. The in-house bakery at this restaurant produces sweet bread rolls and a variety of homemade desserts. The dining room has large windows that face a narrow shoreline park and the lake beyond. It's known for chicken pie, fish fry, and salads, and Kellogg's also serves a wide selection of Finger Lakes wine and beer. You can dine outside on docks that overlook the lake. Kids' menu. | 130 Lakeshore Dr. | 716/394–3909 | Closed mid-Oct.–mid-Apr. | $20–$25 | MC, V.

Koozina's. Italian. Carved out of a section of a former supermarket, this nautical-theme restaurant overlooks the city's busiest intersection. The food is Italian, with a Greek streak. Don't skip the peanut butter pie. | 699 S. Main St. | 716/396–0360 | $18–$26 | AE, D, MC, V.

Lincoln Hill Inn. Continental. This restaurant within walking distance of the Finger Lakes Performing Arts Center is housed in an 1804 farmhouse. Menu items vary seasonally, but always popular is the top-notch prime rib. Open-air dining on covered decks and porches. Kids' menu. | 3365 E. Lake Rd. | 716/394–8254 | Closed Mon. mid-Oct.–mid-Apr. | $12–$25 | AE, MC, V.

Manetti's. Italian. Many consider Manetti's to have the city's best salad bar. Other menu offerings include salmon, pasta, chicken, beef, and veal. Kids' menu. | Parkway Plaza | 716/394–1915 | $10–$22 | AE, DC, MC, V.

Schooners. American. A local favorite that serves generous cocktails, this casual restaurant sports a nautical theme. Best known for boneless prime rib and seafood. Kids' menu. | 407 Lake Shore Dr. | 716/396–3360 | fax 716/396–1297 | Closed Sun. | $9–$20 | MC, V.

Thendara Inn. Continental. This inn, located 5 mi south of town overlooking the east shore of the lake, has four separate dining areas. Upscale meals, including lamb, salmon, and prime rib, are served inside the 1900s Victorian house, and you can get the same menu outside on the wraparound porch. The Boat House on the lake has a more casual menu: sandwiches, salads, barbecue, and chicken. A pianist plays on Saturday. | 4356 E. Lake Rd. | 716/398–2780 | May–Sept., main house 5–7, boat house noon–11 PM. Varying seasonal hours Oct.–Apr. | $15–$30 main house, $5–15 boat house | AE, MC, V.

Lodging

Canandaigua Inn on the Lake. This resort is right on the lake and has sand beaches, a private boat dock, and several surrounding acres of cool green woodland. Entertainment is offered on weekends. Restaurant, bar, picnic area. In-room data ports, some refrigerators, some in-room hot tubs, cable TV. Pool. Exercise equipment. Business services. Pets allowed. | 770 S. Main St. | 716/394–7800 or 800/228–2801 | fax 716/394–5003 | 134 rooms, 44 suites | $65–$250 | AE, D, MC, V.

Econo Lodge. This two-story chain motel is within walking distance of Canandaigua Lake. Complimentary Continental breakfast. Refrigerators, cable TV. Laundry facilities. Business services. Some pets allowed. | 170 Eastern Blvd. | 716/394–9000 | fax 716/396–2560 | 65 rooms | $65–$85 | AE, D, DC, MC, V.

Finger Lakes Inn. Ten landscaped acres and a family activity center give you plenty of elbow room at this hotel. In addition to the standard rooms, there are special family minisuites which include two sleeping areas, one with two double beds and the other with a pull-out sofa bed. Picnic area, complimentary Continental breakfast. Some kitchenettes, some microwaves, some refrigerators, cable TV. Pool. Basketball, volleyball. Pets allowed. | 4343 Eastern Blvd., Rtes. 5/20 E | 716/394–2800 or 800/727–2775 | fax 716/393–1964 | relax@fingerlakesinn.com | www.fingerlakesinn.com | 124 rooms, 4 suites | $39–$118 | AE, D, DC, MC, V.

Greenwoods Bed and Breakfast Inn. Sleep on a queen-size featherbed at this log country inn with individually decorated rooms. The property has three ponds stocked with fish. Picnic area, complimentary breakfast. No room phones. Spa. Business services. No kids under 8. No smoking. | 8136 Quayle Rd., Honeoye | 716/229–2111 or 800/914–3559 | fax 716/229–0034 | 5 rooms | $90–$145 | AE, D, MC, V.

Habersham Country Inn. This Federal-style 1840 inn has a large porch and is surrounded by shady trees. Each room has been furnished differently with reproductions of antiques. Complimentary breakfast. In-room hot-tubs. | 6124 Rtes. 5 and 20 | 716/394–1510 or 800/914–3559 | habershamm@aol.com | www.habershaminn.com | 5 rooms | $85–$160 | AE, V.

Morgan-Samuels Bed and Breakfast. Relax on the enclosed front porch of this 1810 English-style mansion on 42 acres with panoramic views of the lake. All the rooms have fireplaces; three rooms have French doors that open onto balconies. Complimentary breakfast. TV in common area. Hot tub. Tennis. Library. Business services. No pets. No kids. No smoking. | 2920 Smith Rd. | 716/394–9232 | fax 716/394–8044 | 6 rooms, 1 suite | $129–$255 | MC, V.

Super 8. This basic chain is close to the Finger Lakes Performing Arts Center. Complimentary Continental breakfast. Cable TV. Business services. | 333 W. Morris St. | 607/776–2187 or 800/800–8000 | fax 607/776–3206 | 50 rooms | $46–$75 | AE, D, DC, MC, V.

Sutherland House. This 1885 Victorian, about 1½ mi from downtown, was once owned by Henry C. Sutherland, an executive of the Canandaigua Tin Co. who raised beef cattle. His four brothers also built houses on Bristol St. Each room has its own color scheme, and many have king-size beds. | 3179 Rte. 21 S, Bristol St. Extension | 716/396–0375; 800/396–0375 | goodnite@frontier.net.net | www.sutherlandhouse.com | 3 rooms, 2 suites | $85–$185 2-day minimum stay on weekends from mid–May–Dec. 1 | AE, D, MC, V.

Thendara. The sitting room in this Victorian, built between 1900–09 on a bluff overlooking Canandaigua Lake, has oriental rugs and antiques. Some of the rooms have lake views. Restaurant, complimentary breakfast, room service. Cable TV. 9-hole golf course. Dock. Business services. | 4356 E. Lake Rd. | 716/394–4868 | fax 716/396–0804 | 5 rooms | $115–$175 | AE, MC, V.

CANASTOTA

MAP 3, H6

(Nearby towns also listed: Cazenovia, Liverpool, Oneida, Rome, Syracuse)

About 25 mi east of Syracuse on Route 5 and just off Interstate 90 is Canastota, a village founded in 1810. The former world middleweight champion, Carmen Basilio, grew up here, and Canastota is home to the International Boxing Hall of Fame. Ten miles to the west is the village of Chittenango, the hometown of L. Frank Baum, whose books about Oz are celebrated every year with Ozfest.

Information: Greater Canastota Chamber of Commerce | 222 S. Peterboro St., 13032 | 315/697–3677.

Attractions
Canal Town Museum. This museum is an old canal building with period furnishings from the mid-19th century. | 122 Canal St. | 315/697–3451 | Free | Apr.–May and Sept.–Oct., Tues.–Fri. 11–4; June–Aug., weekdays 10–4.

Chittenango Landing Canal Boat Museum. Canal boats were once built and repaired at this 19th-century drydock. Off Route 5, west of Canastota. | 7010 Lakeport Rd., Chittenango | 315/687–3801 | $3 | July–Aug., daily 10–4; May–June and Sept.–Oct. weekends 1–4; Nov.–Apr., by appointment only.

International Boxing Hall of Fame. Photographs, boxing memorabilia, and videos are on exhibit here. | 1 Hall of Fame Dr. | 315/697–7095 | $4 | Mon.–Sat. 9–5, Sun. 9–4.

Old Erie Canal State Park. A path and greenway stretches for 36 mi along the old canal. You can hike, fish, bicycle, canoe, and picnic. Accessible from Routes 5 and 46. | 315/687–7821 | Free | Daily.

ON THE CALENDAR
JUNE: *Ozfest.* This festival in downtown Chittenango honors native son L. Frank Baum, author of *The Wonderful Wizard of Oz.* | 315/684–7320.

CANTON

MAP 3, I2

(Nearby towns also listed: Ogdensburg, Potsdam)

Vermonters settled in Canton in the early 1800s. In 1861, the artist Frederic Remington, whose father edited the local newspaper, was born here. As the home of St. Lawrence University, Canton has become an educational hub for the North Country. The area around Canton has many dairy farms.

Information: **Canton Chamber of Commerce** | Box 369, 13617 | 315/386–8255.

Attractions

Ostrander's Sheep Skin Shop. Four miles outside Canton, you'll find this combination shop and bed-and-breakfast (*see* Lodging, *below*), where Nubian goats, two kinds of sheep, and border collies are bred and raised. You can watch as sheepskin hats, vests, and bath mats are made right in front of you. Owner/innkeepers Al and Rita have been raising sheep for over 35 years. | 1675 State Hwy. 68 | 315/386–2126 | Free | Mid-Oct.–end Jan., daily 10–6; Feb.–mid-Oct., call for hrs.

Silas Wright Museum and St. Lawrence County Historical Association. Silas Wright, a U.S. Senator and governor of New York in the 1830s and '40s, lived in this home built in 1833. Six period rooms illustrate what life was like then. Another room displays changing exhibits. | 3 E. Main St. | 315/386–8133 | Museum free; museum archives $5 | Museum: Tues.–Sat. noon–4; museum archives: Tues.–Sat. noon–4, Fri. 12–8; closed between Christmas and New Year's.

St. Lawrence University. St. Lawrence is a liberal arts–oriented school with just over 2,000 students and about 175 faculty members. Highlights include the Gunnison Memorial Chapel and Griffiths Arts Center. Tours are available. | 23 Romoda Dr. | 315/229–5011 | www.stlawu.edu | Free | Daily.

ON THE CALENDAR
MAY: *Rushton Canoe Races.* Races have taken place here since 1962, as part of a weekend festival. They are named for Canton's J. Henry Rushton, who began building canoes and small boats in 1874. The races are held in Taylor Park, 2 mi outside of Canton. | 315/379–9241.
JUNE: *St. Lawrence County Dairy Princess Parade and Festival.* Dairy displays and fiddlers are among the entertainment at this celebration which also includes a parade, food, and crafts. In Canton Village Park. | 315/386–8255.
AUG.: *Gouverneur/St. Lawrence County Fair.* This weeklong fair has crafts, parade, shows, and music. At the county fairgrounds in Gouverneur, 20 mi south of Canton on Route 11. | 315/287–3010.

Dining

McCarthy's. American. Two large dining rooms offer a choice of casual or formal eating at this restaurant. It's known for chicken and biscuits, nutty melon salad, and lemon broiled steak. Salad bar. Kids' menu. Sunday brunch. | 315/386–2564 | Rte. 11 | Breakfast also available | $10–$14 | D, DC, MC, V.

Meadow's Diner. American. This country diner has been serving three meals a day since the early 1980s. Lunch specials change daily. The meadow burger is a favorite, topped with the "special" gravy sauce. Kids' menu. | 5835 Canton Russell Rd. | 315/386–1139 | Breakfast also available; closed July 4th week | $6–$12 | AE, D, MC, V.

Sergi Italian Restaurant. Italian. The same family has run this downtown eatery since 1966. There are two dining rooms, one candlelit and more elegant, the other quick, friendly, and family-oriented. Veal, chicken, and pasta make up the menu. | 31 Main St. | 315/386–4581 | $9–$15 | MC, V.

Lodging

Best Western University Inn. This rustic chain hotel is located next door to St. Lawrence University. Restaurant, bar. Refrigerators, cable TV. Pool. Golf. Cross-country skiing. Business services. Pets allowed. | 90 Main St. E | 315/386–8522 | fax 315/386–1025 | www.bwcanton.com | 98 rooms | $75–$95 | AE, D, DC, MC, V.

Canton-Potsdam Comfort Suites. This all-suite hotel is approximately 10 mi from the State University of New York at Potsdam and is surrounded by a number of popular fast-food and family-owned restaurants. This spot is popular among business travelers and people in town to visit patients in the nearby hospital facility. No-smoking rooms are available. Complimentary Continental breakfast. In-room data ports, refrigerators, cable TV, in-room VCRs (and movies). Pool. Hot tub, sauna. Gym. Laundry service. | 6000 U.S. 11 | 315/386–1161 | fax 315/386–2515 | 69 suites | $89–$129 | AE, D, MC, V.

Clearview. This one-story brick motel is in a quiet area in Gouverneur, about 20 mi south of Canton. The restaurant, known for its homemade pastas, has been going since 1952; the motel was added in the late 1960s. Restaurant, bar. Cable TV. Pool. Hot tub. | 1180A U.S. 11, Gouverneur | 315/287–2800 | pistoles@northnet.org | 32 suites | $55–$65 | AE, D, MC, V.

Ostrander's Bed and Breakfast. Hidden by the grove of birch and crab-apple trees lining the driveway, this Cape Cod–style abode offers accommodations in guest houses and in the main house (and a sheepskin shop—*see* Attractions, *above*). Explore the 22-acre property following trails that wind around a pond, stone walls, meadows, and forests. All rooms have at least a queen and a twin bed and views that are private, green, and peaceful. The porch is well positioned for catching spectacular sunsets. Complimentary breakfast. | 1675 State Hwy. 68 | 315/386–2126 | 4 rooms | $65 | AE, MC, V.

Windy Hill Motel. With its hilltop perch amid pines and maples, this motel overlooks former farms and meadows. It has barbecue/picnic setups and plenty of room for kids to run around. Laundry facilities. | 6517 U.S. Hwy. 11 | 315/386–8328 | 10 rooms, 2 cabins | $44–$50, cabins $90 | MC, V.

CARMEL/LAKE CARMEL

MAP 3, L9

(Nearby towns also listed: Brewster, Mahopac, North Salem)

Farming was the major source of income in this area in the 1800s and the town of Carmel has a number of historical sites that date to that era, including the Putnam County Courthouse, which has a Greek Revival portico and grand facade. Erected in 1814, today it is the oldest continuously active courthouse in New York and is listed in

CARMEL/
LAKE CARMEL

INTRO
ATTRACTIONS
DINING
LODGING

the National Register of Historic Places. Among other attractions are the town's Old Baptist Cemetery which contains the graves of more than a dozen Revolutionary War soldiers and a statue of local heroine Sybil Ludington, who is often referred to as the "Female Paul Revere" for her courageous nighttime ride across hostile territory during the Revolutionary War to warn her father of a British attack on nearby Danbury, Connecticut. Lake Carmel, located just a few miles north, is a lovely resort area known for its beautiful lake.

Information: Putnam Valley Chamber of Commerce | 1 S. Division St., Peekskill, 10566 | 845/737–3600.

CATSKILL

MAP 3, K7

(Nearby towns also listed: Cairo, Hudson, Hunter, Saugerties, Woodstock)

A favorite among skiers and outdoor recreationalists, Catskill is at the eastern entrance to the Catskill Mountain resort area, and several large resorts keep the community bustling. From 1836 to 1845, Thomas Cole, founder of the Hudson River School, lived here in a house with grounds that sweep down to the river. The house, at Routes 23 and 385, is not open to the public.

Information: Green County Chamber of Commerce | 159 Jefferson Heights Blvd., Catskill, 12414 | 518/943–4222.

Attractions

Catskill Game Farm. This popular attraction boasts tame and exotic animals, including rare wild Przewalski horses. You can visit the animal nursery, pet the llamas and sheep, and see reptiles and a bird garden. There's also miniature golf, a large playground, and rides. About 15 mi from Catskill on Route 32. | 518/678–9595 | www.catskillgamefarm.com | $14.95 | May–Oct. Daily 9–6.

Dining

Fairways. Contemporary. This restaurant on the grounds of the Catskill Country Golf Club in Jefferson Heights is known for fresh seafood, chicken, and broiled steaks. Open-air dining on a covered deck. Kids' menu. | 27 Brooks La. | 518/943–7199 | $15–$20 | MC, V.

Fernwood. Continental. Ten miles west of Catskill is this French country eatery housed in an 1880s building. The dining room is furnished with antiques. Known for veal, shrimp scampi, and linguine *bucaniera*—long, flat noodles drenched in a "buccaneer's" garlic-infused red wine sauce of Roma tomatoes, crabmeat, chunks of lobster, shrimp, and mussels. You can eat outside on a screened-in porch. Kids' menu. | Malden Ave., Palenville | 518/678–9332 | Closed Mon., Tues. No lunch | $25–$30 | AE, D, MC, V.

Stewart House. Contemporary. The 1930s bar, photos of local history, and Victorian ceiling create an interesting atmosphere at this lively bistro restaurant 4 mi from Catskill. Known for steak, seasonal game, fish. Musicians play on Thursday. | 2 N. Water St. | 518/945–1357 | Closed Mon. No lunch | $8–$15 | AE, MC, V.

Lodging

Catskill Mountain Lodge. This lodge 10 mi west of Catskill boasts its own microbrew pub. Some kitchenettes, some refrigerators, cable TV. Pool, wading pool. Playground. | HCR 1, Box 52, Palenville | 518/678–3101 or 800/686–5634 | fax 518/678–3103 | www.catskillmtnlodge.com | 42 rooms, 5 cottages | $70–$150 | AE, D, DC, MC, V.

Friar Tuck Inn. This modern, sprawling resort sits on a private lake. The rooms have mountain views and the grounds include a pheasant preserve. The nightclub features Broadway-style cabaret entertainment. Restaurant, bar (with entertainment). Cable TV. 3 pools. Hot tub. Tennis court. Exercise equipment. Children's programs, playground. Laundry facilities. Business services, airport shuttle. | 4858 Rte. 32 N | 518/678–2271 or 800/832–7600 | fax 518/678–2214 | 550 rooms | $225 | AE, D, MC, V.

Red Ranch. This family-friendly and affordable lodge is minutes off major routes. Picnic area. Some kitchenettes, cable TV. Pool, wading pool. Playground. | 4555 Rte. 32 | 518/678–3380 or 800/962–4560 | 43 rooms | $50–$70 | AE, D, DC, MC, V.

Stewart House Inn. This 1803 home sits on the Hudson River. The rooms are full of antiques. Restaurant, complimentary Continental breakfast. No room phones. | 2 N. Water St., Athens | 518/945–1357 or 800/339–4622 | 4 rooms (1 with shower only) | $90 | AE, MC, V.

Wolff's Maple Breeze Lodge. Hundreds of acres with wood trails and three lakes provide plenty of opportunities for outdoor entertainment at this family-friendly lodge. Rooms are spacious and some can accommodate up to six people. Restaurant, bar (with entertainment). Refrigerators, cable TV. Pool. Tennis. Exercise equipment, boating, fishing. Children's programs, playground. Business services. | 360 Cauterskill Rd. | 518/943–3648 or 800/777–9653 | 48 rooms | $95 | Closed Oct.–May | No credit cards.

CAZENOVIA

MAP 3, H6

(Nearby towns also listed: Auburn, Canastota, Hamilton, Liverpool, Skaneateles, Syracuse)

Among the rolling hills at the southern end of Cazenovia Lake is this village of approximately 3,500 people. Cazenovia can be reached from Route 20, an old east–west highway. Founded in 1794, the village today is home to Cazenovia College and the Lorenzo State Historic Site, an estate with gardens.

Information:**Greater Cazenovia Area Chamber of Commerce** | Box 66, 13035 | 315/655–9243.

Attractions

Chittenango Falls State Park. This state-run park has waterfalls, trails, and 22 campsites. | 2300 Rathbun Rd., off Rte. 13 | 315/655–9620, 800/456–CAMP reservations | $5 per vehicle | Apr.–Nov., daily.

Lorenzo State Historic Site. This 1802 estate has gardens and an arboretum. You can wander the carefully-tended grounds or go inside and see exhibits illustrating the arrival and contributions of Dutch settlers in the area. | 17 Rippleton Rd. | 315/655–3200 | $3 | May–Oct., Wed.–Sat. 10–5, Sun. 1–5.

State Hill Quarry Hill Art Park. Art and land conservation are of equal importance at this unique outdoor exhibit where clay, wood, rock, and any other biodegradable media are transformed into sculptures. Three and a half mi of walking trails wind through the 104 acres. Ample picnic space and parking. One mile east of Cazenovia. | 3883 Stone Quarry Rd. | 315/655–3196 | Free | Daily 10–5.

Toggenburg Ski Center. You'll find 25 trails here, from beginner through black diamond. Ski and snowboard instruction is available to help you tackle the Center's 650-ft vertical drop, as are special lessons for children. There's a restaurant on site. Snowmaking capabilities. Off U.S. 20 W, about 10 mi southwest of Cazenovia. | Fabius | 315/683–5842 | Dec.–early Apr.

ON THE CALENDAR

OCT.: *Apple Festival.* Thousands gather in La Fayette—about 12 mi west of Cazenovia—to celebrate the apple harvest. | 315/677–3644.

Dining

Albert's Restaurant. American. Since 1959 Albert's has been serving a fresh haddock special on Thursday and Friday along with steak and sandwiches all week. The bar and dining room are separate at this popular family spot. Kids' menu. | 5254 Albany Ave. | 315/655–2222 | $9–$13 | AE, D, MC, V.

Brae Loch Inn. Continental. Servers wear kilts at this upscale Scottish country inn with antiques and a plaid carpet. Try the prime rib, the poached Norwegian salmon, or the veal Oscar. You can also eat outside on the lawn facing the lake. Kids' menu. Sunday brunch. | 5 Albany St. | 315/655–3431 | No lunch | $14–$29 | AE, MC, V.

Brewster Inn. Continental. The terrace at this restaurant and inn faces the south side of Cazenovia Lake. Try the veal Atlantis, seasonal fish, rack of lamb, and boneless smoked duck. The restaurant also has a tavern. Sunday brunch, October–June. | 6 Ledyard Ave. | 315/655–9232 | No lunch | $22–$30 | DC, MC, V.

Lodging

Brae Loch. Across from Cazenovia Lake is this Scottish inn with antiques-furnished rooms. Restaurant (*see* Brae Loch Inn), complimentary Continental breakfast. Cable TV. | 5 Albany St. | 315/655–3431 | fax 315/655–4844 | 14 rooms | $100 | AE, MC, V.

Brewster. This elegant, country-style house has three stories overlooking the lake and an equally impressive adjacent carriage house. Some rooms have whirlpool tubs for two, and the restaurant downstairs serves some of the area's most sophisticated Continental cuisine. Restaurant (*see* Brewster Inn), bar, complimentary Continental breakfast. Cable TV. Exercise equipment. Library. Business services. | 6 Ledyard Ave. | 315/655–9232 | fax 315/655–2130 | 17 rooms | $150 | DC, MC, V.

Cazenovia Motel. One mile from the center of town and Lake Cazenovia, and 200 ft from Route 20, this motel is moderately priced and strategically placed. Most rooms have queen-size beds. | 2392 US 20 E | 315/655–9101 | fax 315/655–3288 | 36 rooms | $57–$89 | D, DC, MC, V.

Lincklaen House. This old brick house furnished with antiques has a tavern and a courtyard. It was named after the first Dutch settler to put down roots in the area, and the house's interior reflects the property's historical significance. Dining room, complimentary Continental breakfast. Cable TV. Business services. | 79 Albany St. | 315/655–3461 | fax 315/655–5443 | 18 rooms | $109 | AE, MC, V.

Tall Pines Bed and Breakfast. Surrounded by groves of aged pine trees, this 1850s Victorian is less than 1 mi from town. Rooms and porches have a view of Cazenovia Lake. Breakfast includes tasty homemade granola. Complimentary breakfast. | 4721 Ridge Rd. | 315/655–2690 | $100 | AE, D, MC, V.

CHAUTAUQUA

MAP 3, B7

(Nearby towns also listed: Bemus Point, Jamestown)

Chautauqua is best known for the Chautauqua Institution on Chautauqua Lake. During nine weeks in summer, the Institution offers a rich program of lectures, art exhibitions, outdoor symphonies, theater, dance, and opera. Perhaps what is most special about it, however, is the 856-acre village where all of these activities take place. Founded by Methodists in 1874, the village has changed little since then. No automobile traffic is permitted aside from dropping off and picking up your luggage, and no alcohol is served. The Victorian houses have turrets, multiple gables, and gingerbread woodwork, often painted bright colors.

All types of accommodations are available on the grounds, from bed-and-breakfasts in private homes, to inns, to the five-star Athenaeum hotel, built in 1873.

The Institution's recreational activities complement its cultural opportunities. You can fish, swim, or rent sailboats, motorboats, or canoes from the concessions on the lake, while at the bike shop you can rent bikes for the whole family or even a bicycle built for two. There are miles of paths through woods on which to bike or jog.

Information: **Chautauqua County Visitors' Bureau** | Box 1441, 14722 | 716/357–4569 or 800/242–4569 | ccvb@cecomet.net | www.tourchautauqua.com.

Attractions

Chautauqua Belle. Take a 1½-hour narrated cruise across Lake Chautauqua aboard a 19th-century steam-operated paddle-wheel boat. Off Route 394 in Mayville, 5 mi northwest of Chautauqua. | Lakeside Park, Mayville | 716/753–2403 or 800/753–2506 | Tours daily at 11, 1:15, 3.

The Chautauqua Institution. The Victorian splendor of this self-contained village and cultural education center attracts as many as 180,000 visitors a summer. The Institution reflects the mid- to late-19th-century quest for spiritual self-discovery, and was founded in the belief that everyone should "be all that he can be—and know all that he can know." Today, you can stay on this National Historic Landmark campus and attend lectures and concerts and take courses in everything from philosophy to film. The small winding streets, gas lights, and Victorian architecture make the village a unique vacation spot, and you can also enjoy the attractions of the lake and countryside, which include golf, swimming, tennis, sailing, and biking. Off Route 394 on Chautauqua Lake. | 1 Ames Ave. | 716/357–6200 or 800/836–ARTS | www.chautauqua-inst.org | Admission varies by event; call for specifics | Late June–Aug., tours daily 9–4.

The 6,500-seat, roofed, outdoor **Chautauqua Amphitheater** hosts large events on a first-come, first-served basis. It houses an enormous pipe organ, and is the site of performances by the Chautauqua Symphony Orchestra. Guest artists as diverse as Peter, Paul, and Mary; 10,000 Maniacs; Glenn Miller; and Natalie Cole have performed here. | 716/357–6250.

Four English-language opera performances are presented each season by the Chautauqua Opera Company in **Norton Memorial Hall.** This 1,365-seat Art Deco building was constructed in 1928–29. It is considered the first monolithic concrete structure east of the Mississippi.

In 1875, Chautauqua cofounder John H. Vincent commissioned **Palestine Park,** a complete replica of the Holy Land, including the Sea of Galilee, the Dead Sea, and other landmarks, as a visual aid for teaching biblical history and geography. The park was built on a scale of 1.75 ft per mi. Tours are given twice a week during the summer season.

The **Miller Bell Tower** is the most recognizable landmark on the shore of Chautauqua Lake. Built in 1911, it has since become the symbol of the Institution. Tunes are played by the chime master three or four times a day, and the Miller Bell is rung manually 15 minutes before the amphitheater lectures and evening programs.

The Chautauqua Institution has a wide range of summer **recreation.** At the Sports Club, visitors can rent sailboats and canoes, or dock their own boats. Softball, volleyball, and basketball leagues are also sponsored by the club. The Chautauqua Yacht Club teaches sailing and features weekly races through the Institution's Special Studies Program. The Institution is also associated with four public beaches and eight tennis courts. Bike rentals are available. | The Sports Club: 716/357–6281; Yacht Club: 716/357–4001; beaches: 716/357–6277; tennis: 716/357–6309; bike rental: 716/357–5444.

Lily Dale Assembly. In the mid-1800s, two young girls known as the Fox Sisters sparked a spiritualist movement in New York State. The sisters founded a colony in 1879 on the shores of Lake Cassadaga about 12 mi northeast of Chautauqua where like-minded people could meet and communicate with spirits and participate in other clairvoyant activity. Today, the world's largest spiritualist community has a 10-week summer season, which offers workshops, shopping, dining, a research library, lectures, and a variety of recreational activities, including fishing, swimming, and picnicking. You can go for the day or stay overnight, but call ahead for readings with the most popular mediums. In Lily Dale, off Route 60. | 5 Melrose Park, Lily Dale | 716/595–8721 or 716/595–8722 | fax 716/595–2442 | 24-hr pass $6; evening pass $3 | Late June–Labor Day, daily.

ON THE CALENDAR
AUG.: *Chautauqua Crafts Festival.* Fine crafts and art come to Bestor Plaza at the Chautauqua Institution. | 800/836–ARTS.

Dining

Athenaeum. Continental. The prix-fixe menu at this restaurant rotates every two weeks. The menu features poultry and vegetarian dishes. Dress is formal and you can also eat outside on the porch. | S. Lake Dr. | 716/357–4444 | fax 716/357–2833 | Reservations essential | Jacket required for dinner (excluding Sun.) | Breakfast also available; closed late Aug.–late June | $32 | AE, MC, V.

Blue Heron Inn. Contemporary. About 15 mi southeast of the Chautauqua Institution, you'll find this casual lakefront restaurant serving salads, baby-back ribs, and grilled seafood. Eat outside on the enclosed front porch. | 10412 Main St., Findley Lake | 716/769–7852 | bhinn@cecomet.net | $7–$18 | DC, MC, V.

Dick's Harbor House. American. This family-style restaurant 12 mi northeast of Chautauqua is known for the 8-ft salad bar and the fish fry. Charboiled meats, stews, and casseroles are also popular. No alcohol. | 95 W. Lake Rd. (Rte. 394), Mayville | 716/753–2707 | Breakfast also available | $12–$16 | AE, D, MC, V.

Giambrone's Seafood House. Seafood. This casual, popular tourist spot about 12 mi northeast of Chautauqua overlooks Chautauqua Lake. The menu includes fresh shrimp, lobster, scallops, and clams, as well as prime rib, pastas, and sandwiches. | 7 Water St. (Rte. 394), Mayville | 716/753–2525 | fax 716/753–2522 | Closed Mon., Tues. No dinner | $15–$21 | MC, V.

Rhapsody's Cafe. Continental. Though the napkins here are real fabric and the lights are kept low for intimate dinners, this is really a fairly casual restaurant known for seafood, veal piccata, and French-cut lamb chops. Open-air dining on a deck out back with views of the trees. Kids' menu. No smoking. | 9 Bowman St. | 716/592–5015 | Breakfast also available; closed Sept.–May | $12–$20 | MC, V.

Webb's—The Captain's Table. Contemporary. Dine by firelight in the antiques-furnished dining room or go casual on the deck overlooking the lake at this restaurant in a resort near the Chautauqua Institution. Prime rib, chicken, veal, and fresh seafood are popular, and vegetarian dishes are available. Choose from over 85 wines and 40 brands of imported and domestic beer. Kids' menu. | Rte. 394, Mayville | 716/753–3960 | $12–$30 | AE, D, MC, V.

Lodging

Athenaeum. This grand old Victorian hotel on the grounds of the Chautauqua Institution opened in 1881. The lakefront porch has rocking chairs. Restaurant. 36-hole golf course, tennis. Business services. | S. Lake Dr. | 716/357–4444 or 800/821–1881 | fax 716/357–2833 | www.athenaeum-hotel.com | 157 rooms | $271–$347 | Closed end Aug.–late June | AP | MC, V.

Carey Cottage Inn. The rooms, lobby, and parlor at this four-story Victorian inn in the Chautauqua Institution are decorated with period furnishings. Restaurant, complimentary breakfast. No room phones, no TV, TV in common area. | 9 Bowman Ave. | 716/357–2245 | fax 716/357–9727 | plumbush@yahoo.com | www.chautauquainfo.com | 24 rooms | $70–$140 | Closed Labor day–Memorial Day | AE, D, DC, MC, V.

Maple Springs Lake Side Inn. This gracious Dutch Colonial with porches and fireplaces overlooks Chautauqua Lake, and is 2 mi from the Chautauqua Cultural Center. There is a cross-country skiing trail near the property. Complimentary breakfast. Beach. Snowmobiling. | 4696 Chautauqua Ave., Maple Springs | 716/386–2500 | 7 rooms, 2 suites | $125–$150 | MC, V.

Peek'n Peak Resort and Conference Center. This resort has a wide variety of rooms and suites, for overnight stays or month-long retreats. Some rooms have hand-carved woodwork, stained glass, and fireplaces; some suites have kitchens. The grounds include two 18-hole golf courses, a golf school, and a driving range in summer. In winter, you can try out the 27-slope ski center. 4 restaurants, 2 bars. Cable TV. Indoor-outdoor pool. Gym. 18-hole golf course, driving range, miniature golf, tennis. Gym. Cross-country skiing, downhill skiing. Shops, video games. Playground. | 1405 Olde Rd., Findley Lake | 716/355–4141 | fax 716/355–4542 | peek-peak@aol.com | www.pknpk.com | 212 rooms | $120–$220 | AE, D, DC, MC, V.

St. Elmo Accommodations. When it was built in 1988 to replace the old St. Elmo Hotel that had fallen into disrepair, this building in the center of Chautauqua was designed to fit in with the Victorian homes and buildings that surround it. The rooms have chandeliers and full-size windows, and some have large kitchenettes as well. Kitchenettes, microwaves, cable TV. Driving range, 36-hole golf course, putting green, tennis. Cross-country skiing. Shops. Laundry facilities. Business services. | 1 Pratt Ave. | 716/357–3566, 800/507–5005 reservations | fax 716/357–3317 | careelmo@chautauquaarea.com | www.chautauquaarea.com | 25 suites | $65–$175 | AE, D, MC, V.

The Spencer. The rooms at this Victorian hotel in the heart of the Chautauqua Institution have been inspired by great authors and their works. The Agatha Christie room is decked out with imported fern-print wallpaper, bringing to mind London in the '30s, and the Isabel Allende room has cactus murals on the walls and a warm, South American, desert-hued theme throughout. Outside there is a beautiful garden. Complimentary Continental breakfast. Hot tub. | 25 Palestine Ave. | 716/357–3785 or 800/398–1306 | fax 716/357–4733 | spencer@netsync.net | www.thespencer.com | 22 rooms, 5 suites | $135–$210 rooms, $210 suites | No credit cards.

Webb's Year-Round Resort. Rooms have mahogany furniture and printed curtains at this lakeside resort near the Chautauqua Institution. The property also has a candy shop that sells Webb's homemade candies. Restaurant, bar. Pool. Hot tub. Gym, boating. Shops. Laundry facilities. Business services. | W. Lake Rd. (Rte. 394), Mayville | 716/753–2161 | fax 716/753–1383 | www.webbsworld.com; www.webbscandies.com | 52 rooms | $59–$89 | AE, MC, V.

CLARENCE

MAP 3, C6

(Nearby towns also listed: Amherst, Batavia, Buffalo, East Aurora, Grand Island, Williamsville)

Unlike much of the Buffalo area, the suburb of Clarence has hills and dales that make for an attractive landscape. Route 5, Clarence's main road is a continuation of Main Street that runs east all the way from downtown Buffalo. Clarence is the antiques center of the region, and you will find the large Clarence Antique World and Flea Market here, as well as many shops.

Information: **Clarence Chamber of Commerce** | 8975 Main St., 14031 | 716/631–3888.

Attractions

Clarence Antique World and Flea Market. This is New York State's largest indoor/outdoor antiques market. The over-200-acre complex is made up of many small co-ops and a few large showrooms that sell antiques, collectibles, new merchandise, produce, and more. |

10995 Main St. | 716/759–8483 or 800/959–0714 | fax 716/759–6167 | fleamarket@antique-worldfleamarket.com | www.antiqueworldmarket.com | Free | Sun. 8–4.

ON THE CALENDAR
MAY, NOV.: *Spring Arts and Crafts Show, Fall Arts and Crafts Show.* Craftspeople and artists from the western New York region display their work at these two annual shows. A silent auction is held to benefit the Clarence scholarship fund. At the Clarence Town Park Clubhouse. | 716/741–3605.
JULY: *Bastille Day Picnic.* Clarence's Francophile community turns out every year to celebrate the French Revolution and eat tasty homemade food under the shade trees in the park. You're encouraged to contribute a dish of your own to the festivities. | Clarence Town Park | 716/688–0944.

Dining

Asa Ransom House. Contemporary. Fresh herbs from the garden enhance dishes such as roasted turkey strata, raspberry chicken, and grilled sea bass at this restaurant in an inn. On Fridays and Saturdays, a five-course prix-fixe dinner is served. You can eat outside on a covered porch. Kids' menu. Early bird dinners. No smoking. | 10529 Main St. | 716/759–2315 | Reservations essential holidays | Jacket required | Closed Mon. No lunch Tues., Thurs., Fri., and weekends | $10–$28, $40 prix fixe | D, MC, V.

Tony Rome's Coachman's Inn. American. On Fridays, this restaurant with beamed ceilings and fireplaces serves up a fish fry. At other times, try the steak, charbroiled baby-back ribs, or lobster tail. Entertainment on Fridays and Saturdays. Kids' menu. Early bird dinners. | 10350 Main St. | 716/759–1744 | Reservations essential holidays | Closed Dec. 25 | $10–$20 | AE, D, DC, MC, V.

Lodging

Asa Ransom House. Each room in this 1853 bed-and-breakfast has a distinctive theme and antique furnishings. Most rooms have fireplaces and balconies; several have canopy beds. Restaurant (*see* Asa Ransom House), complimentary breakfast. In-room data ports, cable TV. Business services. No smoking. | 10529 Main St. | 716/759–2315 | fax 716/759–2791 | info@asaransom.com | www.asaransom.com | 9 rooms, 3 suites | $95 rooms, $275 suites | Closed Jan. | AP | D, MC, V.

Village Haven. The grounds at this motel have large oaks and a Victorian gazebo. Some of the suites feature heart-shaped baths and all the rooms have sofas that open up into queen-size beds. Picnic area, complimentary Continental breakfast. Some kitchenettes, microwaves, some in-room hot tubs, cable TV. Pool. Playground. Business services. | 9370 Main St. | 716/759–6845 | fax 716/759–6847 | www.newyorklodging.com | 23 rooms, 10 suites | $50–$75 | AE, MC, V.

CLAYTON

MAP 3, G3

(Nearby towns also listed: Alexandria Bay, Watertown)

Clayton quietly maintains its river-fueled heritage. Settled in 1822, it was once a major shipbuilding port and steamship stop. Later in the 19th century, tourists came here to fish and boat, two of the same activities that still draw people to the area. Today, there's plenty to do in the village, but much of the activity is sedate and museums are its main attractions. The sunsets over its Canadian neighbor Ganonoque can be spectacular.

Information: Clayton Chamber of Commerce | 510 Riverside Dr., 13624 | 315/686–3771 or 800/252–9806 | ccoc@gisco.net | www.thousandislands.com/claytonchamber; www.1000islands.com/clayton.

Attractions

Antique Boat Museum. More than 200 antique boats, engines, and motors make this perhaps the finest collection of old boats in North America. You can also take a ride in a 40-ft antique cruiser. | 750 Mary St. | 315/686–4104 | abm@gisco.net | www.abm.org | $6 | Mid-May–mid-Oct., daily 9–5.

Burnham Point State Park. You can camp, picnic, boat, and fish at this 12-acre park west of Clayton. There are 50 campsites, with 18 electrical hookups, hot showers, and a children's area. | Rte. 12 E, Cape Vincent | 315/654–2324. | www.nysparks.state.ny.us/parks/ | Free; parking $4 | Mid-May–Labor Day.

Cedar Point State Park. This 48-acre park has boat rentals, fishing, and swimming. The camping options include 175 campsites, with 61 electrical hookups, hot showers, a recreation building, and a children's area. Off Route 12 E, west of Clayton. | 36661 Cedar Point State Park Dr., Cape Vincent | 315/654–2522 | www.nysparks.state.ny.us/parks/; www.parknet.com | Free; parking $6 | May–Oct., daily.

Grass Point State Park. Take your pick of boating, fishing, swimming, or camping at this 66-acre island park 5 mi from Clayton in the St. Lawrence River. There are 76 campsites, 19 electrical hookups, hot showers, and a children's area. | Rte. 12 E | 315/686–4472 | www.nysparks.state.ny.us/parks/ | Parking $6 | Mid-May–mid-Sept., daily.

Ferry to Canada. It only takes 10 min to cross from Cape Vincent to Wolfe Island, Ontario, on the only international auto/passenger ferry on the St. Lawrence River. The terminal is at the end of James Street. | Box 116, Cape Vincent | 315/783–0638 | $6 for car and driver, $1 for each additional passenger | May–Oct., daily 8–7:30.

Thousand Islands Museum and Opera House. One special exhibit at this museum in the Town Hall/Opera House is devoted to large muskies, a prized local fish. Other displays focus on life at the turn of the 20th century. The museum also has a large collection of decoys. | 403 Riverside Dr. | 315/686–5794 | $2 | May–Oct., daily 10–4.

Tibbetts Point Lighthouse. One of the oldest lighthouses on the Great Lakes is at the outlet of Lake Ontario. The Coast Guard left in 1981, and the building is now used as a youth hostel. You can visit the grounds, but you cannot climb the lighthouse. It's 12 mi west of Clayton. | 33435 Rte. 6, Cape Vincent | 315/654–2700 (visitors center) | Free | Mid-May–June, weekends 11 AM–sunset; July–Aug., daily 11 AM–sunset; Sept.–late Oct., weekends 11 AM–sunset.

Uncle Sam Boat Tours. Three-hour cruises leave daily to explore the St. Lawrence River. | 604 Riverside Dr. | 315/686–3511 and 800/253–9229 | www.usboattours.com | $15 | June–Labor Day, daily 9:30, 12:30, 3:30.

ON THE CALENDAR

JULY: *Duck, Decoy and Wildlife Art Show.* Artists, carvers, painters, and taxidermists come from all over the country and Canada to show their work at the Recreation Park Arena on East Line Road. | 315/686–5794.

JULY: *French Festival.* The largest festival in the North Country celebrates Cape Vincent's French heritage. | 315/654–2481.

AUG.: *Antique Boat Show and Auction.* This annual show celebrates its finish with an antique boat parade on the St. Lawrence River. Boats are displayed in the water and on land. Includes a flea market, food, and music, at the Antique Boat Museum. | 315/686–4104 | www.thousandislands.com/abm.org.

SEPT.: *Model Train Fair.* You can see working model trains in a variety of different scales and layouts during this fair. Hobbyist items are also on sale. At the Recreation Park Arena. | 315/686–3771 or 800/252–9806.

Dining

Clipper Inn. American. This chef-owned restaurant is upscale but casual. The large and varied menu includes vegetarian dishes, steak, veal dishes, seafood, and chicken. Try the veal Oscar. Kids' menu. Early bird dinners. | 126 State St. (Rte. 12) | 315/686–3842 | Closed Jan.–Mar. No lunch | $13–$25 | AE, D, DC, MC, V.

Foxy's. Italian. Large windows let you look out over the St. Lawrence River as you eat at this waterside restaurant between Clayton and Alexandria Bay. Known for its fresh seafood, veal, pasta, and lasagna, Foxy's also serves steak, chicken parmigiana, and shrimp scampi. There is a video game room for the kids. | 18187 Reed Point Rd., Fisher's Landing | 315/686–3781 | foxys@1000islands.com | www.1000islands.com/foxys | Closed Oct.–mid-May | $6–$16 | D, MC, V.

P. J.'s Riverrat Cafe. American. Mostly families and retirees come to this restaurant and motel halfway between Clayton and Alexandria Bay for the prime rib and fish fry. Other specialties include the Mae West (a fried-turkey dish), shrimp scampi, and seafood Alfredo. The restaurant is only ¼ mi from a public boat ramp. Kids' menu. | 41867 Rte. 180, Fisher's Landing | 315/686–5359 | Closed Nov.–Apr. | $7–$19 | MC, V.

Thousand Islands Inn. Continental. This inn in downtown Clayton is said to be the birthplace of Thousand Island salad dressing. Known for its wild game, the restaurant serves quail and venison, along with fish and veal. The original tin ceiling in the dining room dates from the late 1800s. Kids' menu. Early bird dinners. | 335 Riverside Dr. | 315/686–3030 | Breakfast also available; closed Oct.–Apr. | $18–$24 | AE, D, MC, V.

Lodging

Bertrand's. You'll be right in the middle of the village at this 1930s building close to the shore. Picnic area. Some kitchenettes, cable TV. | 229 James St. | 315/686–3641 or 800/472–0683 | bertrand@gisco.net | 28 rooms | $65–$75 | Closed Jan., Feb. | AE, D, MC, V.

Buccaneer Motel and Bed and Breakfast. This Cape Vincent motel is right on the water, near the ferry to Wolf Island. The rooms have cherry-wood furnishings. Cable TV. Dock. | 230 N. Point St., Cape Vincent | 315/654–2975 | 10 rooms | $65–$85 | MC, V.

Island Boat House Bed and Breakfast. This small bed-and-breakfast on a private island brings to mind croquet, lemonade, and canvas swings. The boathouse has two bedrooms and a private deck with a view of the river and islands. Off Route 12 E, 4 mi east of Clayton. Dock, boating, fishing. | Occident Island, Fisher's Landing | 315/686–2272 or 800/686–

PACKING IDEAS FOR COLD WEATHER

- ❏ Driving gloves
- ❏ Earmuffs
- ❏ Fanny pack
- ❏ Fleece neck gaiter
- ❏ Fleece parka
- ❏ Hats
- ❏ Lip balm
- ❏ Long underwear
- ❏ Scarf
- ❏ Shoes to wear indoors
- ❏ Ski gloves or mittens

- ❏ Ski hat
- ❏ Ski parka
- ❏ Snow boots
- ❏ Snow goggles
- ❏ Snow pants
- ❏ Sweaters
- ❏ Thermal socks
- ❏ Tissues, handkerchief
- ❏ Turtlenecks
- ❏ Wool or corduroy pants

*Excerpted from *Fodor's: How to Pack: Experts Share Their Secrets*
© 1997, by Fodor's Travel Publications

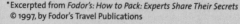

6056 | occident@1000islands.com | www.1000islands.com/occident | 2 bedrooms | $150 | Closed Nov.–Apr. | MC, V.

Martin's Marina and Motel. This rustic motel 3 mi from Cape Vincent caters to those in search of bass, northern pike, walleye, and lake trout. Docks, boating. | 28491 Rte. 6, Mud Bay, Cape Vincent | 315/654–3104 | fax 315/654–4020 | www.marina.com | 6 rooms | $47–$50 | Closed Nov.–Apr. | MC, V.

COBLESKILL

(Nearby towns also listed: Canajoharie, Colonie, Cooperstown)

Cobleskill, which lies along Interstate 88 at the eastern edge of Leatherstocking Country, became a center for agriculture and dairy farming with the advent of rail lines in the area. Today, Cobleskill is home to a two-year state college and about 5,200 people. Nearby Howe Caverns has a famous underground cave that you can explore.

Information: **Schoharie County Chamber of Commerce** | 243 Main St., Schoharie, 12157-0400 | 518/295–7033 | info@schohariechamber.com. | www.schohariechamber.com.

Attractions

Howe Caverns. Take an elevator down 156 ft to reach the caverns. From there, follow paved walkways, and take a boat ride on an underground lake. Grounds include a restaurant, gift shop, and 21-room motel. | R.R. 1, off Rte. 7 | 518/296–8900 | www.howecaverns.com | $12 | Daily 9–6.

Iroquois Indian Museum. One of the mightiest Native American nations of the northeast is celebrated here through displays of ancient and modern artworks, archaeological relics, and ever-changing cultural exhibits and events. | Caverns Rd., Howe Caverns | 518/296–8949 | $7 | July–Aug., Mon.–Sat. 10–6, Sun. 12–5; Apr.–June and Sept.–Dec., Tues.–Sat. 10–5, Sun. 12–6.

Old Stone Fort Museum Complex. Three centuries of rural New York artifacts are located on the grounds of a fort that was raided by the British in 1777. Includes the county's first car, a 1901 Rambler. Revolutionary War reenactments are held on Columbus Day, and Heritage Days are celebrated in August. East of Cobleskill. | R.R. 2, Rte. 30A, Schoharie | 518/295–7192 | fax 518/295–7187 | $5 | May–June, Sept.–Oct., Tues.–Sat. 10–5, Sun. 12–5; July–Aug., Mon.–Sat. 10–5, Sun. 12–5.

Secret Caverns. This unspoiled cave was discovered in 1928 on a rural farm just outside Cobleskill. An hour-long guided tour down windy stairs takes you 85 ft deep and features fossils, domes, and a 100-ft underground waterfall. Since the temperature in the caverns is usually 50°F, walking shoes and a light jacket are suggested. | Secret Caverns Rd., off Rte. 7 | 518/296–8558 | www.secretcaverns.com | $9.50 | Mid.-Apr.–Oct.

ON THE CALENDAR

AUG.: *Annual Sunshine Fair.* Not since 1876, when the fair began, has the town gone a year without this agricultural fair, which includes a midway, animals, thrill shows, and live music. It all takes place at the fairgrounds the second weekend of the month. | 518/234–2123.

Dining

Bull's Head Inn. American. This Colonial, white, frame 1802 building has a restaurant as well as a more casual pub. Prime rib, raspberry chicken, coquilles St. Jacques, and rack of lamb are on the menu. | 2 Park Pl. | 518/234–3591 | Closed Mon. No lunch Sat. | $10–$25 | AE, MC, V.

Lodging

Best Western Inn of Cobleskill. This chain motel is near SUNY-Cobleskill and 10 min from Howe Caverns. Restaurant. Cable TV. Pool, wading pool. | 12 Campus Dr. extension | 518/234–4321 or 800/528–1238 | fax 518/234–3869 | 76 rooms | $124–$139 | AE, D, DC, MC, V.

Gables Bed and Breakfast Inn. These two Victorian homes form a peaceful lodging option amid other turn-of-the-20th-century homes 1 mi from Interstate 88 and a block from Route 10. Most rooms have queen-size beds, and all are decorated in a period style of florals, lace, and wicker. Complimentary Continental breakfast. | 66 W. Main St. | 518/234–4467 | www.nyinn.com | 7 rooms | $70–$100 | MC, V.

Howe Caverns Motel. This motel is right on the grounds of Howe Caverns with views of the mountains and valleys. No-smoking rooms are available. Restaurant (open July–Labor Day). Cable TV. Pool. | Rte. 7, Howe Caverns | 518/296–8950 | fax 518/296–8992 | motel@howe-caverns.com | www.howecaverns.com | 21 rooms | $83–$135 | D, MC, V.

COLD SPRING HARBOR

MAP 3, K9

(Nearby towns also listed: Huntington, Syosset)

One of the north shore's most enchanting towns, Cold Spring Harbor has always been valued for its location on the water. The Matinecock Indians are said to have called it "Wawapex," meaning "place of good water." In 1653, three Englishmen from Oyster Bay bought the land around the harbor from the Matinecocks, and named it Cold Spring after the area's freshwater springs. It became a U.S. Port of Entry in 1799 and, during the mid-1800s, was home to a fleet of nine whaling vessels and numerous ships carrying cargo.

Time has not eroded any of the landscape surrounding this attractive village. As you drive east along the north shore's Heritage Trail, Route 25A, the town's picturesque harbor appears, out of the trees, as a surprise. As you take the turn that brings you up the hill around Cold Spring Harbor the trees are breathtaking, whether in the green of spring and summer or the rich colors of fall.

Once you reach the crest of the hill, it is worth taking time to browse the shops and restaurants on Main Street.

Information: **Huntington Chamber of Commerce** | 151 W. Carver St., Huntington, 11743 | 914/265–3200.

Attractions

Cold Spring Harbor Fish Hatchery and Aquarium. Eight outdoor tanks at this educational center hold the largest collection of native freshwater fish, turtles, and amphibians in New York State. It's 1½ mi from downtown Cold Spring Harbor. | Rtes. 25A and 108 | 516/692–6768 | $3.50 | Daily 10–5.

Cold Spring Harbor Whaling Museum. One of the highlights of the permanent exhibits exploring Long Island's whaling industry is a fully equipped 19th-century whaleboat. Whaling implements, paintings, scrimshaw, and ship models are also on display. | Rte. 25A | 631/367–3418 | $3 | Memorial Day–Labor Day, daily 11–5; Labor Day–Memorial Day, Tues.–Sun. 11–5.

The Gallery. You'll find exhibits on Long Island's history, architecture, and culture at this gallery organized by the Society for the Preservation of Long Island. | 1 Shore Rd. | 631/692–4664 | Jan.–Apr., weekends 11–4.; May–Oct., Tues.–Sun. 11:30–4:30; Nov.–Dec., Fri., weekends 11–4.

Long Island Discovery. Watch a fascinating 28-minute multimedia presentation of Long Island history from the Ice Age to the present. | 334 Main St. | 631/367–7240 | Free | Shows weekdays at 10, 11, and 1; Sat. at 1 and 3.

ON THE CALENDAR
OCT.: *Fall Fair.* Environmental groups and conservationists present exhibits at the fish hatchery, and there are children's games and fishing. | 516/692–6768.

Dining

Inn on the Harbor. Continental.The stately dining room in this Victorian house is a great place to view magnificent summer sunsets over Cold Spring Harbor. Try the rack of lamb with mustard sauce, filet mignon with peppercorn sauce, or sirloin steak with bordelaise sauce. For dessert, there are fruit tarts with seasonal fruit and cheesecake. Kids' menu. Sunday brunch. Dock space. | 105 Harbor Rd. | 631/367–3166 | $18–$32 | AE, DC, MC, V.

Trattoria Grasso III. Italian. Entrées are inspired by Tuscan, Sardinian, and Sicilian cooking, and the wine list is similarly inclusive. You can dine on the porch overlooking the village, or sit at a candlelit table inside, where you'll be surrounded by photographs of Europe and serenaded by live jazz bands on Friday and Saturday nights.Try *branzini,* a Mediterranean fish roasted whole and then filleted at your table. | 134 Main St. | 631/367–6060 | Closed Tues. | $20–$28 | AE, D, DC, MC, V.

Lodging

Swan View Manor. This Victorian house is a block and a half from the center of town and across the street from Cold Spring Harbor. Complimentary tea is served every afternoon. Most beds are queen-size; king-size is available. Complimentary Continental breakfast. No kids under 10. | 45 Harbor Rd. | 631/367–2070 | fax 631/367–2085 | www.swanview.com | 18 rooms, 1 suite | $119–$154 | AE, D, DC, MC, V.

COLONIE

MAP 3, K6

COLONIE

INTRO
ATTRACTIONS
DINING
LODGING

(Nearby town also listed: Albany, Amsterdam, Cobleskill, Schenectady)

This bedroom community, home to Siena College, is just north of Albany.

Information: **Albany County Convention and Visitors Bureau** | 25 Quackenbush Sq., Albany, 12207 | 518/434–1217.

Attractions

Shaker Heritage Society. Maintained by the Shaker Heritage Society, and listed on the National Register of Historic Places, this site includes an 1848 meetinghouse. Shaker founder Ann Lee is buried in the cemetery here. The grounds also include an herb garden, barnyard, and more. | Albany-Shaker Rd. off Rte. 155 | 518/456–7890 | fax 518/452–7348 | www.crisny.org/not-for-profit/shakerwv | $3 | Tues.–Sat. 9:30–4; grounds tours June–Oct., Sat. 11:30 and 1:30.

Dining

Bangkok Thai Restaurant. Thai. Traditional curries are on the menu along with spicy seafood, shrimp spring rolls, and chicken satay.Try the ultra-spicy, rich-flavored Duck Sam-rod. | 8 Wolf Rd. | 518/435–1027 | fax 518/435–1425 | $10–15 | AE, MC, V.

Big House Grill. American.This casual restaurant draws a professional crowd with its specialized microbrews and homey, 1920s-era style. The ribs, pasta, and chicken dishes are popular. Kids' menu. | 112 Wolf Rd. | 518/458–7300 | fax 518/482–3469 | Dinner only Sun. | $12–$22 | AE, D, DC, MC, V.

Century House. American. This restaurant serves classics such as rack of lamb and prime rib with Yorkshire pudding. Another favorite is the Cape Cod pot (lobster, crab, and shrimp). | 997 New Loudon Rd., Latham | 518/785–0834 | No lunch Sat. | $20–$25 | AE, D, DC, MC, V.

Cranberry Bog. American. The outside deck of this restaurant near the airport has a four-season glass-enclosed greenhouse. Inside, the menu is upscale. Try the prime rib, steak, fresh seafood, chicken, pasta, and veal. The breads and desserts are homemade. Open-air dining. Kids' menu. | 56 Wolf Rd. | 518/459–5110 | $15–$30 | AE, D, DC, MC, V.

Dakota. American. Steak and seafood are popular at this restaurant done up in the rustic style of a hunting lodge with Native American artifacts. The restaurant is 5 mi from Albany. Try the prime rib, lobster, chicken, fish. Salad bar. Kids' menu. Sunday brunch. | 579 Troy-Schenectady Rd., Latham | 518/786–1234 | fax 518/786–1374 | www.dakotarestaurant.com | No lunch Mon.–Sat. | $18–425 | AE, D, DC, MC, V.

Scrimshaw. Continental. This restaurant within the Desmond Hotel and Conference Center has 18th-century charm and 400 fine American and European wines to choose from. Pianist. Kids' menu. | 660 Albany-Shaker Rd. | 518/869–8100 | fax 518/869–7659 | Closed Sun. No lunch | $22–$30 | AE, D, DC, MC, V.

Shipyard Restaurant. American. The dining rooms have garden motifs and rustic fireplaces. Try the rack of lamb with roasted garlic, rosemary, and sun-dried tomato demi-glace, or the Maryland-style crab cakes. | 95 Everett Rd. | 518/438–4428 | fax 518/438–2331 | No lunch Sat.–Mon. | $18–$25 | AE, D, DC, MC, V.

Simpson's. American. This casual restaurant in the Desmond Hotel and Conference Center is known for steaks and chicken dishes. | 660 Albany-Shaker Rd. | 518/869–8100 | fax 518/869–7659 | Breakfast also available | $14–$16 | AE, D, DC, MC, V.

Veeder's. Continental. This family restaurant, known for prime rib, lamb, and duck, is proud to be un-trendy. Draws a senior crowd. Salad bar. Kids' menu. Early bird dinners. | 2020 Central Ave. | 518/456–1010 | fax 518/456–1010 | Closed Mon. | $10–$15 | AE, D, MC, V.

Lodging

Inn at the Century. This hotel 10 mi from Albany has rooms done up in burgundy and green with cherry-wood furniture. There is also a nature trail on the property. Restaurant, bar, complimentary breakfast, room service. In-room data ports, some refrigerators, cable TV. Pool. Tennis. Exercise equipment. Business services. Some pets allowed. | 997 New Loudon Rd., Latham | 518/785–0931 | fax 518/785–3274 | 68 rooms | $119–$225 | AE, D, DC, MC, V.

Microtel Inn. This two-story motor lodge is ½ mi from the Albany International Airport and within walking distance of restaurants. In-room data ports, some refrigerators, cable TV. Business services. Some pets allowed. | 7 Rensselaer Ave., Latham | 518/782–9161 or 800/782–9121 | fax 518/782–9162 | 100 rooms | $70–$90 | AE, D, DC, MC, V.

COOPERSTOWN

MAP 3, I6

(Nearby towns also listed: Cobleskill, Oneonta, Richfield Springs)

Located at the southern tip of Otsego Lake (a.k.a. Glimmerglass), Cooperstown is about 30 mi down either Route 80 or Route 28 from the Thruway. The town takes its name from author James Fenimore Cooper's father who settled here in 1786, and Fenimore House is one of the town's attractions.

The most popular Cooperstown draw, though, is the National Baseball Hall of Fame and Museum. You can expect a big crowd for the museum's annual induction ceremony, and you'll need advance reservations for the annual Hall of Fame baseball game or you'll face scalpers' prices. In addition to baseball memorabilia and photographs, the occasional appearance by a major-league player is part of the museum's appeal.

For a break from baseball, check out the Farmers Museum, a step back into a village more than a century old.

Information: Cooperstown Chamber of Commerce | 31 Chestnut St., 13326 | 607/547–9983 | info@cooperstownchamber.org | www.cooperstownchamber.org.

Attractions

Chief Uncas Tours. You can set off on a leisurely cruise on the clear waters of Otsego Lake aboard a classic yacht. | Fair St. | 607/547–5295 | $10 | Mid-May–mid-Oct., daily 9:30–6; mid-May–Labor Day, tours at 10, 11, 6.

Farmers Museum. Craftspeople demonstrate 19th-century trades at this 1845 village and farmstead. The 10-acre site has 26 buildings. The working farm has oxen, chicken, ducks, and Devon cattle. The museum also has the famous Cardiff giant: in the 1800s, the 10-ft-tall, 3,000 lb stone figure was said to be a petrified, prehistoric man or an ancient statue. People came from far and wide to view the "giant," which was eventually proven to be a hoax pulled off by a cigar-maker from Binghamton. Today the giant is displayed much as he was "discovered" by workmen in 1869. One mile north of downtown off Route 80. | Lake Rd. | 607/547–1450 | www.farmersmuseum.org/ | $9 | May–Oct., daily 10–5; Apr. and Nov., Tues.–Sun. 10–4.

Fenimore Art Museum. In addition to James Fenimore Cooper memorabilia and artifacts, this museum has collections of folk art, fine art, and Indian art. Just north of town, off Route 80. | Lake Rd. | 607/547–1400 | www.nysha.org/ | $9 | June–Sept., daily 10–5; Apr.–May and Oct.–Dec., Tues.–Sun. 10–4.

Glimmerglass State Park. You can swim or hike here at this park on the lake. Forty sites are available for camping. In the primitive camping area, there are outhouses and no running water. Concession stand. | 1527 Rte. 31 | 607/547–8662, 800/456–CAMP reservations | $6 per vehicle | May–Oct., daily.

National Baseball Hall of Fame and Museum. Probably the most famous hall-of-fame in the nation, this institution in the heart of downtown Cooperstown is a shrine to America's Pastime. Plaques bearing the pictures and biographies of major-league baseball's luminaries line the walls in the actual Hall of Fame, and the rest of the complex features multimedia displays, exhibits geared for kids, and enough ball-diamond memorabilia to satisfy the most die-hard fan. | 25 Main St. | 888/425–5633 or 607/547–7200 | www.baseballhalloffame.org | $9.50 | May–Sept., daily 9–9; Oct.–Apr., daily 9–5.

Ommegang Brewery. This maker of Belgian-style ales has tours and tastings. | 656 County Hwy. 33 | 607/547–8184 or 800/656–1212 | $4 | Late May–early Sept., weekdays noon–7, weekends 11–7; early Sept.–late May, weekdays noon–5, weekends 11–7.

ON THE CALENDAR

JULY: *Baseball Hall of Fame Weekend.* The National Baseball Hall of Fame inducts new members and there is a Hall of Fame baseball game at Doubleday Field down the street. Advance ticket reservation is required. | 888/425–5633 or 607/547–7200.

JULY–AUG.: *Glimmerglass Opera.* Professional opera offers both matinee and evening performances. At the Alice Busch Opera Theater, Route 80. | 607/547–5704 | www.cooperstown.net/glimmerglass.

SEPT.: *Autumn Harvest Festival.* The Farmers Museum celebrates fall and the harvest every year. | 607/547–1450.

Dining

Doubleday Cafe. American. This baseball-theme café is appropriately near the National Baseball Hall of Fame and Museum. The quiches, fajitas, and cold sandwiches draw a diverse crowd. | 93 Main St. | 607/547–5468 | Breakfast also available | $10–$20 | D, MC, V.

Field of Dreams Steakhouse. American. Four miles outside town, this steak house also serves chicken, seafood, and pasta within its two dining rooms. Baseball photographs both old and new keep the Cooperstown spirit alive. Kids' menu. | 18 Commons Dr. | 607/547–2339 | Closed Tues. | $7–$22 | AE, D, DC, MC, V.

Gabriella's on the Square. Continental. The four dining rooms at this restaurant have tables laid with white tablecloths, flowers, and candles. Known for herb-encrusted rack of lamb, steak au poivre, and crab cakes. Open-air dining. | 161 Main St. | 607/547–8000 | No lunch Nov.–Aug. | $22–$25 | AE, D, DC, MC, V.

Hawkeye Bar and Grill. Continental. This dark, wood-paneled restaurant is in a resort hotel with views of the lake, about three blocks from the Baseball Hall of Fame. Try the herb risotto with fresh vegetables, or the wild mushrooms and pancetta with grilled shrimp. Open-air dining available on the covered back deck. | 60 Lake St. | 607/547–9931 | $20–$30 | AE, MC, V.

Lake Front Restaurant. American. Open-air dining overlooking Lake Otsego in addition to an array of original seafood dishes make this a lovely dining spot. Inside, in the nautical dining room, is a full salad bar and bar. Kids' menu. | 10 Fair St. | 607/547–8188 | Closed Oct.–Apr. | $12–$19 | MC, V.

Pepper Mill. American. This family-style restaurant in a commercial area can accommodate large groups. Known for steak, seafood, and pasta. | 5418 Rte. 80 | 607/547–8550 | No lunch | $11–$32 | AE, D, MC, V.

Lodging

Bay Side Motor Inn. This two-story rustic motel about 7 mi north of Cooperstown is on Otsego Lake. Picnic area. Some kitchenettes, cable TV. Beach, boating. | 7090 Rte. 80 | 607/547–2371 | fax 607/547–5856 | baysideinn@juno.com | www.cooperstown.net/bayside | 29 rooms, 11 cottages | $119–$169 rooms, $190–$285 cottages | Closed Nov.–Apr. | AE, D, MC, V.

Best Western Inn at the Commons. This hotel 4 mi south of the town itself has two two-story buildings, the more recent built in 1999. Picnic area, complimentary Continental breakfast. In-room data ports, microwaves (in suites), refrigerators (in suites), cable TV. Pool. Hot tub. Exercise equipment. Shops. Laundry facilities. Business services. | 50 Commons Dr. | 607/547–9439 | fax 607/547–7082 | 99 rooms, 2 suites | $150 rooms, $179 suites | AE, D, DC, MC, V.

Hickory Grove Motor Inn. This family-owned and -operated inn 2 mi from the Alice Busch Opera Theater has individually decorated rooms, cathedral ceilings, and a picture window facing lake Otsego. You can go paddleboating on the lake. Picnic area. Cable TV. Beach, boating. | 6854 Rte. 80 | 607/547–9874 | fax 607/547–8567 | hgmi@telenet.net | www.cooperstown.net/hickorygrove/ | 12 rooms | $98–$120 | Closed Nov.–mid-Apr. | AE, D, MC, V.

Inn at Cooperstown. Built in 1874, this inn has Victorian woodwork and antique furnishings. You can sit outside on the veranda and, inside, one of the sitting rooms has a fireplace. A trolley that takes you to various sites in Cooperstown stops nearby. Complimentary Continental breakfast. No air-conditioning, no room phones, TV in common area. Business services, free parking. | 16 Chestnut St. | 607/547–5756 | fax 607/547–8779 | theinn@telenet.net | www.cooperstown.net/theinn | 17 rooms, 1 suite | $160 | AE, D, DC, MC, V.

Lake Front. This hotel is just one block from the National Baseball Hall of Fame and Museum on Otsego Lake. The hotel offers a boat tour of the lake and some fantastic sunset views during the summer months. Restaurant. Cable TV. Dock. | 10 Fair St. | 607/547–9511 | fax 607/547–2792 | 44 rooms (15 with shower only) | $135 | MC, V.

Lake 'N Pines. Many of the wood-paneled rooms have private balconies overlooking Otsego Lake at this motel on a hill 1 mi from the Alice Busch Opera Theatre and 7 mi from downtown Cooperstown. Picnic area. Microwaves, refrigerators (in cottages), cable TV. 2 pools. Hot tub, sauna. Beach, boating. | RR 2 | 607/547–2790 or 800/615–5253 | fax 607/

547–5671 | 33 rooms, 3 cottages | $115–$135 rooms, $175 cottages | Closed early Dec.–Mar. | AE, D, MC, V.

Lake View Motel. Six miles north of Cooperstown is this one-story motel on Otsego Lake with its own private beach. The cottages have porches or decks with lawn chairs. Picnic area. Some kitchenettes, some microwaves, cable TV. Beach, dock, boating. | 6805 Rte. 80 | 607/547–9740 or 888/452–5384 | fax 607/547–5080 | www.cooperstownvacations.com | 14 rooms, 5 cottages | $125 rooms, $160 cottages | Closed Nov.–week before Easter | D, MC, V.

Mohican Motel. Two blocks from Main Street, this quite motel overlooks old village homes dating back to the founding of the town. It is made up of three buildings, including a Federal-style colonial building that has been transformed into accommodations. | 90 Chestnut St. | 607/547–5101 | 11 rooms, 2 suites | $74–$135 | Closed Thanksgiving–Easter | D, MC, V.

Otesaga Hotel. This large Georgian Revival hotel on Otsego Lake was built in 1909, and is listed on the National Register of Historic Places. Inside there are chandeliers, and paintings hang on the walls. Outside, a lakeside veranda overlooks the water and the swimming pool. Restaurant. Pool. 18-hole golf course. Dock. Video games. Business services. | 60 Lake St. | 607/547–9931 or 800/348–6222 | fax 607/547–9675 | 125 rooms, 10 suites | $295 rooms, $420 suites | MAP | AE, D, DC, MC, V.

Terrace Motor Inn. Located on Otsego Lake, this modest, one-story motor lodge has roomfront parking and easy access to the water. Downtown Cooperstown and the Baseball Hall of Fame are about ½ mi away. Restaurant. Cable TV. Pool. Dock. | 6439 State Hwy. 80, at Lake Rd. | 607/547–9979 | 15 rooms | $100 | Closed Nov.–Apr. | AE, D, MC, V.

CORNING

INTRO
ATTRACTIONS
DINING
LODGING

CORNING

MAP 3, F8

(Nearby towns also listed: Bath, Elmira, Watkins Glen)

One of the world's glass centers, Corning has an appropriate nickname: Crystal City. Half a million people a year come here to visit the Corning Glass Center. Corning was founded in 1833 and its restored 19th-century Market Street district has shops and restaurants.

Information: Greater Corning Area Chamber of Commerce | 42 E. Market St., 14830 | 607/936–4686 | www.corningny.com.

Attractions

Benjamin Patterson Inn Museum Complex. Guides in period dress show you through this complex of buildings including a log cabin, one-room schoolhouse, barn, and blacksmith shop. The centerpiece is a restored 1796 inn, full of 18th-century furniture and crafts. Five blocks from Market Street. | 59 W. Pulteney St. | 607/937–5281 | $3.50 | Feb.–Dec., weekdays 10–4.

Corning Museum of Glass. About 10,000 of the more than 30,000 glass objects in the museum's collection are on display at any one time. The range of works is enormous: there are recent, contemporary pieces as well as ones made by the Egyptians 3,500 years ago. Catch the Hot Glass Show, a live demonstration of how to make glass. Other highlights include the Hall of Science and Industry and the Steuben Factory. | 1 Museum Way | 607/974–8271 or 800/732–6845 | fax 607/974–8310 | www.cmog.org | $11; special group rates for 20 or more | Daily 9–5 (July–Aug. 9–8).

Market Street. Restored after Hurricane Agnes flooded this street in 1972, the city's main commercial district brings back the late 19th century with brick sidewalks and plenty of trees, more than 20 restaurants, and a number of glass-art studios. A shuttle bus leaves the area for the Corning Glass Center every 20 minutes. | Market St., between Denison Pkwy. and Tioga Ave. | 607/937–5427 | Free | Daily.

Rockwell Museum. This could be the finest collection of Western art in the East, thanks to Corning's Robert F. Rockwell. Works are grouped by three main themes: the Indian, the landscape, and the cowboy. | 111 Cedar St. | 607/937–5386 | $5 | Mon.–Sat. 9–5, Sun. noon–5.

ON THE CALENDAR

MAY: *LPGA Corning Classic.* The best female professional golfers come to the Corning Country Club to play at this event. Two miles from downtown. | 607/962–4441.

Dining

Boomers. American. This casual, family-oriented restaurant known for hamburgers and seafood often draws crowds. Other menu items include: corned-beef sandwiches, chef's salads, tacos, pasta, and Philly steak sandwiches. Kids' menu. | 35 E. Market St. | 607/962–6800 | Breakfast also available | $8–$18 | AE, D, MC, V.

Boomer's Bistro. Eclectic. This restaurant serving filet mignon, steak, and seafood in addition to many Mexican dishes has a touch of Western flare to it in the food and the adornments, which include a frontier painting complete with an authentic bullet hole in addition to a Texas longhorn bull. Dark wood with a brass finish sets the mood in the candlelit booths, where you can try a specialty like yellowfin tuna steak. Kids' menu. | 58 W. Market | 607/936–1408 | $9–$20 | AE, D, DC, MC, V.

London Underground Cafe. Continental. As its name suggests, this restaurant is furnished in British style. The three-level dining room provides plenty of space, and the menu has obvious Brit favorites like fish 'n' chips alongside more classically American burgers, fries, and generous salads. Open-air dining. A pianist plays on Saturday evenings. Kids' menu. Sunday brunch. Beer and wine only. | 69 E. Market St. | 607/962–2345 | $10–$24 | AE, DC, MC, V.

Oliver's Restaurant. Eclectic. Four blocks from Interstate 86, on the first floor of the Days Inn, you'll find a range of finely cooked Mediterranean food, such as pesto and many other non–tomato-based sauces. Classical music or jazz plays while you eat by candlelight, or next to the fireplace. The pastry chef prepares seasonal desserts such as caramel flan. | 58 Ferris St. | 607/936–7020 | Closed Sun. | $10–$25 | AE, MC, V.

Spencer's Restaurant and Mercantile. American. Popular among Corning residents, this rustic, family-oriented restaurant has a large and varied menu that includes chicken and biscuits, steak chops, fish fry, taco salads, seafood, and Italian dishes. Kids' menus. Early bird dinner. | 359 E. Market St. | 607/936–9196 | $6–$14 | AE, DC, MC, V.

Lodging

Best Western Lodge on the Green. This two-story chain hotel is on a 12-acre, parklike lot just west of Corning. You can go fishing next door. Restaurant, room service. In-room data ports, some kitchenettes, cable TV. Pool. Laundry service. Airport shuttle. Pets allowed. | 3171 Canada Rd., Painted Post | 607/962–2456 or 800/528–1234 | fax 607/962–1769 | 135 rooms | $69–$104 | AE, D, DC, MC, V.

Comfort Inn. This two-story hotel is very close to historic Market Street, the Rockwell Museum, and the Benjamin Patterson Inn Museum Complex. Complimentary Continental breakfast. In-room data ports, some refrigerators, cable TV. Pool. Exercise equipment. Business services. | 66 W. Pulteney St. | 607/962–1515 | fax 607/962–1899. | 62 rooms | $95 | AE, D, DC, MC, V.

Days Inn. This chain hotel is just two blocks from the Corning Glass Museum and near historic Market Street. Restaurant. In-room data ports, cable TV. Pool. Exercise equipment. Laundry service. Business services. | 23 Riverside Dr. | 607/936–9370 | fax 607/936–0513 | 56 rooms | $50–$91 | AE, D, MC, V.

Econo Lodge. Roughly 10 mi west of Corning is this chain motel in the suburbs. Complimentary Continental breakfast. Some microwaves, some refrigerators, some in-room hot tubs, cable TV. Business services. Pets allowed (fee). | 200 Robert Dann Dr., Painted Post | 607/962–4444 | fax 607/937–5397 | 61 rooms | $54–$125 | AE, D, MC, V.

Erwin Motel. Seven miles from Corning, and two blocks from Route 15, this U-shaped motel is surrounded by trees, hills, and lots of wildlife—a setting enjoyed by hunters as well as families. Most beds are double, though queen-size is available. Pool. Laundry facilities. | 806 Addison Rd. | 607/962–7411 | fax 607/962–6373 | 25 rooms | $49–$69 | MC, V.

Fairfield Inn. Three stories high and recently renovated, this mid-range chain property is in the Corning suburbs, surrounded by popular restaurants and a few shopping opportunities. Complimentary Continental breakfast, in-room data ports. Cable TV. Pool. Laundry service. | 3 S. Buffalo St. | 607/937–9600 | fax 607/937–3155 | 63 rooms.

Gate House. Offers a country setting, despite itscloseness to the Corning Glass Center and the airport, both of which are within 5 mi of the motel. Restaurant. Cable TV. Laundry facilities. | 145 E. Corning Rd. | 607/936–4131 | 20 rooms (6 with shower only) | $40–$52 | AE, MC, V.

Holiday Inn. This sizable motel is in a light-duty commercial area just 5 min from Corning. Restaurant, bar (with entertainment), room service. In-room data ports, some refrigerators, cable TV. Pool, wading pool. Beauty salon. Exercise equipment. Laundry facilities. Business services. | 304 S. Hamilton St., Painted Post | 607/962–5021 | fax 607/937–4080 | 105 rooms | $124 | AE, D, DC, MC, V.

Lando's Hotel and Lounge. You'll find this hotel in downtown Corning, three blocks from Interstate 86. It's known locally for its lounge and bar, which has live entertainment, dancing lessons, and a light show. The rooms are simple and quiet, even with the festivities taking place downstairs. Video games. | 41 Bridge St. | 607/936–9891 | fax 607/962–5470 | 25 rooms, 5 suites | rooms $35–$50, suites $75 | AE, MC, V.

Radisson-Corning. This three-story hotel is in downtown Corning. No-smoking rooms are available. Restaurant, bar (with entertainment), room service. Some kitchenettes, cable TV. Pool. Business services. Some pets allowed. | 125 Denison Pkwy. E | 607/962–5000 or 800/331–3920 | fax 607/962–4166 | radison@corningny.net | 177 rooms | $105–$169 | AE, D, MC, V.

Rosewood Inn. This restored Tudor-style home is filled with Victorian details and antiques and the parlor has a fireplace. The rooms are individually decorated. Complimentary breakfast. No TV in some rooms. No smoking. | 134 E. 1st St. | 607/962–3253 | 7 rooms | $95–$145 | AE, D, DC, MC, V.

Stiles Motel. Rural, almost pastoral countryside offers a quiet setting around this modest motor inn about 6 mi northwest of Corning. Picnic area. Cable TV. Playground. | 9239 Victory Hwy., Painted Post | 607/962–5221 or 800/331–3920 | 15 rooms | $52 | D, MC, V.

White Birch Inn. Built in 1865 in what has since become the historic section of town, this two-story home is within walking distance of downtown and two blocks from the Rockwell Museum. Rooms are decorated in a country Victorian style, with patchwork quilts, wicker, and oak furniture reminiscent of old America. Complimentary breakfast. No room phones. | 69 E. 1st St. | 607/962–6355 | 4 rooms | $70 | AE, MC, V.

CORTLAND

MAP 3, G7

(Nearby towns also listed: Ithaca, Norwich)

Cortland sits on the eastern side of the Finger Lakes area. The surrounding region is the ski capital of central New York and winter sports activities abound. Cortland, established in 1808, was named for General Pierre Van Cortlandt, the state's first lieutenant governor.

Information: **Cortland County Convention and Visitors Bureau** | 34 Tompkins St., 13045 | 607/753–8463 or 800/859–2227 | cortcvb@mail.odyssey.net.

Attractions

Book Barn of the Finger Lakes. More than 125,000 used and rare books organized into 260 different categories make this the largest bookstore in the Finger Lakes, about 14 mi southwest of Cortland. The farmstead includes three barns built in the 1800s and an apple orchard. | 198 North Rd., Dryden | 607/844–9365 | Free | Mon.–Sat. 10–5:30, Sun. noon–5.

Cortland's Country Music Park and Campground. The huge dance floor, outdoor stage, and statewide Country Music Hall of Fame makes this 13-acre site a country-music mecca for those who can't get to Nashville as often as they'd like. National acts play here four or five times a summer; regional bands fill in the rest of the time. Live country music is played weekends year-round. The park is run by volunteers. | Truxton Rd. off Rte. 13 N | 607/753–0377 | Donations accepted | Daily; call for music schedule.

1890 House Museum. This 30-room Victorian mansion in downtown Cortland was built by wire manufacturer Chester F. Wickwire and is now an informal museum. If you climb the tower, you will get a fine view of the city. | 37 Tompkins St. | 607/756–7551 | $3.50 | Tues.–Sun. 1–4.

Fillmore Glen State Park. This limestone-and-shale glen and park about 20 mi northwest of Cortland has five waterfalls, and a stone-walled swimming pool. Named for President Millard Fillmore, who was born 5 mi to the east, the park also has a replica of the cabin where he was born. Camping is available. | Rte. 38, Moravia | 315/497–0130 | www.nys-parks.state.ny.us/parks/ | Free; parking $5–$6 | Daily.

Skiing. Four popular ski areas nearby provide plenty of downhill and cross-country skiing, as well as snowboarding and snow tubing.

Greek Peak has a 912-ft vertical drop, seven lifts, 29 trails, and night skiing every day. Snowmaking covers 83% of the hill. Downhill and cross-country skiing, snow tubing, and snowboarding. It's 10 mi north of Cortland. | Virgil | 607/835–6111 or 800/955–2754 or 800/365–7669 | Dec.–Apr.

Labrador Mountain, about 12 mi northeast of Cortland, has a 700-ft vertical drop, 22 slopes, five lifts, and night skiing. Snowmaking covers 95% of the area. Lift rates range from $17 to $27. You can ski downhill or cross-country, or go snowboarding. | Rte. 91, Truxton | 607/842–6204 or 800/446–9559 | Dec.–Mar., daily.

Song Mountain Resort, about 13 mi northeast of Cortland, has a 700-ft vertical drop, downhill skiing, and snowboarding on 24 trails. Night skiing every day. Snowmaking covers 75% of the hill. | Off Interstate 81, near Preble | 315/696–5711 or 800/677–7664 | Dec.–Mar., daily.

Toggenburg Ski Center has 25 trails for downhill skiing, snowboarding, and snow tubing, as well as night skiing. About 95% of the hill is covered by snowmaking, and the vertical drop is roughly 650 ft. | Toggenburg Rd., Fabius | 315/683–5842 | Dec.–Mar., daily.

ON THE CALENDAR

APR.: *Central New York Maple Festival.* There is plenty of maple syrup along with other maple products at this festival which also has juried art exhibits. Special train excursions go from Syracuse to Marathon and from Marathon to Cortland. It's 14 mi south of Cortland, in Marathon, exit 9 off Interstate 81. | 607/849–3278 or 607/849–3812.

JUNE–AUG.: *Cortland Repertory Theatre.* Five professional plays or musicals are performed during summer in the turn-of-the-20th-century Pavilion Theatre in Dwyer Memorial County Park, off Route 281 in Little York, 10 mi from Cortland. | 607/756–2627 or 800/427–6160.

OCT: *Great Cortland Pumpkin Festival.* This lively harvest celebration has local bands such as the Old Timers to set the scene, where crafts, hayrides, kids' games, and lots of food are all part of the festivities. Look for the tent where you can sample local micro-brewery beers. It takes place in Courthouse Park, in front of the courthouse, the first full weekend of the month. | 800/859–2227 | Free.

Dining

Benn Conger Inn. Mediterranean. Housed in three large, wood-paneled dining areas within a 1919 Southern Revival mansion, this restaurant serves light-yet-substantial Mediterranean cuisine. The menu changes periodically to take advantage of seasonal produce, but for dinner, anything with seafood is excellent. The kitchen also produces some impressive steaks. Kids' menu. | 206 W. Cortland St., Groton | 607/898–5817 | Reservations essential | Closed Mon., Tues. No lunch | $15–$25 | AE, DC, MC, V.

Hollywood Restaurant. Italian. The star on the door lets you know you've found this restaurant. Inside the walls are covered with more neon-color stars. Try the sautéed broccoli over linguine, the shrimp scampi, or the pasta primavera. | 27 Groton Ave. | 607/753–3242 | $8–$15 | AE, DC, MC, V.

Rocci's. Italian. A family restaurant with white tablecloths just outside downtown Cortland. Baked sausage, New York strip steak, and broiled scallops are popular. Salad bar. | 294 Tompkins St. (Rte. 13 W) | 607/753–0428 | $9–$15 | AE, DC, MC, V.

Rusty Nail. American. Sliding glass doors lead to a private candlelit dining area in this restaurant that also has a lounge area and a bar. Popular dishes include prime rib, chicken, and spareribs. Entertainment on Saturday. Kids' menu. | 3993 West Rd. | 607/753–7238 | No lunch weekdays | $15–$35 | AE, D, DC, MC, V.

Lodging

Benn Conger Inn. Rooms at this early 20th-century mansion on a hill about 10 mi due west of Cortland are furnished with antiques. Restaurant (*see* Benn Conger Inn), bar, complimentary breakfast. Cable TV. Hiking. Airport shuttle. | 206 W. Cortland St., Groton | 607/898–5817 | fax 607/898–5818 | 5 rooms | $120–$220 | AE, DC, MC, V.

Comfort Inn. The guest rooms are larger than usual in this chain hotel. Restaurant, complimentary Continental breakfast. In-room data ports, cable TV. Exercise equipment. Business services. | 2½ Locust Ave. | 607/753–7721 | fax 607/753–7608 | 66 rooms | $84–$139 | AE, D, DC, MC, V.

Downes Motel. This two-story motel is located in a largely commercial area surrounded by restaurants and night sports in Cortland. Ski packages are available. Some microwaves, cable TV. Business services. | 10 Church St. | 607/756–2856 or 800/800–0301 | 42 rooms | $52–$95 | AE, D, DC, MC, V.

Holiday Inn. This chain hotel is located in a fairly busy commercial area. Restaurant. Cable TV. Pool. Exercise equipment. | 2 River St. | 607/756–4431 | 149 rooms | $99 | AE, D, DC, MC, V.

Seven Valley Motel. Choose from an efficiency or a motel room at this family-run property in the residential part of town. Restaurants and shops are within walking distance. | 46 Tompkins St. | 607/753–1515 | 16 rooms, 8 efficiencies | rooms $38, efficiencies $48 | No credit cards.

CROTON-ON-HUDSON

MAP 4, E2

(Nearby towns also listed: Mt. Kisco, Peekskill, Pound Ridge)

The charming village of Croton-on-Hudson has many beautiful country homes, nostalgic shops, and one of the busiest railroad stations north of New York City. Only 5 square mi, the village is home to 7,000 residents. Over the years, Croton-on-Hudson has won fame for its thriving artistic community: world-renowned sculptor Alexander Calder and poet Edna St. Vincent Millay are among the many artists who have lived here.

Information: **Croton Chamber of Commerce** | Box 111, Croton-on-Hudson, 10520 | 914/271–2196.

Attractions

Van Cortlandt Manor. An 18th-century brick manor house is the centerpiece of this beautiful estate on the banks of the Croton River. Also on the grounds of this National Historic Landmark are an 18th-century tavern and tenant house. | S. River Side Ave., off Croton Point Ave. | 914/271–8981 | www.hudsonvalley.org | $8 | Apr.–Oct., Wed.–Mon.; Nov.–Dec., weekends only.

ON THE CALENDAR

JUNE: *Great Hudson River Festival.* This annual summer festival of music, art, and environmental activism was created in 1966 by world-renowned folk singer and activist Pete Seeger to raise funds to build and maintain the *Clearwater,* a 100-ft wooden sailing ship built in 1969. In Croton Point Park, off Route 9 south on Croton Point Avenue. | 914/454–7673.

JULY: *Independence Day Celebration.* Re-live a Revolutionary-era (1799) Fourth of July celebration at Van Cortlandt Manor. Cannon fire begins the festivities and everyone can join in the parade along with the costumed residents of the manor. Patriotic songs and speeches, country cooking and picnics, and demonstrations of military drills and musketry round out the day. | 914/271–8981.

Dining

Casa De Nicota Ristorante. Italian. This intimate dining room serves pasta, steak, and seafood to the gentle, soothing sounds of an indoor fountain. | 441 Albany Post Rd. (Rte. 9A) | 914/271–2920 | Closed Mon. No lunch weekends, Tues. | $8–$22 | AE, MC, V.

Trilogy Restaurant. Eclectic. The main dining room at this restaurant is sophisticated and modern, with black-and-white photographs of New York City and dozens of pillar candles, while the smaller back room is quiet and rustic, with oak beams and a large 19th-century sideboard. Try the ahi tuna sashimi, seared Moroccan salmon, or roast applewood smoked chicken breast. Sunday brunch. | 1 Baltic Pl. | 914/271–2600 | No dinner Mon., no lunch weekends | $15–$25 | AE, MC, V.

Lodging

Alexander Hamilton House. This romantic 1889 Victorian inn in the most historic part of Croton has views of the Hudson River and an outdoor gazebo. Most of the individually decorated rooms have fireplaces. Complimentary breakfast. Some in-room hot tubs. Pool. | 49 Van Wyck St. | 914/271–6737 | www.alexanderhamiltonhouse.com | 7 rooms | $95–$250 | D, DC, MC, V.

CROWN POINT

MAP 3, L4

(Nearby towns also listed: Schroon Lake, Ticonderoga)

The entire area near Crown Point was once known as Ironville, though that name now belongs to a small, nearby village. Crown Point is a quiet town, but the rich bed of iron ore discovered here in the early 1800s once made this a major industrial area. The U.S.

Navy was particularly anxious to use Crown Point's iron ore for its new class of iron-clad ships, such as the *Monitor*. Today, the town offers many historic sightseeing trips, easy access to Vermont via the Crown Point Bridge, and water sports and activities on Lake Champlain.

Information: Ticonderoga Area Chamber of Commerce | 108 Lake George Ave., Ticonderoga, 12883 | 518/585–6619.

Attractions

Crown Point Reservation State Campground. Most of the 64 campsites have views of Lake Champlain, and the park is close to the Crown Point bridge to Vermont. Includes showers. The site is off Route 22, across from the Crown Point State Historic Site. | 518/597–3603 | Call for information | Apr.–Oct., daily.

Crown Point State Historic Site. Since the earliest European explorations of North America, Lake Champlain has been considered an important strategic waterway and both the French and English built forts along its banks. On this peninsula you will find the ruins of both the 1734 French Fort Saint Frederic and the 1759 British Fort Crown Point. Interpretive tours are offered. | 3 mi north of Crown Pointe on Hwy. 17 Rd., RD 1 | 518/597–3666 | $4 per vehicle | May–Oct., Wed.–Sat. 10–5, Sun. 1–5.

Penfield Homestead Museum. Dedicating to preserving the legacy of innovative industrialist Allen Penfield, this museum has exhibits explaining his work using electricity in the process of iron-ore separation. This was the first industrial application of electricity. The museum, 3 mi southwest of Crown Point, also houses many Civil War artifacts and equipment on its 550-acre site. | Country Rte. 2 in Ironville Historic District | 518/597–3804 | $2 suggested donation | Mid-May–mid-Oct., Wed.–Sat. 10–4, Sun. 12–4 (July–Labor Day, daily 10–4).

ON THE CALENDAR

AUG.: *Champ Day*. This festival celebrates Champ, the mythic monster of Lake Champlain, who is believed to live deep in the water and occasionally make an appearance. Includes a giant replica of Champ, pirates, as well as booths and displays on Main Street in Port Henry, just north of Crown Point. | 518/546–3606.

Dining

Frenchy's. American. These picnic tables in the center of town are the perfect spot to eat a Michigan hot dog served with a special tomato-based sauce with onion and spices. Other options are garden burgers and soft ice cream. With these prices you can't go wrong. | Downtown Crown Point, on Main St. | 518/597–3938 | Closed Oct.–Apr. | $1–$4 | No credit cards.

Lodging

Crown Point Bed and Breakfast. This Victorian-era "painted lady" incorporates ten different shades of paint into its exterior, and has hundreds of square feet of high-polish hardwood within. The home was built in 1886 for a banker, but now houses guests in luxurious rooms filled with period antiques. Complimentary Continental breakfast. No air-conditioning, no room phones, TV in common area. No smoking. | Main St. (Rte. 9 N) | 518/597–3651 | fax 518/597–4451 | 5 rooms (1 with shower only), 1 suite | $60–$75 rooms, $100–$130 suites | MC, V.

Harwood Homestead. Seven miles from downtown in the Ironwood section, nestled into a secluded hamlet on 2 acres, sits this 1840 Greek Revival home. Furnished partly with antiques, it still has its original hardwood floors. After your breakfast, you might enjoy a cup of tea on the spacious wraparound porch. It's not within walking distance of any shops or restaurants. Fishing is available. Complimentary Continental breakfast. | R.R. 1 | 518/597–3429 | 3 rooms | $60 | No credit cards.

DELHI

MAP 3, I7

(Nearby towns also listed: Bainbridge, Oneonta, Roxbury, Stamford)

A rural village surrounded by rolling hills and pastures along Route 28, Delhi has a population of barely 3,000. The town, which is Delaware County's government center, has some notable Federal-style architecture.

Information: **Chamber of Commerce** | 114 Main St., 13753 | 607/746–2281.

Attractions

Delaware County Historical Association Museum. The 1797 home of Gideon Frisbee, an original settler of Delhi, this living museum also includes an extensive library, a 19th-century tavern, a barn, and a nature trail. Special events re-create the life of the period. | Rte. 10 2 mi north of Delhi | 607/746–3849 | $3 | Memorial Day–mid-Oct., Tues.–Sun.11–4:30.

ON THE CALENDAR

OCT.: *Harvest Festival.* Held every Columbus Day weekend in Courtyard Square, this small-town festival celebrates the bounty of the autumn harvest with live musical performances, a craft show, and lots and lots of food. | 607/746–6100.

Dining

La Bella Pizzeria. Italian. Locals and college students come here to indulge in thick-crust Sicilian pizza, calzones, strombolis, spicy wings, salads, and subs. Ansel Adams photographs and country music help to give this place character. | Ames Plaza on Rte. 10 | 607/746–3311 | Closed Mon. | $6–$9 | MC, V.

Lodging

Gingerbread House Bed and Breakfast. Built in 1823, this gingerbread-trimmed home sits in the center of town, putting you within walking distance of everything. Inside, the house has retained the Victorian age, with touches like a woodstove and fireplace. All rooms have one double bed. Complimentary Continental breakfast. No room phones, no TV. | 139 Main St. | 607/746–6777 | 3 rooms | $45 | Closed weekdays (Fri.- and Sat.-night stays only) | No credit cards.

DEPOSIT

MAP 3, I8

(Nearby town also listed: Binghamton)

Deposit, in the Southern Tier of the Adirondacks about 25 mi east of Binghamton on Route 17, was founded in 1789. Nearby Oquaga Creek has a state park and campsite, and Oquaga Lake is the site of Scott's Oquaga Lake House resort.

Information: **Deposit Chamber of Commerce** | Box 222, 13754 | 607/467–2556.

Attractions

Oquaga Creek State Park. About 9 mi north of Deposit is this park where you can hike, camp, or swim. After Labor Day, there is no swimming, but you can still camp here. | 5995 County Hwy. 20, Bainbridge | 607/467–4160, or 800/456–CAMP reservations | $6 per vehicle | Memorial Day–Labor Day, daily; Labor Day–Columbus Day, weekends.

JULY: *Lumberjack Festival.* Professional firemen come to Firemen's Field for four days during the third week of the month to participate in events such as log rolling, sawing competitions, and rescue simulations, with winning teams qualifying for a national championship. Pancake breakfasts, canoe races, and games for kids in addition to a Saturday-night parade make it a fun-filled event for all ages. | 607/467–2556.

Dining

Chestnut Inn at Oquaga Lake. American. This secluded place with open-air dining overlooking Oquaga Lake and the surrounding Catskills is 2 mi out of town. Inside, fresh flowers, tablecloths, and dim lighting set the mood for food like lobster tails or filet mignon. Sunday brunch includes smoked salmon and a waffle station. | 498 Oquaga Lake Rd. | 607/467–2500 | Closed 1st 2 weeks Jan. | $22–$35 | AE, D, DC, MC, V.

Lodging

Chestnut Inn. Built in 1928 almost entirely of now-extinct North American chestnut wood, this lakeside resort has easy water access, carefully-tended grounds, and a year-round sunporch. Restaurant, bar. Cable TV, no room phones. Massage. Water sports, boating. Business services. | 498 Oquaga Lake Rd. | 607/467–2500 | fax 607/467–5911 | 30 rooms (20 with shared bath), 5 suites | $99 rooms, $169 suites | AE, D, DC, MC, V.

Deposit Motel. One mile from the center of town, you'll find this quintessential country motel in the Catskill foothills. Pictures of farms and country landscapes surround you inside, while outside the Delaware River is only three blocks away. Rooms have two double beds. Pets allowed. | 44 Oak St. | 607/467–2998 | 12 rooms, 1 suite | $50–$65 | MC, V.

Scott's Oquaga Lake House. This sprawling resort on 11 acres has a private waterfront and plenty of boats, including speedboats and canoes. Activities include weekly cookouts and dancing. Dancing instructors are available to lead you through your paces. Restaurant. No air-conditioning. Two 9-hole golf courses, putting green, tennis. Bowling, hiking. Water sports, boating, bicycles. Children's programs (ages 2–12). Laundry facilities. | 591 Oquaga Lake Rd. | 607/467–3094 | www.scottsfamilyresort.com | 125 rooms, 4 cottages | $107 rooms, $225–$325 cottages (up to 8 people) | Closed mid-Oct.–Memorial Day | AP | D, MC, V.

DIAMOND POINT

MAP 3, L5

(Nearby towns also listed: Bolton Landing, Glens Falls, Lake George Village, Lake Luzerne, Queensbury, Warrensburg)

Diamond Point is on the shores of Lake George, just 5 mi south of Bolton Landing and 3 mi north of Lake George Village. In addition to a wide, sandy beach, the town also has pretty countryside and a trolley that runs from Lake George Village to Diamond Point.

Information: **Lake George Chamber of Commerce** | Box 272, Lake George, 12845 | 518/668–5755.

Dining

McGowan's Restaurant. American. Prime rib, pork, and beef await you here along with a sense of local life: pictures of Lake George and the Adirondacks have hung on the walls since the restaurant opened in 1984. Salads and seafood are also available. You bring your own wine, and there's no corkage fee. Kids' menu. | 3721 Lake Shore Dr. | 518/668–4800 | Breakfast also available | $11–$20 | AE, D, MC, V.

Lodging

Blue Water Manor. Seven miles from the village of Lake George, this 1894 Adirondack-style manor sits on a cliff overlooking Basin Bay. A main draw to this 7-acre resort is the water sports—like swimming, boating, jet-skiing, and fishing—geared toward all abilities. During the evening, there's dancing, live entertainment, and movies in the Manor House. Complimentary breakfast and dinner. Tennis court. Volleyball. Playground. | 4436 Lake Shore Dr. | 518/644–2535 | fax 518/644–2537 | www.bluelagoonresort.com | 74 rooms, 6 suites | $156 | Closed Labor Day–Memorial Day | MAP | MC, V.

Canoe Island Lodge. Lakeside terraces offer views of Lake George at this lodge with rustic cottages. Many of the rooms have fireplaces. Restaurant, bar. Cable TV. Tennis. Beach, docks, water sports, boating. Children's programs (ages 3 and up), playground. Business services. | Lake Shore Dr. | 518/668–5592 | fax 518/668–2012 | www.canoeislandlodge.com/ | 30 rooms in cottages, 6 minichalets, 18 rooms in 2-story lodges | $120–$130 cottage rooms, $144 minichalets, $160 lodge rooms | Closed mid-Oct.–mid-May | No credit cards.

Capri Village. Four and half mi north of the village of Lake George, this resort offers both motel and cottage accommodations. Families come back year after year to sit on the sundeck and hit the beach on Lake George; rooms have either a lake or a pool view. Restaurants and shops are within walking distance. Pool. Basketball, volleyball, beach. | 3926 Lake Shore Dr. | 518/668–4829 | 29 motel units, 29 cottages | $89 rooms, cottages $789–$895 (7-day minimum stay) | MC, V.

Golden Sands Resort Motel. Rooms at this motel on Lake George have easy access to the beach and docks. A few of the rooms have private decks. Picnic area. Some kitchenettes, microwaves, refrigerators, cable TV. Pool. Beach, boating. | 3654 Lakeshore Dr. | 518–668–3294 | www.goldensandsresort.com | 26 rooms | $90–$145 | Closed Labor Day–Memorial Day | MC, V.

Juliana. This one- and two-story motel on Lake George has beautiful views of Buck Mountain. Picnic area. Many kitchenettes, cable TV. Pool. Beach, boating. Playground. | 3842 Lake Shore Dr., Bolton Landing | 518/668–5191 | fax 518/668–9574 | 26 motel rooms, 7 cottages | $72–$110 rooms, $120 cottages | Closed Labor Day–Memorial Day | MC, V.

Treasure Cove Resort Motel. Most rooms at this motel have private balconies with a view of Lake George. The cottages have large living rooms, many with fireplaces and views of the lake. Picnic area. No air-conditioning in some rooms, some kitchenettes, refrigerators, cable TV. 2 pools. Beach, boating, fishing. Video games. Playground. | 3940 Lake Shore Dr., Diamond Point | 518/668–5334 | www.treasurecoveresort.com | 35 rooms, 15 cottages | $105–$131 rooms, $1,195–$1,380 (7-day minimum stay) | Closed mid-Oct.–Apr. | No credit cards.

Trout Lake Club Resort. Some of the rustic, log cabin–style cottages at this family-oriented resort on the lake have fireplaces. You can go hiking nearby. Tennis. Beach, boating, fishing. Video games. Playground. Some pets allowed. | 1 Trout Lake Club Rd., Diamond Point | 518/644–3571 | 44 cabins | $390 (7-day minimum stay) | Closed Oct.–May | No credit cards.

Wide Waters Motel and Cabins. This motel on Lake George maintains a private beach with a dock. No air-conditioning, some kitchenettes, no room phones, no TV. | 4124 Lake Shore Rd. | 518/668–5567 | 4 suites, 10 cabins | $140 suites, $90 cabins | Closed Columbus Day–Memorial Day | No credit cards.

DUNKIRK

MAP 3, B7

(Nearby towns also listed: Fredonia, Westfield)

Dunkirk, a town on one of the few harbors along the east coast of Lake Erie, lies in New York State's newest wine-producing area. Relatively mild winters and glacial soil (left by retreating glaciers in the ice age) make this area south of Buffalo between Silver Creek and the Pennsylvania border perfectly suited for raising grapes. The town was named after Dunquerque in northern France, and was most famous in 1851, when it became the terminus of the longest railroad in the world. Dunkirk's historic lighthouse was built in 1875 and is still operating.

Information: Mayville Area Chamber of Commerce | Box 22, Mayville, 14757 | 716/753–3113.

Attractions

ALCO-Brooks Railroad Display. A 1907 wood-sided boxcar, a locomotive built in Dunkirk, and a restored 1905 wooden New York Central caboose are part of this museum's displays, which showcase the railroading history of western New York. | County Fairgrounds, 1089 Central Ave. | 716/366–3797 | Free | Daily noon to dusk.

Dunkirk Historical Lighthouse and Veterans Park Museum. Downstairs at this museum there are five rooms furnished to show how the lighthouse keeper would have lived, while upstairs, the rooms are filled with exhibits about lighthouses, shipping, and the military. There are Coast Guard boats on display, including a 45-ft buoy tender. You can take a guided tour up to the tower. | 1 Lighthouse Point, off Rte. 5 | 716/366–5050 | $5.50 | Apr.–June and Sept.–Oct., Mon., Tues., and Thurs.–Sat. 10–2; July–Aug., Mon., Tues., and Thurs.–Sat. 10–4.

Evangola State Park. A 4,000-ft sandy beach is one of the highlights of this 733-acre park, 15 mi northeast of Dunkirk, which also has hiking trails, playgrounds, and game areas. You can camp, fish, or picnic. In winter, take advantage of the snowmobiling and cross-country skiing trails. | Rte. 5, Old Lake Shore Rd., Irving | 716/549–1802 or 716/549–1760 | $5 per vehicle | Daily.

Lake Erie State Park. This park, on high bluffs overlooking the lake, has spectacular scenery. If you come for the day, you can swim, picnic, hike, or enjoy the playgrounds. There are also 97 campsites, 10 cabins, and camping amenities. Picnic areas have shelters. The park is 8½ mi from Dunkirk. | Rte. 5 | 716/792–9214 or 800/456–CAMP | www.nysparks.state.ny.us/parks/ | $5 per vehicle; $6 July–Labor day | May–mid-Oct., daily.

ON THE CALENDAR

MAY: *Chautauqua County Annual Arts and Crafts Shows.* At one of the largest arts-and-crafts shows in western New York, you'll find Amish goods, locally grown produce, handmade quilts, handcrafted toys, and plenty more. Second week of the month on Central Avenue. | 716/366–4752.

JULY: *Chautauqua County Fair.* Rides, food, livestock, exhibits, and races at the Chautauqua County Fairgrounds. | 716/366–4752.

Dining

Demetri's on the Lake. Eclectic. Eat Greek or American on the deck overlooking Lake Erie. Entrées such as lamb, chicken souvlaki, prime rib, steak, and seafood go along well with the extensive wine list. The Sunday brunch is wonderfully indulgent. Kids' menu. | 6 Lake Shore Dr. W | 716/366–4187 | $4–$11 | AE, D, MC, V.

Windjammer's. Contemporary. The boat wheel and fish tank in the dining room create a nautical theme at this restaurant overlooking Lake Erie's Chadwick Bay. Part of the Four Points by Sheraton Hotel complex, the restaurant draws a diverse crowd, including many hotel guests. Menu options include filet mignon, grilled pork chops, and chicken Alfredo. | 30 Lake Shore Dr. E | 716/366–8350 or 800/525–8350 | $5–$27 | AE, D, DC, MC, V.

Lodging

Four Points by Sheraton. This four-story hotel looks out over the bay of Lake Erie. Restaurant, bar, room service. In-room data ports, some refrigerators, cable TV. Pool. Hot tub.

Gym. Business services, free parking. | 30 Lake Shore Dr. E | 716/366–8350 or 800/525–8350 | fax 716/366–8899 | 132 rooms | $119–$139 | AE, D, DC, MC, V.

Green Glen Bed and Breakfast. This Queen Anne–style Victorian home, built in 1892, is filled with Victorian antiques. Floral and lace linens help to evoke the period as well, but there's no shortage of modern conveniences. For example, you can check your e-mail in the Internet room. Rooms are large, with four-poster beds and luxurious mattresses. One block from shops and restaurants. Complimentary Continental breakfast. Library. | 898 Main St. | 716/655–2828 | 6 rooms | $75–$135 | No credit cards.

Rodeway Inn. One mi from the center of town, this typical roadside accommodation is only a 2-min drive from Lake Erie. Beds are double or queen size. Complimentary Continental breakfast. Pets allowed ($5 fee). | 310 Lake Shore Dr. | 888/310–5253 or 716/366–2200 | 48 rooms | $55 | AE, D, DC, MC, V.

Southshore Motor Lodge. Both rooms and cottages are available at this motel on 6 rural acres. Picnic area. Many kitchenettes, refrigerators, cable TV, some in-room VCRs. Pool. Playground. Some pets allowed. | 5040 W. Lake Shore Dr. | 716/366–2822 | 2 rooms, 6 suites, 12 cottages | $49–$115 | MC, V.

EAST AURORA

MAP 3, C6

(Nearby towns also listed: Amherst, Buffalo, Clarence, Hamburg, Williamsville)

East Aurora has earned the nickname Toy Town, U.S.A., because it is home to both Fisher Price Toys and a unique toy museum. East Aurora is also the locale of two National Historic Landmarks—the honeymoon cottage of President Millard Fillmore and his wife Abigail, and the Roycroft Campus, an Arts and Crafts movement community founded at the turn of the 20th century by writer and lecturer Elbert Hubbard, in which nine of the fourteen buildings are open to the public. You'll want to have a look inside the Roycroft Inn at the murals painted by Barbizon artist Alex Fournier, as well as original examples of Roycroft Mission-style furniture.

Information: **East Aurora Chamber of Commerce** | 431 Main St., 14052 | 716/652–8444.

Attractions

Elbert Hubbard-Roycroft Museum. This 1910 Craftsman bungalow is filled with the artifacts of Elbert Hubbard, the founder of the colony. | 363 Oakwood Ave. | 716/652–4735 or 716/652–1424 | $2 | June–mid-Oct., Wed. and weekends 2–4; tours by appointment.

Explore and More Children's Museum. Geared to children up to age 10, this museum encourages experimentation, play, and learning in an interactive environment. | 430 Main St. | 716/655–5131 | $2 | Wed.–Sat. 10–4.

Kissing Bridge Ski Area. A favorite with Buffalo residents, this center 20 min from East Aurora has a 550-ft vertical drop, 36 trails, 10 lifts, and annual snowfall of 180 inches. It includes a terrain park and a half pipe for snowboarders. Lessons and ski rentals are available. | Rte. 240, Glenwood | 716/592–4963 or 716/592–4961 | fax 716–592–4228 | kb@pce.net | www.kissing-bridge.com | Mid-Nov.–early May.

Millard Fillmore House. Built by President Millard Fillmore in 1826, this National Historic Landmark has been restored and refurnished to reflect life in the early 19th century. | 24 Shearer Ave. | 716/652–8875 | $2 | June–mid-Oct., Wed. and weekends 2–4; mid-Oct.–May, by appointment.

Roycroft Campus. A center for New York's Arts and Crafts movement, this 14-building community was once home to 500 craftsmen and their shops. | 31 S. Grove St. | 716/652–3333 or 888/769–2738 | fax 716/652–0562 | Free | Daily 10–5.

Toy Town Museum. Rare and one-of-a-kind toys are on display at this museum which also has a collection of Fisher-Price toys from 1930 through 1970. In addition, there is an interactive learning center designed for children. | 636 Girard Ave. | 716/687–5151 | fax 716/687–5098 | www.toytownusa.com | Free | Mon.–Sat. 10–4.

Vidler's 5 and 10 Cent Store. Everything you'd expect to find in an old-fashioned five-and-dime—crafts, housewares, cards, fabrics, and toys—is for sale at this store which has been family-owned since 1930. Four buildings that date to 1890 house the over 15,000-square-ft store. | 680–694 Main St. | 716/652–0481 or 877–VIDLERS | fax 716/655–0631 | www.vidlers5and10.com | Mon.–Thurs. and Sat. 9–5:30, Fri. 9–9, Sun. 12–4.

ON THE CALENDAR

MAY: *Roycroft Elderhostel.* Adults 55 and over attend classes and special tours to learn about the Arts and Crafts movement firsthand on the Roycroft Campus. | 716/652–3333.
JUNE: *Roycroft Summer Festival of Arts and Crafts.* The Roycroft campus hosts an antiques show, a juried art show, and a sale, with live entertainment. | 716/655–1565.
AUG.: *ToyFest.* Notable and historic toys from various periods and manufacturers are on display during this festival that also brings a parade, an antique car show, rides, entertainment, and food to the Toy Museum. | 716/687–5251.

Dining

Old Orchard Inn. American. Housed in a 1901 hunting lodge, this restaurant overlooks a pond and landscaped lawns. Traditional items like chicken pot pie, rack of lamb, and filet mignon fill the menu, complemented by pasta and salmon options. In good weather you can dine beneath an awning on a patio. Kids' menu. | 2095 Blakeley Corners Rd. | 716/652–4664 | $15–$25 | AE, D, DC, MC, V.

Roycroft Inn. Continental. Arts and Crafts furniture is the stage for lamb chops, duck confit, grilled salmon, steaks, and pastas at this restaurant, where, during the summer you can dine on a covered porch. Sunday brunch. No smoking. | 40 S. Grove St. | 716/652–5552 | No lunch Sat. | $10–$22 | AE, D, DC, MC, V.

Lodging

Roycroft Inn. Arts and Crafts furniture made in the Roycroft community fills the rooms at this three-story inn. The single rooms of the early 20th-century inn have been converted to suites, which include a bedroom, sitting room, and bathroom. Restaurant, bar, complimentary Continental breakfast, room service. In-room data ports, in-room hot tubs, cable TV. Business services. No smoking. | 40 S. Grove St. | 716/652–5552, 800/267–0525 reservations | fax 716/655–5345 | 7 rooms, 22 suites | $130–$230 | AE, D, DC, MC, V.

EAST HAMPTON

MAP 3, F2

(Nearby towns also listed: Amagansett, Bridgehampton, Montauk, Sag Harbor, Southampton)

East Hampton, a Long Island village on the South Fork, was founded in 1648 by a group of farmers. Farming remained its main source of livelihood until the mid-1800s when the town began to develop into a fashionable resort.

The village has evolved into a place of charm and grace. Its considerable wealth and Puritan heritage now combine into a particularly understated prosperity, much of the village remaining as it was during the 18th century. Luminaries such as Jackie Kennedy, who spent many childhood days in East Hampton, have enjoyed its beauty and sophistication.

Cooled by the Atlantic Ocean, today it is a thriving summer resort noted for fine food, shopping, and lovely beaches.

Information: **East Hampton Chamber of Commerce** | 79A Main St., 11937 | 631/324–0362 | info@peconic.net | www.easthamptonchamber.com.

Attractions

East Hampton Historical Society. The society operates six local historic sites and museums, including Clinton Academy (circa 1784), Town House (circa 1731), Osborn–Jackson House (circa 1740), and Mulford Farm (circa 1680). | Main St. | 631/324–6850 | Free | July–Labor Day, daily 9–5.

Guild Hall Museum. Changing exhibitions at this fine-arts museum focus mainly on regional artists. There are also lectures, films, music, and the John Drew Theater (*see below*). | 158 Main St. | 631/324–0806 | June–Labor Day, Mon.–Sat. 11–5 (Wed. 11–6), Sun. 12–5; Labor Day–May, Wed.–Sat. 11–5, Sun. 12–5.

John Drew Theater at Guild Hall. Several stage productions a year are put on at this 387-seat theater. Concerts, film festivals, lectures, and readings happen here as well. | 158 Main St. | 631/324–4050 or 631/324–0806 | Call for schedule.

"Home Sweet Home" House. This circa-1680 saltbox house was once home to the 19th-century poet, playwright, and actor John Howard Payne, who wrote the words to "Home Sweet Home." Guided tours lead you through the collections of English ceramics, American furniture, and textiles. The museum is in an historic district, within walking distance of 19th-century windmills, including the Old Hook Mill. | 14 James La. | 631/324–0713 | $4 | May–Sept., Mon.–Sat. 10–4, Sun. 2–4; Apr., Oct.–Nov., Fri.–Sat. 10–4, Sun. 2–4.

Old Hook Mill. Built in 1806 by Nathaniel Dominey, the mill, which once ground corn and wheat, is still operational. | N. Main St. | 631/324–4150 | $2.50 | June–Aug., Mon.–Sat. 10–4, Sun. 2–4.

ON THE CALENDAR

JULY: *East Hampton Antiques Show.* Hobnob with movie stars and television celebrities as you scour through the collections looking for that special item at this show on the grounds of the East Hampton Middle School. | 631/261–4590.

OCT.: *Hamptons International Film Festival.* Preview independent, contemporary, and international documentary films and attend panel discussions with well-known directors, screenwriters, and editors. | 631/324–4600.

Dining

East Hampton Point. Contemporary. You can watch the sun go down over the water through a wall of windows at this restaurant known for its creative menu. The outside tables have umbrellas for shade. Kids' menu. | 295 Three Mile Harbor/Hog Creek Rd. | 631/329–2800 | Reservations essential | $20–$36 | AE, MC, V.

The Farmhouse. French. The dining room is done up like a country farmhouse, with an antique bar and fireplaces. Large parties are no problem here, and there is an extensive wine list to accompany the dry-aged rib-eye steak with garlic mashed potatoes, Farmhouse chicken (a whole baby chicken on a bed of mashed potatoes), or salmon with beet-flavor risotto. Open-air dining on the enclosed patio or the completely open courtyard. Raw bar. Live music. Kids' menu. Early bird dinners. | 341 Montauk Hwy. | 631/324–8585 | No lunch | $18–$25 | AE, MC, V.

James Lane Cafe at the Hedges Inn. Steak. A collection of antique French and English posters brighten the white walls at this 1870s Victorian home with bleached oak floors. Like its sister restaurant, the Palm, the café is well known for its aged prime beef and lobsters (3–6 pounds), as well as crab cakes. Open-air dining in tented/screened garden terrace. Family-style service. Kids' menu. No smoking. | 74 James La. | 631/324–7100 | No lunch | $20–$30 | AE, MC, V.

Laundry. Contemporary. A very large, old laundry machine decorates the patio at this restaurant in a former commercial laundry building. Inside, the brick walls reach up to high ceilings with skylights. Try the grilled shrimp with salsa chutney over frisée and fennel, and grilled scallops in balsamic vinegar reduction with saffron rice and fresh tomato salsa. Open-air dining on patio. Live music Fridays and Saturdays. No smoking. | 31 Race La. | 631/324–3199 | No lunch | $20–$32 | AE, D, MC, V.

Maidstone Arms. Contemporary. One of the chef's signature dishes at this restaurant in a Greek Revival inn is rum-soaked smoked salmon. Try the Long Island lacquered duck, with peanuts, scallions, and dried tangerines. There is a smoking and drinking lounge, as well as the Water Room, which has games, a light menu, and allows cigars. Homemade breads and pastries are on the menu. Open-air cocktail garden. Live music weekends. Kids' menu, pre-theater menu, early bird dinners. Sunday brunch. | 207 Main St. | 631/324–5006 | Breakfast also available | $19–$36 | AE, DC, MC, V.

Nick and Toni's. Mediterranean. The dining room at this restaurant has a wood-burning brick oven where house specialties are cooked daily. The oven's mosaic mural was designed by artist Eric Fischl. Wood-roasted chicken and fish are popular and on Sunday, you can have oven-roasted pizza. Open-air dining on porch. No smoking. | 136 N. Main St. | 631/324–3550 | Reservations essential | $24–$35 | AE, MC, V | No lunch Sun.

The Palm. Steak. The Palm's old-fashioned decor fits perfectly with the building, parts of which were built in 1699. Cramped and usually crowded, the restaurant is well known for its aged prime beef, lobster (3–6 pounds), and other seafood, as well as high prices. Family-style service. No smoking. Free parking. | 94 Main St. | 631/324–0411 | Reservations essential | No lunch | $19–$35 | AE, D, DC, MC, V.

Santa Fe Junction. Southwestern. Rustic wooden walls and beams create a background for the photographs from New Mexico, cacti, and chile-pepper ornaments at this restaurant. Try the seafood faj, a grilled shrimp, scallops, and tuna fajita, and the mango margarita. For desert, there's the banana taco, a variation on the banana split. No smoking. | 8 Fresno Pl. | 631/324–8700 | No lunch | $20–$30 | MC, V.

Lodging

Bassett House–a Country Inn. Built in 1830 as a farmhouse, this Victorian inn is within walking distance of shops and restaurants. Rooms have eclectic antiques, and trees and gardens surround the house. Beds range from twin to queen-size. Some rooms have a fireplace. Complimentary breakfast. Some in-room hot tubs. Pets allowed ($20 fee). | 128 Montauk Hwy. | 631/324–6127 | fax 631/324–5944 | 12 rooms | $195–$275 | AE, D, MC, V.

Centennial House. The rooms in this 1870s house have been individually furnished with Victorian antiques. Outside, behind the rose and herb gardens is a secluded pool. Complimentary breakfast. Cable TV. Pool. Gym. Business services. No kids under 12. No smoking. | 13 Woods La. | 631/324–9414 | fax 631/324–0493 | 4 rooms, 1 cottage | $235–$405 | MC, V.

East Hampton House. This modern hotel on 5 landscaped acres is a pleasant 15-min walk to the ocean. Many kitchenettes, cable TV. Pool, wading pool. Tennis. Gym. Business services. | 226 Pantigo Rd. | 631/324–4300 | fax 631/329–3743 | 52 rooms | $125–$220 | AE, D, MC, V.

Hedges' Inn. Every room is furnished differently at this clapboard inn less than ¼ mi from the beach. Restaurant (see James Lane Cafe), complimentary Continental breakfast. No room phones, TV in common area. Business services. | 74 James La. | 631/324–7100 | fax 631/324–5816 | 11 rooms | $275–$350 | AE, DC, MC, V.

EAST HAMPTON

INTRO
ATTRACTIONS
DINING
LODGING

Hunting Inn. Old elms and maples surround this charming white clapboard inn in the center of town. Each room is individually furnished with reproductions of 18th-century antiques. Restaurant *(see* The Palm), complimentary Continental breakfast. Business services. | 94 Main St. | 631/324–0410 | fax 631/324–8751 | 19 rooms | $275–$350 | AE, D, DC, MC, V.

J. Harper Poor Cottage. Originally a 1648 farmhouse, this luxurious and stylish inn was redesigned in 1910 by famed Arts and Crafts architect Joseph Greenleaf Thorp. The English-style manor house has a beautiful formal garden with boxwoods and 200-year-old wysteria. Rooms have plush furnishings. Complimentary breakfast. Cable TV, in-room VCRs. Pool. Spa. Exercise equipment. Business services. | 181 Main St. | 631/324–4081 | fax 631/329–5931 | info@jharperpoor.com | www.jharperpoor.com | 4 rooms | $325–$450 | AE, DC, MC, V.

★ **Maidstone Arms Inn.** This Greek Revival inn right in the center of town has been in operation since the 1870s. The front porch has wicker rocking chairs and out back, the garden is filled with rhododendrons. Each room is individually furnished with antiques. Restaurant *(see* Maidstone Arms), bar, complimentary Continental breakfast, room service. Some refrigerators, some in-room VCRs. | 207 Main St. | 631/324–5006 | maidstay@aol.com | www.maidstonearms.com | 12 rooms, 4 suites, 3 cottages | $275–$370 rooms, $440 suites, $510–$540 cottages | AE, MC, V.

Mill House Inn. Built in the 1970s as a classic New England Cape Cod saltbox home, this B&B has become anything but typical. Each room has a fireplace and private bathroom, but from there they diverge stylistically, ranging from Asian antiques to nautical to floral. Beds, either queen or king, have featherbeds and high-count cotton sheets that would be hard to leave if it weren't for the savory smell of the professionally cooked brunch wafting up the stairs. Complimentary breakfast. Some in-room hot tubs, cable TV, in-room VCRs. No pets. | 31 N. Main St. | 631/324–9766 | fax 631/324–9793 | www.millhouseinn.com | 8 rooms | $300–$425 | AE, DC, MC, V.

1770 House. Rooms at this inn built in the 1700s have canopy beds and an eclectic personal collection of early American and English antiques. Outside is a patio and yard. Restaurant, complimentary breakfast. Business services. No kids under 12. | 143 Main St. | 631/324–1770 | fax 631/324–3504 | 8 rooms | $165–$350 | AE, MC, V.

Shady Pines Motel. East Hampton is a 5-min drive from this two-story motel surrounded by trees. Cottages are also available and are great for families. Beds are either full or queen with patchwork quilts. Pool. Pets allowed. | 380 Montauk Hwy. | 631/537–9329 | fax 631/537–9328 | 12 rooms, 6 cottages | Call for room rates | AE, MC, V | Closed Jan.–Apr.

EASTPORT/MORICHES

MAP 3, D2

(Nearby towns also listed: Mastic/Mastic Beach, Westhampton Beach)

Originally, Unkechaug Indians claimed this area as home but they maintained good relations with early Colonial settlers who came seeking freedom and land in the mid-1700s.

While the western part of Long Island has become heavily urbanized, eastern Long Island has kept its quiet, rustic charm. The lovely Moriches Bay beaches have the added benefit of being protected from the Atlantic's sometimes rough seas by Fire Island, a barrier island just off the coast. Eastport, where downtown Main Street is home to at least 15 antiques shops, has evolved from the unofficial capital of Long Island duck farming to a "must stop and shop" antiques mecca on the route to the Hamptons.

Information: **Greater Westhampton Chamber of Commerce** | 173 Montauk Hwy., Box 1228, Westhampton, 11978 | 631/288–3337.

Attractions

Shrine of Our Lady of the Island. A dramatic 18-ft granite statue of the Madonna and Child overlooks Great South Bay and Fire Island at this shrine. The 65 acres of grounds include a chapel, landscaped bushes resembling the rosary, and outdoor stations of the cross. Daily masses and group pilgrimages are offered. In Eastport, on the border of Manorville. | Eastport Manor Rd. | 631/325-0661 | Free | Daily.

Dining

Antonacci. Italian. Oldies' music plays at this family-oriented restaurant, 10 mi west of Eastport. Try the angel hair Sarento (angel-hair pasta with fresh clams, shrimp, and mussels in red wine sauce) and penne à la vodka (pasta in pink cream sauce with vodka). Open-air dining on side patio. Raw bar. Sunday brunch. | 234 William Floyd Pkwy., Shirley | 631/395-7011 | $8-$21 | D, MC, V.

Senix Creek Inn. Continental. You can watch boats dock at the marina near this restaurant and sometimes you'll even see the owner buying the fish destined for the broiled or fried seafood platters right off the boats. Try the Senix platter (coconut shrimp, fried calamari, baked clams, and crab cakes served with three different sauces) and the fried cheesecake. Open-air dining on screened deck. Kids' menu. Early bird dinners. Sunday brunch. | 50 Senix Ave., Center Moriches | 516/874-2020 | Closed Mon., Tues. and Labor Day–Memorial Day | $20-$30 | AE, D, DC, MC, V.

Lodging

Victorian on the Bay. The many windows and stark, white walls brighten the rooms of this Victorian-style inn, which sits directly on Moriches Bay. The rooms have featherbeds and views of the water, three have decks. Complimentary breakfast. In-room hot tubs, cable TV, in-room VCRs. Gym. No pets. No kids under 12. No smoking. | 57 S. Bay Ave. | 631/325-1000 or 888/449-0620 | fax 631/325-9659 | rbarone@hamptons.com | www.victorianon-thebay.com | 5 rooms | $200-$350 | D, MC, V.

KODAK'S TIPS FOR NIGHT PHOTOGRAPHY

Lights at Night
- Move in close on neon signs
- Capture lights from unusual vantage points

Fireworks
- Shoot individual bursts using a handheld camera
- Capture several explosions with a time exposure
- Include an interesting foreground

Fill-In Flash
- Set the fill-in light a stop darker than the ambient light

Around the Campfire
- Keep flames out of the frame when reading the meter
- For portraits, take spot readings of faces
- Use a tripod, or rest your camera on something solid

Using Flash
- Stay within the recommended distance range
- Buy a flash with the red-eye reduction mode

From Kodak Guide to Shooting Great Travel Pictures © 2000 by Fodor's Travel Publications

ELLENVILLE

(Nearby towns also listed: Liberty, New Paltz, Walden)

Scenic beauty and hang-gliding are the attractions in this Ulster County village surrounded by the Shawangunk Mountains. The mountains are famous for their ice caves, pine barrens, and glacial formations. A small and compact community, Ellenville traces its history back to New York's canal era. The town has restaurants, shops and government offices, and is one of the best hang-gliding centers in the world. Cragsmoor, a historic artists community, is nearby.

Information: **Ellenville Area Chamber of Commerce** | Box 227, 12428 | 845/647–4620.

Attractions

Sam's Point Dwarf Pine Ridge Reserve. Trees up here (4 mi south of Ellenville) are stunted as a result of the altitude, and hiking up to them is a great workout filled with beautiful mountainscapes. | Sams Point Rd., Cragsmoor | 845/647–7989 | Donations accepted | Daily, dawn–dusk.

ON THE CALENDAR

SEPT.: *Harvest Music Festival Street Fair.* Sponsored by the chamber of commerce, this event has several stages of live music ranging from rock to country to 1950s favorites. There are food vendors and carnival events like a dunking machine all along Main Street. | 845/647–4620 Chamber of Commerce.

Dining

Calloway's Club Restaurant. Continental. Toward the outskirts of town, 1 mi from Route 209, you can dine outside with the Shawangunk Mountains in the background, or inside at candlelit tables. The menu ranges from German entrées such as Wiener schnitzel to lobster tails, pasta, or filet mignon. Homemade desserts like tiramisu are incentive to leave room. Full bar. Kids' menu. | 14 Nevele Rd. | 845/647–1906 | $13–$21 | AE, D, MC, V.

Lodging

Days Inn. Eleven mi south of Ellenville, this two-story chain sits at the intersection of U.S. 209 and Route 17. Complimentary Continental breakfast. Some in-room hot tubs, cable TV. Pool. | 21 Perron Dr. | fax 845/888–2727 | www.daysinn.com | 34 rooms | $50–$90 | AE, MC, V.

Nevele Grande Hotel. A nine-story hotel on sprawling manicured grounds in the mountains, the Nevele operates in the tradition of the famous Catskill resorts, offering a wide variety of sports and outdoor activities, including golfing, skiing, and boating. Restaurant, bar, room service. In-room data ports, cable TV. 4 pools. Hot tub. 27-hole golf course, miniature golf, 15 tennis courts. Gym, horseback riding, boating. Ice-skating, cross-country and downhill skiing, sleigh rides, tobogganing. Shops. Children's programs (ages 3–11). Business services. | 1 Nevele Rd. | 845/647–6000 or 800/647–6000 | fax 845/647–9884 | www.nevele.com | 700 rooms | $105–$165 | AP | AE, DC, MC, V.

ELMIRA

(Nearby towns also listed: Corning, Owego, Watkins Glen)

Settled in 1788, Elmira was the site of one of the battles of the Sullivan-Clinton expedition of 1779, during which a colonial army routed Native Americans who were allied with the British. In the 19th century, the city got its industrial start with lumbering and woolen mills. During the Civil War, there was a prison camp for Confederate soldiers here, and conditions were so bad that thousands of prisoners died.

Elmira's most famous resident was Samuel Clemens (a.k.a. Mark Twain) who spent more than 20 summers in Elmira at Quarry Farm, which belonged to his wife's family. The city has also been known as the "soaring capital of America," since it hosted the first national soaring contest in 1930.

Information: Chemung County Camber of Commerce | 400 E. Church St., 14901-2804 | 800/MARK–TWAIN | fax 607/734–4490 | ccommerc@rr.com | www.chemungchamber.org.

Attractions

Arnot Art Museum. The core collection at this museum comes from Matthias Arnot, who acquired paintings by Brueghel, Rousseau, and others. Other works in the museum include European paintings from the 17th–19th centuries, and American paintings from the 19th and 20th centuries. | 235 Lake St. | 607/734–3697 | $5 | Tues.–Sat. 10–5, Sun. 1–5.

Chemung Valley History Museum. This small local museum downtown has exhibits on the Seneca Nation, Mark Twain, and Elmira's Civil War prison camp. | 415 E. Water St. | 607/734–4167 | $2 | Tues.–Sat. 10–5, Sun. 1–5.

Harris Hill Soaring Site. Gliders and soaring enthusiasts have been coming to this hill since the 1910s. If you're game, you can take a 20-minute sailplane ride. | Harris Hill Park off Rte. 17 | 607/734–0641 or 607/739–7899 | fax 607/732–6745 | www.saoringmuseum.org | Sailplane rides about $65 a person | June–Labor Day, daily 10–6; Apr.–May and Sept.–Oct., weekends 10–6.

Mark Twain Study. Samuel Clemens wrote *The Adventures of Huckleberry Finn* and *The Adventures of Tom Sawyer* at this study built for him by his sister-in-law. The octagonal shape was inspired by a Mississippi riverboat pilothouse. The study is on the campus of Elmira College. | Park Pl. | 607/735–1941 | Free | June–Labor Day, Mon.–Sat. 9–5, Sun. 12–5, or by appointment.

National Soaring Museum. There are 12 antique gliders and a sailplane cockpit simulator on display here. Movies and exhibits explore the sport of gliding. In Harris Hill Park, off Route 17, 15 min from downtown Elmira. | 51 Soaring Hill Dr. | 607/734–3128 | fax 607/732–6745 | www.soaringmuseum.org | $5 | Daily 10–5.

National Warplane Museum. A ready-to-fly B-17 Flying Fortress is the highlight of the collection at this museum with World War II, Korea, and Vietnam warplanes. At the Elmira-Corning Regional Airport, off Route 17. | 17 Aviation Dr., Horseheads | 607/739–8200 | www.warplane.org | $7 | Mon.–Sat. 9–5, Sun. 11–5.

Replica Trolley Tours. Ninety-minute tours of Chemung County leave from the Holiday Inn River View. | 760 E Water St. | 800/627–5892 (MARK TWAIN) | $2 | Departs Tues.–Sat. at 10, 11, noon, 1, and 2:30.

Woodlawn Cemetery. Samuel Clemens, also known as Mark Twain, rests in the Langdon family plot here, with his son-in-law, Ossip Gabrilowitsch, at his feet. A 12-ft-high monument marks the spot (12 ft, in river terminology, is 2 fathoms, or "mark twain"). | 1200 Walnut St. | 607/732–0151 | Free | Daily dawn–dusk.

Next to the main cemetery is the **Woodlawn National Cemetery,** which contains the graves of 2,963 Confederate prisoners who died in the prison in Elmira, as well as the graves of 322 Union soldiers. The Elmira Correctional Facility, at Davis Street and Bancroft Road, sits on the site of the city's Civil War prison camp. | 1825 Davis St. | 607/732–5411 | Free | Daily dawn–dusk.

Zim Center. This was the home of political cartoonist Eugene "Zim" Zimmerman. The center, 5 mi north of Elmira, is now owned by the Horseheads Historical Society. | 2305 Grand Central Ave., Horseheads | 607/739–3938 | Free | By appointment only.

ON THE CALENDAR

MAY: *Arts in the Park.* This juried show allows regional artists to sell their art, which usually includes wood carvings, T-shirts, and paintings. It takes place at Arnot Museum the third weekend of the month. | 607/734–3697.

AUG.: *Chemung County Fair.* Agricultural displays, music, and plenty of food come to Horseheads, 5 mi north of Elmira. | 800/627–5892.

Dining

Anne's Pancakes. American. Come here for some home cookin': country-fried steak, burgers, homemade pies, and rice pudding in addition to the tasty pancakes. | 114 S. Main St. | 607/732–9591 | Breakfast also available; closes at noon weekends | $4–$8 | No credit cards.

Hilltop Inn. American. Elmira's oldest restaurant has been owned by the same family since 1933. Steak and seafood are popular here. Open-air dining. Kids' menu. | 171 Jerusalem Hill Rd. | 607/732–6728 | Closed Sun. Labor Day–Memorial Day. No lunch | $14–$26 | AE, D, MC, V.

Moretti's. Italian. This well-established (1917) neighborhood restaurant in downtown Elmira serves large portions of Italian food, steaks, and chops. Kids' menu. | 800 Hatch St. | 607/734–1535 | No lunch | $8–$30 | AE, D, MC, V.

Pierce's 1894 Restaurant. Continental. This old English–style village inn 15 min from downtown is a top dining experience for the Elmira area. Known for its veal and salmon, the restaurant also serves roasted rack of lamb and châteaubriand. Kids' menu. | 228 Oakwood Ave., Elmira Heights | 607/734–2022 | $15–$28 | AE, D, MC, V.

Lodging

Best Western Marshall Manor. This one-story chain motel is in a country setting 8 mi north of Elmira. Restaurant, bar, complimentary Continental breakfast. In-room data ports, microwaves, cable TV. Pool. Pets allowed. | 3527 Watkins Rd., Horseheads | 607/739–3891 or 800/528–1234 | 40 rooms | $54–$70 | AE, D, DC, MC, V.

Coachman Motor Lodge. Each room at this motel 1½ mi from downtown Elmira has a separate living room. Picnic area. Kitchenettes, cable TV. Laundry facilities. Business services. Pets allowed. | 908 Pennsylvania Ave., Southport | 607/733–5526 | fax 607/733–0961 | 18 rooms | $68–$95 | AE, D, MC, V.

Econo Lodge. This chain motel is about 3 mi from the National Soaring Museum and 10 mi from downtown. Complimentary Continental breakfast. In-room data ports, microwaves, cable TV. Hot tubs. Laundry facilities. | 871 Rte. 64 | 607/739–2000 or 800/446–6900 | fax 607/739–3552 | 48 rooms | $85–$98 | AE, D, MC, V.

Grey Whale Inn. Built on 2 acres in 1897, this Victorian home is within walking distance of antiques shops, and 2 mi from Interstate 86. Cherry and oak woodwork make up the gorgeous floors as well as the staircase. There is a deck off one of the rooms, as well as a full wraparound porch. Complimentary breakfast. | 1101 Maple Ave. | 607/732–3615 | 2 rooms | $55 | No credit cards.

Halcyon Place Bed and Breakfast. Halcyon aptly describes this Federal to Greek Revival transitional home, which was built in 1820. Twelve mi from Elmira, it's just ½ mi from bike paths and the Chemung River. Rooms overlook the aesthetically patterned plantings of the Renaissance herb garden. The original wooden floor panels still remain and period antiques adorn the rooms. In summer, a gourmet breakfast is served in the screened-in porch, and in winter you'll be warmed by the dining room's fireplace. Complimentary breakfast. | 197 Washington, Chemung | 607/529–3544 | www.bbonline.com/ny/halcyon/ | herbtique@aol.com | 3 rooms | $55–$85.

Holiday Inn Riverview. This long brick building overlooks the river and is close to the city's downtown. Restaurant, bar (with entertainment). In-room data ports, microwaves, refrigerators, cable TV. 2 pools, wading pool. Exercise equipment. Laundry facilities. Business services, free parking. Pets allowed. | 760 E. Water St. | 607/734–4211 | fax 607/734–3549 | 150 rooms | $82–$110 | AE, D, DC, MC, V.

Howard Johnson. This two-story chain hotel, 4 mi north of Elmira, sits approximately 15 mi from the Corning Glass Center, and 25 mi from Watkins Glen State Park. Restaurant. In-room data ports, microwaves, cable TV. Pool. Free parking. Pets allowed. | 2671 Corning Rd., Horseheads | 607/739–5636 or 888/895–1403 | fax 607/739–8630 | 76 rooms | $89 | AE, D, DC, MC, V.

ELMSFORD

MAP 4, F4

(Nearby towns also listed: Hartsdale, Hawthorne, Mamaroneck, New Rochelle, Rye, Scarsdale, Tarrytown, White Plains, Yonkers)

This pretty Westchester town nestled between the larger communities of Tarrytown and White Plains was first called Storm's Bridge in the early 1800s, then Hall's Corner in 1840, before being christened Elmsford in 1886. In the century since, the town of 4,000 residents has acquired modern suburban conveniences without losing its small-town spirit.

Information: County Chamber of Commerce | 235 Mamaroneck Ave., Lower Level, White Plains, 10605 | 914/948–2110.

Attractions

Hartsdale Farmer's Market. Vendors gather here on Saturday to sell fresh-grown seasonal produce, flowers, and homemade pies. | 320 Tarrytown Rd. | 914/993–1507 | Free | July–Nov., Sat. 8–2.

Westchester Broadway Theatre. The longest-running year-round Equity theater in New York State presents classic Broadway-caliber productions. The ticket price includes a meal served at your table. | 1 Broadway Plaza, off Clearbrook Rd. | 914/592–2222.

Dining

Ichi Riki. Japanese. Kimono-clad waitresses serve very fresh sushi and other traditional Japanese favorites. Get a mat and try out a private tatami room. | 1 E. Main St. | 914/592–2220 | Reservations essential Fri.–Sun. | Closed Mon. | $13–$25 | AE, DC, MC, V.

Tony La Stazione. Italian. A wood-burning fireplace, hanging plants, copper pots, and large wagon wheels create a country-Italian atmosphere at this train station–turned–restaurant. The menu includes innovative pasta selections along with classic Italian favorites. Kids' menu. No smoking. | 15 Saw Mill River Rd. | 914/592–5980 | $12–$22 | AE, DC, MC, V.

Lodging

Hampton Inn. This seven-floor chain sits less than a mile from I–287 in the center of Elmsford. Complimentary Continental breakfast. Cable TV. Pool. Gym. | 200 Tarrytown Rd. | 914/592–5680 | 156 rooms | $128–$132 | AE, D, DC, MC, V.

Ramada Inn. A convenient suburban setting with easy highway access puts guests near the corporate district, 1 mi from the center of Elmsford, and 5 mi from Tarrytown's historic restorations. Restaurant, bar (with entertainment), room service. Cable TV. Pool. Business services. | 540 Saw Mill River Rd. | 914/592–3300 | fax 914/592–3381 | www.ramada.com | 101 rooms | $99–$159 | AE, D, DC, MC, V.

Saw Mill River Motel. This two-story motel sits just off the parkway, off exit 21, in the center of Elmsford. Refrigerators, cable TV. No pets. | 25 Valley St. | 914/592–7500 | fax 914/592–6461 | 130 rooms | $60–$86 | AE, D, DC, MC, V.

ENDICOTT

(Nearby towns also listed: Binghamton, Owego)

Along with Johnson City and Binghamton, Endicott serves as a gateway to the Finger Lakes region. Shoe manufacturing spurred the growth of this town and its two sister communities of Endwell and Vestal in the late 19th and early 20th centuries. In the early part of the century, Endicott also became home to IBM. Today Endicott boasts one of the best public libraries in the nation.

Information: Broome County Chamber of Commerce | 49 Court St., Box 995, Metro-center, 2nd floor, Binghamton, 13902 | 607/772–8860 | www.spectra.net/broomechamber.

ON THE CALENDAR

JULY: *B.C. Open PGA Tour Golf Tournament.* Four-day professional golf tournament, plus pro-am events in Endicott, north of Binghamton. | 607/754–2482 | www.bcopen. com.

Dining

Julie's Place. American. Connected to an antiques store, this café is ornamented with antique furnishings and serves from a broad menu of traditional favorites like steaks, burgers, and pastas. | 3218 E. Main St. | 607/754–8630 | $8–$15 | AE, D, MC, V.

Lodging

Endicott Inn. One mile from Interstate 86, this three-story inn is in downtown Endicott, so everything is within walking distance. Rooms come with two double beds or one king. Some rooms are adjoining. Complimentary Continental breakfast. Laundry facilities. | 214 Washington Ave. | 607/754–6000 | fax 607/754–6000 | 57 rooms | $40–$45 | AE, D, MC, V.

Executive Inn. This hotel in a mostly residential neighborhood has simple rooms. Some kitchenettes, microwaves, cable TV in some rooms. Business services. Some pets allowed. | 1 Delaware Ave. | 607/754–7570 | 60 rooms, 40 suites | $54–$70 | AE, D, DC, MC, V.

Kings Inn. The rooms in this two-story, two-building complex off I–17 at exit 69, are done in maroon and blue color schemes. Restaurant. In-room data ports, cable TV. Pool. Sauna. Business services, free parking. | 2603 E. Main St., Endwell | 607/754–8020 or 800/531–4667 | fax 607/754–6768 | kingsinn@spectra.net | 60 rooms | $69–$77 | AE, D, MC, V.

FIRE ISLAND NATIONAL SEASHORE

(Nearby towns also listed: Bay Shore, Mastic/Mastic Beach, Patchogue)

On this slender 32-mi-long barrier island, deer roam freely, finding shelter in the thickets, and migrating ducks and geese seek sanctuary in the marshes. One of the outer playgrounds of Long Island's majestic coastlines, Fire Island has six small communities include two lesbian and gay areas, Cherry Grove and The Pines.

In 1964, Fire Island National Seashore was established to protect the only developed barrier island in the United States without roads. Then, in 1980, Congress designated 1,400 acres, including a 7-mi stretch of the island, a national wilderness area. Cars are forbidden on most of the island, which is accessible by ferry, although you can drive to Robert Moses State Park, an extremely popular summer spot.

Information: **Fire Island Ferry Watchill.** The ferry is one of three that goes to Fire Island and departs from a slip in Patchogue. The ferry schedule is reliant upon the season so call for exact schedules. | No ferry service Oct.–Mar. | 631/475–1665.

Attractions

Fire Island Lighthouse. Long Island's tallest lighthouse, built in 1858 on the island's western end. The lighthouse has 192 winding steps and a terrace constructed from the bricks of the original lighthouse that was built in 1826. Exhibits cover the history of the lighthouse. The lighthouse is accessible from Robert Moses State Park, parking lot 5. | 4640 Captree Island | 631/661–4876 | $4 | July–Labor Day, daily 9:30–5.

Robert Moses State Park. The jewel in the park's 875-acre crown is this 5-mi beach with four bathhouses and a nearby boat basin with pump-out and bait stations. One of only two parts of the island you can drive to, the park is open year-round (fields 2 and 5 only). Special summer events include fishing contests. Take the Sagtikos Parkway south to Robert Moses Causeway. | Fire Island | 631/669–0470 | $7 per car; special rates weekends and holidays | Daily dawn–dusk.

Shoreline. With the Atlantic Ocean to the south and the Great South Bay to the north of this long barrier island, the ocean shoreline is one long stretch of magnificent pristine beach. Visitors can enjoy the National Seashore at Sunken Forest and Watch Hill, which are public beaches with rangers and lifeguards. Some parks are restricted to residents. No automobiles are permitted. The largest in a series of small seasonal residential communities is Ocean Beach, which offers some accommodations, restaurants, grocery stores, and shops. Accessible by ferry from Bay Shore. | 631/563–8448 | Call for fees | Daily.

ON THE CALENDAR

AUG.: *Barefoot, Black Tie Gala.* Most people do wear shoes to this fund-raising event for the Fire Island Lighthouse, but some of the men wear boxer shorts with tuxedo jackets. A reggae band supplies the music; there is a buffet and dancing. Shuttle service is available from parking field 5 of the Robert Moses State Park. | 631/321–7028.

FISHKILL

MAP 3, K9

(Nearby towns also listed: Newburgh, Poughkeepsie)

Fishkill's early history is indebted to Madam Brett and her husband Roger, who moved there in 1709 to farm the land. Madam Brett maintained positive relations with the Indians after her husband's death and is said to be one of the first businesswomen in the new world. Her home was used as a storehouse during the Revolutionary War.

Fishkill (Dutch for fish creek) is rich in Revolutionary War–era sites and was the capital of New York State in 1788, during the ratification of the Constitution.

During the 19th century the town was rich in textile mills, farmland, and iron ore mining. Today Fishkill has all the large-town conveniences—lodging, shops, and dining.

Information: **Chamber of Commerce** | 300 Westage, Business Center 100, Fishkill, 12524 | 845/897–2067.

Attractions

First Reformed Protestant Church. The original building, now surrounded by more recent additions, was built in 1731, around when the congregation began. Its history includes serving as a meeting place for the New York Provincial Congress and a prison during the Revolutionary War. | 1153 Main St. | 845/896–9836 | Free.

Madam Brett Homestead. One of the oldest houses in Dutchess County (5 mi southwest of Fishkill), this was home to seven generations of the Brett family from 1709 to 1954. During the Revolutionary War, the homestead was used to store military supplies, and Washington and Lafayette attended a Christmas party here. In 1954, the Daughters of the American Revolution took possession of the house. Inside there is antique furniture and a china collection; outside there are formal gardens and herb gardens. | 50 Van Nydeck Ave., Beacon | 845/831–6533 or 845/896–6897 | www.pojonews.com/enjoy/stories/0830921.htm | $4 | Sept–Dec., 1st Sun. of each month 1–4, or by appointment.

Mount Gulian Historic Site. At this living museum 5 mi southwest of Fishkill, interpreters in period costumes re-create the life of Revolutionary War–era Dutch settlers, African Americans, and Native Americans. | 145 Sterling St., Beacon | 845/831–8172 | $3 | Call for hrs and appointments.

Van Wyck Homestead Museum. This 1732 restored Dutch Colonial home was headquarters for General George Washington's officers from 1776 to 1783. It served as a depot and courtroom as well. Today, costumed guides lead you through the period rooms that also display local archaeological artifacts. | Junction of U.S. 9 and I–84 | 845/896–9560 | $2 | By appointment.

Dining

Harralds. Continental. Fruit trees surround this country inn 12 mi east of Fishkill that serves elegant food, homemade pastries, and complimentary coffee. Smoked *truite au bleu* (trout prepared the instant after it's been killed) is one of the specialties. Veal, beef, and lamb are also on the menu and the extensive wine list includes many modestly priced selections. | 3760 Rte. 52, Stormville | 845/878–6595 | Reservations essential | Jacket required | Closed Sun.–Tues. | $65 (6–course prix fixe) | No credit cards.

Hudson's Ribs and Fish. Seafood. Teak from old lobster boats covers the walls of the main dining room at this eatery, popular for its fresh fish and seafood specials. King crab, shrimp, mussels, lobster, and steaks are regular menu items, complemented by specials like halibut and mahi. For dessert don't miss the popovers with hot strawberry butter; they're legendary. Kids' menu. | 1099 Rte. 9 | 845/297–5002 | No lunch | $15–$21 | AE, D, DC, MC, V.

Inn at Osborne Hill. Contemporary. This building was originally a boarding house, in the 1930s, and is now home to one of the region's finest eateries. Try the pesto grilled salmon, duck marinated in sweet vermouth, and Maryland crab cakes. Extensive wine list. | 150 Osborne Hill Rd. | 845/897–3055 | Closed Sun. No lunch Sat. | $18–$25 | AE, DC, MC, V.

Tutti Quanti. Italian. Exposed brick walls, oak trim, and brass lanterns set the tone at this eatery in the center of the village. Chicken Florentine is a highlight of the menu, which also includes many pastas and traditional dishes. | 1105 Main St. | 845/896–4100 | $9–$16 | AE, D, DC, MC, V.

Lodging

Residence Inn. This long-residence inn is in downtown Fishkill, 100 ft from Interstate 84. Choose from a 750-square-ft studio, or a penthouselike suite. Some have more than one bath and two different levels. All units have full kitchens. Beds range from full to king. They take reservations three months in advance for people who want to stay as long as 30 days or longer. They take reservations for shorter-term visits if the date of the visit is less than three months from the time of the reservation. Complimentary Continental breakfast. Laundry facilities. | 2481 Rte. 9 | 845/896–5210 | fax 845/896–9698 | www.residenceinn.com | 112 studios, 24 penthouses | $139–$145 studios, $145–$165 penthouses | AE, D, DC, MC, V.

Wellesley Inn. Business travelers frequent this hotel at the intersection of I–84 and U.S. 9, less than a mile from the First Reformed Protestant Church and within 20 mi of the Westpoint historical area. Complimentary Continental breakfast. In-room data ports, some

microwaves, cable TV. Pets allowed (fee). | 20 Schuyler Blvd., at Rte. 9 | 845/896–4995 or 800/
444–8888 | fax 845/896–6631 | 82 rooms | $89–$125 | AE, D, DC, MC, V.

FREDONIA

(Nearby towns also listed: Dunkirk, Westfield)

Fredonia, a pretty town just across Interstate 90 from Dunkirk, has several historical
distinctions. The first gas well in the United States was discovered in Fredonia in 1821,
and the first Women's Christian Temperance Union was established here in 1873.
Fredonia State University, a four-year college in the State University of New York
system, gives this small town sophistication and cultural opportunities. The restored
Fredonia Opera House provides music, opera, and theater for all ages. Be sure to drive
by or have coffee at the elegant White Inn on East Main St.

Information: **Fredonia Chamber of Commerce** | Box 566, 14063 | 716/679–1565.

Attractions

Fredonia Opera House. This downtown opera house in a restored 1891 Victorian building
presents a full schedule of live performing arts events, concerts, and films. Guided tours
are available by appointment. | 9-11 Church St. | 716/679–1891 | operahouse@netsync.net
| www.fredopera.org | Call for schedule.

Historical Museum of the Darwin R. Barker Library. The varying exhibits of at this museum
reflect local history. Period furniture, historic documents, photos and portraits, and
genealogical material are also on display. The children's museum has educational programs.
| 20 E. Main St. | 716/672–2114 | Free | Tues. and Thurs. 1–5 and 7–9, Wed. and Fri.–Sat. 1–5.

Michael C. Rockefeller Arts Center. Located on the SUNY Fredonia campus and designed
by I. M. Pei and Partners, the Rockefeller Arts Center is the center of the region's cultural
life. The complex includes three theaters, and an art gallery with over 120 exhibits. | 716/
673–3217 | www.fredonia.edu/rac | Call for schedule.

Dining

White Horse Inn. Continental. Warm and casual, this traditional country inn about 5 mi
south of Fredonia is known for seafood, hand-cut aged steak, and prime rib. Try one of the
dessert specialties: peanut butter pie or tipsy walnut pie. Sun. brunch June–October. | Rte.
60, Cassadaga | 716/595–3523 | $9–$13 | AE, D, MC, V.

White Inn. Continental. This restaurant is part of the Victorian White Inn. Try the White
Inn filet mignon with peppercorns, seafood penne pasta, or chocolate mousse cake. Buf-
fet lunch. | 52 E. Main St. | 716/672–2103 or 888–FREDONIA | inn@whiteinn.com |
www.whiteinn.com | Breakfast also available | $12–$21 | AE, D, DC, MC, V.

Lodging

Brookside Manor Bed and Breakfast. Two mi from downtown and 5 mi from Lake Erie, this
three-story brick Victorian home was built in 1875 on 5½ acres of wooded land that is especially spectacular in fall. Large picture windows and hardwood floors create a sense of spa-
ciousness. Antiques, many of which are family heirlooms, are used in rooms. A gourmet
breakfast is served, and afterward you can relax on the patio. Complimentary breakfast.
| 3728 Rte. 83 | 716/672–7721 | 4 rooms, 1 suite | $75–$80 | MC, V.

Days Inn. This chain hotel offers standard rooms on the east side of town, just south of
U.S. 20. Complimentary Continental breakfast. Cable TV. Free parking. Some pets allowed.
| 10455 Bennett Rd. | 716/673–1351 | fax 716/672–6909 | 135 rooms | $55–$70 | AE, D, DC,
MC, V.

White Inn. Parts of this inn date to 1868, when it was a house owned by the White family. The inn has been in operation since 1919 and the rooms are furnished with Victorian antiques or antique reproductions. Restaurant (*see* White Inn), bar, complimentary breakfast. Some refrigerators, cable TV. Business services. | 52 E. Main St. | 716/672–2103 | fax 716/672–2107 | whiteinn@netsync.net | www.whiteinn.com | 12 rooms, 11 suites | $69 rooms, $150–$179 suites | AE, D, DC, MC, V.

FREEPORT

MAP 4, G8

(Nearby towns also listed: Garden City, New York City, Rockville Centre)

Freeport's busy downtown along the fast-moving Sunrise Highway has residential districts to the north and south that hint at an earlier glory. Originally, the area was inhabited by Indians who were reportedly attracted to its beauty and wealth of seashells or "wampum." Later, notables like bandleader Guy Lombardo and actor Broderick Crawford called Freeport home.

While its bustling downtown shopping area may not be as picturesque as other local waterfronts, its "Nautical Mile" along Woodcleft Canal attracts throngs to its busy wharfs. Here a plethora of waterside restaurants and open-air fish markets serve fresh seafood brought in daily. You can also go fishing, sailing, or cruising in the harbor's surrounding waters.

Information: **Freeport Chamber of Commerce** | 300 Woodcleft Ave., 11520 | 516/223–8840 | www.antonnews.com/communities/freeport/.

Attractions

Cow Meadow Park Preserve. A hiking trail runs through a bayberry thicket at this pleasant 150-acre preserve along saltwater marsh. The marsh is home to over 150 species of nesting, migrating, and wintering birds. There's also a small bird-watching tower. | S. Main St. | 516/571–8685 | Free | Daily 8–6.

Jones Beach State Park. Its 6½ mi of pristine, white sandy beachfront make this beach-park the most famous and popular beach in the New York City region. The 2,500-acre park is loaded with facilities, including bathhouses, piers, a bait station, surf casting, picnic areas, and four basketball courts. From the end of May to mid-September, the restaurant is open, and lifeguards are on duty. There is also an amphitheater where concerts are performed during summer. The park can be reached from the Wantagh and Meadowbrook parkways. | Box 1000, Ocean Pkwy., Wantagh | 516/785–1600 | $7 per car | Daily dawn–dusk.

Long Island Marine Education Center. This annex of the South Street Seaport Museum has interactive exhibits on marine life and trades. | 202 Woodcleft Ave. | 516/771–0399 | $2 | Tues.–Fri. 11–4, Sat. and Sun 1–5.

Woodcleft Canal. Known locally as the "Nautical Mile," this strip along the canal has a national reputation for commercial fishing, charter, and open boats, open-air fish markets, restaurants, and shops with a nautical flavor. | Woodcleft Ave. | 516/223–8840 | Free | Daily.

Dining

Margo and Frank. Seafood. From the casual, water-side dining room you can choose between all of the fruits of the sea, though steaks and chicken are also available. Entrées come à la carte or you can get a meal from soup to nuts. | 379 Woodcleft Ave. | 516/546–3393 | Closed Tues. | $10–$25 | AE, D, MC, V.

Schooner. Seafood. Eat your lobster boiled or steamed at this nautical-theme restaurant with a beautiful view of Woodcleft Canal. Also on the menu are giant lobster tails, steak, and chicken. Early bird dinners. Dock space. No smoking. | 435 Woodcleft Ave. | 516/378–7575 | Closed Mon. and 2nd and 3rd weeks in Jan. | $17–$35 | AE, DC, MC, V.

Lodging

Yankee Clipper Motor Inn. This three-story downtown inn is within walking distance of all the happening restaurants and shops. It's also a two-minute drive from Cowman Park and 5 min from Jones Beach. Most rooms have ocean views and a porch. Laundry facilities. | 295 S. Main St. | 516/379–2005 | fax 516/546–4077 | 36 rooms | $85 | AE, D, MC, V.

FULTON

(Nearby towns also listed: Liverpool, Oswego, Syracuse)

Fulton is on the Oswego River, approximately 11 mi from the river's mouth. The city was settled in the late 1700s and got a boost when the Oswego Canal opened in the 1820s. Thanks to the locks, the river remains a popular passage for recreational boaters. More recently, Fulton has been a center for beer and chocolate making.

Information: Greater Fulton Chamber of Commerce | 41 S. 2nd St., 13069 | 315/598–4231.

Attractions

Thunder Island Amusement Park. This water park has tube slides and body slides, as well as pools and bumper boats. If you'd rather stay dry, there is also miniature golf, go-carts, and a Ferris wheel. | Wilcox Rd. and Rte. 48 | 315/598–8016 | Prices vary per ride | June–Sept., daily noon–10.

ON THE CALENDAR

AUG.: *Fulton Jazz Fest.* During the first weekend in August Canal Landing becomes the site of a four-day music jam. The whole party beckons the big easy, with New Orleans style music and food. | 315/598–6900.

Dining

Lock III. Continental. Windows overlook the Oswego River and canal at this restaurant known for its steak, fresh fish, chicken, and pasta. Salad bar. Jazz music on Friday. Early bird dinners. | 24 S. 1st St. | 315/598–6900 | Reservations essential holidays | $11–$20 | AE, DC, MC, V.

Lodging

Battle Island Inn Bed and Breakfast. This home on 3 wooded acres dates to the 1840s. Rooms, fashioned in a Renaissance Revival style, overlook a well-kept flower garden. A chandelier, a fireplace, and Italian marble floors make it a lovely place to relax. The Oswego River is across the street. Complimentary breakfast. Hot tub. | 2167 State Rte. 48 | 315/593–3699 | www.battle-island-inn.com | 5 rooms | $75–$125 | AE, D, MC, V.

Fulton Motor Lodge. Some of the rooms at this two-story motel have river views. Refrigerators, cable TV. Pool. Exercise equipment. Business services, free parking. Pets allowed. | 163 S. 1st St. | 315/598–6100 or 800/223–6935 | fax 315/592–4738 | 70 rooms | $69–$79 | AE, D, DC, MC, V.

Riverside Motel. This motel is on the Oswego River, close to the intersection of Routes 481 and 57. Restaurant, bar. Cable TV. Pool. | 930 S. 1st St. | 315/593–2444 | fax 315/593–1730 | 70 rooms | $89 | AE, D, MC, V.

GARDEN CITY

MAP 4, G7

(Nearby towns also listed: Freeport, New York City, Rockville Centre)

In 1869, the "Merchant Prince of Broadway," Alexander T. Stewart, put his considerable talents, creativity, and wealth into the creation of a model city, reportedly a century ahead of its time. *Harpers Weekly* said of the venture, ". . . it will be the most beautiful suburb in the vicinity of New York. Godspeed the undertaking!"

By the mid-20th century, the retail stores of Mr. Lord, Mr. Taylor, and Mr. Bloomingdale—who all owned stores modeled after Stewart's—opened along Garden City's Franklin Avenue. Once known as the 5th Avenue of Long Island, an influx of banks, insurance companies, and brokerage houses has since changed the avenue's nickname to the "Wall Street of Long Island."

Today, 7th Street has specialty and food emporiums and gourmet restaurants. Other highlights of the village are the Cathedral of the Incarnation and the Garden City Hotel.

Information: **Garden City Chamber of Commerce** | 230 7th St., 11530 | 516/746–7724.

Attractions

Cathedral of the Incarnation. The cathedral, along with the bishop's house and the St. Mary's and St. Paul's school buildings, were all part of an elaborate memorial for Garden City's founder, A. T. Stewart, built by his wife Cornelia. The bells, bought at the Philadelphia Centennial exposition in 1876, are replicas of the Liberty Bell, and there are 13 of them, one for each of the original colonies. | 50 Cathedral Ave. | 516/746–2955 | Free | Daily.

Eisenhower Park. A special aquatic center only hints at the park's riches, which include 930 acres, seven athletic fields, a batting range, 16 tennis courts (fee), jogging trails, badminton, and shuffleboard. You can picnic or eat at the restaurant in the park. An amphitheater features free concerts. | East Meadow at Steward Ave. | 516/572–0348 | Free | Daily.

Hofstra University. The 240-acre campus arboretum is planted with 7,000 trees of 235 varieties. The university also boasts five exhibition areas that are part of Hofstra Museum, a playhouse, an indoor Olympic-size pool, and more than 1.6 million volumes in its library. West of Meadowbrook Parkway on Hempstead Turnpike. | 1000 Fulton Ave., Hempstead | 516/463–6600 | Free | Daily.

Long Island Children's Museum. Children ages 2 to 12 can inspect a steam engine, climb inside bubbles, ride a wild wheelchair, or preside over the TV news at Long Island's only children's museum. | 550 Stewart Ave. | 516/222–0219 | $5 | Tues.–Fri. 10–4, Sat. 10–5, Sun. 12–5.

Nassau Veterans Memorial Coliseum. Home to trade, consumer, and miscellaneous events such as music events and car, boat, home, market, sport, and pet expos, the coliseum provides a calendar of events. The Coliseum is in Uniondale, 2 mi southeast of Garden City. | 1255 Hempstead Tpk., Uniondale | 516/794–9300 | fax 516/794–9389 | www.nassaucoliseum.com | Call for schedule.

ON THE CALENDAR

MAR. OR APR.: *Antique Car Parade.* Several hundred antique, vintage, and classic cars go on parade on Easter Sunday. | 516/746–7724.
JUNE: *Belmont Stakes.* The final race of the Triple Crown is run at Belmont Park Raceway in Elmont. | 516/488–6000.
OCT.: *Fall Festival Street Fair.* In conjunction with Garden City High School's Homecoming Day parade, there are sidewalk displays, food samplings, music, and entertainment. | 516/746–7724.

Dining

Akbar. Indian. Tables at this restaurant, named after India's King Akbar, who reigned during the 1400s, are set with candles and red, pink, and white tablecloths. Best known for its buffet, tandoori chicken, and prawns asbabi (shrimp grilled over charcoal). Salad bar. Buffet lunch and dinner. Kids' menu. | 1 Ring Rd. W | 516/248–5700 | Reservations essential | $20–$25 | AE, D, DC, MC, V.

Arturo's. Italian. The Venetian murals, French doors, mahogany wainscoting, and polished brass chandeliers create an elegant backdrop at this restaurant, 10 min west of Garden City. Try the rigatoni with porcini mushrooms, Dover sole, veal chop and spaghetti with vodka, and smoked salmon in a light tomato cream sauce. Strolling guitar Sundays–Fridays. | 246–04 Jericho Tpk., Bellerose | 516/352–7418 | $15–$35 | AE, D, DC, MC, V.

Crabtree's. Mediterranean. Flowers and candles decorate the tables at this romantic restaurant that also has a waterfall, 3 mi west of Garden City. The whole-fish entrées are popular, as are the blackened fish, Peking duck, and Monday barbecue. Open-air dining in garden. Pianist on Fridays and Saturdays. Kids' menu. Sunday brunch. No smoking. | 226 Jericho Tpk., Floral Park | 516/326–7769 | Reservations essential weekends | $10–$30 | AE, MC, V.

Orchid. Chinese. This restaurant is done up in opulent red and gold with paintings of birds. The spicy and sweet orange-flavor beef, and the Grand Marnier shrimp are favorites. No smoking. | 730 Franklin Ave. | 516/742–1116 | $20–$25 | AE, MC, V.

Seventh Street Cafe. Italian. Ceiling fans whir above white linen tables and terra cotta floors at this restaurant, which specializes in brick-oven pizza and homemade pastas, like shrimp and porcini mushroom tortellini and farfalle with salmon and Gorgonzola cheese. | 126 7th St. | 516/747–7575 | $10–$15 | AE, DC, MC, V.

Stella Ristorante. Italian. Fresh flowers are brought in daily for the three dining rooms at this restaurant known for veal, homemade pasta, and fish, 3 mi west of Garden City. For dessert, try the gâteau St. Honoré, a vanilla and chocolate mousse cake. | 152 Jericho Tpk., Floral Park | 516/775–2202 | Closed Mon. No lunch Sat. | $22–$28 | AE, D, DC, MC, V.

Victor Koenig's. German. Beer steins and curios give this restaurant 2 mi west of Garden City a traditional European spirit. The menu includes sauerbraten, pot roast with gingersnap gravy and potato dumplings, Wienerschnitzel with potatoes, beef roulade with spaetzle, and Long Island duckling. Kids' menu. | 86 S. Tyson Ave., Floral Park | 516/354–2300 | Reservations essential weekends | $15–$30 | AE, DC, MC, V.

Waterzooi. Belgian. You can choose from Prince Edward Island mussels (the specialty—prepared in 17 different ways), an array of meats, and vegetarian entrées, and eat outside on the deck or inside, where you'd think you were in a Belgian café, as mirrors and clocks surround you. The pastry chef prepares seasonal desserts, such as fruit tarts and coconut crème brûlée. Kids' menu. | 850 Franklin Ave. | 516/877–2177 | $17–$31 | AE, DC, MC, V.

Lodging

Floral Park Motor Lodge. A large modern motel in a residential area minutes from Belmont Park. Complimentary Continental breakfast. Cable TV. Laundry service. Business services. | 30 Jericho Tpk., Floral Park | 516/775–7777 or 800/255–9680 | fax 516/775–0451 | information@www.floralparkmotorlodge.com | www.floralparkmotorlodge.com | 107 rooms | $160–$184 | AE, D, DC, MC, V.

Garden City Hotel. This posh hotel has been in operation since 1874 in a series of buildings, the most recent completed in the 1980s. The many illustrious guests who have stayed here include Charles Lindbergh, who slept at the hotel the night before his transatlantic flight. Restaurant, bar (with entertainment), room service. In-room data ports, some kitchenettes. Pool. Beauty salon, hot tub, massage. Health club. Shops. Business services, airport shuttle. | 45 7th St. | 516/747–3000, 800/547–0400 outside NY | fax 516/747–1414 | www.gch.com | 273 rooms | $250–$350 | AE, D, DC, MC, V.

Long Island Marriott. This 11-story chain hotel is near the Nassau Coliseum and offers 39 guest rooms specifically designed for the business traveller. Restaurant, bar, room service. In-room data ports, cable TV. Pool. Barbershop, beauty salon, hot tub, sauna. Gym. Shop. Business services. Some pets allowed. | 101 James Doolittle Blvd., Uniondale | 516/794–3800 | fax 516/794–5936 | www.marriotthotels.com/dpp/PropertyPage.asp?Marsha-Code=NYCLI | 617 rooms | $135–$299 | AE, D, DC, MC, V.

Wind Gate Inn. Opened in December 1999, this technologically up-to-date inn caters to business travelers, with more families staying on weekends. A common area, equipped with both Internet access and printers, makes it easy to work while away. Beds are king or double. Complimentary Continental breakfast. In-room data ports. | 821 Stewart Ave. | 516/705–9000 | fax 516/705–9100 | www.windgateinns.com | 118 rooms, 12 suites | $143–$159 rooms, $239–$300 suites | AE, D, DC, MC, V.

GARRISON

MAP 3, C1

(Nearby town also listed: Fishkill)

Garrison is on the banks of the Hudson River, just across from the United States Military Academy at West Point. During the Revolutionary War, a chain was stretched across the river from West Point to stop the British from bringing their warships up the Hudson. Garrison has many restored, historic homes, and nearby Boscobel is the most important. The lovely town park along the river has views of majestic cliffs in either direction. Also in the town is the Garrison Art Center, and a theater, The Depot, in the old train station. Bear Mountain State Park is nearby.

Information: **Southern Dutchess Chamber of Commerce** | 300 Westage, Business Center #100, Fishkill, 12524 | 845/897–2067.

Attractions

Boscobel Restoration. This restored Federal-style house stands on a bluff above the Hudson. It was built by Morris Dyckman, a loyalist during the Revolution, who died before it was completed. One of the most meticulously restored mansions in the area, the house contains an elegant staircase and fine collections of furniture, crystal, silver, and porcelain. The orangerie and the grounds are equally noteworthy, with colorful gardens and beautiful views. | Rte. 9D, Garrison-on-Hudson | 845/265–3638 | www.boscobel.org | $8 | Grounds: Apr.–Nov., Wed.–Mon. 9:30–dusk; house (by tour only): Apr.–Nov., Wed.–Mon. 1st tour 10 AM, last tour 4:15 (Dec., last tour 3:15).

Dining

Bird and Bottle Inn. Continental. Meals at this restaurant housed in an inn that dates to 1761, are served by candlelight. Try the roast duckling and rack of lamb. Open-air dining. Sunday brunch. | 1123 Old Albany Post Rd. | 845/424–3000 | Closed Mon.–Wed. No lunch Sat. | $38–$58 | AE, DC, MC, V.

Plumbush Inn. Continental. Each of the dining rooms at this Victorian inn has its own fireplace. Menu options include filet mignon, lamb chops, roast of duck, and shrimp in coconut milk. Sunday brunch. | Rte. 9D, Cold Spring | 845/265–3904 | Reservations essential weekends | Closed Mon., Tues. | $30–$40 | AE, MC, V.

Xaviar's at Garrison. Contemporary. Your six-course wine tasting dinner is served in an elegant turn-of-the-century ballroom with 20 ft ceilings, vaulted French doors, two large fireplaces, and crystal chandeliers. Meals include delights like roast saddle of lamb with rhubarb compote and wild mushrooms and wild rice, breast of Guinea hen with champagne grapes and saffron potatoes, and tartare of hand-harvested scallops. Entertainment

Fridays and Saturdays. Sunday brunch. | Rte. 9D | 845/424–4228 | Reservations essential | Closed Mon.–Thurs. and mid-Jan.–mid-Feb. No lunch | $80 (6–course prixe fix) | No credit cards.

Lodging

Bird and Bottle. This landmark on the old Albany/New York Post Road has 18th-century wood floors, and antique firearms and furniture. Romantic rooms have four-poster or canopied beds. Restaurant, complimentary breakfast. No room phones. Business services. No kids under 12. | Old Albany Post Rd. (Rte. 9) | 845/424–3000 | fax 845/424–3283 | www.bird-bottle.com | 4 rooms | $200 | AE, DC, MC, V.

Hudson House. This three-story clapboard inn is right on the river. It was built in 1832 to house steamboat passengers; the rooms are now individually furnished with antiques. Restaurant. No room phones, no TV. Business services. | 2 Main St., Cold Spring | 845/265–9355 | fax 845/265–4532 | www.hudsonhouseinn.com | 13 rooms | $140–$225 | AE, DC, MC, V.

GENESEO

(Nearby towns also listed: Avon, Canandaigua, Rochester)

Thanks to the State University of New York at Geneseo, this town is now something of an educational center, but it was once an important center of salt mining. The nation's oldest fox hunt, the Genesee Valley Hunt, runs here each fall, and Geneseo is a logical jumping-off point for an excursion to Letchworth State Park. The entire village is listed on the National Register of Historic Landmarks.

Information: Livingston County Chamber of Commerce | 4235 Lakeville Rd., Building 2, Suite A, 14454 | 716/243–2222 or 800/538–7365 | livchamber@aol.com | www.livchamber.com/livchamber.

Attractions

Letchworth State Park. Some of the canyon cliffs that run along the 17 mi of Genesee River Gorge at this park are 600 ft deep. The 14,350 acres also include waterfalls and forest. You can hike, swim, or camp here, and balloon rides are available. It's 10 min from Geneseo. | 1 Letchworth State Park, off I-390 exit 7, Castile | 716/493–3600 or 800/456–CAMP (for cabin or campsite reservations) | www.nysparks.state.ny.us/parks/ | $5 per vehicle | Daily.

Livingston County Historical Museum. This museum housed in a 1838 cobblestone school has Native American artifacts, and collections of old toys, old fire equipment, and Civil War–period objects. | 30 Center St. | 716/243–9147 | Free | May–June, Sept.–Oct., Thurs. and Fri. 2–5; July–Aug., Tues.–Sun. 2–5.

Tired Iron Tractor Museum. More than 100 old tractors along with other farm equipment and toys are on display at this museum 10 minutes from Geneseo. | Rte. 20A, Cuylerville | 716/382–3110 | $3 | May–Oct., daily 10–6.

ON THE CALENDAR

OCT.: *Genesee Valley Hunt.* A grand display of fox hunting, with steeplechase races and pony rides. | 716/243–4218.

Dining

Caroline's at the Glen Iris Inn. Continental. This old-fashioned hotel-style dining room is right near the Middle Falls of the Genesee River. Known for its shrimp specialties. Kids' menu. No smoking. | Letchworth State Park | 716/493–2622 | Breakfast also available; closed Nov.–Mar. | $15–$40 | AE, MC, V.

Conesus Inn. Continental. This restaurant known for its prime rib of beef is on the east side of Conesus Lake, 6 mi southeast of Geneseo. Kids' menu. | 5654 E. Lake Rd., Conesus | 716/346–6100 | Closed Jan.–Apr. No lunch | $10–$40 | AE, D, MC, V.

Lodging

Country Inn and Suites. This two-story building is only ⅛ mi from entrance to Letchworth State Park. Complimentary Continental breakfast. In-room data ports, cable TV. Pool, hot tub. Business services. No pets. | 130 N. Main St., Mt. Morris | 716/658–4080 | fax 716/658–4020 | www.countryinns.com | 60 rooms | $80–$109 | AE, D, MC, V.

Days Inn. This chain hotel is located 2 mi from the State University of New York at Geneseo. Restaurant, bar. In-room data ports, cable TV. Pool. Laundry service. Business services. | 4242 Lakeville Rd. | 716/243–0500 | fax 716/243–9007 | 76 rooms | $56–$75 | AE, D, DC, MC, V.

Greenway Motel. This one-story motel is 2 mi from the northern entrance to Letchworth State Park and right next door to the Greenway, a 90-mi cinder-path trail that runs Lake Ontario to the Pennsylvania border. No-smoking rooms are available. Cable TV. Playground. Laundry facilities. | 6456 Sonyea Rd., Rte. 36, Mount Morris | 716/658–4500 | greenway@wycol.net. | 23 rooms (some with shower only) | $55–$65 | MC, V.

Oak Valley Country Inn. Built in the 1850s, this Federal-style home, once a poorhouse, is now an elegant country inn 1,000 ft from the road, assuring a peaceful stay. Rooms have hand-stenciled borders and beds range from twin to kings. It's 4 mi from Interstate 390, and 1 mi east of Main Street. Complimentary breakfast. Some in-room hot tubs. | 4235 Lakeville Dr. | 716/243–5570 | fax 716/243–0090 | 11 rooms, 2 suites | $90–$150 rooms, $175 suites | AE, D, DC, MC, V.

Some Place Else or Annabel Lee. Two Victorian homes overlooking the Genesee Valley form this bed-and-breakfast. All rooms are designed in varying Victorian styles, from canopy beds to floral wallpaper. Complimentary breakfast. Some in-room hot tubs, cable TV, in-room VCRs (movies). No pets. No kids under 12. No smoking. | 20 Main St. | 716/243–9440 | innkeeper@someplaceelse.com | www.someplaceelse.com | 10 rooms | $80–$200 | AE, D, MC, V.

GENEVA

MAP 3, F6

(Nearby towns also listed: Auburn, Canandaigua, Palmyra, Penn Yan, Rochester, Seneca Falls, Skaneateles, Victor, Waterloo)

Geneva, founded in 1788, is one of the largest cities of the Finger Lakes area. It sits above the northern end of Seneca Lake, one of the biggest Finger Lakes, and a favorite of trout fishermen. Victorian-era retirees settled in Geneva and lived in spacious Greek Revival homes, many of which remain. A cultural and educational center, Geneva is home to Hobart and William Smith colleges. In 1849, at the Medical College of Geneva College (now Hobart), Elizabeth Blackwell became the first woman ever granted a medical diploma in the United States.

Information: **Geneva Area Chamber of Commerce** | 35 Lakefront Dr., 14456 | 315/789–1776 | info@genevany.com | www.genevany.com.

Attractions

Geneva Historical Society Museum. Also known as the Prouty-Chew Museum, this 1829 mansion houses four exhibits of costumes and local history. You can also stop by to pick up directions for walking and driving tours here. | 543 S. Main St. | 315/789–5151 | Museum free; archives $5 | Tues.–Fri. 9:30–4:30, Sat. 1:30–4:30.

Rose Hill Mansion. This restored 1839 mansion with six Ionic columns is one of the finest examples of Greek Revival architecture in America. Many of the Empire-style furnishings were used by the Swam family, who lived here from 1850 to 1890. Guided tours show off the 21 rooms. Outside, the long lawn slopes down to Seneca Lake. | Rte. 96A | 315/789–3848 | $3 | May–Oct., Mon.–Sat. 10–4, Sun. 1–5.

Sampson State Park and Naval Museum. You can swim, fish, boat, and camp at this 1,852-acre park. The on-site museum honors the program at the outbreak of World War II that brought Navy trainees to the shore of Seneca Lake. | Rte. 96A | 315/585–6392, 315/585–6203 park, 800/357–1814 museum | www.nysparks.state.ny.us/parks/ | Free; parking $6 Memorial Day–Labor Day.

Seneca Cruise Company. Tours of Seneca lake and the locks are given for a minimum duration of two hours. | 212 High St. | 315/789–1822, 800/756–7269.

Seneca Lake State Park. The popular park has a marina, swimming beach, picnic areas, and onshore fishing spots. | U.S. 20/Rte. 5 | 315/789–2331 | www.nysparks.state.ny.us/parks/ | Free; parking $5 | Daily.

Smith Opera House for the Performing Arts. Since 1894, this theater has been presenting theater productions and concerts. Tours are available by appointment. | 100 Waterloo-Geneva Rd., off Rtes 5/20 | 315/781–LIVE | Call for schedule.

ON THE CALENDAR

JULY: *Son's of Italy.* Coinciding with the Fireman's Parade, this celebration of Italian heritage includes music, food, and raffles at the Recreation Center. | 315/781–2242.
MAY: *National Lake Trout Derby.* Whoever catches the biggest fish at this competition held every Memorial Day weekend wins $5,000. There are 45 other cash prizes awarded. There is a $25 fee to enter. | 315/781–2195 or 315/789–3464.
AUG.: *Seneca Lake Whale Watch.* The Diaper Derby (a crawling race for toddlers), and the Cardboard Boat Race are among the more usual events at this festival that also has music and entertainment. At Lakefront Park, off Routes 5 and 20. | 315/781–0820 | www.whalewatch.org.

Dining

Belhurst Castle and Lake Spring Manor. Continental. The six ornate dining rooms have beamed cathedral ceilings and mosaic tiled fireplaces. Try the veal piccata, the rack of lamb, or the prime rib. Kids' menu. Sunday brunch. | Rte. 14 S | 315/781–0201 | fax 315/781–0201 | www.belhurstcastle.com | $18–$28 | MC, V.

Emile's. American. Although the exterior looks pretty bland, this casual restaurant's interior is warm, thanks to the wood paneling. The copious menu lists many traditional favorites, including the most popular: prime rib. Salad bar. Kids' menu. | 639 Rtes. 5 and 20, Waterloo | 315/789–2775 | Closed Mon. | $12–$20 | AE, MC, V.

Pasta Only Cobblestone Restaurant. Contemporary. This restaurant housed in a restored 1825 farmhouse is frequented for its innovative Italian menu, seafood, and wood-fired grill cooking. | 3610 Pre Emption Rd. | 315/789–8498 | No lunch Sat.–Mon. | $10–$22 | AE, D, DC, MC, V.

Lodging

Belhurst Castle. This Victorian castle high above Seneca Lake has rooms furnished with antiques. You can even stay in the special tower suite which includes the turret. Restaurant (*see* Belhurst Castle and Lake Spring Manor), bar. Cable TV. Business services. | Rte. 14 S | 315/781–0201 | www.belhurstcastle.com | 8 rooms, 3 suites | $145–$220 rooms, $160–$315 suites | MC, V.

Chanticleer Motor Inn. This motel gives you an inexpensive foothold in the northern area of the Finger Lakes region. Microwaves, refrigerators, cable TV. Pool. Laundry service. Business services. | 473 Hamilton St. | 315/789–7600 or 800/441–5227 | fax 315/781–1850 | 79 rooms | $45–$60 | AE, D, DC, MC, V.

Geneva on the Lake. The grounds at this romantic 1912 building include beautiful formal gardens and there is a terrace overlooking the lake. Inside, antiques furnish the suites. Bar, complimentary Continental breakfast, picnic area. Kitchenettes, refrigerators, cable TV. Pool. Boating. Business services, free parking. | 1001 Lochland Rd., Rte. 14 S | 315/789–7190 or 800/343–6382 | fax 315/789–0322 | www.genevaonthelake.com | 6 studios, 24 one-bedroom suites | $189–$311 studio, $329–$657 1–bedroom suites | AE, D, MC, V.

Ramada Inn Geneva Lakefront. The anchor of the Geneva skyline, this hotel is on the shore of Seneca Lake, close to Seneca Lake State Park. No-smoking rooms are available. Restaurant, bar. In-room data ports, cable TV. Pool. Gym. Laundry services. Pets allowed. | 41 Lakefront Dr. | 315/789–0400 | fax 315/789–4351 | 148 rooms | $69–$149 | AE, D, MC, V.

GLEN COVE

MAP 3, C2

(Nearby towns also listed: Oyster Bay, Port Washington, Roslyn, Syosset)

Since it was established in 1668, Glen Cove's waterfront, woodlands, and varied topography have been constant attractions and it takes only one look at a sunset on Hempstead Harbor to understand why. Once home to J. P. Morgan and F. W. Woolworth, Glen Cove was at the heart of the north shore's Gold Coast. At one time, half of the city's land was taken up by Gold mansions, and the estates of Standard Oil's co-founder, Charles Pratt, and his sons covered more than 1,000 acres. Many of these mansions remain today in and around the more than 300 acres of nature preserves that overlook the harbor.

A varied ethnic population results in year-round festivals that take place throughout Glen Cove. The city is looking to a revitalized waterfront to carry it into the new millennium and development plans are shaping old buildings into new marinas, restaurants, and entertainment facilities.

Information: **Glen Cove Chamber of Commerce** | 14 Glen St., Suite 303, 11542 | 516/676–6666.

Attractions

Garvies Point Museum and Preserve. Prehistoric Indian culture, the science of archaeology, and the area's geological past form the basis of this county-run museum's main exhibits. Woodland thickets, sediments, and meadows fill the preserve's 62 acres overlooking Hempstead Harbor. | 50 Barry Dr. | 516/571–8010 | $1 | Tues.–Sun. 10–4.

Holocaust Memorial and Educational Center of Nassau County. Through its pictorial history of the Holocaust, special exhibits, seminars, and research library, the museum serves as a living memorial to the millions of victims who died at the hands of the Nazis. | 100 Crescent Beach Rd., at Welwyn Preserve | 516/571–8040 | Free | Weekdays 9:30–4:30, Sun. 11–4.

Sea Cliff Village Museum. Displays of documents and photos trace village history at this museum. A scale model of a village Victorian house is also on exhibit. | 95 10th Ave., Sea Cliff (4 mi north of Roslyn) | 516/671–0090 | $1 suggested donation | Weekends 2–5.

Thomas Jefferson. For a taste of Long Island's past, take a narrated brunch or dinner cruise aboard this elegant replica of the paddle steamers that cruised Long Island Sound's Gold Coast in the 19th century. The captain and crew are outfitted in period costumes. | American Phoenix Lines Inc., on the Creek at Shore Rd. | 516/744–2353 | fax 516/821–5508 | Call for hrs.

JUNE: *Greek Village Festival.* This food festival sponsored by the Greek Orthodox Church of the Resurrection brings a flea market, live music, and dancing to Cedar Swamp Road. | 516/676–6666.

JULY: *Waterfront Festival.* U.S. naval ships come into the harbor during this popular event that also has street performers, a floating barge play, an antique car show, a carnival, and fireworks. Food and craft vendors set up their stalls. Tours of Glen Cove mansions are also available. Special buses run from downtown Glen Cove to Morgan Park. | 516/676–2005.

OCT.: *Sea Cliff Mini-Market.* Close to 400 artists and craftspeople display their wares at this event that also has booths for local nonprofit and service organizations. In Sea Cliff, the town next to Glen Cove. | 516/671–0080.

NOV.: *Native American Thanksgiving Feast.* An authentic sweat lodge and demonstrations of American Indian cooking and pottery-making come to Garview Point Museum. There are also films, tools, and demonstrations of corn grinding and spear throwing. | 516/571–8010.

Dining

Barney's. Continental. Housed in a 120-year-old building, this restaurant 20 min from Glen Cove has a decidedly old-country aura. The main dining room downstairs has a fireplace, and there are also two quaint smaller rooms with a bar in the center where you can try the crab cakes, roast duck, or seared ahi tuna. Kids' menu. | 315 Buckram Rd., Locust Valley | 516/671–6300 | Closed Mon. No lunch | $40–$50 | AE, MC, V.

Costello's Pub. American. This bright, cheerful pub has a gas fireplace and tables done in green and white. Known for steak, burgers, chicken, and daily specials. Kids' menu. Sunday brunch. | 248 Sea Cliff Ave., Sea Cliff | 516/676–9403 | $10–$15 | AE, MC, V.

La Bussola. Italian. This romantic restaurant with French doors and lace curtains serves classic Italian dishes of chicken, veal, beef, and fish at candlelit tables. A wooden bar leads into the main dining room. No smoking. | 40 School St. | 516/671–2100 | $30–$35 | AE, D, DC, MC, V.

La Pace. Italian. The walls of this Tuscany-style restaurant are covered in green and beige fabric and adorned with sconces. Fresh roses on the tables, a chandelier, and fireplaces add to the rich feel. Try the fusilli served with cimedirapa (broccoli rabe) and scampi La Pace (sautéed shrimps stuffed with fontina cheese, rolled with bacon, and grilled with mustard sauce). | 51 Cedar Swamp Rd. | 516/671–2970 | No lunch weekends | $25–$30 | AE, DC, MC, V.

Veranda. Italian. Plants and fresh flowers add to the cozy, warm spirit of this restaurant which serves dishes from the northern region of Italy. Fresh fish is popular. For a local treat, try Long Island duck with raspberries and apples. Saturday–Thursday, there is a prix-fixe menu. No smoking. | 75 Cedar Swamp Rd. | 516/759–0394 | $35–$40 | AE, D, DC, MC, V.

GLENS FALLS

MAP 3, L5

(Nearby towns also listed: Bolton Landing, Diamond Point, Lake George Village, Lake Luzerne, Queensbury, Saratoga Springs, Warrensburg)

The tale of Glens Falls's name is poetic enough to be suspicious: once called Wings Falls, after its founder, Abraham Wing, the name became Glens Falls when Wing lost it to Colonel Johannes Glen in a poker game. Whatever the origins of its name, Glens Falls is now the big city of the southeast. With a population of more than 15,000 in the city, and about 25,000 more in surrounding communities (Queensbury and Hudson Falls), this is the only really urban area in this part of the state. While it's actually about

10 mi south and east of the formal boundary of Adirondack Park, its style is clearly Adirondack. Glens Falls has been singled out by national magazines as both a "typical hometown," and as one of the best places in the country to raise a family.

Information: **Adirondack Regional Chambers of Commerce** | 136 Warren St., 12801 | 518/798–1761.

Attractions

Chapman Historical Museum. A visit to the painstakingly restored home of the DeLong family—inhabitants from 1860 to 1910—gives you a glimpse of life in the 19th-century Adirondacks. Exhibits showcase regional history, and an extensive photo collection displays the work of Seneca Ray Stoddard. | 348 Glen St. | 518/793–2826 | $2 | Tues.–Sat. 10–5.

Hyde Collection. One of the finest art museums in the northeastern United States, the Hyde collection features works of such artists as El Greco, Leonardo da Vinci, Rembrandt, Renoir, and Picasso. Antiques and fine period furniture are also displayed, as are temporary exhibits. | 161 Warren St. | 518/792–1761 | Free | Tues.–Sat. 10–5 (Thurs. 10–7), Sun. 12–5.

World Awareness Children's Museum. Children's art from around the world exposes kids and adults to different cultures. | 227 Glen St. | 518/793–2773 | $2 | Tues.–Fri. 10–5, Sun. 10–2.

ON THE CALENDAR

SEPT: *Adirondack Hot Air Balloon Festival.* Hot-air balloons from all over the region take off twice a day, creating a spectacular sight. Weather permitting, third weekend of the month, at the Warren County Airport. | 518/792–2600.

Dining

Davidson Brothers Restaurant and Brewery. American. The menu in this wooded traditional tavern has something for everyone, from pub fare to veggie wraps. Live entertainment and kids' menu. | 184 Glen St. | 518/743–9026 | $6–$14 | MC, V.

Fiddleheads. Contemporary. Antique collectibles and fresh flowers, grown in the back, set the tone at this intimate restaurant, where are served items like herb-encrusted rack of lamb, Maryland crabcakes, filet mignon, and daily fresh seafood specials. | 21 Ridge St. | 518/793–5789 | $15–$25 | AE, D, MC, V.

Lodging

Alpenhaus. Built in the style of an Alpine chalet, this hotel is 1 mi from the Great Escape, in Queensbury, 3 mi from Glen Falls. From your room you will have a view across the road of the Green Mountains. Cable TV. | 851 Lake George Rd. (Rte. 9), Queensbury | 518/792–6941 | 15 rooms | $82–$88 | AE, MC, V.

Landmark. The Landmark's lounge has a fireplace, pool table, and video games as well as music. The motor lodge sits 1 mi northeast of I–87 at exit 17N. Picnic area. Cable TV. 2 pools. Hot tub. Putting green. Exercise equipment. Video games. Playground. Business services, airport shuttle. | Saratoga Rd. (Rts. 9/197), South Glens Falls | 518/793–3441 or 800/541–3441 | fax 518/761–6909 | 74 rooms | $66–$70 | AE, D, DC, MC, V.

Queensbury Hotel. A Victorian hotel in downtown Glens Falls, across from the city park. Restaurant, bar. Cable TV. Pool. Barbershop, hot tub, massage. Exercise equipment. Business services. | 88 Ridge St. | 518/792–1121 or 800/554–4526 | fax 518/792–9259 | 123 rooms | $99–$149 | AE, D, DC, MC, V.

Ramada Inn. This motel at the gateway to the Adirondacks is a good choice if you're traveling on business. Restaurant, bar, room service. In-room data ports, cable TV. Indoor pool. No pets. | 1 Abby La., Queensbury | 518/793–7701 | fax 518/792–5463 | www.ramada.com | 110 rooms | $90–$130 | AE, D, DC, MC, V.

GLOVERSVILLE

(Nearby towns also listed: Amsterdam, Johnstown, Saratoga Springs)

While Gloversville, just outside the Adirondack Park proper, isn't officially part of the Adirondacks, it is dedicated to the Adirondack way of life, and you'll find sporting outfitters here. The town got its start, and its name, from the now much quieter glove-making industry, for which it was once the world capital. Just north of town is Great Sacandaga Lake, an artificial body of water that significantly changed the local landscape. Today, the lake is a good place to fish, swim, or boat.

Information: Fulton County Chamber of Commerce | 2 N. Main St., 12078 | 800/676–3858.

Attractions
Fulton County Museum. Displays trace the history of leather and gloves and the role the glove-making industry played in town. Victorian clothing and 19th-century regional folk art are on exhibit here as well. | 237 Kingsboro Ave., off Rte. 30A | 518/725–2203 | Free | July–Aug., Tues.–Sat. 10–4; May–June and Sept.–Oct., Tues.–Sat. noon–4.

ON THE CALENDAR
OCT.: *Gloversville Firefighters Challenge.* Firefighting teams from all over the country come here to prove themselves in order to make it to the finals in Las Vegas. Competitions include obstacle courses and simulations of real-life situations where life-size dummies are rescued. Kids partake in the fun courses designed for little ones. First weekend of the month in Frontage Road parking lots. | 518/725–3124.

Dining
Salvatore's Italian Pizzeria. Italian. Choose from either thick-crusted Sicilian pizza or thin-crusted New York City style at this popular family spot. Pictures of Italy hang on the wall, but even more noticeable is the Italian horse cart. | 44 N. Main St. | 518/773–7012 | Closed Mon. | $7–$14 | AE, D, MC, V.

Lodging
Lapland Lake Nordic Vacation Center. These housekeeping cottages, 12 mi north of Gloversville, are within walking distance of a private lake, and you can use the canoes and paddleboats. The one- to four-bedroom cottages have enclosed front porches and wood-stoves. Restaurant. Kitchenettes, no room phones, no TV. Hiking, bicycles. Cross-country skiing. | 139 Lapland Lake Rd., Northville | 518/863–4974 | fax 518/863–2651 | www.laplandlake.com | 11 cottages | $98–$187 | DC, MC, V.

Super 8 Motel. This predictable chain motel is 3 mi from downtown Gloversville and 1 mi from Route 29. Beds range from double to kings. Complimentary Continental breakfast. | 301 N. Comrie Ave., Johnstown | 518/736–1800 | 47 rooms, 1 suite | $75 | AE, D, DC, MC, V.

GOSHEN

(Nearby towns also listed: Middletown, Monroe, Newburgh)

This residential community just off Route 17 at exit 124 is Orange County's government center. The center of dairy country, it's also in a region where the soil, known as "black dirt," is particularly rich. Onions are one of the major crops grown in this area. Downtown, Goshen's streets are dotted with 19th-century buildings.

Information: **Orange County Chamber of Commerce** | 40 Mathews St., #103, 10924 | 845/294–8080.

Attractions

Brotherhood Winery. This is America's oldest continually operating winery and some European-style stone buildings date to 1839. Tours, tastings, and festivals are offered. The winery is 30 minutes from Goshen. | 100 Brotherhood Plaza Dr., off Rte. 208 N, Washingtonville | 845/496–9101 | www.wines.com/brotherhood (click on Brotherhood) | $4 | Tours weekends 11–4.

Goshen Historic Track. The oldest harness track in the United States is now a National Historic Landmark. You can watch daily training or take a self-guided walking tour of the premises, but these days races are run only in July. | 44 Park Pl. | 845/294–5333 | Free | Daily.

Trotting Horse Museum. Overlooking the track is this museum and hall of fame dedicated to harness racing. Exhibits include a 3D racing simulator, prints, and paintings. Some of the displays are housed in the original track stables. | 240 Main St. | 845/294–6330 | $7.50 | Daily 10–6.

ON THE CALENDAR

JULY: *Great American Weekend*. The whole town comes together for this festive Fourth of July celebration. Local art and used books are sold, while bake sales and cookouts take place to celebrate the nation's birthday at the Museum of Hall of Fame of Trotter. | 845/294–7741.

JULY: *Harness Racing*. Harness races are held during special weekends at the Goshen Historic Track. | 845/294–5333.

Dining

Ile de France Restaurant. French. Classic French cuisine, such as frog legs and pâté, is served here where 15th-century tapestries line the walls, and each table has roses and a candle. Try a crème brûlée or lemon tart for dessert; everything is baked on the premises. Lunch is less formal and less expensive. | 6 N. Church St. | 845/294–5759 | Closed Sun., Mon. | $17–$28 | AE, D, DC, MC, V.

Lodging

Anthony Dobbins Stagecoach Inn. Built in 1747 as a farmhouse, this quiet Georgian B&B sits peacefully within 4 wooded acres, near the foothills of the Catskills and 1 mi from Interstate 88. Rooms are English and Colonial styles, filled with family antiques, and are named after famous guests, such as the William Penn room. Some rooms have fireplace. Complimentary Continental breakfast weekdays, complimentary breakfast weekends. Library. | 268 Main St. | 845/294–5526 | 7 rooms | $95–$150 | AE.

GRAND ISLAND

MAP 3, C6

(Nearby towns also listed: Amherst, Buffalo, Clarence, Lockport, Niagara Falls, Williamsville)

One of the ways you can drive from the Buffalo area to Niagara Falls is by taking the two spectacular bridges that link Grand Island to the mainland. From the high-arching bridges you can look down on the majestic Niagara River, which parts around this low, flat island as it flows from Lake Erie over Niagara Falls to join Lake Ontario. Once farmland, much of the island is now residential, and many of its inhabitants commute to Buffalo. Beaver Island State Park, at the southern tip of the island, makes a nice place to stop on your way to the Falls.

Information: **Chamber of Commerce** | 1980 Whitehaven Rd., 14072 | 716/773–3651.

Attractions

Grand Lady Cruises. Cruise the Niagara River and Lake Erie while enjoying a brunch, lunch, or dinner. Charters are also available. | 100 Whitehaven Rd. | 716/774–8594 | fax 716/774–8519 | grandlady@grandlady.com | www.grandlady.com | May–Oct., 10–11:30, noon–1:30, 7–9:30.

Martin's Fantasy Island. A wooden roller coaster is one of the over 100 rides at this 80-acre family theme park. The water park includes a wave pool, and there is a petting zoo. | 2400 Grand Island Blvd. | 716/773–7591 | fax 716/773–7043 | $9.95–$16.95 | May–Sept., Tues.–Sun. 11:30–8:30.

River Lea Historic Farm House. This 1849 Victorian farmhouse in Beaver Island State Park was the home of nationally known stock breeder and founder of the Erie County Fair, Lewis J. Allen. Now restored, it has an extensive collection of memorabilia and antique furnishings. | 2136 W. Oakfield Rd. | 716/773–3271 | fax 716/773–4150 | Free | Mar.–June and Sept.–Dec., 3rd Sun. of month 2–4.

ON THE CALENDAR

JUNE: *Island Treasures.* This festival, taking place in the city center between Base Line and Grand Island Boulevard, includes arts, crafts, sales, and more. | Grand Island Blvd., Whitehaven Business District | 716/773–3651.

JULY: *Fourth of July Parade.* Floats, marching bands, and more are brought out to Grand Island Boulevard to celebrate our nation's independence. | 716/733–1900.

Dining

Beach House. American. Two miles north of downtown, this family-style eatery serves Wednesday and Friday fish fries that have earned it such acclaim. The extensive menu offers everything from tacos to subs and wings. Kids' menu and beer and wine available. | 5584 E. River Rd. | 716/773–7119 | $7–$11 | AE, D, MC, V.

Lodging

Chateau Motor Lodge. This family-run lodge 5 mi from Niagara Falls is surrounded by trees and has a picnic area. Nearby restaurants are within walking distance. Beds are queen size. Pets allowed. | 1810 Grand Island Blvd. | 716/773–2868 | fax 716/773–5173 | 17 rooms | $69–$79 | AE, D, MC, V.

GREAT NECK

MAP 3, C2

(Nearby towns also listed: New York City, Port Washington, Roslyn)

The western gateway to the north shore of Long Island, Great Neck is made up of nine villages that sit on a peninsula jutting into Long Island Sound. Ever since Dutch settlers founded the city in 1681, people have been attracted by its tranquil setting and closeness to Manhattan. The mansions here inspired the wealthy estates F. Scott Fitzgerald wrote about in his classic novel *The Great Gatsby.* Today, the city is a thriving residential, shopping, and business area, with Great Neck Plaza, a small village within the greater community, filled with upscale shops, as its hub.

Information: **Great Neck Chamber of Commerce** | 643 Middleneck Rd., 11023 | 516/487–2000.

Attractions

Kings Point Park. The 175 acres at this park hold 5 mi of hiking trails, 26 picnic areas, baseball diamonds, as well as basketball and clay tennis courts. | Steamboat Rd. | 516/477–1383 | Free | Daily.

Saddle Rock Grist Mill. This is one of the few U.S. tidal gristmills still in operation, and a miller is often on hand to distribute samples of ground corn, wheat, and Indian meal. Though it was refurbished in the early 1800s, the mill's records actually date back to 1702. | Grist Mill La. | 516/572–0257 | Free | May 15–Oct. 14, Sun. 1–5.

U.S. Merchant Marine Academy. Officers for the American Merchant Marine and U.S. Naval Reserve come here for training and education. The academy, set on 80 acres of the former Walter P. Chrysler estate, 3 mi southwest of Great Neck, has lovely grounds that include the American Merchant Marine Museum. | 300 Steamboat Rd., Kings Point | 516/773–5000 | Free | Mon.–Fri., 8–4:30.

ON THE CALENDAR

AUG.: *Evenings on the Sound.* On weekends, the Steppingstone Waterside Theater presents a wide variety of live performances including rock concerts, operas, ballets, and fully staged plays, some with well-known performers. A bus runs to the park from various points in town. | 516/487–2000.

Dining

Bruzell's. Contemporary. The Art Deco dining room is done in teal and black at this restaurant. Try the grilled Portobello mushrooms, potato-crusted goat cheese tart, rack of lamb with natural gravy, thin and crispy fried onions, pan-seared Atlantic salmon with citrus beurre blanc, or prime-aged shell steaks. Kids' menu. | 451 Middle Neck Rd. | 516/482–6600 | $14–$25 | AE, D, DC, MC, V.

La Coquille. French. Lace curtains decorate the windows of this restaurant where a harpist plays on Monday. Try the duck à la orange and rack of lamb with a mustard bread-crumb crust. Kids' menu. | 1669 Northern Blvd., Manhasset | 516/365–8422 | Reservations essential Sat. | Jacket required | $30–$35 | AE, DC, MC, V.

Millie's Place. Contemporary. This romantic restaurant has three candlelit dining rooms (one a private party room) with antique furniture. Known for salads and paella, but you could also try the Chilean sea bass with corn and potato hash, and the apple cake. Sunday brunch. No smoking. | 25 Middle Neck Rd. | 516/482–4223 | Reservations essential | $25–$35 | AE, MC, V.

Peter Luger Steak House. Steak. A spacious restaurant paneled in English Tudor style with vaulted ceilings, a stained-glass window, and oak floors. The grilled lobsters with drawn butter come with french fries over ½ ft long. | 255 Northern Blvd. | 516/487–8800 | $30–$50 | No credit cards.

Ristorante Bevanda. Italian. Half a dozen different kinds of fresh fish are served daily at this elegant restaurant with white tablecloths. Also try the veal chops à la Bevanda, which are stuffed with cheese and prosciutto and sautéed in shallots and white wine. No smoking. | 570 Middle Neck Rd. | 516/482–1510 | Reservations essential | $13–$24 | AE, DC, MC, V.

Lodging

Inn at Great Neck. Art Deco motifs dominate the lobby and rooms of this four-story hotel, in the center of Great Neck Plaza, surrounded by shops and restaurants. Restaurant, bar, room service. In-room data ports, minibars, some in-room hot tubs, cable TV, in-room VCRs. Gym. No pets. | 30 Cuttermill Rd. | 516/773–2000 | fax 516/773–2020 | www.innat-greatneck.com | 85 rooms | $215–$325 | AE, D, DC, MC, V.

GREENE

MAP 3, H7

(Nearby towns also listed: Bainbridge, Binghamton, Norwich)

This village about 25 mi north of Binghamton on Route 12, was founded as the town of Hornby in 1798. But in 1806, it was re-named in honor of Revolutionary War hero General Nathaniel Greene. The town's diverse economy includes light and heavy manufacturing, ranging from garments to gardening supplies as well as from metal-casting to industrial machinery.

Information: Greater Greene Chamber of Commerce | 82 S. Shenango, 13778 | 607/656–8225.

Dining
Silo. American. This country restaurant surrounded by rolling hills and gardens is known for steaks, veal, seafood, and chicken. The dining room has floral curtains and country wood furniture. You can stay overnight in one of the three guest rooms. | 203 Morach Rd. | 607/656–4377 | No lunch Mon.–Sat. | $14–$35 | AE, D, DC, MC, V.

GREENPORT

MAP 3, E2

(Nearby towns also listed: Orient Point, Shelter Island)

Clean, uncrowded beaches are one of the treasures found in this charming, old New England–style village on the North Fork. The deep waters of Long Island Sound still summon home tall ships reminiscent of the whaling boats that once harbored in Greenport's safe waters.

When the first settlers arrived here from New England in 1640, Native Americans were living in this area. Beginning in the late 1700s, commercial fishing became one of the town's primary industries. Much later, during Prohibition, the harbor was used for illegal rum-running, and it is said that a few gun battles occurred off Greenport's shores.

Today, the village has quaint shops, and restaurants and the vistas from the wharf area at the end of Main Street can awaken the poet in just about anyone.

Information: Greenport Chamber of Commerce | Box 66, 11944 | 631/477–1383 | www.greenport.com.

Attractions
East End Seaport and Maritime Museum. Exhibits on lighthouses, ships, East End ship-building, and yacht racing are housed in a former Long Island Railroad passenger termi-nal. The museum also sponsors the Lighthouse Cruise, a cruise to the Bug Lighthouse. | 3rd St. (at the ferry docks) | 631/477-2100 | $2 | June–Oct., Wed.–Mon. 10-4.

Railroad Museum of Long Island. The museum, which is housed in a historic 1890 Green-port freight station, exhibits a Reading Railroad track car, a 1907 snow plow, and a 1925 Long Island Railroad caboose. At the Riverhead section, exhibits include two steam engines, a unique passenger car, and a baggage car. | 440 4th St. | 631/727-7920 | www.bitnik.com/rmli/index.html | Donations accepted | Weekends, 10-4.

Shorefront Area. You will find many historic points of interest peppered around quaint shops and restaurants. You can get a great view of the harbor from the wharf area at the foot of Main Street. | Main St. | 631/477-1383 | Free | Daily.

Stirling Historical Society. Maritime exhibits emphasize whaling and oyster industries. Also displayed are whaling tools and oil lamps, as well as a collection of artifacts, furniture, and tools from the 1800s. | 319 Main St. | 631/477–3026 | Donations accepted | July 5–Sept. 6, weekends 1–4.

ON THE CALENDAR

SEPT.: *Greenport Maritime Festival.* For two days, Greenport closes down its main streets for this big festival that includes a chowder-tasting contest, an inner-sea rescue, a regatta, a parade, food vendors, shows, and activities for children. | 631/477–0004.

Dining

Chowder Pot Pub. Seafood. The views of Peconic Bay at this restaurant are best at sunset. As you might guess from the name, chowder is a specialty, complemented by seafood options as well as occasional ribs and steaks. Open-air dining. Live music weekends. Dock space by Shelter Island Ferry. | 104 3rd St. | 631/477–1345 | $15–$28 | AE, MC, V.

Claudio's Clam Bar/Claudio's Restaurant/Crabby Jerry's. Seafood. All three of these restaurants are on the same 2½-acre property on the waterfront. The Clam Bar is right on the dock and serves salads, hot dogs, fried clams, mussels, and soft-shell crab. Claudio's is known for seafood, porterhouse steaks, and lobsters. The old bar in the restaurant dates to the late 1800s. Crabby Jerry's offers self-service with picnic tables on the Main Street Dock. Raw bar. No smoking. | 111 Main St. | 631/477–0627 | $15–$20 | MC, V.

Michael's Restaurant Pub. Contemporary. The original 1937 diner is part of this breezy, relaxed restaurant with outdoor plants and flowers. Try the roasted vegetable quesadillas served with homemade salsa; top sirloin; fresh raspberry peach crisp; or carrot cake with cream-cheese icing. Open-air dining on an enclosed deck and patio. Raw bar weekends. Kids' menu. No smoking. | 212 Front St. | 631/477–9577 | Closed Tues., Wed. | $10–$20 | AE, DC, MC, V.

Lodging

Silver Sands. Some units are just footsteps from the 1,400-ft private beach owned by the Silver Sands. Built in the 1960s, the rooms have '60s period furnishings. Picnic area, complimentary Continental breakfast. Kitchenettes (in cottages), cable TV. Pool. Beach, boating. Video games. | Silvermere Rd. | 631/477–0011 | fax 631/477–0922 | www.greenport.com/silversands | 35 rooms, 15 cottages | $100–$150 rooms, $150 cottages | AE, D, DC, MC, V.

Soundview Inn. All rooms in this modern motel have decks overlooking the waterfront and private beach. Restaurant, bar (with entertainment). Kitchenettes (in suites), refrigerators, cable TV. Pool. Sauna. Tennis. | 57185 North Rd., Rte. 48 at Chaple La. | 631/477–1910 | fax 631/477–9436 | www.greenport.com | 49 rooms, 31 suites | $110–$120 rooms, $150–$300 suites | AE, D, DC, MC, V.

Watson's by the Bay. Built in 1873, this three-story Victorian home sits in a quiet cul-de-sac two blocks from the village, overlooking the Peconic Bay and Shelter Island. Rooms have period antiques and bay views. A favorite pastime is relaxing on the wraparound porch while drinking some of the local wine. Complimentary breakfast. Pool. | 104 Bay Ave. | 631/477–0426 | fax 631/477–8441 | www.greenport.com/watsons | 3 rooms | Call for room rates | Labor Day–Memorial Day | No credit cards.

HAGUE

MAP 3, L4

(Nearby towns also listed: Bolton Landing, Schroon Lake, Ticonderoga)

A small resort town along Lake George, Hague has only 700 regular residents, yet you'll find places to stay along with a number of restaurants. While you're here, look for landforms known as the "Indian kettles," potlike depressions in the rock surface of the surrounding mountains.

Information: **Gore Mountain Regional Chamber of Commerce** | Box 84, North Creek, 12853 | 518/251–2612 | www.goremtnregion.org.

Attractions

Hague Cartoon Museum. On a walk through this museum you'll find nearly 700 framed comic and political cartoons dating back to 1830. "The Yellow Kid," one of the first cartoons, is in the collection. | Graphite Rd. | 518/543–8824 | $3 | Thurs. 7 PM–9 PM; Fri., Sat., and Sun. 2–4; also open by appointment.

Rogers Rock State Public Campground. The winding 2½-mi trail to Rogers Slide ends with a view of Lake George. This basic lakeside campground has 331 sites, a beach, a boat launch, toilets, showers, fireplaces, and picnic tables. | Off Rte. 9 N, in Adirondack Park | 518/585–6746 | $5 per vehicle | Early May–mid-Oct.

Dining

Island View Cafe. American. Opened in the summer of 1998, this chef-owned and -operated place has an outdoor patio overlooking Lake George. Everything on the menu is homemade, from the lavender or vanilla ice cream to pastries. Hamburgers, hot dogs, and chicken fingers are the most popular items at this patriotic eatery, which shares an address with the Old Glory Gifts and Antiques. | Lake Shore Dr. | 518/543–6367 | Breakfast also available; closed Labor Day–Memorial Day | $5–$7 | No credit cards.

Lodging

Hague Motel. You have a range of options here: motel rooms, cottages with views of Lake George, or a housekeeping unit. Most rooms have two double beds. During the summer months, cottages and the housekeeping unit rent by the week. Families return year after year to relax and picnic on the beach. | 9054 Lake Shore Dr. | 518/543–6631 | 4 rooms, 3 cottages, one housekeeping unit | Rooms, $65 cottages, $800 per week, housekeeping unit $700 weekly | No credit cards.

Ruah Bed and Breakfast. This stately, turn-of-the-20th-century B&B is right on the water. The antiques-filled living room has a fireplace and a grand piano. Some of the spacious rooms have huge bay windows and balconies that overlook the lake; all have fireplaces. Complimentary breakfast. | 9221 Lake Shore Dr. | 518/543–8816 | 4 rooms | $105–$170 | AE, D, MC, V.

Trout House Village Resort. The main lodge was built in 1925 and has a large front porch with a view of Lake George. The resort includes 400 ft of private beach. Rooms are individually furnished; the cottages have fireplaces and wood-paneled walls. Picnic area. No air-conditioning, some kitchenettes, some in-room hot tubs, cable TV. Putting green. Beach, docks, boating, fishing, bicycles. | Lake Shore Dr. (Rte. 9 N) | 518/543–6088 or 800/368–6088 | www.trouthouse.com | 4 rooms, 6 cabins, 5 cottages | $79 rooms; $69 day, $425 weekly cabins; $700 cottages (7–day minimum stay) | AE, D, MC, V.

HAMBURG

MAP 3, D5

(Nearby towns also listed: Amherst, Buffalo, East Aurora, Williamsville)

Like much of western New York, Hamburg was originally settled by families moving west from New England. Town historians say the city takes its name from Hamburg, Germany, although legend claims that the first hamburger was made here in 1885. A cook arrived at the Erie County Fair to prepare pork sausages at his concession stand, but the butcher was out of pork; in desperation, the cook substituted ground beef in the buns, and the improvisation became known as hamburgers. Beware of repeating this story, however, as a couple of other towns in the East also have tales about being the birthplace of America's favorite fast food.

Information: **Hamburg Chamber of Commerce** | 8 S. Buffalo St., 14075 | 716/649–7917.

Attractions

Buffalo Raceway. Pari-mutuel harness racing is held at the Erie County Fairgrounds. | 5600 McKinley Pkwy. | 716/649–1280 | fax 716/649–0033 | Free | Feb.–Dec.; call for hrs.

ON THE CALENDAR
APR.: *Springtime in the Country.* More than 200 of North America's finest artisans display handmade items at the Hamburg Fairgrounds Agricenter. | 716/646–1583.
JUNE: *Annual Greater Buffalo Feis.* The Feis (pronounced fesh) includes traditional Irish music, all-day dancing competitions, food, drink, and vocal and soda bread competitions. At the Erie County Agri-Center, South Park Avenue. | 716/827–0223.
AUG.: *Erie County Fair.* Big City county state fair with rides, food, exhibits, and entertainment. | Erie County Fairgrounds | 716/649–3900.

Dining

Daniel's. American. This small, cozy restaurant has white tablecloths and flowers throughout the dining room. The menu includes veal, salmon, and filet mignon. | 174 Buffalo St. | 716/648–6554 | Closed Sun., Mon. No lunch | $15–$22 | AE, MC, V.

Lodging

Stadium View Inn. This single-story hotel, on Highway 62, sits on the western edge of Hilbert College. Cable TV. | 4414 Southwestern Blvd. | 716/649–6206 | 27 rooms | $50–$65 | AE, D, MC, V.

HAMILTON

MAP 3, H6

(Nearby towns also listed: Cazenovia, Norwich, Richfield Springs)

This college town founded in the late 1700s is on Route 12B, a few miles south of Route 20. Home to Colgate University and the Colgate Inn, Hamilton also has many antiques dealers, especially along the stretch of Route 20, where the annual Madison-Bouckville Antiques Show takes place in August.

Information: **Hamilton Chamber of Commerce** | 10 Utica St., 13346 | 315/824–8213.

Attractions

Colgate University. Founded in 1819, this private four-year liberal arts college today has a student population of approximately 2,700. The campus is home to an art gallery, theater, golf course, and sports events. | 13 Oak Dr. | 315/228–1000 | www.colgate.edu | Free | Daily.

Rogers Environmental Education Center. You can walk, bird-watch, or cross-country ski on the variety of trails that cut through the 571 acres here, 11 mi south of Hamilton. There is also a visitors center with exhibits and a library. | 2721 Rte. 80 | 607/674–4017 | www.ascent. net/rogers/ | Free | Sept.–May, weekdays 8:30–4:45, Sat. 1–4:45; June–Aug., weekdays 8:30–4:45, weekends 1–4:45.

ON THE CALENDAR
AUG.: *Madison-Bouckville Antiques Show.* For a long weekend, more than 1,000 antiques dealers cover acres of fields between Madison and Bouckville. On Route 20 about 5 mi north of Hamilton. | 315/684–7320.

Dining

Payne Street Corner. American. This restaurant in the Colgate Inn still has its original chandeliers. Known for crab cakes, chicken asiago, sautéed chicken with broccoli over capellini, and bagel sandwiches. A separate tavern/taproom also serves meals. Sunday brunch. | 1–5 Payne St. | 315/824–2300 | Closed Sun.; taproom open daily | $12–$20 | AE, D, DC, MC, V.

Lodging

Colgate Inn. Built in 1925 in Colonial style, this inn has rooms done up in early Victorian antiques. There are views of the village green and a golf course is just two blocks away. The recreational facilities of Colgate University are available to guests. Restaurant, bar, complimentary Continental breakfast. Some in-room hot tubs, cable TV. Business services. | 1–5 Payne St. | 315/824–2300 | fax 315/824–4500 | 46 rooms | $115–$125 | AE, D, DC, MC, V.

HAMMONDSPORT

MAP 3, F7

(Nearby towns also listed: Bath, Hornell, Naples, Penn Yan)

The center of New York's wine-making industry, Hammondsport lies snuggly between rolling hills and the southern end of Keuka Lake. Hammondsport is also the birthplace of naval aviation. Glenn Curtiss made the world's first pre-announced flight here—a 5,090-ft trip aboard the "June Bug."

Information: **Hammondsport Chamber of Commerce** | Box 539, 14840 | 607/569–2989.

Attractions

Glenn H. Curtiss Museum. Just outside of Hammondsport is this museum honoring Curtiss and his early aviation experiments. He made the first public, pre-announced flight when he flew his June Bug plane more than 5,000 ft outside the village on July 4, 1908. The exhibits include aircraft, engines, and a terrific collection of antique motorcycles. | 8419 Rte. 54 | 607/569–2160 | fax 607/569–2040 | $5 | May–Oct., Mon.–Sat. 9–5, Sun. 11–5; Nov.–Apr., Mon.–Sat. 10–4, Sun. noon–5.

Great Western Winery Visitor Center at the Pleasant Valley Wine Co. Three miles from Hammondsport is one of the largest tourist attractions in the Finger Lakes—the Great Western Winery, the oldest continuous wine maker in the United States. One of the highlights

GETTING BETTER WITH AGE

In 1976, there were 19 wineries in New York; by 1985 that number had grown to 63. Presently there are more than 100. How did New York's wine-making industry grow?

In 1667, French Huguenot settlers planted New York's first grapes in Ulster County. One hundred sixty years later, the first commercial vineyard in the Hudson Valley was planted on what is today Croton-on-Hudson. In 1873, Great Western Champagne took home from Vienna the first gold medal ever to be won by an American wine in a foreign competition.

Although New York State was subject to the laws of Prohibition from the years 1919 to 1933, wineries kept producing, as the market called for sacramental wines and grape juice (surprise, surprise)—the raw material for do-it-yourself wine makers who couldn't wait for the amendment to be repealed.

In 1973, Long Island joined the wine-making scene with the planting of its first commercial vineyard.

© Artville

of its visitors center is a film you can watch from inside a 35,000-gallon wine tank. | 8260 Pleasant Valley Rd. | 607/569–6111 | Free | Jan.–Mar., Tues.–Sat. 10–4; Apr.–Dec., Mon.–Sat. 10–5 (May–Oct., daily 10–5).

Wine and Grape Museum of Greyton H. Taylor. The first wine museum in the nation places an emphasis on 18th-century wine-making equipment. | 8843 Greyton H. Taylor Memorial Dr. (Bully Hill Vineyards), off Rte. 54A | 607/868–4814 | www.bully.com | Free | May–Oct., Mon.–Sat. 9–5, Sun. noon–5.

Dining

Bully Hill Restaurant. Contemporary. This breezy café has a spectacular view of Keuka Lake far below and a wonderful array of sandwiches, salads, and, of course, wines. After all, it's part of the Bully Hill Vineyards. | 8843 Greyton H. Taylor Memorial Dr. | 607/868–3490 | No dinner Sun.–Thurs. No lunch Fri., Sat. | $15–$25 | AE, D, MC, V.

Lakeside Restaurant. American. This 1880s cottage inn on the west side of Keuka Lake was converted into a delightful Victorian-era restaurant. Outside there is a fire pit and 150 seats overlooking the bluff of the lake. Known for prime rib, shrimp, pork *à la russe*, tenderloin with shrimp in a vodka sauce, and *solere scallopes*, scallops wrapped in bacon and served under feta cheese in a sherry sauce. | 800 W. Lake Rd. | 607/868–3636 | $13–20 | AE, D, MC, V.

Snug Harbor. Continental. Perched on the western shore of Keuka Lake is this Victorian-style building with views of the water. Blackened catfish, stuffed trout, chicken marsala, lobster primavera, and prime beef are popular dishes. Overnight stays are available. Kids' menu. Early bird dinner. | 144 W. Lake Rd. | 607/868–7684 | $15–$25 | AE, D, MC, V.

Lodging

Blushing Rosé. This pink Greek Revival and Italianate inn dates to 1843 and even has a cupola. Each of its four rooms is decorated differently with antiques and family heirlooms. A "sister" B&B, the "Amity Rosé," is at 8264 Main Street. Kids over 12 only. Complimentary breakfast. No smoking. | 11 William St. | 607/569–3402 or 800/982–8818 | www.blushingroseinn.com; www.amityroseinn.com | 4 rooms | $85–$105 | No credit cards.

Colonial Shores Cottages. In the heart of the Hamptons, on 2½ tree-shaded acres, you'll find these motel rooms and cottages. There are plenty of activities to keep the kids busy. It's within walking distance of restaurants and shops. Pool. Basketball, volleyball, beach, water sports. | 83 W. Tiana Rd. | 631/728–0011 | fax 631/728–0897 | www.webscope.com/hotels/colonial | 5 rooms, 7 cottages | $225 rooms, $1,400 cottages (7–day minimum stay).

Hammondsport Motel. Some of the rooms at this motel on the southwest edge of Keuka Lake have views of the water. The motel is close to the center of the village and you can swim in public park next door. Cable TV. Docks. | William and Water Sts. | 607/569–2600 | 17 rooms | $57–$63 | MC, V.

HAMPTON BAYS

MAP 3, E2

(Nearby towns also listed: Quogue/East Quogue, Riverhead, Westhampton Beach)

Originally settled in the 1700s, today this seashore community on two tranquil bays has a population of under 8,000. Perfect beaches, wonderful waterways, and fishing facilities attract beach enthusiasts, boaters, and fishermen. Restaurant menus boast fish and seafood caught that day.

As the largest hamlet in the township of Southampton, Hampton Bays has plenty of accommodations, shops, and restaurants.

Information: Greater Westhampton Chamber of Commerce | 173 Montauk Hwy., Box 1228, Westhampton, 11978 | 631/288–3337.

Attractions

Big Duck. You can't miss this unusual landmark on Route 24. Built in the 1930s before the duck industry on the east end of Long Island faded, this 20-ft-tall white duck is made of concrete and plaster. Originally, it was a farm stand; now you can go there to see the spectacular duck or to buy duck paraphernalia. | Rte. 24 | 631/852–8292 | Free | Daily.

Ponquogue Beach–Ocean. Hampton Bays is known for its pristine beaches like this one—600 ft of beach on the Atlantic Ocean. The pavilion houses a food stand, rest rooms, and showers and there are picnic tables and volleyball courts as well. Lifeguards are on duty. | Dune Rd., over Ponquogue Bridge | 631/283–6011 | www.hamptonbaysonline.com | $10 per car | Daily 10–5.

Ponquogue Fishing Pier. This sprawling pier stretches out into beautiful Shinnecock Bay, offering water views and great fishing. The sunsets are fabulous. | Dune Rd., under Ponquogue Bridge | 631/283–6011 | www.hamptonbaysonline.com | Free | Daily.

ON THE CALENDAR

JUNE: *Garden Tour.* The Hampton Bays Beautification Association sponsors self-guided tours of 10–12 gardens. Pick up a map and start at the U.A. Theater parking lot, at the corner of Montauk Highway and Springville Road. | 631/728–3248 | $15.

Dining

Oakland's Restaurant and Marina. Seafood. Every table at this restaurant on the water has a view of the ocean, the bay, or Shinnecock Inlet. Lobster dinners and specials are popular here and you can have your lobster broiled, stuffed, or baked. Try the rare tuna steak. Open-air dining on deck. Raw bar. The live music on weekends ranges from reggae to pop. Dock space. | Dune Rd.; turn left when you come off the Ponquogue Bridge | 631/728–6900 | Reservations not accepted | $35–$45 | AE, D, DC, MC, V.

Villa Paul. Italian. This cozy restaurant downtown has high-back chairs and a fireplace. The emphasis is on northern Italian dishes. Try the veal saltimbocca (veal with prosciutto and mozzarella and wine sauce over spinach) or roast duck with apple-raisin stuffing and black-cherry sauce. Kids' menu. | 162 Montauk Hwy. | 631/728–3261 | No lunch | $15–$25 | AE, MC, DC, V.

Lodging

Hampton Maid. These dark-shingled buildings are nestled in tall pines and overlook the Shinnecock Bay. Rooms have antique-style furniture, wet bars, and decks with views of the garden. The dining room here is a popular breakfast spot. Restaurant, picnic area. Cable TV. Pool. Playground. Business services. | 254 Montauk Hwy. | 631/728–4166 | fax 631/728–4250 | 30 rooms | $165–$480 (2-night minimum weekends) | Closed Nov.–late Apr. | AE, MC, V.

HARTSDALE

(Nearby towns also listed: Elmsford, Hawthorn, Mamaroneck, New Rochelle, Rye, Scarsdale, Tarrytown, White Plains, Yonkers)

This hamlet only a half-hour train ride from New York City combines the old and the new. Beautiful Victorian homes and working farms mingle with two business districts and several shopping centers. There are tennis courts, pools, and a golf course in this town of 10,000 residents, as well as one of the most unusual, if somewhat macabre, attractions around: the Hartsdale Canine Cemetery, one of the first pet cemeteries in the country.

Information: **County Chamber of Commerce** | 235 Mamaroneck Ave. Lower Level, White Plains, 10605 | 914/948–2110.

Attractions

Hartsdale Canine Cemetery. Since 1896 pet owners have laid their beloved animals—well over 100,000 of them—to rest in this apple orchard, which is now the oldest pet cemetery in the country. You'll find not only dogs and cats, but turtles, monkeys, ferrets, and even a lion king. | 75 N. Central Ave. | 914/949–2583 | Free | Mon.–Sat. 8–4:30, Sun. 9–4.

ON THE CALENDAR

JULY: *Irish Heritage Celebration.* One of many in a series of ethnic celebrations, this takes place the second Sunday of the month in Ridge Road Park. Irish dance, live music, food, and arts and crafts. | 914/242–PARK.

Dining

Auberge Argenteuil. French. This lovely Victorian house in a wooded hideaway was once a speakeasy. Now, its romantic setting is popular for weddings and special events. Try the scallop salad, sautéed breast of duck with pine nuts, and finish with one of the special desserts. Sunday brunch. The menu is prix fixe. | 42 Healy Ave., off Central Ave. Rte. 100 | 914/948–0597 | Reservations essential Fri., Sat. | Closed Mon. No lunch Sat. | $39 | AE, D, MC, V.

Villaggio Italiano Pizzeria. Italian. This casual pizzeria, ¼ mi from I–287, has been open since 1977, serving pasta dishes like penne à la vodka, and both thick- and thin-crusted pizza. French, Italian, and domestic wines are available in addition to the full bar. | 389 N. Central Ave. | 914/949–3427 | $10–$17 | AE, D, DC, MC, V.

HAWTHORNE

MAP 3, C2

(Nearby towns also listed: Elmsford, Hartsdale, Mamaroneck, New Rochelle, Rye, Scarsdale, Tarrytown, White Plains, Yonkers)

About 5,000 people live in this Westchester town near White Plains. This beautiful and hilly area is known for its popular restaurants.

Information: **County Chamber of Commerce** | 235 Mamaroneck Ave., LL, White Plains, 10605 | 914/948–2110.

Dining

Gasho of Japan. Japanese. This traditional building surrounded by intricate gardens was transported here from Japan. The filet mignon, chicken, salmon, and lobster are cooked in front of you. Kids' menu. | 2 Saw Mill River Rd. | 914/592–5900 | Reservations essential | $13–$25 | AE, D, DC, MC, V.

Taconic Brauhaus. German. Since the 1970s, this busy restaurant has served up authentic German cuisine (and some American fare) in a lively setting. Known for bratwurst, sauerbraten, and German potato salad. Live music on weekends. | 15 Commerce St. | 914/769–9842 | Closed Mon. No lunch Sun. | $15–$18 | AE, D, DC, MC, V.

Tramanto Restaurant. Italian. Flames within the brick oven pizza greet you at this restaurant which serves classic Italian dishes like pastas, veal, and chicken dishes, not to mention, of course, the brick-oven pizza. | 27 Saw Mill River Rd. | 914/347–8220 | $12–$16 | AE, D, DC, MC, V.

Lodging

Comfort Inn and Suites. Two and a half miles from Interstate 287, this new inn (opened fall 2000) was built to meet the needs of working travelers. Rooms have either two double beds or a king, and all come with kitchenettes. Although it is in a suburban area, it is within walking distance of restaurants and shops. Complimentary breakfast. In-room data ports. Pool. Exercise equipment. Laundry facilities. | 20 Saw Mill River Rd. | 914/592–8600 | fax 914/769–3330 | 55 rooms, 30 suites | Call for room rates | AE, D, DC, MC, V.

HERKIMER

(Nearby towns also listed: Canajoharie, Ilion, Richfield Springs, Utica)

This village on the northern banks of the Mohawk River takes its name from Revolutionary War General Nicholas Herkimer, although the actual historic Herkimer home and historic site are several miles east, near the small city of Little Falls.

Information: Herkimer County Chamber of Commerce | Box 129, 28 W. Main St., Mohawk, 13407 | 315/866–7820 | www.herkimer.org.

Attractions

Herkimer County Historical Society. This Queen Anne–style house has historical displays. There are also dollhouse exhibits and an old jail. | 400 N. Main St. | 315/866–6413 | Free; jail/dollhouses $1 | Weekdays 10–4.

Herkimer Diamond Mines. You'll get a hammer when you visit this mine to try your luck at prospecting. Hammer open the right rocks and you'll find quartz crystals. There is also a gem and mineral shop. | Rte. 28 N, across from the camp ground | 315/891–7355 or 800/562–0897 | $7.50 | Apr.–Nov., daily 9–5.

Herkimer Home State Historic Site. This residence of Revolutionary War General Nicholas Herkimer has been restored. | 200 State Rte. 169, Little Falls | 315/823–0398 | $3 | May–Oct., Wed.–Sat. 10–5, Sun. 1–5.

ON THE CALENDAR
AUG: *Herkimer County Fair.* This typical country fair has animals, tractor pulls, a midway, and fireworks to keep you and the kids entertained for hours. Third week of the month at the fairgrounds. | 315/895–7464.

Dining
Canal Side Inn. French. One hundred yards from the Barge Canal in Little Falls is this warm, provincial restaurant where you can get specialties like steak au poivre, roasted duck with a seasonal fruit sauce, and rack of lamb with herbes de Provence. Overnight accommodations are available in one suite. | 395 S. Ann St., Little Falls | 315/823–1170 | Closed Sun., Mon. No lunch | $20–$25 | D, DC, MC, V.

Lodging
Best Western–Little Falls. This chain motel is near Interstate 90 exit for Little Falls. Restaurant, bar. Cable TV. Video games. Business services. Pets allowed (fee). | 20 Albany St., Little Falls | 315/823–4954 | fax 315/823–4507 | lfbest@ntcnet.com | 56 rooms | $70–$80 | AE, D, DC, MC, V.

Putnam Manor House Bed and Breakfast. An ivy-covered Italianate home from 1902 offers private balconies, a classic Italian-style garden with statuary pieces, as well as antique furnishings. Beds are either king or queen. Within walking distance of restaurants and shops, and only 1 mi from Interstate 90. Complimentary breakfast. In-room data ports, some in-room hot tubs. | 112 W. German St. | 315/866–6738 | fax 315/866–3102 | www.putnammanor.com | 5 rooms | $75–$135 | AE, MC, V.

HILLSDALE

MAP 3, L8

(Nearby towns also listed: Canaan, Catskill, Hudson)

Hillsdale, a beautiful town that borders the Catskill Mountains, dates back to the 1700s. It was here that the legendary Rip Van Winkle is said to have taken his famous 20-year nap. Today this village of 2,000 is anything but sleepy and there is superb skiing and a park nearby.

Information: **Columbia County Tourism Department** | 401 State St., Hudson, 12534 | 800/724–1846.

Attractions

Catamount Ski Area. This ski area has a 1,000-ft vertical drop and 25 trails on 400 acres. | Rte. 23 | 413/528–1262 or 800/342–1840 | fax 518/325–3155 | www.catamountski.com | Dec.–Mar., daily.

Taconic State Park. A brook cascading down in a series of waterfalls is the highlight at this lovely 5,000-acre park. You can fish, hike, swim, boat, and cross-country ski. | Rte. 344, Copake Falls | 518/329–3993 or 800/456–2267 | fax 518/329–0725 | $6 per vehicle | Daily.

ON THE CALENDAR

JAN.: *Chile Contest.* People congregate from the tri-state area at the Catamount Ski Area, where any amateur can enter this chile contest. | 518/824–8213.

Dining

Aubergine. French. Seasonal country cooking is prepared and served in a cozy 1783 Dutch Colonial house. Try the crab boudin with leeks, or the smoked pork chops. | At the intersection of Rtes. 22 and 23 | 518/325–3412 | Closed Mon., Tues. No lunch | $22–$30 | AE, D. MC, V.

Four Brothers Restaurant. Greek. Part of a local family-owned chain, this restaurant has photos of Greece on the wall and serves tasty gyros, pizza, steak, and desserts like baklava. Full bar. | Rte. 23 | 518/325–7300 | $10–$13 | MC, V.

Simmons' Way Village Inn and Restaurant. Continental. Built in the 1850s and filled with antiques, fireplaces, and fresh flowers, this hilltop Victorian home exudes charm and elegance. Try the mussel stew, grilled fruit tenderloin, and seasonal specialties. Open-air dining on patio. Kids' menu. Sunday brunch. Millerton is 17 mi south of Hillsdale. | 33 Main St. (Rte. 44), Millerton | 518/789–6235 | Closed Mon., Tues. No lunch Wed.–Sat. | $17–$28 | AE, D, DC, MC, V.

Swiss Hutte. Continental. This 1800s farmhouse surrounded by a pond and flower and herb gardens is a lovely place to enjoy specialties such as soft-shell crabs, Black Angus beef, and free-range chicken. There is also a patio dining area. Kids' menu. | Rte. 23 | 518/325–3333 | $20–$28 | MC, V.

Lodging

Celerohn Hillsdale Inn. A half mile south of Hillsdale, this inn has 5 acres of lawn and gardens in the Berkshire foothills. If you're with your family you'd do best in an efficiency, while for a romantic getaway you're better off in a regular room. Complimentary breakfast (weekends and holidays only). Pool. Hot tub. | Rte. 22 N | 518/325–3883 | fax 518/325–3883 | sleep@taconic.net | www.celerohn.com | 10 rooms | $65–$175 | AE, D, MC, V.

Inn at Green River. On 1 acre of lush lawn and gardens amid the foothills of the Berkshires sits this 1830 Federal-style home. Some of the rooms have 16-ft cathedral ceilings; from the rooms you'll see the apple orchard or an old cemetery. Some of the beds are poster, and sizes range from twin to king. Breakfast is extravagant and gourmet. Complimentary breakfast. | 9 Nobletown Rd. | 518/325–7248 | www.iagr.com | 4 rooms | $85–$145 | No credit cards.

Linden Valley. All the rooms at this bed-and-breakfast have separate entrances and mountain views. The pond is great for swimming. Complimentary breakfast. Refrigerators, cable TV. Tennis. Beach. Some pets allowed. | Rte. 23 | 518/325–7100 | fax 518/325–4107 | 7 rooms (6 with shower only) | $115–$145 | AE, MC, V.

Simmons' Way Village Inn. Period antiques fill the rooms at this 1854 inn perched on a hill, 16 mi south of Hillsdale. The common room has a television, VCR, and data ports. Restaurant, complimentary Continental breakfast, complimentary afternoon snacks, room service. No room phones. Library. | 53 Main St., Millerton | 518/789–6235 | fax 518/789–6236 | swvi@taconic.net | www.simmonsway.com | 9 rooms | $145–$175 | AE, DC, MC, V.

Swiss Hutte. This 1800s farmhouse is on 12 acres near the Catamount Ski area. Rooms have outdoor porches or balconies so you can enjoy the view. Restaurant (*see* Swiss Hutte), bar. Some refrigerators. Pool. Tennis. Business services. Some pets allowed. | Rte. 23 | 518/325–3333 | 8057@msn.com | www.swisshutte.com | 15 rooms | $110–$170 | MC, V.

HORNELL

MAP 3, E7

(Nearby towns also listed: Bath, Hammondsport)

Hornell, settled in 1799, provides a western entry into the Finger Lakes region and is a favorite destination for hunters. Because of its maple-shaded streets, Hornell is called the Maple City. Alfred University and the State University College at Alfred are nearby.

Information: Address: Hornell Area Chamber of Commerce | 40 Main St., 14843 | 607/324–0310 | www.hornellny.com.

Attractions

Alfred University. This 232-acre campus, 8 mi southwest of Hornell, is home to about 2,500 students. | Saxon Dr., Alfred | 800/541–9229 | www.alfred.edu | Free | Daily.

The **International Museum of Ceramic Art** displays ancient pottery from around the world as well as domestic ceramics. | Ceramics Corridor Innovation Center, Rte. 244 | 607/871–2421 | www.alfred.edu/mus | Free | Tues.–Sun. 10–5.

Stony Brook State Park. A gorge cuts through this 577-acre park and two stream-fed pools proved wonderful spots for swimming. There are bathhouses, hiking trails, playgrounds, picnic areas, campsites, and a tennis court. | 10820 Rte. 365 | 716/335–8111 | www.nys-parks.state.ny.us/parks/ | Free; parking $6 | Daily.

Swain Ski Center. This center southeast of Hornell has a 650-ft vertical drop and 18 trails, the longest of which is 1 mi. Downhill skiing, snow tubing, and snowboarding are available. | Off Rte. 70, Swain | 607/545–6511 | www.swain.com | Lift rates $26–$36 | Nov.–Mar.

Dining

Italian Villa Restaurant. Italian. Since 1958 this restaurant has been in downtown Hornell serving typical Italian fare like homemade lasagna and pasta. Red chairs and red, white, and green awnings add to the spirit. Full bar. Kids' menu. | 196 Seneca Rd. | 607/324–6063 | Closed Sun. | $7–$10 | AE, MC, V.

Rupert's at the Lodge. American. Specialties like "steak Montreal" and chicken imperial as well as open-air dining overlooking well-tended grounds make this an ideal choice for an elegant evening out. Try a homemade pie or pastry, or sample a local wine. Two miles from downtown, and ¼ mi from Interstate 86. Kids' menu. | 7464 Seneca Rd. (on the grounds of Econo Lodge) | 607/324–3000 | Closed Mon. | $12–$20 | AE, D, DC, MC, V.

Lodging

Comfort Inn. This two-story chain hotel has standard rooms less than 1 mi outside of Hornell. Complimentary Continental breakfast. Cable TV. Pool. Exercise equipment. Laundry facilities. Business services, free parking. | 1 Canisteo Sq. | 607/324–4300 | fax 607/324–4311 | 62 rooms | $75–$100 | AE, D, DC, MC, V.

Econo Lodge. A chain motel close to Alfred University and local hunting areas. Restaurant, bar, picnic area, complimentary breakfast. In-room data ports, cable TV. Business services. Pets allowed. | 7462 Seneca Rd. | 607/324–0800 | fax 607/324–0905 | 76 rooms | $60 | AE, D, MC, V.

Saxon Inn. Historic ceramics are on view at the lobby of this two-story inn near Alfred University. Rooms are done up in flower and country decor. Complimentary Continental breakfast. Some refrigerators, cable TV. Business services. | One Park St., Alfred | 607/871–2600 | fax 607/871–2650 | 26 rooms, 6 suites | $95–$110 | AE, D, MC, V.

Sunshine Motel. This hotel is on 2 acres of lawn and trees and within walking distance of shops and restaurants. Rooms have either one or two doubles, and are relatively simple. Relax on the gazebo in the center of the property. | 7433 Seneca Rd. N | 607/324–4565 | fax 607/324–0145 | 14 rooms | $26 | AE, D, DC, MC, V.

HUDSON

MAP 3, K7

(Nearby towns also listed: Cairo, Canaan, Catskill, Saugerties)

Settled in 1783 by whalers from Nantucket and New Bedford, Hudson began its life as a whaling town. By 1790, 25 schooners worked out of here in whaling and the West Indian trade. In the 19th century, Hudson switched to manufacturing, producing machinery, matches, clothing, and cement. The beautiful Federal-style homes bear witness to the town's wealth in that era. But in the 19th century and the first half of the 20th century, Hudson was also famous for another industry: vice. Its red-light district was notorious; today weekenders have restored the old brothel houses. At the western end of main street there are river views from the Parade Hill promenade.

Information: **Columbia County Chamber of Commerce** | 507 Warren St., 12534 | 518–828–4417 | mail@columbiachamber-ny.com | www.columbiachamber-ny.com.

Attractions

American Museum of Fire Fighting. Exhibits and artifacts tell the history of firefighting at this museum 1 mi outside of Hudson. Displays include an apparatus from 1725 and equipment from the Civil War. | 125 Harry Howard Ave. | 518/828–7695 | Free | Daily 9–4:30.

Clermont State Historic Site. Robert R. Livingston, who helped draft the Declaration of Independence, was just one of the illustrious Livingstons who made their home here. Other members of the family served in the Continental Congress and were delegates to the Constitutional Convention. The house reflects the changes made by several generations: it was burned by the British during the Revolutionary War and rebuilt on the original foundations. Further changes came in the 19th century. The rooms are furnished with family heirlooms; there are beautiful examples of decorative objects and of cabinet making. Views of the Catskill Mountains across the river are stunning. Special events are held on July 4th and at Christmas. | Rte. 6 W, off Rte. 9G, Germantown | 518/537–4240 | $3 | Tues.–Sun. 8:30–dusk; tours start at 11.

James Vanderpoel House. This Federal house in downtown Kinderhook, north of Hudson, presents historic exhibits on life in Columbia County. The rooms have plasterwork ceilings and graceful mantelpieces. Pieces by New York cabinetmakers are displayed throughout the house. | 5 Albany Ave., Kinderhook | 518/758–9265 | $3 | Memorial Day–Labor Day, Thurs.–Sat. 11–5, Sun. 1–5.

The **Luykas Van Alen House** is a 1737 restored Dutch farmhouse, and is especially noted for its collection of Hudson Valley paintings. It contains the Ichabod Crane Schoolhouse, a restored one-room schoolhouse. Both this house and the Vanderpoel house are operated by the Historical Society. | Call for hrs Memorial Day–Labor Day, Thurs.–Sat. 11–5, Sun. 1–5.

Martin Van Buren National Historic Site. The 8th president of the United States retired to this estate, Lindenwald. The graceful building was renovated and restored to the way it appeared when Van Buren lived here. Concerts are given here, and nature trails can be found on the peaceful grounds. North of Hudson, off Route 9H. | 1013 Old Post Rd., Kinderhook | 518/758–9689 | Lindenwald house $2; trails free | Spring–Fall, daily 9–4; tours are given every half hour.

Olana State Historic Site. Frederic Church, the foremost artist of the Hudson River School, designed this house himself and his personal vision of Persia produced a house like no other. The interior is an extravaganza of tile and stone, carved screens, Persian rugs, objets d'art, and even a pair of gilded crane lamps. Many of Church's paintings are displayed and his studio is just as it was when he worked there. Outside, you can walk the extensive grounds on carriage roads with views Church himself planned. Olana is 4 mi south of Hudson. | Rte. 9G | 518/828–0135 | $3 | Tours Wed.–Sun. 10, 11, 1, 2, 3; reservations are suggested.

Robert Jenkins House and Museum. This Federal-style home, built in 1811, now houses a museum containing local historic memorabilia. | 113 Warren St. | 518/828–9764 | July–Aug., Sun.–Mon. 1–3.

Shaker Museum and Library. At this museum 15 mi east of Hudson, you can learn about the daily life of the Shakers from one of the largest collections on Shaker culture. Furnishings, tools, machinery, and textiles are on display, with pieces from almost every Shaker community. | 88 Shaker Museum Rd., off County Rd. 13, Old Chatham | 518/794–9100 | www.shakermuseumoldcat.org | $8 | Apr.–Oct., daily 10–5.

ON THE CALENDAR

DEC.: *Winter Walk on Warren St.* Carolers dressed in Victorian costumes, roasted chestnuts, horse carriages, mimes, and Santa Claus help to create holiday spirit. The hot cocoa and punch will help you stay warm. First weekend of the month all along Warren Street. | 518/822–1438.

Dining

Cascades. American. This restaurant, deli, and espresso bar serves a creative breakfast and lunch. Many of the menu items are inspired by western mountain ranges, like the Rocky Mountain sandwich (roast beef and cream cheese on a bagel). Local artists display and sell their work here. | 407 Warren St. | 518/822–9146 | Breakfast also available; no dinner | $5–$8 | AE, D, MC, V.

Rebecca's. Continental. Candles sit on the ivory tablecloths at this quaint restaurant housed in a Victorian building in downtown Hudson. Try the grilled spring lamb chops, the chicken Morocco, or the baked salmon en croûte. Kids' menu. No smoking. | 16-18 Park Pl. | 518/822–9900 | Closed Sun.–Tues. No lunch | $25–$30 | AE, D, DC, MC, V.

Lodging

St. Charles. This three-story Victorian hotel in downtown Hudson has rooms done up in green, burgundy, and mauve. Restaurant (*see* Rebecca's), bar (with entertainment), complimentary Continental breakfast. Cable TV. Business services. Pets allowed. | 16 Park Pl. |

518/822–9900 | fax 518/822–0835 | 34 rooms, 6 suites | $79–109 rooms, $109 suites | AE, D, DC, MC, V.

Warren Inn. Built as a movie theater in the 1920s, it was abandoned until 1958 when it became a motel. Today it overlooks Victorian homes and is filled with antiques and photographs of the Hudson. It's 6 mi from the New York State Thruway, Catskill exit. | 731 Warren St. | 518/828–9477 | fax 518/828–3575 | 14 rooms | $50 | AE, D, DC, MC, V.

HUNTER

MAP 3, K7

(Nearby towns also listed: Cairo, Catskill, Roxbury, Shandaken, Windham)

Hunter is all about the slopes. Nestled in the shadow of Hunter Mountain, the second-highest mountain in the Catskills, it's the oldest of the Catskill ski areas. On winter weekends, thousands of skiers flock to the Hunter Ski Bowl. In other seasons, fairs and special events are hosted here.

Information: **Green County Chamber of Commerce** | 159 Jefferson Heights Blvd., Catskill, 12414 | 518/943–4222.

Attractions

Hunter Mountain Ski Resort. This sprawling resort has a 1,600-ft vertical drop and 53 trails on 250 acres. You can ski, snowboard, and snowtube. In fall and summer, music and theme festivals take place here. | Rte. 23A | 518/263–4223 or 800/for–snow | www.huntermtn.com. | Call for fees | Nov.–Apr.

ON THE CALENDAR

AUG.: *German Alps Festival.* The Hunter Mountain Ski Resort stands in for the Alps at this weekend celebration of music, food, and dancing. | 518/263–4223.
AUG.: *International Celtic Festival.* The highlight of this Irish festival is a parade of 1,000 bagpipers and drummers. Food, step dancing, crafts, and music are also part of the fun at the Hunter Mountain Ski Resort. | 518/263–4223.

Dining

Chateau Belleview. French. This restaurant 5 min east of Hunter has two cozy dining rooms with fireplaces and impressive mountain views. Try the roasted duck, steak au poivre, or chicken breast marsala. You can also eat outside under umbrellaed tables. Kids' portions. | Rte. 23A, Tannersville | 518/589–5525 | Closed Tues. No lunch | $15–$25 | AE, D, MC, V.

Mountainbrook Dining and Spirits. Contemporary. Beneath high wood ceilings and beside a roaring fire, the staff serve the eatery's upscale version of comfort food: grilled filet of tuna with a ginger soy marinade, Black Angus steak with black truffle butter, and an endive and radicchio salad with local goat cheese. Windows overlook Hunter Mountain and the Schoharie Creek. | 23A Main St. | 518/263–5351 | No lunch | $12–$23 | MC, V.

The Prospect. Contemporary. Local cuisine is served in a dining room with panoramic views of Hunter Mountain at this popular restaurant. There's even a fireplace lounge where you can warm up after a day of skiing. Try the locally smoked Catskill rainbow trout or the scaloppine of venison with shiitake mushrooms. There are over 200 wines on the wine list. Jazz weekends. Kids' menu. | Rte. 23A | 518/263–4211 | www.scribnerhollow.com | Breakfast also available | $15–$35 | AE, D, MC, V.

Vesuvio. Italian. Eight miles east of Hunter, antiques fill this eatery with terra-cotta walls and a working fireplace. Artichoke hearts stuffed with crabmeat in a Frangelico sauce and seafood Vesuvio—lobster, clams, mussels, calamari, scallops, and shrimps over pasta—are two representative dishes on the large menu. Early bird dinner menu. Kids' menu. | Goshen Rd., Hensonville | 518/734–3663 | No lunch | $18–$25 | AE, MC, V.

Lodging

Eggery Inn. The wraparound front porch at this farmhouse inn on 13 acres facing the mountains has rocking chairs you can relax in. The rooms, done up in country motifs, have quilts on the beds. The inn is in Tannersville, 3 mi east of Hunter. Complimentary breakfast. No air-conditioning in some rooms, cable TV. | County Rd. 16, Tannersville | 518/589–5363 | fax 518/589–5774 | www.eggeryinn.com | 15 rooms | $95–$125 | AE, MC, V.

Fairlawn Inn. Just ½ mi from Hunter Ski Area, you'll have mountain views from your room. A complete renovation has brought the best of both worlds to this inn: modern-day amenities within a 1900 Victorian-style house furnished with reproduction furniture and Victorian wallpaper. Beds are carved, porcelain, or brass. Complimentary breakfast. In-room data ports. | 6302 Main St. | 518/263–5025 | 9 rooms | $110 | MC, V.

Hunter Inn. This modern hotel is just ¾ mi from the Hunter Ski Resort. Most rooms have balconies and views of the mountains. Complimentary Continental breakfast. Cable TV. Hot tub. Exercise equipment. Video games. Business services. Pets allowed (fee). | Main St. (Rte. 23A) | 518/263–3777 | fax 518/263–3981 | www.hunterinn.com | 41 rooms | $175–$235 | AE, D, MC, V.

Mountain Creek Inn. This inn, once a farmhouse on 8 wooded acres, is 3 mi from Hunter and has an excellent view of Hunter Mountain Ski Area. The Schoharie Creek runs through the property, adding to the country feeling. Choose from a cabin efficiency or a motel room. Beds are either king or queen, and in winter an organic vegetarian breakfast and dinner are served. Complimentary breakfast. In-room data ports. | Rte. 23A | 518/263–4811 | 6 rooms, 2 cabins | $70 | MAP (in winter) | AE, D, MC, V.

Scribner Hollow Lodge. Many of the individually designed rooms at this classic mountain lodge have working fireplaces and exposed beams. The indoor pool and spa area resemble an underground cavern with seven waterfalls, a free-form pool, and water slides. Transportation to Hunter Mountain is available. Restaurant, bar (with entertainment), complimentary dinner, complimentary breakfast, room service. Refrigerators, cable TV. 2 pools, wading pool. Sauna, spa. Tennis. Exercise equipment. Business services, free parking. | Main St. (Rte. 23A) | 518/263–4211 or 800/395–4683 | fax 518/263–5266 | www.scribnerhollow.com | 38 rooms | $270–$400 | AE, D, MC, V.

HUNTINGTON

MAP 3, C2

(Nearby towns also listed: Northport, Oyster Bay, Syosset)

Greater Huntington is made up of 17 communities, including the large urban development in Melville, and the attractive Huntington village. Its original tracts of land were purchased from Native Americans, and its most famous resident, the poet Walt Whitman, was born here in 1819. Later, he founded a local newspaper, the *Long Islander*, which is still published today. The late 1800s and early 1900s saw the development of the north shore's Gold Coast, attracting such estate owners as William K. Vanderbilt, Marshall Field III, and Walter B. Jennings.

Today, the village of Huntington remains at the heart of a township that boasts five navigable harbors, shops, antiques stores, and restaurants.

Information: Huntington Chamber of Commerce | 151 W. Carver St., 11743 | 631/423–6100 | fax 631/351–8276 | staff@huntingtonchamber.com | www.huntingtonchamber.com.

Attractions

Beaches: Town of Huntington. There are five major beaches in Huntington including: Asharoken Beach on Asharoken Road, offering 535 ft on Long Island Sound; Crescent Beach on Northport Bay, off Shore Drive in Huntington; Fleets Cove Beach, off Fleets Cove Road, with 1,600 ft on Northport Bay; Gold Star Battalion Beach, off West Shore Road in Huntington, with 400 ft on Huntington Bay; Hobart Beach, Easton's Neck (off Asharoken Avenue), providing 1,725 ft on Huntington Bay. | 631/261–7574 in season, 631/351–3089 off–season | $10 residents, $15 nonresidents | Daily 9–7:30.

Cinema Arts Centre. A wide range of American and international films show at this independent theater. | 423 Park Ave. | 631/423–3456 or 631/423–7611 | $8 | Call for schedule.

Caumsett State Park. Set in magnificent Lloyd Neck, accessible by taking Rte. 25A west to West Neck Rd., this park covers 1,500 acres and includes a bridle path. You can also hike, go fishing, or cross-country ski. | W. Neck Rd. | 516/423–1770 | Free | Daily 8–6:30.

Eagle Carriage. Horse-drawn carriage tours of the village leave from 1 PM to midnight. | 23 Wall St., Huntington Station, off Rte. 25A (Main St.) | 631/423–4668 | $20–$40 | Apr.–Oct., weekends 7–midnight.

Heckscher Museum of Art. Five centuries of paintings and sculpture are housed in this wonderful example of Beaux Arts architecture just two blocks from downtown Huntington. Guides give gallery talks and there is also a museum shop. | 2 Prime Ave. | 631/351–3250 | $3 suggested donation | Tues.–Fri. 10–5, weekends 1–5.

Henry Lloyd House. This circa 1711 saltbox house was the home of original settlers of the area and the birthplace of Jupiter Hammon, a slave who became a renowned poet. Hikes and guided tours are available. | 41 Lloyd Harbor | 516/673–5476 | $2 | By appointment.

Huntington Historical Society Museums. The society maintains three historic sites in the village of Huntington: Kissam House, circa 1795; David Conklin Farmhouse, circa 1750; and the Huntington Sewing and Trade School, circa 1905. | 209 Main St. (Rte. 25A) | 631/427–7045 | $2 | Tues.–Fri. and Sun. 1–4.

Huntington Village. The active and bustling downtown village is peppered with historic buildings in and around a large array of excellent restaurants and shops. Shopping opportunities include a large independent bookstore, quaint gift shops, trendy boutiques, and antiques stores. | New York Ave. and Main St. (Rte. 25A) | 631/423–6100 | Free | Daily.

Walt Whitman Birthplace State Historic Site. This is the boyhood home of Walt Whitman, whom many believe to be America's greatest poet. The snug house, built by his father, is ingeniously furnished and designed. Whitman portraits, letters, and manuscripts are also on display. The home is on Rte. 110, across from Walt Whitman Mall. | 246 Old Walt Whitman Rd., Huntington Station | 631/427–5240 | $3 | Summer, Mon. and Wed.–Fri. 11–4, weekends 12–5; winter, Wed.–Fri. 1–4, weekends 11–4.

ON THE CALENDAR

MAY: *Renaissance Festival.* A jousting tournament attended by knights and fair damsels is the highlight of this elaborate event held every Memorial Day weekend. The festival, sponsored by the the Unitarian Universalist Fellowship of Huntington, also includes craft vendors and a food court. | 109 Brown's Rd. | 631/427–9547.

JUNE: *Art in the Park.* Almost 200 exhibitors show original ceramics, woodwork, jewelry, photography, and watercolors. There are also artist demonstrations, music, and workshops. Held in Heckscher Park, Prime Ave. and Main St. (Route 25A). | 631/368–0018.

JUNE–AUG.: *Huntington Summer Arts Festival.* Prominent artists perform during this summer festival in Heckscher Park. In the past, performers have included Phoebe Snow, Spalding Gray, and the Gilbert and Sullivan Light Opera Co. | 631/271–8423.

OCT.: *Long Island Fall Festival at Huntington.* This family-oriented event has a carnival and an international food court, as well as arts and crafts. At Heckscher Park. | 631/423–6100.

Dining

Abel Conklin's. Continental. Dark mahogany woodwork shows off the original charm of this 1830s building. Known for aged broiled steaks, sautéed liver, lobsters, and a variety of seafood. Open-air dining on patio. Kids' menu. No smoking. | 54 New St. | 631/385–1919 | Reservations essential Fri., Sat. | No lunch weekends | $27–$40 | AE, MC, V.

Frederick's. Continental. The upstairs room, where dinner is served at the bar, is the quaintest of the three dining rooms at this cozy restaurant in a little house. Try the rack of lamb roasted with rosemary, calf's liver with onions and bacon, and bronzed tuna with pecan and poblano pepper sauce. No smoking. | 1117 Walt Whitman Rd., Melville | 516/673–8550 | Closed Sun. No lunch Sat. | $12–$29 | AE, DC, MC, V.

Panama Hatties. Eclectic. Artful cuisine is served in a relaxed Art Deco setting at this upscale restaurant. Specialties include rare seared tuna; foie gras; New Zealand venison chop and loin with wild rice, cling peaches, and macadamia nuts; pistachio-crusted rack of lamb with roasted eggplant; and couscous cake and mint balsamic sauce. | 872 E. Jericho Tpk., Huntington Station | 516/351–1727 | No lunch | $59 prix fixe | AE, D, DC, MC, V.

Petite on Main. Continental. Ceiling fans revolve above 12 tables dressed in white linens at this cozy downtown restaurant with a blue tin ceiling and cane chairs. Known for filet mignon, the restaurant also serves marinated hanger steak, salmon, and panko (coarse bread crumb)–crusted chicken. Kids' menu. No smoking. | 328 Main St. (Rte. 25A) | 516/271–3311 | Reservations essential weekends | No lunch. Closed Mon. | $30–$35 | AE, DC, MC, V.

Lodging

Abbey Motor Inn. This two-story motel sits between South Huntington and Woodbury. Cable TV. No pets. | 317 W. Jericho Tpk. | 631/423–0800 | 30 rooms | $70 | AE, D, DC, MC, V.

Executive Inn at Woodbury. This four-story chain hotel is close to restaurants, shopping, and movie theaters. Complimentary Continental breakfast. In-room data ports, kitchenettes (in suites), some microwaves, cable TV. Pool. Business services. | 8030 Jericho Tpk., Woodbury | 631/921–8500 | fax 631/921–1057 | 102 rooms, 5 suites | $98–109 rooms, $109 suites | AE, D, DC, MC, V.

Hilton. This five-story upscale hotel 10 minutes from Huntington boasts an atrium and caters to business travelers. Restaurant, bar (with entertainment). In-room data ports, some minibars, cable TV. 2 pools. Hot tub. Tennis court. Exercise equipment. Business services. | 598 Broad Hollow Rd., Melville | 631/845–1000 | fax 631/845–1223 | 289 rooms, 16 suites | $239–$215 rooms, $299 suites | AE, D, DC, MC, V.

Huntington Country Inn. The poet Walt Whitman was born around the corner from this modest, modern hotel. Each room has a cordless phone, CD player, a selection of aromatherapy bath products. Complimentary Continental breakfast. Microwaves, refrigerators, cable TV. Pool. Exercise equipment. | 270 W. Jericho Tpk. | 631/421–3900 | fax 631/421–5287 | www.huntingtoncountryinn.com | 62 rooms | $119–$135 | AE, D, DC, MC, V.

Onesti Motel. This one-story motel sits next door to an Indian restaurant, 1 mi west of Route 110. Cable TV. No pets. | 665 W. Jericho Tpk. | 631/549–5511 | 16 rooms | $50–$60 | No credit cards.

HYDE PARK

MAP 3, K8

(Nearby towns also listed: Kingston, Millbrook, Poughkeepsie, Rhinebeck)

The Hudson River town of Hyde Park dates back to 1702, when an estate on this land was named for Edward Hyde, Lord Cornbury, then the provincial governor of New York. Hyde Park is most famous for being the boyhood home of Franklin Delano Roosevelt.

In addition, it boasts an impressive summer mansion built by one of the Vanderbilts, and the Culinary Institute of America, one of the most respected culinary schools in the world.

Information: **Hyde Park Chamber of Commerce** | 532 Albany Post Rd., 12538 | 845/229–8612.

Attractions

Eleanor Roosevelt National Historic Site at Val-Kill. The First Lady's private retreat is unpretentious and homelike; it holds the museum, and is filled with mementos and photographs. The original house on the site, Stone Cottage, is now a conference center. | Rte. 9G | 845/229–9115 | www.nps.gov/elro/ | $5 | May.–Nov., daily 9–5; Dec–Apr., weekends 9–5 (closed weekdays).

Franklin D. Roosevelt Library and Museum. Photographs, letters, speeches, and memorabilia document FDR's life. A multimedia exhibit examines World War II. The first of the presidential libraries, this building was designed by Roosevelt himself. | 4079 Albany Post Rd. (Rte. 9) | 845/229–8114 | www.fdrlibrary.marist.edu.fdr. | $10 | Nov.–Apr., daily 9–5; May–Oct., daily 9–6; closed Thanksgiving, Christmas, New Year's Day.

Franklin D. Roosevelt National Historic Site. The birthplace and home of the county's 32nd president, the house is just as it was when the Roosevelts lived here, with family furnishings and keepsakes. The grounds include a wonderful rose garden where Franklin and Eleanor are buried. | Rte. 9 | 845/229–9115 | www.nps.gov/hofr/ | $10 | Daily 9–5.

Norrie Point Environmental Site. The site features a freshwater aquarium and a wildlife museum. Environmental educational programs are available. | U.S. 9, Staatsburg | 845/889–4646 | Free | Daily, 8–dusk.

Mills Mansion State Historic Site. A few miles north of Hyde Park on Route 9 is this grand 79-room Beaux Arts mansion that Edith Wharton used as the inspiration for the Trenors' estate in *The House of Mirth*. The original house was built in Greek Revival style in 1832, but in 1895 it was remodeled and expanded by McKim, Mead, and White for Ruth and Ogden Mills. Inside the huge rooms, there are fine furnishings, tapestries, and objets d'art. The grounds sweep down to the Hudson River, making an ideal picnicking spot, and there is a museum store and summer theater and musical events. | Old Post Rd., Staatsburg, 12580 | 845/889–8851 | $3 | Apr.–Labor Day, Wed.–Sat. 10–4:30, Sun. 12–4:30 Labor Day–Oct., Wed.–Sun. noon–4:30.

Vanderbilt Mansion National Historic Site. The grand and imposing 1898 McKim, Mead, and White mansion, built for Frederick Vanderbilt, grandson of Cornelius Vanderbilt, makes a striking contrast with its Roosevelt neighbor. A fine example of life in the Gilded Age, the house is lavishly furnished and full of paintings. Outside there are Italian gardens and the grounds have excellent views of the river. | 4097 Albany Post Rd. (Rte. 9) | 845/229–9115 | www.nps.gov/vama/ | $8 | Daily 9–5.

Dining

American Bounty. Contemporary. Part of the Culinary Institute of America, this informal restaurant surrounded by 150 wooded acres draws people from New York City to sample its regional dishes. Specialties include asparagus-basil risotto, grilled quail "buffalo style," and pan-roasted chicken. | 1946 Campus Dr. | 845/471–6608 | www.ciachef.edu | Reservations essential | Jacket required | Tues.–Sat. 11:30–1 and 6:30–8:30; closed 3 weeks in July, 2 weeks at Christmas | $20–$35 | AE, D, MC, V.

Escoffier Restaurant. French. This elegant Culinary Institute restaurant showcases modern interpretations of classic French dishes such as lobster salad, smoked salmon, and sautéed beef tenderloin. Other specialties include duck liver terrine with mango chutney, seared sea scallops, and snails with basil cream sauce. | 1946 Campus Dr. | 845/471–6608 |

www.ciachef.edu | Reservations essential | Jacket required | Closed Sun., Mon., also 3 weeks in July, 2 weeks at Christmas | $20–$25 | AE, D, MC, V.

St. Andrew's Cafe. Contemporary. The most casual of the Culinary Institute of America restaurants serves nutritionally balanced spa cuisine. The grilled entrées and vegetarian selections are all prepared in ways that accentuate their natural flavors. The wood-fired pizzas are also popular. Open-air dining. | 1946 Campus Dr. | 845/471–6608 | Reservations essential | Closed weekends, 3 weeks in July, and 2 weeks in Dec. | $20–$25 | AE, D, MC, V.

Lodging
Golden Manor. This motel is near FDR's home and library, 1 mi south of downtown. Complimentary Continental breakfast. Some kitchenettes, some refrigerators, cable TV. Pool. | 55 Albany Post Rd. (Rte. 9) | 845/229–2157 | 44 rooms | $40–$60 | AE, D, MC, V.

ILION

MAP 3, I6

(Nearby towns also listed: Canajoharie, Herkimer, Richfield Springs, Utica)

Ilion lies along the southern banks of the Mohawk River just across the river and a few miles west of Herkimer. The village is home to the Remington Firearms Museum, and you can go boating on the river.

Information: **Herkimer County Chamber of Commerce** | Box 129, 28 W. Main St., Mohawk, 13407 | 315/866–7820 | www.herkimer.countychamber.com.

Attractions
Remington Firearms Museum. Both modern and antique guns made by Remington are on display here, as well as gun collectibles, accessories, and apparel. The museum also contains a gift shop. | 14 Hoefler Ave. | 315/895–3301 | Free | July–Aug., weekdays 9–5, Sat. 10–3:30; Sept.–June, weekdays 9–5.

ON THE CALENDAR
JULY: Frankfort Days. A weekend of canoe races and a fishing tournament come to Franklin, southwest of Ilion on Route 5 S. The festival also features crafts, a barbecue, a concert, and a parade. | 315/895–7651.

Dining
Sorrento Pizzeria. Italian. This family-owned and -run downtown spot is the place to get pizza, salad, or subs. You'll also want to leave room for indulgent desserts like cheesecake, fudge, and brownies. | 64 Central Ave. | 315/894–9991 | $4–$7 | AE, D, MC, V.

ITHACA

MAP 3, G7

(Nearby towns also listed: Cortland, Watkins Glen)

Gorges and waterfalls provide plenty of background noise for this city on the southern end of Lake Cayuga. Originally a Cayuga settlement, Ithaca today is a progressive city and home to Ithaca College and Cornell University. For a short time beginning in 1914, Ithaca served as a center for the motion-picture business, but the occasionally slate-color skies drove the industry to the sunnier West Coast.

Information: **Ithaca/Tompkins County Convention and Visitors Bureau** | 904 E. Shore Dr., 14850 | 800/28–ITHACA | www.visitithaca.com.

Attractions

Allan H. Treman Marine State Park. This park north of Ithaca provides access to the Barge Canal and Seneca Lake. There are boat ramps here and you can fish or have a picnic. | Rte. 89 | 607/272–1460 | www.nysparks.state.ny.us/parks/ | $5 per vehicle | May–late Oct., daily.

Bellwether Hard Cider. Learn about one of America's oldest alcohols. | Rte. 96, 1609 Trumansburg Rd. | 607/272–4337 | www.cidery.com | Free.

Buttermilk Falls State Park. Water cascades over 10 falls, dropping close to 500 ft at this park on the southern end of Ithaca. At the base of the falls there is a swimming hole, as well as playing fields and a campground. | Rte. 13 | 607/273–5761, 800/456–CAMP for camping reservations | www.nysparks.state.ny.us/parks/ | Free; mid-May–mid-Oct. parking $5 per vehicle.

Cornell University. With its historic buildings, views of Cayuga Lake, open spaces, and gorges, the campus at this private university founded in 1865 is considered one of the most beautiful in the country. Tours of the campus leave from Day Hall, Tower Road, and East Avenue. | 607/254–4636 | www.cornell.edu | Free | Daily.

The **Cornell Lab of Ornithology** includes 4.2 mi of trails through Sapsucker Woods Sanctuary. Bird artist Louis Agassiz Fuertes named the woods after two yellow-bellied sapsuckers he spotted in the area. In the visitors center, you'll find the Crows' Nest Birding Shop. | 159 Sapsucker Woods Rd. | 607/254–BIRD | Free | Mon.–Thurs. 8–5, Fri. 8–4, Sat. 10–4.

Just north of the university are the **Cornell Plantations,** which include an arboretum, specialty gardens, nature trails, and an herb garden. | 1 Plantations Rd., off Rte. 366 | 607/255–3020 | Free | Apr.–Dec., weekdays 9–4, Sat. 10–5, Sun. 11–5.

The I. M. Pei–designed **Herbert F. Johnson Museum of Art** houses collections of Asian and modern art. The fifth floor offers a wonderful view of Cayuga Lake and the surrounding area. | University Ave. | 607/255–6464 | www.museum.cornell.edu | Free | Tues.–Sun. 10–5.

Ithaca College. This school was first founded as the Ithaca Conservatory of Music in 1892. Until the 1960s, the campus was in a downtown area. Today, the college is on South Hill, overlooking Cayuga Lake, 1 mi south of the center of Ithaca. Tours are available. | Danby Rd., Rte. 96B | 607/274–3011 | www.ithaca.edu | Free | Daily.

Ithaca Commons. This historic center of Ithaca has 23 restaurants as well as specialty book and clothing stores, all set amid statues and landscaped gardens. There's a pavilion where live bands play during summer. | Corner of W. 8th St., Cayuga, and N. Aurora | 607/277–8679 | Free.

Ithaca Farmer's Market. There are 85 stalls at this open-air market where plants, artwork, food, and flowers all come from local residents. | Steamboat Landing on Cayuga Lake | 607/273–7109 | Free | Apr.–Christmas, Sat. 9–2, Sun. 10–2.

Robert H. Treman State Park. Spectacular, rugged Enfield Glen is the highlight of this 1,025-acre park 5 mi south of Ithaca. You can hike, fish, swim, picnic, and camp here. | Rte. 327 | 607/273–3440 | www.nysparks.state.ny.us/parks/ | Free; parking $4 per vehicle mid-May–mid-June, $5 mid-June–mid-Oct. | Daily.

Sciencenter. A walk-in camera and a two-story kinetic ball sculpture are among the 100-plus exhibits at this hands-on museum catering to youngsters. The Sagan Planetwalk honors scientist Carl Sagan. Outside there is a wooden playground. | 601 First St. | 607/272–0600 | $4.50 | Tues.–Sat. 10–5; Sun. noon–5.

Six Mile Creek Vineyard. This boutique winery is in a lovely setting, surrounded by hills 2 mi outside of Ithaca, with a gift shop and picnic facilities. You can take a guided tour or walk around at your own pace. | 1553 Slaterville Rd. | 607/272–WINE | fax 607/277–7344 | Free; $1 tasting fee | Daily noon–5:30, or by appointment.

Taughannock Falls State Park. These 215-ft falls (30 ft higher than Niagara) are surrounded by walls that rise up to 400 ft. Camping and swimming are allowed in season. The park has a wonderful wooden playground for children. | Rte. 89 | 607/387–6739 | www.nys-parks.state.ny.us/parks/ | Free; parking $6 June–Labor Day, $5 Labor Day–Columbus Day | Daily.

Tompkins County Museum and DeWitt Historical Society. A well-organized museum with regular exhibits drawn from a collection of more than 20,000 objects, 3,000 books, and 100,000 photographs. | 401 E. State St. | 607/273–8284 | Free | Museum: Tues.–Sat. 11–5; reference room: Tues., Thurs., Sat. 11–5.

ON THE CALENDAR
JUNE: *Ithaca Festival.* A three-day event with music, food, and crafts at Ithaca Commons and Stewart Park. | 607/273–3646.

JUNE–AUG.: *Hangar Theatre.* Some of the best regional theater in the Northeast is put on here at Cass Park. | 607/273–4497 or 800/284–8422 | $12–$25.

JULY: *Finger Lakes Grassroots Festival.* The music ranges from Cajun and zydeco to African and reggae at this 4-day festival that raises money to fight AIDS. The event is held at the Trumansburg Fairgrounds on Route 96, 10 mi north of Ithaca. | www.grassroots.org | 607/387–5144.

OCT.: *Ithaca Apple Harvest Festival.* This harvest celebration has more than just apples; regional produce, storytellers, bands, puppeteers, baked goods, cider, and other apple products are all part of this downtown event at the Commons. | 607/274–6546.

ITHACA

INTRO
ATTRACTIONS
DINING
LODGING

Dining
Angelina Centini's. Italian. Homemade pasta is served at this casual restaurant in a quaint two-story house in South Hill, just south of Ithaca College. The veal and chicken dishes and the desserts are also popular. Open-air dining is available in a seasonal grape arbor garden. Kids' menu. | 124 Coddington Rd. | 607/273–0802 | Closed Mon. No lunch weekends | $7.50–$17 | AE, D, DC, MC, V.

The Antlers. American. This turn-of-the-20th-century country inn has been turned into an eatery where grill fare is a specialty. Shrimp, chicken, and contemporary pasta dishes round out the extensive menu. Sit in front of the fireplace and drink local wine within the watchful gaze of a large mounted deer head looming above the doorway. | 1159 Dryden Rd. | 607/273–9725 | No lunch | $10–$18 | AE, DC, MC, V.

Dano's. Eastern European. Inside, this downtown restaurant tucked between two storefronts is like a European bistro. Try the daily fish, goulash, or one of the veal dishes. No smoking. | 113 S. Cayuga St. | 607/277–8942 | Closed Sun. No lunch | $14–$22 | AE, DC, MC, V.

Joe's. Italian. Since 1932, this Art Deco Ithaca mainstay has been serving pastas, steaks, and fresh seafood, complemented by a large wine list. | 602 W. Buffalo St., at Rte. 13 | 607/273–2693 | No lunch | $10–$18 | AE, D, MC, V.

John Thomas Steak House. Steak. This restaurant is housed in a two-story farmhouse built in 1848. Steak, chicken, and lobster are popular. In summer, you can eat on the outside deck. | 1152 Danby Rd. (Rte. 96B) | 607/273–3464 | Reservations essential | No lunch | $35–$55 | AE, MC, V.

Moosewood. Vegetarian. Since its founding in 1973, this restaurant downtown has been a pacesetter in the field of creative vegetarian cooking; its cookbooks are known around the nation and the world. The setting is simple and casual. The menu changes daily and everything is prepared from fresh ingredients. A vegan option is always available. You can dine outside on a patio. Beer and wine only. No smoking. | 215 N. Cayuga St. | 607/273–9610 | $10–$14 | MC, V.

Renee's. American. This romantic, lively bistro, just north of downtown, is known for its lamb, grilled steak, seafood, and spectacular desserts. Vegetarian dishes are also on the menu. Beer and wine only. No smoking. | 202 E. Falls St. | 607/272–0656 | Closed Sun. No lunch | $25–$40 | AE, D, MC, V.

Rogue's Harbor Steak and Ale. Contemporary. Five miles from Ithaca is this restaurant in the countryside. The dining room is full of 1830s memorabilia. Try the fried calamari or stuffed pork loin with mushroom sauce, and one of the the homemade desserts. Local wines and microbrew drafts are served. Open-air dining on a covered porch. Sunday brunch. | Rtes. 34 and 34B, Lansing | 607/533–3535 | Closed Mon. | $12–$22 | AE, D, MC, V.

The Station. Contemporary. You can dine in a train car at this former 1850s train station just west of downtown. Popular dishes include the salmon, seafood platter, prime rib, roasted duck, or lamb chops. There are three sleeping cars available for overnight stays. Salad bar. Kids' menu. Early bird dinner. | 806 W. Buffalo St. | 607/272–2609 | Closed Mon. No lunch | $12–$21 | AE, D, MC, V.

Lodging

Best Western University Inn. This modern hotel is ½ mi from Cornell University. Some rooms have fireplaces and cathedral ceilings. Complimentary Continental breakfast. In-room data ports, microwaves, cable TV, in-room VCRs (and movies). Pool. Business services, airport shuttle, free parking. Some pets allowed (fee). | 1020 Ellis Hollow Rd. | 607/272–6100 | fax 607/272–1518 | 94 rooms | $95–$199 | AE, D, DC, MC, V.

Clarion University Hotel. Once the Sheraton's Triphammer Lodge, this remodeled three-story hotel is just south of Route 13 on Ithaca's northern edge. The restaurant is open for breakfast and lunch and the pub serves a dinner menu. 2 restaurants, bar, room service. In-room data ports, cable TV. Pool. Sauna. Business services, airport shuttle, free parking. | 1 Sheraton Dr. | 607/257–2000 | fax 607/257–3998 | 106 rooms | $140–$160 | AE, D, MC, V.

Columbia Bed and Breakfast. Four blocks from downtown, this B&B, designed and owned by an architect, is anything but conventional. Although the original building is Greek Revival from around 1830, it's filled with custom-designed furniture with lots of color in the rooms. Almost all the rooms have gas fireplaces, and works by local artists are displayed throughout. Breakfast is as creative as you'd expect, with dishes like savory French toast. Some pets allowed. | 529 S. Meadow St. | 607/273–3885 | fax 607/277–0758 | 7 rooms | $75.

Comfort Inn. This two-story chain hotel sits just east of Route 13, in the South Hill district. Complimentary Continental breakfast. Some in-room hot tubs, cable TV. | 356 Elmira Rd. | 607/272–0100 | fax 607/272–2405 | 79 rooms | $59–$99 | AE, D, DC, MC, V.

Econo Lodge. Close to shopping malls and restaurants, this chain motel sits on Ithaca's northern end at the intersection of Route 13 and Triphammer Road. Complimentary Continental breakfast. In-room data ports, cable TV. Business services. Pets allowed (fee). | 2303 N. Triphammer Rd. | 607/257–1400 | fax 607/257–6359 | 72 rooms | $76–$102 | AE, D, MC, V.

Grayhaven Motel and Bed and Breakfast. This combination motel and B&B is 3 mi from downtown in a rural, wooded spot great for bird-watching. Sprawled on the lawn are picnic tables and Adirondack chairs, which you might find especially enjoyable after a long hike at one of the nearby trailheads at Buttermilk Falls. Complimentary Continental breakfast (in high season). | 657 Elmira Rd. | 607/272–6434 | 17 rooms | $50–$135 | AE, D, MC, V.

Hanshaw House Bed and Breakfast. This Federal-style country cottage is 5 mi from downtown, assuring you a peaceful stay. A white picket fence surrounds the property, and, inside, antiques furnish the house. Rooms have down comforters and overlook a well-tended garden. After your gourmet breakfast, relax on the patio. Complimentary breakfast. | 15 Sapsucker Woods Rd. | 607/257–1437 or 800/257-1437 | www.hanshawhouse.com | 4 rooms | Call for room rates | MC, V.

Hillside Inn. This three-story hotel is only blocks from Cornell University. The rooms have work desks and rocking chairs. Complimentary Continental breakfast. Cable TV. Free parking. | 518 Stewart Ave. | 607/273–6864 | 41 rooms | $35–$55 | AE, MC, V.

Holiday Inn Executive Tower. The rooms have large windows at this downtown hotel across from Ithaca Commons. In addition to huge two-level penthouse suites, there are no-smoking rooms available. Restaurant, bar, room service. Cable TV. Pool. Exercise equipment. Business services, airport shuttle, free parking. Some pets allowed (fee). | 222 S. Cayuga St. | 607/272–1000 | fax 607/277–1275 | www.harthotels.com | 178 rooms | $99–109 | AE, D, MC, V.

Hound and Hare. In 1829, this colonial house about 1 mi from Cornell University was built on a former military tract in the village of Cayuga Heights. Rooms are done up in Queen Anne style and tea is served on the veranda out back. | 1031 Hanshaw Rd. | 607/257–2821 or 800/652–2821 | fax 607/257–3121 | zsprole@clarityconnect.com | 13 rooms | $75–$150 | AE, D, MC, V.

La Tourelle Country Inn. Three miles from downtown is this three-story hotel in a commercial area. The rooms have dark Mexican wood or lighter, Haitian wood; some have fireplaces. Some refrigerators, some in-room hot tubs, cable TV. Tennis. Hiking. Business services. Some pets allowed. | 1150 Danby Rd. (Rte. 96B) | 607/273–2734 or 800/765–1492 | fax 607/273–4821 | 35 rooms | $125–$250 | AE, MC, V.

Meadow Court Inn. Although this inn is in downtown Ithaca, it's still only 1 mi from Buttermilk Falls State Park. Beds range from double to king. | 529 S. Meadow St. | 607/273–3885 | fax 607/277–0758 | 55 rooms, 5 suites | $75.

Ramada Inn–Airport. This two-story chain hotel is 1 mi from Cornell University and 4 mi from Ithaca College. Bar, room service. In-room data ports, microwaves, cable TV. Pool, wading pool. Exercise equipment. Video games. Business services, airport shuttle, free parking. Some pets allowed. | 2310 N. Triphammer Rd. | 607/257–3100 | fax 607/257–4425 | 120 rooms | $109–$139 | AE, D, DC, MC, V.

Rose Inn. The memorable circular mahogany staircase is one of the highlights of this 1850s white and pale pink bed-and-breakfast on 10 acres of orchards and gardens. All of the rooms have period furniture, goose-down bed covers, and large towels. Three of the suites have fireplaces and sofas. Restaurant, bar, complimentary breakfast, room service. In-room hot tubs, no TV in some rooms, TV in common area. Shops. Business services. No kids under 10. | 813 Auburn Rd. (Rte. 34), Groton | 607/533–7905 | fax 607/533–7908 | info@roseinn.com | www.roseinn.com | 15 rooms, 5 suites | $145–$200 | MC, V.

Statler. Run by Cornell's School of Hotel Management, this nine-story hotel is right on campus, and offers offers access to the recreational facilities of the university. Restaurant, bar, room service. In-room data ports, some kitchenettes, refrigerators, cable TV. Shops, library. Business services, airport shuttle, parking (fee). | 11 East Ave. | 607/257–2500 or 800/541–2501 | fax 607/257–6432 or 800/541–2501 | jh69@cornell.edu | www.hotelschool.cornell.edu/statler/rooms.html | 150 rooms, 17 suites | $150–$375 | AE, D, MC, V.

Super 8. This chain motel is two blocks from downtown, at the intersection of Routes 13 and 96B. Cable TV. Business services. | 400 S. Meadow | 607/273–8088 | fax 607/273–4832 | 63 rooms | $75–$90 | AE, D, MC, V.

Taughannock Farms Inn. Rooms at this Victorian inn built as a home in 1873 have antiques (including some canopy beds) and views of Cayuga Lake. The 12 acres of grounds also overlook Taughannock Falls State Park and you can easily access the park's trails. Restaurant, complimentary dinner. Some room phones, cable TV. | 2030 Gorge Rd., Rte. 89, Trumansburg | 607/387–7711 or 800/982–8818 | www.t-farms.com | 13 rooms, 3 guest houses | $95–$140 rooms, $175–$374 guest houses | AE, D, MC, V.

William Henry Miller Inn. This downtown Queen Anne house built around 1880 has versatile accommodations—suitable whether you're with your sweetheart or your kids—and is popular among parents visiting college kids. It serves an excellent gourmet breakfast, with treats like fresh orange juice, lemon ricotta pancakes, and an assortment of muffins, as well as an evening dessert. Within walking distance of restaurants and shops. Complimentary breakfast. In-room data ports. | 303 N. Aurora St. | 607/256–4553 | www.millerinn.com | 9 rooms | $95–$155 | AE, D, DC, MC, V.

JAMESPORT/AQUEBOQUE/LAUREL

MAP 3, E2

(Nearby towns also listed: Mattituck, Riverhead)

The first European settlers arrived in this area in 1690 and fish oil was the major industry. Later, Methodists set up annual summer camps, first in tents, then in Victorian cottages. In more recent years, the area has become known for equestrian farms and vineyards.

Today the North Fork's westernmost villages are an antiques lover's dream. These quaint New England–style hamlets are also peppered with restaurants and novelty stores, and there is a national golf course here.

Beautiful beaches lie to the south on Great Peconic Bay and to the north on Long Island Sound. During the growing season, you will see nurseries selling colorful flowers and farm stands with just-picked produce.

Information: **Greenport-Southold Chamber of Commerce** | 72250 Main Rd., Greenport, 11944 | 631/477–1383 | www.northfork.org.

Attractions
Iron Pier Beach. Lifeguards are on duty from the end of June through early September along the 480 ft of beachfront on Long Island Sound. | Pier Ave., off Sound Ave. | 631/727–5744 | Parking $5 residents, $10 nonresidents | Late June–Labor Day, daily.

South Jamesport Beach. This beach has 3,000 ft on Peconic Bay, with shallow-water areas for children. Lifeguards are on duty weekends mid-May through the end of June and then daily through early September. | Off Peconic Bay Blvd. | 631/727–5744 | Parking $5 residents, $10 nonresidents | Late June–Labor Day, daily.

Dining
Meetinghouse Creek Inn. Seafood. This cozy restaurant done up like a French country inn overlooks the water. In winter, a fireplace warms the room. The New England clambake comes in a net with lobster, clams, mussels, and oysters and is served with corn on the cob. Other favorites include the cioppino over linguine and strawberry shortcake. A pianist plays on Fridays and Saturdays. Open-air dining on patio. Kids' menu. Early bird dinners. Sunday brunch buffet. Dock space. | 177 Meetinghouse Creek Rd., Aqueboque | 631/722–4220 | $15–$25 | AE, D, MC, V.

Lodging
Motel on the Bay. All the rooms at this motel overlook Peconic Bay and its sandy beach. Some units have full kitchens. Kitchenettes, refrigerators, cable TV. Beach. No pets. | Front St., South Jamesport | 631/722–3458 | fax 631/722–5166 | 17 rooms | $125–$215 | AE, D, MC, V.

JAMESTOWN

MAP 3, B8

(Nearby towns also listed: Bemus Point, Chautauqua, Salamanca)

Jamestown, founded in 1811, is at the eastern end of Chautauqua Lake. One of Jamestown's claims to fame is that it was the childhood home of Lucille Ball. It was here that Ball first performed her wacky comedy acts, which are now commemorated every year during the Lucille Ball Festival. Jamestown's other well-known citizen is Roger Tory Peterson, who wrote and illustrated the world-famous *Peterson Field Guides*, which stunningly document the flora and fauna of various United States regions.

Information: **Jamestown Chamber of Commerce** | 101 W. 5th St., 14701 | 716/484–1101.

Attractions
Fenton Historical Center. Reuben Eaton Fenton, governor of New York from 1865 to 1869, had this Italianate mansion built in 1863. Now it houses Victorian period rooms, and exhibits showcasing the history of Chautauqua Lake, the life and career of Lucille Ball, and Jamestown's Swedish and Italian communities. Also of interest are the archival and genealogical library and Civil War exhibits. | 67 Washington St. | 716/664–6256 | $3.50 | Feb.–late Nov., Mon.–Sat. 10–4; late Nov.–Jan., Mon.–Sat. 10–4, Sun. 1–4.

Lucy-Desi Museum. A collection of Lucille Ball and Desi Arnaz's personal items are on display here in exhibits that follow the lives and careers of the two comedy stars. Several of the exhibits are interactive and there are video presentations. Gift shop. | 212 Pine St. | 716/484–7070 | www.lucy-desi.com | $5 | Mid-May–mid-Oct., Mon.–Sat. 10–5:30, Sun. 1–5; mid-Oct.–mid-May, Sat. 10–5:30, Sun. 1–5.

Panama Rocks Park. The rock outcropping here, 14 mi west of downtown Jamestown, is over 360 million years old and spans 25 acres. There are 60-ft-high cliffs, crevices, and caves which the Native Americans are said to have used as shelter and as places to keep meat fresh in summer. Outlaws are also said to have used the rocks as hiding places. As you hike here, you may also find rare mosses, wildflowers, ferns, and uniquely shaped tree roots. Picnicking is permitted. | 11 Rock Hill Rd., Panama | 716/782–2845 | www.panamarocks.com | $5 | May–mid-Oct., daily 10–5.

Roger Tory Peterson Institute of Natural History. Named for the Jamestown native and noted naturalist, this 27-acre center seeks to educate children about nature. You can hike the wooded trails, or explore the one of the natural history exhibits. The gallery shows a selection of work by Peterson and others. There is also a library and a gift shop. | 311 Curtis St. | 716/665–2473 or 800/758–6841 | fax 716/665–3794 | www.rtpi.org | webmaster@rtpi.org | $3 | Tues.–Sat. 10–4, Sun. 1–5; grounds open daily dawn–dusk.

ON THE CALENDAR
MAY: *Lucy-Desi Hometown Celebration.* This annual celebration of Lucille Ball's comic genius includes tours of the Lucy-Desi Museum, concerts, performances, a scavenger hunt, contests, and more. Held at the Lucy-Desi Museum and other locations. | 716/484–7070.

Dining
The Grainery. Contemporary. At this restaurant 20 mi northeast of Jamestown in an Amish area dishes made with fresh foods gathered from the local countryside are served in a century-old bar fitted out with local antiques. Known for lamb stew and fresh salads. | 1494 Rte. 66, Cherry Creek | 716/287–3500 | $10–$16 | MC, V.

Ironstone. Continental. There are 10 items on the menu for under $10 at this restaurant. Other menu options include salad, seafood, pasta, meat loaf, surf and turf, and prime rib. The outdoor courtyard has seating for 40. | 516 W. 4th St. | 716/487–1516 | Closed Sun. No lunch Sat. | $10–$18 | AE, D, DC, MC, V.

MacDuff's. Eclectic. An intimate dining experience awaits you at this eight-table restaurant with red linen table cloths, Queen Anne chairs with floral upholstery, brass chandeliers and brass wall sconces. The menu leans to the French side with entrées like twin filets in port, Stilton cheese and green peppercorn sauce, and lavender crème brûlée for dessert. Also try the homemade orange ice cream served in a bittersweet chocolate shell and sprinkled with bittersweet chocolate bits. | 317 Pine St. | 716/664–9414 | Closed Sun. No lunch. | $16–$24 | AE, MC, V.

Lodging

Colony Motel. One mile outside Jamestown, you're still within walking distance of restaurants and shops. There is lots of lawn to relax on and some woods for kids to explore in the back. Restaurant. Cable TV. Pool. No pets. | 620 Fairmount Ave. | 716/488–1904 | 45 rooms | $50–$65 | AE, D, DC, MC, V.

Comfort Inn. This two-story chain hotel is just at the edge of town. Complimentary Continental breakfast. Some in-room hot tubs, cable TV. Business services. Some pets allowed. | 2800 N. Main St. | 716/664–592 or 800/453–7155 | fax 716/664–3068 | www.comfortinn.com | 101 rooms | $74–$139 | AE, D, DC, MC, V.

Highland View Farm Bed and Breakfast. At this homey Victorian bed-and-breakfast, 12 mi east of Jamestown, the rooms have antique furniture and lace curtains. The grounds include a pond. Picnic area, complimentary breakfast. | 12693 W. Main St., Randolph | 716/358–2882 | 4 rooms (2 with shared bath) | $50 | Closed Dec.–Mar. | No credit cards.

Hillside Motel. This motel just ¼ mi south of Jamestown is a good choice if you're on a budget. It offers simple, peaceful accommodations amid pines and oak trees on a 5-acre lot. All beds are double. It's ½ mi from Allen Park, and 1 mi from the Lucy-Desi Museum. | 84 Foote Ave. | 716/488–1133 | 12 rooms | $35–$40 | MC, V.

Holiday Inn. This chain hotel is right in Jamestown's downtown business district. Restaurant, bar, room service. In-room data ports, cable TV. Pool. Laundry facilities. Business services. | 150 W. 4th St. | 716/664–3400 or 800/528–8791 | fax 716/484–3304 | 149 rooms | $85–$99 | AE, D, DC, MC, V.

JERICHO

MAP 4, H6

(Nearby towns also listed: Plainview/Old Bethpage, Port Washington, Syosset)

The Quakers gave Jericho its name after the area became a center for their religion in the 1690s. And it is said that the Jericho and Westbury Quakers were among the first New Yorkers to free their slaves as a matter of conscience in the 1770s. In 1940, Jericho still had less than 600 people, but the sparse Quaker farmland gave way to development around 1952 and the area was never the same. Since then, the population has reached over 13,000.

Today, there are restaurants and businesses along Jericho Turnpike, one of the main Long Island arteries and industrial parks near Jericho's border with Westbury.

Information: Hicksville Chamber of Commerce. | 10 W. Marie St., Hicksville, 11542 | 516/931–7170.

ON THE CALENDAR

AUG.: *Lightpath Long Island Classic.* The Lightpath Long Island Classic is a 3-day senior PGA tour tournament held at the Meadow Brook Club in Jericho. The tournament attracts such big names as Palmer, Trevino, Player, Rodriguez, and others. First prize is $225,000. | 516/676–6666.

Dining

Capriccio. Italian. Choose from two different dining rooms at this restaurant that serves northern Italian dishes of chicken, seafood, veal, and pasta. One is very light with big windows, the other is much more like a private club with wood paneling and bar. No smoking weekends. | 399 Jericho Tpk. | 516/931–2727 | Closed Sun. No lunch Sat. | $19–$30 | AE, DC, MC, V.

Frank's Steaks. Steak. Tables at this eclectic restaurant sport tabletop art and are bathed in theatrical spotlights. Popular steak dishes include the skirt steak and the garlic rib eye. If you're not in the mood for steak, try the lobster tails, the Cajun calamari with spicy sauce, or the fillet of salmon topped with diced tomatoes, basil, and garlic. | 4 Jericho Tpk. | 516/338–4595 | No lunch weekends | $30–$50 | AE, D, DC, MC, V.

Maine Maid Inn. Continental. The nine dining rooms at this restaurant in a 1788 building are filled with antiques from different periods. Try the prime rib of beef, roasted Long Island duckling, or lobster. Kids' menu. Early bird dinners. Sunday brunch. | Rte. 106, at Jericho Tpk. | 516/935–6400 | $13–$50 | AE, D, DC, MC, V.

Milleridge Inn. American. Part of a village that includes a carriage house and bakery, this restaurant is a must-see at night during the Christmas season, when it comes alive with thousands of lights, Christmas carolers, and beautiful decorations. Popular dishes include roasted country turkey, and roast center-cut loin of pork with sauerkraut. Live music Christmas and certain holidays. Kids' menu, early bird dinners (late Jan.–early Nov. only). Sunday brunch. | 585 N. Broadway | 516/931–2201 | $15–$25 | AE, D, DC, MC, V.

Lodging

Econo Lodge. This brick and stucco hotel is in a commercial area about 2 mi from the center of Jericho. Rooms are decorated in mauve and lavender and have either two double beds or one king-size. You'll find a family-style restaurant just next door to the hotel. Complimentary Continental breakfast. Cable TV, in-room VCRs, TV in common area. Laundry services. Free parking. No pets. | 429 Duffy Ave., Hicksville | 516/433–3900 | fax 516/433–3909 | www.econolodge.com | 72 rooms | $85–$99 | AE, D, DC, MC, V.

JOHNSTOWN

(Nearby towns also listed: Amsterdam, Canajoharie, Gloversville, Saratoga Springs, Schenectady)

Johnstown was founded in 1763 by Sir William Johnson, an Irish businessman and councilman to the Mohawk Indians who lived in the area. The town now has a population of approximately 10,000 people. In 1781, it was the site of a Revolutionary War battle that took place a few days after General George Cornwallis's 1781 surrender at the Battle of Yorktown. Elizabeth Cady Stanton, a pioneer for women's rights, was born here in the early 19th century.

Information: Fulton County Regional Chamber of Commerce and Industry | 2 N. Main St., Gloversville, 12078 | 518/725–0641 or 800/676–3858 | www.johnstown.com/city.

Attractions

Johnson Hall State Historic Site. This 1763 building was once the home of Sir William Johnson, an early settler in Johnstown. You can tour the house or have a picnic on the grounds. | Hall Ave. | 518/762–8712 | fax 518/762–2330 | $3 | Mid-May–Oct., Wed.–Sat. 10–5, Sun. 1–5.

Knox Mansion Historical Museum. The Victorian mansion of the millionaire industrialist who started Knox Gelatin in the late 1800s contains unusual artifacts from all over the world. A fireplace from an Italian castle dating back to the 1600s now keeps people warm. The living room is stunning, with black walnut woodwork and a grand mahogany staircase. (*See also* Lodging, *below.*) | 104 W. 2nd Ave. | 518/762–5669 | fax 518/725–5250 | Donations accepted.

Dining

Maple Tree Knoll. American. Ten miles outside of Johnstown, this century-old Federal-style building houses one of the area's oldest running restaurants. Lobster tails, pot roast, and

Friday-night buffets guarantee you won't go hungry. Antiques are for sale, and give the restaurant a homey feel. | 2794 State Hwy. 10 | 518/835–3231 | Closed Wed. | $9–$25 | No credit cards.

Union Hall Inn. Continental. Right off Main St., the central artery of Johnstown, a fine dining experience awaits you. Antiques fill the three formal dining rooms in which you may enjoy an unhurried meal, chosen from a small and inventive menu. Try the maple-glazed pork tenderloin, the roasted, herb-crusted rack of lamb, or the fresh seafood special. A side of corn fritters is a must here. And save room for the apple/pear flan. | 2 Union Pl. | 518/762–3210 | Reservations essential | $12–$25 | AE, MC, V.

Lodging

Holiday Inn. This two-story hotel is in a quiet, rural area accessible by exit 28 (Fultonville) off I–90. Once you exit, look for signs to Rte. 30A, which leads you to the hotel. Restaurant, bar (with entertainment), room service. In-room data ports, cable TV. Pool. Laundry facilities. Business services. Some pets allowed. | 308 N. Comrie Ave. | 518/762–4686 | fax 518/762–4034 | jntny@telenet.net | 100 rooms | $65–$104 | AE, D, DC, MC, V.

Olde Knox Mansion Bed and Breakfast. Built in 1898 by Charles B. Knox, the founder of Knox Gelatin, this mansion now houses a museum (*see above*) as well as a one-of-a-kind B&B. Some rooms have antique Victorian beds, but one (by popular demand) has a water bed. Eighteen-karat gold adorns the ceiling in one of the rooms, while a giant Spanish chandelier hangs in the foyer. Eclectic and charming. Complimentary Continental breakfast. | 104 W. 2nd Ave. | 518/762–5669 | fax 518/725–5250 | 4 rooms | $85–$175 | MC, V.

KEENE VALLEY

MAP 3, K3

(Nearby town also listed: Lake Placid)

Keene and Keene Valley are twin towns that border the Giant Mountain Wilderness Area. Both towns also enjoy wonderful views of the "High Peaks"—the largest wilderness area in the park, which includes some of the highest (and therefore most popular) peaks in the Adirondacks, such as Mt. Marcy. Keene Valley has become a popular base camp for hikers and rock climbers, as well as a peaceful place to visit.

Information: Plattsburgh–North Country Chamber of Commerce | Box 310, 7061 Rte. 9, Plattsburgh, 12901 | 518/563–1000.

Attractions

Alpine Adventure, Inc. This guide service provide instruction in and guides for rock climbing, ice climbing, mountaineering, and backcountry skiing for all levels from beginner to advanced. | Rte. 73, Keene | 518/576–9881 | mail@alpineadven.com | www.alpineadven.com | By appointment.

Dining

Keene Valley Ausable Inn. American. This inn serves typical American fare in an English pub setting of knotty-pine paneling, complete with a fireplace. Try hamburgers, filet mignon, or veggie burgers inside or on the patio overlooking Main Street. Full bar. Kids' menu. (*See also* Lodging, *below*.) | Rte. 73, Main St. | 518/576–9584 | $8–$13 | MC, V.

Noon Mark Diner. American. This seven-table, smoke-free, family restaurant is on the north end of town and features photographs of the Adirondacks, shot by the owner's husband. Try the meat and spinach lasagna, broccoli and cheese stuffed chicken, or the broccoli quiche. | Rte. 73 | 518/576–4499 | $6.95–$9.95 | MC, V.

Lodging

Adirondack Rock and River. In addition to a variety of lodging (a lean-to, a bunk room, private rooms), this organization also offers guide service to the high-peaks region. A rock-and ice-climbing school is on the premises. Complimentary breakfast. Hiking. No pets. | End of Alstead Rd., Keene | 518/576–2041 | fax 518–576–9827 | ed@rockandriver.com | 8 rooms (4 with shared bath) | $30–$70 | MC, V.

Bark Eater Inn. Wide floorboards and cobblestone fireplaces set the tone at this spacious 19th-century farmhouse in the Adirondack mountains. The grounds include a polo field and livery stable, and, in summer, there are English- and Western-style riding programs. The innkeepers prepare dinner for those not staying in the inn, depending upon how many guests they are hosting, so call in advance if you are interested. Restaurant, picnic area, complimentary breakfast. No room phones, cable TV in common area. Hiking, horseback riding. Cross-country skiing, downhill skiing. Business services. No smoking. | Alstead Mill Rd., Keene | 518/576–2221 | fax 518/576–2071 | www.barkeater.com | 19 rooms in 3 buildings (7 share baths) | $85–$136 | AE, D, DC, MC, V.

Keene Valley Ausable Inn. Just a few miles from Adirondack Park, where you'll find plenty of trailheads for hiking in summer, ice climbing in winter, is this country inn. Beds are all full or single. (*See also* Dining, *above.*) Complimentary breakfast. | Rte. 73 (Main St.) | 518/576–9584 | 8 rooms | $65 | MC, V.

Keene Valley Lodge. You can hike, ski, climb, or go snowshoeing from the front door of this historic 1910 Victorian lodge. The lounge has a granite fireplace and there is a music room and a large front porch. The beds are covered with quilts and goose-down comforters. Complimentary breakfast. Library. No pets. No smoking. | Rte. 73, Keene Valley | 518/576–2003 | kvlodge@kvvi.net | www.keenevalleylodge.com | 7 rooms (2 with shared bath) | $60–$115 | AE, MC, V.

Snow Goose Lodge. You can bring the whole family to this large turn-of-the-century home that sits on 12 ½ acres of land on the boarder of Adirondack State Park and just 10 mi from Lake Placid's White Face Mountain. With six bedrooms and two pull-out couches, this antiques-filled home sleeps 16 people. For an additional fee, you can hire a private chef. The lodge is accessible from I–87 off exit 30. Kitchenettes, microwaves, refrigerators, cable TV, in-room VCRs, some room phones. Hiking, boating, fishing, cross-country skiing, downhill skiing. Laundry facilities. | Rte. 73, Keene Valley | 800/552–3508 ext. 15 | snowgoos73@aol.com | http://members.aol.com/snowgoos73 | 6 rooms | $1800–$2200 per wk | No credit cards.

Trail's End Inn. Some of the rooms at this secluded 1902 lodge have fireplaces or sleeping porches and some bathrooms have old-fashioned claw-foot tubs. The rustic country-style common areas have wide-board floors and fireplaces. Complimentary breakfast. Kitchenettes (in cottages), some in-room hot tubs. | 518/576–9860 | www.bbonline.com/ny/trailsend/ | 12 rooms, 4 cottages | $75–$125 rooms, $155–$175 cottages | AE, D, MC, V.

KINGSTON

MAP 3, K8

(Nearby towns also listed: Mt. Tremper, Rhinebeck, Saugerties, Woodstock)

This Hudson River city was New York's first capital. Settled by the Dutch in the 1600s, it still has houses dating back to that era in its Stockade District. In the 19th century, Kingston was a thriving commercial port, especially between 1828 and 1898 when the D&H Canal was in operation and coal was shipped here from Pennsylvania for distribution elsewhere. Today, the Rondout area on the river's edge has a lively arts and dining scene, and you can embark on a river cruise from the pier at the foot of Broadway. Kingston is a favorite stop for boaters as well as motorists traveling between New York City and Albany.

Information: **Chamber of Commerce of Ulster County** | 7 Albany Ave., Suite G3, 12401 | 845/338–5100.

Attractions

Delaware and Hudson Canal Museum. This museum 10 mi south of Kingston traces the history of the D&H Canal, an important 19th-century waterway. A brochure outlines a walking tour of the canal's landmark locks. | County Rte. 6A (Monhonk Rd.) off Rte. 213, High Falls | 845/687–9311 | www.canalmuseum.org | $3 | Memorial Day–Labor Day, Thurs.–Sat. and Mon. 11–5, Sun. 1–5; May, Sept.–Oct., Sat. 11–5, Sun. 1–5.

Fred Jay Johnston Museum. In a National Historic district, this Federal-style mansion museum houses 18th-century furniture, art, and everything in between, and is set up as though it were still lived in. | 63 Main St. | 845/339–0720 | $3 | May-Oct., weekends 1–4; group tours by appointment.

Hudson River Maritime Museum and Cruises. You can board this 300-passenger vessel at Roundout Landing at the foot of Broadway for a 2-hr sightseeing tour. You'll enjoy musical accompaniment with the sunset sail. | Under the Rte. 9W bridge, next to the Hudson River Maritime Museum | 845/225–6515 | fax 845/255–3648 | www.hudsonriver-cruises.com | $13 | Closed May 1–Oct. 31; call for exact cruising times.

Hudson River Maritime Museum. Models, artifacts, and photographs illustrate the region's maritime history. There are also changing exhibits of tugboats and antique fishing and sailing craft, and a river cruise to the Rondout Lighthouse. When it is in dock, you can go aboard the *Half Moon,* a replica of Henry Hudson's ship. | 1 Rondout Landing | 845/338–0071 | $3 | May–Oct., daily 11–5.

Hurley Patentee Manor. Just outside Kingston is the village of Hurley where there are a number of stone cottages built in the 17th and 18th centuries. This manor, a 1696 cottage with a 1745 Georgian building attached to it, is the only one open to the public. Inside, the rooms are furnished with period antiques. There is a showroom with reproductions of Colonial furniture. | 464 Old Rte. 209 (County Rte. 29) | 845/331–5414 | $2 | Mid-July–Labor Day, Wed.–Sat. 11-4, Sun.1–5.

Old Dutch Church. This church has been here since 1659 in a series of buildings. The present church dates to 1852 and has windows made in the Tiffany Studios. De Witt Clinton, the first governor of New York, is buried in the graveyard. | Main and Wall Sts. | 845/338–6759 | Free | Weekdays 10–4.

Senate House State Historic Site. This 17th-century Dutch house was the meeting place of the first State Senate. The modern gallery features artwork by John Vanderlyn and others, and has an exhibit on the American Revolution in New York State. | 296 Fair St. | 845/338–2786. | $3 | Apr. 15-Oct. 31, Wed.–Sat. 10–5, Sun. 1–5; Nov.–mid-Apr., by appointment.

Stockade District. Because of land disputes between the Colonists and the Esopus Indians in 1658, Peter Stuyvesant ordered settlers to move up to this bluff, where they built a 1,200 ft x 1,300 ft wall on three sides of an enclave they called Wiltwyck. Twenty-one pre-Revolutionary homes still stand within the stockade area. You can visit homes and sites on which the government of New York State was born. | Between Wall, John, and N. Front Sts. | 845/338–5100 | Free | Daily.

Ulster Performing Arts Center. Local and professional shows are presented on this 1927 vaudeville stage. | 601 Broadway | 845/339–6088 | www.upac.org | Mar.–Dec.; call for schedule.

ON THE CALENDAR

MAY: *Shad Festival.* The first weekend in May marks the season opening of the Maritime Museum with the display of new exhibits and this 2-day festival. There's a fish fry,

musical entertainment, and face painting outside, and you can stroll through the museum. There is an admission fee of around $3. | 1 Roundout Landing | 845/338–0071.
JULY: *Stone House Day.* The village of Hurley, 2 mi south of Kingston, opens up its 17th- and 18th-century stone houses for tours. | 845/331–4121.

Dining

Deising's Bakery. Eclectic. Deising's has been serving American- and European-style breakfast and lunches since 1965. For breakfast, try Belgian waffles or a freshly baked honeynut danish; for lunch you'll choose from hot or cold sandwiches like a vegetarian club. Don't leave without trying the Black Forest double-chocolate cake, with kirsch, fudge, fresh cherries, and whipped cream. | 111 N. Front St. | 845/338–7503 | Breakfast also available. No dinner | $4.50–$7 | www.deisings.com | AE, D, MC, V.

Hoffman House. Continental. You'll enjoy fireside dining in this National Historic Landmark home, built in 1711. Try the aged steak or the special seafood of the day. The homemade pastas are also a treat. A different cheesecake is offered on the dessert menu each day of the week. In summer, ask to sit on the patio. | 94 N. Front St. | 845/338–2626 | $15–$19 | AE, D, DC, MC, D.

Louie's. Continental. Chandeliers, murals, and pictorial screens give the dining room at this Holiday Inn a cosmopolitan spirit. Try the pasta Louis, prepared with black olives, sundried tomatoes, spinach, and basil, or try the rainbow trout amandine. You can hear live music here Wednesdays through Saturdays. Salad bar. Kids' menu. Breakfast also available. | 503 Washington Ave. | 845/338–0400 | $12–$16 | AE, D, DC, MC, V.

Lodging

Black Mansion Lion. Built in the 1880s, this High-Victorian, three-story mansion has views of the Hudson River's Kingston Harbor and the Catskill Mountains. Special touches like stained glass, a domed ceiling, window seats, double-level porches, stunning woodwork, and a lavish breakfast make this a magical place for a getaway. Complimentary breakfast, in-room data ports. | 124 W. Chestnut St. | 845/338–0410 | fax 845/331–5194 | www.theblacklionmansion.com | 5 rooms, 3 suites | $99–$289 | AE, D, MC, V.

Holiday Inn. This two-story chain hotel is ¼ mi off the Kingston exit of I–87, and close to downtown. Restaurant, bar (with entertainment), room service. Cable TV. Pool, wading pool. Hot tub, sauna. Video games. Laundry facilities. Business services. Pets allowed. | 503 Washington Ave. | 845/338–0400 | holiday@mhb.net | 212 rooms | $99–$149 | AE, D, DC, MC, V.

Ramada Inn. A two-story chain hotel off I–87, exit 19, is in a commercial district near to restaurants and shops. Restaurant, bar, room service. Cable TV. Pool. Exercise equipment. Video games. Business services, free parking. | 114 Rte. 28 | 845/339–3900 | fax 845/338–8464 | www.ramada.com | 147 rooms | $105 | AE, D, DC, MC, V.

The Rondout. This Colonial Revival home, built around 1906, is on 2 green and wooded acres with flower gardens, a hammock, and picnic tables. Inside are eclectic portraits, sculptures, and ceramics. No room phones. Some pets allowed. | 88 Westchester St. | 845/331–2369 | fax 845/331–9049 | www.pojonews.com/rondout | 4 rooms, two with private baths | $85–$115 | AE, MC, V.

Super 8. This chain motel, less than a mile from I–87's exit 19, is 10–15 min from the Senate House Museum. Cable TV. Laundry facilities. Business services. Some pets allowed. | 487 Washington Ave. | 845/338–3078, 800/800–8000 reservations | www.super8.com | 84 rooms | $55–$75 | AE, D, DC, MC, V.

LAKE GEORGE VILLAGE

MAP 3, K5

(Nearby towns also listed: Bolton Landing, Diamond Point, Glens Falls, Lake Luzerne, Queensbury, Warrensburg)

If you're looking for people and action in the Adirondacks, this village at the southern end of Lake George is where you want to be. This resort area has over one hundred places to stay, plenty of restaurants, and every kind of amusement under the sun. You can try jet skiing, riding, parasailing and minigolf, along with the more traditional Adirondack sports of swimming, boating, fishing, and hiking.

But the town also has historical significance. Because of its position on Lake George, the village area was inhabited before the European settlers came, and once

© Artville

LAKE GEORGE AREA

If you've got kids from roughly 6–16 years of age and your destination is the Adirondacks, you can save yourself a lot of time by simply heading the car toward the Lake George area. You can simplify things even further by choosing to stay in Lake George Village, the epicenter for kids' entertainment.

Lake George is a 32-mi-long lake known as the Queen of American Lakes; there are, therefore, plenty of water sports available, such as jet skiing, swimming, boating, windsurfing, and angling for both warm- and cold-water fish.

Many area restaurants and hotels are geared toward family vacations, and there are plenty of housekeeping cottages for longer stays. There is a wide variety of simple vacation pleasures, such as factory-outlet shopping, historic sites, balloon flights, and cruises on the Lake George Steamboat Company's three famous ships. You can hike up Prospect Mountain, or visit the Natural Stone Bridge and Caves in Pottersville. What will keep the kids happy, however, is action, and there's plenty of that in the Lake George area.

For starters, the kids might want to spend a few days at the Great Escape and Splashwater Kingdom Fun Park, which is a popular water-theme park. More than 125 rides, shows, and attractions will not only entertain the younger set, but will probably give Mom and Dad a couple of fun-filled days as well. The kids will probably also want to visit the House of Frankenstein Wax Museum, where they'll find interactive wax replicas of their favorite ghouls and monsters. Mom and Dad may be ready for a quiet chair on the lodge porch, but the kids will probably next want to try out Lake George Action Park, where go-carts, laser guns, rides, and more will keep them busy for several more hours.

They're still not tired? Head over to the Lake George Batting Cages on U.S. 9, where they—and you—can choose from several hardball and softball pitches and five different speeds, and see just how good you really are at home plate.

If you haven't worn them out by now, there's still a lot more to try: Water Slide World, indoor rock climbing, mountain biking, horseback riding, and just plain cruising the kid-packed streets of Lake George Village are all awaiting you. And so far, we've only talked about a *summer* vacation. To make the most of your visit to the Lake George area, just remember to bring good walking shoes, a great attitude, and think young.

Towns listed: Bolton Landing, Diamond Point, Glens Falls, Lake George Village, Lake Luzerne, North Creek, Queensbury, Warrensburg.

they arrived, it immediately became a strategic location. Lake George figured prominently in the French and Indian War. You'll find lots of museums, historic sites, forts, and commemorative parks to visit.

Information: Lake George Chamber of Commerce | Box 2722, Lake George, 12845 | 800/705–0059.

Attractions

French Mountain Commons Outlet Center. Within 500 ft of this brand-name outlet mall are three others just like it. The malls are 3 mi south of Lake George Village, at exit 20, off I-87. | 1439 State Rte. 9, #16 | 518/792–1483 | Free | Mon.–Thurs. 10–6, Fri., Sat. 10–8, Sun. 11–5.

Ft. William Henry Museum. This is a restoration of the original French and Indian War fort that James Fenimore Cooper wrote about in *The Last of the Mohicans*. Includes barracks, stockades, dungeons, and fort artifacts. You can take a guided tour or watch the demonstrations. | Canada St. | 518/668–5471 or 800/234–0267 | samfwh@capital.net | $9.30 | May–June and Labor Day–Oct, daily 10–5; July–Labor Day, daily 9–10.

Great Escape and Splashwater Kingdom Fun Park. Five roller coasters are among the 125 rides at this theme park. There is also a water park, a wave pool, and shows that include an ice review. | 1172 U.S. 9 | 518/792–3500 | gescape@capital.net | www.sixflags.com/greatescape | $32.99 | Hrs vary.

House of Frankenstein Wax Museum. More than 50 interactive exhibits of monsters and mayhem are on display here, including such favorites as Frankenstein's Monster, Dracula, and the Wolfman. While children under six are admitted free, you may want to think twice about taking them in. | 213 Canada St. | 518/668–3377 | $6 | Mid-Apr.–mid-Oct., daily 11–11.

Lake George Batting Cages. Five coin-operated baseball and softball pitching machines let you try out your swing on some major- (or minor-) league pitches. | Rte. 9 | 518/668–2531 | $1 for 14 pitches | Mid-May–mid-Sept., daily 10 AM–11 PM.

Lake George Battlefield Picnic Area. The remains of the original Ft. George are here, along with a monument to Jesuit missionary Father Jogues. | Beach Rd. off Rte. 9 | 518/623–3671 | Free; parking $5 | Late June–Labor Day, daily 9–8; early May–late June, weekends 9–5.

Shepard Park. In the summer this lake-side park is teeming with swimmers and in the winter you can stroll on the beach-side walkway. The public park also has a playground. | Canada St. between Amherst & Montcalm | 518/668–5771 | Free.

Lake George Steamboat Co. This company has been taking people out on lake cruises since 1817. Ride aboard the steamboat *Minne-Ha-Ha*, the *Mohican*, the *Lac du Saint Sacrement*, or the brass, glass, and dark-wood-decorated *Sac*; each vessel has its own unique allure. All cruises are narrated. | Steel Pier | 518/668–5777 or 800/553–BOAT | $7.75–$30 | May–Oct., hrs vary.

Million Dollar Beach. This popular swimming beach has a bathhouse, lifeguards, lockers, picnic facilities, and volleyball nets. | Beach Rd., off U.S. 9 | 518/668–3352 | Memorial Day–Labor Day, daily 9–6:30.

Prospect Mountain. A 5-mi corkscrew road takes you most of the way up the mountain and then, from the parking lot, it's just 100 ft to the top where you'll get a view of 100 mi and up to five states. You can also ride a "viewmobile" shuttle to the top. | Canada St., off U.S. 9 | 518/668–5198 or 518/623–3671 | $5 per vehicle | May–Oct., daily 9–5.

Water Slide World. This park, the first water-slide park in the Adirondack region, has more than 35 slides on 12 acres. Food and concessions are available, as are lockers, picnic areas, showers, and life jackets. There is also a gift and sportswear shop. Height restrictions apply for some rides. To get to the park take exit 21 off I-87. | U.S. 9 and Rte. 9L | 518/668–4407 | $20.95 daily, $65 seasonal | Mid-June–Labor Day, daily 9:30–6.

LAKE GEORGE
VILLAGE

INTRO
ATTRACTIONS
DINING
LODGING

ON THE CALENDAR

FEB.: *Lake George Regional Winter Festival.* The races and activities at this event start off with a coronation ball and proceed to international dogsled weight pulls, polar-bear swims, ice sculpting, and snowmobile races. You can also watch the fireworks. | 518/668–2233.

JUNE: *Americade.* If you've got a motorcycle, you'll want to be in Lake George during early June. Over 35,000 motorcycle enthusiasts flock to the area for a weekend of widely assorted activities, including an exposition with over 200 vendors. The big event is a huge motorcycle parade, starting at Million Dollar Beach, and venturing all the way up Prospect Mountain to the summit. | 518/656–3696.

AUG.: *Family Festival.* An old-fashioned street fair with food, games, fun, and items for sale comes to Shepard Park, on Canada Street. | 518/668–5771.

SEPT.: *Jazz Festival.* Jazz groups from all over New York converge at the Shepard Park Bandstand for an end-of-summer bash on the weekend after Labor Day. | 518/668–2616.

SEPT.: *Lakeside Festival.* Food, music, a boat show, and fireworks at Shepard Park. | 518/668–5771.

Dining

Barnsider Smokehouse Restaurant. American. Smoked ribs are the specialty, and if you like them, you might consider buying the bottled barbecue sauce available to go. This family favorite also serves up a hearty breakfast, with pancakes and maple syrup. Open-air dining and full bar. | Rte. 9, just before Waterslide World | 518/668–5268 | Breakfast also available | $6–$24 | AE, D, DC, MC, V.

Contessa Restaurant. Italian. You will have scenic views of Lake George from either the glass-enclosed bar and dining room or the outside patio. The menu has anything from build-your-own pizzas, to a full menu including antipasti and bruschetta, to linguine with a dozen fresh Little Neck clams, to the chicken Valdonstona, a breast sautéed and baked with prosciutto, mozzarella, and mushrooms, in a marsala wine sauce. | 5102 Rte. 9N, Bolton Landing | 518/644–5921 | Columbus Day–May 1 | $10–$18 | AE, D, MC, V.

Log Jam. Continental. This large and cheery restaurant resembles a log cabin. Known for beef, including three cuts of prime rib, onion soup, and barbecued wings. You'll also want to try the Adirondack fries. Salad bar. Kids' menu. | 1484 U.S. 9 | 518/798–1155 | $14–$30 | AE, D, DC, MC, V.

Mama Riso Italian Ristorante. Italian. The hearty, flavorful entrées served here are in direct contrast to the long, lean, and spare dining room in which they are served. Try the homemade linguine served with mussels, shrimp, clams, and squid in marinara sauce, the veal saltimbocca, or the chicken scarpariello served with sausage, olives, and peppers. All meat entrées come with a side of spaghetti or ziti, a salad or soup, and fresh warm bread. Kids' menu. | Rte. 9 at Lake George Rd. | 518/668–2550 | $9–$18 | AE, D, MC, V.

McGowan's Restaurant. American. After crossing the threshold beneath the striped awning of this red-brick, family-style restaurant you will be met with down-home favorites like hot turkey sandwiches, half-pound burgers, and a variety of grilled specialties. The early bird special may include prime rib, broiled scrod, grilled pork chops, or roasted turkey. Kids' menu. | 3721 Lake Shore Dr. | 518/668–4399 | Breakfast served. No dinner Sept.–May | $11–$18 | MC, V.

Montcalm South. Continental. This Adirondack log-cabin restaurant was named for the French General Marquis de Montcalm. There is a large fireplace in one of the three dining rooms. Try the crab cakes, the veal Oscar, or the New England shore dinner with lobster, steamed clams, shrimp, and corn on the cob. Kids' menu. | 1415 Rte. 9 | 518/793–6601 | $12–$30 | AE, D, DC, MC, V.

Lodging

Alpine Village. You can stay in the rustic main lodge or one of the log cabins at this resort right on Lake George with its own beach. Cable TV. Pool. Tennis. Beach, boating. Ice-skating. Playground. | 672 Lake Shore Dr. | 518/668–2193 | www.alpinelg.com | 15 rooms in main lodge, 24 rooms in cabins | $69–$125 lodge rooms, $72–$155 cabin rooms | Closed Dec.–May | AE, D, DC, MC, V.

Amber Lantern Motel. The only thing wrong with this peaceful setting amid dense trees is that there's no lake view. Adirondack-style cabins with knotty-pine interiors offer a privacy that keeps families returning year after year. There are also outdoor social activities, like picnics and barbecues. It's 3 mi from Interstate 87. Some rooms rent weekly. Pool. Playground. | 3601 Lake Shore Dr. | 518/668–4613 | www.lakegeorgenewyork.com/amber | 14 cabins | $45–$75 | Closed Columbus Day–Memorial Day | MC, V.

Best Western of Lake George. This two-story chain motel is decorated in the Adirondack style. You'll find it just 1 mi from the Lake George beaches. Some in-room hot tubs, cable TV. 2 pools, wading pool. Hot tub. Business services. | Exit 21, off I-87 | 518/668–5701 | fax 518/668–4926 | reservations@bestwesternlakegeorge.com | www.bestwesternlakegeorge.com | 87 rooms | $79–$199 | AE, D, DC, MC, V.

Briar Dell Motel. The Briar Dell, which has been run by the same family since 1948, sits up on a hill with cottages overlooking Lake George. Picnic tables are scattered among the shade of aged trees, and there are plenty of water and land activities, like Ping-Pong and horseshoes, to keep your family busy. All rooms have two double beds. It's ¹⁄₁₀ mi from Interstate 87, ³⁄₄ mi from Lake George. Basketball, volleyball, beach. | 3026 Lake Shore Dr. | 518/668–4819 | www.mediausa.com/ny/briardellmotel/ | 22 rooms | $52–$85 | Closed Oct.–May | D, MC, V.

Brookside Motel. The English Brook runs through this 3-acre property and evergreens surround the cabins and motel rooms, only ¹⁄₂ mi from the village of Lake George and the lake itself. Most rooms have two double beds. The Lake George Trolley stops at the driveway. Pool. Playground. | 604 Canada St. | 518/668–3344 or 800/438–6827 | fax 508/448–8942 | www.brooksidemotel.com | 26 rooms, 10 cabins | $59–$84 | Closed Columbus Day–early May | AE, D, MC, V.

Cedarbrook Motel. With the Adirondacks in the background, the town of Lake George a mile away, a pond in the back, and a spacious lawn, you're sure to enjoy Frisbee, picnics, and barbecues here. Rooms are built to feel like a homey cabin, with wood paneling and some fireplaces. Rooms and cottages rent weekly during the summer. Playground. | 3141 Lake Shore Dr. | 518/668–2886 | www.polskimotel.com/in_english.html | 5 rooms, 6 cottages | $69–$89, $169 cottages | Closed Oct.–May | AE, D, MC, V.

Cedarhurst Motel. A quarter mile from town and the lake, this family-owned and -operated horseshoe-shaped motel gets most of its business from families returning year after year. It's within walking distance of a park, and you can picnic, play shuffleboard, and swim on the wooded property. Rooms have either two double beds or a queen. Pool. Basketball. Playground. | 507 Canada St. | 518/668–5002 | 30 rooms | $53–$95 | Closed Oct.–May.

Colonial Manor Lake George Resort. A motel on 5 acres where the Lake George Trolley stops by to take you in to town. Accommodations range from motel rooms to cottages to kitchen suites. All rooms are carpeted and done in an Early American motif. Suites have wood panelled walls. Picnic area. Some kitchenettes, some refrigerators, cable TV. Pool, hot tub. Playground. | 2200 Rte. 9 | 518/668–4884 | www.colonialmanorlg.com/ | 35 rooms, 25 cottages | $82–$150 rooms, $82–$129 cottages | Closed mid-Oct.–mid-May | AE, D, MC, V.

Colonel Williams Motor Inn. The yellow clock tower rising above this family-oriented motel clearly identifies it. The grounds cover 10 acres. Picnic area. Microwaves, cable TV. Pool. Hot tub, sauna. Basketball, exercise equipment. Video games. Playground. | Rte. 9 | 518/668–5727 or 800/334–5727 | 45 rooms | $68–$120 | AE, D, MC, V.

Days Inn. Three miles south of Lake George Village is this two-story chain hotel near many outlet stores. The rooms have large windows. Children under 16 stay free. Take exit 20 off I-87. Restaurant, bar. Cable TV. Pool. Hot tub. Fishing. Business services, free parking. | 1454 U.S. 9 | 518/793–3196 or 800/274–7111 | fax 518/793–6028 | www.daysinn.com | 101 rooms, 3 suites | $126–$136 rooms, $70–$156 suites | AE, D, DC, MC, V.

LAKE GEORGE
VILLAGE

INTRO
ATTRACTIONS
DINING
LODGING

Dutchess. Just north of the village of Lake George is this pleasant motel only 5 to 10 min from Fort William Henry and the cruise ships on Lake George. Picnic area. Some kitchenettes, refrigerators, cable TV. Pool. Tennis. Playground. | Lake Shore Dr. (Rte. 9 N) | 518/668–5264 | 14 rooms, 1- or 2-story | $65–$80 | AE, D, MC, V.

Econo Lodge. A three-story chain motel 1 mi from Lake George Village, with views of Lake George and the surrounding mountains. Cable TV. 2 pools. Hot tub. Business services. No pets. | 431 Canada St. | 518/668–2689 | fax 518/798–3455. | www.econolodge.com | 50 rooms | $80–$123 | Closed Nov.–Apr. | AE, D, MC, V.

English Brook Cottages. On 3½ acres of wooded property, most cottages here have screened-in porches where you can relax after hiking on the nearby trails. Cottages range in size to accommodate two to eight people. Town is 1½ mi and Interstate 87 is 1 mi away. Pool. Basketball. Playground. | 2888 Stage Rte. 9 | 518/668–2434 | 14 cottages | $50–$125 | Closed mid-Oct.–May | AE, MC, V.

Fort William Henry Resort Hotel. This two-level hotel and conference center covers 18 acres overlooking the southern basin of Lake George. Restaurant, bar. Cable TV. 2 pools. Sauna. Miniature golf. Exercise equipment. Bicycles. Shops. Business services. | 48 Canada St. | 518/668–3081 or 800 800/221–9211 | fax 518/668–4926 | info@fortwilliamhenry.com | www.fortwilliamhenry.com | 99 rooms | $150–$179 | AE, D, DC, MC, V.

The Georgian. There is a private beach and a marina at this Lake George Village hotel, the largest in the area. Rooms have views of the lake, the pool, or the courtyard. Restaurant, bar, room service. Some refrigerators, cable TV. Pool. Business services, airport shuttle. | 384 Canada St. | 518/668–5401 or 800/525–3436 | fax 518/668–5870 | www.webny.com/georgian | 164 rooms | $64–$189 | AE, D, DC, MC, V.

Golden Sands Resort. The Adirondack Mountain view from the beach alone makes the trip worthwhile. Although you're 3½ mi from Lake George village (and on the trolley route), there is enough here to keep you and the kids entertained. All beds are queen-size. Adjoining rooms are available, and some rooms have private balconies. Complimentary Continental breakfast. Pool. Beach. | 3654 Lake Shore Dr. | 518/668–2203 | 26 rooms | $80–$140 | Closed Labor Day–Memorial Day | MC, V.

Holiday Inn. This two-story chain hotel is set back 200 ft from the road on a hill. Restaurant, bar, room service. Refrigerators, cable TV. 2 pools, wading pool. Miniature golf. Exercise equipment. Playground. Laundry facilities. Business services. | 2223 Canada St., off Rte. 9 | 518/668–5781 | fax 518/668–9213 | 105 rooms | $161–$210 | AE, D, DC, MC, V.

Howard Johnson. Live music and entertainment happens on weekends at this chain hotel 3 mi from Great Escape amusement park. Restaurant, bar (with entertainment), picnic area. Some kitchenettes, some in-room hot tubs, cable TV. 2 pools, wading pool. Exercise equipment. Business services. | 2 Canada St. | 518/668–5744 | fax 518/668–3544 | 110 rooms, 20 suites | $49–$140 rooms, $79–$200 suites | Closed Nov.–May | AE, D, DC, MC, V.

Lake Crest. This motel is on 1 acre right in the heart of Lake George Village. Cable TV. Pool. Beach. | 366 Canada St. | 518/668–3374 | fax 518/668–2273 | 40 rooms | $98–$189 | Closed mid-Oct.–mid-May | MC, V.

Lake George Boathouse Bed and Breakfast. Eight miles from Lake George Village, on Bolton Landing's Millionaire's row and directly on Lake George, is this grand, 1917 stone-and-wood boat house. Each of the individually appointed rooms has crisp white walls and most rooms have hardwood floors. Some rooms have private walk-out porches so you can bask in the glory of the lake. Complimentary breakfast. Cable TV, no room phones. Lake. Dock, water sports, boating, fishing. No pets. No kids under 12. | 44 Sagamore Rd., Bolton Landing | 518/644–2554 | fax 518/644–3065 | 4 rooms, 1 suite | Rooms, $125–$250; suite $325 | AE, MC, V.

Mohawk Motels and Cottages. You can get king-size beds at this motel in Lake George Village just across the street from a beach. The efficiency suites have living rooms and kitchens. Picnic area. Some kitchenettes, some in-room hot tubs, cable TV. Indoor-outdoor pool. Hot tub, spa. Volleyball. Playground. No pets. | 435 Canada St. | 518/668–2143 or 800–795–6680 | www.mohawkmotel.com | 62 rooms, 7 cottages | $49–$129 rooms, $135–$189 cottages | AE, D, MC, V.

Mohican Motel. This resort complex covers 15 acres. Rooms in the one-story motel are done up in floral fabrics. Restaurant, picnic area. Some kitchenettes, refrigerators, cable TV. 2 pools, 2 wading pools. Hot tub, sauna. Playground. Laundry facilities. | 1545 U.S. 9 | 518/792–0474 | 43 rooms | $42–$185 | AE, DC, MC, V.

Nordick's. This family-operated motel is within walking distance of the center of Lake George Village and has views of the mountains and the lake. Kids 16 under stay free. Restaurant. Refrigerators, cable TV. Pool. | 2895 Lake Shore Dr. | 518/668–2697 or 800/368–2697 | fax 518/668–4514 | info@nordicks.com | www.nordicks.com | 21 rooms | $44–$104 | Closed mid-Oct.–mid-Apr. | AE, D, MC, V.

Roaring Brook Ranch and Tennis Resort. This sprawling mountainside estate has spacious motel-style accommodations. You can go horseback riding or play tennis right on the property. Restaurant, 2 bars. Some kitchenettes, TV. 3 pools. Sauna. 5 tennis courts. Exercise equipment. Horseback riding. Children's programs (ages 4–7). Laundry facilities. Business services. | Rte. 9N S (Luzerne Rd.) | 518/668–5767, 800/882–7665 reservations | fax 518/648–4019 | www.roaringbrookranch.com | 142 rooms | $85–$123 | Closed mid-Oct.–mid-May | MAP | MC, V.

Still Bay. The expansive patio overlooks 300 ft of lakefront at this hotel. The rooms are paneled in wood and have walls of windows that open to let in the lake breezes. A private boathouse provides dock space for boats. Take exit 22 off I–87. Picnic area, complimentary Continental breakfast. Some kitchenettes, cable TV. Beach, dock, boating, fishing. | Lake Shore Dr. (Rte. 9N) | 518/668–2584; 800/521–7511 | stillbay@adrondaknet.com | www.stillbay.com | 22 rooms | $120–$135 (10% discount July–Aug., Sun.–Thurs.) | Closed mid-Oct.–Memorial Day | MC, V.

Sun Castle Villas. The villas have wood-burning stoves and rustic furnishings at this family-friendly resort. Outdoor activities are the main attraction here. The surrounding grounds are lush and inviting. Picnic areas. Kitchenettes, cable TV. Pool. Tennis. Beach, dock, boating. | Box 506, Rte. 9S | 518/668–2085, 518/745–7163 reservations | fax 518/792–3072 | 16 villas (1–2 bedrooms) | $800–$1,375 (7-day minimum stay) | Closed Nov.–Apr. | MC, V.

LAKE LUZERNE

MAP 3, K5

(Nearby towns also listed: Bolton Landing, Diamond Point, Glens Falls, Lake George Village, Queensbury, Saratoga Springs, Warrensburg)

This pleasant town was founded in 1792 under the name of Fairfield. Because of its location on the convergence of the Hudson and Sacandaga rivers, it was once a mill town. Today, tourism is the important industry, and you will find outdoor activities as well as music festivals. Luzerne has been known as part of the "Dude Ranch Trail" for its emphasis on riding stables and ranch-type resorts.

Information: **Chamber of Commerce** | 79 Main St., Box 222, 12846 | 518/696–3500.

Attractions
Bow Bridge. A relic of a type of bridge found throughout New York State in the late 19th century, the Bow Bridge was built in 1895 to cross both the Hudson and the Sacandaga rivers. Though the bridge is actually in nearby Hadley, you can see it from Lake Luzerne. | 518/644–3831 | Free | Daily.

ON THE CALENDAR

JULY: *Lake Luzerne Craft Fair.* Artists of many trades set up stands here and sell their goods, including jewelry, sculptures, paintings, and clothes. The library has a bake sale and book sale. Midmonth at the pavilion next to Wayside Beach. | 518/696–3423.

JULY–AUG.: *Painted Pony Rodeo.* Fill up on chicken, ribs, salad, and strawberry shortcake, then head down to the arena for some serious saddlebronc, bareback, and bull riding. You can also see calf roping and steer wrestling at this summer event, which is generally held three times weekly from July 4th through Labor Day. | 518/696–2421.

JULY–AUG.: *Summer Concerts.* You can hear blues, folk, country, or even choir music at these free summer concerts, which take place every Tuesday night at 7 at the open-air pavilion off Rte. 9N next to the lake. | 518/696–3500.

Dining

Ciro's. Italian. You can get pizza or a more substantial meal at this restaurant. Try the shrimp scampi, seafood marinara, or veal. Kids' menu. | 1439 Lake Ave. | 518/696–2556 | Closed Tues., Wed. Nov.–Mar. No lunch | $7–$14 | MC, V.

Defino's Heritage. Italian. A casual restaurant serving chicken, steak, seafood, and veal. Kids' menu. | 61 Northwood Rd. | 518/696–3733 | Closed Mon., Tues. and mid-Oct.–mid-May; closed Mon.–Thurs. mid-May–June and Labor Day–Columbus Day. No lunch | $7–$11 | MC, V.

Rustic Inn. Eclectic. This Adirondack-style building 5 mi from the village of Lake Luzerne has outdoor seating overlooking Forest Lake as well as a casual indoor dining room. The Italian-American fare includes entrées like veal and chicken parmesan, shrimp scampi, and simpler burgers, pizzas, and sandwiches. Full bar. Kids' menu. | 1338 Lake Ave. | 518/696–2318 | Closed Tues. | $9–$15 | MC, V.

Waterhouse. Continental. Broiled lobster tail, crab-stuffed shrimp, honey-dipped fried chicken, and roasted prime rib are on the menu at this restaurant also known for its Italian specialties. You can dine outside on the deck under umbrellaed tables. Kids' menu. | Rte. 9 | 518/696–3115 | $6–$26 | MC, V.

Lodging

Island View. This one-story motel overlooks the lake. Picnic area. Some kitchenettes, some refrigerators, cable TV. Beach, boating. | 302 Lake Ave. | 518/696–3079 | 10 rooms | $65–$75 | Closed Nov. 1–May 1 | AE, D, MC, V.

Kastner's Motel. Choose from views of Lake Vanare in a motel room, or cottages tucked away into towering maples. Guests return year after year, to enjoy water sports and picnics at this family-oriented resort. Within walking distance of a restaurant; 6 mi from Lake Luzerne. Water sports. Playground. | 188 Hidden Valley | 518/696–2715 | fax 518/696–4669 | 24 rooms and cabins | $50 cabins, $60 motel unit | Closed Oct.–May.

Lake Luzerne Motel. This motel is ½ mi from the village of Lake George and from Saratoga, has rooms with either pool or lake views, and is always full of activity—canoeing, fishing, horseshoes, and water sports being some options. About 90% of the guests have been here before, most of them families. Rooms have a knotty-pine interior and two double beds. Pool. Water sports. | 296 Lake Ave. | 518/696–3012 | www.lakeluzerne.motel | 11 rooms, 11 cottages | $65–$90 | Closed Nov.–Apr. | D, MC, V.

Lamplight Inn Bed and Breakfast. This Victorian inn on 10 acres was built in 1890 as a vacation home. It's just one block from the lake and the Hudson River. Restaurant, picnic area, complimentary breakfast. In-room hot tubs, cable TV, no room phones. Shops. Business services. No pets. No kids under 12. No smoking. | 231 Lake Ave. | 518/696–5294 or 800/262–4668 | fax 518/696–5256 | www.lamplightinn.com | 17 rooms, 5 suites | $110–$229 | AE, MC, V.

Pine Point Cottages. You can go swimming or take paddleboats out on the small, man-made lake in front of this one-story rustic motel. Picnic area. No air-conditioning in some rooms, some kitchenettes, cable TV. Beach. Boating, fishing. Playground. Airport shuttle. | 1369 Lake Ave. | 518/696–3015 | 8 rooms, 10 cottages | $59–$90 rooms, $385–$520 cottages (7–day minimum stay) | Closed Dec.–Mar. | MC, V.

Saratoga Rose Inn & Restaurant. A mile and a half northwest of Lake Luzerne, in nearby Hadley, lies this 1885 Queen Anne home, marked by a bright pink veranda and stunning gardens. Most rooms are done in Victorian motifs, except for the Adirondack room, which suggests a log cabin. All rooms have private baths. Your stay may include dinner. Restaurant, complimentary breakfast. Some in-room hot tubs, no room phones, TV in common room. Business services. No kids under 10. | 4274 Rockwell St., Hadley | 518/696–2861, 800/942–5025 reservations | www.saratogarose.com | mail@sratogarose.com | 6 rooms | $145–$175 | D, MC, V.

LAKE PLACID

(Nearby towns also listed: Keene Valley, Paul Smiths, Saranac Lake, Tupper Lake, Wilmington)

The village of Lake Placid doesn't actually sit on Lake Placid, but is instead on the shores of Mirror Lake, one of the most beautiful of all the Adirondack lakes. (Its namesake lake actually lies north of the village.) Because both the 1932 and 1980 Winter Olympics were held here, Lake Placid is one of the best-known towns in the Adirondacks. But it has been popular since the beginning of the 20th century when the rich and famous first discovered the area and came here to participate in winter sports.

Information: Essex County Visitors Bureau | Olympic Center, 216 Main St., 12946 | 518/523–2445 | www.lakeplacid.com.

Attractions

1932 & 1980 Lake Placid Winter Olympic Museum. A stop by the museum is a fitting way to begin your adventure at Olympic Village. The museum houses the history and legacy of the Olympic Games at Lake Placid with video highlights, uniforms and equipment, and medals. There are also specialty exhibits that change periodically. | 218 Main St. (at the Olympic Ice Center) | 518/523–1655 ext. 226 | www.orda.org/olympic.shtml | $4 | Daily 10–5.

1932 Olympic Rink. This 1,300-person capacity indoor rink was used in the first winter Olympic games in 1932. There is also an outdoor rink. | 218 Main St. | 518/523–1655 ext. 295 | www.orda.org/olympic.shtml | $5 | Dec.–Mar. (depending on weather conditions); call for hours.

John Brown Farm State Historic Site. The passionate abolitionist John Brown lived for a short time on this 244-acre farm. On October 16, 1859, Brown and his followers attempted to spark a slave revolt by taking over the federal arsenal at Harper's Ferry, West Virginia. His two sons and several of his followers were killed, and Brown was tried and executed. His body was brought back and buried here. There are self-guided tours of the farm, a cross-country ski trail, a nature trail, and a picnic area. | 2 John Brown Rd., off Rte. 73 | 518/523–3900 | Free | Nov.–Apr., Wed.–Sat. 10–5; May–Oct., Wed.–Sat. 10–5, Sun. 1–5.

Lake Placid Center For the Arts. Classic films are shown and theater, dance, and music performances are put on here at the largest arts center in the Adirondack region. | 91 Saranac Ave. | 518/523–2512 | lpca@northnet.org | www.lpartscenter.org | $5 for movies; prices vary for other events | July–Aug., Tues.–Sun. 10–5; Sept.–June, Tues.–Sat. 1–5.

Sheffield Speed Skating Oval. You can skate on the oval on which Eric Heiden won his five Olympic golds during the 1980 winter games. | 218 Main St. | 518/523–1655 ext. 253 | www.orda.org/olympic.shtml | $5 | Dec.–March.

Lake Placid Marina Inc. During the 16-mi cruise on Mirror Lake, you'll pass many of the great camps that line the shore. | Mirror Lake Dr., off Rte. 86 | 518/523–9704 | $7.25 | Daily 10:30, 1, 2:30, 4.

Olympic Arena and Convention Center. You can skate or cross-country ski at this center originally built for the 1932 Olympics, and renovated for the 1980 Olympics. There is a museum with exhibits on the property. | 218 Main St. | 518/523–1655 or 800/462–6236 | info@orda.org | www.orda.org | Free | Daily 10–5.

Olympic Sports Complex (Mt. Van Hoevenberg Recreation Area). During the 1980 Olympics, this was the site of the luge, bobsled, cross-country skiing, and biathlon events. If you are here in winter months, you can try a bobsled on wheels, regular bobsled, or a luge. A trolley tour and mountain-biking (with bike rentals) are also offered. | Off Rte. 73 | 518/523–1655 | Bobsled $30, trolley $4 | Call for hrs.

Uihlein Sugar Maple Research–Extension Field Station. An exhibit here explains how maple syrup is made. | 60 Bear Cub Rd. | 518/523–9337 | Free | July–Labor Day, Tues.–Fri. 1–5; mid-Sept.–mid-Oct., Fri. 1–5; late Mar.–Apr., daily 8–5.

Dining

Averill Conwell Dining Room. Continental. Many of Averill Conwell's paintings are hung in this formal, Victorian dining room in the Mirror Lake Inn. Rack of lamb, pan-seared venison, and scallops are popular dishes. You can also eat in a screened-in porch. A pianist plays on weekends. Kids' menu. No smoking. | 5 Mirror Lake Dr. | 518/523–2544 | Breakfast also available. No lunch | $25–$45 | AE, D, DC, MC, V.

Downhill Grill. American. Once you pass the ski jumps in town, you will come to a Western-style building with a two-tiered porch. Inside the paradoxically themed Mexican and ski restaurant you can try various Mexican-American standards like fajitas, enchiladas, or burritos. The drunken salmon in a red wine and chipotle sauce is oft-ordered, and, in line with the eclectic character of this eatery, the fish-and-chips are equally popular. | 434 Main St. | 518/523–9510 | $11–$12 | D, DC, MC, V.

Lake Placid Lodge. Contemporary. Whether you eat on the porch or dine inside by candlelight, you'll have views of the lake and high peaks at this restaurant that was once part of a great camp. Try the roast quail stuffed with pheasant and black-truffle mousse. | Whiteface Inn Rd. | 518/523–2700 | Breakfast also available | $30–$40 | AE, MC, V.

Le Bistro Laliberté. French. This downtown restaurant overlooking the lake serves steak au poivre, crab cakes, and Chilean sea bass. Open-air dining on a covered deck. Kids' menu. | 51 Main St. | 518/523–3680 | Closed Mon. and Tues. in Nov. and Apr. No lunch Oct.–May | $20–$30 | MC, V.

Thirsty Moose. American. At this restaurant in a commercial area near the Olympic Arena, you can order from a diverse menu. Popular dishes include chicken and pasta salad, fresh fish, ribs, sandwiches, and wraps. | 219 Maine St. | 518/523–3222 | Breakfast also available Jan.–Presidents' Day weekend and July–Columbus Day weekend | $15–$20 | AE, MC, V.

Lodging

Adirondack Inn by the Lake. Mirror Lake beach is just a few feet from this one-story building across from the Olympic Arena downtown. Restaurant, bar. Refrigerators, cable TV. 2 pools. Hot tub, sauna. Playground. Business services. | 217 Main St. | 518/523–2424 or 800/556–2424 | fax 518/523–2425 | adkinn@cencom.net | www.lakeplacid.com/adkinn | 49 rooms | $110–$149 | AE, DC, MC, V.

Adirondack Loj. Five miles south of Lake Placid is this campground that was built in 1927. There are tent sites as well as private rooms and a co-ed sleeping loft. The main room has a stone fireplace and homemade breads and soups are served in the dining area. Picnic area. Complimentary breakfast. Library. | Adirondack Lodge Rd. | 518/523–3441 | fax 518–523–

3518 | adkinfo@northnet.org | www.adk.org | 9 rooms, 34 tent sites, 16 shelter sites (lean-tos) | $32–$52 rooms, $18 tents, $21 shelters ($2–$2.50 charge for each additional person in tent and shelter units), $41 per person in 4- to 6-person bunk | AE, D, MC, V.

Alpine Air. All of the rooms at this motel in a commercial area have mountain views and exterior entrances. Picnic area. Cable TV. Pool. | 99 Saranac Ave. | 518/523–9261 or 800/469–3663 | fax 518/523–9273 | 24 rooms (6 with shower only) | $55–$150 | D, MC, V.

Alpine Motor Inn. This motel is on the edge of Lake Placid, near the first green of the Lake Placid Golf Club. Restaurant, bar. Some refrigerators, cable TV. Pool. | 50 Wilmington Rd. | 518/523–2180 or 800/257–4638 | fax 518/523–1724 | 18 rooms | $52–$78 | AE, D, DC, MC, V.

Art Devlin's Olympic. This hotel, named for the famous ski jumper, is three blocks from the Olympic Sports Complex. Complimentary Continental breakfast. Some in-room hot tubs, refrigerators, cable TV. Pool, wading pool. Airport shuttle. Pets allowed. | 350 Main St. | 518/523–3700 | 40 rooms | $48–$128 | AE, D, MC, V.

Best Western Golden Arrow. Rooms have two extra-long double beds at this chain hotel on the lake side of Main Street in the heart of the village. Sliding glass doors open onto private balconies or terraces. Restaurant, bar (with entertainment), picnic area, room service. In-room data ports, in room safes, refrigerators, cable TV. Pool, wading pool. Hot tub, sauna. Gym, racquetball. Boating. Shops. Baby-sitting. Business services, airport shuttle. Pets allowed (fee). | 150 Main St. | 518/523–3353 | fax 518/523–3353 | info@golden-arrow.com | www.golden-arrow.com | 130 rooms | $79–$159 | AE, D, DC, MC, V.

Econo Lodge. This chain motel is 1 mi from town. You'll find queen- and king-sized beds in the standard, comfortable rooms here. Picnic area. Cable TV. Pool. Hot tub. Video games. Laundry facilities. Business services. | Cascade Rd., between downtown and the ski jump complex | 518/523–2817 | 61 rooms | $80–$100 | AE, D, DC, MC, V.

Hilton–Lake Placid Resort. Some of the rooms have balconies overlooking the private waterfront at this three-building complex right in the center of the village. Complimentary rowboats and paddleboats are available if you would like to go out on the lake. Restaurant, bar (with entertainment), room service. Cable TV. 4 pools. Hot tub. Tennis. Gym. Beach, boating, fishing. Video games. Business services. | 1 Mirror Lake Dr. | 518/523–4411 or 800/755–5598 | fax 518/523–1120 | info@lphilton.com | www.lphilton.com | 179 rooms | $149–$169 | AE, D, DC, MC, V.

Howard Johnson. This hotel is made up of four buildings and lies ½ mi west of downtown. Restaurant, bar, picnic area. Cable TV. Pool. Hot tub. Tennis. Cross-country skiing. Pets allowed. | 90 Saranac Ave. | 518/523–9555 | fax 518/523–4765 | 92 rooms | $110–$180 | AE, D, DC, MC, V.

Interlaken. Chef/owner Kevin Gregg will treat you to a Victorian getaway with individually appointed rooms, and a five-course gourmet dinner. The honeymoon suite has a canopy bed and the dining room is panelled in walnut with original tin ceilings. Some rooms overlook the Adirondacks and some overlook the Interlaken's lush gardens. Restaurant, picnic area, complimentary breakfast. No air-conditioning, cable TV, no room phones. Some pets allowed. No kids under 5. | 15 Interlaken Ave. | 518/523–3180 or 800/428–4369 | fax 518/523–0117 | www.inbook.com | interlkn@northnet.org | 11 rooms | $140–$210 | AE, MC, V.

★ **Lake Placid Lodge.** Each of the unique rooms has a stone fireplace and rustic furniture made from twigs and birch bark at this lodge on 3 acres of land right on Lake Placid. Free-standing cabins are also available. Restaurant, bar, picnic area, complimentary breakfast. No air-conditioning in some rooms, in-room data ports, some refrigerators. Business services. Pets allowed (fee). No smoking. | Whiteface Inn Rd., off Rte. 86 | 518/523–2700 | fax 518/523–1124 | www.lakeplacidlodge.com | 17 rooms (5 with shower only), 17 cottages | Rooms $300–$600, cabins $475–$800 | AE, MC, V.

Lake Placid Resort–Holiday Inn. This four-story hotel sits on a hilltop in the center of Lake Placid overlooking Mirror Lake. The more than 1,000 acres of grounds include 45 holes of golf, including both a links and a mountain golf course. In addition to standard rooms, there are chalets, lakeside condominiums, and special rooms with hot tubs and fireplaces available. 4 restaurants, bar, room service. In-room data ports, microwaves, refrigerators, some in-room hot tubs, cable TV. Pool. Hot tub, sauna. 2 golf courses, putting green, tennis. Gym. Beach. Playground. Business services. Pets allowed. | 1 Olympic Dr. | 518/523–2556, 800/874–1980 | fax 518/523–9410. | info@lpresort.com | www.lpresort.com | 199 rooms | $109–$249 | AE, D, DC, MC, V.

Mirror Lake Inn Resort and Spa. Five buildings make up this inn/resort on 8 acres. The rooms have mahogany woodwork, polished walnut floors, and antique furniture. There is a private outdoor ice-skating rink and a 60-ft lap pool with a waterfall and panoramic view of the lake and mountains. Restaurant (see Averill Conwell Dining Room), bar, room service. Refrigerators, cable TV. Pool. Beauty salon, sauna. Tennis. Gym. Beach, boating. Ice-skating. Business services, free parking. | 5 Mirror Lake Dr. | 518/523–2544 | fax 518/523–2871 | info@mirrorlakeinn.com | www.mirrorlakeinn.com | 127 rooms | $160–$285 | AE, D, DC, MC, V.

Mountain View Inn. Rooms at this family-owned and -operated inn have private balconies and views of the lake and the mountains. Cottages are available from June through August. Complimentary coffee. Some microwaves, refrigerators, cable TV. | 140 Main St. | 518/523–2439 or 800/499–2668 | info@lakeplacidlodging.com. | www.lakeplacidlodging.com | 18 rooms | $68–$95 | Closed weekdays Nov.–Jan. | AE, MC, V.

Northway Motel. This two-story motel off Route 86 is within walking distance of the village. No air-conditioning, cable TV. Pool. | 5 Wilmington Rd. | 518/523–3500 or 800/479–2135 | nmotel@aol.com | 14 rooms | $70–$90 | AE, D, MC, V.

Placid Bay Inn. This two-story inn on Lake Placid is decorated with artwork and photographs made by local artists. In addition to the rooms, there are suites and cottages available. The cottages have kitchens, living rooms, two or three bedrooms, and porches facing the lake. You can go canoeing or take a paddleboat out on the lake. Guide services for fishing and hunting are available. Picnic area. Some kitchenettes, cable TV. Pool. Boating, fishing. Cross-country skiing. Playground. | 70 Saranac Ave. | 518/523–2001 | fax 518/523–2001 | reservations@placidbay.com | www.placidbay.com | 19 rooms, 2 cottages | $90–$180 rooms, $150–$200 cottages | AE, D, MC, V.

Ramada Inn. Many of the rooms at this three-story chain motel just off Main Street have views of the lake and mountains. Restaurant, bar. In-room data ports, cable TV. Pool. Hot tub. Exercise equipment. Business services. Some pets allowed. | 12 Saranac Ave. | 518/523–2587 | fax 518/523–2328 | www.ramadalp.com/ | 90 rooms | $75–$119 | AE, D, DC, MC, V.

Schulte's Family Lodge. The photographs on the walls of this motel's coffee shop were taken by Mr. Schulte, co-owner of the motel and an accomplished photographer. From December to March, the motel serves complimentary pastries. Picnic area. Kitchenettes (in cottages), some refrigerators, cable TV, some room phones. Pool. Playground. Some pets allowed. | Cascade Rd. (Rte. 73), near the airport | 518/523–3532 | 15 rooms, 15 cottages | $58–$92 rooms, $48–$95 cottages | AE, MC, V.

Town and Country. This two-story motel is just off Main Street There are also a cottage and an apartment available. Picnic area, complimentary Continental breakfast. Some kitchenettes, refrigerators, cable TV. Pool. Bicycles. | 67 Saranac Ave. | 518/523–9268 or 888/523–6640 | fax 518/523–8058 | info@tcmotorinn.com | www.tcmotorinn.com | 26 rooms | $62–$160 | AE, D, MC, V.

Wildwood. Balconies overlook the lake and mountains at this motel. One of the pools is fed by a natural spring and there are canoes, paddleboats, and rowboats available for use on the lake. Alpine lodge. Picnic area. Kitchenettes (in cottages), refrigerators, some in-room hot tubs, cable TV. 2 pools, wading pool. Hot tub, sauna. Beach, boating. Playground. | 88 Saranac Ave. | 518/523–2624 or 800/841–6378 | fax 518/523–3248 | wildwoodlp@aol.com | www.wildwoodmotel.com | 35 rooms, 6 cottages | $58–$130 rooms, $78–$165 cottages | AE, D, DC, MC, V.

LIBERTY

(Nearby towns also listed: Monticello, Roscoe)

In the pine-clad foothills at the southern edge of the Catskill Mountains is the quiet historic community of Liberty. Thick hilly forests, migrating eagles, and renowned fly-fishing streams teeming with trout attract city dwellers to the town of Liberty, roughly in the center of Sullivan County, a 90-min drive from Manhattan. Sullivan County's lake region stretches to the north of town. The great outdoors is the main attraction here.

Information: **Liberty Chamber of Commerce** | Box 147, 12754 | 845/292–1878 | www.libertyshops.com.

Attractions
New York State Catskill Fish Hatchery. The half-million trout that are raised here each year help stock the state's rivers and lakes. | 402 Fish Hatchery Rd. | 845/439–4328 | Free | Weekdays 8:30–4, weekends 8–noon.

ON THE CALENDAR
MAY: *Kite Festival.* Hundreds of kites from simple children's kites to elaborate professional masterpieces paint the sky with color at Sullivan County Community College in Loch Sheldrake, 8 mi east on Route 52. | 845/434–5750 ext. 4458.

Dining
Piccolo Paese. Italian. Known for its homemade pasta, this eatery specializes in northern Italian cuisine. An elegant wine rack and intimate surroundings make this a romantic spot. Try the stuffed pasta with meat or cheese. | 5 State Rte. 52 E | 845/292–7210 | Reservations essential weekends | No lunch weekends | $16–$24 | AE, D, MC, V.

Lodging
Budget Inn. This two-story motel, off exit 100A on Interstate 17 W, is three blocks from several eateries. Cable TV. No pets. | 2 Oberferst St. | 845/292–6620 | fax 845/292–6620 | 30 rooms | $40–$65 | AE, D, MC, V.

Days Inn of Liberty. This renovated, brick, two-story motel built in the early 1990s is along a commercial strip surrounded by restaurants and one block from Route 17 and 1 mi from golf. Rooms are furnished with burgundy floral fabrics, dark wood, framed prints, and brass light fixtures. Bar, complimentary Continental breakfast. Cable TV. Pool. Video games. Laundry service. Business services. Pets allowed. | 25 Sullivan Ave. | 845/292–7600 | fax 845/292–3303 | www.daysinn.com | 120 rooms | $45–$95 | AE, D, DC, MC, V.

LIVERPOOL

(Nearby towns also listed: Auburn, Canastota, Cazenovia, Fulton, Rome, Skaneateles, Syracuse)

This community on the north side of Syracuse lies along Oneida Lake and is reached from Interstates 90 and 81. Liverpool is home to the Salt Museum and Ste. Marie Among the Iroquois Museum and near Onondaga Lake Park, where a holiday light display is presented for several weeks each winter season.

Information: **Greater Liverpool Chamber of Commerce** | Box 154, 13088 | 315/457–3895.

Attractions

Onondaga Lake Park. The 3-mi-long park includes trails, museums, and a concession stand. During the winter holiday season, you can view "Lights on the Lake," a 2-mi-long drive-through light display that depicts traditional holiday themes and characters. | 106 Lake Dr. | 315/453–6712 or 315/451–7275 | Free | Daily.

Ste. Marie Among the Iroquois Museum This museum recreates a 1657 Jesuit mission and Iroquois roundhouse. Special weekend programs feature costumed interpreters who portray the life and times of the historic mission. | Rte. 370 | 315/453–6767 | $3.50 | May–Dec., Wed.–Sun. noon–7.

Salt Museum. The museum occupies a reconstructed 1800s salt factory. | 1 Onondaga Lake Pkwy. | 315/453–6715 | Free | May–mid-Oct., Tues.–Sun. 11–8.

ON THE CALENDAR

NOV.–JAN.: *Lights on the Lake.* Bring the kids for this 2-mi drive through an illuminated Onondaga Lake Park. They'll love the 50-ft lighting displays with holiday and fairy-tale themes. | Onondaga Lake Park off Rte. 370 | 315/451–7275.

Dining

Christos Restaurant. Greek. Images of the Greek landscape adorn the walls of this casual spot. Gyros, moussaka, and souvlaki are menu staples. The 26-ounce porterhouse steaks also draw customers. Kids' menu | 7608 Oswego Rd. | 315/622–9402 | Breakfast also available weekends | $9–$13 | AE, D, MC, V.

Lodging

Holiday Inn Syracuse/Liverpool. This six-story hotel is just 7 mi from Hancock International Airport in Syracuse and 10 mi from downtown Syracuse. Even closer is Onondaga Lake Park, which is just 1 mi away. Restaurant. In-room data ports. Cable TV. Pool. Hot tub, sauna. Exercise equipment. Laundry services. Business services, airport shuttle. Some pets allowed. | 441 Electronics Pkwy. | 315/457–1122 | fax 315/451–0675 | www.holiday-inn.com | 276 rooms | $150 | AE, D, DC, MC, V.

LOCKPORT

MAP 3, C5

(Nearby towns also listed: Albion, Amherst, Batavia, Grand Island, Medina, Niagara Falls, Williamsville)

As the name suggests, Lockport is a town with a series of five historic operating locks along the Erie Canal. The community is 20 mi northeast of Buffalo. The busy lock system still operates in much the same manner as it did nearly a century ago. The historic district downtown surrounds the canal and locks and you can watch boats move along the canal as huge metal doors control the 50-ft rise and fall of water. Downtown, museums and historic sites trace the heritage of the canal and lock system and the town that grew up around the important waterway.

Information: **Eastern Niagara Chamber of Commerce** | 151 W. Genesee St., 14094 | 800/433–4660 or 716/433–3828 | www.eastniagarany.org.

Attractions

Colonel William Bond House. This 1824 brick house has 12 rooms with pre-Victorian period furnishings and is listed on the National Register of Historic Places. | 143 Ontario St. | 716/434–7433 or 716/434–4795 | Free | Apr.–Dec., Thurs., Sat., Sun. 1–5.

Historic Canal District. This downtown historic district surrounds the canal and lock system and is home to museums, historic homes, shops, and restaurants. Locks 34 and 35 can be viewed from the Big Bridge and Pine Street Bridge. You can also see the upside-down bridge, one of the world's widest bridges, and take a canal tour aboard a sightseeing boat. | North of Main St. downtown via Rtes. 31 and 78 | 716/433–3828 | Free | Daily.

Kenan Center. This Victorian mansion has formal gardens, monthly art exhibits, educational programs, an arena offering sports activities and recreation, and a converted carriage house that presents live musical and theater performances. | 433 Locust St. | 716/433–2617 | Free | Daily 2–5.

Lockport Locks and Erie Canal Cruises. Narrated sightseeing tours cruise the "Grand Old Erie" canal, viewing historic buildings and passing through five of the original 1825 locks. | 210 Market St. | 800/378–0352 or 716/433–6155 | fax 716/433–3679 | $11.50 | Daily 10, 12:30, 3, 7.

Niagara County Historical Society. A diverse collection of artifacts relating to Niagara County history is housed in five buildings. | 215 Niagara St. | 716/434–7433 | Donations accepted | May–Dec., Thurs.–Sun. 1–5; Jan.–Apr., Wed.–Sat. 1–5.

ON THE CALENDAR

JUNE: *Niagara County Strawberry Festival and Carnival.* Includes delectable desserts, arts and crafts, music, and more at the Niagara County Fairgrounds. | 716/434–0939.

JUNE: *Niagara Frontier Art Exhibit.* The Kenan Center presents the juried exhibit of paintings, sculpture, and photography by artists from western New York and southern Ontario, Canada. | 716/433–2617.

JUNE–SEPT.: *Classic Cars Cruise Nights.* Classic and vintage collector cars are on display and deejays play popular musical hits from the 1950s to 1970s on Main Street in Olcott Beach. | 716/778–5537.

Dining

Fieldstone Country Inn. American. This casual restaurant is housed in a stone building with a beamed ceiling and rustic furnishings. Barbecued ribs, steak, and all other entrées include the soup and salad bar. The fall Harvest Platter features roast turkey, stuffing, and all the trimmings. | 5986 S. Transit Rd. | 716/625–6193 | $6–$15 | AE, D, DC, MC, V.

Garlock's. American. This restaurant which sits along the Erie Canal occupies a building that was constructed in 1821 to house canal workers. It's furnished with antiques and collectibles. Kids' menu. | 35 S. Transit St. | 716/433–5595 | No lunch | $10–$25 | AE, D, MC, V.

Village Eatery. Italian. This casual eatery is reminiscent of an Italian bistro café and serves fresh-baked pizza, Italian sandwiches, cappuccino, espresso, and a dessert bar. No smoking. | 429 Davison Rd. | 716/433–0688 | Reservations not accepted | Closed Oct.–Apr. No lunch Sun. | $7–$13 | AE, D, MC, V.

Lodging

Best Western Lockport Inn. This two-story hotel is just 1 mi from historic locks on the Barge Canal and 15 mi from Buffalo International Airport. If you stay in the executive rooms, you'll get a complimentary Continental breakfast. Restaurant, bar. Cable TV. Pool. Sauna. Pets allowed (fee). | 515 S. Transit St. | 716/434–6151 | fax 716/434–5117 | www.bestwestern.com | 95 rooms | $89–$99 | AE, D, DC, MC, V.

Lockport Motel. Rooms at this redbrick, Colonial-style motel are furnished with traditional cherry furniture and a restaurant is nearby. In-room data ports, microwaves, refrigerators, in-room hot tubs. Cable TV. Pool. Business services. | 315 S. Transit St. | 716/434–5595 | fax 716/433–0105 | 59 rooms, 6 suites | $62 rooms, $119–$160 suites | AE, D, DC, MC, V.

LONG BEACH

MAP 4, G8

(Nearby towns also listed: Freeport, Long Beach, Rockville Centre)

Aptly named for its 5-mi-long stretch of pristine, white sandy beach, Long Beach was originally established as a summer resort community in the 1870s. It's still a popular vacation spot and teems with restaurants, nightlife, and shops. The year-round population is 35,000, but in summer the community swells to 50,000.

The focal point of town is the popular 2-mi boardwalk constructed in the early 1900s with the help of elephants from Coney Island's "Dreamland." The pachyderms pulled materials for the boardwalk's pilings along what is known today as Sunrise Highway.

Information: Long Beach Chamber of Commerce | 350 National Blvd., 11561 | 516/432–6000 | www.antonnews.com/communities/longbeach.

Attractions

Boardwalk. Overlooking a beautiful stretch of beach along the Atlantic Ocean, the 2-mi boardwalk is the heartbeat of the community, where you can enjoy live music throughout the summer. On weekends, vendors and entertainers attract lively crowds. | Between New York Ave. and Neptune Blvd. | 516/431–3890 | Free | Daily.

Ocean Beach Park. Stretching for 5 mi along the south end of the island, sun worshipers throng the beach park and play volleyball, surf, swim, and sunbathe—all under the watchful eyes of city lifeguards. Activities include children's playground programs and summer baseball. The city publishes a surfing schedule and provides safety guidelines for use of body boards, and there's an indoor pool at the park. | Magnolia St. at the bay. Entrance between Nevada Ave. and Maple Blvd. | 516/431–1021, 516/431–5533, or 516/431–1810 (summer) | www.longislandnet.com/longbeach | $3 | Daily 9–6.

Rock Hall Museum. Built in 1767 by Josiah Martin, a wealthy West Indian planter, this Georgian Colonial manor was the Hewlett family home for 125 years. The home is now a museum and furnished with period furniture and antiques. | 199 Broadway, Lawrence | 516/239–1157 | fax 516/239–9436 | Free | Wed.–Sat. 10–4, Sun. 12–4.

ON THE CALENDAR

JULY: *Antiques Show.* Fine antiques and vintage collectibles are showcased at this popular annual event held outdoors on Kennedy Plaza across from the City Hall. | 516/261–4590.

JULY: *Arts and Crafts Festival.* This popular event features over 200 artists and crafters, ethnic food, and music along the boardwalk. | 516/431–3890.

Dining

Baja California Grill. Contemporary. This casual and upbeat restaurant is furnished with bright colors and tropical motifs and features patio dining in summer. Music is also the draw here. The owner entertains diners with recorded music that's selected from his personal collection of 3,000 CDs. Popular menu selections include shrimp cocktail, margaritas (10 kinds), and chips with homemade salsa. You can also choose from a variety of chicken wings, including Iguana (very hot with green chile pepper sauce), Buffalo-style, and Shogun (Chinese style) wings. Kids' menu. | 1032 W. Beach St. | 516/889–5992 | $12–$25 | DC, MC, V.

Coyote Grill. Southwestern. Inventive cuisine features crab cakes, lamb-chop dinners, sesame-crusted tuna, and grilled rib-eye cowboy steak served in a Southwestern-style restaurant with adobe walls, tile floors, Native American artifacts, and a dramatic two-sided fireplace that stretches to the ceiling. There's live music in summer and dining on the outdoor deck which overlooks a water channel and bridge. Kids' menu. Sunday brunch. Dock space. | 104 Waterview Rd., Island Park | 516/889–8009 | $16–$23 | AE, MC, V.

Duke Falcon's Global Grill. Eclectic. This restaurant is cozy and intimate with a New York City style and furnished with memorabilia from around the world. The menu features a range of cuisines from nouvelle American to Argentinian and popular dishes include Chilean sea bass and Argentine gaucho steak. There's sidewalk café–style dining in summer. Beer and wine available. No smoking. | 36 W. Park Ave. | 516/897–7000 | $17–$26 | AE, D, DC, MC, V.

Jimmy Hays Filet Mignon. Continental. Relaxed, fun, and lively, this restaurant has upscale furnishings with linen tablecloths. Popular dishes include Black Angus rib-eye steak served over sliced potatoes with spinach florentine, lobster Jimmy (pan-sautéed lobster with lemon, butter, and garlic), chocolate mousse, peach melba, and crème brûlée. You'll find the restaurant on the boardwalk in the Island Park area. | 4310 Austin Blvd., Island Park | 516/432–5155 | No lunch | $30–$40 | AE, D, DC, MC, V.

Kitchen off Pine Street. Eclectic. A unique restaurant with eclectic furnishings that change with the seasons and holidays also hangs works by local artists. You can feast on roasted rack of lamb with ancho chile mashed potatoes and Mexican bean salsa, grilled yellow-fin tuna, and bananas Foster, and also enjoy patio dining in summer. No smoking. | 670 Long Beach Rd. | 516/431–0033 | Reservations essential Sat. | Closed Sun.–Tues. No lunch | $38 prix fixe | AE, DC, MC, V.

Paddy McGee's. Seafood. This restaurant has an old New England classical look with wood beams and old-time photos of the Fulton Fish Market and fishermen. It's known for crab cakes, swordfish, tuna, salmon, large lobsters (call to request special-size orders), and Feast of the Sea, which is a dinner of clams, oysters, mussels, and shrimp. During summer, you can dine outdoors. Kids' menu. Sunday brunch buffet. Dock space. | Barnum Island Wharf, Island Park | 516/431–8700 | Closed Mon.–Wed. Nov.–Mar. | $8–$40 | AE, MC, V.

Lodging

Plantation Motel. Just 2 mi from Long Beach, this two-story motel is in a quiet, residential neighborhood. Several restaurants are within walking distance. Cable TV. No pets. | 4040 Long Beach Rd., Island Park | 516/432–6330 | fax 516/432–6330 | 40 rooms | $85 | No credit cards.

LONG LAKE

MAP 3, J4

(Nearby towns also listed: Blue Mountain Lake, Tupper Lake)

The community is named after Long Lake which is not a true lake but rather a 14-mi-wide section of the Raquette River. It's well known for canoeing, kayaking, and other outdoor sports and for its seaplane service, which is the oldest continuously operating seaplane operation in the Adirondacks. Nearby is Buttermilk Falls and hiking trails lead to the summit of Mount Sabattis.

Information: Town Office Building | Box 496, 12847 | 518/624–3077.

Attractions

Buttermilk Falls. If you're in the area, these beautiful falls are a must-see. Those canoeing down the river will have to pick up the canoe and carry it across 2 ½ mi of shallow water. | 2.1 mi from Rte. 28 north and Rte. 30, on N. Point Rd. | 518/624–3077 | Free | Daily.

ON THE CALENDAR

APR.: *Spring Blossom Fiddle Jamboree.* The whole family will love this event, whether you have an aspiring fiddle player in your clan or just enjoy its down-home sound. Fiddlers from all over the Northeast participate, and there is a featured fiddler. | Long Lake Town Hall, on Rte. 30 | Last Sun. in Apr. | 518/624–3077.

Dining

Island Snack Bar. Fast Food. Dine among the works of local artists in this gallery/eatery, and enjoy a view of Long Lake. Savor a good old-fashioned burger or a delicious chef's salad. | 3 Lake St. | 518/624–2160 | Breakfast also available; no dinner | $3–$6 | No credit cards.

Long View Lodge Restaurant. American. A casual eatery with a view of Long Lake awaits diners here. Try the oven-baked sea scallops or the balsamic-roasted chicken. Kids' menu. | Deerland Rd. | 518/624–3941 | Breakfast also available June–Aug.; no lunch | $11–$20 | D, MC, V.

Lodging

Adirondack Hotel. The last of the original Adirondack 1800s hostelries, this hotel features Victorian-style furnishings with antique beds and furniture. The hotel is known for its reasonable prices and its restaurant, which serves prime rib. Restaurant, bar. No room phones, no TV. No smoking. | Rte. 30 | 518/624–4700 or 800/877–9247 | 18 rooms | $25–$75 | AE, D, MC, V.

Corner Motel. In a residential neighborhood southwest of Long Lake, this single-story motel is just a short jaunt on foot to the lake and a number of eateries. No air-conditioning, refrigerators. Cable TV. Pets allowed. | Rtes. 28 N/30 | 518/624–3571 | fax 518/624–2344 | 6 rooms | $53 | AE, D, MC, V.

Long Lake Motel. All rooms and cottages at this modern small complex feature screened-in patios. Picnic area. No air-conditioning, some kitchenettes, cable TV. Beach. | Rte. 30 | 518/624–2613 | fax 518/624–2576 | jimbriale@aol.com | 8 rooms, 9 cottages | $70–$95 rooms, $500–$950 cottages (7–night minimum stay) | Closed mid-Oct.–mid-May | AE, MC, V.

Sandy Point Motel. A deluxe small lakefront motel with efficiencies that feature screened-in porches and balconies overlooking the lake. No air-conditioning, some kitchenettes, cable TV. Sauna. Beach, dock, boating. | Rte. 30 | 518/624–3871 | 11 rooms | $50–$90 | www.sandy-pointmotel.com | Closed mid-Oct.–mid-May | AE, D, MC, V.

Shamrock Motel and Cottages. This complex, a short walk from several restaurants, includes cottages that rent weekly, efficiency rooms suitable for two, with a required three-night stay, as well as hotel rooms. Each of the cottages has an enclosed porch with views of Long Lake. No air-conditioning, some kitchenettes, refrigerators. Cable TV. Beach, dock, water sports, boating, fishing. Laundry facilities. No pets allowed. | Deerland Rd. | Closed Oct.–May | 518/624–3861 | fax 518/624–9803 | 8 rooms, 11 cottages | $65 rooms, $600 per week for cottages | AE, D, MC, V.

MAHOPAC

MAP 3, C1

(Nearby towns also listed: Brewster, Carmel/Lake Carmel, North Salem)

Some 8,000 residents enjoy the spectacular scenery and historic traditions of this rural Putnam County village near the Taconic State Parkway. Farms, country stores, and other landmarks dot the landscape in this area that was once known as a railroad center and thrived on its milling industries.

Information: **Mahopac Chamber of Commerce** | 925 S. Lake Blvd., 10541-3243 | 845/628–5553.

Attractions

Mahopac Farm. This working farm houses a collection of 19th-century antiques and memorabilia. | Baldwin Pl. Rd., Rte. 6 at Rte. 118, Baldwin Pl. | 845/628–9298 | $3 | Daily 10–6.

DEC.: *Holiday Tree Lighting.* This family-oriented event brings the whole town together. As the Christmas tree is lit, carols are sung, and Santa makes an appearance. | Mahopac Chamber Community Park, intersection of Rtes. 6 and 6 N | 1st Sat. in Dec. | 845/628–5553.

Dining

Heidi's Brauhaus. German. Over-the-top Bavarian furnishings—historic photographs, old-time signs, stuffed pheasants, and you name it—fill the restaurant where you can enjoy traditional German fare and all-you-can-eat specials. Kids' menu. Sunday brunch. | 241 Rte. 6 N | 845/628–9795 | www.heidisbrauhaus.com | Closed Mon., Tues. No lunch Wed.–Sat. | $15–$18 | MC, V.

Marco, a restaurant. Contemporary. Across the street from the lake is this culinary treasure, named for its chef/owner, Marco. From both the aquatic-themed lounge and the main dining room which hosts monthly exhibits from local artists, pour inventive and flavorful dishes like a salad of warm baby black beluga lentils with pancetta, served over greens, or seasonal entrées like wood-grilled New Zealand loin of venison with brandy wild mushroom ragout, sautéed spinach and celery root purée, and scallion potato pancakes. Everything is homemade. | 612 Main St. | 845/621–1648 | No lunch. Closed Mon.–Weds | $19–$27 | AE, MC, V.

Lodging

Budget Motor Inn. For those late-night munchies, you can hoof it to the 24-hour diner next to this two-story, two-building motel complex. Cable TV. Business services. No pets. | 215 Rte. 6 | 845/628–6991 | fax 845/628–4218 | 24 rooms | $52–$58 | AE, D, MC, V.

MALONE

MAP 3, J1

(Nearby town also listed: Massena)

Malone is a community in the northernmost part of the state and is nearly as close to Montreal, Canada, as it is to Plattsburgh, the next-closest town in New York. Malone lies between the foothills of the Adirondack Mountains and the Saint Lawrence River valley. Here you'll find an abundance of clean lakes and rivers, and you'll also be near hiking and camping facilities operated by the New York State Department of Environmental Conservation Service.

Information: **Chamber of Commerce** | 170 E. Main St., 12953 | 518/483–3760.

Attractions

Almanzo Wilder Homestead. The former home of Almanzo Wilder, the subject of Laura Ingalls Wilder's book, *Farmer Boy,* is furnished with period furniture and memorabilia. The home is in Burke, 7 ½ mi northeast of Malone. | Stacy Rd., Burke | 518/483–1207 or 518/483–4516 | www.almanzowilderfarm.com | sallar@slic.com | $4 | Memorial Day–Labor Day, Tues.–Sat. 11–4, Sun. 1–4.

Franklin County Historical and Museum Society. The museum occupies a Victorian home with period furnishings. On exhibit are old maps of northern New York, crafts, and displays on weaving, spinning, and broom making; there's also a genealogy library and country store. | 51 Milwaukee St. | 518/483–2750 | Donations accepted | June–Labor Day, Tues.–Sat. 1–4; Labor Day–May, Sat. 1–4.

Titus Mountain Ski Area. This ski area features 1,200 ft of vertical drop, 26 trails, seven double and triple chairs, racing programs, and snowmaking capabilities. Although Titus is outside Adirondack Park boundaries, it's still considered an Adirondack ski center. | 215 Johnson Rd. | 518/483–3740 or 800/848–8766 | www.titusmountain.com | $21–$25 | Late Nov.–early Apr.

ON THE CALENDAR

JULY: *Malone Auto Show and Flea Market.* Antique and classic hot rods, as well as sports cars from all over New York and Canada, will rev your motor for this event. If you're searching for a part for a vintage car, chances are you'll find it in the flea market. | Malone Recreational Park on State St. | 518/483–3760.

AUG.: *Franklin County Fair.* A county fair with national musical acts delivers old-fashioned, upbeat fun at the Malone Fairgrounds. | 800/709–4895.

Dining

Sansone's Restaurant. Italian. Antiques are scattered throughout this informal eatery. The Italian sampler, which comes with lasagna, spaghetti, manicotti, and chicken strips, is popular. Or you can order these dishes individually. Kids' menu. | 321 E. Main St. | 518/483–9817 | No lunch Sun. | $8–$16 | AE, D, MC, V.

Villa Fiore. Italian. With candlelight and linen tablecloths, this is one of the most formal restaurants in town. The prime rib and zuppa di lobster over pasta are the menu's highlights. Images of Italian cities on the walls add a nice touch. | 18 E. Main St. | 518/481–6557 | $8–$22 | AE, MC, V.

Lodging

Clark's Motel. This single-story motel, built in 1982, is within walking distance to one restaurant and is convenient to Route 11. For those looking for recreation, Titus Mountain is 3 mi to the east. Cable TV. Some pets allowed. | 42 E. Main St. | 518/483–0900 | 19 rooms | $49–$59 | AE, MC, V.

Crossroads Motel. Fluorescent-blue lights trim the outside of this well-maintained strip motel. Among the three themed dining rooms at the motel's popular restaurant is one that's decorated to resemble an apple orchard. There's also a coffee shop, a bowling alley, and a bar. Restaurant, bar (with entertainment). Cable TV. Pool. | Rte. 95 at Rte. 11 | 518/529–7372 | fax 518/529–6755 | 43 rooms | $63–$73 | AE, D, DC, MC, V.

Econo Lodge. This chain motel consists of three buildings and some rooms feature balconies. Restaurant, complimentary Continental breakfast. Cable TV. Pool. Pets allowed. | 227 W. Main St. | 518/483–0500 | fax 518/483–4356 | www.econolodge.com | 38 rooms | $55–$65 | AE, D, MC, V.

Four Seasons Motel. This conventional single-story motel features a horseshoe-shaped configuration and is downtown near a shopping center. Complimentary Continental breakfast. Cable TV. Pool. | 236 W. Main St. | 518/483–3490 | fax 518/483–3490 ext. 133 | 26 rooms | $45–$69 | AE, D, DC, MC, V.

Malone Super 8 Motel. This three-story motel, built in 1994, is next to a restaurant and 2 mi from a 36-hole golf course. In-room data ports. Cable TV, in-room VCRs (and movies). Pets allowed. | 17 Rockland St. | 518/483–8123 or 800/800–8000 | fax 518/483–8058 | www.super8.com | 44 rooms | $66 | AE, D, DC, MC, V.

MAMARONECK

MAP 4, F5

(Nearby towns also listed: Elmsford, Hartsdale, Hawthorne, New Rochelle, Rye, Scarsdale, Tarrytown, White Plains, Yonkers)

This vibrant village of 30,000 grew up around a harbor on Long Island Sound, the second-largest natural small-boat harbor on the east coast. (In fact, its name comes from the

Native American word that means "where the fresh water falls into the salt.") It's only a half-hour from Manhattan, yet it retains all the charm and flavor of a New England seaside village. Local recreational activities include tennis, golf, swimming, and more. You'll also find many quaint antiques shops, fashionable boutiques, and gift shops. In addition, the arts have played a large role in the community's history and such renowned actors as the Barrymores, Mary Pickford, and Douglas Fairbanks have called the area home.

Information: **Mamaroneck Chamber of Commerce** | 1058 Mamaroneck Ave., 10543 | 914/698–4400.

Attractions
Emelin Theater. This theater presents a varied schedule of concerts, cabaret shows, lectures, films, and plays with more than 200 programs each year. | Library La. at Prospect Ave. | 914/698–0098 | Admission varies | Call for schedule.

ON THE CALENDAR
SEPT.: *Mamaroneck Kiwanis Annual Antique Car Show and Flea Market.* Antique cars from across the country are displayed and judged. If cars aren't your thing, hunt for bargains at the enormous flea market. | Harbor Island Park on Boston Post Rd. | 914/698–4400.

Dining
Abis. Japanese. Diners are seated at the sushi bar, small tables, or at the tatami-style seating area where they can enjoy freshly prepared Japanese food at the comfortable, casual restaurant. The sushi deluxe, a sushi and sashimi combination platter, is very popular. Sunday brunch. | 406 Mamaroneck Ave. | 914/698–8777 | Reservations essential weekends | $11–$20 | AE, DC, MC, V.

Charlie Brown's Steakhouse. Steak. With vintage photographs and baseball memorabilia hanging on the walls, this place exudes Americana. Signature dishes include the certified Angus beef and prime rib. Kids' menu. | 181 E. Boston Post Rd. | 914/698–6610 | $10–$16 | AE, D, DC, MC, V.

Chef Antonio. Italian. This dining spot is colorfully adorned with watercolors and the painted ceiling resembles the sky. Popular entrées include chicken *con tadini*, a savory dish of chicken with peppers, sausage, and onions. Kids' menu. | 551 Halstead Ave. | 914/698–8610 | No lunch Sat. | $13–$19 | AE, D, DC, MC, V.

Lodging
Summerfield Suites Hotel. This four-story hotel is just 2 mi from Mamaroneck and a short drive to several restaurants and a mall. A complimentary shuttle to downtown White Plains is available. In-room data ports, kitchenettes, microwaves, refrigerators. Cable TV, in-room VCRs (and movies). Pool. Outdoor hot tub. Gym. Laundry services. Business services. Pets allowed (fee). | 101 Corporate Park Dr., Harrison | 914/251–9700 | fax 914/251–1699 | www.summerfieldsuites.com | 159 rooms | $149–$269 | AE, D, DC, MC, V.

MASSENA

MAP 3, I1

(Nearby towns also listed: Malone, Potsdam)

When the St. Lawrence Seaway was built in the 1950s, Massena gained fame as the home of the Moses-Saunders Power Dam, the largest power plant along the waterway. Founded in 1792, Massena is 5 mi from the huge Eisenhower Lock and is the northeastern gateway to the Thousand Islands region. Although Massena is in the heart of a dairy-farming region, for the most part, the area is supported economically by the New York Power Authority.

Information: **Massena Chamber of Commerce** | 50 Main St., 13662 | 315/769–3525.

Attractions

Coles Creek State Park. This 1,800-acre park offers camping, picnicking, boating, fishing, and swimming. The campgrounds include 235 campsites (147 electrical), a children's area, a recreation building, and a camp store. | Rte. 37, east of Waddington | 315/388–5636 | www.nysparks.state.ny.us/parks/ | Free; parking $6 | Mid-May–mid-Oct., daily.

Robert Moses State Park. This 4,122-acre park provides access to the Moses-Saunders Power Dam and includes a swimming beach, campgrounds with 169 campsites (36 electrical), fishing, a children's area, and a recreation building. | Rte. 37 | 315/769–8663 | www.nysparks.state.ny.us/parks/ | Free; parking $6 | Daily.

St. Lawrence Seaway. Construction of the joint U.S.-Canada Seaway project began in January 1955 and opened to boat traffic in April 1959. More than 1½ billion metric tons of cargo have passed through the $470-million waterway since it opened. A prime time to view ships from the visitors center observation deck is from April to December. | Eisenhower Lock, Rte. 131 | 315/764–3200 | kimberly.l.lydon@sls.dot.gov | www.dot.gov/slsdc.

Dwight D. Eisenhower Lock and Visitors Center. At one of the state's busiest tourist attractions, you can tour exhibits, cargo samples, photos, President Eisenhower memorabilia, and interactive displays and view a video on the seaway's construction. An observation deck overlooks the Eisenhower Lock. The visitors center also provides information on ship transit schedules. | Rte. 131 | 315/769–2422 | Free | Memorial Day–Labor Day, daily 9–9; Oct.–May, weekdays 9–4:30.

Moses-Saunders Power Dam. The 2,960-ft-wide dam is jointly owned by the New York Power Authority and Ontario Hydro. It houses energy-related exhibits and presents a multimedia orientation show, and there's an observation deck. | 830 Barnhart Island Rd. | 315/764–0226 or 800/262–NYPA | www.stl.nypa.gov | Free | Memorial Day–Columbus Day, daily 9:30–6.

ON THE CALENDAR

MAR.: *Cheerleading Contest.* Cheerleading squads from high schools all over St. Lawrence County participate in this annual competition. Fear not: there are food booths aplenty if you're hungry. | Massena High School, 84 Nightengale St. | 315/769–3525.

JUNE: *Heritage Festival.* Local heritage is celebrated with crafts, entertainment, food, and casino games at Massena Arena on Hartehaven Plaza. | 315/769–3525.

AUG.: *Festival of North Country Folklife.* Robert Moses State Park on Route 37 hosts this festival that showcases local folk and ethnic heritage with crafts demonstrations, music, lectures, storytelling, and food. | 315/769–3525.

Dining

Tiffany's Restaurant. American. Old-fashioned booths and black-and-white photos give this eatery, established in the 1970s, its retro appeal. Try the baked ziti with meatballs or the prime rib dinner. Kids' menu. | 46 Main St. | 315/769–9845 | Breakfast also available; no dinner Sun.–Wed. | $5–$12 | AE, MC, V.

Village Inn. Continental. This quiet and comfortable family restaurant dates to the 1950s and serves roast turkey and seafood dinners in four homey dining rooms. Kids' menu. | 181 Outer Maple St., Rte. 37B | 315/769–6910 | Closed Mon., Tues. No lunch Sun. | $10–$16 | AE, MC, V.

Lodging

Econo Lodge Meadow View. The two-story motel has a U-shaped layout with comfortably furnished small rooms and it's just 7 mi from the Eisenhower Lock and Robert Moses State

Park. Restaurant. Microwaves, refrigerators, cable TV. Exercise equipment. Business services. | 15054 Rte. 37 | 315/764–0246 or 800/553–2666 | fax 315/764–9615 | 52 rooms | $78–$95 | AE, D, DC, MC, V.

St. Lawrence Hotel. Built in the late 1950s, this four-story hotel is just 7 mi from Robert Moses State Park. Live entertainment at the hotel's Smokey's Pubhouse on Friday and Saturday nights keeps the joint jumping. Restaurant, bar, dining room, room service. Cable TV. Laundry facilities. Business services. Pets allowed (fee). | 10 W. Orvis St. | 315/769–2441 | fax 315/769–9216 | www.stlawrence.com | 121 rooms | $45–$75 | AE, D, DC, MC, V.

Super 8. This three-story chain motel is near the Eisenhower Lock on the St. Lawrence Seaway. In-room data ports, cable TV. Business services. | 84 Grove St. | 315/764–1065 | fax 315/764–9710 | 42 rooms | $60–$65 | AE, D, DC, MC, V.

MASTIC/MASTIC BEACH

MAP 3, E2

(Nearby towns also listed: Patchogue, Quogue/East Quogue)

Once the home of William Floyd, a signer of the Declaration of Independence, Mastic's tri-hamlet area is 70 mi from Manhattan. Today, the William Floyd Parkway passes through the heart of the Mastic peninsula, which is comprised of three hamlets: Mastic, Mastic Beach, and Shirley. The parkway eventually leads to Fire Island. Like most of Long Island, the peninsula was originally inhabited by Native Americans. Mastic's beaches, vistas, and close proximity to Fire Island make it an ideal vacation spot.

Information: **Chamber of Commerce of the Mastics and Shirley** | Box 4, Mastic, 11950 | 631/399–2228.

MASTIC/
MASTIC BEACH

INTRO
ATTRACTIONS
DINING
LODGING

Attractions

Smith Point County Park. The park offers a campground and camping on the beach, fishing, hunting, picnic areas, and a lovely 5-mi-long pristine beach. | William Floyd Pkwy., at its southern-most end, Shirley | 631/852–1313 or 631/852–1322 | $35 annual pass | Daily dawn–dusk.

William Floyd Estate. This 613-acre site is the ancestral home of William Floyd, a signer of the Declaration of Independence. There are mansion tours and special events, and the grounds include a cemetery and outbuildings. | 245 Park Dr., off the W. Floyd Pkwy., Mastic Beach | 631/399–2030 | Free | Hrs vary.

ON THE CALENDAR
AUG.: *Waldbaum's Balloon Festival of Long Island.* At dawn and dusk, hot-air balloons ascend at the Brookhaven Airport in Shirley. Throughout the day, fireworks, skydiving, kid's entertainment, and big-name performers are featured. | 800/HOT–AIR9 | www.balloonfestival.com.

Dining

Mike's Place Too. American. This sports bar with two dining rooms features furnishings that reflect the seasons of the year and it serves marinated steak, buffalo wings, as well as daily specials. There's karaoke on Saturday nights. Kids' menu. | 1086 Mastic Rd. | 631/281–1169 | $6–$13 | AE, D, DC, MC, V.

Lodging

Smith Point Motel. This L-shaped, one-story, beige building with a brown door is on the William Floyd Parkway, on the way to Smith Point Beach. Some microwaves, some refrigerators, cable TV. Business services. Some pets allowed. | 165 William Floyd Pkwy. | 631/281–8887 | fax 631/395–9584 | 21 rooms | $75 | AE, D, MC, V.

MATTITUCK

MAP 3, E2

(Nearby towns also listed: Jamesport/Aqueboque/Laurel, Riverhead)

Located at Long Island's east end, the Mattituck Inlet originally served as a shortcut for Native Americans traveling inland by canoe. Later, the secluded inlet was favored by rum-runners and early European settlers who used it as a secret and escape route leading to boats docked along the Long Island Sound.

Tourists today find that it's still a secluded hideaway frequented by fishing boats and vacationers. The Matt-A-Mar Marina conducts canoe and kayak tours and also rents boats.

Information: **Greenport-Southold Chamber of Commerce** | Main Rd., Box 66, Greenport, 11944 | 631/477–1383.

Attractions

Matt-A-Mar Marina. This active marina at the mouth of Mattituck Inlet has a year-round restaurant, a snack bar, and a casual café. In addition to the Mattituck Creek Boat Launching Ramp, the marina has 93 slips (40 transient) and guided canoe and kayak tours. | 2255 Wickham Ave. | 631/298–4739 | Free | Daily.

Old Mill. The old mill used to stretch across the inlet and today the historic site includes the Old Mill Inn restaurant and a tavern which was first established in 1821. | 5775 W. Mill Rd. | 631/298–8080 | Free | Daily.

ON THE CALENDAR

JUNE: *June Strawberry Festival.* Along with strawberry shortcake, the popular summer festival features a craft fair, amusement rides, and fireworks. | 631/298–5757 | www.northfork.org.
OCT.: *Mattituck Lioness Club Harvest Fair.* The bounty of autumn is celebrated with homemade food, a farmer's market, and a crafts fair on the village green in the center of town. | 631/734–4269.

Dining

Old Mill Inn. Continental. The restaurant is housed in a gristmill dating to 1821 and features original beams and original mill fixtures and gears. Tables overlook the inlet, you can dine on the outdoor patio in summer and enjoy live music on weekends. Popular dishes include lobster specials and rack of lamb broiled with garlic and rosemary. Kids' menu. Dock space. | 5775 W. Mill Rd. | 631/298–8080 | Closed Mon. | $15–$25 | AE, MC, V.

Touch of Venice. Italian, Seafood. Every table provides a waterfront view at this restaurant known for stuffed artichokes appetizers, entrées such as fresh lobster and shallots sautéed in garlic oil, inventive pasta dishes, and steak dinners. There's open-air dining on the patio in summer and occasional live music. Kids' menu. Dock space. | Matt-A-Mar Marina, 2255 Wickham Ave. | 631/298–5851 | $10–$20 | AE, D, MC, V.

Lodging

Mattituck Motel. Catch some rays down the block at Great Taconic Bay or work on your tennis game at the courts across the street. Afterward, take a stroll to a nearby restaurant. Some kitchenettes, refrigerators. Cable TV. No pets. | 2150 Bay Ave. | 631/298–4131 | 19 rooms | $85–$120 | MC, V.

MEDINA

(Nearby towns also listed: Albion, Lockport, Niagara Falls)

Just before entering the canal town of Medina on Route 31 you might want to make a detour onto Culvert Road where you'll enter a tunnel and see a sign that says you're *under* the Erie Canal. In historic Medina, you can picnic at Canal Park, which is between the Erie Canal and restored buildings on Main Street.

Information: Medina Chamber of Commerce | 433 Main St., 14103 | 716/798–4287.

Attractions

Medina Railroad Museum. Exhibits of railroad, fire protection, and law-enforcement history are displayed in a historic wood freight house that's longer than a football field. The museum also displays scale-model boats, ships, and airplanes. | 530 West Ave. | 716/798–6106 | $5 | Mon.–Sat. noon–7, Sun. 1–5.

ON THE CALENDAR

MAY: *Medina Memorial Day Parade.* Veterans' and community organizations march in this parade, which also features floats and bands at State St. Park. | 716/798–3632.
JUNE–AUG.: *Summer Concert Series.* The series presents Friday-evening concerts and entertainment that draw the community and vacationing boaters to the Canal Basin. | 716/798–4287.

Attractions

Canal Park. You can have a picnic or simply stroll through this canal-side. | Behind Main St. to the end of Pearl St. | 716/798–2323 | Free | Daily.

Dining

Rudy's. American. Don't miss the chicken tender melt at this casual spot known for its sourdough sandwiches and homemade spaghetti sauce. Classic pictures of Elvis, the Beatles, and the cast of *Leave It to Beaver* will induce nostalgia. | 118 W. Center St. | 716/798–5166 | Breakfast also available; no dinner Sun. | $5–$9 | No credit cards.

Lodging

Dollinger's Courtyard. In a commercial area, this single-story motel is just 1 mi from a number of restaurants. Train buffs take note: the Medina Railroad Museum is close, too. Some microwaves, some refrigerators. Cable TV, in-room VCRs (and movies). Pets allowed (fee). | 11360 Maple Ridge Rd. | 716/798–0016 | fax 716/798–9113 | 18 rooms | $58 | AE, D, MC, V.

MIDDLETOWN

(Nearby towns also listed: Monticello, Newburgh, Port Jervis)

Once a bustling railroad town, this small city is convenient to I–84 and Route 17 and offers many shopping, dining, and lodging options. The historic downtown is in the midst of a revival, and some interesting shops and restaurants have taken hold.

Information: Orange County Chamber of Commerce | 40 Matthews St., #103, Goshen, 10924 | 845/294–8080.

MIDDLETOWN

INTRO
ATTRACTIONS
DINING
LODGING

Attractions

Edwin Welling Van Duzer Memorial House. Examine period artifacts and furniture at this 19th-century home. There's also an interesting collection of random Middletown memorabilia. | 25 East Ave. | 845/342–0941 | Free | Wed. 1–5.

JUNE: *The Greek Experience.* This popular ethnic festival features Greek food, dancing, and crafts at the Holy Cross Greek Orthodox Church on Goshen Turnpike. | 845/695–1976.

JUNE: *Orange Classic 10K.* This 10K run is ranked among the nation's top 100 road races and attracts world-class runners. There are also races for kids, food, crafts, and entertainment downtown. | 845/343–8075.

JULY: *Orange County Fair.* This large fair features carnival rides, livestock exhibits, plenty of live entertainment, as well as beauty contests at the Orange County Fairgrounds off Route 17. | 845/343–4826.

Dining

Bistro Zella. Contemporary. This eatery is furnished around an Art Deco theme and from the dining room you can watch the chef through a window. The lounge features a historic back bar and dinner specialties include wild mushroom and potato lasagna, free-range chicken, and sage-crusted loin of pork. | Rte. 211 E | 845/342–1756 | Closed Mon. No lunch | $20–$30 | MC, V.

Casa Mia. Italian, American. This casual, family-friendly Italian restaurant has been a favorite of locals for years. Kids' menu. | Rte. 211 E | 845/692–2323 | Closed Mon. | $15–$25 | AE, DC, MC, V.

New Rusty Nail. Continental. Early American–style furnishings fill this sprawling restaurant that serves steak and seafood dinners and features a big salad bar. In addition to several dining rooms, there's a bar and lounge and entertainment on weekends. Kids' menu. | 50 Dunning Rd. | 845/343–8242 | No lunch Sun. | $13–$29 | AE, D, DC, MC, V.

Olde Erie Brew Pub and Grill. American. The city's railroad history is reflected in the building's design and decorating theme. A 53-ft-long oak bar is the focal point of the dining room where you can enjoy steaks, homemade meat loaf, pasta dishes, and barbecued ribs. There's an extensive selection of microbrewery beers and a late-night menu. | 7 W. Main St. | 845/344–3743 | No lunch Sun. | $15–$30 | AE, MC, V.

Lodging

Holiday Inn Of Middletown. This newer hotel is near the town's industrial and business park at the intersection of Route 17 and Interstate 84. Restaurant, bar, complimentary Continental breakfast. Refrigerators, cable TV. Pool. Sauna. Gym. Laundry services. Business services. | 86 Crystal Run Rd. | 845/343–1474 | www.basshotels.com/holidayinn | 102 rooms | $90–$110 | AE, MC, V.

Howard Johnson Hotel. A mall and movie theater are just across the street from this two-story hotel. Restaurant, bar, room service. In-room data ports. Cable TV. Pool. Laundry facilities, laundry service. Business services. No pets. | 551 Rte. 211 E | 845/342–5822 | fax 845/695–2140 | www.hojo.com | 117 rooms | $75–$95 | AE, D, DC, MC, V.

Super 8 Motel. This L-shaped two-story hotel offers newer accommodations that are near shopping and restaurants off Route 17. Complimentary Continental breakfast. Some in-room hot tubs. Pets allowed. | 563 Rte. 211 E | 845/692–5828 | www.super8.com | 82 rooms | $80 | AE, D, DC, MC, V.

KODAK'S TIPS FOR PHOTOGRAPHING LANDSCAPES AND SCENERY

Landscape
- Tell a story
- Isolate the essence of a place
- Exploit mood, weather, and lighting

Panoramas
- Use panoramic cameras for sweeping vistas
- Don't restrict yourself to horizontal shots
- Keep the horizon level

Panorama Assemblage
- Use a wide-angle or normal lens
- Let edges of pictures overlap
- Keep exposure even
- Use a tripod

Placing the Horizon
- Use low horizon placement to accent sky or clouds
- Use high placement to emphasize distance and accent foreground elements
- Try eliminating the horizon

Mountain Scenery: Scale
- Include objects of known size
- Frame distant peaks with nearby objects
- Compress space with long lenses

Mountain Scenery: Lighting
- Shoot early or late; avoid midday
- Watch for dramatic color changes
- Use exposure compensation

Tropical Beaches
- Capture expansive views
- Don't let bright sand fool your meter
- Include people

Rocky Shorelines
- Vary shutter speeds to freeze or blur wave action
- Don't overlook sea life in tidal pools
- Protect your gear from sand and sea

In the Desert
- Look for shapes and textures
- Try visiting during peak bloom periods
- Don't forget safety

Canyons
- Research the natural and social history of a locale
- Focus on a theme or geologic feature
- Budget your shooting time

Rain Forests and the Tropics
- Go for mystique with close-ups and detail shots
- Battle low light with fast films and camera supports
- Protect cameras and film from moisture and humidity

Rivers and Waterfalls
- Use slow film and long shutter speeds to blur water
- When needed, use a neutral-density filter over the lens
- Shoot from water level to heighten drama

Autumn Colors
- Plan trips for peak foliage periods
- Mix wide and close views for visual variety
- Use lighting that accents colors or creates moods

Moonlit Landscapes
- Include the moon or use only its illumination
- Exaggerate the moon's relative size with long telephoto lenses
- Expose landscapes several seconds or longer

Close-Ups
- Look for interesting details
- Use macro lenses or close-up filters
- Minimize camera shake with fast films and high shutter speeds

Caves and Caverns
- Shoot with ISO 1000+ films
- Use existing light in tourist caves
- Paint with flash in wilderness caves

From *Kodak Guide to Shooting Great Travel Pictures* © 2000 by Fodor's Travel Publications

MILLBROOK

(Nearby towns also listed: Hyde Park, Poughkeepsie)

Located midway between the Hudson River and Connecticut, this picturesque Dutchess County town has long been a retreat for upscale city dwellers. For years, the community has attracted the rich and famous, many of whom have built luxurious weekend and summer homes here. You might spot movie stars like Mary Tyler Moore, Liam Neeson, and Natasha Richardson. The area was originally settled in the 1700s and it combines historic downtown areas with sprawling country retreats tucked into the rural countryside. Shops and restaurants line downtown streets and cluster around the village green. Inviting back roads wind through the picturesque countryside, past rolling farms, country estates, and dense woodlands. There are miles of equestrian and hiking trails. The region is also known as wine country and you'll find wineries tucked down country lanes in the soft hills.

Information: Poughkeepsie Area Chamber of Commerce | 110 Main St., Poughkeepsie, 12601 | 845/454–1700.

Attractions

Mary Flagler Cary Arboretum. This 2,000-acre property has one of the largest perennial gardens in the Northeast and includes more than 1,000 species of plants, a fern glen, miles of trails, and more. Look for the sign at the entrance which says "Institute of Ecosystem Studies" rather than the Mary Flagler Cary Arboretum. | Rte. 44A | 845/677–5359 | Free | Oct.–Apr., weekdays and Sat. 9–4, Sun. 1–4; May–Sept., weekdays and Sat. 9–6, Sun. 1–6.

Millbrook Winery. Among the region's highly acclaimed wineries, Millbrook invites visitors to savor the spectacular views, as well as the chardonnays. Summer weekend programs combine lunch with film screenings and musical performances. | 26 Wing Rd. | 845/677–8383 | fax 845/677–6186 | www.millbrookwine.com | Daily noon–5.

ON THE CALENDAR

JULY: *Millbrook Fire Department Carnival.* Food booths and nightly musical entertainment will entertain kids of all ages at this 3-day event, but the highlight is the parade of firefighters and fire trucks. | Several locations in Millbrook Village | 845/677–3871.

Dining

Allyn's. Continental. The owner-chef at this restaurant housed in a renovated 200-year-old church is so devoted to freshness that all ingredients are obtained locally. The menu includes pan-roasted chicken, grilled duck breast, and seafood dishes. Allyn's has been featured in the *Wine Spectator* as having one of the "finest wine lists in the world" and over 300 wines are listed. Kids' menu. Open-air dining in a perennial garden. Sunday brunch. | 42-58 Rte. 44 | 845/677–5888 | www.allyns.com | Closed Tues. | $30–$35 | AE, D, DC, MC, V.

Old Drovers Inn. Contemporary. During winter months, the dining room at this restaurant gets much of its light from the large fireplace. The menu has old favorites such as rack of lamb and turkey hash, but there are also specialty dishes like sesame-crusted tuna and muscovy duck braised in marsala wine. Sunday brunch. | Old Rte. 22, Dover Plains | 845/832–9311 | fax 845/832–6356 | www.olddroversinn.com | Breakfast also available; closed Tues., Wed.; no lunch Thurs. | $40–$50 | DC, MC, V.

Lodging

Cottonwood Motel. This single-story motel is nestled in a sleepy, residential neighborhood. Stroll to the nearby restaurants or hop in the car to check out some of the antiques shops within 10 mi. Some refrigerators, some in-room hot tubs, cable TV. Business services. Pets allowed. | Rte. 44 | 845/677–3283 | fax 845/677–3577 | 18 rooms, 1 cottage | $105–$145 rooms, $220 cottage | AE, MC, V.

Old Drovers Inn. Cattle herders (aka drovers) bringing in their stock to New York in the 18th century made a stopover at this inn 15 mi southeast of Millbrook. Today, it is one of the oldest continuously operating inns in the United States. Rooms are done in Victorian style and three still have fireplaces. The inn sits on 12 acres of land. Restaurant, complimentary breakfast. No room phones, no TV. Some pets allowed (fee). | Old Rte. 22, Dover Plains | 845/832–9311 | fax 845/832–6356 | www.olddroversinn.com | Closed first 3 weeks Jan. | 4 rooms | $150 | DC, MC, V.

Troutbeck. Surrounded by elaborate landscaping and gardens, this inn on the bank of the Webatuck River has 442 acres of grounds. Inside, the hotel is exquisitely furnished with antiques. The library boasts 12,000 volumes and videotape movies. Ten miles east of Millbrook. Restaurant, bar, complimentary breakfast, cable TV, in-room VCRs. 2 pools. Sauna. Tennis. Library. Business services. | Leedsville Rd., Amenia | 845/373–9681 | fax 845/373–7080 | www.troutbeck.com | 42 rooms, 6 suites | $375 rooms, $475–$600 suites | AE, MC, V.

MONROE

(Nearby towns also listed: Goshen, Newburgh, Warwick)

This residential town offers shopping and dining just off Route 17, exit 130. Monroe is also near Harriman State Park and Sterling Forest.

Information: Orange County Chamber of Commerce | 40 Matthews St., #103, Goshen, 10924 | 845/294–8080.

Attractions

Museum Village in Orange County. The daily life of colonial America is depicted at this recreated living history village. Thirty-five buildings house crafts workshops, old-time equipment, and furnishings. Interpreters dressed in period costumes perform daily activities such as publishing the weekly newspaper, hammering horseshoes in the blacksmith's shop, and throwing pots at the pottery workshop. Special events are offered throughout the year. | 1010 Museum Village Rd., Rte. 17M | 845/782–8247 | www.museumvillage.com | $8 | May–Nov., Wed.–Sun.

Woodbury Common Premium Outlets. This sprawling outlet shopping center is a 1-hr drive north of New York City and among the most popular destinations in the state, attracting about 10 million visitors each year. The parking lots fill quickly, so plan to arrive early in the day. The center offers some 220 stores, including top retailers and fashion-designer outlets. The center is adjacent to Harriman State Park. Take I-87 to Rte. 32, exit 16. | 498 Red Apple Ct., Central Valley | 845/928–4000 | www.chelseagca.com/location/woodbury/wood.html | Free | Mon.–Sat. 10–9, Sun. 10–8.

ON THE CALENDAR
SEPT.: *Civil War Weekend.* Immerse yourself in history during this 2-day Labor Day weekend event, held in Museum Village. If the Civil War reenactments aren't enough, examine Union and Confederate encampments and view a unique period-fashion parade. | 1010 Rte. 17M | Labor Day weekend | 845/782–8247.

Dining
Cafe Fiesta. Mexican. This come-as-you-are family-friendly eatery in Highland Mills offers authentic Mexican fare and is known for traditional dishes, including vegetarian and low-fat renditions. | Rte. 32 | 845/928–2151 | $8–$10 | AE, D, MC, V.

Goodfellows. Italian. This casual bustling restaurant is a local favorite for traditional Italian food such as chicken Romeo: chicken, Italian sausage, broccoli, artichoke hearts, and roasted peppers in a white wine sauce. | 590 Rte. 208 | 845/783–1133 or 845/246–9371 | $7–$18 | AE, D, MC, V.

Rainbow. Italian. This comfortable family restaurant with soft lighting is known for northern Italian cuisine including fresh pasta dishes and seafood dinners. | Rte. 17M | 845/783–2670 | $15–$20 | D, MC, V.

Lodging

James' Motel. This single-story motel is a short stroll to any of the several nearby restaurants. Some microwaves, some refrigerators, cable TV. Some pets allowed. | 370 Rte. 17M | 845/783–9651 | fax 845/783–5765 | 23 rooms | $55–$60 | AE, D, DC, MC, V.

MONTAUK

MAP 3, F2

(Nearby towns also listed: Amagansett, East Hampton)

Located at the easternmost part of the island, Montauk is one of New York's premier seaside resort communities. The popular vacation destination has over 70 hotels, bed-and-breakfasts, and guest houses. It draws vacationers for fishing, water sports, golf, tennis, picturesque coastlines and beaches, shopping, and top-notch restaurants.

In 1792, President George Washington signed an order to build the Montauk Point Lighthouse, the oldest operating lighthouse in the state and the fourth oldest in the country.

Today, 25 marinas launch over 400 charter and party boats. Horseback riding on the beach, nature trails, the world-class Robert Trent Jones golf course, and museums complete the vacationer's paradise.

Information: **Montauk Chamber of Commerce** | Box 5029, 11954 | 631/668–2428.

Attractions

Deep Hallow Ranch. This ranch claims to be the country's oldest cattle ranch and the birthplace of the American cowboy. You can take trail rides on the beach and through the park. There are also pony rides, a petting zoo, and outdoor barbecue dinners. | Theodore Roosevelt County Park | 631/668–2744 | Free | Daily.

Hither Hills State Park. This 160-acre park boasts an 18-hole golf course designed by Robert Trent Jones that's rated as one of the top 50 public courses in the nation by *Golf Digest* magazine. There are golf club and cart rentals, instruction, a driving range, a putting green, and a restaurant. | Old Montauk Hwy. | 631/668–7600 park, 631/668–5000 golf | Free | Daily dawn–dusk.

Montauk Point State Park. President George Washington ordered the building of this lighthouse in 1796. Perched on a bluff, the towering lighthouse overlooks the Atlantic Ocean and the surrounding park includes a scenic drive through the 700-acre preserve. Visitors can climb the 130 steps to the top of the lighthouse and visit the museum in the former light keeper's quarters. | RR2, S. Fairview Ave., at the end of Rte. 27 E | 631/668–2554 | $5 | Daily dawn–dusk.

Theodore Roosevelt County Park. Formerly Montauk County Park, this park is accessible by following the Montauk Highway east through the village just past E. Lake Drive. In the park there are miles of hiking and horseback riding trails as well as a Spanish–American War exhibit. | Montauk Hwy. | 631/852–7878 | Free | Daily, dawn–dusk.

AUG.: *Hamptons Shakespeare Festival.* The annual festival presents one of the bard's famous plays in an attractive park setting at Theodore Roosevelt County Park. | 631/668–2428.

OCT.: *Montauk Chamber of Commerce Annual Fall Festival.* A clam chowder cook-off, clam-shucking contest, hay and pony rides, Long Island wine and microbrew tastings, pumpkin decorating, kids' art contests, antique and classic boat displays, music, and a boat raffle draw crowds to this popular autumn festival. | 742 Montauk Hwy. | 631/668–2428.

Dining

Dave's Grill. Seafood. This unpretentious grill with fresh seafood and local specialties is located at the fishing docks and is popular with locals. There's always a wait for a table. Open-air dining on deck. | 468 W. Lake Dr. | 631/668–9190 | www.davesgrill.com | Reservations not accepted for parties under 6 | Closed Nov.–Apr. No lunch | $20–$29 | AE, D, MC, V.

Gosman's Dock. Seafood. Built on two docks over the water, the popular restaurant offers indoor and outdoor dining. Tables overlook the harbor, Block Island Sound, and, beyond, the ocean. (The bar patio has the best views of the ocean.) Lobster and regional exotic seafood top the menu along with stuffed yellowtail flounder in lobster sauce, and marinated tuna steak. Clam bar. Live concerts Sunday. Kids' menu. No smoking. | 500 W. Lake Dr. | 631/668–5330 | Closed mid-Oct.–mid-Apr. | $14–$21 | AE, MC, V.

Harvest on Fort Pond. Italian, Mediterranean. The glass-enclosed dining room of this restaurant affords stunning views of sunsets glistening on Ft. Pond. Try the calamari salad and the sizzling whole red snapper. There's open-air dining in the herb garden in summer. Family-style service. No air-conditioning. | 11 S. Emory St. | 631/668–5574 | $40–$50 | AE, D, DC, MC, V.

Manor-View. Continental. This newly renovated restaurant has two dining rooms and a Sante Fe look, which includes sandy-color walls. Known for seafood, pasta dishes, and Long Island duckling. Open-air dining under a canopied deck. | 240 Fort Pond Rd. | 631/668–3249 | Closed Nov.–Mar. Closes Mon. No lunch | $25–$40 | AE, MC, V.

Ruschmeyer's. Contemporary. Large windows overlook a lake at this easygoing restaurant with three dining rooms. Alfresco dining under shade trees commands a view of the manicured grounds. The menu changes daily and usually includes inventively prepared veal chops, duck, and tuna. Pianist Friday and Saturday. Kids' menu. | 161 Second House Rd. | 631/668–2877 | Closed Nov.–Apr. | $18–$27 | AE, D, DC, MC, V.

Shagwong Tavern. American. At this restaurant decorated with a nautical theme the menu changes daily and might feature pan-seared rare tuna served over a bed of field greens with ginger dressing and wasabi, and other creatively prepared fare. Open-air dining on patio. Kids' menu. Sunday brunch. | 774 Montauk Hwy. | 631/668–3050 | $15–$25 | AE, D, DC, MC, V.

Lodging

Beachcomber Resort. This modern motel consists of four two-story buildings overlooking the ocean and is an easy walk to the beach. All rooms are apartment-like suites with modern-style furnishings. Kitchenettes, cable TV, in-room VCRs (movies). Pool. Sauna. Tennis. Beach. Laundry facilities. Business services. | 727 Old Montauk Hwy. | 631/668–2894 | fax 631/668–3154 | www.montauklife.com | 88 suites | $75–$400 | Closed Nov.–Mar. | AE, D, DC, MC, V.

Burcliffe by-the-Sea. The small inn consists of efficiencies and cottages; some have ocean views and fireplaces. Picnic area. Kitchenettes, cable TV. Beach. | 397 Old Montauk Hwy. | 631/668–2880 | www.montauklife.com | 7 rooms (5 with shower only) | $75–$250 | No credit cards.

MONTAUK

INTRO
ATTRACTIONS
DINING
LODGING

Driftwood on the Ocean. This contemporary-style motel features Scandinavian furnishings and looks out over sand dunes and the ocean. It's popular with families. Picnic area. Refrigerators, cable TV. 2 pools. Tennis. Beach. Playground. Laundry facilities. Business services. | 2178 Montauk Hwy. | 631/668–5744 or 800/483–7438 | fax 631/267–3081 | www.duneresorts.com | 57 rooms | $160–$255 | Closed late Oct.–May | AE, D, MC, V.

Gurney's Inn Resort and Spa. Located on a 1,000-ft stretch of beach, Gurney's is known for its magnificent views and its spa, which uses saltwater for various therapies. There's a picturesque heated indoor pool with floor-to-ceiling windows looking out to the ocean. 2 restaurants, bar (with entertainment), room service. Refrigerators, cable TV. Pool. Barbershop, beauty salon, hot tub, sauna, spa, steam room. Gym. Beach. Business services. | 290 Old Montauk Hwy. | 631/668–2345 | fax 631/668–2665 | www.gurneysweb.com | 109 rooms, 5 cottages | $400–$500 rooms, $900–$1,800 cottages | AE, D, DC, MC, V.

Hartman's Briney Breeze's Motel. Each room at this two-story motel has a view of Montauk's famed, white-sand beaches. Restaurants and fishing facilities are just a stroll away. Kitchenettes, microwaves, refrigerators. Cable TV. Pool. No pets. | 693 Old Montauk Hwy. | 631/668–2290 | fax 631/668–2987 | www.brineybreezes.com | 44 rooms | $165–$225 | MC, V.

Montauk Yacht Club, Resort and Marina. Surrounded by the Long Island Sound, Montauk Harbor, and the Atlantic Ocean, this luxurious resort is located on an island with its own lighthouse and 232-slip marina. Modern and well-appointed rooms have private terraces. 2 restaurants, 2 bars (with entertainment), room service. In-room data ports, cable TV. 3 pools. 3 tennis courts. Health club, horseback riding, beach, marina, boating. Business services, airport shuttle. | 32 Star Island Rd. | 631/668–3100 or 800/832–4200 (NY) | fax 631/668–3303 | www.montaukyachtclub.com | 107 rooms, 23 villas | $209–$249 rooms, $219–$339 villas | Closed Nov.–early Apr. | AE, DC, MC, V.

Oceanside Beach Resort. After a relaxing day at the beach, what could be better than a stroll to a nearby restaurant or a game of miniature golf? Many rooms have private balconies. Picnic area. Some kitchenettes, some microwaves, refrigerators. Cable TV. Pool. Beach. Some pets allowed. | 626 New Montauk Hwy. | 631/668–9825 | fax 631/668–2784 | obr@montaukmotel.com | www.montaukmotel.com | 30 rooms | $135–$225 | AE, D, MC, V.

Panoramic View. This hotel is tucked into a hillside of pines and overlooks landscaped lawns and flower gardens. Rooms, suites, and cottages all overlook 10,000 ft of private beach. In-room data ports, kitchenettes, refrigerators, cable TV. Pool. Beach. Video games. Laundry facilities. Business services. No kids under 10. | 272 Old Montauk Hwy. | 631/668–3000 | fax 631/668–7870 | www.panoramicview.com | 114 rooms, 14 suites, 3 cottages | Rooms $164–$248, suites $298 cottages $550 | Closed Nov.–Apr. | No credit cards.

Peri's Montauk Bed & Breakfast. An array of antiques from Europe, Asia, and Morocco adds international flavor to the rooms in this two-story Tudor home. Curl up with a good book by the living-room fireplace. Dining room, complimentary breakfast. No room phones, TV in common area. Massage. Bicycles. Library. No pets. No kids under 12. No smoking. | 206 Essex St. | 631/668–1394 | fax 631/668–6096 | www.perisb-bmontauk.com | 3 rooms | $275 | MC, V.

Royal Atlantic Beach Resort. This year-round hotel is two stories high and built of natural wood. It sits along the waterfront and many rooms have views of the ocean. Restaurant, bar, picnic area. Kitchenettes, refrigerators, cable TV. 2 pools. Beach. Business services. | S. Edgemere St., two blocks from the center of town | 631/668–5103 | fax 631/668–4172 | www.montauklife.com | 152 rooms | $149–$189 | AE, D, DC, MC, V.

Wavecrest Resort. This modern complex is situated on a rise so that each room in the four-building complex has an ocean view from the private terrace. Hither Hills State Park is nearby. Kitchenettes, cable TV, in-room VCRs (and movies). Pool. Beach. | Old Montauk Hwy., slightly east of Hither Hills State Park | 631/668–2141 | fax 631/668–2337 | www.wavecrestonocean.com | 65 rooms | $170–$195 | Closed late Oct.–Apr. | AE, D, MC, V.

ONE LAST TRAVEL TIP:

Pack an easy way to reach the world.

Wherever you travel, the MCI WorldCom Card℠ is the easiest way to stay in touch. You can use it to call to and from more than 125 countries worldwide. And you can earn bonus miles every time you use your card. So go ahead, travel the world. MCI WorldCom℠ makes it even more rewarding. For additional access codes, visit **www.wcom.com/worldphone.**

EASY TO CALL WORLDWIDE

1. Just dial the WorldPhone® access number of the country you're calling from.
2. Dial or give the operator your MCI WorldCom Card number.
3. Dial or give the number you're calling.

Canada	1-800-888-8000
Mexico	01-800-021-8000
United States	1-800-888-8000

EARN FREQUENT FLIER MILES

6 "I'm thirsty"s, 9 "Are we there yet"s, 3 "I don't feel good"s,
1 car class upgrade.
At least something's going your way.

Hertz rents Fords and other fine cars. ® REG. U.S. PAT. OFF. © HERTZ SYSTEM INC., 2000/005-00

Make your next road trip more comfortable with a free one-class upgrade from Hertz.

Let's face it, a long road trip isn't always sunshine and roses. But with Hertz, you get a free one car class upgrade to make things a little more bearable. You'll also choose from a variety of vehicles with child seats, Optional Protection Plans, 24-Hour Emergency Roadside Assistance, and the convenience of NeverLost,® the in-car navigation system that provides visual and audio prompts to give you turn-by-turn guidance to your destination. In a word: it's everything you need for your next road trip. Call your travel agent or Hertz at **1-800-654-2210** and mention PC# **906404** or check us out at **hertz.com** or AOL Keyword: **hertz**. Peace of mind. Another reason nobody does it exactly like Hertz.

Hertz
exactly.®

MONTICELLO

(Nearby towns also listed: Liberty, Middletown, Port Jervis)

Sullivan County's largest population center, the village of Monticello is also the county's government seat. It's also considered the gateway to the Catskills resort region and offers large-town conveniences, summer theater, fishing, canoeing, and other sports. It's near the site of the 1969 Woodstock music festival in Bethel.

Information: Sullivan County Chamber of Commerce | 198 Brideville Rd., 12771 | 845/794–2211 | webmaster@sullivanchamber.org | www.catskills.com.

Attractions

Eagle Institute. Guided eagle-watching tours, slide presentations, and children's programs are offered during winter months when eagles migrate to this region. | Rte. 97, Minisink Ford | 845/557–6162 | eagleinstitute@yahoo.com | www.eagleinstitute.org | Field trips $35 | Hrs vary.

Eldred Preserve. This private trout fishing and sporting preserve about 15 mi from Monticello doesn't require a hunting or fishing license; rather, you're charged by the pound for your catch. It also features catch-and-release fishing. | 1040 Rte. 55, Eldred | 845/557–8316 | www.eldredpreserve.com | Memorial Day–Labor Day, daily 8–6; Labor Day–Memorial Day, Wed.–Sun. 8–4.

Fort Delaware Museum of Colonial History. This is a replica of the stockaded fort-settlement that was the first of its kind in the Delaware River valley in 1755. Blockhouses, cabins, and gardens, along with exhibits, films, and demonstrations, give you a glimpse of the everyday life of an 18th-century settler. | Rte. 97, Narrowsburg | 845/252–6660 | $4 | Memorial Day–Labor Day, weekends 10–5:30.

Holiday Mountain Ski Area. Downhill skiing on 15 slopes with eight chairlifts, equipment rentals, snowboarding, and refreshments is offered. There's a Winter Carnival in February and March with special sports and ice-sculpture events and an outdoor barbecue. | 99 Holiday Mt. Rd., off Rte. 17 | 845/796–3161 | Dec.–Mar.

Lander's Delaware River Trips. These guided river trips feature canoeing and rafting with thrilling white-water adventures as well as easygoing floats. Overnight camping packages are available at sites along the river 20 mi from Monticello. | Demauro Rd., Narrowsburg | 800/252–3925 | Apr.–Dec. | www.landersrivertrips.com.

Monticello Raceway. This racetrack has year-round harness racing, a daily-double race, and trifectas and perfectas with wagering. The track also hosts flea markets in spring and summer. | Rte. 17B | 845/794–4100 | www.monticelloraceway.com/ | $1.50 Sun., free Mon.–Wed. | Sun.–Wed.

Woodstock Music Festival Monument. A stone memorial in Bethel roughly 8 mi from Monticello marks the location of the legendary 1969 Woodstock music festival. The concert site, now called "A Day in the Garden," hosts a summer concert series. | Rte. 17B to Hurd Rd. | 845/794–3000 ext. 5010 | Free | Call for concert schedule.

ON THE CALENDAR

AUG.: *A Day in the Garden.* The anniversary of the 1969 Woodstock music festival is celebrated in Bethel, at the original site. Concerts are presented all season with special shows scheduled for the anniversary weekend.

Dining

Eldred Preserve. Continental. This cozy place overlooks trout ponds and offers casual dining with fresh trout almandine, steaks, and sandwiches. Kids' menu. | Rte. 55, Eldred | 845/

557–8316 | www.eldredpreserve.com | Closed Mon., Tues. between Labor Day–Memorial Day | $12–$19 | AE, D, DC, MC, V.

Hana. Japanese, Korean. An authentic Japanese eatery that offers several tranquil dining rooms with an indoor water garden and bar and is known for sushi, sashimi, and tempura. | 166 Bridgeville Rd. | 845/794–3700 | $18–$25 | AE, MC, V.

Tre Alberi. Italian. This quaint eatery offers small tables and soft lighting and is known for traditional Italian fare with freshly prepared pasta dishes, fish, and veal. Full bar. | 110 Rte. 97, Barryville | 845/557–6104 | No lunch | $11–$17 | AE.

Lodging

Econo Lodge. Well-maintained, modest accommodations are near shopping, skiing, and other sports attractions. Complimentary Continental breakfast. Pool. Some kitchenettes, some in-room hot tubs, cable TV. Business services. No pets. | 190 Broadway St. | 845/794–8800 | www.econo.com | 47 rooms | $60 | AE, D, DC, MC, V.

Raceway Motel. Racing fans will be delighted to know that the Monticello Raceway is only ¼ mi from this single-story motel. If you get hungry, a diner is just a short walk away. Cable TV. No pets. | 202 Broadway | 845/794–6500 | 19 rooms | $45–$60 | AE, D, MC, V.

MT. KISCO

MAP 3, C1

(Nearby towns also listed: Croton-on-Hudson, Peekskill, Pound Ridge)

Mt. Kisco is a quaint yet modern town of about 10,000, originally settled in 1719. Its name comes from the Native American term for "muddy place," which refers to the Kisco River flowing through the village. After the railroad was completed in 1847, the community became popular with wealthy city dwellers as a summer retreat. The arts have always played a significant role in the community. The Lawrence Farms Playhouse has featured such stars as Burl Ives, Mildred Natwick, and Henry Fonda.

Information: **Mt. Kisco Chamber of Commerce** | 3 N. Moger Ave., 10549 | 914/666–7525 | mkcc@imr-mkt.com | www.countynet.com/mkcc.html.

Attractions

Caramoor Center for Music and the Arts. The center's Spanish Courtyard and the Venetian Theater resonate with the sounds of some of the world's finest classical and jazz performers. The center displays an extraordinary collection of Renaissance and Eastern art and also features lovely gardens. | 149 Girdle Ridge Rd. | 845/232–5035 | fax 845/232–5521 | www.caramoor.com | Mar.–Dec., Wed.–Sun.

John Jay Homestead State Historic Site. The estate of John Jay, the first Chief Justice of the United States Supreme Court, features period furnishings and traces Jay's life and career. | 400 Jay St. (Rte. 22), Katonah | 914/232–5651 | fax 845/232–8085 | $3 | May–Oct., Wed.–Sat. 10–4, Sun 12–4; Nov.–Apr., by appointment.

Northern Westchester Center for the Arts. This center offers year-round arts activities and performances that appeal to all ages. Events, programs, and workshops explore the creative and expressive arts. | 272 North Bedford Rd. | 914/241–6922 | fax 914/241–0137 | www.nwcaonline.org | Call for schedule.

ON THE CALENDAR

MAY: *Memorial Day Parade.* The entire town turns out for a slice of Americana and some good old-fashioned flag waving. Marchers in this brief parade include community organizations and marching bands. | Memorial Day | 914/666–7525.

Dining

Cafe Antico. Italian. Subdued lighting and fresh flowers at each table set a romantic mood. Try the spaghetti with imported baby octopus or the pasta *bianco e nero,* a black and white spaghetti entrée with calamari and shrimp in a mildly spicy cherry pepper, lobster consumé. The Venetian winged lions at the bar add a nice touch. | 251 Lexington Ave. | 845/242–7490 | $16–$26 | AE, D, DC, MC, V.

Crabtree's Kittle House. Contemporary. This elegant colonial inn outside of Mt. Kisco dates to 1790 and is surrounded by gardens and known for creatively prepared fare such as grilled Hudson Valley foie gras with toasted brioche, candied orange, and Bordeaux syrup. Open-air dining in garden. Live jazz weekends. Kids' menu. Sunday brunch. | 11 Kittle Rd., Chappaqua | 914/666–8044 | No lunch Sat. | $17–$29 | AE, D, DC, MC, V.

Traveler's Rest. Continental. This scenic 1880s spot features European flair with duck ponds and a waterfall and inside, rich wood paneling on the walls, and cozy fireplaces. Known for German specialties such as sauerbraten and also steak and seafood. Kids' menu. | Rte. 100, Yorktown | 845/941–7744 | Closed Tues. No lunch | $28–$35 | MC, V.

Lodging

Holiday Inn. Known as the "Hudson Valley country manor," this two-floor hotel has well-maintained rooms and offers pleasant amenities for both business and leisure travelers. Restaurant, bar (with entertainment), room service. In-room data ports, cable TV. Pool. Laundry facilities. Business services. Pets allowed. | 1 Holiday Inn Dr. | 845/241–2600 | fax 914/241–4742 | www.basshotels.com/holiday-inn | 122 rooms | $150–$170 | AE, D, DC, MC, V.

Ramada Inn. This two-story hotel is just 6 mi from Mt. Kisco and within walking distance of a handful of fine restaurants. For those who prefer the bustling big city, New York City is 40-minute away by train. Restaurant, bar, room service. In-room data ports. Cable TV. Pool. Gym, volleyball. Laundry services. Business services. No pets. | 94 Business Park Dr., Armonk | 845/273–9090 | fax 914/273–4105 | www.ramada.com | 140 rooms | $189 | AE, D, DC, MC, V.

MT. TREMPER

MAP 3, J8

(Nearby towns also listed: Kingston, Woodstock)

Mount Tremper is along the Esopus Creek, known as a blue-ribbon trout stream. The creek attracts fly-fishermen and is a popular spot for tubing and also picnicking along the creek banks.

Information: **Chamber of Commerce** | 21 Tinker St., Woodstock, 12498 | 845/679–8025.

Attractions

Catskill Corners Marketplace. The world's largest kaleidoscope is housed in a converted 60-ft silo next to the historic 1841 Riseley Barn. Visitors step inside the kaleidoscope to view the changing patterns. Other attractions focus on kaleidoscopes, and you can tour the grounds, galleries, shops, and dine at the restaurant. | 5340 Rte. 28 | 845/688–5800 | www.catskillcorners.com | $10 | Mid-Sept.–May, Wed.–Mon. 10–5; June–mid-Sept., daily 10–7.

Dining

Catskill Rose. Contemporary American. There's a funky Art Deco motif inside and a brick courtyard outside for those who prefer to eat alfresco. The energetic restaurant is known for fresh seafood and smoked duck. Kids' menu. | 5355 Rte. 212 | 845/688–7100 | Closed Mon.–Wed. No lunch | $13–$18 | AE, D, DC, MC, V.

La Duchesse Anne. French. This midsize restaurant in a hotel features Victorian furnishings with many antiques and a working fireplace in the center of the dining room. Rack of lamb and *cotriade bretonne* (fish stew) are specialties. Sunday brunch. | 1564 Wittenberg Rd. | 845/688–5260 | www.laduchesseanne.com | Closed Feb., Mar.; Tues. in Apr.–June. No lunch Mon.–Sat. | $15–$35 | AE, D, DC, MC, V.

Spotted Dog. American. Six booths and a play area sit in the front of the authentic fire truck parked in the center of this casual eatery. Try the fire-dog chicken-breast sandwich, served on a croissant with cheddar cheese and garlic sauce. The menu's extensive selection of Mexican dishes includes the popular Frisbee quesadilla with barbecued pork. Kids' menu. | 5340 Rte. 28 | 845/688–7700 | $11–$17 | AE, D, MC, V.

Lodging

La Duchesse Anne. This intimate B&B is surrounded by shade trees and filled with Victorian-style furnishings. Restaurant *(see* La Duchesse Anne), bar, complimentary Continental breakfast. No room phones. Pets allowed. | 1564 Wittenberg Rd. | 845/688–5260 | fax 845/688–2438 | www.laduchesseanne.com | 10 rooms | $90 | AE, D, DC, MC, V.

Lodge at Catskill Corner. Tucked in the Catskill Forest, this inn combines modern luxury with the rustic charm of a log cabin. The rooms have log beds and furniture, and some have fireplaces. Restaurant, complimentary Continental breakfast. In-room data ports, some refrigerators, some in-room hot tubs, cable TV. | 5368 Rte. 28 | 845/688–2828 | www.catskillcorners.com | 27 rooms | $190–$370 | AE, MC, V.

Woodstock Country Inn. The paintings and hand-painted furniture of Woodstock artist Jo Catine are sprinkled throughout this inn in her former home. A heated pool in a wildflower meadow overlooks the Catskill Mountains. The inn is just 6 mi from Mt. Tremper. Complimentary breakfast. Some in-room VCRs, no room phones, no TV in some rooms. Pool. Business services. No pets. No kids under 12. No smoking. | 27 Cooper Lake Rd., Bearsville | 845/679–9380 | info@woodstockcountryinn.com | www.woodstockcountryinn.com | 4 rooms | $145–$250 | D, MC, V.

NAPLES

MAP 3, E7

(Nearby towns also listed: Canandaigua, Hammondsport, Penn Yan)

This tiny village is a tourist favorite, thanks to the picturesque surrounding hills. Naples dates back to 1789 and many original landmarks survive. The area's famous grape pie, made with dark grapes, is only available in fall.

Information: **Ontario County Tourism** | Five Lakes Suite, 20 Ontario St., Canandaigua, 14424-1806 | 716/394–3915 and 877/FUN–IN–NY | fax 716/394–4067 | info@tourismny.com | www.ontariony.com.

Attractions

Arbor Hills Grapery. From chardonnay to spumante, Arbor Hill has been producing quality wines and gourmet foods since 1986. Since it is relatively small, there are no winery tours, but stop in the gift shop to sample the fare. | 6461 Rte. 64 | 716/374–2406 or 800/554–7553 | fax 716/374–9198 | www.thegrapery.com | Free | May–Dec., Mon.–Sat. 10–5, Sun. 11–5; Jan.–Apr., Sat. 10–5, Sun. 11–5.

Cumming Nature Center of the Rochester Museum and Science Center. The environmental center has 6 mi of trails for nature walks, cross-country skiing, and snowshoeing (rentals available). The visitor center has numerous exhibits, including a 300-gallon freshwater tank stocked with rock bass, sunfish, and perch, a tank with four species of painted turtles, a tank with a snapping turtle, and an interactive display of the harvesting practices of the Haudenosaune (the Seneca tribe). | 6472 Gulick Rd. | 716/374–6160 | $4 | Wed.–Sun. 9–5.

Widmer's Wine Cellars. Tastings and tours are offered at one of the largest wineries along the eastern seaboard, which bottles wine under the labels of Widmer, Great Western, and Taylor. | 1 Lake Niagara La. | 716/374–6311 or 800/836–5253 | Free | May–Oct., Mon.–Sat. 10–4, Sun. 11:30–4:30; Nov.–Apr., daily 1–4.

ON THE CALENDAR

SEPT.: *Great Grape Festival.* The festival hosts an arts-and-crafts fair, food concessions, and a grape-pie baking contest at Memorial Town Hall Park on Main Street. | 716/374–2240.

Dining

Bob's and Ruth's/The Vineyard. American. Offers both casual dining in the main dining room and a more formal setting in its Vineyard Room, which is only opened seasonally, with fresh flowers on the table and a view of the vineyards. Daily chicken and beef dinner specials, homemade bread, soups, and desserts are served along with a salad bar. Open-air dining. Kids' menu. | 204 Main St. | 716/374–5122 | Breakfast also available; closed Dec.–Mar. | $7–$20 | MC, V.

Naples Diner. American. Photos documenting the diner's evolution since its opening in 1930 and Naples-area memorabilia give this place its charm. Breakfast all day, delicious cheeseburgers, and the macaroni and cheese keep customers coming back. Try the strawberry-rhubarb pie. | 139 S. Main St. | 716/374–5420 | Breakfast also available; no dinner weekends | $5–$8 | No credit cards.

Naples Hotel. Continental. The restaurant is inside a century-old hotel that's filled with Victorian antiques. Over the years, dignitaries and politicians have given speeches from the front porch. Specialties include German fare, a 16-ounce steak, and fresh seafood. Pianist Friday and Saturday evenings. Kids' menu. | 111 S. Main St. | 716/374–5630 | Call for winter hours | $10–$34 | AE, D, MC, V.

Redwood. American. This comfortable and family-friendly restaurant includes a coffee shop and a dining room and serves home-style fare and fresh-baked pie. Kids' menu. | 6 Cohocton St. | 716/374–6360 | Breakfast also available; closed Mon. | $8–$16 | D, MC, V.

Lodging

Cheshire Inn Bed and Breakfast. Formerly the Landmark Retreat, this 1830 Colonial home is surrounded by 13 acres of farmland and woods 6 mi north of Naples. This Colonial farmhouse has a country-casual decor. Furnishings are country style for relaxed accommodations and rooms come with a view of Canandaigua Lake. Complimentary breakfast. TV and phone in common area. | 6004 Rte. 21 | 716/396–2383 | www.cheshireinn.com | 6 rooms | $75–$125 | MC, V.

Naples Valley Bed & Breakfast. Both rooms at this 1962 Craftsman-style home, furnished with American antiques, have striking views of Canandaigua Lake. The gathering room has a refrigerator, microwave, and VCR for your use. Dining room, complimentary breakfast. TV in common area. Laundry facilities. No pets. No smoking. | 7161 County Rd. 12 | 716/374–6379 | 2 rooms | $95 | No credit cards.

Vagabond Bed and Breakfast. This 8,000-square-ft hotel features eclectic contemporary furnishings, stone floors accented with wood trim, and floor-to-ceiling windows overlooking the lake. The huge building sits on a secluded hilltop and each room is individually decorated. Complimentary breakfast. Some in-room hot tubs, some fireplaces, in-room VCRs (movies). | 3300 Slitor Rd. | 716/554–6271 | www.thevagabondinn.com | 5 rooms | $115–$225 | MC, V.

NEWBURGH

MAP 3, K9

(Nearby towns also listed: Fishkill, Goshen, Middletown)

George Washington had his headquarters in Newburgh from April 1782 to August 1783. It was here that he announced the end of the Revolutionary War and disbanded the army. This historic Hudson River town has lost much of its old architecture to urban renewal, but preservation efforts are saving houses and buildings that remain from the early days. Stewart International Airport is in Newburgh, and the city is convenient to Interstate 87, the United States Military Academy at West Point, and the Storm King Art Center.

Information: Chamber of Commerce | 47 Grand St., 12550 | 845/562–5100.

Attractions

Washington's Headquarters. After the British surrender, George Washington and his wife Martha remained at this site for 1½ years, until the last of the British left New York. The home and grounds were designated a National Historic Site in 1848. Guided tours point out where Washington and his troops lived and worked and the chain of events that marked the Revolutionary War. There are displays of clothing and equipment and special events are held throughout the year. | 84 Liberty St. | 845/562–1195 | $3 | Wed.–Sun. 10–5.

ON THE CALENDAR

JUNE: *The General's Lady.* This festival at Washington's Headquarters celebrates the birthday of Martha Washington with music, food, and craft demonstrations. | 845/562–1195.

JUNE: *Riverfest.* This riverfront celebration at Cornwall Landing, Cornwall-on-Hudson, features music, food, crafts, and boats tours to Bannerman Island, site of a stone castle. | 845/534–4200.

AUG.: *Kites Over the Hudson.* Hundreds of kites fill the air, with free kites distributed to the first 150 kids at Washington's Headquarters. | 845/562–1195.

Dining

Chianti Restaurant. Italian. Large frescos, a Picasso, and wine racks dress up this restaurant, which specializes in northern Italian cuisine. Recommended dishes include the zuppa di pesce, which is a combination of seafood over pasta, and the marinated chicken breast with chardonnay sauce and melted mozzarella. | 362 Broadway | 845/561–3103 | Reservations essential Fri., Sat. | $15–$26 | AE, D, DC, MC, V.

Painter's. American. Housed in one of Cornwall-on-Hudson's historic buildings, this restaurant displays the work of local artists and is known for inventive pasta dishes, seafood, an extensive beer selection, and beer-can chicken (chicken grilled and steamed with beer on the outdoor grill). Open-air dining. Kids' menu. Sunday brunch. | 266 Hudson St., Cornwall-on-Hudson | 845/534–2109 | $8–$19 | AE, D, DC, MC, V.

Lodging

Comfort Inn. This three-story hotel is a short jaunt on foot to a couple of good eateries. Woodbury Commons Outlet Mall and Bear Mountain are approximately 15 mi away. Complimentary Continental breakfast. In-room data ports, some refrigerators, cable TV. Pool. Exercise equipment. Laundry services. Business services. No pets. | 5 Lakeside Rd. | 845/567–0567 | fax 845/567–0582 | www.comfortinn.com | 128 rooms, 2 suites | $99 rooms, $125 suites | AE, D, DC, MC, V.

NEW PALTZ

(Nearby towns also listed: Kingston, Poughkeepsie, Rhinebeck, Walden)

Home to the the State University of New York at New Paltz, this is an energetic college town with eclectic shopping and dining downtown. One of the oldest communities in the nation, the town was founded in the late 1600s by Huguenots who received a land grant from the Colonial governor. Buildings dating to the early 1700s still stand throughout this historic town. It's also a gateway to Minnewaska State Park Preserve, a popular spot among hikers and rock climbers, and the town hosts many crafts fairs and other events.

Information: **New Paltz Chamber of Commerce** | 257½ Main St., 12561 | 845/255–0243.

Attractions

Huguenot Street Old Stone Houses. This collection of stone houses dating from 1692 to 1712 is among the oldest in the nation. Many feature original furnishings and guided tours. | 64 Huguenot St., DuBois Fort | 845/255–1889 | $3–$10 | May–Oct., Tues.–Sun. 9–4.

Locust Lawn. Josiah Hasbrouck's 1814 Federal-style mansion has a striking three-story central hall and a collection of 18th- and 19th-century furniture. The farm museum contains an ox cart that was used to carry supplies to the Continental army at Valley Forge. Nearby is Terwilliger House, a preserved Huguenot-era stone building. Though the home is under restoration until 2002, you can call to arrange an appointment for a tour. | 400 Rte. 32, Gardiner | 845/255–1660 | $7 | Call for hrs, appointments.

Minnewaska State Park Preserve. This park in the Shawangunk Mountains is a favorite of rock climbers. It also offers trails for hikers, and a network of historic carriageways which are now used by mountain bikers, horseback riders, and hikers. With a permit, boating is also available. In winter, the preserve lures cross-country skiers. | 5 mi from the intersection of 299 and Rtes. 44/55 | 845/255–0752 | www.ulster.net/~emeyer/minne.html | $6 per vehicle | Daily dawn–dusk.

State University of New York at New Paltz. On the campus is a theater and an art gallery and, in summer, the Music in the Mountains concert series and the College Summer Repertory Theatre are presented. | Rte. 32 S | 845/257–2121 | www.newpaltz.edu | Free | Daily.

ON THE CALENDAR

MAY, SEPT.: *New Paltz/Woodstock Art and Crafts Fair.* This juried art-and-crafts fair is held Memorial Day and Labor Day weekends at the fairgrounds. It showcases potters, photographers, jewelry designers, and other artists from across the nation and the food is a notch above traditional fair choices, with plenty of vegetarian and unusual choices. | 845/340–3000.
AUG.: *Ulster County Fair.* This county fair has maintained a charming and old-fashioned flavor throughout the years and features livestock exhibits and local crafts at the fairgrounds. | 845/340–3000.

Dining

Hokkaido Japanese Restaurant. Japanese. Dine on sushi beneath lovely handcrafted Japanese lanterns at this informal restaurant. Popular entrées include chicken teriyaki and the house special, spicy noodles. | 18 Church St. | 845/256–0621 | No lunch weekends | $12–$22 | AE, D, MC, V.

Locust Tree Inn. American. Half of this historic building was built in the 1700s and the other half in the 1800s. It's furnished with period pieces and has a beamed ceiling and a massive central fireplace. The dining room has picture windows that overlook a 9-hole golf course. Seafood cioppino (seafood stew in a tomato broth) and grilled Moroccan barbecued lamb with roasted eggplant, sun-dried tomatoes, mint relish, and potatoes galette are specialties. Open-air dining offers a view of the golf course. Sunday brunch. | 215 Huguenot St. | 845/255–7888 | No lunch. Closed Mon., Tues. | $16–$21 | AE, MC, V.

Lodging

Days Inn. This single-story motel is 2 mi east of the State University of New York at New Paltz and equally near to shopping and restaurants. Complimentary Continental breakfast. Cable TV. | 601 Main St. | 845/883–7373 | www.daysinn.com | 20 rooms | $60–$139 | AE, D, DC, MC, V.

Mohonk Mountain House. This noteworthy mountain lodge and resort resembles a Victorian castle and is surrounded by expansive grounds. It sits next to a lake and borders the national forest. Luxurious and spacious rooms are filled with antiques, and many have working fireplaces. The resort's lake has a beach and paddleboats for rent. Hiking trails adjoin the grounds and the resort can arrange for mountain climbing and other outdoor and sporting adventures. Restaurant, room service. No air-conditioning, TV in common area. 9-hole golf course, putting green, tennis. Gym, beach, boating. Ice-skating. Library. Children's programs 2–12. Laundry facilities. Airport shuttle. | 1000 Mountain Rest Rd. | 845/255–1000 or 800/772–6646 | fax 845/256–2161 | www.mohonk.com | 261 rooms | $305–$580 | AE, D, DC, MC, V.

Mountain Rest Bed & Breakfast. This secluded B & B is on 4 wooded acres. Country furnishings accent the dramatic main room with its vaulted ceiling and sunburst windows. Some rooms have exceptional views of the Mohonk Preserve and Hudson Valley. Complimentary breakfast. Some in-room hot tubs, no room phones, TV in common area. Outdoor hot tub. Gym. No pets. No kids under 12. No smoking. | 227 Mountain Rest Rd. | 845/255–7378 | info@mountainrestbnb.com | www.mountainrestbnb.com | 4 rooms | $125–$150 | MC, V.

NEW ROCHELLE

MAP 3, C2

(Nearby towns also listed: Elmsford, Hartsdale, Hawthorne, Mamaroneck, Rye, Scarsdale, Tarrytown, White Plains, Yonkers)

In 1688, when Huguenots purchased large tracts of land in this area, they named it after their French seacoast city of La Rochelle. Because of their proximity to the ocean, early settlers were boatbuilders. One of the oldest cities in the Northeast, New Rochelle was the home to patriot and author Thomas Paine, whose writings profoundly affected public opinion regarding the War for Independence. More recently, it has been known as the home of Rob and Laura Petrie on the TV comedy classic *The Dick Van Dyke Show*. Today, New Rochelle has about 70,000 residents and the city's architecture ranges from serene century-old Victorian homes to ultramodern landmarks.

Information: **Chamber of Commerce** | 557 Main St., 10801 | 914/632–5700.

Attractions

Castle Gallery. Located at the College of New Rochelle, this gallery hosts exhibitions of fine art and contemporary crafts, sculpture, and works in applied design. | 29 Castle Pl. | 914/654–5423 | Free | Tues.–Fri. 10–5, Sat., Sun. 12–4. Closed Mon., major holidays, and weekends in Jan.

Thomas Paine National Historical Association and Museum. This historical attraction includes the farmhouse and former home of Thomas Paine, America's famous patriot and journalist. The Paine Memorial Building contains many historic artifacts. | 983 North Ave. | 914/632–5376 | fax 914/632–9522 | www.thomas-paine.com/tpnha | Donations accepted | Apr.–Oct., Fri.–Sun. 2–5; call for appointment.

JULY: *Japan Air Lines Big Apple Classic LPGA Golf Tournament.* This premier professional golf tournament for women is played at the historic Wykagyl Country Club. At this 72-hole event, 144 top-ranked golfers compete for total prize money totaling more than $850,000. | 800/444–LPGA.

Dining

La Riserva–Trattoria. Italian. This longtime dining spot is a favorite of locals and serves classic Italian fare in four dining rooms. Inside, large French doors and windows and paintings from Rome adorn the walls. Veal scaloppine trattoria with asparagus, roasted peppers, and mozzarella; and angel-hair *abissimarini,* which is angel-hair pasta served in a light cream sauce, with brandy, shrimp, and mushrooms, are popular dishes. Kids' menu. | 2382 Boston Post Rd., Larchmont | 914/834–5584 | No lunch Sat. | $13–$22 | AE, MC, V.

Tandoori–Taste of India. Indian. This restaurant features more than 40 regional Indian dishes, as well as an Art Deco bar and cigar lounge. Specialties are chicken curry, grilled lamb, and seafood. Buffet. Weekend brunch. | 30 Division St. | 914/235–8390 | $10–$28 | AE, D, MC, V.

Lodging

Ramada Plaza. Spacious, traditionally furnished rooms are offered in a multistory hotel that provides easy access to commercial centers of New York City, Westchester County, and Connecticut. Restaurant, bar. In-room data ports, some refrigerators, cable TV. Pool. Exercise equipment. Business services. Free parking. | 1 Ramada Plaza | 914/576–3700 | fax 914/576–3711 | 128 rooms | $157 | AE, D, DC, MC, V.

Residence Inn. From the top floors of this 10-story all-suite hotel you will see Manhattan's skyline and the Long Island Sound. Suites range from studios to two bedrooms and all accommodations have full kitchens. The hotel is accessible by taking the New Rochelle exit (16) off I–95. One restaurant, complimentary breakfast. In-room data ports, microwaves, refrigerators, cable TV, room phones. Outdoor pool. Exercise equipment. Laundry facilities, laundry services. Business services. No pets. | 35 La Count Pl. | 914/636–7888 | fax 914/636–7979 | www.residenceinn.com | 124 rooms | $139–$250 | AE, D, DC, MC, V.

NEW YORK CITY

MAP 3, B3

(Nearby towns also listed: Freeport, Garden City, Great Neck, Rockville Center, White Plains, Yonkers; Hoboken, Jersey City, and Newark, NJ)

New York City sprawls across five boroughs: Manhattan, Queens, Brooklyn, the Bronx, and Staten Island. Over 7 million residents live in this area (which covers a little more than 300 square mi), and additional millions flood in and out of the city each day as commuters.

An endless variety of sights can be found along New York City's busy streets—world-class museums and unusual galleries, breathtaking skyscrapers, historic town houses, vibrant neighborhoods, parks, gardens, and much, much more. Because the city can only grow up, not out, the new simply piles on top of the old; the juxtapositions are endless and amusing—quaint town houses stand shoulder to shoulder with sleek glass towers, gleaming gourmet supermarkets sit around the corner from dusty thrift shops, and chic bistros inhabit the storefronts of soot-smudged warehouses.

New York City is, perhaps above all, a city of immigrants, a "global" town made up of an amazing collection of peoples, gathered from virtually every nation on the planet. Indeed, by the year 1650, barely 25 years after it was settled and when the population was only 4,500, there were already 18 languages spoken in Manhattan. Today, in what sociologists call a "conurbation" of 19.7 million people—encompassing the entire metropolitan New York area, which includes parts of upstate New York, New Jersey, Long Island, and Connecticut—over 90 languages are spoken, and newspapers appear in two dozen of them. No other place on Earth boasts such an amazing polyglot amalgam of people.

It has been less than 400 years since Manhattan grew from a windswept Algonquian oystering station into the most densely populated place in America. The original inhabitants of the area were members of several of the hundreds of autonomous Algonquian bands that hunted and fished in the area. Brooklyn was the territory of the coastal Canarsee tribe, while Staten Island was under the control of roving bands of Lenape tribes.

Giovanni da Verrazano, the official European discoverer of New York, spied the island of Manhattan in 1524, and, a year after Verrazano's visit, Esteban Gomez, a Portuguese Moor sailing for Spain, also sighted the island and the magnificent bay. But it wasn't until Henry Hudson arrived in 1609 that the area was systematically explored by European eyes, when he sailed in search of India up the waterway that would one day bear his name. Hudson's expedition opened the door for Dutch settlement of the area. The Dutch West India company set up the first trading post here in 1615, and in 1624 Peter Minuit is alleged to have purchased Manhattan island from Native Americans for a pittance in beads and trinkets. Conflicts with indigenous peoples and a succession of incompetent or corrupt Dutch governors followed. Peter Stuyvesant, the last Dutch governor of New Amsterdam (as the island was called), inherited a miserable, struggling town in 1647, made considerable headway in improving conditions, and ultimately handed over a thriving city to the British in 1664. The island was promptly renamed in honor of the Duke of York.

From 1776 until 1783, the period of the Revolutionary War, the city was occupied by the British. Manhattan was a haven for British sympathizers, mostly wealthy merchants and shippers who prospered as suppliers to the British army. Insurrectionists who were unable or unwilling to flee suffered the indignities of occupation, including the forced quartering of British troops in their homes. Despite local support, the British occupiers torched Manhattan in 1776, burning a quarter of it, including Trinity Church (home to the first Episcopal congregation in America and today one of the city's best-known landmarks). By the time the Loyalists and British surrendered New York to the Americans on November 25, 1783—eight months after the end of the war—the city was ravaged, it's population decimated (at half its prewar level of 25,000), and its economy in ruins. From Trinity Church to the Battery, the city was a charred swath.

Two years after the surrender, New York City had recovered enough of its grandeur to become the capital of the United States, which it would be for the next five years, from 1785 to 1790. New York continued to rebuild and to grow at an astonishing rate. From 1789 to roughly 1800, the city's population doubled to almost 70,000 people, and Manhattan's devotion to trade was becoming more and more apparent.

By the middle of the 19th century, many of the developments that were to make New York a world-class city were already in place. In 1801, Alexander Hamilton founded the *New York Post*—not the city's first newspaper, but the oldest one still publishing. The New York Stock Exchange began in 1792 with traders gathering under a buttonwood tree near its present-day site of business. In the first decade of the next century, Robert Fulton successfully harnessed steam power, and, with the opening of the Erie Canal in 1825, New York became the nation's busiest seaport, eventually surpassing Philadelphia as a center of business.

European immigrants continued to pour in; an average of 4,000 a year arrived during the 1820s, and 14,000 arrived in 1830 alone. The German revolutions of the 1840s, the Irish Potato Famine of 1846–51, and other political upheavals on the Continent served to spur emigration to America. From 1840 to 1856, 3 million immigrants arrived, representing a never-again-equaled ratio of newcomers to the existing population. All through this period, while some were building fortunes, others were living in filth and squalor, particularly in the Five Points area (the intersection of Baxter, Worth, and Mulberry streets, near present-day Foley Square). Cholera and yellow fever epidemics plagued the city.

For the upper classes, the last decade of the century was indeed the "Gay Nineties," a period of fancy dress balls and social snobbery. However, vast socioeconomic changes were underway that would forever impact the politics of New York. In the first two decades of the new century, a third of Eastern Europe's Jews emigrated (over 1½ million people in all), most to New York City and environs. They joined peasants and laborers from the south of Italy, and continuing influxes from Ireland, Germany, and Russia. In Ellis Island's peak year as an immigrant-receiving station, 1,285,349 people passed through it, sometimes at the astonishing rate of 5,000 a day. By sheer weight of numbers, the new European immigrants tipped the political scales of New York to the left. Many of them, indeed, were socialists and communists fleeing from the oppressive regimes of Europe and, in America, they began to agitate for social and workplace reforms.

In the 1920s, speakeasies and hard partying were the order of the day until it all came crashing down in 1929. Fiorello La Guardia took the city's mayoral reins and repeatedly championed the city in Washington, receiving aid in the form of New Deal public works programs that employed thousands of people. The Triborough Bridge, the Henry Hudson Bridge, the Battery Park Tunnel, and numerous other projects were completed during his terms.

In the two decades following World War II, over 1 million families left New York. Corporate headquarters, which used to be in Manhattan as a matter of course, now decamped to exurban ring cities, lured by lower taxes. As in many American cities, everyone prosperous enough to leave New York seemed to be doing so, until Manhattan was left with a brutally segregated, two-tiered society: the rich, who could afford the high cost of living and the higher taxes, and the poor, who drained the coffers of social welfare funds. Only a government bailout in 1978 protected the city from bankruptcy, and slowly people began to move back to the city during the boom decade of the 1980s.

Today, the city's population—unlike the dwindling population of other major urban centers across America—remains stable and the mood in town is generally confident and optimistic. Like the rest of the country, New York has benefited from the technology and stock market upswing of the 1990s, and gentrification has occurred in much of Manhattan and is now spreading its golden tentacles into other boroughs.

MANHATTAN NEIGHBORHOODS

The map of Manhattan has a Jekyll-and-Hyde aspect. The rational Dr. Jekyll part prevails above 14th Street, where the streets form a regular grid pattern, imposed in 1811. Numbered streets run east and west (crosstown), while broad avenues, most of them also numbered, run north (uptown) and south (downtown). The chief exceptions are Broadway and the thoroughfares that hug the shores of the Hudson and East Rivers. Broadway runs the entire length of Manhattan. At its southernmost end it follows the city's north–south grid; at E. 10th Street it turns and runs on a diagonal to W. 86th Street, then at a lesser angle until 107th Street, where it merges with West End Avenue. Below 14th Street—the area settled before the 1811 grid was decreed—Manhattan streets reflect the disordered personality of Mr. Hyde. They may be aligned with the shoreline, or they may twist along the route of an ancient cow path.

Central Park. This 843-acre patch of rolling countryside is where Manhattanites go to escape from the urban jungle and reconnect with nature. Named a National Historic Landmark in 1965, Central Park offers the city's most soothing vistas and opportunities for just about any activity that a city dweller might engage in outdoors—all right

in the heart of Manhattan. Under the care of the private, not-for-profit Central Park Conservancy, the park is in better shape than ever before. The park is bordered by 59th Street on the south, 5th Avenue on the east, 110th Street on the north, and Central Park West (which is what 8th Avenue becomes north of 59th Street) on the west.

Chelsea. Like its London district namesake, New York's Chelsea maintains a villagelike personality, with a number of quiet streets graced by lovingly renovated town houses. The neighborhood stretches from 5th Avenue west to the Hudson River, and from 14th to 23rd streets (and above). Chelsea has always attracted writers and artists, and embraced a multicultural population for decades; today the area includes an active gay community. The neighborhood is home to lively stores and restaurants on 8th Avenue, and in recent years it has enjoyed an economic boost due to the opening of Chelsea Piers Sports and Entertainment Complex on the Hudson River. The gallery scene thrives west of 10th Avenue from 20th to 29th streets.

East Village. Many regard the East Village—an area bounded by 14th Street on the north, 4th Avenue or the Bowery on the west, Houston Street on the south, and the East River— as the island's most colorful neighborhood. Here, holdouts from the 1960s coexist with a deeply entrenched Eastern European community. Artists, punks, and executives move freely between the Polish and Ukrainian coffee shops, galleries, trendy pasta bars, offbeat shops, and St. Mark's Place—a local thoroughfare for sidewalk vendors.

5th Avenue and 57th Street. One of the world's great shopping districts, 5th Avenue north of Rockefeller Center and 57th Street between Lexington Avenue and 7th Avenue is where you'll find some of the biggest names in New York retailing, as well as the crème de la crème of designer boutiques.

Garment District. For a taste of Manhattan at its most frantic, dive into the Garment District on a weekday, where warehouses, workshops, and showrooms for retail and/or wholesale purchasers of mostly women's and children's clothing share the streets with countless button, fabric, and notions shops. From 6th Avenue to 8th Avenue, and from 31st Street to 41st Street, traffic is perpetually stalled, and if you're not careful, you could well get knocked over by one of the dozens of wheeling garment racks going 25 mph on the sidewalk in all directions.

Greenwich Village. Extending from 14th Street south to Houston Street, and from the piers of the Hudson River east to 5th Avenue, the crazy-quilt pattern of narrow, tree-lined streets known to New Yorkers simply as "the Village" remains true to its 19th-century heritage as a haven for immigrants, bohemians, students, artists, actors, carousers, and tourists. It's one of the best parts of the city to wander in for hours. The Village is still home to one of the largest gay communities in the country (centered on Sheridan Square and Christopher Street).

Harlem. For almost a century, Harlem has been the most famous African-American community in the United States. The fabled Harlem Renaissance in the 1920s resulted from the extraordinary gathering of black novelists, playwrights, musicians, and artists in a community that brought—and kept—them together. From the Depression through the 1960s and '70s, the area was in decline—with the nightclubs no longer a draw for wealthy Manhattanites, and middle-class families fleeing the crime and substandard housing for nearby suburbs. But today, Harlem is experiencing another renaissance, with neighborhoods and old landmarks like the great Apollo Theatre undergoing extensive renovation. Harlem spreads north from 110th Street to about 145th Street (the border of Manhattanville). The most interesting sights on the tourist trail fall roughly between 116th and 135th streets.

Little Italy and Chinatown. Little Italy—a few blocks south of Houston St. between Broadway and the Bowery—is today not as Italian as it used to be. Still, Mulberry Street and its famous—and, in some cases, infamous—eateries are rife with atmosphere. If you head east along Canal Street (the southern border of Little Italy), you will run into the ever-expanding and frenetic **Chinatown** (the area south of Canal on the

East Side), which over the years has spilled into much of the Lower East Side's Jewish neighborhood and Little Italy as well. Chinatown is popular among tourists, but it is also a very real and vital community where about half the city's population of 300,000 Chinese still live. The vast neighborhood has evolved into a virtual marketplace crammed with souvenir shops, tea parlors, and hundreds of restaurants that serve every imaginable type of Chinese cuisine, from real Peking Duck to fast-food dumplings. The narrow streets are packed with shoppers and purveyors of untold varieties of pungent fish and exotic vegetables, and you could easily wander onto a block where you would find not a written or spoken word of English. The main businesses are restaurants and textile and garment factories. Chinatown is bordered by Canal, Worth, and Mulberry streets and the Bowery and Chatham Square, but its thoroughfares are Mott, Pell, and Doyers streets.

Murray Hill to Union Square. Three distinct neighborhoods east of 5th Avenue between 20th and 40th streets—Murray Hill, Madison Square, and Gramercy Park—have preserved some of the historic charm of 19th-century New York: brownstone mansions and town houses, the city's earliest "skyscrapers," shady parks, and, yes, even in New York, some quiet streets. South of Gramercy Park lies Union Square, with its restored park, wonderful Greenmarket, and trendsetting restaurants.

Museum Mile and the Upper East Side. Once called Manhattan's Millionaire's Row, the stretch of 5th Avenue between 79th and 104th streets has been renamed Museum Mile because of the startling number of world-class collections of art and artifacts scattered along its length (some housed in the former mansions of some of the Upper East Side's more illustrious industrialists and philanthropists). It's also still home to more millionaires—and billionaires—than any other street in the city. Whatever you do, don't leave New York without visiting at least a few galleries in the largest art museum in the Western Hemisphere, the Metropolitan Museum of Art, on the Central Park side of 5th Avenue at 82nd Street.

Rockefeller Center and Midtown. Apart from sweeping panoramas from the Hudson River or the New York Bay, no other city scene so clearly says "New York" as the 19-building complex known as Rockefeller Center. These 22 acres of prime real estate (between 5th and 7th avenues and 47th and 52nd streets) contain the Channel Gardens; the GE, Time and Life, and Associated Press buildings; Radio City Music Hall; and plazas, concourses, and street-level shops, virtually forming a city within a city. St. Patrick's Cathedral, Saks Fifth Avenue, and the rest of Midtown's gleaming skyscrapers are just steps away.

Seaport and the Courts. New York's days as a great 19th-century haven for clipper ships are preserved in lower Manhattan at South Street Seaport, centered on Fulton Street at the East River and crowned by the Brooklyn Bridge. Just blocks away, you can take in another slice of New York history by walking the streets of the City Hall district, with its majestic court edifices.

SoHo and TriBeCa. SoHo (short for "south of Houston Street") is bounded on its other three sides by Broadway, Canal Street, and 6th Avenue. This neighborhood has become synonymous with artistic and eclectic elegance, very urban and still very "now." Its streets are clogged year-round with tourists and hardcore shoppers. The area is filled with fairly expensive boutiques and galleries, as well as very trendy restaurants. The marvelous cast-iron buildings, Belgian-block streets and pavements, warehouses that have been converted into multimillion-dollar lofts, and the fascinating ethnic neighborhoods that surround SoHo (Chinatown to the south, Little Italy to the east) have made this area a mecca for tourists and New Yorkers alike. **TriBeCa** (meaning "the triangle below Canal Street") extends roughly as far south as Murray Street and east to West Broadway. Over the past 20 years, both SoHo and TriBeCa have gradually been transformed into lively realms of loft dwellers, galleries, and ultratrendy shops and cafés.

Times Square, the Theater District, and 42nd Street. The place where the ball drops on

New Year's Eve, **Times Square** is one of the city's principal energy centers, and, some might say, one of the crossroads of the world. Perhaps no famous neighborhood in America has gone through a transformation more extreme than Times Square's recent "renovation." Gone (mostly) are the porn purveyors and palaces; swept away is the "sleaze"; now, thousands of tourists swoop in on a daily basis who are so busy looking up at the staggering, Tokyo-esque array of billboards, crawlers, and cranes that they bump into you and each other at every intersection. Some bemoan the loss of the area's vivid, if somewhat kinky, flavor; others herald this extreme and impressive example of urban renewal.

Manhattan's **Theater District** has been the city's—and the nation's—theatrical center since the turn of the 20th century. Thirty or so major Broadway theaters are in the area bounded roughly by 41st and 53rd streets between 6th and 9th avenues. Just a short walk away are Theater Row, a string of intimate off-Broadway houses on the south side of 42nd Street between 9th and 10th avenues, and Restaurant Row (46th Street between 8th and 9th avenues), where critics, actors, directors, playwrights, and spectators come to dine before and after the show.

Bryant Park and the New York Public Library gloriously mark **42nd Street**'s midpoint. Going much farther east on 42nd Street, past 5th Avenue, you'll discover the Beaux Arts beauty of Grand Central Terminal, grandly transformed, à la Washington, DC's Union Station, into a destination in its own right. East of Grand Central is the United Nations headquarters on a lushly landscaped riverside tract just east of 1st Avenue between 42nd and 48th streets.

Upper West Side. The ornate prewar buildings that line the boulevards of Broadway, West End Avenue, Riverside Drive, and Central Park West provide a stately backdrop for glitzy boutiques and the scads of wanna-be soap actors hustling off to their auditions at ABC-TV, not to mention hopeful performers and music aficionados making the pilgrimage to Lincoln Center. A stroll up Columbus Avenue should stretch at least as far as the American Museum of Natural History, whose lavish grounds and pink-granite corner towers occupy a four-block tract. Farther uptown, in Morningside Heights, are the ivied buildings of Columbia University and the Cathedral of St. John the Divine, a magnificent Episcopal church.

Wall Street and the Battery. The historic heart of New York continues to be dominated by Wall Street, which is both an actual Downtown street and a shorthand moniker for the huge and powerful financial community that is clustered around the New York and American stock exchanges. At the tip of Manhattan island, you can gaze across the shimmering harbor to the potent and enduring symbols of America: the Statue of Liberty and Ellis Island.

OUTER BOROUGHS

Driven over the river by astronomical rents, many Manhattanites discovered the outer boroughs—Brooklyn, Queens, the Bronx, and Staten Island—in the late 1970s and '80s. They found sky, trees, and living space among the 19th-century brownstones, converted industrial lofts, Art Deco apartment palaces, and tidy bungalows. They also found fascinating ethnic enclaves and a host of museums and parks. In fact, Manhattan's population of about 1.48 million is smaller than that of either Brooklyn (2 million) or Queens (1.95 million) and only slightly larger than that of the Bronx (1.2 million). Staten Island may be less populous (391,000), but it's 2½ times the size of Manhattan. There are things to see and do in the outer boroughs that you simply won't find in Manhattan, and most are just a subway ride away.

The Bronx. The only one of New York's boroughs attached to the North American mainland, the Bronx has been an emblem of urban decay for the past 30 years, but it is actually as diverse and rich in personality as the rest of the city. The borough is home to a famous botanical garden and a world-renowned zoo. In addition, there's the friendly Italian neighborhood of Belmont; wealthy Riverdale, with its riverside estates; and, of course, Yankee Stadium, the home of the New York Yankees.

Brooklyn. New York City's most populous borough is also its most popular—aside from Manhattan, that is. More people visit Brooklyn than any of the other outer boroughs, and still more come here to live. Several Brooklyn neighborhoods, particularly Brooklyn Heights, Park Slope, Cobble Hill, Carroll Gardens, and Fort Greene, are favored more than ever by young families and professionals, who are drawn by the dignified brownstone- and tree-lined streets, water views, handsome parks, friendly neighborhood businesses, and less-than-frenetic pace of life.

Queens. Home of the La Guardia and John F. Kennedy International airports and many of Manhattan's bedroom communities, Queens is perhaps New York City's most underappreciated borough. It's certainly the most diverse, as the borough's countless ethnic neighborhoods continue to attract immigrants from all over the world. Its inhabitants represent 117 nationalities and speak scores of languages, from Hindi to Hebrew. Queens communities, such as Astoria (Greek and Italian), Jackson Heights (Colombian, Mexican, and Indian), Sunnyside (Turkish and Romanian), and Flushing (Korean and Chinese), are fascinating to explore, particularly if you're interested in experiencing some of the city's tastiest—and least expensive—cuisine. In addition, these areas often feature little-known historic sites, many of them just 10 min by subway from Grand Central Terminal.

Staten Island. Even though Staten Island is officially a part of New York City, it is, to many New Yorkers, the forgotten borough. Its claims to fame are as the city's garbage dump and as the borough perpetually agitating to secede from the city. Settled by Dutch farmers in 1661, Staten Island today still feels provincial and even old-fashioned compared with the rest of the city; indeed, time stands still in the two re-created villages of Richmondtown and Snug Harbor. Although it's less convenient to get here than to the other boroughs, the 20-minute ferry ride across New York Harbor affords phenomenal views of lower Manhattan and the Statue of Liberty—and it's free.

TRANSPORTATION

Airports: The major gateways to New York City are **La Guardia Airport** (718/533–3400) and **JFK International Airport** (718/244–4444), both in the borough of Queens, and **Newark International Airport** (973/961–6000) in New Jersey. Most major carriers serve one or all of these airports.

Airport Transportation: Taxis and shuttle buses from Manhattan serve all major airports. A taxi from Manhattan to La Guardia should cost from $17 to $29 plus tolls (which can be as high as $4) and take 20–40 minutes; a flat fee of $30 plus tolls (which, again, can be as high as $4) is charged to JFK International and the ride is usually 35–60 minutes. Taxis to Newark International cost from $34 to $38 plus tolls ($10) and take 20–45 minutes. The **Gray Line Air Shuttle** (212/315–3006 or 800/451–0455) serves major Manhattan hotels directly to and from the airport. The fare is $12. **Olympia Trails Airport Express** (212/964–6233 or 718/622–7700) buses leave for Grand Central Terminal and Penn Station about every 20 minutes, and 1 World Trade Center (WTC) about every 30 minutes, 24 hours a day. The fare is $10. The **Delta Water Shuttle** (800/533–3779) runs every hour between La Guardia Airport's Marine Air Terminal and 34th and 62nd streets on the East Side, including a stop at Wall Street (Pier 11). The fare is $15, $25 round-trip. Both the M-60 and Q-33 public buses are available from La Guardia Airport and will take you to points connecting to subways that will take you into Midtown. There's a free shuttle bus from Kennedy International Airport to a connecting point with the A train subway line. For information, call **New York City Transit** (MTA; 718/330–1234).

Bus Lines: Long-haul and commuter bus lines feed into the Port Authority Terminal between 8th and 9th avenues from 40th to 42nd streets. **Greyhound Lines Inc.** (212/971–6361 or 800/231–2222) makes runs to many points in the country from the Port Authority Terminal.

Intra-city Transit: The 714-mi subway system operates 24 hours a day and, especially within Manhattan, serves most of the places you'll want to visit. It's cheaper ($1.50 a ride) than a cab and, during weekdays when traffic is especially horrible, it's usually faster than either cabs or buses. The subway is not problem-free, and it's received plenty of bad press over the years, but if you stay alert and keep track of your belongings it's a good way to access most of the tourist points in Manhattan. **Metropolitan Transit Authority (MTA) Travel Information Center** (718/330–1234).

Trains: Amtrak (800/872–7245) trains from points across the United States arrive at Penn Station (W. 31st to 33rd streets, between 7th and 8th avenues). For trains from New York City to Long Island and New Jersey, take the **Long Island Railroad** (718/217–5477) and **New Jersey Transit** (973/762–5100), respectively; both operate from Penn Station. **Metro-North Commuter Railroad** (212/532–4900) trains take passengers from Grand

KODAK'S TIPS FOR PHOTOGRAPHING THE CITY

Streets
- Take a bus or walking tour to get acclimated
- Explore markets, streets, and parks
- Travel light so you can shoot quickly

City Vistas
- Find high vantage points to reveal city views
- Shoot early or late in the day, for best light
- At twilight, use fast films and bracket exposures

Formal Gardens
- Exploit high angles to show garden design
- Use wide-angle lenses to exaggerate depth and distance
- Arrive early to beat crowds

Landmarks and Monuments
- Review postcard racks for traditional views
- Seek out distant or unusual views
- Look for interesting vignettes or details

Museums
- Call in advance regarding photo restrictions
- Match film to light source when color is critical
- Bring several lenses or a zoom

Houses of Worship
- Shoot exteriors from nearby with a wide-angle lens
- Move away and include surroundings
- Switch to a very fast film indoors

Stained-Glass Windows
- Bright indirect sunlight yields saturated colors
- Expose for the glass not the surroundings
- Switch off flash to avoid glare

Architectural Details
- Move close to isolate details
- For distant vignettes, use a telephoto lens
- Use side light to accent form and texture

In the Marketplace
- Get up early to catch peak activity
- Search out colorful displays and colorful characters
- Don't scrimp on film

Stage Shows and Events
- Never use flash
- Shoot with fast (ISO 400 to 1000) film
- Use telephoto lenses
- Focus manually if necessary

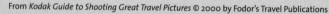

From *Kodak Guide to Shooting Great Travel Pictures* © 2000 by Fodor's Travel Publications

Central Terminal (E. 42nd Street at Park Avenue) to points north of New York City, both in New York State and Connecticut.

Driving Around Town: Prepare yourself—it's no picnic. Rush hour traffic via Manhattan's bridges and tunnels is notorious; plan to arrive and leave only in late morning or early afternoon. Adding to traffic problems, many of the East River bridges are often under repair. Manhattan gridlock and aggressive local drivers can make car travel frustrating, especially in midtown between 14th and 59th Streets. Although road conditions are pretty good, bad weather and detours can cause unexpected bottlenecks and delays.

Parking is scarce on the street, especially in midtown, and illegally parked cars may be ticketed or towed within minutes. If you do find a spot, read signs carefully; parking may be legal only at certain hours on certain days. High rates are the rule for parking lots and garages, some charging $15 for two hours; sometimes hourly rates are lower for longer stays.

In general, the speed limit for city streets is 30 mph, and seat belts are required in both front and back seats. Right turns on red are illegal. Also, if you're planning a night on the town, remember that police can seize the vehicle of any DWI offender, including first-timers.

Bottom line: New York City is best experienced on foot. Subways, buses, and taxis, all of which operate all night, are the surest means of traveling long distances within the city.

Attractions

ARTS AND ARCHITECTURE

Chrysler Building. This Art Deco masterpiece is the favorite building of many New Yorkers. This was the world's tallest building for 40 days, just until the Empire State Building was finished. The Chrysler Corporation moved out back in the mid-1950s, but the building retains the name and the spirit of that company's cars, with "gargoyles" shaped like hood ornaments. There's no observation deck in the Chrysler Building, but you can go into its elegant lobby to see the ceiling mural that portrays themes of transportation and human endeavor. | 405 Lexington Ave., at E. 42nd St. | 212/682–3070 | Free | Daily.

Empire State Building. Arguably the most famous building in America, at 102 stories and 1,250 ft, it's only the fifth-tallest building in the world, but it's still the most elegant and impressive. The two observation decks—one, outdoors on the 86th floor, and the other, glass-enclosed on the 102nd—have wraparound views, with 80-mi visibility on clear days. Don't miss the simulated two-story-tall-screen flight over New York City, "New York Skyride," down on the second floor. | 350 5th Ave., at 34th St. | 212/736–3100; 212/279–9777 Skyride | Observatory $9; "Skyride" $11.50; combination $17 | Daily 9:30–midnight.

Rockefeller Center. One of the greatest achievements in 20th-century urban planning, this stunning confluence of 19 diverse and magnificent buildings is set on 22 acres of the most prime real estate in Manhattan. Included in the acreage: the Channel Gardens; the GE, Time/Life, and Associated Press buildings; the newly renovated Radio City Music Hall; and plazas, concourses, and street-level shops that form a city within a city. | 5th Ave. between 48th and 51st Sts. | 212/632–3975 Rockefeller Center information | Free | Daily.

United Nations. Officially designated an "international zone" and therefore not technically part of the United States, the United Nations Headquarters is a working symbol of global cooperation. The famous narrow 550-ft-tall green-glass Secretariat Building is set like a jewel on the 18-acre riverside tract, forming a complex with the smaller, domed General Assembly Building and the Dag Hammarskjold Library. In season, there is a beautiful rose garden with 1,400 rosebushes and sculptures donated by member nations. Forty-five-min tours in English leave the General Assembly Lobby every 30 min. Children under five are not permitted. | Entrance at 1st Ave. and 46th St. | 212/963–7713 or 212/963–8687 |

www.un.org | $7.50 tours | Tours: daily 9:30–4:45; closed Thanksgiving and several days during year-end holiday season; also closed weekends Jan.–Feb. Schedule may change Sept.–Oct.

Woolworth Building. This 792-ft neo-Gothic tower is one of Manhattan's most imposing commercial buildings, standing as the gem of the Downtown skyline. Built by Cass Gilbert in 1913, it was the world's tallest building until 1930. The ornate lobby features figures carved in the ceiling that include F. W. Woolworth himself counting nickels and dimes. | 233 Broadway, at Park Pl. | 212/233–2720 | Free | Daily.

World Trade Center. The two mammoth twin buildings that make up the World Trade Center are the tallest in New York, and the third tallest in the world. But the World Trade Center is much more than two skyscrapers: it's a miniature city all its own, covering 16 acres, with a daytime population of 140,000. There are seven buildings in all, arranged around a plaza. Underground is a gigantic mall with 70 stores and restaurants. And high above it all is Top of the World, renovated in 1997, a 107th-floor observation deck at 2 World Trade Center. On a clear day, you can see 55 mi from the world's highest outdoor observation platform, known as the Rooftop Observatory. | Tickets booths: 2 World Trade Center (bordered by West, Vesey, Church, and Liberty Sts.) | 212/323–2340 | $13.50 | June–Aug., daily 9:30 AM–11:30 PM; Sept.–May, daily 9:30–9:30.

BEACHES, PARKS, AND NATURAL SIGHTS

Bowling Green. Built in 1733, this is the city's oldest existing public park. In 1771, an iron fence was erected by the British to protect a statue of King George III from rowdy colonists. Five days after the Declaration of Independence was signed, the statue was knocked to the ground. The fence is still there. | Broadway and Battery Pl. | 800/201–PARK | Free | Daily.

Central Park. Without Central Park's 843 acres of meandering, circuitous paths, lovely lakes and ponds, and vast open meadows, New Yorkers might well be even more hyper than they are reputed to be. Every day, thousands of cyclists, in-line skaters, joggers, and walkers make their way through the park on 58 mi of paved pathways or around the reservoir. But there's so much more going on: horseback riding, ice- or roller-skating, rock climbing, softball (on 26 fields), croquet, bird-watching, boating, tennis (on 30 courts), chess and checkers, theater, concerts, dining, skateboarding, and much more. There's a fabulous zoo, renovated in 1988, a castle, a magnificent old carousel, 22 playgrounds, and, of course, the Metropolitan Museum of Art. | 5th Ave. to Central Park W and 59th St. to 110th St. | 212/360–3444 | Free | 30 mins before sunrise until 1 AM.

The Dairy. Built in the 19th century, the Dairy once sat amid grazing cows that produced milk you could purchase by the glass. Today, the attractively painted Dairy contains the Central Park Visitor's Center, which features maps, exhibits and interactive videos on the park's history, and information about park events. | In Central Park, off E. 65th St. | 212/794–6564 | Free | Tues.–Sun.

City Hall Park. Currently, this triangular park is used for picnic lunches and as the finish line for ticker-tape parades. But in its days since the Colonial era, when it was the town common, this charming green spot has witnessed hangings, riots, and demonstrations. | Between Broadway, Park Row, and Chambers St. | 212/408–0100 or 800/201–PARK | Free | Daily.

Washington Square. This 9½-acre park is the spiritual heart of Greenwich Village. It started as a cemetery, primarily for yellow-fever casualties, and an estimated 20,000 bodies lie below. In its day, the park was also the site of public executions. In 1827, it was made into a public park, and it became quite a fashionable area—easy to imagine if you look long enough at the magnificent row houses that line the north side of the square. Today, Washington Square is suffused with playful activity: jugglers and joggers, NYU students and skateboarder, chess players and guitarists, children and dogs, and just about everything in between. Dominating the square is the triumphal Washington Arch, built in 1889 to commemorate the 100th anniversary of George Washington's inauguration. | South end of 5th Ave., between Waverly Pl. and W. 4th St. | 212/408–0100 or 800/201–PARK | Free | Daily.

CULTURE, EDUCATION, AND HISTORY

American Bible Society Gallery/Library. With the exception of the Vatican, this Gallery houses the largest collection of scriptures in the world, with almost 50,000 items in 2,000 languages. | 1865 Broadway, at W. 61st St. | 212/408–1200 | www.americanbible.org | Bookstore and gallery: Mon.–Wed. and Fri. 10–5, Thurs. 10–7, Sat. 10–4; library: weekdays 10–5.

Carnegie Hall. With legendary acoustics and a history richer than any hall in America, this 2,804-seat auditorium was built in 1891 and restored and renovated in 1986. It has has attracted the world's greatest orchestras and conductors from Tchaikovsky to Bernstein, as well as some of the most important jazz and pop performers of the last 100 years. | 154 W. 57th St., at 7th Ave. | 212/247–7800 | $6 for tour and Rose Museum | Tours: Labor Day–end June, Mon., Tues., Thurs., Fri. at 11:30, 2, and 3, performance schedule permitting; Rose Museum: weekdays 9:30–5:30.

Castle Clinton National Monument. Castle Clinton is a circular, red-stone fortress built on an island 200 ft from the shore, originally to defend New York Harbor. Now it's a restored fort, with a fascinating museum, and it serves as a ticket office for ferries to the Statue of Liberty and Ellis Island. | State St. and Battery Pl. in Battery Park | 212/344–7220 | Castle Clinton free; ferry $7 round-trip | Daily 8:30–5.

City Center. Beneath its decidedly eccentric tiled Spanish dome (built by Shriners in 1923) are two theaters. The main stage on the street level features modern dance performances by the likes of Alvin Ailey Dance Company, Twyla Tharp and Dancers, the Martha Graham Dance Company, the Paul Taylor Dance Company, the Merce Cunningham Dance Company, and the Dance Theater of Harlem, while downstairs is the home of the venerable Manhattan Theater Club. | 131 W. 55th St., between 6th and 7th Aves. | 212/581–1212.

City College of New York. City College's neo-Gothic stone towers, arched gates, rolling green lawns, and white terra-cotta trim make it feel like an Ivy League campus, but this has always been a public institution. In fact, tuition was free until the mid-1970s. The neighborhood surrounding the college is especially quiet and charming, with wide sidewalks and lovely row houses. | Convent Ave. and W. 138th St. | 212/650–7000 | Free | Mon.–Thurs., by appointment.

Columbia University. This famous, wealthy, private, coed Ivy League school—New York's first college when it was founded in 1754—has a picturesque main quadrangle, dominated by the neoclassical Butler Library at the southern end and the rotunda-topped Low Memorial Library at the north. | Visitors center: Room 213, Low Memorial Library, north of W. 116th St. and Broadway, between Amsterdam Ave. and Broadway | 212/854–4900 | Tours on weekdays at 11 and 2, except holidays and final-exam period.

Cooper Union. This imposing eight-story brownstone is a tuition-free institution for artists, architects, and engineers. A statue of inventor/industrialist Peter Cooper stands proudly in the square just south of the building. Two galleries in the building are open to the public, offering changing exhibitions during the academic year. | 30 Cooper Sq., at E. 7th St. and 3rd Ave. | 212/353–4200 | Free | Weekdays noon–7, Sat. noon–5.

Federal Hall National Memorial. This memorial and museum stands upon one of the most historic settings in all of New York City, just up the street from the New York Stock Exchange. Federal Hall, built in 1699, once served as the nation's capitol; it was here that the Bill of Rights was adopted and George Washington took his presidential oath in 1789. The second building, erected on the same site in 1842 in the Greek Revival style, was a customs house, then the site of the U.S. subtreasury until 1920. Various Colonial and early Federal artifacts are housed here, along with a statue of Washington on the spot where he took the oath of office. | 26 Wall St., at Nassau St. | Free | Weekdays 9–5.

General Grant National Memorial. Better known as Grant's Tomb, this beautifully positioned memorial, stationed since 1897 across from Riverside Park, was a more popular sight than the Statue of Liberty until the end of World War I. The towering granite mausoleum holds Grant and his wife's twin black-marble sarcophagi, with minigalleries displaying pho-

tographs and Grant memorabilia. | Riverside Dr. and W. 122nd St. | 212/666–1640 | Free | Daily 9–5.

Hamilton Grange National Memorial. Just north of City College in Hamilton Heights is Alexander Hamilton's country retreat, built in 1801. It's one of the few Federal frame houses standing in Manhattan. | 287 Convent Ave., at W. 141st St. | 212/283–5154 | Fri.–Sun. 9–5.

Jewish Theological Seminary of America. Founded in 1887 to train rabbis and scholars of Conservative Judaism, the seminary came to this complex in 1930. There are frequent exhibits in the library; the tower is still undergoing renovations from a major fire in 1966. | 3080 Broadway, at 122nd St. | 212/678–8000 | Free | Mon.–Thurs. 9 AM–10 PM, Fri. 9–2, Sun. 9–5.

Lincoln Center for the Performing Arts. Lincoln Center is the largest performing arts center in the world. It can seat almost 18,000 spectators at one time in its various auditoriums. The $165 million complex was built between 1962 and 1968, with three principal halls grouped around the central Fountain Plaza: the New York State Theater, home to the New York City Opera and the New York City Ballet; the Metropolitan Opera House, home to the great Metropolitan Opera Company and the American Ballet Theater; and Avery Fisher Hall, home to the New York Philharmonic Orchestra. But there is much more. Just south of the Met is Damrosch Park, where open-air festivals are held in the Guggenheim Bandshell. A huge Henry Moore sculpture rests in a reflecting pool just north of the Met, outside the Vivian Beaumont Theater and the smaller Mitzi E. Newhouse Theater, where many acclaimed productions have originated. To the rear is the New York Public Library for the Performing Arts. An overpass leads to the world-famous Juilliard School for music and theater. To the left is the Walter Reade Theater, which screens an eclectic mix of films. An escalator leads down to street level and Alice Tully Hall, home of the New York Film Festival and the Chamber Music Society of Lincoln Center. | 70 Lincoln Center Plaza, on Broadway between W. 62nd and W. 66th Sts. | 212/546–2656 | Free | Daily.

Lincoln Center Guided Tours. One-hour tours are given daily, covering the center's remarkable history and wealth of artwork, including the two gigantic Marc Chagall canvases that grace the Met's outer lobby. Visits to each of the theaters are included, performance schedule permitting. | 212/875–5350 tour information | $9.50 (reservations recommended) | Daily.

Madison Square Garden. Now including the new 5,600-seat Paramount Theater, where mega-productions of *A Christmas Carol* and *The Wizard of Oz* are staged seasonally, Madison Square Garden itself can seat 20,000 people who want to see anyone from Barbra Streisand to Bruce Springsteen, to say nothing of the New York Knicks and the New York Rangers. | Pennsylvania Plaza above Pennsylvania Station, between 7th and 8th Aves., W. 31st to W. 33rd St. | 212/465–6741 | Ticket prices vary | Daily.

Morris-Jumel Mansion. The oldest surviving private dwelling in Manhattan, this pre-Revolutionary Georgian mansion was built in 1765 as a summer villa for British officer Roger Morris and his family. George Washington used it as his headquarters in 1776. The mansion contains nine rooms with magnificent period furnishings, a colonial kitchen, and a beautiful rose garden. | 65 Jumel Terr., at W. 161st St. | 212/923–8008 | $3 | Wed.–Sun. 10–4.

NBC's Studio Tour. NBC has been ensconced in the GE Building for well over 50 years. Daily hour-long tours take visitors through the historic building and onto the sets of *Saturday Night Live* and *Late Night With Conan O'Brien.* | 30 Rockefeller Plaza 50th St., between 5th and 6th Aves. | 212/664–7174 | $17.50 (call for reservations) | Daily 9:30–4:30 | www.nbc.com.

New Amsterdam Theater. The most glorious theater on 42nd Street and the original home of the Ziegfeld Follies, the New Amsterdam was ignored and neglected for decades until the Walt Disney Company decided it wanted a venue in which to stage its own musical productions. In 1997, after a $35 million restoration, the 1,814-seat Art Nouveau theater reopened triumphantly—with a dazzling production of *The Lion King*, which will surely dwell there for years to come. Two hours before each performance, a line for standing-room tickets and cancellations forms. | 214 W. 42nd St., between 7th and 8th Aves. | 212/282–2900 | $25–$85 | Call for show times.

New York Public Library. With 6 million books, 12 million manuscripts, and 2.8 million pictures, this 1911 Beaux Arts masterpiece is one of the greatest research institutions in the world. The best way to enter is to pass between the two stone lions on the 5th Avenue staircase. Free 1-hr tours through the various galleries and magnificently restored reading rooms begin in Astor Hall just past the bronze front doors, Monday–Saturday at 11 and 2. (Sign up at the information desk well in advance.) | 5th Ave. between W. 40th and W. 42nd Sts. | 212/930–0800 | Free | Mon. and Thurs.–Sat. 10–6; Tues.–Wed. 11–7:30.

Schomburg Center for Research in Black Culture. This unique collection of over 5 million books, paintings, documents, photographs, recordings, movies, and videotapes has been housed here since 1980. An expansion and renovation was completed in 1991, and today the Schomburg Center also includes the American Negro Theater and the Langston Hughes Auditorium. | 515 Malcolm X Blvd., at W. 135th St. | 212/491–2200 | Free | Mon.–Wed. noon–8, Thurs.–Sat. 10–6; exhibits: Mon.–Wed. noon–6, Fri.–Sat. 10–6, Sun. 1–5.

New York University. Founded in 1831 by a group of prominent citizens who proclaimed that the institution would serve the common person (as opposed to the Greek- and Latin-obsessed colleges of the day), NYU is today the largest private university in the United States, offering over 2,500 courses and 25 degrees to both graduate and undergraduate students. The school is perhaps best known for its fine film school, whose graduates include Spike Lee, Martin Scorsese, and Ang Lee. Most of the buildings around Washington Square belong to NYU; notice the ubiquitous purple flags. On weekdays during the school year, free tours of the university are given several times a day, Monday–Friday, departing from the Office of Undergraduate Admission. | 22 Washington Sq. N | 212/998–1212 (information), 212/998–4524 (tours) | Free.

Pierpont Morgan Library. A museum as well as a scholarly research center, the Morgan Library has a renowned collection of rare books, manuscripts, and drawings that focus on the history and culture of Western civilization from the Middle Ages to the 21st century. Collection highlights include letters by Thomas Jefferson, handwritten music by Mozart and Beethoven, drawings by da Vinci and Rubens, and original manuscripts by Charlotte Brontë. There are rotating exhibitions in the galleries at the main entrance; beyond these, you'll find the opulent period rooms of Morgan's original library. Free guided tours are conducted weekdays at noon. | 29 E. 36th St., at Madison Ave. | 212/685–0610 or 212/685–0008 | $8 | Tues. and Thurs. 10–5, Fri. 10:30–8, Sat. 10:30–6, Sun. noon–6; closed last 2 weeks Aug.

P.S. 122. If you have had it with the sappy endings of the theater district you may want to head down to this hotbed of irreverence at the corner of 9th Street and First Avenue. This non-profit organization is committed to serving performing artists with authentic and innovative visions and produces the works of such outspokens as Spaulding Gray, John Leguizamo, Paul Zaloom, Danny Hoch, and Karen Finley. | 150 First Ave. | 212/228–4249 | www.ps122.org | Call for ticket prices | Call for specific show times.

The Public Theater. The Shakespeare Workshop was a group of actors who gave free performances of Shakespeare's works, under the direction of Joseph Papp. In 1967, Papp turned what was once The Astor Library into what is now the Public Theater, with an initial run of *Hair*. Today the organization continues to present full seasons of plays and musicals, both at the Lafayette Street location and in Central Park's Delacorte Theater. The Public has hosted a number of important premieres including *A Chorus Line, For Colored Girls . . .*, and *Threepenny Opera*. Before and after a show you can chill out at Joe's Pub on the main floor of the theater. | 425 Lafayette St. | 212/539–8500 | www.publictheater.org.

Staten Island Ferry. One of the best deals in town: This 20–30-min ride across New York Harbor, which provides spectacular views of the Manhattan skyline, the Statue of Liberty, the Verrazano-Narrows Bridge, and the New Jersey coast, is absolutely free. The blue-and-orange ferries embark on various schedules: every 15 min during rush hour; every 20–30 min most other times; and every hour after 11 PM and on weekend mornings. | Departs from the ferry terminal at intersection of Whitehall, State, and South Sts. | 718/390–5253 | Free | Weekdays every 20 mins; weekends every 15 mins; late night–early morning every hr.

Statue of Liberty National Monument. Arguably the most famous monument in America, this treasure still ennobles all those who encounter it. The statue was sculpted by Frederic-Auguste Bartholdi and presented to the United States as a gift from France in 1886. She stands a proud and defiant 152 ft high on top of an 89-ft pedestal on Liberty Island in New York Harbor. Although it may be a long wait (2–4 hrs in summer), the top of the statue is accessible in two ways: An elevator ascends about 10 stories to the top of the pedestal, or you can climb 354 steps to the crown. The line to visit the crown is often closed off by 2 PM, so get there early if you want to make the ascent. The earliest ferry leaves Castle Clinton National Monument at 9:30 (9:15 in summer). The statue's celebrated history, including videos of the view from the crown for those who can't make the wait, are included among the exhibits, along with life-size models of the statue's face and foot for the blind to feel. Pick up ferry service at Castle Clinton, Battery Park, corner of State Street and West Side Highway. | Liberty Island, New York Harbor | 212/363–3200 (statue information), 212/269–5755 (ferry information) | $7 | Ferry service: daily 8:30–4:30 every 20 mins.; schedule subject to change.

Ellis Island Immigration Museum. Today more than 40% of all living Americans can trace their roots to an ancestor who came through Ellis Island, the point of entry for 16 million immigrants from 1892 to 1924. After 36 years of being shuttered, the island's main building reopened in 1990 as the magnificent museum it is today. At its heart is the Registry Room, where immigration authorities tried to ferret out such "undesirables" as polygamists and people suffering from contagious diseases. The Great Hall, where immigrants were registered, features spectacular tiled arches. The Railroad Ticket Office at the back of the main building houses exhibits on "The Peopling of America," which explores 400 years of immigration history, and "Forced Migration," about the slave trade. But the most overwhelming exhibit is the American Immigrant Wall of Honor, where the names of 420,000 immigrants are inscribed along an outdoor promenade with a breathtaking view of the city. You may find the name of an ancestor of yours. | Ferry tickets and service at Castle Clinton, Battery Park, corner of State St. and West Side Hwy. | 212/363–3200 (Ellis Island), 212/883–1986 (Wall of Honor) | Ferry ticket $7 | Daily; ferry service 8:30–4:30 every 20 mins; schedule subject to change.

Theodore Roosevelt Birthplace National Historic Site. The birthplace of our 26th president—and the only one from New York City—was actually demolished in 1916, but this Gothic Revival replica, built in 1923, is a near-perfect reconstruction of the house where Teddy lived until he was 15 yrs old. The house has a fascinating timeline collection of all sorts of Teddyana that weaves through five Victorian period rooms. | 28 E. 20th St., between Broadway and Park Ave. S | 212/260–1616 | $2 | Wed.–Sun. 9–5, with guided tours every hr until 4.

White Horse Tavern. In operation since 1880, this is the famed site where author Dylan Thomas drank himself to death. There is a dispute about just how many shots of scotch he put down that night but estimates hover around 18. Legend has it that Thomas's ghost returns to his favorite corner table, now commemorated with a plaque, and to rotate the table, as he did. | 567 Hudson St. | 212/243–9260 | Free.

Yeshiva University. The oldest and largest Jewish studies center in the country, Yeshiva University was founded in 1886. The main building on campus, called Main Building, has a fanciful facade that combines modern touches with Middle Eastern turrets and minarets. | 2520 Amsterdam Ave., at 185th St. | 212/960–5400 | Free | Daily.
Yeshiva University Museum To reflect the Jewish historical and cultural experience, this museum features rotating exhibits of paintings, ceremonial objects, artifacts, photographs, and architectural models of synagogues around the world. | 15 W. 16th St., between 5th and 6th Aves. | 212/294–8330 | $6 | Sun., Tues., Wed. 11–5, Thurs. 11–8.

MUSEUMS

American Craft Museum. This small museum showcases the works of contemporary American and international artists in mediums such as clay, glass, fabric, wood, metal, and even chocolate. The museum boasts a three-story stairway atrium and the tallest interior museum wall in New York. | 40 W. 53rd St. | 212/956–3535 | www.americancraftmuseum.org | $5 | Tues.–Sun. 10–6 (Thurs. 10–8).

American Museum of Natural History. More than 36 million artifacts, specimens, skeletons, minerals, gems, meteorites, and, yes, dinosaurs fill the museum's 42 exhibition halls. Three awe-inspiring $34 million dinosaur halls are on the fourth floor, but the 50-ft-tall barosaurus is in the Theodore Roosevelt Rotunda. Check out the Rose Center for Earth and Space, home of the spectacular new Hayden Planetarium, the largest virtual-reality simulator in the world. | Central Park W between 77th and 81st Sts. | 212/769–5100, 212/769–5200 tickets | www.amnh.org | $10 suggested donation; with Hayden Planetarium $19; with IMAX $15; all exhibits $25 | Sun.–Thurs. 10–5:45, Fri.–Sat. 10–8:45.

American Numismatic Society. This 132-year-old museum is all about money, with over a million pieces of currency on hand representing every time period, from Ancient Egypt through the Elizabethan era to the present. | Broadway at 155th St. | 212/234–3130 | Free | Tues.–Fri. 9–4:30.

The Asia Society Galleries. In addition to changing exhibitions, this nonprofit educational society hosts lectures, films, and performances. The fabled Rockefeller Collection of Asian Art is housed here permanently. | 680 Park Ave., between 68th and 69th Sts. | 212/249–8950 | www.asiasociety.org | $3 | Tues.–Sat. 10–6.

Children's Museum of Manhattan. The five floors of interactive fun in this creative learning center will wear out your kids. They can crawl, climb, paint, dress up, and even film their own newscasts. | 212 W. 83rd St. | 212/721–1234 | www.cmom.org | $6 | Wed.–Sun. 10–5.

The Cloisters. Nestled on top of a thickly wooded hill in Fort Tryon Park, near the northernmost tip of Manhattan, the Cloisters holds the medieval collection of the Metropolitan Museum of Art in an appropriately monastery-like setting. Austere colonnaded walkways connect French and Spanish monastic cloisters, a 12th-century chapter house, a Romanesque apse, and a French Romanesque chapel. The famous Unicorn Tapestries of the 15th and 16th centuries are here in their full glory, and there are three gorgeous gardens that feature over 250 species of plants similar to those that grew in the Middle Ages. | In Fort Tryon Park, off Henry Hudson Pkwy. | 212/923–3700 | $10 suggested donation | Mar.–Oct., Tues.–Sun. 9:30–5:15; Nov.–Feb., Tues.–Sun. 9:30–4:45.

Cooper-Hewitt National Museum of Design, Smithsonian Institution. Andrew Carnegie built this 64-room house on what, in 1901, were the outskirts of town. From the first-floor study, Carnegie administered his various philanthropic projects. The core of the museum's collection was started in 1897 by the two Hewitt sisters, granddaughters of inventor Peter Cooper. The Smithsonian Institution took over the museum in 1967, and in 1976 the collection of drawings, prints, textiles, furniture, ceramics, and wall coverings was moved to the Carnegie mansion. A three-year renovation of Cooper-Hewitt's exhibition galleries was completed in 2001, and the rotating exhibitions focus on various aspects of historical or contemporary design. | 2 E. 91st St., at 5th Ave. | 212/849–8400 | $8, free Tues. 5–9 | Tues. 10–9, Wed.–Sat. 10–5, Sun. noon–5.

Dyckman Farm House Park and Museum. This original fieldstone building from the 1700s houses a museum of Dutch New York, featuring Dutch and English Colonial antiques. | 4881 Broadway, at 204th St. | 212/304–9422 | Tues., Wed, Sun. 10–5, Thurs. 10–8 | $1 suggested donation.

El Museo del Barrio. "Barrio" is Spanish for "neighborhood," and this museum has been here at the edge of East Harlem, a largely Puerto Rican neighborhood, since 1977. The 8,000-object permanent collection includes pre-Columbian artifacts, objects from the Caribbean and Central and South America, and mostly Puerto Rican art. | 1230 5th Ave., between E. 104th and 105th Sts. | 212/831–7272 or 212/831–7273 | $4 suggested donation | Wed.–Sun. 11–5.

Forbes Magazine Galleries. Housed within the Forbes Magazine Building, these seven galleries display an eclectic array of some of Malcolm Forbes's finest collectibles. It is rumored that only Queen Elizabeth has more Fabergé eggs than Forbes. In the collection are 12,000 toy soldiers, 500 model boats, some of the oldest Monopoly sets, and many historical documents and signed presidential papers, including Abraham Lincoln's Emancipation Proclamation. | 62 5th Ave. | 212/620–2200 | Free | Tues., Wed., Fri., Sat., 10–4.

Fraunces Tavern Museum. Part of a complex built in 1719 that now includes a restaurant and bar, the Fraunces Tavern Museum contains two fully furnished period rooms and other displays of 18th- and 19th-century American history. | 54 Pearl St., at Broad St. | 212/425–1778 | $2.50 | Weekdays 10–4:45.

The Frick Collection. Steel-and-coke baron Henry Clay Frick spent a good deal of time and money gathering a spectacular private art collection, which he eventually housed in this impressive mansion, designed by Thomas Hastings and built in 1913–14. The place still feels like a private home, albeit one with stunning masterpieces—by the likes of Rembrandt, Vermeer, Manet, El Greco, and Whistler—hanging in almost every room. The tranquil indoor courtyard is especially soothing. | 1 E. 70th St., at 5th Ave. | 212/288–0700 | $7 (children under 10 not admitted) | Tues.–Sat. 10–6, Sun. 1–6.

Hispanic Society of America. Paintings and artifacts from the 10th–15th centuries are housed in this museum, built in 1908, including masterpieces by Goya, El Greco, and Velázquez. The library houses nearly a quarter-million books about Spain and Portugal. | Broadway between W. 155th and 156th Sts. | 212/926–2234 | Free | Tues.–Sat. 10–4:30, Sun. 1–4.

ICP/Midtown. The International Center of Photography presents several photography exhibitions every year, usually including selections from the vast permanent collection. | 1133 6th Ave., at W. 43rd St. | 212/860–1777 | $6 | Mon.–Wed. 10–5, Thurs., Fri. 10–8, Sat., Sun. 10–6.

Intrepid **Sea-Air-Space Museum.** This 900-ft aircraft carrier has been retired to become one of the city's most unusual and impressive museums. The array of aircraft displayed on deck ranges from A-12 Blackbird spy planes to helicopters to lunar-landing modules. With *Titanic* mania still lingering, children will enjoy wending their way through the ship's narrow hallways and winding staircases. | Foot of W. 46th St. and 12th Ave., at Pier 86, Hudson River | 212/245–0072 | $12 | May–Sept., weekdays 10–5, weekends 10–6; Oct.–Apr., Tues.–Sun. 10–5 | www.intrepidmuseum.org.

Jewish Museum. This French Gothic mansion facing Central Park boasts one of the largest collections of Judaica in America. Ceremonial objects, paintings, prints, sculpture, photographs, and videos trace the evolution of Jewish culture over the past 4,000 years. The museum also hosts special major exhibitions and retrospectives. | 1109 5th Ave., at E. 92nd St. | 212/423–3200 | $8 | Sun., Mon., Wed., Thurs. 11–5:45, Tues. 11–8 | www.jewishmuseum.org.

Lower East Side Tenement Museum. This museum recalls the immigrant family in their cramped quarters in the land they thought was paved with gold. The tours, which leave on weekdays at 1, 2, and 3 and every 45 min on weekends, chronicle some of the actual families that lived at the Orchard Street address. A video in the basement puts the neighborhood and the home itself in historical context. | 90 Orchard St. | 212/431–0233 | $8 | Tues.-Wed. and Fri. 12–5, Thurs. 12–9, weekends 11–5.

Metropolitan Museum of Art. One of the greatest museums in the world, the Met is the largest museum in the Western Hemisphere, with 1.6 million square ft of gallery space and a permanent collection of over 2 million works of art. With a thoroughness that can be overwhelming, this collection covers 5,000 years of cultural history. Obviously, you can't expect to take it all in during one visit, but do not miss the Egyptian collection, centered around the Temple of Dendur, an ancient temple transported in its entirety from Egypt to a specially designed atrium; and the incomparable collection of European paintings, including 30 Monets, 7 Vermeers, and 17 Cézannes. | 5th Ave. at 82nd St. | 212/535–7710

| www.metmuseum.org | $10 suggested donation | Sun. and Tues.–Thurs. 9:30–5:30, Fri., Sat. 9:30–9.

Museum for African Art. Browse the contemporary and traditional African art in this handsome but small two-story museum. Exhibits change constantly but often include sculpture, ceremonial masks, and textiles. | 593 Broadway | 212/966–1313 | fax 212/966–1432 | museum@africanart.org | www.africanart.org | $5, free Sun. | Tues.–Fri. 10:30–5:30, weekends noon–6.

Museum of the City of New York. The unique history of New York City, from its Native American roots to the complex present-day metropolis, is carefully chronicled in this enormous Georgian mansion, using costumes, furniture, paintings, oral histories, and toys. | 1220 5th Ave., between E. 103rd and 104th Sts. | 212/534–1672 | www.mcny.org | $7 | Wed.–Sat. 10–5, Sun. noon–5.

Museum of Modern Art (MOMA). One of the greatest collections of modern art in the world, MOMA's six stories boast such works as van Gogh's *Starry Night* and an entire gallery devoted to Monet's triptych *Water Lilies*. There are more than 100,000 works on display, from paintings and sculpture to photography and film—six screenings daily. The hushed sculpture garden is one of the most delightful spots in the city. | 11 W. 53rd St. between 5th and 6th Ave. | 212/708–9480 exhibition and film information | $10; Fri. 4:30–8 pay what you wish | Thurs. and Sat.–Tues. 10:30–5:45, Fri. 10:30–8:15 | www.moma.org.

Museum of Television and Radio. If you're hankering to spend an afternoon watching *Gilligan's Island* reruns, or rare pilots of tube favorites such as the lost episode of *I Love Lucy*, this is your place. The museum has collected 75,000 television and radio programs, which are preserved in its permanent collection and available for viewing on one of over 100 personal consoles. There are also two theaters and two screening rooms. | 25 W. 52nd St. | 212/621–6800 | $6 | Tues., Wed., weekends noon–6, Thurs. noon–8, Fri. noon–9.

National Museum of the American Indian. Delve into the history and current cultures of native peoples from throughout the Americas. Literature, films, and crafts tell their stories in this branch of the Smithsonian Institute in Washington D.C. | Alexander Hamilton U.S. Custom House, One Bowling Green | 212/668–6624 | www.si.edu/nmai | Free | Mon.–Sun. 10–5 (Thurs. 10–8).

New York City Police Museum. Here you'll find law-enforcement memorabilia including uniforms, firearms, batons, badges, handcuffs, and confiscated counterfeit money dating back to the Dutch. | 25 Broadway, at Bowling Green | 212/301–4440 | Free | Weekdays 10–6, weekends 10–4 | www.nycpolicemuseum.org.

New York Historical Society. Where else could you see Benjamin Franklin's glasses, Napoleon Bonaparte's signature, 250 Tiffany lamps (the largest collection in the world), and the Louisiana Purchase contract? Concerts and walking tours are now also included in the society's program. | 2 W. 77th St., at Central Park W | 212/873–3400 | $5 suggested donation | Tues.–Sun. 11–5 | www.nyhistory.org.

Solomon R. Guggenheim Museum. One of the beacons of the modernist architectural tradition and Frank Lloyd Wright's only major New York commission, the Guggenheim has a modern collection (nothing earlier than the French Impressionists), with especially strong work by Picasso, Klee, and Kandinsky. Under a 92-ft-high glass dome, a ¼-mi ramp spirals down past rotating exhibits in a manner that some find a bit dizzying. | 1071 5th Ave., at 89th St. | 212/423–3500 | $12; Fri. 6–8 pay what you wish | Sun.–Wed. 9–6, Fri.–Sat. 9–8 | www.guggenheim.org.

    Guggenheim Museum SoHo. This Downtown edition of the famous Uptown museum opened in 1992 and features revolving exhibitions, usually of modern work and a large gift shop. | 575 Broadway, at Prince St. | 212/423–3500 | www.guggenheim.org | Free | Thurs.–Mon. 11–6.

Sony Wonder Technology Lab. Technology and imagination are on tap for all at this interactive technology center. Kids especially will love to play computer specialist, sound engineer, or TV personality. Exhibits pertain to audio, imaging, design, robotics, and networks. Children under eight might need adult assistance. | 550 Madison Ave. | 212/833–8100 | http://wondertechlab.sony.com | Free | Tues.–Sat. 10–6 (Thurs. 10–8), Sun. noon–6 (last entrance 30 mins before closing).

South Street Seaport Museum. This museum without walls fills 11 square blocks on the East River with its cobblestone streets, magnificent historic sailing ships, 18th- and 19th-century architecture, a boat building center, a children's craft center, and much more. Call for details on classes, programs, lectures, events, and cruises. | Visitors center: 12 Fulton St., at South St. | 212/748–8600 | www.southstseaport.com | $6 | Apr.–Oct., Fri.–Wed. 10–6, Thurs. 10–8; Nov.–Mar., Wed.–Mon. 10–5.

Studio Museum in Harlem. This small art museum holds a large collection of paintings, sculptures, and photographs, including the historic Harlem photographs of James Van Der Zee. Exhibits rotate, and there are various lectures and special programs, as well as a splendid gift shop. | 144 W. 125th St., between Lenox and 7th Aves. | 212/864–4500 | $5 suggested donation | Wed.–Thurs. noon–6, Fri. noon–8, weekends 10–6.

Ukrainian Museum. A small East Village gallery celebrating the Ukraine's cultural history, this museum features jewelry, ceramics, folk costumes, and, best of all, hundreds of brilliant-color Easter eggs. | 203 2nd Ave., between E. 12th and 13th Sts. | 212/228–0110 | $3 | Wed.–Sun. 1–5; closed Jan. 7, Orthodox Easter.

Whitney Museum of American Art. Designed by the celebrated Bauhaus architect Marcel Breuer, this striking building—an upside-down ziggurat—showcases mostly 20th-century works. In the permanent collection are Edward Hopper's pristine *Early Sunday Morning* and Alexander Calder's frisky *Circus*, as well as works by contemporary artists such as Matthew Barney and Louise Bourgeois. Special exhibits, including the controversial "Biennial" held every other year, are so interesting and important that they are often jammed. | 945 Madison Ave., at E. 75th St. | 212/570–3676 | $10, Thurs. 6–9 pay as you wish | Tues.–Wed. and Fri.–Sun. 11–6, Thurs. 1–9 | www.whitney.org.

Whitney Museum of American Art at Philip Morris. The Whitney's free Midtown branch features a 42-ft-high sculpture court with spectacular 20th-century sculptures too large to fit into the Whitney's Uptown base. In the adjoining gallery, five shows annually explore all aspects of American art. | 120 Park Ave., at E. 42nd St. | 917/663–2453 | Free | Sculpture court: Mon.–Sat. 7:30–9:30, Sun. 11–7; gallery: Mon.–Wed. and Fri. 11–6, Thurs. 11–7:30.

RELIGION AND SPIRITUALITY

Cathedral Church of St. John the Divine. This Episcopal cathedral is among the most massive in the world. Its cavernous 601-ft-long nave can accommodate 6,000 worshipers, and its 155-ft-tall domed crossing could contain the Statue of Liberty. The stained-glass windows are particularly spectacular, as are the tapestries and artwork. Don't miss the Biblical Garden, a true oasis at the end of the driveway just south of the nave. The Peace Fountain rests in a circular plaza off Amsterdam Avenue at 111th Street. | 1047 Amsterdam Ave., at W. 112th St. | 212/662–2133, box office for concerts; 212/932–7347, tours | $3 public tour; $10 vertical tour (a 12-story climb to the roof of the cathedral) | Daily 9–6. Tours: Tues.–Sat. at 11, Sun. at 1. Vertical tours: 1st and 3rd Sat. of month at noon and 2, reservations required.

Church of the Ascension. This 1841 Gothic Revival brownstone church was designed by Richard Upjohn and features a mural depicting the Ascension of Jesus and stained-glass windows by John LaFarge, as well as a marble altar sculpture by Louis Saint-Gaudens. | 10th St. at 5th Ave. | 212/254–8620 | Free | Daily noon–2; call first.

The Church of Saint Luke in the Field. The church was named in 1820 for the physician evangelist, in recognition of the neighborhood's role as a safe haven from the yellow fever outbreaks that plagued the city's summers in the 1800s. The church continues to play an active role in its Village community and since 1987 has served over 35,000 meals through its HIV/AIDS project, including Saturday dinners and weekend teas. The chapel interior, with checkerboard floors and arching doorways, has been redone since a fire in 1981. | 487 Hudson St. | 212/924–0562 | fax 212/633–2098 | Free.

Grace Church. One of the earliest examples of Gothic architecture in New York City, this regal structure was completed in 1846. Detail work continued after that, a rectory and parish house were built, and the once wooden steeple that stands tall above Broadway is now marble. Likewise, generous donor contributions resulted in the breathtaking east wall, which is almost entirely made of stained glass. The Grace Church School, originally a training ground for choir boys, is now a thriving co-educational private school. | 802 Broadway | 212/254–2000 | Free | Mon.–Tues., Thurs.– Fri. 10–5:30, Wed. 10–7, Sat. 12–4, Sun. 8–8.

St. George's Ukrainian Catholic Church. Originally the Ukrainian Catholic community settled at 20th Street and 1st Avenue, but in 1911, when the congregation grew too large, a new and bigger building was constructed here. In 1978, the current structure was erected, complete with academy, grade school, convent, and rectory, in a Ukrainian Byzantine style. Remarkably, because of the overwhelming response of the faithful, the church was built without incurring any debt. The doorway of the inner entrance has a mosaic depicting the church's patron St. George, slaying a dragon, illustrating the constant struggles of good versus evil. | 30 E. 7th St. | 212/674–1615 | www.brama.com/stgeorge | Free.

St. Mark's Church. Founded in 1779, this Episcopalian church is a community standout and continues its long and generous commitment to its East Village neighbors as well as an outspoken ministry committed to the arts. Two concrete lions flank the church entrance and protect the gardens on the west side and the tiny cemetery on the east. Inside the chapel, stained-glass windows surround you. Besides a regular schedule of religious services, the church is also home to The Ontological-Hysteric Theater, the Poetry Project, and Dancespace Project. | 131 E. 10th St. | 212/674–6377 | www.saintmarkschurch.org.

St. Patrick's Cathedral. Designed by the great 19th-century architect James Renwick, and widely considered his masterpiece, this marble Gothic Revival Roman Catholic church is based on Germany's soaring Cologne Cathedral and took 21 years to build. | 5th Ave. and E. 50th St. | 212/753–2261 | Free | Daily 7 AM–9 PM.

St. Paul's Chapel at Columbia University. This Episcopal brick/terra-cotta/limestone chapel, one of the most impressive buildings at Columbia University, features 24 windows in its dome decorated with the coats-of-arms of prominent old New York families. | Amsterdam Ave., between W. 116th and 117th Sts. | Free | Daily.

St. Paul's Chapel at Fulton Street. This is Manhattan's oldest surviving building. George Washington worshiped here—in fact, there was a prayer service here immediately following his inauguration. The chapel is fronted by a tranquil 18th-century cemetery, a unique flake of open space in the bosom of the bustling financial district. | Fulton St. and Broadway | 212/602–0874 | Weekdays 9–3, Sun. 7–3.

St. Thomas Church 5th Avenue. St. Thomas is an indispensable oasis on one of the busiest stretches of 5th Avenue. The elaborate interior is carved with glorious detail, especially above the main altar. This is a tremendously restorative place to pause and catch your breath, as well as to worship on Sunday. The church proudly features one of the finest boy's choirs in the country. | 1 W. 53rd St. | 212/757–7013 | Free | Daily 7 AM–6:30 PM.

Temple Emanu-El. Constructed in the Byzantine-Romanesque style and nearly completely covered with mosaics, this beautiful Upper East Side synagogue seats 2,500, making it the largest Reform temple in America. | 5th Ave. and E. 65th St. | 212/744–1400 | Free | Daily; no visiting on High Holy Days.

Trinity Church. The first Episcopal congregation in America formed in a church on this site, which was destroyed by fire during the American Revolution. In fact, Richard Upjohn's Gothic Revival edifice, one of New York's best-known landmarks, is the site's third building. Its 280-ft spire made it the tallest building in New York for the entire second half of the 19th century. The church hosts a popular noon concert series. | Broadway at Wall St. | 212/602–0800 or 212/602–0700 | Free; concerts $2 | Daily; concerts most Thurs. at 1.

SHOPPING

Astor Place Hairstylists. A neighborhood barber shop this is not, though there is something quite homey about this famed three-level haircut factory, where your haircut, no matter how complicated the style, will not take more than 10 min, start to finish. There are over 50 stylists but if you're looking for a chic New York do, you may want to head elsewhere. Astor place is great if you want the standard boys haircut, a mohawk, or a crew cut. If you go on a Saturday, be prepared to wait a bit. | 2 Astor Pl. | 212/475–9790 or 212/475–9854 | Mon.–Sat. 8– Sun. 9–6.

Balducci's. It would be a mistake to visit a city as food-oriented as New York without paying homage at one of the city's original and best gourmet-food temples. Browse among the dazzling displays of fruits and vegetables, fish and meat (including $100/lb Kobe beef), over 100 cheeses, more than 50 kinds of bread, and dozens of mouthwatering desserts. When your appetite has been fully cranked up, make a selection from among the first-rate takeout foods, find your way to a bench in nearby Christopher Park (about a block west), and chow down. Try to visit on a weekday to avoid the crowds. | 424 6th Ave., at 9th St. | 212/673–2600 | www.balducci.com | Free | Daily 7 AM–8:30 PM.

Bloomingdale's. One of the few department stores in the world that take up an entire city block, "Bloomie's" is not merely a place to shop, it's an only–in–New York experience. High-quality merchandise prevails, from housewares to designer clothes. | 1000 3rd Ave., at E. 59th St. | 212/705–2000 | www.bloomingdales.com | Free | Weekdays 10–8, Sat. 10–7, Sun. 11–7.

Macy's Herald Square. Allegedly the largest retail store in America, Macy's, like Manhattan itself, is constantly undergoing renovations. You can always expect a certain amount of chaos because there's almost always some sort of special sale going on. But few stores can offer such an array of quality merchandise. The Cellar features a splendid selection of cookware and a lively restaurant, Eatzi's, which makes killer sandwiches. | 151 W. 34th St., at Broadway | 212/695–4400 | www.macys.com | Mon.–Sat. 10–8:30, Sun. 11–7.

Strand Books. The Strand has the best prices and the largest number of used (and not-so-used) books in the city. The original Strand was opened in 1927 on the fabled (and long gone) "Book Row" on 4th Avenue, before the store relocated to its current location. Books throughout the store are mostly half-priced, some considerably less, some just a bit more. This place is any book-lover's dream. | 828 Broadway, at 12th St. | 212/473–1452 | Free | Mon.–Sat. 9:30 AM–10:30 PM, Sun. 11–10:30.

Surma, the Ukrainian Shop. Almost directly across the street from St. George's Ukrainian Catholic Church is this slice of the old country. Surma sells authentic, hand-crafted kilims, porcelain, ceramics, and hand painted icons. Most notable are the painstakingly detailed Ukrainian eggs. It is believed that as long as egg-decorating continues, the world will continue to exist. Should the custom cease, evil in the guise of a monster will envelop and destroy the world. Eggs are available in wood, or painted chicken or goose eggs. You may want to support the tradition. | 11 E. 7th St. | 212/477–0729 | fax 212/473–0439 | Free | Mon.–Fri. 11–6, Sat. 11–4.

Union Square Greenmarket. The largest of the city's two dozen greenmarkets brings farmers and food purveyors from all over the Northeast to appreciative New Yorkers. Crowds (especially large on Saturdays), and more than a few of Manhattan's leading chefs, peruse the shaded stands of fresh produce, homemade cheeses, breads and baked goods, cider, New York State wines, fish, poultry, meat, and pretzels. Longtime denizens of the neighborhood swear that the greenmarket was instrumental in bringing the area from the brink of dangerous slum to a thriving, healthy district. | West and north sides of Union Square Park | 212/477–3220 | Free | Mon., Wed., Fri., Sat. 8–6.

World Financial Center. This four-tower jewel at Battery Park City features nearly a quarter-million square ft of shops and restaurants, as well as the magnificent glass pavilion filled with towering palm trees that overlooks a marina full of yachts and a large riverside plaza. | West St. between Liberty and Vesey Sts., opposite World Trade Center | 212/945–0505 | www.worldfinancialcenter.com | Daily.

SPORTS AND RECREATION

American League Baseball (New York Yankees). Home games for controversial owner George Steinbrenner's legendary team are held at Yankee Stadium in the South Bronx, despite ongoing grumblings from Steinbrenner that he wants to move his team to New Jersey, not to mention Mayor Rudy Giuliani's dreams of a Manhattan stadium. The Yankees have won the World Series in 1996, 1998, 1999, and 2000. | Yankee Stadium, 161st St. and River Ave. | 718/293–4300 or 800/533–3779 (stadium information) | www.yankees.com | Ticket prices vary | Apr.–Oct.

National League Baseball (New York Mets). The Mets continue to have a sizable, devoted following, even after losing to the Yankees in the "Subway Series" of 2000. Mets games are played at Shea Stadium in Flushing, Queens. | Roosevelt Ave., off Grand Central Pkwy. | 718/507–6387 | www.mets.com | Ticket prices vary | Apr.–Oct.

NBA (New York Knickerbockers). Few teams of any sport arouse more passion in New York than the Knicks. Tickets for their games at Madison Square Garden are nearly impossible to come by, but you can call their fan line for a roundup. | 7th Ave. between W. 31st and 33rd Sts. | 212/465–5867 | www.nyknicks.com | Ticket prices vary | Nov.–Apr.

NFL (New York Giants). This hugely popular football team plays at Giants Stadium in the Meadowlands Sports Complex, but don't get your hopes up: Tickets are sold on a season-ticket basis, and even those subscriptions are next to impossible to obtain. Once in a blue moon, a single ticket is available at the stadium box office. | Rte. 3 W, East Rutherford, NJ | 201/935–8111 | www.giants.com | Ticket prices vary | Sept.–Dec.

NFL (New York Jets). This indefatigable football team also plays at Giants Stadium. Most tickets are gone before the season opener. | Rte. 3 W, East Rutherford, NJ | 516/560–8100 | www.newyorkjets.com | Ticket prices vary | Sept.–Dec.

NHL (New York Islanders). To put it kindly, the Islanders haven't had an impressive season since the 1980s. Games are played at the Nassau Veterans Memorial Coliseum. | 1255 Hempstead Tpk., Uniondale | 516/794–4100 | www.newyorkislanders.com | Ticket prices vary | Oct.–Apr.

NHL (New York Rangers). Rangers fans are among the most ferociously devoted sports fans in the area. Tickets to games at Madison Square Garden are scarce. | 7th Ave. between W. 31st and 33rd Sts. | 212/465–6741 | www.nyrfanclub.com | Ticket prices vary | Oct.–Apr.

SIGHTSEEING TOURS

Adventure on a Shoestring. These popular 90-min walking tours through Chinatown, "haunted" Greenwich Village, and Hell's Kitchen are a history-lover's dream. And the price has been five bucks since 1963. One of the very best, nontouristy ways to explore the city. | Call for departure points | 212/265–2663 | $5 | 3–4 jaunts held on weekends, rain or shine.

Circle Line Sightseeing Yachts. An exciting way to get your New York City bearings, this 3-hr, 35-min voyage around Manhattan's circumference is helpfully narrated not by a droning, scripted tape, but by real guides who have a lot to tell you. | Pier 83, W. 42nd St. at 12th Ave. and the Hudson River | 212/563–3200 | $24; $20 for 2-hr Semi-Circle cruise and 2-hr evening cruise | Mar.–mid-Dec., daily, call for hrs (also: May–Oct., nightly, call for hrs; Nov.–Dec., weekend evenings, call for hrs).

Gray Line. Some tours are conducted on replicas of 1930s New York trolleys; others on buses with narration in various languages. There are also cruises and day trips to Atlantic City. | 625 8th Ave., Port Authority Building, ground level | 212/397–2620 | Prices vary | Daily, call for hrs.

Liberty Helicopter Tours. Liberty offers four pilot-narrated tours of Manhattan and environs, ranging from the 4-min "Liberty Sampler" to the 18-min "Big Picture." | Heliport at W. 30th St. and 12th Ave.; also Pier 6 at the Staten Island Ferry | 212/465–8905 | $50–$159 | Midtown: daily 9–9; Downtown: weekdays 9–6.

NEW YORK CITY

INTRO
ATTRACTIONS
DINING
LODGING

New York Doubledecker Tours. London-style double-decker bus tours make stops every 15–30 min at the Empire State Building, Greenwich Village, SoHo, Chinatown, the World Trade Center, Battery Park, South Street Seaport, the United Nations, and Central Park. An Uptown loop (for an additional rate) also includes stops at Lincoln Center and the American Museum of Natural History. You may hop on and off to visit as many attractions as often as you like over a 3-day period. | 33rd St. and 5th Ave. | 212/967–6008 | $20–$30 | Memorial Day–Labor Day, daily 9–4:30; Labor Day–Memorial Day, daily 9–3.

OTHER POINTS OF INTEREST

Brooklyn Bridge. This soaring, graceful, 1,595-ft-long suspension bridge that connects Manhattan to Brooklyn was the longest in the world when it opened in 1883. A walkway across the bridge yields magnificent views of the East River and the skyline. | East side of City Hall Park at intersection of Park Row and Frankfort Sts. | 212/408–0100 or 800/201–PARK | Free | Daily.

Federal Reserve Bank of New York. A gigantic, 14-story, block-long stone building houses the largest stockpile of gold in the world—about $110 billion worth. Free tours, which must be arranged a week in advance, give an overview of the bank's operations, a look at currency processing, and a jaw-dropping visit to the gold vault. | 33 Liberty St., between Nassau St. and William St. | 212/720–6130 | www.nyfrb.org | Free | Tours: weekdays 9:30, 10:30, 11:30, 1:30, 2:30; reservations required at least 1 wk in advance.

Jacob K. Javits Convention Center. Built almost entirely of glass by the renowned architect I. M. Pei and finished in 1986, the Javits Center attracts the most impressive conventions and trade shows to its 1.8 million square ft of floor space on a 22-acre site. | 11th Ave. from W. 34th–39th Sts.; main entrance W. 36th St. and 11th Ave. | 212/216–2000 | Free | Daily.

New York Stock Exchange (NYSE). The NYSE is the largest securities exchange in the world; today, the "Big Board" can handle a trillion shares of stock per day. The third-floor interactive education center has a self-guided tour, touch-screen computer terminals, and live guides to help you wend your way through the apparent chaos you'll see from the gallery overlooking the trading floor. | 20 Broad St., between Wall St. and Exchange Pl. | 212/656–5165 | Free (go early for tickets) | Weekdays 9–4.

South Street Seaport Marketplace. The Seaport's Pier 17 building houses a multitude of upscale shops and restaurants, some of which offer alfresco terrace dining. There are many other shops on the cobbled extension of Fulton Street, which is open only to pedestrians. | Fulton and Water Sts., at East River | 212/732–7678 | www.southstreetseaport.com | Free | Daily.

WALKING TOURS

Walk Through the East Village.

Begin at the beautiful Beaux Arts subway entrance to the **Astor Place Subway Station,** at the wide-open intersection of Astor Place, E. 8th Street, and 4th Avenue. Dip into the station—one of Manhattan's more attractive—for a moment to see the carefully reproduced wall tiles with their beaver motif. On the other traffic island just south of the subway entrance is the famous **Alamo,** a huge black cube sculpted by Bernard Rosenthal that, with pushing from several people, actually rotates. Head east on Astor Place/8th Street, from the Alamo to **St. Mark's Place,** which begins at the intersection of 8th Street and 3rd Avenue. Dozens of bizarre shops—and people—dot the north and south sides of the street between 2nd and 3rd avenues. This is the best block in the country on which to find inexpensive—and rare—compact discs. And if you're interested in viewing the human flotsam and jetsam of the counterculture, there are few better places.

The area along 2nd Avenue north and south of St. Mark's Place was referred to as the Yiddish Rialto in the early part of the 20th century, when eight theaters between Houston and 14th streets showcased Yiddish-language productions of revues, musicals, and melodramas. The only two survivors of that era are the **Orpheum,** just south of St. Mark's Place on 2nd Avenue, and to the north the building that now houses the multiscreen **Village East Cinemas,** between 11th and 12th streets. The largest theater in the complex has preserved an ornate Hebraic ceiling and chandelier. And in 1985, the famous **Second Avenue Deli** on the east side of 2nd Avenue, at 10th Street, proudly committed the sidewalk in front of itself to a series of Hollywood Boulevard–style squares to commemorate Yiddish stage luminaries. Across from the Second Avenue Deli on the west side of 2nd Avenue is the dignified **St. Mark's-in-the-Bowery Church,** an Episcopal church that has also long served as an arts center (Isadora Duncan danced here) and public meeting hall. This is the oldest continually used Christian church building in the city; Dutch governor Peter Stuyvesant and Commodore Matthew Perry are buried here in the ancient churchyard. Head south on 2nd Avenue to 9th Street, where, turning left, walking east, you pass a number of friendly and unusual shops selling housewares, vintage clothing, toys, herbs, coffee, leather goods, and lots more. When you reach 1st Avenue, you'll see on the northeast corner **P.S. 122,** a former public school that is now a complex of spaces for performance art and other avant-garde entertainment. If you continue east, you will be entering what is referred to as **Alphabet City** because the avenues are named A, B, C, and D. This area, formerly a sort of no-man's-land, is transforming itself practically daily into a hip and desirable neighborhood. The blocks are lined with inexpensive (and some quite excellent) restaurants, cafés, and shops. Across from St. Mark's Place on Avenue A is **Tompkins Square Park,** a lush and peaceful haven. Walk back west and follow 7th Street away from the southwest corner of the park. At 1st Avenue, turn left, heading south down to 6th Street, where the entire block is given over to dozens of Indian restaurants competing to serve their very inexpensive fare. Turning right on Taras Shevchenko Place (named for the "Ukrainian Shakespeare"), you'll find one of New York's oldest (1854) bars, **McSorley's Old Ale House,** featuring splendid house ale served at a mahogany bar. This is a lovably stubborn old place: women were not permitted in the bar until a discrimination suit forced civil-rights compliance—in 1970! Just past McSorley's is **Surma, the Ukrainian Shop,** which purveys all manner of Ukrainian handmade goods. Across the street is the beautiful, copper-domed **St. George's Ukrainian Catholic Church.** Turning left, heading west toward 3rd Avenue one confronts the mammoth, brownstone **Cooper Union Foundation Building,** a tuition-free school for artists and architects that overlooks Cooper Square. Head one block west to Lafayette Street. The long block between Astor Place and E. 4th Street contains the famous New York Shakespeare Festival's **Joseph Papp Public Theater,** which, in the 19th century, was the site of the city's first free library. The Public Theater is where such theatrical milestones as *Hair, A Chorus Line,* and *Bring In Da Noise, Bring In Da Funk* were originally staged. Across from the theater is a stretch of four 19th-century Greek Revival houses known as **Colonnade Row.** Head north on Lafayette Street until you're back at Astor Place, then turn left and walk the short block to Broadway. To the south is a "miracle mile" of shops of every description; turn left if you want to go on a spree. But to the north lies **Grace Church,** at the corner of Broadway and 10th Street. Designed by James Renwick, Jr., in 1846, just before he began his masterpiece, St. Patrick's Cathedral, the church's ornate marble tower, topped by a magnificent spire, is visible from dozens of blocks south on Broadway. Inside you'll find relatively comfortable cushioned benches and sumptuous pre-Raphaelite stained-glass windows. You should end your walk at the **Strand Book Store,** the largest secondhand bookstore in the city, with "eight miles of books" and some of the best deals in the country.

A Walking Tour of Greenwich Village.
Begin at Washington Arch in **Washington Square,** at the foot of 5th Avenue on Waverly Place. This populous 9½-acre park, an oasis for locals and tourists alike, is also the seat of New York University, which owns most of the buildings surrounding the square. About

a half block north, on the east side of 5th Avenue, is the quaint **Washington Mews,** a cobblestoned private street where NYU faculty dwell. Continue north and on the west side of 5th Avenue, you'll pass the **Church of the Ascension,** at 10th Street, a handsome Gothic Revival brownstone building. At 12th Street and 5th Avenue, you can stop in the **Forbes Magazine Galleries,** where the unusual personal collection of the late publisher Malcolm Forbes is housed. Particularly striking are the Fabergé eggs that Forbes amassed, and a collection of over 12,000 toy soldiers. Backtrack south two blocks towards the Arch, turn right, and head west on 10th Street, noticing the magnificent town houses that line the street. At Avenue of the Americas (known as "6th Avenue," to natives), turn left to visit the great **Balducci's,** one of the finest gourmet food stores in the country. Across the street is the **Jefferson Market Library,** which at various times in history was a market, a women's prison, and a courthouse. Proceed across the intersection of 6th Avenue and Greenwich Avenue to **Christopher Street,** which begins just off the south end of the library triangle. This has long been the symbolic center of the city's gay and lesbian community. Heading southwest, you'll pass **Gay Street** on the left (named long before the word was attached to a sexual preference), a curved thoroughfare of 19th-century row houses. Continuing along Christopher Street, you'll see the 1831 **Northern Dispensary** building at Waverly Place, which once provided health care to impoverished Village residents. Across the street is **51 Christopher Street,** the site of the historic Stonewall Riots, which launched the modern gay rights movement in 1969. The green triangle in the center of the street is **Christopher Park,** which features a sculpture by George Segal of a gay and a lesbian couple. At the intersection of 7th Avenue, W. 4th Street, and Christopher Street, proceed across 7th Avenue, turn left and head a short block south, turn right onto Grove Street and continue west. The secluded intersection of Grove and Bedford streets holds, on the right side, on the northeast corner, **17 Grove Street,** one of the few clapboard structures remaining in Manhattan. Behind it, at 102 Bedford Street, is **Twin Peaks,** a house from the early 19th century that looks like a Swiss chalet. At Bedford Street, turn left, heading south, and walk until you get to Number 86. Behind this unmarked door is **Chumley's,** a former speakeasy with atmosphere to spare, currently cherished by college students for its beer and burgers. A few blocks farther down at the southwest corner of Commerce at 77 Bedford Street is the **Isaacs-Hendricks House,** the oldest house in the Village. Next door is **75½ Bedford Street,** the narrowest house in the city (9½ ft wide). Turning right on Commerce Street, you come to the intersection of Commerce Street and Cherry Lane, one of the loveliest areas of the entire Village, and home to the perpetually booked **Cherry Lane Theater.** Turn left from Commerce Street onto Barrow Street, and continue to Hudson Street (so named because, before the landfill, this was the bank of the Hudson River). The block to the northwest is still owned by **St. Luke-in-the-Fields,** which served, beginning in 1822, as a country chapel for Downtown's Trinity Church. By now, your feet are probably tired, so before you wander into the winding shopping areas of the West Village, which lie directly to the north, stop in at the legendary **White Horse Tavern,** on Hudson at 11th Street, for some liquid refreshment.

ON THE CALENDAR

The *New York Convention and Visitors Bureau.* has precise dates and times for most of the annual events listed here, and its web site (www.nycvisit.com) has still more information on free activities. | 810 7th Ave. at W. 53rd St. | 212/484–1222 | Weekdays 9–6, Sat. 10–5.

JAN.: *New York National Boat Show.* For 10 days in early January, the Jacob Javits Convention Center gives itself over to an exhibition of the latest in pleasure craft (power- and sailboats), yachts, and all sorts of other seaworthy vessels. | 212/216–2000.

FEB.: *Annual Empire State Building Run-Up.* This invitational event features 150 runners, obviously in optimal cardiovascular condition, who scramble up the 1,576 steps from the lobby of the Empire State Building to the 86th-floor observation deck. | 212/860–4455 (NY Roadrunners Club).

FEB.: *Chinese New Year.* Celebrated over a two-week period, there are now, thanks to Mayor Giuliani's efforts, no fireworks, but still plenty of colorful and extravagant banquets and that famous dragon dance that winds through the narrow streets of Chinatown. | 212/484–1222.

FEB.: *New York Yankees Fan Festival.* You can meet current and former players, bid in a memorabilia auction, and test your swing early in February, at various locations. | 718/293–4300.

FEB.: *Westminster Kennel Club Dog Show.* America's second-longest-running animal event (after the Kentucky Derby), this mammoth show features nearly 3,000 purebred canines and their proud human companions, who take over Madison Square Garden for two days. Be sure to go "backstage" to meet these magnificent creatures. | 7th Ave. at W. 33rd St. | 800/455–3647.

MAR.: *International Asian Art Fair.* Sixty dealers from around the world exhibit furniture, bronzes, carpets, ceramics, sculptures, jewelry, and much more from the Middle East, Southeast Asia, and the Far East. The location varies, so call for information. | 212/642–8572.

MAR.: *St. Patrick's Day Parade.* Every March 17 since 1762, the Irish have taken to the streets for an often-boisterous parade that goes up 5th Avenue, starting at 44th Street, and ending at 86th Street. | 212/484–1222.

LATE MAR.–EARLY APR.: *Triple Pier Expo.* Over 600 dealers of antiques of every vintage come to Piers 88, 90, and 92, displaying everything from art glass to furniture, from books to dolls. The event is also held in November. | Pier 88 is at W. 48th St., Pier 90 is at W. 50th St., and Pier 92 is at W. 52nd St. | 255–0020.

APR.: *Easter Parade.* Just like Judy Garland in the Fred Astaire movie, you can don your Easter bonnet and join the crowd near St. Patrick's Cathedral, on 5th Avenue at E. 51st Street. | 212/484–1222.

APR.: *Macy's Flower Show.* The week before Easter, Macy's creates lush displays inside its flagship store and sets its Broadway windows blooming. | W. 34th St. and Broadway | 212/494–2922.

MAY: *Ninth Avenue International Food Festival.* "Hell's Kitchen" gives itself over to food vendors of every stripe (particularly Hispanic) for two days of food, music, flowers, and agreeable mayhem. | 9th Ave., W. 34th–57th Sts. | 212/484–1222.

MAY: *Washington Square Outdoor Art Exhibit.* For over 50 years, Memorial Day has marked the start of this open-air arts-and-crafts fair, which attracts over 600 exhibitors who set up in Washington Square Park and on surrounding streets. The fair runs for three weekends, from noon to sundown. | University Pl., 3rd St.–12th St. | 212/982–6255.

JUNE–AUG.: *Bryant Park Film Festival.* Every Monday night (weather permitting), movie-lovers of all ages fill Bryant Park behind the New York Public Library's Humanities Center, turning the vast lawn into a picnic ground hours before show time, which is at dusk. Classic, mostly Hollywood movies are screened on a huge outdoor screen. | 6th Ave. between 40th and 42nd Sts. | 212/512–5700 May–Aug., film hot line.

JUNE: *JVC Jazz Festival–New York.* This annual event brings together the giants of jazz as well as newcomers, in some of New York's most prestigious venues: Carnegie Hall, Lincoln Center, and the Beacon Theater, among other theaters and clubs around town. | 212/501–1390.

JUNE: *Lesbian and Gay Pride Month.* Literally hundreds of gay-related events celebrate the diversity of this community, from a sizable film festival to concerts, theater and cabaret events, and much more. It culminates on the last Sunday of the month, in the world's largest gay-pride parade, which winds its way down 5th Avenue and into the West Village for over five hours. | 212/807–7433.

JUNE: *National Puerto Rican Day Parade.* Dozens of wildly energetic bands make 5th Avenue throb while huge crowds cheer them on. | 44th–86th Sts. | 718/665–4009.

JUNE, JULY: *Midsummer Night Swing.* Lincoln Center's picturesque Fountain Plaza is transformed into a huge open-air dance hall. Top big bands fill the summer air with jazz, Dixieland, R&B, calypso, and mambo for dancers of all ages. Dance lessons are given every night. | $11 if you want to dance on the dance floor, free if you don't mind being on the outskirts | Tues.–Sat.: tickets on sale at 6, lessons 6:30, dancing 8–11 | Lincoln Center's Fountain Plaza, Columbus Ave. between 62nd and 65th Sts. | www.lincoln-center.org | 212/875–5766.

EARLY JUNE–MID-AUG.: *Summergarden.* The Museum of Modern Art's glorious sculpture garden becomes an open-air auditorium on Friday and Saturday nights, hosting performances of 20th-century classical music, played by Juilliard School graduates. | 11 W. 53rd St., near 5th Ave. | 212/708–9400.

JULY, AUG.: *Shakespeare in the Park.* Sponsored by the Joseph Papp Public Theater, these performances are held in the magical open-air Delacorte Theater in Central Park. The plays are often cast with high-profile Hollywood/television/Broadway celebrities, and the productions are usually Shakespeare plays, although recent summers have included Thornton Wilder's *The Skin of Our Teeth* and the musical *On the Town.* Tickets are free, but you may well have to wait on line all afternoon. Enter Central Park by the footpath at Central Park W and W. 81st St. | 212/539–8500 or 212/539–8750 (seasonal phone at the Delacorte).

AUG.: *Mostly Mozart Festival.* Free outdoor afternoon concerts and casual indoor evening concerts are held at Lincoln Center, with the festival's orchestra, under the galvanizing baton of Gerard Schwarz, and very special soloists. | Lincoln Center, Columbus Ave. between W. 62nd and 65th Sts. | www.lincolncenter.org | 212/875–5103.

SEPT.: *Feast of San Gennaro.* Twinkling lights festoon Little Italy's Mulberry Street (from Canal to Houston streets) for this festival, the city's oldest and most crowded. Have the carny guess your weight before you eat a couple of sausage sandwiches. | 212/768–9320.

SEPT.: *West Indian American Parade.* New York's largest parade, modeled after the harvest carnival in Trinidad and held in Brooklyn, is the centerpiece of a weekend filled with festivities, beginning with a Friday-night salsa/reggae/calypso party at the Brooklyn Museum of Art and ending Monday afternoon with a giant Mardi Gras–style parade of floats, wildly costumed dancers, and West Indian music and food. | Labor Day weekend | 212/484–1222.

SEPT.: *New York Is Book Country.* Publishers large and small set up booths along 5th Avenue from 48th to 57th streets, and you can preview forthcoming titles, meet authors, listen to readings, play games, and buy all sorts of books. | On 5th Ave. from 48th to 57th Sts. | 212/207–7242 | www.bookreporter.com/nyisbookcountry.

SEPT.–OCT.: *New York Film Festival.* The city's most prestigious film event began in 1963. Movie-lovers and filmmakers alike pack Alice Tully Hall and various other Lincoln Center auditoriums to preview features and shorts from all over the world. Often the stars and filmmakers participate in a panel discussion afterwards. Advance tickets are usually essential; some screenings are sold out a month in advance. | Lincoln Center, Columbus Ave. between W. 62nd and 65th Sts. | 212/875–5610.

OCT.: *International Fine Art and Antique Dealers Show.* One of the world's finest art fairs gathers dealers from Europe and America to display treasures from antiquity to the 20th century. | The Seventh Regiment Armory, Park Ave. at 67th St. | 212/642–8572.

OCT.: *Village Halloween Parade* Started by Greenwich Village mask maker and puppeteer Ralph Lee in 1973, the parade began as a walk from house to house in Mr. Lee's neighborhood and now draws more than 30,000 costumed participants and 2 million spectators. If you don't have a costume, you can volunteer to man one of the large-scale puppets that have become the hallmarks of the parade. | 6th Ave. from Spring to 23rd Sts. | 212/475–3333, ext. 4044 | www.halloween-nyc.com.

NOV.: *NYC Marathon.* The world's largest marathon begins on the Staten Island side of the Verrazano Narrows Bridge and snakes through all five boroughs before reaching the finish line at Tavern on the Green in Central Park. | W. 67th St. and Central Park W | www.nycmarathon.org | 212/860–4455.

NOV.: *Macy's Thanksgiving Day Parade.* A real New York tradition, with gigantic balloons (if it's not too windy) floating down Central Park W from 77th Street. This marks

the official beginning of the Christmas season, with Santa Claus on hand. | From Central Park W and W. 77th St. to Broadway and W. 34th St. | 212/494–4495.
NOV.–JAN.: *The Radio City Christmas Spectacular.* This event has been an annual tradition since 1933. Features the Rockettes, singers, dancers, special effects, a live orchestra, and an appearance by Santa Claus. | Radio City Music Hall, 1260 Ave. of the Americas, between W. 50th and 51st Sts. | 212/247–4777 or 212/307–7171.
DEC.: *Christmas Season.* One of the tallest and most sumptuous Christmas trees in the country is mounted in Rockefeller Center, just above the skating rink, and early each December, thousands of people gather to watch the ceremonial tree lighting, which is telecast live. The city's shop windows, especially those along Fifth Avenue in Midtown, are magnificently decorated, often featuring animated puppets acting out various Christmas stories. The season culminates on New Year's Eve with the famous midnight ball drop in Times Square, which is televised all over the world. Then, in Central Park, a lovely Midnight Run, hosted by the New York Road Runners Club, begins at the perennially festive Tavern on the Green. | 212/632–3975 tree–lighting information; 212/768–1560 Times Square ball drop.

Dining

INEXPENSIVE

Baluchi's. Indian. The spicy food attracts crowds to this dark SoHo dining room decorated in a lush Indian theme. No smoking. | 193 Spring St. | 212/226–2828 | $11–$15 | AE, DC, MC, V.

Carnegie Deli. Delicatessen. This is one of the last of the real Jewish delis. It's very touristy for a reason: the famous mile-high sandwiches provide enough protein for a small army. Try the pastrami sandwich. | 854 7th Ave. | 212/757–2245 | $11–$20 | No credit cards.

Comfort Diner. American. This quintessential diner serves classic comfort food at bright-color booths. Try the macaroni and cheese, meat loaf, and club sandwiches. Kids' menu. No smoking. | 214 E. 45th St.; 142 E. 86th St. | 212/867–4555; 212/426–8600 Uptown | $10–$15 | AE, D, DC, MC, V.

Empire Diner. American. This place is as lively at 4 AM as it is for Sunday brunch. The menu is filled with upscale diner classics. There's a piano, which many patrons use to entertain fellow diners. Open-air dining, patio style with tables in front of the diner. Sunday brunch. Open 24 hrs. | 210 10th Ave. | 212/243–2736 | $9–$19 | AE, D, DC, MC, V.

Floridita Restaurant. Cuban. You'll have to share this large bright dining room with Columbia University students and folks from the neighborhood, around 129th Street. The menu is in English and Spanish and includes breakfast and lunch specials, house specials, and even super house specials. The cafe con leche is out of this world and your best bet is to choose from the extensive list of daily items. The huevos españoles are a treat to the tastebuds. | 3219 Broadway | 212/662–0266 or 212/662–0090 | $6–$18 | D, MC, V.

Harley-Davidson Cafe. American. If you're into bikes, this theme-restaurant can't be beat for the Harley and multimedia displays. Stick to the basics, and the food is passable. Outdoor dining with tables on the sidewalk in front of the restaurant. Kids' menu. | 1370 6th Ave. | 212/245–6000 | $10–$16 | AE, DC, MC, V.

Jackson Hole. American. Huge burgers and milk shakes are standard fare at these neighborhood places, often filled with locals and their kids. The jukebox blasts out 1950s hits. Open-air dining at some locations, with tables on the sidewalk in front of the restaurant. Saturday, Sunday brunch. | 1611 2nd Ave.; 232 E. 64th St.; 517 Columbus Ave.; 521 3rd Ave.; 1270 Madison Ave. | 212/737–8788, 212/371–7187, 212/362–5177, 212/679–3264, or 212/427–2820 | $7–$15 | AE, MC, V.

Joe's Shanghai. Chinese. The Chinatown outpost of this restaurant—the original is in Queens—is always packed. The big round tables make it great for groups. Known for the soup dumplings and traditional Shanghai dishes. | 9 Pell St. | 212/233–8888 | $9–$20 | No credit cards.

Katz's Deli. Delicatessen. The decor hasn't changed much since this deli began serving the Lower East Side in 1888. Though it has never actually been kosher, it is still a real traditional New York Jewish-style restaurant. The Formica tables, vintage advertisements, and indifferent service set the stage. Be nice to the counterman, maybe he'll give you an extra pickle. Known for the corned beef, pastrami, and hot dogs. | 205 E. Houston St. | 212/254–2246 | $10–$19 | AE, MC, V.

Lombardi's. Pizza. Since 1905, the Lombardi family has been serving terrific coal-oven pizza from this crowded storefront in Little Italy. The mozzarella is always fresh and the homemade toppings delicious. | 32 Spring St. | 212/941–7994 | $12–$20 | No credit cards.

Moustache. Middle Eastern. This tiny West Village storefront is always packed with people who love the tasty, inexpensive fare. The flavors are clean and the ingredients always impeccably fresh. There's also a branch in the East Village. Try the "pitzas," Middle Eastern salads, and ouzi, a mix of chicken and vegetables in phyllo dough. | 90 Bedford St.; 265 E. 10th St. | 212/229–2220 West Village; 212/228–2022 East Village | $8–$12 | No credit cards.

Nyonya. Malaysian. This large, busy restaurant has lots of wood and a tropical, Asian feel. The food is interesting, spicy, and authentic, and the menu is lengthy. Try *roti canai, mee siam* (stir-fried rice vermicelli with tofu and shrimp), or *nyonya kari ayam* (chicken with lemongrass and chile paste in coconut curry). | 194 Grand St. | 212/334–3669 | $8–$18 | No credit cards.

Ratner's. Kosher. You can almost hear the pushcart vendors barking their wares outside this Lower East Side institution. The kosher food is accompanied by the best onion rolls in the city and amusingly gruff service. Try gefilte fish, latkas, or blintzes. | 138 Delancey St. | 212/677–5588 | Closed Sat. | $5–$15 | No credit cards.

Republic. Asian. This former warehouse, converted to a hip, airy noodle shop, is decorated with huge black-and-white photographs (of noodles) and wooden benches. The food is cheap and delicious, and the service is extraordinarily fast. Try salmon sashimi salad, fried wontons, or broth noodles. No smoking. Open-air dining with tables on the sidewalk in front of the restaurant. | 37 Union Sq. W | 212/627–7172 | $6–$9 | AE, DC, MC, V.

Second Avenue Deli. Delicatessen. This kosher/meat restaurant offers a real New York deli experience complete with a seasoned staff who love to "kibbitz" with the customers, mile-high sandwiches, and other delights straight from your Jewish grandmother's kitchen. Try the pastrami, corned beef, or chopped liver. | 156 2nd Ave. | 212/677–0606 | Closed Rosh Hashanah, Yom Kippur, Passover | $14–$24 | AE.

Serendipity 3. American. Serendipity invented frozen hot chocolate, and you have to try it to understand how delicious it is. This place is a kiddie favorite, from the huge, goopy sundaes to the special burgers and other fun fare. | 225 E. 60th St. | 212/838–3531 | $7–$18 | AE, D, DC, MC, V.

Siam Grill. Thai. Located in a bustling, theater-filled neighborhood, the authentic, spicy Thai fare is surprisingly good. In addition to the traditional *pad thai,* you'll find seven different curry dishes, including red, green and yellow curries, with a choice of beef, chicken, pork, scallops, or mixed seafood. | 586 9th Ave. | 212/307–1363 | No lunch weekends | $8–$15 | AE, MC, V.

Siam Inn. Thai. The dining room is kitschy but appealing. The food is excellent, spicy, and inexpensive. Known for their seafood, try the soft-shelled crabs. | 916 8th Ave. | 212/489–5237 | Reservations essential Fri. and Sat. | No lunch weekends | $8–$17 | AE, DC, MC, V.

Stage Deli. Delicatessen. The well-known kosher New York deli pickles its own meat and names mammoth sandwiches after celebrities, many of whom have their pictures hanging on the wall. Open-air dining with tables on the sidewalk in front of the restaurant. | 834 7th Ave. | 212/245–7850 | $8–$29 | AE, D, MC, V.

Sweet-N-Tart Cafe. Chinese. Hip Chinatown locals frequent this little basement café. The menu features Cantonese dishes, many of which are unfamiliar to Westerners. Try the fried rice with Chinese sausage, flat noodles, tapioca, and sago shakes. Wide selection of teas. | 76 Mott St. | 212/334–8088 | $4–$10.

20 Mott Street. Chinese. This bustling tri-level restaurant is packed on weekends for dim sum. Waiters parade through the restaurant with tasty items. Some may be unrecognizable but all are worth a try. | 20 Mott St. | 212/964–0380 | $5–$23 | AE, D, MC, V.

Viet-Nam. Vietnamese. This basement dive offers authentic Vietnamese food and friendly service. The decor is nonexistent, and the place is hard to find, but the prices are very low. Try the seafood in black bean sauce, beef with watercress, or the chicken or beef soup with rice noodles. | 11 Doyers St. | 212/693–0725 | $5–$13 | AE.

MODERATE

Alva. American. Named for Thomas Alva Edison, this spot pays proper homage to the American icon with lots of exposed, low-watt bulbs. The bistro food is seductive, and the crowd is hip. Try the grilled herb-crusted salmon, pan-seared duck breast, seared tuna, or the Cuban sandwich. | 36 E. 22nd St. | 212/228–4399 | Closed Labor Day weekend | $18–$29 | AE, DC, MC, V.

Angelo and Maxie's Steakhouse. Steak. The young crowd loves the hefty, artery-clogging portions of beef, and there's a crowded, lively bar and a cigar room in the back. | 233 Park Ave. S | 212/220–9200 | No lunch Sat. | $9–$24 | AE, D, DC, MC, V.

Aquagrill. Seafood. This casual restaurant has a Mediterranean feel and ocean-theme touches, such as shell-covered mirrors. The seafood is exquisitely fresh and simply prepared. Try the grilled fish and the bouillabaisse. Raw bar. Open-air dining on the terrace. Saturday, Sunday brunch. No smoking. | 210 Spring St. | 212/274–0505 | Closed Mon. | $20–$25 | AE, MC, V.

Arqua. Italian. On a quiet TriBeCa corner, this upscale restaurant features cuisine from the Veneto region in northern Italy, serving homemade pastas and gnocchi, artichoke lasagna, pappardella with duck and mushrooms, and braised rabbit in white wine. With its airy dining room and authentic food, it has been pleasing New Yorkers since 1987. | 281 Church St. | 212/334–1888 | No lunch Sun. | $18–$35 | AE, DC, MC, V.

Becco. Italian. It gets very crowded during the pre-theater rush at this northern Italian restaurant, known for osso buco and pasta specials. There's also an amazing wine list: 70 different bottles at $18 apiece. No smoking. | 355 W. 46th St. | 212/397–7597 | Reservations essential for pre-theater menu | $17–$29 | AE, D, DC, MC, V.

Belluno Ristorante. Italian. The attentive staff really care about the food and the customers at this contemporary spot. Try the shrimp martini; risotto with shrimp, scallops and clams; or the veal with porcini and shallots. No smoking. | 340 Lexington Ave. | 212/953–3282 | Closed Sun. | $12–$25 | AE, MC, V.

Bistro du Nord. French. A well-heeled Upper East Side crowd loves the upscale comfort food served here. Try the steak frites, rack of lamb, and roasted salmon. Pre-theater menu. Saturday, Sunday brunch. No smoking. | 1312 Madison Ave. | 212/289–0997 | $16–$27 | AE, DC, MC, V.

Blue Ribbon. Eclectic. Always packed with a regular crowd, this is a favorite place for late-night diners. The menu includes something for everyone, and the offerings at the oyster bar are superb. Try the paella Vasquez, duck club, spicy fish soup, and the banana split. Raw bar. No smoking. | 97 Sullivan St. | 212/274–0404 | Closed Mon. and last 2 wks late summer/early fall. No lunch | $10–$30 | AE, D, DC, MC, V.

Blue Ribbon Bakery. French. This neighborhood bistro offers comfort food with something for everyone. The wide variety of small dishes are perfect for sharing over a glass of wine. Try the country pâté, roasted garlic, sweetbreads, sandwiches, and the banana split. | 33 Downing St. | 212/337–0404 | Closed Mon. | $19–$28 | AE, DC, MC, V.

Blue Ribbon Sushi. Japanese. Leave it to the Blue Ribbon clan to create a fun late-night scene no matter what kind of cuisine it serves. This dark, narrow sushi bar is always packed with a Downtown crowd addicted to the fresh and creative—albeit expensive—sushi. There is also a decent sake selection. | 119 Sullivan St. | 212/343–0404 | Closed Mon. No lunch | $39–$49 | AE, D, DC, MC, V.

Brooklyn Diner USA. American. This place may not have anything to do with its namesake borough, and purists may not agree with the authenticity of the food, but most love the big portions and gooey desserts. Their cheeseburgers were named the best in in New York by *New York* magazine. Try the very popular chicken-liver appetizer. | 212 W. 57th St. | 212/977–1957 | $9–$22 | AE, D, DC, MC, V.

Bryant Park Grill. Contemporary. Windows overlooking Bryant Park transport diners to the treetops while they munch at this restaurant behind the New York Public Library. Midtown working folk flock to the bar after office hours. Open-air dining. No smoking. | 25 W. 40th St. | 212/840–6500 | $18–$26 | AE, D, DC, MC, V.

Cafe de Bruxelles. Belgian. This was the original Belgian restaurant in New York, before they started cropping up all over town. Decorated with wood floors and lacy half-curtains, it is famous for its large selection of mussels, beef stew with beer, and, of course, fries and mayo. Sunday brunch. | 118 Greenwich Ave. | 212/206–1830 | $15–$21 | AE, MC, V.

Cafe Fiorello. Italian. This sophisticated, family-owned Italian trattoria is always bustling before Lincoln Center events. Stick to the simpler dishes, and check out the antipasti bar surrounded by Peter Max paintings. The house special is veal parmigiana. Open-air dining on the sidewalk in front of the restaurant overlooking Lincoln Center. Kids' menu. Saturday, Sunday brunch. No smoking. | 1900 Broadway | 212/595–5330 | $16–$29 | AE, DC, MC, V.

Cafe Luxembourg. French. The food is above average, with some excellent specials, at this chic Art Deco bistro near Lincoln Center. The menu is not extensive, but it's got great basics, such as the roast chicken and steak frites. Changing fish offerings are always a good bet, too. Saturday, Sunday brunch. | 200 W. 70th St. | 212/873–7411 | $19–$29 | AE, DC, MC, V.

Cafe Nosidam. Italian. Watch the ritzy folks who shop Madison Avenue from this European-style bistro decorated with original art. Customers return for the 15 varieties of pasta, including lobster ravioli. Open-air dining on the sidewalk veranda. Sunday brunch. | 768 Madison Ave. | 212/717–5633 | $13–$28 | AE, DC, MC, V.

Calle Ocho. Latin. The huge dining room is wonderfully decorated like a modern Latin fantasy, with beaded curtains, beautiful murals, and a wall of blown glass. The kitchen turns out tasty, upscale versions of traditional Latin American dishes. Try the *chupe*, a Peruvian shrimp chowder with root vegetables, Ecuadoran corn tamales with wild mushrooms and charred beef, and the *bistec* Cuban-style "steak frites" with yucca fries. | 446 Columbus Ave. | 212/873–5025 | No lunch | $15–$24 | AE, DC, MC, V.

Cal's. Mediterranean. There's something for everyone at this stylishly decorated former warehouse. The menu includes some inventive dishes, like risotto, as well as good old standards such as burgers. Small outdoor dining area on the sidewalk in front of the restaurant. | 55 W. 21st St. | 212/929–0740 | No lunch weekends | $15–$20 | AE, DC, MC, V.

Carmine's. Italian. Come hungry to these friendly and large, bustling restaurants where family-style, southern Italian food is king. The old-fashioned mirrors, beautiful dark woodwork, and hardwood floors give it a clean, comfortable feel. The tasty food comes in HUGE portions that are meant to be shared—if the waiter tells you you've ordered too much, believe him. Upfront, there's a crowded bar where you can also order food. Open-air dining on the sidewalk (Uptown location only). The wait can be very long. | 2450 Broadway; 200 W. 44th St. | 212/362–2200, 212/221–3800 | $18–$80 | AE, MC, V.

Chez Michallet. French. This tiny French bistro is on a quiet corner in the West Village. Regulars love the intimacy of the place, as well as the reasonably priced food with Asian accents, like the popular steak au poivre, rack of lamb in a rosemary red wine sauce, and the filet mignon with apple curry sauce and jasmine rice. Pre-theater menu. Beer and wine only. No smoking. Sunday brunch | 90 Bedford St. | 212/242–8309 | No lunch | $19–$33 | AE, MC, V.

Chez Napoleon. French. This family-owned French bistro is known for homey decor and caring service. The classically conceived menu is practically an anthropological document on French food. | 365 W. 50th St. | 212/265–6980 | Closed Sun. No lunch Sat. | $15–$25 | AE, D, DC, MC, V.

Churrascaria Plataforma. Brazilian. This huge meat-lovers' mecca serves the best *rodizio* (various skewered steaks) in town. Don't fill up on goodies from the salad bar, because the parade of roasted meats that follows is mouthwatering. Great for large groups. Known for all-you-can-eat rodizio. | 316 W. 49th St. | 212/245–0505 | Reservations essential | $36 all you can eat | AE, DC, MC, V.

Cibo. Eclectic. Cibo's upscale contemporary dining room offers a variety of northern Italian pasta specialties as well as some eclectic American dishes, such as Maryland crab cakes, filet mignon, and roasted Long Island duck. Saturday, Sunday brunch. | 767 2nd Ave. | 212/681–1616 | www.cibonyc.com | Closed Sun. Memorial Day–Labor Day | $18–$35 | AE, D, DC, MC, V.

Clementine. Contemporary. The sexy front room, complete with a DJ, is a favorite among the Downtown crowd, but the elegant, often busy, back room attracts serious diners. The menu includes updated American classics with lots of regional touches. Try the fried green tomatoes, steamed salmon with risotto, and the lemon icebox cake. | 1 5th Ave. | 212/253–0003 | Reservations essential | No lunch | $15–$25 | AE, D, DC, MC, V.

Cuisine de Saigon. Vietnamese. This is one of the first Vietnamese restaurants in the city. The food is authentic, even if the surroundings are just ordinary. The traditional home cooking is full of lemongrass, seafood, and grilled meat on skewers. | 154 W. 13th St. | 212/255–6003 | Reservations essential weekends | $8–$16 | AE, DC, MC, V.

Dawat. Indian. A sleek dining room and traditional Indian dishes make this a popular choice for Indian food in an upscale setting. Try the tandoori shrimp and whole fish. | 210 E. 58th St. | 212/355–7555 | Reservations essential | No lunch Sun. | $12–$25 | AE, DC, MC, V.

Delegates Dining Room. Eclectic. This fourth-floor restaurant features chefs from different parts of the world on a rotating basis and puts out a lavish lunch buffet each day. This is the U.N., however, and although anyone is welcome to dine, a photo ID is required for entry. Buffet lunch. | 1st Ave. | 212/963–7625 | Reservations essential | Jacket required | Closed weekends. No dinner | $35–$38 | AE, DC, MC, V.

Dolphins. Seafood. New Yorkers rave about the affordable seafood at this tasteful Cooper Square restaurant. There's outdoor dining in a lovely back garden. Saturday, Sunday brunch. | 35 Cooper Sq. | 212/375–9195 | fax 212/375–9197 | No lunch weekdays | $30–$45 | AE, MC, V.

Domingo. Spanish. Placido's powerful tenor is behind this authentic Spanish family restaurant. It features a rooftop terrace, great for intimate dining, and a tapas bar. Try the Argentinian steaks and the rack of lamb. Open-air dining. | 209 E. 49th St. | 212/826–8154 | Closed Sun. No lunch | $39–$46 | AE, D, DC, MC, V.

El Teddy's. Mexican. It's hard to miss El Teddy's with the model of the Statue of Liberty standing on top of the place. Inside, it looks like the fun spot it is, with lots of mosaic tiles and fanciful dioramas. The bar scene is always hopping, due to excellent margaritas. Known for grilled seafood and Mexican dishes. There's also a sidewalk café out front. | 219 W. Broadway | 212/941–7070 | No lunch weekends | $16–$23 | AE, DC, MC, V.

Firemans of Brooklyn. Seafood. This casual, neighborhood mainstay is welcoming, and the food is fresh and tasty, if not particularly innovative. There is a lobster tank and bronze statues of Roy Campanella and Jonny Podres. Try the lobster diablo and the stuffed shrimp. Saturday, Sunday brunch. | 1081 3rd Ave. | 212/838–7570 | $18–$25 | AE, D, DC, MC, V.

First. American. Comfortable round booths, mood lighting, and "industrial" decor help make this spot popular with a stylish Downtown crowd. The tasty food pleases savvy diners and late-night revelers alike. Try the grilled hanger steak, rotisserie free-range chicken, seafood tacos, mussels with Pernod, and s'mores. Sunday brunch. | 87 1st Ave. | 212/674–3823 | No lunch (excluding Sun. brunch) | $16–$24 | AE, MC, V.

Five Points. American. The space, decorated with blond wood, plants, and attractive light fixtures, is appealing, especially for late-night dining. Mediterranean-accented dishes that emerge from the wood-burning stove include grilled Black Angus steak and fire-charred squid stuffed with shrimp and vegetables. Sunday brunch. | 31 Great Jones St. | 212/253–5700 | No lunch (excluding Sun. brunch) | $12–$27 | AE, DC, MC, V.

Florent. French. This chrome-and-aluminum-trimmed diner is attached to a meat market in the newly hip meat-packing district of the West Village. The after-club crowd loves the French comfort food, accompanied by pulsing music, but even at other times Florent is fun. Try the *boudin noir,* fresh fish, and the onion soup. Open 24 hours Fridays and Saturdays. | 69 Gansevoort St. | 212/989–5779 | Closes at 5 AM Mon.–Thurs., Sun. | $10–$17 | No credit cards.

Fraunces Tavern. Continental. Fraunces is set in a historic landmark built in 1763. There's a museum to commemorate the restaurant's history, and the place is really more noted for its Colonial ambience than the uninspired Continental fare. Kids' menu. | 54 Pearl St. | 212/269–0144 | Closed weekends | $35–$41 | AE, DC, MC, V.

Gigino Trattoria. Italian. The cozy ambience here is a welcome change from the industrial TriBeCa neighborhood in which it's located. The cuisine covers both northern and southern Italian and is consistently good. Specialties include the *merluzzo,* codfish with Gorgonzola, mashed potatoes, and tomatoes, and the *petto d'oca,* breast of duck with yams and herbs. Open-air dining on small sidewalk. | 323 Greenwich St. | 212/431–1112 | No lunch weekends | $13–$26 | AE, D, DC, MC, V.

Harbour Lights. American. Some of the best views of the Brooklyn Bridge can be found at the outdoor patio of this South Street Seaport eatery, but unfortunately the food can't compete. Try the charred yellowfin tuna or the swordfish Wellington. Open-air dining. | Fulton Pier 17 | 212/227–2800 | $20–$30 | AE, D, DC, MC, V.

Hasaki. Japanese. Pretty, simple Japanese decor provides serenity, though the often hour-long waits can be frustrating. The sushi is always impeccably fresh and attractively presented. Beer and wine only. No smoking. | 210 E. 9th St. | 212/473–3327 | Reservations not accepted | $33–$39 | AE, D, DC, MC, V.

Home. American. There's a quaint, country-house feel—with wood walls, a tiny open kitchen, and a pretty back garden—at this restaurant where everything is homemade and the simple good food pays homage to the chef-owner's Midwestern roots. Try the blue-cheese fondue, roasted chicken, and sautéed greens with ketchup. There's a nice selection of local wines, and the quiet patio in the garden is open year-round. Saturday, Sunday brunch. Beer and wine only. No smoking. | 20 Cornelia St. | 212/243–9579 | $16–$20 | AE.

I Coppi. Italian. Named for its Tuscan terra-cotta urns, this restaurant has a rustic dining room with a tiny open kitchen, and a bucolic back dining room. The seasonal menu, created by the owner's mother, will transport you to a farmhouse in Tuscany. Try the antipasto, homemade pastas, special soups, and the *spigola ai ferri* (grilled striped bass). Homemade desserts. | 432 E. 9th St. | 212/254–2263 | $18–$25 | AE, MC, V.

I Tre Merli. Italian. Known more for its trendy European crowd than for its northern Italian food, this dark converted warehouse is always full of beautiful people. Over 1,000 wine bottles line the exposed brick walls and the whole front of the restaurant opens up to provide sidewalk dining. Try the herb ravioli with walnut sauce, focaccia sandwiches, and the sea bass with artichoke. | 463 W. Broadway | 212/254–8699 | Reservations essential Fri.–Sun. | $18–$45 | AE, DC, MC, V.

Il Buco. Mediterranean. Chock full of antiques, mismatched tables and chairs, and vintage kitchen gadgets, this former antiques store pulses with energy. The appetizers are served tapas-like, and entrées are simple and tasty. Try the *politetti* (grilled baby octopus) and the fresh-made pastas. | 47 Bond St. | 212/533–1932 | No lunch Sun., Mon. | $25–$30 | AE.

Ithaka. Greek. Simple Mediterranean fare transports you to the seaside towns of the Greek isles, at this crowded neighborhood spot. There's an glass-enclosed garden dining area, plus three outdoor sidewalk tables. | 48 Barrow St. | 212/727–8886 | $16–$24 | AE, DC, MC, V.

Japonica. Japanese. Unpretentious surroundings and excellent sushi have made Japonica a neighborhood mainstay. There are often lengthy waits on the weekends. Try the soft-shell crab and the oysters. | 100 University Pl. | 212/243–7752 | $18–$32 | AE.

Joe Allen. American. This classic Theater District eatery has basic pub grub, but occasional celebrity sightings keep Joe Allen a fun pre- or post-theater choice. Known for steaks and big burgers. Sunday brunch. | 326 W. 46th St. | 212/581–6464 | Reservations essential | $10–$21 | MC, V.

Jubilee. French. This intimate French country bistro is popular with a young European crowd. The food is simple and traditional. Try the five different kinds of mussels and the tuna tartare. Jazz Thursday. Sunday brunch (winter only). | 347 E. 54th St. | 212/888–3569 | No lunch Sat. | $14–$24 | AE, DC, MC, V.

La Belle Vie. French. A casual French theme runs through this busy, neighborhood restaurant with tin ceilings. The menu features bistro staples. Try the rack of lamb and the roast duck. Saturday, Sunday brunch. | 184 8th Ave. | 212/929–4320 | $12–$19 | AE, MC, V.

La Mangeoire. French. Familiar menu items make this a welcome neighborhood spot. The food leans toward Mediterranean specialties that are always good. Try the rack of lamb, shepherd's pie, and the monkfish. | 1008 2nd Ave. | 212/759–7086 | No lunch Sat. | $16–$28 | AE, DC, MC, V.

La Traviata. Italian. This old-fashioned restaurant manages to improve the taste of very basic red-sauced northern Italian fare. Try the Chilean sea bass. There's a balcony facing a garden and a wine cellar. Entertainment Friday, Saturday. Sunday brunch. | 461 W. 23rd St. | 212/243–5497 | Closed Sun. Memorial Day–Labor Day. No lunch Sat. | $10–$24 | AE, DC, MC, V.

Lemon. Eclectic. The entire front of this huge bi-level space opens in summer. Go for the people-watching; the food is secondary. Try the seared rare tuna and the crisp roasted duckling. Open-air dining. Entertainment Thursdays–Saturdays. | 230 Park Ave. S | 212/614–1200 | $15–$20 | AE, DC, MC, V.

Little Doves. American. From the owners of the pricey and romantic Sign of the Dove comes this offshoot, an eatery on the second floor, around the corner from Bloomingdale's. The open kitchen gives the dining room an informal feel. The contemporary American cuisine features entrees like roasted quail stuffed with walnuts in a fig sauce, and seared beef tenderloin, served cold, with frisee of pomegranate sauce. | 200 E. 60th St. | 212/751–8616 | $22–$30 | AE, D, DC, MC, V.

Lola. Eclectic. This elegant restaurant, with Caribbean and Asian accents, continues to be exciting after many years. The room is loud, but it is still romantic, especially when you sit on the softly lighted banquettes. The art is by local artists. Try the fried chicken and the double happiness tuna. Jazz Tuesdays. Blues Wednesday–Saturday. Gospel Sunday brunch. No smoking. | 30 W. 22nd St. | 212/675–6700 | No lunch Sat. | $22–$35 | AE, DC, MC, V.

Luna Piena. Italian. There's a lovely back garden at this Midtown trattoria, opened in 1997, where the simple Italian food is well done and the staff is truly proud of the menu. The seafood pasta and the steak with porcini mushrooms are both good. | 243 E. 53rd St. | 212/308–8882 | $12–$24 | AE, MC, V.

Manhattan Bistro. French. This cozy space in the middle of major SoHo shopping is perfect for a relaxing respite after exploring the neighborhood. Try the pâté or the asparagus salad. Saturday, Sunday brunch. | 129 Spring St. | 212/966–3459 | $8–$16 | AE, MC, V.

Marylou's. Continental. The menu is predictable, but regulars love the ambience at this restaurant. Located in a landmark brownstone, it has a working fireplace and a glass-enclosed garden. Try the seafood platter, grilled swordfish steak, or the linguine pescatore. Sunday brunch. | 21 W. 9th St. | 212/533–0012 | $16–$26 | AE, MC, V.

Mercer Kitchen. Contemporary. This is a fashionable, brick-lined basement space with communal tables as well as private nooks in the chic Mercer Hotel. The menu, conceived by Jean-Georges Vongerichten, divides the food according to which part of the kitchen it comes from. Try the carpaccio of venison from the pantry, seared tuna and wasabi from the pizza oven, and the roasted lobster from the rotisserie. Raw bar. | 99 Prince St. | 212/966–5454 | Reservations essential | $19–$35 | AE, DC, MC, V.

Mezzaluna. Italian. This tiny—somewhat cramped—trattoria provides a nice taste of Italy. The short menu offers updated favorites, and the sidewalk dining is great for people-watching. Try their homemade pizzas from the wood-brick oven. Open-air dining. Beer and wine only. | 1295 3rd Ave. | 212/535–9600 | $20–$26 | AE.

Mezzogiorno. Italian. An outdoor deck opens onto the sidewalk here, providing a great place for hobnobbing with locals. The casual atmosphere and good northern Italian fare attract an eclectic crowd. Try one of the individual pizzas. Open-air dining. | 195 Spring St. | 212/334–2112 | $17–$23 | AE.

Mi Cocina. Mexican. The food is authentically Mexican, but with a decidedly upscale bent at this bright modern restaurant. Try the grilled chicken with poblano chile or the grilled steak. Open-air dining on sidewalk. Kids' menu. Sunday brunch. | 57 Jane St. | 212/627–8273 | Closed 2 wks in Aug. | $19–$32 | AE, DC, MC, V.

Mickey Mantle's Restaurant and Sports Bar. American. Decorated with baseball memorabilia from the sport's beginning until now, this place is heaven for fans of the game. TVs are at various spots around the bar, and there's a large screen in the rear dining room. The food is uninspired but basic, and kids will like it. Known for burgers, ribs, and bowls of Bavarian-style pretzels on the bar. Kids' menu. Open-air dining on the small enclosed sidewalk café. | 42 Central Park S | 212/688–7777 | $10–$26 | AE, D, DC, MC, V.

Miracle Grill. Southwestern. The back garden is among the nicest in New York and a real find in the neighborhood. In summer, there is always a long wait for a table. The reasonably priced menu offers creative dishes inspired by the American Southwest. There's also a branch in the West Village. Try the catfish tacos, Portobello fajitas, and pork chops. | 112 1st Ave., 415 Bleecker St. | 212/254–2353 | No lunch weekdays | $27–$36 | AE, DC, MC, V.

The Odeon. French, American. This American-style brasserie was one of the first TriBeCa hangouts, and it still attracts an artsy Downtown crowd. The food is as good as when it first opened. Try the steak frites and the seared tuna. Open-air dining on sidewalk patio. Kids' menu. Sunday brunch. | 145 W. Broadway | 212/233–0507 | $9–$26 | AE, DC, MC, V.

Osteria al Doge. Italian. Always busy, especially for pre-theater dining, this casual, lively spot feels steps away from the canals of Venice. The menu is reasonably priced for the area. Try the lobster risotto and the calves' liver. | 142 W. 44th St. | 212/944–3643 | No lunch Sun. | $14–$25 | AE, D, DC, MC, V.

Our Place. Chinese. The simple Chinese fare is a cut above most neighborhood restaurants. Try the Peking duck and the Szechuan-style chicken or beef. Early bird dinner Monday–Saturday. | 1444 3rd Ave. | 212/288–4888 | $12–$20. | AE, DC, MC, V.

Oyster Bar. Seafood. Set in the landmark Grand Central Terminal, this restaurant is casual but impressive-looking and the freshness of the seafood is unparalleled. Raw bar. | Vanderbilt Ave. at 42nd St. | 212/490–6650 | Closed weekends | $37–$46 | AE, DC, MC, V.

Pearl Oyster Bar. Seafood. You'll feel like you're at a seaside bar at this cheery storefront restaurant, which serves exceptionally fresh East Coast specialties. Try the steamers, fried cod sandwich, lobster roll, chowder, or the whole grilled fish. | 18 Cornelia St. | 212/691–8211 | Closed Sun. | $17–$25 | MC, V.

Penang. Malaysian. There's usually a wait for a table at this bustling restaurant with a waterfall and a funky Downtown crowd. Try the *roti cani* or mango chicken. | 109 Spring St., 1596 Second Ave., 240 Columbus Ave. | 212/274–8883, 212/585–3838, 212/769–3988 | $8–$20 | AE, MC, V.

Pierre Au Tunnel. French. The cozy fireplace and surroundings are as comforting as the familiar menu. This is a great place for romantic and pre-theater dining. Known for traditional French dishes like *coq au vin* and *cassoulet*. The *tripes à la mode du Caen*, in white wine and Calvados, is a house specialty. | 250 W. 47th St. | 212/575–1220 | Closed Mon. | $35 prix fixe | AE, MC, V.

Pig Heaven. Chinese. The name sounds more like a rib joint than a Chinese restaurant, but the big portions of filling food make it popular among Upper East Side families. Try the chicken *soong* or the pork. | 1540 2nd Ave. | 212/744–4333 | $9–$17 | AE, D, DC, MC, V.

Planet Hollywood. American. This theme restaurant moved to Times Square in 2000, but the music videos and movie clips are still shown 'round the clock. The food is not worth mentioning, but pre-teen girls seem to love the place. | 1540 Broadway | 212/333–7827 | $7–$20 | AE, D, DC, MC, V.

Pó. Italian. This dimly lit, romantic, slightly cramped Village restaurant serves some of the best, and most reasonably priced, food in the city. Mario Batali's creative dishes are inventive and traditional at the same time. Open-air dining at two tables on the sidewalk. Try the white bean ravioli or the black fettuccine. No smoking. | 31 Cornelia St. | 212/645–2189 | Reservations essential | Closed Mon. and 2 weeks in Jan. and Sept. No lunch Tues. | $8–$15 | AE.

Red Cat. Mediterranean. The wood adorning the interior of this country-style restaurant was rescued from an old New England barn. The reasonably priced menu has simple fare dressed up with Mediterranean accents, and is popular with the gallery owners and artists in the neighborhood. Try the mustard-crusted trout. | 227 10th Ave. | 212/242–1122 | No lunch | $16–$28 | AE, MC, V.

Rialto. Contemporary. The pressed-tin ceiling, distressed-wood furniture, and red booths make everyone feel at home at this happening restaurant where everyone is stylish. The basic food is good and satisfying. In summer, there is an attractive garden. Try the roasted garlic soup, marinated yellowfin tuna with Asian spiced fries, and the burgers. Kids' menu. | 265 Elizabeth St. | 212/334–7900 | $14–$20 | AE, DC, MC, V.

Riodizio. South American. The dining room is bright and festive. The all-you-can-eat *rodizio*—chefs bring skewers to the tables and slice off meat—is an experience, as are the potent *caipirinhas*, cocktails made with the rum-like *cachaca*. There is a full à la carte menu. No smoking. | 417 Lafayette St. | 212/529–1313 | No lunch | $15–$31 | AE, MC, V.

Rocking Horse Cafe Mexicano. Mexican. Bright and cheery, this neighborhood favorite is decorated with multicolor tables and walls, and corn-husk light fixtures. The menu is authentic but more upscale than that of most Mexican restaurants. Try the *tamalitos de pato* (tamales with duck confit), *mogo mogo* (plantain and black-bean fritters), and the *posole de mariscos* (seafood in hominy and tomato broth). | 182 8th Ave. | 212/463–9511 | $23–$30 | AE, MC, V.

Rosa Mexicano. Mexican. The festive Mexican decor, with colorful paper cutouts hanging from the ceiling, is the perfect setting for this fun, crowded, margarita-laden scene. The excellent, upscale food goes well beyond the usual Mexican restaurant staples. Don't miss the made-to-order guacamole. | 1063 1st Ave. | 212/753–7407 | Reservations essential | No lunch | $16–$26 | AE, DC, MC, V.

Ruth's Chris Steak House. Steak. The men's-club decor of this newcomer to the New York steak-house scene is appropriate for the meaty menu. Try the cowboy rib-eye steak. | 148 W. 51st St. | 212/245–9600 | No lunch weekends | $55 | AE, DC, MC, V.

Sal Anthony's SPQR. Italian. This quintessential Little Italy dining room has a dependable menu that covers all of the expected southern Italian favorites. Sidewalk open-air dining. Kids' menu. | 133 Mulberry St. | 212/925–3120 | $32–$38 | AE, DC, MC, V.

Salaam Bombay. Indian. The live sitar player on Friday and Saturday evenings gives the dining room an especially exotic feel. The upscale food includes unusual regional dishes. Try the lamb chops and the tandoori shrimp. No smoking. | 317 Greenwich St. | 212/226–9400 | No lunch Sat. | $10–$20 | AE, D, DC, MC, V.

Sarabeth's. American. The soothing, crisp style and delicious baked goods make this one of the most popular brunch spots in town. Dinner is much quieter, and not nearly as good. Try the specialty desserts, like the bread pudding. Also try the oven-roasted lamb with black trumpet mushrooms. Saturday, Sunday brunch. No smoking. | 423 Amsterdam Ave; 1295 Madison Ave. | 212/496–6280, 212/410–7335 | $15–$25 | AE, DC, MC, V.

Savann. Contemporary. The minimalist decor, with an open kitchen and large storefront windows, leaves the food to take center stage. The dining room and the menu are tiny, but everything is well chosen. Try the grilled squid with parsnip horseradish puree, sesame-crusted salmon, and the grilled leg of lamb Napoleon. Homemade pastries. Beer and wine only. No smoking. | 414 Amsterdam Ave. | 212/580–0202 | No lunch weekdays | $34–$40 | DC, MC, V.

Savore. Italian. The food is authentic Italian in this elegant dining room, which is furnished with antiques and polished wood. Try the corn mousse with wild-boar sauce and the vegetable tartare. Homemade baking, pasta. Open-air dining on medium-size sidewalk patio with trees. No smoking. | 200 Spring St. | 212/431–1212 | $14–$20 | AE, D, MC, V.

Screening Room. Contemporary. The menu at this stylish eatery offers interesting takes on American and Italian dishes. The restaurant is attached to two movie theaters that show independent and vintage films. Diners are guaranteed a seat in either theater; a prix-fixe menu/movie ticket is available. Try the grilled prime rib-eye steak and the seafood ceviche whether you've come to see a movie or not. Sunday brunch. | 54 Varick St. | 212/334–2100 | Reservations recommended | No lunch Sat. | $15–$25, $30 prix fixe | AE, D, DC, MC, V.

Shaan. Indian. Wall hangings soften the room and solicitous service softens the customers at this serene Indian restaurant. You'll find authentic and expertly prepared versions of mulligatawny soup and Tandoori rack of lamb marinated in yogurt. Salad bar. Lunch buffet. Entertainment Friday and Saturday. Pre-theater menu. No smoking. | 57 W. 48th St. | 212/977–8400 | $34–$41 | AE, DC, MC, V.

Shabu-Tatsu. Japanese. The food should be good—you cook it yourself with a stove top set into the middle of your own table. The restaurant is clean, modern, casual, and friendly. Try the shabu shabu. Saturday, Sunday brunch. No smoking. | 1414 York Ave. | 212/472–3322 | No lunch weekdays | $10–$20 | AE, D, DC, MC, V.

Shark Bar. Southern. This is a small but very popular spot for drinks as well as for upscale soul food. There's lots of red velvet and woodwork in the dining rooms. The southern-fried, honey-dipped chicken and the turkey meat loaf are specialties. Also known for great Cosmopolitans and Uptowns. Saturday, Sunday brunch. No smoking. | 307 Amsterdam Ave. | 212/874–8500 | No lunch | $13–$19 | AE, D, DC, MC, V.

Steak Frites. French. The namesake dish is always good at this bustling, bistro-style restaurant on Union Square. Specialties include creamed spinach, mussels provençale in white wine, Belgian beers, and crème brûlée for dessert. The wood-accented interior is decorated with paintings by New York artist Ruben Toledo. Open-air dining on sidewalk. Sunday brunch. | 9 E. 16th St. | 212/463–7101 | $32–$40 | AE, DC, MC, V.

Sylvia's. Southern. It's hard to talk about Harlem without making mention of this culinary landmark. Most famous for smothered chicken and barbecued ribs, Sylvia's will make you abandon your diet for the afternoon and dive into all of the southern fixin's, and finish off with peach cobbler. Many of the employees are part of Sylvia Woods's family, which is evident in the kind of service you'll receive. There's a counter and three big dining rooms, but the homey feeling is everywhere. | 328 Lenox Ave. | 212/996–0660 | fax 212/427–6389 | Breakfast served daily | $12–$15 | AE, D, DC, MC, V.

Taormina of Mulberry Street. Italian. Better-than-average Little Italy–style food keeps small, romantic, and private Taormina busy. Try the penne with asparagus and the gnocchi. | 147 Mulberry St. | 212/219–1007 | Reservations essential | $10–$20 | AE, DC, MC, V.

Typhoon Brewery. Thai. This is a favorite after-work hangout. The excellent microbrews are complemented by Thai food that doesn't skimp on the spices, like the wok-charred chicken and crusted Atlantic salmon. No smoking. | 22 E. 54th St. | 212/754–9006 | Closed Sun. No lunch Sat. | $16–$34 | AE, D, DC, MC, V.

Victor's Cafe 52. Cuban. Pre-revolutionary Cuba is the theme at this Theater District favorite. The scent of the delicious food will lure you in, as will the potent cocktails. Try the paella, stone crab Creole, and the suckling roast pig. Pianist Fri.–Sun. | 236 W. 52nd St. | 212/586–7714 | $16–$34 | AE, DC, MC, V.

Vince and Eddie's. American. This spot feels as cozy as being in your own house (if that house is an old Colonial). The seasonal menu is good, with lots of favorites, including calamari and crab cakes appetizers, and main dishes like linguine in a white clam sauce and lamb shank with a cherry sauce. Open-air dining in quiet garden in back of restaurant. Saturday, Sunday brunch. | 70 W. 68th St. | 212/721–0068 | Closed Mon. | $15–$25 | AE, D, DC, MC, V.

Virgil's Real Barbecue. Barbecue. This is a veritable barbecue theme park, with southern decor and dark wood. Luckily the food is actually the real thing. Be prepared to wait. Try the prime rib and the Memphis pork ribs. Kids' menu. No smoking. | 152 W. 44th St. | 212/921–9494 | $11–$25 | AE, MC, V.

Wall Street Kitchen and Bar. American. This Financial District eatery is known mostly for the excellent wine list, offered in a variety of tasting "flights." The food serves mostly to ensure that the after-work crowd doesn't get too drunk. Try the flank steak and the Thai chicken pizza. | 70 Broad St. | 212/797–7070 | Closed weekends | $10–$17 | AE, D, DC, MC, V.

Zarela. Mexican. This festive but sophisticated Midtown restaurant is known for its interesting and authentic dishes. A bar with tables is downstairs, and a quieter dining room is on the second floor. Try the fajitas and the special fish of the day. Entertainment Tuesday–Saturday. | 953 2nd Ave. | 212/644–6740 | No lunch weekends | $14–$19 | AE, DC, MC, V.

EXPENSIVE

Adrienne. French. A 1998 renovation has made this dining room, with its dark wood, even more plush. Elegant, simple, and romantic, Adrienne's formal cuisine is enlivened by numerous Asian accents. Try the seared tuna in rice paper, crisp sweet-water prawns, and the trio of lobster soups. Pianist Tuesday–Friday. Sunday brunch. No smoking. | 700 5th Ave. | 212/903–3918 | Reservations essential | Jacket required | $22–$32 | AE, D, DC, MC, V.

Alison on Dominick Street. Country French. This gem of a restaurant is on a deserted street away from SoHo's throngs. This is a simple, elegant, romantic, spot—great for couples and special occasions. Try the seared foie gras, roast Long Island duck breast, homemade desserts and sorbets, and the Maine lobster stew. Pre-theater menu. | 38 Dominick St. | 212/727–1188 | Reservations essential | Closed 1st week in July. No lunch | $26–$32 | AE, DC, MC, V.

Ambassador Grill. Continental. On the lobby floor of the United Nations Plaza Hotel, the elegant, mirrored room of the Ambassador Grill is a hangout for diplomats and other world figures. The dishes, too, are elegant and include potato-encrusted halibut and duck breast in a peach glaze. Piano bar Thursday–Saturday. Kids' menu. Saturday, Sunday brunch. | 1 U.N. Plaza | 212/702–5014 | $41–$50 | AE, D, DC, MC, V.

Aquavit. Scandinavian. Scandinavian dishes are presented with exceptional purity at this Midtown restaurant. The two dining rooms here both specialize in seafood and game: the street-level café offers a traditional menu, à la carte or a $30 prix fixe; the more formal atrium upstairs has a waterfall to complement the more adventurous and eclectic fare. Sunday brunch. | 13 W. 54th St. | 212/307–7311 | Reservations essential | No lunch Sat. | $53–$58 | AE, DC, MC, V.

Aureole. French. Some of the city's best food is served in the elegant, duplex dining room of this flower-bedecked town house. Expect fabulous dishes, prepared with the freshest seasonal ingredients. Prices are steep, but there's a reasonably priced prix-fixe dinner. The all-tasting menu is adventurous, with six different complementary courses. Known for its game dishes, sea scallop sandwiches, and exquisite desserts. | 34 E. 61st St. | 212/319–1660 | Reservations essential | Jacket and tie | Closed Sun. No lunch Sat. | $69 prix fixe | AE, D, DC, MC, V.

★ **Babbo.** Italian. The bi-level dining room has the feel of an elegant Roman restaurant, with wildflower arrangements and a cheese plate covered with cheesecloth at the waiter station in the middle of the room. The menu is simple yet inventive, with lots of unique pasta dishes and an excellent Italian wine list. Try the pasta-tasting menu, lamb's tongue salad, and the whole fish. | 110 Waverly Pl. | 212/777–0303 | Reservations essential | No lunch | $17–$35 | AE, D, DC, MC, V.

Balthazar. French. This perfect re-creation of a Parisian brasserie—complete with specials written on the mirrors—is a hangout for locals and celebrities who love the casual room, late-night buzz, and excellent French food. Known for the raw seafood, roast chicken, and French specialties. Raw bar. | 80 Spring St. | 212/965–1414 | Reservations essential | $40–$49 | AE, MC, V.

Barbetta. Italian. This century-old Italian restaurant serves traditional Piedmontese specialties in a sumptuously appointed town house. But in the late spring and summer, the real draw is the luxurious outdoor garden, a true oasis in the Theater District. Known for classic northern Italian cooking, white truffles, and homemade pasta. Excellent service. | 321 W. 46th St. | 212/246–9171 | Closed Sun. | $19–$29 | AE, D, DC, MC, V.

Bice. Italian. This Milan import is a favorite among Italian expats. It has a European aura and sophisticated food. Try the *tagliolini* lobster, fettuccine pasta with chunks of lobster, wild mushrooms and tomatoes, or veal Milanese. Open-air dining on sidewalk. | 7 E. 54th St. | 212/688–1999 | $20–$27 | AE, D, DC, MC, V.

Bolivar. Latin. The cheery adobe dining room has South American accents such as chunky glassware and colorful light fixtures. The menu spans the cuisines of Latin America, with many dishes coming from an authentic *parilla* (grill). Try the Peruvian ceviches or grilled Argentinian beef, and lobster *chupe* (soup). | 206 E. 60th St. | 212/838–0440 | $40–$46 | AE, MC, V.

Bolo. Spanish. Creative takes on Spanish staples are tasty and interesting at this festive restaurant, decorated like a colorful hacienda. Try the paella. | 23 E. 22nd St. | 212/228–2200 | No lunch weekends | $24–$40 | AE, D, DC, MC, V.

Bond Street. Japanese. The sleek tri-level space makes full use of trendy black, beige, and white furnishings, and the waitstaff looks as though they just got off from a photo-shoot. Despite the painful hipness, the food is quite good, with exotic sushi offerings not found at other restaurants and admirable dishes from the kitchen. Known for creative Japanese salads, sushi, interesting tempura, and other hot dishes. | 6 Bond St. | 212/777–2500 | No lunch | $18–$26 | AE, DC, MC, V.

Bouley. French. Pass through the retail bakery into this lovely space with exquisite flower arrangements on each table and sheer lamé curtains. David Bouley's cooking brings out the essence of flavors in each dish. Try the crabmeat in an ocean herbal broth, yellowtail with glazed scallions, and the breads. | 120 W. Broadway | 212/964–2525 | Reservations essential | $20–$35 | AE, MC, V.

Bull & Bear Steakhouse. Steak. The menu looks as if it hasn't changed since the Waldorf-Astoria opened in the 1930s—the same goes for the clientele. With its cherry wood accents, it has a businesslike atmosphere. Try the lobster salad with mango, avocado, corn; or the filet mignon with grilled vegetables, potatoes, and balsamic vinegar. Jazz trio Thursday–Friday. Kids' menu. No jeans, no sneakers. | Waldorf-Astoria, 570 Lexington Ave. | 212/872–4900 | No lunch weekends | $26–$38. | AE, D, DC, MC, V.

Cafe Boulud. French/American. This bistro is the hot new venue for acclaimed chef-owner Daniel Boulud's innovative cuisine. There's an extensive wine list and great desserts. Regulars love the menu, which covers both classic fare and more adventurous offerings. Try the heirloom tomato risotto and the duo of roasted duck. | 20 E. 76th St. | 212/772–2600 | No lunch Sun., Mon. | $20–$35 | AE, DC, MC, V.

Cafe Carlyle. Continental. This venerable establishment exudes an old-world sensibility, which is appropriate given the average age of the clientele. Expect white-glove service from the seasoned waitstaff. Known for seasonal specialties. Try the Carlyle chicken hash. Live piano music. | 35 E. 76th St. | 212/744–1600 | Closed Sun. | $20–$40 | AE, DC, MC, V.

Cafe des Artistes. Continental. This gracious and intimate restaurant is most noted for its paintings of nymphs, which adorn the dining room. The largely French menu also has some Hungarian dishes. Saturday brunch. | 1 W. 67th St. | 212/877–3500 | Reservations essential | Jacket required | $25–$35 | AE, DC, MC, V.

Cafe Pierre. Continental. Formal and sedate, this elegant restaurant is in one of New York's premier hotels. Try the sautéed foie gras with sauterne pepper sauce or the seared sea bass with fennel. Homemade pastries. Entertainment nightly. Pre-theater menu (6–7). Sunday brunch. Kids' menu. | 2 E. 61st St. | 212/940–8195 | Reservations essential | Jacket required | $28–$38 | AE, D, DC, MC, V.

Campagna. Italian. The dining room feels like an upscale trattoria, with its comfortable widely spaced tables and wood accents. Many consider Campagna one of the top northern Italian restaurants in the city. Try the roasted halibut with fennel orange and saffron or the tagliolini with lobster and shrimp. | 24 E. 21st St. | 212/460–0900 | No lunch weekends | $17–$32 | AE, D, DC, MC, V.

Capsouto Frères. Contemporary French. This restaurant is on a near-deserted street in TriBeCa. If you can find it, you'll be treated to one of the most romantic dining rooms in town. Try the steak frites and the soufflés for dessert. Open-air dining at medium-size sidewalk café. Saturday, Sunday brunch. | 451 Washington St. | 212/966–4900 | $15–$25 | AE, DC, MC, V.

Castellano. Italian. The staff is truly accommodating, and the northern Italian food is always well executed at this romantic, bi-level, Tuscan-theme eatery with elegant wood panels. Try the ravioli *provinciale* with its tomato and pesto sauce, or the grilled fish of the day. | 138 W. 55th St. | 212/664–1975 | No lunch weekends | $17–$26 | AE, DC, MC, V.

Chelsea Bistro and Bar. French. Bustling with artists and gallery owners, this spot is complete with French waitstaff, a fireplace, indoor terrace, and brass rail along the banquette for a romantic atmosphere. The menu sticks to bistro classics. Try the caramelized onions and herb goat cheese or the hangar steak with fries and vegetables. | 358 W. 23rd St. | 212/727–2026 | No lunch | $17–$23 | AE, MC, V.

Christer's. Scandinavian. An interesting menu makes this is a great choice before a show at Carnegie Hall. Its fishing-lodge decor, with a stone fireplace and exposed wood beams, makes it feel like a cabin. Try the baked salmon and the seasonal game menus. Pre-theater menu (5:30–7). | 145 W. 55th St. | 212/974–7224 | Closed Sun. No lunch Sat. | $25–$35 | AE, DC, MC, V.

Cité. Steak. This dining room is in a cavernous space with impressive flower arrangements and a zinc-topped bar. The French-accented fare is highlighted by a prix-fixe menu that's heavy on meat and with unlimited wine. Wine selections change quarterly. | 120 W. 51st St. | 212/956–7100 | $30 prix fixe | AE, D, DC, MC, V.

Coco Pazzo. Italian. The sophisticated artwork provides a dramatic backdrop to the excellent Tuscan food. The ritzy clientele makes for great people-watching. Try the fish stew and the Black Angus rib-eye steak. | 23 E. 74th St. | 212/794–0205 | Reservations essential | Jacket required | $18–$35 | AE, DC, MC, V.

Coco Pazzo Teatro. Italian. Less formal than its Uptown counterpart, this blue, green, and yellow restaurant, with light-wood accents, is a popular pre- and post-theater spot. Try the steak for two or the *tagliata fiorentina,* a grilled steak with seasonal vegetables. | 235 W. 46th St. | 212/827–4222 | Reservations essential | No lunch weekends | $23–$34 | AE, DC, MC, V.

Cub Room. Contemporary. Upscale country decor and a happening bar scene are the draws at this SoHo restaurant, which serves sophisticated American fare. Fans love the rich, updated-classic desserts. Try seasonal dishes, like veal, crab, or Alaska halibut. No smoking. | 131 Sullivan St. | 212/677–4100 | $23–$30 | AE, MC, V.

Da Sílvano. Italian. The sidewalk café is the place to be seen at this busy brick-walled, upscale trattoria-style SoHo restaurant. The servers whiz by tables with earthy Tuscan classics. Try the *vulcano sivano,* mashed Yukon gold potatoes with porcini mushrooms, and for dessert the *panocotta,* baked heavy cream served with chocolate. Open-air dining on sidewalk. | 260 6th Ave. | 212/982–2343 | $18–$28 | AE, MC, V.

Da Umberto. Italian. The clubby look and excellent Tuscan fare make this a perennial favorite. You'll feel like you entered an elegant northern Italian restaurant. Try the whole baby pheasant or the porterhouse steak à la fiorentina for two. | 107 W. 17th St. | 212/989–0303 | Closed Sun. and week of July 4. No lunch Sat. | $18–$34 | AE.

Demi. Continental. This romantic dining room in the garden level of a town house serves up formal, continental fare. There's a medium-size deck on the second floor of the restaurant. Try the rack of lamb, American red snapper with braised spinach, and the grilled shrimp with asparagus and fresh thyme risotto. Open-air dining. Sunday brunch. | 1316 Madison Ave. | 212/534–3475 | $17–$30 | AE, MC, V.

Destinée. French. A Michelin two-star chef creates updated French dishes in this attractive setting, making it a favorite among the well-heeled locals. The contemporary decor is augmented by original modern art. Try the smoked duck liver in oxtail broth, whole steamed lobster with lobster and garlic sauce, and the roasted herb-crusted rack of lamb. Homemade pastries. No smoking. | 134 E. 61st St. | 212/888–1220 | Closed Sun. | $52–$59 | AE, DC, MC, V.

Duane Park Cafe. Contemporary. This TriBeCa mainstay with lots of fresh flowers has simple decor and a quiet, romantic dining room. Try the seared scallops or the crab-crusted halibut. Weekends get busy. | 157 Duane St. | 212/732–5555 | Closed Sun. and first week in July. No lunch Sat. | $16–$22 | AE, D, DC, MC, V.

Eleven Madison Park. Continental. The cavernous dining room has the feel of a bank at first glance, but once seated and in the hands of the attentive servers, the experience becomes more personal. Huge black-and-white photos of early 20th-century New York decorate the walls. Try the terrine of beef shanks, foie gras and pig's feet, leek and Appenzeller tart, lobster pot-au-feu, and the prime aged rib of beef. | 11 Madison Ave. | 212/889–0905 | Reservations essential | No lunch Sun. | $22–$32 | AE, D, DC, MC, V.

Erminia. Italian. The rustic Italian decor and the restaurant's location in a tiny house on a quiet street make this feel like a romantic country trattoria. The food is hearty and the service is attentive. Try the artichokes sautéed in olive oil and garlic, and the skewer of veal stuffed with prosciutto, pecorino cheese, and pine nuts. Beer and wine only. | 250 E. 83rd

St. | 212/879–4284 | Reservations essential | Jacket required | Closed Sun. and last week June–first week July. No lunch | $16–$32 | AE.

Felidia. Italian. Many hail Felidia as the premier Italian restaurant in New York. The contemporary decor is accented by romantic rustic touches, such as tapestries in the dining rooms, a beautiful wine rack of dark wood, white tablecloths, and dim lighting. Try the osso buco and the homemade pasta. | 243 E. 58th St. | 212/758–1479 | Closed Sun. No lunch Sat. | $25–$35 | AE, D, DC, MC, V.

Fifty Seven Fifty Seven. Contemporary. This room in the grand Four Seasons Hotel is strikingly sleek. With inlaid maple floors, onyx-studded bronze chandeliers, and a contemporary American menu, the restaurant echoes the rest of the building. Creative interpretations of familiar dishes, like lobster Caesar salad, are exceptional, and it's hard to choose between the pepper-crusted tuna niçoise or the herb-roasted veal chop with artichokes and oven-roasted tomatoes. Pianist Thursday–Saturday. Kids' menu. | 57 E. 57th St. | 212/758–5700 | Reservations essential | Jacket required | $53–$58 | AE, DC, MC, V.

Firebird. Russian. This replica of an early 20th-century Czarist mansion is decorated with rich fabrics and lots of gilding. The waitstaff is decked out in pre-revolutionary Russian regalia. The ambience makes the excellent Russian fare taste even better. Try the Ukrainian borscht or the cedar-smoked Alaskan salmon. No smoking. | 365 W. 46th St. | 212/586–0244 | Reservations essential | No lunch Sun.–Tues., Thurs. | $27–$32 | AE, D, DC, MC, V.

540 Park. Contemporary. Come to watch master-of-the-universe types wheel and deal over power breakfasts, or enjoy a sophisticated meal in the elegant dining room. Try the seafood pot pie with herb crust or the grilled Chilean sea bass. They also have a double chocolate pudding for dessert. Kids' menu. Saturday, Sunday brunch. Live cabaret show Tuesday–Saturday (seating begins at 6). | 540 Park Ave. | 212/339–4050 | $22–$36 | AE, D, DC, MC, V.

Follonico. Italian. The farmhouse table at the back is great for large groups, and the food is earthy and delicious at this small, cozy place with lots of dark wood. Try the lobster salad and the osso buco. | 6 W. 24th St. | 212/691–6359 | Reservations essential | No lunch Sat. | $6–$50 | AE, D, MC, V.

Gabriel's. Italian. The artistic crowd from nearby Lincoln Center make this a classy spot for Tuscan fare. The food is uncontrived and well prepared. Try the potato gnocchi with duck ragù or roasted kid. | 11 W. 60th St. | 212/956–4600 | Reservations essential | Closed Sun. No lunch Sat. | $17–$29 | AE, DC, MC, V.

Gallagher's. Steak. Red-checkered tablecloths cover the tables at this quintessential New York steak house, where beef reigns, though pork chops and seafood are also available. The signature dish is the 16-oz sirloin, aged for 21 days at 36 degrees, and cooked to the diner's specifications. | 228 W. 52nd St. | 212/245–5336 | $17–$44 | AE, D, DC, MC, V.

Gascogne. French. A lovely back garden and a homey look make this a favorite spot in the neighborhood. The cuisine is classic country French. Try the foie gras or the cassoulet. Prix fixe and pre-theater menu. Saturday, Sunday brunch. | 158 8th Ave. | 212/675–6564 | $21–$24 | AE, MC, V.

Gotham Bar and Grill. American. After more than 15 years, this remains one of the city's best restaurants, a testament to chef-owner Alfred Portale's many talents. The dining room has 17-ft ceilings, soft lighting, and cast-stone ledges, which give the sense of a garden courtyard. Portale was the first to serve gravity-defying dishes, and he still does it better than anyone else. Menu changes seasonally. | 12 E. 12th St. | 212/620–4020 | Reservations essential | No lunch weekends | $28–$38 | AE, DC, MC, V.

★ **Gramercy Tavern.** Contemporary. Opened by Danny (Union Square Cafe) Meyer, this large and attractive restaurant encompasses three dining areas and a tavern room, with an à la carte menu and a bar. Wooden beams, white walls, and country artifacts lend a rustic feel. The food, courtesy of chef Tom Colicchio, is superb. The prix-fixe menu consists of elegant contemporary American dishes, such as the tuna tartare with sea urchin vinaigrette.

There is also a seasonal menu. No smoking. | 42 E. 20th St. | 212/477–0777 | Reservations essential | $62 prix fixe | AE, DC, MC, V.

Grill Room. American. You'll get some great panoramas of Downtown while you dine on classic American food that matches the monied corporate ambience of the dining room. Try the panfried halibut, then enjoy chocolate souffle. | 225 Liberty St. | 212/945–9400 | Closed weekends | $19–$28 | AE, D, DC, MC, V.

Heartbeat. American. Striking modern decor with rustic touches, including mirrored mosaic columns, cloth walls with stencils of fruit and vegetables, and plenty of blond wood, decorates the dining room of this newcomer. This organic restaurant is in the W Hotel, and the food is surprisingly good considering the kitchen uses no added fat in preparations. The tea selection—and presentation—is wonderful. Try the chopped lobster salad with Peruvian potatoes and black truffles, and the coriander seared duck breast with sweet-potato sauce. | 149 E. 49th St. | 212/407–2900 | $47–$55 | AE, DC, MC, V.

Hudson River Club. Contemporary. Not surprisingly, the menu showcases products from the Hudson River valley. Amid the elegant light-wood decor, try the golden potato ravioli and potato-crusted salmon. Kids' menu. | 250 Vesey St. | 212/786–1500 | Closed Sun. No lunch Sat. | $20–$35 | AE, D, DC, MC, V.

I Trulli. Italian. The excellent cuisine, much of which comes from a domed, wood-burning stove, focuses on the Italian region of Puglia. There is an upscale trattoria feel here, with yellow walls, baskets, and farmhouse furniture. Open-air dining in garden. | 122 E. 27th St. | 212/481–7373 | Reservations essential | Closed Sun. No lunch Sat. | $45–$50 | AE, DC, MC, V.

Il Cortile. Italian. The best bet in Little Italy. The spacious dining room has a huge skylight, and the whole restaurant feels like an Italian piazza. Traditional Italian fare like linguettine with white or red clam sauce and veal scaloppine with fresh tomatoes, wine, and grated provolone is quite satisfying. | 125 Mulberry St. | 212/226–6060 | $40–$47 | AE, DC, MC, V.

Il Monello. Italian. The formal, old-world atmosphere and well-executed northern Italian fare make this a popular, yet elegant, neighborhood choice. The decor is contemporary and the staff is accommodating. Try the lobster ravioli or the veal *monello*, a veal scallopini served with asparagus, cheese, roasted red peppers cooked in white wine. | 1460 2nd Ave. | 212/535–9310 | $18–$35 | AE, DC, MC, V.

Il Nido. Italian. The decor and the food are familiar and well conceived at this classic northern Italian restaurant with excellent service, a devoted clientele, and beautiful fresh flowers. Try the filet mignon or other popular meat dishes. | 251 E. 53rd St. | 212/753–8450 | Closed Sun. | $15–$30 | AE, DC, MC, V.

Jo Jo. French. A somewhat cramped but elegant space is the setting for this celebrated French bistro. Opened in 1991 by star chef Jean-Georges Vongerichten, the buzz in the dining room is still going. The simple, sophisticated menu employs vegetable juices and oils in place of butter. Try lobster tartine in pumpkin seed broth or roast chicken dressed in a ginger-coriander sauce. | 160 E. 64th St. | 212/223–5656 | Reservations essential | Closed Sun. | $19–$36 | AE, DC, MC, V.

Judson Grill. American. An after-work crowd of media types packs this huge Midtown restaurant. Impressive flower displays soften the power look of the room. The seasonal menu includes excellent choices that taste truly fresh and interesting. The service could use a little polishing. Try the seared tuna loin, Black Angus sirloin, and the 10-spice loin of lamb. | 152 W. 52nd St. | 212/582–5252 | Reservations essential | Closed Sun. No lunch Sat. | $19–$34 | AE, D, DC, MC, V.

Kings' Carriage House. English. This continental gem of a restaurant has a romantic, Irish town-house feel, with murals and paintings decorating the walls. The menu, with a mix of Irish and English dishes, may be staid but the service and ambience make for a special meal. Try the medallion of venison or the filet mignon. No smoking. | 251 E. 82nd St. | 212/734–5490 | Reservations essential | No lunch Sun. | $39 prix fixe | AE, MC, V.

La Metairie. French. Beamed ceilings, flower-patterned seat cushions, candlelight, traditional country-French food, and a West Village coziness all come together in this romantic restaurant. The attentive service makes you feel right at home. Favorites include the roasted duck breast and the lobster risotto. Saturday, Sunday brunch. | 189 W. 10th St. | 212/989–0343 | Reservations essential | $16–$25 | AE, D, DC, MC, V.

Larry Forgione's An American Place. American. The restaurant moved to this location in 1999, but chef Larry Forgione still promotes only the best that American cuisine has to offer. Known for the seafood, game, and regional dishes. | 125 E. 50th St. | 212/715–2705 | Reservations essential | Closed Sun. No lunch Sat. | $45–$52 | AE, D, DC, MC, V.

Layla. Middle Eastern. *Arabian Nights* is recalled in fanciful mosaics adorning the walls and ceiling, while a belly dancer spices things up each night. The upscale Middle-Eastern cuisine is satisfying, if somewhat pricey. Try the Moroccan margarita drink and the pomegranate-glazed filet mignon. Open-air dining on an iron patio with a unique lighted floor that looks great at night. No smoking. | 211 W. Broadway | 212/431–0700 | Reservations essential | No lunch Sat.–Thurs. | $20–$28 | AE, DC, MC, V.

Le Boeuf à la Mode. French. The neighborhood crowd enjoys the friendly service and predictable French food. Try the duck à l'orange, rack of lamb, and the daily fish specials. | 539 E. 81st St. | 212/249–1473 | Closed Sun. in July and Aug. | $35 prix fixe | AE, DC, MC, V.

Le Colonial. Vietnamese. The menu's many Asian accents make this restaurant feel truly like a Vietnamese colonial homestead. The upstairs lounge is filled with an attractive crowd. Try the crisp, seared whole red snapper or the sautéed diced breast of chicken. | 149 E. 57th St. | 212/752–0808 | No lunch weekends | $35–$50 | AE, DC, MC, V.

Le Madri. Italian. The dining experience is simple but serious, as is the food, but it all adds up to something special. The surroundings are much like those found in Tuscan restaurants. The look is classic, very warm and inviting, with tapestries on the walls, a painted ceiling, and pillars in the dining room. There is also a sidewalk cafe for warm-weather dining. Try the rigatoni with ragù of tomatoes, the sweet-and-hot Italian sausage, and the grilled steak. | 168 W. 18th St. | 212/727–8022 | Jacket required | $19–$34 | AE, DC, MC, V.

Le Refuge. French. Adorable wooden tables, curtains, and wood floors adorn this French eatery. The menu is pricey, but the dining experience is guaranteed to transport you to France. Try the bouillabaisse. Open-air dining on garden terrace (summer). Saturday, Sunday brunch. | 166 E. 82nd St. | 212/861–4505 | $17–$24 | AE, MC, V.

Lenox Room. Contemporary. This classy, contemporary restaurant attracts a well-heeled crowd that loves the sophisticated, yet relaxed, atmosphere and velvet banquette seating. The menu is New American, taking inspiration from various cuisines. Try the free-range chicken or the large selection of seafood, including the yellowfin tuna tartare. Raw bar. | 1278 3rd Ave. | 212/772–0404 | $19–$32 | AE, DC, MC, V.

Lobster Club. American. This town house feels as cozy as a country home. Lit entirely by candles and fireplaces, the space maintains an urban New York sensibility with the objets d'art decorating the two floors. The restaurant is named for its signature dish and chef-owner Anne Rosenzweig updates comfort-food classics on the fanciful menu. Try the matzo Brie with smoked salmon and dill, meat loaf, or the great macaroni and cheese. No smoking. Kids' menu. | 24 E. 80th St. | 212/249–6500 | $18–$29 | AE, DC, MC, V.

Lumi. Italian. An intimate town-house setting and uncomplicated Italian food please the regulars of this sophisticated restaurant. Try the veal and the ricotta ravioli. Open-air dining on sidewalk, surrounded by a gate made of flowers. | 963 Lexington Ave. | 212/570–2335 | $19–$39 | AE, DC, MC, V.

Lusardi's. Italian. This upscale restaurant, reminiscent of a restaurant in Florence, caters to its equally upscale neighborhood regulars. The northern Italian menu is unchallenging, but unpretentious and good. Try the veal martini and the *rotolo di spinacio,* home-

made pasta filled with spinach and ricotta cheese. No smoking. | 1494 2nd Ave. | 212/249–2020 | No lunch weekends | $16–$26 | AE, D, DC, MC, V.

Maloney & Porcelli. Steak. The fancifully named dishes lean toward huge and meaty portions at this two-story restaurant, which resembles a steak house. Try the Crackling Pork Shank or the Angry Lobster. Saturday, Sunday brunch. | 37 E. 50th St. | 212/750–2233 | $20–$30 | AE, DC, MC, V.

Manhattan Grille. Steak. The admirable menu produces classic steak-house fare with a few surprises. Wood paneling gives the dining room a clubby atmosphere, along with the oriental and Persian rugs, and the Art Deco chandeliers. One of the better steak houses in the city, it's been serving large portions of food since 1983. Sunday brunch. | 1161 1st Ave. | 212/888–6556 | $27–$47 | AE, D, DC, MC, V.

Manhattan Ocean Club. Seafood. With its many nautical touches, this place feels like a luxury ocean liner. Fittingly, the menu comprises delicious offerings from the sea, like seared tuna served with apple-smoked bacon and grouper with roasted pineapple, raisins, and crushed peppercorns. | 57 W. 58th St. | 212/371–7777 | Reservations essential | No lunch weekends | $24–$33 | AE, D, DC, MC, V.

Matthew's. Mediterranean. The billowy white curtains and rattan furniture create a summery, Mediterranean feel, even in the dead of winter. The menu explores Moroccan and other cuisines. Try the tuna tartare or the crab and cod cakes. | 1030 3rd Ave. | 212/838–4343 | $18–$28 | AE, DC, MC, V.

Mesa Grill. Southwestern. This two-tiered lofty space has been transformed into a New York–meets–Southwest fantasy, with lots of bold color and fanciful artwork. The food is exciting, spicy, and delicious and relies more on the chef's invention than on Southwestern traditions. Try the blue corn–dusted squid as an appetizer and follow it with the oven-roasted lamb shank with serrano vinegar brown sugar sauce, served with sweet potato risotto. Saturday, Sunday brunch. | 102 5th Ave. | 212/807–7400 | Reservations essential | $18–$36 | AE, D, DC, MC, V.

Michael's. Contemporary. Hollywood and publishing players power-lunch here, but don't let that stop you from enjoying some fine contemporary American cuisine. The original branch is in Santa Monica and many of the dishes reflect that fact. Try the poached wild Alaskan salmon with braised summer greens, ginger, honshimeji, roasted plum tomatoes, and soy and sesame court bouillon. Though not cheap, you'll find one of the best Cobb salads in town. Kids' menu. | 24 W. 55th St. | 212/767–0555 | Reservation essential | Closed Sun. No lunch Sat. | $26–$35 | AE, D, DC, MC, V.

Molyvos. Greek. This upscale Greek tavern serves excellent food in a space decorated with antique urns and earthy tones. Try the Cretan bread salad, grilled baby lamb chops, and the wild striped bass wood-grilled whole. | 871 7th Ave. | 212/582–7500 | Reservations essential | $18–$24 | AE, D, DC, MC, V.

Monkey Bar. Contemporary. This is an ultra-sophisticated restaurant. Monkeys are everywhere, but thankfully the monkey-less menu provides lots of delicious choices. Try the roasted Amish chicken breast, mustard-crusted rack of lamb, and the roasted cod. | 60 E. 54th St. | 212/838–2600 | Reservations essential | Jacket required | No lunch weekends | $48–$56 | AE, DC, MC, V.

Montrachet. French. This casually chic restaurant offers three dining areas, all painted in muted pastels. The excellent French food is complemented by an outstanding wine list. Known for soufflé, lobster, vegetable terrine, and homemade pastries. | 239 W. Broadway | 212/219–2777 | Reservations essential | Closed Sun. No lunch Mon.–Thurs., Sat. | $22–$33 | AE, D, DC, MC, V.

Morton's of Chicago. Steak. This Morton's outpost continues the tradition of presenting diners with their raw steaks to view before they are cooked. The finished product is uniformly good. | 551 5th Ave. | 212/972–3315 | No lunch weekends | $20–$34 | AE, D, DC, MC, V.

Nino's. Italian. Located somewhat off the beaten path, this stately terra-cotta northern Italian restaurant with modern decor is complete with a trio featuring a pianist, guitarist, and singer and 140 kinds of wine. The excellent service is a pleasure. Try the zuppa di pesce and the homemade pastries. | 1354 1st Ave. | 212/988–0002 | Reservations essential | No lunch weekends | $20–$30 | AE, D, DC, MC, V.

Novita. Italian. The casually elegant, minimalist style, with cherry-wood furnishings, and the excellent Italian menu have made Novita a popular choice among the many interesting Flatiron District choices. Try the porcini mushroom ravioli or the pan-roasted bass. Open-air dining (at lunch only) on sidewalk with five tables. No smoking. | 102 E. 22nd St. | 212/677–2222 | Closed Sun. No lunch weekends | $15–$21 | AE, DC, MC, V.

Oak Room and Bar. Continental. This masculine hangout located in the famous Plaza Hotel is where folks come for cocktails and cigars, but there is a classic American menu. Expect grilled filet mignon and prime rib, cut tableside, and also Dover sole and rack of lamb. If you aren't wearing a jacket and tie, you can order from the Oak Room menu and be served in the bar. Pianist nightly. Pre-theater menu, includes free transportation to theaters. | 768 5th Ave. | 212/546–5330 | Jacket and tie | $47–$56 | AE, D, DC, MC, V.

One If by Land, Two If by Sea. Continental. The food is traditional at this romantic winner set in an opulently restored colonial home. There is a private dining room, and some tables overlook a garden. Try the beef Wellington or, the *côte de boeuf* for two: rib of prime-aged beef in a red wine sauce, served with marrow-stuffed potatoes and Swiss chard. Pianist Friday and Saturday. | 17 Barrow St. | 212/228–0822 | Reservations essential | No lunch | $59 prix fixe | AE, DC, MC, V.

Orso. Italian. A Theater District mainstay where many actors go before and after performances. Orso has mainly pizzas and creative pastas. | 322 W. 46th St. | 212/489–7212 | Reservations essential | $18–$22 | MC, V.

Osterio del Circo. Italian. This festive restaurant is the Italian outpost of the Maccioni clan, responsible for the venerable Le Cirque 2000. The circus theme is reflected in the clownish stuffed-toy monkeys overhead and other theatrical decorations. The sophisticated food is uniformly excellent. Try the ravioli with butter and sage. Open-air dining on sidewalk with 10 tables. | 120 W. 55th St. | 212/265–3636 | Reservations essential | $22–$29 | AE, DC, MC, V.

Palio. Italian. The walls of the incredible bar are painted with a color mural that transports you straight to Siena. The pricey northern Italian food is served in a masculine, wood-paneled room. Try the seasonal risottos, homemade pastas, and the wild-game dishes. | 151 W. 51st St. | 212/245–4850 | Closed Sun. No lunch Sat. | $32–$35 | AE, D, DC, MC, V.

Palladin. French. The sleek, modern, softly lit dining room is a sexy backdrop for the often old-fashioned, country-French fare. The menu includes specialties from the southwestern region of Gascony. Menu changes seasonally. | 224 W. 49th St. | 212/320–2929 | Reservations essential | No lunch Sat. | $28–$36 | AE, D, DC, MC, V.

Palm. Steak. This classic New York steak house is a true original, complete with gruff waiters and celebrity caricatures on the wall. You may be presented with a menu, but the superb beef is the most worthy choice. | 837 2nd Ave. | 212/687–2953 | Reservations essential for 4 or more | No lunch Sat. | $20–$50 | AE, DC, MC, V.

Palm Court. International. This airy columned court, bedecked with plants and flowers, lies off the lobby of the legendary Plaza Hotel and is a New York tradition. The restaurant is most noted for a lovely afternoon tea, and the buffet-style brunch is also a delight. Menu changes seasonally. Sunday brunch. | 768 5th Ave. | 212/546–5350 | Reservations essential for Sunday brunch | $19–$27; brunch $59–$75 | AE, D, DC, MC, V.

Park Avenue Cafe. Contemporary. Authentic American antiques and mismatched place settings don't sound like the trappings for some of the most creative food in the city, but

they are. The whimsical menu will be sure to bring a smile to your lips. Try the tuna and salmon tartare with caviar, swordfish chop, and Mrs. Ascher's steamed vegetable torte. Saturday brunch (winter only). | 100 E. 63rd St. | 212/644–1900 | Reservations essential | No lunch Sat. Memorial Day–Labor Day | $19–$42 | AE, D, DC, MC, V.

Park Bistro. French/Provençal. Hardwood floors, red banquette seating, and black-and-white photos give the place a 1950s Parisian style. Try the sautéed skate or the wild-mushroom ravioli. | 414 Park Ave. S | 212/689–1360 | No lunch weekends | $20–$30 | AE, DC, MC, V.

Park View at the Boathouse. Contemporary. Located in the middle of Central Park, overlooking the lake and Bethesda Fountain, this lovely restaurant offers the best outdoor dining the city has to offer. The food is definitely secondary to the view. Kids' menu. Saturday, Sunday brunch. | In Central Park | 212/517–2233 | Closed Nov.–mid-Mar. | $20–$35 | AE, D, DC, MC, V.

Patria. Latin. Andrew Dicataldo's "nuevo Latino" menu provides bold and spicy offerings, and has spawned a host of devotees and imitators. The dining is spread over two beautiful floors. The best thing available is the chef's tasting menu, which consists of meat, seafood, and salad. | 250 Park Ave. S | 212/777–6211 | No lunch weekends | $59 prix fixe | AE, DC, MC, V.

Periyali. Greek. You'll find loads of plants, lovely furnishings, and some of the best nouvelle Greek food in town here. Glass-enclosed dining in a garden courtyard is available. Try the charcoal-grilled octopus and lamb chops. | 35 W. 20th St. | 212/463–7890 | Closed Sun. No lunch Sat. | $18–$29 | AE, DC, MC, V.

Petrossian. French. Perfect for special occasions, this luxurious, low-lit, Art Deco institution boasts the finest champagne and caviar in town. If fish eggs aren't your thing, there are other French-Russian choices like smoked trout and Arctic venison. Saturday, Sunday brunch. | 182 W. 58th St. | 212/245–2214 | Jacket required | $54–$62 | AE, DC, MC, V.

Picholine. French. Though the Upper West Side is not known for the finest of dining, Picholine can hold its own with any of NYC's top spots. Choose between the front room with its chandeliers and French styling or the more informal back dining area; both are very comfortable. Dishes include Moroccan spiced loin of lamb with vegetable couscous and salmon with horseradish crust, cucumbers, and salmon caviar. No smoking. | 35 W. 64th St. | 212/724–8585 | Reservations essential | No lunch Sun., Mon. | $59–$66 | AE, DC, MC, V.

Post House. Steak. Upscale and clubby, this is one of the more genteel New York steak houses. Most pay little attention to nonbeef offerings, but even the seafood here is well prepared. Try the steak, grilled Atlantic salmon, Cajun rib steak, or the New York sirloin. | 28 E. 63rd St. | 212/935–2888 | No lunch weekends | $18–$27 | AE, D, DC, MC, V.

Primavera. Italian. Stately and wood paneled, this is a clubby backdrop for the worthy northern Italian food and old-world service. The traditional Italian look is captured by the old paintings on the walls. Try the delicious pastas and regional Italian wines. | 1578 1st Ave. | 212/861–8608 | Reservations essential | Jacket required | No lunch | $19–$32 | AE, DC, MC, V.

Provence. French. The appealing country decor is amplified by a pretty back garden. The Provençal cuisine is as lovely as the setting; choose from classics like homemade pate and bouillabaisse, as well as more unique creations like braised rabbit stuffed with leeks, carrots, celery, and foie gras. | 38 MacDougal St. | 212/475–7500 | $19–$27 | AE.

Quilty's. Contemporary. An interesting collection of mounted butterflies—in homage to novelist and lepidopterist Vladimir Nabokov—accent the understated interior. The dining room provides little distraction from the exciting fare from the kitchen. The seasonal menu changes every few months. Sunday brunch. | 177 Prince St. | 212/254–1260 | Reservations essential | No lunch Mon. | $20–$29 | AE, D, DC, MC, V.

Quince. Contemporary. Amid the cozy fireplace and murals from France, the food here is well conceived. Known for the seafood and game in winter, with an emphasis on bright and clean flavors. Open-air dining in garden with flowering quince trees and 14 seats. | 33

W. 54th St. | 212/582–8993 | Reservations essential | Closed Sun., Mon. No lunch Sat. | $62 prix fixe | AE, DC, MC, V.

Rain. Thai. Tropical decor accents this dimly lit space, packed nightly with a young and lively crowd. The creative Thai food at this Upper West Side hot spot is pretty good and reasonably priced. You'll find vegetarian summer rolls, green curry chicken, and spicy charred-beef salad. The East side sister features a similar menu but has simpler decor and a choice of different dining areas. | 100 W. 82nd St., 1059 3rd Ave. | 212/501–0776, 212/223–3669 | $12–$23 | AE, D, DC, MC, V.

Raoul's. French. The lighting at this storefront dining room is subdued, but the energy is often a notch higher. The menu is written in French on blackboards that are brought to the table, and the wine list is huge. The late-night scene at this SoHo institution is legendary. Try the steak au poivre and, for dessert, the warm chocolate torte with raspberries. | 180 Prince St. | 212/966–3518 | No lunch | $17–$30 | AE, DC, MC, V.

Redeye Grill. Contemporary. This large, colorful, and often loud American brasserie features two giant copper shrimp over the fresh seafood choices and red toy planes dangling from the high ceilings. The menu with scores of dishes features everything from sea bass and sushi to rib-eye steak and Wiener schnitzel. Open-air dining on the large sidewalk cafe. Jazz Tuesday–Sat. Sunday brunch. | 890 7th Ave. | 212/541–9000 | $14–$45 | AE, D, DC, MC, V.

Remi. Italian. This is a top choice for wealthy Italian expats. In the bright and airy dining room with a huge colorful painting and ceiling chandeliers, the northern Italian food leans toward the Venetian. Open-air dining for dinner only in a covered atrium. | 145 W. 53rd St. | 212/581–4242 | Reservations essential | No lunch weekends | $21–$28 | AE, DC, MC, V.

René Pujol. French. The comfortable setting and efficient service make this a top choice for pre-theater dining. After the rush, though, the experience is more serene. The intimate, country-French restaurant separates into two dining rooms with working fireplaces. Try the rack of lamb for two or sautéed tuna with crushed peppercorns, red onions, and green lentils. | 321 W. 51st St. | 212/246–3023 | Closed Sun. | $40 prix fixe | AE, DC, MC, V.

San Domenico. Italian. Terra-cotta floors, leather chairs, and earthy hues set an understated, elegant tone in this dining room. The formal northern Italian fare is complemented by a world-class Italian wine list. Past menu choices have included a mushroom and potato tart over a fontina fondue, raviolini filled with sea urchin in a scallop ragù, and a pork fillet with stuffed artichokes and prune sauce. | 240 Central Park S | 212/265–5959 | Reservations essential | Jacket required | No lunch weekends | $20–$40 | AE, DC, MC, V.

Sardi's. American. Food was never the point at this longtime hangout for artists and media moguls. Many people come just to see the framed and famed Abe Hirshfeld caricatures that cover the walls. Try the shrimp à la Sardi, cannelloni, and the chicken à la Sardi. | 234 W. 44th St. | 212/221–8440 | $15–$30 | AE, D, DC, MC, V.

Savoy. French. The downstairs dining room is a cozy, country-French heaven, while the upstairs, which has a prix-fixe menu only, is more private; both have fireplaces. Either way the menu, which changes every couple of weeks, is interesting and lovingly prepared. Try the salt-crusted baked duck. | 70 Prince St. | 212/219–8570 | $20–$30 | AE, MC, V.

Shun Lee. Chinese. In this contemporary, Chinese-inspired setting, the creatively contrived offerings pay homage to their Chinese roots. This is fine Chinese dining at its best. There is also a café in the building with a little cheaper prices. Try the Peking duck or lobster. | 43 W. 65th St. | 212/595–8895 | Reservations essential | Jacket required | $40–$45 | AE, DC, MC, V.

Shun Lee Palace. Chinese. The original outpost of the Shun Lee dynasty continues to win raves for its excellent service and creative Chinese fare. The dining room is a Chinese fantasy with antiques and dragons everywhere. Try the Peking duck and house-special lobster. | 155 E. 55th St. | 212/371–8844 | Reservations essential | $30–$40 | AE, D, DC, MC, V.

NEW YORK CITY

INTRO
ATTRACTIONS
DINING
LODGING

Smith & Wollensky. Steak. Each of the two floors has a sizable dining room filled with wooden tables and hordes of people—mostly men—chowing down on huge hunks of meat. The clamor of the waitstaff and the crowd is surprisingly appealing. The beef is unquestionably good. Wollensky's Grill, entrance at 205 E. 49th Street, open 11:30–2 AM, is a popular after-work watering hole, which also serves food. Grill is open for lunch on weekends. Open-air dining sidewalk patio, enclosed in glass, that can be opened on nice days and seats about 30 people. | 201 E. 49th St. | 212/753–1530 | No lunch weekends | $20–$34 | AE, D, DC, MC, V.

Sonia Rose. French. This quiet, dark, intimate space was designed for romance. The French menu includes many creative specials. Try the poached Norwegian salmon or the tenderloin of beef. No smoking. | 150 E. 34 St. | 212/545–1777 | Jacket required | No lunch Sat.–Mon. | $45 prix fixe | AE, DC, MC, V.

Sparks Steak House. Steak. Despite the usual masculine dark and clubby look of this shrine to beef, Spark's is on top of many steak-lovers' lists due to an exceptional array of wines. This huge space has four private Victorian-style dining rooms with wood paneling. Try the sirloin steak or the jumbo lobsters. | 210 E. 46th St. | 212/687–4855 | Reservations essential | Closed Sun. No lunch Sat. | $21–$32 | AE, D, DC, MC, V.

Spartina. Mediterranean. Simple wood furnishings and exposed brick walls give a chic look to this restaurant. The Mediterranean fare is interesting, with many dishes hailing from Spain. Try the roasted Atlantic salmon or mussels Provençale. Open-air dining on an enclosed sidewalk café that seats about 25. | 355 Greenwich St. | 212/274–9310 | No lunch Sat. | $17–$24 | AE, DC, MC, V.

Sushisay. Japanese. Japanese businessmen and others flock to this understated restaurant for exceptionally fresh sushi and other Japanese dishes. No smoking. | 38 E. 51st St. | 212/755–1780 | Reservations essential | Closed Sun. No lunch Sat. | $22–$35 | AE, DC, MC, V.

Tabla. Indian. Discover truly exceptional Indian-inspired food that defies description in an atrium-like dining room on a second floor. Try the sweet spice and port-glazed sweetbreads, rawa-crusted skate, eggplant stuffed with braised red onion, and the breads from the tandoor oven. There are many exciting vegetarian options. You can also choose the less-formal "bread bar" on the main floor serving more casual food on a first-come, first-served basis. | 11 Madison Ave. | 212/889–0667 | Reservations essential | No lunch weekends | $54 prix fixe; tasting menus $65–$85 | AE, D, DC, MC, V.

Tavern on the Green. American. An old-time tourist spot, Tavern on the Green still retails its magical look, with tiny lights covering the trees surrounding it in Central Park. Inside, there's more glitter, with lots of stained glass and an opulent crystal room filled with twinkling chandeliers. In back, there's a garden room and a patio lined with topiaries that looks out on the park. The mediocre food is really not the point. Entertainment Tuesday–Sunday. Saturday and Sunday brunch. Open-air dining. | Central Park at W. 67th St. | 212/873–3200 | $23–$42 | AE, DC, MC, V.

Terrace in the Sky. Contemporary. This is a somewhat well-kept secret on the upper, Upper West Side. Its locale on the top floor of a Columbia University–owned building provides one of the best views in Manhattan. The once-staid menu has been updated, changing seasonally, to offer meat, fish, and game. The fantastic wine list features French, American, and international vintages. | 400 W. 119th St. | 212/666–9490 | Reservations essential | Jacket required | Closed Sun., Mon. No lunch Sat. | $29–$38 | AE, DC, MC, V.

Trattoria Dell'Arte. Italian. This sleek dining room, with original art on the walls, is a good choice for meals before and after performances at Carnegie Hall across the street. There is an authentic Italian antipasto bar and a great Tuscan rib-eye steak with arugula salad. Saturday, Sunday brunch. | 900 7th Ave. | 212/245–9800 | $42–$49 | AE, D, DC, MC, V.

TriBeCa Grill. American. The classic grill-style menu includes many creative offerings. The space is a converted warehouse owned by Robert De Niro and decorated with paintings by his father. Known for the fish, ravioli, and the duck. Sunday brunch. Kids' menu. | 375 Greenwich St. | 212/941–3900 | No lunch Sat. | $19–$29 | AE, DC, MC, V.

Trionfo. Italian. This is a classic old-world Italian restaurant that's been popular with the theater-going crowd for 15 years. Try the pastas, fish, chicken, lobster salad, and smoked salmon with arugula. Open-air dining on a big sidewalk patio. | 224 W. 51st St. | 212/262–6660 | Reservations essential | $13–$25 | AE, D, MC, V.

21 Club. Contemporary. This former speakeasy has maintained its clubby feel and is still one of the best spots in town for celebrity spotting. Known for the fresh seafood, steak, and the "21" burger. Homemade pastries. Pre-theater menu. | 21 W. 52nd St. | 212/582–7200 | Reservations essential | Jacket and tie | Closed Sun. | $25–$42 | AE, D, DC, MC, V.

Two Two Two. Continental. Fans love the intimacy of the dining room in this small restaurant set in an elegant town house on the Upper West Side. The upscale menu and prices are somewhat unique to the neighborhood. Try the prime rib with black truffles, the rack of lamb, or the beluga caviar. | 222 W. 79th St. | 212/799–0400 | No lunch | $24–$45; prix fixe $39 | AE, D, DC, MC, V.

★ **Union Pacific.** Contemporary. The tranquil dining room has a railroad motif and the open kitchen is surrounded by translucent glass. The prix-fixe menu features intriguing combinations with Southeast Asian accents. Try the black sea bass with sunflower seeds, pomegranate-laquered squab, and the raw scallops with sea urchin. | 111 E. 22nd St. | 212/995–8500 | Closed Sun. No lunch Sat. | $24–$34 | AE, DC, MC, V.

Union Square Cafe. New Yorkers consistently rate Union Square as one of their favorite restaurants—thanks in large measure to executive-chef Michael Romano's crowd-pleasing menu and to the restaurant's unpretentious disposition and friendly service. Mahogany moldings outline white walls hung with bright modern paintings; in addition to the three main dining areas, there's a long bar perfect for solo diners. The cuisine is more-or-less American with a thick Italian accent: for example the signature filet mignon of tuna with Asian slaw can land on the same table as homemade gnocchi in a creamy mushroom sauce. Reservations essential. | 21 E. 16th St. | 212/243–4020 | No lunch Sun. | $19–$29 | AE, D, DC, MC, V.

Veritas. Contemporary. The subdued dining room is defined by clean lines and artistic accents, like the wall display of handblown Italian glass and the mosaics. The menu serves straightforward, seasonal American food with modern touches, and the wine list is exceptional. Try the warm truffled oysters with leeks, fingerling potatoes, and Riesling; pepper-crusted venison; and the salmon with Asian greens and curry emulsion. | 43 E. 20th St. | 212/353–3700 | Reservations essential | No lunch | $68 prix fixe | AE, D, DC, MC, V.

Vong. French/Thai. Potted palms, the gold-leaf ceiling, and patchwork murals set the stage for dazzling dishes of varying sizes, shapes, and colors. The menu, created by Jean-Georges Vongerichten, is an enticing mix of Thai flavors and French dishes. Try the sautéed foie gras with ginger and mango, black bass with wok-fried Napa cabbage, and the lobster with Thai herbs. Pre-theater menu. | 200 E. 54th St. | 212/486–9592 | Reservations essential | No lunch weekends | $20–$40 | AE, DC, MC, V.

Water Club. American. The Water Club is on the edge of the East River and offers a somewhat overrated view of the Manhattan skyline. However, the largely seafood menu has something for everyone in this romantic restaurant with a nautical theme that includes model sailboats and flags. Try the salmon, tuna, scallops, chicken, and veal. Open-air dining on a small terrace overlooking the water (Memorial Day-Labor Day). Piano bar. Sunday brunch. | 500 E. 30th St. | 212/683–3333 | $25–$35 | AE, DC, MC, V.

Willow. French. This charming restaurant, with floor-to-ceiling windows and 19th-century oil paintings, offers a leisurely meal in a pretty room with lots of gold and yellow color schemes. The food is classic French and well prepared. Try the duck confit and the seared tuna with wasabi. Open-air dining on a sidewalk on a lovely tree-lined street. Sunday brunch. No smoking. | 1022 Lexington Ave. | 212/717–0703 | $16–$29 | AE, DC, MC, V.

NEW YORK CITY

INTRO
ATTRACTIONS
DINING
LODGING

Windows on the World. Contemporary. From this dining room, the views of all of Manhattan—and, seemingly, the world—are simply breathtaking. A bonus is that the food is better here than at many touristy spots; the more casual Wild Blue restaurant on the same floor offers a steak-house menu. The wine list and service are exceptional. Try the fillet of buffalo, porcini-crusted halibut, and the silver pot of seafood in ginger broth. Lunch buffet. Dance band Wednesday–Saturday. | 1 World Trade Center | 212/524–7011 | Jacket required | $25–$45 | AE, D, DC, MC, V.

Zoë. Contemporary. Tile floors harken back to the warehouse beginning of the space, but the open kitchen and painted walls are all modern. The menu is always interesting and dining at the "kitchen bar" is a unique experience. Try the crispy calamari or a variety of seafood and game dishes. Saturday, Sunday brunch. No smoking. | 90 Prince St. | 212/966–6722 | No lunch Mon. | $20–$30 | AE, DC, MC, V.

VERY EXPENSIVE

Box Tree. Continental. The prix-fixe continental menu at this ultraromantic restaurant, with candlelight dining, a rose on each table, and intimate service, is familiar enough so as not to interfere with gazing into your loved one's eyes. For an appetizer, try the molasses-glazed duck salad with mango or the rack of lamb with fresh mint sauce. | 250 E. 49th St. | 212/758–8320 | Reservations essential | Jacket required | No lunch Sun. | $86 | AE, V.

Chanterelle. French. Understated but very sophisticated, this excellent restaurant in TriBeCa has a spacious table arrangement, billowy white curtains, and soft peach walls. The French nouvelle cuisine changes every six weeks, but past choices have included cumin-crusted tuna with lemon and leeks and grilled breast of Moulard duck with duck fat béarnaise. | 2 Harrison St. | 212/966–6960 | Reservations essential | Closed Sun. and 2 weeks in Aug. No lunch Mon. | $75 prix fixe | AE, D, DC, MC, V.

★ **Daniel.** French. Daniel Boulud moved his exceptional French restaurant to this bigger, more formal space in 1998. The ornate decor, impeccable service, and exquisite food make this one of the best dining experiences in New York. Try the black sea bass in a crispy potato shell with red wine sauce; salad of Maine crab with mango, coriander, and lime dressing; and seasonal cuisine. Private party space available in banquet room. | 60 E. 65th St. | 212/288–0033 | Reservations essential | Jacket required | Closed Sun. No lunch Mon. | $35–$45 | AE, DC, MC, V.

Four Seasons. Continental. This is New York's power restaurant, especially at lunchtime, when the business giants do their deals. The term "power lunch" was invented by the Grill Room. The Pool Room is a bit less intimidating, with lavish flowers and plants creating a softer effect. As the name suggests, dishes are seasonal, and the pristine American menu evolves accordingly. The delicious low-cal "spa" menu was also invented here. | 99 E. 52nd St. | 212/754–9494 | Reservations essential | Jacket required | Closed Sun. | $39–$50 | AE, D, DC, MC, V.

Harry Cipriani. Italian. Undersized tables and overpriced food don't seem to deter the celebrity-studded crowd that frequents this New York outpost of the Venetian classic. While the signature Bellinis are always great, the food less so. Other dishes include risotto primavera and traditional fish soup. | 781 5th Ave. | 212/753–5566 | Reservations essential | Jacket required | $60–$67 | AE, D, DC, MC, V.

Il Mulino. Italian. People come for the lively old-world charm of this legendary restaurant, where reservations are hard to score. Be careful not to fill up on all the pre-dinner snacks that are presented as soon as you sit down. Daily specials are unbelievably expensive but portions are huge. Known for the veal chop, pasta, and antipasto. | 86 W. 3rd St. | 212/673–3783 | Reservations essential | $59–$75 | AE.

★ **Jean Georges.** French. Chef Jean-Georges Vongerichten's exquisitely pared-down, elegant, and innovative cuisine makes this restaurant one of the best in New York (and possibly anywhere). The fare changes seasonally, but past choices have included Muscovy duck steak with sweet and sour jus and herb-crusted rack of lamb. To get the full experience, though, you should try the $85 tasting menu. Clean, modern lines and plate-glass windows overlooking Central Park make this one of the most stylish rooms in the city. Open-air dining on the medium-size, tree-lined terrace. Sunday brunch. | 1 Central Park West | 212/299–3900 | Reservations essential | Jacket required | $89 prix fixe | AE, DC, MC, V.

La Caravelle. French. In one of New York's most formally opulent dining rooms, owners Rita and André Jammet have been celebrating the good life Parisian-style for 40 years. Walls covered with Jean Pagés murals complement the pink-peach banquettes, while mirrors, flowers, and the Caravelle coat of arms add to the richness. The cuisine is classic and refined, with seasonal selections that change often. Try the pike quenelle with lobster sauce or the assorted soufflés. | 33 W. 55th St. | 212/586–4252 | Reservations essential | Closed Sun. and 1 wk prior to Labor Day | $68 prix fixe | AE, DC, MC, V.

La Côte Basque. French. When Jean-Jacques Rachou's landmark French restaurant moved to new quarters in 1995, many architectural elements of the original restaurant came too—even the revolving door. Patrons of La Côte Basque love it as is, and, like the decor, the cuisine remains classic French. Begin with the trio of pâtés or one of the gossamer soufflés. Try the roast duckling with honey, Grand Marnier, and black-cherry sauce, prepared for two and carved table-side. Homemade pastries. | 60 W. 55th St. | 212/688–6525 | Reservations essential | Jacket and tie | No lunch Sun. | $65 prix fixe | AE, D, DC, MC, V.

Le Bernardin. French. Chef Eric Ripert and owner Maguy LeCoze continue to keep this restaurant at the top of Manhattan's dining spectrum. As the chef is known for his creative fish dishes, try the French seafood specialties, or opt for one of the two tasting menus. The teak-paneled dining room is plush, expansive, and hushed; late-19th-century French oil paintings adorn the walls. | 155 W. 51st St. | 212/489–1515 | Reservations essential | Jacket required | Closed Sun. No lunch Sat. | $77 prix fixe; tasting menus $90 or $120 | AE, DC, MC, V.

Le Cirque 2000. French. Housed in the ornate Villard Houses, Le Cirque 2000 is the place to be seen. The restaurant was transformed in 1997, and fancifully colorful modern elements now attempt to cover the old-fashioned opulence of the original space. The result has been heralded as a design masterpiece by some, a disaster by others. The exquisite French food will take your mind off the celebrities sitting at the next table (who, it seems, always get the preferential treatment). | 455 Madison Ave. | 212/303–7788 | Reservations essential | Jacket and tie | $28–$38 | AE, DC, MC, V.

Le Perigord. French. The dining room of this Sutton Place classic bursts with energy, and the food is traditional French. On a busy night, nonregulars may feel ignored. The new decor is very elegant. Try the homemade foie gras and the Dover sole with mustard sauce. | 405 E. 52nd St. | 212/755–6244 | No lunch weekends | $57 prix fixe | AE, D, DC, MC, V.

Le Régence. French. You'll find an opulent setting in blue and white, with glittery antiques and froufrou touches in abundance. The classic French menu has been enlivened by a new young chef, but many still find the dining room stuffy. Known for the fillet of red snapper, filet mignon of beef, and the roast rack of lamb. Homemade pastries. Kids' menu. Sunday brunch. | 37 E. 64th St. | 212/606–4647 | Jacket required | Closed Mon. | $24–$38 | AE, DC, MC, V.

★ **Lespinasse.** French. Christian Delouvrier (formerly of Les Célébrités) has settled into the opulent, possibly stuffy, Louis XV dining room of the luxurious St. Regis Hotel like an elegant hand into a kid glove. The gilded, trim, extravagant floral arrangements and the roomy—most spacious in the city—seating provide a perfect complement to his seasonal ultra-French menu, which includes a wide selection of game, seafood, and vegetarian fare. Everything is exquisitely prepared and presented with enough pomp to justify the extravagant prices. Menu changes seasonally. Serves breakfast, lunch, and dinner. | 2 E. 55th St. | 212/339–6719 | Reservations essential | Jacket and tie | Closed Sun., Mon. | Tasting menus $78 or $125 | AE, D, DC, MC, V.

Lutèce. French. In 1995, Andre Soltner, the chef and owner of this long-standing temple to French cuisine, passed the toque and whisk to chef Eberhard Muller. The old-fashioned dining room has since been enlivened by lush flower arrangements and subtle, modern touches that only hone the existing charm. The menu has been modernized as well but still retains many of the classic French dishes for which it is known. | 249 E. 50th St. | 212/752–2225 | Reservations essential | Closed Sun. No lunch Mon., Sat. | $64–$72 | AE, D, DC, MC, V.

March. Contemporary. With its working fireplace and burled teak-and-elm wainscoting, this romantic restaurant tucked into a small town house is elegantly understated. The menu has abandoned the "appetizer-entrée" tradition; instead, meals are comprised of a variety of small dishes and they change often. Selections often include a sashimi dish of Japanese yellowfin tuna with olive oil and soy sauce and such luxury offerings as the whimsical "Beggar's Purses," filled with caviar and crème fraîche or lobster and truffles. Try the five-spice salmon, grilled Long Island duck, or the roast rack of lamb with herbed crust. | 405 E. 58th St. | 212/754–6272 | Reservations essential | Jacket required | $66–$72 | AE, DC, MC, V.

Nadaman Hakubai. Japanese. Located in the exclusive Kitano Hotel, this restaurant offers a traditional Japanese dining experience. The memorable, if expensive, à la carte menu comes with exceptional service. Try the tempura and shabu-shabu. No smoking. | 66 Park Ave. | 212/885–7111 | $24–$40 | AE, D, DC, MC, V.

★ **Nobu.** Japanese. Nobu Matsuhisa creates dramatic, contemporary Japanese-inspired food. The vast menu makes deciding which direction to take difficult. One road will take you to classic Japanese sushi and sashimi, among the best in town. Another leads you to contemporary dishes, such as the delicious seared black cod with sweet miso, or Peruvian-style sashimi. | 105 Hudson St. | 212/219–0500 | Reservations essential | No lunch weekends | $60–$71 | AE, DC, MC, V.

Oceana. Seafood. This modern and spacious restaurant is a mecca for those interested in fresh seafood prepared creatively. Try the salmon, Oceana East Coast bouillabaisse, and the excellent pastries. | 55 E. 54th St. | 212/759–5941 | Reservations essential | Jacket required | Closed Sun. No lunch Sat. | $65 prix fixe | AE, D, DC, MC, V.

Parioli Romanissimo. Italian. Housed in a turn-of-the-20th-century brownstone, this long-standing, luxurious restaurant serves good northern Italian dishes to a rich and famous clientele. Regulars love the veal and pasta dishes, which some say are unequaled in the city, and the doting, formal service. | 24 E. 81st St. | 212/288–2391 | Reservations essential | Jacket and tie | Closed Sun. and 2 weeks in Aug. No lunch | $63–$70 | AE, DC, MC, V.

Patroon. American. The lively, ultraplush setting, with its banquette seating, makes the place look as expensive as it is. Patroon is noted for its power lunches and the New American food can be quite good. Try the prime rib of beef for two or the Dover sole. Open-air dining with 50 seats on the rooftop terrace. | 160 E. 46th St. | 212/883–7373 | Closed Sun. No lunch Sat. | $24–$45 | AE, D, DC, MC, V.

Peacock Alley. French. New Yorkers flock to the Waldorf-Astoria to sample Laurent Gras's cooking at Peacock Alley. Gras performs miracles with every course. A savory soup (pumpkin consommé with sweet-and-sour chicken wings, cockscombs, and San Danielle ham) is a triumph, as is a dessert soup (garnished with passion-fruit sorbet and tropical fruit). Tranquil lighting, banquette seating, roomy tables, fine china, professional service, and a comprehensive wine cellar add up to a memorable experience. Entertainment Friday and Saturday. Sunday brunch. | 301 Park Ave. | 212/872–4895 | Jacket required | No lunch Sat. | $64 prix fixe | AE, D, DC, MC, V.

Lodging

INEXPENSIVE

Abingdon Guest House. This inn is in a charming town house with a back garden. Some rooms are decorated with antiques, but some have shared bath. Cable TV. | 21 8th Ave., between

W. 12th and Jane Sts. | 212/243–5384 | fax 401/735–6772 | abingdon@msn.com | www.abing-donguesthouse.com | 9 rooms | $145–$220 | AE, D, DC, MC, V.

Belleclair Hotel. This Beaux Arts–style, Art Deco prewar building is near Central Park, the American Museum of Natural History, Riverside Park, and the Boat Basin. Some refrigerators, cable TV. | 250 W. 77th St., at Broadway | 212/362–7700 | fax 212/362–1004 | www.belleclaire.com | 187 rooms | $119–$229. | AE, MC, V.

Best Western Manhattan. This chain hotel, steps away from the Empire State Building and many restaurants, offers basic amenities, and some of the rooms have Jacuzzi tubs. Restaurant, bar, complimentary Continental breakfast. Cable TV. Barbershop, beauty salon. Exercise equipment. | 17 W. 32nd St., between 9th Ave. and Broadway | 212/736–1600 or 800/528–1234 | fax 212/790–2760 | 178 rooms, 33 suites | $89–$139 rooms, $209 suites | www.bestwestern.com | AE, D, DC, MC, V.

Best Western Seaport Inn. This Best Western is near the East River, Fulton Fish Market, and the South Street Seaport, and convenient to Chinatown, TriBeCa, and SoHo. Complimentary Continental breakfast. In-room data ports, refrigerators, cable TV. | 33 Peck Slip | 212/766–6600 or 800/528–1234 | fax 212/766–6615 | bwseaportinn@juno.com | www.bestwestern.com | 71 rooms | $159–$199 | AE, D, DC, MC, V.

Broadway Bed and Breakfast Inn. Though it isn't the kind where you linger over pancakes in the garden, the Broadway Bed and Breakfast is every bit as friendly and comfortable. Theater hounds can see their fill of Broadway shows, then fall into bed. The homey, brick-walled lobby is lined with stocked bookshelves and photos of Old New York. Restaurant, complimentary Continental breakfast. Some microwaves in suites, refrigerators, cable TV. | 264 W. 46th St., between Broadway and 8th Ave. | 212/997–9200 or 800/826–6300 | fax 212/768–2807 | 28 rooms (15 with shower only), 12 suites | $150–$250 rooms, $250–$295 suites | Closed Jan.–Feb. | AE, D, DC, MC, V.

Carlton Arms. The lobby and guest rooms are covered with original artwork that ranges in theme from Versailles to cows. Many rooms have no bathrooms, and none has phones, TVs, or air-conditioning. But for those with an artistic sensibility and a small budget, this is a good choice. No air-conditioning, no room phones, no TV. | 160 E. 25th St., at 3rd Ave. | 212/679–0680 | www.carltonarms.com | 54 rooms (34 with shower only) | $73–$84 | MC, V.

Chelsea Hotel. This legendary hotel, built in 1884, is most noted for its long history of colorful guests, including Sarah Bernhardt, William S. Burroughs, Hart Crane, Milos Forman, Bob Dylan, and Sid Vicious, who infamously murdered his girlfriend here. The lobby is decorated with artwork from many past visitors. Restaurant. Cable TV. | 222 W. 23rd St., between 7th and 8th Aves. | 212/243–3700 | fax 212/675–5531 | www.chelseahotel.com | 125 rooms, 14 suites | $150–285 rooms, $300–$385 suites | AE, D, DC, MC, V.

Chelsea Inn. The eclectic, country ambience here is a refreshing change from the characterless hotels that dominate this price category. Housed in an old brownstone on a chic Chelsea street, this is a favorite of young budget travelers who appreciate the in-room cooking facilities (some have full kitchenettes; others have just a refrigerator and sink). Rooms, with shared or private baths, are a cozy hodgepodge of country quilts and thrift-shop antiques, with a basket or two of dried flowers in most. A few rooms in back overlook a little courtyard with any ivy-draped fence. Kitchenettes, some refrigerators. | 46 W. 17th St., between 5th and 6th Ave. | 212/645–8989 or 800/640–6469 | 27 rooms (24 with shared bath) | $129–$269 | AE, D, V.

Chelsea Savoy. Spare, but comfortable, this hotel is near many restaurants, cafés, galleries, and shops. It's a convenient location for touring Lower Manhattan. Cable TV. | 204 W. 23rd St., at 7th Ave. | 212/929–9353 | fax 212/741–6309 | 90 rooms | $99–$185 | AE, MC, V.

Cosmopolitan Hotel. This downtown hotel is within walking distance of South Street Seaport, Chinatown, and Little Italy. Some of the best shopping, nightlife, and restaurants in the area are nearby. Cable TV. | 95 W. Broadway, at Chambers St. | 212/566–1900 | www.cosmohotel.com | 105 rooms | $99–$159 | AE, D, MC, V.

Edison. Built in 1930, this modest Art Deco hotel feels like its from another era, especially the coffee shop. Restaurant, bar. Cable TV. Beauty salon. Business services, airport shuttle. | 228 W. 47th St., between Broadway and 8th Ave. | 212/840–5000 or 800/637–7070 | fax 212/596–6850 | www.edisonhotelnyc.com | 790 rooms, 110 suites | $150–$200 rooms, $190–$225 suites | AE, D, DC, MC, V.

The Ellington. Named for one of the area's most famous residents, Duke Ellington, the decor harks back to the bandleader's heyday in the 1930s and '40s. Some rooms have views of Riverside Park, and the hotel is within walking distance of Columbia University. Cable TV. Laundry service. | 610 W. 111th St., between Broadway and Riverside Dr. | 212/864–7500 | fax 212/749–5852 | www.nycityhotels.net | 85 rooms | $120–$280 | AE, D, DC, MC, V.

The Gershwin. Funky decor and a young crowd frequent this Gramercy Park hotel. There's an art gallery on the premises that features new and avant-garde artists, a café that serves breakfast and lunch, and a jazz club. Restaurant, bar. Cable TV. | 7 E. 27th St., between Madison and 5th Aves. | 212/545–8000 | reservations@gershwinhotel.com | www.gershwinhotel.com | 213 rooms, 5 suites | $99–$169 rooms, $225–$250 suites | AE, MC, V.

Herald Square. Housed in the former Life Building, the Herald Square pays homage to its predecessor with framed vintage magazine covers in the hallways. The well-priced rooms are basic, but the service is remarkably attentive for such an inexpensive hotel. In-room safes, cable TV. Airport shuttle. | 19 W. 31st St., between 5th Ave. and Broadway | 212/279–4017 or 800/727–1888 | fax 212/643–9208 | 127 rooms (some with shared bath) | $60–$150 | AE, D, MC, V.

Hotel Deauville. These accommodations are in a turn-of-the-20th-century brownstone near the Empire State Building, Madison Square Garden, and many restaurants. Cable TV. | 103 E. 29th St., at Park Ave. S | 212/683–0990 or 800/333–8843 | fax 212/689–5921 | 53 rooms, 5 suites | $138–$160 rooms, $180 suites | MC, V.

Hotel Stanford. Located on a street known as "Little Korea," this hotel has an authentic Korean restaurant and a mostly Korean clientele. Restaurant. In-room data ports, some refrigerators, cable TV. | 43 W. 32nd St., at Broadway | 212/563–1500 or 800/365–1114 | fax 212/629–0043 | 121 rooms, 30 suites | $130–$160 | AE, DC, MC, V.

Malibu. These are some bare-bones accommodations—just a notch above a youth hostel, but they're some of the cheapest in the city. Some rooms have shared baths, and all have air-conditioning. Located near Columbia University, as well as Riverside and Central parks. Some cable TV. | 2688 Broadway, at 103rd St. | 212/222–2954 | 300 rooms | $49–$129 | No credit cards.

New York's Hotel Pennsylvania. This is the most convenient location for checking out sporting events or concerts at Madison Square Garden, which is directly across the street. It's also a popular hotel for smaller conventions. Restaurant, bar. Cable TV. Barbershop, beauty salon. Shops. Business services. | 401 7th Ave., at 33rd St. | 212/736–5000 or 800/223–8585 | fax 212/502–8712 | 1,705 rooms | $149–$169 | AE, D, DC, MC, V.

Off Soho Suites. Staying at Off Soho Suites is like staying at a bohemian friend's apartment. It looks a little garish from the outside, but this all-suite hotel is near the happening East Village and SoHo. A café serves breakfast and lunch. Restaurant. Some kitchenettes, cable TV. Laundry facilities. | 11 Rivington St., between Chrystie St. and 3rd Ave. | 212/353–0860 or 800/OFF–SOHO | fax 212/979–9801 | www.offsoho.com | 38 suites (10 with shared baths) | $109–$239 | AE, MC, V.

Olcott. This is a generic hotel on a residential street on the Upper West Side, just steps away from Central Park. Kitchenettes, refrigerators, cable TV. | 27 W. 72nd St., between Central Park W and Columbus Ave. | 212/877–4200 | 200 | $125–$145 | MC, V.

Pickwick Arms Hotel. These very basic accommodations, with minimal amenities and low prices, are convenient to the United Nations as well as Midtown sights. Cable TV. | 230

E. 51st St., between 2nd and 3rd Aves. | 212/355–0300 or 800/742–5945 | fax 212/755–5029 | 350 rooms | $105–$130 | AE, DC, MC, V.

Southgate Tower Suite. This all-suite hotel is one block from Madison Square Garden. Restaurant. Kitchenettes, cable TV. Barbershop. Exercise equipment. Laundry facilities. Business services. | 371 7th Ave., at 31st St. | 212/563–1800 or 800/637–8483 | fax 212/643–8028 | www.mesuite.com | 509 suites, 14 studio suites | $164–$270 studio, junior, and 1–bedroom suites; $459–$555 2–bedroom suites | AE, D, DC, MC, V.

Washington Square Hotel. This friendly, family-run hotel is in Washington Square Park near many lively restaurants, jazz clubs, and New York University. The wrought-iron gate out front lends the hotel a bit of a French-courtyard feel. Rooms are small and modern. Restaurant, bar, complimentary Continental breakfast. Cable TV. Gym. | 103 Waverly Pl., between 5th and 6th Aves. | 212/777–9515 or 800/222–0418 | fax 212/979–8373 | www.washington-squarehotel.com | 170 rooms | $121–$174 | AE, MC, V.

Wellington Hotel. The Wellington is near Times Square, Rockefeller Center, shopping, and the Theater District. Some rooms have terraces. 2 restaurants. Cable TV. Laundry service. | 871 7th Ave., at 55th St. | 212/247–3900 or 800/652–1212 | fax 212/581–1719 | www.welling-tonhotel.com | 600 rooms, 100 suites | $165–$195 rooms, $195–$260 suites | AE, DC, MC, V.

Westpark Hotel. The decor is ordinary, but the rooms are of decent size. And it's just a short walk to Lincoln Center, Carnegie Hall, and Central Park. In-room safes, cable TV. | 308 W. 58th St., at Columbus Cir. | 212/246–6440 or 800/248–6440 | fax 212/246–3131 | 88 rooms, 6 suites | $150–$250 rooms, $275 suites | AE, DC, D, MC, V.

Wyndham. The accommodations are basic, but the location—within walking distance of many Midtown attractions like Carnegie Hall, Lincoln Center, Central Park, and premier shopping destinations—can't be beat. Restaurant, bar. In-room data ports, some refrigerators, cable TV. Business services. | 42 W. 58th St., between 5th and 6th Aves. | 212/753–3500 | fax 212/754–5638 | 204 rooms | $145–$165 | AE, DC, MC, V.

MODERATE

Ameritania Hotel 54. Ameritania sports stylish furnishings in an upscale industrial setting. Fixtures include steel columns, brushed metal, black-and white-photography, and modern furniture. Restaurant, bar. Cable TV. | 230 W. 54th St., between Broadway and 8th Ave. | 212/247–5000 or 800/66–HOTEL | fax 212/247–3313 | www.nychotels.net | 208 rooms, 12 suites | $99–$255 rooms, $175–$375 suites | AE, D, DC, MC, V.

Bedford Hotel. The central location is convenient to Broadway theaters and Midtown restaurants. The old-fashioned brick building in residential Murray Hill has a cozy wood-paneled lobby. Restaurant, bar, complimentary Continental breakfast. Some refrigerators, cable TV. Laundry facilities. Business services. | 118 E. 40th St., between Park and Lexington Aves. | 212/697–4800 | fax 212/697–1093 | www.bedfordhotel.com | 136 rooms, 58 suites | $215 rooms, $285–$300 suites | AE, DC, MC, V.

Beekman Tower. This traditional Art Deco, all-suite hotel is in a quiet, residential neighborhood, very close to the United Nations. Restaurant, bar (with entertainment). In-room data ports, kitchenettes, microwaves, cable TV. Exercise equipment. Laundry facilities. Business services. | 3 Mitchell Pl., at 49th St. and 1st Ave. | 212/355–7300 or 800/637–8483 | fax 212/753–9366 | 174 suites | $209–$293 studio and 1–bedroom suites, $254–$321 2–bedrooms | www.mesuite.com | AE, DC, MC, V.

Belvedere Hotel. Renovated in 1997, the Art Deco Belvedere now offers modern conveniences in the heart of the Theater District. Restaurant. Cable TV. Laundry service. | 319 W. 48th St., between 8th and 9th Aves. | 212/245–7000 | www.newyorkhotel.com | 400 rooms | $160–$250 | AE, D, DC, MC, V.

Bentley Hotel. An ultramodern feel is created by simple, unique design elements in all of the one-of-a-kind rooms. Some rooms have panoramic East River views. Restaurant, bar,

room service. Cable TV. | 500 E. 62nd St., at York Ave. | 212/644–6000 | fax 212/207–4800 | 157 rooms, 40 suites | $245–$265 rooms, $350 suites | AE, D, DC, MC, V.

Best Western Woodward. The atmosphere is pleasant and service congenial at this modern hotel, just five blocks from the Museum of Modern Art. It's also near Lincoln Center and the Theater District. Room service. Some refrigerators, cable TV. Business services. | 210 W. 55th St., between Broadway and 7th Ave. | 212/247–2000 or 800/528–1234 | fax 212/ 581–2248 | 180 rooms (20 with shower only) | $189–$269 | www.bestwestern.com | AE, D, DC, MC, V.

Box Tree. Box Tree is in a luxurious brownstone, and each room has unique decor. There is a romantic feel, with a fireplace in every room. On weekends, a $100 credit toward dinner in the on-site Box Tree restaurant is included in the room price. Restaurant, complimentary Continental breakfast. | 250 E. 49th St., between 2nd and 3rd Aves. | 212/758–8320 | 13 suites in 2 town houses | $240–$340 | AE, MC, V.

Clarion Fifth Avenue. Clean accommodations, a pleasant, helpful staff, and the convenient east Midtown location make this a popular choice. Restaurant. In-room data ports, cable TV. Business services. | 3 E. 40th St., at 5th Ave. | 212/447–1500 or 800/CLARION | fax 212/213–0972 | www.clarionhotel.com/hotel/ny201 | 189 rooms | $299–$359 | AE, D, DC, MC, V.

Comfort Inn. The hotel offers standard chain accommodations and is one block from the Empire State Building and close to both Midtown and Lower Manhattan. The light wood-paneled lobby has a huge silk-flower display. Restaurant, complimentary Continental breakfast. Some microwaves and refrigerators, cable TV. Business services. | 42 W. 35th St., between 5th and 6th Aves. | 212/947–0200 | fax 212/594–3047 | www.comfortinnmanhattan.com | 131 rooms | $214–$234 | AE, D, DC, MC, V.

Crowne Plaza–United Nations. This Crowne Plaza is in a quieter locale than its Midtown West sister. The 1931 landmark building was formerly the Tudor Hotel. Fancy touches include a pianist in the lobby and Italian marble in the bathrooms. Restaurant, bar, room service. Minibars, cable TV. Massage, spa. Exercise equipment. Business services. | 304 E. 42nd St., between 1st and 2nd Aves. | 212/986–8800 or 800/879–8836 | fax 212/986–1758 | www.crowneplaza-un.com | 300 rooms, 14 suites in 2 towers | $159–$349 rooms, $489 suites | AE, D, DC, MC, V.

Days Hotel. This lodging is on a rather dreary stretch of 8th Avenue, but it's very convenient to all parts of the city. Restaurant, bar. Cable TV. Business services. | 790 8th Ave., between W. 48th and 49th Sts. | 212/581–7000 or 800/325–2525 | fax 212/974–0291 | www.daysinn.com | 367 rooms | $195–$230 | AE, D, DC, MC, V.

Doral Park Avenue. Its upscale style distinguishes this comfortable hotel on a quiet stretch of Park Avenue from others in the area. There is a mural at the front desk and marble floors throughout. Restaurant, bar. Minibars, cable TV. Spa. Exercise equipment. Business services. | 70 Park Ave., at 38th St. | 212/687–7050 or 877/99–DORAL | fax 212/808–9029 | www.doralparkavenue.com | 188 rooms, 3 suites | $224–$399 rooms, $700–$1,300 suites | AE, D, DC, MC, V.

Doubletree Guest Suites. This hotel is right in the heart of Times Square and is convenient to the Theater District. Restaurant, bar, room service. In-room data ports, minibars, refrigerators, cable TV. Exercise equipment. Laundry facilities. Business services. | 1568 Broadway, at 47th St. and 7th Ave. | 212/719–1600 | fax 212/921–5212 | www.doubletree.com | 460 suites | $269–$499 | AE, D, DC, MC, V.

Dumont Plaza. This is a somewhat ordinary hotel, but it's convenient to all Manhattan sights. Check out the small garden and its water fountain and mural. Restaurant, room service. In-room data ports, kitchenettes, microwaves, cable TV. Exercise equipment. Laundry facilities. Business services. | 150 E. 34th St., at Lexington Ave. | 212/481–7600 or 800/637–8483 | fax 212/889–8856 | www.mesuite.com | 247 suites | $194–$309 studio, junior, and 1–bedroom suites, $403–$575 2–bedroom suites | AE, D, DC, MC, V.

Eastgate Tower Suites. The flowered gazebo and patio are welcoming and attractive features of this hotel, in a relatively quiet section of the city. Restaurant, bar. In-room data ports, kitchenettes, microwaves, cable TV. Health club. Business services. | 222 E. 39th St., between 2nd and 3rd Aves. | 212/687–8000 or 800/637–8483 (in NY) | fax 212/490–2634 | www.mesuite.com | 188 suites | $234–$264 | AE, DC, MC, D, V.

Empire Hotel. This hotel is directly across from Lincoln Center and a short walk to Central Park. The rooms are comfortable, if somewhat small. Restaurant, bar, room service. In-room data ports, cable TV, in-room VCRs (and movies). Business services. | 44 W. 63rd St., at Broadway | 212/265–7400 | fax 212/315–0349 | www.empirehotel.com | 375 rooms | $160–$260 | AE, D, DC, MC, V.

Essex House. The marble, flower-laden lobby is truly grand. The guest rooms are comfortable and plush and many have views of Central Park. 2 restaurants, bar, room service. In-room data ports, minibars, cable TV, rental VCRs. Spa. Gym. Business services, parking ($33 per day). | 160 Central Park South, between 6th and 7th Aves. | 212/247–0300 or 800/645–5697 (reservations) | fax 212/315–1839 | www.essexhouse.com | 517 rooms, 80 suites | $265–$625 rooms, $425–$975 suites | AE, D, DC, MC, V.

The Franklin. This is an intimate, European-style hotel with canopy beds in the guest rooms. It's six blocks from the Metropolitan Museum of Art in a residential neighborhood. Complimentary Continental breakfast. Cable TV, in-room VCRs (and movies). | 164 E. 87th St., between 3rd and Lexington Aves. | 212/369–1000 or 877/847–4444 | fax 212/369–8000 | www.franklinhotel.com | 50 rooms | $249–$269 | AE, MC, DC, V.

Gracie Inn. You're steps from Gracie Mansion (the home of New York City's mayor) at this quaint guest house, on a quiet, residential street. Complimentary Continental breakfast. Kitchenettes, cable TV. | 502 E. 81st St., at York Ave. | 212/628–1700 | fax 212/628–6420 | www.the-gracieinn.com | 12 suites | $179–$299, $349–$600 penthouse suites | AE, D, DC, MC, V.

Gramercy Park Hotel. The hotel, built in the 1920s and on the edge of charming and picturesque Gramercy Park on a quiet street, offers basic accommodations. It has a hip reputation, even though it seems to attract lots of families. Check out the bar. Restaurant, bar. Refrigerators, cable TV. | 2 Lexington Ave., at 21st St. | 212/475–4320 or 800/221–4083 | fax 212/505–0535 | www.gramercyparkhotel.com | 350 rooms, 160 suites | $175–$190 rooms, $220–$260 suites | AE, D, DC, MC, V.

Helmsley Middletowne. Try a room with a balcony at this hotel, near the United Nations. Helmsley hotels are famous for their lavishness, and this antiques-filled hotel is no exception. In-room data ports, some refrigerators, cable TV. Business services. | 148 E. 48th St., between Lexington and 3rd Aves. | 212/755–3000 or 800/221–4982 | fax 212/832–0261 | www.helmsleyhotels.com | 192 rooms, 43 suites | $175–$280 rooms, $265–$565 suites | AE, D, DC, MC, V.

Helmsley Windsor. This property is smaller than the other New York Helmsley hotels. The staff is friendly, and the large rooms are filled with very contemporary furniture and extremely mirrored bathrooms. Complimentary Continental breakfast. Cable TV. Business services. | 100 W. 58th St., between 5th and 6th Aves. | 212/265–2100 or 800/221–4982 | fax 212/315–0371 | www.helmsleyhotels.com | 245 rooms, 92 suites | $170–$240 rooms, $280–$630 suites | AE, D, DC, MC, V.

Hilton and Towers at Rockefeller Center. Modern decor and decent-size guest rooms in a variety of color schemes are the results of a 1999 renovation at this large Midtown hotel. It's in a perfect locale for 5th Avenue shopping. Restaurant, bar. In-room data ports, minibars, cable TV. Gym. Shops. Business services. | 1335 Avenue of the Americas (6th Ave.), between W. 53rd and 54th Sts. | 212/586–7000 | fax 212/315–1374 | www.hilton.com | 2,086 rooms | $209–$560 | AE, D, DC, MC, V.

Holiday Inn–Downtown. Stay in the heart of vibrant Chinatown in this Holiday Inn, which is also convenient to SoHo, TriBeCa, and Lower Manhattan. The lobby is full of cityscape

paintings and flowers along the escalator. Restaurant, bar. In-room data ports, some refrigerators, cable TV. | 138 Lafayette St., between Howard and Canal Sts. | 212/966–8898 or 800/HOLIDAY | fax 212/966–3933 | www.holidayinn-nyc.com | 227 rooms | $199–$269 | AE, D, DC, MC, V.

Hotel Avalon. The elegant lobby, with Italian marble floors and pillars and a working fireplace, is joined by comfortable rooms, some with Jacuzzi tubs and their signature 5-ft ergonomic body-pillow. Restaurant, bar, complimentary Continental breakfast. Cable TV. Laundry service. Business services. | 16 E. 32nd St., between 5th and Madison Aves. | 212/299–7000 or 888/HI–AVALON | www.theavalonny.com | 20 rooms, 80 suites | $225 rooms, $275–$400 suites | AE, DC, MC, V.

Hotel Beacon. The Beacon is in a classic prewar building, steps away from the American Museum of Natural History, Lincoln Center, and Central Park. Kitchenettes, cable TV. Laundry facilities. | 2130 Broadway, at 75th St. | 212/787–1100 or 800/572–4969 (reservations) | fax 212/724–0839 | www.beaconhotel.com | 217 rooms, 100 suites | $175 rooms, $250 suites | AE, D, DC, MC, V.

Howard Johnson Plaza. This Theater District hotel has a certain charm, despite very basic amenities. Restaurant, bar. Cable TV. Business services. | 851 8th Ave., between W. 51st and 52nd Sts. | 212/581–4100 or 800/654–2000 | fax 212/974–7502 | www.hojo.com | 300 rooms | $99–$499 | AE, D, DC, MC, V.

Jolly Hotel Madison Towers. Most branches of this boutique chain are in Italy, but this one is only a few blocks from the Empire State Building. Four business meeting rooms were introduced in 2000. Restaurant, bar. In-room data ports, minibars, cable TV. Business services. | 22 E. 38th St., at Madison Ave. | 212/802–0600 or 800/225–4340 | fax 212/447–0747 | www.jollymadison.com | 245 rooms, 7 suites | $210–$350 rooms, $450 suites | AE, DC, MC, V.

Kimberly. For a nominal additional price, weekend guests at this pretty, four-star hotel can enjoy a sunset or brunch cruise on the Hudson on the hotel's private yacht, weather permitting. Some rooms have balconies. 2 restaurants, bar (with entertainment). Minibars, cable TV. Spa. Laundry facilities. Business services. | 145 E. 50th St., between Lexington and 3rd Aves. | 212/755–0400 or 800/683–0400 | fax 212/486–6915 | www.kimberly.com | 26 rooms, 132 suites | $259–$449 rooms, $450–$1,000 suites | AE, D, DC, MC, V.

The Mayflower. Some rooms have park views at this West Side hotel, directly across from Central Park. It's just three blocks away from Lincoln Center. Restaurant, bar. In-room data ports, cable TV. Exercise equipment. Business services, parking ($35 per day). Pets allowed. | 15 Central Park W, between W. 61st and 62nd Sts. | 212/265–0060 or 800/223–4164 | fax 212/265–5098 | www.mayflower.com | 365 rooms, 200 suites | $190–$400 rooms, $260–$400 suites | AE, D, DC, MC, V.

The Metropolitan. Located in a distinctive 1960s high-rise, this hotel provides basic amenities and convenience to Midtown. Restaurant, bar. In-room data ports, refrigerators, cable TV. Barbershop. Gym. Business services. Pets allowed. | 569 Lexington Ave., at E. 51st St. | 212/752–7000 or 800/836–6471 | fax 212/758–6311 | www.loewshotels.com | 722 rooms | $299–$369, rooms, $378–$1,000, suites | AE, D, DC, MC, V.

The Michelangelo. An Italian influence permeates this hotel in everything from the black-and-white marble to the pastries served in the lounge. Each room is different, with sleigh beds in some suites. The location is convenient to the Theater District and the Museum of Modern Art. Restaurant, bar, complimentary Continental breakfast, room service. In-room data ports, minibars, cable TV. Exercise equipment. Business services. | 152 W. 51st St., at 7th Ave. | 212/765–1900 or 800/237–0990 | fax 212/541–6604 | www.michelangelohotel.com | 178 rooms, 52 suites | $225–365 rooms, $335–$1,400 suites | AE, D, DC, MC, V.

Millenium Hilton. The class act of Downtown, this sleek, black monolith is across the street from the World Trade Center. The modern, beige-and-wood rooms have a streamlined look, with contoured built-in desks and night tables; almost all have expansive views of landmark buildings and either the Hudson or the East River. The health club has an Olympic-size pool with windows that look out on St. Paul's Church. Restaurants, bar, room service. In-room data ports, minibars, cable TV. Pool. Spa. Gym. Children's programs, 12 and under. Business services. | 55 Church St., between Fulton and Dey Sts. | 212/693–2001 or 800/445–8667 (reservations) | fax 212/571–2316 | www.hilton.com | 504 rooms, 57 suites | $139–$400 rooms, $550–$700 suites | AE, D, DC, MC, V.

Murray Hill East Suites. This clean, comfortable all-suite hotel is on a quiet street near the United Nations and Midtown. Kitchenettes, cable TV. Gym. Laundry facilities. | 149 E. 39th St., between Lexington and 3rd Aves. | 212/661–2100 or 800/222–3037 | fax 212/818–0724 | 120 suites | $199–$559 | AE, DC, MC, V.

New York Helmsley. This modern Theater District hotel comes with an indoor foyer for taxi pick up and drop off. Restaurant, bar (with entertainment). In-room data ports, some refrigerators, cable TV. Business services. | 212 E. 42nd St., between 2nd and 3rd Aves. | 212/490–8900 or 800/221–4982 | fax 212/986–4792 | www.helmsleyhotels.com | 780 rooms, 20 suites | $175–$310 rooms, $500–$900 suites | AE, D, DC, MC, V.

New Yorker Ramada. This hotel, in a turn-of-the-20th-century building, went through a complete refurbishment in 1995, which decreased the number of guest rooms to provide more spacious accommodations and a tower floor with all suites. 2 restaurants, bar, room service. Some kitchenettes, cable TV. Business services, parking ($35 per day). | 418 8th Ave., between W. 34th and 35th Sts. | 212/971–0101 or 800/RAMADA | fax 212/629–6536 | www.nyhotel.com | 1,000 rooms, 150 suites | $169–$199 rooms, $225 suites | AE, D, DC, MC, V.

Novotel. The seventh-floor Sky Lobby overlooks the lights of Times Square, and the hotel will assist guests in purchasing theater tickets for the many popular shows that are playing nearby. The white limestone building, built in 1984, has French-style rooms decorated with paintings and photographs. Restaurant, bar (with entertainment). In-room data ports, cable TV. Exercise equipment. Business services. Pets allowed. | 226 W. 52nd St., at Broadway | 212/315–0100 or 800/221–3185 | fax 212/765–5369 | www.novotel.com | 480 rooms | $219–$339 | AE, D, DC, MC, V.

Paramount. This Philippe Starck–designed hotel is the ultimate in cool creativity. The rooms are very small, but the space is so interestingly carved and fashionably hip; travelers feel treated as if they were paying higher prices. Restaurant, 2 bars. In-room data ports, minibars, cable TV, in-room VCRs (and movies). Gym. Business services. | 235 W. 46th St., between Broadway and 8th Ave. | 212/764–5500 or 800/225–7474 | fax 212/575–4892 | 600 rooms, 13 suites | $155–$580 rooms, $350–$1,200 suites | AE, D, DC, MC, V.

Plaza Fifty. Located near Rockefeller Center and 5th Avenue, the suites here have separate sitting areas. In-room data ports, kitchenettes, microwaves, refrigerators, cable TV. Exercise equipment. Business services. | 155 E. 50th St., at 3rd Ave. | 212/751–5710 or 800/ME–SUITE | fax 212/753–1468 | www.mesuite.com | 209 rooms, 135 suites | $252–$281 rooms, $299–$564 suites | AE, DC, MC, V.

Radisson New York East Side. With renovations completed in the fall of 2000, this very modern hotel, full of marble and glass, is convenient to the United Nations, Midtown, and the Theater District. Restaurant, bar (with entertainment). Some microwaves and refrigerators, cable TV. Exercise equipment. Business services. | 511 Lexington Ave., at 40th St. | 212/755–4400 or 800/448–4471 | fax 212/751–4091 | www.radisson.com | 675 rooms, 26 suites | $239–$339 rooms, $339–$650 suites | AE, D, DC, MC, V.

Ramada Milford Plaza. This Ramada is in the heart of the Theater District and close to Times Square. Restaurant, bar. In-room data ports, cable TV. Exercise equipment. Business services. | 270 W. 45th St., at 8th Ave. | 212/869–3600 | fax 212/944–8357 | www.ramada.com | 1,300 rooms | $144–$194 | AE, D, DC, MC, V.

Renaissance New York. Art Deco style, attractively comfortable rooms, and professional service are draws at this hotel, just off Times Square. Restaurant, bar (with entertainment),

room service. In-room data ports, minibars, cable TV, in-room VCRs. Massage. Exercise equipment. Business services. | 714 7th Ave., between 47th and 48th Sts. | 212/765–7676 | fax 212/765–1962 | www.renaissancehotels.com | 305 rooms | $225–$390 | AE, D, DC, MC, V.

Roosevelt Hotel. Named for Teddy Roosevelt, the hotel has an opulent, Neoclassical lobby, resplendent with marble floors, glittering chandeliers, and Corinthian columns. The spacious rooms were renovated in 1997. Restaurant, bar, room service. Cable TV. Health club. | 45 E. 45th St., between Madison and Vanderbilt Aves. | 212/661–9600 | fax 212/885–6168 | www.theroosevelthotel.com | 999 rooms, 41 suites | $169–$320 rooms, $350–$1,800 suites | AE, DC, D, MC, V.

Salisbury. This contemporary, European-style hotel with friendly service is near shopping, Carnegie Hall, and Central Park. Complimentary Continental breakfast. In-room data ports, some refrigerators, cable TV. Laundry facilities. Business services. | 123 W. 57th St., between 6th and 7th Aves. | 212/246–1300 or 888/692–5757 (reservations) | fax 212/977–7752 | nyc-salisbury@worldnet.att.net | www.nycsalisbury.com | 320 rooms, 60 suites | $259 rooms, $299–$399 suites | AE, D, DC, MC, V.

San Carlos. This very simple hotel, with pleasant service, is convenient to the United Nations, Museum of Modern Art, and other Midtown sights. Restaurant, complimentary Continental breakfast. In-room data ports, some kitchenettes, microwaves, cable TV. Laundry facilities. | 150 E. 50th St., between Lexington and 3rd Aves. | 212/755–1800 or 800/722–2012 | fax 212/688–9778 | sancarlos@pobox.com | www.sancarlos.com | 75 rooms, 76 suites | $195–$215 rooms, $245–$325 suites | AE, D, DC, MC, V.

Shelburne Murray Hill. This modern hotel is set in a quiet Murray Hill neighborhood, close to businesses and the Theater District. Many of the nice-size rooms have views of the East River and the Chrysler Building, and some have balconies. Restaurant, bar. In-room data ports, kitchenettes, microwaves, cable TV. Exercise equipment. Laundry facilities. Business services. | 303 Lexington Ave., between 37th and 38th Sts. | 212/689–5200 or 800/637–8483 | fax 212/779–7068 | www.mesuite.com | 263 suites | $205–$450 | AE, D, DC, MC, V.

Regal U.N. Plaza. This modern, chrome-and-glass tower offers fine views of United Nations Headquarters and the surrounding area. Rooms are simple but quiet and nice. Restaurant *(see* Ambassador Grill), bar. In-room data ports, minibars, refrigerators, cable TV. Pool. Massage. Tennis. Gym. Business services. | 1 U.N. Plaza, 44th St., between 1st and 2nd Aves. | 212/758–1234 or 800/228–9000 (reservations) | fax 212/702–5051 | www.unplaza.com | 427 rooms, 45 suites | $259 rooms, $500–$625 suites | AE, D, DC, MC, V.

Time. Rooms are tiny, but the hotel, very near Times Square, is as sleek and trendy as they come. There's a popular restaurant as well. All the rooms are either yellow, red or blue, with matching furniture and sheets. Restaurant, bar, room service. Minibars, cable TV, in-room VCRs. Gym. Laundry facilities. | 224 W. 49th St., between Broadway and 8th Ave. | 212/246–5252 | fax 212/245–2305 | www.thetimehotel.com | 165 rooms, 28 suites | $289–$509 rooms, $339–$689 suites | AE, D, DC, MC, V.

Wales. Set in an Uptown residential neighborhood convenient to Central Park and several major museums, this hotel has a restaurant known for brunch. The old English-style suites are big and very elegant. Restaurant, complimentary Continental breakfast and afternoon refreshments. Cable TV, in-room VCRs (and movies). Laundry service. Business services. Some pets allowed. | 1295 Madison Ave., between 92nd and 93rd Sts. | 212/876–6000 or 877/847–4444 (outside NYC) | fax 212/860–7000 | hotelwales@aol.com | www.unique-hotels.com | 92 rooms, 40 suites | $269 rooms, $429 suites | AE, MC, V.

EXPENSIVE

Algonquin. Eighteenth-century English decor and a clubby atmosphere permeate this hotel, which became famous for the many literary and theatrical personalities who frequented the bar in the 1920s, most notably "The Algonquin Roundtable." Old English decor graces the rooms, with antique furniture to match. Popular with business travelers. Restaurant, bar, complimentary Continental breakfast. Refrigerators (in suites), cable TV. Laundry service. Business services. | 59 W. 44th St., between 5th and 6th Aves. | 212/840–6800 or 800/ 548–0345 | fax 212/944–1419 | www.camberlyhotels.com | 165 rooms, 15 suites | $289–$399 rooms, $369–$629 suites | AE, D, DC, MC, V.

Barbizon Hotel and Towers. This New York landmark was renovated in 1996, and the hotel now has a pool. The guest rooms are decorated in pastel and earth tones, and the spacious bathrooms have white marble, pedestal sinks, and halogen lighting. In-room data ports, minibars, cable TV. Pool. Hot tub. Gym. Business services. | 140 E. 63rd St., between Lexington and 3rd Aves. | 212/838–5700 or 800/223–1020 | fax 212/888–4271 | www.thebarbizon.com | 300 rooms, 12 suites | $295–$495 rooms, $500–$650 suites | AE, D, DC, MC, V.

Benjamin Hotel. The Benjamin is an understated all-suite hotel, particularly suited to business travelers. Rooms have work stations with high-speed Internet access, fax and copy machines, and web TV. Some rooms have private terraces. Restaurant, bar. Cable TV. Laundry service. Business services. No pets. | 125 E. 50th St., between Lexington and 3rd Aves. | 212/715–2500 or 888/4BENJAMIN | fax 212/715–2525 | www.thebenjamin.com; www.mesuite.com (reservations) | 209 suites | $320–$770 | AE, D, DC, MC, V.

★ **The Carlyle.** European tradition and Manhattan swank come together at New York's most lovable grand hotel. Everything about this Madison Avenue landmark suggests refinement, from the Mark Hampton–designed rooms, with their fine antique furniture and artfully framed Audubons and botanicals, to the first-rate service. Many guests head straight to the Bemelmans Bar, named after Ludwig Bemelmans, the illustrator who drew the beloved children's book *Madeline*; he created the murals here. Others come just to hear such singers as Barbara Cook or Bobby Short perform at the clubby Cafe Carlyle, the quintessential cabaret venue. Restaurant *(see* Cafe Carlyle), bar, room service. In-room data ports, minibars, microwaves, some in-room hot tubs, cable TV, in-room VCRs (and movies). Massage. Gym. Laundry service. Business services. Some pets allowed. | 35 E. 76th St., between Madison and Park Aves. | 212/744–1600 or 800/227–5737 | fax 212/717–4682 | 196 rooms | $375–$650 | AE, DC, MC, V.

Casablanca. Humphrey Bogart would be right at home in this Moroccan-theme hotel with its wild, over-the-top decor, complete with a mural of the desert. It's just off Times Square. Restaurant, bar, complimentary Continental breakfast and afternoon snacks, room service. In-room data ports, refrigerators, cable TV, in-room VCRs (and movies). Laundry service. Business services. | 147 W. 43rd St., between Broadway and 6th Ave. | 212/869–1212 or 888/922– 7225 (reservations) | fax 212/391–7585 | casahotel@aol.com | www.casablancahotel.com | 48 rooms (8 with shower only) | $265–$375 | AE, DC, MC, V.

Crowne Plaza. Just off Times Square, this is a good location for exploring Midtown sights and the Theater District. Each room has either city views or river views. Restaurant, bar. Minibars, refrigerators, cable TV. Pool. Gym. Laundry service. Business services. | 1605 Broadway, between 48th and 49th Sts. | 212/977–4000 | fax 212/333–7393 | www.crowneplaza.com | 770 rooms | $189–$299 | AE, D, DC, MC, V.

Drake Swissôtel. This elegant hotel provides free transportation to Wall Street for its business clientele. There are desks in the rooms, some of which have river views. Restaurant, bar, room service. In-room data ports, minibars (in suites), cable TV. Spa. Health club. Laundry service. Business services. | 440 E. 56th St., between Madison and Park Aves. | 212/421– 0900 or 800/372–5369 | fax 212/371–4190 | www.travelweb.com/thisco/swiss/9404 | 396 rooms, 98 suites | $265–$600 rooms, $650–$1,000 suites | AE, D, DC, MC, V.

Fitzpatrick Manhattan. More than half of the units are suites at this cozy hotel just south of Bloomingdale's, and all have emerald carpets and traditional dark-wood furniture. The publike bar at the heart of the hotel is as welcoming as any in Dublin. Restaurant, bar, room service. In-room data ports, some refrigerators, cable TV. Laundry service. Business services, airport shuttle. | 687 Lexington Ave., between 56th and 57th Sts. | 212/355–0100 or 800/ 367–7701 | fax 212/355–1371 | fitzusa@aol.com | www.fitzpatrickhotels.com | 92 rooms, 52 suites | $179–$199 rooms, $365 suites | AE, D, DC, MC, V.

Grand Hyatt. This big, glitzy hotel overlooking Grand Central Terminal is a convenient location for commuters and other travelers who come through the station. Some of the rooms have balconies, some have sofa sleepers, and some have views of 42nd Street. Restaurant, bar (with entertainment), room service. Refrigerators (in suites), cable TV. Laundry service. Business services. | 1 E. 42nd St., between Park and Lexington Aves. | 212/883–1234 or 800/223–1234 | fax 212/697–3772 | www.hyatt.com | 1,347 rooms, 55 suites | $345 rooms, $600–$800 suites | AE, D, DC, MC, V.

Helmsley Park Lane. The Helmsley Park Lane, which occupies prime real estate overlooking Central Park, is close to Carnegie Hall, the Museum of Modern Art, and superb 5th Avenue shopping. Restaurant, bar, room service. In-room data ports, refrigerators, cable TV. Laundry service. Business services. | 36 Central Park S, between 5th and 6th Aves. | 212/371–4000 or 800/221–4982 | fax 212/319–9065 | sales@helmsleyparklane.com | www.helmsleyhotels.com | 640 rooms | $315–$380 | AE, D, DC, MC, V.

Hotel Delmonico. Some suites have city views at this hotel. Lots of plush fabrics and chandeliers adorn the lobby. Bar. Some kitchenettes, microwaves, cable TV. Business services. | 502 Park Ave., at 59th St. | 212/355–2500 or 800/821–3842 | fax 212/755–3779 | www.hoteldelmonico.com | 158 suites | $325–$490 1–bedrooms, $595 2–bedrooms | AE, D, DC, MC, V.

Hotel Elysée. This pleasant boutique hotel prides itself on personal service. It's in an old building with traditional European decor. Rooms have views of Madison Avenue. Restaurant, bar, complimentary Continental breakfast and afternoon snacks, room service. Microwaves, cable TV, in-room VCRs (and movies). Business services. | 60 E. 54th St., between Madison and Park Aves. | 212/753–1066 or 800/535–9733 | fax 212/980–9278 | http://members.aol.com/elysee99 | 99 rooms | $325–$525 | AE, DC, MC, V.

★ **Inn at Irving Place.** Each elegantly appointed room in this landmark town house has a view of either the inn's gardens or Gramercy Park. Located on a quiet street near Union Square, it is convenient to all Downtown sights. Restaurant, bar, complimentary Continental breakfast and afternoon snacks, room service. In-room data ports minibars, refrigerators, cable TV, in-room VCRs (and movies). Laundry service. Business services. No kids under 12. | 56 Irving Pl., between 17th and 18th Sts. | 212/533–4600 or 800/685–1447 | fax 212/533–4611 | inn@irving.com | www.innatirving.com | 12 rooms (2 with shower only) | $300–$500 | AE, DC, MC, V.

Inter-Continental. The guest rooms have lots of amenities, including luxurious marble bathrooms. The Midtown location is convenient for business travelers. Restaurant, bar. In-room data ports, minibars, cable TV. Massage. Exercise equipment. Business services, parking ($38 per day). | 111 E. 48th St., between Park and Lexington Aves. | 212/755–5900 or 877/508–9890 | fax 212/644–0079 | www.interconti.com | 683 rooms | $385–$535 | AE, D, DC, MC, V.

Iroquois. Originally opened in 1923, the Iroquois received a $10 million face-lift in 1998 and now competes with the other upscale boutique hotels in town. There is a room dedicated to James Dean, who lived at the hotel from 1951 to 1953. Restaurant, bar, complimentary Continental breakfast, room service. Cable TV. Spa. Health club. | 49 W. 44th St., between 5th and 6th Aves. | 212/840–3080 or 800/332–7220 | fax 212/719–0006 | www.iroquoisny.com | 115 rooms | $275–$325 | AE, D, DC, MC, V.

Kitano Hotel. Guests at the Kitano enjoy contemporary comfort with a Japanese sensibility. Some suites are designed with tatami mats and Japanese bathrooms, and there's an art gallery on the premises. 2 restaurants, bar, complimentary Japanese tea. Cable TV. Laundry facilities, laundry service. | 66 Park Ave., at 38th St. | 212/885–7000 or 800–KITANO NY | fax 212/885–7100 | www.kitano.com | 149 rooms, 18 suites | $315–$450 rooms, $500–$1,400 suites | AE, D, DC, MC, V.

Le Parker Meridien. A European ambience is created here with painted ceilings and classically appointed guest rooms. Great location near Carnegie Hall, 57th Street, and 5th

Avenue shopping. The restaurant in the hotel specializes in wonderful breakfasts. Restaurant, bar, room service. In-room data ports, cable TV. Pool. Hot tub. Health club. Business services, parking ($39 per day). Small pets allowed. | 118 W. 57th St., between 6th and 7th Aves. | 212/245–5000 or 800/543–4300 | fax 212/708–7477 | www.parkermeridien.com | 700 rooms | $350–$450 | AE, D, DC, MC, V.

The Lombardy. This property is a short walk away from Carnegie Hall and shopping on 57th Street. Restaurant, bar, room service. In-room data ports, some kitchenettes, microwaves, refrigerators, cable TV. Exercise equipment. Laundry service. Business services. | 111 E. 56th St., between Lexington and Park Aves. | 212/753–8600 or 800/223–5254 (reservations) | fax 212/754–5683 | www.hotellombardy.com | 105 rooms, 60 suites | $225–$280 rooms, $395 suites | AE, DC, MC, V.

Lyden Gardens. This quaint hotel is situated on a quiet street in an upscale residential neighborhood, close to shopping and restaurants. Some of the rooms have terraces, while others have garden views. There are desks in every room. Kitchenettes, microwaves, cable TV. Business services. | 215 E. 64th St., between 2nd and 3rd Aves. | 212/355–1230, 212/320–8022, or 800/637–8483 | fax 212/758–7858 | www.mesuite.com | 133 suites | $309–$339 | AE, DC, MC, V.

Lyden House. This is a very small hotel with basic services, but the guest rooms are spacious, and it's convenient to Midtown sights, shopping, and restaurants. Many kitchenettes, microwaves, cable TV. Laundry facilities. | 320 E. 53rd St., between 1st and 2nd Aves. | 212/888–6070 or 800/637–8483 | fax 212/935–7690 | www.mesuite.com | 81 rooms, 8 suites | $305–$345 | AE, D, DC, MC, V.

Manhattan Club. Guest rooms are spacious, understated, and elegant at this Midtown hotel, near Carnegie Hall, Lincoln Center, and the Museum of Modern Art. Microwaves, refrigerators, cable TV, in-room VCRs. Business services. Pets allowed (deposit). | 200 W. 56th St., at 7th Ave. | 212/707–5000 or 800/NYC–2121 | fax 212/707–5140 | www.manhattanclub.com | 165 suites | $350–$450 | AE, DC, MC, V.

The Mansfield. This stylish, boutique hotel, with ebony-wood floors, Belgian linens, and CD players in all of the rooms, is one block from Times Square. Complimentary Continental breakfast. Refrigerators, cable TV, in-room VCRs (and movies). Business services. | 12 W. 44th St., between 5th and 6th Aves. | 212/944–6050 or 800/255–5167 | fax 212/764–4477 | www.boutiquehg.com | 123 rooms (36 with shower only), 24 suites | $295–$375 rooms, $455 suites | AE, MC, V.

Marriott–East Side. Polished wood and marble floors gleam in the lobby of this 35-story luxury hotel renovated in 2000. The rooms have desks and new furnishings, and some have balconies. Restaurant, bar. In-room data ports, minibars, cable TV. Exercise equipment. Laundry service. Business services. | 525 Lexington Ave., between 48th and 49th Sts. | 212/755–4000 or 800/228–9290 | fax 212/751–3440 | www.marriotthotels.com | 650 rooms | $289–$299 | AE, D, DC, MC, V.

Marriott–Financial Center. This hotel has European decor, with polished mahogany and marble floors. Some of the burgundy-carpeted rooms have views of the Hudson River. All have desks and fax machines. Restaurant, bar. In-room data ports, minibars, microwaves, cable TV. Pool. Massage. Gym. Business services. | 85 West St., between Albany and Carlisle Sts. | 212/385–4900 or 800/228–9290 | fax 212/227–8136 | www.marriotthotels.com | 504 rooms | $359–$399 | AE, D, DC, MC, V.

Marriott Marquis. This Midtown Marriott is a huge, bustling hotel, with slick glass elevators and comfortable guest rooms. All of the rooms open onto a soaring atrium. There is a revolving bar on the seventh floor that looks out on the lights of Times Square. 4 Restaurants, 3 bars, room service. In-room data ports, minibars, cable TV. Hot tub. Exercise equipment. Business services, parking ($35 per day). | 1535 Broadway | 212/398–1900 or 800/228–9290 | fax 212/704–8930 | www.marriotthotels.com | 1,946 rooms, 58 suites | $200–$400 rooms, $500–$2,500 suites | AE, D, DC, MC, V.

★ **Mercer.** The chic, minimalist design at this boutique hotel attracts a clientele to match. Many rooms have deep marble tubs, and all have CD players. Restaurant, bar. Cable TV, in-room VCRs. | 147 Mercer St., between Mercer and Prince Sts. | 212/966–6060 or 888/918–6060 | fax 212/965–3838 | 71 rooms, 4 suites | $375–$500 rooms, $925 suites | AE, D, DC, MC, V.

Millennium Broadway. The lobby is sleek and dramatic, with black marble floors; rich, African-mahogany walls; enormous, outrageously stylized paintings of fleshy, classical figures; and striking flower arrangements. Modern rooms are splashed with leather and suede; appliances are high-tech chrome; and everything is black, brown, and gray. The white-tile bathrooms, in contrast, are nothing special. Restaurant, bar. In-room data ports, minibars, cable TV. Massage. Exercise equipment. Laundry facilities. Business services. | 145 W. 44th St. | 212/768–4400 or 800/622–5569 | fax 212/789–7688 | www.mill.bdwy.com | 752 rooms | $295–$395 | AE, D, DC, MC, V.

Morgans. Fresh flowers and a VCR grace the Andree Putman–designed guest rooms which are styled in muted earth tones. The bar at this chic, contemporary hotel attracts a hip, New York crowd, but overall, the mood of this boutique hotel is serene. Bar, complimentary Continental breakfast, room service. In-room data ports, minibars, refrigerators, cable TV. Business services. | 237 Madison Ave. | 212/686–0300 or 800/334–3408 | fax 212/779–8352 | 78 rooms, 35 suites | $380–$525 rooms, $530–$675 suites | AE, DC, MC, V.

New York Marriott–World Trade Center. Many rooms have excellent views of the Hudson River, New York harbor, and the downtown skyline at this Downtown Marriott, which is especially convenient for bankers and traders with business in the area. Some of the elegant rooms are duplexes. All have desks and lounge areas, and some even have pianos. Restaurant, complimentary Continental breakfast, bar, room service. In-room data ports, minibars, cable TV. Pool. Massage. Gym, racquetball. Business services. | 3 World Trade Center, on West St., between Liberty and Vesey Sts. | 212/938–9100 or 800/228–9290 | fax 212/444–3444 | www.marriotthotels.com | 820 rooms | $399–$429 | AE, D, DC, MC, V.

Omni Berkshire Place. The rooms here are modern and larger than average, and there's a lounge with a fireplace on the second floor. Restaurant, bar, room service. In-room data ports, minibars, cable TV. Exercise equipment. Laundry facilities. Business services. | 21 E. 52nd St., between 5th and Madison Aves. | 212/753–5800 or 800/790–1900 | fax 212/754–5018 | www.omnihotels.com | 396 rooms | $359 | AE, D, DC, MC, V.

Roger Williams. This small, stylish hotel with sleek furnishings is in a quiet area of town just north of Madison Square and south of busy 34th Street. Great for business travelers. The rooms, which have CD players, are small, but the hotel is convenient to the Flatiron District and all Downtown sights. Complimentary Continental breakfast. In-room data ports, cable TV, in-room VCRs (and movies). Business services. | 131 Madison Ave., between 30th and 31st Sts. | 212/448–7000 or 877/847–4444 | fax 212/448–7007 | www.uniquehotels.com | 200 rooms (20 with shower only) | $329–$950 | AE, D, DC, MC, V.

Royalton. The Philippe Starck–designed Royalton features sleek, contemporary rooms, some with fireplaces or balconies, and the Vodka Bar in the lobby attracts a fashionable crowd. The penthouse has a terrace. Restaurant, bar, room service. In-room data ports, minibars, refrigerators, cable TV, in-room VCRs (and movies). Exercise equipment. Business services. Some pets allowed. | 44 W. 44th St., between 5th and 6th Aves. | 212/869–4400 or 800/635–9013 | fax 212/869–8965 | 168 rooms | $315–$580 | AE, DC, MC, V.

Sheraton Manhattan. This big, modern hotel, which seems always to be under renovation, has all of the standard amenities. Guest rooms are comfortable and well-appointed, and come with desks. Restaurant, bar, complimentary Continental breakfast, room service. In-room data ports, minibars, microwaves, cable TV. Pool. Gym. Laundry service. Business services. | 790 7th Ave. | 212/581–3300 or 800/325–3535 | fax 212/262–4410 | www.sheraton.com | 650 rooms | $335–$459 | AE, D, DC, MC, V.

Sheraton New York Hotel and Towers. This Midtown Sheraton is large, with a helpful staff. Rooms are standard but quite comfortable. 2 restaurants, 1 bar (with entertainment). In-room data ports, minibars, cable TV. Pool. Gym. Business services. | 811 7th Ave. | 212/581–1000 or 800/325–3535 | fax 212/262–4410 | www.sheraton.com | 1,750 rooms | $335 | AE, D, DC, MC, V.

Sheraton Russell. A converted prewar building provides a charming, intimate setting for this small chain hotel. Many rooms have fireplaces. Restaurant, bar, complimentary Continental breakfast. In-room data ports, minibars, microwaves, cable TV. Pool. Exercise equipment. Business services, parking ($28 per day). | 45 Park Ave. | 212/685–7676 or 800/325–3535 | fax 212/889–3193 | www.sheraton.com | 146 rooms, 26 suites | $325 rooms, $625 suites | AE, D, DC, MC, V.

Sherry Netherland Hotel. Opened in 1927, the Sherry Netherland retains an air of privacy, solicitude, and stately elegance. The hotel overlooks Central Park. Guest rooms are spacious and homey (in a really expensive sort of way). Some suites have dining areas, fireplaces, and marble baths. Restaurant, bar. Cable TV, in-room VCRs. Barbershop, beauty salon. Gym. | 781 5th Ave. | 212/355–2800 or 800/247–4377 | fax 212/319–4306 | www.sherrynetherland.com | 168 rooms | $310–$450 rooms, $595–$1400 suites | AE, D, DC, MC, V.

The Shoreham. The stately old Shoreham was renovated in 1999 and is now sleekly modern, with brushed metal and black furniture. A single red rose in each guest room is an elegant touch. Complimentary Continental breakfast. In-room data ports, cable TV, in-room VCRs (and movies). Laundry service. Business services, parking ($24 per day). | 33 W. 55th St. | 212/247–6700 or 877/847–4444 | fax 212/765–9741 | www.shorehamhotel.com | 176 rooms, 18 suites | $345–$455 rooms, $380–$540 suites | AE, D, DC, MC, V.

Soho Grand. The public spaces in this trendy SoHo hotel don't disappoint. There's a grand staircase leading to a hip lounge and the super-cool staff is dressed in black. The light-color rooms, however, are merely basic. There are terraces in the suites. Restaurant, bar. In-room data ports, minibars, cable TV. Massage. Exercise equipment. Business services. Pets allowed. | 310 W. Broadway | 212/965–3000 or 800/965–3000 (reservations) | fax 212/965–3200 | www.sohogrand.com | 369 rooms, 4 penthouse suites | $349–549 rooms, $1,299–$1699 suites | AE, D, DC, MC, V.

Stanhope Park Hyatt. Built in the 1920s, this regal 17-story hotel is a New York institution, offering guests old-world luxury and prestige directly across from the Metropolitan Museum. Restaurant, bar, room service. In-room data ports, kitchenettes (in some suites), minibars, cable TV. Exercise equipment. Laundry facilities, laundry service. | 995 5th Ave. | 212/288–5800 or 800/233–1123 | fax 212/517–0088 | www.hyatt.com | 92 rooms, 48 suites | $325–$450 rooms, $420–$900 suites | AE, D, DC, MC, V.

Surrey. This very private, sophisticated boutique hotel is just steps away from Central Park and major museums, and has one of the top restaurants in New York. Restaurant *(see* Cafe Boulud*)*, bar, room service. In-room data ports, microwaves, cable TV, in-room VCRs (and movies). Exercise equipment. Laundry facilities. Business services. Small pets allowed ($300 deposit). | 20 E. 76th St. | 212/288–3700 | fax 212/628–1549 | www.mesuite.com | 130 rooms | $284–$325 | AE, DC, MC, V.

"W" New York. Completed in 1998, this hotel has an upscale "urban-rustic" feel. The rooms and public spaces use all-natural materials. Restaurant *(see* Heartbeat*)*, 2 bars. Minibars, cable TV. Spa. Health Club. Laundry facilities, laundry service. Business services. | 541 Lexington Ave. | 212/755–1200 | fax 212/644–0951 | www.starwoodhotels.com | 712 rooms | $399 rooms, $489–$1,100 suites | AE, D, DC, MC, V.

Warwick. Built in 1925 by William Randolph Hearst, this hotel is decorated in a European style with Asian accents. The 33-story building features some great views of Manhattan. Some rooms have antique furniture, tapestries, or balconies. Restaurant, bar. Cable TV. Exercise equipment. Laundry service. Business services. | 65 W. 54th St. | 212/247–2700 or 800/

223–4099 | fax 212/957–8915 | 350 rooms, 72 suites | $295–$325 rooms, $335–$750 suites | AE, DC, MC, V.

Westbury. British formality meets congeniality at the Forte Hotel chain's New York outpost. Leather banquettes look out on Madison Avenue at the clubby Polo Bar and Restaurant. Rooms and suites have a lived-in country-English look, with floral chintz, oriental rugs, and mahogany furnishings. Restaurant, bar, room service. In-room data ports, cable TV. Exercise equipment. Business services. Pets allowed. | 15 E. Madison Ave. | 212/535–2000 or 800/321–1569 | fax 212/535–5058 | 228 rooms, 52 suites | $325–$500 | AE, D, DC, MC, V.

VERY EXPENSIVE

★ **Four Seasons.** An impressive soaring marble lobby, an elegant bar, spacious rooms, and panoramic city views make this one of the top choices in the city. There's a fax machine in every room. Restaurant (see Fifty Seven Fifty Seven), bar, room service. In-room data ports, minibars, cable TV, in-room VCRs. Massage. Gym. Business services. Some pets allowed. | 57 E. 57th St. | 212/758–5700 or 800/332–3442 | fax 212/758–5711 | www.fourseasons.com | 370 rooms, 61 suites | $585 rooms, $1,350 suites | AE, D, DC, MC, V.

Gorham New York. This private boutique hotel with attentive service is in Midtown, just blocks from the Museum of Modern Art and Carnegie Hall. The small, cozy lobby has modernist couches. The large-size rooms are newly renovated with marble bathrooms. The suites have whirlpools; penthouses have balconies. In-room data ports, kitchenettes, microwaves, cable TV. Exercise equipment. Business services. | 136 W. 55th St. | 212/245–1800 or 800/735–0710 | fax 212/582–8332 | www.gorhamhotel.com | 114 rooms | $400 rooms, $440 suites | AE, DC, MC, V.

Inter-Continental Central Park South. Enjoy old-world elegance and luxurious style at this Central Park South hotel, formerly the Ritz Carlton. Many rooms have views of the park. Some suites have balconies, and there are desks in all the rooms. Restaurant, bar. In-room data ports, minibars, cable TV. Exercise equipment. Laundry service. Business services. | 112 Central Park S | 212/757–1900 | fax 212/757–9620 | http://new-york.interconti.com | 207 rooms, 26 suites | $439–$575 rooms, $550–$910 suites | AE, D, DC, MC, V.

★ **The Lowell.** This lovely small hotel, situated on a stately, residential block on the Upper East Side, is close to Madison Avenue shopping and many restaurants. Thoroughly upscale, the hotel has been operating since 1928 and is a designated historical landmark building. Most suites have woodburning fireplaces, some have terraces, and all have fully equipped kitchens. Restaurants, bar. In-room data ports, kitchenettes (in suites), minibars, refrigerators, cable TV, in-room VCRs (and movies). Exercise equipment. Business services. | 28 E. 63rd St. | 212/838–1400 or 800/221–4444 | fax 212/319–4230 | lowellhtl@aol.com | www.small-hotel.com/lowell | 21 rooms, 47 suites | $485–$495 rooms, $585–$815 suites | AE, D, DC, MC, V.

The Mark. This very exclusive boutique hotel has exquisitely appointed guest rooms. The rooms have English and Italian decor, with chairs, sofas, fancy linens, and beds. Restaurant, bar, room service. In-room data ports, cable TV, in-room VCRs (and movies). Exercise equipment. Laundry service. Business services. No pets. | 25 E. 77th St. | 212/744–4300 or 800/843–6275 | fax 212/744–2749 | www.themarkhotel.com | 120 rooms, 60 suites | $500–$600 rooms, $600–$2,500 suites | AE, D, DC, MC, V.

★ **New York Palace.** The reinvented Palace is one of New York's most upscale hotels. The rooms are plush and stylish in bright colors, with desks and electronic controls for lights and temperature control. Some suites have balconies, and many have views of nearby St. Patrick's Cathedral. The tower level on the most upper floors offers 24-hour butler service. 2 restaurants (see Le Cirque 2000), room service. In-room data ports, refrigerators (in suites), cable TV. Massage. Health club. Laundry service. Business services. Pets allowed. | 455 Madison Ave. | 212/888–7000 or 800/697–2522 | fax 212/303–6000 | hrihotel@haven.ios.com | www.newyorkpalace.com | 900 rooms, 104 suites | $475–$600 rooms, $900–$1,000 suites | AE, D, DC, MC, V.

Peninsula New York. The lobby of this 1905 Beaux Arts building features a vast marble staircase and a lavish carved ceiling. The hotel was renovated in 1998, making it even more luxurious. The Penn Top bar provides a dramatic view of the city, and the spa is first class. Restaurant (*see* Adrienne), bar, room service. In-room data ports, minibars, cable TV. Pool. Hot tub, spa. Gym. | 700 5th Ave. | 212/247–2200 or 800/262–9467 | fax 212/903–3949 | pny@peninsula.com | www.peninsula.com | 200 rooms, 42 suites | $550–$690 rooms, $750–$1,950 suites | AE, D, DC, MC, V.

The Pierre. Run by the Four Seasons chain, the Pierre is the ultimate in elegance. Since the 1930s, it has occupied its 5th Avenue post with all the grandeur of a French château. The public areas drip with chandeliers, handmade carpets, and Corinthian columns. The king-size guest rooms are resplendent with traditional chintz fabrics and dark-wood furniture; bathrooms have Art Nouveau fixtures. Service is first rate. Restaurants (*see* Cafe Pierre, The Rotunda), bar (with entertainment), room service. In-room data ports, minibars, cable TV. Barbershop, beauty salon, massage. Exercise equipment. Laundry service. Business services. Pets allowed. | 2 E. 61st St. | 212/838–8000 or 800/743–7734 | fax 212/940–8109 | www.fourseasons.com | 149 rooms, 53 suites | $430–$655 rooms, $695–$5,050 suites | AE, D, DC, MC, V.

Plaza Athénée. Based on the original Paris hotel, this version sports traditional French decor, with antique furniture in the rooms. Some suites have balconies. Restaurant (*see* Le Régence), bar, room service. In-room data ports, refrigerators, cable TV. Exercise equipment. Laundry service. Business services. Pets allowed. | 37 E. 64th St. | 212/734–9100 or 800/447–8800 | fax 212/772–0958 | www.plaza-athenee.com | 124 rooms, 26 suites | $440–$600 rooms, $1,100–$3,600 suites | AE, D, DC, MC, V.

Plaza Hotel. The most famous hotel in New York, this huge châteaulike building on the edge of Central Park was the home to the children's book character Eloise. The lobby is always bustling with tourists and visitors to the Oak Room restaurant and bar, the Palm Court restaurant, shops, and more. Guest rooms are done in classic style, complete with double-height ceilings. 3 restaurants, 2 bars, room service. In-room data ports, minibars, refrigerators, cable TV. Barbershop, beauty salon, massage, spa. Laundry service. Business services. | 5th Ave. at Central Park S | 212/759–3000 or 800/759–3000 | fax 212/759–3167 | plaza@fairmont.com | www.fairmont.com | 692 rooms, 112 suites | $405 rooms, $495–$1,500 suites | AE, D, DC, MC, V.

Regency Hotel. The Regency—known as a hotel for top business executives—provides classically appointed guest rooms and excellent service. The luxurious suites have French doors, desks, and fax machines. The decor is modern, with light-color wallpaper to match the wood in the rooms. Restaurant, room service. In-room data ports, kitchenettes (in suites), refrigerators, cable TV, in-room VCRs. Barbershop, beauty salon, massage. Gym. Laundry service. Business services. | 540 Park Ave. | 212/759–4100 or 800/233–2356 | fax 212/826–5674 | 362 rooms, 185 suites | $425–$595 rooms, $750–$1,200 suites | AE, D, DC, MC, V.

Rihga Royal. The hotel is part of a deluxe Japanese chain, and all of the suites have marble bathrooms, with separate showers and tubs, as well as fax machines. They are also large, with French doors; some have balconies. Restaurant, bar (with entertainment), room service. In-room data ports, minibars, refrigerators, cable TV, in-room VCRs. Gym. Laundry service. Business services. No pets. | 151 W. 54th St. | 212/307–5000 or 800/937–5454 | fax 212/765–6530 | 496 suites | $425–$575 | AE, D, DC, MC, V.

St. Regis Hotel. Elegant, antiques-laden guest rooms line the halls of this exquisite, Beaux Arts building, which has been restored to its original splendor. The restaurant is one of the best in town. Restaurant (*see* Lespinasse), bar, room service. In-room data ports, cable TV, in-room VCRs. Barbershop, beauty salon, massage. Gym. Shops. Laundry service. Business services, parking ($40 per day). | 2 E. 55th St. | 212/753–4500 or 800/325–3535 | fax 212/787–3447 | www.stregis.com | 220 rooms, 92 suites | $520–$590 rooms, $950–$1,400 suites | AE, D, DC, MC, V.

Trump International Hotel and Tower. Located across from Central Park, the hotel offers excellent, personalized service. The rooms are very comfortable, and all have sitting areas. The restaurant is world-class. Restaurant *(see* Jean Georges), bar, room service. In-room hot tubs, in-room data ports, some kitchenettes; minibars, microwaves, refrigerators, cable TV, in-room VCRs (and movies). Pool. Massage. Gym. Laundry service. Business services. | 1 Central Park W | 212/299–1000 or 888/448–7867 (reservations) | fax 212/299–1150 | www.trump-intl.com | 168 rooms, 130 suites | $445–$550 rooms, $650–$1,100 suites | AE D, DC, MC, V.

"W" Court. This restored hotel is in a quiet residential neighborhood, in an older building, yet the decor in the lobby is modern and elegant. The rooms are beautiful, and some have balconies. Restaurant, bar. Kitchenettes (in suites), refrigerators, cable TV. Laundry service. Business services. | 130 E. 39th St. | 212/685–1100 or 877/946–8357 | fax 212/889–0287 | www.starwoodlodging.com | 155 rooms, 53 suites | $455 | AE, D, DC, MC, V.

"W" Tuscany. The Tuscany, set in the peaceful Murray Hill neighborhood, is a bit smaller and more intimate than her sister, the "W" Court. Rooms are unusually spacious and uncluttered, with walk-in closets, down-cushioned chaise longues, and contemporary high-style. Restaurant, bar, room service. Minibars, refrigerators, cable TV. Business services. | 120 E. 39th St. | 212/686–1600 or 800/22–DORAL | fax 212/779–7822 | www.starwoodlodging.com | 106 rooms, 16 suites | $475 | AE, D, DC, MC, V.

Waldorf-Astoria. Built in 1931, the Waldorf-Astoria still retains many of its original details. The expansive lobby is truly a period piece, with its 20-ft-high clock, very high ceilings, and four black-marble columns. There is also a men's store and a jeweler. The tower level provides ultraexclusive amenities like Jacuzzis, balconies, and full kitchens. 4 restaurants (*see* Bull & Bear Steakhouse, Peacock Alley, Oscar's), 3 bars, room service. In-room data ports, minibars, refrigerators, cable TV. Barbershop, beauty salon, massage. Gym. Shops. Laundry service. Business services. | 301 Park Ave. | 212/355–3000 or 800/WALDORF | fax 212/872–7272 | www.waldorfastoria.com | 1,219 rooms | $435–$525 | AE, D, DC, MC, V.

BRONX

ATTRACTIONS

Bronx Museum of the Arts. The museum's permanent collection contains 20th-century works on paper by African, African-American, Latin, Latin American, South Asian, and Asian-American artists. There are rotating exhibits of contemporary works by international artists, many of which focus on the cultural and social history of the Bronx. | 1040 Grand Concourse, at 165th St. | 718/681–6000 | $3 suggested donation, free Wed. | Wed. 12–9, Thurs.–Sun., 12–6.

Bronx Zoo. The 265 acres and 4,000 animals of the Bronx Zoo (now officially called the International Wildlife Conservation Center), which opened in 1899, make it the world's largest urban zoo. About 600 species are represented, mostly in naturalistic settings, usually separated from you by no more than a moat. At the children's petting zoo nothing comes between you and the many furry creatures. Among the best exhibits at the Center are: "Jungle World," an indoor tropical rain forest with five waterfalls, flowering orchids, and pythons; and "Wild Asia," where tigers and elephants roam 40 acres of open meadows and dark forests. | 2300 Southern Blvd. | 718/367–1010 or 800/937–2868 | www.wcs.org | $9; children's zoo $2; parking $6 | Apr.–Oct., weekdays 10–5, weekends 10–5:30; Nov.–Mar., daily 10–4:30.

Edgar Allen Poe Cottage. From 1846 to 1849, this was the last home of the great American writer. Now it's filled with exhibits detailing Poe's life and times. | Poe Park, 2460 Grand Concourse | 718/881–8900 | fax 718/881–4827 | $2 | Sat. 10–4, Sun. 1–5.

Fordham University. Originally a Jesuit college when it opened in 1841, Fordham now has nearly 6,000 undergraduates enrolled here, and a second campus near Lincoln Center. Enter the Rose Hill Campus grounds via Bathgate Avenue to see Old Rose Hill Manor Dig, the

University Church, whose magnificent stained glass was donated by King Louis Philippe of France shortly before his death in 1850, and Keating Hall, the Collegiate Gothic fortress at the center of Edward's Parade quadrangle. The Rose Hill campus is home to Fordham College at Rose Hill, the College of Business Administration, Ignatius College, the Graduate School of Arts and Sciences, and the Graduate School of Religion and Religious Education. | Rose Hill campus, 441 E. Fordham Rd. | 718/817–1000 | www.fordham.org.

The New York Botanical Garden. This 250-acre garden, founded in 1891, was modeled after the Royal Botanical Gardens in Kew, England. It's spectacular in every season. In spring, there's the Peggy Rockefeller Rose Garden with its 2,700 bushes of 230 varieties. In summer, the Arlow Stout Daylily Garden is spectacular. There's a restored rock garden, an azalea glen, a pine grove, 40 acres of trails through natural forest, and a great deal more. Narrated tram tours (tickets $4, departing every 30 minutes) transport you across the vast grounds. There's also a children's adventure garden with a hedge maze and all sorts of indoor and outdoor activities. If you don't want to drive or take the subway, a NYBG Shuttle operates on weekends Apr.–Oct. It departs from the Metropolitan Museum of Art and from the American Museum of Natural History and costs $7 roundtrip, $4 one-way. Reservations essential. | 200th St. and Kazimiroff Blvd. | 718/817–8700 | www.nybg.org | $3; Garden Passport (all admissions and tram tour) $8; free Wed., Sat. 10–noon | Apr.–Oct., Tues.–Sun. and Mon. holidays 10–6; Nov.–Mar., daily 10–4.

Pelham Bay Park. This enormous park, one of the city's most versatile and the largest, was named after Englishman Thomas Pell, who bought land in the area in 1654. Its 2,765 acres are filled with wildlife, from fish and frogs to owls and ospreys and even seals. There are tennis courts, baseball diamonds, a track, golf courses, a playground, and a stable. Orchard Beach, a Robert Moses creation, is one of the park's supreme highlights. This white-sand crescent on Long Island Sound draws crowds, largely from the Bronx. The main entrance is at Bruckner Boulevard and Middletown Road. | Bruckner Blvd. and Middletown Rd. | 718/430–1890 or 718/885–3466 | www.nyc.gov/parks.

Bartow-Pell Mansion Museum and Gardens. This country home, built in 1836, is filled with period furnishings and surrounded by stately sunken gardens. | 895 Shore Rd. N, in Pelham Bay Park | 718/885–1461 | Wed. and weekends noon–4.

Valentine-Varian House. Imagine the Bronx as a more rural, tranquil place as you wander through this 18th-century fieldstone house constructed in Georgian vernacular style. Exhibits trace the history of the borough from the Native American period through the Revolution. | Varian House Park, 3266 Bainbridge Ave. | 718/881–8900 | $2 | Sat. 10–4, Sun. 1–5.

Wave Hill. This 28-acre nonprofit environmental center, overlooking the Hudson River, was formerly the estate of conservation-minded financier George Perkins. It has been rented at various times to Theodore Roosevelt, Mark Twain, and Arturo Toscanini, and was donated to the city in 1960. There are 18 acres of gardens, including greenhouses and magnificent wildflower and aquatic habitats, guided walks, and an art museum, and concerts are held here. | 249th St. and Independence Ave. | 718/549–3200 | $4, free Nov. 16–Mar. 14 | Tues.–Sun. 9–5:30; closed Jan. 1 and Dec. 25.

Yankee Stadium. This mammoth 57, 545-seat stadium was built in 1923, and it resounds with the screams of Yankees fans who watched their heroes win 23 World Championships. | E. 161st Street and River Ave. | 718/293–6000.

ON THE CALENDAR

OCT.: *Halloween on Haunted Walk.* Master puppeteer Ralph Lee's human-size walking pumpkin and tap-dancing skeletons join his other creepy creations at this spooky extravaganza. Dress up and join the fun. | New York Botanical Garden, 200th St. and Kazimiroff Blvd. | Sun. before Halloween | 718/817–8700 | www.nybg.org/events.

DINING

Dominick's. Italian. Crowds line up outside this simple spot, one of the best restaurants on Arthur Avenue. Seating is at at communal tables; there's no menu—the waitstaff just reels off the kitchen's offerings of the evening. Garlic is the predominant flavor (you can even smell it in the street). A bottle of Chianti is all you need. | 2335 Arthur Ave. | 718/733–2807 | $25–$34 | No credit cards.

Emilia's. Italian. This is another classic among the Italian eateries on Arthur Avenue. The style is no-frills but the food is satisfying, especially the seafood *pescatore*, a seafood sampler, and the sambuca. | 2331 Arthur Ave. | 718/367–5915 | Closed Mon. | $10–$20 | AE, D, MC, V.

Lobster Box. Seafood. On City Island with a view of the Long Island Sound, the setting is perfect for eating seafood—especially on the outdoor terrace—even if the food is only okay. | 34 City Island Ave., City Island | 718/885–1952 | Closed Jan.– Feb. | $16–$40 | AE, D, DC, MC, V.

Mario's. Italian. You'll find excellent pizza, in addition to more substantial Italian dishes, at this Arthur Avenue favorite, frequented by locals. | 2342 Arthur Ave. | 718/584–1188 | Closed Mon., last 2 weeks in Aug., and first wk in Sept. | $12–$18 | AE, D, DC, MC, V.

LODGING

Le Refuge Inn Bed & Breakfast. This three-story Victorian-style home dating to the 17th century is in a residential neighborhood. City Island's beaches are a stroll away. Restaurant, complimentary Continental breakfast. Some refrigerators, some room phones. No pets. | 620 City Island Ave. | 718/885–2478 | fax 718/885–1519 | 6 rooms, 2 suites | $96–$120 rooms, $160–$190 suites | AE.

BROOKLYN

ATTRACTIONS

Brooklyn Academy of Music. The country's oldest performing arts center is home to the Brooklyn Philharmonic, but it also has groundbreaking operatic, dance, and theatrical performances. The main performance spaces include a 2,000-seat opera house and the 900-seat Majestic Theater. The venue now includes a movie theater complex. | BAM Opera House, BAMcafe, and BAM Rose Cinemas: 30 Lafayette Ave. (between Ashland Pl. and St. Felix St.), Fort Greene; BAM Harvey Theater: 651 Fulton St. (between Ashland and Rockwell Pl.) | 718/636–4100 | www.bam.org.

Brooklyn Botanic Garden. One of the headiest and most restorative experiences in New York City is these 52 acres lovingly divided into seasonal attractions. There are the mammoth greenhouses, the Cranford Rose Garden, and a special Fragrance Garden designed with consideration for people with visual impairments. (You are encouraged to rub the various herbs until their aromas are released on your fingers.) Other unique attractions are the voluptuous Japanese Garden and a cherry arbor that overwhelms the senses each spring. The Steinhardt Conservatory, a complex of greenhouses with carefully controlled "environmental" wings, showcases the plant life of desert, tropical, aquatic, and temperate zones. | 1000 Washington Ave. | 718/623–7200 | $3, free Tues. | Apr.–Sept., Tues.–Fri. 8–6, weekends 10–6; Oct.–Mar., Tues.–Fri. 8–4:30, weekends 10–4:30.

Brooklyn Children's Museum. Among the kid-friendly attractions at this fully interactive museum are tunnels to crawl through and animals to pet, as well as plenty of other exhibits. This is the oldest children's museum in the country. | 145 Brooklyn Ave., at St. Marks Ave. | 718/735–4432 | $4 suggested donation | Mon. and Wed.–Thurs. noon–5, Fri. noon–6:30, weekends 10–5.

Brooklyn Heights. Named for its enviable hilltop position, Brooklyn Heights was New York City's first suburb, connected to the city originally by ferryboat and eventually by subways and the Brooklyn Bridge. The area sprang to life in the 1820s when construction rapidly transformed the Heights into a fashionable upper-middle-class community. By the 1940s and '50s the area attracted a more bohemian crowd, especially writers, including W. H. Auden, Carson McCullers, Christopher Isherwood, Truman Capote, Arthur Miller, Richard Wright, and Norman Mailer. During the 1960s the Heights was declared a historic district—New York's first. Bounded by Columbia Heights and the Brooklyn-Queens Expressway to the west and north, to the east by Court St. and Cadman Plaza W, and to the south by Atlantic Avenue. To get there by subway, take the A train to High Street or take the No. 2 or 3 train to Clark Street.

Brooklyn Museum of Art. This is the second-largest art museum in New York City, with 1½ million pieces in its permanent collection. The Egyptian Art Collection features an entire sarcophagus, and the American Painting and Sculpture Galleries hold works by Winslow Homer, Gilbert Stuart, and John Singer Sargent. The outdoor Sculpture Garden features 19th-century architectural artifacts. But the museum's temporary exhibits are also among the best in the area. | 200 Eastern Pkwy. | 718/638–5000 | $4 suggested donation | Wed.–Fri. 10–5, weekends 11–6; first Sat. of every month 11–11.

Brooklyn Public Library. Built in 1941, this Neoclassical edifice resembles an open book. Its spine faces Grand Army Plaza and the building's two wings open like pages onto Eastern Parkway and Flatbush Avenue. The 15 bronze figures over the entrance represent characters in American literature. | Grand Army Plaza at the intersection of Flatbush Ave. and Eastern Pkwy. | 718/230–2100 | www.brooklynpubliclibrary.org | Free | Mon.–Thurs. 9–8, Fri.–Sat. 9–6, Sun. 1–5.

Coney Island. Here are the famous boardwalk; 2½ mi of beach; an enormous amusement park; New York's only aquarium; and nearby Brighton Beach, a fascinating and utterly transporting Russian enclave. Although the area has undergone a considerable decline since its heyday in the early 1900s, it's still a great place to experience the sights, sounds, and smells of summer: fried clams, foot-long hot dogs, suntan lotion (make that sunscreen), carnival madness, and, of course, the famous Cyclone roller coaster and Wonder Wheel. To get there by subway, take the F or D train to W. 8th Street station. | Surf Ave., from Ocean Pkwy. to 37th St. | 718/266–1234.

Aquarium for Wildlife Conservation. Penguins, walruses, otters, and seals relax on a replication of the Northern Pacific coast, and a 180,000-gallon seawater complex hosts beluga whales in New York City's major aquarium, set on an appropriately marine spot alongside Coney Island beach. Dolphins and sea lions perform in the Aquatheater. | Boardwalk at W. 8th St. | 718/265–3474 | $9.75 | Weekdays 10–5:15, weekends 10–6:15.

Sheepshead Bay. Although this port has a handy fleet of boats that whisks devout anglers out to sea to some secret fishing holes, this salty old neighborhood in southeastern Brooklyn is most famous for its seafood restaurants, in particular, the legendary Lundy's. To get there by subway, take the D or Q train to Sheepshead Bay Road.

Montgomery Place. Wedged between 8th Avenue and Prospect Park W, this one-block street in Park Slope is one of the finest thoroughfares in Brooklyn. Amble along and see the picturesque town houses designed by the Romanesque Revival architect C. P. H. Gilbert. | Free | Daily.

New York Transit Museum. Naturally, the Transit Museum is underground, in a 1938 subway station. The museum contains full-size classic subway cars dating back to the turn of the 20th century. There are also antique turnstiles, trolley models, and exhibits on the history of the subway system. Volunteers dressed as subway conductors give tours. | Decommissioned subway station at Boerum Pl. and Schermerhorn St. | 718/243–3060 | www.mta.nyc.ny.us/museum | $3 | Tues.–Fri. 10–4, weekends noon–5.

Prospect Park. The great Frederick Law Olmsted and Carter Vaux began construction of this park in 1866, and considered it superior to what they'd done with Central Park (which was just being completed at the time). One reason they favored Prospect was because there would be no streets dividing the park, and no skyscrapers bordering it. A number of restoration projects are planned or in progress. While guided tours are given, mostly April–November, it's rewarding just to wander the park's winding paths and undulating

hills. Key attractions include the Tennis House, the Kate Wollman Center and Rink (open for ice-skating November through March), and the Wildlife Center. | Bordered by Parkside Ave., Ocean Ave., Flatbush Ave., and Prospect Park W and SW | 718/965–8999 or 718/438–0100 | www.prospectpark.org.

ON THE CALENDAR

SEPT.: *Concert in the Garden.* Staged in the A. T. White Memorial Amphitheater, this concert's setting is almost as serene as its music. Relax amid Brooklyn Botanic Garden's delights and enjoy classical music performed by a full ensemble. | 1000 Washington Ave. | 718/623–7200.

DINING

Al Di La. Italian. This storefront trattoria with farmhouse tables wins raves from many Park Slope residents. There are also a lot of Manhattanites who cross the river to enjoy the modest Italian menu. Topping the choices are homemade pastas and steak *tagliata*. | 248 5th Ave., Park Slope | 718/783–4565 | Closed Tues. | $12–$20 | MC, V.

Cucina. Italian. One of the classiest restaurants in the Park Slope neighborhood, Cucina is not only elegant, with two candlelit dining rooms, but the menu is top-notch. Included among the selections are filet mignon, salmon, and striped sea bass. Antipasto bar. Kids' menu. | 256 5th Ave., Park Slope | 718/230–0711 | No lunch | $36–$45 | AE, D, DC, MC, V.

Embers. Continental. This crowded Bay Ridge steak house delivers prime meat at discount prices, as well as food ranging from Italian to French. | 9519 3rd Ave., Bay Ridge | 718/745–3700 | $15–$20 | MC, V.

Gage and Tollner. Contemporary. Original gas lights cast a flickering light on mahogany-paneled walls in the dining room of this landmark downtown restaurant. It all feels a bit like the turn of the 20th century. Traditional fare is served here: steaks, seafood, and a few pasta dishes. | 372 Fulton St., Downtown | 718/875–5181 | Closed Sun. No lunch Sat. | $18–$26 | AE, D, DC, MC, V.

Giando on the Water. Italian. The food doesn't really live up to the magnificent views this Williamsburg restaurant offers from its perch on the water, overlooking the Manhattan skyline. Although seafood is its claim to fame, the penne with vodka cream sauce and the veal chops are hits too. Pianist Friday and Saturday nights. | 400 Kent Ave., Williamsburg | 718/387–7000 | $20–$30 | AE, D, DC, MC, V.

Harvest. Southern. This unpretentious spot in Brooklyn's thriving Cobble Hill neighborhood serves terrific Southern food. The gumbo excels, and above-average crab cakes are lightly breaded and not trumped up with filler. Try the shredded pork platter in molasses marinade and order the homemade apple pie for a comforting conclusion. The intimate setting is a perfect complement to the food: downstairs, an open kitchen, zinc-topped bar, brick walls, and a red neon sign reading EATS say it all. Upstairs, blue-and-white checked cloths, hand-stenciled sheaths of wheat, and antique fruit labels adorn the cozy dining room. Breakfast. Sunday Brunch. Kids' menu. | 218 Court St., Cobble Hill | 718/624–9267 | Closed Mon. | $10–$18 | AE, DC, MC, V.

Henry's End. American. A cozy interior with an exposed brick wall and friendly service make this a Brooklyn Heights mainstay. The menu has some unexpected offerings, including wild game. | 44 Henry St., Brooklyn Heights | 718/834–1776 | No lunch | $16–$28 | AE, D, DC, MC, V.

Lundy Brothers. Seafood. This huge, famous, Sheepshead Bay restaurant closed in the 1970s, but reopened in splendor in the '90s. The menu is all about seafood. The Short Diner special, which includes but is not limited to lobster, chicken, chef's vegetables, potatoes, and fruit pie or ice cream, is delicious and filling, but the oysters and clams are also on the "must-taste" list. This open kitchen restaurant has stained-glass lamps hanging from the ceiling. | 1901 Emmons Ave., Sheepshead Bay | 718/743–0022 | Reservations essential | $16–$40 | AE, D, DC, MC, V.

Marco Polo. Italian. Exquisite service and a quiet environment make this one of the nicest restaurants in Caroll Gardens. The menu is good, if not exciting, and there's an elegant, old-worldliness to the place that draws diners. Appetizers include baked clams, Portobello mushrooms con polenta, oysters Rockefeller, stuffed artichokes, and escargot bourguignonne. Pianist, Wed.–Sun. | 345 Court St., Carroll Gardens | 718/852–5015 | $13–$25 | AE, DC, MC, V.

Peter Luger's. Steak. This New York institution, which looks like a German beer hall, is one of the best places in the city for beef. Don't miss the porterhouse. | 178 Broadway, Williamsburg | 718/387–7400 | $25–$50 | No credit cards.

River Cafe. American. Stunning views of the East River, the Brooklyn Bridge, and the Manhattan skyline make this a prime spot for romance. The food is good enough to take your mind off the view for a minute or two. The Sunday brunch menu highlights include fruit-wood-smoked whitefish, iced jumbo shrimp, and fried Ipswich clams, just to name a few. Pianist Mon.–Sun. Sunday brunch. | 1 Water St. | 718/522–5200 | Reservations essential | Jacket required | $70 prix fixe | AE, DC, MC, V.

Sunset Landing. Northern Italian. Regulars love the traditional fare served at this popular eatery formerly known as Abbracimento on the Pier. Try the Sunset Landing pasta, with shrimp, veal, and pasta in an oyster sauce, or the coconut shrimp. Pianist Fri., Sat. Sunday brunch. | 2200 Rockaway Pkwy. | 718/251–5517 | Reservations essential | $18–$36 | AE, DC, D, MC, V.

Tommaso's. Italian. This family-owned Bensonhurst restaurant serves home-style food the way Mama used to make it. Opera Thursday through Sunday evenings. | 1464 86th St., Bensonhurst | 718/236–9883 | No lunch | $13–$25 | AE, MC, V.

LODGING

Awesome Bed & Breakfast. Each room in this B & B in the Metrotech area, Brooklyn's main commercial district, exudes originality. Artists designed them with themes ranging from Ancient Madagascar to the Dragon's Palace. Complimentary Continental breakfast. No room phones, no TV. No pets. No smoking. | 136 Lawrence St. | 718/858–4859 | fax 212/858–4892 | www.awesome-bed-and-breakfast.com | 5 rooms | $110–$160 | MC, V.

Bed and Breakfast on the Park. This beautiful Park Slope brownstone was built in 1892 for George Bricklemyer, a whiskey mogul in his time. Every level of the house has wood paneling—some is African mahogany—stained glass, and parquet floors. Cable TV. | 113 Prospect Park W, between 6th and 7th Sts., Park Slope | 718/499–6115 | 7 rooms (2 with shared bath) | $125–$300 | No credit cards.

Brooklyn Marriott. Some rooms at this Downtown Marriott overlook the East River and the Brooklyn Bridge. Nine major subway lines are within one block. Restaurant, bar. Mini-bars, cable TV. Pool. Health club. | 333 Adams St., Downtown | 718/246–7000 | fax 718/246–0563 | 374 rooms | $185–$259 | AE, D, DC, MC, V.

Comfort Inn. Formerly the Gregory Hotel, this four-story hotel, built in 1926, is in a residential neighborhood, but is a short trek to all the action—two blocks from a subway station and 7 mi from Manhattan. Restaurant, bar, complimentary Continental breakfast. In-room data ports. Cable TV. Business services. No pets. | 8315 4th Ave. | 718/238–3737 | fax 718/680–0827 | www.comfortinn.com | 64 rooms, 6 suites | $169–$199 rooms, $219–$279 suites | AE, D, DC, MC, V.

Foy House. This Edwardian structure is Brooklyn's oldest bed and breakfast. The original owners of this houses were the Foy sisters, a wild pair of Wall Street workers who made their home a lavish social center in the Roaring '20s. Complimentary Continental breakfast. | 819 Carroll St., Park Slope | 718/636–1492 | 3 rooms (2 with shared bath) | $95–$125 (2-night minimum).

QUEENS

ATTRACTIONS

American Museum of the Moving Image. This entire museum is devoted to the technology, art, and history of the movie and television industries, with a collection that includes a Zoetrope (the giant spinning disk on which the first movies were shown) and costumes worn by Marlene Dietrich, Marilyn Monroe, and Robin Williams. There's a 190-seat theater, a 60-seat screening room, and 25,000 square ft of exhibition space. Hundreds of classic films are shown annually. | 35th Ave. at 36th St., Astoria | 718/784–4520 | $8.50 | Tues.–Fri. noon–5, weekends 11–6.

Flushing Meadow Corona Park. At 1,257 acres, this is by far Queens's largest park. It began, inauspiciously enough, as a swamp; then it was a garbage dump. It wasn't until the 1939 World's Fair that the park came into its own. Then, from 1946 until 1950, it served as the meeting ground for the newborn United Nations, and in 1964 it was the site of another World's Fair. The Queens Museum of Art and the Unisphere are still here from those fairs. | Grand Central Pkwy. to Van Wyck Expy., and Union Tpk. to Northern Blvd. | 718/760–6565 or 718/699–4209.

Queens Museum of Art. Painting and sculpture exhibits from classical to 20th-century are displayed on a rotating basis, but perhaps the museum's most famous attribute is the Panorama, on permanent view. This 9,000-square-ft highly detailed scale model of the city's five boroughs includes nearly every building, and is constantly updated. Follow signs through the park, across from Unisphere. | New York City Building, Flushing Meadow Corona Park, 111th St. at 49th Ave. | 718/592–5555 | $5 suggested donation | Tue.–Fri. 10–5, weekends noon–5.

New York Hall of Science. Considered one of the nation's finest science museums, the Hall of Science invites children and other would-be researchers to experiment with 160 hands-on exhibits, including everything from laser beams to microbes. | 111th St. and 48th Ave., in Flushing Meadow Corona Park | 718/699–0005 | $7.50; parking $6 | July–Aug., Tues.–Sun. 9:30–5, Mon. 9:30–2; Sept.–Dec., Tues. and Wed. 9:30–2, Thurs. and Fri. 9:30–5, weekends 11–5.

Shea Stadium. When this 55,777-seat stadium—home of the New York Mets—is filled, even nearby La Guardia airport's comings and goings are drowned out. | 126th St. and Roosevelt Ave. | 718/507–8499.

Isamu Noguchi Garden Museum. A large, open-air garden and two floors of gallery space hold more than 250 of Noguchi's pieces in stone, bronze, wood, clay, and steel. Videos document his long career. | 32-37 Vernon Blvd., Long Island City | 718/721–1932 | fax 718/278–2348 | www.noguchi.org | $4 suggested donation | Apr.–Oct., Wed.–Fri. 10–5, weekends 11–6.

Queens Botanical Garden. These lovely 39 acres of specialized plantings have a remarkably calming effect on visitors. This is the home of the city's largest rose garden, and also of bird and bee gardens, a pine cove, and magnificent formal gardens that flank the central mall. | 43-50 Main St. | 718/886–3800 | Tues.–Fri. 8–6, weekends 8–7.

Socrates Sculpture Park. Once an illegal dump site, this 4.3-acre park is devoted to large-scale public sculptures. Beyond the massive artworks a superb view of the river and Manhattan skyline awaits you. | Vernon Blvd. at Broadway, Long Island City | 718/956–1819 | Free | Daily 9–sunset.

ON THE CALENDAR

AUG.: *Hong Kong Dragon Boat Races.* Rowing teams from all over the country bring their eye-popping vessels to compete in this event. Other highlights of the weekend include martial-arts demonstrations, traditional dances, and an ethnic food court. | Flushing Meadow Park, Meadow Lake | 718/539–8974.

DINING

Elias Corner. Greek. There's always a line at this Astoria hot spot, where what's lacking in ambience is made up for in flavor. A meal including the tender grilled octopus appetizer and any of the market fresh fish entrées, accompanied by a bottle of Greek wine, is a fine way to spend an evening, romantic or otherwise. There's a charming garden in the back. | 24-02 31st St. | 718/932–1510 | No lunch | $15–$18 | No credit cards.

Jackson Diner. Indian. This popular Jackson Heights restaurant outgrew its tiny diner digs in 1998 and moved to a larger space down the block. In addition to enlarging the dining room, the owners hired architects and designers to create a more modern space with spice-color, earth-tone accents. Neighborhood folk and Manhattanites alike flock here for cheap, spicy, authentic Indian fare served in generous portions. | 37–47 74th St., Jackson Heights | 718/672–1232 | $10–$20 | No credit cards.

Karyatis. Greek. One of the oldest and most elegant of Astoria's Greek restaurants, airy multilevel Karyatis is perfect for a festive evening of live music and professional service. Whole grilled fish of the day, wonderful vegetables, and skillfully executed sauces (especially the traditional *avgolemono*, or egg-lemon) lead the list. | 35–03 Broadway, Astoria | 718/204–0666 | $20–$39 | AE, DC, MC, V.

Manducatis. Italian. This restaurant serves excellent pasta and has a surprisingly good wine list. It's a family-run business, all the way up to the family photos on the walls. Favorite dishes include the Shrimp *à la Ida* and the fried calamari. Of course, the home-made pastas are great. | 13–27 Jackson Ave., Long Island City | 718/729–9845 | Closed Sun. July–Aug. and last 2 weeks in Aug. No lunch Sat. | $9–$24 | AE, DC, MC, V.

Marbella. Spanish. This is a fun, family-owned restaurant, offering nothing but classic dishes from Galicia. The seafood with green sauce, shrimp with garlic, or the sea bass cooked in garlic and parsley and served in a white wine sauce are among the specials. Harpist Friday through Sunday. Parking. | 220–33 Northern Blvd., Bayside | 718/423–0100 | $12–$20 | AE, DC, MC, V.

Park Side. Italian. The food in this classic restaurant will leave you full for days. There are six rooms, seating 180 people total: the Marilyn Monroe room, one of two garden rooms, and the oak panel room are the nicest. | 107-01 Corona Ave., Corona | 718/271–9274 | $10–$25 | AE, DC, MC, V.

Piccola Venezia. Northern Italian. The food is pricey, especially for the outer boroughs, but fans say it is as good and authentic as it gets. Astoria native Tony Bennett calls it one of his favorites. Try classic fare like linguine with clam sauce or fettuccine Alfredo. The fish dishes are especially good. | 42-01 28th Ave., Astoria | 718/721–8470 | Closed Tues. and July 24–Aug. 24 | $19–$29 | AE, DC, MC, V.

Ubol's Kitchen. Thai. You'll know that the subway ride to Astoria is well worth it as soon as you dig into a tangy and spicy green papaya salad or the spicy squid salad. There's a variety of vegetarian entrées and all the house specials cooked in a clay pot are especially tasty. | 24-42 Steinway St. | 718/545–2874 | No lunch Mon.–Tues. | $7–$11 | AE, MC, V.

Water's Edge. American. Eating here makes you feel as if you're dining on an exclusive island. There is seating for up to 400 people, and from many tables you'll get beautiful views of Manhattan. Although the cuisine is labeled "American," there is a strong Continental essence to the well-prepared dishes. Some favorites include roasted rack of Lamb, English peas, and crab cakes. Free water shuttle. Open-air dining. Pianist Mon.–Sat. The restaurant offers a free water shuttle free from the 34th St. pier in Manhattan, on the East River. | East River and 44th Dr., Long Island City | 718/482–0033 | Reservations essential | Closed Sun. No lunch Sat. | $55 prix fixe | AE, D, DC, MC, V.

LODGING

Best Western. This Best Western is at JFK Airport, about 40 minutes to Manhattan. The rooms are basic, with simple furnishings. Restaurant, bar. In-room data ports, cable TV. Exercise equipment. Business services, airport shuttle. | 138-10 135th Ave., Jamaica | 718/322–8700 | fax 718/529–0749 | www.hilton.com | 333 rooms | $149–$265 | AE, D, DC, MC, V.

Crowne Plaza La Guardia. These basic accommodations, convenient to La Guardia Airport, are about 30 min from Manhattan. Desks with bright lighting, phones with data port, a comfortable sitting area, and a second phone by the bed are among the convenient in-room amenities if you need to do any business during your stay. Restaurant, bar. In-room data ports, some refrigerators, cable TV. Pool. Hot tub. Gym. Laundry facilities. Business services, airport shuttle. | 104-04 Ditmars Blvd., East Elmhurst | 718/457–6300 | fax 718/899–9768 | www.crowneplaza.com | 358 rooms (200 with shower only) | $129–$259 | AE, D, DC, MC, V.

Holiday Inn–JFK. This is a serviceable airport hotel, near JFK Airport. The design is basic, with off-white walls, printed linens, and a table and chair. Restaurant, bar, complimentary Continental breakfast. Cable TV. Pool. Hot tub, sauna. Gym. Business services, airport shuttle. | 144-02 135th Ave., Jamaica | 718/659–0200 | fax 718/322–2533 | 360 rooms | $159–$169 | AE, D, DC, MC, V.

Holy Family Bed & Breakfast. Situated in a 1924 town house, this B&B is affiliated with a Catholic family ministry, and is just a 3-min subway ride from midtown Manhattan. Or if you prefer, stroll two blocks and simply gaze at the Manhattan skyline from Gantry Plaza State Park. Feel free to use the full kitchen. Dining room, complimentary Continental breakfast. Library. Business services. No pets. | 10-11 49th Ave., Long Island City | 718/392–7597 | fax 718/786–3640 | www.bnbfinder.com/holyfamily | 4 rooms | $120–$300 | AE, MC, V.

Marriott La Guardia. This large, comfortable facility is convenient to La Guardia Airport and surrounding attractions. Among the closest are Queens Museum of Art (3 mi), Shea Stadium (2 mi), Yankee Stadium (7 mi), and Midtown Manhattan (6 mi). Restaurant, bar. In-room data ports, cable TV. Pool. Hot tub. Exercise equipment. Business services, airport shuttle. Pets allowed. | 102-05 Ditmars Blvd., East Elmhurst | 718/565–8900 | fax 718/898–4995 | www.marriotthotels.com/LGAAP | 436 rooms | $179 | AE, D, DC, MC, V.

Sheraton La Guardia East Hotel. This 16-story hotel, just 3 mi from La Guardia Airport, is within walking distance of Shea Stadium and the USTA National Tennis Center. Restaurant, bar, complimentary Continental breakfast. In-room data ports, minibars, some refrigerators, cable TV. Exercise equipment. Laundry services. Business services, airport shuttle. No pets. | 135-20 39th Ave. | 718/460–6666 | fax 718/445–2655 | www.sheraton.com | 164 rooms, 9 suites | $179–$250 rooms, $250–$300 suites | AE, D, DC, MC, V.

STATEN ISLAND

ATTRACTIONS

Conference House. Also known as Billopp House, this manor house was built by British naval captain Christopher Billopp in 1675. Its primary claim to fame is as the site of the only attempted peace conference during the American Revolution. | 7455 Hylan Blvd., Tottenville | 718/984–2086 | $2 | Mar.–Dec., Fri.–Sun. 1–4 (for guided tours).

High Rock Park in the Greenbelt. This is one of the best areas for bird-watching in the New York City area, with a peaceful 86-acre section of the vast park known as Greenbelt (nearly 2,000 contiguous acres in the center of Staten Island). Don't be surprised by the many school groups that come here. | 200 Nevada Ave., Egbertville | 718/667–2165 | Daily.

Historic Richmondtown. In 1685 Dutch, French, and English settlers founded Richmondtown, which is now the site of 26 historical buildings dating from 1690 to 1890. The oldest-known elementary school building in the country, Voorlezer's House, and a reconstructed 19th-century store, Stephens General Store, are two primary attractions. In summer, costumed craftspeople re-create a 19th-century village, but winter here has its charms, as well: from January to April, there are tavern concerts in a period tavern lit only by candles and heated (very well) only by a wood-burning store. | 441 Clarke Ave., Richmond and Arthur

Kill Rds. | 718/351–1611 | $4 | Apr.–June and Sept.–Dec., Wed.–Fri. and Sun. 1–5; July–Aug., Wed.–Fri. 10–5 and weekends 1–5; Jan.–Mar., call for hrs.

Jacques Marchais Museum of Tibetan Art. A full replica of a Buddhist temple, this museum holds a major collection of Tibetan art, including bronzes, sculptures, scrolls, paintings, and ritual artifacts. | 338 Lighthouse Ave., between New Dorp and Richmondtown | 718/987–3500 | $3 | Apr.–Nov., Wed.–Fri. 1–5; Dec.–Mar., shorter hrs or by appointment.

Snug Harbor Cultural Center. Originally a home for aged sailors in the 1840s, today there are 28 buildings on 83 acres of park land, which serve as performing arts facilities, as well as the homes of the Staten Island Botanical Garden and the Staten Island Children's Museum. | 1000 Richmond Terr., Livingston | 718/448–2500 or 718/815–SNUG | Daily 8–dusk.

Staten Island Zoo. This small zoo is best known for its "Serpentarium," which features reptiles and especially rattlesnakes; its aquarium, home to sharks and shrimp; an outdoor pool with flamingos; and an indoor re-creation of a tropical forest. The African Savannah at Twilight spotlights roaming tigers and leopards. Warning: the feeding schedules may sound enticing, but they are definitely not for the faint of heart. | 614 Broadway, Barrett Park, W. New Brighton | 718/442–3100 | $3, free Wed. 2–5 | Daily 10–4:45.

ON THE CALENDAR

OCT.: *Staten Island Half Marathon.* This annual event is the final race of the New York Road Runners Grand Prix series of half marathons held in each of the city's five boroughs. To accommodate Manhattanites, the race starts near the ferry terminal. | 212/860–4455.

DINING

Aesop's Tables. Contemporary. Though Manhattan dwellers don't often venture to Staten Island, this New American restaurant near the ferry is a good choice for a first excursion. Its pretty garden overlooks the Manhattan skyline, and the contemporary food is reasonably priced and well prepared. The menu changes daily. Look for dishes such as bacon-wrapped monkfish medallions and pan-seared duck breast with winter squash and pancetta risotto. Sunday brunch. | 1233 Bay St., Rosebank | 718/720–2005 | $14–$26 | AE, D, DC, MC, V.

LODGING

Harbor House Bed & Breakfast. This three-story B&B, built in 1890 in a residential neighborhood, is a short bus ride to the ferry. Each cozy room has a "New York" name, and is furnished with an eclectic mix of antique and contemporary furniture. (For example, the Staten Island suite has a full kitchen and a Victorian claw-foot bathtub). Harbor House attracts a varied clientele, including Europeans and Australians, who appreciate the low price and the safe neighborhood. Complimentary Continental breakfast. No pets. No smoking. | 1 Hylan Blvd. | 718/876–0056 | www.nyharborhouse.com | 11 rooms | $59–$150 | D, MC, V.

NIAGARA FALLS

MAP 3, C5

(Nearby towns also listed: Amherst, Buffalo, Grand Island, Lockport, Medina, Williamsville)

Niagara Falls, on the border of the United States and Canada, is one of the most famous tourist attractions in the world, and certainly one of the most beautiful.

You'll probably want to see the U.S. side first. Park in the lot on Goat Island near the American Falls and walk along the path beside the Niagara River, which becomes more and more turbulent as it approaches the big drop-off of nearly 200 ft. Be sure to go down to the lower level of Goat Island so you can get up close to Bridal Veil Falls itself—but don't fall in; every year there are newspaper accounts of people boating, swimming, or picnicking along the river who get caught up in the fast-flowing Niagara River and swept over the falls.

After enjoying the falls from the U.S. side, you can walk or drive across Rainbow Bridge to the Canadian side, where you can get a far view of the American Falls and a close-up of Horseshoe Falls. You can park your car for the day in any of several lots on the Canadian side, and hop onto one of the People Mover buses, which run continuously to all the sights along the river. If you want to get close to the foot of the falls, the *Maid of the Mist* boat takes you close enough to get soaked in the spray.

Information: **Niagara Falls Area Chamber of Commerce** | 345 3rd St., 14303 | 716/285–9141 | www.nfachamber.org.

Attractions

Aquarium of Niagara. Dive into a world of discovery with over 1,500 aquatic animals, including sharks, piranha, sea lions, and moray eels. The aquarium has sea-lion demonstrations daily and an outdoor harbor-seal exhibit. | 701 Whirlpool St. | 716/285–3575 or 716/692–2665 | fax 716/285–8513 | www.niagaranet.com/niagara/ | $7 | Late May–early Sept., daily 9–7; early Sept.–late May, daily 9–5.

Artpark. Niagara Falls's premier performing arts center offers reasonably priced, world-class musical theater, dance, classical, pop, and jazz concerts. The center is in a 202-acre state park in Lewiston, 7 mi north of the falls. | 150 S. 4th St., Lewiston | 716/754–9000 or 800/659–7275 | www.artpark.net | Call for schedule.

Bedore Tours. Full service tours of the falls, nearby parks, and observation spots. | 454 Main St. | 716/285–7550 or 800/538–8433 | www.niagarafallslive.com/bedore_tours_inc.htm | Daily.

Castellani Art Museum. Dedicated in 1990, this museum at Niagara University houses a permanent collection of 3,000 works. Styles range from the Hudson River School to Abstract Expressionism, and mediums include sculpture, drawing, and photography. There is also a substantial Pre-Columbian collection. | Rte. 104 W, Lewiston | 716/286–8200 | Free | Wed.–Sat. 11–5, Sun. 1–5.

Devil's Hole State Park. You can hike to the Niagara Falls gorge in this park overlooking the New York State Power Plant. You can also fish. Rest rooms are closed in winter. Follow signs from Robert Moses Parkway. | Devil's Hole State Park | 716/278–1770 | Free | Daily dawn–dusk.

Ft. Niagara State Park. You'll find picnic tables, shelters, swimming, nature programs, hiking, fishing, tennis, a boat-launch site, and a playground in this park, which surrounds Ft. Niagara. In winter there is cross-country skiing, snowmobiling, and sled slopes. In Youngstown, 10 mi north of Niagara Falls. | Rte. 18F | 716/745–7273 | June–Labor Day, $5 per vehicle; rest of the year, free | Daily.

Old Ft. Niagara provides an introduction to the fort's 300-year history with cannon and musket firings, historical reenactments, 18th-century military demonstrations, and archaeological programs. The fort's buildings date from 1726, and include a French castle. There's a museum shop and snack bar. In Youngstown, 10 mi north of Niagara Falls. Follow signs from Robert Moses Parkway. | Ft. Niagara State Park, Youngstown | 716/745–7611 | $6.75 | Jan.–Mar., daily 9–4:30; Apr., daily 9–5:30; May, weekdays 9–5:30, weekends 9–6:30; June, weekdays 9–6:30, weekends 9–7:30; July–Aug., daily 9–7:30; Sept., weekdays 9–5:30, weekends 9–6:30; Oct., daily 9–5:30; Nov.–Dec., daily 9–4:30.

Historical Society of the Tonawandas. Housed in an old railroad station circa 1870, the exhibits at this regional historical society include studies of Native Americans and the Erie Canal. | 113 Main St., North Tonawanda | 716/694–7406 | Free | Wed.–Fri. 10–4:45.

***Maid of the Mist* Boat Tour.** View the three falls from up close during a spectacular 1½-hour ride on this world-famous boat tour. Waterproof clothing is provided. To get to the boat launch, take the elevator in the Prospect Point Observation Tower, which descends to the base of the falls. | 151 Buffalo Ave., Prospect Park | 716/284–8897 | www.maid-ofthemist.com | $9.50 | Apr.–Memorial Day, 9:45–5:45; Memorial Day–Aug., 9–7:45; Aug.–Sept., 9–7; Sept.–late Oct., 9:45–4:45, weekdays only.

Niagara Falls Convention and Civic Center. Events include everything from rodeos to concerts. | 305 4th St. | 716/286–4769 | Call for schedule.

Niagara Power Project Visitor Center. Niagara Falls generates power at one of the largest hydroelectric plants in the world. The self-touring visitors center has hands-on exhibits and computer games and an explanation of how hydroelectric power is generated. | 5777 Lewiston Rd. (Rte. 104) | 716/285–3211 | Free | Daily 9–5.

Niagara Reservation State Park. This state park around Niagara Falls includes Prospect Point, Goat Island, Luna Island at Bridal Veil Falls, and Three Sisters Island. Witness the nightly illumination of the falls from here, and check out the visitors center and the Observation Tower and elevator, which takes you to the base of the falls. Follow signs from Robert Moses Parkway. | Niagara Reservation State Park | 716/278–1770 | fax 716/278–1744 | $5 per vehicle | Daily.

The **Prospect Park Visitor Center** provides tourist information, exhibits, a garden, and a snack bar. The giant-screen "thrill film" *History of Niagara* gets your attention with a virtual-reality helicopter simulator ride. | Prospect Park | 716/278–1796 | Free | Sun.–Thurs. 8–8:15; Fri.–Sat., 8–10:15.

The **Prospect Point Observation Tower** offers dramatic views of all three falls. A glass-walled elevator takes you above the falls and descends to the base for a boat tour. At the Niagara Reservation on the U.S. side of the falls. Follow signs from Robert Moses Parkway. | Prospect Park | 716/278–1762 | 50¢ | Daily.

Schoellkopf Geological Museum exhibits and shows relate to the 435 million-year geological history of the Niagara Gorge and the 12,000 years of the falls' recession. Follow signs from Robert Moses Parkway. | Schoellkopf Geological Museum | 716/278–1780 | $1 | Apr.–Memorial Day, 9–5; Memorial Day–Labor Day, 9–7; Labor Day–Oct., 9–5.

Goat Island provides access to Three Sisters Islands and Top of the Falls restaurant. It's a wonderful spot for a quiet walk and a close-up view of the rapids. | 716/278–1762.

Cave of the Winds Trip is a guided excursion along special walkways at the base of Bridal Veil Falls. Waterproof clothing is provided. | Cave of the Winds Facility Building, Goat Island | 716/278–1730 | $6 | May–mid-Sept., daily 8–8.

Niagara's Wax Museum of History. Exhibits of life-size wax figures depict events in the area's history. | 301 Prospect St. | 716/285–1271 | $4.95 | Daily 9:30 AM–11 PM.

Rainbow Air Inc. Observe the falls from a different angle: hover above them on this 10-min helicopter ride. | 454 Main St. | 716/284–2800 | fax 716/298–8179 | www.rainbowair-inc.com | rai@macronet.com | $50 | Mid-May–Oct., daily 9–dusk (weather permitting).

Reservoir State Park. This day-use facility has hiking, picnicking, fishing, and playing fields. At the junction of Routes 31 and 265. | Reservoir State Park | 716/278–1762 | Free | Daily.

Whirlpool State Park. Set near the falls, this park has nature trails, fishing, and hiking. Follow signs from Robert Moses Parkway. | Whirlpool State Park | 716/278–1770 | Free | Daily dawn–dusk.

Wintergarden. Over 7,000 trees are housed in this glass-enclosed botanical garden, making it a popular place for wedding ceremonies. | Rainbow Center, Rainbow Blvd. | 716/286–4940 | Free | Daily 9AM–10PM.

ON THE CALENDAR

APR.: *Earth Week Celebration.* Celebrate Earth Day at the aquarium. Presentations and special family activities are planned for an entire week. | Aquarium of Niagara, 701 Whirlpool St. | 716/285–3575.

JUNE: *Colonial Niagara District National Historic Landmark Celebration.* A celebra-

NIAGARA FALLS

INTRO
ATTRACTIONS
DINING
LODGING

tion of the area's designation as a national historic landmark. Includes guided trail tours, historic interpreters in period costumes, and more. In Lewiston, 7 mi north of Niagara Falls. | Artpark, 150 S. 4th St., Lewiston | 800/659–7275.

Dining

Alps Chalet. American. Although you won't actually have a view of the Alps, you will be in a Swiss-style building that has a fireplace and a patio, and is styled with dark wood, fake pine trees, and many photos of actual Alpine mountains. The menu ranges from chicken cordon bleu to barbecue and surf and turf. Kids' menu. | 1555 Military Rd. | 716/297–8990 | www.alpschalet.com | Closed Mon. No lunch Tues.–Thurs. | $9–$15 | AE, MC, V.

Buzzy's New York Style Pizza & Restaurant. Pizza. Buzzy's, an institution since 1953, serves up 30 different pies and calzones. For the adventurous eater, the chicken wings—fresh, not frozen—come with blue cheese dip and a choice of 10 sauces, including one called Suicide. | 7617 Niagara Falls Blvd. | 716/283–5333 | $6–$15 | AE, MC, V.

Clarkson House. American. Along with delicious steaks and lobsters, there's a lot of history in this restaurant, which housed in an antiques-filled 19th-century building. Kids' menu. | 810 Center St., Lewiston | 716/754–4544 | Reservations essential weekends | $11–$38 | AE, D, MC, V.

Como Restaurant. Italian. Since 1927, the Antonacci family has been serving traditional dishes from the south of Italy like veal à la Francesca, chicken cacciatore, and veal parmigiana. The interior evokes Italy with a stone fireplace and grapes hanging from the ceiling. Sunday brunch. Kids' menu. | 2220 Pine Ave., U.S. 62A | 716/285–9341 | www.fallscasino.com/como | $8–$18 | AE, D, MC, V.

Crown Chinese Buffet. Chinese. This family-owned restaurant serves Cantonese, Szechuan, and Hunan delicacies as well as sushi. The seafood and spareribs are favorites. | 7325 Niagara Falls Blvd. | 716/283–7080 | $6–$15 | AE, MC, V.

Hard Rock Cafe. American. It's the view that's unusual at this Hard Rock Cafe, located just 500 ft from the brink of the falls. Other than that it's the usual burgers and rock-and-roll memorabilia. | 333 Prospect St. | 716/282–0007 | Reservations not accepted | $15–$20 | AE, D, DC, MC, V.

John's Flaming Hearth. American. Forget the usual men's club steak-house decor: John's serves its New York strip steak and filet mignon in haute surroundings. Enjoy the elegance of red-velvet booths (the Voltaire Room), high-backed chairs surrounded by mirrors and chandeliers (the Gold Room), or a garden atrium (Anna's Room). Try the herb-crusted lamb, salmon with lobster, or daily specials. Entertainment Saturday. Kids' menu. Early bird dinners. | 1965 Military Rd. | 716/297–1414 | $12–$20 | AE, D, DC, MC, V.

Macri's Palace. Italian. This casual spot is in the heart of Niagara Falls's Little Italy, in the City Market farmers' market. The specialty is southern Italian dishes like pasta and chicken parmigiana, but they also serve seafood. Kids' menu. | 755 W. Market St. | 716/282–4707 | $20–$25 | AE, MC, V.

Olde Fort Inn. Continental. This colonial inn in Youngstown is known for barbecued ribs, Angus beef, and Maryland crab cakes. Bread and desserts are homemade. Near Artpark in Youngstown, 15 mi south of Niagara Falls. Early bird dinners. Friday fish fry. Kids' menu. | 110 Main St., Youngstown | 716/745–7141 | www.youngstownnet.net/oldefort.htm | Closed Mon. No lunch | $10–$25 | AE, MC, V.

Red Coach Inn. Continental. This cozy English tavern in the traditional Red Coach Inn has something most pubs can't claim: a spectacular view of the falls' upper rapids. Try the slow-roasted prime rib of beef or a broiled, 8-oz lobster tail with black-pepper fettuccine. The main dining room has a cozy stone fireplace; the patio, for outdoor dining in summer, is strewn with flowers. Kids' menu. | 2 Buffalo St. | 716/282–1459 | www.redcoach.com | $15–$20 | D, DC, MC, V.

Riverside Inn. Continental. Breathtaking views of Niagara Gorge and amazing sunsets make this a popular honeymooners' dining spot. Try the aged Angus beef or the Maine lobster. Entertainment. Kids' menu. Early bird dinners. | 115 S. Water St., Lewiston | 716/754–8206 | $9–$30 | AE, D, DC, MC, V.

Lodging

Best Western Inn on the River. This chain motel is on the Niagara River, 4 mi north of the falls. Complimentary Continental breakfast is served. Restaurant, bar (with entertainment), room service. Cable TV. Pool. Sauna. Dock. Video games. Laundry facilities. Business services. | 7001 Buffalo Ave. | 716/283–7612 | fax 716/283–7631 | www.bestwestern.com | 150 rooms | $99–$129 | AE, D, DC, MC, V.

Best Western Summit Inn. This comfortable chain is in a quiet suburban setting just minutes from shopping and a casino. Restaurant, bar. Cable TV. Pool. Sauna. Business services. Pets allowed. | 9500 Niagara Falls Blvd. | 716/297–5050 | fax 716/297–0802 | www.bestwestern.com | 88 rooms | $89–$109 | AE, D, DC, MC, V.

Chateau Motor Lodge. This motel on Grand Island, 5 mi from the falls, offers affordable, basic rooms with contemporary furnishings. Some kitchenettes, microwaves, cable TV. Some pets allowed. | 1810 Grand Island Blvd., Grand Island | 716/773–2868 | fax 716/773–5173 | 17 rooms | $50–$80 | AE, D, MC, V.

Comfort Inn at The Pointe. They say you can feel the mist from the falls here, at this modern chain just 500 ft away. Some rooms have a view of the river. Restaurant, complimentary Continental breakfast. Some in-room hot tubs, cable TV. Shops, video games. Business services. | 1 Prospect Pointe | 716/284–6835 or 800/284–6835 | fax 716/284–5177 | 118 rooms | $118–$139 | AE, D, DC, MC, V.

Driftwood Inn Motor Lodge. This low-budget motel offers affordable rooms. Some refrigerators. Pool. | 2754 Niagara Falls Blvd. | 716/692–6650 or 800/500–1765 | 20 rooms | $34–$87 | AE, D, MC, V.

Econo Lodge. This chain near a factory-outlet mall has standard rooms, some with a pool view. Some deluxe rooms have hot tubs and king-size beds. Some in-room hot tubs, cable TV. Pool. Business services. | 7708 Niagara Falls Blvd. | 716/283–0621 | fax 716/283–2121 | www.econolodge.com | 70 rooms | $109–$149 | AE, D, DC, MC, V.

Elizabeth House. This three-story, Georgian-style home built in 1922 has a backyard, deck, patio, and pool. On chilly days, you can curl up with a book in the library or listen to music in the sunroom. Rooms have floral-pattern fabrics, lace insets in the windows, and antique furnishings. Complimentary breakfast. Cable TV in common area. Pool. Library. | 327 Buffalo Ave. | 716/285–1109 | www.elizabethhousebandb.com | info@elizabethhousebandb.com | 4 rooms (2 with shared bath) | $60–$100 | AE, MC, V.

Fallsview Travelodge Hotel. True to Niagara Falls's honeymoon tradition, some rooms have king-size beds and red, heart-shaped hot tubs. Just one block east of the falls, this property in a brown-brick building has some rooms with views of the upper Niagara River. Restaurant, bar. Some refrigerators, cable TV. Business services. Pets allowed. | 201 Rainbow Blvd. | 716/285–9321 or 888/515–6375 | fax 716/285–2539 | www.niagarafallstravelodge.com | 193 rooms | $89–$199 | AE, D, DC, MC, V.

Hanover House. Artist Paul Hanover, known for his paintings of Niagara and Adirondack scenery, keeps his studio in this enchanting Victorian B&B. Lovely period furnishings brighten the rooms. The many common areas—library, tea nook, living room, sunporch, and dining room—make for homey retreats after a day of sightseeing. Complimentary breakfast. No pets. No kids under 8. No smoking. | 610 Buffalo Ave. | 716/278–1170 or 877/848–0543 | 5 rooms | $120–$130 | MC, V.

Holiday Inn–Grand Island. This resort-type hotel with an adjacent golf course and marina is on Grand Island, about 12 mi south of Niagara Falls. Some rooms have views of the Niagara River. Restaurant, bar. Cable TV. 2 pools, wading pool. Hot tub, massage. Gym. Playground. Business services. | 100 White Haven Rd., Grand Island | 716/773–1111 or 800/465–4329 | fax 716/773–1229 | www.basshotels.com/holiday-inn | 262 rooms | $129–$159 | AE, D, DC, MC, V.

Howard Johnson Inn at the Falls. You can walk to Cave of the Winds, the Casino Niagara, the Niagara Aquarium, and many other attractions from this chain motel. Restaurant. Some in-room hot tubs, cable TV. Pool. Sauna. Laundry facilities. Business services. | 454 Main St. | 716/285–5261 or 800/282–5261 | fax 716/285–8536 | 82 rooms | $95–$229 | AE, D, DC, MC, V.

Linda Ann's House Bed & Breakfast. Here's a B&B that doesn't take itself too seriously. In fact, fun is serious business in the common room: kick back amid the 1950s memorabilia and enjoy the billiard table, soda bar, big-screen TV, and sauna. Complimentary breakfast. Some refrigerators, cable TV. No pets. No smoking. | 745 4th St. | 716/285–7907 | www.lindaannsbb.com | 4 rooms | $65–$165 | No credit cards.

Manchester House. Dating to 1903, this cozy Victorian B&B is less than a mile from the falls. Relax in the common sitting room with books, board games, and a spinet piano. You can even get acquainted with the Manchester House's friendly resident cat. Complimentary breakfast. Cable TV in common area. No pets. No kids under 6. No smoking. | 653 Main St. | 716/285–5717 or 800/489–3009 | fax 716/282–2144 | www.manchesterhouse.com | 3 rooms | $60–$100 | D, MC, V.

Park Place. Once the home of Union Carbide founder James G. Marshall, this B&B was built and furnished in the Arts and Crafts style. An antique Chickering piano for guest use, a veranda, and a dining-room fireplace will warm your heart, soul, and toes. This home is an easy walk to Horseshoe and American waterfalls as well as the Rainbow Bridge and Goat Island. Complimentary breakfast. No pets. No smoking. | 740 Park Pl. | 716/282–4626 or 800/510–4626 | 4 rooms | $60–$105 | AE, MC, V.

Portage House. This no-frills motel is a good budget choice near Artpark and other Lewiston attractions. Cable TV, no room phones. | 280 Portage Rd., Lewiston | 716/754–8295 | fax 716/754–1613 | 21 rooms | $50–$60 | AE, D, MC, V.

Rainbow House Bed & Breakfast. Antiques, hand-painted furniture, and Niagara Falls memorabilia give this turn-of-the-20th-century B&B its gracious appeal. Its location on the Seaway Trail—the 454-mi scenic National Recreational Trail that parallels Lake Erie, Lake Ontario, and the St. Lawrence Seaway—makes it an ideal stopover for bikers and backpackers looking for a little luxury. Honeymooners also love this spot. A wedding chapel on the premises lets them have the ceremony, reception, and honeymoon all in one place. Complimentary breakfast. Cable TV in common area. No pets. No kids under 9. No smoking. | 423 Rainbow Blvd. S | 716/282–1135 or 800/724–3536 | fax 716/282–1135 | www.rainbowhousebb.com | 4 rooms | $60–$100 | MC, V.

Ramada Inn at the Falls. You can hear the cascading falls from this hotel, which is within walking distance of the U.S. falls and Canadian border. Shopping, restaurants, and many other attractions are just a few blocks away. There's a tour desk and gift shop in the lobby. Restaurant, bar. Cable TV. Pool. Hot tub. Business services. | 240 Rainbow Blvd. | 716/282–1212 or 888/298–2054 | fax 716/282–1216 | 217 rooms, 8 suites | $60–$95 rooms, $95–$150 suites | AE, D, DC, MC, V.

Ramada Inn–Fourth Street. This chain hotel is within walking distance of area attractions. Some rooms have hot tubs. Tours leave from the lobby. Restaurant. Cable TV. Pool. Laundry facilities. Business services. | 219 4th St. | 716/282–1734 or 800/333–2557 | fax 716/282–1881 | 112 rooms | $49–$169 | AE, D, DC, MC, V.

Red Coach Inn. Established in 1923 and modeled after the Old Bell Inn in Finedon, England, this inn has wood-burning fireplaces and a spectacular view of Niagara Falls's upper rapids. Unique guest rooms—with names like the London Room, Bristol Suite, and Windmere Suite—are furnished with antiques, and there are 12 large, luxurious suites. Old-world service includes champagne and a cheese tray presented when you arrive. Restaurant, bar, complimentary Continental breakfast, room service. Kitchenettes (in suites), cable TV. Business services. | 2 Buffalo Ave. | 716/282–1459 | fax 716/282–2650 | www.redcoach.com | 2 rooms, 12 suites | $79–$159 rooms, $119–$219 suites | AE, D, DC, MC, V.

Sands Hotel. This motel is a budget-price alternative for travelers who want a comfortable room and a convenient location for sightseeing. Not just a cookie-cutter roadside motel, this place has retro charm with low-key, friendly service. Picnic area. Refrigerators, cable TV. Pool. | 9393 Niagara Falls Blvd. | 716/297–3797 | www.travelbase.com/destinations/niagara-falls/sands-motel/ | sands-motel@travelbase.com | 17 rooms | $28–$75 | AE, D, DC, MC, V.

Thriftlodge. This budget option is within walking distance of a factory-outlet mall and close to all area attractions. Just 4 mi from Niagara Aquarium, Cave of the Winds, Niagara Casino, and Falls Mall of the Mist. Picnic area. Refrigerators, some in-room hot tubs, cable TV. Pool. Laundry facilities. Business services. | 9401 Niagara Falls Blvd. | 716/297–2660 or 888/515–6375 | fax 716/297–7675 | www.thriftlodge.com | 45 rooms | $45–$100 | AE, D, DC, MC, V.

NORTH CREEK

MAP 3, K4

(Nearby towns also listed: Blue Mountain Lake, Bolton Landing, Schroon Lake, Speculator, Ticonderoga, Warrensburg)

If it's the outdoors you want, look no farther than North Creek, a small town wholly located within the Adirondack Park, between the mountains and the Hudson River Gorge. Since the early part of the 20th century, North Creek has been the kind of place people think of when they envision vacationing in the Adirondacks: a great base for skiing, hiking, mountain biking, white-water rafting, canoeing and kayaking, and viewing pretty mountain scenery.

Information: Gore Mountain Regional Chamber of Commerce | Box 84, 12853 | 518/251–2612 | www.goremtnregion.org.

Attractions

Gore Mt. Garnet Mine. The Gore Mountain mine, started in 1878, is one of the largest garnet mines in the world. Guided tours include a walk through an open-pit mine 800 ft below ground. Tours leave from the Gore Mountain Mineral Shop. | Burton Mine Rd. | 518/251–2706 | $3 | June–Labor Day, Mon.–Sat. 9–4.

Hudson River Rafting Co. Choose from a variety of river-rafting adventures, with trips leaving from Cunningham's Ski Barn. | 1 Main St. | 518/251–3215 or 800/888–7238 | $75 per person for a full day of rafting | Apr.–Aug, daily at 9 AM, Sept.–Columbus Day, weekends and holidays at 9 AM.

Skiing. The Adirondacks boast some of the finest skiing in the Northeast. With high peaks, steep slopes, and an abundance of snow, it's not surprising that the Adirondacks and skiing have been synonymous for decades.

The state-owned and operated **Gore Mt. Ski Center** has a 2,100-ft vertical drop and 62 trails, offering some of the longest (up to 1½ mi) runs in the East. Has a wide variety of trails, snowmaking, a detachable high-speed triple chair, a quad chair, and a detachable high-speed heated gondola. | Peaceful Valley Rd. | 518/251–2411 or 800/342–1234 | info@gore-mountain.com | www.goremountain.com | Nov.–Apr., daily; June–mid.-Oct., weekends for gondola.

The four-season **Garnet Hill Ski Lodge and Cross-Country Ski Center** relies heavily on cross-country skiing. With over 120 inches of snow each year, skiing is often available into the spring. Visitors can cross-country ski a 4-mi route downhill and be shuttled back to the lodge. There are 56 km of groomed trails. Offers night skiing, lessons, rental equipment, and a ski shop. There are no alpine downhill trails. In summer, swimming, boating, and tennis are available. In North River, 5 mi west of North Creek. | 13th Lake Rd., North River | 518/251–2444, 518/251–2821, or 800/497–4207 | Daily.

Upper Hudson River Railroad. This scenic railroad offers unparalleled views of the Hudson. The 2-hr, round-trip excursion runs along an 8½-mi section of the former Adirondack Branch of the D&H Railroad. | 3 Railroad Pl. | 518/251–5334 | $10 | May–Oct.

ON THE CALENDAR

MAY: *Annual Whitewater Derby.* The white-water derby is a gathering for canoeing, kayaking, and camping on the Upper Hudson River. There's also a music festival and a street fair with rides, food, and game booths. | Rte. 28 | 518/251–2612 or 800/896–5428.

SEPT.: *Teddy Roosevelt Festival.* This annual event, held along Main Street, commemorates Teddy Roosevelt's train ride from the Adirondacks to Washington, D.C., to take office as president. Music, a parade, activities for children, train rides, and a barbecue are all part of the celebration. | 518/251–2612 | Free.

Dining

Casey's North Restaurant & Tavern. American. Try the blackened salmon—or any of the other sandwiches, nachos, soups, steaks, or salads—at this casual, lodge-style restaurant. Friendly, capable servers and reasonable prices make it a preferred destination for families after a day on the slopes. If you're busy, order a boxed lunch to go. | 3195 Rte. 28 | 518/251–5836 | $6–$14 | AE, MC, V.

Trapper's Tavern. Continental. After a day on the mountain, unwind in front of the large stone fireplace at this rustic eatery in the Copperfield Inn. Exposed beams, deer-antler chandeliers, and a wooden bar set Trapper's apart from Gardens, the more formal of the inn's two restaurants. A pub-style menu is served from noon until midnight. | 307 Main St. | 518/251–2500 or 800/424–9910 | $7–$15 | AE, MC, V.

Lodging

Black Mountain Ski Lodge. This family motel is located in a quiet country setting just minutes from Gore Mountain Ski Center. A dark-wood exterior and wood-paneling walls in the guest rooms give it a rustic chalet look. Restaurant. Some refrigerators, cable TV. Pool. Playground. Pets allowed. | 2999 Rte. 8 | 518/251–2800 | www.blackmountainskilodge.com | 25 rooms | $41–$51 | AE, D, MC, V.

Copperfield Inn. This white clapboard inn at the base of Gore Mountain has a living room with fireplace and other inviting public spaces. Gardens restaurant serves a Continental menu in a setting of chandeliers and crystal; the more casual tavern/sports bar serves pub food and has live music nightly. Guest rooms have pull-out loveseat sofas and marble bathroom floors. Suites have marble bathrooms, hot tubs, and spacious living rooms, some with a view of the Hudson River. Restaurant. Pool. Beauty salon, outdoor hot tub, massage, sauna. Tennis. Health club. | 307 Main St. | 518/251–2500 or 800/424–9910 | www.copperfield-inn.com | 24 rooms, 7 suites | $120–$230 rooms, $175–$355 suites | AE, D, DC, MC, V.

Garnet Hill Lodge and Crosscountry Ski Center. This rustic Adirondack inn overlooks mountains and a pristine private lake, and was built in the tradition of the Adirondack great camps, with hewn beams and posts and a front porch spanning the length of the house. Located 5 mi from Gore Mountain Ski Center, the lodge accommodates guests in five distinctive buildings. The Log House is an Adirondack lodge with a view of the lake and mountains, and a cozy fireplace area surrounded by sofas and rocking chairs. The Big Shanty is a turn-of-the-20th-century Adirondack house set on a hill above the lake. Curl up next to the stone fireplace, surrounded by shelves of old books and rustic yellow birch log pillars. Larger groups can be accommodated in the few guest rooms at The Birches (set in a grove of white birch trees), the Tea House, and the Ski Haus. Restaurant. TV in common room. Sauna. Tennis. Hiking, beach, boating, fishing, bicycles. Cross-country skiing. Business services. Pets allowed in Ski Haus. | 13th Lake Rd. | 518/251–2821 or 800/497–4207

| fax 518–251–3089 | garnet@netheaven.com | www.garnet-hill.com | 29 rooms (26 with bath) | $72–$125 | MC, V.

Goose Pond Inn. This lovely, antiques-filled B&B, built in 1894, is just 1 mi from Gore Mountain. Set on bucolic grounds bordered by stone walls, the inn overlooks a pond that is home to the owner's two tame geese. Free shuttle to the mountain is available. Complimentary breakfast. No TV in some rooms, TV in common area. | 196 Main St. | 518/251–3434 or 800/806–2601 | www.goosepondinn.com | 4 rooms | $70–$115 | No credit cards.

Inn at Gore Mountain. Set on 6 acres of white birch and pine, this mountain retreat enchants outdoor enthusiasts year-round. Its proximity to Gore Mountain Ski Area (the inn is just 500 ft from the ski area's access road) make it perfect for a winter stay. And the many hiking and biking trails, as well as the nearby Hudson River, keep it busy all year. A family-friendly attitude prevails: half of the rooms include bunk beds, and children under 8 stay free. Restaurant. Cable TV. | 711 Peaceful Valley Rd. | 518/251–2111 | inngore@superior.net | 16 rooms | $49–$75 | MC, V.

NORTH SALEM

(Nearby towns also listed: Brewster, Carmel/Lake Carmel, Mahopac)

Home to about 5,000 people, North Salem has some of the prettiest rural landscapes in northern Westchester County, complete with gently rolling hills, streams, ponds, horse farms, narrow winding roads, and lovely old houses. The area was a camp for General de Rochambeau and his French troops after their victory in Yorktown that ended the Revolutionary War. Shortly thereafter, North Salem bustled with factories and mills, churning out everything from dairy and lumber products to tools and clothes. The town is also known for its contribution to the early-American circus; residents founded the first touring circus syndicate, which made its way throughout the United States and South America. Their travels introduced new circus animals—including the hippopotamus—to American audiences.

Information: Brewster Chamber of Commerce | 31 Main St., Brewster, 10509 | 845/279–2477 | www.brewsterchamber.com.

Attractions
Hammond Museum and Japanese Stroll Gardens. This cross-cultural center features changing exhibitions related to Eastern and Western cultures, as well as a 3½-acre Japanese stroll garden that is beautiful in all seasons. There is also a café with outdoor dining on a tree-lined terrace. | Deveau Rd. | 845/669–5033 | www.hammondmuseum.org | $4 | Wed.–Sat. noon–3.

North Salem Vineyard. Westchester's only vineyard and winery has 18 acres of grapes, planted by George Naumburg almost 35 years ago. | 441 Hardscrabble Rd. | 845/669–5518 | www.north-salemvineyard.com | Free | Weekends 1–5 and by appointment.

ON THE CALENDAR
AUG.: *Wine and Food Festival.* Twelve Hudson Valley wineries, three restaurants, and several farms offer tastes of the region in celebration of 30-plus years of growing wine grapes in North Salem. | North Salem Vineyard | 845/669–5518.

Dining
Auberge Maxime. French. Set amid rolling tree-covered hills, this elegant French restaurant serves up such specialties as roast duck with berry medley and braised lamb shank. The elegant interior is warmed by candlelight, white tablecloths, floral draperies, and

upholstered seats. Dine outside on the terrace for a view of the manicured grounds and hills beyond. | 721 Titicus Rd. | 914/669–5450 | www.aubergemaxime.com | Jacket required | Closed Wed. | $23–$29 | AE, DC, MC, V.

Purdys Homestead. Contemporary. This restaurant has the sophistication of the city minus the attitude. The 18th-century farmhouse with three fireplaces has been updated to look sleek and welcoming. Try the rainbow trout or the buttery breaded chicken breasts flavored with chives. The elaborate Sunday brunch brims with oysters, foie gras, omelettes, crêpes, poached salmon, and grilled lamb. | 100 Titicus Rd. | 914/277–2301 | Closed Mon. | $25–$29 | AE, D, DC, MC, V.

NORTHPORT

MAP 4, I5

(Nearby town also listed: Huntington)

The Matinecock Indians were the first inhabitants of what is today one of north-shore Long Island's oldest and most charming villages. Originally known as Cow Harbor, Northport was incorporated in 1895 and today is a thriving, picture-postcard village on Route 25A's Heritage Trail.

A true nautical village, Northport's scenic harbor area is filled with Victorian houses, some built by old sea captains. The downtown shopping area is south of the harbor, and another shopping area is hidden away to the north in Northport's historic district.

Information: **Northport Chamber of Commerce** | 316 Main St., 11768 | 631/754–3905 | www.northportny.com.

Attractions

Centerport Beach. This small beach stretches 230 ft along Northport Bay on Long Island Sound. Facilities include picnicking in the pavilion area, a senior center, a playground, an aid station, outdoor showers, and small boat racks. Off Little Neck Road. | Centerport Beach, Centerport | 631/261–4207 or 631/261–7574 (in season) | Free | June–Labor Day, daily.

Crab Meadow Beach. Basketball and volleyball courts, a playground, a restaurant, a snack bar, a boardwalk, outdoor showers, and an aid station are set along 1,000 ft of beachfront on Long Island Sound's Northport Bay. | 447 Waterside Ave. | 631/261–7574 | Fee | June–Labor Day, daily.

Eaton's Neck Lighthouse. Built in 1799, the 50-ft tower on the Coast Guard Station is open for group tours only with advance reservations. | Lighthouse Rd. | 631/261–6959 | Free | Weekends.

Northport Historical Society and Museum. Built by Andrew Carnegie in 1914 as the village library, this structure now houses exhibits on the history, culture, and geography of Northport and its environs. There's also walking tours of Northport, educational programs, lectures, and a museum shop. | 215 Main St. | 631/757–9859 | Tues.–Sun. 1–4:30.

Suffolk County Vanderbilt Museum and Planetarium. William K. Vanderbilt's 24-room Moroccan-style mansion called Eagles Nest sits on 43 lovely acres overlooking Northport Harbor and houses collections that Vanderbilt acquired as he traveled throughout the world. The adjacent planetarium is one of the best equipped in the nation, featuring a 60-ft sky theater. Sky shows are held regularly. In Centerport, 3 mi southeast of Northport. | 180 Little Neck Rd., Centerport | 631/854–5555 | $8 | Tues.–Sat. 10–5, Sun. noon–4.

Sunken Meadow State Park. This 1,200-acre beachfront state park features three 9-hole golf courses. It also boasts a plethora of playgrounds, basketball courts, softball fields, and trails and offers cross-country skiing. There are bicycle trails, a driving range, a 3-mi beach, showers, a soccer field, an aid station, tournaments, and children's shows. Take Sunken Meadow Parkway north and follow signs for the park. | Sunken Meadow State Pkwy. | 631/269–4333 | $7 | Daily dawn–dusk.

ON THE CALENDAR
APR.: *Earth Day.* Budding conservationists will love the village's Clean the Bay event, when the fire department scuba team dives into the harbor to clean out debris. There are recycling demonstrations, entertainment, and refreshments. | 631/754–3905.
MAY: *Spring Maypole Celebration.* Dancers from the local ballet school teach children to dance around the maypole. Refreshments are offered. | 631/754–3905.
SEPT.: *Cow Harbor Day.* Events include a world-class 10K run.
NOV.: *Winterfest.* This annual winter holiday celebration takes place the day after Thanksgiving with a tree lighting in the waterfront Village Park and kicks off the holiday shopping season. Carolers and Santa's helpers serve hot chocolate. | 631/754–3905.

Dining

Mill Pond Inn. Continental. Giant picture windows provide a view of the waterfront at one of the last waterside restaurants in Centerport. The quaint little dining room in this turn-of-the-20th-century building retains its original charm. Try the homemade lobster bisque or mixed seafood platters with lobster tail, stuffed shrimp, and baked clams; other specialties include broiled fillet of flounder and blackened catfish. The cheesecake and other desserts are homemade. The Mill Pond is also home to the oldest piano lounge on Long Island, open Thursday–Sunday after 9 PM. Kids' menu. Sunday brunch. Free parking. On Route 25A in Centerport, 7 mi east of Northport. | 437 E. Main St., Centerport | 631/261–5353 | Closed Mon. | $16–$28 | AE, D, DC, MC, V.

Pumpernickels Restaurant. German. This cozy restaurant at the entrance of beautiful Northport village is known for its sauerbraten and seafood. The dining room has lots of candles and fresh flowers. There's often live music on weekends. | 640 Main St. | 631/757–7959 | $13–$20 | AE, D, DC, MC, V.

Sea Shanty. Seafood. Chances are you'll wait for one of the 10 tables here, but you won't be disappointed with the seafood—or the water view, which extends across the harbor. This casual spot is known for baked clams, flounder with crabmeat stuffing, crab cakes, fried calamari, and seasonal soft-shell lobsters plucked right out of the harbor. Service is family style. Kids' menu. Beer and wine only. | 16 Woodbine Ave. | 631/261–8538 | Reservations not accepted | $10–$18 | AE, D, DC, MC, V.

Ship's Inn. American. Sit in a candlelit booths and dig into mussels marinara, crab cakes, soft-shell crabs, or prime rib (on Wednesdays). The ship theme is heightened with polished mahogany and brass nautical details. Kids' menu. Early bird dinners. Sunday brunch. Dock space. No smoking. Free parking. | 78 Main St. | 631/261–3000 | $13–$22 | AE, D, DC, MC, V.

Lodging

Hampton Inn. This five-story motel, 3 mi south of Northport, is convenient to North Shore businesses and shopping areas. It is 2 mi from the Long Island Railroad and 10 mi from the ocean. Hamlet Golf and Tennis Club, home of the Hamlet Challenge Cup, is a mile away. Refrigerators, cable TV. Gym. Laundry services. No pets. | 680 Commack Rd., Commack | 631/462–5700 or 800/426–7866 | fax 631/462–9735 | www.hampton-inn.com | 144 rooms | $110–$150 | AE, D, DC, V.

NORWICH

MAP 3, H7

(Nearby towns also listed: Bainbridge, Cortland, Greene, Hamilton)

This small city on Route 12 is about 60 mi south of the New York Thruway at Utica, and almost 40 mi north of Binghamton. Norwich is home of the Northeast Classic Car Museum, the Chenango County Historical Society Museum, and some local galleries.

Information: Chenango County Chamber of Commerce | 29 Lackawanna Ave., 13815 | 607/334–1400 or 800/556–8596 | www.chenangony.org or www.chenangony.com.

Attractions

Chenango County Historical Society Museum. Here you'll find handicrafts of early settlers, Native American artifacts, and Chenango Canal history. On Route 23. | 45 Rexford St. | 607/334–9227 | $2 suggested donation | Wed.–Fri. and Sun. 1–4.

Northeast Classic Car Museum. This museum has a classic and antique car collection. | 24 Rexford St. | 607/334–AUTO or 800/556–8596 | www.classiccarmuseum.org | $7 | Daily 10–5.

ON THE CALENDAR

AUG.: *Chenango County Fair.* For more than 150 years, Chenango Countyites have been gathering annually to show off their livestock and enjoy rides, food, and local entertainment. | 607/334–1400.

Dining

Nina's Pizzeria. Pizza. Locals frequent this family-owned restaurant for its fresh Italian-American cooking at reasonable prices. Nina's offers classic dishes as well as pizzas and desserts. | 32 Broad St. | 607/334–6278 | $6–$15 | AE, MC, V.

Lodging

Fred's Inn. Previously just a steak house, Fred's expanded in 1998 to include lodging as well. You'll find tasteful motel-style rooms with parking just steps from your door. Restaurant, room service. In-room data ports, refrigerators, microwaves, some in–room hot tubs, cable TV. No pets. | 5149 Rte. 12 | 607/334–9282 | fax 607/336–6767 | 13 rooms | $99–$159 | AE, D, DC, MC, V.

Howard Johnson Hotel. This chain hotel is located in the historic downtown area. Restaurant, bar. Some in-room hot tubs, some refrigerators, cable TV. Pool. Business services. Some pets allowed (fee). | 75 N. Broad St. | 607/334–2200 | fax 607/336–5619 | www.hojo.com | 83 rooms, 4 suites | $69–$99 rooms, $159 suites | AE, D, DC, MC, V.

Super 8. This three-story member of the chain was built in 1990 and offers standard rooms, just off Rte. 12, about 1 mi north of town. Picnic area, complimentary Continental breakfast. Refrigerators (in suites), cable TV. | 6067 Rte. 12 | 607/336–8880 | fax 607/336–2076 | 41 rooms, 4 suites | $90 rooms, $100 suites | AE, D, DC, MC, V.

NYACK

MAP 4, E3

(Nearby towns also listed: Piermont, Spring Valley, Stony Point, Suffern, Tarrytown)

Nestled along the west bank of the Hudson River, the historic village of Nyack is only 35 min from Manhattan, yet it retains a small-town charm that seems reminiscent of the 19th century. It has only 7,000 residents, and it's streets are lined with gorgeous Victorian homes. The quaint downtown has delightful antiques shops and several fine dining spots.

The arts have long played an important role in Nyack, which was the birthplace of American artist Edward Hopper. Today Hopper's house is a community cultural center and exhibit space that is open year-round. Nyack was also the longtime home of stage actress Helen Hayes, and there is a thriving theater named in her honor. Other show-business favorites, including comedienne/talk show host Rosie O'Donnell, have also chosen this beautiful riverside village over the hustle and bustle of New York City.

Information: Rockland County Office of Tourism | 3 Main St., 10960 | 845/353–5533 | www.rockland.org.

Attractions

Hopper House. Visit artist Edward Hopper's childhood home, now a community center and exhibition space. Built in 1858 by Hopper's grandfather, this Federal-style house with a view of the Hudson River was owned by the famed painter until his death in 1967. It was saved from ruin by a group of Nyack citizens in 1971. | 82 N. Broadway | 845/358–0774 | $1 suggested donation | Thurs.–Sun. 1–5.

Hudson Valley Children's Museum. There are more than 10 hands-on exhibits here, including "The Hudson River Dive," which explores the ecology of the Hudson. | 21 Burd St. | 845/358–2191 | fax 845/358–2642 | www.hvcm.org | $5 | Tues.–Sat. 10–5, Sun. noon–5.

Helen Hayes Performing Arts Center. Named for famed actress and native resident Helen Hayes, this theater hosts dramatic, dance, and musical performances, as well as community outreach programs and a school for gifted youth. | 117 Main St. | 845/358–6333 | fax 845/358–6846 | www.helenhayespac.org.

ON THE CALENDAR
AUG.: *Annual Crab Festival.* Put on a bib, grab a mallet, and sample some tasty crustaceans at this festival. Learn the secrets of crab preparation or take a lesson in conserving the local ecology from the Hudson River Foundation. | Memorial Park | 845/358–4973.

Dining

Ichi Riki. Japanese. The private tatami rooms and a bustling sushi bar draw large crowds to this comfortable, reliable spot. Known for sushi, tempura, and other traditional Japanese dishes. | 110 Main St. | 845/358–7977 | Reservations essential Fri.–Sun. | Closed Mon. No lunch weekends | $13–$25 | AE, MC, V.

King and I. Thai. This busy restaurant has standard decor, but an excellent, varied menu, including crispy duck and steamed dumplings. Try the weekend specials. No smoking. | 93 Main St. | 845/353–4208 | $11–$18 | AE, MC, V.

Restaurant X. Contemporary. Fireplaces warm this rustic restaurant overlooking picturesque ponds and gardens. Try crispy salmon roll tempura, Pacific ahi tuna, or classic beef Wellington. There's a deck to hang out on before dinner. Kids' menu. In Congers, 7 mi north of Nyack. | 117 N. Rte. 303, Congers | 845/268–6555 | fax 845/268–6608 | www.xaviars.com | Closed Mon. No lunch weekends | $19–$26 | AE, MC, V.

River Club. Seafood. This restaurant's interior, with paintings of Hudson River sidewheelers, complements the sweeping views of the river, marina, and Tappan Zee Bridge. Popular dishes include salmon Wellington and chicken Arezzio (chicken breast sautéed with pine nuts and spinach). There's a covered deck on the water for warm-weather dining. Sunday brunch. | 11 Burd St. | 845/358–0220 | Closed Mon. | $12–$19 | AE, D, DC, MC, V.

Lodging

Best Western. Conveniently located near the New York Thruway and the Hudson River, this chain motel has a three-story conference room/lobby area enclosed in smoked glass. The family-style restaurant is open 24 hours. Restaurant, bar (with entertainment). Cable TV.

| 26 Rte. 59 | 845/358–8100 | fax 845/358–3644 | www.bestwestern.com | 80 rooms | $89–$110 | AE, D, DC, MC, V.

Comfort Inn. This three-story, standard member of the chain is 5 mi from downtown Nyack and 5 from the Tappan Zee Bridge. Restaurant, bar, complimentary Continental breakfast. Some refrigerators, cable TV. Pool. Gym. Laundry facilities. Business services. No pets. | 425 E. Rte. 59, Nanuet | 845/623–6000 or 800/228–5150 | fax 845/623–9338 | www.choicehotels.com | 102 rooms | $85–$90 | AE, MC, V.

Nyack Motor Lodge. This two-floor local standby is across the street from the Palisades Mall and has been in business since 1975. At the junction off Rte. 303 and NY 59. Complimentary Continental breakfast. Cable TV. Pool. Pets allowed. | 110 Rte. 303, West Nyack | 845/358–4100 | fax 845/358–3938 | 125 rooms | $55–$70 | AE, DC, MC, V.

Super 8. This pleasant Tudor-style motel offers reasonable rates and is convenient to major highways. All single rooms have king-size beds and recliners. In-room data ports, cable TV. Business services. | 47 Rte. 59 | 845/353–3880 or 800/800–8000 | fax 845/353–0271 | 43 rooms | $68–$113 | AE, D, DC, MC, V.

OGDENSBURG

MAP 3, I2

(Nearby towns also listed: Canton, Potsdam)

Known simply as "the Burg," this industrial town at the junction of the Oswegatchie and St. Lawrence rivers is the oldest settlement in northern New York, and the only U.S. city on the St. Lawrence Seaway. Founded in 1749 as a post for French trappers, about half of its present population is of Canadian origin. During an unsuccessful attempt to wrest Canada from Great Britain in 1837, Ogdensburg was a major staging area for American sympathizers.

Information: **Greater Ogdensburg Chamber of Commerce** | 1020 Park St., 13669 | 315/393–3620 | chamber@gisco.net | www.ogdensburgny.com.

Attractions

Ft. Wellington National Historic Site. This site gives you a sense of what life was like at a British fort in the mid-1840s. Ft. Wellington was built to protect transportation along the St. Lawrence River during periods in the 19th century when Canada's existence was repeatedly threatened. Period rooms are furnished to their 1846 appearance, and costumed guides provide historical interpretation. In Prescott, Ontario, 4 mi west of the International Bridge. | 379 Van-Koughnet St., Prescott | 613/925–2896 | www.parkscanada.pch.gc.ca | $3 | May–Sept., daily 10–5.

Frederic Remington Art Museum. One of New York's prime tourist destinations, this museum has a collection of 77 major oil paintings, 16 bronze sculptures, and other works by Canton native Frederic Remington, who captured the Old West with his art. | 303 Washington St. | 315/393–2425 | fax 315/393–4464 | www.remington-museum.org | $4 | May–Oct., Mon.–Sat. 9–5, Sun. 1–5; Nov.–Apr., Wed.–Sat. 11–5, Sun. 1–5.

Greenbelt Riverfront Park. This downtown walkway along the St. Lawrence River has numerous historic plaques marking sites from the War of 1812 and the Battle of Ogdensburg. | Riverside Ave. | 315/393–1980 | Free | Daily.

Jacques Cartier State Park. This 461-acre park has camping, picnicking, fishing, and swimming. Includes 93 campsites (22 electrical), showers, flush toilets, a children's area, and a camp store. | Rte. 12, Morristown | 315/375–6371 or 315/375–8990 | www.nysparks.state.ny.us/parks/ | Free; parking $6 | Mid-May–mid-Oct., daily.

Library Park Historic District. The Library Park Historic District is an architecturally significant collection of 19th-century buildings of some of Ogdensburg's oldest buildings, including the brick, early Federal-style Parish House and another built of Potsdam sandstone. Local industrialist David Parish completed construction of his home, known as the "Red Villa," here in 1810. Today it houses the Frederic Remington Art Museum. | 303–323 Washington St. and 100–112 Caroline St. | Free.

Ogdensburg-Prescott International Bridge. Stretching from Ogdensburg, New York, to Prescott, Ontario, the Bridge is the 18th-longest suspension bridge in the world. | 1 Bridge Plaza | 315/393–4080 | www.ogdensport.com | $2 toll | Daily.

Robert C. McEwen U.S. Customs House. This structure, with walls of Berea Sandstone, was built in 1870 to be used as a post office and customs house. During its life, the building housed the town post office, a federal coutroom, the revenue collector's office and the special agent of the treasury department. Today the building stands vacant, but it's worth a look for history buffs. It was put on the National Register of Historic Places in 1977. | 127 N. Water St. | Free | Daily.

Upper Canada Village. This re-creation of a rural riverfront village from the 1860s includes demonstrations by people in period costumes. Among the buildings are a woolen mill, gristmill, hotel, and sawmill. On Route 2 E in Ontario, Canada. | RR 1 | 613/543–3704 or 800/ 437–2233 | www.parks.on.ca/village | $14.95 (Cdn) | May–Oct., daily 9:30–5.

ON THE CALENDAR
JULY: *International Seaway Festival.* This weeklong festival includes a carnival, fishing derby, antique car show, 3-hr parade, nightly concerts, and fireworks. | 315/393–3620.
AUG.: *Frederic Remington Pro Rodeo.* This three-day event includes a Texas barbecue, dance, and concert. | Ogdensburg International Airport, Rte. 812 | 315/393–3620.

Dining
Donut King. American. Fuel up on sugar and caffeine at this no-frills, affordable restaurant with quick service. Try the bottomless cup of coffee with a chocolate-covered donut. | 715 Canton St., Seaway Shopping Center | 315/393–7631 | $1–$5 | No credit cards.

Gran-View. Continental. Family dining goes upscale at this restaurant with a wonderful view of the St. Lawrence River. Specialties include chateaubriand, shrimp scampi, and veal dishes. Entertainment Friday and Saturday. Kids' menu. Sunday brunch. | 6765 Rte. 37 | 315/393–4550 | www.1000islands.com/granview/granview.htm | Breakfast also available; closed late Dec. | $12–$36 | AE, D, DC, MC, V.

Sholette's Steak and Ale. Steak. This casual place is known for steaks, but the huge menu offers plenty of choices, including a salad bar. Dine in the sports memorabilia–theme dining room or in the enclosed sunroom. Sholette's delivers to all local motels. Kids' menu. | 1000 Linden St. | 315/393–5172 | $20–$25 | AE, D, MC, V.

Stone Fence Dining Room. Italian. Though this restaurant is in a hotel, it's a popular destination in its own right. The all-you-can-eat pasta buffet on Friday night is such a hit with locals that reservations are essential. Choose between the casual but elegant dining room with high ceilings or outdoor seating on the patio in summer. Sunday brunch. | 7191 Hwy. 37 | 315/393–1545 | Closed Oct.–Apr. | $8–$15 | AE, D, MC, V.

Lodging
Days Inn. This single-story member of the chain is at the junction of Rtes. 37 and 68, near the Frederic Remington Art Museum and the St. Lawrence River. Restaurant, bar. Cable TV. Pets allowed (fee). | 1200 Paterson St. | 315/393–3200 or 800/329–7466 | fax 315/393–6098 | dheren@bbs.tsf.com | www.daysinn.com | 29 rooms | $45–$75 | AE, D, DC, MC, V.

Gran View Quality Inn. With a wonderful view of the St. Lawrence River, this motel-restaurant facility comes by its name honestly. The riverside property covers 14 acres, with a large outdoor pool and poolside bar, and volleyball courts overlooking the river. Restaurant, bar (with entertainment), picnic area. In-room data ports, cable TV. Pool. Volleyball, dock. Business services. | 6765 Rte. 37 | 315/393–4550 or 800/392–4550 | fax 315/393–3520 | granview@1000islands.com | www.1000islands.com/granview | 48 rooms | $69–$89 | AE, D, DC, MC, V.

Ramada Inn/River Resorts of Ogdensburg. This two-story motel in downtown Ogdensburg was renovated in 1996. Boaters appreciate its 42-slip marina as well as its views of the Oswegatchie and St. Lawrence rivers. There's live entertainment or a DJ in the lounge on Friday and Saturday nights. Restaurant, bar with entertainment. Complimentary Continental breakfast, room service. Cable TV. Pool. Spa. Gym. Laundry facilities. Some pets allowed. | 119 W. River St. | 315/393–2222 or 888/298–2054 | fax 315/393–9602 | 76 rooms | $59–$129 | AE, MC, V.

Rodeway Inn. This chain hotel overlooking the St. Lawrence Seaway has clean, spacious rooms at an affordable price. Picnic area. Cable TV. Pool. Dock. | 6801 Rte. 37 | 315/393–3730 | fax 315/393–3520 | 20 rooms | $54–$74 | AE, D, MC, V.

Stone Fence Motel. This property has guest rooms in four buildings, all surrounded by the namesake stone wall. Two buildings have standard motel rooms, and one offers riverside rooms with large balconies overlooking the St. Lawrence. The fourth building has lofts with full kitchens that can sleep six–eight guests. Restaurant, picnic area. Cable TV. Pool. Hot tub, sauna. Tennis. Docks, boating. Laundry facilities. Pets allowed. | 7191 Riverside Dr. | 315/393–1545 or 800/253–1545 | fax 315/393–1749 | stonefence@1000islands.com | www.1000islands.com/stonefence | 31 rooms, 8 suites | $79–$135 | AE, D, DC, MC, V.

Way Back Inn. This B&B, built in 1800 and surrounded by lovely gardens, is nestled in a sleepy residential neighborhood overlooking the St. Lawrence River. Wake up to breakfast served in the cheerful solarium. Unwind later in the day with wine, cheese, and dessert. Complimentary breakfast. No pets. No kids. No pets. No smoking. | 247 Proctor Ave. | 315/393–3844 | 2 rooms | $60 | No credit cards.

Windjammer Friendship Inn. You can sit by this motel's pool overlooking the St. Lawrence River and watch the huge ships pass by. Rooms are standard, with double or king-size beds. Restaurant, picnic area. Pool. | Rte. 37 | 315/393–3730 or 800/392–4550 | fax 315/393–3520 | windjammer@1000islands.com | www.1000islands.com/windjammer | 22 rooms | $54–$64 | Closed Nov.–Apr. | AE, D, MC, V.

OLD FORGE

MAP 3, I4

(Nearby towns also listed: Blue Mountain Lake, Boonville)

Old Forge, in Adirondack Park, is a village at the start of the Fulton Chain of Lakes. In years past, it was a hub for wealthy travelers, who arrived by train, then continued by boat to their Adirondack hotels and summer homes. Today it attracts vacationers with plenty of year-round activities including restaurants, museums, musical performances, and a water park.

Information: **Tourist Information Center** | 3140 Main St., Box 68, 13420 | 315/369–6983.

Attractions

Adirondack River Outfitters. This guide service will take you on a rafting adventure in three different Adirondack locations. The class III and IV rapids on the Hudson River in spring are for the adventurous. If you want tamer waters, try summer family rafting and tubing on the Sacandaga River. All trips include shuttle, equipment, guides, snacks, and drinks. Hot meals are served after some trips. Take exit 21 off I–87. | Rte. 9N S | 800/525–RAFT | www.aroadventures.com | Call for hrs.

Adirondack Scenic Railroad. Relive the golden age of railroading when the Adirondack Line was the way the rich and famous made their way from New York City, Boston, and other locations to their grand Adirondack summer homes. Take a 1-hr train trip through undisturbed forests and scenic wilderness on the Wilderness Local (you may encounter train robbers along the way), which leaves from Old Forge on Tuesday. The Grand Limited, which runs from Utica to Old Forge, visits historic villages and passes through glorious countryside. The rail station is off Route 28 in Thendara, 1.6 mi southwest of Old Forge. | Thendara Railroad Station | 315/369–6290 or 315/724–0700 | www.adirondackrr.com | $7 | Early May–late Oct.; call for hrs.

Arts Center/Old Forge. The Arts Center is a nonprofit, educational organization formed to celebrate Adirondack arts and artists. Each year, the Arts Center sponsors exhibits, performances, artists' receptions, and special events focusing on Adirondack traditions and artists. Classes and workshops for children and adults teach everything from watercolor and basket weaving to poetry. | 3260 Rte. 28 | 315/369–6411 | fax 315/369–2431 | arts@telenet.net | Free, excluding some major exhibitions | Mon.–Sat. 10–4, Sun. noon–4.

Enchanted Forest/Water Safari. New York's largest water park is much more than a water park. Highlights include a tidal-wave pool and the Amazon, a family tube ride. For the adventurous, there's the Wild Waters water slide. For the little ones there are 14 traditional amusement rides and five themed areas; circus shows are offered twice daily. | Rte. 28 N, Adirondack Mountain | 315/369–6145 | www.watersafari.com | safari@telenet.net | $20 | June–Labor Day, daily 9:30–7.

Forest Industries Exhibit Hall. This museum, in a small, unimposing building, demonstrates the importance of forestry to the Adirondack region. A variety of dioramas depict forest management, recreational activities, and wildlife management. | 3311 Rte. 28 | 315/369–3078 | nela@telenet.net | Free | Memorial Day–mid-June, weekends noon–5; mid-June–Labor Day, weekdays 10–5, weekends noon–5; Labor Day–Columbus Day, weekends noon–5.

McCauley Mt. This year-round mountain sports center offers both downhill and cross-country skiing in winter. This 100-acre area has 22 trails with a vertical drop of 700 ft. In summer there's a chairlift ride, picnic area, and deer-feeding exhibit. | 300 Bisby Rd. | 315/369–3225 or 315/369–6983 | central@telenet.net | www.adirondacktravel.com | $22 for all-day skiing; $4 for lift.

Old Forge Hardware. This authentic, old-time general store was founded in 1900. It lives up to the name "general store" with shelves filled with items ranging from maps, canoes, and clothing to feed, housewares, snowshoes, and lumber. There's also a mail-order business. | 104 Fulton St., Rte. 28 | 315/369–6100 | Free | Mon.–Sat. 8–5, Sun. 9–5.

Old Forge Lake Cruise. Take a 25-mi round-trip cruise or stop in the village of Inlet to shop and eat and take the next boat back. Most cruises are 2–2½ hrs. Historic navigated cruises and romantic dinner cruises are available. | Main St. Dock, Rte. 28 | 315/369–6473 | www.old-forgecruises.com | cruises@telenet.net | $9–$12.50; $32.50 for dinner cruise | Memorial Day–Columbus Day, daily 9 AM–8 PM.

T and M Equestrian Center. Horseback riding, pony rides, and guided rides along wooded trails. Riders on the trail must be at least 4 yrs old. In Inlet, 10 mi north of Old Forge. | Rte. 28, Inlet | 315/357–3594 | Free | Memorial Day weekend–Columbus Day, daily 9–6.

Tickner Canoe Rental/Tickner's Adirondack Canoe Outfitters. Rent a canoe for paddling down the waterways of the Moose River. Drop-offs are available. You might like to try paddling down the Moose River and returning via the Adirondack Scenic Railroad. | Rte. 28, Old Forge | 315/369–6286 | Mid-June–mid-Sept., daily 8:30–6.

ON THE CALENDAR
JUNE: *Classic Car Show.* Give dad a treat by taking him to this annual event held on the Saturday of Father's Day weekend. More than 100 cars of all vintages are here, from

antiques to hot-rods. The fun kicks off with a car parade through Old Valley forge on Friday night. | 315/942–2251 | 9–3 | $2.

Dining

Big Moose Inn. Continental. Enjoy elegant lakeside dining in this turn-of-the-20th-century building. Try fillet of beef Oscar, Alaskan king crab legs, and fruit of the sea. There's also outdoor lakeside dining at umbrella-covered tables. | 1510 Big Moose Rd., Eagle Bay | 315/357–2042 | $14–$30 | AE, MC, V.

Farm Restaurant. American. This spot serves up classic diner food, including an all-day breakfast of eggs, sausage, home fries, and pancakes. It's filled to the brim with fascinating antiques from the days when it was part of a working farm. Check out the old record books signed by diners in the 1910s, '20s, and '30s. In Thendara, 1.6 mi southwest of Old Forge. | Rte. 28, Thendara | 315/986–4724 | Closed Sun., Mon. and late Oct.–early May | $5–$10 | No credit cards.

Frankie's. Italian. Tucked away on Main Street behind Walt's Diner in Fern's Complex, this classic Italian restaurant complete with checkered tablecloths has a cheerful, no-nonsense style. Try the vodka rigatoni or the chicken parmigiana along with a selection from the extensive wine list. Kids' menu. | Fern's Complex, Main St. | 315/369–2400 | Closed Mon. (and Tues. in winter) No lunch | $11–$18 | AE, MC, V.

Keyes Pancake. American. Soups, sandwiches, burger baskets, chicken 'n' biscuits, and bottomless cups of coffee are the specialties. Keyes is a great place to take the kids, or to go if you've got a yen for breakfast any time of day. Kids' menu. | Main St. | 315/369–6752 | $5–$10 | D, MC, V.

Old Mill. Continental. Prime rib and stuffed chicken breast are served up in this converted mill ½ mi south of Old Forge. Outside there's a huge working waterwheel, and the dining room has an inviting stone fireplace and vaulted ceiling. Kids' menu. | 315/369–3662 | Closed Nov., Dec., and 2nd weekend in Mar. No lunch Mon.–Sat. | $20–$30 | MC, V.

Riley's Restaurant at Water's Edge. Italian. Gorgeous lake views set this unpretentious restaurant apart. Try the chicken marsala, broiled swordfish, or shrimp scampi. Browse the library or relax in the lounge while you wait for a table. | Rte. 28 | 315/369–2484 | $7–$16 | AE, MC, V.

Steak House. Steak. This informal restaurant is 1 mi south of downtown Old Forge. In addition to the sirloin, check out the daily specials. Beer and wine are served in the lounge. | Rte. 28 | 315/369–6981 | $6–$15 | AE, MC, V.

Lodging

Best Western Sunset Inn. This property, 2 mi from public lakeside beaches and a water park, has standard, modern rooms. The lobby has hanging plants and Greek statues, and the pool has an attached sundeck. Picnic area. Cable TV. Pool. Hot tub, sauna. Tennis. Cross-country skiing, downhill skiing. Playground. Pets allowed. | 2752 Rte. 28 | 315/369–6836 | www.best-western.com/best.html | 52 rooms | $79–$103 | AE, D, MC, V.

Big Moose Inn. This large and rustic 1902 Adirondack inn sits on the lakeshore and has a central fireplace, a cozy lounge, a front porch with rockers, a floating gazebo with checkerboards, and a deck for dining near the lake. Some rooms have a lake view. Restaurant (see Big Moose Inn), complimentary Continental breakfast. Dock, boating, fishing. | 1510 Big Moose Rd. Eagle Bay | 315/357–2042 | fax 315/357–3423 | bigmoose@telenet.net | www.bigmooseinn.com | 16 rooms | $48–$145 | Closed Apr. | AE, MC, V.

Clark's Beach Motel. Clark's is a popular destination for snowmobilers and has large, two-story, fully furnished family units with four double beds, a living and dining room, stocked kitchen, and private porches facing the lake. Double rooms are also available. A snowmobile trail is at the edge of the property, so on weekends it can get a little noisy. The lounge has magazines and games. Some kitchenettes, some microwaves, some refrigerators, cable TV. Indoor pool, lake. Hiking. Beach, dock, boating, fishing. Cross-country skiing, snowmobiling. Pets allowed. | Rte. 28 N | 315/369–3026 | 42 rooms | $52–$70 | MC, V.

Country Club Motel. Set on spacious grounds next to Thendara Golf Course and snow-mobile trails, the Country Club Motel offers comfortable budget rooms with wood furniture and gold quilts on the beds. In Thendara, 1.6 mi southwest of Old Forge. Some refrigerators, cable TV. Pool. | Rte. 2 | 315/369–6340 | fax 315/369–6650 | www.oftimes.com/ccm | 27 rooms | $40–$80 | AE, D, DC, MC, V.

Covewood Lodge. This quiet, relaxing spot 15 mi northwest of Old Forge is on Big Moose Lake in the middle of a wildlife sanctuary. Cottages have one to seven bedrooms, fireplaces, and full-service kitchens; two-bedroom apartments have glassed-in living rooms with porches. No air-conditioning, kitchenettes, no room phones. Lake. Tennis. Dock. Cross-country skiing. Library. Playground. Laundry facilities. | Big Moose Lake, Eagle Bay | 315/357–3041 | fax 315/357–5902 | webmaster@covewoodlodge.com | www.covewoodlodge.com | 3 apartments, 17 cottages | $900–$1,105 apartments (7–day minimum stay in summer), $650–$1,625 cottages (7–day minimum stay in summer, studio to 7 bedrooms) | No credit cards.

Eagle Creek Cottages. Situated on eight private, wooded acres, these cottages (about 8 mi northeast of Old Forge), are named after trees—Balsam, Hemlock, Pine, and Spruce. Pillows, blankets, and cleaning supplies are available, but bring your own sheets, towels, and soap. Kitchens. Microwaves, refrigerators. Some pets allowed. | Kopps Rd. | 315/357–4134 | 4 cottages | $50–$80 | No credit cards.

The Narrows. Some of these cottages, overlooking the First Lake Channel, are at the water's edge. Others are set back in the trees. All have outdoor fireplaces and picnic tables, and there is a play area for children. Explore the lake in a canoe, paddleboat, or rowboat. Less than a mile from Old Forge, these cottages are an easy walk to the beach, tennis courts, boat tours, churches, grocery stores, shops, and theater. No pets. | Hollywood Hills Rd. | 315/369–6458 | www.thenarrowsofoldforge.com | narrows@telenet.net | 1 house, 8 cottages | $275–$575 weekly | No credit cards.

19th Green Motel. This motel is on spacious, tree-lined grounds next to a golf course. Guest rooms are large and some have queen-size beds. Picnic area. Microwaves, refrigerators, cable TV. Pool. Video games. | 2761 Rte. 28 | 315/369–3575 | 13 rooms | $40–$80 | AE, D, DC, MC, V.

North Woods Inn and Resort. This 1890 great camp–style resort is set on 4th Lake, the largest of the Fulton Chain of Lakes. Guests stay in the rustic lakeside lodge with modern facilities, or in surrounding motel units, also on the lake. Restaurant, bar. Some in-room hot tubs, cable TV. Pool. Gym, beach, dock. | 4th Lake, Rte. 28 | 315/369–6777 | fax 315–369–2575 | www.northwoodsinnresort.com | nrthwoods@telenet.net | 22 rooms | $95–$175 | AE, DC, MC, V.

Pine Knoll Motel. Set among pine trees, this motel overlooks Old Forge Lake and the Adirondack Mountains. Grocery stores, shops, restaurants, and churches are all within walking distance. Accommodations are in rooms or fully furnished cabins, some of which sleep up to seven. Golf, boat tours and rentals, hiking, and chairlift rides. Some kitchenettes, some refrigerators, cable TV. Lake. Tennis. Beach, dock. Pets allowed. | S. Shore Dr. | 315/369–6740 | 22 motel rooms, 3 cottages | $65–$74 rooms, $67–$80 cottages | MC, V.

Sugarbush Bed & Breakfast. Flourishing gardens and emerald lawns envelop this delightful, two-story white clapboard B&B. Built in the 1800s by John Serman, a signer of the Declaration of Independence, it was once a boys' school. Now it's a refuge for those seeking more tranquil pleasures, like strolling through its apple orchard. Complimentary breakfast. Library. | 8451 Old Poland Rd., Barneveld | 315/896–6860 or 800/582–5845 | 6 rooms | $75–$90 | AE, D, MC, V.

Van Auken's Inne. Built in 1891 as a boardinghouse for lumberjacks, this historic country inn is easily identified by its over-long two-story porch with rockers. Guest rooms have antiques and quilts. In Thendara, 1.6 mi south of Old Forge Restaurant. Complimentary Con-

tinental breakfast. Cable TV. | 108 Forge St., Thendara | 315/369–3033 | vanauks@telenet.net | www.vanaukensinne.com | 12 rooms | $65–$85 | Closed Apr., Nov. | MC, V.

Water's Edge Inn and Conference Center. This rustic lodge with modern amenities is on the shores of Old Forge Pond, the beginning of the Fulton Chain of Lakes. The standard rooms have balconies, some overlooking the lake and the gorgeous setting. Just north of the New York Thruway. Restaurant, bar. Cable TV. Pool. Library. Business services. | Rte. 28 | 315/369–2484 | fax 315/369–6782 | 61 rooms, 8 suites | $65–$185 rooms, $99–$185 suites | AE, MC, V.

OLEAN

MAP 3, C8

(Nearby towns also listed: Salamanca, Wellsville)

Olean, founded in 1804, is a community of 20,000, nestled in the hills formed by receding glaciers. The town is a hub for St. Bonaventure University, two community colleges, and the manufacturing of everything from Cutco knives to Drusser Rand turbines. Facing the tree-lined town square, the old public library, a National Historic Landmark, has been converted into a Continental restaurant. From Olean there is a paved path for walking, bicycling, or in-line skating along the meandering Allegheny River. Olean is south of the Southern Tier Expressway at exit 25.

Information: **Olean Area Chamber of Commerce** | 120 N. Union St., 14760 | 716/372–4433.

Attractions
Cuba Cheese Shop. Home of an award-winning cheddar (it won a gold medal at the New York State Fairgrounds dairy contest), mozzarella, and Old York cheddar spread, Cuba Cheese offers over 100 varieties of imported and domestic cheeses. There's also a cheese history exhibit. In Cuba, 15 mi east of Olean. | 53 Genesee St., Cuba | 716/968–3949 or 800/543–4938 | www.cubacheese.com | info@cubacheese.com | Free | Mon.–Sat. 9–5, Sun. 10–4.

Friedsam Memorial Library. St. Bonaventure University's Friedsam Memorial Library houses a significant collection of art and rare books. Among the many pieces are Rembrandts, Rubenses, and Bellinis, in addition to Chinese porcelains, rare books, American Southwest and pre-Colombian pottery, and a collection of contemporary art. | St. Bonaventure University campus | 716/375–2323 or 716/375–2000 | Mon.–Thurs. 8–12 AM, Fri. 8–6, Sat. 10–6, Sun. 12–12.

Rock City. Sometimes called the Eighth Wonder of the World, Rock City, perched atop the Allegany Mountains, is the world's largest exposure of quartz conglomerate, displayed in towering rocks, some of them several stories high. You can now walk through the "streets" of Rock City's huge boulders, explore Native American fortresses, picnic, and visit the gift shop and mineral room. Wear casual clothes and shoes fit for hiking. | 505 Rock City Rd. (Rte. 16 S) | 716/372–7790 | $4.50 | May–June, daily 9–6; July–Aug., daily 9–8; Sept.–Oct., daily 9–6.

ON THE CALENDAR
JULY–AUG.: *Olean's Hottest Weekend.* Bid for chairs at a charity auction, and enjoy a free all-day concert, a classic car show, food, art and more. | 716/372–4433.

Dining
Beef 'N' Barrel. American. Beef 'N' Barrel is known for its generous portions, in-house bakery, and friendly staff. Juicy roast beef is carved up and served on hard homemade rolls with kummelwick seeds at four stations. Solid oak doors, beams, and panels give the dining room

a colonial look. The soups, roast-beef dinner, and pot-roast sandwich are also specialties. Kids' menu. | 146 N. Union St. | 716/372–2985 | Closed Sun. | $6–$16 | AE, D, DC, MC, V.

Old Library. Continental. This National Historic Landmark was built with funds from Andrew Carnegie as the town library. Its was converted to a restaurant in 1983, and retains most of its original architecture and feel. Dine amid some original furnishings, many antiques, leaded glass, a rotunda, and a marble frieze that extends through the foyer. Old Library is known for prime rib, scampi, and veal dishes. Kids' menu. Early bird dinners. Sunday brunch. | 116 S. Union St. | 716/372–2226 | fax 716/373–2226 | www.oldlibraryrestaurant.com | $8–$26 | AE, D, DC, MC, V.

Lodging

Castle Inn. This 1950s property offers a resort-type atmosphere next to St. Bonaventure University. Rooms are standard with king-size beds. Restaurant, bar (with entertainment), picnic area, complimentary breakfast. Some refrigerators, cable TV. Pool. 9-hole golf course. Bicycles. Business services. | 3184 Rte. 417 (W. State Rd.) | 716/372–1050 or 800/422–7853 | fax 716/372–4745 | 160 rooms | $59–$95 | AE, D, DC, MC, V.

Gallets House Bed and Breakfast. This impossibly romantic Victorian home in Allegany has a 100-ft wraparound porch and rooms furnished with antiques. The Mary Elizabeth room is circular and surrounded by windows. Stroll the grounds, where a goldfish pond and a stream with a small waterfall add to the tranquillity. One modern touch: All guest rooms come with CD players and soft music CDs. Allegany is 4 mi north of Olean. Complimentary breakfast. Some in-room hot-tubs. | 1759 Four Mile Rd., Allegany | 716/373–7493 | fax 716/806–0384 | www.e-localad.com/olean/gallets.html | gallets@netsync.net | 5 rooms | $75–$110 | AE, MC, V.

Hampton Inn. This motel is within 5 mi of Rock City Park, St. Bonaventure University, Olean Center Mall, and several area restaurants. Cable TV. Gym. Laundry service. No pets. | 101 Main St. | 716/375–1000 | fax 716/375–1279 or 800/426–7866 | 76 rooms | $69–$84 | AE, D, DC, V.

Motel De Soto. Less than 1 mi from St. Bonaventure University and the Allegheny River, this motel has more than just location going for it. The staff prides itself on providing comfortable accommodations and congenial, efficient service at low prices. Cable TV. Pool. | 3211 W. State Rd. | 716/373–1400 or 800/325–0043 | fax 716/373–3196 | 75 rooms | $40–$51 | AE, MC, V.

Old Library Bed and Breakfast. This Victorian home facing the tree-lined main square, next to the Old Library restaurant, has original oak, mahogany, and maple woodwork from 1895, including parquet floors. Guest rooms have period antiques; one suite has a four-poster bed and one has a brass bed. Restaurant, complimentary breakfast. In-room data ports, cable TV. Business services. | 120 S. Union St. | 716/373–9804 | fax 716/373–2462 | 6 rooms, 2 suites | $65–$75 rooms, $115–$125 suites | AE, D, DC, MC, V.

ONEIDA

MAP 3, H6

(Nearby towns also listed: Canastota, Rome, Syracuse, Utica)

This small city off Route 5 and the Thruway was settled in 1834, and is the site of the Mansion House, the former Oneida Community's utopian experiment. The Community was a religious sect, led by John Humphrey Noyes, whose followers believed that the second coming of Christ had already occurred, and that a new Eden could be born on Earth. Their fundamental beliefs were Perfectionism, and that each person, under the arch of Christianity, must achieve excellence and a communal nature. Each adult was married to all other community members of the opposite sex, were housed in group quarters, and supported themselves with the production of silk thread, animal traps, canned fruits and vegetables, and silverware. The group incorporated in 1880 as Oneida Community, Ltd., and today Oneida is one of the foremost names in tableware. A few miles away in Verona, the Oneida Indian Nation runs Turning Stone Casino, which has around-the-clock gambling, a hotel, and restaurants. A few miles north, on the eastern end of Oneida Lake, Sylvan Beach has amusements in the warmer months, and Verona Beach has a state park on the lake and campsites.

Information: **Madison County Tourism** | Box 1029, Morrisville, 13408 | 315/684–7320.

Attractions

Cottage Lawn Museum. The Madison County Historical Society offers tours of an 1850 Gothic Revival cottage with period furnishings. | 435 Main St. | 315/363–4136 | mchistorical@bhin-surance.com | $2 | Mon.–Fri. 9–4, June–Sept. Mon.–Sat. 9–4.

Mansion House. The three-story brick Mansion House and 33 acres of lawns were the home of the 19th-century utopian Oneida Community, founded in 1848 by the religious followers of John Humphrey Noyes. The National Historic Landmark house contains apartments occupied by residents (some descendents of the original community members), so you can see inside the house only on guided tours. | 170 Kenwood Ave. | 315/363–0745 | www.onei-dacommunity.org | $5 | Tours Wed. and Sat. 10 and 2, Sun. at 2.

Sylvan Beach. This amusement park near Oneida Lake has rides and games. | 112 Bridge St. | 315/762–5212 | Free | Apr.–June, weekends, June–early Sept., daily, call for hrs.

Turning Stone Casino. The Oneida Indian Nation's casino, hotel, and restaurant complex is a huge curved white concrete and glass structure that looks like the Guggenheim Museum on steroids. When you're finished at the tables, there's golf, shops, and many other amusements. You must be at least 18 years old to be on the gambling floor. In Verona, 4 mi east of Oneida. | 5218 Patrick Rd., Verona | 800/771–7711 or 315/361–7711 | www.turning-stone.com | Free | Daily, 24 hrs.

Vernon Downs. This harness-racing track has featured live competition since 1953. | Rte. 31, Vernon | 315/829–2201 | www.vernondowns.com | $2; $3.50 clubhouse | Apr.–Oct., Wed.–Sat. Call for hrs.

Verona Beach State Park. Located on Oneida Lake, this state-run park has 45 campsites. | Rte. 13 N | 315/762–4463 or 800/456–CAMP (reservations) | $6 per vehicle | Apr.–Oct., daily.

International Boxing Hall of Fame. Two 1950s hometown world boxing champs inspired local residents to honor the sport of boxing with a museum filled with memorabilia, awards, and casts of boxers. The annual induction ceremony is a major event in the boxing world. | 1 Hall of Fame Dr. | 315/697–7095. www.ibhof.com | $4 | 9–5, daily.

ON THE CALENDAR

SEPT.: *Craft Days.* Craft exhibitors and artisans set up shop at the Madison County Historical Society Museum. Held the weekend after Labor Day. | 435 Main St. | 315/363–4136.

Dining

Turning Stone Casino Resort. Eclectic. With six restaurants to choose from, including a steak house, trattoria, buffet, and ice cream shop for dessert, this is a good place to come with groups or picky eaters since everyone will find something. Try the Emerald Restaurant for sandwiches, steaks, and quesadillas; the Peach Blossom for specialties from the Orient; and sandwiches, pizza, and soups from Delia Cafe. | 5218 Patrick Rd. | 800/771–7711 | $6–$26 | AE, D, DC, MC, V.

Lodging

Comfort Suites. You can place bets without leaving your room with a remote control, or in the lobby since you'll be right next to Vernon Downs, a harness racetrack. Bet on a good future in one of six honeymoon suites, or sit by the fire at one of two track-side suites. Standard suites are one large room arranged into sleeping and sitting areas. Restaurant, bar, complimentary Continental breakfast, room service. In-room data ports, microwaves, refrigerators, some in-room hot tubs, cable TV. Pool. Hot tub, sauna, steam room. Gym. Video games. | 4229 Stuhlman Rd., Vernon | 315/829–3400 | fax 315/829–3787 | www.comfort-suites.com | 175 suites | $89–$149 | AE, D, DC, MC, V.

Governor's House Bed & Breakfast. This pristine four-story brick house was built in 1848 to be the state capitol. The town, however, lost out by one vote to Albany, and the building was used as a tourist house and private residence thereafter. Restored in 1995, the home now has spacious rooms furnished with period antiques and two parlors. You'll feel right at home using the fully stocked guest kitchen and large video library. Complimentary breakfast. Cable TV. Library. Laundry services. Some pets allowed. No smoking. | 50 Seneca Ave., Oneida Castle | 315/363–5643 or 800/437–8177 | www.bbhost.com/govhouse | 5 rooms | $76–$155 | AE, D, MC, V.

Inn at Turning Stone. This former Super 8 is now owned by Turning Stone Casino, 1 mi away. Guests can take advantage of a free shuttle to the casino or free parking at the casino, and can also use the casino's pool and spa. In Verona, 5 mi east of Oneida. Complimentary Continental breakfast. Cable TV. | 5558 W. Main St., Verona | 315/363–0096 | fax 315/363–2797 | 63 rooms | $98–$110 | AE, D, MC, V.

Oneida Community Mansion House. This mammoth three-story brick home once belonged to the Oneida Community, a utopian religious group founded in 1848. Built in stages between 1861 and 1914, Mansion House's scale—over 200 rooms and 93,000 square ft— illustrates the needs of a society living as one family. Today the building is primarily occupied by private residences, a museum, and eight large guest rooms, which have quilts and wooden post beds. The grounds include lawns and gardens covering more than 33 acres. Some refrigerators, cable TV. Library. No pets. | 170 Kenwood Ave. | 315/363–0745 | fax 315/361–4580 | www.oneidacommunity.org | 8 rooms | $80 | MC, V.

Super 8. This chain motel is convenient to such attractions as the Turning Stone Casino, Vernon Downs racetrack, and the International Boxing Hall of Fame. Rooms are spacious, and some have recliners. Complimentary Continental breakfast. In-room data ports, cable TV. | 215 Genesee St. | 315/363–5168 | fax 315/363–4628 | www.super8.com | 39 rooms | $55–$95 | AE, D, DC, MC, V.

Turning Stone Casino Resort. This resort hotel on the grounds of the Turning Stone Casino has guest rooms with dramatically lit marble bathrooms, contemporary furniture, and matching pink, yellow, and blue bed coverings and curtains. Rooms also have bathrobes and wine glasses. 6 restaurants. Pool. Beauty salon, spa. Gym. Shops, video games. Business services. | 5218 Patrick Rd., Verona | 800/771–7711 | www.turning-stone.com | 255 rooms, 30 suites | $109–$149 rooms, $174 suites | AE, D, DC, MC, V.

ONEONTA

MAP 3, I7

(Nearby towns also listed: Bainbridge, Cooperstown, Delhi, Roxbury, Stamford)

Founded in 1780, this city along Interstate 88 by the Susquehanna River is home to Hartwick College and the State University College at Oneonta, with their respective art and science museums. Oneonta is also home to the National Soccer Hall of Fame.

Information: Otsego County Chamber of Commerce | 12 Carbon St., 13820 | 607/432–4500.

Attractions

Gilbert Lake State Park. You'll find 221 campsites, 33 cabins, swimming, boat rentals, hiking trails, fishing, and a concession stand here. | Rte. 12 | 607/432–2114 or 800/456–CAMP (reservations) | $6 per vehicle | Daily.

Hanford Mills Museum. This museum includes a restored farmhouse and a water-powered working gristmill and sawmill. | Rte. 10, East Meredith | 607/278–5744 | $6 | May–Oct., daily 10–5.

Hartwick College. Founded as a seminary in 1797 in accordance with Lutheran minister John Christopher Hartwick's last will, today Hartwick College is a four-year, private, nondenominational liberal arts school with over 1,400 students. | West St. | 607/431–4200 or 607/431–4030 | www.hartwick.edu | Daily.

The **Yager Museum** displays fine art, folk art, and Native American artifacts. | Yager Building, Hartwick College | 607/431–4480 | www.hartwick.edu/museum | Free | Oct.–May, Tues., Thurs., Fri., Sat. 11–4; Wed. 11–9; Sun. 1–4; June–Sept., Tues.–Sat. 11–4, Sun. 1–4.

National Soccer Hall of Fame. This interactive, hands-on (and feet-on) museum features memorabilia, equipment, trophies, photographs, and more. | 18 Stadium Cir. | 607/432–3351 | www.soccerhall.org | $7.50 | Daily 10–7.

State University of New York College at Oneonta. This 4-yr state college was established in 1889 and became a founding member of the State University of New York system in 1948. The 250-acre main campus is home to approximately 5,000 full-time undergraduate students. | 116 Alumni Hall | 607/436–3500 or 800/SUNY–123 | www.oneonta.edu | Free | Daily.

The university's **Science Discovery Center of Oneonta** is a hands-on science museum. | Physical Sciences Bldg. | 607/436–2011 | www.oneonta.edu/~scdisc | Free | Thurs.–Sat. noon–4.

ON THE CALENDAR

SEPT.–OCT.: *Farmer's Market.* Enjoy live music while you shop for fresh produce, herbs, and crafts at this weekly event. Saturday, from 9 to 2 on Main Street. | 607/643–0059.

Dining

Brooks' House of Bar-B-Que. American. The original Brooks' House opened in 1961, and it's still owned by the same family. Today, it serves up spareribs, chicken, and seafood to as many as 600 customers a day. | 5560 Rte. 7 | 607/432–1782 | Closed Mon. | $4–$13 | D, MC, V.

Cathedral Farms. Continental. Country meets upscale dining at this restaurant/inn on the site of a turn-of-the-20th-century farm. Try the Black Angus prime rib, the Maryland crab cakes, or the breast of duck smoked on the premises. There are several dining rooms to choose from—the sunny atrium room, the sky-frescoed Crystal Room, and the enclosed porch overlooking the lawn where peacocks stroll. Sunday brunch. | 4158 Rte. 23 | 607/432–7483 | www.cathedralinn.com | Closed Mon., Tues. No lunch Mon.–Sat. | $15–$25 | AE, MC, V.

Christopher's Restaurant and Country Lodge. Continental. Settle into a table or booth amid the carved-wood bears for a meal of thick bone-in steak, chops, or seafood. There's also overstuffed sandwiches, build-your-own burgers, and pizza. Guest rooms are available. Dine on the outside porch in summer. | Rte. 23 | 607/432–2444 | www.christopherslodging.com | $18–$26 | AE, DC, MC, V.

Farmhouse Restaurant. Continental. Enjoy fireside dining in a century-old farmhouse. Try the salad bar, which has greens, peel-and-eat shrimp, soups, and homemade bread. Specialties include steaks, chops, and seafood, but the Farmhouse also has vegetarian dishes. Kids' menu. Sunday brunch. | 4158 Rte. 23 | 607/432–7374 | www.farmhouserestaurant.com | No lunch Mon.–Sat. | $20–$30 | AE, MC, V.

Sabatini's Little Italy. Italian. Sabatini's serves up large portions of pasta, antipasto, and brick-oven pizza. The dining room has cozy booths and a fireplace. | Rte. 23 | 607/432–3000 | www.sabatinislittleitaly.com | No lunch weekends | $20–$25 | AE, D, DC, MC, V.

Lodging

Cathedral Inn. Country goes upscale at this inn on the site of a turn-of-the-20th-century farm. Guest rooms have Ralph Lauren sheets and comforters and French pedestal sinks. Cathedral Inn is two blocks from the National Soccer Hall of Fame. Restaurant (*see* Cathedral Farms), room service. Cable TV. Pool. Hot tub. Business services. No smoking. | 4158 Rte. 23 | 607/432–7483 | fax 607/432–6368 | www.cathedralinn.com | 15 rooms, 4 suites | $125 rooms, $180–275 suites | AE, DC, MC, V.

Christopher's Country Lodge. No two rooms are alike at this cozy lodge. Quirky details abound, such as painted armoires, carved wooden lamps, Adirondack-style twig furniture, and antler chandeliers. Restaurant. Cable TV. No pets. | Rte. 23 (I–88, exit 15) | 607/432–2444 | 28 rooms | $75–$180 | AE, MC, V.

Holiday Inn. This hotel is near the interstate, about 10 mi east of the National Soccer Hall of Fame. Restaurant, bar (with entertainment), picnic area, room service. In-room data ports, microwaves, cable TV. Pool, wading pool. Video games. Laundry facilities. Some pets allowed. | Rte. 23 | 607/433–2250 | fax 607/432–7028 | www.holiday-inn.com | 120 rooms | $139–$179 | AE, D, DC, MC, V.

Knott's Motel on the Lake. This 6-acre property on Goodyear Lake has some lakefront rooms. Each floor has its own patio. Picnic area. Kitchenettes (in cottages), some room phones, cable TV. Tennis. Beach, boating. | 2306 Rte. 28 | 607/432–5948 | fax 607/433–2266 | www.cooperstownchamber.org/knotts | 25 rooms, 10 cottages | $68–$98 rooms, $100–$110 cottages | D, MC, V.

Rainbow Inn. Spacious, comfortable rooms with king- or queen-size beds are the norm here. Some rooms have water beds and hot tubs. You're welcome to use the sundeck and barbecue pit. Less than 1 mi from downtown, the inn is a short walk to area restaurants. Some microwaves, some refrigerators. Cable TV, in-room VCRs. No pets. | 5690 State Hwy. 7 | 607/432–1280 | 28 rooms | $58–$178 | www.therainbowinn.com | MC, V.

Super 8. This chain motel is across from a movie theater and shopping mall, and approximately 1 mi from the National Soccer Hall of Fame, 2 mi from Hartwick College, and 2½ mi from the State University of Oneonta. Complimentary Continental breakfast. Cable TV. Laundry facilities. Business services. Some pets allowed. | 4973 Rte. 23 | 607/432–9505 | www.super8.com | 60 rooms | $53–$107 | AE, D, DC, MC, V.

ORIENT POINT

MAP 3, E1

(Nearby towns also listed: Greenport, Riverhead)

Located at the easternmost tip of the Long Island's North Fork, Orient Point is a charming 18th-century seaside village. Along with its neighbor, East Marion, it is a photographer's dream. Still very much a rural hamlet, Orient Point is surrounded by water to the north and south, and its environs consist of farmland and undeveloped wetlands. The area's tranquillity is symbolized by the Orient Point Lighthouse, which sits quietly in the bay, recalling the ships it has led home safely.

The Corchaug Indians inhabited the area in 1661, when six English families settled here and called the area "Oysterponds" because of the rich reservoirs of shellfish.

Information: Greenport Chamber of Commerce | Box 66, Greenport, 11944 | 631/477–1383 | www.greenport.com.

Attractions

Cross Sound Ferry. Sit back and relax on this high-speed ferry service between New London, Connecticut, and Orient Point, at the tip of beautiful North Fork of Long Island. The ferry dock at Orient Point is at the end of Route 25. | 860/443–5281 | www.longisland-ferry.com | $34 1-way with car, $10 per passenger without | Departures every hr between 7 AM and 9 PM, with an additional ferry departing at 9:45 PM.

Orient Beach State Park. With 45,000 ft of water frontage on Gardiner's Bay, this beach is nestled beside a rare seaside forest with red cedar, black-jack oak, and prickly-pear cactus. Enjoy swimming, fishing, picnicking, hiking, and biking. Arrangements can be made for pavilion rentals and catering. | N. Country Rd., Rte. 25 | 631/323–2440 | Free; parking $5–$7 | Daily, dawn–dusk.

Oysterponds Historical Society. The village of Orient Point literally wraps around this wonderful collection of buildings, which depict early everyday life of the area. See the 19th-century Village House, Hallock building exhibits, Old Point Schoolhouse, 18th-century Orange Webb House, and the Red Barn. | Village La. | 631/323–2480 | $3 | June–Sept., Thurs., Sat., Sun. 2–5.

Dining

Orient by the Sea. American. A nautical theme pervades this casual restaurant, set in a marina that overlooks Gardiner's Bay. Lots of picture windows offer a lovely bay view. Try the twin lobster special or the broiled combo, which includes lobster tail, stuffed flounder, shrimps, and scallops. There's open-air dining on the deck. Kids' menu. Dock space. | Main Rd. | 631/323–2424 | Closed winter | $17–$25 | D, DC, MC, V.

Lodging

Quintessentials Bed & Breakfast. Fresh flowers, chocolates, and maximum pampering await you at this antiques-filled Victorian home set amid lush gardens. Indulge in extras such as massage, reflexology, facials, and body wraps. For the more active, bicycles are available. Complimentary breakfast. Library. No pets. No smoking. | 8985 Main Rd., East Marion | 631/477–9400 or 877/259–0939 | www.quintessentialsinc.com | 14 rooms | $150–$200 | AE, MC, V.

OSWEGO

MAP 3, G5

(Nearby town also listed: Fulton)

Located at the mouth of the Oswego River and the northern end of the state canal system, Oswego has long been a major freshwater port. Its military importance was recognized as early as 1722, and for decades it served as a strategic outpost for the United States. It was also the home of the only refugee settlement for Jews who were escaping the Holocaust. Today Oswego caters to a large number of boaters and anglers.

Information: **Greater Oswego Chamber of Commerce** | 156 W. Second St., 13126 | 315/343–7681 | www.oswegochamber.com.

Attractions

Energy Center. This information center run by two area power plants exalts the wonder of nuclear power. You can see a 40-ft scale model of a nuclear plant and exhibits on radiation and transmission distribution. It's 6 mi east of Oswego. | E. Lake Rd. | 315/342–4117 | Free | Sept.–Apr., weekdays 10–4; May–Oct., Mon.–Sat. 10–4, Sun. noon–4.

Fair Haven Beach State Park. This popular swimming area is located on Lake Ontario. The 865-acre park is also used for camping, picnicking, hiking, boating (rentals), and fishing. Facilities include 185 campsites (44 electrical), flush toilets, showers, a children's area, recreational building, and camp store. In Fair Haven, 16 mi southeast of Oswego. | Rte. 104A, Fair Haven | 315/947–5205 | www.nysparks.state.ny.us/parks/ | Free; parking $6 | Daily.

Ft. Ontario State Historic Site. The British built a fort here, and the French captured and destroyed it in the 1740s. The British then built another fort, which they eventually handed over to the United States in the late 1700s. Reenactments and festivals are staged throughout the summer. Military drills are performed July 1–Labor Day. | 1 E. 4th St. | 315/343–4711 | $3 | May–Oct., Wed.–Sat. 10–5, Sun. 1–5.

The **Safe Haven Exhibit** presents the story of the United States' only camp for Holocaust survivors during World War II. In 1944, the U.S. allowed 982 European Holocaust escapees and survivors to seek shelter here at Fort Ontario, a former army camp surrounded by a chain-link fence topped with barbed wire. | Head Start Building, Fort Ontario Park | 315/343–1971 | www.syracuse.com/features/safehaven | Free | Memorial Day–Labor Day, Sun. 1–4.

H. Lee White Marine Museum. Artifacts reflect local history and include a real birch-bark canoe, an old dugout canoe, and some wall-size murals. Parked outside is the *Nash*, a U.S. Army tug (an LT-5) that is a veteran of the D-Day invasion of Normandy. The collection is odd but memorable; pieces range from a wooden mallet for breaking ice on the rigging of a ship to the U.S. Navy manual on meat preparation. At the end of the pier. | W. First St. | 315/342–0480 | $2 | June and Sept., daily 1–5; July–Aug., daily 10–5.

New York State Salmon River Fish Hatchery. More than 4½ million fish are raised here (chinook and coho salmon, and brown, rainbow, and steelhead trout). Self-guided tours run through the incubation area, spawning house, and fish pens. In Altmar, about 20 mi east of Oswego. | Rte. 22 N, Altmar | 315/298–5051 | Free | Mar.–Nov., daily 9–4.

Oswego Speedway. Opened in 1951, this track has seen many a race in its day. Come see stock cars and limited and super modifieds cruise to the finish. | Rte. 104 | 315/342–0646 | www.oswegospeedway.com | $5 | Call for schedule.

Richardson-Bates House Museum. Walk through six period rooms patterned after 1890s lifestyles. Exhibits focus on county history. | 135 E. 3rd St. | 315/343–1342 | $4 | Jan.–Mar., Tues.–Fri. 10–5; Apr.–Dec., Tues.–Fri. 10–5, weekends 1–5.

Selkirk Shores State Park. This 980-acre park offers camping, picnicking, hiking, boating, snowmobiling, fishing, swimming, and bicycling. Facilities include 148 campsites (86 electrical), flush toilets, showers, a children's area with playground, a recreational building, and a store. In Pulaski, 10 mi northwest of Oswego. | 7101 Rte. 3, Pulaski | 315/298–5737 | www.nysparks.state.ny.us/parks/ | $6; parking an additional $6 | Daily.

Tioga Scenic Railroad Excursions. Meals and trips available; fall foliage tours are especially scenic. | 25 Delphine, off Rte. 17 | 607/687–6786 | July–Oct., weekends 1 PM.

ON THE CALENDAR

MAY: *Lake Ontario Bird Festival.* Attend demonstrations and sightings related to the massive bird migrations that take place along the eastern shore of Lake Ontario. | Mexico Point State Park, off Rte. 104B | 315/349–8322.

JULY: *Oswego County Fair.* A full lineup of country-western and other musical performances highlights this annual county fair. | 315/343–FREE.

JULY: *Oswego Harborfest.* This 4-day music festival on the Port of Oswego features an art show and tall ships. | 315/343–FREE | www.oswegoharborfest.com.

Dining

Admiral Woolsey's. Contemporary. Enjoy a harborside view at this restaurant perched at the end of the Oswego River. The five-page menu offers plenty to choose from, but the broiled trout is a specialty. | E. 1st St. | 315/342–4430 | $19–$25 | AE, D, DC, MC, V.

Canale's Ristorante. Italian. Gorge on a huge plate of pasta at this relaxed restaurant known for big portions. Private booths and a bar add intimacy. Kids' menu. | 156 W. Utica St. | 315/343–3540 | No lunch weekends May–Sept. | $7–$20 | AE, DC, MC, V.

Rudy's Lakeside Drive-In. American. Set on the shores of Lake Ontario for more than half a century, this casual eatery is a local institution. Fresh fish, sandwiches, burgers, and ice cream are menu staples. If you're brave, try Rudy's signature Texas Hot Sauce. Takeout available. | Washington Blvd. | 315/343–2671 | Closed Oct.–Feb. | $2–$8 | AE, MC, V.

Vona's. Italian. Southern Italian dishes like veal parmigiana and baked lasagna are the specialties of this pleasant, family-style restaurant. There's also a cocktail lounge. Kids' menu. | W. 10th and Utica Sts. | 315/343–8710 | No lunch weekends | $7–$27 | AE, DC, MC, V.

Lodging

Battle Island Inn. Snuggle up with down pillows and comforters at this luxurious inn, and awake to breakfast served in the gracious dining room. A meticulous three-season garden rings the house. Stroll through it or enjoy it from the shaded porch. Complimentary breakfast. Cable TV. No pets. No smoking. | 2167 Rte. 48 N, Fulton | 315/593–3699 | fax 315/593–3699 | www.battle-island-inn.com | 6 rooms | $50–$125 | AE, MC, V.

Best Western Captain's Quarters. All guest rooms have a view of historic Oswego Harbor. Queen- and king-size beds and family suites are available. Restaurant. In-room data ports, cable TV. Pool. Hot tub. Exercise equipment, fishing. Business services. | 26 E. 1st St. | 315/342–4040 | fax 315/342–5454 | www.bestwestern.com | 93 rooms | $88–$108 | AE, D, DC, MC, V.

Black Creek Farm Bed & Breakfast. Twenty acres of grounds and extensive gardens encircle the main house and the homey guest house. Enjoy the view of the 2-acre stocked pond or go exploring in the available paddleboat. The innkeepers grow their own strawberries, blueberries, apples, pears, peaches, walnuts, and filbert nuts. Children under 12 can only stay in the guest house. Twenty miles southwest of Oswego. Complimentary breakfast. No pets. No smoking. | 13615 Mixer Rd. Red Creek | 315/947–5282 | 3 rooms, 1 guest house | $75–$100 room, $125 guest house | No credit cards.

Days Inn. This is the closest hotel to the Oswego Speedway. Restaurant, complimentary Continental breakfast. Some in-room data ports, refrigerators, cable TV. Laundry service. Business services. | 101 Rte. 104 E | 315/343–3136 or 800/329–7466 | fax 315/343–6187 | 44 rooms | $55–$125 | AE, D, MC, V.

Econo Lodge Riverfront. This modern motel has standard rooms that overlook Oswego Harbor. Restaurant. Refrigerators, cable TV. Laundry services. Business services. | 70 E. 1st St. | 315/343–1600 | fax 315/343–1222 | 93 rooms | $75–$150 | AE, D, MC, V.

Oswego Inn. This quiet country inn is run like a bed-and-breakfast. Don't be deceived by the old-fashioned rooms; they conceal such modern touches as in-room data ports and cable TV. The work of local artisans depicting Oswego County scenes adds a personal touch. Complimentary Continental breakfast. In-room data ports, refrigerators, cable TV. Business services. No smoking. | 180 E. 10th St. | 315/342–6200 or 800/721–7341 | fax 315/343–6234 | www.pos.net/oswego/inn/index.htm | 13 rooms | $55–$65 | AE, D, MC, V.

Portly Angler Lodge. This lodge caters to salmon fishers in fall (September and October), snowmobilers in winter, and kayakers in spring. In true fishing-lodge style, the three log buildings are filled with rustic, rough-hewn furniture. The large guest rooms with over-size bathrooms accommodate up to six people. There's a gathering room with fly-tying tables and 550 ft of shoreline on the Salmon River. In Pulaski, 30 mi east of Oswego. | 24 County Rte. 2A, Pulaski | 315/298–4773 | www.theportlyanglerlodge.com | 39 rooms | $45–$68 | Closed mid-May–July | AE, MC, V.

OWEGO

MAP 3, G8

(Nearby towns also listed: Binghamton, Elmira, Endicott)

This Southern Tier village is about 20 mi west of Binghamton on Route 17, at the confluence of several rivers. Here you'll find Tioga Gardens and a scenic railroad.

Information: Tioga County Chamber of Commerce | 188 Front St., 13827 | 607/687–2020.

Attractions

Tioga County Historical Society Museum. This museum includes folk art and local history displays. | 110 Front St. | 607/687–2460 | Free | Tues.–Sat. 10–4.

Tioga Gardens. Stroll around the Japanese gardens, conservatory, and greenhouse. | 2217 Rte. 17C | 607/687–5522 or 800/649–0494 | Free | Daily.

Tioga Scenic Railroad. Take a 2-hr, 22-mi round-trip (Oswego to Newark Valley) excursions aboard a vintage 1900s train. There's a museum as well. | 25 Delphine St. | 607/687–6786 | www.tiogascenicrailroad.com | $9 | July–Oct., weekends, call for hrs. Trips depart at 1 PM.

ON THE CALENDAR

JUNE: *Strawberry Festival.* Strawberry lovers, this is for you. The succulent red fruit is the centerpiece of all activities at this annual festival, which includes a parade, crafts, music, and food. At Owego Marketplace. | Owego Marketplace | 607/687–2556.

JUNE: *Concerts in the Park.* Every summer, the Tioga County Council on the Arts sponsors a series of free night concerts. Pack a picnic and some lawn chairs, and bring the family. Performances cover the musical spectrum, from polka to big band to blues. | 607/687–0785 | July–Aug., Wed. 7 PM.

AUG.: *Tioga County Fair.* This county fair has agricultural exhibits, rides, and entertainment. At the Tioga County Fairgrounds. | Tioga County Fairgrounds, Main St. (Rte. 17C) | 607/687–7440 or 800/671–7772.

Dining

Riverside Tavern. American. Located in the Treadway Inn and Conference Center, this is an affordable, relaxed place for drinks, appetizers, or burgers. Stop in on the weekend for live music. | 110 Rte. 17C | 607/687–4500 | $5–$8 | AE, MC, V.

Lodging

Holiday Inn Express. This two-story suburban property, renovated in 1999, overlooks the Susquehanna River. Some rooms have river views. You can also walk to area restaurants and shops, and a small park around the corner where you can do a little fishin'. Complimentary Continental breakfast. In-room data ports, cable TV. Pool. Gym. Laundry service. Business service. No pets. | 20 Hickory Park Rd. | 607/687–9000 or 800/465–4329 | fax 607/687–3034 | 74 rooms | $74–$89 | www.basshotels.com/hiexpress | AE, MC, V.

Sunrise Motel. This roadside motel offers affordable rooms 2 mi west of Owego. Rooms have two double or one queen-size bed, a round table, and a desk. There's a coffee shop on site. Picnic area. Cable TV. Some pets allowed. | 3778 Waverly Rd. | 607/687–5666 | 20 rooms | $49 | AE, D, MC, V.

Treadway Inn and Conference Center. This Susquehanna River property is a popular spot for conferences and weddings. Guest rooms are modern and comfortable, but the highlight is the well-groomed grounds. Restaurant, bar (with entertainment), room service. Cable TV. Pool. Exercise equipment. | 1100 Rte. 17C | 607/687–4500 | fax 607/687–2456 | www.owegotreadway.com | 96 rooms | $96 | AE, D, DC, MC, V.

OYSTER BAY

MAP 4, H5

(Nearby towns also listed: Glen Cove, Syosset)

This quaint town sits on an inlet off Long Island Sound. Its history can be traced to 1615, when a Dutch explorer, impressed by its bountiful shellfish, named the area Oyster Bay. The hamlet's distance from Long Island's more urbanized areas has helped preserve a small-town feel.

The area's most famous resident was President Teddy Roosevelt, who built his residence, Sagamore Hill, in 1885. Not all its visitors had such positive pedigrees, however. It is reported that Oyster Bay was the last port of call for Captain Kidd before he was arrested and hanged in Boston, and a local cook, Mary Mallon, received lots of publicity in 1906 after being dubbed Typhoid Mary. Singer Billy Joel is the town's most recent claim to fame.

Information: Chamber of Commerce | 120 South St., Box 21, 11771 | 516/922–6464 | www.oysterbay.org.

Attractions

Planting Fields Arboretum. The home of insurance magnate William Robertson Coe from 1910 to 1955, Planting Fields is now an arboretum of 409 acres, including 160 of gardens and plant collections and the rest lawns and woodlands. Two greenhouse complexes nurture native plants. | Planting Fields Rd. | 516/922–9201 or 516/922–9200 | $4 per car | Daily 9–5.

    Coe Hall. Located at Planting Fields Arboretum, this magnificent Tudor manor was the home of William Robertson Coe. The house is filled with period furnishings and antiques, including windows from the home of Henry VIII's second wife, Anne Boleyn. Daily tours. | Planting Fields Rd. | 516/922–0479 | $4 | Daily 9–5.

Raynham Hall Historical House Museum. The history of this Colonial saltbox structure dates from the American Revolution through the town's affluent Victorian period. It was home to three generations of the Townsend family, renowned merchants and ship traders. Sally Townsend is responsible for tipping off her father to the fact that a certain Benedict Arnold was going to betray his country. Today many of the original family furnishings are in the house, and there are rotating exhibits of Civil War memorabilia and holiday decorations. | 20 W. Main St. | 516/922–6808 | $2 | Tues.–Sun. 1–5.

Sagamore Hill National Historic Site. This 23-room Victorian was Theodore Roosevelt's family home. Often called the summer White House, it was President Roosevelt's cherished family retreat. | Cove Neck Rd. | 516/922–4447 | www.nps.gov/sahi | $5 | Daily 9:30–4.

MAKING A MINT

In the early 1800s, much of the world's peppermint was grown in Asia. Around 1833, a peddler found some peppermint plants growing wild in Wayne County, New York, and distilled it. Farmers in the area caught on, followed suit, and sold their product to store owner Hiram Hotchkiss of Phelps, New York. It wasn't long before Hotchkiss had 1,200 pints of the oil, so he took it to New York City where merchants rejected him, thinking the oil wasn't pure. Hotchkiss trudged back to Phelps, tested his stock, and, after confirming that it was, indeed, pure, decided to ship some to Hamburg, Germany, a center for worldwide distribution of such oils. The Germans agreed to buy Hotchkiss's goods and, in turn, sold it to some of those same merchants in New York City who had rejected it.

    Wayne County on the shore of Lake Ontario was thereby established as a primary source of the oil. Nearly every farmer in the county was soon growing and distilling the stuff, and Hotchkiss, who moved to nearby Lyons, New York, became known as the Peppermint King. Although the peppermint-growing industry moved to the Midwest around 1900, Lyons still remembers its heritage by holding "Peppermint Days" every year in July.

© Artville

Theodore Roosevelt Memorial Bird Sanctuary and Trailside Museum. Located just down the road from Sagamore Hill, Theodore Roosevelt's family home, this bird sanctuary is the perfect legacy of this environmentally active president. There's a cemetery on the grounds where Roosevelt is buried. | 134 Cove Rd. | 516/922–3200 | Free | Daily 8:30–4:30.

ON THE CALENDAR

SEPT.: *Annual Bluefish Tournament.* Anglers of all ages participate in this annual event. Winners receive plaques and gift certificates at the post-tournament tailgate party. | 516/797–4123.

OCT.: *Oyster Festival.* This arts-and-crafts show held downtown in the central business district includes oyster-shucking contests, a 5K run, and a historic boat exhibit. | 516/922–6464 or 516/624–8082.

Dining

Canterbury Ales Oyster Bar and Grill. American. This family bistro and grill serves everything from horseradish honey mustard salmon and Japanese ahi tuna to Parmesan- and herb-crusted chicken and wild game. You'll also find 99 beers from around the world. Raw bar. Kids' menu. Sunday brunch. | 46 Audrey Ave. | 516/922–3614 | $10–$23 | AE, DC, MC, V.

Mill River Inn. Contemporary. This quiet restaurant, known for grilled fish and steak, has romantic touches such as a fireplace, white linen, fresh flowers, and candlelight. Try sautéed Hudson Valley foie gras; rack of lamb grilled with rosemary and served with poached pears and spinach; or pork chops stuffed with Swiss chard, roasted peppers, and pecorino cheese. No smoking. | 160 Mill River Rd. | 516/922–7768 | Reservations essential | No lunch | $17–$32; $55–$65 prix fixe (weekends) | AE, DC, MC, V.

Oyster Bay Railz. American. Open until 1 AM, this is the place to indulge those late-night cravings for burgers, chicken wings, mozzarella sticks, and other not-so-healthy foods. Grab a beer, play darts or pool, catch the game, or enjoy live music on weekends. | 115 Audrey Ave. | 516/624–6911 | $6–$7 | AE, MC, V.

Steve's Pier I. Continental. Set right on the Long Island Sound, this spot is full of maritime memorabilia such as an 8-ft replica of the USS *Rotterdam* and a stuffed 9-ft hammerhead shark. The flame-roasted lobster is seasoned with a special Pier 1 blend and cooked in a custom-made broiler at over 1,000°F, and rumor has it that the result is the tenderest and tastiest lobster you'll find anywhere. Open-air dining on deck. Live music Friday in winter. Kids' menu. In Bayville, 10 mi north of Oyster Bay. | 33 Bayville Ave., Bayville | 516/628–2153 | www.stevespierone.com | $21–$38 | AE, D, DC, MC, V.

Lodging

East Norwich Inn. A comfortable modern hotel in a country setting, this inn has Tudor-style accents and standard rooms, suites, and a cottage. The cottage has a full kitchen. In East Norwich, 1.3 mi south of Oyster Bay. Complimentary Continental breakfast. In-room data ports, some kitchenettes, cable TV. Pool. Sauna. Gym. Business services, free parking. | 6321 Northern Blvd., East Norwich | 516/922–1500 or 800/334–4798 | fax 516/922–1089 | www.eastnorwichinn.com | 72 rooms, 5 suites, 1 cottage | $115–$130 rooms, $185–$260 suites, $210–$260 cottage, $185–$220 apartment | AE, D, DC, MC, V.

PALMYRA

MAP 3, F6

(Nearby towns also listed: Canandaigua, Geneva, Rochester, Victor, Waterloo)

Founded in 1789, this former bustling canal town is surrounded by dairy farms and orchards. Palmyra is the birthplace of Mormonism and the home of founder Joseph Smith. It wasn't until Brigham Young crossed the U.S. with his followers that Mormonism was established in Utah. As a special place for Mormon followers, Palmyra still bustles with the annual Hill Cumorah Pageant in July. The town of Lyons, 12 mi east of Palmyra, was the home of the H.G. Hotchkiss Company, the world's largest producer of peppermint oil from 1839 until its close in 1990.

Information: Wayne County Office of Tourism | Dept. TG98, 9 Pearl St., Box 131, Lyons, 14489 | 315/946–5469 or 800/527–6510.

Attractions

Alling Coverlet Museum. This museum has the largest collection of handwoven coverlets in the nation. You'll also find quilts, miniature rugs, and a gift shop. | 122 William St. | 315/597–6737 | Free | June–Sept., daily 1–5.

The Amazing Maize Maze at Long Acre Farms. This 5-acre living board game called "The Amazing Maize Maze" takes about 90 min to negotiate. Also on the grounds are smaller mazes, a farm market, play area, animals, an ice cream shop, and tractors. In Macedon, 4 mi south of Palmyra and 12 mi east of Rochester. Hours change with the length of the day, so call ahead. | 1342 Eddy Rd., Macedon | 315/986–9821 | www.longacrefarms.com | $7.00 | Late July–Oct., call for hours.

Mormon Historic Sites and Bureau of Information. This is perhaps the best place to learn about the beginnings of the Mormon religion. It is where Joseph Smith is said to have received golden plates from the angel Moroni (it was from these plates that the Book of Mormon came). A 40-ft monument stands on the hill. Guided tours last 25 min. | 603 Rte. 21 | 315/597–5851 | Free | Mon.–Sat. 9–7, Sun. 11–7.

The **Joseph Smith Home** is where Smith lived until he was 22 years old, 8 yrs after he is said to have received his first vision in the Sacred Grove behind the house. Smith, the founder of Mormonism, was born in Vermont in 1805, and came here with his family in 1815. | 29 Stafford Rd. | 315/597–4383 | Free | Mon.–Sat. 9–6, Sun. 1–6.

The first 5,000 copies of the Book of Mormon came off the press at the **E. B. Grandin Print Shop** from 1829 to 1831. An early copy of the book and many copies in different languages are on display here. | 217 E. Main St. | 315/597–5982 | Free | Mon.–Sat. 9–5, Sun. 11–7.

Palmyra Historical Museum. This museum in the former St. James Hotel houses 18th-century furniture, Erie Canal artifacts and artwork, toys, and Victorian-era portraits. | 132 Market St. | 315/597–6981 | Free | June–Oct., Tues.–Thurs. 1–4.

Phelps General Store Museum. The Phelps family ran this store from the 1860s until the 1940s. There's an odd collection of rooms upstairs, where an eccentric Sybil Phelps, the daughter of founder Julius Phelps, lived without utilities until 1976. | 140 Market St. | 315/597–6981 | Free | June–Sept., Sat. 1–4.

ON THE CALENDAR

JULY: *Hill Cumorah Pageant.* Enjoy one of the nation's largest outdoor theater productions, with a cast of 600 and outdoor seating for 9,000. Each of the seven performances is free. | 315/597–5851.

JULY: *Peppermint Days.* Music, exhibits, dancing, and the Peppermint Princess honor the village's roots as a worldwide center for peppermint oil production. | 800/527–6510.

SEPT.: *Canaltown Days.* This festival recalls the heyday of the Erie Canal with tours, music, and food. | 315/597–6700.

SEPT.: *Lumberjack Festival.* This two-day event includes lumberjack breakfasts, competitions, and greased-pole climbing. | 315/986–3732.

Dining

Zero's Hot Dog Stand. Casual. You can order something besides a hot dog here, but that would be sorely missing the point. A local favorite, especially with kids, this is easy on your wallet. | 623 E. Main St. | 315/597–5654 | $2–$8 | No credit cards.

Lodging

Liberty House Bed & Breakfast. Built in the 1840s on the site of a blacksmith shop, this graceful three-story gingerbread home with a wraparound veranda has served as a Baptist parsonage, a private home, and, since 1997, a B&B. The Liberty House is a relaxed place with a friendly resident dog that welcomes families. Complimentary breakfast. Cable TV. No pets. No smoking. | 131 W. Main St. | 315/597–0011 | 3 rooms (2 with shared bath) | $65–$85 | www.libertyhousebb.com | No credit cards.

Quality Inn. The rooms are standard, but the view is not. This property in Newark, 9 mi east of Palmyra, is right on the barge canal, providing wonderful scenes of passing boats. Restaurant, bar (with entertainment), picnic area. Cable TV. Indoor pool. Gym. | 125 N. Main, Newark | 315/331–9500 | fax 315/331–5264 | 107 rooms | $89–$99 | AE, D, DC, MC, V.

Wayne Villa. This stone inn with a spacious lawn offers affordable, standard rooms. In Macedon, 6 mi west of Palmyra. Picnic area. Kitchenettes, cable TV. Playground. | 344 Rte. 31, Macedon | 315/986–5530 | 17 rooms | $40–$54 | D, MC, V.

PATCHOGUE

MAP 4, L7

(Nearby town also listed: Westhampton Beach)

The seaport village of Patchogue was at one time the last stop east on the Long Island Railroad for vacationers. Its premier status as *the* summer resort continued until the early part of the 20th century, when motor cars, transporting tourists ever farther east, contributed to its decline as a tourist mecca.

Today ferries run on the Patchogue River to transport vacationers to nearby Fire Island points Watch Hill and Davis Park. Patchogue village and many local organizations are working together to rebuild and reinvigorate the village's appeal to travelers.

Europeans settled Patchogue in 1664, when the Unkechaug Indians sold nine pieces of land to Governor Winthrop of Connecticut. The early European settlers took advantage of local water power and operated grist, saw, and other mills, producing paper, wool, carpet, twine, and lace. Eventually, the area developed a beautiful seaport and village.

Information: **Village of Patchogue** | 14 Baker St., Box 719, 11772 | 631/475–4300 | fax 631/475–4314.

Attractions

Shorefront Park. A public park along the shore with a playground, picnic area, and band-shell where there's live music in the summer. | Smith St. | 631/475–4314 | Free | Daily, dawn to dusk.

ON THE CALENDAR

JUNE–AUG.: *Concerts at the Bandshell.* Come down to the Shorefront Park on Saturdays and Sundays to hear live jazz, swing, rock, and folk music. | 631/475–4314.
SEPT.: *Clam and Crab Festival.* This festival offers exhibits, seafood, entertainment, boat displays, and craft vendors. | 631/475–0121.
NOV.: *Thanksgiving Parade.* This holiday parade along the river is held the weekend before Thanksgiving. | 631/475–0121.

Dining

Bellport. Contemporary. Antique iron chairs and painted tables fill the three open and bright dining rooms at this country restaurant, 4 mi east of Patchogue. Try the grilled marinated

Angus rib-eye steak, grilled buttermilk chicken breast with hush puppies and tamarind sauce, jumbo Louisiana crab cakes, or the corn-crusted oysters. Live music on holidays. | 159 S. Country Rd., Bellport Village | 631/286–7550 | www.donaldshaw.com/thebellport | $15–$23 | MC, V.

Brick House Brewery. American. Brick House Brewery serves pub food in the oldest commercial building in Patchogue—a large brick building with a slate gable roof. The building was once a stop on the underground railroad. Keeping the historic flavor, the brewery has retained the original ceilings in the Tap Room and has exposed a lot of the original brick. The upstairs dining room doubles as a beer museum. Try the house sampler with wings, chicken fingers, and onion rings with blue cheese, horseradish, and barbecue sauce. There's outdoor dining in the garden. Live music Wednesday–Saturday. Comedy on Tuesday night. Kids' menu. Sunday brunch. | 67 W. Main St. | 631/447–2337 | $12–$21 | AE, DC, MC, V.

Chowder House. Seafood. Housed in a former hotel, this casual restaurant packed with sports memorabilia is within walking distance of the water. The seafood dishes are popular; try the seafood bisque and Manhattan chowder, crab cakes, or broiled seafood plates. Four miles east of Patchogue. Open-air dining on a porch. Kids' menu. Sunday brunch on patio. | 19 Bellport La., Bellport | 631/286–2343 | $22–$32 | AE, MC, V.

Louis XVI. French. With perhaps some of the best reviews of any Long Island restaurant to its credit, Louis XVI's reputation begins with its opulent decor, which, in the style of the palace at Versailles, is done with lots of glass and chandeliers. Don't miss the lobster, crabmeat, or salmon salad. Try also the potato-encrusted red snapper, venison Wellington, and Marie Antoinette Doll (a chocolate dessert with marzipan, a chocolate skirt, and chocolate sorbet). There's open-air dining on the patio with beautiful views of Great South Bay. Sunday brunch. | 600 S. Ocean Ave. | 631/654–8970 | Jacket required | Closed Mon. | $45–$55, $63 prix fixe menu | AE, D, DC, MC, V.

Reese's 1900. American. Reese's 1900, housed in a turn-of-the-20th-century building, has been a Suffolk County meeting place for over 25 years. Reese's is known for the fisherman's platter of fried shrimp and scallops. Try 55 mph chile—spicy and topped with melted cheddar, onions, and sour cream—as well as sandwiches such as The Rachel (hot pastrami on rye, with sauerkraut and bubbling Swiss cheese). No smoking. | 70 N. Ocean Ave. | 631/289–1900 | Reservations not accepted | Closed Sun. | $6–$15 | AE, DC, MC, V.

Lodging

Inn at Medford. This two-story motel, built in 1976 and renovated in 1999, was designed in the Southwestern adobe style. The spacious, comfortable rooms have modern amenities, and a golf course and marina are just 2 mi away. 4 mi north of Patchogue. Bar, complimentary Continental breakfast, room service. Some refrigerators, cable TV. Pool. Business services. | 2695 Rte. 112 (Long Island Expressway, exit 64), Medford | 631/654–3000 or 800/626–7779 | fax 631/654–1281 | 76 rooms | $129–$149 | AE, D, DC, MC, V.

PAUL SMITHS

MAP 3, J3

(Nearby towns also listed: Lake Placid, Saranac Lake, Tupper Lake, Wilmington)

This small community was named after Appollos (Paul) Smith, a famed Adirondack guide. Smith established a hotel whose reputation for hospitality gave rise to Paul Smiths College, known for its degrees in hotel management and the culinary arts. It is the only private college within the boundaries of the Adirondack Park.

Information: **Chamber of Commerce** | 30 Main St., #3, Saranac Lake, 12983 | 518/891–1990.

Attractions

Paul Smiths College. With degrees in culinary arts and hospitality, natural resources and environmental technology, this lakeside campus is home to a small population of students who enjoy a 14–1 student-to-teacher ratio and plenty of outdoor recreation. The hotel and restaurant run by the school is in the town of Saranac Lake. | Rtes. 86 and 30 | 518/327–6211 | www.paulsmiths.edu | Campus tours Mon.–Sat. 10–2.

White Pine Camp. President Calvin Coolidge used this great camp as the "Summer White House" in 1926. Also known for its outstanding architecture, White Pine Camp has guided tours that take about two hours and cover the grounds and all 20 buildings. Check out the stuffed-animal collection, bowling alley, and the Japanese teahouse on a small island, which can be reached by an arched stone bridge. Off Route 86, 12 mi northwest of Saranac Lake. | White Pine Rd. | 518/327–3030 | wpinecamp@aol.com | www.whitepinecamp.com | $9 | Mid-May–mid-Oct., tours at 10 AM and 1:30 PM; visitors allowed only during tour hrs.

ON THE CALENDAR

AUG.: *Adirondack Wildlife Festival.* Wildlife rehabilitators and educators bring a variety of interesting species to the park visitors center. Includes music, food, and interpretive walks. | 518/327–3000.

Dining

St. Regis Restaurant. American. This Adirondack-style restaurant has been around since 1964, and has a wooden interior covered with old snow shoes and skis. The main dining room has a fireplace and mountain views, and there's also a luncheonette café. They specialize in steaks and seafood, but be sure to try the stuffed pork chop or come by on Sunday night for the roast turkey dinner. Kid's menu. | Rte. 86 | 518/327–9454 | Closed Tues. | $8–$14 | No credit cards.

Lodging

Lodge on Lake Clear. Accommodations at this 25-acre resort range from simple lodge rooms in a century-old inn to chalets, cabins, and lakeside cottages. Many are fully furnished and have fireplaces and can sleep up to twelve adults. Great for groups and families. Restaurant, bar. Some kitchenettes, some microwaves, some refrigerators, some in-room hot tubs, no TV in some rooms, some room phones. Beach, boating. | Rtes. 186 and 30, Lake Clear | 518/891–1489 or 800/442–2356 | www.lodgeonlakeclear.com | 4 rooms, 5 suites, 2 chalets, 2 cabins, 4 cottages | $99–$149 rooms, $189–250 suites, $325–$750 chalets and cabins | AE, MC, V.

White Pine Camp. White Pine Camp has hosted many prominent guests since it was built in 1907. This historic Adirondack "great camp" was known as the 1926 "Summer White House" after President Calvin Coolidge enjoyed a vacation here. White Pine House is also known for its outstanding architecture and location, on 35 acres of Lake Osgood shoreline amid majestic pines. Grounds include a bowling alley, and Japanese teahouse. Cabins are fully furnished; some can sleep 6–8 adults. Off Route 86, 12 mi northwest of Saranac Lake. Picnic area, kitchenettes, refrigerators, no TV, no room phones. Lake. Hiking, beach, dock, boating, fishing. Cross–country skiing. No pets. | White Pine Rd. | 518/327–3030 | info@ whitepinecamp.com | www.whitepinecamp.com | 9 cabins | $140–$275 nightly; $900–$1700 weekly | MC, V.

PEEKSKILL

MAP 3, C1

(Nearby towns also listed: Croton-on-Hudson, Mt. Kisco, Pound Ridge)

Overlooking the beautiful Hudson River, Peekskill is a pretty village filled with Victorian homes and turn-of-the-20th-century architecture. Today about 20,000 residents enjoy the gorgeous vistas and old-time feel of this north Westchester spot. Settled in the early 1600s, Peekskill is named after a Dutch trader named Jan Peek, who moved his family near the "kill" (Dutch for "creek") and built a trading post known as "Peek's kill." In its early years the town was an important market and harbor community; during the Revolutionary War it served as the hub for militiamen from New York and New England. By the Civil War, the town had become a prominent industrial center where stoves, iron products, plows, and many other items were made.

Information: **Peekskill/Cortland Chamber of Commerce** | 1 S. Division St., 10566 | 914/737–3600.

Attractions

Paramount Center of the Arts. The Paramount Center offers a variety of arts performances year-round. It has 1930s-era theater seats and a historic marquee. | 1008 Brown St. | 914/739–2333 | fax 914/736–9674 | www.paramountcenter.org | Call for schedule.

Peekskill Museum. This museum, established in 1946, is in a Victorian home, built by a prominent local lawyer in 1877. It has some fine artifacts conveying Peekskill's history, and has for the most part remained in-state, with original fixtures and ornaments of resident families. | 124 Union Ave. | 914/736–0473 | www.peekskillmuseum.org | $1 | Sat. 1–3 PM and by appointment.

A HANDFUL OF LAKES

Native American legend holds that the Finger Lakes came to be when the Great Spirit blessed the land and left hand imprints behind in the soil. Geologists say a retreating glacial sheet of ice clawed the north–south valleys and left behind enough glacial debris to dam the rivers at the northern end. The lakes do, of course, resemble fingers—well, except for one (Keuka Lake is Y shape). To keep the finger analogy alive, picture Keuka Lake as a slingshot dropped by the nearby fingers.

The area's tourist bureau considers 11 lakes to be Finger Lakes. The six that are more than 10 mi long emerge as the major ones. Here are the lakes, from west to east, with their Native American names (if applicable), length, and depth:

Conesus ("Always Beautiful"]: 9 mi long, 59 ft deep.
Hemlock (not named by Native Americans): 8 mi long, 98 ft deep.
Canadice ("Long Lake"): 3 mi long, 91 ft deep.
Honeoye ("Finger Lying"): 5 mi long, 30 ft deep.
Canandaigua ("The Chosen Place"): 16 mi long, 262 ft deep.
Keuka ("Canoe Landing"): 22 mi long, 157 ft deep.
Seneca ("Place of Stone"): 36 mi long, 632 ft deep.
Cayuga ("Boat Landing"): 40 mi long, 435 ft deep.
Owasco ("Crossing Place"): 11 mi long, 177 ft deep.
Skaneateles ("Long Lake"): 15 mi long, 350 ft deep.
Otisco ("Waters Much Dried Away"): 6 mi long, 66 ft deep.

AUG.: *Peekskill Celebration: Ships and Sails.* This citywide celebration features tall-ship cruises, coast-guard demonstrations, pleasure-craft regattas, a parade, live music, arts and crafts, and a fireworks display. | 914/737–3600.

Dining

Crystal Bay. Eclectic. Arrive by land or by sea to this fun restaurant overlooking the Hudson River. It's known for crab cakes, lobster, and a huge brunch buffet. There's open-air dining on the patio, and live music on weekends. Kids' menu. Sunday brunch. Dock space. | 5 John Walsh Blvd., Charles Point Marina | 914/737–8332 | Closed Mon. No lunch Sat. | $9–$24 | AE, DC, MC, V.

Division Street Grill. Contemporary. In keeping with Peekskill's recently developed art scene, this restaurant has a "downtown" sensibility without the attitude. Choose from specialties like the prawns with garlic, tomato, and heavy cream, the Chilean sea bass wrapped in a potato crust, and the scallops with curried coconut milk, fennel salad, and lemongrass. | 26 No. Division St. | 845/739–6380 | $18–$25 | AE, MC, V.

Monteverde at Oldstone. Continental. This romantic restaurant, housed in a 1773 mansion, has period lamps and chandeliers. There's also alfresco dining with views of the Hudson. Known for beef, veal, seafood. | 28 Bear Mountain Bridge Rd. | 914/739–5000 | Closed Tues. No lunch Sat. | $23–$28 | AE, DC, MC, V.

Susan's. Contemporary. This warm and cozy spot in the downtown arts district has a country-French look, with checkerboard floors and pig memorabilia on the walls. Susan's serves a salmon strudel baked in pastry and a grilled breast of duck with dried-cherry sauce. Kids' menu. | 12 N. Division St. | 914/737–6624 | Closed Sun., Mon. | $18–$25 | AE, DC, MC, V.

Lodging

Peekskill Inn. This inn offers panoramic views of the Hudson River, and many of the rooms have outdoor terraces on which to enjoy the breathtaking scenery. Restaurant, bar, complimentary Continental breakfast, room service. Cable TV. Pool. Some pets allowed. | 634 Main St. | 914/739–1500 or 800/526–9466 | fax 914/739–7067 | www.peekskillinn.com | 53 rooms | $80–$93 | AE, D, DC, MC, V.

PENN YAN

MAP 3, F6

(Nearby towns also listed: Canandaigua, Geneva, Hammondsport, Naples, Watkins Glen)

Legend has it that this town's unusual name was a compromise between settlers from Pennsylvania and New England (Yankees), who could not agree on anything else. Sitting at the north end of one of the branches of Keuka Lake, the village is centrally located for the entire Finger Lakes region. Founded in 1787, Penn Yan is today home to Birkett Mills, the world's largest producer of buckwheat products. Today Penn Yan has a large Mennonite and Amish community that came from Lancaster and Ohio during the 1970s after capitalizing on the sale of their valuable real estate holdings, and moving in search of a more remote, private home.

Information: Yates County Chamber of Commerce | 2375 Rte. 14 A, 14527 | 315/536–3111 or 800/868–9283 | info@yatesny.com | www.yatesny.com.

Attractions

Keuka Lake State Park. This 621-acre park has snowmobiling, picnic spots, camping, hiking, boating, fishing, and swimming. In Bluff Point, 7 mi west of Penn Yan. | 3370 Pepper

PENN YAN

INTRO
ATTRACTIONS
DINING
LODGING

Rd., off Rte. 54A, Bluff Point | 315/536–3666 | www.nysparks.state.ny.us/parks/ | Free; $5 per vehicle | Daily.

The Viking Spirit. Take a leisurely ride across Keuka Lake on this two-tier boat. Catering available or BYO. Leaves from the Viking Resort. | 680 East Lake Rd. (Rte. 54) | 315/536–7061 | www.vikingresort.com.

Keuka Lake Wine Trail (800/440–4898 | www.fingerlakes.net/keukawines) includes seven area wineries. **Dr. Konstantin Frank's Vinifera Wine Cellars** (9749 Middle Rd., Hammondsport, about 10 mi southwest of Penn Yan | 607/868–4884 or 800/320–0735 | fax 607/868–4888 | frankwines@aol.com | www.drfrankwines.com | Free | Mon.–Sat. 9–5, Sun. noon–5) was founded in 1962 by Dr. Konstantin Frank, who pioneered the growth of European grape varieties in the eastern United States. A renovation project allows the **Heron Hill Winery** (9249 Rte. 76, Hammondsport | 800/441–4241 | fax 607/868–3435 | www.heronhill.com | info@heronhill.com | Free | Mon.–Sat. 9–5, Sun. noon–5) to handle many more visitors than in the past. The **Keuka Spring Vineyards** (273 E. Lake Rd. (Rte. 54) | 315/536–3147 | www.keukaspring.com | Free | June–mid-Oct., Mon.–Sat. 10–5, Sun. noon–5; Apr.–May, mid-Oct–Nov., Fri.–Sun. 10–5) offers tastings of its 14 varieties of wine, a gift shop and picnic area. **McGregor Vineyard** (5503 Dutch St., off Rte. 54 | 607/292–3999 or 800/272–0192 | www.linkny.com/~mcg | Free | Apr.–Nov., daily 10–6; Dec.–Mar., daily 11–5; sunset tastings July–Aug., Fri.–Sat. 6 PM–8 PM) has an excellent view of Keuka Lake.

Oliver House Museum. A small museum devoted to local history, this is run by the Yates County Genealogical and Historical Society. It was the home of a succession of physicians in the Oliver family. | 200 Main St. | 315/536–7318 | Free | Weekdays 9:30–4:30.

Outlet Trail. The Outlet hike-and-bike trail follows an abandoned 1884 railroad track along a 6-mi linear park connecting Keuka and Seneca lakes. | Boat Launch at Water and Keuka Sts.; trail ends at Seneca St., Dresden | 315/536–3111 or 800/868–9283 | Free | Daily.

ON THE CALENDAR

JULY: *Yates County Fair.* Get down and dirty at this 5-day festival, which includes a demolition derby, tractor pull, and community tug-of-war. | 315/536–3111.

Dining

Miller's Essenhaus. American. A Mennonite staff offers wholesome, homemade, and filling meals such as orange-glazed roast pork, chicken and biscuits, and ham loaf. The building is new but the wood floors, copper lights, handmade quilts, and Mennonite photos create a homey feel. Buffet dinner Thursday, buffet breakfast and lunch Saturday. No smoking. | 315/531–8260 | Breakfast also available; closed Sun. | $8–$16 | AE, D, MC, V.

Lodging

Colonial Motel. This local landmark has been a motel since the late 1800s, and it retains much of the original Adirondack architecture, including the original clapboard sidings. Units are fully furnished efficiencies which are ideal for families or longer term stays. Kitchenettes, refrigerators, cable TV. | 175 W. Lake Rd. | 315/536–3056 | 17 rooms | $75–$95 | AE, D, MC, V.

Feather Tick 'n Thyme. This romantic 1890s Victorian is set on 80 acres of rolling farmland in the Finger Lakes wine country. A wraparound porch, stone walkways, and gardens overlooking a creek make it impossible to stay indoors. But if you must, the luxurious rooms are furnished with lovely period antiques and reproductions. Complimentary breakfast. No pets. | 7661 Tuttle Rd. | 607/522–4113 | fax 607/522–4651 | 4 rooms | $75–$95 | No credit cards.

Finton's Landing. Stenciled walls, quilt-covered beds, hardwood floors, and shutters give this Federal-style B&B on Keuka Lake its quaint appeal. In summer, enjoy a healthy breakfast with the chirping birds on the front porch. Then head off for some blueberry picking, a winery tour, and a hike along the old Fall Brook Railroad. Complimentary breakfast. No pets. No kids under 14. No smoking. | 661 E. Lake Rd. | 315/536–3146 | 4 rooms | $99–$109 | MC, V.

Fox Inn. Rooms at this Greek Revival House are filled with both antiques and modern luxuries such as Internet access for guests. Some even have hot tubs. The two-room suite is good for two couples or two families. There's a lovely rose garden on the property. Picnic area, complimentary breakfast. Some in-room hot tubs, cable TV, in-room VCRs, no room phones. No smoking. | 158 Main St. | 315/536–3101 or 800/901–7997 | fax 315/536–7612 | 6 rooms (1 with shower only), 1 suite | $75–$150 | AE, MC, V.

Viking Resort. This resort about 6 mi south of Penn Yan is on the eastern shore of Keuka Lake, and has private docking facilities. It's home base for the *Viking Spirit* cruise, which takes visitors out on Keuka Lake. Three- and six-bedroom cottages are popular for family reunions. Picnic area. Some kitchenettes, refrigerators, cable TV. Pool. Hot tub. Beach, dock, boating. Pets allowed (fee). | 680 E. Lake Rd. | 315/536–7061 | fax 315/536–0737 | viking@vikingresort.com | www.vikingresort.com | 42 rooms, 35 apartments | $65–$140 rooms, $180–$212 apartments | Closed mid-Oct.–Apr. | No credit cards.

PIERMONT

(Nearby towns also listed: Nyack, Spring Valley, Stony Point, Suffern, Tarrytown)

This attractive town on the west bank of the Hudson River is known for its lovely views and acclaimed fine dining that brings people from miles away. Visitors can enjoy hiking in Tallman Mountain State Park. As the town's name suggests, boating is also a major activity.

Information: Rockland County Office of Tourism | 3 Main St., Nyack, 10960 | 845/353–5533 | www.rockland.org.

Attractions

Fly Wheel. Founded in 1992, Piermont's first artist-run gallery strives to exhibit the finest work of tri-state-area artists. | 223 Ash St. | 845/365–6411 | Free | Thurs. and Sun. 1–6, Fri. and Sat. 1–9.

Tallman Mountain State Park. This 689-acre park along the Hudson River has 3 mi of hiking trails, a pool, picnic areas, ball field with track, tennis courts, and basketball. Migratory birds and bird-watchers are attracted to the 500-acre Piermont Marsh, part of Hudson River National Estuarine Research Reserve. | Rte. 9 W, Sparkill | 845/359–0544 | $5 per car June–Labor Day; pool $2 | Daily dawn–dusk.

Dining

Freelance Cafe and Wine Bar. Eclectic. This intimate main-street bistro serves contemporary American cuisine with French and Italian touches. Try the Pacific ahi tuna served rare with a wasabi crust or the roast duckling orange-caramel. Rotating exhibits of art hang in the black-and-white interior. Starters include Alsatian onion tart with crème fraîche and wild-mushroom ravioli. | 506 Piermont Ave. | 845/365–3250 | Reservations not accepted | $18–$22 | No credit cards.

The Mariner. Seafood. A tiered dining room offers sweeping views of the Hudson and the Tappan Zee Bridge. Known for crabs, oysters, steaks. Try filet mignon of tuna with teriyaki plum sauce or mussels steamed with tomatoes and herbs. Open-air dining on patio. Raw bar. Kids' menu. Dock space. | 701 Piermont Ave. | 845/365–1360 | Reservations essential Fri. and Sun.; reservations not accepted Sat. | $16–$39 | AE, MC, DC, V.

Lodging

Holiday Inn. This hotel is 3½ mi from Nyack's antiques and restaurant district, 5 mi from the Tappan Zee Bridge, and 10 mi from Bear Mountain State Park. With three meeting rooms, it's geared toward the business traveler and is within a few miles of area businesses such as Volvo, Verizon, and IBM. Restaurant, bar, complimentary Continental breakfast, room service. In-room data ports. Cable TV. Pool. Sauna. Gym. Laundry service. Business services. | 329 Rte. 303, Orangeburg | 845/359–7000 or 800/243–8287 | fax 845/359–7196 | 167 rooms | $109–$154 | AE, MC, V.

PLAINVIEW/OLD BETHPAGE

MAP 3, C2

(Nearby towns also listed: Jericho, Plainview, Syosset)

Both Plainview and Old Bethpage are unincorporated villages in the greater township of Oyster Bay. Originally known as Manetto Hill Farm, Plainview was named in 1885. Today the area, which was mostly flat farmland when originally settled, is a pretty residential district broken only by the occasional strip mall and horse farm. The area is home to the Old Bethpage Restoration Village, which is a re-created pre–Civil War Long Island farm community resting on a beautiful 200-acre site.

Information: **Huntington Chamber of Commerce** | 151 W. Carver St., Huntington, 11743 | 631/423–6100 | fax 631/351–8276 | staff@huntingtonchamber.com | www.huntingtonchamber.com.

Attractions

Bethpage State Park. A 1,500-acre park boasts one of the country's best public golf complexes (Black Course) and polo fields. The Black Course will be home to two U.S. Opens in the coming years. There are picnic areas and bridle paths. Take Bethpage Parkway and follow signs. | 99 Quaker Meeting House Rd., Farmingdale | 516/249–0700 | Free | Daily dawn–dusk.

Old Bethpage Village Restoration. This 200-acre pre–Civil War farm village is well worth the visit. The site is pastoral, with soft rolling hills and lovely meadows, and the original structures were moved to this spot from other parts of Long Island. Buildings include two general stores, nine residences, a schoolhouse, a tavern, a church, and a working farm with animals. Interpreter staff are dressed in period costumes and love sharing their knowledge. Call for ongoing events. Take the Long Island Expressway to exit 48, and go 1 mi south. | 1303 Round Swamp Rd. | 516/572–8401 | $6 | Mar.–Dec., Wed.–Sun.

ON THE CALENDAR
JULY: *Old-Fashioned Independence Day Celebration.* This unusual 4th of July celebration at the Old Bethpage Village Restoration is mid-1800s style, so leave your six-packs at home. There's a picnic, choral music, and children's games. | 516/572–8400.
DEC.: *Holiday Traditions and Candlelight Evenings.* Christmas in the 1800s comes to life with entertainment and traditional music of the period, magic lantern shows, and a visit from St. Nick. At Old Bethpage Village Restoration. | 516/572–8400.

Dining

56th Fighter Group. Continental. This fun World War II–theme restaurant sits on a local airport runway with real planes and jeeps out back. Watch planes take off and land while you dig into the steaks, chops, and seafood. Big band music piped throughout the restaurant further sets the World War II–era mood. Kids' menu. Early bird dinners. Sunday brunch. No smoking. | Rte. 110, Republic Airport Gate 1, E. Farmingdale | 631/694–8280 | Reservations essential | $17–$29 | AE, D, DC, MC, V.

Morgo's Dynasty. Chinese. Though its focus is on classic Hunan and Szechuan dishes, Morgo's has expanded to include sushi. As an incentive to get that extra spring roll, Morgo's will throw in a free lottery ticket for orders over $20. Takeout and delivery available. | 1163 Old County Rd. | 516/942–8688 | $15–$30 | AE, MC, V.

Lodging

Marriott Melville. The Melville business district is 3 mi from this Marriott, which is also close to the Adventureland Amusement Park. For shopping, try the nearby Walt Whitman Mall. Some rooms have wet bars and satellite TV. In Melville, 5 mi northeast of Farmingdale. Restaurant, bar (with entertainment), room service. In-room data ports, cable TV. Pool. Hot tub. Exercise equipment. Video games. Business services. | 1350 Old Walt Whitman Rd., Melville | 631/423–1600 | fax 631/423–1790 | www.marriott.com | 374 rooms, 24 suites | $219–$229 rooms, $249 suites | AE, D, DC, MC, V.

Residence Inn. Situated within 3 mi of major area businesses such as Lockheed Martin, Northrup/Grumman, and Lilco, this hotel is geared primarily toward business travelers. For recreation, a 9-hole golf course and tennis courts at Bethpage State Park are just ½ mi away. The ocean is about 10 mi away. Restaurant, bar, complimentary breakfast, room service. In-room data ports, some kitchenettes, cable TV, in-room VCRs. Pool. Hot tub, sauna. Gym. Baby-sitting. Laundry facilities, laundry service. Business services. Pets allowed (fee). | 9 Gerhard Rd. | 516/433–6200 or 800/331–3131 | fax 516/433–2569 | 165 suites | $135–$214 | www.residenceinn.com | AE, MC, V.

PLATTSBURGH

MAP 3, L2

(Nearby towns also listed: Ausable Chasm, Wilmington)

Located at the mouth of the Saranac River, Plattsburgh has a long military history and is therefore home to many historic artifacts. Named for pioneer Zephaniah Platt, who settled here shortly after the American Revolution, Plattsburgh is today a city known for year-round recreation. Visitors should walk the Heritage Trail, beginning downtown, and pass the city's historic homes and waterfront.

Information: Plattsburgh-North Country Chamber of Commerce | 7061 U.S. 9, Box 310, 12901 | 518/563–1000 | chamber@westelcom.com | www.northcountrychamber.com.

Attractions

Alice T. Miner Colonial Collection. William Miner, a railroad industrialist in the 1920s, lived in the small northern New York town of Chazy, where his wife followed her passion for collecting period and miniature furniture, china, porcelain, glass, and textiles. Mrs. Miner's collection filled 15 rooms, leading to the creation of the Miner Museum, housed in her Colonial Revival grey stone mansion. Grounds include gardens. In Chazy, about 12 mi north of Plattsburgh. | 9618 Main St., Chazy | 518/846–7336 | $3 | Tues.–Sat. 10–4; closed Jan.

Ausable Point State Park. You'll find a sandy beach and 123 campsites, 43 with electric hookup. | 3346 Lake Shore Rd. | 518/561–7080 or 518/563–4431 | Memorial Day–mid-Sept., daily.

Champlain Monument. A gift to the city from France in 1909, the monument commemorates the 300th anniversary of the voyage of Samuel de Champlain. | In Riverwalk Park, downtown | 518/563–1000 | Free | Daily.

Cumberland Bay State Park. This state park, for day use and camping, includes a 2,700-ft sandy swimming beach, 200 campsites, a playground, volleyball courts, playing fields, horseshoes, and picnic areas. | 152 Cumberland Bay Rd. | 518/563–5240 or 518/563–4431 | www.nysparks.com | $5–$20 | Memorial Day–mid-Sept., daily.

Juniper Boat Tours. Scenic tours of area islands and sunset dinner/dance cruises are offered aboard the M/V *Juniper*. | 2 Dock St. | 518/561–8970 or 800/388–8970 | $10–$30 | June–Sept., daily 1–3 and 6–10.

Kent-Delord House Museum. In the late 1700s the Delord family were avid travelers who brought treasures back to New York from the far corners of the world. This wonderful collection of these treasures, housed in a landmark Colonial farmhouse, recalls both the family and their era. The museum includes an exhibit on Fanny Delord Hall, a "healer" who patented Fanoline, a medicine reputed to cure "eczema, fever-sores, catarrh, piles, burns, blisters, corns, chapped hands and lips." | 17 Cumberland Ave. | 518/561–1035 | $3 | Mar.–Dec., Tues.–Sat. noon–4; rest of the year by appointment.

Macdonough Monument. A recognized landmark and gathering place along the River Walk, this obelisk commemorates an 1814 naval encounter between the United States and Great Britain. | City Hall Pl. | 518/563–7704 | Free | Daily.

Plattsburgh City Beach. America's largest freshwater beach offers concessions, picnic facilities, and Jet Ski and paddleboat rentals. | Cumberland Head Rd. | 518/563–4431 and 518/563–4431 | $4 per vehicle | Memorial Day–mid-Sept., daily.

State University of New York College at Plattsburgh. This medium-size college offers 50 programs in the liberal arts and sciences, professional studies, and business. | 101 Broad St. | 518/564–2000 | www.plattsburgh.edu | Free | Daily.

ON THE CALENDAR

SEPT.: *Battle of Plattsburgh Commemorative Weekend.* A 2-day reenactment of one of the most pivotal battles of American history when the U.S. troops, outnumbered ten to one, beat back the British navy from the Bay of Plattsburgh, preventing their control of Lake Champlain and, hence, the whole of New England. Many of the battles heroes were black slaves, freed fifty years before the Emancipation Proclamation. The weekend features authentic period food and crafts and a host of spin-off events.

JULY: *Mayor's Cup Race and Landlubbers Festival.* Starting with a week of free outdoor movies and entertainment, wagon rides and live music, and culminating in a 100-sailboat race across Lake Champlain, this is one of summer's most popular, and fun, events.

AUG.: *Redford Picnic.* This old-time country fair is centered around this original, 1855, tractor-powered merry-go-round. Period crafts and games, antiques, and down-home food.

Dining

Anthony's Restaurant and Bistro. Continental. This rustic old farmhouse has two restaurants under its roof. Choose from more casual fare in the loungey piano bar and bistro, or a more formal affair in the brick and wood trimmed dining room with white tablecloths and candles. Both menus have fresh seafood and grill specialties; the bistro is on the lighter side, the main dining room has dishes like roast duckling and rack of lamb. The piano bar is keyed up from Wednesday–Saturday. Kids' menu. | 538 Rte. 3 | 518/561–6420 | No lunch weekends | $8–$14, bistro, $12–$25 dining room | AE, D, DC, MC, V.

Royal Savage Inn. American. This restaurant is in a converted barn with a view of the Salmon River. Look for specialties like maple cider chicken, seafood chardonnay, London broil, turkey dinner, and, for vegetarians, the Mediterranean pasta. Senior citizen specials are offered on Thursdays. Kids' menu. | 4107 U.S. 9 | 518/561–5140 | Closed Jan.–Easter | $15–$20 | AE, D, DC, MC, V.

Lodging

Comfort Inn. This two-story motel in Plattsburgh's business district is a short walk to major shopping centers. Fishing, boating, a public beach, and a golf course are all within 5 mi. Restaurant, bar, complimentary Continental breakfast. Kitchenettes. Cable TV. Pool. Outdoor hot tub, sauna. Laundry service. No pets. | 411 Rte. 3, at I–87 | 518/562–2730 or 800/ 228–5150 | fax 518/563–1562 | 111 rooms | $81–$108 | www.comfortinn.com | AE, MC, V.

Days Inn. This chain hotel offers affordable rooms near Lake Champlain. The three-story brick building is on Plattsburgh's main road. Picnic area. Cable TV. 2 pools. Hot tub. Exercise equipment. Business services. | 8 Everleth Dr. | 518/561–0403 or 800/544–8313 | fax 518/ 561–4192 | www.daysinn.com | infor@daysinn-plattsburgh.com | 112 rooms | $56–$75 | AE, D, DC, MC, V.

Econo Lodge. This two-story motel is 1 mi from Lake Champlain and 5 mi from a snow-mobiling area and a golf course. For those looking for indoor entertainment, Champlain Centre Mall is just ½ mi away. Restaurant, bar, complimentary Continental breakfast. Cable TV. Pool. Business services. Pets allowed. | 528 Rte. 3 | 518/561–1500 or 800/553–2666 | fax 518/563–3144 | www.econolodge.com | 98 rooms | $49–$57 | AE, MC, V.

Holiday Inn. This chain hotel is only 60 mi from Montreal at the intersection of Interstate 87 and Route 3 at exit 37. Restaurant, bar, room service. In-room data ports, cable TV. Pool, wading pool. Hot tub. Exercise equipment. Video games. Business services. Some pets allowed. | 412 Rte. 3 | 518/561–5000 | fax 518/562–2974 | www.holiday-inn.com | 102 rooms | $69–$79 | AE, D, DC, MC, V.

Inn at Smithfield. This Best Western hotel is located between two malls. Rooms have balconies, some with pool views. Some rooms have recliners. From the Adirondack Northway (I–87), take exit 37. Restaurant, bar, room service. In-room data ports, cable TV. Pool. Exercise equipment. Laundry facilities. Business services. Pets allowed. | 446 Rte. 3 | 518/561– 7750 | fax 518/561–9431 | www.bestwestern.com | 120 rooms | $66–$99 | AE, D, DC, MC, V.

Stonehelm. This friendly budget property in a residential area is near campsites, hiking, and the beach. Restaurant, bar, picnic area. Some refrigerators, cable TV. | 72 Spellman Rd. | 518/563–4800 or 800/443–4344 | fax 518/562–1380 | 40 rooms | $40–$50 | AE, D, MC, V.

PORT JEFFERSON

MAP 3, D2

(Nearby towns also listed: Riverhead, Stony Brook)

Because of its port and deep harbor, Port Jefferson has long served as a gateway to Long Island. The Setauket Indians were the first to live here and they began selling the land to settlers in the mid-1600s. By the time of the Revolutionary War, the town was home to many patriots, and during the War of 1812, the harbor was attacked. In 1836, the local residents named the village after Thomas Jefferson and several years later began construction of a large dock. The area had once been named "Drowned Meadow" because it was so marshy, and during the building of the dock, landfill was added to what is now Main Street. Shipbuilding was Port Jefferson's major industry until the size and weight of ships required larger shipyards in the late 1800s.

Since then, it has become a tourist mecca. Across from its busy harbor, restaurants, souvenir shops, antiques stores, and art galleries abound. Waterfront estates, charming Victorians, and old sea captains' homes crowd its downtown. Along its cliffs lies some of the most cherished real estate on Long Island, including such prestigious neighborhoods as Belle Terre.

Information: **Great Port Jefferson Chamber ofCommerce** | 118 W. Broadway (Rte. 25A), 11777 | 631/473–1414 | www.portjeff.com.

Attractions
Ferry to Bridgeport, Connecticut. Instead of driving, you can relax on this passenger ferry that runs across the Long Island Sound to Bridgeport and back. Ferries arrive and depart from

the active and bustling Port Jefferson harbor docks. | 102 W. Broadway (Port Jefferson Harbor) | 631/473–0286 | www.bpjferry.com | $13 walk-on; $36 with vehicle | Call for schedule.

Mather House Museum. Learn about shipbuilding at this site which includes the mid-19th-century home of shipbuilder John Mather, a marine barn and sail loft, and a tool shed with early shipbuilding tools. There is also a country store, butcher and barbershop, a craft house with pre–Civil War furnishings, and perennial and herb gardens. | 115 Prospect St. | 631/473–2665 | www.portjeff.com/pjmuse.html | $2 suggested donation | Sat.–Sun. 1–4; July–Aug., Tues. Wed., Sat., Sun. 1–4.

Tall Ships. Several historic tall ships dock at Port Jefferson Harbor and offer tours and daytime sunset sails. Contact the Long Island Seaport Eco Center. | Port Jefferson Harbor | 631/474–4725 | www.lisec.org | $1 suggested donation; sails $15 | Call for hrs.

Theatre Three. Live productions take place throughout the year at this 400-seat professional theater. | 412 Main St. | 631/928–9100 | fax 631/928–9120 | www.theatrethree.org | Call for schedule.

ON THE CALENDAR
JULY: *Port Jefferson Lions Festival.* Celebrate the July 4th holiday with fireworks, games of chance, live music, food, and rides. | 631/331–2832 | $8.

Dining
Dockside. Seafood. Etched-glass windows overlook the harbor at this spacious family-style restaurant known for its seafood. The dining room sports a nautical theme and there is a saltwater fish tank by the bar. Open-air dining on deck. A pianist plays Friday through Sunday. Kids' menu. Sunday brunch. | 111 W. Broadway | 631/473–5656 | fax 631/473–0195 | $15–$35 | AE, D, DC, MC, V.

25 East American Bistro. American. Part of the dining room has been built directly over the water at this haborside restaurant in the Danford's on the Sound. Pastas, buttered Maine lobster with rice pilaf, and the porterhouse steak are favorites. Open-air dining is available on the Admirals Deck. Kids' menu. Sunday brunch. | 25 E. Broadway (Rte. 112) | 631/928–5200 | fax 631/928–3528 | www.danfords.com/restaurant.html | Breakfast also available | $16–$29 | AE, D, DC, MC, V.

Village Way. American. The ship's stern just outside this restaurant 100 ft from the harbor is a Port Jefferson landmark. Inside, you'll find a child-friendly, casual restaurant serving seafood, beef, and pasta. Try the stuffed shrimp, steak, shrimp scampi, and salmon stuffed with crabmeat. Open-air dining on patio. Live music Thursday–Saturday. Kids' menu. Early bird dinners. Sunday brunch. | 106 Main St. | 631/928–3395 | fax 631/928–3458 | $16–$26 | AE, D, DC, MC, V.

Lodging
Danfords Inn on the Sound. This inn near a marina on the harbor has spacious rooms with antiques and views of Long Island Sound. Restaurant, room service. Some kitchenettes, cable TV. Exercise equipment. Library. Business services. | 25 E. Broadway | 631/928–5200 or 800/332–6367 | fax 631/928–9092 | www.danfords.com | 85 rooms, 7 suites | $159–$179 rooms, $209–$389 suites | AE, D, DC, MC, V.

PORT JERVIS

MAP 3, A1

(Nearby towns also listed: Middletown, Monticello)

This railroad city at the meeting place of the Neversink and Delaware rivers is bordered by New Jersey and Pennsylvania. It is a small and aging city, with some lovely Queen

Anne homes dotting its residential streets. Products used all over the world such as airport runway lights, lipstick, and the first biodegradable pen made from corn are produced here. You will find most conveniences here, including lodging, food, and shopping.

Information: **Tri-State Chamber of Commerce** | 5 S. Broome St., 12771 | fax 845/856–6695 | www.tristatechamber.org.

Attractions

Gillinder Glass Museum and Factory. Tour one of the county's oldest glass-making factories and learn about the history of glass. | Erie and Liberty St. | 845/856–5375 | fax 845/858–2687 | www.gillinderglassstore.com | $4 | Weekdays 9:30–5:30, Sat. 9:30–4, Sun. noon–4; tours 10:15, 12:30, 1:30. No tours in July.

ON THE CALENDAR
AUG.: *Little Worlds Fair.* This kid-friendly country fair has crafts, food, entertainment, and games. | 845/985–2500.

Dining

Cornucopia. German. The interior of this restaurant known for its large selection of schnitzels and bratens is done in dark wood. Salad bar. | 176 U.S. 209 N | 845/856–5361 | Closed Mon. No lunch weekends | $10–$30 | AE, D, DC, MC, V.

Flo-Jean. Continental. This Port Jervis landmark serves drinks and food on an outdoor deck perched above the water. Inside, there are musical instruments and a wide array of antiques, including dolls, doll carriages, and trinkets hanging from every beam. The Long Island duck and stuffed sole are popular. Kids' menu. | 2 Pike St. | 845/856–6600 | Closed Mon, Tues., and Mar.–Dec. No lunch Wed., Thurs. | $18–$25 | AE, D, MC, V.

Lodging

Comfort Inn of Port Jervis. The rooms at this chain motel off I–84 have pull-out sofa beds. Restaurant, complimentary Continental breakfast. Cable TV. Pool. | 40 Greenville Tpk. | 845/856–6611 | fax 845/856–5299 | 104 rooms | $60–$80 | AE, D, DC, MC, V.

PORT WASHINGTON

MAP 4, G6

(Nearby towns also listed: Glen Cove, Huntington, Plainview, Roslyn)

This area was originally settled in 1674, and early residents made their living farming oysters and raising cattle until the 20th century when the sand and gravel industry took off. In fact, 90% of all the skyscrapers in New York City were made with Port Washington sand.

The community is made up of four villages, parts of two others, and a large unincorporated area. If you walk down Main Street, you'll find many antiques and collectibles stores, gift shops, and old buildings. At the end of the hill, you'll come to the town dock and the Port Washington Harbor with its tall ships bobbing in the water.

Information: **Glen Cove Chamber of Commerce** | 14 Glen St., Suite 303, Glen Cove, 11542 | 516/676–6666.

Attractions

Sands Point Preserve. You'll find this 216-acre preserve at the tip of the Port Washington Peninsula overlooking Long Island Sound. Once part of a Gold Coast estate, the grounds today include natural and landscaped areas, with forests, meadows, lawns, shore cliffs, and freshwater ponds. Tours through the mansions are available as well as nature tours and science exhibits. | 95 Middle Neck Rd., Sands Point | 516/571–7900 | $2 preserve; $5 mansion.

Sands Willets House. The kitchen, the oldest part of this house, was built in 1735 by the Sands family who were early settlers in the area. In 1845, Edmund Willets, an abolitionist and Quaker, bought the house and his descendants lived here until 1967. Open by appointment only. | 336 Port Washington Blvd. | 516/365–9074 | www.cowneck.org | Call for hrs.

ON THE CALENDAR

MAY: *HarborFest Dock Day.* Tall-ship exhibitions and concerts mark this annual celebration of environmental awareness and Port Washington's nautical heritage. At the town dock (Main Street). | 516/883–6566.

OCT.: *Pride in Port Day.* The Main Street Parade is one of the highlights of this event which also includes a homecoming football game, senior citizens' luncheon, dinner, and a dance. | 516/883–6566 or 516/767–8657.

Dining

Diwan. Indian. The many windows at this two-floor restaurant provide a view of Manhassett Bay. If you eat dinner upstairs, you'll have evening views of a pond and marina. Try the rack of lamb barbecued in the clay tandoori oven. Lunch buffet and weekend dinner buffets. Sunday brunch. | 37 Shore Rd. | 516/767–7878 | fax 516/944–5743 | $13–$26 | AE, D, DC, MC, V.

Finn MacCool's. Irish. Part restaurant, part post-work social pub, Finn's has the feel of an old-world tavern with lots of wood and a noise level that rises as the evening wears on. You can get hearty homemade stews, pub sandwiches, and, of course, a wide variety of domestic and imported beers. | 205 Main St. | 516/944–3439 | $8–$12 | AE, D, DC, MC, V.

Pastavileti. Italian. Modern interpretations of Italian classics like chicken parmigiana and veal scaloppine dominate the ever-changing menu here. The main dining area is well-lit and spacious, with linen table coverings and a few potted plants. | 2 Shore Rd. | 516/883–9067 | $12–$20 | AE, D, DC, MC, V.

Yamaguchi. Japanese. The weekend crowds at this restaurant attest to the authenticity and freshness of the sushi and sashimi. Japanese paintings line the walls and on weekends, the employees wear traditional Japanese clothing. | 63 Main St. | 516/883–3500 | Reservations essential weekends | Closed Mon. No lunch weekends | $10–$25 | AE, DC, MC, V.

POTSDAM

MAP 3, I2

(Nearby towns also listed: Canton, Massena, Ogdensburg)

This town on the Raquette River is near the northern reaches of the Adirondacks and serves as an eastern gateway to the Thousand Islands region. It was founded in 1802 and today is home to two large universities: Clarkson and the State University of New York at Potsdam.

Information: **Potsdam Chamber of Commerce** | Potsdam Civic Center, 13676 | 315/265–5440 | www.potsdam.ny.us.

Attractions

Adirondack Park. This entrance at the northwest edge of the 6.1-million-acre park takes you past Catamount Mountain and Carry Falls Reservoir before you hit scenic Route 3, which takes you to Tupper Lake and Lake Placid to the east. | 518/668–9238 | Free | Daily.

Potsdam Public Museum. The highlight of this museum is the Burnap Collection of English pottery, which dates from 1700–1870. Most of the other exhibits focus on the decorative arts. | 2 Park St. | 315/265–6910 | Free | Labor Day–Memorial Day, Tues.–Sat. 10–5.

State University of New York at Potsdam. About 4,000 undergraduates and graduates attend this university primarily known for its Crane School of Music. The Gibson Gallery presents regularly changing exhibits of regional, national, and international artists' work and has a sculpture park. | 44 Pierrepont Ave. (Rte. 56) | 315/267–2000 | www.potsdam.edu | Free | Daily.

ON THE CALENDAR
JULY: *Summer Festival.* Kids will love this festival's "rubber ducky" race. There's also live music, crafts, and an antique auto show. | 315/265–5440.

Dining
French's 1844 House. Continental. As its name suggests, this farmhouse was built in 1844, and it is still owned by the same family. The menu includes traditional steak dinners as well as interesting seafood specials and vegetarian entrées. If you eat on the deck, you'll have views of open fields and wildlife. Kids' menu. | 6885 U.S. 11 | 315/265–9896 | Closed Sun., Mon. No lunch | $14–$21 | AE, D, DC, MC, V.

Tardelli's. Italian. All the sauces are homemade at this restaurant known for pasta and veal. Italian paintings hang on the walls. Kids' menu. | 141 Market St. | 315/265–8446 | Closed Sun. No lunch Sat. | $5–$20 | AE, MC, V.

Lodging
Clarkson Inn. This inn is in downtown Potsdam, along the Racquette River and only minutes from SUNY-Potsdam and Clarkson. The lobby includes a sitting room with a fireplace and a tearoom where breakfast is served. The rooms have Victorian-style furniture. Restaurant. In-room data ports, cable TV. Business services. | 1 Main St. | 315/265–3050 or 800/790–6970 | fax 315/265–3050 | www.potsdam.ny.us/theclarksoninn | 40 rooms | $85–$110 | AE, MC, V.

Smalling Motel. Room sizes vary at this one-story motel, set far from the road on well-landscaped grounds. Picnic area. Cable TV. Pool. | 6775 Rte. 56 | 315/265–4640 | fax 315/265–4614 | mjsmall@northnet.org | 15 rooms | $50 | AE, MC, V.

Wedgewood Inn. This basic motel is right in the town of Potsdam and about 2 mi from State University of New York at Potsdam. Refrigerators, cable TV. No pets. | 6570 Rte. 56 | 315/265–9100 | 15 rooms | $90–$100 | AE, D, MC, V.

POUGHKEEPSIE

MAP 3, K9

(Nearby towns also listed: Fishkill, Hyde Park, Millbrook, New Paltz)

Poughkeepsie served as the state capital briefly during the Revolutionary War, and it was here that New York State ratified the Constitution in 1788. It has several historic districts, and is home to prestigious Vassar College. Poughkeepsie also offers large-city convenience, including major shopping malls, lodging, and services.

Information: **Poughkeepsie Area Chamber of Commerce** | 1 Civic Center Plaza, 12601 | 845/454–1700.

Attractions
Bardavon 1869 Opera House. The home of the Hudson Valley Philharmonic is the oldest opera house in the state. The beautifully restored auditorium has an active program of

theater, music, dance, and drama. There are performances on most weekends. | 35 Market St. | 845/473–5288 | fax 845/473–4259 | www.bardavon.org | $15–$30 | Oct.–June, call for schedule.

James Baird State Park. The manicured 18-hole championship golf course at this park is open to the public. You can also hike, cross-country ski, or visit the nature center. | 122D Freedom Rd. | 845/452–1489 | Free | Daily dawn–dusk.

Locust Grove. When Samuel F. B. Morse, the inventor of the telegraph, bought this house built around 1830, he remodeled it into a Tuscan-style villa. It still contains all the possessions and keepsakes of the family that lived there after him. There is also an interesting exhibit of telegraph equipment and other artifacts. The grounds have hiking trails. | 370 South Rd. (U.S. 9) | 845/454–4500 | fax 845/485–7122 | Park free; guided house tours $5 | Daily; guided tours available May–Thanksgiving, daily.

Vassar College. Begun as a women's college in 1861, Vassar has since gone co-ed. Today around 2,250 students attend this well-respected liberal-arts college. It was the first college to have an art gallery and today, the Frances Lehman Loeb Art Center contains a huge collection from all periods. Other highlights of the campus include the Tiffany windows in the chapel, and the Warthin Geological Museum. With its lakes, gardens, and old trees, the campus itself makes a lovely place for a walk. | Raymond Ave. | 845/437–7000 | www.vassar.edu | Free | Daily.

Windsor Vineyards. Wine and champagne are made here, and tastings are available. | 26 Western Ave. | 845/236–4233 | Free | Tastings Fri., Sat., Mon. 10–5, Sun. noon–5.

Dining

Banta's Steak and Stein. Steak. This restaurant on the Poughkeepsie border serves ribs, seafood, and steaks in an American Colonial–style dining room. A banjo band plays Monday. Kids' menu. | 9 Mall Plaza, Wappingers Falls | 845/297–6770 | $13–$28 | AE, DC, MC, V.

Le Pavilion. French. Classical music plays and French paintings hang on the walls at this restaurant in a 200-year-old farmhouse surrounded by well-tended grounds. The dishes make use of local ingredients. You can also dine on an open-air patio. Kid-friendly selections. | 230 Salt Point Tpk. | 845/473–2525 | Closed Sun. and 2 weeks in July. No lunch | $25–$35 | AE, D, DC, MC, V.

Milanese. Italian. Widely-spaced tables draped with crisp linens in the main dining area here allow for an intimate dinner without a lot of distractions or noise from neighbors. The extensive menu has homemade soups, fresh green salads, and entrées that include stuffed pasta shells in tomato sauce and filet of sole with lemon-herb butter and wine sauce. | 115 Main St. | 845/471–9533 | Closed Mon. | $7–$15 | AE, D, DC, MC, V.

O'Sho Steakhouse. Japanese. Wrought-iron window grates and tea-garden landscaping outside set the stage for the tranquil, Zen-like demeanor of the main dining area here. Lots of blond wood, translucent window-glass, and an artificial waterfall serve as a backdrop while several chefs prepare sushi and hibachi dishes at your table. Along with the fish, the menu features salads with O'Sho's special ginger dressing, as well as less adventuresome options like filet mignon. | 763 South Rd. | 845/297–0540 | No lunch Sat.–Sun. | $12–$25 | AE, D, MC, V.

River Station Restaurant. Steak. The wood-paneled walls at this restaurant have plenty of windows to let you get a good view of the riverfront. Regulars love the baby-back ribs and say the meat is "fall-off-the-bone tender." Aged steaks are a specialty here and there is a variety of seafood served as well. Open-air dining. Kids' menu. | 1 Water St. | 845/452–9207 | www.riverstationrestaurant.com | Reservations essential holidays | $25 | AE, D, DC, MC, V.

Spanky's. Cajun. You can get zesty Cajun and Creole classics like seafood jambalaya and chicken gumbo at this restaurant, housed in a historic building with high, embossed-tin ceilings, exposed brick walls, and lots of potted greenery. There's a full bar and two separate dining areas, and if you'd prefer something with a little less kick, the menu also offers more pedestrian fare like tuna steaks and barbecued ribs. | 85 Main St. | 845/485–2294 | $10–$15 | AE, D, DC, MC, V.

Lodging

Best Inn. This friendly, two-story chain hotel is only three blocks from Vassar College. Complimentary Continental breakfast. In-room data ports, cable TV. Pool. Business services. | 62 Haight Ave. | 845/454–1010 | fax 845/454–0127 | 41 rooms | $90–$110 | AE, D, DC, MC, V.

Courtyard by Marriott. Rooms at this chain hotel 4 mi from Vassar College have large work desks with PC ports. Restaurant, bar. Some in-room data ports, some refrigerators, cable TV. Pool. Hot tub. Exercise equipment. Laundry facilities. Business services. | 2641 South Rd. (Rte. 9) | 845/485–6336 | fax 845/485–6514 | www.courtyard.com | 149 rooms, 12 suites | $80–$130 rooms, $180–$200 suites | AE, D, DC, MC, V.

Econo Lodge. This basic chain hotel is about a 10-min drive to Vassar College, and good for folks coming for interviews or campus tours. Complimentary Continental breakfast. In-room data ports, some refrigerators, cable TV. Laundry facilities. Business services. Pets allowed. | 2625 South Rd. (U.S. 9) | 845/452–6600 | www.econolodge.com | 111 rooms | $100 | AE, D, DC, MC, V.

Holiday Inn Express. This chain hotel is in a residential area, 2 mi north of the commercial district. Complimentary Continental breakfast. Cable TV. Pool. Business services. Pets allowed. | 341 South Rd. (Rte. 9 and Sharon Dr.) | 845/473–1151 | fax 845/485–8127 | www.basshotels.com | 121 rooms | $109 | AE, D, DC, MC, V.

Inn at the Falls. The two-story windows in the common room at this inn look out upon Wappinger Creek and falls. Each room is furnished in a different style that ranges from contemporary to European to country, and has its own distinct character. Complimentary Continental breakfast, room service (breakfast only). In-room data ports, refrigerators, some in-room hot tubs, cable TV. Business services. | 50 Red Oaks Mill Rd. | 845/462–5770 | fax 845/462–5943 | www.inn-at-the-falls.com | 24 rooms, 12 suites | $155–$170 rooms, $195 suites | AE, D, DC, MC, V.

Poughkeepsie Travel Lodge. This two-story member of the chain is 2.2 mi from Vassar College. Restaurant, bar, picnic area. Some kitchenettes, refrigerators, cable TV. Pool. Tennis. Business services. Pets allowed. | 313 Manchester Rd. (Rte. 55) | 845/454–3080 or 800/578–7878 | fax 845/452–2516 | www.travelodge.com | 100 rooms | $45–$85 | AE, D, DC, MC, V.

Sheraton. Set right in the center of Poughkeepsie, this hotel is within walking distance of the Bardavon Opera House. Restaurant, bar. Cable TV. Exercise equipment. Business services, free parking. | 40 Civic Center Plaza | 845/485–5300 | fax 845/485–4720 | www.sheraton.com | 175 rooms, 9 suites | $129 | AE, D, DC, MC, V.

POUND RIDGE

MAP 4, H2

(Nearby towns also listed: Brewster, Croton-on-Hudson, Mt. Kisco, Peekskill)

On the very eastern edge of New York, Pound Ridge almost straddles the Connecticut line and actually maintains a strong New England feel. The small community has its origins in a land purchase from local Indians in 1646 and then a land grant from William III in 1697 and was officially founded in the early 1800s. Eventually, the area become known as "Basket Town" due to a thriving cottage industry that provided many of the baskets that were used by nearby oyster fishers to pack and ship their harvest out of the area. Today, there are a few small businesses, but Pound Ridge is predominantly a quiet, bedroom community of commuters to nearby Bridgeport and Danbury, Connecticut, and White Plains. The cool waters of Long Island Sound—less than 10 mi away—offer watery, beachside respite for weekend trips.

Information: **Peekskill/Cortland Chamber of Commerce** | 1 S. Division St., Peekskill, 10566 | 914/737–3600.

Attractions

Muscoot Farm. This vintage farm is now a county park, with a lively roster of seasonal special events. Check out the huge draft horses and colorful chickens, and attend demonstrations of blacksmithing, maple sugaring, and sheep-shearing. Eleven mi northeast of Pound Ridge. | Rte. 100, Somers | 914/232–7118 | fax 914/232–1731 | www.westchesterny.com | Free | Daily 10–4.

Trailside Nature Museum, Ward Pound Ridge Reservation. This resource center north of Pound Ridge has a collection of Native American artifacts, as well as hiking trails and picnic areas. | Off Rte. 121 S, Cross River | 914/763–3993 | Free; parking $6 | Wed.–Sun. 9–4.

Dining

Inn at Pound Ridge. Continental. Inside this mid-19th-century house is a formal dining room serving fresh fish, duck, and rack of lamb. You can also dine in the Garden Room, which has ground to ceiling windows. Kids' menu. Sunday brunch. | 258 Westchester Ave. | 914/764–5779 | Reservations essential weekends | No lunch Sat. | $40 | AE, DC, MC, V.

L'Europe. French. Veal chops and rack of lamb are among the favorites at this restaurant with a country French–style dining room. Open-air dining. Kids' menu. Six mi west of Pound Ridge. | 407 Smithridge Rd., South Salem | 914/533–2570 | Closed Mon. | $45 | AE, DC, MC, V.

QUEENSBURY

MAP 3, L5

(Nearby towns also listed: Bolton Landing, Diamond Point, Glens Falls, Lake George Village, Lake Luzerne, Saratoga Springs, Warrensburg)

Together the twin cities of Glens Falls and Queensbury make up a major Adirondack cultural center, with opera, a symphony, and museums, as well as the usual Adirondack activities. Once part of the great northern wilderness, Queensbury was a favorite hunting and fishing spot of the Iroquois. The British chose to settle here in the mid-1700s because the area was on a well-traveled path to Canada.

Information: **Warren County Tourism Department** | 2760 Municipal Center, 1340 State St., Lake George, 12845 | 518/761–6366 or 800/95–VISIT.

Attractions

Rock Sport Indoor Climbing. The 4,000 square ft of climbing walls here boast a 35-ft vertical ascent. If you are a novice, you can take a lesson. | 138 Quaker Rd. | 518/793–4626 | $15 for instruction on the first day; $8 per day thereafter; equipment rental $6 | Weekdays 4–10, weekends noon–6.

West Mountain Ski Resort. The ski trails here have a vertical height of 1,010 ft. Primarily a day ski center for local families, the resort also offers extensive night skiing on all but a few of the 22 slopes. Includes snowmaking, two double chairs, a triple, and three surface lifts. Offers 4- and 8-hr "start anytime" lift tickets. | West Mountain Rd. | 518/793–6606 | Mid-Dec.–mid-Mar.

ON THE CALENDAR

SEPT.: *Adirondack Balloon Festival.* Up to 100 balloons in wild shapes and styles float high in the sky throughout the weekend, especially at dawn and dusk. There's also rides, music, crafts, and food. The event takes place at Adirondack Community College and Floyd Bennett Memorial Airport. | 518/761–6366 or 800/365–1050 | www.adirondackballoonfest.org.

NOV.: *North Country Festival of Trees.* Every Thanksgiving weekend, designer Christmas trees, wreaths, centerpieces, and a gingerbread village go on display at the Highland Family Golf Center. Breakfast with Santa and a senior luncheon are also part of the event. | 518/798–0170.

Dining

Mangy Moose. American. Large burgers on hearty, cracked-corn buns and an outdoorsy, Adirondacks theme in the dining room make this whimsically-named spot popular with both families and sportsmen. Several TVs in the lounge area broadcast sporting events, and the rough wood planking in the dining area gives the place a rough-and-ready feel. Though burgers are king here, try siding your sandwich with some of the Moose's unusual sweet-potato fries. | 4 S. Western Ave. | 518/792–7175 | $6–$10 | AE, MC, V.

Montcalm Restaurant. Continental. The three dining rooms of this rustic log cabin restaurant hold about 180 hungry folks who come to dine on prime rib, seafood, and pasta. Specialties include the veal Oscar, sautéed and topped with crab meat, bordelaise, and béarnaise sauce. All desserts are made on the premises, including the pecan pie and the flourless chocolate cake. | Rte. 9, Queensbury | 518/793–6601 | $13–$26 | AE, D, DC, MC, V.

Lodging

Brown's Welcome Inn. This simple, one-story drive-up motel offers affordable rooms and is located near several restaurants. Picnic area. Some refrigerators, cable TV. Pool. Playground. | 932 Lake George Rd., Queensbury | 518/792–9576 or 800/780–7047 | 20 rooms (5 with shower only) | $85–$100 | Closed Columbus Day–Memorial Day | AE, D, MC, V.

Ramada Inn. This two-story chain hotel is only a 10-min drive from West Mountain Ski Resort. Restaurant, bar, picnic area, room service. In-room data ports, some kitchenettes, cable TV. Pool. Business services. | Abby La. (I–87, exit 19) | 518/793–7701 | fax 518/792–5463 | www.ramada.com | 110 rooms | $59–$149 | AE, D, DC, MC, V.

Super 8. This chain motel is just off Interstate 87 and 3 mi away from local skiing areas. Complimentary Continental breakfast. Cable TV. No pets. | 191 Corinth Rd. (I–87, exit 18) | 518/761–9780 or 800/800–8000 | fax 518/761–1049 | www.super8.com | 59 rooms | $89–$95 | AE, D, DC, MC, V.

QUOGUE/EAST QUOGUE

MAP 3, E2

(Nearby towns also listed: Hampton Bays, Riverhead, Westhampton Beach)

Quoque is one of the oldest communities on Long Island and part of the Greater Westhampton area. Today, thanks to the stately Victorians nestled along its tree-lined streets and the contemporary mansions along the ocean on Dune Road, Quoque has become one of the most desirable residential areas in the Hamptons, known for opulent living.

East Quogue was settled in 1686 and was originally known as "Fourth Neck." When the railroad came in the 19th century, it changed East Quogue from a hamlet of solitary farms into a summer resort. The acres of farmland and pine forest, beautiful bay, and ocean beaches, along with vibrant Main Street shopping and lively nightlife, are still attractions today.

Information: Greater Westhampton Chamber of Commerce | 173 Montauk Hwy., Box 1228, Westhampton Beach, 11978 | 631/288–3337.

Attractions

Dune Road Public Beaches. There's public beach access all along the Dune Rd. strip. Some have snack-bars. | Dune Rd., Quogue | 631/653–5143 | $10 | Daily.

QUOGUE/
EAST QUOGUE

INTRO
ATTRACTIONS
DINING
LODGING

Quogue Wildlife Refuge. There are over 300 acres with 7 mi of self-guided trails at this wildlife preserve managed by the State Department of Environmental Conservation. The Nature Center has exhibits and a library. | 3 Old Country Rd., Quogue | 631/653–4771 | Free | Mar.–Thanksgiving, Tues., Thurs., and weekends, dawn to dusk.

ON THE CALENDAR

SEPT.: *Country Jamboree and BBQ.* This community event features barbecued food and live country music. | 516/653–5143.

Dining

Dockers. Seafood. People stop in at this casual, lively waterfront restaurant on their way home from the beach just across the road. Try the Black Angus aged steak, the clambake, or the lobster (they've got them up to 5 lbs). The large deck overlooking the bay has good views of the sunset. Raw bar. Live music on Tuesdays and Friday through Sunday. Early bird dinners. | 94 Dune Rd., East Quogue | 631/653–0653 | Reservations not accepted | Closed week after Labor Day–week before Memorial Day | $15–$40 | AE, D, DC, MC, V.

Inn at Quogue. American. This restaurant is housed in a building that dates to the late 18th century. Try the salmon poached in fish broth with spices and fennel and served with diced potatoes, string beans, and other vegetables. For dessert, there is homemade cheesecake with fresh berries, or strawberry layer cake. Open-air dining in enclosed sunroom. | 47 Quogue St., Quogue | 631/653–6800 | Reservations essential weekends | No lunch | $18–$26 | www.innatquogue.com | AE, D, DC, MC, V.

New Moon Cafe. Southwestern. This rustic, noisy restaurant has bright colors and lots of windows. Try the barbecued brisket, smoked with mesquite and served with Texas pinto beans and corn-on-the-cob. Occasionally there is live guitar music, keyboards, and a singer. Sunday brunch. Kids' menu. | 524 Montauk Hwy., East Quogue | 631/653–4042 | $12–$24 | AE, D, MC, V.

Stone Creek Inn. French. You can't miss this huge white building on Montauk Highway. On the menu, you'll find dishes such as grilled yellowfin tuna, garlic roasted rack of lamb, and tiny cheese ravioli in mussel and chive broth. Kids' menu. | 405 Montauk Hwy., East Quogue | 631/653–6770 | fax 631/653–6782 | No lunch | $20–$30 | AE, D, DC, MC, V.

Lodging

Inn at Quogue. The core of this inn was built in 1785 as a family residence, and it became a summer boardinghouse in 1871. The 15 rooms in the main house were recently renovated

KODAK'S TIPS FOR USING LIGHTING

Daylight
- Use the changing color of daylight to establish mood
- Use light direction to enhance subjects' properties
- Match light quality to specific subjects

Dramatic Lighting
- Anticipate dramatic lighting events
- Explore before and after storms

Sunrise, Sunset, and Afterglow
- Include a simple foreground
- Exclude the sun when setting your exposure
- After sunset, wait for the afterglow to color the sky

From *Kodak Guide to Shooting Great Travel Pictures* © 2000 by Fodor's Travel Publications

under the supervision of Ralph Lauren's design team. Beaches are nearby, and you can borrow towels and beach chairs from the inn. Restaurant, bar. Some kitchenettes, cable TV. Pool. Spa. Tennis. Beach, bicycles. Baby-sitting. Pets allowed. | 47-52 Quogue St., Quogue | 631/653–6560 | fax 631/653–8026 | www.innatquogue.com | 67 rooms, 2 cottages | $200–$300 rooms, $550–$800 cottages | AE, D, MC, V.

RHINEBECK

(Nearby towns also listed: Hyde Park, Kingston, Saugerties, Woodstock)

Just off U.S. 9 and across the river from Kingston is Rhinebeck, an affluent village full of picture-perfect Georgian and Victorian houses. Once known as "violet town" because hothouse violets were grown here, the village today has restaurants, craft and jewelry shops, and the oldest inn in the area, the Beekman Arms. Rhinebeck's Dutchess County Fairgrounds hosts the annual Dutchess County Fair as well as important crafts and antiques fairs.

Information: Rhinebeck Chamber of Commerce | Box 42, 12572 | 845/876–4778.

Attractions

Montgomery Place. On the banks of the Hudson River, north of Rhinebeck, lies this 23-room house that was once the the Livingston family estate. The original building was Federal, but in the mid-19th century, it was remodeled into a Greek Revival mansion. The grounds include a visitors center, hiking trails, orchards, and a farm stand. The rose garden is notable. | River Rd., Annandale | 845/758–5461 | $6 | Apr.–Oct. 31, Daily 10–5, closed Tues.; Nov.–Dec., Sat.–Sun. 10–4; Dec.–mid-Dec., Sat.–Sun, 10–5.

Rhinebeck Aerodrome Museum. All of the vintage aircraft at this unusual museum still fly. The collection includes a reproduction of Charles Lindbergh's *Spirit of St. Lewis* and fighter planes from World War I. The Fokker DR-1 triplane was the favorite of the Red Baron, and the Spad was flown by Eddie Rickenbacker. Sunday air shows feature these craft, and it's possible to take open-cockpit rides. Airshows 2 PM Saturday mid-June through mid-October. | 44 Stone Church Rd. | 845/752–3200 | fax 845/758–6481 | www.oldrhinebeck.org | Museum $5; weekend air shows $10 | Mid-May–Oct., daily 10–5.

Wilderstein. This appealing residence was built in Italianate style for Thomas Suckley; later on, Queen Anne elements were added by his son. The main-floor interiors and stained-glass windows were designed by J. B. Tiffany. The house still contains family furniture and keepsakes. The grounds, which are being progressively restored, were designed by Calvert Vaux. In summer, tea is served on the side porch. | 330 Morton Rd. | 845/876–4818 | fax 845/876–3336 | www.wilderstein.org | $5 | May–Oct., Thurs.–Sun. noon–4.

ON THE CALENDAR

JUNE: *Great Hudson Valley Balloon Race and Air Show.* Dozens of hot-air balloons fill the spring sky during this aerial spectacle. Rides and races plus food and venders. | 845/463–6000.

JUNE: *Hudson Valley Wine and Food Festival.* Montgomery Place hosts wine tastings and cooking demonstrations. | 845/758–5461.

AUG.: *Dutchess County Fair.* The livestock includes sheep, cows, goats, and chickens at this annual fair that also has a carnival, local crafts, parades, food, and hundreds of exhibits. At the Dutchess County Fairgrounds, Route 9. | 845/876–4001.

Dining

Beekman 1766 Tavern. American. Inside this popular restaurant, you'll be surrounded by 18th-century fixtures and portraits. The seafood, mahi-mahi tuna, and linguine are specialties. Dine in the glass-enclosed greenhouse. Sunday brunch. Kids' menu. | 4 Mill St. | 845/871–1766 | $18–$25 | AE, DC, MC, V.

Marco Polo's. Italian. Dishes are prepared in a wood-burning brick oven at this restaurant housed in a renovated church with cathedral ceilings. The homemade pasta and pizza are popular. Open-air dining. | 37 Montgomery St. | 845/876–3228 | $10–$25 | AE, D, DC, MC, V.

P. J. McGlynn's American Steak House. Continental. You won't get lamb any fresher than at this restaurant because they raise their own sheep. The dining room inside this mid-19th-century building has a fireplace and many original furnishings. Aged steaks and Yankee pot roast are also specialties. Kids' menu. Sunday brunch. | 147 Rte. 9 | 845/758–3102 | $12–$18 | AE, D, DC, MC, V.

Red Hook Inn. Contemporary. This 1841 Federal building north of Rhinebeck has original furnishings and photographs of the town in the 19th century. Cheeses are made on premises and the menu changes regularly. You can dine on the front porch as well. Kids' menu. Guest rooms. | 74-60 S. Broadway, Red Hook | 845/758–8445 | Closed Mon. No lunch | $15–$20 | AE, D, MC, V.

Lodging

Beekman Arms. This is said to be the oldest operating inn in the United States. Rooms have been rented and meals have been served every single day since 1776. Guest rooms are furnished with antiques, and some have working fireplaces. There's also a Colonial tap room and a greenhouse dining room. Restaurant, bar. No air-conditioning in some rooms, cable TV. Business services. | 63-87 Mill St. | 845/876–7077 | www.beekmanarms.com | 63 rooms | $85–$145 | AE, D, DC, MC, V.

Red Hook Inn. The five rooms inside this pleasant 1841 Federal building have period antiques. The suite has a separate sitting area and a pullout couch that can be used for two more adults. Restaurant, bar. No room phones, TV in common area. No pets. No smoking. | 74-60 S. Broadway, Red Hook | 845/758–8445 | 4 rooms, 1 suite | $75–$125 | AE, D, MC, V.

Village Inn. Across from a wine grove, this conventional motel is ½ mi south of the intersection of Hwy 308 and Rte. 9, and just as far from the center of Rhinebeck, across from a wine grove. Complimentary Continental breakfast. Some refrigerators, cable TV. | 6260 U.S. 9 S | 845/876–7000 | fax 845/876–4756 | 16 rooms | $60–$74 | D, MC, V.

RICHFIELD SPRINGS

MAP 3, I6

(Nearby towns also listed: Canajoharie, Cooperstown, Hamilton, Herkimer, Ilion, Utica)

Richfield Springs, north of Cooperstown on Route 20, is known for its mineral springs, which, in their heyday, drew visitors from far and wide to enjoy its healing properties. It was known as the Great White Sulphur Springs among Native Americans who gathered here for ceremonies. Later it was used as a deluxe spa, the remains of which can be seen in Spring Park, where the spring still runs to this day.

Information: **Richfield Area Chamber of Commerce** | Box 909, 13439 | 315/858–2553.

Attractions

Petrified Creatures Museum. You can pan for fossils in this area that was covered by the Devonian Sea over 300 million years ago. More than 40 different types of invertebrates have been identified here. | Rte. 20 | 315/858–2868 | $8 | May–Sept., daily.

Dining

Garland Restaurant. Contemporary. Set in the old town bank, this restaurant serves fine contemporary fare with a French flair. Marble walls, beveled glass, and lots of private nooks, including a table for five in the vault, are a unique setting for dishes like the Garland filet mignon topped with a pasilla sauce, Portobello mushrooms, and feta cheese. | 118 Main St. | 315/858–5811 | $12–$20 | D, MC, V.

Lodging

Fountain View. This one-story wood building is on a hillside overlooking a park, pond, and illuminated fountain. About a mile from town of Richfield Springs. Refrigerators, cable TV. | 3607 Rte. 20 | 315/858–1360 | 16 rooms | $70–$80 | Closed Dec.–Mar. | AE, D, MC, V.

Village Motel. This owner-operated roadside motel overlooking Spring Park, home of the mineral springs, has been open since 1954. Rooms are quiet and simple. Picnic area. Cable TV. No pets. No smoking. | 168 E. Main St. (Rte. 20) | 315/858–1540 | www.cooperstown.net/villagemotel | 11 rooms | $75–$90 | D, MC, V.

RIVERHEAD

MAP 3, D2

(Nearby towns also listed: Hampton Bays, Orient Point, Port Jefferson, Quogue/East Quogue, Westhampton Beach)

The town of Riverhead was established in 1792 between the North and South Forks of Long Island, with the Peconic River and Great Peconic Bay bordering the town on the south and Long Island Sound on the north. Riverhead started out as a farming village, but thanks to its miles of beaches and nearby woodlands, today the town's main industry is tourism. Agriculture is still a key factor in Riverhead's economy however, and visitors can see crops ranging from potatoes to grapes being tended in the fields surrounding town. There are roughly 24,000 permanent residents of Riverhead, but the population swells exponentially during the summer months when tourists descend on the town.

Information: Chamber of Commerce | 524 E. Main St., Box 291, 11901 | 631/727–7600 | www.riverheadli.com/coc.

Attractions

Atlantis Explorer Environmental Boat Tours. Interact with marine wildlife on this 2½-hour boat tour down the Peconic River. Certified naturalists explain the geological history of the Peconic Estuary system and discuss local flora and fauna. There's also a shoreline walking tour. | 431 E. Main St. | 631/208–9200 | $17 | www.atlantismarineworld.com | Apr.–Oct.

Peconic River Herb Farm. This working riverfront farm on 13 acres west of Riverhead grows over 700 varieties of plants including herbs and heirloom vegetables, beautiful shrubs, and roses. Wander through the trail gardens or visit, in season, their market. | 2749 River Rd., Calverton | 631/369–0058 | fax 631/369–6179 | www.prherbfarm.com | Free | Apr.–Oct., 9–4.

Riverhead Foundation for Marine Research and Preservation. The foundation operates a stranding/rescuing program for Long Island's sea creatures. A Preview Center features 12 fresh- and saltwater tanks depicting the ecology of Long Island waters. There's also a special touch tank. | 428 E. Main St. | 631/369–9840 | www.riverheadfoundation.org | $4 suggested donation | Weekends 10–5.

Riverhead Raceway. Come check out NASCAR racing, late models, chargers, super pro trucks and spectator drag racing. Open since 1949, this is one of the oldest tracks in the country. Admission varies per event, so call ahead for exact rates. | Old Country Rd. | 631/727–0010 | www.riverheadraceway.com | Apr.–Sept.

Splish Splash. Ride an inner tube down the 1,300-ft-long Lazy River past waterfalls, geysers, and wave pools at this 60-acre water park. Other attractions include Monsoon Lagoon, Mammoth River Ride, and Kiddie Cove. There are three pools, a beach area, and two restaurants. A changing room with lockers is also available. | 2549 Splish Splash Dr. | 516/727–3600 | fax 631/727–6868 | www.splishsplashlongisland.com | $24 | Memorial Day–Labor Day, daily 10–6.

Tanger Outlet Stores. There's over 170 brand-name factory stores to choose from in this set of two outlet complexes. A free trolley runs between the two. | Old Country Rd. | 631/727–7600 | Free | Daily.

ON THE CALENDAR
OCT.: *Riverhead Country Fair*. Most of downtown Riverhead is taken over by this fair that includes a carnival with food and craft vendors, entertainment, pony rides, boat rides, and contests for everything from the best jams and jellies to the largest pumpkin. | 631/727–1215.

Dining
Digger O'Dells. American. This restaurant serves shepherd's pie, a hearty dish of beef, carrots, onions, and peas topped with golden brown mashed potatoes; Jack Daniels filet mignon; and king-cut prime rib. If you are looking for a drink to accompany your dinner, they have classic Irish beers on tap including Harp, Killians Red, and Guinness. Live music on Fridays and Saturdays. Kids' menu. | 58 W. Main St. | 631/369–3200 | $11–$19 | AE, D, DC, MC, V.

Meeting House Creek Inn. Continental. Popular seafood dishes keep them coming to this waterside restaurant 4 mi east of Riverhead. Known for steaks, pasta, mako steaks, and Cajun fish. Open-air dining on patio. Pianist Fri., Sat. Kids' menu. Sun. brunch. | 177 Meeting House Creek Rd., Aquebogue | 631/722–4220 | $13–$20 | AE, D, MC, V.

Lodging
Budget Host Inn. This standard member of the chain is set on 6 acres 6 mi from the Splish Splash water park. Take exit 71 off the Long Island Expressway. Picnic area. Some kitchenettes, cable TV. Pool. Business services. | 30 E. Moriches Rd. | 631/727–6200 | fax 631/727–6466 | www.budgethost.com | 68 rooms | $79–$129 | AE, D, DC, MC, V.

Ramada Inn East End. This hotel, 10 min from the ocean and next door to the outlet centers, was rated "Gold Key" by Ramada, meaning it is among the best in the chain. Restaurant, bar, room service. In-room data ports, cable TV. Pool. Business services. | 1830 Rte. 25 | 631/369–2200 | fax 631/369–1202 | www.ramada.com | 100 rooms | $99–$189 | AE, D, DC, MC, V.

Wading River. You'll find this modest one-story brick motel just west of Riverhead on 5 landscaped acres. Picnic area. Some kitchenettes. Pool. | 5890 Middle County Rd., Wading River | 631/727–8000 | 32 rooms | $96–$112 | AE, D, DC, MC, V.

ROCHESTER

MAP 3, E5

(Nearby towns also listed: Albion, Avon, Canandaigua, Geneseo, Geneva, Palmyra, Victor)

The third-largest city in the state, Rochester has endured economic downturns to maintain its niche as a high-tech and industrial center with broad and sophisticated cultural and entertainment offerings. Founded in 1803, Rochester prospered early on as an agricultural-based "Flour City," thanks to the mill-powering waters of the Genesee River, which runs through the middle of town. Its location on Lake Ontario and proximity to the Erie Canal allowed for high trade levels and population growth. As the Midwest took over wheat production, however, Rochester adapted by evolving into a horticultural "Flower City," housing some remarkable nurseries. Kodak, Xerox, and Bausch and Lomb all set up shop here, with varying degrees of prosperity. Though, today, the city has a modern look, Greek Revival architecture still survives.

Information: **Visitors Information Center** | 45 East Ave., Suite 400, 14604-1102 | 716/546–3070 or 800/677–7282 | www.visitrochester.com.

Attractions

The Center at High Falls. You can see High Falls, at 96 ft the tallest of the city's three waterfalls, from a pedestrian bridge at this educational and entertainment complex that was once the city's major flour milling center. The center's Laser, Light and Fireworks Spectacular lights up the falls nightly from May to early October. | 60 Brown's Race | 716/325–2030 | Free | Tues.–Sat. 10–4, Sun. noon–4.

George Eastman House. This Georgian mansion was the home of the founder of Eastman Kodak and has been restored to its early 1900s appearance. The International Museum of Photography and Film offers changing exhibits on the history of photography, film technology, and literature. There are evening film programs Wednesday through Sunday at 8. | 900 East Ave. | 716/271–3361 | www.eastman.org | $6.50 | May, daily 10–4:30; June–Apr., Tues.–Sat. 10–4:30, Sun. 1–4:30. Garden tours May–Sept.

GeVa Theater. The city's only resident professional theater stages about nine shows a year in this brick-and-limestone building that was once the Naval Armory. | 75 Woodbury Blvd. | 716/232–GEVA | www.gevatheatre.org | Call for schedule.

Hamlin Beach State Park. Twelve miles northwest of Rochester is this 1,243-acre park with nature trails, cross-country skiing, camping, picnicking, fishing, and swimming. | 1 Camp Rd., Hamlin | 716/964–2462 | www.nysparks.state.ny.us/parks | Free; parking $6 | Daily.

Highland Park. Rochester's first public park, Highland Park was established in 1888, and is the home of Rochester's hugely popular Lilac Festival each spring. The park itself is home to over 500 varieties of lilacs, and over 1,200 individual lilac shrubs. Walking paths criss-cross the park, and there are a number of shelters for picnickers and barbecue enthusiasts, as well as an ice-skating rink and two softball fields. | At the intersection of South and Highland Aves. | 716/256–4950 | Free | Daily, 6 AM–11 PM.

Lamberton Conservatory. Built in 1911, the Conservatory houses stunning exhibits of flowering plants from around the world, ranging from arid desert species to lush tropical vegetation. The Conservatory is open year-round, and the exhibits and displays change regularly. | Highland Park | 716/234–4769 | Free | Wed.–Sun.; May–Oct. 10–6, Nov.–Apr. 10–4.

Mount Hope Cemetery. One of the nation's oldest cemeteries (1838), Mount Hope includes the graves of Frederick Douglass (off East Avenue near the northern end of the cemetery) and Susan B. Anthony (off Indian Trail Avenue on the far northern end). The Friends of Mt. Hope Cemetery offers guided tours on Sundays May–October. | 791 Mt. Hope Ave. | 716/461–3494 | www.zipcon.com/~trey/mthope.html | Free | Daily dawn–dusk; tours May–Oct., Sun. 2 PM and 3 PM.

Museums of the Landmark Society. The Landmark Society oversees two important Rochester museums (716/546–7029 | www.landmarksociety.org).

The **Campbell-Whittlesey House Museum** (123 S. Fitzhugh | (716) 546–7028 | $3 | Mar.–Dec., Fri.–Sun. 12-4) is an 1835 Greek Revival home in the city's oldest neighborhood. The elegant parlors and restored kitchen, pantry, and cold storage room show what life was like for a wealthy flour miller's family during the high-water days of a once booming Erie Canal.

The **Stone-Tolan House Museum** (2370 East Ave. | 716/546–7029 | $3 | Mar.–Dec., Fri.–Sun. noon–4) is the oldest house in Monroe County and the Stone family began running a frontier tavern here in 1805. The grounds include an orchard and smokehouse.

Rochester Institute of Technology. More than 13,000 students attend RIT, an institution known for its engineering and applied sciences programs. Highlights of the campus include the National Technical Institute for the Deaf and the Bevier Gallery. On-campus tours are available. | One Lomb Memorial Dr. | 716/475–6736 or 716–475–2411 | www.rit.edu | Free | Daily | 716/475–6736.

Rochester Museum and Science Center. Family-oriented activities at this museum focus on science and technology, nature, and the cultural heritage of the area. Of special note are an exhibit on the Seneca Nation, an opened 1873 Time Capsule, and the Strasenburgh Planetarium. | 657 East Ave. | 716/271–4320 | fax 716/271–5935 | www.rmsc.org | $6 | Mon.–Sat. 9–5, Sun. noon–5.

Seabreeze Amusement Park. This park on the shore of Lake Ontario has been open since 1879. Today it has water rides, four roller coasters, a carousel, and live shows. | 4600 Culver Rd. | 716/323–1900 or 800/395–2500 | www.seabreeze.com | $15.50 unlimited rides | Mid-June–Labor Day, Sun.–Thurs. noon–10, Fri.–Sat. noon–11.

Seneca Park Zoo. The Rocky Coasts exhibit at this zoo along the Genesee River gorge provides an underwater look at polar bears, penguins, and sea lions. Above ground, you'll spot some African elephants and orangutans, among other beasts. There's a barnyard petting zoo for kids and an area where children can touch turtle shells, snakeskins, antlers, and other items. | 2222 St. Paul St. | 716/266–6846 | $4 | Daily 10–5.

Strong Museum. A must-see, especially for children, this museum specializes in everyday American history and folk art. Don't be surprised if you come across an exhibit on Jell-O, Barbie, or GI Joe. Children can scan groceries, visit an old-fashioned ice-cream parlor, ride a carousel, and eat in a 1950s diner. | One Manhattan Sq. | 716/263–2700 or 716/263–2702 | www.strongmuseum.org | $6 | Mon., Tues., Wed., Thurs., Sat. 10–5; Fri. 10–8; Sun. noon–5.

Susan B. Anthony House. Susan B. Anthony, a dedicated women's rights activist, lived in this Victorian home during the most politically active years of her life. In 1872, she and several other women were arrested for voting here in Rochester. | 17 Madison St. | 716/235–6124 | www.susanbanthonyhouse.org | $6 | Memorial Day–Labor Day, Tues.–Sun. 11–5; Labor Day–Memorial Day, Wed.–Sun. 11–4.

Tour Boats. Many companies in the Rochester area offer tours of the Eric Canal and other waterways. | 877/386–4676 | www.rochgetaway.com.

Colonial Belle runs narrated tours up to 3 hrs long on the Erie Canal in boats that hold up to 246 people. Meals must be preordered. Ten miles southeast of Rochester. | 400 Picket's Landing, Fairport | 716/223–9470 | $12–$15; $18.95 lunch cruise; $23.95 dinner cruise | May–Oct., Tues.–Sat., noon, 2:30, 6:30; Sun. noon and 3.

The *Sam Patch* **Tour Boat** travels the upper Genesee River and the Erie Canal holding up to 49 passengers. Built in 1991, the 54-ft *Sam Patch* is a replica of the 19th-century ships which were towed, in their day, by teams of mules. Trips leave from the Schoen Place dock in Pittsford, 9 mi southeast of Rochester. | 12 Cornhill Terr., Suite 7 | 716/262–5661 | www.sampatch.org | $11 for 90-min cruise; $17.50 lunch cruise; $32.50–$38.50 dinner cruise | May–Oct., Mon.–Fri. noon, 3, 6:30; Sat.–Sun. noon, 2, 4, 6:30.

University of Rochester. This private school founded in 1850 enrolls 7,700 students. The music, medicine, optics, and laser technology programs are strong. | Wilson Blvd. | 716/275–5911 | www.rochester.edu | Free | Daily.

Each year the **Eastman School of Music,** one of the best of its kind in the nation, presents around 700 concerts by guest artists, faculty members, and students. | 26 Gibbs St. | 716/274–1100 (24–hr concert information) | www.rochester.edu/eastman | Free | Daily.

Among the artists represented at the **Memorial Art Gallery** are Mary Cassatt, Paul

Cézanne, Winslow Homer, Henri Matisse, and Claude Monet. | 500 University Ave. | 716/473–7720 | $5 | Tues. noon–9, Wed.–Fri. 10–4, Sat. 10–5, Sun. noon–5.

Victorian Doll Museum and Chili Doll Hospital. More than 3,000 dolls dating from the mid-1800s to the present day are on hand at this museum 15 mi west of Rochester. | 4332 Buffalo Rd., North Chili | 716/247–0130 | $2 | Feb.–Nov., Tues.–Sat. 10–4:30; Dec., Tues.–Sat. 10–5.

Warner Castle. This ivy-covered, castellated Gothic building was originally the private residence of local attorney and newsman H.G. Warner. Today the castle serves as the headquarters for the Rochester Civic Garden Center, a horticultural-education group. The grounds surrounding the castle are divided into dozens of fantastic gardens, including rock and herb gardens. | 5 Castle Park | 716/473–5130 | Free | Tues.–Thurs. 9:30–3:30, Sat. 9:30–12:30; Closed Sun.–Mon. and Fri.

ON THE CALENDAR

MAY: *Lilac Festival.* Approximately 1,200 lilac bushes bloom in Highland Park. | 10–8 | 716/256–4960 | www.lilacfestival.com.
JUNE: *Fairport Canal Days.* This two-day festival has arts, crafts, music, and canal cruises. In Fairport, a suburb of Rochester. | 716/234–4323 | www.fairportcanaldays.com/.
JUNE: *Rochester Harborfest.* This event has tall ships, entertainment, fireworks, and food. Shuttle buses leave from Dewey Avenue for the waterfront. | 716/865–3320.
JULY: *Corn Hill Arts Festival.* Music and arts and crafts squeeze into the Corn Hill neighborhood off Exchange Boulevard and Plymouth Avenue. | 716/262–3142.
JULY: *Monroe County Fair.* Agricultural exhibits, crafts, rides, and entertainment come to the Dome Center in Henrietta, south of Rochester. | 716/334–4000.

Dining

Bangkok Restaurant. Thai. Authentic cuisine and a full vegetarian menu are served at this restaurant within walking distance of many downtown landmarks. The seafood dishes are popular; try the salt-and-pepper squid. Beer and wine only. | 155 State St. | 716/325–3517 | fax 716/325–3538 | Closed Sun. | $10–$15 | D, DC, MC, V.

Cartwright Inn. American. When this restaurant west of Rochester first opened, most of its clientele came in by horse-drawn buggy. Today, you can choose from more than 50 items on the menu, including fresh lobster or the clam chowder. Kids' menu. Early bird dinners. | 5691 W. Henrietta Rd., West Henrietta | 716/334–4444 | fax 716/334–8925 | $10–$30 | AE, DC, MC, V.

Daisy Flour Mill. American. All of the original equipment is still in place in the 1848 gristmill that houses this restaurant. The kitchen is known for its beef and seafood. Entertainment on Saturday. Early bird dinners. | 1880 Blossom Rd. | 716/381–1880 | fax 716/381–0899 | www.daisyflourmill.com | Reservations essential Sat. | Closed Sun. No lunch | $15–$40 | AE, D, MC, V.

Dinosaur Bar-B-Que. Barbecue. This roadhouse restaurant serves its barbecue quickly. Live blues Wednesday through Saturday. | 99 Court St. | 716/325–7090 | fax 716/325–7125 | Reservations not accepted | Closed Sun. | $10–$22 | AE, D, MC, V.

Edwards. French. Arguably one of the best of Rochester's downtown restaurants, Edwards has five dining rooms, each of them differently, and lavishly, furnished. Try the shrimp Edwards: shrimp stuffed with dill, feta, and ricotta wrapped in prosciutto with jalapeño butter and served over angel-hair pasta. Other specialties include duck and aged steaks. A pianist plays on Saturdays. | 13 S. Fitzhugh | 716/423–0140 | fax 716/423–2223 | www.edwardsrestaurant.com | Closed Sun. | $30–$40 | AE, D, MC, V.

Grill at Water Street. Contemporary. This restaurant overlooking the river is popular for upscale business lunches. Try the marinated-duck spring rolls and the eggplant and artichoke soup. Steaks, pasta, and fresh fish dishes are also on the menu. Over 1,000 labels make up the extensive wine selection. Open-air dining in a small park overlooking the river. | 175 N. Water St. | 716/454–1880 | fax 716/325–5004 | www.grillatws.com | Closed Sun. No lunch Sat. | $18–$28 | AE, D, DC, MC, V.

India House. Indian. This casual restaurant with Indian paintings and music serves an all-you-can-eat lunch buffet from 11:30 AM to 2:30 PM. Kids' menu. No smoking. | 998 S. Clinton Ave. | 716/461–0880 | $8–$20 | AE, D, DC, MC, V.

Mario's Via Abruzzi. Italian. Mario's is known for fresh seafood. A strolling accordion player serenades diners on Saturday evenings. Sunday brunch. | 2740 Monroe Ave. | 716/271–1111 | fax 716/271–1149 | www.mariosviaabruzzi.com | $15–$25 | AE, D, MC, V.

Newport House Restaurant. Continental. This pleasant waterside restaurant has two decks overlooking Newport Marina. Try the tenderloin of beef with bacon, mushrooms, and blue cheese. Come by on Wednesday nights for the all-you-can-eat pasta bar, or on Thursdays for the all-you-can-eat surf and turf special. Raw bar. Entertainment Fridays and Saturdays. Sunday brunch. | 500 Newport Rd. | 716/467–8480 | fax 716/266–1056 | www.newporthouse.com | $11–$25 | AE, MC, V.

Olive Tree. Greek. This Greek restaurant is housed in a 19th-century building that received an Excellence in Design Award from the American Institute of Architects. The menu includes contemporary and traditional Greek dishes, with plenty of broiled fish and lamb specialties, along with vegetarian entrées. Open-air dining on the sidewalk. | 165 Monroe Ave. | 716/454–3510 | www.olivetreerestaurant.com | Closed Sun. No lunch Sat. | $10–$20 | AE, MC, V.

Raj Mahal. Indian. Peek through the glass window before entering to see a chef prepare the breads, chicken, and seafood at this restaurant. Lamb vindaloo is popular, but if you're not used to spicy foods, ask them to keep it mild. Other specialties include tandoori chicken or shrimp, and chicken tikka. Buffet lunch. | 324 Monroe Ave. | 716/546–2315 | fax 716/546–4078 | www.rajmahalrochester.com | $7–$15 | AE, D, DC, MC, V.

Richardson's Canal House. French. This 1818 inn in a suburb southeast of Rochester is the oldest of its kind on the Erie Canal. Both elegant and informal meals are available. The menu changes seasonally and often includes chicken, lamb, beef, and fish. The outdoor terrace overlooks the canal. | 1474 Marsh Rd., Pittsford | 716/248–5000 | www.frontiernet.net/~rchi | Closed Sun. No lunch | $38 | AE, DC, MC, V.

Spring House. Continental. Meals have been served at this Colonial landmark and former Erie Canal inn since 1822. The four-story-southern-style brick building is surrounded by a patio and gardens. Try the chicken Ketchikan, a boneless breast, sautéed and topped with béarnaise sauce, or the lobster Thermidor. Open-air dining. Kids' menu. | 3001 Monroe Ave. | 716/586–2300 | fax 716/586–2395 | Closed Mon. | $18–$28 | AE, DC, MC, V.

Tokyo Japanese Restaurant and Steak House. Japanese. The waiters are dressed in Japanese costumes and the chefs are fun to watch at this restaurant known for sushi and hibachi dishes. Samurai swords and Japanese paintings hang on the walls. Kids' menu. No smoking. Ten miles south of Rochester. | 2930 W. Henrietta Rd. | 716/424–4166 | No lunch Sun. | $10–$21 | AE, D, MC, V.

Village Coal Tower. American. The Friday-night fish fry is popular at this homey, friendly restaurant housed in a tower once used in the mid-1800s to store coal for the canal. Hamburgers and salads are also on the menu. The restaurant is in a southeast suburb of Rochester. Open-air dining. Kids' menu. | 9 Schoen Pl., Pittsford | 716/381–7866 | Breakfast also available | $8–$10 | No credit cards.

Lodging

Brookwood Inn. This hotel is in a quiet suburb of Rochester, two blocks from the Erie Canal, and is popular with corporate travelers. You can easily reach the nearby bicycle path along the canal from the hotel. Restaurant, bar, room service. In-room data ports, cable TV.

Pool. Hot tub. Exercise equipment. Bicycles. Business services. | 800 Pittsford-Victor Rd., Pittsford | 716/248–9000 or 800/426–9995 | fax 716/248–8569 | 108 rooms | $119–$199 | AE, D, MC, V.

Comfort Inn–West. This five-story brick hotel is located near Kodak Park, three major malls, and about 30 restaurants. Red Lobster, Bob Evans, Applebee's, Olive Garden adjacent. King suites and double rooms available. Continental breakfast. In-room data ports, some in-room hot tubs, cable TV. Barbershop, beauty salon. Baby-sitting. Business services. Some pets allowed. | 1501 Ridge Rd. W | 716/621–5700 or 800/892–9348 | fax 716/621–8446 | www.comfortinn.com | 83 rooms | $75–$140 | AE, D, DC, MC, V.

Courtyard by Marriott. This modern, three-floor hotel has a courtyard area and solarium. Located 5 mi west of Rochester in the town of Brighton. Restaurant, bar, room service. In-room data ports, cable TV. Pool. Hot tub. Exercise equipment. Laundry facilities. Business services, airport shuttle. | 33 Corporate Woods, Brighton | 716/292–1000 | fax 716/292–0905 | 149 rooms | $100–$149 | AE, D, DC, MC, V.

Dartmouth House Bed and Breakfast. Each of the four rooms at this 1905 English Tudor house has been individually furnished, and some have king-size beds. The common areas have beamed ceilings and there is a cozy library/sitting room. This bed-and-breakfast is within walking distance of the George Eastman House. Complimentary breakfast. Cable TV. Library. Business services, airport shuttle. No kids under 12. | 215 Dartmouth St. | 716/271–7872 and 800/724–6298 | fax 716/473–0778 | www.dartmouthhouse.com | 4 rooms | $115 | AE, D, MC, V.

Days Inn–Victorian. This two-story brick hotel is in the Preservation District on East Avenue, a street lined with beech trees and broad lawns. The hotel is within walking distance of the George Eastman Museum and the Strong Museum. King-size beds are available. Complimentary Continental breakfast. In-room data ports, cable TV. Hot tub. Exercise equipment. Business services, airport shuttle. | 384 East Ave. | 716/325–5010 or 800/559–8039 | fax 716/454–3158 | www.daysinn.com | 128 rooms (60 with shower only) | $54–$150 | AE, D, DC, MC, V.

Econo Lodge–Brockport. This chain motel 15 mi west of Rochester has some connecting rooms and some efficiencies. Complimentary Continental breakfast. Some kitchenettes, some microwaves, cable TV. Pool. Playground, laundry facilities. Business services. Pets allowed. | 6575 4th Section Rd. (junction of Rtes. 19 and 31), Brockport | 716/637–3157 | fax 716/637–0434 | www.econolodge.com | 39 rooms | $52–$90 | AE, D, DC, MC, V.

Econo Lodge–Rochester South. Some rooms at this three-story chain hotel off Interstate 90 (exit 46) have king-size beds and in-room video games. Continental breakfast. Some in-room hot tubs, cable TV. Laundry facilities. Business services, airport shuttle. Some pets allowed. | 940 Jefferson Rd. | 716/427–2700 | fax 716/427–8504 | www.econolodge.com | 102 rooms | $58–$65 | AE, D, MC, V.

Four Points Sheraton. This downtown hotel overlooking the Genesee River has an enclosed skyway that connects you to the convention center. Rooms have double or king-size beds. Restaurant, bar, room service. In-room data ports, cable TV. Pool. Exercise equipment. Shops. Laundry facilities. Business services. Some pets allowed. | 120 E. Main St. | 716/546–6400 | fax 716/546–3908 | www.fourpoints.com | 466 rooms, 10 suites | $129–$149 | AE, D, MC, V.

428 Mount Vernon. The couple who run this bed-and-breakfast are known for their home-made chocolate scones. All rooms have antique furniture and private baths. The B&B is in a restored 1917 home on 2 wooded acres, within walking distance of the University of Rochester. Complimentary breakfast. Cable TV. | 428 Mount Vernon Ave. | 716/271–0792 | fax 716/271–0946 | 7 rooms | $115 | AE, D, MC, V.

Hampton Inn–South. This five-story chain hotel is 4 mi from downtown Rochester, 3 mi from the Rochester Institute of Technology, and 2 mi from the University of Rochester. Complimentary Continental breakfast. In-room data ports, cable TV. Business services. Some pets allowed. | 717 E. Henrietta Rd., off I–390, Brighton | 716/272–7800 | fax 716/272–1211 | www.hamptoninn.com | 113 rooms | $75–$95 | AE, D, DC, MC, V.

Holiday Inn–Airport. This chain is right next to the airport and 4 mi from downtown. Restaurant, bar (with entertainment), room service. In-room data ports, cable TV. Pool. Hot tub. Exercise equipment. Laundry facilities. Business services, airport shuttle. Some pets allowed. | 911 Brooks Ave., Gates | 716/328–6000 | fax 716/328–1012 | www.holiday-inn.com | 280 rooms | $89–$139 | AE, D, DC, MC, V.

Hyatt Regency. The pool area at this luxury hotel downtown has a glass wall with a view of the surrounding area. The lobby is marble. Restaurant, bar, room service. In-room data ports, cable TV. Pool. Hot tub. Exercise equipment. Business services, airport shuttle, parking (fee). | 125 E. Main St. | 716/546–1234 or 800/233–1234 | fax 716/546–6777 | www.hyatt.com | 335 rooms | $190–$240 | AE, D, DC, MC, V.

Lodge at Woodcliff. Bi-level suites and rooms with king-size beds are available at this upscale lodge on a wooded hill in an Erie Canal community. The lodge also hosts special murder-mystery evenings. No-smoking rooms are available. Restaurant, bar. In-room data ports, refrigerators, minibars, cable TV. Indoor-outdoor pool. Sauna. 9-hole golf course, tennis. Laundry service. Pets allowed. | 199 Woodcliff Dr., Fairport | 716/381–4000 or 800/365–3065 | fax 716/381–2673 | www.woodclifflodge.com | 232 rooms, 12 suites | $145 rooms, $175–$350 suites | AE, D, MC, V.

Marriott–Airport. This Marriott, 6 min from the airport and 10 min from downtown, is popular among business travelers. Restaurant, bar. In-room data ports, room service, cable TV. Pool. Hot tub. Exercise equipment. Business services, airport shuttle. Some pets allowed. | 1890 W. Ridge Rd., Greece | 716/225–6880 | fax 716/225–8188 | 210 rooms | $130–$150 | AE, D, DC, MC, V.

Marriott–Thruway. This five-story chain hotel is in a suburban setting 15 min from downtown and the airport. Many of the rooms were designed specifically for business travelers. Rooms have video games. Restaurant, bar (with entertainment), room service. Some refrigerators, cable TV. 2 pools. Hot tub, sauna. Putting green. Business services, airport shuttle. | 5257 W. Henrietta Rd. | 716/359–1800 | fax 716/359–1349 | 299 rooms, 5 suites | $115–$160 | AE, D, DC, MC, V.

Microtel. This chain hotel with compact rooms is 2 mi from the Rochester Institute of Technology. Cable TV. Business services. Some pets allowed. | 905 Lehigh Station Rd., Henrietta | 716/334–3400 or 800/999–2005 | fax 716/334–5042 | www.microtelinn.com | 99 rooms | $56 | AE, D, DC, MC, V.

Oliver Loud's. When this property, 6 mi southeast of Rochester on the Erie Canal, was restored, every effort was made to copy the original wallpaper, borders, and mouldings from 1812. Rooms have reproduction furniture and paintings. The common room has a fireplace and there are rocking chairs on the porch that overlooks the canal. Restaurant (see Richardson's Canal House), complimentary Continental breakfast. Cable TV. Business services. No kids under 12. | 1474 Marsh Rd., Pittsford | 716/248–5200 | fax 716/248–9970 | 8 rooms | $135–$155 | AE, DC, MC, V.

Radisson. The lobby of this chain hotel next to the Rochester Institute of Technology has a grand piano and overstuffed sofas. Some rooms have balconies; connecting rooms are available. Restaurant, bar (with entertainment), room service. In-room data ports, some microwaves, some refrigerators, cable TV. Pool. Exercise equipment. Business services, airport shuttle. | 175 Jefferson Rd. | 716/475–1910 | fax 716/475–9633 | 171 rooms | $89–$149 | AE, D, MC, V.

Ramada. This three-story hotel was fully renovated during its changeover to Ramada in 2000. Located 5 mi south of Rochester in the town of Henrietta, and about ½ mi from Marketplace Mall. Restaurant, bar, complimentary Continental breakfast. In-room data ports, room service, cable TV. Pool. Business services, airport shuttle. Some pets allowed. | 800 Jefferson Rd. | 716/475–9190 or 888/298–2054 | fax 716/424–2138 | 145 rooms | $76–$88 | AE, D, MC, V.

Red Roof Inn. Rooms have balconies at this chain hotel close to the intersection of Interstates 90 and 390 and 7 mi south of downtown Rochester. Some rooms have king-size beds and recliners. Cable TV. Business services. Pets allowed. | 4820 W. Henrietta Rd., Henrietta | 716/359–1100 | fax 716/359–1121 | www.redroof.com | 108 rooms | $56–$76 | AE, D, DC, MC, V.

Residence Inn by Marriott. The studio and loft suites have fully equipped kitchens and some have fireplaces at this all-suite hotel south of Rochester. The penthouse suites have two king-size beds, two bathrooms, and pull-out couches. Complimentary Continental breakfast. In-room data ports, kitchenettes, cable TV. Pool. Hot tub. Laundry facilities. Business services, airport shuttle. Some pets allowed (fee). | 1300 Jefferson Rd., Henrietta | 716/272–8850 | fax 716/272–7822 | www.residenceinn.com | 112 suites | $100–$145 | AE, D, DC, MC, V.

Strathallan Hotel. This all-suite hotel is in a quiet residential area within walking distance of the George Eastman House. The suites range in size from studios to one bedrooms and apartments. Restaurant, bar (with entertainment), complimentary breakfast, room service. In-room data ports, refrigerators, cable TV. Beauty salon. Exercise equipment. Video games. Business services, airport shuttle. | 550 East Ave. | 716/461–5010 or 800/678–7284 | fax 716/461–3387 | www.strathallan.com | 156 suites | $129–$149 | AE, D, MC, V.

Trail Break Motor Inn. You'll find this no-frills motel in a residential area about 2 mi south of Rochester. Refrigerators, cable TV. Pets allowed. | 7340 Pittsford-Palmyra Rd., Fairport | 716/223–1710 | fax 716/271–2147 | 32 rooms | $40–$59 | AE, D, MC, V.

Twenty Woodlawn Bed and Breakfast. There are only two rooms in this 1882 Victorian house: the Rose Room, which has imported English floral wallpaper and a rosebud chandelier with antique stained glass; and the Morning Room, which has an antique iron bed. Outside, there is an English cottage garden. The bed-and-breakfast is 5 mi southeast of Rochester. Complimentary breakfast. | 20 Woodlawn Ave., Fairport | 716/377–8224 | fairportbb@aol.com | www.nycanal.com/bandb/woodlawn | 2 rooms, 1 with shared bath | $75–$90 | No credit cards.

Wellesley Inn–North. King-size beds are available at this hotel in a shopping and business district 3 mi northwest of Rochester. Complimentary Continental breakfast. In-room data ports, some refrigerators, cable TV. Business services. Some pets allowed. | 1635 W. Ridge Rd., Greece | 716/621–2060 or 800/444–8888 | fax 716/621–7102 | www.wellesleyinnand-suites.com | 93 rooms (2 with shower only), 4 suites | $65–$90 | AE, D, DC, MC, V.

Wellesley Inn–South. This branch of the Wellesley is on the southern edge of the city, very close to the Erie Canal. Complimentary Continental breakfast. In-room data ports, cable TV. Business services. Some pets allowed. | 797 E. Henrietta Rd. (Rte. 15A), Brighton | 716/427–0130 | fax 716/427–0903 or 800/444–8888 | www.wellesleyinnandsuites.com | 92 rooms, 4 suites | $70–$90 | AE, D, DC, MC, V.

ROCKVILLE CENTRE

MAP 4, G8

(Nearby towns also listed: Freeport, Garden City, Long Beach, New York City)

In the mid-1700s, after the last of the local Indians had left, the first settler to this area, Michael DeMott, built a mill on a stream. But the village wasn't established until 1893, 140 years later.

Today, the heavily traveled routes of Sunrise Highway and Merrick Road run through the heart of the downtown shopping area, and yet, just north and south of these roads, there are residential areas with large green yards, wraparound porches, and tree-lined streets. Rockville Center has 200 acres of parkland and is just minutes away from some of the south shore's most beautiful beaches and parks.

Information: **Chamber of Commerce** | Box 226, 11570 | 516/766–0666 | www.ci.rockville-centre.ny.us.

Attractions

Hempstead Lake State Park. There are 775 acres of park along this beautiful lake just north of Rockville Center. You can camp, saltwater fish, swim, and hike. Facilities include ball fields, a bicycle path, a boating ramp, picnic areas, a food service, and a bathhouse. In winter, you can cross country ski. | Peninsula Blvd., West Hempstead | 516/766–1029 | Free; parking $5 | Daily dawn–dusk.

Village Shopping Area. In downtown Rockville Center, along two highly trafficked roads and several smaller side streets, there are many restaurants and shops, both large and small. | Sunrise Hwy. and Merrick Rd. | Free | Daily.

ON THE CALENDAR

MAR.: *St. Patrick's Parade.* Pipe bands, mounted police, and Irish wolfhounds all participate in this parade down Maple Avenue the Saturday after St. Patrick's Day. | 516/678–9338.

OCT.: *Halloween Rag-A-Muffin Parade.* Over 2,000 children and adults show up for this costume parade the Sunday before Halloween, which includes one segment with families marching together. The parade starts at the village green on Maple Avenue at Morris Avenue. | 516/678–9338.

NOV.: *10K Road Race.* Since the 1970s, over 1,000 runners have been racing through the village streets on the second Saturday in November. Residents stand in front of their houses to cheer the competitors on. The race starts at Park Avenue between Merrick Road and Sunrise Highway. | 516/678–9338.

Dining

Bigelow's. Seafood. This local take-out landmark has been serving some of the best seafood around for over 60 years. Friendly staff will serve you at the counter, or you can take the fried Ipswich clams with fries to go. Try the fried shrimp or the red or white chowder. | 79 N. Long Beach Rd. | 516/678–3878 | fax 516/763–1950 | Reservations not accepted | $8–$15 | No credit cards.

Buon Giorno. Italian. With warm, low lighting, this restaurant, 10 mi west of Rockville Centre, has original artwork hanging on the walls, and is a nice place for a quiet, romantic dinner. The kitchen is known for its veal scaloppine, homemade pasta, fish, and chicken. | 476 Merrick Rd., Lynbrook | 516/887–1945 | Reservations essential weekends | Closed Mon. | $12–$30 | AE, D, DC, MC, V.

Cafe Riviera. Italian. Italian music plays in the background at this romantic restaurant with a cozy fireplace. Try the squid-ink linguine (black linguine with mixed seafood in a fresh tomato sauce) or the Dover sole amandine (broiled and served with white beans, carrots, peas, and corn). | 208 Sunrise Hwy. | 516/678–1996 | Closed Mon. | $20–$30 | AE, DC, MC, V.

Catfish Cafe. Cajun/Creole. Dishes here blend exotic spices with the cooking styles of many different cultures, including French, Indian, West Indian, and Spanish. Try the catfish cakes with jalapeño rémoulade sauce, Catfish Named Desire (panfried fillets in a lemon-pepper corn flour crust), Miss Mary-Ann's Chicken, or Mumbo Gumbo with sausage. The restaurant is 2 mi west of Rockville Center. Live music on Wednesdays and Fridays. Kids' menu. No smoking. | 172 Merrick Rd., Lynbrook | 516/599–0137 | Closed Mon., Tues. No lunch | $20–$30 | AE, D, DC, MC, V.

Focaccia Grill. Italian. Clouds are painted on the ceiling and there is a 55-gallon tank of tropical fish at this restaurant, 2 mi west of Rockville Centre. The menu has daily specials such as polenta-crusted red snapper and linguine with sausage, broccoli rabe, and sun-dried tomatoes. | 323 Merrick Rd., Lynbrook | 516/593–5858 | Closed Mon. No lunch | $22–$30 | AE, D, DC, MC, V.

George Martin. Contemporary. Prepare for crowds at this upscale bistro that serves aged New York sirloin, as well as pasta and seafood. | 65 N. Park Ave. | 516/678–7272 | fax 516/594–9356 | No lunch weekends | $13–$27 | AE, MC, V.

International Delight Cafe. American. This casual, noisy restaurant serves hearty fare including salad platters, burgers, and homemade gelati. Try the Belgian waffles. | 241 Sunrise Hwy. | 516/766–7557 | Reservations not accepted (excluding large parties) | $8–$12 | No credit cards.

Maier's Brick Cafe. American. Booths run down one side of this cozy, sports-theme, family-oriented pub. The menu is American and German. Try the chicken pot pie, the sauerbraten, or the Wienerschnitzel. The café is 2 mi west of Rockville Centre. Sunday brunch. | 157 Lakeview Ave., Lynbrook | 516/599–9669 | $15–$25 | AE, D, DC, MC, V.

Nick's Pizza. Italian. The made-to-order pizza is the main draw at this casual family restaurant with high tin ceilings and opera or oldies playing in the background. The ravioli specials and the desserts are also good. Beer and wine only. | 272 Sunrise Hwy. | 516/763–3278 | Reservations not accepted | $10–$25 | AE, DC, MC, V.

Raay-nor's Cabin. Southern. The fried chicken and ribs are popular at this local landmark that's been around since the 1940s. From the outside you'd think you're entering a log cabin; the inside has the same flavor with aged wood paneling. Menu items include pot pies and certified Angus beef. The restaurant is ½ mi east of Rockville Centre. Kids' menu. | 550 Sunrise Hwy., Baldwin | 516/223–4886 | fax 516/223–8163 | www.lirestaurants.com/raaynors | $9–$18 | AE, D, DC, MC, V.

Tuscany. Contemporary. This cozy, romantic restaurant has dim lighting and light jazz playing in the background. Try the grilled ostrich smothered in sun-dried cherry sauce. For dessert, try white chocolate crème brûlée. You can call to be put on the list for special wine-tasting dinners. No smoking. | 187 N. Long Beach Rd. | 516/763–9313 | Closed Mon. | $20–$30 | AE, MC, V.

Lodging

Holiday Inn. Sandwiched between the Long Island Railroad Station and the ever-busy Sunrise Highway, this five-story standard member of the chain trades in peace and quiet for convenience and reliability. Restaurant, bar, room service. In-room data ports, some refrigerators, cable TV. Business services. Pets allowed ($15). | 173 Sunrise Hwy. | 516/678–1300 or 800/HOLIDAY | fax 516/465–4329 | www.holidayinn.com | 100 rooms | AE, D, DC, MC, V.

ROME

MAP 3, I5

(Nearby towns also listed: Canastota, Liverpool, Oneida, Syracuse, Utica)

Rome lies on the Mohawk River about 10 mi north of Interstate 90. The Oneida were the first to live in this area, and because it lay on the route linking the Atlantic Ocean with the Great Lakes, British and French fur traders came here in the 1600s to trade for black beaver pelts. In the 1750s, the British built Fort Stanwix, which the Americans then took over during the Revolutionary War. And it was here, in 1817, that the first portion of the old Erie Canal was dug. Today approximately 40,000 people live in Rome.

Information: **Rome Area Chamber of Commerce** | 139 W. Dominick St., 13440 | 315/337–1700 | www.romechamber.com.

Attractions

Delta Lake State Park. You can swim or camp at this state-run park. | 8797 Rte. 46 | 315/337–4670 or 800/456–CAMP (reservations) | www.nysparks.stat.ny.us/ | $6 per vehicle | May—Oct., daily.

Erie Canal Village. At this re-created 19th-century canal settlement, you can see a tavern, blacksmith shop, settler's house, and one-room schoolhouse. There are several museums, including a cheese museum housed in a former cheese factory, a carriage museum that has horse-drawn vehicles, and a canal museum with displays about the construction of, and life along, the canal. A trip aboard a re-created packet boat gives a taste of 19th-century water travel. | 5789 New London Rd. | 315/337–3999 or 888/374–3226 | www.eriecanalvillage.com | $6 | Memorial Day–Labor Day, Wed.–Sat. 10–5, Sun. noon–5.

Fort Rickey Children's Discovery Zoo. There is a large petting area at this zoo that houses native and exotic animals. | New London Rd. (Rte. 46) | 315/336–1930 | $7.50 | Memorial Day–Labor Day, daily 10–5.

Fort Stanwix National Monument. Living-history programs include a military drill with 18th-century weaponry at this reconstruction of the fort built by the British in 1758 to protect the strategic Oneida Carrying Place—a 1-mi area over which boats had to be carried on the route from the Atlantic Ocean to the Great Lakes. | 112 E. Park St. | 315/336–2090 | www.nps.gov/fost | Free; parking $2 | Apr.–Dec., daily 9–5.

Woods Valley Ski Area. With a 500-ft vertical drop, three lifts, and several beginner and intermediate trails, this is a popular hill for novices. Twelve miles north of Rome. | Rte. 46, Westernville | 315/827–4721 or 315/827–4206 | Closed Mon. | Dec.–Mar.

ON THE CALENDAR

JULY: *World Series of Bocce.* More than 100 teams compete in these matches held at the Toccolana Club. | 1412 E. Dominick St. | 315/337–1700 or 315/339–3609.

Dining

Michelina's. Continental. This restaurant inside The Beeches, a 1920s brownstone estate on 52 landscaped acres, is known for steak, seafood, lobster, and pasta. Sunday brunch. | 7900 Turin Rd. (Rte. 26) | 315/336–1700 | fax 315/336–7270 | Breakfast also available; closed Mon. | $9–$18 | AE, D, DC, MC, V.

Savoy. Italian. Checkered cloths cover the tables at this restaurant known for homemade pasta, fresh seafood, and steak. The Savoy is run by the same family who runs The Beeches. A pianist plays Wednesdays, Fridays, and Saturdays. Kids' menu. | 255 E. Dominick St. | 315/339–3166 | www.thebeeches.com/savoy.html | No lunch weekends | $7–$19 | AE, D, DC, MC, V.

Lodging

Beeches Paul Revere Lodge. This lodge is part of The Beeches estate which includes 52 landscaped acres and the family that runs it has been in the hotel business since 1908. Rooms are done in French-country style. Restaurant (*See* Michelina's). In-room data ports, refrigerators, cable TV. Pool. Business services. Some pets allowed (fee). | 7900 Turin Rd. | 315/336–1776 or 800/765–7251 | fax 315/339–2636 | www.thebeeches.com | 75 rooms | $69 | AE, D, DC, MC, V.

Quality Inn. Some rooms at this chain hotel have balconies and sofa beds. Connecting rooms are also available. Restaurant. Cable TV. Pool. Laundry facilities. Business services. | 200 S. James St. | 315/336–4300 | fax 315/336–4492 | 104 rooms | $89 | AE, D, DC, MC, V.

ROSCOE

(Nearby town also listed: Liberty)

The site of the protected Esopus Creek, one of the most famous angling rivers in the Northeast, Roscoe is known as "Trout Town, USA." Fly-fishermen make pilgrimages to this Sullivan County community to fish for rainbow, brook, and brown trout.

Information: **Chamber of Commerce** | P.O. Box 443, 12776 | 607/498–5222.

Attractions

Catskill Fly Fishing Center and Museum. This non-profit center 4 mi east of Roscoe is wholly devoted to the preservation of the sport of fly-fishing and the delicate ecological environment that makes the sport possible. The center maintains a vast collection of fishing accoutrements, antique flies, and fishing-related artwork. The center also conducts outreach and educational programs throughout the year. | Old Rte. 17, off Exit 94 | 914/439–4810 | $3 | Apr.–Oct., daily 10–4; Nov.–Mar.; call for hours.

ON THE CALENDAR

JAN.: *Livingston Manor Ice Carnival.* Ice-skating, ice-carving and snow sculptures, and dog-sledding demonstrations are part of this carnival in Livingston Manor, about 9 mi east of Roscoe. | 914/439–5225.

Dining

Roscoe Diner. American. Your quintessential upstate diner, the Roscoe has been under the same family ownership since 1969. The menu has a bit of everything, starting with omelettes for breakfast, soups and sandwiches for lunch, and hearty steaks, seafood, and chicken dishes for dinner. Kids menu. | Old Rte. 17 | 607/498–4405 | $8–$24 | AE, D, DC, MC, V.

Lodging

Roscoe Motel. Some rooms have views of the water at this quiet motel along the Beaverkill River. Picnic area, complimentary Continental breakfast. Some refrigerators, cable TV. Pool. Pets allowed. | Old Rte. 17 | 607/498–5220 | 18 rooms | $45–$60 | AE, MC, V.

ROSLYN

(Nearby towns also listed: Glen Cove, Great Neck, Port Washington)

Roslyn boasts an attractive downtown, well-known restaurants, and charming residential areas. Its valley setting at the head of Hempstead Harbor is reported to have reminded early residents of a Scottish castle area named Roslin.

In addition to trendy boutiques, Roslyn is home to approximately 100 pre–Civil War buildings. However, its tree-lined Main Street and quiet family life have not been untouched by some of the ill effects of urbanization. Traffic remains a problem in Roslyn as it does in most of Nassau County today.

Information: **Glen Cove Chamber of Commerce** | 14 Glen St., Suite 303, Glen Cove, 11542 | 516/676–6666.

Attractions

Clock Tower. This stunning clock tower, the town landmark, was acquired in 1895. | Main St. and Old Northern Blvd. | Free | Daily.

Nassau County Museum of Art. This Georgian brick mansion is on 145 manicured acres of the Frick estate. The permanent collection has 600 works from 19th and 20th century European and American Artists. There is also the Tee Ridder Miniatures Museum, a collection of 26 miniature rooms made by Madeline "Tee" Ridder. | Old Museum Rd. | $4 | Tues.– Sun. 11-5.

ON THE CALENDAR

OCT.: *Craft As Art Festival*. Long Island's best attended and most comprehensive crafts event showcases handcrafted original designs in precious jewelry, toys, and musical instruments by more than 100 craft-artists from every region of the United States. At the Nassau County Museum of Art. | 516/484–9337 or 973/746–0091.

Dining

Bryant and Cooper Steak House. American. The owners of this traditional steak house buy prime meat and age it themselves. You may prefer to dine here on weekdays when it is less crowded. | 2 Middle Neck Rd. | 516/627–7270 | No lunch weekends | $15–$35 | AE, D, DC, MC, V.

Classico. Italian. Paintings by local Port Washington artists hang on the walls and the tables are spread with linen clothes at this Tuscan-style restaurant a mile northeast of Roslyn. Try the Dover sole with mornay sauce or rabbit roasted with rosemary and potatoes. Live music on Saturdays. | 1042 Northern Blvd., Roslyn Estates | 516/621–1870 | No lunch Mon., Tues. | $18–$28 | AE, D, DC, MC, V.

George Washington Manor. American. George Washington is said to have eaten in this mansion that dates back to 1740. The menu has traditional food including prime rib, fillet of sole, and salmon, and there also is a four-course prix-fixe menu. Buffet on major holidays. Sunday brunch. No smoking. | 1305 Old Northern Blvd. | 516/621–1200 | $15–$22 | AE, D, DC, MC, V.

Jolly Fisherman and Steak House. Seafood. Waiters in tuxedoes serve simple dishes such as broiled fish at this restaurant with white linen tablecloths, fireplaces, and paintings of old Roslyn. Kids' menu. | 25 Main St. | 516/621–0055 | Closed Mon. | $18–$35 | AE, D, DC, MC, V.

La Marmite. Continental. This formal restaurant has a glass front and several dining areas. The menu includes staples such as Caesar salad, shrimp cocktail, and rack of lamb, along with newer selections such as ostrich carpaccio and boneless quail stuffed with wild rice and goose liver. La Marmite is 4 mi south of Roslyn. Sunday brunch. | 234 Hillside Ave., Williston Park | 516/746–1243 | Jacket required at dinner | No lunch weekends | $14–$28 | AE, DC, MC, V.

La Parma. Italian. One of three La Parmas, this well-known southern Italian restaurant 4 mi south of Roslyn draws crowds. It's noisy, but the portions are ample and you can go into the kitchen and watch the food being prepared. Try the chicken or veal parmigiana, or the shrimp La Parma. | 707 Willis Ave., Williston Park | 516/294–6610 | Reservations not accepted (except for holidays) | $30–$40 | AE, DC, MC, V.

Riverbay Seafood Bar and Grill. Seafood. The extremely fresh seafood is the reason there are long waits and crowds at this bright, airy restaurant 4 mi south of Roslyn. Raw bar. Sunday brunch. | 700 Willis Ave., Williston Park | 516/742–9191 | No lunch Sat. | $15–$22 | AE, DC, MC, V.

Lodging

Roslyn Claremont. Most of the suites at this hotel have king-size four-poster canopy beds and sitting rooms with fireplaces. Restaurant, bar, room service. In-room data ports, minibars, cable TV. Gym. Business services. | 1221 Old Northern Blvd. | 516/625–2700 or 800/626–9005 | fax 516/625–2731 | info@www.roslynclaremonthotel.com | www.roslynclaremonthotel.com | 75 rooms | $209–$345 | AE, D, DC, MC, V.

ROXBURY

(Nearby towns also listed: Cairo, Delhi, Hunter, Oneonta, Stamford, Windham)

Roxbury is a quiet village in the heart of the Catskills. John Burroughs, the American nature writer, spent his youth here, as did railroad magnate, Jay Gould.

Information: **Roxbury Town Hall** | Main St., Roxbury 12474 | 607/326–7641.

Attractions

Burroughs Memorial. Just outside Roxbury is this memorial to American naturalist John Burroughs (1837–1921), an early environmentalist whose books changed the way many Americans looked at the natural world. | Burroughs Memorial Rd. | 607/326–7908 | Free | Daily dawn–dusk.

Ski Plattekill. This resort on 75 acres has 32 trails and a 1,200-ft vertical drop. In summer the resort is a leading mountain biking venue, with 60 mi of trails. | 1 Plattekill Mt. Rd. | 607/326–3500 | www.plattekill.com | $34.

ON THE CALENDAR

SEPT.: *Extreme Phat Tire Festival.* Mountain-bike races for all ages and skills levels take place at the Ski Plattekill resort. | 607/326–3500.

OCT.: *Oktoberfest.* This traditional German celebration includes mountain-bike races, foliage sky rides, and bike and tent sales. At Ski Plattekill. | 607/326–3500.

Dining

Bud's Country Store and Restaurant. American. The country-style restaurant is like home to many locals. The kitchen is on display as breakfast or lunch is prepared in front of you. Popular dishes that keep the locals coming back are their sandwiches, cheese burgers, French toast, and omelettes. | Main St. | 607/326–3663 | No Dinner | $3–$4 | No credit cards.

Hitching Post. American. Lots of bare wood and low lighting gives this family-friendly restaurant about 8 mi northeast of Roxbury a mild roadhouse-y feel. The menu is loaded with well-prepared favorites like burgers and fries, hearty steak-and-potato dinners, and shareable appetizer baskets. | Rte. 23, Grand Gorge | 607/588–6389 | $6–$10 | MC, V.

Lodging

Brennans Hillview Inn. This four-unit motel renovated in Fall 2000 features clean, well-maintained rooms with deluxe rooms available. Conveniently located only 2 mi from Belleayre Mountain and 8 mi from Roxbury. Reservations recommended. None. | Brushing Road Main St., Fleischmanns | 845/254–9810 | 4 rooms | $50–$75 | No credit cards.

Tait's Colonial Motel. This modest, family-run motel is practically the only game in town in tiny Grand Gorge, about 8 mi northeast of Roxbury. It's a single story with room-front parking, and guest rooms are outfitted with standard wood-veneer motel furniture. There are a few fast-food restaurants nearby, and the town's small enough to make walking anywhere feasible. Cable TV. | Rte. 23, Grand Gorge | 607/588–6122 | 14 rooms | $55–$65 | AE, D, MC, V.

T-Bar Country Inn. The two-story building has a restaurant, bar, lounge, and liquor store on the first floor with rooms available on the top level. Restaurant. | Rte. 30 | 607/326–7501 | fax 607/326–4909 | 7 rooms | $37–$40 | MC, V.

RYE

(Nearby towns also listed: Elmsford, Hartsdale, Hawthorne, Mamaroneck, New Rochelle, Scarsdale, Tarrytown, White Plains, Yonkers)

Rye is the oldest permanent settlement in Westchester County. It was founded in 1660 when a small group of settlers with ties to Rye, England, made a treaty with the Mohegan Indians. For centuries, farming, raising livestock, and oystering in Long Island Sound were major occupations. By the mid-19th century, Rye had become a popular summer resort for city dwellers looking to beat the heat. The advent of commuter trains and parkways in the 1920s brought a rush of suburbanites to the village, and in 1942 Rye was incorporated and became Westchester's sixth city. Today, 15,000 people live in this suburban community with tree-lined streets.

Information: **Rye City Chamber of Commerce** | 110 Willett Ave., 10573 | 914/939–1900.

Attractions

Playland Park. One of the oldest amusement facilities of its type in the country, this park on Long Island Sound has retained some of its original rides (its carousel was built in 1915). You can also swim, boat, fish, or have a picnic. | Playland Pkwy. (I–95, exit 19) | 914/925–2701 | fax 914/925–0668 | www.ryeplayland.org | 75¢–$4 per ride; multiple ticket books are available; parking $4.

Dining

Belluscio's Restaurant. Italian. This family-friendly restaurant has fireplaces in the dining room. The pizza, pasta, and seafood are popular, and there are weekend specials. | 352 Midland Ave. | 914/967–5634 | Closed Mon. No lunch | $11–$23 | AE, MC, V.

La Panetiere. French. The formal dining room inside this French country house has exposed ceiling beams and antiques. Traditional dishes of lobster, scallops, lamb, fish, and poultry are prepared with fresh, seasonal ingredients. | 530 Milton Rd. | 914/967–8140 | fax 914/921–0654 | www.lapanetiere.com | Jacket required | No lunch Sat. | $24–$32 | AE, DC, MC, V.

Lodging

Courtyard by Marriott. This four-story chain is 1 mi from Rye Playland. Suites have king-size beds and separate dining and living area. Restaurant. In-room data ports, cable TV. Pool. Hot tub. Gym. | 631 Midland Ave. | 914/921–1110 or 800/266–1953 | fax 914/921–1110 | www.courtyard.com | 145 rooms, 12 suites | $100–$185 | AE, D, DC, MC, V.

SACKETS HARBOR

(Nearby town also listed: Watertown)

Settled in 1800, this village on Lake Ontario was the site of two naval battles during the War of 1812. Many of its buildings date from the early 1800s and while Sackets Harbor is a popular cruising destination, land-going travelers are beginning to find it as well.

Information: **Sackets Harbor Visitors Center and Chamber of Commerce** | 301 W. Main St., 13685 | 315/646–2321 or 315/646–1700 | shvisit@gisco.net | www.1000islands.com/sacketsharbor.

Attractions

Old McDonald's Children's Farm. Part of a 1,200-acre working farm, Old McDonald's has been devoted to educating children about farm life for more than a decade. Places like Goatsville and Bunnyville are popular for young children. There's a miniature golf course, too. | 14471 Rte. 145 | 315/583–5737 | www.1000islands.com/mcfarm/oldmac.htm | $5 | May–Oct., daily 10–6.

Sackets Harbor Battlefield State Historic Site. During the War of 1812, two battles were fought here between the British and the Americans. The harbor served as headquarters for divisions of the army and navy. Today the site includes a nicely restored commandant's house, which dates to 1850. Guides reenact camp life in summer. | 505 W. Washington St. | 315/646–3634 | $1 | May–Oct., Wed.–Sat. 10–5, Sun. 1–5; grounds open daily.

Sackets Harbor Heritage Area Visitors Center. Displays focus on the harbor's role in the War of 1812. | 301 W. Main St. | 315/646–2321 | www.1000islands.com/sacketsharbor | Free | Call for hrs.

Seaway Trail. This is the Discover Center for the Seaway Trail, a 454-mi marked route that follows the the coastlines of Lake Erie, the Niagara River, Lake Ontario, and the St. Lawrence River. Designed to be an alternative to major highways, the trail takes you past historic sites. | Corner of Ray St. and W. Main St. | 315/646–1000 | fax 315/646–1004 | seaway@north-net.org | www.seawaytrail.com | $4 | Daily 10–5.

Westcott Beach State Park. You can camp, boat, fish, swim, and picnic at this 319-acre park. There are 169 campsites (85 electrical), flush toilets, showers, picnic sites, and a camp store. | 505 W. Washington St. | 315/938–5083 | www.nysparks.state.ny.us/parks/ | Free; parking $5 | Mid-May–mid-Oct., daily.

ON THE CALENDAR

JULY: *Can/Am Festival.* Highlights of this festival include reenactments of the War of 1812 bombardments. At the Sackets Harbor Battlefield State Historic Site. | 315/646–2321.

Dining

1812 Steak and Seafood Co. Contemporary. Try the London broil à la 1812 at this restaurant right in the middle of the village's historic district. Kids' menu. Early bird dinners. | 212 W. Main St. | 315/646–2041 | $10–$24 | AE, D, MC, V.

Tin Pan Galley. Contemporary. This is actually two restaurants in one; upstairs dining begins at 5:30 PM daily, and breakfast and lunch are served downstairs or outside. Salads and sandwiches are popular. Try the grilled Portobello mushroom sandwich. You can dine outside in a New Orleans–style flower garden with wrought-iron gates and a stone archway. | 110 W. Main St. | 315/646–3812 | $9–$15 | AE, D, MC, V.

Lodging

Candlelight Bed and Breakfast. This 1832 Georgian red brick home is a next door to the Sackets Harbor Battle Field State Historic Site and a 3-min walk to restaurants, shops, and the Seaway Trail. Rooms have period antiques, four-post beds, and quilts; two have water views, the other looks out onto the village. Complimentary breakfast. TV in common area. Business services. No pets. No kids under 18. No smoking. | 501 W. Washington St. | 315/646–1518 or 800/306–5595 | candlebb@imcnet.net | www.imcnet.net/candlelight | 3 rooms | No credit cards.

Ontario Place. Some rooms have views of the harbor at this hotel with a range of accommodations. In addition to standard rooms, there are minisuites with refrigerators, microwaves, and in-room hot rubs, and special suites for up to five people. In-room data ports, some microwaves, some refrigerators, some in-room hot tubs, cable TV. Bicycles. Business services. | 103 General Smith Dr. | 315/646–8000 | fax 315/646–2506 | hotel@imc-net.net | www.imcnet.net/ontario_place/hotel.htm | 38 rooms, 1 suite, 1 apartment | $74–$150 rooms, $175 suite, $325 apartment | AE, D, DC, MC, V.

SAG HARBOR

(Nearby towns also listed: Bridgehampton/Water Mill, East Hampton, Southampton)

The South Fork village of Sag Harbor has been a port since the early 1700s. Along with New York City, it was one of the first ports of entry in the United States in 1789.

Originally Sag Harbor thrived through its whaling industry and West Indian trade, and its streets are lined with the homes of early colonists, whaling captains, and wealthy industrialists. Today its history, old trees, inviting homes, restaurants, and shops make it one of the most popular historic Long Island villages. Unfortunately though, this charm and popularity has spawned an increase in year-round traffic.

Information: **Chamber of Commerce** | Box 2810, 11963 | 631/725–0011.

Attractions

Custom House. Built circa 1800–20, this beautifully appointed historic house museum was the home of the Dering family of Sag Harbor. Mr. Dering was the port's first U.S. Custom's Master, and the house was also used as a custom office. Historical documents and period furnishings are on display. | Garden St. | 631/725–0250 | $3 | July–Aug., daily, 10–5; Sept.–June, Sat.–Sun, 10–5.

Morton National Wildlife Refuge. This 187-acre refuge overlooking Peconic Bay has beaches and woody bluffs that are home to the piping plover, a large variety of terns, osprey, waterfowl, wading birds, and deer. | Noyack Rd. | 631/286–0485 | $4 per car | Daily.

Sag Harbor Whaling and Historical Museum. An historic boat collection, ship models, tools, period furnishings, and oil paintings are on display at this whaling museum housed in a striking Greek Revival structure. The house was originally built for shipowner Benjamin Huntting and his family in 1845; years later it was converted to a Masonic temple, which still occupies its second floor. | Garden and Main Sts. | 631/725–0770 | $3 | Mid-May–Christmas, Mon.–Sat. 10–5, Sun. 1–5.

ON THE CALENDAR
JULY: *Band Concerts.* The Sag Harbor Community Band plays music from Sousa to Strauss at the American Legion Patio on Bay Street. | 631/725–0011.

Dining
American Hotel. French. This formal dining room has alcoves, plenty of antiques, and pictures of Abraham Lincoln and George Washington on the walls. Try the rack of lamb, grilled lamb chops, roast pheasant, or lobster Thermidor. | 25 Main St. | 631/725–3535 | No lunch weekdays | $20–$32 | AE, D, DC, MC, V.

B. Smith's. Eclectic. There's a busy bar scene at this restaurant facing the harbor. Try the pork chops with fried plantain, ancestral gravy, and greens, or ribs with B's sweet success sauce. Open-air dining on the patio has seating for 150. Raw bar. Live music occasionally. Sunday brunch. Dock space. | 1 Bay St. | 631/725–5858 | Closed mid-Oct.–Memorial Day | $18–$30 | AE, D, MC, V.

Beacon Restaurant. Contemporary. This casual restaurant overlooking the harbor serves French and American food with an Asian influence. Popular menu items include soy-glazed salmon grilled in Thai peanut sauce, rock shrimp hash, and crème brûlée Napoléon. Open-air dining on the deck. | 8 W. Water St. | 631/725–7088 | Reservations not accepted | Closed Tues.–Wed. No lunch | $20–$35 | AE, MC, V.

Il Capuccino. Italian. Chianti bottles hang down from the ceiling over red-and-white-checked tablecloths at this restaurant known for homemade ravioli, seafood, and garlic bread. Kids' menu. | 30 Madison St. | 631/725–2747 | No lunch | $15–$25 | AE, DC, MC, V.

Spinnaker's. Eclectic. Try local seafood, steaks, and pasta served in a dining room with a tin ceiling. There's a prix-fixe meal on weeknights that includes salad, a main course, and dessert. Piano bar on Saturdays. Kids' menu. Sunday brunch. | 63 Main St. | 631/725–9353 | $20–$30, prix fixe $13 | AE, DC, MC, V.

Lodging

American Hotel. An 1846 Gothic Revival home houses both an excellent French restaurant (*see* above) and a handful of luxurious guest rooms full of antiques dating back to the town's days as a center for the whaling trade. There's a cigar lounge, a gift shop, and a wrap-around porch with an excellent view of the water. Sag Harbor's quaint historic downtown area is within a three-block walk. Dining room. No in-room TVs. | 25 Main St. | 631/725–3535 | www.theamericanhotel.com | 8 rooms | $145–$295 | AE, D, DC, MC, V.

Barcelona Inn. All rooms have kitchenettes and queen-size beds. This small complex of family-owned and -operated efficiencies is a mile from Sag Harbor Village, next to the Sag Harbor Golf Course and State Park. Cable TV. No pets allowed. | Rte. 114 | 631/725–0714 | 42 rooms | $95–$125 | No credit cards.

Sag Harbor Inn. This two-story inn built in the late 1980s is only three blocks to Main St., where you will find restaurants and shops. Complimentary Continental breakfast. Outdoor pool. No pets allowed. | W. Water St. | 631/725–2949 | fax 631/725–5009 | 6 rooms | $185–$275 | AE, MC, V.

SALAMANCA

MAP 3, C8

(Nearby towns also listed: Jamestown, Olean)

Salamanca, on the broad Allegheny River, has the distinction of being the only United States city on a reservation belonging to Native Americans. The region was settled by the Seneca Nation, one of the five tribes in the formidable Iroquois Federation. You won't want to miss the small but state-of-the-art Seneca Iroquois National Museum.

South of Salamanca is Allegany State Park, and 11 mi north is Ellicottville, a small village that is home to a popular ski resort.

Information: **Salamanca Area Chamber of Commerce** | 696 Broad St., 14779 | 716/945–2034.

Attractions

Allegany State Park. The park bills itself as "The Year-Round Park," and because it has a full slate of all-season activities, the title seems appropriate. The largest, and wildest, member of the New York State park system, Allegany State Park covers 65,000 acres, and has more than 85 mi of hiking trails. These trails range from short, easy strolls, to an 18-mi trek over rugged terrain. You can also fish in the lakes and streams; camp year-round; rent rowboats, paddleboats, or mountain bikes; go horseback riding; play tennis; and play miniature golf on two courses. In winter, you can cross-country ski, snowmobile, and go tobogganing. There are snack bars, a restaurant, picnic areas, and three gift shops in the park. Among many other planned activities, the park hosts a series of free summer concerts held in the Quaker Beach area. | 2373 Rte. 1 | 716/354–9101 or 800/456–CAMP | $6 per vehicle | Daily.

Holiday Valley Resort. This resort in a small town 11 mi north of Salamanca has 52 slopes, 12 lifts, a vertical drop of 750 ft, a ski school, and ski-out-your-back-door accommodations. In summer, the ski center transforms into a vacation spot with an 18-hole golf course, a golf school, tennis courts, mountain biking, and three swimming pools. Lodging on premises. | Rte. 219, Ellicottville | 716/699–2345 | fax 716/699–5204 | www.holidayvalley.com | skiing@holidayvalley.com | Daily.

Nannen Arboretum. Begun in 1977 as an adjunct to the Cornell Cooperative Extension facility, this arboretum today occupies 8 acres on which over 400 unique trees and shrubs grow. Includes an extensive herb garden with 300 species, and a popular Japanese meditation garden. The arboretum is 11 mi north of Salamanca. | 28 Parkside Dr., Ellicottville | 716/699–2377 or 716/945–5200 | dswaciak@cce.cornell.edu | Free | Daily dawn–dusk.

Salamanca Rail Museum. This fully restored 1912 passenger depot offers a fascinating look at the history of the Erie Lackawanna Railroad, whose anticipated arrival led to the creation of the city of Salamanca. Exhibits include artifacts, memorabilia, and an extensive collection of vintage photographs. Includes a high-ceiling waiting room, and an old-fashioned ticket office. | 170 Main St. | 716/945–3133 | Free | Apr.–Dec., Tues.–Sat. 10–5, Sun. noon–5 (May–Sept., also Mon. 10–5).

Seneca Iroquois National Museum. The prehistory, history, and current culture of the Seneca Nation, Keeper of the Western Door for the Iroquois Confederacy, is explored at this museum on the Allegany Indian Reservation. Permanent exhibits include clan animal displays, a partially reconstructed longhouse, and traditional Iroquois pieces such as baskets, corn-husk items, beadwork, and silverwork. | 794-814 Broad St. | 716/945–1738 | www.seneca-museum.org | seniroqm@localnet.com | $4 | Apr.–Sept., Tues.–Sat. 10–5, Sun. noon–5; Oct.–Dec. and Feb.–Apr., weekdays 9–5.

ON THE CALENDAR

JULY: *North American Iroquois Veterans Association Pow Wow.* This event acknowledges and honors Native American veterans with dancing, music, contests, food, and more. Held at Veterans Park on Broad Street. | 716/945–2034 | www.naiva.homestead.com/powwow.html.

Dining

Balloon's Restaurant. American. Striped awnings and cozy booths set a casual tone at this restaurant 11 mi north of Salamanca. Burgers, salads, and mozzarella sticks are popular, and there is a vegetarian menu as well. On the weekends, you can sample Tex-Mex food and listen to jazz bands. Open-air dining on sidewalk. | 20 Monroe St., Ellicottville | 716/699–4162 | fax 716/699–5659 | $4–$20 | MC, V.

Ellicottville Brewing Company. Continental. This trendy, rough-hewn microbrewery 11 mi north of Salamanca draws a young crowd. The shepherd's pie is popular, and the menu also includes English fish-and-chips and Westphalian German sausages charbroiled and served with potato perogies, sauerkraut, and German potato salad. You can eat outside in the German beer garden which has a brick patio and vines climbing the walls. Tours of the brewery are available. | 28A Monroe St., Ellicottville | 716/699–2537 | www.ellicottville-brewing.com | Closed several weeks after Easter | $10–$18 | AE, MC, V.

The Hearth. Contemporary. Golfers and skiers frequent this restaurant with a view of the ski slopes and golf courses of the Holiday Valley Resort, 11 mi north of Salamanca. Try the venison medallions dressed with blackberry sage sauce and served with jasmine rice and haricots verts. A wide selection of wines are available as well as locally brewed Ellicottville Buchan Nut Brown Brew. | Holiday Valley Rd., Ellicottville | 716/699–2345 | www.holiday-valley.com | $14–$20 | AE, D, DC, MC, V.

Red Garter Playhouse. Continental. This restaurant known for steak, ribs, seafood, and pasta has a view of Salamanca and the Allegheny River. Open-air dining on the deck. | 716/945–2503 | Reservations essential | $9–$20 | AE, D, MC, V.

Lodging

Dudley Motor Inn. Rooms at this motel close to the Allegany State Park have views of the surrounding hills. Restaurant. Cable TV. | 132 Main St. | 716/945–3200 | 47 rooms | $46–$89 | AE, D, DC, MC, V.

Inn at Holiday Valley. Located at the base of the Sunrise Quad ski lift, this inn is of absolute convenience for skiiers. Rooms have two queen beds and patios or balconies. Suites have the luxury of fireplaces, hot tubs, and cathedral ceilings. Seven mi north of Salamanca. Complimentary Continental breakfast. Some minibars, some refrigerators, some in-room hot tubs, cable TV. Indoor-outdoor pool. Massage, sauna, spa. Exercise room. Cross-country skiing, downhill skiing. Library. | Rte. 219, Ellicottville | 716/699–2345 or 800/323–0020 | 95 rooms, 7 suites | $102–$118 rooms, $165–$186 suites | AE, D, DC, MC, V.

Jefferson Inn of Ellicottville. This Victorian home with a wraparound Greek Revival porch is within walking distance of shops, restaurants, and bars in Ellicottville, 11 mi north of Salamanca. You can stay in B&B rooms, a luxury suite, or one of the two self-contained efficiency suites suitable for families with small children or pets. Complimentary breakfast is included in bed-and-breakfast rooms only. Some kitchenettes, no TV in some rooms, TV in common area. Some pets allowed. No smoking. | 3 Jefferson St., Ellicottville | 716/699–5869 or 800/577–8451 | fax 716/699–5758 | jeffinn@eznet.net | www.thejeffersoninn.com | 5 rooms, 2 suites | $140 (2–night minimum stay) | AE, D, MC, V.

Myers Hotel and Steak House. This hotel was built in the early 1900s and has a large front porch. The interior is made of American chestnut wood, and the rooms have antique furniture. Most rooms have king-size beds. No-smoking rooms are available. Dining room, bar. Cable TV. | 460 Wildwood Ave. | 716/945–3153 | 6 rooms | $65 | D, DC, MC, V.

SARANAC LAKE

MAP 3, K3

SARANAC LAKE

INTRO
ATTRACTIONS
DINING
LODGING

(Nearby towns also listed: Lake Placid, Paul Smiths, Tupper Lake, Wilmington)

This village of 5,000 people sits on small Flower Lake (the Saranac Lakes are to the west) and has a wealth of outdoor recreational opportunities. Settled in the early 1800s, Saranac Lake remained a remote community through the 19th century, relying economically mostly on logging, and guiding the occasional intrepid hunter or fisherman. But when a doctor discovered the healing properties of an Adirondack vacation in Saranac Lake in the 1800s, the village suddenly boomed, becoming home to the world-renowned Trudeau Sanitorium, several hotels, and a score of what became known as "cure cottages" (large boardinghouses with comfortable porches), many of which are still available for a restful vacation.

Information: Saranac Lake Area Chamber of Commerce | 30 Main St., 12983 | 518/891–1990 | besttown@northnet.org | www.saranaclake.com.

Attractions
Meadowbrook State Public Campground. The sites at this campground 4 mi southeast of Saranac Lake are quiet and private. You can also go boating and canoeing. | Rte. 86, Raybrook | 518/891–4351 | Camping $10 per day | May–Labor Day, daily.

Mt. Pisgah Municipal Ski Center. There is one main slope at this ski center owned by the village of Saranac Lake that has been in operation since the 1920s. Snowmaking. | Mount Pisgah Rd. | 518/891–0970 | $10–$15 | Dec.–Apr.

Robert Louis Stevenson Memorial Cottage. In 1887, the author of *Dr. Jekyll and Mr. Hyde* spent a year here being treated for tuberculosis. Today, this quaint farmhouse holds a collection of Stevenson memorabilia. | 11 Stevenson La. | 518/891–1462 | $2 | July–mid-Sept., Tues.–Sun. 9:30–4:30.

Six Nations Indian Museum. Native American art, crafts, and artifacts are on display at this museum dedicated to preserving the culture of the Six-Nation Confederacy—the Mohawks, Oneida, Onondaga, Cayuga, Seneca, and Tuscarora. The museum is 14 mi northeast of Saranac Lake. | Rte. 30, Onchiota | 518/891–2299 | redmaple@northnet.org | $4 | July–Labor Day, Tues.–Sun. 10–5.

ON THE CALENDAR

FEB.: *Winter Carnival.* This weeklong festival held the first two weeks of February is the oldest winter carnival in the country. There is a lighted ice palace, sporting events, theater, fireworks, a Saturday carnival parade, and other unusual events throughout the town of Saranac Lake. | 518/891–1990 or 800/347–1992.

JULY: *Willard Hanmer Guideboat, Canoe, and War Canoe Races.* Races along Lake Flower are held in guide boats, canoes, kayaks, rowing shells, and war canoes (solo, tandem, and eight-person). Includes a picnic, along with other events. | 518/891–1990.

SEPT.: *Adirondack Canoe Classic.* A 90-mi, 3-day competitive canoe race from Old Forge to Saranac Lake. | 518/891–1990 or 800/347–1992.

Dining

A. P. Smith Restaurant. American. This training facility and restaurant in the Hotel Saranac is run by Paul Smiths College students. Wood chandeliers hang over candlelit tables and classical music is usually playing in the background. Try the chicken muscadet, New York strip steak, crispy salmon, or rack of lamb persillé (with chopped parsley and garlic). On Thursdays, there is an international buffet. Baked goods are prepared daily. Kids' menu. Sunday brunch. No smoking. | 101 Main St. | 518/891–2200 | Breakfast also available | $12–$25 | AE, D, DC, MC, V.

Belvedere Restaurant. Italian. This casual, family-style restaurant serves up hearty dishes like pasta, veal parmesan, strip steaks, and the Odd Couple surf and turf combo of steak and lobster tails. There's a lounge and pool table. | 57 Bloomingdale Ave. | 518/891–9873 | No lunch. Closed Mon. | $8–$27 | No credit cards.

Lodging

Adirondack Comfort Inn. This modern two-story inn was built in 1992 on extensive grounds across from Lake Flower. Grounds offer direct access to snowmobiling trails. Picnic areas. In-room data ports, cable TV. Pool, pond. | 148 Lake Flower Ave. | 518/891–1970 | 69 rooms | $65–$115 | AE, D, DC, MC, V.

Adirondack Motel. Rooms at this two-story motel have views of Lake Flower. Standard rooms and suites with fireplaces are available, as well as efficiencies with kitchenettes. Picnic area, complimentary Continental breakfast. In-room data ports, some kitchenettes, refrigerators, cable TV. Dock, boating. Pets allowed. | 23 Lake Flower Ave. | 518/891–2116 or 800/416–0117 | fax 518/891–1405 | www.adirondackmotel.com | 14 rooms | $45–$150 | AE, D, DC, MC, V.

Hotel Saranac of Paul Smiths College. The Grand Hall on the second floor of this hotel in the center of town is a replica of the foyer of the Davanzati Palace in Florence, Italy. The architect replaced the Italian coats-of-arms with regional icons such as a snowshoe and a mounted deer. Students from Paul Smiths College are trained here alongside professional staff. Rooms are cozy. Restaurant, bar. Cable TV. Business services. | 101 Main St. | 518/891–2200 or 800/937–0211 | fax 518/591–5664 | www.hotelsaranac.com | 92 rooms | $59–$119 | AE, D, DC, MC, V.

Lake Flower Inn. This small one-story motel on Lake Flower has lake access and is close to a public boat launch and snowmobiling trails. Some of the rooms have views of the water; the pool overlooks the lake. Picnic area. In-room data ports, cable TV. Pool. Dock. Some pets allowed. | 15 Lake Flower Ave. | 518/891–2310 or 888/628–8900 | 14 rooms | $42–$92 | MC, V.

Lake Side. Rooms have views of Lake Flower at this motel with a private swimming and picnic area. You can also fish or rent canoes and paddleboats and there is a 50-ft heated pool. No-smoking rooms are available. Picnic area. Cable TV. Pool. Beach, boating, fishing. Pets allowed. | 27 Lake Flower Ave. | 518/891–4333 | 22 rooms | $45–$89 | AE, D, DC, MC, V.

The Point. Originally the home of William Avery Rockefeller, this exclusive inn evokes the spirit of the great Adirondack camps. The rooms are filled with antiques, custom-made beds, and stone fireplaces. All meals are served on the premises, including black-tie dinners on Wednesdays and Saturdays. The price includes free use of the canoes, rowboats, speedboats, sailboards, and a classic 30-ft Hackercraft. Hiking, beach, boating. Library. | HCR 1 Buck 65 | 518/891–5674 or 800/255–3530 | 11 rooms | $950–$1,700 | Closed mid-Mar.–mid-Apr. | AP | AE, MC, V.

Sara-Placid Motor Inn. This motel just across from Lake Flower offers a variety of accommodations from standard rooms to housekeeping apartments with decks. The motel provides free paddleboats that you can take out on the pond. Picnic area, complimentary Continental breakfast. No air-conditioning in many rooms, some kitchenettes, cable TV. Tennis. Boating. Ice-skating. | 120 Lake Flower Ave. | 518/891–2729 or 800/794–2729 | fax 518/891–5624 | capital.net/com/placid | 20 rooms | $99–$175 | AE, D, DC, MC, V.

Saranac Inn Golf and Country Club. Established at the turn of the 20th century, the Saranac Inn Golf and Country Club was designed by Seymour Dunn, a well-respected Scottish architect and professional golfer. The inn is home to a world-famous championship golf course, and offers a golf package which includes lodging and two rounds of golf with cart. Rooms overlook the first tee. Restaurant. Cable TV. Driving range, 18-hole golf course, putting green. | Rte. 30 | 518/891–1402 | fax 518/891–1309 | golf@saranacinn.com | www.saranacinn.com | 11 rooms | $125 | Closed Nov.–Apr. | AE, MC, V.

SARATOGA SPRINGS

MAP 3, K5

(Nearby towns also listed: Albany, Amsterdam, Glens Falls, Gloversville, Johnstown, Queensbury, Schenectady)

Mineral-water springs first brought Native Americans and, later, American settlers to this area in the Adirondack foothills. Saratoga Springs was founded in 1773, and by the mid-19th century, society people were coming for the waters, and the gambling. When the Saratoga Race Course was built in 1864, the city really took off. While the city suffered a decline during the first half of the 20th century, it has since been revitalized. One of its biggest attractions is the Saratoga Performing Arts Center, where festivals are held in summer.

Information: **Saratoga County Chamber of Commerce** | 28 Clinton St., Saratoga Springs 12866 | info@saratoga.org | www.saratoga.org | 518/584–3255.

Attractions

Batten Kill Rambler Scenic Train. During a 14-mi, 2½-hour ride from Salem to Cambridge, the train crosses rivers and journeys through farmland and hamlets. The train leaves from Salem, 15 mi north of Saratoga Springs. | 223 Main St. (Rte. 22), Salem | 518/692–2191 | fax 518/692–0271 | www.nenyrail.com | $10 | July–mid Oct.; call for hrs.

Historic Congress Park. The "Spirit of Life" sculpture by Daniel Chester French is one of the highlights of this city park at the southern end of downtown. The park also includes Italian gardens and the Canfield Casino, a former gambling hall that now houses the Historical Society of Saratoga Springs. | Broadway | 518/584–6920 | fax 518/581–1477 | www.saratogahistory.org | $3 | Daily.

National Bottle Museum. This state-chartered museum has a collection of 2,000 bottles dating to the 1700s, videos of glassblowing, a research library, and a gift shop. The museum is 7 mi south of Saratoga Springs. | 76 Milton Ave., Ballston Spa | 518/885–7589 | fax 518/885–0317 | www.crisny.org/not-for-profit/nbm | $2 suggested donation | June–Oct., daily 10–4; Nov.–May, weekdays 10–4.

National Museum of Racing and Hall of Fame. Exhibits at this museum focus on the history of racing, horse breeding, and Saratoga Springs. There is also a research library, and the museum offers educational programs. The lobby exhibit is free of charge. | 191 Union Ave. | 518/584–0400 | fax 518/584–4574 | www.racingmuseum.org | $7 | Mon.–Sat. 10–4:30, Sun. noon–4; during the race meet, daily 9–5.

Petrified Sea Gardens. This National Natural Landmark features a half-billion-year-old exposed ocean reef and fossils. Self-guided tours. | 42 Petrified Sea Gardens Rd. | 518/584–7102 | www.squonk.net/psg | $3 | May–June and Sept.–Oct., Thurs.–Sun. 11–5; July–Aug, daily 11–5.

Saratoga Equine Sports Center. Offers harness racing, simulcasting, dining, concession stands, and an air-conditioned clubhouse. | Nelson Ave. | 518/584–2110 | fax 518/583–1269 | www.saratogaraceway.com | $3 clubhouse; $2 grandstand | Feb.–Nov.; call for schedule.

Saratoga Harness Racing Museum and Hall of Fame. Houses exhibits, antiques, and a library devoted to trotters. | 352 Jefferson St. | 518/587–4210 | Free | July–Aug., Tues.–Sat. 10–4; Sept.–June, Thurs.–Sat. 10–4.

Saratoga Lake. An 8½-mi-long, 1½-mi-wide lake about 5 mi from Saratoga on Route 9P. You can fish and rent boats, and there is a beach for swimming. | 28 Clinton St. | 518/584–3255 | www.saratoga.org | Daily.

Saratoga National Cemetery. The nation's 116th national cemetery, one of six in the state, opened in 1999, 11 mi east of Saratoga Springs. It will serve as final resting place for 175,000 veterans. Tours by arrangement. | 200 Duell Rd., Schuylerville | 518/581–9128 | fax 518/583–6975 | mfisher@cem.va.gov | www.cem.va.gov/saratogahtm | Free | Daily dawn–dusk.

Saratoga National Historical Park (Battlefield). The 1777 Battle of Saratoga was fought 12 mi southeast of Saratoga Springs on this site. The battle was a turning point of the American Revolution because it ended with the British Army offering their first surrender in the field. The site includes a 9½-mi road tour and a visitors center. You can also cross-country ski and bicycle here. | 648 Rte. 32, Stillwater | 518/664–9821 | fax 518/664–3349 | www.nps.gov/sara | $4 per vehicle | Grounds daily; visitors center daily 9–5; tour road open to cars Apr.–mid-Nov., daily.

Saratoga Monument. The three statues in the niches of this this monument built in 1877 to commemorate the centennial of the Battle of Saratoga are of Generals Schuyler, Gates, and Morgan. The fourth niche, where a statue of Benedict Arnold would have gone, has been deliberately left empty and cannot be entered. | 53 Burgoyne St. | 518/664–9821 | fax 518/664–3349 | www.nps.gov/sara | Free | Fri.–Sun., 9–4:30.

The **General Philip Schuyler House** was destroyed by the British in 1777, and rebuilt by Schuyler and his soldiers in 29 days. Includes some original furnishings. | 1072 Rte. 4 S, Schuylerville | 518/664–9821 | Free | June–Sept, Wed.–Sun. 10–4:30; tours every half hr.

The **John Neilson House** is the only structure standing that was here at the time of the battle. It might have served as headquarters for Benedict Arnold. Interpretive programs are offered. | Between Rtes. 4 and 32, Schuylerville | 518/664–9821 | fax 518/664–3349 | www.nps.gov/sara | Free | Fri.–Sun., 9–5.

Saratoga Race Course. Every year thoroughbreds compete for six weeks from late July to September. | 267 Union Ave. | 518/584–6200 | www.nyra.com | Parking $1; admission $1 | Late-July–early Sept. Sat.–Sun., gates open at 11; call for weekday schedule.

Saratoga Spa State Park. Developed in the 1930s for the study and therapeutic use of the famous mineral springs, this 2,200-acre park listed on the National Historic Register also has sports facilities and centers for the performing arts. At Hayes Springs the water rises 15 ft, and there are brick and stone walkways throughout the park. A 9- and an 18-hole golf course, two pools, and clay and asphalt tennis courts are among the sports facilities; you can also cycle and picnic. The park is also home to the Gideon Putnam Hotel, and the Spa

Little Theater, which offers fall, winter, and spring theater. | S. Broadway (U.S. 9) | 518/584–2535 | fax 518/587–8804 | $5 per vehicle.

Located on the grounds of Saratoga Spa State Park, the **Lincoln Mineral Baths** offer massage, mineral baths, and other spa treatments. Appointments are required. | 65 S. Broadway (U.S. 9) | 518/584–2011 or 518/584–3000 | www.gideonputnam.com | Mineral bath $16; herbal massage $21; half-hour massage $40 | July–Aug., Sun.–Fri. 9–4, Sat. 9–4:30.

The **National Museum of Dance** is the only museum devoted exclusively to professional dance. The Hall of Fame honors top dancers, choreographers, and costumers. Summer School for the Arts dance classes are available for public viewing. | 99 S. Broadway (U.S. 9) | 518/584–2225 | fax 518/584–4515 | www.dancemuseum.org | $3.50 | June–Nov., Tues.–Sun. 10–5.

The **Saratoga Performing Arts Center** is the region's premier performing-arts center. It is the summer home of the New York City Ballet and the Philadelphia Orchestra. Popular music shows are also put on in summer. | Between U.S. 9 and Rte. 50 | 518/587–4427 | fax 518/584–5181 | www.spac.org | Box office Mon.–Sat. 10–6.

Skidmore College. Approximately 2,200 students attend this four-year co-educational college founded in 1903 that offers an interdisciplinary curriculum. The college sponsors year-round cultural events and entertainment, and is the summer home of the New York State Writer's Institute. | 815 N. Broadway | 518/580–5000 | www.skidmore.edu | Free | Daily.

Urban Heritage Area Visitor's Center. You can get regional travel information and brochures at this center, which also houses exhibits on local history. | 297 Broadway | 518/580–0980 | www.saratoga.org/visitorcenter | Free | Mon.–Sat. 9–4.

Willard Mountain Ski and Ride Center. There are 18 trails and a 550-ft vertical drop at this ski area. Other facilities include a ski school, cafeteria, shop, and bar. 16 mi east of Saratoga Springs. | 77 Intervale Rd., Greenwich | 518/692–7337 | fax 518/692–9287 | www.willardmountain.com | Dec.–late Mar.

Yaddo. Artists, writers, and musicians from all over the country come to this artists' colony to work. The estate was originally built in 1899 by the philanthropist Spencer Trask as a gift to his wife, Katrina. Although you cannot visit the house, you can tour the Italian gardens on the grounds. There is a formal rose garden with fountains, as well as an informal rock garden. | Union Ave. (Rte. 9P) | 518/584–0746 | fax 518/584–1312 | Free | Daily dawn–dusk.

ON THE CALENDAR
JUNE–AUG.: *Saratoga Performing Arts Center.* The New York City Ballet and the Philadelphia Orchestra put on summer performances here. Jazz, rock, and pop concerts are hosted as well. | 518/587–3330.
JULY–AUG.: *Lake George Opera Festival.* An all-English-language opera festival featuring guest performers and Opera Insights with the artistic director. Each production is performed three times during the monthlong season. The festival is held in Saratoga Springs at the Sara Toga Spa State Park | 28 Sherman Ave., Glen Falls | 518/584–6018.
JULY–AUG.: *Saratoga Polo Club.* The club hosts a world-class polo competition and other special events. Events are at Whitney Field and Lodge Field. | 518/584–8108.
JULY–SEPT.: *Thoroughbred Racing at Saratoga Race Course.* The big races at the nation's oldest thoroughbred racing venue are the Whitney Handicap, the Breeders Cup, and the Travers. | 518/584–6200.

Dining
Chez Pierre. French. French paintings decorate the walls at this homey restaurant in a European inn 8 mi north of Saratoga Springs. The dining room has a fireplace and the kitchen is known for veal, rack of lamb, and fish. Kids' menu. | 340 U.S. 9, Gansevoort | 518/793–3350 | fax 518/798–1165 | Closed Mon. No lunch | $16–$25 | AE, MC, V.

Chez Sophie Bistro. French. This gleaming 1950s diner looks very American, but the menu is all French. Known for duckling, veal, steak, and a different fish daily. The restaurant is

4½ mi south of Saratoga. | 2853 U.S 9, Ballston Spa | 518/583–3538 | fax 518/583–3436 | Closed Mon. No lunch | $21–$30 | AE, DC, MC, V.

Eartha's Court Street Bistro. Contemporary. Local artists did the designs inside this funky restaurant in an old building painted purple. Vintage liquor ads hang on the walls, and a young, hip crowd comes for the fresh seafood and pasta. Try the marinated breast of duck. | 60 Court St. | 518/583–0602 | fax 518/583–9507 | Closed Mon., Tues. No lunch | $18–$24 | AE, D, DC, MC, V.

43 Phila. Contemporary. Caricatures of guests and Campari posters vie for space at this upscale bistro known for small tables and innovative food. The menu includes sea bass, prime steaks, ribs, and duck. Try the crab cakes with spicy coleslaw. On a side street. | 43 Phila St. | 518/584–2720 | fax 518/584–2896 | $21–$35 | AE, D, DC, MC, V.

Hattie's. Southern. Since 1938, this restaurant has been serving fried chicken, ribs, pork chops, jambalaya, and other Southern dishes. At night, Hattie's is bright with purple and pink lighting and checkered tablecloths. The overhead fans and banging screen door will make you feel like you're in the South. Try the ribs in Key lime tartar sauce. The menu also has vegetarian dishes, and you can eat outside in the New Orleans–style courtyard patio. | 45 Phila St. | 518/584–4790 | www.hattiesrestaurant.com | Reservations not accepted July–Aug. | Breakfast also available July–Aug.; closed Mon., Tues. in Sept.–June; no lunch | $12–$17 | AE, MC, V.

Olde Bryan Inn. American. This Colonial tavern-restaurant has big fireplaces and exposed beams. Three levels provide seating for 150. Known for sandwiches, fresh seafood, chops. Kids' menu. | 123 Maple Ave. | 518/587–2990 | fax 518/587–4316 | $14–$22 | AE, D, DC, MC, V.

Parting Glass. Irish. This traditional Irish pub has live music, darts, and a toy box for kids. Known for soups, stew, and corned beef and cabbage. | 40-42 Lake Ave. | 518/583–1916 | fax 518/587–8138 | Breakfast also available | $8–$12 | MC, V.

Ripe Tomato. American. You'll find this casual restaurant surrounded by trees on 2 acres about 5 mi south of Saratoga. The menu includes pasta, steak, and seafood. Try the Ripe Tomato roast pork, orecchiette alla vodka, or seafood Fridays. Open-air dining in covered café. Kids' menu. | 2721 U.S. 9, Malta | 518/581–1530 | fax 518/581–9241 | www.ripetomato.com | $10–$17 | AE, DC, MC, V.

Sperry's. Contemporary. The 1930s Art Deco design at this restaurant on a narrow side street includes a black-and-white tile floor. Try the soft-shell crab, Maryland crab cakes, swordfish, or steaks. The restaurant also has a garden. | 30½ Caroline St. | 518/584–9618 | fax 518/584–0342 | $20–$25 | AE, D, DC, MC.

Wallie's of Greenwich. American. This old school restaurant has been in business under the same family since 1919. They serve the regular crowd-pleasers of steak and seafood, but their prime rib is especially popular. Kids' menu. Early bird dinners. Twenty miles east of Saratoga. | 56 Main St., Greenwich | 518/692–7823 | Closed Mon.–Tues., closed Mon. only Mid–July–Aug.). No dinner Sun. | $15 | AE, D, MC, V.

Lodging

Adelphi Hotel. Rooms at this four-story downtown hotel built in the late 19th century have high ceilings, tall windows, and original woodwork; all have been individually decorated with antique furniture. On the second floor, there is a 90-ft porch that overlooks bustling Broadway. Hand-painted stencils line the walls of the lobby and the café/lounge has a three-story mural of an 1880s Saratoga hotel courtyard. Complimentary Continental breakfast, room service. Cable TV. Pool. | 365 Broadway | 518/587–4688 | fax 518/587–0851 | www.adelphihotel.com | 21 rooms, 18 suites | $120–$215 | Closed Nov.–Apr. | AE, MC, V.

Gideon Putnam Hotel and Conference Center. This hotel, built in the 1930s, is right on the grounds of the Saratoga Spa State Park, and some of the rooms have views of the park. The special porch suite has French doors that open into a screened porch overlooking the park. Restaurant, bar (with entertainment). Cable TV. Pool. Business services. | 24 Gideon

Putnam Rd. | 518/584–3000 or 800/732–1560 | fax 518/584–1354 | www.gideonputnam.com | 114 rooms, 18 suites | $119–$265 rooms, $135–$480 suites | AE, D, DC, MC, V.

Grand Union Motel. This one-story drive-up motel in a residential area was built in the 1950s and provides no-frills lodging. Picnic area. In-room data ports, cable TV. Pool. Pets allowed (fee). | 120 S. Broadway | 518/584–9000 | fax 518/584–9001 | www.grandunionmotel.com | 64 rooms | $69–106 | AE, MC, V.

Holiday Inn Saratoga. This four-story chain is in downtown Saratoga Springs. Restaurant, bar, room service. In-room data ports, some in-room hot tubs, cable TV. Pool. Gym. Laundry facilities. Business services. Pets allowed. | 232 Broadway | 518/584–4550 | fax 518/584–4417 | hisara@capital.net | www.hisaratoga.com | 168 rooms | $85–$129 | AE, D, DC, MC, V.

Inn at Saratoga. This Victorian inn built in 1848 has an old-fashioned hand-operated elevator and rooms done in Victorian style. The cocktail lounge overlooks busy downtown Broadway. Restaurant, complimentary Continental breakfast, cable TV. | 231 Broadway | 518/583–1890 or 800/274–3573 | fax 518/583–2543 | www.theinnatsaratoga.com | 38 rooms | $110–$150 | AE, D, DC, MC, V.

Roosevelt Suites. This complex, 6 mi southwest of Saratoga Springs, has a variety of lodging available on 16 acres of manicured grounds. There are rooms with views of the grounds and easy access to the pool, deluxe rooms with balconies, and one- and two-bedroom suites inside the Val-Kill Pool House. The pool house has spa facilities including a sauna, massage service, and a lap pool. You can borrow videotapes from the library in the lobby. Restaurant, bar, picnic area, complimentary Continental breakfast. In-room data ports, refrigerators, some in-room hot tubs, cable TV, in-room VCRs. Pool. Tennis. Business services. | 2961 U.S. 9, Ballston Spa | 518/584–0980 or 800/524–9147 | fax 518/581–8472 | www.saratoga.org/roosevelt | 39 rooms, 13 suites | $165–$225 rooms, $225–$300 suites | AE, D, MC, V.

Sheraton–Saratoga Springs. This high-rise hotel complex is in downtown Saratoga, 1 mi from the racetracks and 2 mi from the Performing Arts Center. Restaurant, bar (with entertainment), room service. Cable TV. Pool. Sauna. Gym. Business services. | 534 Broadway | 518/584–4000 | fax 518/584–7430 | www.sheraton.com | 235 rooms, 5 suites | $94–$229 | AE, D, DC, MC, V.

Springs Motel. This two-story, two-building motel is in the business area near the visitors center. Rooms have two double beds only. No-smoking rooms are available. Expect room rates to double in August for the peak racing season. Refrigerators, cable TV. Pool. | 189 Broadway | 518/584–6336 | fax 518/587–8164 | 28 rooms | $80 | AE, MC, V.

Westchester House Bed and Breakfast. Rooms have antique furnishings at this bed-and-breakfast within walking distance of downtown and the track. The Victorian house was built in 1885 and there is a garden on the grounds. Complimentary Continental breakfast. In-room data ports. No smoking. | 102 Lincoln Ave. | 518/587–7613 | www.westchesterhousebandb.com | 7 rooms | $100–$175 | Closed Dec., Jan. | AE, D, MC, V.

SAUGERTIES

MAP 3, K8

(Nearby towns also listed: Catskill, Kingston, Rhinebeck, Woodstock)

The streets of Saugerties are lined with Queen Anne and Victorian houses and the downtown shopping area, especially on Main St. and Partition St., includes several worthy antiques stores. Saugerties was once a thriving riverfront town, famous for building racing sloops and single-masted sailing ships. Fine paper, leather, and canvas were also manufactured here. In 1994, the town drew attention when it hosted the second Woodstock festival.

Information: **Chamber of Commerce** | 7 Albany Ave., Kingston, 12401 | 845/338–5100.

Attractions

Opus 40 and Quarryman's Museum. This 6½-acre bluestone sculpture/environment was built by a single man on the site of an abandoned quarry. Harry Fite spent 37 years creating sculptures, levels, paths, passages, steps, and pools—he called it Opus 40 because he thought it would take 40 years to finish. The museum houses a collection of 19th-century artifacts. | 7480 Fite Rd., High Woods | 845/246–3400 | www.opus40.org | $5 | Memorial Day–Columbus Day, Fri.–Sun. noon–5.

ON THE CALENDAR

JULY: *Winterhawk Bluegrass Festival.* This annual family-oriented music festival is held 30 mi northeast of Saugerties at Long Hill Farm in Hillsdale, on Route 23. | 800/724–1846.

SEPT.: *Hudson Valley Garlic Festival.* During the last weekend of the month, more than 45,000 people gather in Saugerties at the Cantine Field for this "stink fest." All the foods at this fair have something to do with garlic, from pastas to pestos, to even coffee spiked with a dash of it. | 845/246–3090.

Dining

Cafe Tamayo. Contemporary. Antiques abound in this 1864 building with wood-burning fireplaces and a hand-carved bar. The kitchen uses fresh local and regional ingredients. Goat cheese, organic chicken, freshly smoked pork products, foie gras, and duck are a few of the items that come from farmers throughout the Hudson Valley. Open-air dining on a garden patio. Sunday brunch. | 89 Partition St. | 845/246–9371 | www.cafetomayo.com | Closed Mon., Tues. No lunch Wed. | $20–$30 | D, MC, V.

Lodging

Cafe Tamayo. These three bed-and-breakfast rooms, upstairs from the café, are filled with antiques and brass beds. The suite has two double beds and a sitting area. Since the café isn't open for breakfast, you get vouchers for your meal around the corner. Restaurant. No room phones, no TV. No pets. No smoking. | 89 Partition St. | 845/246–9371 | 2 rooms, 1 suite | $85 rooms, $125 suite.

Comfort Inn. This two-story chain motel in a residential area is just off the New York State Thruway's exit 20, about 2 mi from village shops. Some rooms have king beds and recliners. Complimentary Continental breakfast. In-room data ports, microwaves, some in-room hot tubs, cable TV. Business services. | 2790 Rte. 32 | 845/246–1565 | fax 845/246–1631 | 66 rooms | $65–$89 | AE, D, DC, MC, V.

SAYVILLE

MAP 3, D2

(Nearby town also listed: Patchogue)

When Easthampton resident John Edwards returned from the French and Indian War, he passed by the land along Great South Bay and decided, in 1871, to build a home there—Sayville's first. By 1830, Sayville had become a leading exporter of pine to New York City. Later it was known as the oyster capital of the United States. Sayville also became a well-known seaside resort town because visitors were attracted by its large Victorian homes and its proximity to Fire Island. Today, you can catch the ferry from Sayville's Watch Hill Ferry Terminal and travel across Great South Bay to Fire Island. Nearby West Sayville's West Avenue Dock has views of the tranquil bay.

Information: **Chamber of Commerce** | Montauk Hwy. and Lincoln Ave., Box 235, Sayville 11782 | 631/567–5257 | fax 631/218–0881 | www.sayville.com.

Attractions

Watch Hill Ferry Terminal and the Davis Park Ferry. Catch the ferry to Watch Hill, Fire Island, from this pier in Patchogue. Call ahead for seasonal schedule. | West Ave., Patchogue | 631/475–1665 | $5.50 | Mid-May–mid-Oct.

Long Island Maritime Museum. A 19th-century oystering vessel is on display at this museum 1½ mi west of Sayville. Changing exhibits focus on boating and maritime history. There is also a small local craft collection. | 86 West Ave., W. Sayville | 631/854–4974 | $3 suggested donation | Mon.–Sat. 10–4, Sun. noon–4.

Old Edward's Homestead. The homestead has been restored and furnished to its 1785 condition. Photographs, quilts, whale oil and gas lamps, and a local history collection are on display. The general store sells old-time merchandise. | Collins Ave. | 631/563–0186 | Free | Oct.–June, daily 9–5.

ON THE CALENDAR
AUG.: *Seafood Festival and Craft Show.* The Long Island Maritime Museum hosts a craft show and music. Seafood is served. | 631/854–4974 or 631/447–8679.

Dining

Le Soir. French. The tables are spread with white linens at this restaurant housed inside a Tudor-style building 1¾ mi east of Sayville. Try the lobster with whisky sauce, duck à l'orange, or the rack of lamb. In winter, game dishes are on the menu. | 825 Montauk Hwy., Bayport | 631/472–9090 | Closed Mon. No lunch | $20–$32 | AE, MC, V.

Riverview. Seafood. A wall of windows overlooks the Great South Bay at this restaurant known for its seasonal menu of fresh seafood and salads. Inside, the dining room has fireplaces and carousel horses; outside there is a gazebo and boat docking area. The restaurant is 3½ mi west of Sayville. Open-air dining on patio. Live music on Fridays and Saturdays in winter. Kids' menu. Sunday brunch. Dock space. | 3 Consuelo Pl., Oakdale | 631/589–2694 | Reservations essential Fri., Sat. | No lunch Sat. | $20–$30 | AE, D, DC, MC, V.

Snapper Inn. Seafood. The oldest working sailboat on the Great South Bay (it dates to 1813) is tied up at the dock by this restaurant 3½ mi west of Sayville. The inn's own boat fishes 5 days a week for tuna, fluke, striped bass, bluefish, and weakfish, and freshly caught fish is on the menu. The lobster, lamb chops, and chocolate bread pudding with caramel sauce are popular. A gorgeous lawn with a bar stretches between the restaurant and the river. Kids' menu. Sunday brunch. Dock space. | 500 Shore Dr., Oakdale | 631/589–0248 | Closed Mon. | $25–$40 | AE, D, DC, MC, V.

Lodging

Best Western MacArthur. The indoor heated pool, hot tub, and fitness center at this chain hotel 7 mi north of Sayville are enclosed in glass and surrounded by tropical plants and a patio garden. The restaurant has brass railings, mahogany wood, and English memorabilia. Restaurant, bar, complimentary Continental breakfast. In-room data ports, cable TV. Pool. Hot tub. Business services, airport shuttle. | 1730 N. Ocean Ave., Holtsville | 631/758–2900 | fax 631/758–2612 | 134 rooms | $139–$149 | AE, D, DC, MC, V.

Holiday Inn MacArthur Airport. This friendly chain hotel 6 mi south of Sayville was voted number one of the 127 Holiday Inns in the region. It is particularly busy with business travelers during the week. Restaurant, bar (with entertainment), room service. In-room data ports, cable TV. Pool. Exercise equipment. Business services, airport shuttle. | 3845 Veterans Memorial Hwy., Ronkonkoma | 631/585–9500 or 800/422–9150 | fax 631/585–9550 | www.holiday-inn.com | 289 rooms | $159–$249 | AE, D, DC, MC, V.

SCARSDALE

MAP 4, F4

(Nearby towns also listed: Elmsford, Hartsdale, Hawthorne, Mamaroneck, New Rochelle, New York City, Rye, Tarrytown, White Plains, Yonkers)

This idyllic, upscale Westchester town of 17,000 is filled with beautiful homes and land-scaped estates. One of the most popular local recreational activities is golf, a fact attested to by the numerous golf courses in the area.

Information: **Chamber of Commerce** | 864 Scarsdale Ave., 10583 | 914/725–1602.

Attractions

Greenburgh Nature Center. This 33-acre woodland preserve has trails, ponds, orchards, a maple sugaring site, and gardens. There is also a 21-room manor house with a petting zoo that is home to more than 100 specimens. | 99 Dromore Rd. | 914/723–3470 | $4 | Manor house Sat.–Thurs. 10–5; animal museum Sat.–Thurs. 9:30–noon and 1–4:30; grounds daily dawn–dusk.

Scarsdale Historical Society. The society presents a wide variety of programs including lectures, workshops, trips, a country fair, and December candlelight tours. On the grounds are the Cudner-Hyatt House Museum, a traditional two-story clapboard farmhouse, and an 1828 Quaker meetinghouse. The society's library houses more than 2,500 books and documents which may be used by appointment. | 937 Post Rd. | 914/723–1744 | fax 914/723–2185 | Cudner-Hyatt House Museum $3; 1828 Quaker Meeting House Museum $1.50 | Wed.–Fri. 1:30–4:30.

Weinberg Nature Center. The 7½ acres at this center include a variety of habitats. There is also a trailside museum and an outdoor Native American village on the grounds. | 455 Mamaroneck Rd. | 914/722–1289 | www.audobon.org/chapter/ny/scarsdale/weinberg | Free | Trails daily, dawn–dusk; nature center Wed.–Sun 9–5.

Dining

Scarsdale Metro. Eclectic. The quintessential Long Island diner with quick waitresses, mirrored walls, and plenty of things to choose from on the menu. Greek specialties, steaks, seafood, sandwiches, and omelettes. Sunday brunch. Kids menu. | 878 Scarsdale Ave. | 914/713–0309 | $12–$22 | AE, D, DC, MC, V.

SCHENECTADY

MAP 3, K6

(Nearby towns also listed: Albany, Amsterdam, Colonie, Saratoga Springs, Troy)

Schenectady, a city on the Mohawk River west of Albany, was founded in 1661 by the Dutch. Many of its original 18th- and 19th-century buildings are still standing in the Stockade district where the Dutch first settled. Today it is an industrial city of 65,000, home to General Electric and Union College.

Information: **Schenectady Chamber of Commerce** | 306 State St., 12305 | www.schenectadychamber.org | 518/372–5656 or 800/962–8007 | fax 518/370–3217.

Attractions

Historic Stockade District. Some of the houses in this district, among the oldest continuously occupied neighborhoods in the nation, date back to the early 1700s. Walking tour information is available through the historical society and chamber of commerce; both are located in the neighborhood. | Off State St. | 518/374–0263 or 518/372–5656 | fax 518–

370–3217 | www.schenectadychamber.org | Schenectady Museum and visitors center Tues.–Fri. 10–4:30, weekends noon–5; Chamber of Commerce weekdays 8–5; Schenectady County Historical Society weekdays 1–5, Sat. 9–1.

Proctor's Theatre. This restored 1926 vaudeville movie house listed on the National Historic Register is a 2,700-seat theater with a year-round schedule of Broadway shows performed by national touring companies. Also hosts popular and classical music performances, dance performances, and second-run movies. | 432 State St. | 518/346–6204 | fax 518/346–2468 | www.proctors.org.

Schenectady Museum. This museum includes a planetarium, hands-on exhibits, and live reptiles. | 15 Nott Terr. Heights | 518/382–7890 | fax 518/382–7893 | www.schenectadymuseum.org | Museum $3.50; museum and planetarium $5.50 | Tues.–Fri. 10–4:30, weekends noon–5.

Union College. This small, highly selective liberal-arts and engineering college was founded in 1795. The campus covers 100 acres that include woodlands and formal gardens, and it hosts lots of art exhibits and theater performances. The hockey team plays in Division I. | 807 Union St. | 518/388–6131 or 518/388–6004 (arts information) | www.union.edu | Free | Daily.

ON THE CALENDAR
FEB.: *Mardi Gras Celebration.* Just because you're not in New Orleans doesn't mean you can't enjoy Mardi Gras—check out this one-night display of zydeco musicians and Cajun food at the historic Proctor's Theatre. | 518/382–3884 | www.proctors.org.
MAY: *Festival of Nations.* Food, crafts, dance, and exhibits celebrate world cultures at the Schenectady Museum. | 518/382–7890 | fax 518/382–7893.
JULY–AUG.: *Central Park Concert Series.* Outdoor concerts feature local, national, and internationally known musicians. | Central Park | Sun. 3 PM | 518/292–0368.
SEPT.: *Annual Stockade Walkabout House and Garden Tours.* A guide leads you on tours through restored homes in the 300-year-old Stockade neighborhood. | 518/374–0263.

Dining
Carlton Restaurant. Steak. This restaurant serves prime rib and filet mignon on candlelit tables with white tablecloths. The Carlton is a surprisingly well-kept secret. | 1605 Becker St. | 518/393–0726 | Closed Tues. No lunch weekends | $12–$22 | AE, D, DC, MC, V.

Glen Sanders Mansion Restaurant. Contemporary. The menu changes every three months at this restaurant housed in an elegant colonial mansion on the Mohawk River, about 2 mi northwest of Schenectady. Depending on the season, you might find shellfish, sea bass, rack of lamb, or tenderloin beef. Sunday brunch. | 1 Glen Ave., Scotia | 518/374–7262 | fax 518/374–7391 | $18–$28 | AE, D, DC, MC, V.

Olde Dater Tavern. American. Once a stagecoach stop, this circa-1700s home now houses an intimate dining room with a fireplace. The seasonal menu is written on the blackboard and usually includes seafood, beef, and chicken dishes. The tavern is 9½ mi northeast of Schenectady. | 130 Meyer Rd., Clifton Park | 518/877–7225 | Closed Mon. | $18–$24 | AE, DC, MC.

Van Dyke Restaurant and Brewery. Contemporary. Several different dining rooms in this 1800s Victorian building offer a choice of formal or more casual ambience, but all with the same menu. If you choose the formal option, you will be served by tuxedoed waiters. The shrimp cocktail, calamari, salads, and sandwiches are popular. Try the macadamia nut–crusted fresh salmon fillet, or andouille sausage–wrapped filet mignon. Sunday brunch. | 237 Union St. | 518/381–1111 | fax 518/382–5564 | No lunch Sat. | $10–$30 | AE, D, DC, MC, V.

Lodging
Best Western Rotterdam. This chain hotel in a suburban area of Schenectady is near Interstate 90. King-size beds are available; the suites have three double beds. Restaurant,

bar, room service. Cable TV. Pool. Business services. | 2788 Hamburg St. | 518/355–1111 | fax 518/356–3817 | 50 rooms, 6 suites | $85–$95 rooms, $100–$130 suites | AE, D, DC, MC, V.

Days Inn. This chain motel is downtown, within walking distance of Union College and Proctor's Theater. King-size beds are available. Complimentary Continental breakfast. In-room data ports, cable TV. Pets allowed. | 167 Nott Terr. | 518/370–3297 | fax 518/370–5948 | www.daysinn.com | 68 rooms | $80–$100 | AE, D, DC, MC, V.

Glen Sanders Mansion Inn. Many of the rooms at this Colonial-style inn built in 1995 have balconies overlooking the mansion gardens. Others have double-French doors that open onto a patio, and some rooms have fireplaces. It is 2 mi northwest of Schenectady on the Mohawk River. Restaurant *(see* Glen Sanders Mansion Restaurant), bar, complimentary Continental breakfast, room service. In-room data ports, cable TV. | 1 Glen Ave., Scotia | 518/374–7262 | fax 518/374–7391 | www.glensandersmansion.com | 20 rooms, 2 suites | $119 rooms, $185–$285 suites | AE, D, DC, MC, V.

Holiday Inn. This four-story chain hotel is in downtown Schenectady. King-size beds are available and the suites have wet bars, conference tables, and pull-out sofa beds. Restaurant, bar, room service. In-room data ports, cable TV. Pool. Hot tub. Exercise equipment. Airport shuttle. Some pets allowed. | 100 Nott Terr. | 518/393–4141 | fax 518/393–4174 | www.holiday-inn.com | 181 rooms, 3 suites | $84–$114 rooms, suites $159 | AE, D, DC, MC, V.

Ramada Inn. This five-floor member of the chain is 5 minutes' walk to downtown Schenectady, and across the street from Union College. Restaurant, bar, room service. In-room data ports, cable TV. Pool. Hot tub. Exercise equipment. Laundry facilities. Business services. | 450 Nott St. | 518/370–7151 | fax 518/370–0441 | www.ramada.com/ramada.html | 170 rooms | $79–$106 | AE, D, DC, MC, V.

SCHROON LAKE

MAP 3, K4

(Nearby towns also listed: Bolton Landing, Crown Point, Hague, North Creek, Ticonderoga)

Schroon Lake is a picturesque resort community just off Interstate 87 in the southeastern Adirondacks. It was established in the mid-1800s and was at one point a logging town. Main Street now has numerous shops, various restaurants, and antiques stores.

Information: **Schroon Lake Chamber of Commerce** | South Ave., Box 726, 12870 | 518/532–7675 | schroonlake@adirondack.net | www.schroonlake.org.

Attractions
Natural Stone Bridge and Caves. Take a 1-hr, self-guided tour of the natural caves, grottoes, waterfalls, and gorge at this park 9 mi south of Schroon Lake. There is also a rock shop, snack bar, and gemstone mining exhibits. You can fish, or picnic, and even rent sturdy shoes, in case you didn't come prepared. | 535 Stone Bridge Rd., Pottersville | 518/494–2283 | www.stonebridgeandcaves.com | $8.50 | Memorial Day–Columbus Day, daily 9–7.

Public campgrounds. Camping is very popular in this peaceful but active area of the Adirondacks.
Eagle Point State Campground's location on Schroon Lake draws boaters. | U.S. 9 S | 518/494–2220 | $3 | Daily.
Paradox Lake is a sheltered, 4-mi lake popular with paddlers. It has many isolated bays, peninsulas, and channels. | 518/532–7451 | Free | Daily.

SEPT.: *Adirondack Marathon.* Four hundred to 500 runners participate in this 26.2-mi race around Schroon Lake. The race begins on Main Street. | 888–SCHROON | www.adirondackmarathon.org.

Dining

Terrio's Carriage House. Continental. Hundreds of antiques like old fishing implements, saddles, farm equipment, musical instruments, and its namesake, a full horse-drawn carriage hanging from the ceiling, make this the most unique dining establishment in the area. The menu features steaks, seafood and poultry dishes, and the house special of two filet tenderloins of beef topped with crab and béarnaise sauce. Check out Tuesday lobster night, Thursday steak nights and the Sunday night prime rib special. Kids' menu. | Rte. 9N | 518/532–7700 | Closed Nov.–Feb., Mon.–Tues. only. Open 7 days Feb.–Oct. | $15–$23 | AE, D, MC, V.

Lodging

Davis Motel and Cottages. This motel right on Schroon Lake has a beach and rowboats you can rent. The accommodations range from standard rooms to cottages. The cottages have living rooms, kitchens, and two or three bedrooms, along with porches overlooking the lake. All linens and dishes are included. Picnic area. Some kitchenettes, cable TV. Pool. Basketball, hiking, volleyball, beach, dock, boating, fishing. Cross-country skiing, snowmobiling. Playground. | Rd. 1 | 518/532–7583 | fax 518/532–0158 | www.adirondack. net/tour/davis | 20 rooms, 9 cottages | $46–$76 rooms, $610–$685 cottages (7–day minimum stay, 2–4 people) | AE, MC, V.

SENECA FALLS

MAP 3, F6

(Nearby towns also listed: Auburn, Canandaigua, Geneva, Skaneateles, Waterloo)

Some say that Seneca Falls, a canal town on man-made Van Cleef Lake, served as the model for Bedford Falls in the movie, *It's a Wonderful Life.* Settled in 1787, it became the birthplace of women's rights in 1848 when Elizabeth Cady Stanton, who lived here, organized the first women's rights convention. Today it has several historic sites and nearby wineries.

Information: Seneca County Tourism | Box 491, 13148 | 800/732–1848 | windmill@ seneca.org | www.seneca.org.

Attractions

Cayuga Lake State Park. This 190-acre park on the lake has a swimming beach, bathhouse, playground, campground, and trails. You can also fish here. | 2678 Lower Lake Rd. | 315/568–5163 | www.nysparks.state.ny.us/parks/ | Free; parking $6 | Daily.

Cayuga-Seneca Canal. This canal connects the Erie Canal near the Montezuma Wildlife Refuge with Cayuga and Seneca lakes. The portion connecting the two lakes runs right through Seneca Falls. The New York State Canal Corp. provides information on cruising the canal. | 9 Seneca St. | 800/4–CANAL–4 or 315/568–5797 | Free | Daily.

Cayuga Wine Trail. Ten wineries are part of this trail that circles Cayuga Lake. Most are clustered on the western shore, in the towns of Romulus, Ovid, and Interlaken. The Cayuga Wine Trail organization sponsors various events throughout the year. | Fayette | 800/684–5217 or 315/549–7075 | www.cayugawine.com | Free | All wineries open for tours May–Nov., daily.

Montezuma National Wildlife Refuge. For an introduction to these wetlands, take the 3½-mi Wildlife Drive, which begins at the visitors center. Pick up a brochure listing the 320 species of birds that have been identified at the 7,000-acre Montezuma site since 1938. The entrance is at the north end of Cayuga Lake, 5 mi east of Seneca Falls. | U.S. 20/Rte. 5 | 315/568–5987 | www.fws.gov/r5mnwr | Free | Daily dawn–dusk; center weekdays 10–3, weekends 10–4.

National Women's Hall of Fame. The hall honors distinguished American women, with portraits, recordings, and photographs. The collection is not very extensive and can be seen in 30 minutes. | 76 Fall St. | 315/568–8060 | fax 315/568–2976 | www.greatwomen.org | $3 | May–Oct., Mon.–Sat. 9:30–5, Sun. noon–4; Nov.–Apr. Wed.–Sat. 10–4, Sun. noon–4.

Seneca Falls Historical Society Museum. This museum has Victorian-era rooms and local history exhibits. | 55 Cayuga St. | 315/568–8412 | fax 315/568–8426 | $3 | Sept.–June, weekdays 9–4; July–Aug., weekdays 9–4, weekends 1–4.

Women's Rights National Historical Park. Exhibits, films, and talks explore the development of the women's rights movement. | 136 Fall St. | 315/568–2991 | fax 315/568–2141 | $2 | Daily 9–5.

The **Elizabeth Cady Stanton House** is the meticulously restored home of one of the leaders of the women's rights movement. Amelia Bloomer, the reformer who first introduced pants for women, was a frequent guest. | 32 Washington St. | 315/568–2991 | fax 315/568–2141 | $1 | Mar.–Oct., Wed.–Sun. noon–4.

The **Wesleyan Chapel Declaration Park** is the site of the 1848 women's rights convention, which produced the Declaration of Sentiments. Its words are etched on a 140-ft-long water wall nearby along with the names of the 300 signers (both men and women). All that remains of the chapel are a piece of the roof and fragile walls. | 126 Fall St. | 315/568–2991 | www.nps.gov/wori | Free | Daily.

ON THE CALENDAR
JULY: *Convention Days Celebration.* Celebrates the first Women's Rights Convention with speeches, reenactments, music, fireworks, and food. The event is held at the Wesleyan Chapel Declaration Park. | 315/568–8412.

Dining

Knapp Vineyard and Restaurant. Contemporary. This restaurant is in a vineyard with flower and vegetable gardens, the latter providing much of the fresh produce the kitchen uses. Try the fried green tomatoes with shrimp rémoulade, the Sicilian tuna, or the tenderloin of Angus beef. Dine on the outdoor patio overlooking the garden. Located 14 mi south of Seneca Falls on the Cayuga Wine Trail. | 2770 County Rd. 128 (Ernsberger Rd.), Romulus | 607/869–9271 | fax 607/869–3212 | www.knappwine.com | Closed Jan.–Mar. No dinner Mon.–Wed. | $15–$21 | AE, D, MC, V.

Lodging

Guion House Bed and Breakfast. This 1876 home is one block from the downtown historic district and the Women's Rights National Historical Park. Rooms are attractively decorated, and there is no elevator. Ask about age restrictions. Complimentary breakfast. No smoking. | 32 Cayuga St. | 315/568–8129 or 800/631–8919 | 6 rooms | $69–$85 | D, MC, V.

Van Cleef Homestead Bed and Breakfast. Lawrence Van Cleef, the first permanent settler in the village, built this Federal-style home in 1825. All the rooms have private baths. There are pets in the home. Complimentary breakfast. Pool. | 86 Cayuga St. | 315/568–2275 or 800/323–8668 | 3 rooms | $70–$90 | MC, V.

SHANDAKEN

(Nearby towns also listed: Cairo, Hunter, Windham)

Shandaken means "rapid waters," and the town is on Esopus Creek, famous for wild trout fishing. Also home to the highest mountain in the Catskills, it shares the region's rich history and mountainous beauty. It's a favorite spot among hunters and fishermen, and near to skiing at Belleayre and Hunter. The town is at the crossroads of Routes 42 and 28.

Information: Chamber of Commerce | 21 Tinker St., Woodstock, 12498 | 845/679–8025.

Attractions

Belleayre Mountain. Located in the Catskill Forest Preserve, approximately 2½ hours by car north of the George Washington Bridge, Belleayre is the only mountain in the area that has a natural division, with one section for expert skiers and another for intermediates and beginners. There are 133 acres of skiable terrain with 35 trails that can be used for hiking in summer. The summer months also feature cultural programs and concerts, and Belleayre Mountain's Pine Hill Lake offers swimming, boating, and fishing. In October there is a Fall Festival. | Off Rte. 28 at Highmount | 845/254–5600 or 800/942–6904 | belleayr@catskill.net | www.belleayre.com | Nov.–Apr.

Catskill Park. Catskill Park was designated in 1904 as a state treasure. It's got 700,000 acres of public and private land, and some of the wildest country south of Maine. There are 200 mi of marked trails, campgrounds, ponds, lakes, and mountains. | Rtes. 28 and 212 | 845/256–3000, Dept. of Environmental Conservation, Ulster County | www.catskillpark.com | Free | Daily.

Shandaken Theatrical Society. Area performers produce a show each season: a spring musical, a summer melodrama, a fall comedy or drama, and a winter holiday event. Past performances include *Cabaret, Harvey,* and *The Sound of Music.* | Church St., Phoenicia | 845/688–2279 | $10 | Call for schedule.

ON THE CALENDAR

JULY–AUG.: *Belleayre Music Festival.* Jazz, folk, country, classical, rock, Broadway, and opera artists from across the country appear at Belleayre Mt. Ski Center, Highmount. | 800/942–6904.

Dining

Auberge des 4 Saisons. French. This charming and elegant eatery looks like a French country inn. Try the baby lamb, steak au poivre, roasted duck with wild rice, or ravioli with Portobello mushrooms. | 178 Rte. 42 | 845/688–2223 or 800/864–1877 | No lunch | $15–$30 | AE, MC, V.

Café on Main. Continental. The menu changes weekly at this small café with canteloupe-color walls, but you'll always find fish and vegetarian entrées. Located 25 mi south of Shandaken in Margaretville. | Main St., Margaretville | 845/586–2343 | $11–$20 | AE, MC, V.

Loretta Charles Natural Wood Grill. Eclectic. Most dishes involve seafood in this rustic dining room with wood-burning fireplace and a view of Esopus Creek. The blackboard menu changes weekly, but includes such dishes as shrimp grilled Thai style with hot chiles and garlic, served with basmati rice. | Rte. 28 | 845/688–2550 | Closed Mon.–Wed. No lunch | $16–$23 | MC, V.

Pine Hill Arms Hotel. Continental. There are two dining rooms in this 100-year-old country inn; a traditional Catskill Mountain Room with rustic barn–wood siding, and a greenhouse room. It's known for charcoal-broiled steaks and blackened red snapper, a wide range of desserts, and a hearty, country-style breakfast. Shandaken is 5 mi away. | Main St., off Rte. 28 W, Pine Hill | 845/254–9811 | www.pinehillarms.com | vkonefal@catskill.net | Closed Wed. No lunch | $10–$20 | AE, D, MC, V.

Lodging

AppleTree Inn. Hunters, hikers, and anglers stay at this inn 30 mi west of Interstate 87. Picnic area. Some kitchenettes, refrigerators. No pets. | Rte. 28 | 845/688–7130 | www.apple-treeinn.homepage.com | 4 rooms, 3 efficiencies | $49–$59 | AE, D, MC, V.

Auberge des 4 Saisons. This charming French country inn with a wood-burning stove and noted restaurant is perched on a running stream. With its many activities on the grounds, including swimming, tennis, hiking, and fishing, it's more like a resort than just an inn. The rooms are country style, and many have balconies. Restaurant (See Auberge des 4 Saisons), bar, picnic area, complimentary breakfast. No air-conditioning, cable TV. Pool. Tennis. Hiking, fishing. Playground. Some pets allowed. | 178 Rte. 42 | 845/688–2223 or 800/864–1877 | 30 rooms | $85 | AE, MC, V.

Birch Creek Inn. Architect Henry Morton designed this antiques-filled inn in 1896. It's nestled in the woods, bounded by streams, stone bridges, and slate walks. A vintage billiard room contains a pool table, piano, and board games. Complimentary breakfast. Some refrigerators, cable TV. Hiking. No smoking. | Rte. 28, Pine Hill | www.abirchcreekinn.com | 845/254–5222 | fax 845/254–5812 | 9 rooms, 1 cottage | $85–$145; cottages $155 | AE, D, MC, V.

Copper Hood Inn and Spa. This is a small and elegant full-service spa and fitness center, situated in Catskill Park. Rooms are furnished in old European style, with Louis XVI and country pine furnishings. There are goats and sheep on the property. Picnic area, room service. Cable TV. Pool. Hot tub, massage. Exercise equipment. Tennis. Cross-country skiing. Library. Playground. Business services. | 70-39, Rte. 28 | 845/688–2460 | fax 845/688–7484 | www.copperhood.com | 19 rooms | $270–$285 (spa, food, and accommodation package inclusive) | AE, MC, V.

Margaretville Mountain Inn. Located on 6 country-farm acres, this bed-and-breakfast is a 1896 Queen Anne Victorian, situated atop Margaretville Mountain overlooking the Catskill Mountain State Park. Rooms are decorated in a Victorian style. Complimentary breakfast. Cable TV, no room phones. Playground. Some pets allowed (fee). No smoking. | Margaretville Mountain Rd., Margaretville | 845/586–3933 | www.catskill.net | 7 rooms | $65–$120 | AE, MC, V.

River Run Bed & Breakfast. This Queen Anne Victorian has wicker furniture and original stained glass from 1887. One suite is decorated with '50s memorabilia and has two bedrooms, two baths, and a full kitchen. Located 10 mi west of Shandaken. Dining room, picnic area. No air-conditioning, some kitchenettes, some in-room VCRs, no TV in some rooms, TV in common area. Library. Pets allowed. No smoking. | Main St., Fleischmanns | 845/254–4884 | www.catskill.net/riverrun | 8 rooms, 1 suite | $95–$120 | AC, MC, V.

SHELTER ISLAND

MAP 3, E2

(Nearby towns also listed: Greenport, Sag Harbor)

A picturesque island nestled in the bay between Long Island's North and South forks, Shelter Island feels like old New England, with its pristine beauty and relaxed pace.

White sandy beaches along the bay rest under soft rolling hills, and delightful inns, quaint shops, and superb dining line the streets. The 2,000-acre Mashomack Nature Preserve is a draw for hikers, bird-watchers, and nature enthusiasts.

Information: **Chamber of Commerce** | Box 598, 11964 | 631/749–0399 or 800/9–SHELTER.

Attractions

Mashomack Nature Preserve. This glorious preserve boasts over 2,000 acres of forest and an abundance of hiking trails through salt and fresh wetlands. | 79 S. Ferry Rd. (Rte. 114) | 631/749–1001 | www.shelter-island.org/mashomack | $2.50 suggested donation | Apr.–Oct., Wed.–Mon. 9–5. Closed Tues.; Nov.–Mar., Wed.–Mon. 9–4. Closed Tues.

ON THE CALENDAR

AUG.: *Annual Arts and Crafts Show.* This event, held on the Shelter Island School grounds, includes a wide array of arts-and-craft vendors and demonstrations. | 631/749–0399.

Dining

Chequit Inn. Continental. Built in 1872, this 35-room, Victorian country inn is also home to a kid-friendly restaurant. Try the fettuccine with smoked chicken, Gorgonzola, and spinach in a light cream sauce. There is open-air dining on the porch and the tree-shaded patio. Kids' menu, early bird dinners in winter. Sunday brunch. | 23 Grand Ave. | 631/749–0018 | $20–$35 | AE, MC, V.

Michael Anthony's. Eclectic. Try the fried calamari with cilantro, soy, and field greens. You'll dine by candlelight overlooking the waters of Dering Harbor. | 13 Winthrop Rd. | 631/749–3460 | Reservations essential | Closed Jan.–Mar. No lunch | $20–$30 | AE, MC, V.

Ram's Head Inn. Contemporary. Built in 1929, the Ram's Head Inn is surrounded by sweeping lawns and gardens, and you can eat outside on a porch and patio overlooking the har-

KODAK'S TIPS FOR PHOTOGRAPHING PEOPLE

Friends' Faces
- Pose subjects informally to keep the mood relaxed
- Try to work in shady areas to avoid squints
- Let kids pick their own poses

Strangers' Faces
- In crowds, work from a distance with a telephoto lens
- Try posing cooperative subjects
- Stick with gentle lighting—it's most flattering to faces

Group Portraits
- Keep the mood informal
- Use soft, diffuse lighting
- Try using a panoramic camera

People at Work
- Capture destination-specific occupations
- Use tools for props
- Avoid flash if possible

Sports
- Fill the frame with action
- Include identifying background
- Use fast shutter speeds to stop action

Silly Pictures
- Look for or create light-hearted situations
- Don't be inhibited
- Try a funny prop

Parades and Ceremonies
- Stake out a shooting spot early
- Show distinctive costumes
- Isolate crowd reactions
- Be flexible: content first, technique second

From *Kodak Guide to Shooting Great Travel Pictures* © 2000 by Fodor's Travel Publications

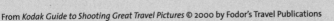

bor. The menu changes seasonally and incorporates local produce, seafood, and game. Try the roasted fall squash salad with mushrooms, or the ragout of free-range Long Island duck with an apple-cider glaze. Live jazz Sunday, July–Labor Day. Kids' menu. Limited dock space. | 108 Ram Island Dr. | 631/749–0811 | $35–$50 | AE, MC, V.

Lodging

Chequit Inn. The renovated 1870s main building has large romantic suites with antique Georgian furnishings and hardwood floors. This is a quiet getaway. Located in downtown Shelter Island. Restaurant, complimentary Continental breakfast. No air-conditioning in some rooms, in-room data ports, some in-room VCRs, room phones, no TV in some rooms. No pets. No smoking. | 23 Grand Ave. | 631/749–0018 | fax 631/749–0183 | www.shelteris-landinns.com | 33 rooms, 4 suites in 3 buildings | $80–$225 rooms, $150–$225 suites | AE, MC, V.

Dering Harbor Inn. Ride the ferry to this resort hotel located ½ mi south of Shelter Island on Teconic Bay. With contemporary furnishings and wall-to-wall carpeting, suites have one or two bedrooms and private decks. Restaurant, bar, picnic area. Some kitchenettes, some microwaves, some refrigerators, cable TV, some in-room VCRs, room phones. Pool. 2 tennis courts. Volleyball. Laundry facilities. No pets. | 13 Winthrop Rd. | 631/749–0900 | www.der-ingharborinn.com | 4 rooms, 26 suites in 5 buildings | $200–$275 | Closed May–Oct. | AE, D, MC, V.

Pridwin. This rambling, old-fashioned family-friendly resort is across the street from the bay and great for water-sports lovers. In summer, you can enjoy your meals on the deck, and there's outdoor dancing at night. The rooms are simple but comfortable, and the cottages are quaint. Restaurant, bar (with entertainment), complimentary breakfast. Refrigerators (in cottages). Pool. Tennis. Beach, docks. Video games. | Shore Rd. | 631/749–0476 or 800/273–2497 | fax 631/749–2071 | www.pridwin.com | 40 rooms, 8 cottages | $133–$180 rooms, $213 cottages | Closed Nov.–Apr. | AE, D, MC, V.

Ram's Head Inn. This lovely 1929 inn has traditional country interiors, rolling landscaped grounds, and a private beach. Rooms are bright and sunny, furnished in Early American style with colorful flowered wallpaper. Some have views of the ocean and lawns. Restaurant, bar, complimentary Continental breakfast. No air-conditioning, no TV in some rooms, TV and VCR in common room. Sauna. Tennis. Beach. Playground. No smoking. | Ram Island Dr. | 631/749–0811 | www.shelterislandinns.com/ramshead/ | 17 rooms (4 with shared bath) | $125–$290 | AE, V.

Sunset Beach. Every room has a terrace with a view at this hotel overlooking Shelter Island Bay. The downstairs restaurant, which is directly across the street from the island's most popular beach, is a hot spot. Restaurant, bar, picnic area, complimentary Continental breakfast. Some kitchenettes, cable TV. Beach. Business services. | 35 Shore Rd. | 631/749–2001 | 20 rooms | $150–$295 | May–Sept. | AE, D, MC, V.

SKANEATELES

MAP 3, G6

(Nearby towns also listed: Auburn, Geneva, Liverpool, Seneca Falls, Syracuse, Waterloo)

One of the most attractive and active villages of the Finger Lakes region, this resort town was founded in 1794 and presides over the north end of the lake of the same name. The lake is exceptionally deep (350 ft) for its length (15 mi) and is known for its beauty and cleanliness.

Information: **Skaneateles Area Chamber of Commerce** | Box 199, 9 E. Lake St., 13152 | 315/685–0552 | skaneateles-chamber@worldnet.att.net | www.skaneateles.com.

Attractions

Mid-Lakes Navigation Co. This is the tourist information center for the area. Find out about sightseeing, lunch, dinner, and wine-tasting cruises, mostly on Skaneateles Lake and the Erie Canal. Mailboat cruises are also available; Skaneateles has one of the few remaining U.S. mail runs by boat, as Mid-Lakes Navigation Co. delivers mail to people living on and around the lake. | 11 Jordan St. | www.midlakesnav.com/MLN/ | 315/685–8500 or 800/545–4318 | May–Sept. daily, 9–9.

Skaneateles Historical Society Museum. This small museum, in a former creamery building, includes exhibits on the lake's history, dairy farming, and the teasel, a plant used by woolen mills. | 28 Hannum St. | 315/685–1360 | Free | June–Labor Day, Thurs.–Sat. 1–4; Labor Day–May, Fri. 1–4.

ON THE CALENDAR

JULY–AUG.: *Polo Matches.* Weekly games take place at the Skaneateles Polo Club on Sundays at 3 PM, some of which are linked to various charities. | Sun. 3 PM | 315/685–7373.

AUG.: *Antique and Classic Boat Show.* This annual display draws boat owners from across North America to the north end of Skaneateles Lake. | 315/685–0552.

AUG.–SEPT.: *Skaneateles Festival.* Enjoy a five-week presentation of all different kinds of music by well-known performers. Brochures with venues and times can be picked up at the Mid-Lakes Navigation Co. | 315/685–7418.

NOV.–DEC.: *Dickens Christmas.* Between Thanksgiving and Christmas, the downtown is decorated for the season with a Charles Dickens's *A Christmas Carol* theme. | 315/685–2268.

Dining

Bluewater Grill. American. The menu looks simple, but the meals are generous and tasty. The Grill is known for chowder, gumbo, seafood, ribs, chicken, and salads. There is open-air dining on both an upper and lower deck, both overlooking the water. | 11 W. Genesee St. | 315/685–6600 | $6–$20 | AE, MC, V.

Doug's Fish Fry. Seafood. There aren't many frills here, but there's likely to be plenty of hungry patrons. Doug's serves seafood, including steamed lobster and clams, as well as frankfurters, ice cream, beer, and wine. There's outdoor picnic area dining and takeout. | 8 Jordan St. | www.dougsfishfry.com/ | 315/685–3288 | Closed first 2 weeks in Jan. | $6–$8 | No credit cards.

Johnny Angel's Heavenly Hamburgers. American. If you're really hungry, this is a fine place to go for very informal dining. Try the fresh handmade burgers, and the homemade soups and salads. It's across from the water. | 22 Jordan St. | 315/685–0100 | fax 315/685–3298 | www.johnnyangels.com | Breakfast also available | $5–$12 | AE, MC, V.

Krebs. Continental. This rambling old house, which originally sat 25, has been expanded and now seats 150. There is also a cocktail lounge and sitting rooms, all furnished with tavern furniture and antiques from the early 1900s. The tables are dressed in white linen (as are the waitresses!) and adorned with fresh flowers. Try the lobster Newburg, prime rib, and the homemade desserts. This restaurant is widely known for its traditional seven-course dinner. | 53 W. Genesee St. | 315/685–5714 | www.thekrebs.com | Closed Nov.–Apr. No lunch Mon.–Sat. | $35–$40 | AE, D, MC, V.

Mandana Inn. Seafood. You'll find this former stagecoach tavern on the west shore of Skaneateles Lake and fresh seafood—like shrimp scampi, mussels, and cod—on the menu. Kids' menu. | 1937 W. Lake Rd. | 315/685–7798 | fax 315/685–6490 | Closed Jan.–Mar.; Apr.–May closed Mon.–Thurs.; Memorial Day–Labor Day closed Mon.–Wed.; Sept.–Dec. closed Mon.–Thurs. No lunch | $15–$20 | AE, MC, V.

Millard's at the Summit. American. This historic 1840 building offers a wonderful view of one of the most beautiful Finger Lakes. Cajun specials are featured every third Thursday of the month. Known for its pork and vegetarian meals. Open-air dining on a two-tier deck, overlooking the lake. | 1715 E. Lake Rd. | 315/673–2254 | www.skaneateles.com/millards | Closed Mon. May–Sept. No lunch Tues.–Sat. | $15–$24 | AE, MC, V.

Rosalie's Cucina. Italian. Rosalie's is one of the region's most popular fine restaurants, and tables are likely to be full by 6 PM on a Saturday. The veal scallops and yellowfin tuna steak are worth any wait. Autographs of former diners adorn the walls; huge mirrors make the dining area look larger than it is. | 841 W. Genesee St. | 315/685–2200 | www.skaneateles.com/rosalies | No lunch | $18–$35 | AE, D, MC, V.

Sherwood Inn. Continental. This restaurant offers a regional menu. Try the herb-crusted rack of lamb, yellowfin tuna, or grilled salmon. | 26 W. Genesee St. | 315/685–3405 or 800/374–3796 | $18–$25 | AE, MC, V.

Lodging

Arbor House Inn. Built around 1850, this brick Federal building has antiques of the same period and hardwood floors. There are some oriental rugs. The master suite has a king-size bed, gas fireplace, private sunporch, adjoining sitting room, and double hot tub with separate shower. Complimentary breakfast. In-room data ports, some in-room hot tubs, cable TV, in-room VCRs, room phones. No pets. No kids under 9. No smoking. | 41 Fennell St. | 351/685–8966 | fax 315/685–6104 | www.arborhouseinn.com | 5 rooms | $135–$175 | AE, D, MC, V.

Bird's Nest. Located about ½ mi east of the village on U.S. 20, this hotel is surrounded by 58 acres of countryside, with a pond for fishing and hiking trails. Picnic area. Some kitchenettes, some in-room hot tubs, refrigerators, cable TV. Pool. Some pets allowed. | 1601 E. Genesee St. | 315/685–5641 | www.skaneateles.com/birdsnest | 30 rooms | $49–$135 | D, MC, V.

Hobbit Hollow Farm Bed and Breakfast. This comfortable 100-year-old Colonial Revival house sits on 300 private acres of woods and meadows and has great views of Skaneateles Lake. There are vibrant murals in the inn's common areas, as well as a sunroom for relaxing, porches, four-poster beds in guest rooms, and multiple fireplaces. Complimentary breakfast. In-room data ports. No kids. | 3061 W. Lake Rd. | 315/685–2791 | fax 315/685–3426 | www.hobbithollow.com | 5 rooms | $120–$270 | AE, D, MC, V.

Lady of the Lake. From the porch of this Queen Anne Victorian in downtown Skaneateles, you can see the north end of Skaneateles Lake. The Stella Room, named for the woman who built the house in 1900, has a king-size bed, pastel oriental rug, and Victorian antiques. Located 17 mi south of Interstate 90. Dining room, complimentary breakfast. TV in common area. Lake. Library. No kids under 8. No smoking. | 2 W. Lake St. | 315/685–7997 or 888/685–7997 | fax 315/685–7997 | www.ladyofthelake.net | 3 rooms | $110–$130; 2–night minimum stay weekends May 15–Oct. 15 | AC, D, MC, V.

Sherwood Inn. Built as a stagecoach stop in 1807, each room has been restored and is in keeping with the original style. The rooms are furnished with antiques and oriental rugs. Some guest rooms overlook the lake. Restaurant, bar, complimentary Continental breakfast. In-room data ports. Library. Business services. | 26 W. Genesee St. | www.thesherwoodinn.com | 315/685–3405 or 800/374–3796 (reservations) | 19 rooms, 1 suite | $85–$170 rooms, $275 for 4–bedroom suite | AE, MC, V.

SMITHTOWN

MAP 3, D2

(Nearby towns also listed: Northport, Port Jefferson, Stony Brook)

Legend says that the boundaries of Smithtown township were determined by an unusual bargain between Richard Smythe and the Nesaquake Indians in which Smythe was to receive as much land as he could cover riding his bull from sunrise to sunset.

After the Revolutionary War, the Blydenburgh family established a milling complex called New Mills at the site of what is now Blydenburgh Park. And in 1790, President George Washington, on a tour of Long Island, stopped at Widow Blydenburgh's Tavern to water his horse, and, in his diary, referred to her establishment as a "decent house."

Information: **Smithtown Chamber of Commerce** | 1 W. Main St., 11787 | www.smith-townchamber.org; www.smithnetny.com | 631/979–8069.

Attractions

Blydenburgh Park. This 588-acre facility offers rowboat rentals, picnic facilities, hiking, horseback trails (no rentals), and fishing. Several restored historical buildings are open to the public. Saltwater fishing (no license required). Horseback riding permits are required to use trails. | Veterans Memorial Hwy. | 631/854–3713 | Free | Daily.

Caleb Smith State Park Preserve. Over 500 acres of trails (one of which accommodates wheelchairs), bird walks, and cross-country ski trails are 1 mi west of Smithtown. Also home to a nature museum. Fly-fishing through mid-October. Family programs. | Jericho Tpk. | 631/265–1054 | Apr.–Sept., $5 per car before 4 PM | Apr.–Sept., Tues.–Sun. 8 AM–sunset; Oct.–Mar., Tues. and Thurs.–Sun. 8 AM–sunset.

ON THE CALENDAR

JUNE: *Nature Fair and Wildlife Festival.* Exhibits on ecology/environment, children's games, bee-keeping, guided walks, museum tours, and butterfly and birds of prey exhibits take place at the Sweetbriar Nature Center. | 631/979–6344.
AUG.: *Smithtown Fiddle Jamboree.* Bring folding chairs to traditional Scottish, Irish, and bluegrass/Cajun fiddle music at the Smithtown Brush Barn. | 631/385–7363.

Dining

Bonwit Inn. Continental. The Bonwit offers fine dining in an old building with a cozy bar and sunny dining rooms. It's known for Greek salad and seafood. Early bird dinners. Sunday brunch buffet (except in summer). | 1 Commack Rd. and Vanderbilt Pkwy., Commack | 631/499–2068 | $15–$30 | AE, D, DC, MC, V.

Country Kitchen. American. You can order breakfast all day at this family-style restaurant. A popular dish is smothered chicken, which consists of chicken breasts topped with sautéed onions, mushrooms, and Wisconsin cheese. | 77 Rte. 111 | 631/366–5271 | Breakfast available | $7–$13 | AE, MC, V.

La Mascotte. French. This small dining room with a fireplace is reminiscent of a Swiss chalet house or a country French home outside of Paris. Try roasted Long Island duck with fresh fruits and roasted lamb with garlic-herb crust. Save room for the crème brûlée. There's an extensive wine list. No smoking weekdays. | 3 Crooked Hill Rd., Commack | 631/499–6446 | No lunch weekends | $25–$35 | AE, D, DC, MC, V.

Lodging

Econo Lodge. This chain hotel is off the main highway in an industrial area, 3 mi from a shopping mall and restaurants. Bar, complimentary breakfast. Cable TV. | 755 Rte. 347 | 631/724–9000 | 39 rooms | $78–$83 | AE, D, DC, MC, V.

Hampton Inn. This chain hotel is close to downtown, and convenient to public transportation, including bus service, rail service, and MacArthur Airport. The rooms are neat and basic. Complimentary Continental breakfast. In-room data ports, some refrigerators, cable TV. Business services. | 680 Commack Rd., Commack | 516/462–5700 | fax 516/462–9735 | 144 rooms | $155–$180 | AE, D, DC, MC, V.

Marriott Hotel Islandia. This 10-floor hotel located close to the Long Island Expressway is a 20-min drive from the beach. Executive suites are huge rooms with combined sleeping and sitting areas. Restaurant, bar (with entertainment). In-room data ports, some microwaves, some refrigerators, cable TV, in-room VCRs, room phones. Pool. Sauna. Laundry service. Business services, airport shuttle. | 3635 Express Dr. N, Hauppauge | 631/232–3000 | fax 631/232–3029 | www.marriott.com | 277 rooms | $159–$209 | AE, D, DC, MC, V.

Sheraton–Long Island. Situated on a main road, this Sheraton is close to shopping, movie theaters, the airport, and the ocean. Restaurant, bar (with entertainment), complimentary Continental breakfast, room service. In-room data ports, cable TV. Pool. Hot tub. Exercise equipment. Business services, airport shuttle. | 110 Vanderbilt Motor Pkwy. | 631/231–1100 | fax 631/231–1143 | 209 rooms | $159–$199 | AE, D, DC, MC, V.

Wyndham Wind Watch Hotel. This hotel has a concierge to help you with travel plans. It's about 3 mi south of Smithtown, 7 mi north of Islip MacArthur Airport, and ¼ mi east of Interstate 495. Restaurant, bar, picnic area, complimentary Continental breakfast, room service. In-room data ports, cable TV. 2 pools. Hot tub, massage, 2 saunas. Health club. Basketball, volleyball. Video games. Playground. Laundry service. Business services, airport shuttle. | 1717 Motor Pkwy., Hauppauge | 631/232–9815 | fax 631/232–9853 | www.marriott.com | 355 rooms, 5 suites | $159–$199 | AE, D, DC, MC, V.

SOUTHAMPTON

MAP 3, E2

(Nearby towns also listed: Bridgehampton/Water Mill, East Hampton, Hampton Bays, Sag Harbor)

The town of Southampton was established in 1640 by English colonists and was the first settlement in New York State. It has a decidedly Colonial feel and, armed with maps obtained from the Chamber of Commerce, visitors enjoy walking tours that pass the Historical Museum and the Old Halsey Homestead, where English General Erskine had his headquarters during the American Revolution.

Southampton village boasts 7 mi of unspoiled white beaches and its waters attract both boaters and fishermen. Shinnecock is a popular diving spot and windsurfers enjoy the Three Bays: Shinnecock, Peconic, and Noyac.

Downtown Southampton village simply oozes chic. Charming shops along beautiful and historic tree-lined streets pepper the village and the Job Lane's shopping district.

Information: **Southampton Chamber of Commerce** | 72 Main St., 11968 | www.southamptonchamber.com | 631/283–0402 | fax 631/283–8707.

Attractions

Old Halsey House. The Old Halsey Homestead was built in 1648 by town founder Thomas Halsey. Today it's a museum that includes furniture from the 17th and 18th centuries. | 189 S. Main St. | 631/283–2494 | $2 | Mid-June–Sept. 7, Tues.–Sun. 11–5.

Parrish Art Museum. This museum features 19th- and 20th-century art, a sculpture garden, and lectures, workshops, and concert performances. | 25 Job's La. | 631/283–2118 | $2 suggested donation | Mon.–Sat. 11–5, Sun. 1–5.

Southampton Campus of Long Island University. In summer, the campus hums with jazz and popular concerts. Other organizations sponsor a variety of activities for adults and children including plays, art shows, concerts, readings, and workshops. | 239 Montauk Hwy. | 631/283–4000 | Admission varies | Daily.

Southampton Historical Museum. The museum boasts seven historic sites including a whaling captain's home built in 1843. There is also a country store, an old-fashioned drugstore, a pre–Revolutionary War barn, and a blacksmith shop. | 17 Meeting House La. | 631/283–2494 | $3 | Mid-June–Sept., Tues.–Sat. 11–5, Sun. 1–5.

AUG.: *Southampton Shakespeare Festival.* For 2 wks each August, professional actors perform outdoors in Southampton's Agawam Park. Plays are free. Actors also host Camp Shakespeare, a workshop for kids. | 631/267–0105.

SEPT.: *Pow Wow.* Traditional Native American tribal dances, crafts, and ceremonies take place Labor Day weekend on the Shinnecock Reservation. | 631/283–6143.

Dining

Armand's. Continental. Eat great pasta by candlelight with a lovely wooded view. Try also the scampi and the fabulous garlic focaccia knots. Pianist Saturday. Sunday brunch. | 1271 Noyac Rd. | 631/283–9742 | Dec.–Feb., closed Tues.–Weds. Mar.–Nov., Closed Tues. No lunch weekdays | $15–$25 | MC, V.

Basilico. Mediterranean. This trendy spot serves daily specials of homemade pasta, fresh fish, and classic meats. The dining room is lit with candles and done in wood and terra-cotta tiles. | 10 Windmill La. | 631/283–7987 | Reservations essential | $35–$50 | AE, D, DC, MC, V.

Coast Grill. Seafood. Set in a marina, this rustic restaurant is known for no-attitude and serious food. Try the pepper-crusted tuna with sesame noodles or the grilled swordfish with spiced lime papaya puree. The steak, lamb, and buffalo filet mignon also get rave reviews. | 1109 Noyac Rd. | 631/283–2277 | Weekends only Oct.–May; No lunch | $35–$45 | AE, MC, V.

Golden Pear. American. Place your orders at the counter of this tiny café, and then sit at one of 12 tables to be served. It's known for pasta, chile, vegetable lasagna, and interesting combo sandwiches. No alcohol. | 97–99 Main St. | 631/283–8900 | Breakfast also available; no dinner | $10–$20 | AE, MC, V.

John Duck Jr. American. The restaurant has been a family business for over 100 years. It's in a converted farmhouse on top of a terraced hill, and there are five dining rooms, one of which is a glassed-in porch. Seafood, steak, roast Long Island duckling, and local produce make up the menu. Kids' menu. Sunday brunch. | 15 Prospect St. | 631/283–0311 | Closed Mon. | $15–$25 | AE, D, DC, MC, V.

Le Chef. French. This busy little bistro is warm and welcoming. Try the rack of lamb, lobster with tomato cognac cream sauce, or veal scaloppine with wild mushroom sauce. | 75 Jobs La. | 631/283–8581 | $20 prix fixe | AE, DC, MC, V.

Lobster Inn. Seafood. Nautical and rustic, the building was an old marina and boat sale shop before it was turned into a family-friendly and very popular restaurant serving local fish. All dining is outdoors under a tent with a lovely view of the water. Salad bar. No air-conditioning. | 162 Inlet Rd. | 631/283–1525 | Reservations not accepted | $25–$35 | AE, D, DC, MC, V.

Mirko's. Eclectic. Mirko's has been reviewed as one of the area's best-kept secrets. It has a country inn feel, and is known for shrimp, pork, and the chef's special sauces. Try pan-seared calamari with a lemon, garlic, and sherry sauce. Open-air dining on patio. | Water Mill Sq., Water Mill | 631/726–4444 | www.mirkosrestaurant.com | Reservations essential | $45–$55 | AE, DC, MC, V.

Peter's Backstreet. American. For over 40 years, Peter's has been serving fresh seafood and steak in a relaxed setting with an eclectic mix of decorations. Walls are covered with old photographs, political buttons, and baseball cards. | 56 Nugent St. | 631/283–8082 | No lunch | $20–$25 | AE, MC, V.

Red Bar Brasserie. French. The 1930s roadhouse that houses this popular restaurant has been renovated, but the wonderful casement windows lined with candle sconces remain. Try grilled salmon with local corn, or grilled pepper tuna with steamed baby bok choy. | 210 Hampton Rd. | 631/283–0704 | Closed Tues. No lunch | $35–$45 | AE, MC, V.

Savanna's. Continental. Savanna's home is in a building that was the original town hall for Southampton. The dining room has wainscoting, ceiling fans, and lots of candlelight.

Try the Chilean sea bass and horseradish-crusted yellowtail snapper. There is dining on the patio. Weekend brunch. | 268 Elm St. | 631/283–0202 | No lunch weekdays | $20–$40 | AE, D, DC, MC, V.

75 Main. Eclectic. This old clapboard building in the middle of town has a light and airy interior, not to mention a martini menu and cigars for aficionados. The busy bar scene and music and dancing (after 11 pm) on Friday and Saturday nights are popular, and the internationally accented menu offers delicacies like the duck and roast vegetable spring roll, with tamarind barbecue sauce and jimica slaw, or the grilled Nova Scotia salmon over Beluga lentils, Swiss chard, and red-onion marmalade. Brunch, Kids' menu, pre-theater menu. | 75 Main St. | 631/283–7575 | www.75main.com | $20–$30 | AE, MC, V.

Station Bistro. French. Set in a former 1903 railroad station, the Bistro has a vaulted ceiling and a cheery yellow, plum, and off-white interior. Try herb-crusted bass, Dijon-crusted rack of lamb, and roasted Long Island duck with raspberry and roasted shallot sauce, and don't skip the baked fruit tarts or the chocolate Chambord cake. Open-air dining on screened porch. | 50 Station Rd., Water Mill | 631/726–3016 | Reservations essential Fri.– Sat. | Jacket required | Closed Mon.–Thurs. | $35–$45 | AE, MC, V.

Lodging

Arlington Shores. View a gorgeous Hamptons sunset from the common balcony at this condominium resort located 10 mi west of Southampton in Hampton Bays on Shinnecock Bay. Standard condos have a queen-size bed, kitchen, private bath, and oak floors. Stay for a week, a month, a season, or even a year. Shuttle provided to train or bus stops. Picnic area. No air-conditioning, kitchenettes, microwaves, refrigerators, cable TV. Pool. Tennis. Volleyball. No pets. | 40 Penny La., Hampton Bays | 631/723–6000 | fax 631/723–4517 | arlington-shores@aol.com | 28 condominiums | $150–$350 | AE, MC, V.

The Atlantic. This 1950s-style hotel has totally renovated deluxe rooms, and is about 4 mi from town center. Maple wood and stainless steel furniture give the rooms a streamlined clean look. Some kitchenettes, cable TV. Pool. Business services. Pets allowed. | 1655 Rte. 39 | 631/287–0908 | fax 631/283–4625 | 70 rooms | $180–$290 | AE, MC, V.

Bel-Aire Cove Motel. The quiet Bel-Aire Cove is right on the waters of Shinnecock Bay, 8 mi west of Southampton and 3 mi south of the Montauk Highway. Picnic area, complimentary Continental breakfast. Some kitchenettes, some microwaves, refrigerators, cable TV, room phones. Pool. Volleyball. Pets allowed. No smoking. | 20 Shinnecock Rd., Hampton Bays | 631/728–0416 | fax 631/728–9426 | www.bel-airecove.com | 19 rooms | $100–$150 | AC, D, DC, MC, V.

The Bentley. This modern mini-resort has some rooms overlooking the Peconic Bay. All suites have a private patio or deck. Set on 4½ acres, the property has a kidney-shaped pool with a large sunning deck and a tennis court. Picnic area, complimentary Continental breakfast. Kitchenettes, cable TV. Pool. Tennis. Laundry facilities. Business services. Pets allowed. | 161 Hill Station Rd. | 631/283–6100 | fax 631/283–6102 | 38 suites | $200–$390 | AE, D, DC, MC, V.

The Capri. This modest-yet-modern, privately-owned motel is 3 mi from the beach, and ½ mi from the downtown area. All guest rooms face the pool in the central courtyard of the property. Restaurant. Some refrigerators, cable TV. Pool. Business services. Pets allowed. | 281 Rte. 39A | 631/283–0908 | fax 631/283–6496 | 33 rooms | $140–$250 | AE, D, MC, V.

Easterner Motel. Nestled on 2 acres in the Shinnecock Hills (5 mi west of downtown Southampton), this motel has handmade contemporary furniture, and two extra-long double beds in each room. Kitchenettes, some microwaves, refrigerators, cable TV, room phones. Pool. Tennis court. No pets. | 639 Montauk Hwy. | 631/283–9292 | www.hamptons.com/easternermotel | 8 rooms in 4 cottages | $125–$250 | Closed Labor Day–Memorial Day | AE, MC, V.

The Ivy. This renovated 1800s home has a large brick-floored living room with bright yellow printed chairs and a baby-grand piano. Mirrors dot the hallways to the upstairs bedrooms, which are individually decorated in rich fabrics of various colors. Large comfortable beds with plush comforters are inviting after a day at the beach (less than 2 mi away) or shopping in downtown Southampton (less than 1 mi away). Complimentary breakfast. Pool. No TV in some rooms. | 244 N. Main St. | 631/283–3233 | fax 631/283–3793 | theivy@earthlink.net | www.theivy.com | 5 rooms (2 with shower only) | $135–$325 | AE, D, DC, MC, V.

Mainstay. Every bedroom here features antique iron beds and country pine furniture. A 15-min walk will get you to Main Street, Southampton. Complimentary Continental breakfast. No air-conditioning, no TV in some rooms. Pool. Business services. No smoking. | 579 Hill St. | 631/283–4375 | fax 631/287–6240 | elizmain@hamptons.com | www.hamptons.com/mainstay | 8 rooms (3 with shared bath) | $125–$300 | AE, D, MC, V.

1708 House. This early 18th-century antiques-filled bed-and-breakfast is in the center of town. There are three public rooms, a card room, and a parlor. The rooms are all adorned with antiques in keeping with the original 1708 style. Dining room, complimentary Continental breakfast. No kids. No smoking. | 126 Main St. | www.1708house.com | 631/287–1708 | fax 800/287–3593 | 6 rooms, 3 suites, 3 cottages | $175–$395 rooms, $250–$395 suites, $375–$475 cottages | AE, MC, V.

Southampton Inn. This modern luxury hotel, decorated in upscale country casual, features landscaped grounds and a patio courtyard. Bar (with entertainment). In-room data ports, some refrigerators, cable TV. Pool. Tennis. Business services. Exercise equipment. Video games. | 91 Hill St. | 631/283–6500 or 800/832–6500 | fax 631/283–6559 | www.southamptoninn.com | 90 rooms | $189–$349 | AE, MC, V.

Southampton Village Latch Inn. Set on 5 acres near town and the beach, this hotel is owned and run by a collective of local artists, and the decor reflects their tastes. The rooms and suites are theatrically furnished with Burmese puppets, masks from New Guinea, African artifacts, and Tibetan rugs. Complimentary Continental breakfast. Some refrigerators, cable TV. Pool. Tennis. Business services. Pets allowed. | 101 Hill St. | 516/283–2160 or 800/545–2824 | fax 516/283–3236 | www.villagelatch.com | 72 rooms | $195–$550 | AE, D, MC, V.

SOUTHOLD

MAP 3, E2

(Nearby towns also listed: Greenport, Mattituck)

Southold, which was settled in 1640, originally consisted of an area that included Riverhead, Shelter Island, Southampton, and all the north shore of Long Island from Orient Point to Wading River. The distances and conditions of travel in those days were the major reasons for the town's division. Later, when the colonial ties to Mother England were severed, the heady atmosphere of liberty and freedom deepened desires for more local autonomy.

The community of Southold remains at the heart of Long Island's North Fork with its wineries and beautiful farmland. Like its neighboring villages and hamlets, it exudes New England charm. Back in 1757, a young surveyor from Virginia, George Washington, recommended that a lighthouse be built off Cliff Lot to assist sailors who had to face the perilous glacier boulders just below the surface of Long Island Sound's Deadman's Cove. This lighthouse still stands atop a 110-ft bluff.

Information: **Greenport-Southold Chamber of Commerce** | Main Rd., Box 66, Greenport, 11944 | www.greenportsouthold.org | 631/477–1383. .

Attractions

Historic Museums of Southold. The complex is home to the Ann Currie-Bell Home, which has antique dolls and toys, costume collections, and period rooms. The Thomas Moore House is a mid-19th-century carriage house and blacksmith shop. The Old Bayview School (circa

1821) has been restored to its 1914 appearance. The Prince Building has historical records that date to the 17th century. | At Main Rd. and Maple La. | 631/765–5500 | Donations accepted | Wed., Sat., Sun. 1–4.

Horton Point Lighthouse and Nautical Museum. The dangers of a rocky cove were noticed by a young surveyor named George Washington in 1757, and his recommendation to build a lighthouse came to fruition in 1847. Operated by the Southold Historical Society, it features a nautical museum with sea captains' journals, sea chests, paintings, and maps, as well as public barbecue grills on the grounds. | Lighthouse Rd. | www.longislandlighthouses.com | 631/765–5500 or 631/765–3262 | $2 suggested donation | Memorial Day–Columbus Day, weekends 11:30–4.

Southold Indian Museum. Permanent exhibits of Native Americans record cultural evolution beginning from 10,000 years ago. The museum includes a large collection of artifacts and handiwork of Inuit, Middle and Far Western Native Americans, and Central and South American native tribes. | Main Bayview Rd. | www.i2.i-2000.com/~skindoc | 631/765–5577 | $1 suggested donation | Weekends 1:30–4:30, weekdays by appointment.

ON THE CALENDAR

SEPT.: *Annual North Fork Jazz Festival.* Jazz greats including pianist Bill Charlap, vocalist Melissa Walker, and trumpeter Clark Terry have performed at the Southold High School auditorium stage for this one-night event. | 631/734–7696.

Dining

Coeur des Vignes Restaurant Francais & L'Hotel. French. The name of this family-run restaurant in the heart of Long Island's wine country translates as "heart of the vines," fitting for this romantic spot with lace curtains, candlelight, and fine china—and of course an extensive wine cellar. Duck breast, seared and served under pistachio and honey, leads off the menu, which also includes braised sweetbreads, lobster, and filet mignon. Sunday brunch. | 57225 Main Rd. | 631/765–2656 | Closed Tues. | $18–$30 | AE, D, DC, MC, V.

Ross' North Fork. American. This local favorite is in a cement-block contemporary building. The dining room is done in beautiful burgundy and gray colors accented by wine racks and wine art. It is known for local wine and cuisine. Try the baked oysters in garlic and Pernod, the pumpkin Chardonnay soup, the summer lobster stew, and the seasonal cobblers, pies, and cakes for dessert. Kids' menu. | Rte. 48, between Horton's La. and Young's Ave. | 631/765–2111 | Closed Mon. and Jan.–mid-Feb. | $35–$45 | AE, DC, MC, V.

Seafood Barge. American. The "barge" offers sweeping views of the bay and the Hamptons. The chef prepares sushi by blending traditional ingredients with fresh local catches. Try the pan-seared local fish or the grilled salmon over lobster succotash with sweet-potato sticks. No smoking. | 62980 Main Rd. | 631/765–3010 | $15–$26 | AE, DC, MC, V.

Lodging

Santorini Beach. This hotel is on 17 acres of a private enclave with 800 ft of serene beach. All the rooms are furnished with European artwork and accessories. Restaurant, complimentary Continental breakfast. Cable TV, some room phones. Pool, wading pool. Basketball. Beach. Pets allowed. | 3800 Duck Pond Rd., Cutchogue | www.santorinibeach.com | 631/734–6370 | 45 rooms | $179–$345 | AE, D, MC, V.

Sound View Inn. On a 1,400-ft private beach with complimentary chaises and umbrellas, this inn has standard deluxe bedrooms with a back door opening onto a deck overlooking the water. Suites, studios, and luxury apartments also available. Restaurant. Some kitchenettes, refrigerators, room phones. Pool. Sauna. Golf privileges, 4 tennis courts. | Rte. 48, Greenport | 631/477–1910 | fax 631/477–9436 | www.greenport.com/soundinn/welcome.htm | 18 rooms, 31 suites | $110–$120 rooms, $150–$300 suites | D, DC, MC, V.

SPECULATOR

(Nearby towns also listed: North Creek, Warrensburg)

Only 625 people live in this small hamlet that thrives on tourism of the quiet kind. There are no outlets here, but Speculator is close to three wilderness areas, with hundreds of miles of trails for bikers, hikers, and snowmobilers. Speculator is also home to Camp-of-the-Woods, a religious retreat established in the 1930s that holds seminars on Christianity and promotes global evangelism.

Information: Speculator Chamber of Commerce | Box 184X, Elm Lake Rd., 12164 | 518/548–4521 | www2.telenet.net/community/adrkmts/.

Attractions
Sacandaga Pathways. Informational signs describe the flowers, trees, and foliage along this 1-mi walk beside the Kunjamuk River. There is also a picnic area. | Rte. 30 N, at the city park | 518/548–4521 | Free | Closed Dec.–Mar.

ON THE CALENDAR
FEB.: *Annual Big East Snow Cross Championship.* Snowmobile races are held on trails in Piseco, 8 mi from Speculator. Anyone with a snowmobile can enter. | 518/548–4521.

Dining
Zak's Waterfront. Contemporary. This restaurant with a mildly nautical theme has a small back deck and game room for the kids. The dishes are imaginative, with influences that range from Italian to Mexican to Cajun. Try the prime-rib bracciole, stuffed with black wild rice, fresh herbs, and mozzarella cheese, or the paella of chicken, sausage, shrimp, scallops, clams, and mussels. | 306 Woods Hollow Rd., Mayfield | 518/883–8351 | $15–$20 | D, MC, V.

Lodging
Cedarhurst Motor Lodge. This motor lodge is convenient to winter and summer recreation. It's about 500 ft from the public beach at Lake Pleasant and a mile from the Oak Mt. Ski Center. The property adjoins a network of snowmobile trails. Picnic area. Cable TV. | Rtes. 8 and 30 | 518/548–6064 or 518/548–8427 | lodge@klink.net | www.cedarhurstmotor-lodgespeculator.com/ | 10 rooms | $45–$65 | AE, D, DC, MC, V.

SPRING VALLEY

(Nearby towns also listed: Nyack, Piermont, Stony Point, Suffern, Tarrytown)

This Suburban Rockland County town of 20,000 is near the Palisades Interstate Parkway, surrounded by lush green hillsides. Spring Valley is a harmonious mix of the old and the new: modern businesses, shopping malls, delightful boutiques, and notable restaurants are near lovely parks and historic buildings.

Information: Rockland County Office of Tourism | 3 Main St., Nyack, 10960 | 845/353–5533 | www.rockland.org. **Nyack Department of Tourism** | 10 Piermont Ave., Nyack, 10960 | 845/638–5800.

Attractions
Historical Society of Rockland County. Features exhibits documenting the history of the area. | 20 Zukor Rd., New City | 845/634–9629 | fax 914/534–8690 | $4 | Tues.–Sun. 1–5.

ON THE CALENDAR

SEPT.: *Annual Street Fair.* Vendors of arts and crafts, jewelry, clothing, and food fill downtown Spring Valley. You can participate in games, or dance to a live band. | 845/426–3897.

Dining

El Bandido Mexican Restaurant. Mexican. Authentic Mexican food is the fare at this brightly colored, festive restaurant. Specialties include chicken, beef, or bean enchiladas and burritos, served with rice and beans. | 196 E. Rte. 59 | 845/425–6622 | Reservations not accepted | $11–$21 | AE, D, DC, MC, V.

Lodging

Hilton Pearl River. This sumptuously grand hotel offers a taste of France nestled in 17 picturesque acres. It is built along the edge of the Blue Hill Golf Course, 45 min from Newark and La Guardia International Airports. Elegantly decorated, the lobby has a grand piano, traditional hearth fireplace, and overstuffed chairs. Restaurant, bar (with entertainment). In-room data ports, refrigerators, cable TV. Pool. Hot tub. Exercise equipment. Laundry facilities. Business services. | 500 Veterans Memorial Dr., Pearl River | 845/735–9000 | fax 845/735–9005 | www.hilton.com | 150 rooms | $139–$189 | AE, D, DC, MC, V.

Nanuet Inn. Located less than 2 mi outside of Spring Valley and just a few hundred yards off I–87 at exit 14. Cable TV, room phones. Pool. Laundry facilities. Pets allowed. | 260 W. Rte. 59, Nanuet | 845/623–0600 | 120 rooms | $125 | AE, D, DC, MC, V.

Susse Chalet. This pleasant lodging offers affordable rates 8 mi from White Plains and 20 mi from New York City. Complimentary Continental breakfast. Cable TV. Pool. Laundry facilities. | 100 Spring Valley Marketplace | 914/426–2000 | fax 845/426–2008 | 105 rooms | $70–$77 | AE, D, DC, MC, V.

STAMFORD

MAP 3, J7

(Nearby towns also listed: Delhi, Oneonta, Roxbury, Windham)

A congenial town in the heart of the Catskills, Stamford is known for its mountain air, old boardinghouses, and crafted-wood products. Known as the "Queen of the Catskills" at the height of the resort era of late 19th and early 20th centuries, Stamford was the home to nearly 40 hotels, many of which still stand today. It lies near Scotch Ski at the crossroads of Routes 10 and 23.

Information: **Stamford New York Chamber of Commerce** | Box 166, 12167-0166 | 607/652–3673 | stmfrdcoc@aol.com.

Attractions

Lansing Manor. A restored manor house and estate offers a glimpse of life in a mid-19th century Dutch immigrant household. It's 40 mi southwest of Albany on the Schoharie Creek in the northern Catskill Mountains. | Rte. 30, North Blenheim | 518/827–6121 or 800/724–0309 | Free | May–Oct. daily 10–5.

Mine Kill State Park. Picnic, hike, swim, or hit the nature trails here 20 min northeast of Stamford. In winter, you can cross-country ski or ride a snowmobile. | Rte. 30, North Blenheim | 518/827–6111 | Free | Daily.

Zadock Pratt Museum. Pratt's restored homesite, filled with antiques and memorabilia, shows what life was like in the 1850s. Pratt was a talented entrepreneur who began as a harness maker and tanner, became a community leader, and served in the state and federal governments. | Main St. (Rte. 23), Prattsville | 518/299–3395 | www.prattmuseum.com | Free | May–Oct., Wed.–Sun. 1–4.

Pratt's Rocks. Local entrepreneur Zadock Pratt himself had this relief carved. The Civil War monument is dedicated to his son, George Pratt. Hike to see the mountainside carvings of Pratt, his son, and his favorite horse on the cliff face. | Main St., Rte. 23 | 518/299–3395 | Free.

ON THE CALENDAR
OCT.: *Scarecrow Festival.* Hundreds of people compete to build the best scarecrow. Corn stalks and ribbons are placed throughout the downtown area while vendors pile into the town green. | 800/652–7869.

Dining
John's Tavern and Restaurant. American. The moose head mounted above the bar completes the rustic decor here. Traditional fare includes burgers, sub sandwiches, rack of lamb, and lobster tails. | 87 Main St. | 607/652–7389 | $4–$21 | No credit cards.

Lodging
Belvedere Country Inn. This old-fashioned inn has L-shaped suites with three beds, and standard rooms with one or two double beds. The public pool is less than 1 mi down the road and skiing, golf, hiking, and bike trails are nearby. Restaurant, bar (with entertainment), picnic area. No air-conditioning. No TV in some rooms. No pets. | 10 Academy St. | 607/652–6121 | fax 607/652–6121 | belsusan@yahoo.com | 12 rooms, 12 suites | $40–$60 | AE, D, MC, V.

STONY BROOK

MAP 3, D2

(Nearby towns also listed: Port Jefferson, Smithtown)

Stony Brook is one of the most historic and picturesque Long Island villages along the north shore's Heritage Trail. In Revolutionary times, Washington's spy ring operated in the area and its gristmill was regularly visited by British soldiers for supplies.

The attractive downtown area was the country's first planned business center. It consists of approximately 30 Colonial-style shops guarded by old-fashioned street lamps that surround a small park overlooking the picturesque harbor.

Information: **Greater Port Jefferson Chamber of Commerce** | 118 W. Broadway, Port Jefferson, 11777 | 631/473–1414.

Attractions
Museums at Stony Brook. This group of museums includes the History Museum, which depicts interior design from the late 1600s through the 1930s; the Carriage Museum, displaying 100 horse-drawn carriages; and the Art Museum, which houses a collection of works by Long Island artist William Sidney Mount. | Main St. and Rte. 25A | 631/751–0066 | www.museumsatstonybrook.org | $4 | Jan.–June and Sept.–Nov., Wed.–Sat. 10–5, Sun. noon–5; July–Aug., Mon.–Sat. 10–5, Sun. noon–5.

State University of New York at Stony Brook. The campus has been recognized as one of America's top three public research universities. Its hospital has been ranked one of the 100 best and is a major teaching facility. The campus is home to Staller Center for the Arts. | 100 Nichols Rd. | 631/689–6000 | Free | Daily.

Staller Center for the Arts. Located on the campus of the State University of New York at Stony Brook, this is the county's primary performing arts center and is active year-round. Many of its productions are by student groups. | 100 Nichols Rd. | 631/632–7230 or 631/632–7235 | Call for schedule | www.stallercenter.com.

JUNE, OCT.: *Kids Day.* The day includes games, refreshments, ice cream, and pony rides. | 631/689–8172.

OCT.: *Scarecrow Competition and Halloween Celebration.* Contestants display scarecrows near Village Center shops; the public gets to vote for winners. | 631/751–2244.

Dining

Country House. American. This big, white Victorian set on a hill at the entrance of Stonybrook Village was built in 1710. The restaurant is listed with two historical societies, and includes many of the building's original 12-pane windows. There's a nice lounge and a beautiful large fireplace that was once used as an oven. Try the special aged-steak menu, the Long Island duck with apple walnut and sausage stuffing, or the lobster royale (diced lobster meat stuffed into the cleaned shell with shrimp and scallops and served with risotto). | Rte. 25A and Main St. | 631/751–3332 | Reservations essential for dinner | $25–$35 | AE, DC, MC, V.

Lotus East. Chinese. This restaurant is elegant and gracious; the Chinese motif is accented by white tablecloths and burgundy napkins. Try General Tso's chicken, tangerine beef, and raspberry shrimp or chicken. | 416 N. Country Rd., St. James | 631/862–6030 | $8–$18 | AE, DC, MC, V.

Mirabelle. French. Terrific reviews have not spoiled this elegant yet cozy little farmhouse restaurant known for creative preparation of classic dishes. Try the duck in two courses and the ginger almond tart. Homemade pastas and desserts, including ice cream. Open-air dining on patio. | 404 N. Country Rd., St. James | 631/584–5999 | Reservations essential | Closed Mon. No lunch weekends | $25–$40 | AE, D, DC, MC, V.

Three Village Inn. American. Built in 1751, this historic building near the harbor retains much of its original design and decor. The staff dress in colonial costume and are especially festive around the holidays. Specialties include roast prime ribs of beef, New England seafood pie, and basil-crusted salmon fillet. Kids' menu. Sunday brunch. | 150 Main St. | 613/751–0555 | www.threevillageinn.com | Breakfast also available | $25–$36 | AE, DC, MC, V.

Lodging

Miss Scarlet's Bed and Breakfast. French Provincial and English Country antiques fill this cottage-style bed-and-breakfast, about 3 mi east of Stony Brook. In-room data ports, some refrigerators, cable TV, some in-room in-room VCRs. No pets. No kids ages 3–11. No smoking. | 305 California Ave., Port Jefferson | 631/928–5064 | fax 631/928–3067 | www.miss-scarletts.com | 3 rooms | $98–$135 | AE, MC, V.

Three Village Inn. You can stay in the main white clapboard house or in one of the small outlying private cottages that overlook Stony Brook Harbor. Each room has been decorated in Laura Ashley patterns, and has a fireplace and a brick patio. Restaurant, bar, picnic area. Cable TV. Business services. | 150 Main St. | 631/751–0555 | fax 631/751–0593 | inn3vi@aol.com | www.threevillageinn.com | 26 rooms, 6 cottages | $139–$184 | AE, DC, MC, V.

STONY POINT

MAP 3, B1

(Nearby towns also listed: Nyack, Piermont, Spring Valley, Suffern, Tarrytown)

Set above the Hudson River, this picturesque Rockland County town of 13,000 has a hilly landscape dotted with boutiques and eateries. Local attractions include the Hudson's oldest lighthouse and Stony Point Battlefield, where General "Mad Anthony" Wayne defeated British troops.

Information: Rockland County Office of Tourism | 3 Main St., Nyack, 10960 | 845/353–5533 | www.rockland.org.

Attractions

Bear Mountain State Park. The portion of the park that lies in Stony Point has lakes that you can swim in during summer and ice-skate on in winter. Other park areas include nature, hiking, and biking trails, boat rentals, cross-country skiing, a dock on the Hudson for mooring small craft, lake and river fishing access, swimming, a zoo, museum, playground, and ski jumps. | Rte. 9 W, Bear Mountain | 845/786–2701 | www.nysparks.state.ny.us | Free; parking $6 | Daily 8 AM–dusk.

Stony Point Battlefield State Historic Site. The battlefield, 25 mi north of Manhattan, is the only Revolutionary War battleground in Rockland County. It is also the home of the oldest lighthouse on the Hudson River, which was restored in 1995. | Park Rd. off Rte. 9 W | 845/786–2521 | www.lhric.org/spbattle/spbattle.htm | Free | Mid-Apr.–Oct., Wed.–Sat. 10–5, Sun. 1–5.

ON THE CALENDAR

JULY: *Wayne Day Carnival.* The Stony Point Fire Department's annual fund-raiser celebrates General Wayne's Revolutionary War victory over the British with rides, games, and music. | 845/786–3386.

Dining

Fiesta Cancun. Mexican. Try the chicken and beef fajitas at this family-owned Mexican joint near the marina. | 90 S. Liberty Dr. | 845/429–9363 | $11–$18 | AE, D, MC, V.

Lodging

Stony Point Motel. Located 3 mi from the Palisades Parkway and about 10 mi from restaurants and shops, this motel has dinettes in each room. Some kitchenettes. No pets. | 87 S. Liberty Dr. | 845/942–0681 | 32 rooms | $45–$60 | AE, D, MC, V.

SUFFERN

MAP 4, C3

(Nearby towns also listed: Nyack, Piermont, Spring Valley, Stony Point, Tarrytown)

This little town is the gateway to the foothills of the Catskills. Situated in Rockland County near the New Jersey border, Suffern's tree-lined residential streets include some lovely Victorian homes from the 1800s. Downtown bustles with boutiques, restaurants, and offices. Although it is only about 30 min from New York City, it feels a million miles away.

Information: Suffern Chamber of Commerce | Box 291, 10901 | 845/357–8424. **Rockland County Office of Tourism** | 3 Main St., Nyack, 10960 | 845/353–5533 | www.rockland.org.

Attractions

Suffern Village Museum. View an ever-expanding exhibit of Suffern artifacts and photographs, dating from the 17th century up through World War II. Items on display include Native American tools, Revolutionary War pieces, and artifacts relating to the village's founder, John Suffern. | 61 Washington Ave. | 845/357–3667 | Free | Sun. 2–4 except holiday weekends, or by appointment; closed July and Aug.

ON THE CALENDAR

JUNE, AUG., SEPT.: *Annual Street Fair.* The downtown business district shuts down for this 1-day sale, and 150 antiques, clothing, and jewelry vendors from all over the state set up their wares. There's also clowns, face painting, and a Dixieland band. | 845/357–8424.

Dining

Carmichael's Ristorante. Italian. This stylish restaurant has a clublike ambience and special cigar nights. It's known for innovative pasta, seafood, and chicken dishes. Live music Friday. | 150 Lafayette Ave. | 845/369–0100 | No lunch Sun. | $20–$30 | AE, DC, MC, V.

Lodging

Holiday Inn. This hotel is at the crossroads between New York City and the Catskill Mountains, 15 mi from the historic Hudson Valley. The hotel sits just off the New York State Thruway (I–87/287) at exit 14B. Restaurant, bar, room service. In-room data ports, some kitchenettes (in suites), in-room hot tubs, cable TV. Pool. Hot tub, sauna. Exercise equipment. Video games. Laundry facilities. Business services. | 3 Executive Blvd. | 845/357–4800 | fax 845/368–0471 | 243 rooms | $120 | AE, D, DC, MC, V.

Sheraton Crossroads Hotel. Party all night at the in-house dance club of this 22-floor hotel. It's 5 mi south of Suffern in Mahwah, New Jersey, and less than 1 mi from the New York State Thruway (I–87). 2 restaurants, bar, complimentary Continental breakfast, room service. In-room data ports, cable TV. Pool. Sauna. 2 tennis courts. Health club. Shop. Pets allowed. | 1 International Blvd., Mahwah, NJ | 201/529–1660 | fax 201/529–4709 | www.starwood.com | 221 rooms, 4 suites | $129–$179 | AE, D, DC, MC, V.

Wellesley Inn. This inn about 2 mi from the center of Suffern offers very basic rooms and limited services. It is near I–87 and I–287. Complimentary Continental breakfast. Microwaves, cable TV. Laundry services. Business services. Some pets allowed. | 17 N. Airmont Rd. | 845/368–1900 | fax 845/368–1927 | 95 rooms | $89–$99 | AE, D, DC, MC, V.

SYOSSET

MAP 3, C2

(Nearby towns also listed: Cold Spring Harbor, Glen Cove, Huntington, Jericho, Oyster Bay, Plainview/Old Bethpage)

The Matinecock Indians sold this area in 1648 to a Welsh settler, Robert Williams, but the land was not cleared for farming for another 100 years, when a few Dutch families formed a small farming community there. Later, when Theodore Roosevelt wanted to avoid being noticed, he would take the train to Syosset instead of Oyster Bay and ride his horse home through the cover of the Syosset woods.

Today, pines and other trees still line its attractive streets and backroads, and the town may have gotten its name from an Indian word, "suwasset," meaning "place in the pines." A lovely residential community sitting between Woodbury and Muttontown, Syosset has maintained a good deal of its early charm. A few shopping areas dot its landscape, including a main shopping district on Jackson Avenue with restaurants and the local train station.

Information: **Syosset Chamber of Commerce** | c/o Owen Photography, 45 Jackson Ave., 11791 | 631/364–6650 | fax 631/351–8276 | mail@syossetchamber.com | www.syossetchamber.com.

Attractions

Syosset United Artists Cinema. This cinema is actually in Woodbury. It is the last single-screen theater with a balcony in Nassau County. | 7500 Jericho Tpk., Woodbury | 631/364–0700 | $8.

Wetlands "Discovery" Cruises. The Ward Melville Heritage Organization runs these cruises. The cruise on the 35-passenger pontoon boat *Discovery* is joined by a naturalist from the State University of New York at Stony Brook, who educates passengers on the wetlands. |

Depart from Boatworks, off Shore Rd. | 631/751–2244 | www.wardmelvilleheritage.org | $15 | Hrs vary depending on season and tides. Closed Nov.–Apr.

ON THE CALENDAR
DEC.: *Holiday Lighting Ceremony*. This celebration in downtown Syosset includes entertainment by the high-school choir and a local dance group, and a countdown to the menorah and Christmas tree lighting. | 631/423–6100.

Dining
Nostalgia Diner. American. Mahogany furniture and loveseat booths make this place comfortable. Try the Texas wrap, a fajita filled with sliced steak and sautéed mushrooms, onions, and peppers. Also try the homemade pies. Breakfast served all day. | 407 Jericho Tpk. | 516/364–1977 | Breakfast also available | $7–$21 | AE, D, MC, V.

Lodging
Best Western Woodbury Inn. This Best Western is 1 mi north of the Long Island Expressway and less than 2 mi east of Syosset, in Woodbury. Complimentary Continental breakfast. In-room data ports, some kitchenettes, some microwaves, some refrigerators, some in-room hot tubs, cable TV, in-room VCRs. Pool. No pets. | 7940 Jericho Tpk., Woodbury | 516/921–6900 | fax 516/921–6908 | www.bestwestern.com/woodburyinn | 85 rooms | $89–$99 | AE, D, DC, MC, V.

SYRACUSE

MAP 3, G6

(Nearby towns also listed: Auburn, Canastota, Cazenovia, Fulton, Liverpool, Oneida, Rome, Skaneateles)

Founded in 1789, today Syracuse is the largest city in Leatherstocking Country. Home to Syracuse University and its sports venue Carrier Dome, Syracuse also hosts the annual two-week State Fair, a showcase for New York's agriculture. The city is in the geographic center of New York State, at the intersection of Interstate 81 and the Thruway (Interstate 90). Syracuse also has Le Moyne College, Onondaga Community College, the State College of Forestry, a symphony orchestra, zoo, and art and historical museums.

Information: Greater Syracuse Chamber of Commerce | 572 S. Salina St., 13202 | 315/470–1800.

Attractions
Beaver Lake Nature Center. This area has a nature preserve, lake, trails, and exhibits. | 8477 E. Mud Lake Rd., Baldwinsville | 315/638–2519 | $1 per vehicle | Daily.

Burnet Park Zoo. Visit more than 1,000 animals and birds, many in re-created habitats. | 1 Conservation Pl. | 315/435–8511 | $5 | Daily 8–sunset.

Erie Canal Museum and Syracuse Urban Cultural Park Visitors Center. This museum illustrates Erie Canal and Syracuse history. | 318 Erie Blvd. E | 315/471–0593 | Free | Daily 10–5.

Everson Museum of Art. A collection of American art in various media is displayed. There is also a children's gallery and a café. | 401 Harrison St. | 315/474–6064 | www.everson.org | $2 | Tues.–Fri. and Sun. noon–5, Sat. 10–5; first Thurs. of each month noon–7:30 (excluding July, Dec.).

Green Lakes State Park. This is a state-run campground with 137 sites, lakes for swimming, a concession stand, boat rentals, and hiking trails. It's 10 mi east of Syracuse. | Rte. 5 in Fayetteville | 315/637–6111 or 800/456–CAMP (reservations) | $6 per vehicle | May–Oct., daily.

International Mask and Puppet Museum. Masks and puppets of different cultures and areas of the world are displayed at this museum. Exhibits change bimonthly. The museum also has a hands-on art studio, puppeteer performances, and an international craft gift shop. | 518 Prospect Ave. | 315/476–0466 | fax 315/677–3263 | www.syr.edu/~pbarfoot | $3 | Wed. 2–5, Sat. 10–3.

Landmark Theatre. This vintage, ornate theater hosts touring Broadway shows, classic films, and concerts. | 362 S. Salina St. | 315/475–7979 | Weekdays 10–5, and by appointment.

Museum of Science and Technology. Get your senses going by taking a simulator ride that imitates downhill skiing or a roller coaster. You can also learn about stars in the planetarium or watch an IMAX film. | 500 S. Franklin St. | 315/425–9068 | fax 315/425–9072 | $5; IMAX $9.75 | Tues.–Sun. 11–5 and Mon. holidays.

Onondaga Historical Association Museum. Here you'll find county historical exhibits, maps, paintings, photos, and the Greater Syracuse Sports Hall of Fame. | 321 Montgomery St. | 315/428–1864 | Tues.–Sat. noon–4.

Syracuse University. This major university was founded in 1870 as a private, coeducational institution and today offers undergraduate and graduate programs to more than 18,000 undergraduate and graduate students, as well as big-time sports. The University offers several dozen courses of study including performing arts, nursing, law, and architecture. | University Ave. at University Pl. | 315/443–1870 | www.syr.edu | Free | Daily.

The **Carrier Dome** is the university's venue for football and basketball games. | 900 Irving Ave. | 315/443–2121 or 888/DOMETIX | www.carrierdome.syr.edu | Call for schedule; tours by appointment.

ON THE CALENDAR

JUNE: *Balloon Festival.* Held the second weekend in June at the Jamesville Beach Park, this festival includes 40 hot-air balloons, entertainment, food, and crafts. | 315/435–5252 or 800/234–4SYR.

JULY: *Open-air concerts.* The Syracuse Symphony performs in various venues. | 315/424–8222.

AUG.: *Scottish Games.* Join in traditional Scottish games, and enjoy costumes and entertainment. | 315/252–5676, 315/470–1910, or 800/234–4SYR.

AUG.–SEPT.: *New York State Fair.* This is a massive 2-wk showcase for the state's agriculture, and also has vendors, entertainment, and a midway. | 315/487–7111.

SEPT.: *Golden Harvest Festival.* This weekend-long event at the Beaver Lake Nature Center includes music and crafts. | 315/638–2519.

SEPT.: *Syracuse International Air Show.* Planes are everywhere—on the ground and in the air—at the Syracuse Hancock Airport. | 315/454–3263.

SEPT.–MAY: *Syracuse Stage.* A half dozen plays are performed in a season. Admission is $15–$38. | 315/443–3275.

DEC.: *Lights on the Lake.* This drive-through light show at Onondaga Lake Park features extensive holiday displays. | 315/451–PARK or 315/453–6712.

Dining

Brooklyn Pickle. Delicatessen. This downtown, all-American deli has oversize sandwiches, hearty soups, and generous salads. Every paper-wrapped sandwich arrives topped with tangy pickle chips. Order at the counter, then sit at a booth or a table. No smoking. | 2222 Burnet Ave. | 315/463–1851 | Breakfast also available; closed Sun. | $6–$10 | No credit cards.

Captain Ahab's. Seafood. Enjoy casual dining in rooms with fish tanks, plants, and nautical items. The menu has steaks, prime rib, and extensive seafood selections. There is dining on the patio in an enclosed garden. Salad bar. Kids' menu. | 3449 Erie Blvd. E | 315/446–3272 | No lunch Sat. | $16–$35 | AE, D, DC, MC, V.

Coleman's. Irish. Originally opened in 1933 after the repeal of Prohibition, this restaurant has two main entrances: a regular heavy oak door; and a miniature replica for the "wee people who come directly from Ireland and do not have to pass through immigration because the authorities do not believe the truth of legend." Inside there is dark oak woodwork, multihued stained glass, and detailed appointments. The traditional Irish menu includes Guinness beef stew and pork Wellington. Entertainment most Fridays and Saturdays. Kids' menu. There is also patio dining in a casual setting. | 100 S. Lowell Ave. | 315/476–1933 | www.colemansirishpub.com | $35–$50 | AE, D, DC, MC, V.

Fred Grimaldi's Chop House. Continental. This chop house has been serving steak and seafood since 1989. Kids' menu. | 6400 Yorktown Cir., East Syracuse | 315/437–1461 | No lunch weekends | $18–$30 | AE, D, DC, MC, V.

Glen Loch Mill. Continental. This restaurant has a rustic feel, and you can eat outside on a deck overlooking a brook and a working waterwheel. Dishes include pasta primavera, filet mignon, oven-roasted Long Island duckling, and shrimp scampi. Raw bar. Dinner theater Fridays and Saturdays in winter. Kids' menu. Sunday brunch. | 4626 North St., Jamesville (near Fayetteville) | 315/469–6969 | Closed Mon. No lunch Mon.–Sat. | $18–$25 | MC, V.

Green Gate Inn. American. This 1861 Victorian house has a cupola on top and two separate dining areas inside. Both are decorated in period style, and open for a casual bite of tavern fare for lunch or for a more formal evening meal. The menu includes steaks, seafood and veal dishes, and daily specials such as chicken and biscuit, beer-battered haddock, and prime rib. Kids' menu. Sunday brunch. | 2 Genesee St., Camillus | 315/672–9276 | No lunch Sat. | $13–$30 | AE, D, MC, V.

Inn Between. Continental. This spacious 19th-century house has an herb garden from which the kitchen gets its seasonings. Try the shrimp, lobster, and scallops served in a phyllo shell, or grilled tenderloin medallions topped with lobster, crab meat, asparagus, and béarnaise sauce. | 2290 W. Genesee Tpk., Camillus | 315/672–3166 | www.inn-between.com | Closed Mon. No lunch | $17–$20 | AE, MC, V.

Pascale's. Contemporary. Much of the food here is prepared in the wood-burning grill. Try the Asian chicken or the lobster. The restaurant has an airy setting and original artwork. | 204 W. Fayette St. | 315/471–3040 | Closed Sun. No lunch Mon., Sat. | $18–$40 | AE, DC, MC, V.

Pastabilities. Continental. It's serve-yourself cafeteria-style lunch at this downtown Syracuse restaurant that attracts a bohemian and university crowd. Dinner is full service, and there's always fresh pasta with unique sauces. You can eat outside on the sidewalk or in the back courtyard. | 311 S. Franklin St. | 315/474–1153 | No lunch weekends | $14–$24 | AE, D, DC, MC, V.

Phoebe's Garden Cafe. American. You can sit down to bistro-style dining in the foliage-filled sunroom out back, or take in a more casual atmosphere in the front dining room with its large windows overlooking the sidewalk. Both parts of the restaurant serve from the same menu. Try the London broil, or the scrod Christopher. Don't skip the crème brûlée. Sunday brunch. | 900 E. Genesee St. | 315/475–5154 | $16–$25 | AE, DC, MC, V.

Plainville Farms. American. Eat in a country setting in the town of Cicero, 7 mi north of Syracuse's center, amid a hydroponic (grown in water, without soil) horticulture display. The specialty here is turkey and more turkey. Try the roast turkey dinner and the turkey noodle soup. (There's also some fish on the menu.) Don't skip the homemade chocolate chip cookies and deep-dish apple pie. Kids' menu. No smoking. | 8450 Brewerton Rd., Cicero | 315/699–3852 | $10–$12 | D, MC, V.

Spinning Wheel Restaurant. Steak/Seafood. Family-owned and operated, the Spinning Wheel serves a mean prime rib and a seafood platter overflowing with shrimp, scallops, clam strips, and haddock. Everything comes with soup, salad, potato or pasta, and a loaf of bread with homemade butter. Dine indoors or on the enclosed deck. | 7384 Thompson Rd., North Syracuse | 315/458–3222 | $8–$13 | AE, D, DC, MC, V.

Top O' the Hill. Italian. Fine dining and banquet facilities are available in this chalet-style building. Local produce is used to provide upscale dining amid ski-lodge surroundings.

SYRACUSE

INTRO
ATTRACTIONS
DINING
LODGING

Try the hot seafood antipasto and the veal parmigiana. Entertainment Friday. | 5633 W. Genesee St., Camillus | 315/488–2400 | Closed Mon. No dinner Sun. | $10–$28 | AE, D, DC, MC, V.

Treehaven Cafe. American. Eat in or take out at the Treehaven, whose menu ranges from omelets and bagels to gourmet sandwiches with a full salad bar. Try the roast beef roaster: a roast beef sandwich topped with apple slices, spinach leaves, bacon, red onion, roasted red peppers, cheddar cheese, and a horseradish glaze. | 232 Harrison St. | 315/476–2980 | fax 315/476–2980 | Breakfast also available; closed weekends; no dinner | $3–$6 | No credit cards.

Twin Trees. Italian. The Twin Trees legacy began in 1956, when Don Ross, Sr., opened the original Twin Trees restaurant here. In addition to serving what's been voted the best pizza in Central New York, Twin Trees has prime rib and seafood entrées. Kids' menu. | 1100 Avery Ave. | 315/468–0622 | No lunch | $8–$20 | AE, D, DC, MC, V.

Lodging

Bed and Breakfast Wellington. This 1914 home has hardwood floors, two Mercer tile fireplaces, oriental rugs, and lots of antiques. A gourmet chef serves a several-course breakfast on weekends. Located 1 mi north of downtown, 3 mi south of Syracuse Airport, and 1 mi east of the Carousel Center Mall. Dining room, complimentary breakfast. In-room data ports, some microwaves, cable TV, in-room VCRs. Library. Free parking. No pets. No smoking. | 707 Danforth St. | 315/474–3641 | fax 315/474–2557 | innkeepers@bbwellington.com | www.bbwellington.com/ | 5 rooms | $75–$125 | AE, D, DC, MC, V.

Best Western–Marshall Manor. This chain is south of Syracuse, near I–81. It's convenient to area attractions, including Toggenburg Ski Center and Syracuse University. The accommodations are basic, but comfortable. Restaurant, bar. Cable TV. Business services. | Rte. 80, Tully | 315/696–6061 | fax 315/696–6406 | 44 rooms | $59 | AE, D, DC, MC, V.

Best Western Syracuse Airport Inn. Located next to Syracuse Airport, this hotel has standard rooms and suites. Restaurant, bar, complimentary Continental breakfast. Cable TV. Pool. Airport shuttle. No pets. | Syracuse Airport | 315/455–7362 | fax 315/455–6840 | www.bestwestern.com | 95 rooms | $78 | AE, D, DC, MC, V.

Cambridge Inn. Kids will love the outdoor minizoo here, with its peacocks, ostriches, pygmy goats, deer, and pheasants. Located 8 mi west of Syracuse in Camillus. Picnic area, complimentary Continental breakfast. Refrigerators. Cable TV. Pets allowed. | 2382 W. Genesee Tpk., Rte. 5 W, Camillus | 315/672–3022 | 10 rooms | $79–$89 | AE, D, MC, V.

Comfort Inn. This four-story motel near the I–90 and I–690 junction is just west of Syracuse. There's a restaurant across from the parking lot. Complimentary Continental breakfast. Exercise room. Video games. Business services. | 7010 Interstate Island Rd. | 315/453–0045 | fax 315/453–3689 | 109 rooms | $89–$99 | AE, D, DC, MC, V.

Courtyard by Marriott. This three-story hotel is approximately 9 mi from Syracuse University and 25 mi from Turning Stone Casino. A number of golf courses are about 5–20 mi away. The rooms here are basic unadorned chain-hotel style. Restaurant. In-room data ports, refrigerators (in suites), cable TV. Pool. Hot tub. Exercise equipment. Laundry facilities. Business services. | 6415 Yorktown Cir., East Syracuse | 315/432–0300 | fax 315/432–9950 | 137 rooms, 12 suites | $99 rooms, $120 suites | AE, D, DC, MC, V.

Craftsman Inn. Appropriately named, this inn has Arts and Crafts– and Mission-style furniture. Receive 10% off entrées and a complimentary glass of house wine or draft beer at the restaurant on weeknights. Located 3 mi east of Syracuse. Restaurant, bar, complimentary Continental breakfast. In-room data ports, some microwaves, some refrigerators, some in-room hot tubs, cable TV. Gym. Laundry service. No pets. No smoking. | 7300 E. Genesee St., Fayetteville | 315/637–8000 | fax 315/637–2440 | craftman@dreamscape.com | www.someplacesdifferent.com/craftsman.htm | 65 rooms, 25 suites in 2 buildings | $84–$89 rooms, $125–$150 suites | AE, D, DC, MC, V.

Cresthill Suites. Opened in 2000, this motel has a convenience store where you can get a complimentary movie rental and a business center with free access to computers and fax machines. Studio suites have two beds, kitchenettes, and living areas with sofas and TVs. Complimentary Continental breakfast. In-room data ports, kitchenettes, microwaves, refrigerators, cable TV, in-room VCRs (and movies). Pool. Gym. Shops. Laundry facilities. Business services. | 6410 New Venture Gear Dr., East Syracuse | 315/432–5595 | fax 315/432–5686 | www.cresthillsuites.com | 86 suites | $94–$149 | AE, MC, V.

Dickenson House on James. This upscale 1924 English Tudor inn sits on a stretch of opulent homes known as Millionaire's Row, about 2 mi east of downtown Syracuse. Each room has a theme ranging from Cape Cod/Nantucket to Scottish. The loft suite has vaulted ceilings, a mahogany kitchen, fireplace, and marble bath. Complimentary breakfast. In-room data ports, cable TV. Library. No pets. No smoking. | 1504 James St. | 315/423–4777 | fax 315/425–1965 | www.dickensonhouse.com | 4 rooms, 1 suite | $99–$120 rooms, $350 suite | AE, D, MC, V.

Econo Lodge. Located approximately 4 mi from downtown Syracuse, this roadside lodge offers affordable rooms near exits for both I–90 and I–81. There are also five restaurants within walking distance. Complimentary Continental breakfast. In-room data ports, cable TV. Business services. Some pets allowed. | 401 7th North St., Liverpool | 315/451–6000 | fax 315/451–0193 | 83 rooms | $49–$79 | AE, D, DC, MC, V.

Embassy Suites. All the rooms in this quiet suburban five-story suite hotel overlook a garden atrium, which includes waterfalls and streams. It's close to downtown Syracuse. Restaurant, bar, complimentary breakfast. In-room data ports, kitchenettes, cable TV. Pool. Exercise equipment. Laundry facilities. Business services. Some pets allowed. | 6646 Old Collamer Rd., East Syracuse | 315/446–3200 | fax 315/437–3302 | 215 suites | $139 | AE, D, DC, MC, V.

Fairfield Inn by Marriott. Nestled in between two other Marriotts, this three-story hotel is convenient to restaurants and attractions, including golf courses, Syracuse University, and the Burnet Park Zoo. Complimentary Continental breakfast. In-room data ports, cable TV. Pool. Laundry facilities. Business services. | 6611 Old Collamer Rd., East Syracuse | 315/432–9333 | 135 rooms | $65 | AE, D, DC, MC, V.

Golden Tulip Genesee Inn Hotel. You'll be minutes from downtown Syracuse and Syracuse University at this modern hotel with huge arching windows. Rooms have Mission-style furniture. Restaurant, bar, room service. In-room data ports, cable TV. Business services. Pets allowed. | 1060 E. Genesee St. | 315/476–4212 or 800/365–HOME | fax 315/471–4663 | 96 rooms | $99 | AE, D, DC, MC, V.

Hampton Inn. Located in a major business and industrial section of the city, this four-story chain hotel has standard rooms and is convenient to many area restaurants and attractions. Complimentary Continental breakfast. In-room data ports, cable TV. Business services. | 6605 Old Collamer Rd., East Syracuse | 315/463–6443 | fax 315/432–1080 | 116 rooms | $84 | AE, D, DC, MC, V.

Holiday Inn at Carrier Circle. This two-story hotel is built on a hill, 10 min by car from downtown Syracuse, near Interstate 90, exit 35. The rooms are spacious. Restaurant, bar (with entertainment), room service. Cable TV. Pool. Hot tub. Exercise equipment. Business services. Some pets allowed. | 6555 Old Collamer Rd. S, East Syracuse | 315/437–2761 | fax 315/463–0028 | www.holiday-inn.com | 203 rooms | $109 | AE, D, DC, MC, V.

Holiday Inn at Farrell Road. Renovated in 1997, this two-story hotel sits near the intersection of I–90 and I–690, about 10 mi from Syracuse University. Restaurant, bar (with entertainment), room service. In-room data ports, cable TV. Pool. Exercise equipment. Business services. Pets allowed. | 100 Farrell Rd. | 315/457–8700 | fax 315/457–2379 | www.holiday-inn.com | 152 rooms | $149 | AE, D, DC, MC, V.

Holiday Inn at Four Points. This eight-floor Holiday Inn is just south of I–90 at exit 37 and was completely renovated in 1998. Restaurant, bar (with entertainment). In-room data ports, room service. Cable TV. Pool. Hot tub. Exercise equipment. Video games. Business services. Pets allowed. | 441 Electronics Pkwy., Liverpool | 315/457–1122 | fax 315/451–1269 | www.holiday-inn.com | 280 rooms | $120 | AE, D, DC, MC, V.

John Milton Inn. Right off the Thruway at exit 35, this two-story motel sits northeast of Syracuse, near the airport. Complimentary Continental breakfast. Cable TV. Business services. Pets allowed. | 6578 Thompson Rd. | 315/463–8555 or 800/352–1061 | fax 315/432–9240 | 54 rooms | $40–$50 | AE, D, DC, MC, V.

Knights Inn. Stay here for spacious rooms just 5 mi from Syracuse University. Complimentary Continental breakfast. Some kitchenettes, cable TV. Business services. Some pets allowed. | 430 Electronics Pkwy., Liverpool | 315/453–6330 or 800/843–5644 | fax 315/457–9240 | 82 rooms | $50 | AE, D, DC, MC, V.

Radisson Plaza Hotel Syracuse. Built in 1924, this downtown hotel is listed as an historic building, and the interior is done in keeping with the original era. The guest rooms however, are modern and spacious. Restaurants, 2 bars (with entertainment). In-room data ports, cable TV. Pool. Barbershop, beauty salon, hot tub. Exercise equipment. Shops. Business services. | 500 S. Warren St. | 315/422–5121 | fax 315/422–3440 | 487 rooms | $109 | AE, D, DC, MC, V.

Ramada Inn. This two-story building is north of the the city, about 15 min by car from downtown. Restaurant, bar, room service. Cable TV. Pool. Exercise equipment. Business services. | 1305 Buckley Rd., North Syracuse | 315/457–8670 | fax 315/457–8633 | 150 rooms | $109 | AE, D, DC, MC, V.

Red Roof Inn–Syracuse. You'll be close to the Syracuse State Fairgrounds here. Rooms are spacious and modern, and fast food is right outside your door. Cable TV. Business services. Pets allowed. | 6614 N. Thompson Rd. | 315/437–3309 | fax 315/437–7865 | www.redroof.com | 115 rooms | $60 | AE, D, DC, MC, V.

Residence Inn by Marriott. Built in 1991, this hotel is convenient to area attractions and dining. There are also several golf courses in the area and two restaurants within walking distance. All guest accommodations are suites, and there is an outdoor sports courtyard in the center of the hotel with a pool, tennis, basketball, and volleyball courts. Picnic area, complimentary Continental breakfast. Kitchenettes, cable TV. Pool. Hot tub. Tennis. Basketball, exercise equipment, volleyball. Laundry facilities. Business services. Pets allowed (fee). | 6420 Yorktown Cir., East Syracuse | 315/432–4488 | fax 315/432–1042 | 102 suites | $122 studio suites, $142 2–bedroom suites | AE, D, DC, MC, V.

Sheraton University Hotel and Conference Center. This high-rise, full-service hotel is adjacent to the main campus of Syracuse University. Restaurant, bar (with entertainment). In-room data ports, some refrigerators, cable TV. Pool. Hot tub. Exercise equipment. Business services. | 801 University Ave. | 315/475–3000 | fax 315/475–3311 | 231 rooms and 18 suites | $142 | AE, D, DC, MC, V.

Super 8. Renovated in 2000, this three-story building offers basic rooms less than 5 mi from Syracuse University and the downtown area. There are several restaurants within walking distance. Picnic area, complimentary Continental breakfast. In-room data ports, cable TV. Business services. | 421 N. 7th St., Liverpool | 315/451–8888 | fax 315/451–0043 | 99 rooms | $45–$65 | AE, D, DC, MC, V.

University Towers Hotel. This downtown high-rise near Syracuse University's main campus has basic rooms with the usual modular motel furnishings. It is 3 min by car from the Syracuse Mall. Restaurant, bar. Cable TV. Pool. Sauna. Video games. Business services. | 701 E. Genesee St. | 315/479–7000 | fax 315/472–2700 | 280 rooms | $79 | AE, D, DC, MC, V.

Western Ranch Motor Inn. The restaurant serves home-cooked meals at this hotel about 6 mi west of downtown Syracuse. Restaurant. Some refrigerators, cable TV, room phones. Laundry facilities. Pets allowed. | 1255 State Fair Blvd. | 315/457–9236 | fax 315/457–9236 | 42 rooms | $59–$89 | AE, D, MC, V.

Wyndham Syracuse. Located in an East Syracuse business district, this hotel sits in front of a row of restaurants ranging from McDonalds to fine dining. Restaurant, bar (with entertainment), room service. In-room data ports, some refrigerators, cable TV. Indoor-outdoor pool. Hot tub. Exercise equipment. Laundry facilities. Business services, airport shuttle. Pets allowed. | 6301 Rte. 298, East Syracuse | 315/432–0200 | fax 315/433–1210 | www.wyndham.com | 248 rooms, 2 suites | $139 rooms, $275 suites | AE, D, DC, MC, V.

TARRYTOWN

(Nearby towns also listed: Elmsford, Hartsdale, Hawthorne, Mamaroneck, New Rochelle, New York City, Nyack, Piermont, Rye, Scarsdale, White Plains, Yonkers)

Set on the banks of the majestic Hudson River, Tarrytown is a gorgeous spot with a rich artistic history. In the mid-1600s this Westchester County village was settled by the Dutch, who called it "Tarwe," which means "wheat." Filled with boutiques, antiques shops, art galleries, restaurants, bed-and-breakfasts, and beautiful area parks, Tarrytown is a popular tourist destination. The American writer Washington Irving, whose classic works include *Rip Van Winkle* and *The Legend of Sleepy Hollow* (a neighborhood of Tarrytown), lived here; his wonderful house, Sunnyside, is now a tourist attraction.

Information: Tarrytown/North Tarrytown Chamber of Commerce, Sleepy Hollow Chamber of Commerce, Tarrytown and Sleepy Hollow | 80 S. Broadway, 10591 | 914/631–1705 | fax 914/631–1512 | www.sleepyhollowchamber.com.

TARRYTOWN

INTRO
ATTRACTIONS
DINING
LODGING

Attractions

Kykuit. Situated on a hill surrounded by gardens and sculptures, the grounds of this estate run close to 400 acres. Home to four generation of Rockefellers, Kykuit has breathtaking views of the Hudson River, extensive stone terraces, formal gardens, and glorious fountains. It is adjacent to the Rockefeller State Park Reserve and accessible only by shuttle bus from Philipsburg Manor. (See listing below.) | 381 N. Broadway | 914/631–9491 | fax 914/631–0089 | www.hudsonvalley.org | $20 | Late Apr.–early Nov., by appointment only. Closed Tues.

Lyndhurst. Overlooking the Hudson River in Tarrytown, Lyndhurst is America's premier Gothic Revival mansion. Visitors are free to tour the mansion and stroll the 67 landscaped acres. It also includes a turn-of-the-20th-century bowling alley and an original child's play house, open for children to play in today. | 635 S. Broadway | 914/631–4481 | fax 914/631–5634 | www.lyndhurst.org | $9 | Mid-Apr.–Oct., Tues.–Sun. 10–5; Nov.–mid-Apr., weekends 10–4.

Old Dutch Church of Sleepy Hollow. Built in 1685, this church is the oldest church in New York State. It figures prominently in Washington Irving's *The Legend of Sleepy Hollow.* Adjacent to the church is the famous Sleepy Hollow Cemetery. | 430 N. Broadway, Sleepy Hollow | 914/631–1123 | www.rctodc.org | Free | Grounds daily; church by appointment.

Philipsburg Manor. This working 18th-century farm is in Sleepy Hollow on the banks of the Pocantico River. Tours at Philipsburg Manor are conducted in 18th-century costume. | 381 N. Broadway, Sleepy Hollow | 914/631–8200 | fax 914/631–0089 | www.hudsonvalley.org | $8 | Open weekends in March. Apr.–Oct., Wed.–Mon. 10–5. Nov.–Dec., Wed.–Mon. 10–4. Closed Jan.–Feb.

Tarrytown Music Hall. This National Historic landmark, designed by Philip Edmunds and built in 1885, is now a cultural arts center that presents theater, concerts, and opera. It is one of the oldest standing "legitimate" theaters in Westchester County. The theater's interior combines the Victorian workmanship and design with the playfulness of Art Deco. | 13 Main St. | 914/631–3390 | Call for schedule.

Sunnyside. Tours are available of the restored and charmingly picturesque home of Washington Irving, whose writings include *The Legend of Sleepy Hollow* and *Rip Van Winkle.* | W. Sunnyside La. | 914/631–8200 | www.hudsonvalley.org | $8 | Mar., weekends 10–5; Apr.–Oct., Mon. and Wed.–Sun. 10–5; Nov.–Dec., Mon. and Wed.–Sun. 10–4.

Rockefeller State Park Preserve. Hiking trails, fishing ponds, carriage paths, woodlands, and lush meadows make up the nearly 1,000 acres of this park 4 mi northeast of Tarrytown. The wetlands portion of the preserve is home to a number of migratory bird species, and the area is particularly popular among photographers and bird enthusiasts. | Rte. 117 | 914/631–1470 | $5 per car | Daily, 8–sunset.

ON THE CALENDAR

MAY: *Spring Crafts Show.* Hundreds of artists from across the United States showcase fine contemporary crafts on the grounds of the famed mansion, Lyndhurst. A fall crafts show is held in September. | 914/631–4481.

AUG.: *Sunnyside Jazz Festival.* Hear live jazz by world-class performers outside at Sunnyside, the historic home of author Washington Irving. | 914/631–8200.

OCT.: *Sleepy Hollow Legend Weekend.* Events include storytelling, candlelighting ceremonies, shadow-puppet shows, harvesting activities, video presentations, and of course, the possibility of an appearance by the town's famous ghost—the Headless Horseman. | 914/631–8200.

DEC.: *Holiday Candlelight Tour.* Enjoy traditional 19th-century holiday celebrations, including carol singing and readings of Washington Irving's *Tales of Old Christmas.* At Sunnyside. | 914/591–8763 or 914/631–8200.

DEC.: *St. Nicholas Day.* Celebrate the Dutch tradition of St. Nicholas Day at Colonial Philipsburg Manor. Meet St. Nick in his dramatic bishop's hat and long beard and learn why Santa fills your stocking on Christmas. | 914/631–3992 or 914/631–8200.

Dining

Bellas Restaurant. Greek. This small stucco restaurant with booths and a coffee counter serves Greek specialties for lunch, dinner, and breakfast all day. | 5 S. Broadway | 914/332–0444 | Breakfast also available | $3–$15 | No credit cards.

Caravela. Brazilian. This small, informal, but critically acclaimed restaurant features a nautical decor. Try the paella stocked with shrimps, clams and mussels, chicken, and sausage, or the fresh cod, shrimp, scallops, and clams in fennel and saffron broth. Outdoor dining at sidewalk tables. Kids' menu. | 53 N. Broadway | 914/631–1863 | Reservations essential Sat. | $15–$20 | AE, D, DC, MC, V.

Equus. Continental. A grand experience awaits at this luxurious restaurant, located inside the Castle at Tarrytown, a century-old mansion set on a 10-acre estate. Choose from three dining rooms: the historic Oak Room transported from France; the Tapestry Room; and the Garden Room, which has breathtaking views of the Hudson River. There is also an outdoor terrace. The cuisine is French-influenced. Try the brioche with smoked salmon, the chilled sweet-pea soup, and the lobster and goat cheese cannelloni. Kids' menu. Sunday brunch. | 400 Benedict Ave. | 914/631–1980 | Breakfast also available | $54 prix fixe | AE, D, MC, V.

Maison Lafitte. Continental. River views and a quiet ambience characterize this elegant restaurant, set in a 1902 mansion. Try the crêpe Riviera, a seafood crêpe filled with lobster, crabs, shrimp, and scallops, or the veal chops, which are stuffed with Parma prosciutto, Swiss cheese, chives, and shallots. | 25 Studio Hill Rd., Briarcliff Manor | 914/941–5787 | $16–$29 | AE, D, MC, V.

Rudy's Beau Rivage. Continental. Pleasant views of the Hudson River make this stately Victorian mansion a nice spot for brunch or dinner. Try the seafood "gold of Naples," capon maison, veal piccata, or the chicken marsala. The outdoor dining area overlooks the Hudson River. Kids' menu. Sunday brunch. | 19 Livingston Ave., Dobbs Ferry | 914/693–3192 | www.rudysbeaurivage.com | Closed Mon., Tues. | $10–$20 | AE, MC, D, V.

Santa Fe. Southwestern. Locals flock to this restaurant for its fresh specialties and festive atmosphere. Try the conch fritters, a tropical shellfish specialty served with Caribbean tartar sauce, or the *Cochinita Pibil,* a classic dish from the Yucatan, consisting of boneless pork marinated in sour Seville orange juice with achiote (Mayan spices) and slow cooked in banana leaves. Over 30 premium tequilas are on the menu. Kids' menu. | 5 Main St. (Rte. 9) | 914/332–4452 | $10–$16 | AE, D, DC, MC, V.

THE MARVELOUS MANSIONS OF WESTCHESTER COUNTY

"Be it ever so humble, there's no place like home" goes the saying, but there is nothing even remotely humble about many of the sprawling estates of Westchester County.

These particular home-sweet-homes were very sweet, indeed, for some notable Americans, from industrialists like the Rockefellers to literary figures such as Washington Irving, who opted for the gorgeous greenery and spectacular shorelines of Westchester instead of the hustle and bustle of New York City. A tour of any one of these marvelous mansions will bring new meaning to Dorothy's famous mantra, "There's no place like home." In truth, there are very few places like these homes.

Probably the most spectacular of them all is Kykuit, the six-story stone mansion, which was home to four generations of Rockefellers. The first-floor rooms are open to the public, as are the gorgeous gardens with their extraordinary Hudson River vistas and extensive collection of superlative 20th-century sculpture (acquired by Governor Nelson Rockefeller).

The 2-hr tour of the estate, which departs from Sleepy Hollow April–November, is so popular that it is often booked solid months in advance.

Another worthwhile stop on the estate tour is Philipsburg Manor in Sleepy Hollow, a colonial farm and trading site built in the 1700s. The property, once owned by the Philipse family, includes the manor house, a barn (complete with farm animals), a completely restored and fully operational gristmill, and a wooden dam you can walk over. Visitors can witness demonstrations of Colonial-era carpentry techniques and farming chores (there's a sheep-shearing demonstration), and picnicking is welcome.

Another dazzling domicile in the area is Lyndhurst, the ultra-opulent Gothic-style mansion that was home to three of the 19th century's most famous financiers: William Paulding, who was mayor of New York City during the 1830s; merchant George Merritt; and railroad tycoon Jay Gould. This exceptional estate, open to the public in summer months only, overlooks the flowing Hudson River just south of the Tappan Zee Bridge. Built in 1838, the mansion sits on a 67-acre landscaped plot and is filled with fascinating furnishings, books, artwork, and other period artifacts.

The Van Cortlandt Manor, the Revolutionary War–era estate of a prominent colonial family in Croton-on-Hudson, is both elegant and educational. You can tour the gorgeously furnished home, a separate kitchen house, and lovely gardens and picnic areas, as well as the 17th-century tavern on the property. George Washington and General Lafayette were entertained here (and you thought they were all work and no play!) and you will be, too. There are frequent demonstrations of Revolutionary-era trades, including weaving, brick making, open-hearth cooking, and much more.

Not as elaborate but just as delightful is Sunnyside, the happy home of famed American author Washington Irving. Overlooking the Hudson River, this warm and cozy estate where the author lived from 1836 to 1859 contains furnishings and personal possessions from around the time he penned many of his classic stories. The site includes delightful landscaped grounds and a picnic area.

Lodging

Alexander Hamilton House. Rooms in this Victorian house have floral spreads, iron beds, and some antique furniture; some have fireplaces and views of the Hudson River. Breakfast is served in your room at a table for two. Located 12–15 mi north of Tarrytown in Croton-on-Hudson. Complimentary breakfast. In-room data ports, some microwaves, some refrigerators, some in-room hot tubs, cable TV, some in-room VCRs. Pool. Shop. No pets. No smoking. | 49 Van Wyck St., Croton-on-Hudson | 914/271–6737 | fax 914/271–3927 | www.alexanderhamiltonhouse.com | 8 rooms | $100–$250 | AE, D, DC, MC, V.

Castle at Tarrytown. This magnificently restored castle, built in 1910 on 10 hilltop acres overlooking the Hudson River, is now an exclusive inn. The rooms are appointed with antiques and four-poster beds. There's a two-night minimum stay on weekends. Restaurant (*see* Equus, *above*), room service. In-room data ports, in-room safes. Pool. Tennis. Gym. | 400 Benedict Ave. | 914/631–1980 | fax 914/631–4612 | www.castleattarrytown.com | 39 rooms, 9 suites | $300 rooms, $375–$495 suites | AE, MC, V.

Courtyard by Marriott. This pleasant hotel is near the Hudson River, the historic Sleepy Hollow district, and I–87 and U.S. 9. The rooms are outfitted with the usual modular pieces. Restaurant, bar. Cable TV. Pool. Hot tub. Exercise equipment. Laundry facilities. Free parking. | 475 White Plains Rd. | 914/631–1122 | fax 914/631–1357 | www.courtyard.com | 139 rooms, 19 suites | $149–$175 rooms, $189 suites | AE, D, DC, MC, V.

Krogh's Nest. Perched on a hill above Hartsdale, the Kroghs (pronounced "crows") have been in business since 1986. This 1896 Center Hall Victorian has antique Colonial trimmings. Dining room, complimentary breakfast. Cable TV. | 4 Hillcrest Rd., Hartsdale | 914/946–3479 | ckrogh'snest@aol.com | www.bbchannel.com/bbc/p216636.asp | 2 rooms | $75 | AE.

Tarrytown Hilton. This beautifully landscaped historical building is nestled in the Hudson River valley, close to the mysterious neck of woods made famous by Washington Irving's *The Legend of Sleepy Hollow*. The rooms are simple and functional. Rates drop by as much as $50 on weekends. Restaurant, bar (with entertainment), complimentary Continental breakfast, room service. In-room data ports, cable TV. 2 pools, wading pool. Hot tub, massage. Tennis. Exercise equipment. Playground. Business services. | 455 S. Broadway | 914/631–5700 | fax 914/631–0075 | www.hilton.com | 247 rooms, 3 suites | $180 | AE, D, DC, MC, V.

Tarrytown House. Built in the mid-1800s, this estate overlooks the majestic Hudson River valley. Most rooms overlook the extensive gardens and beautiful wooded areas, and many rooms have outdoor terraces with views of the valley. Tarrytown House is a noted conference center. Restaurant, complimentary breakfast. In-room data ports, cable TV, in room VCRs (and movies). 2 pools. Hot tub. Tennis. Gym, racquetball. Business services. | E. Sunnyside La. | 914/591–8200 or 800/553–8118 | fax 914/591–7118 | tarrytownhouse@dolce.com | www.dolce.com | 148 rooms | $109–$190 | AE, D, DC, MC, V.

Westchester Marriott. There's a beautiful atrium here with an indoor pool and a full-service health club, and some rooms overlook the pool/courtyard. The hotel is within a short drive of several restaurants. Restaurant, bar (with entertainment). Cable TV. Pool. Beauty salon, hot tub, massage. Gym. Business services. | 670 White Plains Rd. | 914/631–2200 | fax 914/631–7819 | 444 rooms | $109–$225 | AE, D, DC, MC, V.

TICONDEROGA

MAP 3, L4

(Nearby towns also listed: Bolton Landing, Crown Point, Hague, Schroon Lake)

Ticonderoga is an Iroquois Native American term, meaning "land of many waters." The town of Ticonderoga is indeed between many waters, bordering both Lake George and Lake Champlain, with the LaChute River running through the town. A key attraction for visitors is Fort Ticonderoga, where reenactments make history come alive. Although

Ticonderoga was, for a long time, known for being a center of pencil- and paper-making factories, today it is probably best known as the point of embarkation for the Fort Ticonderoga Ferry, which runs between New York and Vermont.

Information: Ticonderoga Area Chamber of Commerce | 108 Lake George Ave., 12883 | 518/585–6619.

Attractions

Ft. Ticonderoga. Originally named Fort Carillon when it was built by the French in 1755, this fort was captured by the British in 1759 and renamed Fort Ticonderoga. Today the site on Lake Champlain presents living-history demonstrations which include cannon-fire drills, fife-and-drum exhibitions, encampments, and reenactments. | 518/585–2821 | $10 | May–June and Sept.–Oct., daily 9–5; July–Aug., daily 9–6.

Ft. Ticonderoga Ferry. Cross Lake Champlain to Shoreham, Vermont, in 6 min. This ferry service has been in operation since the mid-1700s. | Shorewell Ferries, Inc., Rte. 74 W | 802/897-7999 | May–Oct., daily 7 AM–8 PM.

Heritage Museum. Learn about the industrial history of Ticonderoga through exhibits, demonstrations, and a self-guided tour. | Montcalm St. at Bicentennial Park | 518/585–6366 | Free | July–Aug., daily 10–4; mid-May–July, Sept.–mid-Oct., weekends 10–4.

Mount Defiance. View Ft. Ticonderoga from up above. During the Revolutionary War, patriots pushed heavy cannons to the top of this mountain in order to destroy the fort before the English could get to it. The motto was: "Where a goat can go, a man can go. Where a man can go, a cannon can go." | Mt. Defiance St. | 518/585–6619 | www.fort-ticonderoga.org | $10 | Early May–late Oct. daily 9–5 (July–Aug. 9–6).

Putnam Pond State Public Campground. Putt's Pond, as it is called locally, is a campground and beach with hiking, boating, and fishing. In Adirondack Park. | Off Rte. 74 | 518/585–7280.

Replica of Hancock House. This reproduction of John Hancock's Boston home houses the Ticonderoga Historical Society. Includes a research library and museum. | 3 Wicker St. | 518/585–7868 | ths@capital.net | Free | Wed.–Sat. 10–4.

ON THE CALENDAR
JULY: *The Best Fourth in the North.* Ticonderoga celebrates July 4th weekend with parades, carnivals, chicken BBQs, strawberry socials, live local bands, an Elvis impersonator, and fireworks. | 518/585–6619.

Dining

Carillon Restaurant. Steak. Try the seafood pot pie or the roast duckling with raspberry sauce at this casual steak and seafood spot. Order lighter food choices in the lounge. | 61 Hague Rd. | 518/585–7657 | Closed Wed. | $12–$21 | AE, D, DC, MC, V.

Hot Biscuit Diner. American. Homemade, all-American food is served at this casual dining spot. Try the chicken and biscuit, with vegetables and gravy, and the homemade strawberry shortcake. Kids' menu. | 428 Montcalm St. | 518/585–3483 | Breakfast also available; no dinner Sun. | $9–$15 | MC, V.

Lodging

Circle Court Motel. The Circle Court, situated at the top of Ticonderoga village, is within walking distance of the lakes and the river. There's also a public park nearby with waterfalls and springs. Refrigerators, cable TV. Pets allowed. | 440 Montcalm St. | 518/585–7660 | 14 rooms | $57–$62 | AE, MC, V.

Super 8 Motel. Located ¼ mi from downtown Ticonderoga, this hotel has extremely basic rooms. Picnic area, complimentary Continental breakfast. In-room data ports, cable TV. No pets. | Rte. 9 N | 518/585–2617 or 800/800–8000 | fax 518/585–3521 | www.super8.com | 39 rooms | $50–$89 | AE, D, DC, MC, V.

TROY

MAP 3, L6

(Nearby towns also listed: Albany, Colonie, Schenectady)

This onetime seat of the Industrial Revolution is north of Albany, on the east bank of the Hudson River. Troy has a population of 55,000 and is noted for historic architecture, restaurants, and Rensselaer Polytechnic Institute.

Information: **Rensselaer County Chamber of Commerce** | 31 Second St., 12180 | info@renscochamber.com | www.renscochamber.com | 518/274–7020.

Attractions

Arts Center of the Capital Region. This not-for-profit center for arts instruction has two gallery spaces where local and regional artists show their work. | 265 River St. | 518/273–0552 | fax 518/273–4591 | Free | Mon.–Sat. 9–5.

Bennington Battlefield State Historic Site. This National Historic Landmark was the scene of the British Army's defeat by American forces during General Burgoyne's invasion from Canada in 1777. Offers picnicking and views of Vermont's Green Mountains. | Rte. 67, RD2, Hoosick Falls | 518/686–7109 (summer) or 518/279–1155 | Free | June–Sept., daily 10–7.

Grave of "Uncle Sam" Wilson. Samuel Wilson, a local meat packer who supplied beef to the U.S. Army in the War of 1812, is buried at Oakwood Cemetery. Soldiers interpreted the government stamp "U.S Beef" to mean "Uncle Sam's" beef, and thus was born the inspiration for Uncle Sam, America's white-haired personification. | Oakwood Ave. | 518/272–7520 | Free | Daily 8–4:30.

Junior Museum. Engage in interactive, hands-on programs for kids in science, history, and art. | 105 8th St. | 518/235–2120 | fax 518/235–6836 | www.juniormuseum.org | $5 | Fri.–Sat. 10–5.

Rensselaer County Historical Society. Located in a historic house in Troy, this site has a museum, gallery, gift shop, and research library. | 59 2nd St. | 518/272–7232 | fax 518/273–1264 | www.rchsonline.org | $3 | Museum Tues.–Sat. 10–4; research library Tues.–Fri. 1–4, Sat. 10–4.

Rensselaer Polytechnic Institute. Founded at Troy in 1824, this is the oldest technological university in America, with 6,000 students specializing in engineering, architecture, and management. | 110 8th St. | 518/276–6000 | www.rpi.edu | Free | Daily.

Russell Sage College. This private, four-year, liberal-arts women's college was founded in 1916, and today has a student population of approximately 1,000. It hosts public speakers, art exhibits, and concerts. | 45 Ferry St. | 518/244–2000 | fax 518/244–6880 | www.sage.edu | Free | Daily.

Troy's RiverSpark Visitor Center. This center offers an orientation to the surrounding area attractions and has historical exhibits. | 251 River St. | 518/270–8667 | fax 518/270–1119 | www.rpi.edu/tildacarroll/tvc | Free | May–Sept., Tues.–Fri. 10–6, weekends 10–5; Oct.–Apr., Tues.–Sat. 11–5.

Troy Savings Bank Music Hall. This restored 1875 hall is internationally acclaimed by conductors and musicians for its fine acoustics. There's a full lineup of classical, popular, and jazz concerts in winter, spring, and fall. | State and 2nd Sts. | 518/273–0038 | fax 518/273–1564 | www.troymusichall.org | $20–$25 | Sept.–May; call for schedule.

ON THE CALENDAR

JUNE: *Riverfront Arts Festival.* Enjoy music, performances, art demonstrations, and crafts on Father's Day weekend in Riverfront Park. | 518/273–0552.

DEC.: *The Victorian Stroll.* Downtown Troy puts on its 100-yr-old finery in music, costume, crafts, food, and entertainment, just in time for Christmas. | 518/274–7020.

Dining

Café Allegro. Eclectic. The food has Mediterranean, Spanish, Mexican, Japanese, and Italian influences, while the restaurant itself has a New York City ambience. Try the rack of lamb, the yellowfin tuna, or the South American sea bass. In fall, if you're daring, try the ostrich and antelope. | 33 2nd St. | 518/271–1942 | fax 518/271–1942 | No lunch | $25 | AE, MC, V.

The Capehouse. Seafood. This downtown Troy institution serves lots of fish and shellfish, as well as some beef, veal, and chicken entrées. There is a raw bar as well as a full bar. | 254 Broadway | 518/274–0167 | fax 518/274–0167 | Closed Sun., Mon. | $25 | AE, D, DC, MC, V.

Crooked Lake House. American. This restaurant exudes rustic elegance in the tradition of the Adirondack great camps. It's known for rack of lamb, venison, antelope, and vegetarian specialties. Sunday brunch. Big band Saturday, vocalist Friday. | Rtes. 43 and 66, Averill Park | 518/674–3894 | Nov.–Apr., Closed Mon–Thurs.; May–Oct., closed Mon.–Wed. Lunch on weekends only | $30 | AE, DC, MC, V.

Gregory House. Continental. Housed in an 1830 inn, this elegant candlelit eatery is known for veal, lamb, and seafood. | Rte. 43, Averill Park | 518/674–3774 | fax 518/674–8916 | Closed Mon. No lunch | $50 | AE, D, DC, MC, V.

Loporto's. Italian. This casual multilevel restaurant is known for its fresh seafood and veal. Try the veal medallions stuffed with crab, provolone, and basil, or the veal with capers, artichoke hearts, mushrooms, and plum tomatoes. | 85 4th St. | 518/273–8546 | Closed Sun., Mon. No lunch Sat. | $35 | AE, D, DC, MC, V.

Old Daley Inn. American. The Old Daley is a local institution known for steak and prime ribs. The dining room is small and there is a rathskeller in the basement. | 499 2nd Ave. | 518/235–2656 | fax 518/235–3275 | No lunch Sun. | $20 | AE, D, DC, MC, V.

Paolo Lombardi's. Italian. Veal dishes are the specialty of the house at this restaurant 7 min south of downtown Troy. The dining room has cathedral ceilings and walls made primarily of glass. | 104 W. Sand Lake Rd., Wynantskill | 518/283–0202 | fax 518/283–0243 | No lunch Mon.–Sat. | $33 | AE, D, DC, MC, V.

River Street Café. Eclectic. Exposed wood, natural brick, and mahogany lend a historic ambience to this restaurant on the river. The eclectic fare melds flavors of the Southwest and the Mediterranean. Try the prime sirloin topped with brown butter sauce or the diver's sea scallops. | 429 River St. | 518/273–2740 | Closed Sun.–Mon. No lunch | $32 | MC, V.

Tavern at Sterup Square. American. Take your meal in the glass-enclosed dining room, on the terrace, or in the more casual adjacent tavern. The tavern serves hearty meat sandwiches and homemade soups, but if you opt for something fancier in the other two areas, try the pancetta antelope tenderloin, the *scampi in carrozza* (sautéed jumbo shrimp on a "carriage" of Tuscan bread with grilled yellow and red tomatoes), or the sea scallop gazpacho martini (lime-and-cilantro-marinated sea scallops, wood grilled and served on a seven-vegetable gazpacho with crisp corn tortillas). Sunday brunch. Kids' menu. It's 9 mi northeast of Troy. | 2113 Rte. 7 | 518/663–5800 | www.sterupsquare.com | Jacket required | $21 | AE, D, DC, MC, V.

Troy Pub and Brewery. Contemporary. This brewpub in a restored river warehouse has an extensive menu and is full of local memorabilia, antiques, and old photos. Try the chicken wings, fried green tomatoes, burgers, fresh salmon, catfish, or black-collar stout pie. | 417-419 River St. | 518/273–BEER | fax 518/273–4838 | Reservations not accepted weekends | $18 | AE, MC, V.

Villa Valenti. Italian. The casual decor doesn't distract from the delicious homemade pastas. The menu is traditional Italian fare. Try the homemade spumoni for dessert. Full bar. Takeout available. | Rte. 150, W. Sand Lake | 518/283–1291 | $30 | AE, D, DC, MC, V.

Lodging

Best Western Inn. This independently owned hotel is in downtown Troy. Complimentary breakfast, picnic area. In-room data ports, cable TV. Pool. Exercise equipment. Video games. Laundry facilities. Airport shuttle. | 1800 6th Ave. | 518/274–3210 | fax 518/274–3294 | www.bestwestern.com | 152 rooms | $69 | AE, D, DC, MC, V.

Super 8 Motel. This motel is within walking distance of the Riverboat Cruises on the Hudson River. The major Vermont ski resorts are 30 mi away. The basic, affordable rooms are in downtown Troy. Complimentary Continental breakfast. Cable TV. | 1 4th St. | 518/274–8800 | fax 518/274–0427 | 76 rooms | $47–$90 | AE, D, DC, MC, V.

Susse Chalet. Flanked by two restaurants, this four-story hotel sits 15 min by car from downtown Troy. Complimentary Continental breakfast. In-room data ports, cable TV. Pool. Laundry facilities. Business services. | 124 Troy Rd., East Greenbush | 518/477–7984 | fax 518/477–2382 | www.sussechalet.com | 105 rooms | $72 | AE, D, DC, MC, V.

TUPPER LAKE

MAP 3, J3

(Nearby towns also listed: Lake Placid, Long Lake, Paul Smiths, Saranac Lake)

Another Adirondack town named for a lake other than the one on which it sits, Tupper Lake is actually on Raquette Lake. A former logging town, Tupper Lake is now a quiet vacation spot with plenty of outdoor activities.

Information: **Tupper Lake Chamber of Commerce** | 60 Park St., 12986 | 888/TUP–LAKE.

Attractions

Fish Creek Pond State Public Campground. Located near the St. Regis Canoe Wilderness Area, this campground has 355 campsites, hiking, fishing, ponds, lakes, and lots of activities for kids. | Rte. 30 N | 518/891–4560 | $5 day use per vehicle; $16 per night for campsite; $2.50 camping registration fee | Mid-Apr.–mid-Nov., daily.

Historic Beth Joseph Synagogue. Jewish peddlers in the Adirondack region built the Beth Joseph Synagogue in 1905 as a place of worship. Now listed on the National Register of Historic Places, the synagogue has been restored and contains art exhibits. It also hosts concerts and other activities. | Corner of Mill and Lake Sts. | 518/359–9594 | Free | July–Aug., weekdays 1–3.

Junction's Main Street. Located on the village's west side where the remains of the old railroad tracks cross Main Street, this part of Tupper Lake was once called The Junction. Buildings dating from the town's early days as a logging and transportation center, including the Grand Union Hotel on Depot Street and the Armour meatpacking house, are well preserved. The Goff–Nelson Library on Lake Street houses a large collection of photographs and accounts of Tupper Lake's early history. | Main St. | 888/887–5253 | Free | Daily.

ON THE CALENDAR

JUNE: *Flatwater Weekend.* A strenuous 9 mi race and 40 mi marathon highlight this event, which also features canoes and kayak guide boats. | 518/359–3328.
JULY: *Adirondack Festival of American Music.* This monthlong festival held at various locations around Saranac Lake includes music workshops and concerts for all ages. | 518/891–1057.
JULY: *Tinman Triathlon.* The three legs of this event include a 1.2-mi swim, a 56-mi bike course, and a 13.1-mi run ending in Tupper Lake. | 518/359–3328.
JULY: *Woodsmen's Field Days.* Skills and crafts related to the lumber industry are demonstrated during this colorful event at Tupper Lake Municipal Park. Draft horses

pull logs, chain-saw artists sculpt, and modern-day lumberjacks demonstrate chopping and ax throwing. | 518/359–3328 or 518/359–9444.

Dining

Dumas' Restaurant. American. This charming and rustic family-style restaurant offers diners a taste of real home cooking: grilled ham-and-cheese sandwiches, burgers, steaks, chops, spaghetti, and seafood. Just north of Tupper Lake on Route 3. | Rte. 3, Childwold | 518/359–2540 | fax 518/359–8409 | Breakfast also available | $7–$10 | MC, V.

Lumberjack Inn. American. This rustic family restaurant in downtown Tupper Lake harks back to the old lumber-camp days with antique chain saws and cans, buck saws, and frying pans hanging on the wall. Meals are hearty, including four-egg omelets, pancakes, tuna and turkey melts, spaghetti, steaks, and the Friday-night special—a fish fry. | 76 Main St. | 518/359–2910 | Breakfast also available | $8–$12 | D, MC, V.

Mountain Valley Pizza. Italian. This little restaurant serves sandwiches, barbecued ribs, pasta dishes, wings and, of course, pizza, all at an affordable price. | 99 Park St. | 518/359–2233 | $8–$12 | No credit cards.

Pine Grove Restaurant. American. The restaurant's country-rustic decor is accented by plenty of ponderosa pine, and local wildlife art adorns the walls. Enjoy sandwiches, burgers, steaks, and chops at a table or at the bar. | 166 Main St. | 518/359–3669 | Closed Tues. | $8–$12 | AE, D, MC, V.

The Wawbeek. American. Enjoy fine dining in the heart of the Adirondacks on the decks or inside with a view of Upper Saranac Lake. The Wawbeek serves top-quality beef, venison, and fish, among other more exotic specials. North of town off Route 30. | 553 Panther Mountain Rd. | 518/359–2656 | Reservations essential | $17–$26 | AE, DC, MC, V.

Lodging

Cold River Ranch Bed and Breakfast. Set amid 100 acres of forest at the northern end of the High Peaks region of the state, this ranch offers guest rooms and various riding packages, including trips into the mountains and the wilderness area of Adirondack Park. Complimentary breakfast. Horseback riding. | Rte. 3 between Saranac Lake and Tupper Lake | 518/359–7559 | fax 518/359–9761 | 6 rooms | $35 | DC, MC, V.

Cranberry Lake Lodge. This simple but comfortable hotel/motel is set directly on the lake, next to a marina which offers boat rentals. Some rooms have balconies overlooking the lake. Restaurant, bar. Cable TV. Dock. | 7202 Rte. 3, Cranberry Lake | 518/848–3301 | fax 518/848–9675 | cranlodge@aol.com | www.cranberrylakelodge.com | 23 rooms | $54–$82 | AE, DC, MC, V.

Hauser's Haven. This three-bedroom square-timber cottage with a fully equipped kitchen and fireplace sits across from the public beach just a few miles outside of Tupper Lake. It rents by the week. Picnic area. Kitchenettes, microwaves, refrigerators, cable TV, no room phones. Beach. Playground. | 113 Washington St. | 518/359–9007 | 1 cottage | $375 week | Closed Oct.–May | No credit cards.

Journey's End. These wood-frame lakefront cottages (one, two, and three bedrooms) sit on a 17th-century estate about 2 mi south of Long Lake off Route 30. Additional features include a dock, courtesy canoe, and grills. Picnic area. Kitchenettes, microwaves, refrigerators, cable TV, in-room VCRs. Beach, water sports. | Rte. 30, Long Lake | 518/624–5381 or 888/624–5381 | 4 cottages | $550–$675 week | Closed Nov.–May | D, MC, V.

Longview Lodge. Built in 1929 and restored in 2000, this country inn features rooms with hardwood floors and antiques. You'll also find a pool table, private dock, courtesy canoes, and a beach on Long Lake. Adjoining the lodge are two seasonal one-bedroom cottages. Complimentary Continental breakfast. Cable TV. Beach, water sports. | Deerland Rd., Long Lake | 518/624–2862 | 17 rooms, 2 cottages | $55–$80 rooms, $510 per week for the cottages | AE, MC, V.

Pine Terrace Motel and Resort. Located on Big Tupper Lake, this property consists of 20 cottages with pine-wood interiors. There is golf and hiking next door. Picnic area. No air-conditioning, some kitchenettes, refrigerators, cable TV. Pool, wading pool. Tennis. Boating. Pets allowed. | 94 Moody Rd. | 518/359–9258 | fax 518/359–8340 | 20 cottages | $45–$75 | AE, DC, MC, V.

Shaheen's Motel. Convenient to hiking, skiing, canoeing, and other outdoor activities, this motel is also close to Tupper Lake. Guest rooms can be adjoining, and family units are available. Most are wood paneled with forest views. Picnic area, complimentary Continental breakfast. No air-conditioning in some rooms, refrigerators, cable TV. Pool. Miniature golf. Playground. | 314 Park St. | 518/359–3384 or 800/474–2445 | fax 518/359–3384 | shaheens@capital.net | www.shaheensmotel.com | 31 rooms | $39–$78 | AE, D, DC, MC, V.

Sunset Park Motel. All rooms in this quiet motel overlook Tupper Lake. The motel is next to a park with basketball, tennis, and volleyball courts. Adirondack hiking and mountain-bike trails are also nearby. Picnic area. No air-conditioning, some kitchenettes, cable TV. Beach, dock, boating. Some pets allowed. | 71 De Mars Blvd. | 518/359–3995 | fax 518/359–9577 | sunsetpk@org.net | 11 rooms | $55–$70 | Closed Jan.–Apr. | AE, DC, MC, V.

Tupper Lake Motel. Within walking distance of a supermarket and restaurants, and less than a mile from Tupper Lake, this motel has comfortable modern rooms that overlook a kidney-shaped pool. Complimentary Continental breakfast. No air-conditioning. In-room data ports, refrigerators, cable TV. Pool. Business services. | 259 Park St. | 518/359–3381 or 518/359–3382 | fax 518/359–8549 | info@tupperlakemotel.com | 18 rooms | $40–$63 | AE, DC, MC, V.

Wawbeek on Upper Saranac Lake. Built in 1880 as a great camp, this turn-of-the-20th-century lodge is set deep in the woods, east of the village of Saranac Lake, on 40 acres. Visitors can enjoy a meal at the Mountain House Lodge, sampling country-French and American cuisine. Tennis. Beach. | 553 Panther Mountain Rd. | 518/359–2656 or 800/953–2656 | fax 518/359–2475 | wawbeek@capital.net | www.wawbeek.com | 18 rooms, 5 cabins | $155–$250 rooms, $245–$420 cabins | AE, MC, V. .

UTICA

MAP 3, I5

(Nearby towns also listed: Herkimer, Ilion, Oneida, Richfield Springs, Rome)

This city on the Mohawk River/Barge Canal saw its industrial heyday in the early 20th century. In downtown Utica, the maker of Saranac beer, F. X. Matt Brewing Co., gives tours of its beer-making facilities and tastings in an old tavern. The Munson-Williams-Proctor Institute displays a large collection of fine art, and the Utica Zoo is home to many animals. Utica also boasts a number of colleges.

Information: Mohawk Valley Chamber of Commerce | 520 Seneca St., 13502 | 315/724–3151.

Attractions

Children's Museum. Kids will love the hands-on exhibits and crafts. | 311 Main St. | 315/724–6128 | $2.50 | Tues.–Fri. 10–5, Sat. 10–4:30, Sun. noon–4:30.

Hamilton College. The third-oldest college in New York, Hamilton was founded in 1793 as the Hamilton-Oneida Academy and rechartered as a private, 4-yr college in 1812. The school's 1,300-acre campus (8 mi southwest of Utica) has several buildings listed on the National Register of Historic Places. | 198 College Hill Rd., Clinton | 315/859–4011 | www.hamilton.edu | Free | Daily.

Munson-Williams-Proctor Institute. This fine-arts museum is noted for its works by Thomas Cole. | 310 Genesee St. | 315/797–0000 | Free | Tues.–Sat. 10–5, Sun. 1–5.

Oneida County Historical Society. This museum showcases the history of Mohawk Valley and Utica. | 1608 Genesee St. | 315/735–3642 | Free | Tues.–Fri. 10–4:30, Sat. 11–3.

Saranac Brewery Tour Center. On tours of the F. X. Matt Brewing Co., you ride a trolley, learn about the beer-making process, and get to taste samples. | 80 Varick St., at Court St. | 315/732–0022 or 800/765–6288 | www.saranac.com | $3 | Tues.–Fri. 10–4:30, Sat. 11–3.

Upstate New York Italian Cultural Center and Museum. You'll find folk art and sculpture exhibits, as well as a library/archive and a gift shop. Italian-language and cultural classes are offered. | 668 Catherine St. | 315/684–9502 | Free | Weekends 1–4:30.

Utica College of Syracuse University. This 4-yr, private, coeducational school, founded in 1946, is part of Syracuse University. It offers undergraduate degrees as well as continuing education programs. Today, around 1,600 students attend school on the suburban 140-acre campus. | 1600 Burrstone Rd. | 315/792–3111 or 315/792–3006 | Free | Daily.

Utica Zoo. Primates, big cats, reptiles, and hoofed mammals all call this zoo home. | 99 Steele Hill Rd. | 315/738–0472 | www.uticazoo.com | $4.25 | Daily 10–5.

ON THE CALENDAR
JULY: *The Boilermaker.* America's largest 15K road race, the Boilermaker winds its way through the city and attracts world-class runners. Be sure to register in advance if you plan to run. | 315/724–7221 or 800/426–3132 | www.boilermaker.com.

Dining
Dominique's Chesterfield Restaurant. Italian. This family restaurant with a full-service bar serves traditional and Utica regional Italian dishes such as chicken riggies (bite-size boneless breast of chicken, served with hot cherry peppers, cheese, onion, and white wine in a marinara sauce) and greens morelle (escarole, prosciutto, cheese, and hot cherry peppers tossed together and sautéed). Unique desserts are offered each night. The well-lit dining area features Tiffany lamps, marble accents, and a tin ceiling. | 1713 Bleecker St. | 315/732–9356 | $10–$17 | AE, MC, V.

Hook, Line and Sinker. Seafood. This quiet restaurant with private party rooms (3.4 mi southwest of Utica) serves fresh, grilled tuna, Atlantic lemon sole, and certified Angus aged steaks. Fridays, the restaurant has live entertainment. Salad bar. Kids' menu. | 8471 Seneca Tpk., New Hartford | 315/732–3636 | No lunch Sat. | $15–$25 | AE, D, DC, MC, V.

Horned Dorset. French. This restaurant, housed in a Victorian building 23 mi south of Utica, has a fireplace, antiques, and oil paintings of Dorset sheep. Tables are set with formal white linen. House specialties include boneless loin of lamb with black currant sauce, and veal horned Dorset, the house specialty. Classical guitarist weekends. | Main St., Leonardsville | 315/855–7898 | www.horneddorset.com | Closed Mon. No lunch | $27–$29 | AE, MC, V.

Joey's Restaurant. Italian. Pictures of Italy and Frank Sinatra adorn the walls of this cozy family restaurant. Diners often chat and intermingle, but only until Joey tells them to "sit down and eat before dinner gets cold." The menu includes greens, fried calamari, homemade pasta, veal, chops, and seafood. | 815 Mohawk St. | 315/724–9769 | Closed Sun. | $8–$15 | MC, V.

Pescatore's Restaurant. Italian. This lively family restaurant features pasta, veal, and shrimp dishes along with Italian pastries for dessert. The atmosphere is "Little Italy" with Sinatra tunes and Italian maps, plates, and pictures decorating the walls. Every Thursday is Godfather Night when all the dishes are named for characters in the movie, such as Don Corleone chicken. | 705 Albany St. | 315/733–9027 | Closed Sun. | $8–$12 | MC, V.

Thornberry's Restaurant. Continental. Set in a restored Victorian carriage house filled with antiques, Thornberry's is directly behind the Stanley Performing Arts Center in downtown Utica. You'll find continental, Italian, and American dishes. Popular choices include chicken Sonoma (grilled chicken on bed of fettuccine and sun-dried tomatoes topped with feta cheese, toasted walnuts, and a basil-pesto cream sauce); coq au vin; and Saranac strip steak (New York strip grilled, topped with a mushroom-and-honey-beer sauce and frizzled onions). | 1011 King St. | 315/735–1409 | Closed Sun. | $10–$20 | AE, D, DC, MC, V.

Lodging

Adam Bowman Manor. Once a stop on the Underground Railroad, this 1823 brick Federal manor is now a comfortable B&B. Each guest room is spacious and graced with antiques; two have private baths and two share a bath. On weekends, afternoon tea is served. While in an urban location, the building is nestled amid parklike grounds. Complimentary breakfast. Cable TV. | 197 Riverside Dr. | 315/735–6756 or 315/724–7266 | fax 315/738–0276 | 4 rooms (2 with shared bath) | $50–$75.

Best Western Gateway Adirondack Inn. Right off the Thruway exit 31, approximately 7 mi from the Oneida County Airport and 25 mi from downtown Utica, this two-story Best Western was built in 1960 in a business area. All rooms have double or king-size beds. Family suite available. Complimentary Continental breakfast. Cable TV. Exercise equipment. Video games. Business services. Some pets allowed. | 175 N. Genesee St. | 315/732–4121 | fax 315/797–8265 | 89 rooms, 1 suite | $109–$129 rooms, $139–$169 suite | AE, D, DC, MC, V.

Country Motel. The 4.75 acres surrounding this one-floor motel makes it feel like it's in the country, but it's actually in a residential part of the city. Convenient to public transportation and city attractions. Picnic area. In-room data ports, cable TV. Pond. | 1477 Herkimer Rd. | 315/732–4628 | fax 315/733–8801 | 25 rooms | $36–$65 | AE, D, MC, V.

Holiday Inn of Utica. Tucked off Interstate 90 in the Utica Business Park, this hotel has a landscaped courtyard with an outdoor pool. Standard rooms include a desk, chair with reading light, and 25-inch color TV. The hotel is close to area attractions, including the Utica Zoo, the Saranac Brewery Tour Center, the Baseball Hall of Fame in Cooperstown, the Boxing Hall of Fame in Canastota, and the Adirondack Scenic Railroad in nearby Utica. Restaurant, bar (with entertainment), room service. In-room data ports, cable TV. Pool. Exercise equipment. Video games. Laundry facilities. Business services. Pets allowed. | 1777 Burrstone Rd., New Hartford | 315/797–2131 | fax 315/797–5817 | www.holiday-inn.com | 100 rooms | $110–$129 | AE, D, DC, MC, V.

Iris Stonehouse B&B. This 1930 English Tudor on the National Register of Historic Places boasts leaded-glass windows and a fireplace for snowy winter days. All rooms have private baths, and the Queen room has become renowned for its "great shower"—six side sprays with a traditional showerhead above. The B&B is in a quiet residential neighborhood with easy access to Interstate 90, exit 31, and Routes 5, 8, and 12. Complimentary breakfast. No room phones, TV in common area. | 16 Derbyshire Pl. | 315/732–6720 or 800/446–1456 | fax 315/797–5134 | 4 rooms | $60–$90 | D, MC, V.

Pratt Smith House B&B. This 1815 brick Colonial on 22 acres is in a wooded residential area on the north edge of Utica. You'll find wide plank floors, antiques, private baths, and a view of the city and valley. Complimentary breakfast. Cable TV. | 10497 Cosby Manor Rd. | 315/732–8483 or 800/941–2337 | 2 rooms | $55–$60 | No credit cards.

Radisson–Utica Centre. This slightly upscale hotel is in the heart of downtown Utica, close to shopping, the Munson-Williams-Proctor Institute Museum, and the F. X. Matts Brewery. Relax next to the tropically landscaped indoor pool. Each room has double or king-size beds. Restaurant, bar (with entertainment). In-room data ports, refrigerators, cable TV. Pool. Barbershop, beauty salon, sauna. Exercise equipment, health club. Shops, video games. Business services. Some pets allowed. | 200 Genesee St. | 315/797–8010 | fax 315/797–1490 | www.radisson.com | 158 rooms | $119 | AE, D, DC, MC, V.

Red Roof Inn–Utica. A mile north of downtown Utica in a business area, this two-floor hotel is close to many restaurants. All rooms are furnished with either two full-size beds or a king-size bed. Cable TV. Business services. Some pets allowed. | 20 Weaver St. | 315/724–7128 | fax 315/724–7158 | www.redroof.com | 112 rooms | $65–$82 | AE, D, DC, MC, V.

Rosemont Inn Bed & Breakfast. The 1864 three-story brick Italian Victorian with a cupola on top is on the National Register of Historic Places and in the heart of Utica's downtown Historic District. The B&B features two large porches and private bathrooms with claw-foot tubs and showers. Complimentary breakfast, no room phones, TV in common area. | 1423 Genesee St. | 315/792–8852 or 800/883–0901 | www.borg.com/~rosemont | 7 rooms | $99–$145 | MC, V.

Sugarbush Bed and Breakfast. This English Colonial country home was built in 1807 as a school for boys on an 8-acre lot, 10 mi north of Utica. Today, the building's past lives on with Early American furnishings and antiques. Rooms are decorated in English country style, and vary from a suite with a sitting room to a double. Complimentary breakfast. No room phones, no TV in some rooms. Pond. Tennis, volleyball, cross-country skiing. No smoking. | 8451 Old Poland Rd., Barneveld | 315/896–6860 or 800/582–5845 | www.bedbreakfastnys.com/sugarbus.htm | 5 rooms, 2 suites | $55–$145 | AE, D, MC, V.

VICTOR

MAP 3, E6

(Nearby towns also listed: Avon, Canandaigua, Geneva, Palmyra, Rochester)

Though surrounded by farms, Victor is only 25 min southeast of Rochester. The area was once home to 4,500 Native Americans until their settlement was destroyed by the French in 1687, and today it remains one of the more notable Native American historic sites in the state.

Information: **Ontario County Tourism** | 20 Ontario St., Five Lakes Suite, Canandaigua, 14424-1806 | 716/394–3915 or 877/FUN–IN–NY | www.ontariony.com.

Attractions

Ganondagan State Historic Site. Wander down the trails of this 17th-century Seneca Nation settlement and gaze at the modern displays and videos detailing different aspects of Native American life. West on Boughton Hill Road to Victor-Holcomb Road. | 1488 Victor Holcomb Rd. | 716/924–5848 | Free | Daily 8 AM–dusk; visitors center May–Oct., Wed.–Sun. 9–5.

ON THE CALENDAR

JULY: *Native American Dance and Music Festival.* The festival celebrating Native American traditions is generally scheduled for the third weekend in July and held at the Ganondagan State Historic Site. There's dancing, music, storytelling, food, and more. | 716/742–1690 or 716/924–5848 | www.ggw.org/ganondagan.

Dining

Mickey Finns. American. Sitting along the old New York Central railroad bed, the restaurant is in an 1800s brick building which was originally part of the Victor Flour Mill complex. A warm and casual experience is created with brick walls, oak booths, a four-sided bar, Tiffany lamps, and a stone fireplace. The varied menu includes light fare (salads, soups, sandwiches, burgers), hearty entrées (filet mignon, chicken parmesan, shrimp scampi, rainbow trout), and vegetarian dishes. Eighteen different draft beers are available in frosted mugs. | 14 Railroad St. | 716/924–0530 | www.mickeyfinns.com | No lunch Sun. | $12–$20 | AE, D, DC, MC, V.

Victor Grilling Company. American. Several fireplaces and impressionistic landscape paintings on the walls give this restaurant an air of country romance. Bring your appetite, as portions are huge. Try the tuna wrapped in bacon, the certified Angus aged sirloin, or any of the grilled meats. | 75 Coville St. | 716/924–1760 | Closed Mon. and 1 week in Jan. No lunch | $16–$25 | AE, D, DC, MC, V.

Lodging

Exit 45 Motel. You can't get much more "no-frills" than this rural one-floor motel built in the 1950s. Rooms have either doubles or king-size beds. Bar. Cable TV. Business services. | 7463 Victor-Pittsford Rd. | 716/924–2121 | 34 rooms | $40–$100 | AE, D, MC, V.

Safari House Bed & Breakfast. The Safari House is truly unique with its 12 wooded acres and nature trail that are home to geese, ducks, deer, mink, and wild turkey. Inside, the large pecan-paneled common room with bar and fireside conversation pit displays 36 mounted trophies, including a 9-ft grizzly bear. One guest rooms is decorated in an African safari theme, while the other two are suites with cathedral ceilings, fireplaces, decks, and private entrances. Complimentary breakfast, some refrigerators, some in-room hot tubs, cable TV. | 94 Deer Crossing | 716/924–0250 | www.safarihouse.com | 3 rooms | $95–$175 | No credit cards.

Sunrise Hill Inn. This inn on 40 acres of open land (5 mi west of Victor) has a three-story building, housing the lobby and restaurant, and external corridors connecting separate buildings with guest rooms. Restaurant, bar. In-room data ports, cable TV. Pool. Business services. Some pets allowed. | 6108 Loomis Rd., Farmington | 716/924–2131 or 800/333–0536 | fax 716/924–1876 | www.e-localad.com/canandaigua/sunrisehill.html | 104 rooms | $40–$90 | AE, D, MC, V.

WALDEN

MAP 3, K9

(Nearby towns also listed: Goshen, Middletown, Newburgh)

Located at the intersection of Routes 52 and 208, Walden is a small residential village alongside the Wallkill River, not far from Stewart International Airport. Well-tended Queen Anne homes surround a downtown shopping center. If you are interested in horses, Alnoff Farms on Searsville Road is worth a visit.

Information: **Montgomery Chamber of Commerce** | 2357 Albany Post Rd., 12586 | 845/778–0514.

Attractions

A Beautiful Balloon. Southwest of Walden, float peacefully in a hot-air balloon over scenic countryside and farmlands surrounding Goshen and Warwick. Flights are available year-round at sunrise and 2 hrs before sunset. Call to schedule and for launch sites. | 973/335–9799 | www.balloon-rides.com | $75.

ON THE CALENDAR

JAN.–DEC.: *The Orange County Farmers Museum.* The Farmers Museum hosts a variety of events; prior years' programs included Model A Ford shows, tractor pulls, fife & drum musters, cider-making demonstrations, and Civil War reenactments. | 850 Rte. 17K | 845/457–5671 | www.new-york-inns.com/attractions-ny.html.

Dining

Loughran's. American. You'll find daily chalkboard specials, prime rib, and fresh seafood at this Hudson Valley Irish pub. Live music Wednesdays, Fridays, and Saturdays. On Route

94, south of Walden and east of the Routes 208 and 94 intersection. | Rte. 94 at School-house Rd., Salisbury Mills | 845/496–3615 | www.frontiernet.net/~loughran | $8–$13 | AE, D, MC, V.

Lodging

B&B on Mills Road. This country ranch B&B has large comfortable rooms, a gazebo, and mountain views. Guests often sit on pillows in the living room while playing board games in front of the crackling fireplace. In the morning, there's a deluxe Continental breakfast including quiche and homemade muffins, and in the evening, cheese and crackers are served. One guest room has a private bath; the other two share. Central to all Hudson Valley activities. Complimentary Continental breakfast. | 94 Mills Rd. | 845/778–2070 | fax 845/778–1223 | bbmillsroad.cjb.net | 3 rooms (2 with shared bath) | $75–$115 | No credit cards.

Harvest Inn Motel. This country motel in the small town of Pine Bush is just a few miles outside of Walden. As you enter the large lobby, you are greeted by a small waterfall, fire-place, and grand piano. Many rooms have mountain views. A mini–wedding suite is avail-able, and the Magnolia suite has a four-poster bed. Garden gazebo. Cable TV. Pool. | 96 Boniface Dr., Pine Bush | 845/744–5700 | www.harvestinnmotel.com | 39 rooms | $65–$100 | AE, D, MC, V.

WARRENSBURG

MAP 3, K5

(Nearby towns also listed: Bolton Landing, Diamond Point, Glens Falls, Lake George Village, Lake Luzerne, North Creek, Queensbury, Speculator)

Warrensburg is a small Adirondack town of 4,100 people with a full slate of outdoor activities. Called "The Gateway to the Adirondacks," Warrensburg has long been known for its natural beauty, from the pure sparkling water to the lush green forest and unspoiled wilderness. Cultural attractions, as well as historic sites and special events, round out Warrensburg's reputation as a charming, quiet town with a lot to do.

Information: **Warrensburg Chamber of Commerce** | 3847 Main St., 12885 | wcc@adiron-dack.net | www.warrensburgchamber.com | 518/623–2161.

Attractions

Hickory Ski Center. Winter sports thrive at this small scenic ski resort at the junction of the Hudson and Schroon rivers. There's a lodge, tavern, 15 beginner-through-expert slopes, natural snow, and lessons available to help you navigate the Center's 1,200-ft vertical drop. Kids welcome. | Rte. 418 W | 518/623–2825 | Dec.–Apr., weekends, depending on weather conditions.

Schroon River. Canoeing, kayaking, and tubing are favorite activities here, and the White Water Rafting Company rents equipment for all your floating needs. | Rte. 28, The Glen | 518/494–7478 or 800/867–2335 | www.wildwaters.net | $20–$40 | Apr.–Columbus Day.

ON THE CALENDAR

JULY: *Arts, Crafts, and Collectibles Festival.* Held on the weekend following 4th of July, the festival features only handcrafted items including quilts, ceramics, pottery, jewelry, and wood crafts. | Senior Citizen Center, 3847 Main St. | 518/623–2161 | www.warrens-burgchamber.com.

OCT.: *World's Largest Garage Sale and Foliage Festival.* Locals and out-of-towners (over 500 vendors in all) sell their wares from sidewalks, porches, and garages. You'll find plenty of bargains, and parking is available at the county fairgrounds with a shut-tle bus service to town. | Main St. and Stewart Farrar Ave. | First weekend in Oct. | 518/623–2161.

Dining

Friends Lake Inn. Contemporary. This 1860 inn (11 mi north of Warrensburg) is a must-stop on any Adirondack itinerary. The inn has a tin roof, original woodwork, period wallpaper, and three dining rooms, one with a lake view and fireplace. The menus change seasonally, but notable staples include the marinated rack of lamb, the beef tenderloin, and the sea bass. | Friends Lake Rd., Chestertown | 518/494–4751 | www.friendslake.com | Breakfast also available; no lunch | $19–$28 | AE, DC, MC, V.

Grist Mill on the Schroon Limited. American. Dine on venison medallions, salmon, prime rib, and salads in this former mill that offers a wonderful view from where it has overhung the rapids of the Schroon River since 1824. There is a mill museum on site. | 100 River St. | 518/623–8005 | Closed Mon., Tues., and Columbus Day–Mother's Day. No Lunch | $8–$23 | AE, MC, V.

Lodging

Country Road Lodge. Situated on the Hudson River and 35 scenic acres, the lodge also borders extensive state forest lands. Its location in the Adirondack Mountains offers many opportunities for hiking, skiing, biking, canoeing, antiquing, and sightseeing. Two rooms have private baths, the other two share a bath. Winter weekend packages are available. Complimentary breakfast, no room phones. Hiking, cross-country skiing. | 115 Hickory Hill Rd. | 518/623–2207 | fax 518/623–4363 | www.countryroadlodge.com | 4 rooms (2 with shared bath) | $72 | No credit cards.

Friends Lake Inn. Gaze out upon a gorgeous mountain lake from the Adirondack-style porch of this luxurious inn 7 mi north of Warrensburg. Each room is decorated differently with colorful quilts and spreads, and some rooms have lake views and Jacuzzi baths. The most deluxe room has a private entrance, a king-size bed, a large bathroom with a steam shower and Jacuzzi, a wet bar, a stone fireplace, and a screened balcony. Common areas include a heated pool and pool house, and a lakefront area with canoe and paddleboats. Restaurant. TV in common area. Pool. Hot tub. Hiking. Beach, boating. Cross-country skiing. Library. Business services. | Friends Lake Rd., Chestertown | 518/494–4751 | fax 518/494–4616 | friend@netheaven.com | www.friendslake.com | 17 rooms | $195–$375 | AE, MC, V.

Merrill Magee House. This 19th-century country estate is surrounded by trees and gardens. Each room has a fireplace and a different garden herb theme, and is furnished with antiques and quilted linen. | 10 rooms. Restaurant, complimentary breakfast. Pool. Hot tub. No smoking. | 2 Hudson St. | 518/623–2449 | www.merrillmageehouse.com | $115–$125 | AE, D, MC, V.

CAR RENTAL TIPS

- ❑ Review auto insurance policy to find out what it covers when you're away from home.
- ❑ Know the local traffic laws.
- ❑ Jot down make, model, color, and license plate number of rental car and carry the information with you.
- ❑ Locate gas tank—make sure gas cap is on and can be opened.
- ❑ Check trunk for spare and jack.
- ❑ Test the ignition—make sure you know how to remove the key.
- ❑ Test the horn, headlights, blinkers, and windshield wipers.

*Excerpted from *Fodor's: How to Pack: Experts Share Their Secrets*
© 1997, by Fodor's Travel Publications

WARWICK

(Nearby towns also listed: Goshen, Monroe, Spring Valley)

Warwick's quaint downtown shopping district is surrounded by the famous Pine Island black dirt farming region, known for its celebrated onion crop. Warwick is also near Sugar Loaf, an arts-and-crafts village with dozens of shops and restaurants.

Information: Chamber of Commerce | Box 202, 10990 | 845/986–2720 | www.warwickcc.org.

Attractions

Sugar Loaf Village. The village of Sugar Loaf is a scenic 10 min drive east from Warwick, and is made up of more than 60 shops and artists' studios. Painters, sculptors, and other craftspeople ply their trade and sell their wares here, some in buildings dating back to the mid 1800s. | Kings Hwy. | 845/469–9181 | www.sugarloaf.hvnet.com | Free | 11–5; Closed Mon.

ON THE CALENDAR

JUNE: *Around the World in 60 Miles.* This annual event celebrates the Shawangunk Wine Trail. The tour of the trail includes tastings and wine-making demonstrations at seven regional wineries (accessible from Interstate 84, exits 16, 17, and 18). You begin at any of the participating wineries, and then makes a circuit, following the grape cluster signs from one winery to the next. | 845/255–2494, 845/258–6020, or 845/496–9101.

AUG.: *Onion Harvest Festival.* Enjoy Polish foods, crafts, and performances by polka king Jimmy Sturr and his orchestra as part of this weekend-long festival. | County Rte. 1, Pine Island | 845/986–5004.

SEPT.–OCT.: *Applewood Orchards and Winery.* During the months of September and October, pick your own apples and pumpkins. | 82 Four Corners Rd. | 845/988–9292 | www.applewoodorchards.com.

OCT.: *Applefest.* The streets of Warwick close for this fall harvest festival; hundreds of vendors sell food and crafts, and you can sample apple pies baked by the most famous local chefs. | 845/986–2031.

Dining

Ye Jolly Onion Inn. American. This landmark eatery is about 7 mi northwest of Warwick, in the heart of Pine Island's famous black dirt region. The restaurant is known for meats, fish, and seasonal vegetables. Salad bar. Full bar. Early bird specials Wednesday–Friday. | Rte. 1, Pine Island | 845/258–4277 | www.yejollyonioninn.com | No lunch Mon.–Sat. | $15–$25 | MC, V.

Lodging

Warwick Valley Bed and Breakfast. This B&B in a 1900s Colonial Revival home is in the historic tree-lined district of Warwick. Decorated with an eclectic combination of antiques and country furnishings, the spacious guest rooms include private baths and sitting areas. The dining room has individual tables or the breakfast area can be set with a common table to share conversations with other guests. Complimentary breakfast. In-room data ports, cable TV. Business services. No pets. | 24 Maple Ave. | 845/987–7255 or 888/280–1671 | fax 845/988–5318 | www.wvbedandbreakfast.com | 4 rooms | $100–$125 | AE, D, MC, V.

WATERLOO

(Nearby towns also listed: Auburn, Canandaigua, Geneva, Palmyra, Seneca Falls, Skaneateles)

Waterloo, along the Cayuga-Seneca Canal between Cayuga and Seneca lakes, is surrounded by farmland, wineries, lakes, and canals. First settled in 1800, the town is rich in historical significance. The Church of Jesus Christ of Latter-Day Saints was formed here in 1830 on the Peter Whitmer Farm, about 3 mi south of downtown. In addition, Waterloo was formally recognized in 1966 by the U.S. Congress as the birthplace of Memorial Day.

Information: Seneca County Tourism | Box 491, 2020 Rtes. 5 and 20, Seneca Falls, 13148 | 800/732–1848 | windmill@seneca.org | www.senecachamber.org.

Attractions

McClintock House. The McClintocks, a Quaker family, helped plan the first Women's Rights Convention, which was held in nearby Seneca Falls in 1848. Their house, renovated in 2000, is now part of the National Women's Rights Historical Park based in Seneca Falls. | 14 E. Williams St. | 315/568–2991 | $4 | Call for hours.

Peter Whitmer Farm. The Church of Jesus Christ of Latter-Day Saints was organized here in 1830. The farm includes a reconstructed 1810 log home. | 1451 Ox Rd. | 315/539–2552 | www.mormons.org/daily/history/1820_1831/fayette_eom.htm | Free | Daily.

Prime Outlets. The center has more than 100 brand-name outlet stores. | 655 Rte. 318 | 315/539–1100 | www.primeoutlets.com | Free | Mon.–Sat. 10–9, Sun. 11–6.

Terwilliger Museum. This small historical museum details Native American history and offers a peek at life in the 1920s. Each of the five rooms of the museum is furnished in the styles of five different eras. | 31 E. Williams St. | 315/539–0533 | www.waterloony.com/library.html | Free | Tues.–Fri. 1–4.

Waterloo Memorial Day Museum. The museum presents the village's case for being the birthplace of Memorial Day. Evidently, the holiday, then celebrated with a parade, speeches and prayer, first happened here on May 5, 1866. One hundred years later, Congress and President Lyndon B. Johnson declared the village the holiday's place of origin. | 35 E. Main St. | 315/539–9611 | www.waterloony.com/mdaymus.html | Free | July–Sept., Tues.–Fri. 1–4, Sat. 10–2; or by appointment.

ON THE CALENDAR

MAY: *Memorial Day.* In Waterloo, the birthplace of Memorial Day, the holiday is held on the traditional date of May 30th and is a solemn commemorative event rather than a celebration. Events include a parade and a ceremony at the cemetery. | 315/539–9131 | www.waterloony.com.

Dining

Abigail's Restaurant. American. This large, sunny restaurant sits beside the Seneca-Cayuga Canal with a deck and dining room that overlook the water. Try the broiled whitefish. The menu includes a wide selection of Finger Lakes wines. | 1978 Rtes. 5 and 20 | 315/539–9300 | No lunch Sat. | $12–$14 | AE, D, DC, MC, V.

Lodging

Holiday Inn. This comfortable chain hotel is near an outlet mall and surrounded by a number of popular restaurants. Many rooms overlook a courtyard with a tennis court and heated swimming pool. King-size beds available. Restaurant, bar (with entertainment), room service. In-room data ports, cable TV. Pool. Hot tub. Tennis. Exercise equipment. Laundry facilities. Business services, free parking. Pets allowed. | 2468 Rte. 414 | 315/539–5011 | fax 315/539–8355 | 147 rooms | $80–$159 | AE, D, MC, V.

Microtel Inn and Suites. This two-story hotel with inside corridors was built in 1999 and is situated between Waterloo and Seneca Falls. It's on Routes 5 and 20 near the intersection of Route 414. In-room data ports, cable TV. Free parking. Pets allowed. | 1966 Rtes. 5 and 20, Seneca Falls | 315/539–8438 | fax 315/539–4780 | 48 rooms, 21 suites | $65–$71 rooms, $73–$75 suites | AE, D, DC, MC, V.

WATERTOWN

(Nearby town also listed: Sackets Harbor)

The Black River churns through this city, founded in 1799. Today, Watertown's location 11 mi east of Lake Ontario and 22 mi south of the St. Lawrence River makes the town a fine staging area for someone who wants to be equidistant from a number of the region's outdoor recreation and cultural attractions. Rafting, fishing, hiking, and winter sports abound in and around Watertown. The U.S. Army's Fort Drum neighbors the town, and much of the area's economic activity is tied to the military base.

Information: Greater Watertown Chamber of Commerce | 230 Franklin St., 13601 | 315/788–4400 | fax 315/788–3369 | chamber@imcnet.net | www.watertownny.com.

Attractions

American Maple Museum. This small museum 30 mi east of Watertown presents the history of maple-syrup making in North America. If you have a sweet tooth, it's worth the trip. | 81 Main St., Croghan | 315/346–1107 | $2 | July–mid-Sept., Mon.–Sat. 11–4; mid-Sept.–mid-Oct., Mon., Fri., Sat. 11–4; mid-Oct.–Nov., by appointment.

Jefferson County Historical Society Museum. Housed in an 1876 Tuscan-style villa, this museum exhibits period furnishings, Native American artifacts, and a 1910 Babcock automobile made in Watertown. | 228 Washington St. | 315/782–3491 | Free | May–Nov., Tues.–Fri. 10–5, Sat. noon–5; Dec.–Apr., Tues.–Fri. 10–5.

Long Point State Park. This 23-acre park, 15 mi west of Watertown at Point Peninsula (near Three Mile Bay), has 87 campsites (19 electrical), flush toilets, showers, a children's area, picnicking, boating, and fishing. | County Rte. 57, Point Peninsula | 315/649–5258 | www.nysparks.state.ny.us/parks/ | Free; parking $5 | May–mid-Sept., daily dusk–dawn.

Roswell P. Flower Memorial Library. The library's collection numbers 200,000 books and includes a large number of genealogy materials. | 229 Washington St. | 315/788–2352 | Free | Mon. 9:15–9, Tues.–Fri. 9:15–5.

Sci-Tech Center of Northern New York. Visit this hands-on science museum and learn the physics of light, sound, and electricity. | 154 Stone St. | 315/788–1340 | $4 | Tues.–Sat. 10–4.

White-water Rafting. The Black River has exciting rafting during the warm weather seasons. **ARO Adventures** (Box 649, Rte. 28, Old Forge | 315/369–3536 or 800/525–7238. | www.aroadventures.com | Apr.–Oct.; call for hours) runs 4-hr trips down the Black River. Trips offered by the **Hudson River Rafting Co.** (424 Newell St. | 315/782–7881 and 800/888–RAFT | hudson@netheaven.com | www.hudsonriverrafting.com | Admission varies | Apr.–Oct.; call for hrs) range from ½-hr to daylong excursions on the Black, Ausable, Hudson, and other rivers. 8 mi west of Watertown, **Whitewater Challengers** (Rte. 126, Dexter | 800/443–RAFT | wcrafting@microserve.net | www.wcrafting.com | Apr.–Oct.; call for hrs) offers white-water rafting for ages 14 and up.

Zoo at Thompson Park and Conservancy. You'll find wildlife habitats and trails, with an emphasis on North American animals. There's a children's farm, picnic pavilion, and swimming pool on site. | 1 Thompson Park | 315/782–6180 | $4 | Daily 10–5.

ON THE CALENDAR

JULY: *Black River Festival.* Hosts kayaking along the Black River, and lots of family events on the Riverwalk. | 315/788–2538.

JULY: *Jefferson County Fair.* More than 180 yrs old, this county fair is the oldest annual one in the nation. | Alex Duffy Fairgrounds, Coffeen St. | 315/782–8612 or 315/782–5698.

JULY: *Riverfest.* Enjoy frog jumping, entertainment, food, fireworks, and a pet parade along the banks of the Black River. | 315/493–3590.

SEPT.: *Lumberjack Festival.* Watch wood-cutting and truck- and tractor-pulls 30 mi east of Watertown. | Rte. 126, Croghan | 315/376–2213 or 800/724–0242.

Dining

Ann's Restaurant. Italian. Family owned, Ann's offers contemporary Italian and American cuisine like Nunzio's Sicilian Feast (a garlic pasta sampling with petite filet mignon, sautéed shrimp, and chicken breast), along with prime rib, gourmet sandwiches, and homemade desserts. Breakfast buffet also available Sundays. Directly in front of the Salmon Run Mall, near Interstate 81, exit 45. | Arsenal Street Rd. | 315/788–4402 | $4–$16 | AE, MC, V.

Art's Jug. Italian. This very popular dining destination in the greater Watertown area offers take-out service. They specialize in Italian entrées, steaks, seafood, chicken, veal, prime rib, and pizza. Wine and beer available. | 820 Huntington St. | 315/782–9764 | No lunch | $7–$16 | AE, D, MC, V.

Benny's Steak House. Italian. This family-owned, home-style Italian-American restaurant serves big steaks and seafood in a casual setting. Entertainment on Fridays, and kids' menu on Saturdays. | 1050 Arsenal St. | 315/788–4110 | $8–$20 | AE, D, MC, V.

Cavallario's Cucina. Pizza. Cavallario's opened the Watertown location after a 35-yr tradition of serving homemade pasta and pizza in Alexandria Bay. Eat in or take out. | 140 Eastern Blvd. | 315/788–9744 | www.1000-islands.net/cavallarios | Closed Sun. | $7–$15 | AE, MC, V.

Partridge Berry Inn. Continental. This old country inn with vaulted ceilings is one of the most refined dining experiences in northern New York. Veal cordon bleu, and Oscar-style chicken lightly sautéed and topped with crabmeat, asparagus, and béarnaise sauce are house specialties. Kids' menu. Sunday brunch. | 26561 Rte. 3 | 315/788–4610 | www.partridgeberryinn.com | No lunch Mon.–Sat. | $12–$19 | AE, MC, V.

Sboro's Restaurant. Italian. The winner of the 1998 NY State Beef Backer's Award, Sboro's offers simple, yet sophisticated Italian-American dishes, including a variety of fresh fish, lobster, steaks, chicken, veal, and pasta dishes. Try the antipasto or bruchetta bread appetizer. Sboro's also features local microbrewed beer and homemade desserts. | 836 Coffeen St. | 315/788–1728 | Closed Sun. No lunch | $10–$18 | AE, D, MC, V.

Lodging

Allen's Budget Motel. This traditional one- and two-story motor inn is near Salmon Run Mall and the Fort Drum military base. Free morning coffee is available in the office, and a 24-hr restaurant is nearby. On Route 342 near exit 48 off Interstate 81. In-room data ports, some kitchenettes, refrigerators, cable TV. | 24019 Rte. 342 | 315/782–5319 or 800/545–4184 | www.1000islands.com/allens | 21 rooms | $40–$48 | AE, D, DC, MC, V.

Best Western Carriage House Inn. This chain inn has helpful service, comfortable rooms, and a relaxing sundeck. The inn is convenient to local attractions, including the Sci-Tech

Center and the Thompson Park Zoo. Restaurant, bar (with entertainment), room service. Some minibars, some in-room hot tubs, cable TV. Pool. Barbershop, beauty salon, sauna. Business services. | 300 Washington St. | 315/782–8000 | fax 315/786–2097 | bestwest@imc-net.net | www.bestwestern.com | 150 rooms, 10 suites | $76–$125 | AE, D, DC, MC, V.

Davidson's Motel. Eight acres of forrested grounds, complete with two beaver ponds, make for lovely strolling around this one-level motel. Rooms are rather bland, but have the basics. Picnic area. Cable TV. Pool. | 26177 Rte. 3 | 315/782–3861 | fax 315/786–0599 | 20 rooms | $45–$49 | AE, D, MC, V.

Days Inn–Watertown. This six-story chain hotel is in the heart of Watertown's shopping district, and is connected to a Denny's fast-food restaurant. Rooms are furnished with two double or one king-size bed. Restaurant, bar, room service. Some refrigerators, cable TV. Pool. Gym. Business services, airport shuttle. | 1142 Arsenal St. | 315/782–2700 | fax 315/785–9877 | 135 rooms | $69–$89 | AE, D, MC, V.

Econo Lodge. Prefabricated, functional, and basic, this one-floor hotel is a study in bland corporate-chain American roadside accommodation. Picnic area, complimentary Continental breakfast. Refrigerators, cable TV. Pool. Laundry facilities. Pets allowed. | 1030 Arsenal St. | 315/782–5500 | fax 315/788–7608 | www.econolodge.com | econo@imc.net | 60 rooms | $63–$68 | AE, D, MC, V.

George's Backroom. Just west of the Watertown Airport in downtown Sackets Harbor is the exclusive George's Backroom with a balcony overlooking the waterfront. The VIP lodging consists of one large suite with fireplace, king-size bed, full kitchen, and sitting area. While the property is separate from the Ontario Place Hotel, reservations are made with the Ontario Place. Kitchenette, cable TV. Hot tub. | 208 W. Main St. | 315/646–8000 or 800/564–1812 | www.1000-islands.net/index7.htm | 1 suite | $125 | AE, D, DC, MC, V.

The Inn. This two-floor 1960s strip motel is notable for its spacious rooms that come with either two double or one queen-size bed. Cable TV. Pool. Video games. Laundry services. Pets allowed. | 1190 Arsenal St. | 315/788–6800 | fax 315/788–5366 | 96 rooms | $60–$70 | AE, D, MC, V.

Lucky Star Ranch. Lucky Star is a private estate on 4,500 acres of unspoiled wilderness in the Thousand Islands Region. There, you'll find a wide variety of natural habitats with nature and wildlife trails. Both the main house and the lodge overlook the lake and offer elegant interiors with European-style country living. All guest rooms have private baths, but phones are in the common areas. Three daily meals are included. From Memorial Day through Labor Day, special packages are available at $50 per night, 6-night minimum stay. Complimentary meals. Cable TV in common area, no room phones. Hiking, boating, fishing. | 13240 Lucky Star Ranch, Chaumont | 315/649–5519 | fax 315/649–3097 | www.luckystar-ranch.com | 6 rooms | $205 | AE, MC, V.

Microtel Inn. This two-floor hotel is on the north side of Watertown, within shouting distance of the Thousand Islands. Rooms have queen-size beds only. Cable TV. Video games. Pets allowed. | 8000 Virginia Smith Dr. | 315/629–5000 and 800/447–9660 | fax 315/629–5393 | microtel@gisco.com | 100 rooms | $49 | AE, D, MC, V.

New Parrot Motel. This affordable motel is in a commercial area. Rooms are simple, with either a king-size bed or two doubles. Picnic area. Some refrigerators, cable TV. Pool. Pets allowed. | 19325 Washington St. | 315/788–5080 or 800/479–9889 | 26 rooms | $48–$68 | AE, D, MC, V.

Ramada Inn. This chain hotel off I–81 has a lounge, a large dining room, and a café overlooking the pool area. Standard rooms come with either king-size, or two double beds. Restaurant, bar (with entertainment), dining room, room service. In-room data ports, cable TV. Pool. Shops. Baby-sitting. Laundry service. Business services, airport shuttle. | 6300 Arsenal St., at exit 45 | 315/788–0700 | fax 315/785–9875 | 145 rooms | $50–$80 | AE, D, DC, MC, V.

WATKINS GLEN

(Nearby towns also listed: Bath, Elmira, Hammondsport, Ithaca, Penn Yan)

Catharine Creek, a famous trout stream, flows into Seneca Lake at Watkins Glen. In town, you can fish on a 300-ft pier on the lakefront or take a stroll through Watkins Glen State Park, one of the state's premier natural wonders. Surrounding the town are the Finger Lakes National Forest and plenty of wineries.

Information: Schuyler County Chamber of Commerce | 100 N. Franklin St., 14891 | 800/ 607–4552 | www.schuylerny.com.

Attractions

Captain Bill's Seneca Lake Cruises. The Captain runs meal cruises and 10-mi lake trips from the bottom of Franklin Street. | 1 N. Franklin St. | 607/535–4541 | $7.75 | July–early Sept., daily 10–8 on the hr; May–June and early Sept.–Oct., daily, 10–8.

Farm Sanctuary. This 175-acre working farm and educational center houses hundreds of livestock and other animals brought from slaughterhouses and stockyards and nursed back to health. You are encouraged to pet the animals. Tours are every hour, on the hour. | 3100 Aikens Rd. | 607/583–2225 | www.farmsanctuary.org | $2 | June–Aug., Wed.–Sun. 10–4; May and Sept.–Oct., weekends 10–4.

Finger Lakes National Forest. The only real forest in the region, this park runs along a ridge 9 mi north of Watkins Glen between the southern ends of Cayuga and Seneca lakes. At 16,000 acres, it is one of the smallest of the 76 national forests. There are around 33 mi of easy-to-moderate hiking trails, and spaces for camping, horseback riding, fishing, and hunting. In winter you can cross-country ski and ride a snowmobile. | 5218 State Rte. 414, Hector | 607/546–4470 | $5 | Daily; visitors center weekdays 8–4:30, Sat. noon–4.

Glen Vintage Auto Museum. Plenty of zippy cars, like Austin Healeys, Morgans, Triumphs, Porsches, and others that recall the heyday of the American Grand Prix, are parked here. Be sure to check out James Bond's Aston Martin from *Goldfinger.* | N. Franklin St. | 607/ 535–9088 | $3 | May–Sept., daily noon–8.

Montour Falls. This small industrial community, 1 mi south of Watkins Glen, is surrounded by seven glens. Chequagua Falls, dropping 165 ft, is a visual treat at the foot of Main Street. The falls are lit at night and can be seen well from a pedestrian bridge near the crest of the falls. The village's National Historic District is made up of a group of 24 buildings dating back to the 1850s. | 14891 Rte. 14 | 607/535–7367 | Free | Daily.

Watkins Glen International Raceway. "New York's Thunder Road" is loud from June to October. Depending on how much you love fast cars and roaring engines, the season's highlight is the NASCAR Winston Cup Series race in mid-August. | 2790 Rte. 16 | 607/535–2481 | www.theglen.com | Admission varies per event | Hrs vary per event.

Watkins Glen State Park. This park's main entrance is in the village of Watkins Glen, near the south end of Seneca Lake, off Route 14. Campgrounds are scattered around the beautiful creek and its waterfalls. The waters of Glen Creek drop about 500 ft in 2 mi, in nearly 20 waterfalls. The 1½-mi gorge trail runs parallel to the water and 300-ft cliffs border the creek. One bridge spans 165 ft over the water. There is also an Olympic-size pool. | Franklin St. | 607/535–4511 | www.nysparks.state.ny.us/parks/ | Free; parking $5 | Daily.

Winery tours. The Seneca Lake Wine Trail includes many, but not all, of the area's wineries. Most of the 21 wineries are clustered around the southern third of Seneca Lake, northeast and northwest of Watkins Glen. Tours are based out of Penn Yan (25 mi north of Watkins Glen). | 315/536–9996 | fax 315/531–8292 | www.senecalakewine.com | slwa@eznet.net | Hrs vary by winery.

Chateau Lafayette Reneau (14841 Rte. 414 N, Hector | 607/546–2062 | Free | Apr.–Nov., Mon.–Sat. 10–6, Sun. 11–6; Dec.–Mar., Mon.–Sat. 10–5, Sun. 11–5) is a beautiful, friendly winery 9 mi north of Watkins Glen. The view of Seneca Lake is gorgeous, and the wine is award-winning.

A tour of the **Glenora Wine Cellars** (5435 Rte. 14, Dundee | 607/243–5511 or 800/243–5513 | fax 607/243–5514 | Free | Mon.–Sat. 10–5, Sun. noon–5), about 9 mi north of Glen Watkins, includes a "Vine to Wine" video tour.

ON THE CALENDAR

MAY–SEPT.: *Watkins Glen International.* This is world-class auto racing. | 607/535–2481.

JULY: *Finger Lakes Wine Festival.* Virtually all the area wineries are represented at this festival that takes place at Watkins Glen International Race Track. Schedule includes music, seminars, and tastings. | 2790 Rte. 16 | 607/535–2481.

AUG.: *NASCAR Racing.* Thousands of fans and top drivers appear at the state's only NASCAR Winston Cup race. | 2790 Rte. 16 | 607/535–2481.

Dining

Castel Grisch. German. This restaurant feels like a cross between a Swiss chalet and a French castle. There's a winery on site, and a large dining terrace with a view of Seneca Lake. Specialties include Wienerschnitzel, spaetzle, and fresh-baked strudel. Sunday brunch. | 3380 County Rd. 28 | 607/535–9614 | fax 607/535–2994 | www.fingerlakes-ny.com/castelgrisch | Closed Jan.–Mar., except Valentine's Day weekend | $14–$23 | AE, D, MC, V.

Franklin Street Grill. American. Franklin Street is downtown, a few blocks north of the entrance to Watkins Glen State Park. Before the International Raceway was built in the late 1940s, cars would race through the village past the restaurant, providing exciting mealtime entertainment. Known for its steaks and seafood. Kids' menu. | 413 Franklin St. | 607/535–2007 | Closed Sun. Feb.–May | $8–$22 | AE, D, MC, V.

Seasons Restaurant. American. This restaurant in a former hotel, renovated in 1998, is known for strip steak, seafood, and dinner salads. In winter, two cozy fireplaces warm up the dining room. Kids' menu. | 108 N. Franklin St. | 607/535–4619 | $15–$24 | AE, D, MC, V.

Wildflower Cafe. Contemporary. This upscale-yet-casual eatery is housed in a brick-and-wood building, close to the entrance of Watkins Glen State Park. Oak and brass touches and stained-glass windows adorn the interior. The kitchen's specialties are rack of lamb, salmon, and duck. Kids' menu. | 301 N. Franklin St. | 607/535–9797 | www.wildflower-cafe.com | $14–$24 | AE, MC, V.

© Artville

NOT ALL OF THEM GET AWAY

The Eastern Lake Ontario Basin is considered by many to be one of the best freshwater fisheries in the world. Current state records for lake trout and chinook, coho, and Atlantic salmon have been set in the area.

If you're interested in fishing while visiting the area, you can expect to find brown and lake trout moving toward the shore in April, and walleye and steelhead running inland in May and early June. Small and largemouth black bass are found in June and July, and king, coho, and Atlantic salmon are found in the tributaries from late summer through November.

Steelheads, walleye, and brown and lake trout can be found in both the spring and summer, and salmon and trout can be found during deepwater fishing in summer. Look for northern pike and yellow perch under the ice of bays and marshes in winter.

Lodging

Bellevue. This small, rural motel has a large lawn and views of Seneca Lake. Rooms have either queen-size, king-size, or double beds. Picnic area. Kitchenettes, refrigerators. | 3812 Rte. 14 | 607/535–4232 | 7 rooms, 1 apartment, 5 cottages | $55–$85 | Closed late Nov.–mid-Apr. | AE, D, MC, V.

Cherry Orchard Bed & Breakfast. Overlooking Seneca Lake, this B&B is set in a cherry orchard and vineyard. The contemporary rooms have private baths and a view of either the lake, the orchard, or Fox Run Golf Course; some rooms have a private entrance. The Cherry Orchard is approximately 4 mi north of Watkins Glen on Route 14. Restaurant, complimentary breakfast. Spa. | Rte. 14 | 607/535–7785 or 607/535–9330 | www.cherryorchard.com | 6 rooms | $95–$125 | AE, MC, V.

Inn at Glenora Wine Cellars. This luxurious inn (12 mi north of Watkins Glen) was built in 1999 as an addition to a working winery on the Seneca Lake Wine Trail. Most rooms overlook Seneca Lake from the west bank, and the inn's restaurant serves regional cuisine from around the world. Restaurant, picnic area. Some in-room hot tubs, cable TV. | 5435 Rte. 14, Dundee | 607/243–9500 and 800/243–5513 | www.glenora.com | 30 rooms | $100–$225 | AE, D, MC, V.

Longhouse Lodge. This one-story hotel, sitting atop a hill off State Route 14 just north of Watkins Glen, affords views of Seneca Lake from both the rooms and the deck and gazebo. Standard rooms have king-size or double beds, and deluxe rooms have refrigerators and VCRs. Free movies are available in the lobby. Complimentary Continental breakfast. Some microwaves, some refrigerators, some in-room VCRs. Pool. | 3625 Rte. 14 | 607/535–2565 | www.longhouselodge.com | 21 rooms | $69–$125 | D, MC, V.

Seneca Lake Watch Bed and Breakfast. This Queen Ann Victorian B&B has second- and third-floor watch towers overlooking Seneca Lake. The rooms are large with modern private baths. The common area has a telephone, fireplace, and piano. Complimentary breakfast, picnic area. No room phones, cable TV and VCR in common area. Water sports. | 104 Seneca St. | 607/535–4490 | www.bbhost.com/senecalakewatchbb/ | 5 rooms | $65–$125 | AE, MC, V.

WELLSVILLE

MAP 3, E8

(Nearby town also listed: Olean)

Wellsville, the largest community in Allegany County, was named in 1855 after Gardner Wells, one of the town's original landowners. Oil has been produced here since 1879 and was the area's primary industry until 1958. Today Wellsville is an important regional education center. It's the home to a branch of Alfred State University, and within a 15-min drive of two other colleges: Houghton College and Alfred University. In addition, Wellsville has the distinction of hosting one of the nation's oldest hot-air balloon rallies, first held in 1975.

Information: Wellsville Area Chamber of Commerce | 114 N. Main St., 14895 | 716/593–5080 | fax 716/593–5088 | wacoc@vivanet.com | www.wellsvilleny.com/chamber.htm.

Attractions

Dyke Street Museum. This museum, housed in an old firehouse, displays memorabilia, clothing, furniture, quilts, Native American relics, and census and genealogical records. | 116 E. Dyke St. | 716/593–1404 | Free | June–Oct., Wed. 1–4 or by appointment.

Mather Homestead Museum. This century-old home on 1½ acres of land includes a library, memorial park, and a 1930s-era room. | 343 N. Main St. | 716/593–1636 | Free | Wed. and Sat. 2–5 or by appointment.

JULY: *Wellsville Balloon Rally.* A week of activities starts with the Annual Balloon Rally parade featuring specialty balloons where spectators can go down on the field and get close to the hot-air creations. In conjunction, the 2-day Main Street Festival has over 100 craft and specialty vendors, as well as music, children's activities, and a hot-dog-eating contest. | 716/593–5080 | wellsville.balloonrally.com.

Dining

Texas Hot Restaurant. American. This family restaurant grills up tasty hot dogs and filling hamburgers with all the fixin's. | 132 N. Main St. | 716/593–1400 | Breakfast also available | $2–$9 | No credit cards.

Lodging

Long-Vue Motel. This standard one-story motel with outside corridors has a breathtaking view of the valley below. Some microwaves, some refrigerators, cable TV, in-room VCRs. | Rte. 417 W | 716/593–2450 | fax 716/593–2450 | 19 rooms | $65–$100 | AE, MC, V.

Victorian Pines Bed and Breakfast. This small bed-and-breakfast has a quaint, Victorian air about it, as well as modern amenities. Complimentary breakfast. Hot tub. No smoking. | 3148 Riverside Dr. | 716/593–3923 | fax 716/593–3923 | 4 rooms | $57–$90 | MC, V.

WEST POINT

MAP 3, K9

(Nearby towns also listed: Newburgh, Stony Point)

America's oldest and most distinguished military academy, West Point, is on the bluffs overlooking the Hudson River. The academy has been the training ground for U.S. Army officers since 1802. Distinguished graduates include Robert E. Lee, Ulysses S. Grant, and Douglas MacArthur. The museum at Thayer Hall houses one of the world's foremost collections of military memorabilia and equipment. Uniforms, weapons, field equipment, flags, and American military art are on display. There are also galleries depicting the history of West Point, and on the grounds you'll find memorials, cannons, and restored forts, such as Ft. Putnam. Admission to West Point is free, although there is a fee for tours. The visitors center and museum are open daily.

Information: West Point Visitor Center | Building 2107, 10996 | 845/938–2638.

Lodging

★ **Hotel Thayer.** This stately brick hotel on the grounds of the U.S. Military Academy is steeped in history and tradition and has welcomed military and civilian guests for 70 yrs. The public rooms are highlighted by marble floors, iron chandeliers, military portraits, and leather furnishings. Guest rooms have standard appointments, and many have views of the river and West Point grounds. Restaurant, lounge. In-room data ports, cable TV. Tennis court. Business services. | Rte. 9W | 845/446–4731 or 800/247–5047 | fax 845/446–0338 | 125 rooms | $150–$170 | AE, MC, V.

WESTBURY/OLD WESTBURY

MAP 4, H7

(Nearby town also listed: Garden City)

This 2½-square-mi village with its harmonious mingling of ethnicities is a convenient hour from Manhattan and an easy jaunt to some of Long Island's loveliest beaches.

WESTBURY/
OLD WESTBURY

INTRO
ATTRACTIONS
DINING
LODGING

Incorporated in 1932, Westbury lacks the old money of Old Westbury, but has highly regarded restaurants, and hosts the Westbury Music Fair. The town is also quite close to two of Long Island's largest shopping areas, the Mall at the Source and Roosevelt Field.

Old Westbury, strictly a wealthy residential community, is one of the least-populated areas of Nassau County, due to zoning requirements. Its historical roots date to 1657, when Captain John Seamann bought 12,000 acres from the Algonquin Indians. Later, in 1700, Quakers fleeing persecution settled in the area, naming their settlement Westbury after their home town in England. Over time, estates replaced the farms of early settlers and today horse trails wind along its soft rolling hills

Information: **Garden City Chamber of Commerce** | 230 7th St., Garden City, 11530 | 516/746–7724.

Attractions

Cradle of Aviation Museum. Opened in 2001, the museum recalls a time when Long Island was "The Cradle of Aviation." Displays include a Republic A-10 Thunderbolt II, a supersonic F-14 Tomcat, a Grumman's F6F Hellcat, and one of only three existing original Apollo lunar modules. | Museum La., Mitchel Field, Garden City | 516/572–0410 | www.cradleofaviation.org | Admission varies per event | Hrs vary per event.

Old Westbury Gardens. One of the few former Long Island estates still intact, this Gold-Coast mansion built by financier-sportsman John S. Phipps is open to the public. Tours of the beautiful 100-acre property showcase the home's original furniture, the family's art and belongings, and the extraordinary formal manicured gardens and grounds. | 71 Old Westbury Rd., Old Westbury | 516/333–0048 | $10 | Apr.–mid-Dec., Wed.–Mon. 10–5; call for holiday events in Dec.

Westbury Music Fair. This theater-in-the-round holds a capacity of 2,700, and attracts musical performers and pop artists of all genres. | Brush Hollow Rd. (on I–495, near exit 40 W | 516/334–0800 | www.musicfair.com | Admission varies | Call for schedule.

ON THE CALENDAR

AUG.: *Scottish Games.* Participate in games and contests, such as a caber toss and tossing the shear. Enjoy Highland Fling demonstrations, Scottish food, bagpipes, and crafts. | 516/333–0048.

NOV.: *Long Island Festival of Trees.* Purchase or simply view beautiful designer-decorated trees (over 150 displayed), wreaths, and holiday crafts. | 516/378–2000.

DEC.: *First Night.* Tour a former Gold Coast mansion beautifully decorated for the Christmas season with over 100,000 twinkling lights adorning the building and grounds. Storytelling and games for children on Nanny Night. | Old Westbury Gardens, Old Westbury | 516/333–0048.

Dining

Cafe Baci. American, Italian. This bright, fun-but-occasionally-noisy restaurant lined with sunny windows serves such large portions of veal, chicken, and pasta that you may want to split a dish with a friend. | 1636 Old Country Rd. | 516/832–8888 | $9–$18 | AE, DC, MC, V.

Cafe Spasso. Italian. At night, pink neon lights make the place ½ mi east of Old Westbury gleam. The rigatoni in vodka sauce, tortellini da Vinci (cheese tortellini with mushrooms and shrimp in pink cream sauce), calamari, and mussels marinara are local favorites. | 307 Old Country Rd., Carle Place | 516/333–1718 | Reservations not accepted | $15–$20 | AE, DC, MC, V.

Churrasqueira Bairrada. Portuguese. Judging from the crowds, the public and critics agree on this restaurant (4.4 mi southwest of Old Westbury). Get there early and brave the noise to taste the delicious barbecued chicken, steaks, and homemade potato chips. | 144 Jericho Tpk., Mineola | 516/739–3856 | Closed Mon. | $14–$20 | AE, DC, MC, V.

Giulio Cesare. Italian. Enjoy fresh seafood in an upscale dining room dotted with wine bottles and white linen. | 18 Ellison Ave. | 516/334–2982 | Reservations essential | Closed Sun. No lunch Sat. | $15–$30 | AE, MC, V.

Piping Rock. Italian. This elegant restaurant, known for steak, seafood, and pasta, was recently renovated after a fire destroyed the building in 2000. Try the Piping Rock Chicken: sautéed breast of chicken topped with eggplant, prosciutto, and mozzarella. Raw bar. Salad bar. Live music Thursday–Saturday. Kids' menu. No smoking. | 130 Post Ave. | 516/333–5555 | $25–$35 | AE, DC, MC, V.

Rialto. Italian. This florally accented restaurant (2 mi from Westbury) has two dining areas: one casual; and the other candlelit and romantic. House specialties include veal chops with portobello mushrooms, snapper, and tuna steaks. | 588 Westbury Ave., Carle Place | 516/997–5283 | Closed Sun. No lunch Sat. | $17–$28 | AE, DC, MC, V.

Westbury Manor. Continental. This restaurant sits on 6 acres of landscaped gardens with ponds, waterfalls, and gazebos. The dining room has antique heirlooms, plush upholsteries, and finished wood. The fish, rack of lamb for two, and pasta are well renowned. Guitarist Tuesdays; pianist Wednesday–Sunday. Long Island Expressway, exit 39, Glen Cove Road, S for 1.8 mi, turn left onto Jericho Turnpike, Route 25B E, ³/₁₀ mi. | Jericho Tpk. | 516/333–7117 | www.scottobrothers.com | $15–$32 | AE, DC, MC, V.

Lodging
Howard Johnson Inn. The three-story inn, remodeled in 1999, is just ¼ mi from Westbury Music Fair. The full breakfast includes French toast, waffles, and pancakes. All guest rooms have in-room coffeemakers, irons and ironing boards, and hair dryers. Complimentary breakfast. In-room data ports, cable TV. Pool. Fishing. Free parking. | 120 Jericho Tpk. | 516/333–9700 or 800/406–1411 | fax 516/333–9393 | 80 rooms | $111–$139 | AE, D, DC, MC, V.

WESTFIELD

MAP 3, B7

(Nearby towns also listed: Chautauqua, Dunkirk, Fredonia)

As the home of Welch's grape juice, the town of Westfield calls itself the grape-juice capital of the world. Antiques and craft shops and Federal-style mansions built in the 1820s are reminders of the town's rich history.

Information: Westfield Chamber of Commerce | 19 W. 2nd St., 14787 | 716/326–4000.

Attractions
Chautauqua Institution. The Institution presents over 2,000 events each season, including the symphony, opera, chamber music, visual arts, dance, theater, open-enrollment classes, and programming for young people. | 1 Ames Ave., Chautauqua | 716/357–6200 or 800/836–2787 | fax 716/357–6369 | www.chautauqua-inst.org | June–Sept.

ON THE CALENDAR
JULY–AUG.: *Westfield Antique Show.* An annual antiques show is held in late July or early August. | 718/326–4185 | www.landmarkacres.com.

Dining
Ye Hare 'n Hounds Inn. American. Overlooking Chautauqua Lake, the inn opened as a restaurant in 1921. Traditional seafood, steak, veal, poultry, and lamb dishes are served amidst English decor, fireplaces, and candlelight. Homemade desserts and breads. | 64 Lakeside Dr., Bemus Point | 716/386–2181 | www.madbbs.com/users/tanka | No lunch | $14–$40 | AE, D, MC, V.

Lodging

Candlelight Lodge Bed and BreakfastName. Built in 1851, this Italianate-style brick Victorian mansion is listed on the National Register of Historic Places. The B&B has spiral walnut staircases, arched windows, and fireplaces. Rooms feature Victorian furnishings and private baths. You are within walking distance of antiques shops, stores, and restaurants, and the Chautauqua Institute is 15 min away. Nearby are Lakes Erie and Chautauqua water sports, downhill skiing, and winery tours. An expansion, Captain Storm's House, is expected to open in the summer of 2001. Picnic area, complimentary breakfast. Some kitchenettes, some microwaves, cable TV, no room phones. Hiking, cross-country skiing. | 143 E. Main St. (Rte. 20) | 716/326–2830 | www.landmarkacres.com/page5 | 8 rooms | $65–$155 | Closed Jan.–Feb. | MC, V.

Sugar Shack Bed and Breakfast/Country Cottage. This small bed-and-breakfast, nestled on 30 acres of Lake Erie waterfront, is also a working farm. Complimentary breakfast is served with real maple syrup and fresh fruit spreads, both made on the premises. You can tour the maple production facilities and a grape farm. The property has a private swimming area, three stocked ponds, and nature trails. Restaurant, picnic area, complimentary breakfast. Cable TV. Hiking. Beach, fishing. Laundry facilities. | 7904 Rte. 5 | 716/326–3351 or 888/563–4324 | www.vinetime.com/vinewood | 3 rooms | $75–$100 | AE, D, MC, V.

William Seward Inn. This fully restored 1837 country inn is bathed in vivid hues and classic fabrics. Rooms are furnished with period antiques or reproductions. Some deluxe rooms have double Jacuzzis, while others are warmed with gas log fireplaces. Restaurant, complimentary breakfast. Some in-room hot tubs, no room phones. No kids under 12. No smoking. | 6645 S. Portage Rd. | 716/326–4151 or 800/338–4151 | fax 716/326–4163 | wmseward@cecomet.net | www.williamsewardinn.com | 12 rooms | $70–$185 | AE, D, DC, MC, V.

WESTHAMPTON BEACH

MAP 3, E2

(Nearby towns also listed: Hampton Bays, Quogue/East Quogue, Patchogue, Riverhead, Southampton)

One could say that the "Hampton mystique" began in beautiful Westhampton Beach. In 1870, residents began renting out rooms to travelers who reached the area on the newly constructed Long Island Railroad. Soon the practice spread to the rest of the Hamptons and it was not long before the Hamptons was a resort area of renown. In fact, so many seasonal visitors have fallen in love with Westhampton's manicured lawns, beautifully cultivated gardens, and mystical waters that it has become one of the fastest-growing year-round communities on eastern Long Island.

Westhampton's excellent restaurants, sophisticated shops, nightlife, and magnificent ocean beaches attract the rich and famous, as well as those who just enjoy the good life. A scenic drive not to be missed is Dune Road east to Hampton Bays. Simple beach houses mixed with extravagant mansions of stunning architecture are magnificently juxtaposed under the blue Hampton skies.

Information: **Greater Westhampton Chamber of Commerce** | Box 1228, 173 Montauk Hwy., Westhampton, 11978 | 631/288–3337.

Attractions

Cupsogue Beach County Park. The park includes 1 mi of beachfront on Moriches Inlet. There are lifeguards from the end of May to early September, as well as a pavilion with a snack bar and rental sand chairs, and limited camping facilities. | Dune Rd. | 631/852–8111 or 631/852–8112 | $8 | Daily 8:30–6.

Hampton Synagogue. Attractive landscaping and formal gardens surround this beautiful synagogue. | 154 Sunset Ave. | 631/288–0534 | Free | Services Fri. 4:30 and 5:30, Sat. 9 and 4:30, Sun. 9.

Westhampton Day Spa. The popular spa is at the Westhampton Bath & Tennis Center. | 231 Dune Rd. | 631/288–2500, ext. 2841 | Prices vary per service | Tues.–Sat. 10–9, Sun. 9–6.

Westhampton Historical Museum. The house, built in the early 1800s, has temporary exhibitions and a permanent collection of photographs of early Westhampton Beach. | 11978 Mill Rd. | 631/288–1139 | Admission varies per event | Hrs vary per event.

ON THE CALENDAR

JAN.–DEC.: *Performing Arts Theater.* You'll find a variety of musical and theatrical performances. Call for program and schedule. | Long Tree Pond Development, 42 Drew Dr., Eastport | 631/325–8624.
OCT.: *Harvest Festival.* The festival includes a boat show, maritime crafts, vendors, and rides. | 11978 Main St. | 631/668–2428.

Dining

Dora's. Eclectic. You're one of the family at this carpeted, down-home establishment with mostly booth seating. Plaques and paintings of the town in the 1930s hang from the old-wood walls. The menu features a wide range of dishes—from duck and beef Wellington to pasta and seafood. Kids' menu. Early bird dinners (excluding Sat.). | 105 Montauk Hwy. | 631/288–9723 | $15–$25 | AE, D, DC, MC, V.

Rene's Casa Basso. Italian. Sculptures dot the front and side lawns of this upscale, traditional restaurant. To enter, you walk under the swords of two concrete 12-ft-tall fencing musketeers, revealing a miniature castle complete with mythological figures. Food is both northern and southern Italian, and the pasta, seafood, veal, and steaks only complement this truly unique dining experience. | 59 Montauk Hwy. | 631/288–1841 | Reservations essential | Closed Mon. No lunch | $16–$30 | AE, MC, V.

Starr Bogg's. Seafood. The dining room of this upscale restaurant has a spectacular view of the beach and ocean and is accented with artwork, crystal, and white linen. Watch from the deck and bar as the sun sets into the ocean. The menu changes daily. Go Mondays for the lobster bake. Open-air dining on a deck. | 379 Dune Rd. | 631/288–5250 | Reservations essential | Closed mid-Oct.–mid-May | $24–$35 | AE, MC, V.

Tierra Mar. French. This romantic restaurant is warmed by a fireplace in winter and enlivened by a garden room in summer. Chef Todd Jacobs, well known on Long Island, prepares exquisite salmon and exotic game such as Ostrich Carpaccio (fillet of ostrich seared on the grill) and baby antelope. Raw bar. Winter Sunday brunch. No smoking. | 213 Dune Rd. | 631/288–2700 | $22–$40 | AE, DC, MC, V.

Lodging

1880 House. Filled with antiques, this 100 year-old B&B features guest rooms with private baths and a fireplace in the common area. Two rooms have an adjoining sitting room, and the third is a suite in an old converted barn. The ocean beach is just a 5 min walk away. Complimentary breakfast. Pool. Tennis. Hiking, water sports. | Two Seafield La. | 631/288–1559 or 800/346–3290 | fax 631/288–0721 | 3 rooms | $100–$200 | AE, MC, V.

WESTHAMPTON
BEACH

INTRO
ATTRACTIONS
DINING
LODGING

WHITE PLAINS

(Nearby towns also listed: Elmsford, Hartsdale, Hawthorne, Mamaroneck, New Rochelle, New York City, Rye, Scarsdale, Tarrytown, Yonkers)

This city's 50,000 residents live amid a dynamic mixture of new and old in the heart of Westchester County. Founded in 1735, White Plains became a major crossroads during the Revolutionary War, after General George Washington out-maneuvered British General Lord Howe here. Today, important historical sites sit next to modern shopping malls, corporate centers, and suburban homes, separated only by wooded and winding roads.

Information: County Chamber of Commerce | 235 Mamaroneck Ave., #Ll, 10605 | 914/ 948–2110.

Attractions

Washington's Headquarters and Museum. Visit the site of General George Washington's 1776 headquarters during the final hours of the Battle of White Plains. Tours, musket demonstrations, and other activities take place. Nearby is the Miller Hill Restoration, the excavated and restored earthworks built by George Washington's troops during the battle. | 140 Virginia Rd. | 914/949–1236 or 914/242–6324 | www.historytrail.com | $3 | By appointment only.

ON THE CALENDAR

OCT.: *Westchester Crafts Show.* This annual fair represents some of the best crafters in the region. | 914/285–4050.

Dining

Bengal Tiger. Indian. Serving White Plains since 1974, the Bengal Tiger offers traditional dishes including lamb vindaloo and vegetarian dishes. The interior of the restaurant reflects an exotic past when every meal was a feast. | 144 E. Post Rd. | 914/948–5191 | whiteplains.com/dine.html | $11–$23 | AE, MC, V.

Café Michelangelo. Italian. This warm Italian restaurant is known for its welcoming atmosphere. The lighting is low, tables are well-spaced, and the service is efficient but obtrusive. The menu feaures classic Italian dishes like lasagna, fettuccine Alfredo with grilled chicken or shrimp, and chicken parmigiana. | 208 Underhill Ave., West Harrison | 914/428–0022 | Closed Mon. | $9–$25 | AE, D, DC, MC, V.

Dawat. Indian. Ornate puppets and statues adorn the interior of this classy Indian favorite. Their enormous lunch buffet is packed with inventive dishes. Buffet lunch. Kids' menu. Sunday brunch. | 230 E. Post Rd. | 914/428–4411 | www.dawat.com | No lunch Fri.–Sun. | $16–$21 | AE, DC, MC, V.

Olliver's. American. This local watering hole serves basic pub food and has a busy bar scene. Live DJ on Thursdays, Fridays, and Saturdays. | 15 S. Broadway | 914/761–6111 | Closed Sun. | $13–$20 | AE, D, DC, MC, V.

Reka's. Thai. Authentic Thai artifacts adorn this welcoming restaurant serving traditional Royal Thai cuisine. Try escargot Thai style and wild boar jungle style with Thai eggplant. Sunday brunch. | 2 Westchester Ave. | 914/949–1440 | Reservations essential weekends | Closed Mon. No dinner Sun. | $10–$20 | AE, DC, MC, V.

Lodging

Crowne Plaza. This pleasant, upscale 12-story hotel close to major highways has bathrobes and double and king-size beds. Executive rooms available. Restaurant, bar. In-room data ports, cable TV. Pool. Hot tub. Exercise equipment. Laundry facilities. Business services, air-

IT'S REVOLUTIONARY: THE WAR FOR INDEPENDENCE IN WESTCHESTER COUNTY

In many ways, a trip through the lovely landscapes of Westchester County is a journey back in time. Some of the most pivotal battles of America's fight for independence were waged here, and many of the most important patriots of the Revolution called the area home. Local historical sites honor the great men and women who won the freedom Americans enjoy today.

In October 1776, one of the largest battles of the war took place in what is today the picturesque town of White Plains. Although General George Washington's troops were outnumbered by British General Lord Howe's, Washington managed to outmaneuver the British commander and escape through White Plains to assume a nearly impregnable position. If Washington had not been able to slip through with his men, the war—and America's independence—probably would have ended right there. Afterward, Howe could never explain how and why he let Washington get away, but it was a turning point in the war.

Numerous sites in White Plains commemorate this famous battle. At Washington's 1776 Headquarters, on Virginia Road in North White Plains, you can view Revolutionary War relics and attend lectures and see reenactments of the famous battle. Nearby is the Miller Hill Restoration site, where you can see restored earthworks built by Washington's troops. There are also battle plans, diagrams, and other artifacts from the battle that changed American history.

When it comes to notable patriots, few have a more prominent place in history than Thomas Paine, a leader in the colonial drive for independence and author of *Common Sense,* a publication that cemented the colonists' resolve for freedom. You can visit the Thomas Paine Cottage in New Rochelle, a museum that houses Paine's personal effects and memorabilia, and the Thomas Paine National Historical Association, which displays some of his original writings.

Another important patriot was John Jay, the first Chief Justice of the United States Supreme Court in 1789. The John Jay Homestead in Mount Kisco is where Jay and four generations of his descendants lived. This historic site includes original furnishings, artifacts, and beautiful gardens, as well as a fine American portrait collection.

No tour of Revolutionary-era Westchester would be complete without a trip to St. Paul's Church National Historic Site in Yonkers. The event that made this site famous was the Great Election of 1733, which led to the establishment of a free press in colonial America. This setting helped to establish the basic freedoms we as Americans enjoy today and that are outlined in the Bill of Rights. In fact, there is a Bill of Rights Museum in the building, complete with a working model of an 18th-century printing press, as well as dioramas depicting many aspects of colonial-era life. This historic building also served as a military hospital during the Revolutionary War and housed a courtroom where Aaron Burr practiced law.

port shuttle. | 66 Hale Ave. | 914/682–0050 | fax 914/682–7404 | www.crowneplaza.com | 401 rooms | $189–$249 | AE, D, DC, MC, V.

Doral Arrowwood. This luxury resort and conference center less than 1 mi from the Hutchinson Parkway at exit 28 has gorgeously landscaped grounds. Many of the rooms have balconies and screened-in porches with lovely views. Restaurant, bar, room service. In-room data ports, some microwaves, cable TV. 2 pools. Hot tub, massage, spa. Driving range, 9-hole golf course, putting green, 4 tennis courts. Gym, racquetball. Business services, airport shuttle. | Anderson Hill Rd., Rye Brook | 914/939–5500 | fax 914/323–5500 | www.arrowwood.com | 374 rooms | $149–$179 | AE, D, DC, MC, V.

Esplanade at White Plains. The Esplanade Hotel is in the center of White Plains in Westchester County. The hotel offers 38 overnight guest rooms as well as 200 apartments for extended stays. Restaurant. Cable TV. Exercise equipment. Free parking. | 95 S. Broadway | 914/761–8100 | www.esplanadecorporate.com/index.htm | 38 rooms | $109 | AE, D, MC, V.

Hilton Rye Town. This posh hotel 3 mi east of White Plains is convenient to major highways and the Westchester County Airport. All rooms have double or king-size beds. Many have balconies, and some have bathrobes and wet bars. Connecting rooms available. Restaurant, bar. In-room data ports, cable TV. 2 pools. Hot tub. Tennis. Exercise equipment. Business services. | 699 Westchester Ave., Rye Brook | 914/939–6300 | fax 914/939–5328 | www.hilton.com | 438 rooms | $119–$365 | AE, D, DC, MC, V.

Ramada Inn. This reputable chain (10 mi north of White Plains) in the quaint village of Armonk, has easy access to nearby Westchester and New York City. Room have double or king-size beds. Restaurant, bar (with entertainment), picnic area. Complimentary Continental breakfast. In-room data ports, microwaves, cable TV. Pool. Exercise equipment. Laundry facilities. Business services, airport shuttle. | 94 Business Park Dr., Armonk | 914/273–9090 | fax 914/273–4105 | 140 rooms | $79–$169 | AE, D, DC, MC, V.

Renaissance Westchester. This hotel, spread out on 30 wooded acres, is just 35 min from Manhattan. All rooms have either two double, two queen-size, or a king-size bed. Some have sofas and plants. Restaurant, bar, room service. In-room data ports, refrigerators, cable TV. Pool. Hot tub. Tennis court. Exercise equipment. Business services. | 80 W. Red Oak La. | 914/694–5400 | fax 914/694–5616 | www.renaissancehotels.com | 357 rooms | $135–$205 | AE, D, DC, MC, V.

Summerfield Suites Hotel. This all-suite, four-story hotel is close to downtown White Plains and many Westchester corporate campuses. On Corporate Park Drive at the intersection of Interstates 287 and 684 with the Hutchinson River Parkway. Complimentary Continental breakfast. Kitchenettes, cable TV. Pool. Hot tub. Exercise equipment. | 101 Corporate Park Dr. | 914/251–9700 | 159 rooms | $109–$339 | AE, D, DC, MC, V.

Westchester Residence Inn by Marriott. This 16-floor, all-suite hotel in downtown Westchester specializes in extended-stay accommodations. With the corporate offices of IBM, Kraft/Philip Morris, Lockheed Martin, Pepsico, and Texaco within 7 mi, it's geared toward business travel. Suites have two double or king-size beds. Restaurant, complimentary Continental breakfast, room service. In-room data ports, kitchenettes, cable TV. Gym. | 5 Barker Ave. | 914/761–7700 | fax 914/761–0136 | www.residenceinn.com | 133 suites | $179–$205 | AE, D, DC, MC, V.

WILLIAMSVILLE

MAP 3, C6

(Nearby towns also listed: Amherst, Buffalo, Clarence, East Aurora, Grand Island, Hamburg, Lockport, Niagara Falls)

The Village of Williamsville is the only incorporated town in the township of Amherst. Two prominent features of the town are the north campus of the Erie Community College system and a town park with an old red mill (off Main Street at Spring Street). The town park runs along the course of a river on both sides of Main Street. Take an ice-cream break and wander through the restored water-run mill from 1811, in front of which smiling couples take their wedding pictures.

Information: **Amherst Chamber of Commerce** | 326 Essjay Rd., Suite 200, 14221 | 716/632–6905.

Attractions

Western New York Railway Historical Society. The museum preserves western New York's railroad heritage through the restoration and preservation of depots, steam engines, cabooses, other locomotives, and displays of railway artifacts. Call or check the Web site for a calendar of events. | 86 S. Long St., Buffalo | 716/633–7002 | www.trainweb.org/wnyrhs | Donation suggested | Hrs vary by event.

ON THE CALENDAR

JULY: *Old Home Days.* The village celebrates its heritage at this annual festival with live music, games, and a giant parade. | Island Park, 5565 Main St. | 716/632–4120.
JULY, AUG.: *Lebanese Festival.* This Lebanese heritage festival has music, dancing, food, a special dinner dance, and a bazaar. | St. John Maron Church, 2040 Wehrle Dr. | 716/634–0669.

Dining

Buffalo Brew Pub. American. The gray roadhouse at Main and Transit streets has an "old pub" interior that includes an 80-ft bar, a stone fireplace, and a dartboard. The menu includes French onion soup, chile con carne, chicken wings, burgers and sandwiches, fish-and-chips, barbecued baby-back ribs, salads, and an extensive beer list. | 6861 Main St. | 716/632–0552 | fax 716/632–1336 | www.buffalobrewpub.com | $5–$13 | AE, D, DC, MC, V.

Daffodil's. Contemporary. This restaurant with its fireplace feels like a country club. Try the pork tenderloin medallions or the classic surf and turf. Pianist Friday nights. | 930 Maple Rd. | 716/688–5413 | Jacket and tie | No lunch weekends | $16–$29 | AE, DC, MC, V.

Jenny's Ice Cream. American. This small ice-cream parlor in the center of Williamsville is lined with freezers from which they serve homemade ice cream plain and simple. No smoking. | 78 E. Spring St. | 716/633–2424 | Closed Nov.–Mar. | $2–$6 | No credit cards.

Old Red Mill Inn. American. This railroad-theme restaurant used to be part of a dairy farm. The restaurant's railroad theme began with the addition of a caboose, followed by a couple of dining cars. After enjoying a meal of certified-Angus prime rib or surf and turf, you can tour the old farm's many rooms filled with antiques and early farm implements. Kids' menu. Sunday brunch. | 8326 Main St. | 716/633–7878 | $10–$35 | AE, D, DC, MC, V.

Lodging

Fairfield Inn Buffalo/Williamsville. This three-story hotel with exterior and interior corridors features guest rooms with work desks and in-room movies; ironing boards and cribs are available. Complimentary breakfast. In-room data ports, some refrigerators, cable TV. Pool. Business services, free parking. | 52 Freeman Rd. | 716/626–1500 | fax 716/626–1500 | fairfieldinn.com/buf1 | 135 rooms | $56 | AE, D, DC, MC, V.

Heritage House Country Inn. This two-story, Victorian-style inn has individually furnished rooms, some with king-size and four-post beds. Picnic area, complimentary Continental breakfast. Some kitchenettes, microwaves, some refrigerators, cable TV. Business services, airport shuttle, free parking. Some pets allowed. | 8261 Main St. | 716/633–4900 or 716/283–3899 (reservations) | fax 716/633–4900 | www.wnybiz.com/heritage | 53 rooms | $54–$100 | AE, D, DC, MC, V.

Residence Inn by Marriott. This two-story chain hotel near Dunlop and Dupont (10 mi from Lake Erie) specializes in extended-stay suite accommodation. Rooms in the suites have various combinations of double, queen-size, and king-size beds, and some have two levels, two baths, and pull-out beds. Complimentary Continental breakfast. In-room data ports, some kitchenettes, microwaves, cable TV. Pool. Exercise equipment. Laundry facilities. Business services, airport shuttle, free parking. Some pets allowed (fee). | 100 Maple Rd. | 716/632–6622 | fax 716/632–5247 | 112 suites | $120–$150 | AE, D, DC, MC, V.

WILMINGTON

MAP 3, K2

(Nearby towns also listed: Lake Placid, Paul Smiths, Plattsburgh, Saranac Lake)

While many believe that Whiteface Mountain is in Lake Placid, the famous ski center is, in fact, in Wilmington. A fairly typical Adirondack town, Wilmington has plenty of outdoor activities, and many places to eat, sleep, shop, and visit.

Information: Whiteface Mountain Regional Visitors Bureau | Box 277, Rte. 86, 12997 | 518/946–2255 or 888/944–8332.

Attractions

High Falls Gorge. A spectacular 700-ft waterfall and ancient granite cliffs more than a billion years old are highlights of the self-guided tour of this gorge. It was created as the Ausable River cut through the granite base of Whiteface Mountain. Nearby are a shop, restaurant, and picnic areas. | Rte. 86 at Wilmington Notch | 518/946–2278 | highfallsgorge@lakeplacid.ny.us | www.highfallsgorge.com | $6 | Daily 9–5; Closed Mid-Nov.–Mid Apr.

Santa's Home Workshop. This simple theme park (2 mi northwest of Wilmington) with rides and live reindeer is ideal for small children. Santa and his helpers talk with children, while elves practice their crafts in shops around the park. | 12946 Whiteface Mountain Memorial Hwy., North Pole | 518/946–2211 or 800/488–9853 | www.northpoleny.com | $11.95 | Mid-June–Labor Day, weekdays 9:30–4:30; Labor Day–Columbus Day, weekends 10–3:30; call for hrs in Nov. and Dec.

YOUR CAR'S FIRST-AID KIT

- Bungee cords or rope to tie down trunk if necessary
- Club soda to remove stains from upholstery
- Cooler with bottled water
- Extra coolant
- Extra windshield-washer fluid
- Flares and/or reflectors
- Flashlight and extra batteries
- Hand wipes to clean hands after roadside repair
- Hose tape
- Jack and fully inflated spare
- Jumper cables
- Lug wrench
- Owner's manual
- Plastic poncho—in case you need to do roadside repairs in the rain
- Quart of oil and quart of transmission fluid
- Spare fan belts
- Spare fuses
- Tire-pressure gauge

*Excerpted from *Fodor's: How to Pack: Experts Share Their Secrets*
© 1997, by Fodor's Travel Publications

Whiteface Mountain. Though only the fifth highest in the region, Whiteface Mountain is probably the best-known mountain in the Adirondacks. A tour of the area isn't complete without a drive up Veterans' Memorial Highway, which climbs 8 mi through forest and alpine country to the top of the mountain. Once you reach the peak, leave your car in the parking lot and ride the elevator. If you're feeling energetic, hike to the summit for a truly spectacular 360-degree view. Snack bar. | 12997 Veterans' Memorial Hwy. | 518/523–1655 or 800/462–6236 | fax 518/946–2223 | info@orda.org | www.orda.org | $8 per car and driver | Mid-May–June, daily 9–4; July–Labor Day, 8:30–5; Labor Day–Columbus Day, 9–4.

Whiteface Mountain Ski Center. Whiteface, owned by the State of New York and operated by ORDA (Olympic Regional Development Authority), is one of the biggest ski centers in the East, with 66 slopes and trails that drop 3,216 vertical ft. Whiteface offers an unmatched view from the top (you can see nearly 100 mi), and a variety of ways to the bottom, from expert to novice slopes and some just for kids. There's a ski school, snowmaking, rentals, and restaurants. | Rte. 86 | 518/946–7171 or 800/462–6236 | $46 | Mid.-Nov.–Apr.

ON THE CALENDAR

SEPT.: *Whiteface Mountain Scottish Highland Festival.* Held on a Saturday in early September, the festival features piping, drumming, Highland dancing, Celtic harps, Celtic fiddles, spinning and weaving, Scottish heavy athletics competition, clan tents, and Scottish imports and food. | 518/946–2223 or 518/946–2223.

Dining

Ratskeller. German. Connected with the Willkommen Hof B&B, Ratskeller has a dining room that is centered around a German *Kachel* (oven with tables). It also features a traditional German *Stamtisch* (corner booth) and an English-style bristle dartboard. Imported beers and wines are available. | Rte. 86 | 518/946–7669 or 800/541–9119 | Reservations essential | Closed Sun. No lunch | $7–$25 | MC, V.

Wilderness Inn #2. American. A mile and a half southwest on Route 86, this restaurant, which serves hearty steaks, chops, chicken, and fresh seafood, is surrounded by forest. Knotty-pine walls, antique figurines, and a doll collection dress up the interior. Bi-level open-air dining. Salad bar. Kids' menu. | Rte. 86 | 518/946–2391 | Closed Wed. Sept.–June, and first 3 weeks in Nov. | $11–$19 | D, DC, MC, V.

Lodging

Deer's Head Inn. While known mainly as a restaurant, this inn in the center of small Elizabethtown (12 mi northwest of Wilmington) has four comfortable guest rooms. The two-story 1808 structure that houses the inn still retains its original architectural detail and some original woodwork. Rooms have private baths and two double or full-size beds. Restaurant. | Court St., Elizabethtown | 518/873–9903 | fax 518/873–9903 | marko@willex.com | 4 rooms | $45–$65 | AE, D, MC, V.

Howard Johnson Resort Inn. This resort inn with mountain views on Lake Placid was the 1999 Howard Johnson Property of the Year. Many of the rooms have balconies and there are free rowboats, paddleboats, and canoes; a game room; and nature trails. Restaurant, picnic area. Pool. Hot tub. Golf privileges, tennis. Hiking, water sports, fishing. Pets allowed (fee). | 90 Saranac Ave., Lake Placid | 518/523–9555 or 800/858–4656 | hojolkpl@north-net.org | 92 rooms | $78–$150 | AE, D, DC, MC, V.

Hungry Trout Motor Inn. Rooms at this motel on the west branch of the Ausable River, close to Whiteface Mountain Ski Center, have mountain views. Two-room suites with kitchenettes are available. Restaurant. Cable TV. Pool, wading pool. Cross-country skiing. Playground. Pets allowed. | 12997 Rte. 86 | 518/946–2217 or 800/766–9137 | fax 518/946–7418 | www.hungrytrout.com | 22 rooms | $54–$139 | Closed Apr., Nov. | AE, D, DC, MC, V.

Ledge Rock at Whiteface Mountain. This upscale motel, named for the ledges on the mountain directly behind the building, is on 100 acres across the road from Whiteface Mountain. Rooms have mountain views, and two double or a queen-size bed. Picnic area. Some microwaves, some refrigerators, cable TV. Pool, pond, wading pool. Boating. Playground. Pets allowed. | Rte. 86, at Placid Rd. | 518/946–2302 or 800/336–4754 | fax 518/946–7594 | ledgerock@whiteface.net | 18 rooms | $50–$159 | AE, D, DC, MC, V.

Whiteface Chalet. This three-story replica of a Swiss chalet surrounded by serene woods was built in 1959 and faces Whiteface Mountain. Rooms have double-size beds only. Second-floor rooms have balconies, and deluxe rooms which sleep up to six are available. Restaurant, bar. No air-conditioning in 1 room, cable TV. Pool. Tennis. Playground. Airport shuttle. | 12997 Springfield Rd. | 518/946–2207 or 800/932–0859 | whiteface.chalet@whiteface.net | 16 rooms | $59–$79 | AE, D, DC, MC, V.

Willkommen Hof B&B. The two-story European-style *gasthof,* or "guest house," was built in 1920 at the foot of Whiteface Mountain. There are rooms with private baths, shared baths, and a three-room suite. You'll also find a large cedar sauna, a year-round outdoor spa, and on-site bicycling and jogging trails. The breakfast includes apple pancakes and blintzes. Restaurant, complimentary breakfast. Hot tub. Hiking, fishing, cross-country skiing. Business services, free parking. Pets allowed (fee). | Rte. 86 | 518/946–7669 or 800/541–9119 | www.lakeplacid.net/willkommenhof | 8 rooms (six with private bath), 1 suite | $58–$115 rooms, $125–$154 suite | MC, V.

WINDHAM

MAP 3, J7

(Nearby towns also listed: Cairo, Hunter, Roxbury, Stamford)

Once a private club attracting politicians and business leaders, Windham still retains something of an exclusive air. It's a favorite spot for hunters and hikers, and lodging options range from intimate inns and converted Victorian homes to a sprawling resort and modern hotels.

Information: **Windham Chamber of Commerce** | South St., Box 613, 12496 | 518/734–3852 | www.windhamchamber.org.

Attractions

Ski Windham. In addition to 34 trails for downhill skiing, this resort has year-round events and autumn lift rides for beautiful views of the changing colors of the Catskills. A shuttle bus operates from the town area. | C. D. Lane Rd. | 518/734–4300 or 800/729–4766 | www.ski-windham.com | Late Dec.–Mar.

Windham Chamber Music. All concerts are at the Windham Civic Centre with past performances featuring the Meridian String Quartet, the Borealis Wind Quartet, and other chamber music. | Main St. | www.windhamny.com | $15 | July 4th–Labor Day, Sat. 8 PM.

ON THE CALENDAR

SEPT.: *Windham's Autumn A-Fair.* A town-wide celebration of fall in the Catskills is held on a weekend in late September. Events have included music, pony rides, a petting zoo, cider making, beekeeping, maple syrup demonstrations, cloggers, fiddlers, and hay-wagon rides. | 515/734–3852 or 877/294–6342 | www.windhamny.com.

Dining

Chalet Fondue Restaurant. German. Enjoy German-Swiss-American cuisine like sauerbraten and Wienerschnitzel, as well as steaks, chicken, and seafood amid authentic alpine decor, soothing candlelight, and crackling fireplaces. Extensive beer and wine list. | Rte. 296 | 518/734–4650 | www.windham-area.com/chaletfondue.htm | Closed Tues. No lunch | $10–$24 | AE, DC, MC, V.

La Griglia. Italian. This family-style Italian restaurant has three dining rooms, a full bar, and nice views of the Windham Country Club's 9th hole through the large windows in the main dining areas. Kids' menu. Sunday brunch. | Rte. 296 | 518/734–4499 | Closed Tues. No lunch Mon.–Sat. | $15–$20 | AE, DC, MC, V.

Thetford's Restaurant. American. Serving the Windham area since the mid-60s, Thetford's offers a selection of salmon, T-bone steak, and specialties which could include roast Long Island Duck or sautéed red snapper. In the Pub, you can order a 10-oz burger. The casual dining room has white walls with dark wood beams and seats 140. The restaurant is occasionally closed on Monday or Tuesday during the off-season of April and May. | Rte. 23 | 518/734–3322 | www.windham-area.com/thetford's.htm | $6–$25 | AE, D, MC, V.

Lodging

Albergo Allegria. This two-story Victorian inn nestled in the Catskill Mountain Forest Preserve is furnished with period wallpaper and antiques. Lounge in wicker furniture on the porches or stroll in the gardens. The 12 guest rooms, named for the 12 months of the year, have down comforters and plush carpeting. Four suites are named after the four seasons, and the master suite has a king-size bed with a featherbed, a double Jacuzzi, and an antique wedding certificate from 1899. The five carriage-house suites, each named for a different herb, have king-size beds, 15-ft cathedral ceilings with skylights, double whirlpool tubs, and marble gaslight fireplaces. These suites face wild thyme fields and have their own courtyard, garden view, and outdoor lounge. Complimentary breakfast. Some in-room hot tubs, cable TV, some in-room VCRs. Hot tub. Library. Business services. | 43 Rte. 296 | 518/734–5560 or 800/625–2374 | fax 518/734–5570 | mail@albergousa.com | www.albergousa.com | 14 rooms, 7 suites | $73–$153 rooms, $103–$233 suites | MC, V.

Apple Tree Bed & Breakfast. The Apple Tree, just ½ mi from Windham, is an 110-year-old Victorian B&B with a wraparound porch. Furnished with a combination of antiques, traditional American, and Italian pieces, the two rooms and one suite have private baths. A sample breakfast menu includes eggs Benedict or Farmers Market French Toast, juice, and fresh pastries. Children are welcome. Special nonweekend, nonholiday, and summer rates are available. Complimentary breakfast. Hiking. | Rte. 296, Hensonville | 518/734–5555 | www.windham-area.com/appletree.htm | 2 rooms, 1 suite | $85–$185 | MC, V.

Hotel Vienna. This Austrian-theme hotel is nestled in the mountainous Catskill State Park, near miles of hiking and mountain-biking trails. All rooms have solid cherry furniture, lace curtains, beamed ceilings, and sliding doors to a private, tiled balcony. Complimentary Continental breakfast. Air-conditioning, cable TV. Pool. Hot tub. Business services. | 107 Rte. 296 (I–87, exit 21) | 518/734–5300 or 800/898–5308 | fax 518/734–4749 | www.thehotelvienna.com | 30 rooms | $80–$160 | MC, V.

Redcoat's Return. In a valley in the northern Catskill Mountains just 20 min from Ski Windham, the Redcoat's Return has the ambience of an English country inn and restaurant. Seven rooms have private baths, the other five rooms share three baths. Dinner is available on weekend evenings in the book-lined dining room. Complimentary breakfast. Cable TV in common area, no room phones. Hiking, cross-country skiing. | Dale La., Elka Park | 518/589–6379 or 518/589–9858 | 12 rooms (5 with shared bath) | $80–$105 | AE, D, MC, V.

Windham Arms. This classic, family-oriented inn, built in 1800, has wood-trimmed rooms with two double or one queen-size bed. Some rooms have courtyard views and other have full mountain views from private terraces. Restaurant. No air-conditioning in some rooms, cable TV. Pool. Putting green, tennis. Spa. Gym. Video games. Playground. Laundry facilities. Business services. | Rte. 23 | 518/734–3000 or 800/946–3476 | fax 518/734–5900 | www.windhamarmshotel.com | 50 rooms | $70–$330 | AE, D, MC, V.

WOODSTOCK

MAP 3, K8

(Nearby towns also listed: Catskill, Kingston, Mt. Tremper, Rhinebeck, Saugerties)

Woodstock has been an artists' colony ever since Ralph Radcliffe Whitehead established the Byrdcliffe Art and Crafts Colony here in 1902. Shortly thereafter, the Art Students League opened its summer school in Woodstock. In 1910, the Woodstock Artists Association was founded, and in 1916 Harvey White launched a series of music and dance festivals at the breakaway Maverick Colony. Today, many artists and craftspeople still live and work in the area, and Sundays, the Maverick Colony hosts summer chamber music concerts. Fine shops, delectable food, and eccentricity are all part of Woodstock's charm. Aging hippies and baby boomers, families, and musicians share the sidewalks with hordes of tourists. But don't ask a native to point you toward the Woodstock concert site. While Woodstock got the notoriety, the famous 1969 music festival was actually held in Bethel, 60 mi away.

Information: Chamber of Commerce | 21 Tinker St., 12498 | 914/679–8025.

Attractions

Opus 40. Harvey Fite put 37 years into the making of this 6-acre outdoor sculpture that was created in the rock bed of an abandoned bluestone quarry. The architectural creation is an assemblage of curving bluestone walkways, swirling terraces, and finely fitted ramps around pools, trees, and fountains. There's also the Quarryman's Museum containing 19th-century tools. Six miles from Woodstock, Opus 40 is sometimes closed for special events, so call ahead or check the website. | 50 Fite Rd., Saugerties | 845/246–3400 | www.opus40.org | $5 | Memorial Day–Columbus Day, Fri.–Sun. and holiday Mon. noon–5.

Woodstock Artists Association Gallery. This gallery has been showcasing new and local artists in ever-changing exhibitions since 1920. | 28 Tinker St. | 845/679–2940 | Free | Thurs.–Mon. noon–5.

ON THE CALENDAR

MAY: *Woodstock Renaissance Fair.* Crafts, music, readings, theater, costumes, and food abound at this noncommercial fair. Downtown. | 845/679–7148.

WOODSTOCK: A GENERATION'S DEFINING MOMENT

In August 1969, some 500,000 people spent 3 days of peace, love, and music at Yasgur's Farm, a rolling field and amphitheater in the Sullivan County hamlet of Bethel. Just a couple of miles down Hurd Road off Route 17B, at the end of a residential and rural road, the field is still there. A simple monument marks the site. In the late 1990s, the field and surrounding properties were purchased by a local businessman.

Locals remember the famous weekend, when Route 17 became a parking lot, muddy kids washed themselves off in driveways with garden hoses, and Joan Baez's voice (among others) drifted through the chilly night air. They remember the rain and the helicopters and the unprecedented mess the 3-day rock concert made.

Each year, on the festival's anniversary, pilgrims come to the site to remember. They leave wildflowers at the monument, take pictures, and try to tell their kids what the event meant for them individually, and for their generation.

© Artville

JUNE–SEPT.: *Maverick Concert Series.* The country's oldest continuously running summer chamber music series is held in the Maverick Hall, a 1916 structure built in the woods outside of Woodstock. | 845/679–8217.

Dining

Al's. American. This casual and family-friendly place has been a fixture of Phoenicia (12 mi west of Woodstock) for some 60 years. It's known for its summer outdoor clambakes, fresh seafood, shellfish, and vegetarian offerings. Early bird specials. | 10 Main St., Phoenicia | 845/688–5880 | No lunch Tues.–Weds., Sun. | $15–$20 | AE, D, MC, V.

Bear Cafe. Contemporary American. This streamside restaurant 3 mi west of Woodstock has a horseshoe bar adjoining two dining areas, one outdoors. Try the pan-seared scallops with pepper sauces and kale with garlic, or the swordfish with fire-roasted sweet peppers, olives, and oregano. Sit on a patio that's about as close to the water as you can get without falling in. | 295 Tinker St., Bearsville | 845/679–5555 | Closed Tues. No lunch | $14–$22 | MC, V.

Joshua's. Continental. This bistro is one of the oldest eateries on Woodstock's main street. It's known for its Middle Eastern, fresh seafood, and inventive vegetarian selections. Brunch. | 51 Tinker St. | 845/679–5533 | $15–$25 | AE, MC, V.

New World Home Cooking Co. Eclectic. The *Hudson Valley Magazine* & *Metroland* proclaimed New World the "Best New American Restaurant in 1999." The space is big and filled with art and color; a large bar and a sapphire-and-stainless-steel open kitchen complete the picture. Food is prepared without using "zappers," deep-fat fryers, excessive thickeners, or MSG. The dinner menu includes a sampler with Creole mustard shrimp, Spanish manchego cheese, Sicilian olive salad crostini, smoked Maine mussels, roasted chorizo, and escabèche vegetables. You'll also find chicken Punjabi, Thai barbecued fish, and Cajun peppered shrimp. Between Saugerties and Woodstock, 3½ mi east of downtown Woodstock. | 1411 Rte. 212, Saugerties | 845/246–0900 | www.newworldhomecooking.com | $7–$22 | AE, D, DC, MC, V.

Lodging

Twin Gables. This comfortable, turn-of-the-century Victorian bed and breakfast in the center of Woodstock has been operated by the same family for many years. Fresh flowers perfume all rooms, and shops, restaurants, and live music are within strolling distance. No room phones. TV in common area. No pets. No smoking. | 73 Tinker St. | 845/679–9479 | fax 845/679–5638 | www.twingableswoodstockny.com | 9 rooms (6 with shared bath) | $52–$92 | AE, D, MC, V.

Woodstock Country Inn. Amid acres of rolling meadows, woods, and the Catskill Mountains, this B&B was built as the home of Woodstock artist Jo Cantine—several of her paintings and examples of her hand-painted furniture are displayed in the common room and bedrooms. The four guest rooms offer mountain views, a porch or deck, private entrances, private baths, and fireplaces. A heated pool is in the meadow with mountain views. Skiing is nearby at Hunter, Windham, and Belleayre mountains. Off-season rates are available. Complimentary breakfast. Cable TV. Pool. Hiking. | Cooper Lake Rd. | 845/679–9380 | woodstockcountryinn.com | 4 rooms | $150–$250 | MC, V.

YONKERS

MAP 3, C2

(Nearby towns also listed: New York City, Scarsdale, Tarrytown, White Plains)

Home to almost 200,000 people, Yonkers is a modern city of shopping malls, corporate parks, and fine golf courses. While many know it for the excitement of the famous

YONKERS

INTRO
ATTRACTIONS
DINING
LODGING

harness racing at Yonkers Raceway, the city is steeped in history. The city's name is a derivation of Van Der Donck, a Dutch nobleman who bought land in the area in the mid-1600s. The name underwent many changes until the area became known as "The Yonkers Land" and then simply, Yonkers.

A bustling city amid its smaller, quainter, neighbors on the Hudson, Yonkers was made famous by author Thornton Wilder as the home of Dolly Levi, the main character in his play, *The Matchmaker,* which became the hit musical, *Hello, Dolly!* A bit of city, suburbs, and country all rolled into one, Yonkers sits on the border of the Bronx and is just minutes away from Manhattan.

Information: **Yonkers Chamber of Commerce** | 20 S. Broadway, 10701 | 914/963–0332.

Attractions

Hudson River Museum of Westchester. This museum displays changing exhibitions of 19th- and 20th-century American art. The museum's specialty is combining the elements of art, history, and science into its shows. | 511 Warburton Ave. | 914/963–4550 | $3 | Wed.–Sun. noon–5.

Philipse Manor Hall State Historic Site. Frederick Philipse III, a wealthy merchant and loyalist to the British crown, began building this house in the 1680s. The historic home, the oldest in Westchester County, features some of the finest surviving American Rococo architecture and decor. | 29 Warburton Ave., at Dock St. | 914/965–4027 | Free | Wed. and Thurs. 11–2, Sun. 2–5, or by appointment.

St. Paul's Church National Historic Site. The parish that built St. Paul's church was established in 1665. The present fieldstone-and-brick Georgian church, begun in 1763, was used by British and Hessian soldiers as a military hospital during the Revolutionary War. This building was the site of events that led to the freedom of the press in colonial America during the 1700s, and now contains the Bill of Rights Museum. It's in Mount Vernon, about 2 mi east of Yonkers. | 897 S. Columbus Ave., Mount Vernon | 914/667–4116 | Free | Weekdays 9–5.

Yonkers Raceway. This harness-racing track opened in 1899. | 810 Central Ave. | 914/968–4200 | Free; parking $2 | Hrs vary per event.

ON THE CALENDAR

JUNE: *Westchester County Fair.* This family event has more than 50 games and rides, as well as live entertainment, free shows, food posts, and a merchandise mart. | Yonkers Raceway | 914/968–4200.

SEPT.: *Yonkers Riverfest.* Great family fun, this musical and cultural event takes place on the magnificently restored Yonkers Pier, the oldest recreational pier on the Hudson River. There are ferry rides, entertainment, and food. Near the train station. | 914/377–FEST.

Dining

Hunan Village. Chinese. Dine on specialties such as clams in black-bean sauce, "vegetarian monk," and filet mignon with black pepper sauce, amid a colorful interior design that incorporates Chinese artifacts and artwork. | 1828 Central Park Ave. | 914/779–2272 | $10–$20 | AE, DC, MC, V.

J. J. Mannion's. Irish. A crowd of regulars enjoys classic pub food and pints at this comfortable neighborhood spot. Known for burgers, shepherd's pie, and pasta. Sunday brunch. | 640 McLean Ave. | 914/476–2786 | No dinner Sun. | $10–$22 | AE, D, DC, MC, V.

Mount Olympus. Greek. There's a festive air at this family-oriented restaurant, from the wall murals to the chatty servers. You can get pitas full of spicy lamb and other Greek favorites, or opt for one of the menu's Italian or American offerings. | 1 Fort Hill Rd. | 914/961–4677 | $8–$12 | AE, D, DC, MC, V.

Tum Raa. Thai. There are only six tables in the tiny dining area of this otherwise spartan, no-frills, family-run restaurant, so get cozy. The menu features the usual spicy and super-hot concoctions, including peanut soup and chicken and pork satay. A handful of seafood options rounds out the menu. | 629 McLean Ave. | 914/965–1800 | $7–$12 | AE, MC, V.

Lodging

Holiday Inn. This well-kept chain hotel, built in the 1960s, is 15 mi from New York City and 2 mi from downtown Yonkers. Rooms come with either a double, two doubles, or a king-size bed. Restaurant, bar (with entertainment), room service. In-room data ports, cable TV. Pool. Exercise equipment. Business services. | 125 Tuckahoe Rd. | 914/476–3800 | fax 914/423–3555 | 103 rooms, 3 suites | $93–$195 | AE, D, DC, MC, V.

Royal Regency Hotel. The three-story hotel is near the Tappen Zee Bridge and close to the Metro train station. Each room has a work desk, and whirlpool suites are available. The lounge is open nightly for cocktails and music. Take exit 6 W off Interstate 87 (New York State Thruway) or the Tuckahoe Road exit from the Sprain Brook Parkway. Restaurant, bar, complimentary Continental breakfast. In-room data ports, some in-room hot tubs. Exercise room. Free parking. | 165 Tuckahoe Rd. | 914/476–6200 or 800/251–3858 | fax 914/375–7017 | www.royalregencyny.com | 91 rooms | $109 | AE, D, MC, V.

Index

Notes

Notes

Notes

TALK TO US

Fill out this quick survey and receive a free *Fodor's How to Pack* (while supplies last)

1 Which Road Guide did you purchase?
(Check all that apply.)
- ❏ AL/AR/LA/MS/TN
- ❏ AZ/CO/NM
- ❏ CA
- ❏ CT/MA/RI
- ❏ DE/DC/MD/PA/VA
- ❏ FL
- ❏ GA/NC/SC
- ❏ ID/MT/NV/UT/WY
- ❏ IL/IA/MO/WI
- ❏ IN/KY/MI/OH/WV
- ❏ KS/OK/TX
- ❏ ME/NH/VT
- ❏ MN/NE/ND/SD
- ❏ NJ/NY
- ❏ OR/WA

2 How did you learn about the Road Guides?
- ❏ TV ad
- ❏ Radio ad
- ❏ Newspaper or magazine ad
- ❏ Newspaper or magazine article
- ❏ TV or radio feature
- ❏ Bookstore display/clerk recommendation
- ❏ Recommended by family/friend
- ❏ Other:_____

3 Did you use other guides for your trip?
- ❏ AAA
- ❏ Compass American Guide
- ❏ Fodor's
- ❏ Frommer's
- ❏ Insiders' Guide
- ❏ Mobil
- ❏ Moon Handbook
- ❏ Other:_____

4 Did you use any of the following for planning?
❏ Tourism offices ❏ Internet ❏ Travel agent

5 Did you buy a Road Guide for (check one):
- ❏ Leisure trip
- ❏ Business trip
- ❏ Mix of business and leisure

6 Where did you buy your Road Guide?
- ❏ Bookstore
- ❏ Other store
- ❏ On-line
- ❏ Borrowed from a friend
- ❏ Borrowed from a library
- ❏ Other:_____

7 Why did you buy a Road Guide? (Check all that apply.)
- ❏ Number of cities/towns listed
- ❏ Comprehensive coverage
- ❏ Number of lodgings   ❏ Driving tours
- ❏ Number of restaurants ❏ Maps
- ❏ Number of attractions ❏ Fodor's brand name
- ❏ Other:_____

8 Did you use this guide primarily:
- ❏ For pretrip planning   ❏ While traveling
- ❏ For planning and while traveling

9 What was the duration of your trip?
- ❏ 2-3 days   ❏ 11 or more days
- ❏ 4-6 days   ❏ Taking more than 1 trip
- ❏ 7-10 days

10 Did you use the guide to select
- ❏ Hotels   ❏ Restaurants

11 Did you stay primarily in a
- ❏ Hotel   ❏ Hostel
- ❏ Motel   ❏ Campground
- ❏ Resort   ❏ Dude ranch
- ❏ Bed-and-breakfast   ❏ With family or friends
- ❏ RV/camper   ❏ Other:_____

12 What sights and activities did you most enjoy?
- ❏ Historical sights   ❏ Shopping
- ❏ Sports   ❏ Theaters
- ❏ National parks   ❏ Museums
- ❏ State parks   ❏ Major cities
- ❏ Attractions off the beaten path

13 How much did you spend per adult for this trip?
- ❏ Less than $500   ❏ $751-$1,000
- ❏ $501-$750   ❏ More than $1,000

14 How many traveled in your party?
___ Adults   ___ Children   ___ Pets

15 Did you
- ❏ Fly to destination   ❏ Rent a van or RV
- ❏ Drive your own vehicle ❏ Take a train
- ❏ Rent a car   ❏ Take a bus

16 How many miles did you travel round-trip?
- ❏ Less than 100   ❏ 501-750
- ❏ 101-300   ❏ 751-1,000
- ❏ 301-500   ❏ More than 1,000

17 What items did you take on your vacation?
- ❏ Traveler's checks   ❏ Digital camera
- ❏ Credit card   ❏ Cell phone
- ❏ Gasoline card   ❏ Computer
- ❏ Phone card   ❏ PDA
- ❏ Camera   ❏ Other

18 Would you use Fodor's Road Guides again?
- ❏ Yes   ❏ No

19 How would you like to see Road Guides changed?

- ❑ More ❑ Less Dining
- ❑ More ❑ Less Lodging
- ❑ More ❑ Less Sports
- ❑ More ❑ Less Activities
- ❑ More ❑ Less Attractions
- ❑ More ❑ Less Shopping
- ❑ More ❑ Less Driving tours
- ❑ More ❑ Less Maps
- ❑ More ❑ Less Historical information
- ❑ Other:_____

20 Tell us about yourself.

❑ Male   ❑ Female

Age:
- ❑ 18-24   ❑ 35-44   ❑ 55-64
- ❑ 25-34   ❑ 45-54   ❑ Over 65

Income:
- ❑ Less than $25,000   ❑ $50,001-$75,000
- ❑ $25,001-$50,000   ❑ More than $75,000

Name:_____   E-mail:_____

Address:_____   City:_____ State:_____ Zip:_____

Fodor's Travel Publications
Attn: Road Guide Survey
280 Park Avenue
New York, NY 10017